P9-AGA-610

LORRAINE MOTEL

ROOM 306

BATHROOM
WINDOW

PARKING
LOT

ANNEX

ROOMING
HOUSE

JIM'S
GRILL

CANIPE'S

Drawing By Adam Schneider

SOUTH MAIN STREET

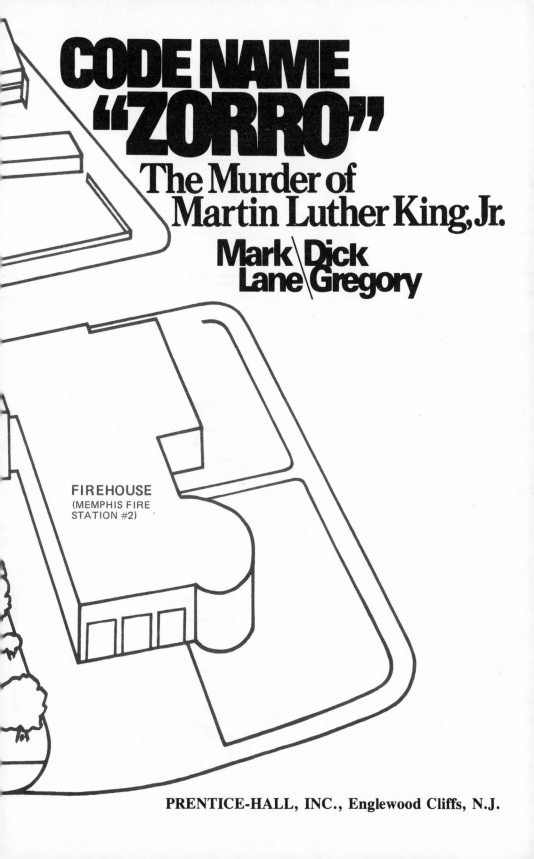

CODE NAME "ZORRO"

The Murder of Martin Luther King, Jr.

Mark Lane \ Dick Gregory

FIREHOUSE
(MEMPHIS FIRE
STATION #2)

PRENTICE-HALL, INC., Englewood Cliffs, N.J.

Quotation from "Letter from Birmingham Jail,"
abridged from pp. 77, 78, 83-84, 92, 100 of "Letter
From Birmingham Jail"—April 16, 1963—in *Why We
Can't Wait* by Martin Luther King, Jr., copyright © 1963
by Martin Luther King, Jr. By permission of Harper &
Row, Publishers, Inc.
"I Have a Dream," by Martin Luther King, Jr.,
copyright © 1963 by Martin Luther King, Jr., reprinted
by permission of Joan Daves.
Quotation from "I've Been to the Mountaintop," by
Martin Luther King, Jr., copyright © 1968 by the Estate
of Martin Luther King, Jr., reprinted by permission of
Joan Daves.
Quotation from "The Drum Major Instinct," by Martin
Luther King, Jr., copyright © 1968 by Martin Luther
King, Jr., Estate, reprinted by permission of Joan Daves.
Eulogy of Dr. Martin Luther King, Jr., Atlanta, Georgia,
April 9, 1968, by Benjamin E. Mays, reprinted by
permission of Charles Scribner's Sons from *Born to
Rebel: An Autobiography,* by Benjamin E. Mays,
copyright © 1971 by Benjamin E. Mays.

Code Name "Zorro" The Murder of Martin Luther King, Jr.
by Mark Lane/Dick Gregory
Copyright © 1977 by Mark Lane and Dick Gregory
All rights reserved. No part of this book may be
reproduced in any form or by any means, except
for the inclusion of brief quotations in a review,
without permission in writing from the publisher.
Printed in the United States of America
Prentice-Hall International, Inc., London
Prentice-Hall of Australia, Pty. Ltd., Sydney
Prentice-Hall of Canada, Ltd., Toronto
Prentice-Hall of India Private Ltd., New Delhi
Prentice-Hall of Japan, Inc., Tokyo
Prentice-Hall of Southeast Asia Pte. Ltd., Singapore
Whitehall Books Limited, Wellington, New Zealand
10 9 8 7 6 5 4 3 2 1

Library of Congress Cataloging in Publication Data

Lane, Mark.
  Code name "Zorro".

  Includes index.
  1. King, Martin Luther—Assassination. I. Gregory,
Dick, joint author. II. Title.
E185.97.K5L3   364.1'524'0973   77-4448
ISBN 0-13-139600-5

Contents

PART SIX / THE STATE OF TENNESSEE VS. JAMES EARL RAY

PART SEVEN / KALEIDOSCOPE

PART EIGHT / FOR A DAY IN COURT

Postscript by Mark Lane   272

Appendix

PART ONE
NINE YEARS AGO

Chapter One

ON THE DEATH OF GREAT MEN

by Mark Lane

Nine years ago Dr. Martin Luther King, Jr., the greatest civil rights protagonist in modern American history, was murdered in Memphis, Tennessee. Subsequently James Earl Ray was arrested and charged with the crime. Ray insisted that there had been a conspiracy and that after Dr. King's death he discovered that he had been an unwitting implement of that conspiracy.

No trial, or other public proceeding, has occurred since April 4, 1968, the day Dr. King was killed, which permits us to evaluate the evidence in the case. Ray entered what he has referred to, not without some supporting evidence, as an induced plea of guilty. A prearranged and rehearsed hearing was conducted without cross-examination or challenge by the defense. It raised more questions than it answered. Ray publicly contended, much to the embarrassment of his own lawyer, the Tennessee Attorney General, and the trial judge, that there had been a conspiracy to kill Dr. King. No one asked him what he meant or asked him to elaborate.

In this book, Ray's explanation of that provocative assertion will be explored. I have spent many hours with him at Brushy Mountain Penitentiary in Petros, Tennessee. I was the first person to visit him after his incarceration there in 1976, and I have met with him there for several hours as recently as February 1977. His view is presented here, as are the results of my own investigation into his allegation. Ray is an intelligent and articulate man not without a sense of humor, some of it self-directed, some of it poured upon those who have assessed his role in the murder. I think that the reader will only be able to evaluate Ray's participation in the events of April 4, 1968, in Memphis after hearing Ray's account of the events and when that exposition is placed in its full context.

The troubling events surrounding the murder of Dr. King encompass much that is beyond the range of perception or knowledge of James Earl

Ray. A minor publishing industry developed after the murder. Much of the work it produced did little more than obfuscate the essential truth, through the promulgation of an army of irrelevant data and flawed reasoning.

With the exception of the incipient investigation of the murder by the Select Committee on Assassinations of the House of Representatives the only examination of the events in the nine years that have passed is a secret inquiry conducted primarily by a police agency that vowed to destroy Dr. King and a recent Department of Justice review of the work of that police agency. Such investigations can hardly be expected to win the confidence of the American people. It is, therefore, not surprising that just before this book was completed a national poll conducted by George Gallup disclosed that fewer than one out of five Americans believed the official version of the events—that James Earl Ray was the lone assassin of Dr. Martin Luther King, Jr.

That is why Dick Gregory and I decided that this book must be written now. So much new and profoundly disturbing evidence has come to light since 1968—some of it uncovered by Greg, some by me, some by other investigators—that the matter cries out for reconsideration by the most eminent of all juries, the American people.

Greg and I decided to divide the task of preparing the manuscript along purely practical lines. Greg knew King—was deeply involved in his work. I, on the other hand, had ready access to extensive documentation through the files of the Citizens Commission of Inquiry, which I now head. So it was decided that Greg should be primarily responsible for writing the first part of the book, the part dealing with Martin Luther King and events leading up to his murder, and that I should be primarily responsible for the later parts of the book, those dealing with the murder and its aftermath.

Through the work of Dick Gregory, Martin Luther King becomes alive again for the readers of this book. Greg stood with Dr. King in Birmingham and in a score of other cities throughout the Deep South, and in the Deep North of Chicago as well. Dr. King's assassination was a moment of history that traumatized this country, for in his life he was for a moment the conscience of mankind. Greg's work and Martin's words remind us again that not just a symbol died that day in Memphis. A man who could think, and inspire, and lead, and love, and be hurt was killed.

My task was different from Greg's. I have undertaken to tell the story of some particularly significant events that preceded the murder, to relate the evidence that we have uncovered about the murder, and to describe the efforts to suppress information that leads inexorably toward the prime suspects in the murder.

3

If the American people are not satisfied with the official rendition of the events, then they evidently spurn as well the quasi-official efforts by writers Ray refers to as "novelists." Who are these writers, and why might they have chosen to ignore some of the relevant evidence?

The death of great men often leaves behind a tumultuous wake that may inundate those who have stood too close to the event, or who may have inadvertently seen too much. In this case witnesses who lived in the rooming house from which the shot was presumably fired were unintentional witnesses to that moment of history. The rooming house was, if not what unkind fiction writers refer to as a flophouse, something akin to it. Those who were forced by events to live there were, for the most part, ill prepared to withstand societal pressures designed to alter their testimony, to forget their unmistakable observations, and to remain silent about official discrepancies. One of them, perhaps potentially the most important witness of all, remains today—nine years after the event—in a Tennessee mental institution which she said she was placed in as punishment for seeking to tell the truth.

In life as in drama, minor characters may be swept away by great events they do not understand and cannot even begin to comprehend. The real actors in the drama of Memphis, messengers who felt called upon to relate what they had seen, suffered grievously; some are suffering still. For those of us who were not witnesses that day, the suffering is of a different nature and of a different degree. We are, all of us, poorer for the death of Dr. King. We suffer still from the injury done to our right to know about events that have been contrived to shape our lives. If a major political and social leader may be murdered without a proper inquiry into the circumstances, our constitutional rights are in jeopardy. We have the power, I am convinced, to influence our own collective destiny. First, I believe, we must secure and understand the facts.

This book, we hope, will contribute to that body of knowledge essential to the mastering of the relevant evidence. Only when we know what things are may we hope to transform them into what they should be. Humans possess that unique ability. William Hazlitt perhaps said it best:

Man is the only animal that laughs and weeps; for he is the only animal that is struck by the difference between what things are and what they ought to be.

Chapter Two

NINE YEARS AGO
by Dick Gregory

Martin Luther King and I fought together on the battlefield for human justice. This is where I learned to respect him as a leader, to admire him and love him for what he was doing for humanity. Martin had a tremendous influence on my life, on my commitment to nonviolence, and on my commitment to the struggle for human justice.

A convention of frozen food executives at the Playboy Club in Chicago started me on the road to fame in show business. My new status led to my first involvement in the civil rights movement of the 1960s.

I was a participant in most of the "major" civil rights demonstrations of the early sixties, including the March on Washington and the Selma-to-Montgomery March. During these marches, I was called an outside agitator so many times I went to check out my birth certificate to make sure I wasn't born in Iceland or someplace else. And the FBI used to infiltrate all of our marches, but we could always spot them by looking at their feet. Like whoever heard of walking fifty miles wearing patent leather shoes and white socks!

Under the leadership of Dr. King, I became totally committed to nonviolence, and I was convinced that nonviolence meant opposition to killing in any form. I felt the commandment, "Thou Shalt Not Kill," applies to human beings not only in their dealings with each other —through war, lynching, assassination, murder, and the like—but in their practice of killing animals for food and sport. Animals and humans suffer and die alike. Violence causes the same pain, the same spilling of blood, the same stench of death, the same arrogant, cruel, and brutal taking of life.

I, along with millions of other blacks, was born into the world accepting certain negatives. I expected to be treated as less than a human being. Martin made the suffering and problems we blacks had undergone through so many years clamor for attention. He made it clear that we no longer had to accept a condition of servitude and second-class citizenship.

5

The moments I spent with Martin were many things. They were pleasant, stimulating, honest, and humorous. He enjoyed my jokes. Through him I was able to meet, associate with, and exchange ideas with many others who shared our concerns and convictions. My only regret is that my moments with him were not more relaxed. There was rarely an opportunity for lazy, reflective conversation. Either a demonstration beckoned, or I was rushing to entertain at some fund-raising event—or both.

I watched Martin as he grew large and vital on the American scene. And I watched and listened as a few powerful Americans attempted to make the world believe that what he was doing was wrong—that he was "picking on" America. They fought back by accusing Martin of being everything except what he really was—one of the most brilliant, dedicated, and admired spokesmen and leaders for the fight to gain humanity that this world has ever known. The FBI hated King with a passion. A clever criminal could have called the FBI and told them that King was organizing a march on one side of town, waited five minutes for all the agents to get there, and then have an open season robbing the banks on the other side of town.

I watched Martin as he dealt with issues concerning the plight of the poor and oppressed. I watched as he dealt with violence and injustice in America, and as he pointed out the country's lack of moral leadership. Then I saw him become the conscience of America.

Today, nine years after his death, Martin Luther King, Jr., is still the conscience of America. I shall never forget how upset America was when he began his vigorous, adamant, and extremely vocal opposition to the Vietnam War. Through him I came to understand that a commitment to nonviolence is more than marching for a cause and singing "We Shall Overcome," or turning the other cheek when one was slapped by a Southern sheriff.

Clearly, those who feared for King's life and safety were not paranoid. His violent death in Memphis is proof. And the "white folk watchers" in the black community have been ever and acutely aware of what Mr. Charlie will and will not tolerate. When King left off antagonizing bigots and Klansmen and began attacking defense spending and pointing out the inconsistency between claiming to be a Christian country and committing unspeakable atrocities in Vietnam, they saw the gauge on the social Geiger counter go wild. Danger! Danger! Danger! was the only possible interpretation.

King, they felt, had crossed that invisible line separating black folks' business from white folks' business. The governmental policy makers, the industrial giants, the shakers and movers of American society do not use public accommodations. It was barely relevant to them whether or not blacks were served at Woolworth's counter, or where they sat on the bus. King was no longer a darky preacher leading the country in a rousing prayer meeting. He was attacking the power elite.

Nine years have lapsed since the assassination of Martin Luther King. Sufficient time has passed to make it possible for one to look back realistically at Memphis, April 4, 1968, to scrutinize the events that led to a motel balcony, to a sniper's shot, and culminated with a life and promise felled, a dream deferred.

It may be debatable that time heals wounds, but there is no doubt that it does place events in proper perspective, allowing one to study them without the drama and emotion of the moment, which must inevitably color them.

Momentous changes have occurred on the American scene. The Vietnam War is over. Richard Nixon was catapulted to the Presidency and then toppled by Watergate. Bobby Kennedy and J. Edgar Hoover, respectively King's staunchest ally and most bitter foe, are dead now, as is Lyndon Johnson who was tortured by the same war—if for different reasons.

Yes, it has been nine years since that fateful day, April 4, 1968. Let us move back in time until we are there.

I was in the State of California, campaigning for the Presidency of the United States and lecturing at various colleges. Earlier in 1968 I had become a write-in candidate for the nation's highest office, with Mark Lane as my running mate.

At a little after 4 P.M. that day, California time, I was driving with a friend to Hartnell College where I was scheduled to deliver a lecture. Our conversation was interrupted by a radio bulletin. Martin Luther King had been shot in Memphis!

I began to remember Martin, clearly, vividly. I remembered his sweet innocence and his warm, gentle smile. I thought of the time when he and I had been riding on a plane and he expressed concern about my personal safety.

"Now Gregory," he said, "I want you to be careful. I'm just afraid they're gonna kill you."

I answered, "If they do, Doc, will you preach my funeral?" He said, "I sure will."

We continued our drive to Hartnell College in silence. Even now I can feel the numbness, still remember my disbelief.

Finally we arrived at the school. Standing up before an audience was the last thing I felt like doing that night. But, of course, I had to go out there and explain as best I could how I saw the situation. Many people were in the audience only because they wanted to know my thoughts and my opinions of the day's events. They knew Martin and I were friends and that I held him in great esteem.

At my lecture that night I realized for the first time that America was in trouble with her young white kids. I was surprised to see the effect King had on them. They had grown up hearing about him, seeing him on television, and being influenced by his national presence. No matter what J. Edgar Hoover, or their own mommas and daddies may have said about King, these young white kids knew he was not wrong and he was not bad. Martin was a living denial of all the racist myths perpetrated in the white community about black folks. Martin didn't lie, he didn't cut, he didn't steal, and he wasn't on welfare. These young white kids learned some truths about black folks from Martin Luther King, and he had a more profound impact on their minds and lives than anything they had heard around the family dinner table.

Martin Luther King had become a victim of violence while preaching nonviolence and it raised a crucial question. When I heard the conclusive word of his death at my hotel that night, the question became even more compelling.

Would the concept of nonviolence, already under brutal attack by many blacks and whites, die with King? Would black awareness and black progress be buried with him? Would the tremendous strides toward awakening the conscience of America to the plight of the poor and the oppressed be halted? Had Martin lived and died in vain? Was it possible that violence had conquered nonviolence?

For the first time since the news of King's being shot, I smiled, a reflective smile, sad and bittersweet, and I recalled the words of Gandhi.

My creed for nonviolence is an extremely active force. It has no room for cowardice or even weakness. When a man is fully ready to die he will not even desire to offer violence. History is replete with instances where, by dying with courage and compassion on their lips, men converted the hearts of their violent opponents.

King had faced his attackers; he did not beg, or scream, or whimper.

Martin Luther King, Jr., was laid to rest in the spirit which defined his days among us.

It was a poor folks' funeral, as sad as it was beautiful. I knew then there would never be another Martin Luther King, Jr., and further, that there did not need to be. A little bit of Dr. King resided in the heart and soul of every American. He had awakened it and brought it out into the open. He did what he had been placed on earth to do. There was no need for subsequent imitations of his life. America is a better place because Dr. King lived. History may prove him to have been his country's salvation.

Ironically, President Johnson was unable to attend Dr. King's funeral because he had to meet his generals and talk about Vietnam. Still I imagine the President spoke from the heart when he said, "We are shocked and saddened by the brutal slaying tonight of Dr. Martin Luther King. . . . I ask every citizen to reject the blind violence that has struck Dr. King, who lived by nonviolence."

I shall never forget the reaction of white America that night. The looks of horror, disbelief, embarrassment, and guilt. The haunting question was written on every face, "How will black folks react?" I saw it on California Governor Ronald Reagan's face on television. Black folks in California saw it too, and I really believe his tearful expression of personal shock and horror was largely responsible for keeping things cool in Watts.

The account of the assassination printed in *The New York Times* was typical of the press response throughout the country.

The 39-year-old Negro leader's death was reported shortly after the shooting by Frank Holloman, director of the Memphis police and fire departments, after Dr. King had been taken to St. Joseph Hospital.

"I and all the citizens of Memphis," Holloman said, "regret the murder of Dr. King and all resources at our and the state's command will be used to apprehend the person or persons responsible."

The police broadcast an alarm for "a young white male," well dressed who was reported to have been seen running after the shooting. . . . Policemen poured into the area around the Lorraine Motel on Mulberry Street where Dr. King was shot. They carried shotguns and rifles and sealed off the entire block, refusing entry to newsmen and others.

Dr. King had been in his second-floor room throughout the day until just about 6:00 P.M. central standard time (7 P.M. New York Time).

Then he emerged in a silkish-looking black suit and white shirt. He paused, leaned over the green iron railing and started chatting with an associate, Jesse Jackson, who was standing just below him in a parking lot.

Mr. Jackson introduced Dr. King to Ben Branch, a musician who was to play at a rally Dr. King was to address two hours

9

later. As Mr. Jackson and Mr. Branch told of Dr. King's last moments later, the aide asked Dr. King:

"Do you know Ben?"

"Yes, that's my man!" Dr. King glowed.

They said Dr. King then asked if Mr. Branch would play a spiritual, "Precious Lord, Take My Hand," at the meeting that night.

"I really want you to play that tonight," Dr. King said. The Rev. Ralph Abernathy, perhaps Dr. King's closest friend, was just about to come out of the room.

A loud noise burst out.

Dr. King toppled to the concrete passageway floor and blood began gushing from a wound.

Someone rushed up with a towel to stem the flow of blood. Rev. Samuel Kyles of Memphis placed a spread over the fallen head of the Southern Christian Leadership Conference. [Kyles was to have hosted a dinner for King and his associates that night before the rally.]

Mr. Abernathy hurried up with a larger towel. And then the aides waited, while policemen rushed up within minutes. In what seemed to be ten or fifteen minutes, an ambulance arrived.

"He had just bent over," Mr. Jackson went on bitterly, "I saw police coming from everywhere. They said, 'Where did it come from?' and I said, 'Behind you.' The police were coming from where the shot came."

Mr. Branch, who is from Chicago, said the shot had come from "the hill on the other side of the street." He added:

"When I looked up, the police and the sheriff's deputies were running all around. The bullet exploded in his face."

"We didn't need to call the police," Mr. Jackson declared, "they were here all over the place."

PART TWO

MARTIN LUTHER KING AND HIS MISSION

Chapter Three

MARTIN AND CORETTA KING

by Dick Gregory

Born: January 15, 1929, a boy child in the city of Atlanta. A black boy child. Of course the birth record in Atlanta was different. They had to put, Born: A boy child. A negro. Few people on this planet were aware that on January 15, 1929, a boy child would be born on this planet Earth to an environment and to a family that would touch the spirit of this boy child to the extent that another spirit would develop. A boy child was born on January 15, 1929. His name was Martin Luther King, Jr.

Martin Luther King reached the lives of each and every black person in America. He also affected the attitudes of nearly all white people living in America. He was loved and he was hated. His name and his face were known to just about every person living in the United States. He had been on the pages of every magazine and newspaper in the country. No other black person in America ever received as much attention in the media as Martin Luther King. The radio and television networks covered each and every demonstration led by King, and they followed the progress of the civil rights movement with dedication. Dr. King was a hero of the press. He was easily accessible to it and he always provided the dramatic impact that a hungry press was anxious for.

At the height of the civil rights movement, one could easily detect the optimism that had swept through black communities around the nation. Phrases such as "Black is Beautiful" and "Hey Brother" became a part of the new sense of black pride. Black people in America were changing. Fear began to disappear from the hearts of many older folks living in the South; for the first time in their lives, many black men and women were not afraid to stand up for their rights, to say to white people what they would no longer tolerate. The end to segregation was a reality because of Martin Luther King. This one man had more impact on the attitudes of black Americans than any other person in contemporary history.

This is not the place to try to give a full-scale biography of Martin Luther King, and still less, the history of the black civil rights movement.

I'd rather try to convey what the man and the movement meant to black people in America. But a few dates and facts may be helpful as background. King was ordained a Baptist minister in 1947. A graduate of Morehouse College, he continued his education also attending Boston University and The Crozer Theological Seminary in Boston, Massachusetts, gaining a Ph.D. in 1955. In 1957, he received a D.D. from the Chicago Theological Seminary. By that time he had already sprung to national prominence for the leading part he played in the black boycott of buses in Montgomery, Alabama, in 1956. This nonviolent protest against the bus lines' mistreatment of black passengers resulted in the jailing of more than ninety black protesters including King. The local court naturally found King guilty. He appealed the decision. Meanwhile, the bus lines, which were going broke, dropped the charges. It was a great victory, both for King and for the principle of nonviolence.

The next year, an impressed Congress passed the first civil rights legislation since 1875, and Martin Luther King founded the Southern Christian Leadership Conference (SCLC), the organization which was to be his main vehicle for promoting black civil rights in the years to come. Through the remaining years of the 1950s and the early 1960s, the SCLC, along with The Congress of Racial Equality (CORE) and the Student Non-Violent Coordinating Committee (SNCC), with the blessings of the older, more established organizations such as National Association for the Advancement of Colored People (NAACP) made the tactic of nonviolent protests as familiar to Americans as their morning breakfast cereal.

In April of 1963, this movement reached a kind of crescendo when Dr. King led an enormous protest march in Birmingham, Alabama. More than 2,500 black demonstrators were arrested. Three months later he led an even bigger march in Washington, D.C. In terms of mass demonstrations, probably the high point of the civil rights movement was that march. I'll deal with both these dramatic events in greater detail in later chapters. Within a year, the most extensive civil rights legislation in United States history, The Civil Rights Act of 1964, had been enacted into law. That same year, King was awarded the Nobel Peace Prize.

During the next four years, King continued his struggle for equality on many fronts, but by 1968 he had become convinced that still another mass demonstration was needed. This was to be The Poor People's March on Washington. He was deeply involved in plans for this event when, in the spring of 1968, he interrupted his work to go to Memphis, Tennessee, to lend his support to the striking sanitation workers there. On April 4, while standing on the balcony of his Memphis motel room, Dr. King was shot and killed. He had made the final sacrifice for the great cause to which he had devoted his life.

But then Martin Luther King had made many sacrifices during the period of time he spent organizing black people and leading demonstrations. He spent a lot of time away from his home in Atlanta, Georgia. His wife Coretta spent many nights alone with their four children. There was not much time for fun and recreation for a man who was putting his whole life into fighting for human rights. Every time Martin Luther King led a march, every time he felt the pain of a police nightstick against his body, and every hour he spent in jail helped black Americans wake up to the problems that existed and helped black America hold its head up high. It was a difficult time in Martin Luther King's life. There were many sleepless nights in strange hotels. There were thousands of strange phone calls and letters criticizing the civil rights movement. There were constant threats of death to Martin Luther King, members of his family, and many of his aides. Every day that Martin Luther King walked the streets, and every night when he lay down to rest, the reality of death was his shadow. But King learned to deal with the notion that death was a possibility, and he knew that fear would only make those around him afraid. King was not fearful of death; at least I can say that I never saw him show the strain and pressure that would normally burden a man faced with such grim prospects. It was his calmness and consistently positive attitude that made those around him feel comfortable. When word of possible danger was made known, Martin Luther King never panicked. He knew how to handle situations with whatever kind of tact was necessary. He was a master when it came to dealing with the pressures that were forever surrounding him. For these reasons, millions of people loved and respected Dr. King. Those who never got a chance to march in a demonstration or see King in person were with him in spirit. They knew him as their leader, and with the help of newspapers and television, Martin Luther King became the most well-known black person in America.

There were, of course, black Americans who felt that the black struggle might be more effective without King's nonviolent approach. Some of them tried to get King to change, but his beliefs were too strong for him to be swayed in any other direction. The efforts of these more radical civil rights advocates were short-lived. Allegiance to Martin Luther King was steadfast. Even through times when it seemed that nonviolence was ineffective, the people who believed in King's methods stood behind him. We used to get a kick out of hearing the Northern black guy who would say ''I can't go down South because I'm too violent.'' Yet this cat was scared to talk back to his own white paper boy! It is ironic that

14

King's nonviolent movement brought on a violent reaction from much of white America. They were reacting to a type of attitude they didn't understand. America is accustomed to using violence as a tool to obtain whatever goal it is trying to reach, and for that reason it could not accept masses of black people acting peacefully in order to get their point across. Many whites felt Martin Luther King must have been planning something else. They just couldn't believe that this nonviolent approach was for real. Examples of the violence that stalked the nonviolent movement were spread throughout King's career. In January of 1956, less than two months after he became leader of the Montgomery, Alabama, bus boycott someone threw a bomb onto the porch of his home; no one was hurt. Two days before Christmas in 1956, blacks and whites rode integrated buses together for the first time. An unidentified gunman fired a shotgun blast into the front door of King's home; there were no injuries. On January 27, 1957, someone threw a bomb on King's porch; it did not explode. On September 3, 1958, King was arrested and charged with loitering while on his way to a Montgomery, Alabama, legal hearing involving his close friend and fellow civil rights advocate, Reverend Ralph D. Abernathy. On November 17, 1958, as Dr. King was signing copies of his new book *Stride Toward Freedom* in a Harlem bookstore, a black woman by the name of Mrs. Izola Ware Curry stabbed him in the chest with a steel letter opener, barely missing his heart. King was hospitalized for thirteen days in a Harlem hospital. On May 21, 1961, a mob of 1,000 angry whites upset over the Freedom Rides menaced Dr. King and 1,500 blacks holding a meeting at the First Baptist Church in Montgomery, Alabama. The National Guard escorted the blacks back to their homes. On September 28, 1962, during a Southern Christian Leadership Conference convention in Birmingham, a man who described himself as a member of the American Nazi Party hit Dr. King in the face twice, causing swelling and bruises. King did not press charges. The man was fined twenty-five dollars and sentenced to thirty days in jail. On June 30, 1963, people who were displeased by his nonviolent policies threw eggs at his car as King went to speak at a Harlem church. On June 18, 1964, Dr. King charged St. Augustine, Florida, police with brutality after they used cattle prods and beat people who tried to desegregate a motel. He asked President Lyndon B. Johnson to send in federal marshals. On January 18, 1965, as Dr. King registered at a previously all-white hotel in Selma, Alabama, a member of the National States Rights Party, punched and kicked him. The twenty-six year old assailant was sentenced to sixty days in jail and fined $100. On August 5, 1966, as Dr. King led marchers past angry white residents of Chicago's Southwest Side, he was struck in the head by a rock. He stumbled, but continued to march. Later a knife thrown at him missed and struck a white youth in the neck. On April 4, 1968, Martin Luther King was killed.

The violence that confronted King from the time he first led the civil rights movement up to the time of his death convinced many blacks to abandon their nonviolent beliefs. Though violence produced only temporary gains, many blacks felt it was the right direction to take. They felt they had been patient too long. It was the white police reaction and response to the rioting and violence that forced many blacks to reconsider King's methods, although they knew that King's way was not just for the benefit of those living, but was aimed at affecting unborn generations of black people.

One of the traits that made Martin Luther King popular as a leader and as a newsmaker was his dynamic speaking ability. He was a brilliant man with a widely diverse educational background and the soul of a country preacher. King reached millions with his echoing voice that made one feel a chill just listening to him. His choice of words was always perfect. He taught the world that it was both morally wrong and psychologically harmful to hate anyone. He believed that hate did more harm to the hater than it did to the hated. He urged people to try to solve the racial problems of the world through love and goodwill. He told parents to teach their children to fight injustice with an open heart and with an open mind. Martin Luther King believed that this was the only solution to the problems that plagued black America.

Despite his constant struggle to unite blacks and whites through nonviolence, and though he lost his life trying, some whites in America refused to give Martin Luther King his due respect. On the day of his funeral in Atlanta, many retail stores did business as usual, completely ignoring the fact that one of the greatest men that had ever lived had been shot to death. Most of white Atlanta was completely uninvolved in the sorrowful memorial that was taking place that day. Two major department stores did close, but many blacks felt it was not out of respect for King, but because they feared violence might break out if they stayed open. Governor Lester Maddox allowed all state employees to go home from work at two o'clock in the afternoon for what he called ''security reasons.'' Many city workers were not required to come in to work at all because their employers were trying to protect them from possible harm from angry blacks. But for blacks who had been around to see Dr. King fight for equality and for an end to segregation, it was a good feeling to see his mule-drawn coffin being pulled down the downtown streets, passing stores and restaurants that King himself had helped to integrate.

There are people who dedicate their lives to helping other people. We seem to take so much from them and give so little in return. We could always criticize Martin, but Martin never criticized the masses. He never complained that the crowds were not large enough, or that there weren't enough people supporting the cause in the black communities. But I guess that's part of being a leader; to lead a group of people who are so hungry for freedom and justice that all they see are the injustices and you. You weren't a man, you weren't a human being. You were something that wasn't supposed to get tired. You weren't supposed to get hungry, you weren't supposed to go to sleep, you weren't supposed to die. We need you; we need you here; we need you there. Hey Martin, come over here and help us. If you would just come they would listen to us. What about the other side? What about the family? Take a few minutes at home. Take the day off Martin, and rest. The family; no, we always forget about that. We talk about Mahatma Gandhi, but who was his wife? Who were his children? You were forced to give us so much. There was another side. There was a Coretta. There was a very warm side. There was Martin the father, Martin the husband. And it's like every other human being who meets another human being, and falls in love and gets married.

When Martin Luther King first met Coretta Scott they were both in Boston. It was 1951. She was twenty-four years old, fresh out of Antioch College and studying at the New England Conservatory of Music. King was working on his doctorate degree in theology at Boston University. After two years of dating, they were married. Coretta Scott had thought earlier, and had even said to her friends, that she and Martin would probably not think seriously of marriage. She was an accomplished concert singer and didn't think that being the wife of a minister would be her style. But, she soon changed her mind. They were married at her parents' home in Marion, Alabama. Their first child, Yolanda, was born two years later. Just two weeks after her birth, the Montgomery bus boycott began, and with it, the start of King's rapid rise to leadership and prominence. The couple's first son, Martin Luther King III, was born in 1958, followed by Dexter three years later, and Bernice in 1963. Coretta King spent a lot of time at home with the children during their preschool years. She spent her free time with local club work and singing with her church choir.

Coretta King was deeply involved in her husband's work. She taught their children about the civil rights movement and the importance of their father's involvement in it. She took her knowledge of the civil rights movement and expanded her own ideas. She was a member of the Women Strike for Peace movement where she, along with fifty other American women, went to the seventeen-nation disarmament conference in Geneva to encourage world peace. She even used her talents as a singer to benefit the movement. Not long after Martin Luther King was awarded the Nobel Peace Prize his wife said, "My life is either the church or the struggle for civil rights." Mrs. King did a series of cross-country freedom concerts which were solo singing engagements to raise money for the Southern Christian Leadership Conference. From 1965 until Martin Luther King's death, Coretta King barely saw a day pass without the threat of death surrounding her husband. She developed a philosophy that helped her live with the reality that he could be killed because of his commitment to the human struggle. She said, "If something does happen, it would be a great way to give oneself to a great cause."

Coretta King became involved in nearly every activity that her husband took part in; even after his death she continued to emphasize the need to carry on the movement. The Southern Christian Leadership Conference named her to its board of directors. Many felt that she would now emerge to carry on King's work. But those who knew Coretta King knew that she had always been out in front during all the demonstrations, during all the sit-ins, and throughout the entire movement. She was never just a behind-the-scenes companion. Coretta King was a strong, black woman who had long realized the necessity of her husband's work. She also knew the importance of her own association with it. She had stamina and patience. She was able to see ahead just as her husband did, to the time when injustice and segregation would be a thing of the past. It was this vision and the hope of a brighter tomorrow that allowed her to stand beside Martin Luther King in his fight for a better world.

Coretta King had suffered many periods of fear and grief long before her husband was killed. When King was stabbed she had flown to New York City to be with him. She always told the children what was going on, and she prepared herself for anything that could happen. She fully realized that danger was indeed a part of her husband's sacrifice.

Coretta King had become a well-known figure in the civil rights movement. Her name was a symbol of dignity, and her face mirrored the reflections of a woman dedicated to building her life around helping to solve the problems of the poor and the unfortunate. Coretta King's reputation as a hard worker with a genuine desire to keep the movement strong was evident as one read newspapers and listened to the news on television and radio. Reporters were beginning to mention her more and more, and many discovered that Coretta King provided a separate story, but one which would lead back to her husband—a story that would explain how important it was that she existed, how relevant she was to the entire civil rights struggle. Americans know who Martin Luther King's wife was because she made herself known through her involvement with him and with the movement. But it wasn't only this involvement that made her stand out. There were other wives of civil rights leaders who marched and demonstrated; even others who went to jail fighting for an end to segregation and racial inequality. I'm sure Coretta King helped to give these other wives strength and courage.

Chapter Four

KING AND KENNEDY CALL
by Dick Gregory

In May 1963 I received a call from Martin Luther King asking me to come to Birmingham. Then I received a call from President John F. Kennedy, asking me not to go.

I was at the height of my show business career and my involvement in the civil rights movement had grown to the point where I had become aware of a lot of things I was never aware of before. In the early days of the civil rights movement, I would get phone calls to come down South and perform. I had all the normal fears that one would have about going into the South. I had been told about the Ku Klux Klan, but the connection between the KKK, and the police, and the federal agencies had never been established. I think that was probably the most horrifying thing for me to find out—that it wasn't just the Klan.

Then I really started realizing the problems that black folks have in the South. I mean, that once the arm of the law grabs you, there is no way out. They could make you say things that you didn't want to say. They could say, "We can do this to your family; we can do this to your mother; we can get your wife fired from her job; or your father fired; or you're going to lose your home." It's amazing that the black folks had the strength and courage to stand up and push, because in America's wildest imagination, we could hardly believe that many of the things that were happening, actually happened. America could see the beatings and the jailings, but the political maneuvers behind the scenes were just as vicious and they fascinated me almost as much as they bothered me. It fascinated me when I went South, as informed as I always thought I was. It was almost as if I was not an American black, but was living on another planet, listening to someone say, "This is the way they treat them people."

Of course, it didn't just happen where it was obvious, as in Georgia,

20

Alabama, and Mississippi; it happened all over the country. Probably the one big difference between the black reaction in the North and the black reaction in the South was that black folks in the North weren't scared to walk down the street. This is the reason that the civil rights movement wasn't as effective up North—because we tried to use the same tactics that they were using in the South. The tactic in the South was to get a large crowd to walk down the street, because black people there were scared to walk down the street alone. This same tactic was followed in the North; we could have used ninety percent of our energy doing other things.

We were really trying to get that crowd to improve the news coverage. The one thing the press always asked us was, "How many people do you think you'll have for the demonstration?" For the evening news they had certain deadlines, and so they would come up and ask us to demonstrate early so it could be on the evening news. The press was managing our affairs, making things happen.

There was a certain type of closeness, in a hostile way, between black and white folks in the South. The whites had to dislike blacks for what was going on, but in the process of change, blacks became human. The movement started exposing our feelings, and making us human to the whites. When you are ill and your body goes numb, and then you start healing, you start tingling and the numbness gives way to real feeling again. I looked at the events, at black people showing their feelings, and saw a certain amount of beauty because years from now it would be different.

I knew the effect that those Southern street demonstrations were having on the young white kids. They would say, "Mommy, how come they let us treat them like that?" There was no more saying, "Oh, they're happy." There was no more Beulah singing in the kitchen. The old black man who worked around the house used to smile because his true feelings were hidden from white America. Now those feelings weren't hidden anymore.

There was an individual emerging who was becoming more than just a leader to black folks. Martin Luther King was more than just a leader in America—he was recognized worldwide. I started feeling the power and the effect of Martin by the way people talked of him. As much as certain people in the system tried to put him down, they always dealt with him with respect because of the way he carried himself. He was always the same.

I had such respect for everybody in the movement, I would never go to a demonstration until I was asked, and I would always call the leadership so they wouldn't think they were infringing on me because they looked at me as a celebrity. When I would go someplace, the cameras would go. I didn't want to go in without being officially invited. The first thing I would do, when I got into town, was brief myself, because the press would tend to walk away from the local leaders and start asking me questions. In the process of doing this, I became very familiar with situations. When I was picked up at the airport, they put it in my ear—what's happening, who's in jail, what the situation is.

King asked me to come to Birmingham, and I said, "Yes, Martin, I'll come." There had been strong rumors that the Birmingham problem was about to be resolved. President Kennedy and the city officials had worked out a deal, and there was speculation that King might be jumping the gun and ruining the deal. But I felt good because I was tired of white folks working out deals for black folks and I felt that King had to be in Birmingham and had to lead that movement. Whatever deal might have been worked out was no more.

We were to come in and solve this problem. The big problem in Birmingham was the police—Sheriff Bull Connor among others—and they became one of the main issues.

Arthur Hanes, the mayor of Birmingham, wasn't an issue to me because I didn't confront his side of the city. I confronted the Bull Connor street demonstration side—the hoses. The fire hoses had a tremendous effect on me because I had always loved firemen, and I used to follow firemen. I felt that the fire departments in America were making a mistake not to disassociate themselves from the white government. This eventually proved to be true, because in the North, when the firemen answered an alarm in the black community, bricks were thrown at them—at black and white firemen. The firemen couldn't be disassociated from the hosings down South. You kind of expected it from the police, but not from firemen. Firemen always seemed to have been good guys.

Firemen and fire hoses have become symbolic of black repression. This is the first time it ever hit us blacks; it had never happened before. This was the first time hoses were used against us. They had been used often in America's history, for crowd control, but now they were used against people who had thought firemen were heroes. The force of the hoses would sweep those kids around the corner.

The most horrible photograph that came out of Birmingham was that of the dog biting the black man in the rump, grabbing his pants. They tell me that he was one of the few blacks who didn't get bitten. It just made a beautiful picture. All the dog got was the pants, but that picture had a most significant effect on black folks and their relationship with dogs. The older black person always had to have a dog. *Someone* had to be below you. To watch dogs kiss folks on television really turned off black folk, because we had to keep that dog *a dog*. The dog had to eat the scraps, the dog could never be caught up on the couch and *the dog was the dog*.

Until Birmingham, the largest percentage of false alarms turned in, in major cities in America, were in black communities. This was before black folks started outnumbering white folks all through the cities, and living in distinct areas. There was something so beautiful, peaceful, and competent about the firemen's attitudes that you'd put in false alarms just to have them show up. After Birmingham, the false alarms decreased considerably in the black communities; it became something that you didn't want to see. The firemen and dogs are just examples of the tremendous emotional impact of the events in Birmingham.

When I got the call from Martin and he asked me if I would come down, I said, "Yes, Martin, I'll come." I was always scared when I had to go into the South—not the type of scared so that you wouldn't go, but the type of scared knowing that it can be your last time; you can be killed. The FBI, and the local police, and the state police were so vicious that anything could happen. My secret ambition, when I was a kid, was to be an FBI agent. I thought that was the epitome—higher than a fireman —and then the whole scene crumbled. I could see the FBI doing illegal things. No one had to tell me about it; I watched it happening.

When I went into Birmingham, what a funny feeling—only white police met me and asked me a bunch of questions when I got off the plane. The hostility from the press was unbelievable. Black folks had always accepted the white press as being factual. We were never in it so we could never document it if it wasn't factual. Until the civil rights movement, during which we started seeing our news being twisted and turned around, with hostile, vicious headlines, we had believed in the white press.

All over the world, Birmingham was making front pages—but in Birmingham, the stuff wasn't on the front page, it was on page three or four. The front page was just business as usual.

I had told Martin I would be there, and that a very interesting thing had happened. I had gotten a call from President Kennedy, but wasn't at home at the time. It was really interesting because Lil, my wife, said when I came home, "Where have you been!" She never snapped at me like that. I said, "Well, why?" She said, "Because President Kennedy has been trying to get you—he's called this house three or four times." I said, "I don't want to talk to him." Lil said, "He said he's going to wait up at the White House until you call him." I said, "But it's three o'clock in the morning, he's not going to wait up, no way, he's probably got a tie line anywhere he is—you really think he's waiting up in the White House?'' She said, ''Yes, I talked to him personally and he told me it is very important that he talk to you.'' So I said, ''I don't want to talk to him anyway.'' I was getting ready to go to bed and she really had an attitude. She said, ''Well, you're not going to bed—you're not going to sleep.''

I really don't want to say I was drunk, because my life has changed so much, but I was. I'd been out drinking all day and Lil said, ''Well, you're not going to sleep until you call the President.''

Many years later, when Gerald Ford was in the White House, a call came from the White House; I wasn't home. About a week later a letter came from the White House saying they had called, that the President had wanted to ask Dick Gregory about something, and Lil said, ''Oh, God, I can't believe I forgot the White House, I meant to tell you the White House had called!'' I thought about the time Kennedy had called. I said to Lil, ''I would never have thought that there would be a day the White House would call and you would just forget about it.'' I guess that's growing up, or whatever you would call it.

I had to call President Kennedy, though, that night. The note said, ''Call Operator 18, Washington, D.C., the White House,'' and so I called Operator 18. I really was surprised, because when I said, ''Dick Gregory,'' Kennedy said, ''Oh, yes, Dick, I've been waiting for your call. I have a problem and I wonder if you'll help me with it?''

Martin had announced that I was going to Birmingham. President Kennedy said, ''Do me a favor and don't go down to Birmingham, because I feel that Dr. King is wrong. We reached a settlement there, and everything is going to be fine—your going there will create problems.'' So I said, ''I know Dr. King, and I know a lot of things are changing in the South that never started changing until Dr. King got involved. So I told Dr. King I'm coming down, and I'm going down, and I don't think he would have called me if he didn't need me and the last person who is going to put me in a trick is Dr. King.'' The President said that he wished that I wouldn't go. Then he said, ''Why don't you just wait for seven days? I'm sure the whole problem will be solved.'' I said, ''I told Dr. King that I'm going on Monday, and that's tomorrow—and I'm going.

''I want to go, you know. When I see what's happening to black folks on television, with the news, and the fire hoses, and whatever deal between white folks that's been made, the streets are where I need to be, and where I'm going.'' And Kennedy said, ''Well, I'm sorry you feel that way, Dick, but thanks for returning my call.'' Next day I got on a plane and flew to Birmingham with Jim Sanders, a brilliant comedy writer. All through the South, he was always with me. He was always arrested with me, but never got his name mentioned in the paper. When we got off the plane and met with King's people, I said that I really had to meet with Martin and tell him about the call I had from the President, because I thought it was serious and that there might be danger when we got to the 16th Street Baptist Church rallying point.

Chapter Five

BIRMINGHAM
by Dick Gregory

When we arrived at the church, I had a strange feeling, seeing the police surrounding the church. I think it went back to my childhood. My mother had told me about the lions eating the Christians and I thought that that period would never recur in history. I thought no one would ever violate the church. But then I saw the way the cops surrounded the church and realized how dangerous it could become to them if it were used as a water trough where people could gather to drink up the ideas of change. The church leaders said, "Until we rid ourselves of certain pressures, we will never find our true spiritual power." We can be happy belonging to an organized religion—it helps us put off the battle, it comforts us. But there's a universal God inside us and there are certain things that the inside of us will not tolerate, even if it means a confrontation to the extent of injury or death.

While I observed the activities in the church, my fear left me. I looked outside the church and what had been hate, and bigotry, and white evilness became fear. I was seeing the same expressions on their faces that I used to see on black folks' faces. They were afraid because officers of the law, knowing what a potential danger one person is, were now dealing with thousands, and, not knowing and not understanding non-violence, saw black folks losing their fear. The power was turning, and the police and their dogs were in trouble.

Those cops who "knew their niggers" suddenly realized that maybe they didn't know them. Cops used to say to black folk, "Get on down the street, boy," and now some black folks said, "Maybe I'm not going on down the street." The Southern cop was forced to do something that he had never done before; to deal with black folks that weren't scared, that couldn't be intimidated. Nobody seemed to mind getting bitten by a dog when there were three thousand people around to help.

A leadership was being developed that was above and beyond mere celebrity; Martin Luther King, the Southern Christian Leadership Conference (SCLC), and young people with new, different minds. Black kids listened to the news and gained a new awareness—their conscious mind was no longer locked into getting off the street when they saw white folks coming. Black folks got off the street not necessarily because all white folks wanted them to do that, but they didn't know which ones did and which ones didn't. I was looking out of the church at those cops, waiting to tell Dr. King about the call from the President, when someone said, "We've got a big march ready to leave, and we're trying to hold it, but the kids won't wait. The kids won't wait, and they're ready to go and take the streets downtown."

There were all groups and ages, but most of them were kids. I got arrested with one kid who was four years old. The whole town was under siege. This time, it was not business as usual in the whole town, white or black. Birmingham was the biggest thing happening in the world, on this planet Earth, and everybody was coming in from all over the world to cover it. Jim Sanders and I had to run out of the church to get in front of the group, and no sooner had we stepped off the sidewalk and walked across the street than we were arrested.

We were arrested for parading without a permit, but they didn't tell us at that time what the charge was. They just said, "You're under arrest," and they lined up the paddy wagons, and arrested close to 800 people at that particular affair.

There were so many blacks in the jail, this was the first time most of the niggers in Birmingham were eating good. There was a strong white reaction to the mass jailings; everybody was afraid. "What are we going to do with these blacks in jail? Do we feed them, and what about the whites there?" There was a big debate about whether we were going to get fed. The paper work of arresting so many was mountainous.

A white detective came over to me and said, "Dick Gregory, I'd like to talk to you. This is just a job for me but I really admire what you're doing and I know from what I see here that this whole thing is going to break. I'm one of the people who will be glad, but I have a job, and a wife, and a family, so I guess I'm part of it. I'm going to tell you about your rights, and I have some questions that I want to ask you, and you don't have to answer." I said, "I don't mind answering." "You don't have to. Do you understand your rights?" and he read them to me. "Do you choose to answer these questions?" I said "Yes." I sat down and it almost turned into a comedy. He thought I would be hostile with him after he had poured his whole soul out and that was a heck of a thing for a white cat to do.

He said, "What's your name?" I told him, "You know." "Where

do you live?'' I told him. He said, ''At what time did you get arrested?'' I said, ''I don't know.'' He approximated a time. He asked, ''What street did you get arrested on?'' I said, ''I don't know.'' He stared at me. ''What was the name of the church that you came from?'' At that time I didn't know, having just gotten to town. I said I didn't know. The detective said, ''Well, who were the people you were arrested with?''

I said, ''Jim Sanders, who came to town with me.'' The detective asked, ''Where's he from?'' ''Chicago,'' I answered. He asked, ''Who were the local people?'' I said, ''I don't know 'em.'' He began to think I was pulling his leg—he *really* thought this and he really had an attitude because he said, ''Now, wait a minute, I told you you didn't have to answer any questions, and you told me you wanted to.'' I said, ''You really won't believe this, but I don't know anything. I just got off the plane and I haven't been in this town an hour and here I'm in jail now.''

We were moved into the cell block, and rumors started that King had been killed and that there were bombings in town. None of this was happening at that time but these were things that people were bringing back to us. There were more rumors from people in jail, and we were worried about being hungry, and then they told us King was arrested. When you're in jail, you're totally out of the mainstream. You can't find out anything for yourself. The jail kept getting more and more crowded. That day I think two thousand people were arrested.

The youngest kid in jail was about four, sucking his thumb. I got to thinking about my kids at home, and I walked over to this little kid, and asked him his name, and he told me, and I asked him what he was in for, and he tried to say ''Freedom'' but he couldn't; all he could say was ''Teedom.'' He just looked around at the rest of the people in the cells, and everybody ignored him; he stood there by himself, sucking his thumb. He was waiting for his mother to come and get him. I don't even know if his mother knew he was there.

The biggest crowds we had were young people. I was way back in the cell block, and there was a commotion up front. I told Jim Sanders, ''I'm going up front to see what's going on.''

Somebody was coming into the cell block, and the young kids wouldn't let them close the door. That's when I went up to the front of the cell block, and the jailer was yelling, ''You close this door! We'll get this door closed!'' He ran out, and I said to the youngsters, ''You know we're really not in here to hassle around this door, so we better just close this door.'' The kids moved back, and I stood next to the door, with my hands around the bars, and forgot that I was in jail. I was at home with the kids and Lillian, and I had drifted out of that jail cell in my mind; meanwhile

28

the jailer had just come back with help to get the cell door closed. I was the only person standing up there and he hit me across the knuckles. I had my hands around the bars, and when he hit me with that nightstick, I still didn't realize I was in jail. I opened up the cell door and leaped out on him and spit in his face and balled up my fists and knocked him down and—God, what did I do that for? They ran outside, and came back in with baseball bats, and cue sticks, and just about anything you could think of and I was fighting for my life. I'm sure the only reason I wasn't killed was that the hallway was too narrow and no one could draw back on me, and there were too many cops in there. There were about twenty-five, all shouting and beating me.

The door opened to a small hallway which led to a larger passageway. The kids started pouring out of the open cell door, and then the battle was really on. I was trying to stop the jailers, yelling, "Wait a minute, man!" and they didn't want to hear anything from me. We battled our way all the way into an office outside. Then there was screaming about a jail break, and somehow we ended up fighting back inside. I kept telling the kids to get back in the jail, and we pushed our way back in. I fell unconscious in the hallway and they just pulled me back into the cell.

The jailers were scared to come in. As long as we were back in the cell block, they were happy; they would settle for that. I went to the back of the cell and Jim Sanders said, "Damn, man, they just finished whopping somebody's ass up front," and I said, "That somebody's ass was whopped was mine!" We sat and talked the rest of the night in the cell, dozing on and off. When I woke, my arm was swollen; I had been severely battered. My hand, arm, neck and back were swollen and the kids were really concerned then because they saw how big my arm had gotten and knew the pain I was in.

The rumors started getting out about my beating, and people outside started hearing about it. That morning the federal agents came in from the Justice Department and asked me what had happened. I told them that I had been beaten up in the jail and then they decided to let me out. King had decided to come out. I didn't want to go to the doctor there and I didn't want to talk to the government. I did not want to talk to the agents but I knew I had to talk with someone because of the call from the White House. Then I decided to fly to Chicago and hold a press conference and tell what happened, and how I felt that the White House was not living up to its duty to show that this was not going to be tolerated any more.

At first, no federal troops came in; Kennedy's policy was strictly hands off. Finally, after many arrests, they knew our civil rights had been violated, and the federal government could get involved. I finally talked to the FBI in Chicago, went back to Birmingham, and stayed a week. There was so much going on; a lot of violence, and a lot of innocent people getting beaten up, and a lot of people losing their jobs.

I saw Martin Luther King at the Gaston Motel, which was bombed, but fortunately he had quietly left the day before. The Gaston Motel was his headquarters. I looked at the police around the motel and questioned the people around me to see if it was safe enough. There were so many bombings, and other violence, that I had a premonition. This was before the 16th Street Baptist Church got blown up, when the four little girls were killed.

Angela Davis went to that church as a little girl. Those were her friends that were killed. Nobody knows that side of the story; they just know Angela grown, but she's from Birmingham and that was her church and those were her friends that were killed.

I was invited to the home of A. D. King, Martin's brother, in Birmingham. His house was also bombed. I was considered a celebrity, and people invited me into their homes because they wanted to know what was going on in the world, how the movement was viewed outside of the South, and what other celebrities would be coming down to help. When I went to A. D.'s house for dinner, there were police sitting outside. Every black leader's home was surrounded by police.

Nothing could happen to A. D. unless the police were involved. They were watching the house. If SCLC headquarters were blown up, officers would be nearby. It was impossible for anyone to do anything without the police knowing about it. There were so many of them around.

The Gaston Motel was the nerve center, for a while, of the Birmingham movement. At the meetings were Fred Shuttlesworth, Ralph Abernathy, Hosea Williams, C. T. Vivian, of course Martin, and a great force, Jim Bevel. Many other people came in and out. I told King at the Gaston that I was worried about the police attitude around the motel. I thought that anytime that motel could go up in smoke, and wondered if there were enough security personnel. Martin said that he felt there was enough security. I didn't feel scared but I felt that the whole motel would go up in smoke and kill everybody in it.

I never understood why the federal government would tolerate the illegal actions of the local and state police. The intimidation of the black population could be seen. In most places, it was the white mob you had to worry about; in Birmingham, it was the police. What would happen to people who live in Birmingham after all this was over with, with that kind of hatred in the police department? What would happen to blacks who had to testify in various trials?

There was no doubt that the problem was going to be resolved. It was costing Birmingham too much money, and costing America too much prestige. Everything changed from that time in Birmingham, the turning point in the civil rights movement. The things that finally got all the black folks involved were things that shocked black folks—the fire hoses, the dogs, and children being beaten and jailed.

We knew that things would happen to the martyrs, to King and the leadership, but seeing dogs bite children, and fire hoses knocking down little kids—this was more than any normal person could take. It was a reaction against white America, against white, racist America. America had to deal with what would happen to her children. White Americans could easily hate an evil, militant black cat who was making demands on folks, and even some black folks didn't like that; but when it came to hurting children, Birmingham was the turning point in the movement.

Martin asked me to come to Birmingham and the President asked me not to go. The black folks in Birmingham were doing more than they should, and it was time for me to do what I could. So I said, "Yes, Martin, I'll come."

Chapter Six

"PEARLS BEFORE SWINE"

by Mark Lane

On May 10, 1963, it appeared that peace might come to the embattled city of Birmingham, Alabama. The two score bombings that had torn apart the city and set whites and blacks against each other passionately were, it was thought, a remembrance of a troubled and violent recent past. As homes, and churches, and meeting halls owned by blacks had been blown to pieces by dynamite, the anger of the black community began to focus upon the failure of the local and federal police authorities to determine who had planted a single bomb. Arthur Hanes, the Mayor of Birmingham and one of its leading segregationists, had been an FBI agent. Years later testimony revealed that the FBI itself had played a part in the campaign to elect him Mayor. When the bombings began, there was hope that Clarence Kelley, the newly-appointed Special-Agent-in-Charge of the FBI office in Birmingham, would act. However, during the years he occupied that position, not a single bomber was found, not a single case was solved. After Mr. Kelley moved to a new assignment, as Special-Agent-in-Charge of the FBI office in Memphis, Tennessee, his successor in Birmingham was no more effective.

Dr. King and his associates and the thousands who had witnessed for equality by marching in the streets of Birmingham, by kneeling-in in segregated churches, and by demonstrating at its city jail the previous month, had won a victory. The walls of apartheid had cracked and Birmingham, previously denounced by Dr. King as "the most thoroughly segregated big city in America," had at last agreed to change.

Dr. King greeted the new moment with a new approach. He said, "The city of Birmingham has reached an accord with its conscience. The acceptance of responsibility by local white and Negro leadership offers an example of a free people uniting to meet and solve their problems." He called upon the black community in Birmingham to "accept this achievement in the right spirit" and to understand that it was not that they had won a narrow victory but rather that a victory had been won "for democracy and the whole citizenry of Birmingham." Dr. King added, "We must respond to every new development in civil rights with an understanding of those who have opposed us, and with an appreciation of the new adjustments that the new achievements pose for them."

The same page of the *Birmingham News* that carried those concilia-tory and healing words also reported that United States Senator Lister Hill urged President John F. Kennedy and Attorney General Robert F. Ken-nedy to use their "influence and power" to remove Dr. King, Dick Gregory, and other "outside agitators" from Birmingham, charging "that these professional agitators have provoked and led demonstrations and lawlessness in open defiance of state and local laws and court orders."

The *Birmingham News* that day also carried a headline announcing "All But 119 of Arrested Children Free." The story reported that most of the 1,400 children arrested the previous week in demonstrations had been released on a $300 bond while some children remained in the county jail and others at "emergency quarters at the State Fair Grounds."

Another story on the same page said that "a special report from the Jefferson County Grand Jury commended the Birmingham police de-partment, and Sheriff Mel Bailey and his officers 'for the fine manner in which they have carried out their duties in the difficult situation which has existed here the last several days.' The commendation signed by the grand jury foreman stated 'We feel fortunate in having law enforcement officers of this caliber.' " One column removed from the commendation release was the news story that an FBI investigation was underway into the beating of Dick Gregory in the Birmingham Jail. Clearly all was not well in the city but Dr. King, buoyed by the agreement, was hopeful that it signified change.

Reverend Wyatt Tee Walker, the executive director of the Southern Christian Leadership Conference, was concerned that the new agreement might further anger some segregationists and drive them to acts of violence. When several white men were observed, according to Reverend Walker, "casing the Gaston Motel" late that evening, he reported that activity to the police and asked for police protection. The Birmingham police officials agreed to "keep a watch on the motel."

Later that evening Roosevelt Tatum, a black resident of Birmingham, was in the vicinity of 12th Street and Avenue H. He reported that at approximately 11:30 P.M. he saw a police car slow down and then park on 12th Street directly in front of the residence of the Reverend A. D. King.

Tatum said that "a uniformed police officer . . . got out of the car, [and] walked behind the police car to Reverend King's house."

Tatum said that because he was curious about this late night visit by the local police to the home of Martin Luther King's brother, he remained in the shadows silently observing the events that were unfolding before him. The officer, according to Tatum, "walked to the front porch, at a moderate pace, stooped and placed a package at the right side of the steps of Reverend King's house," ran back to the car and entered it. Then "the driver of the police car tossed something out the window of the auto" and it landed, Tatum said, "approximately two or three feet from the sidewalk directly in front of the King residence." Almost immediately after the object landed there was an explosion that Tatum said knocked him to the ground. A second explosion took place. Tatum said he stood up, and as he approached the wreckage, saw a police car arrive "as if they were investigating." The two dynamite bombs had been effective. They demolished a corner of the home, and blew off almost half the roof and the living room wall.

At approximately the same time that dynamite tore apart the residence of A. D. King, the area in the Gaston Motel where his brother, Martin, had been staying was destroyed by another powerful dynamite blast. Two bombs exploded there, one through the registration office wall, directly below Room 30 where Dr. Martin Luther King, Jr., had been staying. Three women and a man were injured by this blast at the Gaston Motel. Dr. King had left the motel earlier to return to Atlanta.

According to some observers, Roosevelt Tatum entered into what was left of the King house and helped the children escape through the wreckage. Later Tatum told A. D. King what he had seen immediately before the explosions. A. D. King telephoned the FBI office in Birmingham and two agents reported to Reverend King's house to meet Tatum. They took him to the FBI office and immediately began to question him.

We may never know the presumed target of those Saturday night bombings in Birmingham since it is difficult to enter into the disturbed minds of the bombers and to know what their thinking process may have been. However, to many in the black community of Birmingham, it seemed apparent that attempts had been made to assassinate Dr. Martin Luther King, Jr.

The agreement for peace had been abrogated and for five hours hundreds of angry blacks filled the streets. It was Saturday night and the bars had been serving for hours a local homemade brew, called *Joe Louis* to describe its knockout potential. As the police moved into the streets they were targets of rocks and bricks. A white-owned taxicab was turned over and set on fire. The police reinforcements arrived with the dreaded police dogs. This time the anger and the resolve of the blacks was so high that the dogs, used to intimidate and assault the demonstrators during the previous weeks, merely provoked more anger and greater resolve. The police almost immediately withdrew the dogs. The response to the possible attempt upon the life of Dr. King was but a precursor on a local level of what was to come to the nation five years later on April 4, 1968. It made, therefore, the response to Dr. King's murder almost predictable. President Kennedy, alarmed by the bombings and by the reaction to them, issued a statement on Sunday in which he said that he was sending Assistant Attorney General Burke Marshall to Birmingham that evening to join with Assistant Deputy Attorney General Joseph Dolan and other Justice Department officials he had sent to Birmingham that morning. He said that he had also instructed Secretary of Defense Robert McNamara "to alert units of the armed forces trained in riot control and to dispatch selected units to military bases in the vicinity of Birmingham."

In addition, President Kennedy nationalized the Alabama National Guard. He explained these emergency actions by stating "I am deeply concerned about the events which occurred in Birmingham, Alabama, last night. The home of Reverend A. D. King was bombed and badly damaged. Shortly thereafter, the A. G. Gaston Motel was also bombed. These occurrences led to rioting, personal injury, property damage and various reports of violence and brutality." The response to the bombings by the President and his action in immediately sending high-level Department of Justice officials to the scene, together with the presence of a frightened but determined eyewitness to one of the bombings, gave the leaders of the movement the impression that, at long last, law and order might return to Birmingham.

Martin King returned with plans to lay nonviolent siege to the city. Together with Reverend Fred Shuttlesworth he prepared a bill of rights for Birmingham residents, including equal job opportunities in the large white-owned department stores, a realistic schedule for school desegregation, immediate lunch counter integration, and the appointment of a committee of blacks and whites to discuss the ongoing problems.

Two hundred and fifty blacks sought service at various lunch counters. Sheriff Bull Connor said he would "fill the jail full" and twenty demonstrators were arrested that day. The next day they were sentenced to six months in jail, the maximum provided by the trespassing statute. Other store owners declined to call the police and Bull Connor, powerless to make further arrests, said "We had to let them sit in. It's a disgrace." However, before the week was over more than seventy-five nonviolent demonstrators had been arrested. Some blacks and many white liberals urged Dr. King to leave town and initiate a thirty-day truce. But Martin King, his belief in the white legal structure more tenuous than ever before, pressed on. Easter was approaching and he urged blacks not to purchase new outfits, to boycott the downtown stores, and to attend church on Easter Sunday in blue jeans. He said that he would remain in Birmingham. "The time is always wrong for some people," he said. "The cup of endurance has run over."

The importance of Roosevelt Tatum's statement was not lost upon the federal authorities in Washington. As the Klan rallied in Birmingham and as Dr. King proclaimed that the time would never be more right for a commitment to nonviolent action, Tatum was taken to the office of an Assistant Attorney General in Washington and questioned at length. He said that for three days beginning on Tuesday, May 14, he was interrogated by Justice Department employees and two men he could describe only as "Washington lawyers." He also said that a member of Congress from New York was present during part of the questioning.

Upon his return Tatum was questioned by FBI agents in the Birmingham office and subjected to polygraph examination. He later reported upon what he considered to be the odd conduct of the agents who had administered the "lie detector" test. They had, he said, told him to answer each question negatively so that they could get a proper reading when he did not tell the truth. Because the questions he was asked did not pertain to the events that he observed on the evening of May 11, he said he was not suspicious at the time. He was told, he recalled later, to answer "no" to all questions about his "family life" and "the names of his children." He said he did so, and when the polygraph examination was completed the agents required him to sign a statement admitting that he had made false statements. He said he was told that if he did not do so he would be prosecuted. He signed the statement.

Tatum had been employed at the Choctaw Pipe Company. His closest friend was his roommate and fellow worker at the pipe company, Morris Teasley. Teasley offered a form of corroboration for many of Tatum's observations. On May 12, Tatum told him that he had seen the police officers place and throw the dynamite at the King house. Teasley recalled that Tatum told him how he had been tricked into making false statements during the polygraph examination. One example Teasley recalled was that Tatum said that he was told by the agent, "When we ask you if you have a child named 'Bronco' you say no." When Tatum was asked that question he told Teasley that he answered "no" and then the agent said that he could send him to jail for lying. Teasley observed, "They tricked him on that. But why? But why?"

On June 27, a federal grand jury was drawn in Birmingham for the United States District Court for the Northern District of Alabama. The drawing had been scheduled for July and the premature move was marked by another departure from custom. A deputy marshal is traditionally assigned to conduct that routine task. On this occasion the U.S. Marshal, Peyton Norville, selected the names of the jurors himself in the court of U.S. District Court Judge Clarence Allgood. Later in a conversation with Chief Deputy U.S. Marshal Daniel Moore, Norville said "Well, I have put my son-in-law on the grand jury." According to Moore, Norville explained to him that he had just "written in his name at the bottom of the list. I didn't select it. I just wrote it in."

In a subsequent investigation into a peripheral matter (an effort to remove Chief Deputy Moore for "speaking out too freely, particularly with regard to the illegal manipulation of the grand jury"), a Department of Justice report to the Administrative Assistant Attorney General confirmed the charge that "the then Marshal, Mr. Norville, knowing his son-in-law to be a qualified voter, wrote his name on a piece of paper and put it into the box."

Moore later said that he believed that the grand jury had been organized improperly for one reason. "It was," he told me, "to get Tatum. To indict him. He was a problem. They had to get him out of the way."

On July 26, 1963, Macon Weaver, the United States Attorney with jurisdiction in Birmingham wrote to the Department of Justice "requesting authority to prosecute one Roosevelt Tatum 'for making false statements to the FBI.' " Upon receipt of that request Assistant Attorney General Herbert J. Miller, Jr., responded for the Department of Justice. He wrote that the Department had concluded that "this is not an appropriate vehicle for prosecution" and advised against the prosecution of Roosevelt Tatum as recommended by the local federal authorities under Title 18, Section 1001.

The grand jury convened in Birmingham, nevertheless, and indicted Roosevelt Tatum. The minutes remain secret but an attorney, Orzell Billingsley, who represented Tatum was permitted to read them a decade ago and make contemporaneous notes. The notes reveal that among the witnesses to appear before the grand jury was James Edward Lay, a Civil Defense Captain, who said that "the Negro population of the City of Birmingham is under my supervision," and testified that "it is not the prevailing view by Negroes that the bombing was done by police officers."

A police officer who drove a police car apparently testified that he was at the scene "before the second explosion" and that he did not normally patrol the area involved.

The first FBI agent to testify said that Tatum had told him of his observations on May 11, the night of the bombing. The same agent was later recalled to state that he talked with Tatum on July 3.

Another witness testified that he lived near A. D. King's house and that he did see a police car parked in front of that house. He said he saw only one officer in the car at that time.

Another local FBI agent testified about his "investigation of Negroes" and about "their resentment."

The FBI polygraph examiner, brought in from his assignment in Memphis, testified that he did ask a series of routine questions of Tatum "about his family" and "other routine things" and that he did talk with Tatum "for about one hour before the examination was given."

It appeared that substantial portions of Tatum's statement had received some corroboration even by hostile witnesses before a hostile grand jury. A police car was in the area, although not ordinarily assigned to patrol that area. It was parked in front of the King residence and when it was observed by one witness at that time there was only one occupant in it. Tatum was talked to at length before the polygraph examination was given and was asked routine questions about his family at the outset of the examination. Together with the direction from the Department of Justice not to prosecute, the improper selection of the grand jury, and the inflammatory and irrelevant information submitted to the grand jury, it seemed very unlikely that Tatum could be indicted.

On August 20 the home of Arthur Shores was bombed in Birmingham. Shores, a black lawyer, had represented two black students who had enrolled earlier that summer at the University of Alabama. Following that bombing U.S. Attorney Macon Weaver issued a public statement. The federal authorities in Birmingham had until that time been unable to solve a single bombing. Now Weaver felt that he had at last located a certifiable culprit. The *Birmingham News* carried a front-page story under the headlines "False Charges Brought Attack on Police." The story reads:

U.S. Atty. Macon L. Weaver, in an unprecedented disclosure of Justice Department secrets, today said "false charges" that two policemen bombed a Negro minister's home in May resulted

directly in the violent aftermath of Tuesday night's bombing of Negro Attorney Arthur Shores' home.

After a fourteen-paragraph story which condemned Tatum, the U.S. Attorney referred at last to the bombing of the Shores home. He said "The FBI is working, as always, closely with the local police department to bring to the bar of justice the perpetrators of this crime against society."

The following day in a front-page story under the headline "Jury to Probe Negro's Lie" Judge Allgood said, according to the *Birmingham News*, "He will ask a federal grand jury to consider charges against a Negro who falsely alleged that Birmingham police bombed a Negro minister's home last May." If the newspaper report is accurate the good judge had evidently determined and publicly reported that Tatum had "falsely" implicated the police even before he was indicted.

The following week Roosevelt Tatum was indicted by the federal grand jury in Birmingham under Title 18, Section 1001, for making a false statement to the FBI. In the minds of the Birmingham black community, the connection between the local police, the U.S. Attorney's Office, the FBI, and the federal judiciary was never more clearly established. In the past there was the hope that the federal authorities might act as a restraining force against local police excesses but the indictment of Roosevelt Tatum shattered such hopes, particularly since it so closely followed President Kennedy's decision to send his Justice Department representatives to Birmingham. A presidential election was approaching; the black community, isolated and alone, had reason to feel alienated from the white system of justice.

Surely other witnesses would be afraid to come forward no matter what they saw. The government had indicted the one person who had come forward and said he was witness to a bombing. Upon reflection Orzell Billingsley said; "Why, no witness would dare open his mouth after they got Roosevelt for telling the truth. You'd have to be crazy to. They could do anything they wanted, bomb in broad daylight with a crowd watching and people would be too scared to say who did it. Man, to make a truthful statement to the FBI after that was like casting pearls before swine."

Approximately two weeks later the Sunday school at the 16th Street Baptist Church was blown up by dynamite. Four little black girls, Denise McNair, eleven years old, and Cynthia Wesley, Carol Robertson, and Addie Mae Collins, all fourteen years old, were killed.

President Kennedy sent Burke Marshall back to Birmingham and a special force of fifteen FBI agents was on the scene. The Justice Department said it would undertake the most vigorous manhunt since John Dillinger was captured.

Martin King delivered a moving epitaph. He said the four children "have something to say to each of us in their death, to every minister of the gospel who has remained silent behind the safe security of stained glass windows, to every politician who has fed his constituents with the stale bread of hatred and the spoiled meat of racism." He added, "We must be concerned not merely about who murdered them but about the system, the way of life, the philosophy which produced the murderers."

Roosevelt Tatum's case was to be tried in the continuing hysteria that was Birmingham before an all-white jury under the direction of Judge Allgood. His lawyer, Orzell Billingsley, had undertaken to handle the defense of some 3,000 persons who had been arrested in the previous weeks, a trial load so awesome that no lawyer could have adequately performed if he had been given ten years to do so.

He began by challenging the grand jury which returned the indictment against Tatum, charging quite accurately that blacks had been denied service on that panel. Billingsley was convinced then that Tatum was innocent, and now, in retrospect, he remains even more convinced that Tatum had told the truth and had been tricked. The record reveals that Tatum appeared in Judge Allgood's court on the morning of November 18, 1963. His lawyer was excused so that he could try another case that morning with the understanding that he would return to try the Tatum case at 2 o'clock that afternoon. Yet the afternoon session began with Billingsley entering the plea of guilty while Tatum stood silently by.

The lawyer was not present on the day of sentence and Roosevelt Tatum, standing alone, was sentenced by Judge Allgood to a penitentiary for one year and one day.

Today the lawyer cannot recall why Tatum, who insisted that he was innocent even on the day that the guilty plea was entered, pleaded guilty. He does recall the oppressive atmosphere, the hopelessness, and the isolation that marked those bitter days. He believes that the system coerced the plea.

It is impossible to determine with certainty whether or not Tatum was a reliable witness. Yet the federal and local police record remains intact. The chilling fact remains that the only person convicted in connection with a Birmingham bombing was a man who came forward as a witness, Roosevelt Tatum. If his plea was not freely entered into, but was a result of the hopelessness of the situation, then this attempt to murder Dr. King bears, in its legal conclusion, a remarkable similarity to the legal conclusion of the case against James Earl Ray, the man who allegedly did kill him.

Toward the end of 1964 Roosevelt Tatum was released from prison. He left Birmingham, where he could not find a job, to look for work in New York City. Before leaving his friends and his family he said that he had told the truth about the bombing of A. D. King's house. His friends say that he insisted that he would keep on telling the truth, whatever the cost.

He died in 1970, at the age of 46.

Chapter Seven

BIRMINGHAM JAIL
by Dick Gregory

Birmingham demonstrated how thoroughly American society was insulated against realizing what it had become. Birmingham forced America to face some terrible truths about itself. The world joined hands in outrage when television cameras recorded the grim pictures of children being clubbed and waterhosed, and dogs turned loose on nonviolent marchers. That's why the Lassie TV show got more hate mail from the ghetto than anyplace else.

At the same time, Birmingham was the wedge; it offered the opportunity for King and his followers to prove how powerful nonviolence was. And it made America recognize itself, the mightiest nation on earth, as a country whose practices were inconsistent with its creed. It exposed America as grossly hypocritical, woefully insensitive to the needs and plight of its minorities, its poor, and its old.

Countless numbers of us went to jail in Birmingham. I never did worry about staying in jail too long back in the 1960s because in those days I was earning more than a million dollars a year. So I knew the Internal Revenue was going to see to it that I didn't stay in jail too long. I remember the crowded jail cells and the inhumane treatment that was, for some of us, an introduction to Southern hospitality. Surprise lit the faces of the authorities when they realized how many we were and how unconditionally committed we were to going to jail and even dying, if necessary, to prove our utter dedication to the philosophy of nonviolence.

It was from such an inhospitable cell that King wrote his classic open letter to the clergy, entitled simply "Letter From Birmingham Jail." This letter was a response to eight white clergymen who wrote a public statement criticizing King for what they termed "unwise and untimely" demonstrations. In the reply, addressed to "My Dear Fellow Clergymen," King cleanly excised the meat, the nitty-gritty of the principles of Judaism, Christianity, and nonviolence, and proved them interchangeable.

Moving away from the American establishment as a target of criticism, King, here for the first time, dealt with the flaws and shortcomings of the church in America.

King said the church could do no more than reflect America, and that America, in turn, reflected the church. He saw the church as the moral barometer of the nation. He felt that religious institutions must be dedicated to humanity, equality, and justice; that this dedication was prerequisite to the development of a society in which all men and women could develop their highest potential.

I share with King the idea that America can be no worse than its churches. I would like to see American religious institutions become so clean and pure and just that the country could pattern after them, thus becoming all that it has ever claimed, striven, and hoped to be.

But we must let King's words of April 1963 speak for his position.

MY DEAR FELLOW CLERGYMEN:

. . . But more basically, I am in Birmingham because injustice is here. Just as the prophets of the eighth century B.C. left their villages and carried their "thus saith the Lord" far beyond the boundaries of their home towns, and just as the Apostle Paul left his village of Tarsus and carried the gospel of Jesus Christ to the far corners of the Greco-Roman world, so am I compelled to carry the gospel of freedom beyond my own home town. Like Paul, I must constantly respond to the Macedonian call for aid. . . .

. . . Perhaps it is easy for those who have never felt the stinging darts of segregation to say, "Wait." . . . But when you have seen vicious mobs lynch your mothers and fathers at will and drown your sisters and brothers at whim; when you have seen hate-filled policemen curse, kick, and even kill your black brothers and sisters; when you see the vast majority of your twenty million Negro brothers smothering in an airtight cage of poverty in the midst of an affluent society; when you suddenly find your tongue twisted and your speech stammering as you seek to explain to your six-year-old daughter why she can't go to the public amusement park that has just been advertised on television, and see tears welling up in her eyes when she is told that Funtown is closed to colored children, and see ominous clouds of inferiority beginning to form in her little mental sky, and see her beginning to distort her personality by developing an unconscious bitterness toward white people; when you have to concoct an answer for a five-year-old son who is asking, "Daddy, why do white people treat colored people so mean?"; when your first name becomes "nigger," your middle name becomes "boy" (however old you are) and your last name becomes "John," and your wife and mother are never given the respected title "Mrs."; when you are harried by day and haunted by night by the fact that you are a Negro, living constantly at tiptoe stance, never quite knowing what to expect next, and are plagued with inner fears and outer resentments; when you are forever fighting a degenerating sense of "nobodiness"—then you will understand why we find it difficult to wait. There comes a time when the cup of endurance runs over, and men are no longer willing to be plunged into the abyss of despair. I hope, sirs, you can understand our legitimate and unavoidable impatience. . . .

. . . So the question is not whether we will be extremists, but what kind of extremists we will be. Will we be extremists for hate or for love? Will we be extremists for the preservation of injustice or for the extension of justice? In that dramatic scene on Calvary's hill three men were crucified. We must never forget that all three were crucified for the same crime—the crime of extremism. Two were extremists for immorality, and thus fell below their environment. The other, Jesus Christ, was an extremist for love, truth, and goodness, and thereby rose above his environment. Perhaps the South, the nation, and the world are in dire need of creative extremists.

. . . Let us all hope that the dark clouds of racial prejudice will soon pass away and the deep fog of misunderstanding will be lifted from our fear-drenched communities, and in some not too distant tomorrow the radiant stars of love and brotherhood will shine over our great nation with all their scintillating beauty.

Yours for the cause of peace and brotherhood,
MARTIN LUTHER KING, JR.

Chapter Eight

"I HAVE A DREAM"
by Dick Gregory

The March on Washington on August 28, 1963, was a drama of epic proportions. I will never forget it. It was wall-to-wall black folks and white folks, over a quarter of a million of us. I had never seen so many black folks and white folks together this side of a race riot. No event in human history was so feverishly anticipated, so fervently hoped for before it became reality. None has been so thoroughly analyzed, discussed and dissected when it was over. We made our point to the world—that the civil rights of black Americans must be respected.

It is not difficult to extract from the great panorama of the day the single most awesome, most inspiring, most moving aspect. What has come to be known as King's "I Have a Dream" speech was easily the gem that sparkled most brightly.

Those who were not present and have had to rely on published versions of the speech, however textually accurate, will never know the precise flavor. King's mood, the exhilaration he exuded are elements that cannot be reproduced on the printed page.

It seemed as if the very cells of his body were charged with new life and renewed spirit. As if the magic of the day, the nobility of the cause had been transformed into a potent elixir and absorbed into the very cells of his body, infusing him with optimism, courage, and joy. It was contagious. All of us there, black, white, young, old, rich, poor, Jew, Gentile, and Muslim caught King's spirit. Spontaneously, it was as if we all knew that after today we would never be the same, that whatever lay ahead: suffering, uncertainty, doubt, fear—even death—nothing would ever turn us around. We found a vigor, a lightness of heart, a gladness of soul that we had not brought with us, but which, miraculously, we were all privileged to take away.

Opponents of the March and its goals hoped for violence. We disappointed them. It was a picnic. I remember the March On Washington mainly because it was the only march I participated in that I wasn't arrested in. As a matter of fact, the March On Washington set a record for an American city. It was the first time that a civil rights march was held that the police arrested more criminals that day than civil rights marchers. It was a day of jubilee.

I can see Martin now, walking to the podium, 'midst thunderous applause, waiting patiently until it was over, and then, with simplicity, honesty and human warmth saying:

Five score years ago, a great American, in whose symbolic shadow we stand today, signed the Emancipation Proclamation. This momentous decree came as a great beacon light of hope to millions of Negro slaves who had been seared in the flames of withering injustice. It came as a joyous daybreak to end the long night of their captivity.

But one hundred years later, the Negro still is not free; one hundred years later, the life of the Negro is still sadly crippled by the manacles of segregation and the chains of discrimination; one hundred years later, the Negro lives on a lonely island of poverty in the midst of a vast ocean of material prosperity; one hundred years later, the Negro is still languished in the corners of American society and finds himself in exile in his own land.

So we've come here today to dramatize a shameful condition. In a sense, we have come to our nation's capital to cash a check. When the architects of our republic wrote the magnificent words of the Constitution and the Declaration of Independence, they were signing a promissory note to which every American was to fall heir. This note was the promise that all men, yes, black men as well as white men, would be guaranteed the unalienable rights of life, liberty, and the pursuit of happiness.

It is obvious today that America has defaulted on this promissory note insofar as her citizens of color are concerned. Instead of honoring this sacred obligation, America has given the Negro people a bad check; a check which has come back marked "insufficient funds." We refuse to believe that there are insufficient funds in the great vaults of opportunity of this nation. And so we've come to cash this check, a check that will give us upon demand the riches of freedom and the security of justice.

We have also come to this hallowed spot to remind America of the fierce urgency of now. This is no time to engage in the luxury of cooling off or to take the tranquilizing drug of gradualism. Now is the time to make real the promises of democracy; now is the time to rise from the dark and desolate valley of segregation to

the sunlit path of racial justice; now is the time to lift our nation from the quicksands of racial injustice to the solid rock of brotherhood; now is the time to make justice a reality for all God's children. It would be fatal for the nation to overlook the urgency of the moment. This sweltering summer of the Negro's legitimate discontent will not pass until there is an invigorating autumn of freedom and equality.

Nineteen sixty-three is not an end, but a beginning. And those who hope that the Negro needed to blow off steam and will now be content, will have a rude awakening if the nation returns to business as usual. There will be neither rest nor tranquility in America until the Negro is granted his citizenship rights. The whirlwinds of the revolt will continue to shake the foundations of our nation until the bright day of justice emerges.

But there is something that I must say to my people, who stand on the warm threshold which leads into the palace of justice. In the process of gaining our rightful place, we must not be guilty of wrongful deeds. Let us not seek to satisfy our thirst for freedom by drinking from the cup of bitterness and hatred. We must forever conduct our struggle on the high plane of dignity and discipline. We must not allow our creative protest to generate into physical violence. Again and again we must rise to the majestic heights of meeting physical force with soul force; and the marvelous new militancy, which has engulfed the Negro community, must not lead us to a distrust of all white people. For many of our white brothers, as evidenced by their presence here today, have come to realize that their destiny is tied up with our destiny. And they have come to realize that their freedom is inextricably bound to our freedom. We cannot walk alone. And as we talk, we must make the pledge that we shall always march ahead. We cannot turn back.

There are those who are asking the devotees of civil rights, "When will you be satisfied?" We can never be satisfied as long as the Negro is the victim of the unspeakable horrors of police brutality; we can never be satisfied as long as our bodies, heavy with the fatigue of travel, cannot gain lodging in the motels of the highways and the hotels of the cities; we cannot be satisfied as long as the Negro's basic mobility is from a smaller ghetto to a larger one; we can never be satisfied as long as our children are stripped of their selfhood and robbed of their dignity by signs stating "For Whites Only"; we cannot be satisfied as long as the

Negro in Mississippi cannot vote and a Negro in New York believes he has nothing for which to vote. No! no, we are not satisfied, and we will not be satisfied until "justice rolls down like waters and righteousness like a mighty stream."

I am not unmindful that some of you have come here out of great trials and tribulations. Some of you have come fresh from narrow jail cells. Some of you have come from areas where your quest for freedom left you battered by the storms of persecution and staggered by the winds of police brutality. You have been the veterans of creative suffering. Continue to work with the faith that unearned suffering is redemptive. Go back to Mississippi. Go back to Alabama. Go back to South Carolina. Go back to Georgia. Go back to Louisiana. Go back to the slums and ghettos of our northern cities, knowing that somehow this situation can and will be changed. Let us not wallow in the valley of despair.

I say to you today, my friends, so even though we face the difficulties of today and tomorrow, I still have a dream. It is a dream deeply rooted in the American dream. I have a dream that one day this nation will rise up and live out the true meaning of its creed, "We hold these truths to be self evident, that all men are created equal." I have a dream that one day on the red hills of Georgia, sons of former slaves and the sons of former slave owners will be able to sit down together at the table of brotherhood. I have a dream that one day even the state of Mississippi, a state sweltering with the heat of injustice, sweltering with the heat of oppression, will be transformed into an oasis of freedom and justice. I have a dream that my four little children will one day live in a nation where they will not be judged by the color of their skin but by the content of their character.

I have a dream today!

I have a dream that one day down in Alabama — with its vicious racists, with its governor having his lips dripping with the words of interposition and nullification—one day right there in Alabama, little black boys and black girls will be able to join hands with little white boys and white girls as sisters and brothers.

I have a dream today!

I have a dream that one day "every valley shall be exalted and every hill and mountain shall be made low. The rough places will be made plain and the crooked places will be made straight, and the glory of the Lord shall be revealed, and all flesh shall see it together."

This is our hope. This is the faith that I go back to the South with. With this faith we shall be able to transform the jangling discords of our nation into a beautiful symphony of brotherhood. With this faith we will be able to work together, to pray together, to struggle together, to go to jail together, to stand up for freedom together, knowing that we will be free one day. And this will be the day. This will be the day when all of God's children will be able to sing with new meaning—"My country 'tis of thee, sweet land of liberty, of thee I sing. Land where my fathers died, land of the pilgrim's pride, from every mountainside, let freedom ring." And if America is to be a great nation, this must become true.

So let freedom ring from the prodigious hilltops of New Hampshire; let freedom ring from the mighty mountains of New York; let freedom ring from the heightening Alleghenies of Pennsylvania; let freedom ring from the snowcapped Rockies of Colorado; let freedom ring from the curvaceous slopes of California. But not only that. Let freedom ring from Stone Mountain of Georgia; let freedom ring from Lookout Mountain of Tennessee; let freedom ring from every hill and molehill of Mississippi. From every mountainside, let freedom ring.

And when this happens, and when we allow freedom to ring, when we let it ring from every village and every hamlet, from every state and every city, we will be able to speed up that day when all God's children, black men and white men, Jews and Gentiles, Protestants and Catholics, will be able to join hands and sing in the words of the old Negro spiritual: "Free at last. Free at last. Thank God Almighty, we are free at last."

Chapter Nine

"A FAR DEEPER MALADY"
by Mark Lane

Dr. King had become the most prestigious leader for liberation in recent American history. Future historians would in all probability consider this Southern black preacher, the son of a Southern black preacher, along with Abraham Lincoln. While others devised the "black is beautiful" slogan, a phrase which Dr. King admired little, in the ghettos of Montgomery and Birmingham and Selma and Jackson and Atlanta and Chicago, poor blacks looked toward Dr. King and said he was proof that they were not inferior. They said he had proved as well that they were not born to be victims; that by working together they had the power to control their own destiny, to shape their own lives.

In the spring of 1967, Dr. King risked all that he had achieved, his national reputation, a working relationship with the American news media, with black leaders and other national leaders, and the financial security of his Southern Christian Leadership Conference (SCLC). On that day he committed the SCLC to a formally sealed compact which unanimously condemned the war in Vietnam as "politically and morally unjust" and pledging to do "everything in our power" to end it.

A few days later, on April 4, 1967, Dr. King called upon all blacks and "all white people of good will" to boycott the war by becoming conscientious objectors to military service. He outlined a program designed to "begin the long and difficult process of extracting ourselves from this nightmarish conflict." He likened the use of new weapons against the farmers of Vietnam to the testing of "new tortures in the concentration camps of Europe" by the Nazis. Dr. King bitterly assailed American military policy from the standpoint of the Vietnamese peasants who

> **watch as we poison their water, as we kill a million acres of their crops.**
>
> **They must weep as the bulldozers roar through their area**

50

preparing to destroy the precious trees. They wander into the hospitals, with at least twenty casualties from American firepower for one Vietcong-inflicted injury.

So far, we may have killed a million of them—mostly children. They wander into the towns and see thousands of the children, homeless, without clothes, running in packs on the streets like animals. They see the children degraded by our soldiers as they beg for food. They see the children selling their sisters to our soldiers, soliciting for their mothers.

Dr. King added, "If America's soul becomes totally poisoned, part of the autopsy must read Vietnam."

One year later to the day, he was dead.

Dr. King's call for action to end the war was greeted with a chorus of public denunciation created by many of the nationally known leaders, including black opinion makers.

In an article published in *Reader's Digest,* a nationally known black communicator charged that Dr. King had created "doubt about the Negro's loyalty to his country." He had become "persona non grata to Lyndon Johnson," and he added that King's former friends in Congress will probably not be "moved by him the way they were in the past."

He then wrote that "talk of Communists influencing the actions and words of the young minister" had been revived. He added, "I report this not to endorse what King and many others will consider a 'guilt by association' smear, but because of the threat that these allegations represent to the civil rights movement." He wrote that since Dr. King had involved himself in "a conflict where the United States is in direct combat with Communism," he had imperiled chances for needed legislation to protect civil rights workers in the South and to ban housing discrimination.

The executive director of a national black organization agreed. He said that "urgent domestic programs of civil rights and the issue of the war in Vietnam should remain separate." The Jewish War Veterans (JWV) sharply attacked King. In reference to his comparison between German and American methods, the JWV charged, "It is utterly incredible that Dr. King's denunciation of our government should manifest itself in such an ugly parallel."

Another national black organization reported that its board of directors had voted unanimously against the proposal by Dr. King to "merge the civil rights and peace movements." The board called Dr. King's efforts "a serious tactical mistake" and added, "we are not a peace organization."

Senator Jacob Javits, a leading Republican liberal, said King's statement is "certainly bound to be resented by the country which is deeply involved in the war and which feels it can certainly do justice by the Negro at one and the same time."

Lyndon Johnson told a cabinet member, "That goddamn nigger preacher may drive me out of the White House." While Dr. King never evidenced such a desire, his call for peace, begun that day in early April and continued through the last year of his life, may have played an important part in President Johnson's decision not to seek reelection. It was the war and the growing opposition to it that led to Johnson's somewhat involuntary retirement.

What the President said with characteristic bluntness in private, the leading news media put more acceptably and more publicly.

Dr. King's last year on earth began in turmoil. He appeared to stand almost alone as a withering torrent of apparently orchestrated abuse engulfed him. He had expected that his public dissent from the war would create controversy. He had been advised that donations to the SCLC might sharply diminish and that public figures, major newspapers, and even some black leaders would express their displeasure. He was, nevertheless, unprepared for the depth of hostility he witnessed.

He was almost bewildered and thoroughly frustrated by the unthinking response to his call for an end to the war. He had reason to be frightened. For he appeared to stand almost alone, and to those who detested him, he appeared more helpless and vulnerable than ever before. Yet if he was frightened by the savage nature of the attacks, he never expressed that fear privately, and publicly his initial opposition to the war was honed through his almost prophetic reasoning into an analysis of the nature of American imperialism.

At that moment, and for the days that were left to him, his thoughtful bravery and his grace while under fire were never more apparent. Those who hid behind their shield of Congressional immunity, protected by a biased media and supported in their endeavors by the awesome power of the intelligence organizations, called into question *his* manhood and challenged *his* courage. Yet he was not blinded by panic. In private he wept as the reckless attacks against him increased. Yet through the tears of frustration, no doubt swollen by self-pity and righteous indignation, he saw the problem more clearly. He understood the goals of those who opposed him and took the full measure of their power.

And then he spoke. In 1967, a few months before he was murdered, he said:

The war in Vietnam is just a symptom of a far deeper malady within the American spirit. And if we ignore this sobering reality,

we will find ourselves organizing clergy and layman concerned committees for the next generation. They will be concerned with Guatemala and Peru; they will be concerned about Thailand and Cambodia; they will be concerned about Mozambique and South Africa. We will be marching for these and a dozen other names and attending rallies without end unless there is a significant and profound change in American life and politics.

Dr. King had been to the mountain top. And from the panoramic perception afforded by the lofty height, he set aside personal concerns for self and shared his view with those who could still hear him through the mounting din of false analysis.

He was a dangerous man. He had perceived some dangerous truths and he was so struck by the meaning of his discoveries that he incautiously, almost recklessly, spoke to us of what he had learned.

His words almost a decade ago spoke to the developing efforts for national liberation in Southeast Asia, in Latin America, and in Africa. If we need not march off to rallies to protest American involvement there, then some small credit must be given to his words and his actions.

Newsweek reported in its news columns that Dr. King's opposition to the war was brought about because "he saw black students defecting to [Stokely] Carmichael and white liberals increasingly deserting civil rights causes for peace parades." *Newsweek* continued, "He considered his role as a Nobel peace laureate, a clergyman, even a prophet." Emmet John Hughes, writing in *Newsweek,* said, under a heading "A Curse of Confusion" and a sub-heading "False Image," King "achieves perhaps the greatest irony in his ·fancy that the civil rights movement can be strengthened by enlisting the moral passions exacted by Vietnam. . . . He propagates, even more remarkably, a confusion of moral and political values."

A nationally known black writer offered another motive for Dr. King's opposition to the war.

Some say it was a matter of ego—that he was convinced that since he was the most influential Negro in the United States, President Johnson would have to listen to him and alter U.S. policy in Vietnam.

Perhaps Reverend Bernard Lee of Atlanta, Dr. King's close friend and aide, had better reason than most to understand why King had spoken out against the war. The Reverend Lee recently recalled a day in the Spring of 1967. "Martin and I were traveling to Jamaica. He was going to finish a book that he had been working on. Martin always carried a couple of really heavy suitcases. Never had any clothes in them, really. They were filled with books and magazines and various kinds of documents that he would study."

The Reverend Lee said that before boarding the plane they stopped at a restaurant. Both ordered dinner. Dr. King had stopped off at a newsstand to pick up an armload of current magazines. The food arrived and both men began to eat. While he ate, Dr. King looked through the magazines. The Reverend Lee said, "When he came to *Ramparts* magazine he stopped. He froze as he looked at the pictures from Vietnam. He saw a picture of a Vietnamese mother holding her dead baby, a baby killed by our military. Then Martin just pushed the plate of food away from him. I looked up and said, 'Doesn't it taste any good?' and he answered, 'Nothing will ever taste any good for me until I do everything I can to end that war.'

"That's when the decision was made. Martin had known about the war before then, of course, and had spoken out against it. But it was then that he decided to commit himself to oppose it. When we got back from Jamaica that is what he did."

When he returned to the United States, Dr. King embarked upon a militant program designed to gain political and economic rights for blacks. He continued and increased the marching and organizing in Chicago, announced a twenty-city boycott campaign against companies with discriminatory hiring policies and began to mobilize white college students for work in political education campaigns.

Dr. King said that the war was morally wrong and itself a barrier to the realization of the dreams of black people. "Many of the very programs we are talking about," he said, "have been stifled because of that war in Vietnam. I am absolutely convinced that the frustrations are going to increase in the ghettos of our nation as long as the war continues."

Dr. King pointed out that blacks were serving in Vietnam in disproportionate numbers. Twice as many blacks as whites died each day in Vietnam in relationship to their numbers in the whole population.

He answered those who insisted that he should work only in the civil rights movement with but two sentences. He said he opposed segregation, and that he would refuse to segregate his principles. He said the war was wrong, and that he would oppose it until it ended.

Dr. Martin Luther King, Jr., in the
Birmingham Jail, April 1963

Ebony Magazine

"I Have a Dream."
Dr. Martin Luther King, Jr., addressing the March on
Washington, August 28, 1963

Ebony Magazine

Dr. Martin Luther King, Jr.,
receiving the Nobel Peace Prize from
King Olav V of Norway,
in Oslo, Norway, December 10, 1964

Ebony Magazine

Dr. Martin Luther King, Jr., visiting Dick Gregory in jail in Chicago, August 1963

Ebony Magazine

Dr. Martin Luther King, Jr., and Reverend Ralph Abernathy, 1967

Andy Young and Dr. Martin Luther King, Jr., 1968
Ebony Magazine

Chapter Ten

THE LAST CAMPAIGN
by Dick Gregory

Martin Luther King had become the true voice of America. When you read the United States Constitution, you hear all the beautiful things we teach in our grade schools, and our high schools, and colleges of what America should be all about. Martin brought those dead words alive. America needed a voice; America needed millions to speak out and yell; America needed to be heard the world over, and it was—through Martin's commitment. Through his suffering and unselfish attitude when it came to helping others, Martin earned the right to be that voice. Not just to be the spokesperson for black America, but he spoke for what the true, real, America should have been speaking about and sounding like. Because of that, every section of the country and the world that was having problems and was reaching out and crying for help was reaching for Martin. Come Martin, help us Martin, be with us Martin, lead with us. If you were here we could survive. Yes, we could survive. Oh God, if we could just get Martin here it would be all over. The white folks would listen to him. If we could get Martin here we could raise enough money. If we could get Martin here he would say it like it's supposed to be said. Martin Luther King developed into the real, true, honest voice of America. Because of him, every town, village, and city in America where there was suffering going on called on King for help. It wasn't just black folks who needed him. The Jews, the Gentiles, the Catholics, the Irish, the Baptists, the old and the young, men and women; they were all calling for Martin. Come and help us, talk to us, give us some encouragement. Tell us what we would not accept anyone else telling us. Tell us Martin, tell us rich, white, sophisticated folks what this America is all about. Because he was the voice for an entire nation, King was always in demand. As important as Memphis was, it came at a bad time.

The need for King to return to Memphis in April 1968 to help the striking garbage workers came at an inconvenient time. Martin Luther King was getting ready to do something that neither he nor any other civil rights leader had tried to do before. He was preparing for the Poor People's Campaign and March on Washington. Never before had masses of poor folks come together and talked about being poor and disadvantaged. This was different from all the other marches and demonstrations that Martin Luther King had led. Organizing a one-day march was simple. King had proven to America and the world that large numbers of black people could be organized for short periods of time. Many of the people participating in King's previous marches were not the poor and the hungry, but mainly middle-class people, celebrities, and working folks. This was going to be different. This time the force would come from a different group of people. The ones without jobs, people without enough food to feed their families, and the people whose faith in the American system had been shattered because of years of discrimination and injustice. The Poor People's March on Washington would go down in history as the biggest demonstration that the nation's capital had ever been confronted with—and it would be nonviolent. Imagine Dr. King coming into Washington, D. C., with thousands of poor people of all colors quietly asking America for a chance to be part of that respected segment of society reserved for the chosen few.

King knew that the Poor People's March would need a lot of careful planning. Everything had to be just right or it would not work. All things had to be considered. A lot of money would be needed, and King himself would be influential in raising funds. People might be reluctant to contribute to a cause that seemed as farfetched as thousands of poor folks marching into the nation's capital. King would have to convince both blacks and whites that it would work. And even if the money were raised, there were so many other problems that would have to be considered with so many people living in such close contact for an undetermined length of time. Husbands and wives would be together. Some pregnant women would come to Washington and give birth while they were there. Others might become pregnant, and there would be the problem of having the proper medical care available for them. There would be sickness, and problems of taking care of young children. Everyone would have to be fed properly, and while all these necessary things had to be taken into account, King still had the burden of watching out for government *agents provocateurs*. They might try to undo all the hard work and effort that had gone into the planning of this demonstration. King knew that he had a big job waiting ahead of him, and he was hoping everything would work out. He knew that if the Poor People's March was a success, black people and poor folks of all colors would be on their way to a better life.

The two things that upset the Establishment most about Martin Luther

King were the fact that he came out against the war in Vietnam and his plan for a Poor People's March in the nation's capital. King's plan to bring thousands of people into Washington, D.C., would broaden his base from civil rights to human rights. He would not only be concerned with equality under the law for blacks, but for all citizens who were not getting a chance to earn their fair share of what America had to offer. They would demand jobs and decent wages. This would be a new era in American history.

Many whites have always had a basic fear of black people, and that fear alone makes them resist anything that even appears as though it might have an effect on them. If Martin Luther King's bringing poor folks to the capital was going to jeopardize their jobs, or their life styles, then they didn't want the Poor People's March to take place. The government, too, was worried about masses of poor people pitching tents in Washington. What would this do to America's reputation in other countries? What would this do to our image as the richest nation in the world? What about those countries who were not aware of America's racial problems and problems of poverty and hunger? A Poor People's March on Washington would be an absolute embarrassment to the President of the United States and his entire Cabinet. It would be an embarrassment to all of America. The United States has always been able to hide its poor. People with no jobs, no homes, and no money have always been separated from the rest of American society. There are vagrancy laws that keep these people from being on the street. When they are caught mingling with the so-called decent people, they can be picked up and taken to jail for loitering.

White reaction to the planned Poor People's March was astonishing. A headline in *Reader's Digest* magazine a few days before King was killed read: "The United States may face a civil crisis this April when a Poor People's Army pitches camp in the nation's capital." The article stated that authorities must be prepared for the worst: a Washington paralyzed by a so-called Poor People's Army. At the White House, the Justice Department, the Pentagon, and the Metropolitan Police Headquarters, dozens of conferences were held to coordinate strategy. All of Washington knew, from the President on down, that if King's Poor People's March really took place, there was a possibility that nearly anything might happen. It could not be predicted, and the government with all its methods of tapping phones and sending out spies did not know how to prepare to handle this massive demonstration that was about to take place. The press was busy trying to find out each and every detail of the march. What would happen if the police told them to move? What if the government ordered an end to the demonstration? What if the police used force to physically remove the crowd? Was there a possibility of violence? And more than anything else, could this thing work without Martin Luther King?

It did work. Ralph Abernathy and other SCLC leaders led thousands into Washington, D.C. They lived in tents through the sweltering summer heat and through many days of hard rain. They were determined to make their voices heard, and they did it without chaos or violence. America had to listen.

PART THREE

CODE NAME "ZORRO"

Chapter Eleven

HOOVER'S FBI
by Mark Lane

The torrent of violence that greeted the nonviolent protesters in Birmingham dramatized again the problem that had beset the civil rights movement from the beginning: *Why was the law not being adequately enforced?* No one was naive enough to expect much help from local law-enforcement agencies in the Deep South, but what about the FBI, the federal agency sworn to uphold the Constitution and enforce the laws of the land on behalf of *all* the people? With its already broad criminal investigative authority, backed by a growing body of Supreme Court decisions and Congressional legislation on civil rights, surely the FBI had all the power necessary both to defend the legal rights of protesters and to arrest the lawbreakers who confronted them with acts of violence.

Why, then, was the law not being adequately enforced? FBI apologists, of course, said that the problem was too big, that the Bureau's manpower was inadequate to cope with widespread civil disorders. Yet the complex problems can hardly be understood solely in those terms. Who were the men who made up J. Edgar Hoover's FBI? What were their motives and how dedicated were they really to enforcing *all* the laws for *all* the people? Since Hoover's death the American public has already learned some of the dismaying answers to these questions. In three consecutive chapters, beginning here, we shall examine these questions again and try to determine what bearing their answers might have on the murder of Martin Luther King, Jr.

Although books have been written by FBI agents, and reports have been made by committees of the Congress detailing the aberrations, eccentricities, and illegal acts of J. Edgar Hoover's FBI, little has been done to effect a cure.

The reformation of the FBI cannot be achieved by the passing of Hoover. His fifty-year tenure was longer than the reign of most monarchs, and certainly longer than that of most dictators. Hoover was able to devise a classic carrot-and-stick employment bureaucracy, so that

60

employees of the FBI became enmeshed in a system that left them little opportunity for free thinking. According to one former employee we talked to, "All the agents ever talked about was ball games and women. And their house. The house that they'd just bought. And their pay raise; mainly their pay raise. Talk about pay raise until you'd go crazy."

On November 27, 1976, I interviewed Arthur Murtagh at his home in Constable, New York. Before retiring, he had been a Special Agent of the FBI, for twenty years and nine months.

Murtagh, who now practices law in Constable and teaches at Clarkson College, had testified before the House Select Committee on Intelligence, chaired by Otis Pike, Democrat of New York, generally called the Pike Committee. Informing the Committee that he had "loyally served the Bureau for twenty years," and that he had been "assigned to the FBI's internal security intelligence squad in Atlanta for 10 years," he hoped he "could give this Committee insight into the Bureau's intelligence practices not from the theoretical viewpoint of a policymaker but from the practical viewpoint of a field agent."

Murtagh said, "It is possible for the structures of an organization such as the Bureau to be responsible for much wrongdoing without any measurable culpability on the part of individuals working in the lower levels of the organization." He gave one example:

I was at one time asked to obtain through my informants handwriting samples of a gentleman who is now a member of your body, the Honorable Andrew Young of Atlanta [now United States Ambassador to the UN]. I was also asked to obtain handwriting samples of several of his associates in Dr. Martin Luther King's Southern Christian Leadership Conference. I was an agent with a lot of experience at the time this request came to me from my superiors. I was aware that the manner in which the request was made was such that the information was to be used for one of the illegal purposes of the Bureau.

Murtagh also said that he was requested to order his informant in the SCLC to steal some stationery. The agent surmised that the plan was to effect a blackmail with forged love letters from "Andy Young to somebody's wife." Murtagh told his superior that "those fellows at SCLC will laugh at you." Although Hoover's interest in sexual blackmail is well-known, one wonders how seriously love letters on SCLC stationery would have been viewed.

Murtagh "flatly refused to comply" with the request, made after regular working hours, "orally in private." He turned to his supervisor, who was known among the agents as "Colonel Klink," and told him

". . . he could tell his counterpart at the Bureau who had called him on the WATS line seeking the information that I knew damn well it was going to be used in an unrecorded counterintelligence operation to destroy Mr. Young's chances of getting elected to the House of Representatives." The request came only a few days after Mr. Young had announced that he was seeking a seat in the House. Murtagh threatened to go to the Civil Service Commission or to somehow publicize it, so his supervisor backed down and said, "We will make some other arrangement." Assuming that the Bureau failed in this attempt on Mr. Young because his "supervisor had no other source at that time who could get the information for him," Murtagh also remarked that "no record of the above incident" would be found "in the Bureau files."

In an unsigned response to Mr. Murtagh's testimony, the FBI said: ". . . a review of the files disclosed no information to support Murtagh's allegation and that personnel, who would be knowledgeable of such a request of Murtagh, had no recollection of any such request. FBI headquarters files did not contain information which would substantiate Murtagh's allegation."

Murtagh added, in his testimony, that "if the same request had been made to most agents who had reached [my] level in the Bureau . . . they would have routinely complied with their supervisor's request, simply because they would have gone through a process which would have eliminated all those who saw anything wrong with the type of activity contemplated by their supervisor."

An agent with years of Bureau experience explained how this mind set was achieved. Because the Bureau was "exempt from Civil Service" regulations, it was free to set up its own criteria for the selection and training of personnel. Murtagh, in his testimony, confirmed that "Mr. Hoover was able over a period of nearly 50 years to bring in thousands of carefully selected agent-personnel who were as politically disposed to the right as he was and then through a personnel system, which offered no possibility at all for an agent to question Hoover's ethics or methods, to force thousands of those selected to leave the Bureau in utter disgust simply because they had no avenue through which they could air grievances involving unethical or illegal conduct."

The process of breaking down an agent's resistance to objectionable activities was, besides that of selection, one of occasional choices. Murtagh told me, "The average agent on a day-to-day basis might have to falsify a record for some purpose to keep the Bureau from some little scandal, but they'd go through 20 years and they might not have to, to any great extent. Except in the little administrative things. They'd have to lie about how many hours they'd worked. They broke 'em in on that kind of lying, and then when they got to the point where they had to lie for something big, their character—their self-respect—had been deteriorated. Agents said to one another, 'I have absolutely no respect for myself. I am a broken man.' Another was reported to have said, 'When I shave I close my eyes.' ''

An example of this debilitating dictatorship is the weight program of the Bureau. Arthur Murtagh suffered personally because, although he did not look or feel overweight, he did not accord with a chart provided to the Bureau by an insurance company.

Hoover was a very clever man—he was a clever dictator. He knew that if he could divide and conquer he'd be successful in controlling people. One of the things he used was the weight program. If we just talked about the weight program we'd laugh about it because it in itself was of no importance, but it accomplished the purpose of dividing the troops. Some people couldn't get their weight down to chart weights. The charts were such that it was an absolute impossibility for some of us to get to it. They were later done away with by the insurance company that had recommended them. And they weren't even used the way the company said they should be used.

The weight requirement obviously never applied to Hoover, or to John Moore, who was directly under him. Murtagh's supervisior asked him his weight every day—and Murtagh insisted on telling the truth. ''My supervisor would come and say, 'What do you weigh, Art? You're supposed to weigh 168.' I'd say I weighed 182 or 187. *And he put down 168.*''

Transfers to undesirable posts were used as punishment. This device was used so arbitrarily and capriciously that the lower echelons in the Bureau developed a defense against it. Murtagh's noncompliance with the weight charts was eventually discovered and he was ordered transferred. ''By the late fifties and sixties, the internal workings of the Bureau had broken down. If Hoover wanted to punish somebody, the manipulators under him would create a kind of cushion between him and us. They'd transfer us—but they'd give us the best damn transfer that we could get!'' Murtagh was transferred from Charlotte, North Carolina, to Atlanta, Georgia.

Hoover's methods of control of over 7,000 agents were worthy of

Machiavelli. He always cited national security and efficient law enforcement. In creating the Bureau, Hoover invented an institution that presented a polished, competent exterior to the public, an exterior hard-won by rigid rules of conduct and secrecy. Murtagh testified, "Secrecy served many useful purposes to the Bureau. It made it impossible for the public or Congress to know anything about what was going on internally. It gave the Bureau operation an aura of mystery and created a type of fear and respect for the Bureau which I personally feel is unhealthy in a society that strives to be both democratic and open."

The FBI's unsigned response to Murtagh's testimony was:

Annual appropriations [for the FBI] were based on Hoover's testimony before Congressional Committees which were at liberty to examine all areas of the Bureau's operations in conducting their inquiry for budget justification. As members of the Congress and representatives of the people, Committee members have always been in a position to know of the Bureau's internal as well as external operations and to make Congress and the general public aware of their observation *within their prescribed mandate and subject to the rules of confidence* [*emphasis added*].

Budgets of individual investigations never find their way into reports accessible to the public, however. Murtagh told me that a reluctant FBI was prompted, perhaps constrained, by the media to act after the murder of three civil rights workers in Mississippi. The investigation was designed to find the bodies he said. Murtagh was told by a supervisor that the Bureau spent $250,000 a day for over three months.

"We had about seventy agents on the case, and agents in the field, U-2 flights taking pictures, and about 150 backup agents in the state of Mississippi doing work that was directly related to recovering leads. It was a massive investigation." Ultimately the bodies were found when an informant was paid $10,000 for the location of each of the bodies.

Murtagh said that in a "normal criminal investigation, the Bureau should get high marks, in things like bank robbery, car thefts, kidnappings—there was some doctoring of statistics, but those things were played straight. But," added the same agent, "it was when they got into the intelligence area, an area with political overtones, that things began to break down. The Bureau's approach was so predominantly right that they might look at an ordinary citizen as a threat to the internal security of the United States. Anybody who wore a beard, in the mid-sixties—they'd take pictures of people in parades and pick the ones with beards—they were the dangerous ones."

An agent who had served in Detroit informed me that the "Two Squad," which was usually an intelligence squad, had conducted an investigation of Walter Reuther because of President Eisenhower's appointment of Reuther to an atomic energy conference in Europe. "The Bureau had to give him a clearance—the Bureau didn't call it that." The agent, in discussing the Reuther investigation with veteran "Two Squad" members, found that

> the famous Walter Reuther letters which were used against Reuther and published in the papers back in the thirties were actually written by a guy who is now a vice-president of General Motors. They were forgeries.
>
> When Reuther was trying to organize the CIO, back in the thirties, there were riots and several people were killed and a lot of people went to the hospital. During the riots Reuther made a trip to Russia, about 1932 or 33, and during the riots, these letters came out in local papers, and they were allegedly written by Walter Reuther, from Moscow, praising the Communist system.
>
> Reuther denied that he had written the letters—and there is information in the Bureau files to show that this General Motors guy had. I don't know whether the Bureau worked with this guy, using the FBI laboratories to create forgeries, or whether he wrote them independently and the Bureau found out about it. But at any rate, the Bureau never told anybody about this. They let Reuther bear the burden of the allegation. This extreme rightist approach is typical of Bureau history.

A Special Agent commented that when the FBI had to deal with other than "ordinary criminal behavior," it applied its own standards to formulate a judgment as to correct and moral politics. "Walter Reuther was a rabble-rousing labor leader by the Bureau's standards."

Two agents were assigned to investigate the applications of two young women who had applied for clerical positions with the Bureau in Atlanta. "They had worked in a rag-rendering plant in the mid-sixties. They had had a dispute and won it through the National Labor Relations Board. The investigation on their background went up to the Bureau, and Clyde Tolson wrote across it, 'What are we doing, fooling around with people who've been connected with labor unions? Close immediately.' They were denied jobs on the basis that they had something to do with labor unions—this was in the mid-sixties."

An agent who had been with the Bureau for many years remarked that, to J. Edgar Hoover, the Bureau was the "Seat of Government," and that the head office in Washington, D.C., was therefore referred to by agents as "SOG." Hoover regarded Presidents as transients passing through his administration. "Now to the average agent, after he'd been in fifteen or twenty years, there wasn't any government other than the Bureau. Kennedy couldn't have brought Hoover down, Johnson didn't bring 'im down, and Nixon didn't dare to bring him down—I don't think Nixon wanted to." He added, "Nobody dared cross him, he had built an impregnable dictatorship. It's still there today."

Because the primary mandate of the Bureau was to protect the Bureau's image, agents often were placed in humiliating situations to fulfill this mandate. An agent who had served in Atlanta recalled the plane crash at Orly Field in Paris, in which 130 prominent Atlanta citizens were killed.

The Bureau wanted to get a lot of good publicity out of that situation; they wanted to get in on the identification of the bodies and the French government didn't want to let them in. So we flew the identification crew from the Bureau over to France and then we had to go through Atlanta and collect pantyhose and shoes and bras and things like that and get the sizes from the various families.

Well, the families were all in mourning, and some of these mansion houses were under the control of lawyers, and we had to go through the lawyers in order to get permission to get in. Now this was pertinent information—you've got inheritance rights, was the person actually on the plane, or did they miss it—there was nothing wrong with collecting it.

But we kept having conferences—they had used all the agents in the office—and the conferences didn't concern solution of the case—they dealt with this guy who was the head of the identification unit, who wanted to get a promotion in the Bureau. He was an assistant director who wanted to be an associate director, and he needed this case to go to Hoover as a great publicity success. The only way it could be a great publicity success would be if the press and those involved in the investigation said it was.

So two days after the investigation was finished, we got a call from the Bureau, and this guy, back from France, called in all the Atlanta agents and said, "Gentlemen, I talked to [the assistant director], and he wants us to go back out to the families, and make under pretext some second contact or third contact with them, and subtly suggest to them that they write a letter to the FBI Director, thanking him for the FBI's part in solving this case."

They were still in mourning! And I walked out with some

agent, saying, "I'll be damned—I'm not going to cover those leads." I just didn't do it! And some of the other agents didn't do it. Most agents would do it, so that would be enough. Then they could satisfy the Bureau.

Now everyone knew what was going on. The telephone operator talked to me about how rotten it was that they'd ask us to do that sort of thing. Demoralization took place. That was a prelude to [the attempt at] bringing down Dr. King by taking stuff off the wiretap and feeding it to the press. It's all part of the same process. You would have to have a control system and restructure the organization so that the Orly crash incident wouldn't happen. So that a guy wouldn't dare do it!

Another agent reported that the FBI had its own kind of "dirty tricks" operation.

We had files—counterintelligence files where you had to periodically submit schemes for counterintelligence. I had a guy, working under me, to whom this intelligence file was assigned. He was thirty-nine years old—one of the wildest, drinkingest, women-running-around guys that I have ever known. He would come in the office half crocked nearly every morning.

The intelligence files came up for review every ninety days. So every ninety days he would say—and he used that awful language, he used to swear all the time—slam it down—"I'VE GOT TO WRITE ANOTHER SO-AND-SO!!" Then he'd come over to me a few minutes later and say, "Hey, give me some ideas," And I would get the steno, and out of the blue think of some kind of a scheme that would satisfy the Bureau. And we'd send it up as a proposal. Every ninety days you had to send something in telling them something dirty we were going to do, in order to accomplish the purpose of counterintelligence.

Any kind of scheme would do—it didn't make any difference. They were directed against the Klan as well as against blacks in civil rights, but mostly against blacks.

The Bureau had a penchant for forged letters, and for attacking people on the sex angle. Sex seemed to be—because they were all from the right wing, churchgoing moralists—they figured that's the way you blackmail somebody.

An agent remarked that this attitude was prevalent in areas other than the Bureau.

Nothing surprised me about Watergate—there were no surprises. Nor did it surprise my wife. She was privy enough to all that was going on in the Bureau. We watched the Watergate hearings and we said, "Why doesn't he ask this question? Why doesn't he ask that question?" And the reason they didn't ask the questions was evidenced by what Senator Baker said to McCord once.

He said to McCord, "What I'd like you to do now is go home"—it was Friday—"and think over the weekend what questions we should ask you." Baker could see that he didn't know enough about what was going on to know what kind of questions to ask. I wished to God I could talk to Baker.

They should have gotten some advice. But where could they go to be briefed? Anyone who filters up through the system, and particularly in the Bureau, and in the government generally, goes through this culturization process. By the time he gets to the top, it's very doubtful if his perceptions will be accurate—if he'll be able to see what's going on. He's up there because he wants promotions, he wants power, he's gone through the system, and he has compromised himself.

Murtagh told me a story to illustrate how far this "compromise" could extend.

We had jurisdiction in selective service matters, and a guy we'll call "Pedro" was arrested in Chicago and he didn't have a draft card with him. So the police turned him over to the FBI, and Chicago called Detroit, and they said, "Pedro says he's registered with Board 91 on Taylor Street in Detroit." So the supervisor made the phone call, and he made a mistake and didn't check the right board. There are four on Taylor Street and he checked three, not the one Pedro was registered at.

He told Chicago that the guy wasn't registered. Well, Pedro was of a minority, and this was before the *Miranda* warning, and Pedro was brought before a Federal District judge and asked if he was registered and he said, "Yes, I registered at Taylor Street," and some FBI agent testified, "No, he didn't," and they sent Pedro to jail for eighteen months.

The Bureau didn't find out about this until over two years after it happened. Pedro's number came up at Board 91, and they wanted to know where Pedro was, so they could induct him. They looked for him, and couldn't find him, so they turned the case over to the FBI—told them to find Pedro. They searched the indices and found that—Jesus, we put Pedro in jail for *not* being registered, now we're looking for him because he *was* registered. WE MADE A MISTAKE!

I was with a group of agents in the squad room when this one agent—a loudmouthed little guy whom no one liked—he certainly didn't measure up to my idea of what an agent is—came running into the room showing this to everyone. We all knew the supervisor had made a mistake. He had eight kids. He was going to get transferred.

Then there was a closed-door conference in the supervisor's office—something very unusual. Then this supervisor walks out, and walks into his supervisor's office. And then, nothing happens for another two years.

We hear no more about it until a guy—Charlie—was testifying—he was an accountant for the Bureau—testifying in Grand Rapids, in Federal District Court, and somebody said something derogatory or unfavorable to the Bureau or about the Bureau's investigation and Charlie didn't ask the prosecuting attorney for an opportunity to refute the testimony. It wasn't very important—at least he didn't think so. By the time he got back to the office he had been transferred, because this thing had hit the wire and had gotten to Hoover's office, and the Bureau had been criticized and this guy hadn't defended the Bureau. Hoover transferred him—by teletype. Charlie, normally very reflective, was absolutely beside himself, and he wasn't going to take the transfer.

He quit, took another job, there were lots of jobs at that time. The thing kept stewing at him all the time, "this goddamn Bureau is doing these things to people." We all knew about a lot of things—not as bad as Pedro's—but there were all kinds of coverups on a day-to-day basis. We spent more time covering things up, even in the fifties—a lot more time writing memos covering things up, creating the record—than investigating. It certainly was the more important part of the work.

Anyway, Charlie was bothered so much that he went to a priest, and out of the confessional told him this Pedro thing, and that the Bureau had covered it up. So the Catholic priest, as I got the story, went to Washington, and went to the Bureau. The Bureau, up to this time, knew nothing about Pedro. But the cat was out of the bag, and somebody else knew about Pedro. So the Bureau came to Detroit and the supervisor and his supervisor and the little guy who had found the truth were called into the boss's office. I know all the details of this because the little guy came to see me after he quit.

The boss said, "What's this story about Pedro?" My supervisor says, "Jeez, boss, I don't remember any case like that at all," and his supervisor says, "I don't remember any case like that," and the little guy says, "You lying sons of bitches, you told me to take that case and put all that information about the previous investigation in the details, and to put all the other stuff in the synopsis, and that the Bureau wouldn't catch it because they don't read the details, and that would cover it up." I saw the damn door close with the three of them in the room when it was being talked about!

The supervisor said to the little guy, "We never knew anything about that; you must have just slipped and not put it in the synopsis."

The boss ordered them to go down to the files to see if they could find it. So they started walking down into the files and the two guys were walking on either side of this little guy—his supervisor and his supervisor's supervisor. This little tiny guy, with bulging eyes and great big teeth, was telling them about the case, and they both turned to him and said, "Now, for Christ's sake, don't! We'll tell him we can't find it." Even at this late date they were still lying.

The little guy says, "What do you mean, we can't find it? The damn thing's down there! We talked about it!" The supervisor says, "We never talked about it!" They find the file and bring it back, and the two supervisors persist in stating that they know nothing about it at all.

So the little guy took out his credentials, and his badge and his gun, and threw them down in front of the boss, and said, "If I have to work with a bunch of lying bastards like this, guys, you can take this gun, and credentials, and badge, and do so-and-so with it!" And the boss says, "Well, don't get hot—you're entitled to have it checked out. Who do you know who can tell your side of the story?" The little guy said that he had told the guys in the squad room about it, and named five of us. I wasn't named, for some reason. All five named said they didn't know anything about it, they'd never heard of it. But we'd all discussed it, and we knew as much about that in the Detroit office as we did about the Kennedy killing.

So the little guy said to me later, "When I knew they were all going to lie, I figured—my brother-in-law has a sugar business in Charleston, and offered me a job with $500 more than I was getting in the Bureau, so I figured I was better off to get away from those lying bastards."

I offered to go to the office and write a memorandum and

bring it to the boss—this was back about '55 or '56—and blow the whistle on the whole goddamn thing. He said, "Nah, it wouldn't do any good. You can't fight that kind of system." He didn't want me to do it. He said, "I wouldn't take the job back from the Bureau even if they gave it to me." I said, "Okay, if you don't want to do it, we won't do anything about it."

Later, I walked into the office, and saw this one agent, one of the five named, alone there, and went up to him, and said, "Hi, how ya doing?" and he said, "Fine, how are you?" and I said, "Why in Christ's name did you and those other guys throw him to the wolves? He wasn't a nice guy, I didn't like him myself, but why would you lie, and let him get it?"

He said, "Well, the supervisor has eight kids. There's the moral basis. The supervisor couldn't afford the transfer and the little guy could."

And this takes us back to Watergate. Who outside of the Bureau would know the questions to ask? Even those inside the Bureau, asking questions, were not able to get the truth—if they wanted it.

They didn't ask the right questions because they're part of the system and they know which questions to ask, so that they can shape the story the way they want it to come out. That's the way it's done. That's the secret of the whole thing.

Chapter Twelve

ONE MAN
by Mark Lane

When he testified before Otis Pike's Select Committee on Intelligence, Arthur Murtagh wept as he told the Committee of his years of frustration and pain.

Although now retired and on a pension, Murtagh knows he could have retired at a higher grade with a larger pension if he had been more cooperative.

When Murtagh failed the weight program, he was transferred. He said,

> **They had methods worked out so that they could manipulate the transfers and they could kind of cushion the blow. What it amounted to was that the guys who were trying to enforce Hoover's rules had to deal with us because we had so much on them and the organization that they didn't dare fire us. They were afraid that we'd blow the whistle and the whole thing would blow up.**
>
> **When I was transferred to Atlanta, I went in and told him "I got a royal rooking in Charlotte. My wife isn't going to move down here until spring, and I need to get on per diem where I can make extra money." He sent me off to Macon, Georgia, to stay for five months on nine dollars a day, which was a lot of money in those days. I got a room at the YMCA—the cheapest one I could get. And I stayed there; there was no work. I was an extra man on the totem pole—just somebody farmed out to cool off. You know, they figured I was madder than hell and if they left me there I'd cool down. They didn't dare fire anybody, because they might have to face the issues before a Civil Service board. They didn't want to be in a position where they'd have to answer for anything because they knew they were wrong in what they were doing.**
>
> **So I was in the YMCA in Macon, at seven dollars a week and**

actually making money. There were five agents there. I'd go in, in the morning, and anything they didn't want to do, I'd do. But they didn't need me—I mean they could've gotten along without me. I stayed there five months and I read, I read everything that I could find about dictatorships. I read the life of Martin Luther, and his difficulties with the Pope. I was Catholic and I had gone to a Lutheran college in Pennsylvania. I just went to the library and got all that I could find of the dictators throughout history, from Genghis Khan down to Adolf Hitler. I read and read, about Catherine the Great, Frederick the Great, the Tudor Dynasties, and the French revolution. Authoritarian systems, and "Jesus," I said to myself, "Hoover read all this stuff. Or he knew about it." The Bureau was a medieval dictatorship. . . . This is the Justice Department of the United States. The Bureau is an integral part of the Justice Department, and yet it is autonomous—no controls, no influence over it, getting stronger and stronger, and the core, Mr. Hoover's people, zombies. There was never any thought of whether anything was right or wrong—if Hoover said it was right, it was right. He was becoming godlike to a lot of us, particularly the old timers.

I saw this as a very dangerous thing. I used to talk to my colleagues in Birmingham during the civil rights troubles, and say, "Look, there will be a Congressional investigation of the FBI and the whole house of cards will come down. This can't work in a democracy, the way he's trying to run it." And they would always say, "You're right, Art, but there's nothing we can do about it."

Everything in the Bureau was secondary to how one was going to survive as an agent. The work itself was secondary. The questions were always who was going to get clobbered; was somebody going to go to the press; were they going to blow the lid on the Bureau? We had to do our work, cover our leads. But the interests of the agents centered around—if the Bureau comes down, are my kids going to be able to hold their heads up at school?

In 1960 I made up my mind. I decided I'd stay in the Bureau and I'd get to retirement, but I wouldn't violate the law, and I wouldn't lie. That was a hard order to come by in the Bureau.

The other agents tolerated me—"Art's a nice guy, but he's crazy, you know, he won't roll with the punches, he calls the shots the way they are." I had one boss who told me, "Art, I have a lot of respect for your principles, but you have to decide"—this was in 1968—"whether to give up your principles or get out of the Bureau. There's no room in the Bureau for a man of principle."

These circumstances, through the years, got me to a point where, by the time I retired, I was just washed out. I wasn't healthy. I had an intestinal tumor that had probably been there as much as fifteen or twenty years, and it was never taken care of because I kept moving around all the time.

Because of the stand Murtagh took, he was never compelled to commit perjury.

I think it was a matter of policy. The Bureau thought nothing of lying to protect itself. The main tool by which Hoover controlled his seven thousand men. But it didn't work, and resulted in the ultimate downfall of the Bureau.

Why did I make that decision in 1960? Well, I have seven kids, and my education, even though I graduated from law school, is not such that I can go out and get a comparable job anywhere.

Here's another part of the Bureau structure: the public was told that the Bureau had lawyers and accountants, but they hired football players and bank tellers with B.A. degrees and night school attendees who worked in the Bureau as clerks and just barely got enough hours together to get a degree. The Bureau would then make an agent of them, and they'd jump from $7,500 a year to $18,000 in a matter of a few months; they had no hope of getting anything comparable to that on the outside, because they had no particular expertise that they could sell. Only 7 percent of the work force in the Bureau were lawyers and accountants.

Even though I was a part of that 7 percent, my family background made me Depression-oriented. I had a great lack of confidence in myself, in my ability to make it in life.

The Murtagh family had arrived from Ireland in 1841 and settled in the upper New York State area. The family had never been able to make money or get any real security. Murtagh was sickly as a child, and his development was very slow.

At fourteen years old, I only weighed seventy-two pounds. I had something wrong with my throat. Every winter I had tonsilitis three of four times. I'd sit in school and fall asleep. I was in the first grade for two years and the second grade for a year and a half.

When I got into the seventh grade my mother finally decided I

74

was sick. This wasn't through ignorance; it was a lack of medical care and lack of money. We owed the doctor $86.00 through the Depression and I used to hear my mother and father talking about how they couldn't pay the doctor.

Finally I came home one Friday, while in the seventh grade, at noon. My mother counted around the table, and I wasn't there. One of the eight was gone. She came up, put her hand on my head and said, "My God, you've got a fever! It must be 106!" And then they called the doctor.

That was the first time I saw the doctor, that I could remember, in six or seven years. The doctor said he thought I had tuberculosis and would die. They took the tonsils out, and I bled for months.

Then I went back to school and in the seventh grade I put on weight and grew taller and began to be able to learn. I got to where I could read a little.

I couldn't read at all, before that; I couldn't even read the newspaper, and I was in the seventh grade. Once my aunt gave me a *Saturday Evening Post,* and it took me three days to read a four-page article about some American scientists that went to Russia.

Then I went to high school and had a sense of being intelligent. I did fairly well in high school. I was in the honor society and in areas where I didn't have to read—like math—I got straight A's. Then into college and the service, and out of the service into more college, and then law school. I finally got to be a very accurate reader, although very slow. But once I've read something, it's memorized.

All of my youthful problems affected me terribly; I was almost twenty-one when I finished high school. This can't be the sort of thing that builds confidence in a young man. By thirty I was a lawyer and admitted to the New York State Bar.

I went into the Bureau because I wasn't sure I could make it elsewhere. I also wanted to make some money—still Depression-oriented. I drive old cars—because I won't be in debt. I've never used credit of any kind. I've been frugal my whole life. All of this has something to do with my unwillingness to give up something that was sure financial security—the Bureau.

I knew what was wrong, and not to be corrected. Trying to correct it at the time, while I was in the Bureau, would have been hopeless and disastrous. So I waited.

When the Watergate break in first appeared in the news, Murtagh's first question to himself was "What part did the Bureau and Nixon have in it?"

Murtagh waited some more. "I had never criticized the Bureau publicly. But then the Senate Watergate hearings started and I watched them for about three days and I said this is it, the whole house of cards is coming down and I'm going to be there when it falls."

Murtagh wrote to *The New York Times* to offer what information he had, especially with regard to the illegal activities involved in the Martin Luther King investigation. A *Times* reporter went up to see Murtagh, who said, "that was the beginning of the world beating a pathway to my door. Two weeks don't pass before someone calls or comes to see me . . . sometimes there are two or three a week."

Murtagh's interest, as he has consistently told all the media and the Pike Committee, is in a "complete restructuring" of the Bureau. "Without that, we'd just be treading water."

Murtagh wants to be sure that the abuses of the enforcement and intelligence agencies are made public.

Unless the younger generation learns about this, they're going to forget, and think they can wash it all clean with Mr. Clean. We could put Jesus Christ at the top of the Bureau and he could not change it unless the structure is changed.

Those who have to carry out the dirty work, Murtagh feels, are the ones who need an opportunity to speak out. "Who knows about wrong-doing in government? Is it the guys at the top, or is it the clerks and secretaries at the bottom? Who knew that there was a wiretap on King? Who typed some of the memos? Some of the stenos and clerks came to me at different times—they knew that the system was rotten."

Murtagh believes that a thorough reconstruction of the Bureau will achieve what the Bureau had promised its recruits:

A due process system would work—it would be fair and better than secrecy, and the resulting image would make them proud to have their kids go to school and say they were an FBI agent's children.

Chapter Thirteen

THE OBSESSION
by Mark Lane

The United States Senate, through its Select Committee to study Governmental Operations with respect to Intelligence Activities (popularly known as the Church Committee) concluded in its final report:

> **The Committee finds that covert action programs have been used to disrupt the lawful political activities of individual Americans and groups and to discredit them, using dangerous and degrading tactics which are abhorrent in a free and decent society. . . . The sustained use of such tactics by the FBI in an attempt to destroy Dr. Martin Luther King, Jr., violated the law and fundamental human decency.**

The Senate Committee which issued the report represented the disparate philosophies and politics found within the Senate. Among the members of the Select Committee were liberals such as its Chairman, Frank Church, Walter F. Mondale, moderates such as Howard Baker, and conservatives such as its Vice Chairman, John G. Tower, and Barry Goldwater.

The chilling language of the Committee report is underscored by the refusal of the FBI to make available to the Select Committee evidence regarding its most extreme programs to destroy Dr. King.

For example, the Committee learned that Hoover's pathological obsession with Dr. King was so grand that even after Dr. King was murdered the FBI continued its attempts to discredit him and his widow, Coretta King. During March 1969, the Congress was considering a resolution to declare Dr. King's birthday a national holiday. The Crime Records Division of the FBI recommended briefing members of the relevant Committee of Congress considering the resolution because "they were in a position to keep the bill from being reported out of Committee" if "they realize King was a scoundrel." Assistant FBI Director Cartha De Loach wrote, "This is a delicate matter—but can be handled very cautiously." Hoover wrote back, "I agree. It must be handled *very cautiously*."

The following month the Atlanta Field Office submitted a recommendation for a counterintelligence program "in the event the Bureau is inclined to entertain counterintelligence action against Coretta Scott King and/or the continuous projection of the public image of Martin Luther King." Hoover evidently had determined that the time was not right for the suggested action against Mrs. King or Dr. King's memory. He therefore informed the Atlanta office that "the Bureau does not desire counterintelligence action against Coretta King of the nature you suggest at this time." The Select Committee was unable to secure any information about the nature of the proposed program because the FBI, which ostensibly it was investigating, decided not to share the evidence with the members of the Senate Committee. The Select Committee reported only "the nature of the proposed program has not been revealed to the Committee."

On November 18, 1975, Frederick A. O. Schwarz, Jr., chief counsel, and Curtis R. Smothers, minority counsel of the Church Committee, testified before the Committee regarding the results of their investigation. In questioning them, Senator (now Vice President) Mondale summarized the evidence "and the tactics they [the FBI] used [against Dr. King] apparently had no end." He then made specific reference to the methods employed by Hoover and his associates against King. "They included wiretapping. They included microphonic surveillance of hotel rooms. They included informants. They included sponsoring of letters signed by phony names to relatives and friends and organizers. They involved even plans to replace him with someone else whom the FBI was to select as a national civil rights leader." The record reveals that, as Mondale continued, counsel confirmed the accuracy of his summary, on occasion offering additional information.

Senator Mondale: It also included an indirect attempt to persuade the Pope not to see him [King].

Mr. Schwarz: And many other people.

Senator Mondale: It directed him [an FBI employee] to persuade one of our major universities not to grant him [King] a doctorate degree.

Mr. Schwarz: That is correct. I think there were two universities.

Senator Mondale: It included an attempt to send him a letter prior to the time he received the Nobel Peace Prize, which Dr. Martin Luther King and close associates interpreted to mean a suggestion that King should attempt suicide.

Mr. Schwarz: That's right. Included in that were materials which the Bureau had gathered illegally or improperly through tapes and bugs and so forth.

Mondale then responded to his partial accounting of the evidence: "I must conclude that apart from direct physical violence and apart from illegal incarceration, there is nothing in this case that distinguishes that particular action much from what the KGB does with dissenters in that country. I think it is a road map to the destruction of American democracy."

Hoover began to travel that road regarding Dr. King during February 1962. The Church Committee said that it could not determine if "Hoover's animosity toward Dr. King" influenced the FBI's decision to initiate a "COMINFIL" (Communist infiltration) investigation of him "without full access to the Bureau's files." Again, the FBI had decided not to share the evidence with the Senate Committee authorized to investigate it. In January 1962, the Southern Regional Council released a report which was critical of the failure of the FBI to take action during civil rights demonstrations in Albany, Georgia. The report was updated and issued in November 1962. Press reports about the document were forwarded to the FBI office in Washington, D.C. FBI regulations seemed to require that the specific allegations in the report be examined. The Bureau rules provided that allegations about FBI misconduct had to be investigated and that "every logical lead which will establish the true facts should be completely run out unless such action would embarrass the Bureau." The FBI's determination to secure, as the Bureau so oddly put it, "true facts" appeared to be tempered by a Catch-22 clause. How could an honest investigation of a valid charge of FBI misconduct not embarrass the Bureau? In this instance the conundrum was avoided as the FBI decided to conduct no investigation of the charges, to describe the report as "slanted and biased" even before the full report was received, and to begin an investigation of its author instead.

Soon after the report was issued, Dr. King was quoted in the press as having said that he agreed with the conclusions in the report and that the FBI had failed to adequately investigate civil rights violations in Albany. He said:

One of the great problems we face with the FBI in the South is that the agents are white Southerners who have been influenced by the mores of the community. To maintain their status, they have to be friendly with the local police and people who are promoting segregation.

Every time I saw FBI men in Albany, they were with the local police force.

The SAC of the Atlanta FBI office immediately notified headquarters about those remarks. The FBI concluded that Dr. King's comments ''would appear to dovetail with information'' the Bureau knew of ''indicating that King's advisors are Communist Party (CP) members and that he is under the domination of the CP.'' To Hoover and his associates any criticism of the FBI was proof that a critic was a Communist. The Bureau officials decided to meet with Dr. King in order to ''set him straight.'' After considerable thought was given as to who should contact King it was decided that he should be contacted by both Assistant FBI Director William Sullivan and Assistant FBI Director Cartha De Loach ''in order that there be a witness and there can be no charge of provincialism inasmuch as Cartha De Loach comes from the South and Mr. Sullivan comes from the North.'' Two telephone calls were made to the busy and often hectic office of the SCLC in Atlanta. King was not in on either occasion and when he failed to return the calls De Loach wrote:

It would appear obvious that Rev. King does not desire to be told the true facts. He obviously used deceit, lies, and treachery as propaganda to further his own cause. . . . I see no further need to contacting Rev. King as he obviously does not desire to be given the truth. The fact that he is a vicious liar is amply demonstrated in the fact he constantly associates with and takes instructions from [a] . . . member of the Communist Party.

While the FBI officials were upset when Dr. King criticized them, they became enraged when he ignored them. William Sullivan was the head of the Domestic Intelligence Division during the harassment of Dr. King. He later testified that Hoover ''was very upset about the criticism that King made publicly about our failure to protect the Negro in the South against violations of the Negro civil liberties'' and that ''I think behind it all was the racial bias, the dislike of Negroes, the dislike of the civil rights movement.''

Hoover detested criticism, blacks, and movements for change. Dr. King epitomized all that threatened Hoover's tenuous hold on reality. The FBI's unholy war against Dr. King was on. Before it ended Dr. King would lie dead on a motel balcony in Memphis.

In May 1962, the FBI included Dr. King's name on ''Section A of the Reserve Index'' as a person to be rounded up and imprisoned in the event of a national emergency.

During October 1962, the FBI began an investigation of the Southern

Christian Leadership Conference (SCLC) and of its president, Dr. King. The FBI conducted the investigation under a provision in its manual captioned COMINFIL—an acronym for Communist Infiltration. That provision authorized investigations into "Legitimate Noncommunist Organizations that are Communist Infiltrated" in order to determine the extent of the alleged Communist influence. If the FBI excesses visited upon Dr. King and his associates were a road map to the destruction of democracy, the assumption that the government, through its federal police, had the right to examine, through methods legal or illegal, the constitutionally protected exercises of citizens constitutes the compass that pointed the way. Yet it was that basic assumption that Hoover shared with President John F. Kennedy, Attorney General Robert F. Kennedy, President Lyndon B. Johnson, and others in positions of influence including Burke Marshall, Nicholas Katzenbach, and Byron R. White. The wide-ranging investigations into the SCLC and of Dr. King were conducted with the knowledge of the Attorney General in 1962. The investigation which was largely carried out through the illegal use of electronic surveillance and through the use of informants was predicated upon the suspicion that one of Dr. King's advisers was a Communist. Fourteen years after the investigation began Burke Marshall, the Assistant Attorney General for Civil Rights from 1961–65, testified that he "never had any reason to doubt [the FBI's] allegation concerning" the adviser. He added that the charges against the adviser were "grave and serious."

After Hoover and Attorney General Robert F. Kennedy conferred, President Kennedy decided to send Marshall to meet with Dr. King and urge him to disassociate from his adviser. Marshall did meet with Dr. King and Andrew Young. When Young later testified before the Church Committee he said that Marshall said at the meeting that the FBI had informed the Justice Department that there was in fact Communist influence in the civil rights movement and had explicitly mentioned the adviser. When Young asked Marshall for proof that the adviser was a Communist he said that he had none, and that he "couldn't get anything out of the Bureau."

Proof was still lacking thirteen years later. The Church Committee concluded that it was shown no evidence that demonstrated that the adviser was a member of the Communist Party at any time during the entire FBI COMINFIL investigation. The failures of the Church Committee were numerous. It failed to secure what were likely the most relevant and illuminating FBI documents; it failed to publish many of the documents that it did receive with the exception of a few excerpts; it failed to publish the testimony of those who appeared before it. Yet perhaps its greatest failure was its reluctance to challenge the concept that the government has the right, indeed the obligation, to monitor the lawfully protected actions of the people.

Burke Marshall occupied a position in the Justice Department which imposed upon him the primary responsibility for the administration of equal justice to those struggling for equal rights. Dr. King and his associates felt that it was to Marshall that they must look for protection against those violently committed to segregation. They saw Marshall and the two Kennedys as a bulwark against the excesses of the local police and the Hoover regime. In the end it appeared that both the Kennedy and Johnson Administrations shared with Hoover the belief that the government had the duty to determine which private citizens could give lawful advice to other private citizens. Starting from that premise, which contemplates governmental intrusion into private sectors of life, all that remained to be determined were the methods to be utilized and the extent of the intrusions.

The most sensitive survivors of the Kennedy and Johnson Administrations shrink when they are informed of the details of the war that Hoover launched against Dr. King. Sensitive as they are and as appalled as they may be when they hear of the atrocities in the trenches, the singularly important fact that emerges from the investigation by the Church Committee is the inescapable conclusion that they, the technicians in the Kennedy and Johnson administrations, had declared war against Dr. King.

The Church Committee wrote:

The extent to which Government officials outside of the FBI must bear responsibility for the FBI's campaign to discredit Dr. King is not clear. Government officials outside of the FBI were not aware of most of the specific FBI actions to discredit Dr. King. Officials in the Justice Department and White House were aware, however, of the investigation, of Dr. King; that the FBI had written authorization from the Attorney General to wiretap Dr. King and the SCLC offices in New York and Washington; and that the FBI reports on Dr. King contained considerable information of a political and personal nature which was "irrelevant and spurious" to the stated reasons for the investigation. Those high executive branch officials were also aware that the FBI was disseminating vicious characterizations of Dr. King within the Government; that the FBI had tape recordings embarrassing to Dr. King which it had offered to play to a White House official and to reporters; and that the FBI had

offered to "leak" to reporters highly damaging accusations that some of Dr. King's advisers were communists. Although some of those officials did ask top FBI officials about these charges, they did not inquire further after receiving false denials. In light of what those officials did know about the FBI's conduct toward Dr. King, they were remiss in failing to take appropriate steps to curb the Bureau's behavior. To the extent that their neglect permitted the Bureau's activities to go on unchecked, those officials must share responsibility for what occurred.

Perhaps the ultimate irony is found in the current evaluation of that period by the FBI. Testifying for the Bureau in an appearance before the Church Committee, the Deputy Associate Director, James Adams, said, "I see no statutory basis or no basis of justification for the activity . . . as far as the activities which you are asking about, the discrediting, I know of no basis for that and I will not attempt to justify it."

Yet at the time the unjustified and illegal programs were not challenged. FBI Assistant Director William C. Sullivan testified that he "never heard anyone raise the question of legality or constitutionality, never." Sullivan was in charge of the program.

He told the Church Committee:

No holds were barred. We have used [similar] techniques against Soviet agents. [The same methods were] brought home against any organization against which we were targeted. We did not differentiate. This is a rough, tough business.

He also said:

This is a common practice, rough, tough, dirty business. Whether or not we should be in it or not, that is for you folks to decide. We are in it. To repeat, it is a rough, tough, dirty business, and dangerous. It was dangerous at times—that is, dangerous to the persons who are being affected, not to the Bureau persons—when you are trying to disrupt someone's family life. It was dangerous at times, no holds were barred. We have used that technique against foreign espionage agents, and they have used it against us.

The FBI, employing almost every intelligence-gathering technique in its arsenal, collected information about Dr. King, his family, his activities, his plans and his associates.

During September 1963, the FBI conducted a survey of Dr. King's home and the New York office of the SCLC. On October 7, Hoover requested permission from Attorney General Robert Kennedy for a wiretap "on King at his current address or at any future address to which he may move" and "on the SCLC office at the current New York address or to any other address to which it may be moved." On October 10, Kennedy signed the request and on October 21 he also approved Hoover's request to wiretap the SCLC's Atlanta office. In making his application to Kennedy, Hoover did not allege that any criminal conduct might be uncovered. He cited only the "possible Communist influence in the racial situation." Predictably Hoover interpreted the Attorney General's permission to wiretap King "at any future address" broadly and therefore placed wiretaps on telephones in hotel and motel rooms where King stayed and on the telephones of friends with whom he stayed temporarily. Telephones in the homes and offices of Dr. King's advisers were also wiretapped. In addition to wiretapping, the FBI placed concealed microphones in Dr. King's motel and hotel rooms in an "attempt" to obtain information about the private activities of King and his advisers for use to "completely discredit" them.

Tape recordings made on these occasions were "improved" at the FBI electronics laboratory and then played for friendly reporters. This technique was employed in an effort to develop "friendly" news sources which would publish derogatory information about Dr. King and to discourage objective reporters from writing fair stories about him.

On a personal note I might add that similar techniques were utilized against me by the FBI as I looked into the assassinations. FBI agents have made similarly "improved" and fabricated material available to contacts in the news media, to members of Congress, and to the late President Lyndon B. Johnson.

The Church Committee, through the efforts of Senator Richard Schweiker, discovered through the questioning of James Adams that in 1966, just after *Rush to Judgment* was published, a request was made by the White House for "personal data information and dossiers," on seven Warren Commission critics. Adams admitted that the request was not a normal one, since it bypassed the Attorney General. Adams explained:

This is not a normal procedure. It is not the procedure followed today. There was a period of time where, at the President's directions, Mr. Hoover reported more directly to him in certain areas, and it was apparently a feeling that he did not want the Attorney General to know certain things.

Adams agreed, when specifically asked by Sen. Schweiker, that a dossier did include documents regarding the sexual activities of a critic.

Schweiker understood that the technique employed by the FBI against Dr. King and his associates was also used against Warren Commission critics. He said:

> I think what concerns the committee is that whenever you get to the nitty-gritty of investigations—and it doesn't relate to the Warren Commission, I will leave that alone—we get back to something like a photograph or a tape recording or some letter referring to some kind of human weakness or failing that is really very irrelevant to the investigation, is sandwiched in here. It just seems to me that it was a tactic. This just happens to be the Warren Commission I singled out, but it was a tactic that was used rather frequently as a lever, or for reasons which I am trying to discover, as an instrument of investigative policy. Would you differ with that or dispute that? What rationale would you use? Do we use sexual activities as a standard criterion for investigations?

Schweiker added:

> And my question is, how is that relevant to being a critic of the Warren Commission? What standard do we use when we just pass photographs of sexual activities to the White House? Is this a normal proceeding when a dossier is requested? Is this normally included, or did they specifically request photographs of this kind, or what light can you shed on this?

And the FBI's Deputy Associate Director replied:

> I can't shed much. I know they requested information on him. I think there was other material concerning that individual of a security nature that was included. Why the information in that respect was submitted I am unable to answer. I do know at the time there was a lot of concern following the Warren Commission report. Had all the answers been explored? Was the Soviet Union involved? Was Cuba involved? And who were the critics who now are attacking this? But I have seen nothing which would explain the rationale for requesting the material.

When Schweiker asked, "What other purpose would a photograph of this nature have, other than to discredit critics?" Adams replied, "I can't answer that."

I have explored this rather personal area at some length because unhappily it does not belong to the past alone. Even as I worked on this book during the closing days of 1976, the documents referred to by

Senator Schweiker were being circulated among members of the Washington press corps, primarily to "friendly" FBI news sources and to various members of the Congress. The purpose—to discourage the Congress from responding to the call for a thorough inquiry into the murder of Dr. King and President Kennedy by attempting to discredit a man who has issued that call.

Thus the techniques used by the FBI to discredit Dr. King during his life are presently being used to discredit those who wish to learn about his death.

A microphone concealed in a hotel where King stayed picked up sounds of a party at which he was present. According to the Department of Justice, the tape recording indicated sexual activity. The problem with the tape, it has been conceded, is that it did not really relate King to the sexual activity and one could barely hear King's voice. Hoover and his friend Clyde Tolson decided to send the tape to Coretta King in an effort to cause the family to break up. William Sullivan testified that the tape was intended to precipitate a separation between Dr. King and his wife in the belief that the separation would reduce his stature.

Hoover ordered the FBI laboratory to "improve" or doctor the tapes so that Dr. King's voice could be clearly heard in a context that would prove embarrassing. The tape was then sanitized, that is, all fingerprints were removed from it. It was placed in a package which was also sanitized and then mailed to the SCLC. Hoover ordered that the tape be mailed "from a Southern state." Accordingly, an FBI agent flew to Florida with the small package, mailed it and then flew home. Hoover evidently reasoned that King would be emotionally weakened from the confrontation with his wife and the impending separation. He therefore ordered that a letter be sent to Dr. King, a letter that Dr. King and his advisers interpreted to mean that he would be publicly exposed if he did not commit suicide within the next thirty-four days. The letter was dispatched thirty-four days before Dr. King was scheduled to receive the Nobel Prize.

Hoover's conceived plot was seriously flawed. It was white-oriented and bureaucratically programmed. It certainly did not contemplate the problems and strengths of the civil rights movement. Hoover, Tolson, and Sullivan, for all their intelligence-gathering devices and their techniques and equipment for surveillance, had not even begun to understand the pace and priorities of the movement. Hoover knew that a personal tape addressed to him would be on his desk and analyzed shortly after its arrival.

The arrival of a tape at the Atlanta office of the SCLC was not a signal event. Tapes came in all the time. The SCLC was collecting tape recordings of Dr. King's speeches. This one took its place near the bottom of a substantial pile of tapes, packages, and letters. Eventually the tape was listened to. Coretta King heard it as did Dr. King. He read the letter as well. The sanitizing had removed FBI fingerprints, the old typewriter that had been used could not be traced, and the postmark read Florida, not Washington, D.C. However, to Dr. King the origin was clear. This ultimate scurrilous action—including what he believed (and many others have since come to believe) was a clear suggestion that he kill himself —could have come, he reasoned, only from J. Edgar Hoover.

The following day Dr. King met with Ralph Abernathy and Andrew Young. He had the tape played for them. Sadly, King said that he then knew that he could never again trust the FBI to protect him.

Chapter Fourteen

THE DESTROY KING SQUAD

by Mark Lane

J. Edgar Hoover's attitude toward civil rights activitists was evident from the first. FBI Special Agent Arthur Murtagh had served in Georgia in the early sixties. He told me that the ways the Bureau had chosen to deal with this delicate and potentially dangerous matter were hardly satisfactory:

> **This was in Albany, Georgia, in the early sixties, during demonstrations. I observed, in court, Dr. King, and Asa Kelly, the mayor, and the Judge—a Federal District judge whom I had investigated for the job—the mayor, the judge and I were the only white people in the crowded courtroom. Constance Motley, now a District Judge in New York, represented Dr. King.**

King and the city of Albany were seeking cross-injunctions against one another. FBI agents were dispatched from Atlanta to Albany to investigate the demonstrations.

> **The personnel situation at Albany was unbelievable. We had a guy at the office nicknamed RN. . . . He was a Special Agent in Charge (SAC). RN was forty-five years old then. He had come up in the Bureau when it expanded from 600 to 6,000. He was not excessively bright.**
>
> **Nobody had any respect for RN. He got interested in women when he hit the big salary, just about the time we hit Albany, Georgia. . . . If this had gotten to the Bureau, it would have resulted in forty or fifty agents being transferred from Atlanta.**
>
> **His behavior could have been reported. But it wasn't—the personnel structure of the Bureau was so decayed that an agent could challenge a supervisor with, "You can't do it to me—the consequences are too severe!"**

RN was SAC of the task force that went down to Albany. Another character in this story is nicknamed SF, the local agent in charge, in the field, what we call a resident agent. There was another local agent also, but he didn't count for anything—this Albany agent was second in command to RN when he came down. There were five agents in Albany when this case went to court, and RN and SF were pitted against the other three agents. They hated each other vehemently. . . . Some of it was religious-oriented. They couldn't stand being in the same rooms together, the three and the two.

The two brought down to Albany forty agents, and set up an office in the Holiday Inn, collecting information on the King demonstrations.

SF called the shots. He was better equipped to be the Grand Cyclops of the Ku Klux Klan. When he met me at the office, he said, "You want to be careful here. I just talked to my wife, and I told her not to come downtown. Be sure to keep all the doors locked. We've got an explosive situation—just don't take any chances, whatever you do. You can't tell how long it'll be before this thing blows sky high!" I went out later to find out what he was talking about—one hundred bedraggled, beaten-down blacks, surrounded by about four hundred policemen, who were marching around the block once or twice a day in protest against not being able to use the library.

SF controlled the Bureau's response to these activities. The civil rights cases in the Bureau, including police brutality cases, went through the office with special handling. They were even on different colored paper—green.

An agent familiar with this procedure explained, "The Bureau handled civil rights cases by collecting information and turning it over to the Civil Rights Division of the Justice Department in a type of preliminary communication." Agents were not empowered to interview, in a police brutality case, the sheriff, the officer, or the victim until the Bureau responded to the preliminary communication and ordered the interview. The Bureau's response was always very specific, naming those to be interviewed, and ordering that the agent inform the interviewer that the investigation had been ordered by a particular Assistant Attorney General, head of the Criminal Justice Division of the Department of Justice.

"The reason we told them that was because Hoover didn't want to be connected with any civil rights investigations," Murtagh said.

This was the only time when we told anyone that the Justice Department was ordering us to conduct an investigation. In any other kind of case, the Bureau would be glad to take credit—shipping, interstate commerce—we'd let someone know we were saving their ship or their trucks.

Hoover wanted to minimize the responsibility of the Bureau for civil rights. His way of doing it was to have guys like SF in key positions throughout the states. He didn't have to pick them and put them there—the system caused them to gravitate there. His type was a racist who didn't want any part of civil rights, and wouldn't ask the right questions.

Arthur Murtagh added,

The whole thing was structured so that we weren't going to scratch the surface on the civil rights cases, unless we were forced into it as we were in Philadelphia. Bobby Kennedy had, at that time—it was unheard of—a bunch of bearded assistants, who would go out to interview the blacks who had sent in civil rights complaints, and they would ask them what had happened. They would get a different story from the one we were giving on the green sheets at the Bureau.

King got word of this, and three or four blacks told me, and other agents, this—they were terrified of SF. He was a good guy to sit down with and talk to—as long as you were white—but he instructed all the new men who came to Albany not to shake hands with any black people—he said, "We don't do that down here!"

The situation was getting quite active—the Klan was shooting into houses at night, and burning churches. SF was manipulating the civil rights investigation. Dr. King called a news conference and said that the FBI wasn't doing its job.

Well, I was there, and I know that the FBI wasn't doing its job—it didn't surprise me; and I don't suppose that it surprised the Bureau—but that was the beginning of the vendetta against King. From that time on, the concentration of effort against King was greater than any other single investigation that I saw take place at the Bureau and I saw a lot of them in twenty years. There was a crew of people who did almost nothing for a period of seven or eight years, except investigate King and try to destroy him.

Murtagh said that while the anti-King effort came mostly out of the Atlanta office, it also came out of the New York and Washington field offices, and "some other" offices had a part in it.

It was an organized vendetta. They were going to get King in one way or another.

At first, it was difficult for Murtagh and other agents to perceive the anti-King effort as a personal one: "I thought that it was just that the Bureau was anti-civil rights and that King represented the movement.

I knew enough about the phony Communist domination theory on King to know that it had no validity. In fact, the whole Communist scare, even through the fifties, fell flat on its face because it didn't have any substance. I don't mean that there weren't some Communists, but they never were in a position to do us internal harm of any significance, and most agents that knew what was going on would agree with that.

Murtagh saw a shift from efforts against Roy Wilkins, Whitney Young, James Farmer, Stokely Carmichael, H. "Rap" Brown, and Huey Newton, to an intense concentration on King. "The Bureau was even considering trying to substitute a leader that they could control. I saw many memoranda on this—they were going to try to take over the movement and direct it from the Bureau. But they couldn't get to first base," Murtagh said.

Murtagh worked with two men in the Atlanta office who were in charge of the wiretaps on Dr. King.

There was Al Santinella and Bob Nichols. I liked them both—and I could never agree, but we were gentlemanly and pleasant with one another. Al I had a lot of respect for. A quiet guy, with little to say—but I could tell from the little bit he did say, that he was anti-King in the early sixties, and by the time the whole thing was over, he felt that the Bureau [performance] was a travesty, that they shouldn't have taken King in. He told me, years later, that he didn't think the Bureau had any substantive grounds for the wiretap on King, and that he was satisfied that King wasn't involved in any Communist movement, which could have justified the wiretap. And I think that he never approved of the peddling of the information, to the media, from the wiretap, which in fact was a clear violation of the law. I think he would not have done it by himself.

The Bureau maintained a two-bedroom apartment in the Peach Street Towers in Atlanta, close to the office, where the wiretap surveillance on King was conducted. "In that apartment, one of the rooms had panels; the whole room was filled with wiretap equipment. They had a man there all the time, twenty-four hours a day, monitoring the equipment and recording things he thought were pertinent," Murtagh said.

This was all about King. They wrote down every word that transpired over the King telephone, and identified all of the people involved. It was estimated one time that there were five or six thousand people that the wiretap actually got information on—people that called him. My own doctor was in that file.

My doctor, a white man, was active in the King movement. He and his wife were both graduates of Harvard Medical School. We were neighbors and good friends.

I found his name when going through the wiretap files one time—all of it was longhand notes. There was a string of file cabinets twenty or more feet long, starting with Day One in the wiretap, and every single communication that took place. This was a form—the number called from, the number of the person who answered. Identity of the person; what was said. And so on. The files were in a special room, the room I worked in for eleven years.

Murtagh's squad was not just criminal or intelligence, but a hash of both. "We called it the security squad. We handled racial matters, applicant investigations, even antitrust. Very bluntly—I hate to say this—the more intelligent, better-educated would be apt to be on this squad. If there was an investigation where one had to talk to bankers —they would need someone who could handle that kind of work, someone smooth. The ex-ball player would go in the bank robbery squad."

Wiretaps, when conducted legally, are performed at the order of an appropriate judge or official, after a showing of probable cause. The use of information received from wiretaps as evidence is so restricted and subject to challenge by a good defense attorney that it often seems hardly worth it. Murtagh said that the justification for the wiretap on King was based on an investigation that had been conducted before the wiretap was begun.

You'd have to have a whole staff to investigate just that area.

I think this happened. Bobby Kennedy was Attorney General and he signed the order permitting the wiretap. There were agents, oriented to the right, who investigated King in New York and found a lawyer working with him. . . . [The lawyer] had had a flirtation with the Communist Party back in the late forties. He'd been to meetings and worked with the CP in New York, so you would say that he was connected with it and at that time probably subscribed to some of the CP concepts.

Whether [the lawyer] changed his view is neither here nor there. I don't think he had that much influence over Dr. King—and the things that he encouraged, King had a perfect right legally to do, and had nothing to do with Communist domination or influence. To be a dangerous Communist, you'd have to steal government secrets and feed them to the Russians.

But if you encourage a bus boycott in Montgomery, is that Communist or not? It may cause riots and riots are associated with Communist activity. Discord in the community is an opportunity for the Communists to take over. That may be true, part of the Communist doctrine and tactics.

But labor unions demonstrate also, and there could be a riot—it depends on who pushes first, who shoots first.

I never saw anything to indicate that King was influenced to create riots. Whether what was in King's mind was also in [the lawyer's] mind when they decided to demonstrate, I don't know.

Remember in Birmingham, when the Catholic priests begged King not to demonstrate, that it would create chaos? I could see that it would create chaos. But I wouldn't see any other way, how the situation in Birmingham would change without chaos. As long as demonstrations were prevented in Birmingham, the segregationists could not be broken. If the segregationists started to riot, then they were the "Communists," as far as I was concerned.

I saw it that way, and so did a few agents. But most of the agents, in the early sixties, figured this to be Communist rabble-rousing.

The Bureau carefully refrained from instructing its agents on any of King's or the Southern Christian Leadership Conference's ideology. It preferred instead to place a convenient label on that behavior. King achieved a melding, peculiarly for the American people, of Christian principles and Gandhian demonstrations of nonviolent civil disobedience. He knew, through long years of study and prayer, exactly what his ideals were and their sources; and he used this blend to force the Constitution to come alive.

This thrilling revitalization and its origins were treated by the Bureau with the deepest ignorance. One agent assigned to listen to King's conversations commented, after listening to King and . . . [the lawyer] that King had "stood fast" against a suggestion by . . . [the lawyer] that

King rehire a SCLC aide he had fired for unsavory political connections. The agent was so impressed with King's obvious dominance that he taped the conversation and took it home, and played it for his agent friends.

"This guy was an ex-football player with no real politics," a friend of his said. "He said, 'I'd always thought that King was just a dumb nigger, couldn't write a speech, couldn't make up his own mind. But he stood fast on all counts!' " His friend added, "The ball player's racism was so pervasive that he couldn't conceive of an intellectual being black. He wouldn't listen to his speeches. He shut them off when King was on the radio."

Of course, agents had to attend King's speeches; his movements were covered at all times. "But they wouldn't listen to the speeches; they thought they'd been written by someone else," said Arthur Murtagh.

Lively debate ensued between those agents willing to discuss Dr. King. Murtagh said, "One of the agents and I had a sparring match about King's alleged flirtation with Communism and what it meant, and the agent felt, at first, that King was some kind of a devil. There was a code name for King—Zorro." Zorro, the Spanish word for *fox,* was a legendary masked figure in the Spanish Old West, popularized by a television program of the late fifties; a nobleman in disguise, he was a political Robin Hood.

"Zorro" was followed and spied upon constantly, and concerted efforts were made to humiliate King. Murtagh related how his own doctor had been involved:

> **The wiretap had been on for a long time. King had been awarded the Nobel Prize, and a banquet was planned for King, to be in Atlanta, to which world dignitaries would be invited, thousands of people. It would be a testimonial.**
>
> **Bill Sullivan, an Assistant Director of the Bureau, from Hoover's office, came into the Atlanta office and called a field conference for security. I never heard of a field conference for security. The Bureau always has the agents go back to the Bureau—even from the West Coast. They don't send Assistant Directors out to the field—they bring the troops in.**
>
> **So they were coming to Atlanta to have a field conference on security, and they had one. But none of the security agents met Sullivan. There was no meeting. There was no discussion.**
>
> **I walked into the squad room in the morning and the agent came out of the meeting room and said, "They're going to get Zorro now! Sullivan's in there and we're really going to get him!"**

Sullivan was in there with the supervisor we called Colonel Klink, which was the best characterization we could give him; when he came out, because he was so much a Colonel Klink, he couldn't resist telling me how he was hobnobbing with the big shots. "I'm going out with Sullivan," he said. "We're gonna fix King this time."

I went out, and went about my work, and came back in, and Klink was back, saying, "We really laid it on."

Klink told Murtagh that he hadn't gone in with Sullivan to see Ralph McGill, editor of the Atlanta *Constitution,* a highly respected newspaper, but that Sullivan had been "closeted with McGill for an hour and a half."

"I don't think you'll find McGill giving King any favorable treatment from now on," said Klink to Murtagh.

A week later, Murtagh went to see his doctor. The doctor said, "Art, I'm glad you came in. I wanted to ask you something."

The doctor had accompanied the Archbishop of Atlanta to the Vatican II conference in Rome because the Archbishop was very ill. He died soon after at the age of forty-nine.

The doctor told Murtagh, "I went in to see the Archbishop a few days ago, and he was in bed, and he asked me why two FBI men from Washington would come to see him, and try to dissuade him from making a speech—the main testimonial speech for Dr. King at the banquet."

The doctor said that he didn't know why, and the Archbishop said they told him that there was going to be an exposé of King that would embarrass the Church if they had anything to do with him. He had better withdraw his support of King.

"Also," Murtagh continued, "the chief rabbi of Atlanta called the Archbishop, and said that two men from the Bureau in Washington had come to see him."

The Archbishop responded, "I respect Dr. King's public position on race, and I think he is a great leader in that area, and I intend to go ahead with the speech."

Murtagh supposed that Sullivan and Colonel Klink told prominent citizens and the press that they had something devastating on King —something, perhaps, from the wiretap. "I think they were clever enough. Divulging the material would be a crime. They probably merely made implications."

Although Murtagh was assigned to the King investigation, he did not work on the wiretap. "I told Klink I wouldn't do it. I thought the damn thing was illegal. And I knew the bastards were using it illegally. One time King was in a house and they called the fire department on him.

Reported a fire in the house, to harass him. All child's play. They mailed him things—a tape to his wife.

The bugging of King was so constant that his hotel rooms were bugged in advance of his arrival, and an agent said, "He was even bugged in Sweden when he went to collect the Nobel Prize."

PART FOUR

PRELUDE TO MURDER

Chapter Fifteen

MARCH 28, MEMPHIS
by Mark Lane

In March 1968, Martin Luther King was stepping up his activities in preparation for the Poor People's March, which was to begin April 29. The plan was to amass a multiracial army of the poor to "stay-in" the nation's capital until "human dignity" concessions were wrenched from a government then pouring billions of dollars into the Vietnam War. King's daring plan was attacked strongly by black moderates, including Bayard Rustin and Roy Wilkins. It marked a shift from civil rights to economic issues. It was this same shift in politics that brought King, somewhat reluctantly, to Memphis. Although he had wanted to devote all of his time to building a successful Poor People's March, King's new politics would not allow him to ignore the call for help from a nascent union of mostly black sanitation workers in Memphis. The workers were on strike for union recognition, an end to racial discrimination on the job, and better wages and working conditions. The strikers had gained the united and militant support of the entire black community and a handful of white sympathizers.

King's help was requested by SCLC member Reverend James Lawson, the leader of the Memphis Strike Strategy Committee. A plan was formulated—King would send in aides James Bevel, James Orange, Tyrone Brooks, Andy Young, and Hosea Williams to prepare a massive march in Memphis which would draw national attention to the strike. King's aides recruited the help of an organized militant black group, the Invaders. This group had repeatedly brought hundreds of black students to earlier marches. The Invaders were helpful at times, provocative at others.

On the day of the March 28 demonstration, a crowd of 8,000 people, spanning many blocks, awaited Dr. King's arrival. Reverend Lawson noticed many marchers he had never seen at strike sessions or civil rights demonstrations directly at the front of the march.

Shortly after the march began, the first windows were broken. In some areas, looting began before the marchers entered the area. According to eyewitness reports, police just watched this looting and did nothing to stop it until the marchers came through.

Soon the police entered, viciously and indiscriminately attacking the demonstrators. Dr. King's party commandeered a passing car and was taken by a police escort to the Holiday Inn Rivermont Hotel.

At a press conference the next day, King vowed to return to show that his tactics of mass nonviolent action were still viable. The violence in Memphis gave black Establishment spokesmen more ammunition with which to attack King's Poor People's March. The day before King was killed, NAACP executive director Roy Wilkins scored King in a story in the Memphis *Press-Scimitar*, saying he doubted that the SCLC leader could keep the Washington march nonviolent. "If a maverick at the rear ranks of the march decides to throw a brick through a window, there's nothing Dr. King up front can do to stop it."

The official explanation of the Memphis march-turned-riot is that the violence and looting were probably triggered by the Invaders. But a black reporter for *Newsday*, Les Payne, has turned up evidence which adds a new dimension to the matter.

In an article entitled, "FBI Tied to King's Return to Memphis," Payne reached his conclusion in three steps:

1) Several FBI informants and at least one Memphis police undercover agent were among the most active members of the Invaders.

2) According to some witnesses, the Invaders led the March 28 riots which attempted to discredit King.

3) According to Jesse Jackson and Andrew Young, "Dr. King would never have returned to Memphis if the violence had not happened."

This seemingly farfetched thesis must be considered seriously when viewed in the context of the FBI's campaign to destroy Dr. King and their COINTELPRO (Counterintelligence Program) tactics to provoke and disrupt black groups. One FBI memo admitted the use of agents provocateurs ". . . in harassing and impelling criminal activities. . . ." During the late sixties, FBI provocateurs in the black movement repeatedly urged and initiated violent acts. In the Memphis setting, turning a nonviolent march into a riot would have furthered the FBI's goal of discrediting King.

In his *Newsday* article, Payne wrote, "One of the informants [in the Invaders] reportedly planned a large portion of the group's violent confrontations." The undercover policeman, who is still a member of the Memphis force, was at the scene of the violence on the day of the riot. He was a very active and vocal member of the group. A former leader of the Invaders told Payne:

He had a 7.62 Russian automatic rifle and he was armed every time we were armed. He was always suggesting actions that we should take; I never saw him physically attack anyone. But he was one of the most provocative members of the Invaders.

The group was apparently so well penetrated that, according to Payne, "Police and FBI officials were regularly provided with detailed information about the group's plans, activities and meetings." A source went on to tell him, "They knew what went on at Invaders' meetings. It was as if they had a tape recorder there."

Detective Ed Redditt, a member of the Memphis Police Department in 1968, described another agent provocateur within the Invaders in a conversation with me last year:

He left the police department . . . and the word was that he went to Washington, D.C. Then a couple of years after the King slaying I ran face to face with him in downtown Memphis. He was wearing a disguise.

When Redditt stopped and confronted the man, the former infiltrator pretended to be someone else, but finally acknowledged his true identity. "He acted very mysterious, saying that he was now with the Central Intelligence Agency, and begged me not to blow his cover," Redditt told me.

The infiltration of the Invaders touched directly on Dr. King. According to Payne, the undercover agent who carried around the automatic rifle was also part of an Invaders security detail for King. This detail left the Lorraine Motel—for unexplained reasons—just thirty minutes before King was killed.

As the head of the strike strategy committee, Reverend James Lawson tried to work with the Invaders during and after the strike. It was not always easy.

Lawson spent most of a 2½ hour interview with Jeff Cohen, an able investigator residing in Los Angeles, discussing the now-defunct group. "From the beginning, I said publicly at mass meetings that I thought the Invaders were provocateurs."

Reverend Lawson invited an Invader representative to join the broad-based strategy committee. The committee had to deal with the survival needs of the strikers and their families, plus the boycott of downtown merchants, daily marches, and tactical issues. Lawson said, "The Invaders made it difficult for us to do the work that was on top of us. They wanted to rearrange the agenda to make room for their rhetoric. It seemed like they wanted to create havoc.'' He continued:

At a time when we were strong and dynamic, when the strike was freezing up the downtown area, when our boycott was 97 percent effective, according to *Business Week*, when the business community was putting pressure on the Mayor to settle, when our weaponry was obviously effective, why then would you want to change strategy? It would be another story if your weapons weren't working. Why would these guys come around at public meetings, yelling about burning down and killing honkies? They talked nonsense.

Lawson remembered that on March 28 he confronted a man described as a "Beale Street crook," haranguing the crowd to remove the posters from the sticks and use them as spears.

Immediately after the riot, Reverend Lawson launched an investigation into who was behind the violence. After studying photographs and conducting interviews, he concluded that much of the violence was instigated by known Beale Street muggers and crooks. "They may or may not have been paid provocateurs, but they are all not Invaders," he told Cohen.

Lawson takes the issue of FBI provocation of the Invaders and others very seriously. He still wonders about a threat he received in the mail.

A few days after Martin's death, I received a package in the mail that had my picture and a bullet taped to it. It read something like, "We've got one for you too, nigger-preacher." Although I showed it to no one but my wife, I soon got a call from [Memphis Police Director] Holloman on some matter and he said, "I understand you got a package." That's when, for some reason, I was convinced it came from the Invaders and that the FBI was in on it. It's funny, I didn't suspect the Memphis police. Probably because Holloman worked for the FBI for so many years.

One of the leaders of the Invaders, John B. Smith, told Jeff Cohen that:

The marching contingent, not the leadership, could have been infiltrated. They were mostly eighteen- and nineteen-year-olds. It's very possible that the FBI hired people to throw rocks and bricks. It's also possible that a paid provocateur would have then proclaimed, "I'm an Invader." Remember too, if someone got up and spoke loudly at a meeting, that didn't mean that they were part of the leadership.

Smith disagreed with Payne's statement that the Invaders provided a four-man security force for Dr. King, but he offered an explanation:

We provided no security for King at the Lorraine. There was a heavy-set, brown-skinned, baldheaded guy named Barracuda, who, along with three or four others, played a security role. They were probably not from Memphis. At least I hadn't seen them before . . . or since. They wore cutoff Levi jackets and could easily have been mistaken for Invaders.

The confusion about the Levi-jacketed security detail parallels the situation in certain places where anyone who wore a black leather jacket was considered a member of the Black Panther Party.

While Smith contests some of Payne's specifics in his defense of the Invaders' leadership, he would be surprised if the FBI did not provoke violence to discredit King. "Knowing how they tried to destroy Dr. King, I'd be shocked if they did not have a hand in it. But the premise that the FBI had to go through the Invaders' leadership to hurt King is wrong."

In an account published by the black-oriented *Tri-State Defender,* Coby Smith, formerly a senior member and adviser to the Invaders and now an administrator at State Tech Institute, called the *Newsday* article "not completely accurate." Coby Smith claimed that he and other Invaders were aware of infiltrators in the organization long before King's death. He said that although the Invaders decided not to take part in the march, many people were donning Invader jackets because "they were very easy to make." His comments agree with John B. Smith's that there were people posing as Invaders who could have provoked the march to violence.

The FBI's role in Memphis just prior to the assassination is a huge and ominous question mark. Most Americans believe that the FBI investigates crimes. But revelations about the COINTELPRO operation indicate that the FBI has been committing them.

Dr. King's nonviolent movement in Memphis had been jeopardized by a series of events, culminating in the massive use of weapons, tear gas, clubs, and mace by the police under the direction of Frank Holloman, against the marching black population of Memphis. The fact that some of the violence was initiated, or at the least was said to have been initiated by some of the demonstrators, created a crisis for King's movement. He had little choice. It appeared that he was constrained to return to Memphis, to preach nonviolence yet again and to carry off a successful demonstration as witness to his deeply-held beliefs.

King was under fire from almost all of the traditional national black leaders for having called for an end to the war in Vietnam. The federal police had weakened his movement through numerous illegal efforts that enjoyed uneven success. FBI-infiltrated groups of young "militants" condemned him for his adherence to nonviolence in the face of continued and unabated violence directed against him and those who marched with him.

Liberal publications and friends who had formerly supported him had turned against him. Andrew Young, a black minister who had served in the Southern Christian Leadership Conference with King, now the United States Ambassador to the United Nations, told the Church Committee:

It was a great burden to be attacked by people he respected, particularly when the attacks engendered by the FBI came from people like Ralph McGill. He sat down and cried at *The New York Times* editorial about his statement on Vietnam, but this just made him more determined. It was a great personal suffering, but since we don't really know all that they did, we have no way of knowing the ways that they affected us.

If a meaningful and nonviolent march to Washington on April 22, 1968, appeared to be crucial to Dr. King, it seemed on March 28 that a similar action in Memphis was required as a precursor.

On March 29 the local press in Memphis removed any doubt. On that day the Memphis *Commercial Clarion* stated,

Yesterday's march, ostensibly a protest on behalf of the city's striking sanitation workers, was generally considered to be a "dress rehearsal" by Dr. King for his planned march on Washington April 22.

The Domestic Intelligence Division of the FBI, in a memorandum circulated the previous day, stated:

A sanitation strike has been going on in Memphis for some time. Martin Luther King, Jr., today led a march composed of 5,000 to 6,000 people through the streets of Memphis. King was in an automobile preceding the marchers. As the march developed, acts of violence and vandalism broke out including the breaking of windows in stores and some looting.

This clearly demonstrates that acts of so-called nonviolence advocated by King cannot be controlled. The same thing could happen in his planned massive civil disobedience for Washington in April.

The memorandum was accompanied by an "action" directive which read:

ACTION

Attached is a blind memorandum pointing out the above, which if you approve, should be made available by Crime Records Division to cooperative news media sources.

The memorandum was initiated by Hoover and carried his approval in the form of the "O.K." written by him. On the memorandum the notation, "handled on 3/28/68," was evidence that the suggestion had been given to "cooperative news media sources."

The Memphis *Commercial Clarion* was the first news media to publish an article that resembled the memorandum written by FBI agents. The Memphis *Commercial Appeal* the next day picked up the "dress rehearsal" phrase and reported:

Dr. Martin Luther King, Jr., came to Memphis to star in what was billed as a "dress rehearsal" for his April 22 "Poor People's Crusade" on Washington. By his own nonviolent standards, the rehearsal was a flop.

The article then presented the other point that had been made by the FBI news writers. "The question being asked in Memphis, the nation and the world is whether—with the increasing militancy of the black youth—anyone can say with certainty that a nonviolent demonstration will stay that way."

That same day *The New York Times* published an editorial entitled "Mini-Riot in Memphis . . ." which made the same point:

The disorder in Memphis that left store windows on Beale Street smashed and one Negro youth dead exposes the danger in drawing large numbers of protesters into the streets for emotional demonstrations in this time of civic unrest. The Rev. Dr. Martin Luther King, who organized the Memphis march, is organizing a "Poor People's Campaign" for Washington, D. C., next month. None of the precautions he and his aides are taking to keep the capital demonstration peaceful can provide any dependable insurance against another eruption of the kind that rocked Memphis.

Chapter Sixteen

MARCH 29, MEMPHIS AND WASHINGTON
by Mark Lane

On March 29 the Domestic Intelligence Division of the FBI drafted another "news story" and recommended that that article should also be furnished to cooperative news sources. It read:

> **Martin Luther King, during the sanitation workers' strike in Memphis, Tennessee, has urged Negroes to boycott downtown white merchants to achieve Negro demands. On 3/29/68 King led a march for the sanitation workers. Like Judas leading lambs to slaughter [sic], King led the marchers to violence, and when the violence broke out, King disappeared.**
>
> **The fine Hotel Lorraine in Memphis is owned and patronized exclusively by Negroes, but King didn't go there for his hasty exit. Instead, King decided the plush Holiday Inn Motel, white owned, operated and almost exclusively patronized, was the place to "cool it." There will be no boycott of white merchants for King, only for his followers.**

The FBI agents even provided a headline for the story; "Do As I Say, Not As I Do." The news story was accompanied by an internal Bureau memorandum, bearing the caption of its Counterintelligence Program, which read as follows:

> **The purpose is to publicize hypocrisy on the part of Martin Luther King. Background: Martin Luther King has urged Negroes in Memphis, Tenn., to boycott white merchants in order to force compliance with Negro demands in the sanitation workers' strike in Memphis. On March 28, 1968, King disappeared. There is a first-class Negro hotel in Memphis, the Hotel Lorraine, but**

King chose to hide out at the white owned-and-operated Holiday Inn Motel.

Recommendation: The above facts have been included in the attached blind memorandum, and it is recommended it be furnished to a cooperative news media source by the Crimes Records Division for items showing King is a hypocrite. This will be done on a highly confidential basis.

That document bore Hoover's approval as well. He wrote on it "O.K., H" which indicated his approval of the plan.

When the Church Committee examined the document it reported that the notation "handled" appeared on the document, but that the date next to the word "handled" was illegible on the copy of the document furnished to the Senate Committee by the FBI and that "we have not yet seen the original document."

Since the FBI maintained that the date of handling was April 3, 1968, the FBI was also able to maintain that its program was not put into effect in this instance. Dr. King arrived in Memphis on April 3. Yet the blurred date, the refusal of the FBI to furnish a clear copy or the original document, and the history of FBI officials in hastily putting programs against Dr. King into action immediately after they were approved by Hoover for fear of Hoover's wrath if they failed to do so, raises serious questions. The Church Committee, however, did not confront those questions.

Instead of closely questioning the FBI agent who wrote "handled" on the memorandum, in an effort to determine how he had acquitted himself of his responsibility to furnish the article to a "cooperative news media source" on "a highly confidential basis" before he wrote the note signifying that he had done so, the Church Committee asked the FBI to investigate. The Committee then reported, "The FBI questioned the agent who wrote 'handled' on the memorandum and informed the Committee that he did not recall the memorandum, and did not know whether 'handled' indicated that he had disseminated the article or simply cleared the memorandum through the Crime Records Division of the FBI." Since in intelligence jargon "handled" means that the job has been done, the doubt suggested by the FBI investigation as to what "handled" meant in this instance hardly seems justified. It also appears rather unlikely that an FBI agent who may have played an important part in moving Dr. King from the relative safety of the imposing and isolated Rivermont Holiday Inn to a very vulnerable location at which he was, in fact, killed the next day would "not recall" the incident or his own actions relevant to it.

106

Perhaps the best evidence presently available regarding the action taken by the FBI in reference to the promulgation of its own news article can be gleaned by an examination of the news media reports. For, in this instance, the proof of the plotting is in the reading.

The day after the agent noted that the matter had been "handled," the Memphis newspapers began referring to Dr. King's "posh" room at the Rivermont Holiday Inn. In an article the Memphis *Commercial Appeal* even disclosed the exact cost of the room, referring to it as "Dr. King's $29-a-day room at the Holiday Inn Rivermont."

The Memphis police reporters in contact with Frank Holloman began to speak of King's betrayal as evidenced by his "posh" accommodations at the Rivermont. The political reporters in contact with the Mayor made similar observations. According to Kay Pittman Black, a reporter for the Memphis *Press-Scimitar,* "there was even resentment in the Invader group about him staying at this fancy hotel." Ms. Black had covered all aspects of the sanitation strike and the visits to the city that Dr. King had made. The Church Committee offered the conclusion that "Dr. King always stayed at the Lorraine when he visited Memphis; with the exception of his prior visit." That conclusion, however, was not based upon an investigation by the Committee, but upon its acceptance of the assertion of the FBI and of one other person. Clearly, a cursory examination of hotel registration records might have revealed the facts.

When Ms. Black was told that it was alleged that Dr. King had always stayed at the Lorraine in the past, she said, "No. He did not. I covered his every visit to this city—even before the strike. He stayed at the Claridge, the big hotel downtown, right across from City Hall. The SCLC and Dr. King had almost an entire floor there. They had never stayed at the Lorraine. Not that I know of. In fact when I was told, I guess it was on April 3, that he was to be at the Lorraine, I was at the AME building. I spent a great deal of time there and it was my specific duty to keep up with Dr. King, to know when he was to arrive, to know where he was staying."

Ms. Black said that the coordinator of the sanitation workers' strike told her that King "would not be at the Rivermont—that he would be staying at the Lorraine as a commitment to patronize small black-owned businesses, as opposed to staying at a white-owned hotel." Ms. Black added, "I know it was the first time that I ever heard of Dr. King being at the Lorraine Motel because at that time I didn't even know where that hotel was. I knew, I guess, that it was generally in the black area, but I didn't actually know where it was located. I went over there in the morning and I sat in the coffee shop and talked to Andy Young and Jim

Bevel and Jesse Jackson. And that was the first time I saw the Lorraine Motel and I followed Dr. King closely whenever he was in Memphis.''

The FBI memoranda had accomplished their tasks. Dr. King had returned to Memphis to lead a nonviolent march for the sanitation workers and to salvage his national movement and his projected Poor People's Crusade. He was compelled to do so, at least partially due to the FBI memorandum of March 28 and the wide circulation given to that memorandum, at first in Memphis, and then throughout the country.

Senator Robert C. Byrd led the efforts in Congress to condemn Dr. King and said that he should be enjoined from carrying out the planned demonstration in Washington. He referred to Dr. King as a ''self-seeking rabble-rouser'' and predicted that King, if not stopped, would be responsible for ''violence, destruction, looting and bloodshed'' in Washington.

Approximately seven years later the origin of Senator Byrd's vehement attack upon Dr. King became evident as the Church Committee secured access to various FBI memoranda. On January 19, 1968, Cartha De Loach, then a high-ranking FBI official, reported to Hoover's personal friend and FBI colleague, Clyde Tolson, that he had met with Senator Byrd. According to the De Loach memorandum, Byrd had expressed concern over Dr. King's plan for demonstrations in Washington and said that it was time that ''King met his Waterloo.'' De Loach's memorandum states that Byrd asked if the FBI would prepare a speech about Dr. King which he could deliver on the floor of the Senate.

The speech, which was delivered on March 29, 1968, by Senator Byrd, now the leader of the Democratic Party in the Senate, was vehement. Although Dr. King was the victim of the violence, Byrd said:

Yesterday, Mr. President, the nation was given a preview of what may be in store for this city by the outrageous and despicable riot that Martin Luther King helped to bring about in Memphis, Tennessee.

He continued:

In Memphis, people were injured, stores were looted, property was destroyed, terror reigned in the streets, people were beaten by hoodlums, at least one Negro youth is known to have been killed, and massive rioting erupted during a march which was led by this man. It was a shameful and totally uncalled for outburst of lawlessness undoubtedly encouraged to some considerable degree, at least, by his words and actions, and his presence. There is no reason for us to believe that the same destructive rioting and violence cannot, or that it will not, happen here if King attempts his so-called Poor People's March, for what he

108

plans in Washington appears to be something on a far greater scale than what he had indicated he planned to do in Memphis.

Almost all who admired Dr. King as well as those who despised him or were indifferent to his work agreed that he was a man of great personal courage. From his upholstered chair in what its members are pleased to refer to as the most exclusive club in the world, Byrd attacked Dr. King's commitment and questioned his courage.

When the predictable rioting erupted in Tennessee, Martin Luther King fled the scene. He took to his heels and disappeared, leaving it to others to cope with the destructive forces he had helped to unleash.

Returning to his theme of Dr. King's "flight" from danger again and again, Byrd said:

King intends to create a black hole of despair with people packed together with pigs and chickens in a "shanty town" lacking sanitation. Surely he must know that to change hearts it is not necessary to turn stomachs. It can be assumed that, however, if yesterday's flight by King from the disorder he had helped to generate was any indication of what he might do here, the "Messiah" himself will not share the squalor he plans and that instead he will be conducting a lay-in at a posh Washington hotel to dramatize some imaginary discrimination there.

Had the speech been prepared on Hoover's private stationery, the clues regarding its conception would have been little more apparent. The word "Messiah" figured prominently in FBI jargon regarding Dr. King. A high-level FBI memorandum suggested that the FBI create its own black "messiah" to replace Dr. King. The allegation that Dr. King would conduct a "lay-in" at a Washington hotel might be construed as a reference to the then still secret war against Dr. King waged through FBI sexpionage tactics.

The reference to the "posh Washington hotel" may have been a device calculated by the FBI to embarrass Dr. King and drive him from the Holiday Inn Rivermont Hotel into the more modest Lorraine. If so, the United States Senate was employed, along with the local newspapers in Memphis, in an effort to move Dr. King to the location at which he was ultimately murdered. Byrd charged that "King lovingly breaks the law like a boa constrictor." He continued,

Apparently the hoodlums in Memphis yesterday followed King's advice to break laws with which they did not agree. This has been a cardinal principle of his philosophy—a philosophy

109

that leads naturally to the escalation of nonviolence into civil disobedience—which is only a euphemism for lawbreaking and criminality and which escalates next into civil unrest, civil disorder, and insurrection.

Mr. President, I have previously urged, in discussing this matter with the Justice Department, that the Federal Government seek a court order to enjoin Martin Luther King and his pulpitless parsons from carrying out their planned poor people's campaign in the Nation's Capital. In the light of yesterday's bloody chapter of violence which erupted with the visit of Martin Luther King to Memphis, I again urge that the Federal Government take steps to prevent King from carrying out his planned harassment of Washington, D. C. An ounce of prevention is worth a pound of cure. It is time for our Federal Government —which in recent years has shown itself to be virtually spineless when it comes to standing up against the lawbreakers, the hoodlums, and the Marxist demonstrators—at least to let the Nation know, in no uncertain terms, that it will not allow this Nobel Peace Prize winner to create another Memphis in the city which serves as the seat of the Government of the United States.

Byrd was joined by other Senators and Representatives who, no doubt, without understanding that they were doing so, followed closely the script that the FBI had prepared just the day before. Among those who focused upon the Memphis riot to demand executive action to bar the demonstration were senators Strom Thurmond, John Stennis, and various members of the House. Among those who "saw the possibility of violence" in Washington and who opposed Dr. King's march were Senator Edward W. Brooke, described by the media as "the nation's highest Negro office holder," and Senator Howard Baker, who said that "the March on Washington is like striking a match to look in your gas tank and see if you're out of gas."

Senator Strom Thurmond echoed Byrd's remarks and then revealed that he too may have been privy to an FBI briefing or two.

. . . I call upon President Johnson to make public the information about King which is available to him. This information is openly talked about in Washington. References to it have appeared in the newspapers. I challenge the administration to let all the citizens of this country know what kind of a man King really is, and what his true purpose is.

The campaign of vilification of Dr. King raged on unabated in the Senate, far from the slums of Memphis where children of sanitation workers suffered from malnutrition, were ill clothed, and attended substandard schools.

Senator Stennis had a word of advice for those and other "colored" people:

I want to give a word of advice and counsel to the colored people and to any others who may be inclined to come to Washington from Mississippi. It is to stay out of the march. Nothing good for them or from anyone else can come from it. They run the risk that harm can come from it. They run the risk that harm can come to any individual or any group. I mean by that the possibility of personal injury and violence in the course of any demonstrations that may get out of hand.

Dr. King returned to Memphis. The riot required that he return to confront yet again the twin evils of economic and racial discrimination.

The FBI had prevailed. Dr. King was to return not just to Memphis but to the Lorraine Motel.

Chapter Seventeen

APRIL 3 AND 4, MEMPHIS

by Dick Gregory

Reading Martin Luther King's final message to America and reflecting on his last day of life was a profoundly emotional experience for me. As I re-read it and listened to it so many times on tape, the feeling recurs, that King betrayed in his comments a premonition of the vicious experience creeping up on him. The tone and content of the message suggests that he believed his life might end soon.

I try to reconstruct in my own mind how he may have been feeling that night in Mason Temple in Memphis. Was he sad, weary, but determined to fight on to the end? Was he lonely, misunderstood but still unwavering in his convictions? I wonder what went through his mind as he stood there, knowing the stark hatred many aimed at him and his cause. And I wonder if his thoughts were with his family; those I had met, his brother, A. D., his mother, Alberta, his father, Daddy King, his children, and Coretta; and those I didn't know.

And I listen again to the touching segment of his speech in which he drew an analogy between his reasons for being in Memphis and the Bible parable of the Good Samaritan.

King related how he and Coretta were in Jerusalem where they rented a car to Jericho, taking the same road traveled by the Good Samaritan and the victim of highway robbery that he befriended. As they drove along the ancient road King said he saw the application of the parable to contemporary American life.

I was struck by King's keen perception of the lesson of the parable. The question, he said, must be what will happen to my brother if I don't stop to help him—not what will happen to me, what will I lose, if I do help him. He posed the question to his audience, told them that his position was not what might he lose if he joined the sanitation workers in their dispute, but rather what terrible consequences might result if he failed to help them.

If Martin could return and sit down with me, there are a million things I'd want to say to him. But, if the time were very short and I had to choose one topic, it would be this:

Martin, I want you to know how grateful I am that you stopped. That you encountered a sick, mortally wounded society as you traveled the road of life and you refused to ignore it; that you offered a helping hand. Thank you for stopping in Memphis, Birmingham, in Selma and St. Augustine, in Cleveland, Ohio, and Chicago. You stopped, you interrupted your life to speak out against the War in Vietnam.

I would go on,

Thank you, Martin, for ensuring that we need never ask the tragic question that too often follows neglect of duty: "Would this have happened if. . ." Because of you, we don't have to go to the back of Birmingham's buses, we don't have to say "If Martin had stopped here, the buses and the schools and the stores and the restaurants would be desegregated now," because you came and they are. We don't have to say "If Martin Luther King had stopped to help with voter registration there would be more black voters in the country," because you did stop and there are.

Because of you, Martin, I can give thanks that I, as an American and human being, will never have to pose that question. Because you stopped, a thousand potential tragedies were eliminated before they could be set in motion. I'm glad I don't have to say, "If only King had been there, this might not have happened," because you were there, and it didn't happen.

I reflect on your final message and know it is one from which unborn generations will derive meaning and inspiration. How I wish I could have been in the audience that last night of your life. I wish I could have been there to listen as you delivered your talk, to watch as you touched your face with your finger in a characteristic gesture, as you moved your shoulders to make sure your coat hung properly. I'm sorry I missed your smile as your eyes swept the crowded auditorium, as you recognized so many of the folks and welcomed the ones who listened to you for the first time.

I wish I had been there to hear the following brilliant farewell message, although none of your listeners knew it was goodbye.

Dr. Martin Luther King's final words to America were spoken at Mason Temple, Memphis, Tennessee, on April 3, 1968. The next day he was murdered, but his vision for a humane world order will never die. Excerpts from his address follow.

I'VE BEEN TO THE MOUNTAINTOP

. . . if I were standing at the beginning of time, with the possibility of a general and panoramic view of the whole human history up to now, and the Almighty said to me, "Martin Luther King, which age would you like to live in?"—I would take my mental flight by Egypt through, or rather across the Red Sea, through the wilderness on toward the promised land. And in spite of its magnificence, I wouldn't stop there. I would move on by Greece, and take my mind to Mount Olympus. And I would see Plato, Aristotle, Socrates, Euripides and Aristophanes assembled around the Parthenon as they discussed the great and eternal issues of reality.

But I wouldn't stop there. I would go on, even to the great heyday of the Roman Empire. And I would see developments around there, through various emperors and leaders. But I wouldn't stop there. I would even come up to the day of the Renaissance, and get a quick picture of all that the Renaissance did for the cultural and aesthetic life of man. But I wouldn't stop there. I would even go by the way that the man for whom I'm named had his habitat. And I would watch Martin Luther as he tacked his 95 theses on the door at the church in Wittenberg.

But I wouldn't stop there. I would come on up even to 1863, and watch a vacillating President by the name of Abraham Lincoln finally come to the conclusion that he had to sign the Emancipation Proclamation. But I wouldn't stop there. I would even come up to the early thirties, and see a man grappling with the problems of the bankruptcy of his nation. And come with an eloquent cry that we have nothing to fear but fear itself.

But I wouldn't stop there. Strangely enough, I would turn to the Almighty and say, "If you allow me to live just a few years in the second half of the Twentieth Century, I will be happy." Now that's a strange statement to make, because the world is all messed up. The nation is sick. Trouble is in the land. Confusion all around. That's a strange statement. But I know, somehow, that only when it is dark enough, can you see the stars. And I see God working in this period of the Twentieth Century in a way that men, in some strange way, are responding—something is happening in our world. The masses of people are rising up . . . whether they are in Johannesburg, South Africa; Nairobi, Kenya; Accra, Ghana; New York City; Atlanta, Georgia;

Jackson, Mississippi; or Memphis, Tennessee—the cry is always the same—"We want to be free."

And another reason that I'm happy to live in this period is . . . we're going to have to grapple with the problems that men have been trying to grapple with through history, but the demands didn't force them to do it. Survival demands that we grapple with them. Men, for years now, have been talking about war and peace. But now, no longer can they just talk about it. It is no longer a choice between violence and nonviolence in this world, it's nonviolence or nonexistence.

That is where we are today . . . Now, I'm just happy that God has allowed me to live in this period, to see what is unfolding. And I'm happy that he's allowed me to be in Memphis. . . .

Now we've got to go on to Memphis just like that. I call upon you to be with us Monday. Now about injunctions: We have an injunction and we're going into court tomorrow morning to fight this illegal, unconstitutional injunction. All we say to America is, "Be true to what you said on paper." If I lived in China or even Russia, or any totalitarian country, maybe I could understand the denial of certain basic First Amendment privileges, because they hadn't committed themselves to that over there. But somewhere I read of the freedom of assembly. Somewhere I read of the freedom of speech. Somewhere I read of the freedom of the press. Somewhere I read that the greatness of America is the right to protest for right. . . . This is what we have to do.

. . . Always anchor our external direct action with the power of economic withdrawal. Now we are poor people, individually, we are poor when you compare us with white society in America. We are poor . . . collectively, that means all of us together, collectively we are richer than all the nations in the world. . . . Did you ever think about that? . . . That's power right there, if we know how to pool it.

We don't have to argue with anybody. . . . We don't need any bricks and bottles, we don't need any molotov cocktails, we just need to go around to these stores, and to these massive industries in our country, and say, "God sent us by here, to say to you that you're not treating his children right. And we've come by here to ask you to make the first item on your agenda—fair treatment, where God's children are concerned. Now, if you are not prepared to do that, we do have an agenda that we must follow. And our agenda calls for withdrawing economic support from you."

. . . up to now, only the garbage men have been feeling pain, now we must kind of redistribute the pain. . . .

I remember when Mrs. King and I were first in Jerusalem. We rented a car and drove from Jerusalem down to Jericho. And as soon as we got on that road, I said to my wife, "I can see why Jesus used this as a setting for his parable." It's a winding, meandering road. It's really conducive for ambushing. You start out in Jerusalem, which is about 1200 miles, or rather 1200 feet above sea level. And by the time you get down to Jericho, 15 or 20 minutes later, you're about 2200 feet below sea level. That's a dangerous road. In the days of Jesus it came to be known as the 'Bloody Pass.' And you know, it's possible that the priest and the Levite looked over that man on the ground and wondered if the robbers were still around. Or it's possible that they felt that the man on the ground was merely faking. And he was acting like he had been robbed and hurt in order to seize them over there , lure them there for quick and easy seizure. And so the first question that the Levite asked was, "If I stop to help this man, what will happen to me?" But then the good Samaritan came by. And he reversed the question: "If I do not stop to help this man, what will happen to him?"

That's the question before you tonight. Not, "If I stop to help the sanitation workers, what will happen to all of the hours that I usually spend in my office every day and every week as a pastor?" The question is not, "If I stop to help this man in need, what will happen to me?" "If I do not stop to help the sanitation workers, what will happen to them?" That's the question. . . .

It really doesn't matter what happens now. I left Atlanta this morning, and as we got started on the plane, there were six of us, the pilot said over the public address system, "We are sorry for the delay, but we have Dr. Martin Luther King on the plane and to be sure that all of the bags were checked, and to be sure that nothing would be wrong with the plane, we had to check out everything carefully and we've had the plane protected and guarded all night."

And then I got into Memphis and some began to say the threats, or talk about the threats that were out. What would happen to me from some of our sick white brothers?

Well, I don't know what will happen now. We've got some

difficult days ahead. But it doesn't matter with me now. Because I've been to the mountaintop. And I don't mind. Like anybody, I would like to live a long life. Longevity has its place. But I'm not concerned about that now. I just want to do God's will. And He's allowed me to go up to the mountain. And I've looked over. And I've seen the promised land. I may not get there with you. But I want you to know tonight, that we, as a people will get to the promised land. And I'm happy, tonight. I'm not worried about anything. I'm not fearing any man. Mine eyes have seen the glory of the coming of the Lord.

April 4, 1968

Morning comes too quickly to suit the two tired men who sleep in the motel room. The night before both had participated in a long, emotion-charged rally. One was the main speaker and the other a kind of advance man.

One of them opens his eyes and realizes that the light coming through the window near the edge not covered by the heavy drapes is a sign of morning. It is indeed time to get up, and this, like many mornings, is one where both men would have liked to have been able to rest a while longer.

Ralph Abernathy sits up in his bed, and there is a creaking sound as he swings his feet over the edge of the bed to the floor. He sits there for a long moment and then succumbs to the inevitable. Stretching and yawning at the same time, he rises.

Then he glances in the bed next to his and sees that his friend is still sound asleep. He would like so much not to have to wake him, but there's a lot of work that has to be done, and they could not sleep late.

"Michael," he says in a kind, quiet voice. "Michael, come on now, it's time to get up." The response is prompt, though the voice is still heavy with sleep.

"Yes, David," he replied without making any motions to get out of bed.

"It's time to get up now. . . . You know we can't win this nonviolent revolution in bed. It's time to rise and shine. The early bird gets the worm."

Michael is fully awake now, and though he really isn't ready to get up, he is alert and jovial.

"Aw, David," he teases, "you're still a farmer. I'm never gonna get that Alabama soil out of you!"

They tease back and forth, lightly and easily, in a familiar pattern. It is a typical beginning to an ordinary day. I talked with Ralph Abernathy at great length about his private relationship to Dr. King. I wanted to know more than the story of two men who were professional colleagues and who shared a philosophy that is unique in our violence-prone society—the philosophy of nonviolence.

Among other things, I learned that King called Abernathy by his middle name, David; and that Ralph privately addressed King by his real name, which was Michael. (King was christened Michael Luther but when he was six years old his father changed both their names to Martin Luther.) It interests me that King's original given name was Michael. This name, historically, is as eminent as that of Martin Luther. Michael, the archangel, according to the Bible, will be a leader in the war between God and Satan. It seems to me that King fulfilled the name of Michael more than that of Martin Luther. The legal act of changing his name to Martin did not alter the destiny of Michael. For it was certainly King's perception that he was engaged in a battle between good and evil.

Ralph Abernathy's reflections to me about King added another dimension to the man many have viewed as a saint, savior, and humanitarian. Because of Ralph's love for King, he was able to reveal a type of personal warmth when he recalled important times that he had spent with him. The events that took place on April 4, 1968, prior to the moment when King was shot, were typical of the daily routine of these two men.

After getting up that morning, they each showered and shaved as they had to get ready for an important meeting where they would discuss the forthcoming Poor People's March on Washington. Getting organized was never a problem. Though Ralph was always the first to get up, he was frequently the last to get dressed because while King would be dressing, he would request Ralph to make phone calls and take notes for him. It was Ralph's job to make sure everything was done right and on time. There was no man in whom King had greater confidence.

They held the meeting right at the motel. They were meeting with the leaders of a local militant group called the Invaders. A march held the week earlier had been disrupted by persons claiming to be Invaders who had infiltrated the ranks of the peaceful marchers and begun rioting when the group reached downtown Memphis. Police had intervened and the march had to be called off. Andy Young reported that the Invaders were asking the SCLC to pay them $50,000 and give them five automobiles. Abernathy recalls vividly King's response.

"This movement will exclude any person or group who uses violence as a tactic, as a strategy, or as a way of life." King, says Abernathy, was adamant that SCLC would not pay blackmail to any person or group for any reason.

King and Abernathy had not eaten breakfast that morning before the meeting. Normally, their first meal was around noontime. They were both hungry after leaving the meeting and they decided to have lunch in their room. Each ordered fried catfish and salad. When the waitress brought their meal to the room, Abernathy was annoyed that she had not gotten the order right. She had all the fish on one plate, along with two bowls of salad. Abernathy was about to send her back to get the order straight when King told him not to worry about it. Abernathy recalls King saying to him, "Leave her alone, David, it doesn't matter. You and me can eat from the same plate."

The two men spent the afternoon with other SCLC members, making plans, mapping strategy. Reverend Samuel Kyles, a Memphis minister who was in charge of the garbage workers' boycott, was one of those who came. King's brother, A.D., had come from Lexington to particpate in the boycott and rally. Abernathy remembers King teasing Jesse Jackson. "Look, Jesse, you can't take that whole band out to Sam's house tonight." SCLC had been invited to Reverend Kyles' home for dinner before the scheduled rally. "Sam's wife can't feed the whole bunch. And you be sure to dress up a little tonight, OK, Jesse? No blue jeans, all right?"

Abernathy was the next in line for the teasing that was going on. One of the ministers accused him of taking almost as long to introduce King at the rally the night before as it took King to give the main address.

King had spoken the night of April 3rd, and that address came to be known as the now famous "Mountaintop Speech." It had been cold and dreary in Memphis; there were even tornado warnings. King did not think that people would turn out to hear him because of the bad weather, so he requested Abernathy to go to the Mason Temple and speak in his place. "You go ahead and speak for me tonight," he told Ralph. "I'll stay here and relax." Abernathy asked Jesse Jackson to go with him that night, and when they arrived at the church they were amazed at the large number of television cameras and reporters who were waiting outside in the cold and the rain. Abernathy was surprised that such a large number of press people were there. He looked inside and saw that about three hundred people were inside the enormous church that could seat three thousand. It was at that point that he decided that King, not himself, should be there to speak. He quickly went to a telephone and called the motel. King was hesitant at first, but realizing that all these people had come out despite the severe weather warnings, he told Ralph he would be there. The church was very near the motel, and it was not long before King arrived.

After Abernathy's introduction, King came onstage. His opening words that night were, "I want everybody here to know that Ralph David Abernathy is the closest and dearest friend I have in the world!" He went on to give his historic address, but in Ralph Abernathy's gallery of memories, King's public acknowledgment of the devotion he felt for his chief lieutenant were the words that shone most brightly that night.

Abernathy was often described as King's "behind the scenes man," or "his assistant." It was only when I talked with Ralph and learned of their many private conversations that I realized how very much Ralph Abernathy meant to Martin Luther King.

"David," King would say, "I want you to know how much I appreciate your loyalty. I get all the attention from the press, but you're just as important to the movement as I am. I couldn't do my work if you were not here with me. Life is very arbitrary in choosing who will be idolized, who will be the leader. People often forget that a leader is no stronger than his foundation, the often invisible people who give him support. I'll never forget that, David. The newspapermen, the cameramen, some of our own SCLC colleagues may forget it, but I want you to know that I *never, never* will forget it." Abernathy recalls that during King's words to him, he felt that King was looking for a way to repay Ralph for all the work he had done. But Ralph said he always replied this way: "I don't want anything more, Michael, I just want to be here working with you. I'm pleased and satisfied about what I can do for you." Envy and jealousy were never present in the relationship between Ralph David Abernathy and Martin Luther King, Jr.

It is still April 4th, and King's mother, Alberta King, was elated at the fact that her two sons, Martin and A. D., were together this day, chatting and sharing precious memories. King had gone to his brother's room at the motel while Ralph rested in Room 306. Around two-thirty that afternoon, King rang Ralph in the room and told him how happy he was that his brother had come, and that they had just both spoken with their mother over the telephone. King always shared these kinds of personal joys with his friend Ralph.

Around five o'clock King and Abernathy prepared to leave the Lorraine Motel for the dinner which was planned at Samuel Kyles' home. Abernathy, at King's direction, had phoned Mrs. Kyles and had been reassured that it was indeed a soul food feast that awaited the hungry SCLC corps. They were all hungry, and Kyles' wife, who they had all heard was a terrific cook, had prepared a dinner that included roast beef, collard greens, chitterlings, black-eyed peas, cornbread, and fried chicken. Kyles' wife also told Abernathy that the dinner would be at six o'clock, not at five o'clock as he had told them.

Confronted with this discrepancy, Kyles admits a little sheepishly that he wanted to make sure they got there on time. Everyone, after all, was aware of "Colored Peoples' Time," meaning that blacks were notoriously late. Kyles said he simply wanted to insure that they would not be late for the special meal.

Now the two men are in Room 306 alone. Both have changed clothes and are freshening up. Both King and Abernathy splash on some Aramis after-shave lotion. Abernathy told me that he remembered saying something about the lotion being a real necessity because King had just used a depilatory shave powder that fouled the air in the room. He said that the two of them often joked about the smell left by King's shaving solution.

King goes out to the balcony leading from the room. Jesse Jackson is on the ground below. They talk about the music to be played tonight. King turns to Jackson's companion, Ben Branch, an organist from Chicago. "Be sure and play my favorite song tonight, okay?" Branch assures King that he will play the familiar tune "Precious Lord, Take My Hand."

Abernathy, meanwhile, continues to rub Aramis into his cheeks. He hears a noise, reminiscent of a firecracker popping. He looks to the balcony and sees King's knees collapse. "All I could see was his feet," said Abernathy as he recalled that fateful night. Abernathy immediately ran toward King and saw the blood as he lifted the head of his friend and looked into his eyes. Ralph believes that King did see and hear him that night. He recalls saying to King, "Michael, its going to be all right, don't you worry now because everything's going to be all right. I'll get help, don't worry. . . ."

All the rest has been recorded a thousand times. One thing sticks in Abernathy's mind though. It is Andy Young's voice saying, "It's over, it's over. . . ." Ralph told me that he kept telling Andy, "No, it's not over, it's not over."

It was Ralph Abernathy who stayed with King's body the rest of the night. It was Abernathy who stayed in the operating room though doctors and nurses had told him that he would have to leave. The world was shocked and the press was looking for Ralph Abernathy to talk to about what had happened. But Ralph Abernathy never left the side of his friend's body that night. It was he who was called to the morgue to identify the body. "I remember something that hurt me more than anything else that night. . . . I remember going to that morgue and seeing my good friend with a brown paper tag hooked to his toe. I'll never forget that sight."

PART
FIVE

THE
MURDER

Chapter Eighteen

APRIL 4, MEMPHIS
by Mark Lane

Directly across the street from the Lorraine Motel was a large rectangular building which served Memphis as Fire Station Two. From the rear of the building, which was built on an embankment, one was afforded a fine view of the Lorraine and, because it was raised high above the street, an almost eye-level view of the motel's second floor balcony. For some days the police had utilized Fire Station Two as a command post. It was ideal because it was so near the motel, had an unobstructed view of the scene in the motel court and of most of the rooms which faced the fire station, and because it provided cover for the police. During the previous week, on March 28, a march from Clayborn Temple, led by Dr. King, was interrupted by window breaking. The police then moved into the demonstrators. Police attack dogs were replaced by the first mass use of mace in the nation against peaceful demonstrators. The police charged the marchers, using night sticks and tear gas, and firing weapons. A sixteen-year-old boy, Larry Payne, was shot and killed. Two hundred and eighty people were arrested and at least sixty were injured by police violence. The state legislature mandated a nightly curfew at 7 o'clock and 4,000 members of the National Guard moved into Memphis.

The feeling in the black community against the city officials, who would not consider the minimal demands of the sanitation workers, and the police, who were at best unsympathetic to their fellow city employees, most of whom were black, was exacerbated by the brutal attack upon the demonstrators. The Invaders, a militant black youth group, demanded that the police be removed from the scene. Reverend Samuel Kyles asked the police to assign Ed Redditt, a black Memphis detective, to provide security for Dr. King. Redditt was assigned and set up the police command post at the fire station because of its proximity to the Lorraine and because it provided security from the Invaders and others who wanted no police, black or white, on the scene.

A very interested observer in the police surveillance of the Lorraine Motel and Dr. King and his associates was Floyd Newsum, an intelligent, articulate supporter of his fellow city employees. Floyd Newsum, a black fireman for the city of Memphis, was stationed at Fire Station Two. Newsum had marched with the sanitation workers. He had walked with and listened to Dr. King. He had been for many years an activist in the struggle for equal rights in Memphis. When I spoke to him recently he had just celebrated his forty-fourth birthday. His daughter lives at home; one son, who has a masters degree in art, teaches art at the University of Houston while his other son is completing work for his doctorate at the University of Michigan.

On April 3, 1968, Newsum saw Detective Redditt at the fire station. That evening Newsum went to the Mason Temple to hear Dr. King, who had just returned to Memphis. Newsum saw Redditt at the rally that evening as well. Then Dr. King spoke. Newsum was deeply moved by King's words and those words still haunted him as he returned to his home that Wednesday night. He entered his home at approximately 10:30 that evening and "I found a message to call into the Fire Department; to call my lieutenant, Lt. Smith." He called Smith who ordered him not to report to Station Two the next morning but insisted he report to Station Thirty-one "on detail." A detail is a temporary transfer that is traditionally arranged so that a fire company with a surplus of men, or at least more personnel than are required for the task, can temporarily assign one or more employees to an understaffed company. Newsum told me, "I worked on a truck company. Our company simply could not operate with less than five men. On April 3rd our company was a company consisting of five men. When they detailed me out of Two they made that equipment inoperable, unless they sent someone in to replace me." Smith told Newsum that he did not know why he had been detailed to Thirty-one but that Newsum definitely had been ordered to report there in the morning and that he was not to report to Two.

On the morning of April 4th, Newsum reported to Thirty-one. He was assigned to a pumper company, a company that required four people to operate the equipment. He was the fifth man in the unit. He learned later that day that Thirty-one was sufficiently overstaffed to detail a man elsewhere. "During the entire period that I was at Thirty-one a man was detailed to another station."

He told me that on April 4th, "I asked the question over and over as to why I had been detailed. It just did not make any sense from a fire department personnel management viewpoint." Later, when Newsum learned of Dr. King's murder he cried. And in the agony of that moment, he said, "The fact that I had been detailed out so suspiciously became more important to me."

"Of course," he said, "the police knew who I was and that I supported the sanitation workers and Dr. King." Newsum explained how he knew that the Memphis police were tracking him.

I was definitely under police observation before April 4th. All during the movement I carried a little transistor radio that picked up police and fire calls. Just about everyone in the movement knew that I had that little radio with me all of the time which means, of course, that people outside the movement had access to that fact as well. One day we were conducting a sit-in at the council chambers. When I walked into City Hall a police officer transmitted over the police radio channel the fact that I was there. The voice on the other end asked if the officer was sure that it was me and he answered that he was reasonably sure. The officer was then instructed to make a picture of me. Then the officer reported, "He's got his radio and he might be listening to us."

An independent examination of Newsum's file confirmed the charge that he had been placed under police surveillance before April 4th.

Two weeks later Newsum decided to seek a leave of absence from the Fire Department or, in the alternative, to resign. He was deeply troubled about his transfer and the murder of Dr. King and wondered if the two events were somehow related. He asked to see the Chief of the Fire Department, but Deputy Chief Gerald Barnett made it clear to him that he would not be able to see the Chief. Newsum then submitted his letter of resignation to Barnett, who left the room and then returned a moment later. Barnett then told Newsum that he could see Chief Hamilton. Hamilton asked him why he was resigning. Newsum said, "I sensed that he was happy, very happy, that I was leaving the department." Newsum told me, "After I came out of the Chief's office I saw Barnett and I said, 'I asked you before and you never did answer me, you never did give me any kind of reason. Now that this is settled, now that I have resigned and my resignation has been accepted by the Chief, now will you tell me why I was moved on April 4th?' Barnett said, 'All I can tell you is that you were moved at the request of the police.' "

When Abby Mann interviewed Barnett in 1976 he was at first vague about Newsum's allegation, didn't recall that conversation with Newsum eight years earlier, and added, "Without going up there [to Fire Department headquarters] and briefing myself on the personnel records I might tell you a story. I might be mistaken. Why don't you call up and talk to Chief Williams about that. He's sitting up there with the records." When Mann asked the question again Barnett said, "He's got me mixed up with some other Chief." I asked Chief Williams if the personnel records supported Newsum's charge about being transferred and he replied, "Our records show that Mr. Newsum was detailed, I mean detailed from one place to another. And our records show that he was on April 4, 1968, he was detailed to what we say is Fire Station 31. But it doesn't give a reason."

I asked if the records revealed that there were only two black firemen at Fire Station Two and that both had been detailed out to other stations on April 4th. "Well, yes," said Chief Williams, "And they both were detailed to another station. The other one was named Wallace." I asked if he had any idea why the temporary transfers had taken place. "We try to keep the fire department balanced by details. To even up the personnel to take care of the shortage at a fire station." I then asked whether Thirty-one, to which Newsum had been transferred, had been short? He answered, "Well, like I say, a number of them were short that day. No, Thirty-one was not short. It wasn't below maximum strength." As for Wallace, "He was detailed to number Thirty-three, which is at the airport." Was Thirty-three short that day? "No, I don't think it was."

Well, was there a shortage of personnel at Two immediately after the two black firemen were detailed out on April 4 to other stations which were not short? "Yes, there was. In fact one man had to be detailed in, they were so short." When was this other man detailed in? "April 4, the day that Mr. Newsum was detailed out."

I told Chief Williams that Newsum had told me that Barnett had informed him that his transfer was the result of a police department request. Williams responded, "We had a fire and police director by the name of Holloman in 1968, at the time that King was killed. If Newsum was detailed out because of a police request it would have to come from Mr. Holloman, the director at that time. He was over the fire and police departments."

I spoke to Robert Walker, the current director of the Fire Department, told him what I had learned about the temporary transfers of Newsum and Wallace on April 4, 1968, and asked if he had any explanation for the odd events. "I think the records will reflect that those men were temporarily assigned to other stations and I think the reason might have been that there was a lot of tension, with the black-white issue there. And I think there had been a few occasions where they were harassed. I think it was this kind of tension that existed at the moment." I asked if the transfer was for the purpose of protecting Newsum and Wallace. "Yes. Right. In other words it was to relieve them of the tension that was being built up in the neighborhood." I told Walker that Newsum had been told that the police department had requested the transfer.

It's kind of bad that Mr. Holloman was the fire and police director at that time. Now we have separate directors, one over fire and one over police. It could have been that an agreement was worked out. I don't know what his thoughts were at that time. But it could have been that they were using Two as a stakeout by the police and possibly the FBI. I have been told that there were FBI people at the firehouse. You could call the FBI to check that out. I'm sure they keep the records. I know they were using it as a lookout post because the Lorraine Motel is near, in the vicinity of it.

During my next meeting with Newsum I told him that Walker had told me, in essence, that both he and Wallace had been detailed out due to the racial tension and to protect them. Newsum laughed and said,

I don't believe that was the reason. I never had been threatened. I never was harassed. In fact I felt quite comfortable at Station Two. I felt a lot more comfortable there than where I was sent to. Two is in a black community and I was transferred from there into a totally white community where I was the only black in the company. I was then with a group of men I didn't know. That was a crucial time, a very difficult time, and I was very uncomfortable there. In fact, I was so upset about that new assignment and so uncomfortable there that I called the Chief on April 4th and asked how long I had to remain there and asked to be returned to Two. There just is no way that they could have thought that they were doing me a favor, protecting me or making me more comfortable by transferring me. I am sure that I was not moved because of considerations of my safety.

Members of the fire companies stationed at Fire Station Two often sit outside the station during pleasant weather. They sit or stand around on a small patch near the rear of the firehouse, overlooking the Lorraine, or on a bench near the front of the station on South Main Street. If Newsum had been at the rear of the station on April 4th he might have seen Dr. King when he was shot. He might have responded by running toward the front of the station and looking to his right. If so, he probably would have seen the killer emerge from the rooming house door just a few yards down the street.

If Newsum had been sitting on a bench in front of the station, had he looked down South Main, he probably would have seen the murderer emerge from the rooming house.

Newsum was an activist. One cannot predict what his response might have been, but it certainly is possible that he might have interfered with the flight of the murderer from the scene, or at least have observed the man and perhaps his vehicle and reported that information to the police.

However, for reasons not yet adequately explained by the Memphis police and fire authorities, Newsum was not there. At Thirty-one all Newsum could do upon learning of Dr. King's death was to cry.

While Newsum was the only committed activist at Fire Station Two on April 3, he was not the only black fireman stationed there; N. E. Wallace was also assigned to Two at the time. On April 3 his company officer, R. T. Johnson, told him not to report to Station Two on April 4 for he too had been detailed out. Wallace asked Johnson why he was being transferred and Johnson told him, "Well, we hear that you have been threatened. You know, we don't want anything to happen to you."

Wallace told me that to his knowledge he had never been threatened while at Two and that he was certainly not afraid that anything would happen to him if he remained there. "That was a black community; there was another black in our station house and I felt comfortable there. I don't believe that I was threatened."

He said that approximately two and a half months after King was killed he was reassigned to Station Two and that he was never threatened or harmed after he returned.

I asked Wallace if he ever believed that the real reason that he had been transferred was because he had been threatened. "I've got my doubts. I always did have. I never believed I was being transferred for my own good." Prior to April 4th Wallace was in a position to observe the various strangers who appeared in and about Two. "I saw the two black detectives, Redditt and the other one. And there were also white men there in street clothes. People said they were FBI but you can't tell from just looking."

On April 4th there were no black firemen in Fire Station Two, since the only two blacks had been assigned elsewhere.

Detective Ed Redditt was at Two, however, and he was in charge of stationary security for King. His radio provided him immediate access to the mobile units in the vicinity. Assigned to assist him was a Memphis police officer, W. B. Richmond.

Redditt said, "The day of King's assassination I was at the firehouse. I could identify everybody who came and went. I knew the SCLC personnel, I knew Dr. King, I knew the cars, I knew the license plate numbers."

I asked if he had always provided security when King came to town. "Right," he answered, "So I knew who to look for. I knew the local Klansmen by sight. I knew the Invaders, the ministers, the militant groups, everyone involved in the leadership of the sanitation strike." I asked Redditt what his plan was in case of an attempt on Dr. King. "My thing was this. If something occurred in my sight Richmond would remain there, at the rear of the Firehouse, overlooking the motel. I would run to the front. I run a little bit faster, and I would try to cut off anybody in front. Richmond could radio a perimeter of security, a moving task force." I asked Redditt what the stationary security consisted of. "Just me and Richmond, that was the total security."

I asked Redditt how many police officers had provided stationary security for King in the past. "Normally we had ten, but this time it was reduced to two."

Redditt was at the airport when King arrived. He remembers one woman, no doubt still reacting to the police violence at the March 28th march, who said, "We don't want no security. We don't need no police." Redditt approached a black minister and said that he had come to provide security and the minister responded, "We don't need any security." Redditt said, "I could feel the anxiety and the bitterness because of the police macing and beating. I could understand this feeling, the reason that they didn't want any police around. But I said, 'Well I'm going to get him to the Lorraine' and I got in front of the car in which Dr. King was traveling and we proceeded on down to the Lorraine and when we got there, I saw him up the steps." A police inspector was at the Lorraine and he asked Redditt what the black leaders had said. Redditt informed the inspector that the situation was very touchy and that some people in King's party did not want the police around. As they were talking, Redditt recalls that someone walked up to them and said, "We don't want no police around him. Get the hell out of there." The inspector took out his radio and called back to headquarters; "Okay, pull out," came the response from headquarters. Redditt was surprised. "I couldn't understand what the police were doing. It always is the function of the police to provide protection for people who are threatened even if some of the people around them don't want it. That's the way it always was. But with Holloman there it was different all of a sudden. I told the inspector," Redditt later said, "I need to have some type of security for King. We can't just walk away after all the threats and violence." According to Redditt, the inspector asked, "Well, what do you want to do?" and Redditt replied, "Well, there at the firehouse at least we can see if it's open; if it looks out adequately on the motel. At least we can go there and establish stationary security. We won't even be seen." The inspector replied "OK, do what you want to do."

Redditt established a command post at the firehouse. The normal complement of ten men had been reduced to two until approximately four o'clock on the afternoon of April 4th.

According to Redditt, "About an hour and a half, no more than two hours before Dr. King's assassination, Lt. Arkin, who was in intelligence, came down to the station. He said, 'Ed, they want to see you at headquarters.' " Redditt was reluctant to leave his post, to abandon the entire security operation to Richmond. Redditt had difficulty leaving since his plan to cut off a potential escape from the scene, should there be an attempt on King's life, was predicated upon a functioning team of at least two men. Arkin told Redditt that Holloman himself had ordered him to report to him at headquarters. "So what could I do? I got into the car with Arkin, leaving Richmond all alone, and we proceeded to headquarters." Upon arriving at police headquarters Redditt was taken into the conference room.

"It was like a meeting of the Joint Chiefs of Staff. In this room, just before Dr. King was murdered, were the heads and the seconds in command of I guess every law enforcement operation in this area you could think of. I had never seen anything like it before. The Sheriff, the Highway Patrol, Army Intelligence, the National Guard. You name it. It was in the room."

Redditt recalled that, "I walked right in and Holloman addressed me at once. He said, 'Ed, there's a contract out on you.' I said, 'What do you mean?' I couldn't understand why I was there at this top-level meeting and why I was being told about a contract on me in front of that whole group. The whole thing didn't make any sense."

Redditt said that Holloman then introduced him to a man in the room dressed in civilian clothes. Redditt remembers very clearly that Holloman, indicating a man at the conference table said, "Ed, this gentleman is from the United States Secret Service in Washington, D.C. He has secured information from the Highway Patrol in Mississippi that a group in Mississippi has a contract out to kill you. This group has let the contract out to a hit man from St. Louis to get you. That hit man may be here in Memphis now. He, [indicating the Secret Service man again] has just flown down from Washington to give me this information."

The events and assertions were moving too quickly for Redditt to calmly evaluate them. A top-level police mini-convention to which he had been summoned to be informed that the United States Secret Service had sent its representative by plane from Washington to warn of a three-state conspiracy to kill him, a relatively unknown local detective, was difficult to assess and impossible for him to believe.

Later he told me that he could not believe that the United States Secret Service, which is primarily obligated to provide protection for Presidents, Vice Presidents, members of their families, and candidates for the two highest elective offices, had taken a real interest in him. Upon reflection he also found it somewhat troubling to consider that if the Secret Service in Washington really did have information that someone was stalking the streets of Memphis presumably armed with a gun and motivated by a contract to kill him that the agent in Washington would pick up the telephone and ask his secretary to book passage for him on the next convenient flight to Memphis, rather than report the threat by telephone at once to the responsible persons in Memphis. In fact, nothing about the story rang true. On reflection, and without the perspective afforded by the inexorable passing of time and events, in that room crowded with the police elite, all Redditt knew was that something was terribly wrong.

Holloman continued, "So, Ed, in order to protect you, I have personally made reservations for you and your family at the Rivermont Holiday Inn. You and your family are to move in there right now for your safety."

Redditt told me, "My first thought was that Dr. King was going to be leaving the Lorraine shortly and that I should be there. Then I thought about my mother-in-law who was really quite ill. I knew that if she heard this rumor that I had been threatened and if she had to move, it might be very bad for her. Anyway I knew that Richmond couldn't handle it alone there at the station house and besides I was the one that knew the people, the cars, the license numbers and I was the one that could spot trouble." Redditt responded to Holloman. "Sir, I'm not going. You can't stop a contract. If there is one on me I'll just stay on the streets and try to be cautious. But I won't involve my family. My family will stay at home. I'll stay on the streets. If they're going to get me let them get me on the streets while I'm nowhere near my family."

Holloman answered sharply, "Redditt you are going to the Rivermont with your family. That's an order and there is nothing to discuss."

Redditt made one more effort. He told Holloman that his mother-in-law was too sick to be moved and too sick to be left alone. Holloman thought for a moment and said "All right. You just go home and stay there." Redditt asked if he could finish his assignment at the Lorraine first. Holloman said, "You are going home. You are going home now. That's an order."

Redditt drove home with Memphis police officers. When they drove up in front of Redditt's house, the Memphis police informed him that they were going to stay in his house with him. At that point it became clear to Redditt that their assignment quite obviously was to watch him, not guard the house.

I thought they might sit outside in unmarked cars, maintaining radio contact with each other and with me, and in that way provide some protection. But their orders apparently were to stay in the house with me. That way they could watch me but they couldn't protect me. If someone threw a bomb in a window those two officers would just have been two more casualties. Then I really knew something was wrong. I sat in the car and thought about Dr. King. I had been with him so much, everytime he came to Memphis, I had heard him speak so often that I was practically one of his disciples. I thought about him at the Lorraine without adequate protection. I didn't want to leave the car, to go into the house, because I thought that the presence of the other officers was going to upset my mother-in-law. So we sat in the car for a few minutes and then the radio announced that Dr. King had been shot.

Redditt ran into the house as soon as he heard the news.

I thought that it would be too much of a shock for my mother-in-law. Anyway the excitement of having the police there watching me didn't help. And we thought she didn't have a radio. We were trying to keep the news from her. But she did have a small transistor radio and she heard that he had been killed. The next night she screamed out "Dr. King, Dr. King, Dr. King. God, take me instead of Dr. King." And she died. She died of grief.

I asked Redditt when he returned to work and how the contract story was finally disposed of. "It was Thursday, April 4, that they ordered me to go home. I called Thursday to see if I could participate in the homicide investigation. I called Friday. I called Saturday. When I called Sunday, the basic investigation was over and they ordered me to go back to work. The contract? Nothing else has ever been said about the contract on my life."

When Redditt was removed from the scene, only W. B. Richmond, then a Memphis patrolman, now a sergeant, was left on the scene. My interview with him was less than satisfactory. I began by introducing myself and then saying, "I've been told that you were the one police officer who was a witness to the murder of Dr. King." He responded, "I'd like to know who gave you my phone number." I told him that I had found it in the telephone book following his name. Then he said, "I have nothing to talk to anybody about the King killing because I don't know anything about it." He denied that he was at or near the Lorraine Motel on April 4; he denied he had been in a stake-out with or without Ed Redditt; and he denied that he had been near the fire station that day. When I asked him what observations he had on April 4, he said, "I had none." When I asked him how far from the Lorraine Motel he was when Dr. King was shot he said that he was "at police headquarters" and added, "I didn't hear the shot."

It was clear to me that Richmond had not told the truth to me. He told me that he had been "talked to by the Department of Justice" during the first part of July 1976. "They're the only people I'm supposed to talk to about it. I don't know anything about the man's killing." He told me that he had told the Department of Justice "the same things that I told you." Weeks later when I returned to Memphis I spoke with Richmond again. This time he told me that he had been at the firehouse and that he was there when King was killed. He said he had talked to his supervisors who said that he should give me that information. He said that was all he remembered about the murder.

Later two investigators for the Citizens Commission of Inquiry interviewed two firemen who were present when King was shot. One of them, Charles E. Stone, said, "And Lt. Redditt, I believe that was his name, was gone and the other boy was here. Only one was here at the time of the shooting."

The other fireman, William B. King, said,

Well, it was around six o'clock when it happened. We had a warning test and at six o'clock the alarm goes off. So I know it was right at six o'clock when he was shot. He had come out to the banister. He was standing there talking to his chauffeur who was on the ground. The chauffeur was on the ground and all of a sudden he kind of looked up, at least it looked like he looked up and there was this noise and he fell. And there were several people crying at the motel and this one guy come out, just fell down and started crying and crying. There was a lot of emotion at that time. We heard a lot of policemen shouting and hollering over there because the door was shut and I forget the exact words that was said but there was a lot of emotion. And I

think we all ran to see who was shot. And then this policeman, Richmond, he got on the phone and made a call. Well, in no time he left.

Since Richmond had a radio, which could have provided immediate access to the police mobile units in the area as well as to headquarters, it is difficult to understand why he did not use it. It becomes even more puzzling in light of the plan that Redditt had promulgated and shared with Richmond. That plan called for Redditt to cover South Main Street and for Richmond to use the radio to alert the mobile units. One must concede that Richmond could not have done both. The mystery lies in trying to determine why he attempted neither.

If the elaborate charade, which included the removal of Redditt and the detailing of Newsum and Wallace, was designed to strip away the security just before Dr. King was killed, in order to facilitate the escape of the sniper, it was an ultimately successful plan. The murderer fled, unobserved and unimpeded.

Chapter Nineteen

APRIL 4, ATLANTA
by Mark Lane

Arthur Murtagh, the veteran FBI agent, said,

> The day that King was shot, I was at the office, leaving for the day, with an FBI agent who was at the supervisory level. He was a young man, twenty-nine to thirty-two years old, handsome, nice dresser—reasonably intelligent and the women were crazy about him in the office. He was friendly with me.
>
> We heard the announcement, that King had been shot, as we were preparing to leave. This agent jumped for joy, literally leaped in the air, yelling, "They got Zorro! They got the son of a bitch! I hope he dies!"
>
> As we punched our salmon-colored cards out, the agent explained to me how King was nothing but a "goddamn Communist" troublemaker anyway. Then we heard that King had died. Again, he was elated. He just went crazy with joy.
>
> I said, "For Christ's sake, they killed a great leader," and as we walked to the parking lot, we had a discussion. The agent told me how King had been ruining the United States; that he was dividing our people; that he was Communist-dominated; and that "if the lazy goddamned niggers had worked, instead of demonstrating, they could make it just like anybody else in this country—for example, the Italians and the Irish!"

Following the murder of Dr. King a number of American cities were set on fire. The Attorney General was able to view part of the conflagration in Washington, D.C. A federal decision was made to investigate the crime. Murtagh said that the Department of Justice called upon the FBI to investigate. Hoover sent the request to the SAC in Atlanta. The SAC there turned it over to the intelligence unit—the Destroy King Squad. The very people who had illegally harassed him when he was alive, including the agent who celebrated when he died, were really in charge of the investigation. Memphis had the early lead material. The Bureau in Washington directed the early stages of the investigation. But it was directed out of Atlanta by the Destroy King Squad after a day or two.

Teletype leads would come in, and the case supervisor would assign the leads to various agents. "Now the assigning of leads would make a lot of difference," said Murtagh. "Up until civil rights were pushed hard in the sixties, I was never assigned to civil rights work at all. Only when they got to the point where they had to get some answers would they assign anybody like me. They had been assigning old-time Southern agents to handle civil rights cases."

How did the fact that those assigned to investigate King's death had been members of the get-King Squad affect that effort? "I think they might not have gotten the right answer on a lot of these things simply because there was no will to get the right answer," said Murtagh. "They didn't want to ask the right questions. The feeling against King, in the Bureau, was so strong," said Murtagh, that if the Bureau had had advance information of an assassination plot against King,

and no one else knew about it—they would sit on it. And let King get killed.

The Bureau wanted to get the investigation wrapped up and get out of it. I think there was sentiment in the Bureau, also—an extreme sentiment, at all costs, to keep the blacks from making any inroads.

I would not depend on an investigation, by the people I knew, to be very accurate. Statements came out from the Bureau, within twenty-four hours of each killing, that there was no conspiracy involved in the deaths of President Kennedy, Dr. King, and Bobby Kennedy.

I talked about conspiracy in Atlanta regarding King, and thought about it in the Kennedy case. I was told that we weren't to think about conspiracy. Our jurisdiction was very flimsy anyway, since King wasn't a government official. What were we doing investigating it?

I feel it was a political decision. I don't think the crime was ever investigated. In fact, I'm convinced it was never investigated. It wasn't investigated like the Mississippi killings, it wasn't investigated like the Hoffa disappearance. It wasn't even investigated as well as King was, when he was alive. I think eventually, if everybody keeps pushing, eventually some way, sometime, the whole thing will break open—you'll probably find a conspiracy.

Maybe it's a movement. You've got to be able to think in terms of the fiendish minds of people in counterintelligence. If we're right, the King killing was some kind of a counterintelligence scheme, cooked up by somebody and it could be anybody. It could be anyone who could manipulate things in such a way to get them to happen. I think it can be done, and I think it was done.

There are too many questions about Oswald and Ray. How did they get all the way across the country? And where the hell did the money come from? How did they have their identities covered? No guy like Ray can do that sort of thing on his own. It just didn't happen that way.

Chapter Twenty

DIRECTOR HOLLOMAN
by Mark Lane

On July 27, 1976, my close friend Abby Mann and I interviewed Frank Holloman in his Memphis office. Holloman was then the director of Future Memphis, Inc., a corporation established by one hundred leading businesses in Memphis to "cut off trouble before it begins" and to create a better image for Memphis. He was at first reluctant to talk about the King assassination. "The reason I resigned as director of fire and police," he told us, "was so that I would not have to answer questions about that case." Yet, Abby was persuasive and with a minimum shifting of emphasis regarding his credits and a somewhat more substantial but temporary shift of his perspective, he convinced Holloman that he was a sympathetic listener, and perhaps an advocate of Holloman's cause as well. For example, Abby did not spend a great deal of time explaining that he had written the American film classic *Judgment at Nuremberg* or that he had been a close friend of Dr. King. Instead, he pointed to the fact that he created *Kojak*, a fact which often has caused Abby to wince but caused, in this setting, a warm and welcoming smile across Holloman's face. Abby's most impressive moment came when he referred to the chairman of the Church Committee as "somewhat of an extremist," followed quickly by his observation that "it is easy to criticize the FBI but where would we be without it." As I pondered that proposition for a moment, I saw Holloman melt and heard him ask Abby, "Well, what can I tell you that will help you?"

Abby explained that he was writing an objective screenplay for NBC-TV on the life of Dr. King and that while the program would not dwell on his death, quite naturally it would refer to it. He introduced me as his assistant in the project and said that I had done some research on the subject and would like to ask him a few questions. Holloman stared at me for a moment or two and we were both aware, I believe, that I had not offered my own police-oriented credentials.

Abby began to ask Holloman about the March 28th demonstration and Holloman responded:

There was a large number of people involved; a large number of school students. From early morning until the time of the actual step-off of the march we were receiving numerous reports of students moving from their school areas to the area where the march was to start. When the march started Dr. King stepped out. He was in the lead. And behind him violence did break out. They began to break windows. We felt we had no alternative at that point except to stop the march. We ordered the march stopped and ordered dispersal of the crowd. The crowd at that point in the rear was completely out of hand and we did have to use tear gas in order to disperse the crowd. I do recall the break out, then the fight, then the riot situation developed all over town.

Abby asked, "There was a boy killed later, wasn't there?" Holloman replied, "Yes . . . he was dying in the south, as I recall it was in the south part of the city in which there was a connection with looting as I recall. It was controversial as to whether or not there was a justifiable killing. We thought it was a justifiable defense of a policeman's life because the policeman thought his life was in danger."

I asked Holloman what his assessment of the situation was just before Dr. King came to Memphis. "What were the feelings and what were the police problems in terms of potential racial conflicts?" Holloman said that "From the time of the first riots until he returned, the feelings in the community were naturally very high. He came back for the purpose of making a successful march. We felt that there was a danger to Dr. King by information that we received that there would possibly be more violence and possibly violence toward him. And so we felt so strongly about it that we went to the federal court in order to seek an injunction against the march which was scheduled whenever it was, I've forgotten." I asked, "What was the information you received about violence which would happen against King?" Holloman answered, "It was an accumulation of intelligence information we had received. I will not be more specific on that." I asked Holloman what security was afforded to Dr. King by the police in the light of the potential violence against him. He answered, "The security we provided for him was a peripheral security because his people refused personal on-the-scene security." Holloman then pointed to my tape recorder and said, "Turn this off a minute." Holloman's warm tone had cooled a bit. By dramatically altering the course of the discussion to more general and less troublesome areas such as his police background, his "absolutely down the middle neutral position" regarding the strike and other trying events, Abby and I were able to secure his permission to turn on the tape recorder again.

Soon after the recording device was reactivated, I told Holloman that Ed Redditt had told me that he had always been in charge of security every time King came to Memphis. I asked Holloman if Redditt had been correct. Holloman stared at me and, in a harsh and almost angry manner that is quite noticeable when the tape is played, asked me, "Did you talk to Ed Redditt himself?" I said that I had and then again asked if Redditt had always been in charge of providing police security for King and if he had been in charge on April 4th. Holloman replied, "He could have been. I don't recall though." I then told Holloman what Redditt had told me about the exchange that took place between them in the conference room just before the murder of Dr. King. Holloman said, "I arranged for him to go to a hotel." I asked Holloman if there had been a threat to kill Redditt and he answered:

Yes, yes. I got a report on the line for it and immediately pulled. See, I had been in court due to actual time I was in court until five o'clock. I think it was four, in federal court, and I came back in the office. I was then advised. I didn't know about this until I got back to my office. Shortly after I got back to the office I was then advised that a threat had been made against Redditt's life. I immediately ordered Redditt to my office. I cannot tell you frankly where the report came from. I don't know the source. I can't say. Some people say it was the Secret Service. Some say it was somebody else. I frankly do not know. As far as I recall it came from a substantial source that convinced me that it was true. So I immediately called him into my office, told him what the report was and then told him that his life was invaluable as far as I was concerned and that I would take every effort to protect him. And I made arrangements to have him placed in a motel in Memphis under an assumed name together with his entire family which he did not want to do because Ed Redditt is a brave man. But I told him there was no choice, that his life was in danger and I was going to do what I could to protect it. Ah, this was after five o'clock. At 6:01 as I recall I was still in my office by myself handling some work cleaning out my desk before I went home when the report came that Dr. King had been killed.

I asked, "When Redditt left your office was it your understanding that he would then be going home or to the motel but not to the Lorraine Motel?" Holloman said, "Right." I inquired, "Well, was he at that point in charge

141

of security at the Lorraine for the police department? I don't mean the peripheral TAC [Tactical] squad which had its own operation but I mean the on-the-scene.'' Holloman said, ''At that point I cannot say whether he was or not. If he says he was I have no reason to question that as to whether or not he was in charge. He was not in charge of the operation. Let's put it that way.''

I reported that Redditt said that there was only one other person with him, a fellow officer. I asked Holloman if Redditt was replaced by anyone else. He answered ''Was he what?'' ''Replaced at the scene by anyone else at the Lorraine Motel?'' I asked again. Frank Holloman responded, ''I do not recall because at that point in time I was I had handled this particular thing. I was sitting there trying to do some work on my desk when 6:01, which was less than an hour, this happened, so I don't know. I was never in that direct contact. I had been in court all day and it happened; as far as a replacement, frankly I do not know.'' I asked Holloman if it was unusual for him to be notified that there was a contract out on a police officer. He answered, ''There was never any contract. I mean there was no contract. It isn't that dramatic in the modern day organized crime. I just was advised that a certain organization was going to kill him.'' I asked, ''Organization? Do you remember which it was?'' Holloman answered, ''Yes, but I'm not going to reveal it. It was an organization. Not locally. Not local; not a local organization.''

I wondered if Holloman had ever considered what might appear to some to be obvious; that the death threat about Redditt was developed for the purpose of stripping away King's security. Holloman answered firmly, not to say repetitively, ''Absolutely not. No way. No possible way. No way.''

In fact, the death threat, real or contrived, was responsible for Redditt's removal and that removal was useful, perhaps critical, to the murderer in his escape from the scene. I asked Holloman why the only two black firemen at Fire Station Two had been removed from that assignment on the very day of the murder. He said, ''I never heard about that. No. And I would say there's absolutely no connection with any of it. So for whatever reason he may have been transferred, he was not there in the first place with the King operation.'' When I informed Holloman of Newsum's information regarding his transfer, he answered ''I don't think it would be true. I knew what was happening as far as the police department was concerned. And I knew of no orders, no instructions of any kind. And I don't believe that it would have gone through except through me. And it did not.''

I again asked Holloman if he recalled the original source of the threat to Redditt's life. He said:

No. I don't recall. And so you're going into something that I haven't thought about before. I just cannot recall. I guess the events—of the shock of the next hour. That's really completely in my memory, as far as that part was concerned. And I don't recall. I do know it came from a reputable source. I would say an agency. Whether it was the Secret Service, I frankly cannot tell you right now. I couldn't testify to that fact.

I asked, "If it was the FBI you probably would have remembered it?" Holloman answered:

Not necessarily. No, not necessarily. No it could have been the FBI, it could have been the Secret Service—it's just right there it's a blank. I don't recall. The source was so positive, and so reliable, that I immediately took action. In spite of what was going on at that time, I believed it. And that's the reason I took the action that I did.

Almost immediately after Holloman gave that answer he picked up the microphone and tossed it towards me, saying, "All right, put that thing off for good now."

There is much that is troubling about Holloman's explanation of the events. Why is he reluctant to release the name of the organization that conspired to kill Redditt? Holloman had said that he felt that Dr. King was in danger and that he believed that there might be violence directed against him. Why then was the police detail reduced to two men on April 4, 1968? He then reduced the detail to one man. Under the circumstances why did he not replace Redditt if he truly believed that Redditt had to be removed? Why did he take no action to apprehend those responsible for conspiring to kill one of his police officers, a crime, from the viewpoint of law enforcement officials, more serious than any other? How could he fail to remember the agency or bureau that flew a representative into Memphis to warn him about the threat to Redditt?

Redditt was certain when he talked to me that Holloman identified the agent on April 4th as a representative of the Secret Service. Yet, Redditt later conducted an independent inquiry and discovered, not at all to his surprise, that the Secret Service had dispatched no one to Memphis that day and that the officials there had never even heard of the threat to Redditt's life. If Holloman could remember his source, his allegation could be verified or proven to be untrue. His loss of memory, due, he asserts, to the "shock" of learning of the death of Dr. King, is both convenient and speaks of a sensitive man deeply committed to the law.

If one secures the threshhold impression that Holloman's failure to take adequate precautions was due to his lack of experience or that his memory was erased due to the personal grief that he experienced when a man he respected was murdered, an examination of his background may alter that concept.

Holloman had been with the FBI for a quarter of a century. He was the Special Agent in Charge (SAC) of the FBI office in Atlanta, where Dr. King lived and where his church and family were; he had been SAC at the FBI office in Jackson, Mississippi; he had been the SAC at the Memphis office, as well, when many of the problems which led to the strike were developing. During eight of Holloman's years with the Bureau, he worked in the FBI headquarters in Washington, D.C.

Holloman said of that period, "I was the Inspector in Hoover's office. You might say the Inspector-in-Charge of his office."

When Abby asked him about the charges made by the Church Committee about the numerous illegal and immoral actions of the Hoover FBI, many of which emanated from that office when Holloman was the Inspector-in-Charge, Holloman said, "I have nothing to apologize for that we ever did when I was there. What we did we had to do and it was proper to do it. J. Edgar Hoover was a friend of mine and I saw nothing that he did that was wrong."

It is in view of Hoover's pathological hatred of Dr. King, an obsession which led him to commit numerous crimes in order to destroy him, and which apparently did not trouble Holloman, that one must evaluate Holloman's claim of amnesiac shock occasioned by Dr. King's death.

Chapter Twenty-One

APRIL 5, MEMPHIS
by Mark Lane

Wayne Chastain, now a practicing lawyer in Memphis, was a reporter for the Memphis *Press Scimitar*, one of the two major daily newspapers at the time of the assassination of Dr. King.

After the police concluded that the shot had been fired from the bathroom window in the rooming house, Chastain came across an unpublished photograph in the newspaper's files. Taken by an Associated Press photographer from the bathroom window, it showed the Lorraine Motel balcony as the sniper would have seen it if the shot had been fired from there.

Chastain noted that the view was obscured by branches from trees growing on the embankment between the rooming house and the motel.

Later that day he discussed that oddity in the case with Kay Black, another reporter for the Memphis *Press Scimitar*. Chastain told me that although the picture was puzzling he paid little attention to it, "because at that time I believed the shot had come from that window. I believed that the police were right about that."

Chastain has continued to maintain a growing file on the case and has talked with many witnesses since. "Now I no longer believe the shot came from there. Now I think that picture and those trees take an added significance," he told me.

Later Kay Black received a telephone call from William B. Ingram, the former mayor of Memphis. Ingram had called to inform Black that the city was cutting down the trees on the embankment between the rooming house and the motel. She later told me, "Now, I hadn't been in the rooming house looking through that bathroom window but I do recall Wayne Chastain having said that he didn't see how someone could shoot through the trees to the motel. He said that he was puzzled how a clear shot could have been fired because he didn't see how you could see through the branches."

I asked Ms. Black if she could describe the trees.

I was over there all the time after Dr. King and his regiment arrived because I was covering the black community during the strike. I would go over there and have coffee with people if anything was happening. And it was spring and the normal thing was to be in the parking lot, the motel court. Right above the lot, on this embankment there was sort of an overgrown place. And of course I noticed it. There were a good sized amount of trees there—and they made a screen, more or less between the motel and the rooming house. They were between ten and twelve feet tall. Oak trees, and perhaps willows.

I asked Ms. Black if, in her judgment, the trees would have interfered with a shot from the bathroom window to the motel balcony. "Well, it occurred to me that they might, and on reflection I think they might have. That is why Mayor Ingram called, I think. They provided very substantial screening. And they were possibly important evidence and they were being cut down just as the investigation began."

Ms. Black determined that the city of Memphis had arranged for the trees to be cut down and had ordered the city sanitation department to remove them. She said that Ingram had called her in the morning. She reported the information to her desk and that afternoon she visited the murder scene. "And those trees were down. The screen was gone. There was just no way any longer to know if that shot could have been possible."

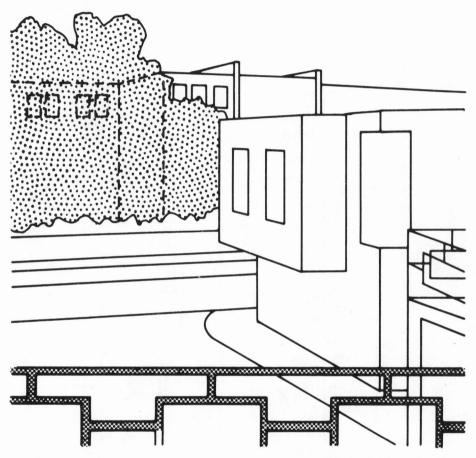

Drawing By Adam Schneider

The view from the balcony in front of Room 306 at the Lorraine Motel. The building to the left rear is 422½ South Main Street. The rear of the building which faces the motel is completely blocked by bushes and trees and cannot be seen from the Lorraine Motel. Yet it is that building that provides the entrance to the rooming house. One may pass through 422½ South Main and then enter the building which does overlook the Lorraine Motel.

The entrance to the rooming house at 422½ South Main provides internal access to the building to its left. It was alleged by the prosecution that Ray entered 422½, from which the Lorraine Motel could not be seen, walked through it to the next building, and secured a view of the Lorraine Motel balcony from the bathroom to the rear of that building. How Ray could have known of the internal connection between the two buildings and that the building housing Jim's Grill was part of the rooming house has not been explained.

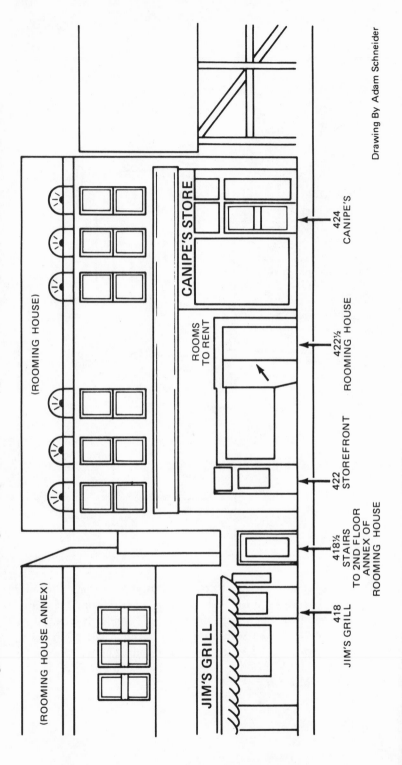

Drawing By Adam Schneider

PART SIX

THE STATE OF TENNESSEE VS. JAMES EARL RAY

Chapter Twenty-Two

THE CASE AGAINST RAY
by Mark Lane

On March 10, 1969, in Division III of the Criminal Court of Shelby County, Tennessee, James Earl Ray entered a prearranged plea of guilty in the murder of Dr. King. Judge W. Preston Battle accepted the plea after Ray's attorney, Percy Foreman, had worked out the arrangements with Memphis Attorney General Phil Canale, the prosecuting attorney.

Canale explained to the jurors:

It is incumbent upon the State in a plea of guilty to murder in the first degree to put on certain proof for your consideration.

We have to put on proof of what we lawyers call the proof of the corpus delicti which is the body of the crime. We will also put on several lay witnesses or police officers to fill you in on certain important aspects of this case, and then we will introduce certain physical evidence through these witnesses, and Mr. Beasley, or Mr. Dwyer will question these witnesses, and Mr. Beasley will give you an agreed stipulation of facts that the State has gotten up which contains what the State would prove by witnesses if this went to trial, and you will have the benefit of all that information through this stipulation of fact which has been agreed to by the State and by the Defendant as to what the State would prove if this matter went to trial.

Before the morning had ended and the jurors excused for lunch, the case against James Earl Ray for the murder of Dr. King had been spelled out in detail.

Several witnesses were called and questioned by Robert Dwyer, an Assistant Attorney General. Foreman did not object to any question put to any witness, even when the question was leading and improper. Foreman did not cross-examine any witness.

The first witness called was Reverend Samuel Kyles. He said he had

148

known Dr. King for more than ten years. He had been with him in Room 306 of the Lorraine Motel for approximately forty-five minutes. "I had gone to pick Dr. Martin Luther King, Jr., up to go home, go to my house at 2215 South Parkway East for a soul food dinner." Dwyer asked, "Was Dr. King alive and in good health and in good spirits at that time and at that location?" Kyles answered affirmatively.

Dwyer asked Kyles what took place at 6:00 P.M.

Fairly close to 6:00 P.M. we were going to leave for dinner. Dr. Abernathy was also in the room. Dr. King came out. I was still in the room. He came out on the balcony and was greeting some of the people who were in the courtyard, and he came back in the room, I believe to get his coat, and the both of us came out together, and we stood at this point on the balcony for about three minutes greeting some people who also were going to dinner with us. And we stood together there about three or four minutes, and I turned to my right to walk away and said I was going and get my car and take some of the people who were going to dinner.

I got approximately 5 or 6 steps away from him and I heard what I now know to be a shot, and I looked over the railing. I thought it was a car backfiring, or something, and when I realized what had happened, I turned back to my left and saw Dr. King lying in a position thusly with a tremendous wound in his right side. He was laying in this position with the wound here [indicating].

Kyles said that when the shot was fired he looked in the general direction of the rooming house. "Yes, I looked over there because there were bushes and things."

Kyles was asked to describe the wound that had been inflicted upon Dr. King.

It tore this much of his face away that I could see, and I also noticed that the shot had cut his necktie, just cut right off at that point.

I remember that because he had been trying to find out—he thought somebody was playing a trick in the room—he couldn't find his necktie and he finally did find it, and we had had some conversation about his shirt and his necktie.

Kyles was asked if he had attended the funeral of Dr. King and he replied that he had.

Through the testimony of the first witness the state had established that Dr. King was shot at approximately 6:00 P.M. on April 4, 1968, and that he subsequently died.

Chauncey Eskridge, a Chicago lawyer who had represented Dr. King, testified next. He said that he had been "standing in the courtway looking up at door 306" at about 6:00 o'clock in the evening when Dr. King came out of his room. He said that soon "the sound came from my right ear and said 'Zing!' " He agreed with Kyles that the sound came from the general direction of the rooming house and that when he looked there he did not see anybody moving. Eskridge said that he had gone to the hospital with Dr. King and later attended his funeral.

Eskridge's testimony broke no new ground and was corroborative of Kyles' statement.

The state called no other eyewitnesses to the murder of Dr. King.

The next witness was Dr. Jerry Thomas Francisco, the Medical Examiner for Shelby County. He testified about the autopsy that was performed on Dr. King's body.

The examination revealed a gunshot wound to the right side of the face, passing through the body into the neck, through the spinal cord at the base of the neck, with the bullet lodging beneath the skin near the shoulder blade on the left.

Q. Cause of death was what, Dr. Francisco?

A. A gunshot wound to the cervical and thoracic spinal cord.

Q. In your medical opinion, how soon did death occur from that wound?

A. Shortly after death, shortly after injury.

Q. Did you recover anything from the body, Dr. Francisco?

A. Yes.

Q. I am going to show you an object and ask you if you can identify those, Dr. Francisco.

A. Yes.

Q. And what is that, please, sir?

A. This is the bullet that was removed from the body at the time of the autopsy.

Q. What, if anything, did you do with that bullet, Dr. Francisco, that you recovered?

A. This bullet was identified by number and delivered to a representative of the police department.

Francisco said that the bullet had angled downward from right to left passing through the chin, the base of the neck, and the spinal cord into the back. Francisco offered the opinion that the angle of the bullet through the body was consistent with a shot having been fired from the rooming house.

Francisco did not state that he knew where Dr. King had been standing, which direction he had been facing, or if he had been leaning over when he was shot, thereby considerably reducing the value of his opinion as to the origin of the shot.

Inspector N. E. Zachary of the Memphis Police Department testified that he had been the inspector in charge of the Homicide Bureau on April 4, 1968. He was at police headquarters when Dr. King was shot and when he heard that news on a radio broadcast he immediately went to the Lorraine Motel and began assigning men to the investigation. He then went to Main Street, he said, and stopped in front of the Canipe Amusement Company.

I found a package rolled up in a bedspread which consisted of a blue briefcase and a Browning pasteboard box containing a rifle.
At that particular time I put a guard on it with instructions to let no one touch it or move it until we could take photographs of it.

He said that the package had been wrapped in a bedspread when he found it. Zachary identified various articles that had been in the package including a box, a rifle that had been in the box, a pair of binoculars, a case for the binoculars, a pair of undershorts, a shaving kit, two cans of Schlitz beer, a hair brush, a transistor radio, a pair of pliers, a hammer, a paper bag, a copy of the *Commercial Appeal*, a Memphis newspaper, and some cartridges. He testified that he gave the evidence "to the FBI sometime around 10:00 P.M. that night" by delivering the material to "Mr. Jensen of the Memphis FBI." Zachary answered affirmatively when asked, "The purpose of turning these objects that you have identified here over to the FBI was to be sent to Washington for its examination, Inspector Zachary?"

Robert Jensen testified that on April 4, 1968, he was the Special Agent in Charge (SAC) of the Memphis Division of the FBI. He said that at about 6:05 P.M. he was told that Dr. King had been shot. He testified, "I called my Washington headquarters to advise them of the information which I had received, and then subsequently dispatched men to assist in the investigation." He said that he assigned agents to the investigation "probably around 6:30." The twenty-five minute hiatus, unexplained by the testimony or by subsequent official Bureau statements, leads to the conclusion that there was no federal effort to close off the area to prevent the murderer's escape. Since the city of Memphis borders on the states of Arkansas and Mississippi, both just minutes away, no local police blockade was likely to prove effective.

Jensen said that at 10:00 o'clock that evening he was in the offices of the Memphis Police Department. At that time, he said, "certain evidence was turned over to me." Dwyer inquired about the evidence.

Q. I am going to ask you, Mr. Jensen, to look at—there is a green spread here, here is some pliers and a hammer, here is a rifle, here is some shaving articles, binoculars, beer cans, newspaper, tee shirt, shorts, there is a transistor radio over there [indicating].

I will ask you if those objects were turned over to you by Inspector Zachary of the Memphis Police Department?

A. Yes, they were.

Q. And the purpose of that was what, sir?

A. In order that I could send them to our laboratory for examination.

Q. And did you do that, Mr. Jensen?

A. Yes, I did.

Q. And can you tell us briefly how that was done, sir?

A. Yes. The evidence was taken over to my office, was personally wrapped under my supervision, and when all the material was wrapped, I dispatched an agent to Washington to physically carry the material to the laboratory."

Jensen said that FBI agents discovered that a man named Eric S. Galt had registered at the Rebel Motel, although he did not say and was not asked for the date of that registration. He said that Galt had been driving a white Mustang. He testified that the FBI had discovered that the rifle had been sold by the Aeromarine Supply Company in Birmingham. Jensen said that the Mustang was discovered on April 11th. He said that the pliers and hammer may have been purchased from a hardware store in Los Angeles and that the tee shirt and shorts had been laundered in Los Angeles as well.

He then said that the FBI investigation culminated in the arrest of James Earl Ray. At that point Dwyer excused Jensen and said, "That is all the proof the State cares to offer at this time, if the Court pleases, except some stipulations by Mr. Beasley."

Through the testimony of witnesses the state had offered evidence that Dr. King had been shot on April 4, 1968, that he subsequently had died, that the shot had come from the direction of a clump of bushes and the rear of a rooming house, and that a package had been discovered near the entrance to the front of the rooming house. In addition, a witness had testified regarding the presence in Memphis of Eric S. Galt and his vehicle.

After a brief recess, the jurors were returned to the courtroom to listen to a lengthy narration by Assistant Attorney General James Beasley. He began, "May it please the Court, Gentlemen of the Jury, I propose at this time to narrate to you gentlemen a stipulation of the facts and evidence that the State would prove in addition to the testimony that you heretofore heard in the trial of this cause." Beasley contended that the state could prove that Ray had rented a room in the rooming house.

The State would show in the course of its proof, Gentlemen of the Jury, through Mrs. Bessie Brewer, who was employed as manager of this rooming house, that on the afternoon of April the 4th, between 3:00 and 3:30 P.M. in the afternoon, the Defendant appeared here at Mrs. Brewer's office or apartment that was used as an office in this rooming house. Under the name John Willard he requested a room for a week.

He added, "He was taken to room 5-B which is located in this section [indicating]. The Defendant did rent this room for a week from Mrs. Brewer." Beasley said that the state could prove that Ray had purchased Bushnell binoculars from Ralph Carpenter at the York Arms Company located one mile north of the rooming house.

A witness, Elizabeth Copeland, could testify, Beasley said, that between 4:30 and 4:45 P.M. a white Mustang parked near and to the south of the Canipe Amusement Company and was still there at 5:20 P.M. when she left the area.

Beasley said,

At approximately 6:00 P.M., Mr. Stephens heard the shot coming apparently through this wall from the bathroom. He then got up, went through this room out into the corridor in time to see the left profile of the Defendant as he turned down this passageway which leads to an opening with a stairwell going down to Main Street.

According to Beasley, Guy Warren Canipe and two customers were in the Canipe establishment and "saw the back of a white man going away from that area in a general direction on down Main Street, observing momentarily thereafter a white Mustang pull from the curb, head north on Main Street with one occupant."

The package found in front of Canipe's, Beasley said, was wrapped in the green bedspread, previously identified, and contained the rifle, the binoculars and the other items in evidence. Beasley said that a crime scene search of the bathroom in the rooming house by officers of the Memphis Police Department "found marks in the bottom of the tub consistent with shoe or scuff marks" and that

The sill of this window in the bathroom was observed by Inspector Zachary to have what appeared to be a fresh indentation in it. This sill was ordered removed, was cut away, was subsequently sent to the FBI for comparison, and the proof would show through expert testimony that the markings on this sill were consistent with the machine markings as reflected on the barrel of the 30.06 rifle which has heretofore been introduced to you gentlemen.

Beasley said the state could prove that Ray had purchased the 30.06 rifle that had been found in the package outside Canipe's Store and that he had used the pseudonym Harvey Lowmeyer when he bought the rifle in Birmingham.

The evidence would prove, said the prosecutor, that Ray had purchased the white Mustang for $1,995 on August 30, 1967, then using the name Eric S. Galt. At that point Beasley said that the evidence would prove that Ray entered Mexico on October 7 and remained there until the middle of November 1967. He said the State's proof would locate Ray in Los Angeles, New Orleans, and Birmingham in the intervening weeks. The State knew when Ray drove from Los Angeles to New Orleans and who accompanied him. The State knew that Ray was a customer of the Home Service Laundry Company located at 5280 Hollywood Boulevard and was prepared to offer Mrs. Mary Lucy Panella to testify that Ray brought his laundry in quite regularly between December 1967 and early March 1968. She was able, Beasley said, to identify her laundry marks on the undergarments found in the package.

Beasley continued,

Mr. Avidson, Rodney Avidson, who operated the dance studio at Long Beach, California, would testify with reference to knowing the Defendant as Eric S. Galt during the period from December the 5th until February the 12th while Mr. Galt was taking dancing lessons at his place of business.

Through the testimony of Mr. Thomas Reeves Lau, the State

would show that the Defendant, under the name of Eric S. Galt, enrolled in the International School of Bartending there in Los Angeles, and he attended this school from January the 19th until March the 2nd, when he graduated. We were able to obtain a photograph in color reflecting the graduation picture from Mr. Lau, which you will see does show the Defendant along with Mr. Lau, who was standing, as you gentlemen view the picture, to the Defendant's left and is holding the diploma in front of him with the name, Eric S. Galt.

Ray drove from Los Angeles to New Orleans and then spent the night of March 22, 1968, at the Flamingo Motel in Selma, Alabama, Beasley said.

The prosecutor continued:

We would show through Mr. Jimmy Garner, who operates a rooming house in Atlanta, Georgia, that he rented a room to the Defendant under the name Eric S. Galt on March the 24th, 1968; that he collected a week's rent and subsequently on March the 31st, collected a second week's rent from the Defendant as Eric S. Galt; that at the time of collecting the rent on March the 31st, that the Defendant did write his name out as Eric S. Galt on an envelope, and this envelope was subsequently turned in in the course of this investigation.

That on the morning of April the 5th, Mr. Garner went into the room that had been rented to the Defendant as Eric Galt, and for purposes of changing the linen, at that time he found a note in substance saying, "I have to go to Birmingham. I will be back later to pick up my, within about a week, to pick up my television set and my other articles"; that on April the 14th of 1968, some ten days after the murder in Memphis, Mr. Garner did give permission to the members of the Atlanta FBI office to make a search of the premises there at his rooming house which had the room which had subsequently been rented to the Defendant.

Mrs. Annie Peters would be called by the State to testify with reference to the operation of the Piedmont Laundry, which is located around the corner from Jimmy Garner's rooming house; that on April the 1st, the Defendant, as Eric Galt, left certain laundry and cleaning there; that on the morning of April the 5th, 1968, at around mid-morning, he returned and picked up this laundry and dry cleaning.

At that point those jurors who were observant realized that the prosecutor had taken them beyond the date of the murder. For the next twenty minutes Beasley spoke of the recovery of the white Mustang and of Ray's trip to Toronto, to London, to Portugal and his return to London where he was arrested by Detective Sgt. Phillip F. Birch of New Scotland Yard.

Toward the conclusion of his indictment of Ray the Assistant Attorney General offered the testimony of the FBI experts. He began with an assessment of the relevant fingerprints.

Mr. George J. Bonebrake, who has been working with fingerprints since 1941, would testify that at 5:15 A.M., April 5th, 1968, he received the following items as has been heretofore testified to; that is, the rifle, the items that, from the bag, that were delivered to him by the representative from the Memphis FBI office, with reference to this material from the front, recovered from the front of Canipe's Amusement place here, that he found a print of sufficient clarity, fingerprint of sufficient clarity on the rifle itself; he found another print of sufficient clarity for identification on the scope, the Redfield scope mounted on the rifle; he found a print on the after-shave bottle, which is in the little packet that was obtained or purchased from the Rexall Drug Store in Whitehaven, Tennessee, which was part of the items that we have heretofore mentioned to you. He found a print on the binoculars. He found a print on one of the Schlitz beer cans. He found a print on the front page of the April 4th issue of the Memphis *Commercial Appeal.* That on April the 17th he received this map of Mexico which was, the State would have shown, was obtained from the room, Jimmy Garner's rooming house in Atlanta; that he found prints of sufficient clarity on that map for identification purposes; that he started an extensive investigation through fugitive files consisting of some 53,000 fingerprint cards, and on April the 19th he identified all the above-mentioned prints that I have mentioned to you from these items as being identical with the records bearing the name and photograph of James Earl Ray.

An alert juror might have noticed that the State did not allege that Ray had left behind a fingerprint in the room that he had allegedly rented in the rooming house or in the bathroom from which the State alleged the shot had been fired.

Beasley then moved to what might have been the most difficult evidence for Ray to contend with. If the ballistics established that the bullet taken from Dr. King's body was fired from a rifle that had been

156

purchased by Ray, the case against him would begin to take shape. Beasley now spoke slowly and loudly, his voice emphasizing the importance of his words.

Mr. Robert A. Frazier, the chief, firearms identification unit at the FBI, with 27 years' experience, would testify as to examination and firing of this rifle, 30.06, that has been heretofore introduced.

He examined the cartridges, the hull from the chamber of this rifle, the slug removed from the body of Dr. Martin Luther King, Jr., and would testify as to his conclusions as follows:

The death slug was identical in all physical characteristics with the five loaded 30.06 Springfield cartridges found in the bag in front of Canipe's. The cartridge case had in fact been fired in this 30.06 rifle. That the death slug removed from the body contained land and groove impressions and direction of twist consistent with those that were in the barrel of this rifle.

This, to the jurors straining for the damning and conclusive evidence, to the reporters seeking, quite literally, the smoking gun, was the climax of the undefended case against James Earl Ray. His rifle had killed Dr. King.

Beasley then appeared to establish as fact that allegation yet again. He added that Frazier had

also made microscopic comparison between the fresh dent in the sill of the window at the bathroom, 422½ South Main, and concluded that the microscopic evidence in this dent was consistent in all ways with the same microscopic marks as appear on the barrel of this rifle, 30.06 rifle.

The veteran lawyers in the courtroom smiled to themselves in much the same manner as professional magicians do when they observe an audience puzzled by a simple but well performed trick.

Moments later Beasley turned from the jury to Judge Battle and said, "If the Court pleases, that covers our stipulation."

This then was the case against James Earl Ray, fully and thoroughly presented by his prosecutors, uninterrupted by his counsel, and unrestrained by the rules of evidence.

Chapter Twenty-Three

THE DEFENSE
by Mark Lane

There is the truth. And there is the legal truth. It is not unusual for both truths to coincide. Yet the law, in its majesty, recognizes that this will not always be the case. The theoretical responsibility borne by the prosecution is to prove the guilt of the defendant, not by a fair preponderance of the evidence, but beyond a reasonable doubt. Therefore, continuing in a theoretical vein, a juror who was inclined to believe that the defendant was guilty—who had arrived at what was the truth for him but who was not convinced of the defendant's guilt beyond a reasonable doubt, would be obligated to vote for an acquittal.

For most Americans the technical problems confronting the prosecuting authorities in Memphis are of less concern than an examination of the facts which may lead to the truth. Yet those two areas of concern merge, entangle with one another, and make a clear understanding of the circumstances of the crime difficult to comprehend. It is because Ray pleaded guilty that the record of the crime is so barren. Had Ray been tried, certainly had he testified at the trial, the record would have been studded with, if not all or almost all of the relevant facts, a fair history of the events which had been tested in the crucible of cross-examination.

The search for the truth in this matter must, I believe, commence with an exploration of the anatomy of the guilty plea: its origin, its development, and the manner of its execution. In order to evaluate that bargained plea in the appropriate context it is necessary to assess the legal and technical validity of the case against Ray. For if he did kill Dr. King but the state was unable to prove that he did, then Ray is innocent under our understanding of the law. More important perhaps is the certain knowledge of the defendant and his attorney of this peculiar and marvelous dichotomy in our system of justice. In this chapter we will evaluate the viability of the case against Ray. If we conclude that the state could not have proved Ray's guilt beyond a reasonable doubt we will be constrained to examine his charge that his plea was improperly coerced.

Shortly after his arrest in England, Ray wrote to Arthur Hanes, Sr., the former mayor of Birmingham, and F. Lee Bailey of Boston, requesting that they each consider representing him. Bailey declined and Hanes accepted. Bailey explained that his friendship with Dr. King created a conflict of interest which barred him from representing Ray. Hanes had successfully represented defendants in the highly-publicized murder of Viola Liuzzo, a civil rights worker who had been slain in the South. Apparently Ray had been aware of that defense and of Hanes' skill and his empathy with Southern jurors. He wrote to Hanes from London:

Dear Mr. Hanes,

I am writing this letter from London, England. I am being held here on a charge of passport fraud, also I think for Tenn. in the Martin King Case. I will probably be returned to the U.S. about June 17, and would like to know if you would consider appearing in my behalf? So far [three days] I have only been permitted to talk to police and also have not seen any papers except a headline today. By accident, stating I had given an interview to a Mr. Vinson, which is false. Most of the things that have been written in the papers about me I can only describe as silly. Naturally I would want you to investigate this nonsense before committing yourself. For these reasons and others which I won't go into I think it is important that I have an attorney upon arrival in Tenn. or I will be convicted of whatever charge they file on me before I arrive there. An English attorney came to see me today and said he would also write to you. I don't know your address is why I am sending this letter to the bar asso. The reason I wrote you is I read once where you handled a case similar to what I think may be filed on me also whatever the papers might say. I don't intend to give any interviews until I have consulted with an attorney. In the event you can not practice in Memphis would you contact an attorney their who would?

Sincerely

R. G. Sneyd

P.S. Among the many names they have me booked under this one so if you should correspond use this one, address on envelope.

William Bradford Huie, an Alabama writer, almost immediately contacted Hanes and suggested that he would pay Ray a substantial sum for the exclusive rights to his story. Huie pointed out to Hanes that the sum could be used to pay lawyers' fees. Hanes left for England having decided both to represent Ray and to attempt to arrange a tri-party contract among himself, Ray, and Huie. Such a contract was agreed upon by the parties.

Hanes and his son, Arthur Hanes, Jr., diligently pursued leads, many of which were being developed by a private investigator, Renfro Hays.

I spent days at the Hanes law offices in Birmingham sorting through the voluminous investigative reports, trial briefs and working papers that the lawyers had prepared. They were kind enough to allow me to photocopy all those documents I considered to be relevant and I subsequently spent weeks studying that material. I also made available copies of that material to the Select Committee on Assassinations of the House of Representatives, with the permission of the Hanes law firm.

Interviews with the two lawyers and a thorough examination of their trial preparation work led me to conclude that they were ready for the trial. I began to defend against criminal prosecutions twenty-five years ago. In the course of hundreds of trials, including prosecutions for murder, manslaughter, conspiracy to overthrow the government, conspiracy to blow up the Statue of Liberty, the Washington Monument, and the Liberty Bell, and conspiracy to seize federal property at Wounded Knee, South Dakota, I have come to understand and cope with our system of justice and to respect the vagaries of the jury system. I understand as well, I believe, the special problems imparted to the defense in an unpopular case, especially when the difficulties are compounded by extensive and prejudicial pretrial publicity. After taking into account the unusual problems posed for this defense by extralegal considerations, I believe that the essential case against Ray was so flawed that it would have been difficult for the jury to have returned a verdict of guilty. Had the case been tried the state would have undertaken the responsibility of proving beyond a reasonable doubt that James Earl Ray fired a rifle from a bathroom window of a rooming house and that the bullet from that rifle struck and killed Dr. Martin Luther King, Jr. This, I believe, the state could not do, partially due to the paucity of evidence linking Ray to the crime and partially due to the affirmative defense that had been established by the investigation conducted on his behalf.

Experienced trial lawyers know that there are no easy cases in which victory for either side is assured in advance of trial. In cases involving capital punishment, as in this one, the awful possibility of the ultimate penalty tends to diminish feelings of ebullience that defense counsel might otherwise experience following multiple assessments of the evidence. Yet in spite of the highly prejudicial publicity surrounding the charges against the defendant, and in spite of the awesome potential should the defendant be convicted, Arthur Hanes, Sr., and his son and their client shared a quiet optimism and a cautious confidence. That confidence was threatened primarily by the defense lawyers' everpresent fear that the state might be holding some decisive evidence in reserve. In this case such fears were groundless. All the authorities knew and much of what they suspected had been offered to the media and commented on repeatedly.

The case against Ray, all that could be proven and in addition all that the state said could be proven—although on occasion it lacked the evidence to follow through on that boast—was presented by the authorities on March 10, 1969, and fully reflected in the previous chapter.

Witnesses who testified offered evidence that Dr. King had been killed on April 4, 1968, on the balcony of the Lorraine Motel from a shot fired from the general direction of a clump of trees and bushes at the rear of a rooming house beyond the vegetation.

A pathologist established that a bullet was taken from Dr. King's body and he offered a vague and, as we have seen, poorly based opinion as to the possible origin of the bullet. A police inspector told of a package found on South Main Street, two blocks from Dr. King's location at the Lorraine Motel balcony, and he described its contents. The FBI SAC in Memphis said that the package had been received by the Bureau later that day.

At that point the Memphis prosecutor abandoned the usual method of presenting important evidence through the testimony of witnesses and offered instead his own unsworn and sometimes unsupported allegations about what the evidence would show. This technique is regularly and properly utilized by prosecuting attorneys for the purpose of offering an opening statement but in the ordinary course of events such a statement is not construed as evidence and is followed by witnesses whose testimony is considered as evidence. Thus the jurors may test the allegations of the accuser against the testimony of the witnesses. In addition, of course, in an ordinary trial the witness is subjected to cross-examination, a device which often proves useful in arriving at the facts. In Memphis there was no cross-examination and for the most part the evidence was not offered through the testimony of witnesses.

To the uninitiated jurors and the reporters the nice distinctions and precise language of the law no doubt proved misleading. The prosecutor alleged that the FBI firearms expert with 27 years of experience "would testify" that "the death slug [the bullet taken from Dr. King's body] was identical in all physical characteristics" with the cartridges found in the package in front of Canipe's. All that Frazier, the Bureau expert, had said was that both the bullet that killed King and the cartridges in the package were a common variety of 30.06 ammunition. That is not very dissimilar from a fingerprint expert testifying that the killer had ten fingers on two hands, five on each, and that the subject was similarly equipped. Then the prosecutor added that Frazier "would testify" that "the death slug removed from the body contained land and groove impressions and direction of twist consistent with those that were in the barrel of this [Ray's] rifle." To those without trial experience in assault and homicide cases, that allegation appeared conclusive or at least terribly damaging to Ray's claim that he had not killed Dr. King. Yet a knowledgeable defense lawyer would have welcomed that report and might have been tempted to call Frazier as a defense witness if the prosecution failed to call him as theirs.

As a bullet moves through a rifle barrel it spirals. Microscopic indentations which comprise the rifling inside the barrel cause that effect and remove particles from the jacket of the bullet. If the bullet is not substantially demolished a comparison with another bullet test-fired from the same weapon may yield conclusive results. The language of the government's firearms experts is standard, and their recitation is pro forma. In case after case the experts recite the conclusions that "my examination of this bullet proved beyond doubt that this bullet was fired from this weapon to the exclusion of all other weapons in the world." Any statement short of that one is considered to be valueless to the prosecution. In this case a substantial portion of the bullet remained intact. An expert who saw it but was not allowed to examine it under a microscope said that the bullet was sufficiently undamaged to permit a positive finding regarding the weapon from which it was fired. The failure of the state to prove that the "death slug" was fired from what was alleged to be Ray's rifle reflected very poorly upon the case against Ray.

The prosecutor sought to overcome this essential weakness in the case by stretching Frazier's identification of the mark on the bathroom window sill. Beasley said that Frazier would testify that the dent on the window sill "was consistent in all ways" with the marks on what was alleged to be Ray's rifle. No doubt, had Frazier been subjected to cross-examination he would have conceded that what he meant was that any metal object similar to the rifle barrel in question could have caused the dent. His refusal to inform the state that "Ray's" rifle did cause the dent meant that the state could neither prove that the rifle fired the bullet that killed Dr. King nor that it had been in the rooming house from where the shot was allegedly fired. Beasley's indications to the contrary may have been useful to obfuscate the record and mislead the jurors and the press in 1969, but upon sober reflection and in the context of the evidence now available his comments appear to have been a somewhat desperate prosecutorial effort to give the impression that there was a substantial case when in fact there was not.

If the state could not prove that the rifle fired the shot or that it had even been in the bathroom or elsewhere in the rooming house, the evidence that seemed to establish Ray's ownership of the rifle was rendered almost worthless. I believe that the state could have proven that Ray purchased the rifle from the Aeromarine Supply Company in Birmingham. Further, Ray told me that he had done so. Yet even if that weapon was judged to be the murder weapon by competent experts, proof of Ray's guilt would depend upon additional factors. Proof of ownership of a weapon employed in a murder case does not establish the owner as a criminal. In this case the state could not even establish any links between the defendant, James Earl Ray, and the bullet which killed Dr. King.

The state claimed that it could prove that Ray had been in the rooming house before the murder, during the murder, and immediately after the murder. For those assertions Beasley relied upon statements which he said were made by eyewitnesses. It is interesting to note that as the mythology of the case against Ray developed it became conventional wisdom to allege that Ray left fingerprints and palm prints around the rooming house. William Bradford Huie, whose book, *He Slew the Dreamer*, is discussed in Chapter 26 told Ray that his prints were found in Room 5 and in the bathroom. This inclined Ray to believe that his defense would be more difficult than he had conceived. In his book Huie wrote:

> **Part of the time between 4:30 and 6:01 P.M. Ray watched for Dr. King leaning out of the window of Room 5. Evidence of this comes from fingerprints and from the fact that, after the murder, a chair and table in Room 5 were found to have been moved to the window.**

Huie added that "a print of the heel of his [Ray's] palm was found on the bathroom wall." Huie informed Percy Foreman, Ray's lawyer, of his discovery and later Foreman declared in an article he wrote in *Look* magazine in April 1969 that Ray had left behind both fingerprints and palm prints and that he, Foreman, knew why. Foreman wrote, "he wanted to escape, but he didn't want to lose credit. As further precaution against such dreaded loss, he left his fingerprints in the side room that he had rented, and his palm print in the bathroom from which he fired the shot.''

Huie, Foreman, and the many representatives of the news media who relied upon them for the facts, were wrong. The prosecution did not charge that Ray's fingerprints or palm prints had been found in the rooming house. At the outset, the Memphis police alleged that the shot had been fired from the bathroom window and that the killer had left scuff marks in the bathtub and a palm print on the wall over the tub. Captain Dewell Ray of the Internal Security Division of the Memphis Police Department and Sergeant Jim Papia discovered the palm print soon after the shot had been fired. Later, under the direction of Inspector Zachary, the chief of homicide, the palm print was dusted and examined. Fingerprints in Room 5 were also dusted and examined. Subsequently the state concluded that neither the fingerprints in Room 5 nor the palm print in the bathroom were left behind by Ray. On March 10 the prosecution made an apparent and deliberate effort to avoid the question. While Beasley considerably stretched, not to say entirely deformed, the statements of eyewitnesses in order to prove that Ray had been in the rooming house, he abandoned any effort to link either the fingerprints in Room 5 or the palm prints in the bathroom to Ray. Yet if the scuff marks in the tub and the palm print on the wall were evidence left behind by the killer, as the police had previously charged, it might be useful to discover whose hand matched the print. If the police did make such a determination they declined to reveal it.

With Ray's attorney and his biographer going far beyond the prosecutor and the evidence in their zeal to prove his guilt while the facts indicated that the case against Ray was largely conjectural, his hopes for an adequate defense diminished.

As we have seen, Beasley relied to a considerable extent upon Mrs. Bessie Brewer, the manager of the rooming house, to establish Ray's presence in the rooming house before the shot was fired and he relied upon her entirely for his assertion that Ray, using the name John Willard, requested a room for a week. Beasley said that the state would prove, through Mrs. Brewer, that Ray had entered the rooming house ''between 3:00 and 3:10 P.M. in the afternoon'' and that ''the defendant appeared here at Mrs. Brewer's office or apartment.'' Yet Mrs. Brewer never made such a statement. Mrs. Brewer consistently refused to identify Ray as the man she rented the room to and as the man who used the name John Willard. She refused to make any such statement, written or verbal, in spite of the pressure upon her to do so. As Beasley, the Assistant Attorney

General, made those declarations to the jury and to the press, Phil Canale, the Attorney General, sat at the prosecution table.

Years later, Pamela Spack and Leona Zanetti, two researchers for the Citizens Commission of Inquiry, interviewed Canale. Canale admitted then that Mrs. Brewer had never identified Ray. He said, "Mrs. Brewer did not positively identify Ray as being the Willard who had checked in there. She said she said she never looked him full in the face or anything like that. That was her testimony."

The state alleged that only one other witness could place Ray in the rooming house. According to Beasley, Charles Q. Stephens, a resident of the rooming house, heard the shot and went "out into the corridor in time to see the left profile of the defendant as he turned down this passageway." But Stephens did not make a positive identification of Ray. He only said the man looked "very much like" an FBI picture of Ray. That modest assertion was challenged by other statements, including earlier statements made by Stephens himself.

Approximately one week after Dr. King was killed I visited Stephens in the room which he shared with Grace Stephens, his wife. At that time he told me that he had seen the man who fled from the bathroom just after the shot was fired. He said that the man was "very small, quite short and certainly not heavy." He also told me that he had been the primary source for the artist's portrait of the presumed killer which was at that time being circulated by law enforcement authorities. Ray is five feet, ten inches tall and in no manner resembles the artist's drawing. At that time I was unable to ask Stephens directly if the man who fled after the shot was fired was James Earl Ray, since Ray was not a police suspect then, and his name was not known. After Ray was apprehended I sought to question Stephens again but by then Stephens had been placed in jail by the Memphis authorities and held as a material witness. Canale explained why Stephens had been held: "He had a reputation for being an alcoholic and he frequented places that we thought if somebody had it in their mind to harm him they could." Although Pamela Spack and Leona Zanetti pressed Canale for an explanation, he could think of no other. He added only, "So we talked to him and his lawyer about putting him in protective custody, which he agreed to; then later on he got tired of sitting over at the jail and requested that he be released and he was." Canale added that "We were worried to some extent about his personal safety and we considered he was a material witness in the case although I think we could have presented the case adequately without him."

However, Canale did not tell the court in 1969 that Stephens was an alcoholic who should be imprisoned for his own protection. He filed an affidavit with Judge Battle in which he swore that he was concerned that Stephens "might leave the state and not testify." Based upon that affidavit Stephens was held involuntarily in prison under a $10,000 bond. The record reveals that Stephens did ask to be released on numerous occasions but that Canale refused. Stephens finally secured counsel and brought a writ of habeas corpus before a judge other than Battle. Judge William W. O'Hearn ruled that the incarceration of Stephens was "illegal" and ordered him to be freed at once. In contesting that ruling Beasley argued that the prosecution has no other witnesses who can "testify to the same material facts."

For two weeks before Stephens had been placed in jail police officers had been assigned to be with him all day and night. As soon as he was released the officers began to accompany him again around the clock. Canale later admitted that no one had ever threatened Stephens in any way. In retrospect it appears that the Memphis authorities were less concerned about protecting their witness from harm than they were about protecting him from interviews, particularly with the team of defense lawyers and their investigator.

Stephens was a disabled veteran with a severe drinking problem. Apparently he was drunk when the shot that killed Dr. King was fired. His wife told me in the week following the assassination that "Charlie didn't see anything. He couldn't have. He was on the bed trying to sleep one off." That statement received independent corroboration from James M. McCraw. The month before the plea of guilty was entered by Ray two investigators questioned McCraw. They prepared a rather odd document entitled "Statement of James M. McCraw" in which McCraw began speaking in the first person and then was referred to in the third person. The document, in its entirety, reads as follows:

> On April 4, 1968, I was driving for Yellow Cab Co. and was dispatched to 422½ So. Main St. to pick up a fare. When I arrived at this address, I double parked as there were cars and trucks parked at the curb. I observed a Cadillac auto, owned by Mr. Jones, owner of Jim's grill on So. Main, 526-9910. I also observed two white Mustangs parked at the curb and several delivery trucks. All of this traffic was parked on the East side of So. Main St. facing North. A woman who ran the rooming house directed Mr. McCraw to a certain room, stating that the occupant of that room directed that a cab be called. The door of the room was open and McCraw went in the room and found Charles Stephens lying on the bed fully clothed, he was in a very

drunken condition. Stephens was well-known to McCraw, as he had picked him up many times before. Mr. McCraw refused to transport Stephens as a fare because of his drunken condition. McCraw stated that Stephens could not get off the bed. Mr. McCraw left the rooming house, got back into his cab, made a U-turn went South on South Main St. When Mr. McCraw got to the corner of So. Main and Calhoun Sts. the dispatcher said that Mr. M. L. King had been shot and for all cabs to stay out of the So. Main area. Mr. McCraw, after he got back into his cab, received a call to Frankie and Johnny's Boat Store on the Mississippi River at the Bridge. Mr. McCraw estimates that he was in the rooming house about three minutes and that from the time he left the rooming house until the time the dispatcher called about King being shot was about two minutes.

McCraw has driven Stephens to many liquor stores through the city at many different times. Stephens drank all kinds of whiskey or beer. Mr. McCraw could not tell whether Stephens drank more on the first and fifteenth of the month as he [Stephens] was a heavy drinker at all times.

McCraw's statement, ignored by Beasley when he ostensibly presented the facts in the case to the jury, provides strong support for Grace Stephen's earlier comment to me. The gravamen of the declaration made by the taxi driver is that Stephens, the only man who the state said could identify Ray as the fleeing gunman, was drunk on his bed two to five minutes before Dr. King was killed. The statement, of course, also raised the question of not one but two white Mustangs in front of the rooming house entrance.

Lloyd Jowers, the proprietor of Jim's Grill, located on the street level floor of the rooming house, was interviewed by Memphis police authorities on February 6, 1969, at four o'clock in the afternoon. Almost a year had passed since the murder and the state and defense were making last-minute preparations for the trial. Jowers, who was to be a prosecution witness, told two local investigators, according to their written statement, that "Charlie Stephens was drunk on April 4, 1968, in the afternoon." The report added that Jowers "remembers because Stephens and his landlady were having trouble about Stephen's rent."

Thus further corroboration for Mrs. Stephen's statement was available to the police and prosecution.

At this point the state's case against Ray crumbled. There was no reliable evidence that placed Ray in the rooming house at any time. No reliable witness would testify to his presence there before the shot was fired. The only witness who on occasion identified Ray as the man who fled through the corridor, and who had previously described a different man in size and facial characteristics, was evidently too drunk to observe the culprit and could not have seen him from his position on the bed, in any event. No fingerprints or palm prints placed Ray in the rooming house and indeed those that were located seemed to point in another direction which evidently was not explored by the police. No evidence demonstrated that Ray's rifle had fired the bullet which struck Dr. King and there, too, the evidence appeared to point in another direction which arrarently the police also failed to examine.

Although neither Beasley nor Canale mentioned her, Grace Stephens was an important witness. She was sober on the afternoon of April 4, 1968, and she was in her room at the rooming house. She heard the shot. She said, "At about six o'clock I heard a shot. I cannot tell where the shot came from. I know it echoed in the arcade beneath my window."

She said, "Right after the shot a man left the bathroom and went down the hall and down the steps to Main Street. I saw the man as he passed the door of my room. My guess of this man's age was in his fifties. This man was not quite as tall as I am. He was small-boned built. He had on an Army-colored hunting jacket unfastened and dark pants." She said that the man also wore a "plaid sport shirt." The man, Mrs. Stephens said, had "salt and pepper colored hair." She added, "He had something long in his right hand but I cannot swear what it was." She said that she heard "screaming at the motel" and that later reporters came to their room. Police officers did not visit her room for four hours. When they did arrive, she said, she accompanied them to Police Headquarters where she gave a statement to Inspector Zachary.

At last the Memphis authorities apparently had uncovered a reliable witness. Yet when Ray was arrested her statement was inconvenient. Ray was taller than average and Mrs. Stephens had described a man approximately five feet, five inches tall. Ray was well-built and muscular and she described a small-boned man. Ray was in his thirties and she described a man twenty years older.

While Charles Stephens was illegally held in jail by Memphis authorities, Grace Stephens was illegally taken from her home by other Memphis authorities and placed in a mental institution. Tennessee law requires that a commitment proceeding be initiated by a relative, guardian, licensed physician, or the director of a health and welfare institution. The proceeding against Mrs. Stephens was initiated by an assistant administrator at a hospital in Memphis. While the law required that the subject be notified in writing by mail of the proposed commitment hearing, that was not done in this case. Notice was not given to relatives as required by law. After Mrs. Stephens was illegally placed in the mental institution, the Memphis prosecutors removed her records from the hospital, according to her lawyer, C. M. Murphy.

Murphy also charged that his client had no history of mental illness and that she was able to care for herself. He said that the Memphis prosecuting attorneys committed her to safeguard their case against Ray. While one of the two prosecutors denied the allegation, he said that he did not know who really was behind the effort to commit her. Murphy said,

The reason she was placed in the psychiatric hospital was because her testimony would have been unfavorable to the position taken by the Shelby County attorney general [Memphis prosecutor] and his staff.

She was not mentally ill at the time and has at no time since been mentally ill. She charges further that although she was a material witness and that she informed the Memphis police . . . as to the details of her knowledge, such information was deliberately concealed . . . and she was unlawfully shuttled off to the psychiatric department of the city of Memphis' hospitals.

In 1970, two years after Mrs. Stephens was committed, Murphy brought an action for her release. A reporter for the *Washington Post* who attended the hearing said that Mrs. Stephens, "was heavily sedated" and that she "stared blankly." He reported as well that "attorneys say that ordinarily she is bright, articulate, and reads a great deal and that she completed three years of college."

Murphy was struck by the evident deterioration of his client. He said that a doctor at the mental institution had said in January 1969, two months before the Ray case came to trial, that her condition did not warrant commitment and that she should be released. Despite the evaluation by the institution's psychiatrist that her condition would "decline and deteriorate" if she was not released at the time of the evaluation in 1969, she was not released and she remains at the institution now, almost a decade after her incarceration.

Charles Stephens originally offered evidence which cast doubt upon the state's case against Ray. He was incarcerated and was released after he recanted. Mrs. Stephens has not recanted. When she was visited at the institution where she is confined she was asked if she remembers what she saw on April 4, 1968. She answered with a sad smile, "Oh yes. I remember what I saw and who I saw run away. That's why I'm here, you know."

The tragedy of April 4, 1968, apparently did not end that day.

Chapter Twenty-four

THE AFFIRMATIVE CASE
by Mark Lane

The defendant in a criminal case need not offer any evidence. He need not testify. The jurors may not draw any conclusion from his failure to testify. The defendant is not obligated to offer an alibi or an affirmative defense. He need not present the testimony of a single witness. The defendant may rest secure that if the state fails to prove his guilt beyond a reasonable doubt the jury will acquit him.

It is generally advisable for defendants and their attorneys to remind the jury of these components that comprise the presumption of innocence and then to place no reliance upon such shibboleths for in all probability the jurors will not.

While the state was unable to prove that Ray was in the rooming house, that he had fired a weapon, or even that the weapon which he had purchased fired the shot which killed Dr. King, curious jurors might be interested in trying to comprehend his strange behavior.

Ray had purchased the rifle in Birmingham under an assumed name. He had purchase binoculars shortly before Dr. King was killed and both the rifle and the binoculars and other articles were tossed to the sidewalk near the entrance to the rooming house within minutes of the firing of a rifle. Ray had registered at the Rebel Motel the previous night using a pseudonym. And while Ray had traveled by automobile from Los Angeles to New Orleans and from Canada to Mexico, he appeared to have no legal and visible means of support.

Had there been a trial the defense might have faced a dilemma. If the charge against Ray had not been dismissed by the trial judge after the presentation of the prosecution's case, the defense would have been constrained to determine whether Ray should testify. Very likely Battle, given his disposition to convict, would not have granted a defense motion based upon the failure of the state to present a *prima facie* case. While such a motion perhaps merited a serious hearing it seems doubtful, in a case of this magnitude, that it might be considered by the court. Through the cross-examination of the prosecution witnesses the defense in all probability would have established in the minds of the jurors that the overblown promises made by Beasley could not be sustained by evidence. A well-planned defense seeks to answer the questions that remain for the jurors when a prosecution case dissolves. Although it is not necessary for jurors to have a reasonable alternative theory of the crime presented to them in order to acquit, indeed it is contrary to law even to suggest that the defense has such a burden, it is generally helpful for the defense to suggest that the crime may have been committed in another way. Similarly while the defendant need not explain where he was when the crime was committed—it theoretically being sufficient for the finding of innocence that the state be unable to prove that he was an activist at the scene of the crime at the appropriate moment—if the defendant can make a showing as to his actual whereabouts without jeopardizing his legal defense it is often useful to do so.

After talking with the relevant witnesses and after reading interview reports and official records comprising the entire defense and prosecution cases, I am convinced that the state was not prepared to prove that Ray was in the rooming house on April 4, 1968. I am equally convinced that he was there shortly before Dr. King was killed. Ray, himself, told me that he had been in the rooming house earlier in the day and that he had in fact registered that day. He told me

I signed the name John Willard in the registration book. I was really amazed when the prosecutor never mentioned that at the mini-trial. They said that the registration book was lost.

It is difficult to imagine how the registration book, an important, almost an essential document in the case against Ray, could have disappeared. The police were at the rooming house within minutes after the shot was fired and questioned the occupants of the house shortly thereafter. They were seeking information about who had occupied the various rooms that day. The registration book was an obvious prime target of their search. Ray's handwritten registration was the only evidence that the state could use to prove his presence there. Yes the prosecuting authorities made no reference to that document and relied upon poor Mr. Stephens instead.

I asked Ray if he could understand the disappearance of the book. He said, "I don't know for sure but I can guess that maybe there is something else in that book, perhaps someone else who registered, that they don't want anyone to know about. It would have to be something important for them to give up the only evidence that could prove I was in that rooming house."

Ray's narrative of the events that led to the murder of Dr. King involve him in the commission of a number of crimes. If he admitted in court that he had committed those crimes he might have been prosecuted and the cumulative penalties that could be invoked against him for those crimes, when added to the penalty for the crime of escaping from jail and then added to the time that he owed the State of Missouri at the time of his escape, might have kept him in jail for the rest of his life. Yet Ray was anxious to testify at his trial in order to deny that he shot King or even knew that King would be shot. His first attorneys, who were confident that Ray would be acquitted, were reluctant to place him on the stand.

Ray did testify in an action that he subsequently brought against Foreman, Huie, and Hanes, Sr. On that occasion he testified that he had not fired the shot that killed Dr. King. Ray was willing to accept the risk that he might be required to spend a substantial portion of his life in jail for the opportunity to explain how he was used, without his knowledge, by those who murdered Dr. King. It is in this light that one must examine the statements by Huie and Foreman that Ray wanted to be caught so that he could proclaim that he murdered King. Both said that Ray's glory was in letting the whole world know of his guilt. Yet, as we have seen, Ray has insisted that he was innocent, denied that he shot King, and proclaimed himself to be an inglorious and unwitting dupe of others.

Ray's explanation to me of his movements through the United States from Canada to Mexico, his purchase of a rifle in Birmingham, and ultimately his presence in Memphis on April 4th in the vicinity of the murder scene is either basically true, or the intricate and comprehensive work product of a brilliant mind. For the narrative explains in a cohesive fashion all of Ray's otherwise inexplicable actions. Ray's relationship with a man he refers to only as Raoul becomes the Rosetta Stone of the defendant's odyssey.

According to Ray he fled to Canada after escaping from the Missouri penitentiary in Jefferson City. While in Montreal, he said, he "let the word get around" in the Neptune Tavern, a bar that welcomed seamen, that he had been in trouble in the United States and that he was seeking identification papers and money. Ray made it plain that he had been involved in criminal activities and was willing to undertake similar low-risk activities if his needs could be met. According to Ray a man he subsequently referred to as Raoul approached him and indicated that he could provide adequate documents and sufficient funds if Ray helped him to accomplish various projects. After a series of meetings Ray said the two men reached an agreement.

In furtherance of that agreement Ray began to surreptitiously deliver articles across the border from Canada to the United States and from the United States to Mexico. Ray was not told, and he states that he did not ask, about the contents of the packages. He, of course, presumed that he was smuggling contraband from one country to another.

Ray said that for one episode Raoul paid him $3,000 in cash. According to Ray, Raoul suggested that he go to Alabama from Montreal. "I didn't want to go back to the United States," Ray said to me. "Raoul told me he operated out of New Orleans and that he wanted me to help him in that area. He said I should go to a place near New Orleans and he suggested Mobile." According to Ray he chose Birmingham over Mobile because "I'm allergic to salt air." He added, "When you're living underground a bigger city is safer than a smaller one and Birmingham is bigger than Mobile." Raoul told Ray to buy a car in Birmingham.

In September 1968, Ray wrote, "I suppose I became involved in the plot to kill King when I took those packages into the United States from Canada. I would think it had all been decided before the car was bought in Birmingham, as no one would have given me $3,000 in Birmingham just to haul narcotics across the border. But nobody told me about any planned murder of King or anyone else." Subsequently Raoul arranged for Ray to drive his white Mustang into Mexico after Raoul had exchanged the spare tire in the Mustang for another one. After Ray had cleared Mexican customs Ray's tire was returned by Raoul who removed the one that Ray had driven across the border. "I never thought I was smuggling a spare tire," Ray told me later. "Obviously something was in the tire."

Ray said to me that Raoul gave him $2,000 in cash for that episode. "It was all in twenty-dollar bills. And he said he would have $12,000 more for me to go into a business within another country and he would also have a passport for me." Ray told me that Raoul said "he would probably need me in about two or three or four months. This was in October 1967. He said I should call him at his New Orleans telephone number once in a while. I told him that I would be in Los Angeles and he said that he would write to me there."

Ray said that approximately four months before Dr. King was killed he returned to New Orleans to meet Raoul in a tavern on Canal Street on the border of the French Quarter. At that time Raoul told Ray that he would have a job for him to do in about three months and that it was to be Ray's last assignment. "He told me that when that job was done he was going to give me $12,000 and all the documents that I would need to travel wherever I wanted to outside of the States. He wouldn't tell me what the job was, told me not to ask about it, and gave me $500 in cash," Ray said.

Ray also told me that subsequently Raoul contacted him and told him to meet him in New Orleans on March 20, 1968, less than two months before King was killed. When Ray arrived in New Orleans he said he was told that Raoul had gone to Birmingham and that he expected Ray to meet him there in two days. Ray arrived a day late in Birmingham since he became confused and took a highway to Montgomery by mistake.

Raoul and Ray traveled to Atlanta together. There, according to Ray, Raoul "told me that he wanted me to buy a large-bore deer rifle with a telescopic sight. He said that if the rifle was approved of by the buyers that I was to get about a dozen more and also about 200 cheap rifles. The good one had to be new, the others they didn't care about."

Ray said that since he had Alabama identification it might be better if he went back to Birmingham to buy the rifles. Raoul agreed. Ray said, "We met in Birmingham and Raoul and I got the address of a rifle place, Aeromarine Supply, out of a newspaper advertisement, which said they had a lot of rifles." According to Ray, Raoul gave him about $750 and told him to buy the large-bore deer rifle. Ray purchased a rifle and showed it to Raoul in a Birmingham motel. He said Raoul was displeased—"said it was the wrong kind." Raoul pointed out to Ray the rifle that he preferred from the catalogue and Ray called the store and said that he wanted to exchange it. Ray exchanged rifles. Raoul told him, he said, to meet him "in Memphis on April 3 in the evening at the Rebel Motel and to bring the rifle." Ray said that he did meet Raoul as planned and that he was told that he was to go back to Birmingham in a few days to purchase some more rifles and "a lot of cheap foreign rifles so that they could be shipped to New Orleans." Ray said that "before he left he said I should meet him the next day at four o'clock in the afternoon at a rooming house at 422½ South Main Street. He wrote down the address and said to meet him in the bar downstairs if he was not in the rooming house." Ray said that he met Raoul in Jim's Grill on the afternoon of April 4, 1968, and that subsequently they went together to a room in the rooming house. "When we got there Raoul said we would be there for a few days 'so bring the Mustang around and get your stuff out of it and bring it up here.' He also said to get a pair of infrared binoculars at York Arms, a store that was nearby." Ray did purchase binoculars but the sales clerk told him that the store did not carry the infrared variety.

Ray said that when he returned to the rooming house he brought his suitcase to the room. "I also brought the bed spread from the car since I was going to have to sleep in the room for a few days."

Quite obviously Ray's location at the time the shot was fired remains the single most important question in considering the case against him. It has been pointed out that he has vacillated when asked to establish that locale. Ray conceded the accuracy of that accusation when I inquired and

175

now he explained it this way. As in the case with much of the evidence, this matter has neither been tested by cross-examination nor has it been offered in a courtroom under oath.

"I wanted to testify at the trial. Lawyers can say and the judges can agree that if you don't testify it can't be held against you. But jurors want to see you. They want to hear the defendant talk. I didn't kill King and I wanted to testify. Toward the end of our arrangement, when it was breaking down, old man Hanes came in to see me. He said, 'Huie wants to know where you were when King was shot.' I was surprised that Huie didn't ask me long before. I might have told him then. Now I said, 'Tell Huie it could have happened this way.' Then I told him a story about me waiting in the car, Raoul running down the steps and jumping in the back seat of the car. I said 'Tell Huie that Raoul pulled a sheet over him in the back seat.' I mentioned a sheet because Huie is so interested in the Klan I thought he would appreciate it. It never happened that way at all. The next morning young Hanes came in to see me. He said Huie is mad. 'He doesn't want to know how it could have happened, he wants to know how it did happen.' I just sort of smiled. I wasn't going to give away my testimony to the other side in advance."

I asked Ray if he would tell me where he was when Dr. King was murdered.

"Yes, I'll tell you. It looks now as if I may not get a trial at all so I'll tell you what happened."

Our conversation took place in the library of the Brushy Mountain Penitentiary. I was the first visitor to see him after the United States Supreme Court had denied his application for a trial.

He said, "I was sent out of the rooming house eight or ten times that day. I was almost never in there. As to the bathroom I'm not sure I was ever in there at all. It had no special meaning for me at the time. But I was in and out of the room I had rented all day—mostly out of it."

I asked why his fingerprints had not been found in the room. "Well," he said, "the doors did not have door knobs for one thing. They had a hole to stick a finger through and a leather strap to pull."

Ray returned to the narrative. "I was sent to the drugstore, to the gun shop, twice to the place that sold binoculars, to taverns. Late afternoon I was sent to a gas station to check out the car, to get air in the spare tire. I did that and drove back toward the rooming house on South Main. The place was filled with police, blocking off the street. Something had happened and I knew I had to get out of there. I was a fugitive and I could not afford to get stopped by the police. I turned down a street before the rooming house and started to drive away. I was later told that a police officer waved me on through but I don't remember that happening."

I asked Ray where he went. He said, "I began to drive toward New Orleans. I had the car radio on and the announcement came that King had been shot. It was dark by then. Maybe about seven o'clock when I heard that news. But even then I wasn't sure about what had happened. I didn't even know that the Lorraine Motel was behind the rooming house. I didn't know that King was staying there. I didn't even know that King was in town."

I asked Ray when he determined for the first time that he had some involvement with the events that led to Dr. King's death. "Well, I kept on driving and then the news report came over the radio about King being shot and the suspect, a white man, had escaped from the area in a white Mustang. I was driving a white Mustang. I had just left the area. It wasn't hard at that time for me to put two and two together and decide that I was it." Ray said, "Then I just wanted to get far away from Memphis. I had good reasons to leave. I wanted to get away from the police. A convict, a fugitive wanted for killing King. I didn't think I had a chance. Anyway, even if I did I still owed time to Missouri and there would be the additional time for escaping. I had to get away before I was caught by the police or anyone else."

According to Arthur Hanes, Jr., Ray was fleeing for his life. "He knew all of a sudden that he was in deep trouble. I think it was not just the authorities Ray feared. He was afraid that Raoul or Raoul's friends might kill him. He knew by then, of course, that he'd been set up and he feared that as an important link to the killers he imposed a real threat. He was afraid that they would kill him."

Certain elements of Ray's explanation of the events are subject to independent verification. I have been able to establish that Ray had been at the motels and restaurants that he spoke of and that he was there during the time frame that he gave. Yet those facts do not establish the validity of his essential claim that another was involved and directed him. Ray could have woven the fabric of his conspiracy story around the framework of a real set of facts. There are, I suggest, three areas of inquiry which might tend to confirm or challenge the essence of his story.

If Raoul was not a source of substantial funding for Ray during his months as a fugitive, what was the source?

Was the package containing evidence that would inexorably lead to him left on the sidewalk rather than placed in the Mustang?

Did he exchange rifles at the Aeromarine Supply Company after conferring with another as he claimed?

There has been speculation about how Ray's trips around the country and his trips to Europe were financed. Novelists have offered theories. The FBI conducted a relatively thorough investigation and was unable to establish any proof that Ray had been financed from the time of his escape from the prison at Jefferson City, Missouri, until the time of his arrest in London in any fashion other than Raoul, as Ray claimed. If Ray did receive substantial funds from other sources, those sources have escaped detection.

The troubling presence of the package containing evidence tending to link Ray to the crime creates a serious logical problem. If Ray acted alone, used the weapon that he purchased in Birmingham, and then was motivated to flee quickly from the scene, why did he take the time to pack the weapon in a cardboard box and then place his bulky belongings in a bedspread? Indeed, why had he not left the articles not required to kill Dr. King in the trunk of the Mustang before he fired the shot? If he was going to carry the rifle, binoculars, radio, clothing, and other articles from the bathroom, taking precious time to wrap them up, why did he leave them on the sidewalk? Why did he not just throw them in the Mustang parked a few feet away? The gratuitous placement by Ray of evidence that would, without doubt, lead to him is inexplicable. Ray's narrative of the events has the virtue of offering a rational explanation.

If Ray had discussed the characteristics of the rifle that he had purchased from the Aeromarine Supply Company with another who considered it to be unsuitable for the intended use, and then Ray exchanged the rifle for a more accurate or more powerful weapon, his narrative takes on an added authority. It is sometimes necessary for a juror to enter the mind of a defendant to determine if his testimony meets the crucial test of reasonableness. Since you, the reader, may be the only jury that James Earl Ray will ever have, an examination by you of his mental process at the time of purchase of the presumed murder weapon is important. Does it not seem likely that had Ray purchased the rifle with the intent of using it to murder Dr. King that he would have decided upon the weapon in advance of entering the store in order to spend as little time as possible with the store personnel? According to the state's hypothesis, the first overt act that Ray committed in his solitary plan to kill Dr. King was the purchase of a suitable weapon. Would Ray have not sought to complete that task expeditiously so that the salesperson might be less likely to identify him subsequently? Yet Ray, for some reason, did return to the Aeromarine Supply Company to exchange the weapon for a much more powerful and accurate one. Ray has told us of his view of the transaction with the Aeromarine Supply Company in Birmingham. Robert Wood and Donald Wood were the proprietors of the company on

March 29, 1968. According to Donald Wood, on that day Ray told him he was going deer hunting with his brother and that he needed a rifle for that purpose. Ray later recalled that he had said he was to hunt deer with "my brother-in-law." With the exception of that discrepancy, Wood fully corroborates Ray's narrative and provides, as well, details which tend to confirm essential elements in the narrative. Wood said that Ray looked over a number of rifles, seemed confused by the array of rifles available, and appeared to know even less about deer hunting. Ray selected a Remington Gamemaster. Wood affixed a telescopic sight to the .243 caliber weapon while Ray waited.

During the afternoon, Wood received a telephone call from Ray. Ray said that he required a "heavier gun" and that he wanted to exchange the weapon he had just purchased for a more powerful one. Wood agreed. He was, however, puzzled since the weapon he'd sold earlier in the day was more than adequate for deer hunting. Wood pointed out that he would prefer to make the exchange the next day when he would have time to mount the telescopic sight on the weapon he purchased. Ray agreed.

Wood said that Ray returned the following morning and chose a more powerful weapon, a Remington 30.06 rifle which fired a bullet that weighed approximately as much as the bullet for the .243 Remington.

Ray's account of the transaction at Aeromarine was confirmed both by Donald Wood and his father Robert Wood. Only the mysterious Raoul can corroborate or challenge Ray's account of why he exchanged weapons and risked a second visit to the location of his first overt act in the murder of Dr. King. We are left to ponder this question—Why did Ray exchange rifles unless someone advised him to do so after he had made the initial purchase?

Ray's explanation, whether truthful or not, claims the virtue of being reasonable. It also enjoys another distinction. During the nine years that have passed since that day it remains the only explanation of the prolonged transaction.

In-depth interviews with potential witnesses, an examination of all of the voluminous working papers prepared by the original defense lawyers and their investigation, and days spent with Hanes senior and junior provided me with some insight into what might have been the affirmative case for the defense even had Ray not testified.

Arthur Hanes, Jr., a Princeton graduate and a sophisticated and urbane young Birmingham trial lawyer in 1968, told me what all trial lawyers know. "Hell, it wasn't our job to find out who killed King. We were there to defend Ray." This is the credo of the trial lawyer and it is, I suggest, an entirely proper approach when the role of the defense lawyer is examined in context. Students of history may be appalled by what may appear to be, and by what in fact may be, a cavalier attitude toward the facts. Yet, since historical truth is arrived at in one fashion and justice in the courtroom in another, the obligation of those who participate in a search for the truth is quite different from the responsibility of participants in the search for justice. The judicial experience as we practice it relies theoretically upon an impartial and wise judge, an impartial and open-minded jury, a state devoted to the discovery of evidence demonstrating the guilt of the defendant, and a defense dedicated to refuting that case. Should the defense lawyer abandon his traditional role and strike out on his own to learn and reveal the "truth," the delicate balance devised to create a fair and equal contest fails. It is for others to explore the facts to discover the truth. The suitable defense lawyer is an advocate for his client's case. It is in this light that the case, as seen and presented by the defense lawyers, should be understood.

Had Ray been tried, very likely the defense would have offered a serious challenge to several elements of the state's case. The jurors would have been required to determine if the shot was fired from the bathroom window; when and by whom the package that seemed to incriminate Ray was placed on the sidewalk; whether there was a deliberate police effort to allow Ray to escape from the scene; if the FBI deliberately allowed Ray to escape from the country before advertising their interest with him; why Ray's prints were not found in the bathroom; whether the bullet that killed Dr. King came from the rifle Ray had purchased; could the state prove that Ray had pulled the trigger that resulted in the fatal wound.

Among the most intriguing questions presented by the case against Ray as the lone killer are those that flow from the presumption that Ray rented a room at 422½ South Main in order to have a clear shot at Dr. King. Dr. King had not stayed at the Lorraine during his most recent visits to Memphis prior to April 1968. While the FBI had, since March 29, 1968, sought to drive King into that motel, Ray, presumably, would not have been aware of those efforts.

The prosecution alleges that once Ray learned that King was to be at the Lorraine it was obvious that a room at 422½ South Main would provide the perfect sniper's nest. In retrospect the casual observer might agree. However, an examination of the area either from the balcony at the Lorraine or from South Main Street reveals the true complexity created by the geography and topography of the site. From the Lorraine Motel balcony, it is not possible to see the building at 422½ Main Street. The rear of the building facing the Lorraine is entirely hidden by trees and bushes. From the Lorraine, one cannot even know that 422½ exists. The perspective afforded by an examination from South Main Street of the buildings located there does not reveal that by entering the 422½ address one will be able to see the Lorraine. A person familiar with the inner structure of the buildings might know that by entering 422½ and passing through a jerry-built impermanent corridor constructed of tin sheets and wood which connects 422½ with a separate building to its south a view of the Lorraine could be arranged. It is, of course, not impossible to enter the rooming house on South Main and arrive at a window which provides a view of the Lorraine balcony. It is, however, difficult to know that such a feat can be accomplished without advance knowledge of the connection between the two buildings and without knowing that the building south of 422½ is also a rooming house managed by the proprietors of the 422½ South Main establishment. The jurors might have been troubled by the failure of the prosecution to contemplate the curious complexity of the problem. They might have been stunned by the possibility that Ray had either inadvertently stumbled into a solution without even understanding the problem or that he had, as he had stated, been guided to the scene by someone with knowledge who had solved the problem for him.

If the jurors believed that Ray had managed to get to the bathroom window without help, as the prosecution had alleged, they would then have been confronted with the question of the origin of the shot. If the state had proof that the shot was fired from that window, it has not yet proffered it. It may very well be that a serious study of the autopsy documents, including contemporaneous notes, photographs, and X-rays, taken together with eyewitness testimony which may reconstruct the exact posture of Dr. King when he received the fatal bullet, will establish the angle of entry and thus the origin of the shot. In the absence of scholarly work by experts armed with the authority of the power of subpoena, who can say that he is content that the origin of the bullet is known? It is in this gray area of conjecture that the defense might have made significant gains. There were those in the Lorraine Motel courtyard and those on the balcony with Dr. King who believed that the shot may have been fired from a clump of bushes and scrub trees on the embankment between the rooming house and Dr. King and beneath the rooming house windows. As I have observed in the case of similar statements made by witnesses in the murder of President Kennedy, earwitness testimony is generally less reliable than eyewitness testimony. It is often difficult to identify the origin of a sound with precision. By contrast, it is relatively simple to state where one saw an event occur. There is some additional evidence which supports the defense theory that the shot was fired not from the bathroom window but rather from the bushes and trees on the embankment. This evidence, developed by the defense, should be examined as cautiously and evaluated as carefully as the evidence and statements proffered by the prosecution. This evidence, as in the case of the prosecution's allegations, has not been subjected to the crucible of cross-examination.

Solomon Jones was the driver of the car which transported Dr. King in the Memphis area. The vehicle had been made available by a local funeral parlor. In a statement Jones gave to the Memphis police authorities who questioned him on February 3, 1969, ten months after the murder, Jones said, "On the day of the shooting, I was on the ground beside the car, which was parked on the west side of the motel; I was on the north side of the car." While Jones was quoted by the police in an unsigned statement as having said, "Everybody was running and the yard was full of police, I was unable to tell who, if anyone, ran from the bushes." He had made earlier statements, some of them almost contemporaneous with the event, with a different emphasis. Jones told Renfro Hays, the defense investigator, and prior to that, news reporters at the scene, that he saw someone run from the bushes on the embankment immediately after the shot was fired. Jones said that the man had "something white" across his face. At one point Jones said that the man carried something in his hand.

On April 5, 1968, the morning following the murder, the Memphis *Commercial Appeal* quoted Jones as saying that just after the shot was fired he saw a man "with something white on his face" leave "a thicket across the street." Yet the police did not interview Jones until ten months had passed. Corroboration for the original observations made by Jones was furnished by Harold Carter. Carter lived at 422½ South Main. On April 4, 1968, he sat on a cardboard box on the embankment just in front of the clump of bushes and trees. If a shot was fired from that area he should have heard it. If a man fled from the area he might have observed him.

Carter was interviewed by Hays on August 25, 1968. He said,

That afternoon I was sitting out on the vacant lot behind the rooming house with Dude Wheeler and another man who works on the river. We were sitting there on some cardboard next to some bushes watching the people over at the Lorraine Motel as there was a lot going on over there. Just before six o'clock Dude and the other fellows left but Dude was supposed to come back. Then two men standing on the ground by the Lorraine Motel started calling up asking for someone to get Dr. King to the door. A man, I guess he was King, came out the door and came to the

rail and started talking to these men on the ground. At the same time I heard some one walking behind me from the other side of the bushes. I thought it was Dude Wheeler coming back and I didn't even look around. Then there was a loud shot from the bushes right beside me. I looked around and saw the man running away, north—I did not see his face. He was about my size and he must have been young because he moved fast. He had on dark clothes with a high necked white sweater. He had a rifle or shotgun in his hand. When he got to the northwest corner of the lot he took the stock off his gun and threw it in some bushes and put the barrel under his jacket and stepped down on a barrel and down to the sidewalk. Everyone was running to the motel then. And he just walked on away from them.

Carter told Hays that he was not anxious to become involved in the case. For that reason he made no voluntary statement to the police. However, during the evening of April 4th police officers interrogated all of the residents of 422½ South Main. Carter said that when the police asked him what he had been doing at the time of the murder and what he observed, he answered them truthfully. The officers then took him to police headquarters where he was interviewed by detectives. Carter said he told the detectives about the origin of the shot and of the man who fled from the bushes. Carter said, "They called me a damn liar!" After the detectives had made it plain to Carter that his allegations were not acceptable, he was left alone for awhile.

When they talked to me again I told them I didn't know anything, I never got around to telling them where the gunstock was. I have nothing to hide about this, I never saw that man before or since that I know of. If the police had treated me like a human being I would have told them everything I knew.

Carter later signed a statement which was witnessed by Hays in which he said that he was reluctant to sign a statement about his observations "because I don't want to be thrown in jail like Charlie Stephens was."

On June 19, 1968, *The New York Times* published a review of some of the evidence by Martin Waldron, a veteran investigative reporter. The story ran under the headline "Evidence Hints a Conspiracy in Slaying of Dr. King."

Waldron began:

From the moment of the assassination of the Rev. Dr. Martin Luther King, Jr., on April 4 evidence has accumulated to suggest that he was the victim of a conspiracy. Several bits of evidence

**indicate more than one person may have been involved in Dr.
King's slaying. Others point to the possibility that the murder
may have been a hired killing.**

Waldron considered the official response to the evidence tending to
establish conspiracy.

**The Federal Bureau of Investigation has refused to comment.
Attorney General Ramsey Clark has said several times that the
FBI has not uncovered any evidence of a conspiracy.**

**Mr. Clark said, however, that the investigation did not end
with the arrest of James Earl Ray in London on June 8. If others
are involved, he said, the FBI will find them.**

During the halcyon days of 1968, before the United States Senate had
informed us that the FBI destroyed evidence, suborned perjury and
committed perjury to prevent the Warren Commission from learning who
killed President Kennedy, and operated as well a squad determined to
destroy Dr. King, it was easier to believe that the FBI might be interested
in finding the assassins. Mr. Clark's assurances were no doubt comfort-
ing to many. But to a few, including Ray, his two lawyers and his one
investigator, the evidence that raised doubts for Waldron had raised
serious questions for further exploration.

The first matter that Waldron addressed himself to as one which
indicated ''that there may have been a conspiracy'' was ''a vivid description broadcast over the Memphis police radio network on the night of
April 4 of an automobile chase that never took place.''

The broadcast, made at the time Ray was fleeing from the city
southward, attempted to establish the flight of the alleged assassin to the
northeast.

Arthur Hanes, Sr., told me that he had listened to the official recording of the Memphis police radio broadcasts for the evening of April 4. He
had taken handwritten verbatim notes of the broadcast which he gave to
me. At 6:10 P.M. the radio broadcast the message ''6:10—Information
subject [or suspect] may be in late model Mustang going north on Main.''
Hanes said, ''Now where did they get that information from. There is not
a single witness who they can produce who claims that they saw anyone
get into a white Mustang and leave the scene.''

At 6:36 the police radio broadcast this message. ''6:36—60 at Jackson and Hollywood. Mobile unit. East on Summers—from Highland
exceeding speed limit. Blue 66 Pontiac going over 75 mph. Three white
males in blue Pontiac. North on Jackson.'' And at 6:48 the radio broad-

cast this message. "White Mustang is shooting at Pontiac. Austin Peay. Approaching the road going into Naval Base." While the police concentrated upon an apocryphal gun battle in one part of town, according to Ray, he drove out of town in the opposite direction.

To this date, no adequate official explanation of the police radio broadcast has been offered. When I asked Frank Holloman, who had been the director of the police department on April 4, 1968, for an explanation he said, "Oh, it is nothing serious. It was just a teen-ager involved in a prank." That appears to be the official explanation. I asked Holloman if the teen-ager was arrested and prosecuted for obstruction of justice since quite possibly he had aided a murderer escape from the area. While Holloman paused for a moment, I asked if the teen-ager's radio license had been revoked. Holloman appeared troubled by the questions and then answered, "I don't recall if we ever found out who it was. If we didn't, then we couldn't arrest him." I agreed with Holloman's logic and asked how the police could learn the age of the suspect from the radio broadcast without learning his identity. Holloman pondered the question for a long moment and then said, "Well maybe we did locate him and that's how we got his age. I just don't know."

Had the case been tried while Hanes and Hanes represented Ray, the defense would have been prepared to explore this area of evidence that indicated the possibility of conspiracy. An examination of the broadcasts by the police over the two frequencies they employed revealed false or inexplicable references to the fleeing white Mustang at 6:10 P.M., 6:12 P.M., 6:35 P.M., 6:48 P.M., and 6:53 P.M., as well as a reference to an abandoned Mustang at 5:42 P.M. Approximately twenty minutes before the shot was fired a broadcast stated that "Tac 11 [Tactical Squad] has witness who saw white Olds pull away from Lorraine before police arrived."

The broadcast at 7:37 P.M. said "complete curfew in effect." Exactly ten minutes later the police reported "Tac units to start cruising from Lorraine. Homicide has completed investigation." There is very little evidence to dispute the police assertion that less than two hours after Dr. King had been murdered the police had finished their work. The unexamined clues, the unfollowed leads, the unexplored circumstances that led toward a conspiracy to kill Dr. King remain today unexamined, unfollowed, and unexplored by those in Memphis or in the Department of Justice.

Martin Waldron was concerned by evidence showing that Ray, using the alias Eric S. Galt, left "a trail of free spending" indicating that he had been financed by others. The Hanes law firm also focused upon that matter. Ray explained that he was paid by Raoul and he quite specifically supplied the amounts paid, the dates and places of payment, the denominations of the bills and the services that he performed. The FBI, through news leaks attributed by *The New York Times* to "quoted FBI 'sources,'" responded that Ray had probably robbed a bank in Alton, Illinois, on July 13, 1967, and taken $20,000. Waldron wrote that "other evidence indicates that Ray may have been living in Toronto at this time." In any event, Ray was never charged with the crime and the only evidence of his possible involvement in that crime was the statement of one woman in the bank who allegedly said that one of the two robbers resembled photographs of Ray. There exists no reasonable explanation of Ray's funding for the period of time preceding the murder of Dr. King, other than Ray's own explanation. While his explanations may not be accurate, they remain unchallenged by a viable prosecution alternative.

Waldron was also concerned that Ray used four aliases in Canada and in his trips about the United States and ultimately to Europe. The names Ray operated under were Ramon George Sneyd, Eric S. Galt, Paul Bridgman and John Willard. All four men exist. All four men live in Toronto. All four men are approximately the same height and weight as James Earl Ray, and like Ray, all four have dark hair. All four men give the appearance of being the same age as Ray. The evidence indicates that Ray used the name Galt in Birmingham, Atlanta and Los Angeles; the name Willard in Memphis; the name Sneyd in Toronto and London; the name Bridgman in Toronto.

The question that troubled Waldron and the defense attorneys is how did Ray, unknown in Canada, assemble documents from four men who resembled him physically and who did not even know each other. Did Ray have assistance in choosing the aliases? The prosecution failed to investigate this intriguing question and failed to comment upon it when presenting the case against Ray. Indeed neither the jurors nor the trial judge were informed of any of the distressing details which might have discommoded the case against Ray as the lone assassin. The unexplained false radio broadcasts, Ray's unexplained well-financed trips, the unexplored four remarkable aliases, the unrefuted evidence that indicated that the shot may have originated from a place other than the bathroom window, and the difficulty in knowing that by entering 422½ South Main one could arrange for a view of the motel balcony were neither commented upon by Ray's prosecutors when they presented the case against Ray to the court and jury nor alluded to by Ray's lawyer, the renowned Percy Foreman of Houston, Texas.

Indeed, why did Ray plead guilty when the state would have had a most difficult and perhaps an impossible task of establishing a *prima facie* case against him, and when such a strong affirmative defense was available to him? And why did Foreman, Ray's trial counsel, offer no resistance to an arrangement which sent his client to jail for ninety-nine years in a state where the death penalty had not been carried out for many years?

Chapter 25

THE PLEA
by Mark Lane

Those who assert that Ray alone killed King offer as proof Ray's plea of guilty. That plea, however, can not be dispositive of the many and serious questions raised by the evidence. When closely examined, the plea itself, in fact, tends to support the other evidence of a prearranged plan to murder Dr. King and to cover up the evidence of that conspiracy.

When Ray entered his plea before Judge Battle, he stated that there had been a conspiracy to murder Dr. King. He has consistently held to that position. Over the years he has told all of his attorneys that there had been a conspiracy. He made that statement to the Hanes defense team, to their successor, Percy Foreman, and to the lawyers who have since represented him. He explained the details of the conspiracy to his lawyers and to Huie before he entered the plea and he elaborated upon those details when he spoke with me later.

The curious circumstances surrounding the arrangement for the guilty plea hardly do credit to our oft-repeated claims of due process in difficult cases and raise yet additional questions. Was a deliberate effort made to induce Ray to plead guilty so that the full facts might be successfully concealed? An examination of the development of the various episodes that led to the courtroom ritual in which the guilty plea was offered and accepted may provide the answer.

Ray was imprisoned in the Shelby County Jail in Memphis in maximum security until he pleaded guilty. During the months that he was jailed, bright lights were kept on him twenty-four hours each day. Closed circuit cameras monitored his every move. Guards were present in the cell with him while other guards watched him from the other side of the bars. Microphones in the cell picked up and magnified every sound that he made. Even his breathing was heard. Months later when Ray described the conditions in the cell during a civil suit against Foreman and Huie he testified, "As I stated, maximum security jail, lights on twenty-four hours a day, steel plates over the windows, two television sets watching me all the time . . . no fresh air." Ray testified that his conversations with his attorneys were overheard by the guards. He said that the listening devices were so sophisticated that the guards "could hear a roach walk across the floor." Ray said that Foreman "often spoke very loudly when talking with him." I was always warning Mr. Foreman about talking so loud. A lot of times he would talk loud on purpose so they [the guards] could hear him. A lot of times he had them sign documents as witnesses." Ray said that he did not wish to speculate about which conversations the guards had overheard. "I think you would have to talk to the guards to find out what they heard and what they didn't hear." He did say that on one occasion "one of them told me he heard some of Mr. Foreman's conversations one time."

Two months after Ray had been confined under the extraordinary conditions imposed by the Memphis authorities, Arthur Hanes, Sr., filed a motion requesting an order directing the Shelby County Sheriff to "cease and desist from the use of television lights, cameras and microphones to constantly surveille the Defendant." The attorney said that "the presence of said illumination and surveillance has deprived Defendant of the opportunity to rest or sleep and has a tendency to cause Defendant to be nervous and disturbed and constitutes an electronic form of cruel and unusual punishment."

The Attorney General, Phil Canale, filed an answer stating that the television cameras were required "as a security measure to protect the defendant Ray as well as to keep the defendant Ray from effecting an escape."

During 1976, Leona Zanetti and Pamela Spack, two investigators with the Citizens Commission of Inquiry, interviewed Phil Canale. They asked him about the presence of microphones in Ray's cell. He replied:

Well, we had a big hearing on that down there when, ah, one of his lawyers filed something, some motion about the fact that he was, ah, his health was going bad, and surveillance and everything, and we had a hearing, and, ah, the doctor testified, the jailers testified, and, ah, we had a full blown hearing on it. As I recall it there was always some light in the cell there . . . I think Hanes also said that he had to lie on the floor to talk to Ray because the place was bugged. Well, there was never any indication of bugs, I never heard of any, anything that came out of the cell. I'm sure that I would have heard it if anything came out of there, you know. But yes, I think there was some illumination in there at all times.

However, that same year the United States Court of Appeals for the Sixth Circuit concluded that Ray's prison conversations had been monitored and that such electronic surveillance was "improper."

Eight years before, on November 22, 1968, Judge Battle had ruled that "the security complained of is for the benefit of the defendant" and that "the measures taken for the security and protection of the defendant are reasonable."

Two months after Hanes had applied to Judge Battle for some relief from the oppressive jail conditions, Michael Eugene, an English solicitor who had been appointed to represent Ray's rights in London, saw Ray. He was astonished by the deterioration in Ray's condition. He said that Ray looked sick, weak, and nervous.

When James Earl Ray pleaded guilty, a reporter from the Chicago *Daily News* interviewed his brother, John Ray. John said that he had doubted that his brother would plead guilty but that the strain of being under constant observation in his cell by guards and closed circuit television must have affected him. "All the time he has spent up there in his cell may have affected his mind. He can't even go to the bathroom in private."

When I interviewed Jerry Ray, another brother, in December 1976, he said that Foreman's efforts to convince James to plead guilty were substantially aided by the defendant's condition.

He couldn't sleep. Those bright lights on all the time. Always being looked at. No air conditioning. No fresh air. Never any daylight. Never any night. I guess it was kind of like a concentration camp. You ended up doing things you ordinarily wouldn't do. James was sort of out of his mind at the time. He hadn't seen outside, even through a window, for four months. Never knew whether it was night or day. It was the kind of conditions that big shots in this country are always complaining about in other countries."

In *Spandau,* a remarkable prison book, Albert Speer, the convicted Nazi war criminal, discussed the conditions to which he was subjected as a military prisoner. Speer had been sentenced at Nuremberg to serve a twenty-year term. He explained that "the prison regulations are strict" because another convicted war criminal had just hanged himself. To prevent another death, his cell was not entirely darkened. He wrote that at first "the cell is poorly illuminated at night by a light placed outside." Speer added "at night we live in twilight." Later in his imprisonment at Spandau all of the lights were extinguished before ten o'clock. Indeed the rules required, he wrote, "that all cells had to be dark at ten o'clock."

The experience at Spandau, the ultimate maximum security military prison, was not pleasant. Yet Speer, in describing the conditions there, wrote of his regular visits with other prisoners which occurred many hours each day, his work in the garden with the other prisoners, the walks in the courtyard, the window in his cell which permitted a view of the stars at night, and fresh air both night and day.

In my view all prisons that I have seen offer artificial and brutalizing experiences. Yet Speer, a major war criminal, was not subjected to the dehumanizing denial of sensory perception that the elaborately contrived circumstances imposed upon James Earl Ray. If the torture that Ray was subjected to was not designed to weaken his resistance and to drain his resolve it nevertheless should have been quite clear to counsel, the prosecutors and the court that such a result was predictable, indeed, very likely inevitable.

It appears that the most important decision that Ray made after his arrest was to discharge the Hanes defense team and retain Percy Foreman. I believe that the father and son team was adequately prepared to represent Ray at trial and that the evidence against him was minimal and insufficient to convict him. Once Foreman entered the case the inexorable march toward a deal—the guilty plea and a ninety-nine year sentence—was underway.

Arthur Hanes, Sr., remembers quite clearly his last day as attorney for Ray. "We learned of it on Sunday, November 10. We, Art Junior and I, went to the jail to see Ray at about 8:30 at night. The guard said the Sheriff wanted to see me. I went to the Sheriff's office and they showed me a Xerox copy of a handwritten note from Ray. It said 'Dear Mr. Hanes, I thank you for all you've done for me, however I've decided to change lawyers and obtain other counsel. Sincerely, Jim.' I said, 'Well, Percy Foreman was in his cell four or five hours today while you were driving here from Birmingham.' "

Hanes added, "Foreman had the original of my letter from Ray. How he was allowed to get in there and see my client about our case I never did find out for sure."

A substantial question also remains as to why Foreman visited Ray in his Memphis jail cell. On a January 2, 1976, CBS-TV broadcast an interview of Foreman conducted by a CBS reporter, Dan Rather. Rather asked Foreman how he got into the case. The following colloquy ensued:

Foreman: His brother, Jerry, had written me almost from the beginning, asking me to get in the case, and I refused—until I had a letter from James Earl Ray himself. And when he asked me to

come, I did go from Texas to Memphis, and talked with him, and I was employed.

Rather: You're aware that he now says that—James Earl Ray, that is—that he never asked you to get into the case?

Foreman: No, I wasn't aware of that. That's the first I ever heard of it. I have his letter.

Rather: If Mr. Foreman had his letter, he does not have it now. We asked to see it. We were told it had been lost.

When I asked Ray why Foreman had made that initial visit to him in November 1968, he said, "I really don't know. I was surprised to see him. Of course, I knew he was a famous lawyer. He told me that several times. He said he had tried a thousand murder cases, that almost no one ever went to jail and that just one was executed. He said that my case was the easiest one that he had seen."

Ray prepared a statement of his case in affidavit form from his cell in the Memphis Criminal Court on August 31, 1970. In that document, he explained his relationship with Foreman.

On or about November 10th, 1968, Mr. Percy Foreman, a Texas licensed attorney came to Shelby County Jail and asked to see me.

I agreed to see Mr. Foreman although I never contacted him directly or indirectly requesting any type of legal assistance.

After the amenities I saw that Mr. Foreman had the contracts I had signed with Mr. Hanes and Mr. Huie.

I asked his opinion of them. Mr. Foreman came right to the point, he said he had read the contracts and had concluded that the only thing Hanes and Huie were interested in was money. He said they were personal friends and if I stuck with them I would be barbecued.

I told Mr. Foreman I was concerned with certain aspects of the contracts, such as the inference of a trial date deadline, but that since I had signed the document there wasn't much I could do.

Mr. Foreman replied there was something I could do, that he could break the contracts if I hired him. Since I had been taken advantage of due to a lack of education in such matters.

I asked him what his position would be if I did engage him in relation to contracts with book writers and retaining a Tennessee licensed attorney.

He said there would be no stories written until after the trial was over and that it was necessary that Tennessee licensed counsel be retained to advise and assist with Tennessee laws.

I also asked Mr. Foreman how he would finance the trial. He said let him worry about that. That when the trial was over he would make a deal with some book writer but that he wouldn't compromise the defense with pretrial deals.

He said that his fee would be $150,000 for the trial and appeals, if necessary, and that as a retainer he would take the 1966 Mustang I had, which I signed over to him. Mr. Foreman also asked me to sign over to him a rifle the prosecution was holding as evidence. Although there was a question of ownership, I also signed this item over to him. I then wrote out a statement for Mr. Foreman dismissing Mr. Hanes and stating I would engage Tennessee counsel.

During November 1969, when Ray testified against Foreman in a civil suit, he said much the same thing.

Ray: Mr. Foreman came to jail. I will explain the surroundings. When Foreman came to the jail, evidently, my brother, someway, had contacted him when they found out they were going to make an effort to keep me off the stand. So Mr. Foreman come to jail and it was a complete surprise to me. He asked if I would let him in to see me and I said to let him in. When Mr. Foreman came to talk with me he had these contracts in his hand. He had them all, all my previous contracts, so after just some general conversation Mr. Foreman mentioned these contracts and I asked him what he thought of the contracts and he told me that the only thing Mr. Hanes and Mr. Huie was interested in was money. He said he studied those contracts and if I stuck with them I would be barbecued. That's Mr. Foreman's lingo for the electric chair.

Q: What else did Mr. Foreman say about those contracts?

Ray: Well, he didn't . . . we didn't discuss them deeply. We didn't go into any legal reasons, anything legal. The only thing he said, he said Mr. Hanes and Mr. Huie had been friends a long time and that's why they got involved in these contracts. That's what he said.

Q: What did Mr. Foreman propose at that time?

Ray: Well, he told me if he had been on the case to start with or if he was on it now he would never . . . would never become involved with no contracts on books until after the trial was over and he told me if he took the case we could forget about the books until the trial was over.

Q: Did you employ Mr. Foreman as your attorney?

Ray: Yes, I employed him . . . I got him.

Q: When?

Ray: At that time, going in that conversation, after he made those charges and I was just . . . it was just enough substance in what he said to make me believe it and, of course, what give me the impression he had plenty of money to finance the cause without compromising the case to book writers and I thought maybe it was a possibility Mr. Hanes didn't have that much money. I agreed to discharge Mr. Hanes.

Q: Just sort of get down to telling us what you said and what Mr. Foreman said in that conversation about the contracts, the contracts of employment as well as the book contracts. Did you employ Mr. Foreman?

Ray: Yeah. As far as Mr. Foreman, he said I would pay him $150,000 straight fee and he would handle all the appeals until the trial was over, carry it all the way to the United States Surpeme Court. I agreed to that and we made two or three other arrangements. One, that it would be necessary to hire a Tennessee counselor. I even stipulated this in the paper I wrote up relieving Mr. Hanes.

Q: What was the stipulation about hiring Tennessee counsel?

Ray: The paper is on record down there in Shelby County Court about the necessity of hiring Tennessee counselors.

Q: Was any Tennessee counsel hired?

Ray: No, there never was any counsel hired.

While Ray has been consistent regarding his dealings with Foreman, the latter has vacillated. Foreman had originally stated that Ray's brothers, John and Jerry, asked him to enter the case. Later he said that Jerry alone had invited him. On November 11, 1968, he told Martin Waldron of the *New York Times* that Jerry and John had forwarded a request, evidently an oral one, from James. Later he told Dan Rather that he had received a letter from Ray. Ray's denial that he had sent a letter, together with Foreman's inability to produce it, tends to support Ray's version of the events.

The brothers, Jerry and John Ray, said that they met Foreman for the first time on the day that Foreman also met James in his Memphis jail cell. Jerry told me that "the only time my dad ever saw Foreman was when Foreman was in St. Louis, he saw us all together. My mother is dead. My dad and John and me saw Foreman in St. Louis once. But John and me saw Foreman in Memphis. We would go over to Memphis to see James and we'd see Foreman. This is after he was the lawyer for James. I never did see him until the day he became James' lawyer."

I asked Jerry if Foreman talked about the defense for James.

Not much. He used to have us come over to his hotel room and he'd send down for a bottle of Scotch, he liked Scotch, and he'd drink and tell me about all these other cases he won. Then he'd say this would be the easiest case he ever had. He said my brother's case would be. He said they had no real evidence against James. He said, "They have no actual evidence." He said, "I've got guys out before where they had evidence against them but they don't have evidence against James."

On November 11, 1969, Foreman testified in an action brought against him by James Earl Ray. He said of John and Jerry Ray, "I had not met them officially or personally except over the telephone, in telephone conversations prior to the Sunday morning that I came." The morning he referred to, he explained, was the day that he met James Earl Ray in prison. Foreman then testified that he did not talk to Huie until "approximately a week later." Unexplained by that testimony is how Foreman was able to secure the contracts among Hanes, Huie, and Ray before meeting any of them.

Foreman has said that within an hour of reading about Ray's arrest in London he ordered his secretary to begin a file on the case so that he would be prepared in the event that someone asked him to enter the case. Foreman has often boasted that he has represented more than 1,000 persons accused of murder and that he has only lost one man to the executioner. Major newspapers and national magazines have repeated that allegation as fact.

Not as thoroughly publicized was Foreman's indictment by a federal grand jury in Dallas in July 1975, for conspiring to obstruct justice and for obstructing juctice. Indicted with him were Nelson Bunker Hunt and W. Herbert Hunt, both sons of the millionaire H. L. Hunt. In essence the grand jury charged that the Hunts employed two men to conduct alleged wiretapping and that Foreman was given "a secret payment of $100,000" in order "to guarantee the silence of prospective witnesses." The indictment charged that the Hunt brothers paid the $100,000, which constituted Foreman's fee, to prevent his two clients (the men employed by the Hunts) from telling the truth to the grand jury. The charge against Foreman was that, in 1970, he conspired to pay witnesses to go to jail rather than permit them to tell the full truth about the principals involved with them in the criminal conspiracy. Foreman allegedly participated in the crime to secure a large sum of money for himself and in order to protect the other members of the conspiracy. He never informed his clients that he was really serving another master. According to a story written by Martin Waldron in *The New York Times,* Senator Eastland took an interest in the case:

There have been widespread allegations that political pressure was brought in Washington to keep the Hunts from being prosecuted. Senator James O. Eastland of Mississippi, the chairman of the Senate Judiciary Committee, made several inquiries about the case to the Justice Department. Senator Eastland has vigorously denied reports that he was paid $50,000 to do this.

As the case against the defendants began, Foreman stated that he was too ill to participate. After Senator Eastland had expressed a concern, those defendants on trial, including Nelson Bunker Hunt, were permitted to plead no contest to reduced charges and fined. Foreman's case has not yet come to trial, as of this writing, March 18, 1977.

In 1969, James Earl Ray had charged that Foreman, perhaps acting on behalf of an unknown principal, had maneuvered him into a position in which he was forced to remain silent about the principals involved in a criminal conspiracy. Ray went to jail, remained silent, and the principals were not revealed.

The next year, according to a federal grand jury, Foreman entered into a conspiracy on behalf of principals unknown to his clients. Not until Foreman's case is tried, or until civil cases raise and dispose of the outstanding questions, can we pass upon the validity of the indictment against him. The plea entered by his codefendants, however, does not weaken the viability of the grand jury's indictment nor does it threaten the viability of Ray's account of his relationship with Foreman.

After Foreman became Ray's attorney by dazzling him with his almost unblemished record of victories, and by assuring him that no book or magazine contracts would be entered into and all previous ones revoked, according to Ray, Foreman embarked upon a campaign for more book contracts. In his August 31, 1970, affidavit, Ray wrote:

During this early period of Mr. Foreman's tenure he once suggested I confirm, in writing, some theories being propounded

by another novelist, one George McMillan who, in collaboration with a phrenologist, was writing another novel concerning the case.

Mr. Foreman said the pair would give us $5000.00 to use for defense purposes. I rejected this suggestion.

Then later Mr. Foreman transported a check to the jail for $5000.00 for me to endorse. He had received the check from the novelist William Bradford Huie and that would I let him have the money to give to Nashville attorney, John J. Hooker, Sr. as a retainer fee. I agreed to this.

Also during this period I suggested to Mr. Foreman that rather than printing more pre-trial stories we instigate some type legal action to prevent the publishing of stories, especially the more rancid type articles such as was appearing in *Life* magazine.

Mr. Foreman rejected this suggestion saying: "Why stir up a barrel of rattlesnakes." Still, later, on or about Jan. 29th, 1969, Mr. Foreman transported a contract to the jail and advised me to sign it. "See contract Ct. records."

Mr. Foreman saying it would take considerable funds to finance the suit and pay John J. Hooker, Sr.'s fee.

On or about February 3rd, 1969, Mr. Foreman transported still another contract to the jail and advised me to sign it. He told me the law suit was progressing well, that he could prove I was innocent, and the trial would start in the near future.

I also signed this document being reassured because the document stipulated that Mr. Foreman would represent me at "trial or trials" pending in Shelby County, Tennessee: in exchange for me signing the document. "see contract Ct. records."

There was no mention of "cop-outs" in the contract and it seems "cop-outs" are not legally classified as trials in Tennessee.

Foreman testified on November 11, 1969, that he did not "do business" regarding the publication of books until "about the 25th of January 1969," and that he did so then only because "Ray ordered me to do so." The testimony continues:

Foreman: I mentioned selling some pictures to *Life* Magazine and I made the contact with *Life* and *Life* sent a man to see me, the Senior Editor of *Life* that I am acquainted with and I relayed my conversation to Mr. Ray and Mr. Ray said, "Well, we have started with Mr. Huie and with *Look*. I don't see any reason to be contacting or communicating with anyone else. Why don't you get in touch with Mr. Huie?"

Q: And that was the last week in January?

Foreman: It was about the 25th of January, my best judgment. I only say that because it was three or four days before the 29th of January and from the time around the 25th to the 27th of November until the 29th of January, I had no communication, conversation, written or otherwise, with Mr. Huie and didn't intend to have any.

Q: After your discussion with Mr. Ray when did you contact Mr. Huie?

Foreman: I would just have to estimate this but it was sometime between the 25th of January and the 29th of January, I would guess possibly the same day.

Q: And when did you agree upon a contract—there is one written out and dated, but did you agree on a contract at that time that was later put in written form?

Foreman: I never discussed any terms or contracts except the assignment from James Earl Ray to me dated January 29, of which I just presented you a copy and I would not have taken all of the rights of Ray as they had been reconveyed to him save at his request.

Foreman testified that although Huie was writing stories stating that Ray was guilty it was "absolutely not" damaging to the defense since Ray had agreed before January 29, 1969, to plead guilty. Ray has consistently denied that he agreed to plead guilty during January 1969. A contract signed by Foreman and Ray on February 3, 1969, tends to support Ray's contention. That contract obligates Foreman to represent Ray at a trial or at trials presently pending. In exchange for that agreement, Ray gave all of his rights to the Huie book, including possible motion picture rights, to Foreman. It seems unlikely that Foreman could have extracted those rights from Ray in consideration of Foreman's silent appearance at Ray's side while he entered the plea of guilty.

Foreman's sworn statement that he had not talked to Huie about his interest in the book prior to January 25, 1969, was challenged by Huie. In the book, *He Slew the Dreamer*, Huie wrote:

Early on Wednesday morning, November 27, 1968, I met Mr. Foreman at the statue of the Texas Ranger at the Dallas airport. We drove to Fort Worth, where he made a brief courtroom

appearance. Then we had lunch, and altogether, we talked for several hours.

According to Huie, Foreman wanted Hanes out of the contract so that he "could have what Hanes had had." Huie said that Foreman told him, "So you get Hanes out and let me in, then, goddamn it, get to work and write us a good book and make us a good movie and make us some money."

Considerations as to how and why Foreman entered the case are important and interesting, but the attention of a serious inquiry must focus upon what he did after he became the attorney of record. I believe that the record reveals that Foreman was not prepared to go to trial. The implications of that statement are awesome, especially since during the period when he should have but failed to make a thorough examination of the facts, he was assuring Ray and his family that he was going to try the case and win it. Foreman's conduct constrains one to consider the nature of his commitment.

Young defense lawyers are often appalled when they learn that their client has a rather protracted yellow-sheet indicating a substantial criminal record. Experienced trial lawyers understand that such a record may be useful if it portrays a defendant very different from the one likely to have committed the crime in question. Ray had a not insubstantial record of petty thefts and robberies. Yet his *modus operandi* did not indicate that he would kill. A thorough examination of his record by the FBI revealed one fist-fight. He never fired a weapon at a human being. Percy Foreman might have made much of Ray's nonviolent background. Instead of probing that record, Foreman dismissed the subject stating that "all of a man's cells change every five years." Therefore, Foreman reasoned, past character attributes and previous experience and actions are irrelevant since each five years "a new man" with all new cells emerges like a moth from a chrysalis. Foreman's pseudoscientific analysis, offered quite seriously, might have been amusing had the circumstances been different.

This cavalier attitude characterized Foreman's approach to the evidence. When Judge Battle accepted Foreman as Ray's lawyer he made it plain that the case was to be tried in the near future. He ordered Foreman to prepare for trial quickly and indicated that he would be loathe to grant any additional delay.

Foreman knew that in order to be ready he would be required to secure and study the voluminous Hanes files, debrief Hanes, Sr., and Jr., quickly, interview Hays, their investigator, and send his own investigators into the field at once. Foreman evidently took none of those essential and basic steps.

Arthur Hanes, Sr., told me that on the Sunday that Foreman became counsel he spoke with Foreman about the files.

Hanes, Sr., also told me that upon being discharged by Ray he did want to be paid for the services that he had rendered. Subsequently, however, he said that he had offered all of his files and full cooperation to Foreman without charge.

Foreman called us on a Monday morning and said he was coming to Birmingham that afternoon. That was about three or four weeks after we were relieved of the case, about the end of November 1968. We said "fine." He told us his flight number and Art, Jr., met him at the airport and brought him to the office. We showed him what we had, advised him he was welcome to everything he could see. We said, "You can have it all; you're the trial lawyer now." We tried to outline the case for him, to tell him what we knew. He didn't seem to be too interested. We offered him everything we had. He took nothing with him.

Arthur, Jr., interjected at that point, "He wasn't interested in the case. He wanted to drink some Scotch, eat some dinner, and talk about his famous cases. He also told us about how he made speeches all over the country."

I asked both lawyers how much time Foreman spent looking at the thousands of pages of documents, reports, photograph interviews, and trial briefs that comprised the Ray file in the Hanes office. Arthur, Sr., said "about ten minutes." He added, "then we took him to dinner. We called and made reservations for him because he said he wanted to go to Miami. We took him to the airport and put him on a plane to Miami. We offered him our files. He could have taken the originals. The whole thing. He was welcome to. If he had wanted photocopies we would have made them. He didn't want anything."

I asked Hanes, Sr., what he thought of Foreman's actions. He said, "My judgment is that the man never even considered trying the case. Far as I can ascertain he never prepared and he never investigated. He never considered giving James Earl Ray a trial. For what reason, I don't know."

Renfro Hays said that he was never asked by Foreman to share the results of his investigation. Foreman, nevertheless, said that the Hays investigation was worthless.

Foreman's description of his investigation was made under oath. He testified, "I investigated the case and had the case investigated. As a matter of fact I spent, I don't know how much money." He said that he questioned James Earl Ray about the crime "anywhere from thirty to seventy-five hours." The difference between thirty and seventy-five is considerable. If Foreman had questioned Ray two hours a day from the time he was retained until he pleaded Ray guilty he would not have had sufficient time to have amassed seventy-five hours of interrogation. Foreman was ill for a good portion of that time and in Memphis, where Ray was imprisoned, only rarely.

Ray told me that Foreman never asked him if he had fired the shot on April 4th, or if he had been in a conspiracy with others to kill Dr. King. Foreman confirmed Ray's assertion. Manuel Chait, a staff correspondent for the St. Louis *Post-Dispatch,* reported on March 11, 1969, following the guilty plea, that "after the sentencing Foreman, answering questions from reporters, said he never had asked Ray specifically whether he had been involved in a conspiracy." And Jerry Lipson, a staff writer for the Chicago *Daily News,* reported on that same day that "throughout his tenure as Ray's lawyer, the bear-sized Texan said, he never discussed the slaying directly. 'I never asked Ray that question,' he said, when asked if Ray had told him he had pulled the trigger." It is apparent to me that the most significant aspects of the case are: Was there a conspiracy to murder Dr. King? And did Ray pull the trigger? Yet the only two men who participated in the conferences, Foreman and Ray, both state that Foreman never inquired about either.

Ray told me that he recalled vividly one occasion when Foreman did touch upon the case in a conversation with him.

> **Foreman came to see me and he brought a batch of pictures with him. He had about ten or fifteen pictures. Most of them were pictures of Cubans or that's what they looked like to me. They were all white except one. Foreman said to me, "These are people that the FBI wants to get out of circulation." He said that the FBI said they were pro-communist or anti-communist and that the FBI wanted me to identify one or more of them. I told Foreman that I did not want to get involved in making a false ID. He said the FBI wanted an ID of one or more of them, that they wanted to get them out of circulation. I said I would not identify any of them. He looked at me and said that if I picked one out and said he shot Martin Luther King the FBI would arrest him and transport him to Memphis. I said, "No, I don't want to get involved in that type thing for various reasons." When it was clear that I was not going to make a false identification Foreman**

said to me, "Is that your last word on the subject?" and I answered, "Yes." Then he left.

I asked Ray if any of the men looked familiar to him. He thought for a moment and I remembered again his style. He had said he would give me leads to follow and refute false charges that had been made against him but that he was not an informer and would not finger anyone. Then he said, "I recognized one picture. It was a man who may have been a Klan member. I never met him but I think I did see his picture in a newspaper. There was another picture that was familiar. It is hard to recognize a person and make a certain identification from a snapshot. But Foreman showed me a picture from the FBI of three men in Dallas. Just after Kennedy was killed. The three looked like they were under arrest. One of them looked like, and might have been, Raoul."

I have seen the photograph Ray referred to. In the photograph three men in Dealy Plaza, Dallas, appear to be under arrest, shortly after the assassination of President Kennedy. No available Dallas police department record makes reference to such an arrest and the names of the three men, apparently in police custody, have not been revealed by the local or federal police authorities. One of the men in that photograph, the smallest and the slightest of the three, bears a striking resemblance to the artist's sketch of the presumed murderer of Dr. King. The sketch was utilized by the local and federal police in a search for the murderer. It was created by an artist employed by a Memphis newspaper in conjunction with witnesses who said they saw the man flee through the rooming house corridor and from the rooming house just after the shot was fired.

As we talked in the small library of the Brushy Mountain Penitentiary Ray recalled another occasion when Foreman had discussed a peripheral aspect of the case with him. The atmosphere was relaxed for the warden, Stonney Ray Lane (not related to either Ray or me), had been most hospitable in arranging for a comfortable room where Ray and I could talk without interruption or surveillance. Warden Lane had met me at the gate and had driven me to the maximum security section of the prison where Ray was confined. Will Rogers once said that he never met a man he didn't like. I never understood how that could be. In any event I never saw a prison that I did like. But Warden Lane proved a kind and considerate host and Ray and I talked on in relative calm and isolation.

Ray said, "One time Foreman came into the cell with a long list of places that had been robbed: banks, supermarkets, insurance companies. It was quite a long list with maybe fifty or sixty places on it. He said the list came from the FBI. I don't know if the FBI gave it to him or Huie got it from the FBI to give to him. He told me once, 'Huie's got real good connections with the FBI. Even better than mine. Huie can get things from the FBI in three or four hours that would take me three or four days to get.' "

Ray said that Foreman asked him to look over the list. "He wanted me to check off the places that I had robbed from the FBI list of unsolved crimes. Foreman said 'the FBI wants to be able to explain your source of money.' It was the craziest thing I ever seen. I told him 'I got the money from Raoul. He paid me for various jobs that I did.' Foreman said that the FBI wanted me to check off some of the places from the list. I just looked at him and said 'If I cop out to robbing a place I didn't rob someone is going to put me under oath and I won't be able to supply the details when they ask about them.' He said 'Yeah, that's right' and he finally put that long list away."

Ray recalled other subjects that the two men discussed as well.

Then at a later date when attorney Foreman visited me he had several duplicated typewritten sheets of paper with him; one clause in the sheets cleared the novelist William Bradford Huie and *Look* magazine of damaging my prospects for a fair trial because of their pretrial publishing ventures; another clause, that if I stood trial I would receive the electric chair.

I told Mr. Foreman that Mr. Huie and *Look* magazine were able, legally and financially, to look out for their own interest.'

Mr. Foreman's monologue was very strident that day in insisting that I sign the papers as I had to ask him several times to lower his voice to keep the guards, and open mike, from overhearing our conversation.

On November 11, 1969, when Foreman testified in a civil action brought against him in the United States District Court in Tennessee he was asked, "Who did your investigating work for you?" He answered, "Oh, different people. I had a number of students from the university at Memphis and I had—." Since he never finished answering, the attorney inquired, "Could you give us some names please?" Foreman, however, had no names to offer. He said, "I don't know the names. My god-amighty, man, they were students. There were at least seven or eight of them." Foreman was then asked if he had "any investigators that were not students." He testified, "I don't use investigators except students. Wherever there is a college my investigators are always students and preferably senior students. I would not believe a private investigator, under oath, anywhere in America." Later Foreman was asked if he could remember the name of at least one of his investigators in the James Earl

Ray murder case. He replied, "I never knew the names of the student investigators." Foreman was asked how he could have known that his investigators were reliable since he knew nothing about them, not even their names. How did he know, he was asked, that they might not give any information they uncovered to the prosecution. Foreman said, "Yes, sir, that's why I hired them, because a man has to have character to stay four years in law school or medical school." He continued, "They have spent four years in college and it takes character to make that."

Before a few minutes had passed Foreman said that "there were about six or eight" from the school. He secured them through the services of a teacher, he thought, but he added, "I don't remember the names of a single teacher there. I am in a trial all the time. I don't try to remember anything like that." It soon became apparent that Foreman could not even remember the name of the school from which the "at least seven or eight" or "about six or eight" students whose names he did not know had been referred by a teacher or teachers he could not remember.

Foreman's cavalier attitude toward the investigation of a capital case is startling. A trained and skillful investigator can make the difference between a conviction and an acquittal. Neither senior students nor trained investigators can function on their own. The investigators must, of course, conduct their inquiries into the areas considered to be relevant and potentially rewarding by the trial counsel. Their work becomes valuable only at the point of production—in the court room. Had Foreman worked closely with the investigators, he would have been able to evaluate their work, know what discoveries they made, and certainly he would have remembered some of their names. It is not necessary to speculate about the anonymous investigators who apparently developed not a single lead. Foreman later said that he did all of his own investigating and never relied upon others. Hugh Stanton of the public defender's office in Memphis served as cocounsel with Foreman. During November 1976 investigators for the Citizens Commission of Inquiry asked if his colleague, Percy Foreman, used any investigators in the Ray case. He answered, "No, he did not to my knowledge." When Stanton was asked what Foreman did do for the investigation, he was unable to think of a single contribution. Eventually he answered, "Why don't you ask him that. I'm not going to sit here, honey, and tell you what somebody else did."

Several months after Foreman's investigation had been completed and his client imprisoned at a Tennessee penitentiary to serve a ninety-nine year sentence, Foreman, while testifying, was asked if he had ever talked to Charles Q. Stephens and his wife, Grace. Charles Stephens was the only eyewitness against Ray, and his wife might have been the most important witness for Ray. Foreman did not know who they were; he asked if they were the owners of the rooming house. Foreman eventually admitted that he had not talked to either Mr. or Mrs. Stephens.

One of the lawyers who represented Ray after Foreman was discharged told me that Renfro Hays had been very anxious to assist Ray even while Foreman represented him. He said that Hays sent McCraw, the taxi driver, to see Foreman so that the new trial counsel might be informed that Stephens was drunk shortly before Dr. King was shot. During his testimony, Foreman acknowledged that he spoke with Mc-Craw, whose name he could not remember. He said, "I talked to the cab driver that hauled him [Stephens] away from there." Actually McCraw told Foreman that he did not "haul him [Stephens] away" because Stephens was too drunk. Foreman had finally remembered a witness, although not by name, but he had forgotten the point of the witness' assertion. According to Foreman's successor, McCraw said that after he told Foreman that the state's only witness was too drunk at the crucial moment to be reliable Foreman said only, "Don't tell this to Stanton." Foreman had finally come across an important allegation for the defense and he was apparently determined not to share that evidence with his co-counsel.

The evidence reveals a sad and shameful story. Foreman, for reasons not now known, had not adequately prepared to try the murder case although he constantly assured his ill-educated client and his brothers that he was more than ready for the easiest of all conflicts.

According to Ray, Foreman began a campaign to convince him to plead guilty soon after Ray had entered into a binding contract with him. Ray said he recalled the arguments Foreman advanced quite clearly.

Mr. Foreman gave me the following reasons why a guilty plea was necessary:

(One) He said the media had already convicted me and cited the pretrial articles written in *Life* magazine and the *Reader's Digest*, with the help of government investigative agencies as examples.

He also cited various articles printed in the local press, particularly the story in the *Commercial Appeal* dated November 10th, 1968, just two days before trial date.

Further, Foreman cited the record of the Amicus Curiae Committee saying neither the committee or trial judge would attempt to halt publicity unless it reflected on the prosecution case.

(Two) Foreman suggested, speciously, that it would be in my financial interest to plead guilty.

(Three) That the prosecution had promised a witness considerable reward money for testifying against me, that this witness had already been given a raise in a welfare check he was receiving from the government, that the prosecution was also paying his food and wine bills.

Further, that two Memphis attorneys had signed a contract with his alleged witness for 50 percent of all revenue he received for his testimony. They in turn would look out for his interest.

Mr. Foreman also gave me the following reasons why the prosecution wanted, and would therefore let me plead guilty:

(One) That the Chamber of Commerce was pressuring the trial judge and the Attorney General's office to get a guilty plea as a long trial would have an adverse effect on business, boycotts and such.

Further, that the chamber wasn't unhappy about Dr. King being removed from the scene—hence the acceptance of a guilty plea.

(Two) That trial judge Battle was concerned about the effects a trial would have on the city's [Memphis] image, and that the judge had even dispatched his Amicus Curiae Committee Chairman, Mr. Lucian Burch, to persuade some SCLC members to accept a guilty plea.

Ray told me that he had listened very carefully to Foreman's arguments and that he replied that he had wanted to stand trial. "I also remembered that he told me that it was an easy case to win. I thought we would win but even if we might lose I wanted to stand trial. Hanes knew that and they were ready. Now I know that I had made a terrible mistake firing them." Ray said:

Later, after considering all that Mr. Foreman had told me I said I still wanted to stand trial.

I told Foreman I agreed that the media had had an adverse effect on the prospects of my receiving a fair trial but I didn't think the public any longer believed every fabrication they read or saw on TV— therefore a possible fair jury verdict.

Mr. Foreman's reply was that if I plead guilty he could get me a pardon, after two or three years, through the office or Nashville attorney, John J. Hooker, Sr., as a relative of Mr. Hooker would then be Governor.

John J. Hooker, Sr., was a well-respected member of the Tennessee bar. His son was at the time a candidate for the office of Governor of

Tennessee. The political prognosticators predicted that Hooker could not lose. Foreman's association with Hooker, who later represented both Huie and Foreman when Ray brought a civil action against them, was related to Ray as the clincher in Ray's subsequent pardon application if he would but cooperate and plead guilty. Hooker, Jr., never did become governor; he was defeated. Yet his candidacy played an important part in ultimately convincing Ray to plead guilty.

On February 13, 1969, Foreman wrote a letter to Ray. In that letter Foreman said that there was a "little more than a 99 per cent chance" of a death penalty and a "100 percent chance of a guilty verdict." Ray began to wonder what had happened to "the easiest case" Foreman had ever encountered. Ray said that when he told Foreman he expected to be acquitted, Foreman replied that the prosecution could rig the jury. According to Ray, Foreman said, "the court clerk had been on the job for eighteen or twenty years." Ray said, "I was considering trying to relieve Mr. Foreman and get another attorney who would let me have a jury trial, but Judge Battle said that I was going to trial with Mr. Foreman and that was it. In other words, I was caught between Judge Battle and Mr. Foreman."

Even under those circumstances Ray decided to risk a jury trial. Ray said that he continued to give leads to Foreman and that Foreman refused to explore them.

One time I told him that the police had made a statement that I was not within four miles of Dr. King when he was shot. So I told Mr. Foreman about that. Later he told me he called Mr. Holloman, the director of the police department but that Mr. Holloman would not let him have the statement. I said, "Why don't we get a discovery proceeding so we can force him to give us the statement," and Mr. Foreman said, "If we do that he might destroy the statement." I knew it wasn't logical but what could I do.

Ray said he felt trapped, caught between the judge who would not permit him to get another lawyer and his own attorney who insisted that he plead guilty. During this most difficult time, Ray was unable to sleep due to the constant bright illumination of his cell and unable to speak frankly to his attorney except in whispers due to the microphones in the cell which the trial judge had solemnly asserted were placed there for his own security.

Ray said that Foreman explained to him that if the state could prove that he had been involved in any criminal conduct, and that Dr. King died as a result of that conduct, that Ray could be convicted and executed as if he had fired the fatal shot. According to Ray, Foreman said that even if Ray had not known that there was a conspiracy to kill Dr. King he could be convicted because he had been part of it. "He told me that if they could prove I was just an accomplice I would be just as guilty as the other party."

Foreman was apparently discussing the legal concept of felony murder. If several men agree to participate in the robbery of a store, and all agree that none of them is to be armed and that none will harm any other person, and in the midst of the robbery one of the robbers pulls out a gun and kills anyone, either the proprietor, a bystander, or a fellow robber, all of the survivors may be tried for first-degree murder under the concept of felony murder. The theory is based upon the agreement to commit a felony and the death of anyone during the commission of the felony. Foreman extended the concept, Ray said, to cover his case. Ray had purchased a rifle illegally, and transported it across state lines in order to participate in the illegal sale of arms abroad. If anyone died as a result of that effort, Ray was led to believe, he was legally guilty of the murder.

At last Ray began to believe that he might be legally guilty even if he had not known of the conspiracy to kill Dr. King and even if he had not fired the fatal shot, as long as there actually was a conspiracy. Ray knew that he had participated in a criminal conspiracy to smuggle guns out of the country. He believed that one of those guns may have killed Dr. King.

Finally, Ray said, Foreman said, "If you force me to go to trial I will get that Negro judge Ben Hooks as co-counsel."

In an affidavit he filed with the Memphis Criminal Court, Ray said:

> **I knew from newspaper accounts that Mr. Hooks had resigned a judgeship to accept a position with SCLC.**
>
> **Therefore I told Foreman that having Mr. Hooks as a co-counsel would be a clear conflict of interest, more so than the grounds attorney F. Lee Bailey refused the case on. Foreman's reply was that as chief counsel he had the right to pick co-counsel.**
>
> **By this time Mr. Foreman had finally got the message over to me that if I forced him to trial he would destroy—deliberately —the case in the courtroom.**
>
> **I didn't know how he would fake the trial until I read the article he wrote for *Look* magazine, published April 1969.**
>
> **It was also my belief that I would only receive one trial—that appellant cts. probably wouldn't be looking too close for technical error in case of conviction—therefore I didn't want the one trial faked.**

On March 9, 1969, Foreman sent a letter to Ray which had the effect of assuring him that he would be given a potentially large sum of money if he did not alter his agreement to plead guilty to murder the following day and "if the plea is entered and the sentence [of 99 years] accepted and no embarrassing circumstances take place in the court room."

On March 10, 1969, James Earl Ray, accompanied by his lawyer, Percy Foreman, appeared before Judge Battle and pleaded guilty. Battle asked Ray if he was pleading guilty to murder in the first degree because he was "legally guilty of murder in the first degree as explained to you by your lawyers." Ray answered, "Yes, *legally* guilty, uh-huh." Foreman then addressed the court and jury.

> **Gentlemen of the Jury, I am Percy Foreman, permitted by his honor to appear, and it is an honor to appear, in this court for this case.**
>
> **"I never expected, hoped or had any idea when I entered this case that I would be able to accomplish anything except perhaps save this man's life.**
>
> **"All of us, all of you were as well-informed as I was about the facts of this case due to the fact that we have such an effective news media, both electronic and press and magazines. Took me a month to convince myself of that fact which the Attorney General of the United States and J. Edgar Hoover of the Federal Bureau of Investigation announced last July; that is, just what [Attorney] General Canale told you, that there was not a conspiracy.**

At the first opportunity to speak Ray said:

Ray: Your honor, I would like to say something too, if I may.

The Court: All right.

Ray: I don't want to change anything that I have said. I don't want to add anything onto it, either. The only thing I have to say is, I don't exactly accept the theories of Mr. Clark. In other words, I am not bound to accept the theories of Mr. Clark.

Foreman: Who is Mr. Clark?

Ray: Ramsey Clark.

Foreman: Oh.

Ray: And Mr. Hoover.

Foreman: Mr. who?

Ray: Mr. J. Edgar Hoover. The only thing, I say I am not—I

agree to all these stipulations. I am not trying to change anything. I just want to add something onto it.

The Court: You don't agree with those theories?

Ray: I meant Mr. Canale, Mr. Foreman, Mr. Ramsey Clark. I mean on the conspiracy thing. I don't want to add something onto it which I haven't agreed to in the past.

Foreman: I think that what he is saying is that he doesn't think Ramsey Clark's right or J. Edgar Hoover is right.

I didn't argue them as evidence in this case. I simply stated that underwriting and backing up the opinions of [Attorney] General Canale, that they had made the same statement. You are not required to agree or withdraw or anything else.

The Court: You still—your answers to those questions that I asked you would be the same?

Ray: Yes, sir. The only thing is I didn't want to add anything onto them. That was all.

The Court: There is nothing in these answers to those questions I asked you, in other words, you change none of those?

Ray: No, sir. No sir.

The Court: In other words, you are pleading guilty and taking 99 years, and I think the main question here that I want to ask you is this:

Are you pleading guilty to murder in the first degree in this case because you killed Dr. Martin Luther King under such circumstances that would make you legally guilty of murder in the first degree under the law as explained to you by your lawyers?

Ray: Yes, sir, make me guilty on that.

The Court: Your answers are still yes?

Ray: Yes, sir.

The Court: All right, sir, that is all.

Ray had remained loyal to the only concept which he said might legally establish his guilt. There was a conspiracy, and because there was, he was *legally* guilty. The incurious attitude of the judge while the defendant stated in open court that others were involved in the murder remains inexplicable nine years later. After the plea was entered, Judge Battle sentenced Ray to 99 years in a state penitentiary. The judge then addressed the jury and the press. He said:

The question might arise in many minds, "Why accept any plea at all? Why not try him, try to give him the electric chair?"

Well, I have been a judge since 1959, and I myself have sentenced at least seven men to the electric chair, maybe a few more. My fellow judges in this County have sentenced several others to execution. There has been no execution of any prisoners from Shelby County in this state since I took the Bench in 1959. All the trends in this country are in the direction of doing away with capital punishment altogether.

Well, that certainly explained why the state was eager for the plea, but left in doubt those who wondered why Ray's attorneys had arranged a deal which secured the maximum sentence for Ray.

The Judge, who had refused to inquire about the conspiracy to kill Dr. King when Ray invited him to do so, then discussed the absence of conspiracy.

It has been established by the prosecution that at this time they are not in possession of any evidence to indict anyone as a coconspirator in this case. Of course, this is not conclusive evidence that there was no conspiracy. It merely means as of this time there is not sufficient evidence available to make out a case of probable cause against anybody. However, if this defendant was a member of a conspiracy to kill the decedent, no member of such conspiracy can ever live in peace or lie down to pleasant dreams, because in this state there is no statute of limitations in capital cases such as this. And while it is not always the case, my 35 years in these criminal courts have convinced me that in the great majority of cases, Hamlet was right when he said, "Murder, though it hath no tongue, will speak with most miraculous organ."

Judge Battle had kind words to offer about Percy Foreman for he had played a decisive role in arranging for the guilty plea.

The defendant is represented by able and eminent counsel. All his rights and all the safeguards surrounding him have been zealously and conscientiously observed and adhered to.

The Judge felt called upon to praise the system of justice that had brought about such an irrefutably fair result.

I cannot let this occasion pass without paying tribute to Tennessee, Southern, American and Western Free World Justice and security which was truly a team effort involving scores and even hundreds of persons.

Having defended Foreman, Tennessee, the South, and the Western Free World, Judge Battle closed with a modest eulogy for Memphis.

> **This court, nor no one else, knows what the future will bring, but I submit that up to now we have not done too badly here for a "decadent river town."**
>
> **If I may be permitted to add a light touch to a solemn occasion, I would like to paraphrase the great and eloquent Winston Churchill, who, in defiant reply to an Axis threat that they were going to wring England's neck like a chicken, said, "Some chicken, some neck."**
>
> **I would like to reply to our Memphis critic, "Some river, some town."**
>
> **Is there anything else?**

What else could there be?

Ray was transferred to a state penitentiary to begin serving his long sentence. As soon as he was removed from the oppressive and blinding atmosphere of the Memphis jail he wrote a letter to Judge Battle.

> **Dear Sir,**
>
> **I wish to inform the honorable court that the famous Houston Attorney Percy Fourflusher is no longer representing me in any capacity. My reason for writing this letter is that I intend to file for a post-conviction hearing in the very near future and don't want him making any legal moves unless they're in Mr. Canale's behalf.**
>
> **Sincerely,**
> **James Earl Ray**

He later submitted a sworn statement to the Memphis Criminal Court explaining what happened to him after he wrote the letter.

> **After I wrote the March 13th letter to Judge Battle indicating I would ask for a trial, corrections Commissioner Harry Avery strongly advised me not to seek a trial.**
>
> **He said if I didn't I would be treated like any other prisoner and would be released from isolation at the end of the prescribed six weeks. But if I persisted in asking for a trial he couldn't promise anything—he said he was speaking for the highest authority.**

Just one week after Judge Battle had sentenced Ray, he granted an interview to Bernard Gavzer of the *Washington Post*. In that interview, Battle said that he accepted the plea because "had there been a trial, there could have been the possibility, in such an emotionally charged case, of a hung jury." He added that Ray "could have perhaps been acquitted by a jury." So much for justice in this part of the Western Free World.

On April 15, 1969, *Look* magazine, in an article by Percy Foreman, credentialed as "attorney for James Earl Ray," purported to prove that Ray acted alone in the murder of Dr. King. Foreman offered his theories, claiming that he had spoken with Ray for "40 hours" and concluding that Ray "didn't tell me any of this: it is what I believe he thinks." On October 10, 1976, Foreman was interviewed by Roger Aldi, an intelligent and informed newsman. For the first time Foreman was pressed to provide some details. A transcription of that part of the program follows.

> **Aldi: Mr. Foreman, from a defense perspective, from what I could gather, there is no way to trace the bullet that killed Dr. King to the rifle that James Earl Ray admittedly did purchase in Birmingham.**
>
> **Foreman: It is true that the, uh, . . . there were no ballistics, that was an FBI report on that bullet. But that is not the only way to get convicted of murder.**
>
> **Aldi: The state's only real witness to place James Earl Ray at the scene at the time of the murder apparently was dead drunk at the time.**
>
> **Foreman: Well, you've been reading a bunch of things that have been collected by somebody with a Jewish name—I forget his name, uh, and all of this—what you're probably doing is rewriting the book.**

When the program was broadcast, Aldi interjected the following comment at this point:

> **I don't know what book Mr. Foreman was referring to but his answers to other questions about evidence that might have proved James Earl Ray innocent were dismissed in a similar manner. And the situation did not get better when I asked him about what he reportedly told James Earl Ray before the decision to plead guilty.**

Their dialogue continued:

> **Aldi: Did you ever tell James Earl Ray that the state would get some kind of blue ribbon jury, and it was a sure conviction?**
>
> **Foreman: Now listen, Mr. Aldi—I'm tired of listening to this horse shit. I told your James Earl Ray exactly what it was my**

duty to tell him. And I pointed it out to him—sometime while I was on this case in Memphis there were at least five or six major cases tried with serious verdicts. And each one of them—I didn't tell him anything. I discussed with him whatever was in the papers about the other cases.

On January 14, 1970, James Earl Ray, in his lonely cell in a Tennessee penitentiary learned that Arthur Hanes, Sr., his first trial attorney in the case, had been quite ill. He wrote to him:

Dear Arthur,

I have read in the paper where you have been a little under the weather.

I trust those young nurses will have you back in condition before you receive this letter.

Sincerely,

James Earl Ray

P.S. At least you don't have Percy Foreman for a doctor.

PART
SEVEN

KALEIDOSCOPE

Chapter Twenty-Six

"THEY/HE SLEW THE DREAMER"

by Mark Lane

During the eight years that followed Ray's initial effort to secure a trial, after entering a plea of guilty before Judge Battle, a few books have been written purporting to tell the truth about the events of April 4, 1968. Perhaps the two most important books on the subject are *He Slew the Dreamer*, by William Bradford Huie, and *The Making of an Assassin*, by George McMillan. One can, on occasion, tell a book by its cover. The titles of both books about James Earl Ray make it quite clear that the authors were convinced of his guilt. Huie said that after Ray was arrested, "I decided to try to persuade him to sell me information." He wrote to Ray that "if you want to deal with me, I will have a contract drawn for us to sign, and I will pay you a substantial sum of money." He told Ray in that introductory letter that "Americans yearn to know the whole truth about why and how" the murder of Dr. King was accomplished. In many letters to Huie, Ray described in exquisite detail his view of the conspiracy to murder Dr. King. Yet, although Huie's book was published in 1970, on December 25, 1976, *The New York Times*, in a front-page story headlined "Conspirator Hunted in Dr. King Slaying," published an article which said "In March 1969, when Mr. Ray pleaded guilty to killing Dr. King, he told the court that he did not agree with statements by the prosecution and by his own defense attorney that there was no conspiracy involved. However, Mr. Ray has never explained what he meant." Evidently, a problem had arisen somewhere between Ray's telling of the tale to Huie and its publication by Huie.

There is no doubt that Ray understood that his prospective biographer, Huie, had prejudged the case against him even before he had begun his inquiry. In the first letter sent by Huie to Ray, through his attorney Arthur Hanes, Sr., he wrote, "Obviously you were involved in

Dr. King's murder." Later, when Percy Foreman tried to insinuate George McMillan into the scene by arranging yet another publishing deal, this one between McMillan and Ray, the defendant, this time exercising sound discretion, declined. Foreman had brought McMillan to the jail cell, but Ray refused to see him.

Why did Ray enter into a business arrangement with Huie when he suspected, not without reason, from the outset that Huie's prejudice might overcome the facts? Ray explained in testimony offered by him in the Federal District Court in an action that he subsequently brought against Huie and others.

> **Well, the only reason I signed this contract there, well, I was under obligation to Mr. Hanes. He made three trips to London and I didn't have no money to pay him. I think I had $150, something like that, so I, originally, suggested that Mr. Hanes try to raise the defense money or something, but he thought the book would be best and so I more or less had to go along with the recommendations of the attorneys and I signed the contract in order to raise money for the defense. Mr. Hanes didn't want to get involved in—in the pauper's—in other words, more or less Court appointed people to work on the defense. That's one reason I signed the contract.**

Later Ray testified about the new book contract that involved both Huie and Foreman.

> **This here was a little different, the way I got involved with Mr. Foreman and the way I got involved with Mr. Hanes. After Mr. Hanes had been dismissed at the recommendation of Mr. Foreman, I—I—Mr. Foreman told me there couldn't be any contracts until after the trial was over. He also made the statement in open Court, I think, that he wasn't going to—Mr. Foreman made the statement he wasn't going to pan his profession to the press, or something of that nature, so I was under—I was under the impression there wouldn't be no contract when Mr. Foreman took the case until after the trial was over.**

> **Q. After you were under that impression there would be no contracts with Mr. Foreman—are you talking about book contract or some other kind of contract?**

> **A. No, book contract with Mr. Huie, he—we discussed this when he took over the case. That was one of the stipulations, that contract bookwriting wouldn't interfere with the trial. Mr. Foreman said he had enough—in other words, enough money**

that he wouldn't get obligated with book rights to finance the case, in other words, Mr. Foreman financed the case on his own until the trial was over and then he could get his money.

Q. Then subsequent to that, about how long was it until you did sign the contracts with Mr. Foreman and Mr. Huie, or did you?

A. Yes, I did, but this—Mr. Foreman, he—these contracts came up in a more or less—another money matter—do you want—I would have to explain that to start with.

Q. Go ahead and explain it.

A. Like I said, Mr. Foreman made the public statement that he could finance the case himself until the trial was over and he would have me sign a contract for the book to pay him off and his fee was supposed to be $150,000 and he would take care of all expenses and finance the jury trial and everything but after he had been on the case, I am not positive now, I will say two or three weeks, and he came to see me and he told me he was going to hire one of the best attorneys in Tennessee. He talked to several of them and he mentioned Mr. Hooker here, Senior, personally, and so he told me it was going to take quite a bit of money, so I thought maybe he was hinting around wanting more money for the contract. Of course, I know attorneys like money. I said, I told him to just take all that contract when this trial was over and go ahead and hire Mr. Hooker or whoever you want to as long as we can get the right kind of trial.

So, sure enough, a few days later he came up with a contract with Mr. Huie, and Mr. Foreman said he was—the contract would give, I think, Mr. Foreman sixty percent and Mr. Huie forty percent, so I signed it under those—believing that we were going to have all these high powered attorneys and everything. What we got was the Public Defender.

The contract among Huie, Ray, and Hanes stated that it was "for the purpose of establishing the truth" regarding "the assassination of Martin Luther King, Jr.," and "the alleged participation of Ray therein." It was entered into during July 1968. Three months later Huie told the press that "Ray delivered to me a first installment of 10,000 words written in longhand, a month ago. Since then he has delivered 10,000 words more." Quite clearly Ray cannot be held accountable for the failure of communication upon which *The New York Times* commented.

When Huie testified on his own behalf in the federal action filed against him by Ray he made a most intriguing disclosure. He testified that he originally planned to call the book "They Killed the Dreamer" and that later the title was changed to "He Killed the Dreamer." Huie was incorrect. He had originally entitled the book "They Slew the Dreamer" and then changed the title to "He Slew the Dreamer." Quite obviously there had been a change in concept from a book seeking to prove a conspiracy to one asserting that Ray acted alone.

When he testified as a defendant in November 1969, Huie sought to explain how and why the change had occurred. He was asked who had made the decision to change the title.

> **I did. You see, all publishing plans and interests in the King case, many people sitting in New York assumed from the beginning that Ray didn't make the decision to kill Dr. King, meaning conspiracy. Gallup Poll showed eighty-four percent of the people in the United States wanted to believe in conspiracy as regards murders of Jack Kennedy or Bobby Kennedy or Dr. King. All publishers and editors want is books about conspiracy. They want you to prove conspiracy and show conspiracy.**

Actually the Gallup Poll did not measure what the American people "wanted to believe" regarding a conspiracy; it was intended to reflect what the people did believe.

Huie then volunteered a bit of testimony which was quite surprising, perhaps astonishing, to me.

> **As an aside, if I may, I was offered $250,000, not returnable, by a group of publishers soon after the murder of Jack Kennedy to write the first of the books questioning the Warren Commission Report, what was to be the Warren Commission Report, the authoritative statement. I went to Texas with private detectives who worked with me before and we worked for two weeks and came back and talked to the Attorney General, Bobby Kennedy, and I convinced myself that Jack Kennedy was killed by Lee Harvey Oswald and that Oswald never met Jack Ruby, his own assassin, before in his life. Therefore, I couldn't write a book that would have been economically profitable, and, therefore, had to decline the money because I simply believed Oswald acted alone and Bobby Kennedy, the Attorney General, whose office had all the facts that had been released, believed it and therefore, I don't know why I should disbelieve it.**
> **I went along on this business of a Ray conspiracy reluctantly,**

so all of the projections as to what the Ray story might be worth was based on the assumption that they did kill the dreamer. That there was a "they" in the story, and early in the story, I, myself, reluctantly, went along on a conspiracy.

On occasion one comes across a joint venture in the publishing industry where a hardcover firm and a paperback company do a contract together for a book. However, in the highly competitive book publishing industry groups of publishers do not usually join together to publish a work. I remember the period prior to the publication of the Warren Report quite well. During that period almost every major publisher in the United States declined to publish my book based on the subject and it was not until after a conservative English firm in London agreed to publish *Rush to Judgment* that an American publisher did publish the book. It is safe to say that major publishers in the USA were not anxious to publish books questioning the Warren Commission Report during 1964. The advance offered to me by an American publisher was $5,000 for world rights to my book, not $250,000. It is true that after 1966 when *Rush to Judgment* was published and became the number one best-selling book in America that year, and the next year in paperback form, other manuscripts on the subject were more easily able to find publication. Yet, Huie's testimony was in relationship to a much earlier time, a period prior to the publication of the Warren Report itself. More troubling is the assertion that his two-week inquiry into the assassination of President Kennedy disposed of all of the troubling questions. Thirteen years later most Americans, including a majority of the members of the Congress, are still not satisfied.

Huie continued with his testimony.

I went along with the theory. There were several bits of evidence. The first thing I found that seemed to indicate to me that someone other than Ray made the decision to kill Dr. King—I never had any doubt from the beginning that Ray was the murderer himself, but the question was in my mind whether Ray himself made the decision to kill. So I believed, for several weeks in August and September, oh, until early in November, until Ray took the step to postpone the trial. For instance, I believed that someone other than Ray had made the decision. That was a mistake. I made a horrible mistake because I went along with the conspiracy theory for a while. I could not find any evidence that other people were involved and Ray, who had failed to provide me or anyone any

believable evidence that anyone else was involved, so I had to change my plans and inform everybody, magazine publishers, book publishers and everybody, which I did, I think, possibly, around December 1st, that I couldn't travel on a conspiracy; that I could not identify any person; I couldn't sustain a proposition that someone other than James Earl Ray made the decision to kill Dr. Martin Luther King. I had to back off and I would never have written anything else about Ray except that I had already committed myself and already made a mistake and I had to try to correct it and it is something that is a very grave disappointment to me.

Huie's statement that ''I never had any doubt from the beginning that Ray was the murderer'' places in rigid context his approach to the evidence in the case. In this respect he shared with George McMillan (whose work we will explore fully in the next chapter) a prejudice that precluded the consideration of the delicate shading of testimony. Huie and McMillan operated from a commitment to preconceptions. The prosecuting authorities in Memphis, Huie, and McMillan continually observed that major portions of the evidence had to be rejected because they did not fit in with what had been presumed—the lone guilt of Ray. Thus, the official version of the events could hardly be distinguished from the epistle published by those claiming to possess independent judgment. Huie then explained why he decided that there had been no conspiracy.

The postponement—Ray's desire to postpone the trial was one of the things that caused me to decide, because I thought the decision to postpone the trial was very ill-advised from Ray's point of view.

Although Huie said that the desire to postpone the case was ''one of the things'' that brought about his decision that there had been no conspiracy, he, at that time, offered no other consideration that led him to that conclusion. The determination to seek a continuance in this case, as in most pending matters, was made by trial counsel, not by the defendant. While such a decision may have been ill-advised, it is difficult to understand how such an application could logically have any bearing on the question of whether or not there had been a conspiracy to murder Dr. King. In the absence of some more substantial argument proffered by Huie his dramatic change is, in my opinion, unconvincing.

According to Huie's testimony, before he contracted to write *They* or *He Slew the Dreamer*, he entered into an agreement with *Look* magazine through its Vice President and general counsel, John F. Hardy. "At that time we foresaw two articles," he testified. He added, "They paid me $10,000 on what I was anticipating writing at that time."

Huie did write two articles for *Look* which were published in November 1968, three months after Ray's first installment of 10,000 words reached him and more than two months after the second installment was in his hands. Since Huie had solved the John F. Kennedy assassination in two weeks, even though ten months and 25,000 interviews by the FBI were required to assist the Warren Commission to its conclusion, two or three months to look into Ray's allegations would seem to be more than adequate for him. He evidently thought so. His first article was entitled, "The Story of James Earl Ray and the Conspiracy to Kill Martin Luther King." The second, "I Got Involved Gradually and I Didn't Know Anybody Was to be Murdered." In the November *Look* articles Huie makes it quite apparent that he believes that a conspiracy took the life of Dr. King and Ray was utilized, perhaps unwittingly, by that conspiracy.

In April 1969, *Look* published a third article by Huie. This story, "Why James Earl Ray Murdered Dr. King" reflected Huie's new position. In his appearance in the Federal Court in Memphis Huie, when asked how much *Look* paid him for all the articles responded, "*Look* paid me $62,871.85." A conclusion can be drawn from Huie's testimony that *Look* paid him $5,000 for each of the first two articles in which Huie stated that there was a conspiracy and more than $50,000 for the third and shortest article which he entitled "Why James Earl Ray Murdered Dr. King." It would appear, therefore, that Huie successfully rebutted his earlier testimony in which he claimed that publishers only desire and, therefore, pay handsomely for conspiracy stories.

It is, I suggest, truly instructive to make at least a cursory examination of Huie's three magazine articles before looking at the book which he later published.

In the first article, published on November 12, 1968, Huie described Ray's escape from the Missouri State Penitentiary at Jefferson City, his trip to Canada, and his fateful meeting with a blond Latin, approximately thirty-five years of age, to whom Ray referred only as Raoul.

Ray wrote to Huie that after arriving in Canada he did not plan to return to the United States. Huie asserted that Ray wrote that his decision to remain out of the country was "certain." Ray's efforts, according to Huie, were directed toward securing a passport and sufficient funds to leave Canada for Europe.

McMillan, and other supporters of the theory that Ray broke out of jail solely for the purpose of assassinating Dr. King, could not be expected to believe Ray's assertion. Huie, however, wrote, "I believe it's true that he never intended to return to the United States."

According to Huie, Ray frequented the Neptune Tavern in Montreal where he "sort of let the word get around that he had had a little trouble down in the States, that he was looking for I.D. and capital, and just might be available for activities that didn't involve too much risk." This, said Huie, "resulted in a contract." The contract was with Raoul. According to Ray, he and Raoul met at least eight times during the next three weeks to explore Raoul's suggestion that identification papers and cash might be provided to Ray if he assisted in various efforts. Ray said that he had just about run out of funds at that point. He held up the manager of a house of prostitution and stole approximately $800. Of that effort Ray said, "I hated to take a risk like that, but I figured that if I held up a whorehouse they probably wouldn't report it, and I guess they didn't."

While developing a relationship with Raoul, Ray met and cultivated a relationship with a Canadian woman who he had hoped would assist him in securing a passport.

Between August 8 and August 21, 1967, Ray met with Raoul at least five more times.

Huie wrote that Raoul had offered a six point deal to Ray:

One—They were to meet in Windsor on August 21, 1967, at the railroad station.

Two—Ray was to furtively transport packages for Raoul in a series of border crossings between the United States and Canada in his used car.

Three—Ray was then to travel to Alabama by surface transportation (train or bus) after selling the car.

Four—Ray would receive from Raoul living expenses and a sum to purchase an appropriate automobile.

Five—After Ray had undertaken and accomplished several more tasks Raoul would provide $12,000 and a passport and other means of identification.

Six—Raoul required that Ray remain incurious about the projects and seek to secure no information that Raoul did not provide voluntarily.

According to Huie, Ray later explained the dilemma that had confronted him and informed Huie that he was in a quandary. He was more than reluctant to return to the United States and face the possibility of being returned to the penitentiary in Missouri. However, he had almost no money left and he had been unable to secure adequate identification. He said that he had agreed to meet Raoul in Windsor but was planning to ask the Canadian woman who lived in Ottawa if she would help him get a passport.

223

Later Ray told me the same thing. He said, "I had sworn to myself never to come back to the U.S., to this snake pit. If the Canadian woman was willing to arrange for me to get a passport I never would have come back. If she said she would help me then I never would have met Raoul in Windsor, I never would have bought the rifle in Birmingham and I never would have been in Memphis on April 4th."

Huie sought to check out each of the allegations made by Ray. In almost every instance Huie went to the address indicated by Ray, found the relevant witnesses, and was satisfied that Ray had been truthful.

Huie met and interviewed the Canadian woman. He was evidently overcome with her beauty for he made repeated references to her appearance. He wrote that he was surprised that such a very attractive woman could have been interested in James Earl Ray. Later when I told Ray that I wanted to interview his Canadian friend he smiled and asked, "Is that because she's an important witness or because you believe Huie's description of her?" He added, "She isn't beautiful at all. She is a real nice person and just an average-looking middle-class woman." I said Huie had gone on at some length about her beauty and Ray answered "Well, she is beautiful compared to him."

Huie wrote that he met and interviewed the Canadian woman. Huie's published account of that interview is in all major respects identical with what Ray told me had transpired. Ray had driven to Ottawa to see her. As they drove around the capital city she pointed out where she worked and various other government buildings in the vicinity, including the nearby headquarters of the Royal Canadian Mounted Police. Thus did Ray discover that his Canadian friend was a government employee. He had almost decided to risk telling her the truth, or part of it, in an effort to enlist her in his plan to receive a passport. He was about to ask her if she would swear on an official government form that she had known him for two years. The proximity of the government buildings, the Mountie headquarters and his discovery that she worked for the government caused him a moment's panic. He decided not to ask for her help. The alternate plan, to meet Raoul, had suddenly become the only viable route.

The Canadian woman said that when Ray left her "He said he had to meet a man in Windsor." He wrote to her, planned to meet her when she took her vacation, but a brief stop in Memphis intervened and they never met again. The romantic-tragic parting between Ray and his Canadian friend was but a precursor to the monumental tragedy that was to follow.

It is apparent that Huie accepted as fact the major portions of Ray's lengthy statement, and that in addition he was satisfied that Ray's allegations, which were readily subject to verification, had been verified by his own inquiries. In most instances Huie gave the impression that he believed Ray and in some instances he stated that he did. The title of the article gave further credence to the belief that Huie believed that there had been a conspiracy to murder Dr. King. Yet it was not until the second *Look* article, which appeared two weeks later, that Huie publicly offered his conclusions.

Huie said that he had communicated with Ray for two months and had traveled throughout the United States and into Canada in an effort to verify Ray's allegations. He decided, he said, that the conspiracy to murder Dr. King began approximately eight months before King was shot. He concluded that "Ray was drawn unknowingly into this plot" during August 1967 in Montreal. He added that two weeks before the assassination Ray "did not know" that there was a plot to kill King or that the conspiracy was in any way aimed at King. Huie assured his readers that he knew more about the conspiracy to murder Dr. King than he was able to publish at that time. Some other evidence proving the conspiracy could, he stated, be released at the trial.

Huie wrote that the outline of the conspiracy to assassinate King began to become "visible" to him. He explained that if it was not clear to the readers it was only that he "could not reveal all that I have found to be true" about the conspiracy to murder Dr. King. What he discovered, said Huie, about "this plot" to murder Dr. King, he could reveal only after the trial.

There was no trial. Huie was, therefore, at liberty to share with America the additional, and no doubt sensational, details of the evidence that he had uncovered regarding the conspiracy against the United States of America.

However, in his third article published in *Look* in April 1969, Huie instead assured us that Ray acted alone or was involved in a "little conspiracy." Huie added that if there had been a little conspiracy, "I now believe that James Earl Ray was probably its leader not its tool or dupe." Huie never did enlighten us regarding the evidence he had previously uncovered, and the draconic conspiracy against our entire nation had been transformed into a small one if one existed at all. Huie certainly had the right, indeed the obligation, to inform us of his new insights and of the evidence that had led him to shun his previous conclusions. Yet he offered with his new conclusions no new evidence upon which they could be based. It appeared that Huie had simply changed his mind and was not prepared to share with his readers the reason for that dramatic metamorphosis.

Huie asserted that Ray killed Dr. King because he wanted "status among criminals and their guards," since he knew he would spend many years in prison. Huie also claimed that Ray killed Dr. King because he

225

expected Alabama Governor George C. Wallace to be elected President on November 5, 1968, "and that President Wallace would promptly pardon the murderer of Dr. King." These two motives offered so firmly by Huie appear to be mutually exclusive. And these two important sentiments attributed to Ray by Huie appear in a form that sharply contrasts with the manner that Huie had adopted, and was so faithful to, in the first two articles. Huie did not quote Ray directly in the April article regarding his motivation, nor did he state that Ray had been his source. Yet Huie offered no other source for his startling conclusion. From a relatively careful author who quoted accurately and in context and who had conducted his own not inconsiderable research, most of which he was anxious to permit his readers to participate in, Huie had been transformed into an author who offered his own conjectures.

Huie concluded his curious article by stating that Ray "deliberately" placed his possessions, including a rifle with his fingerprints on it, and other items, including a transistor radio which he knew carried his prison identification number, on the sidewalk. He did this, said Huie, because he wanted to leave "his calling card" so that the FBI and all of America would know that he had killed Dr. King.

If Ray did want the FBI to know, why is it that thirteen days after the FBI laboratory in Washington, D.C., had received Ray's rifle and binoculars with his fingerprints on them and Ray's radio which "clearly bore his prison I.D. No. 00416" that the FBI was not looking for Ray? Why had the FBI not picked up Ray's calling card? Almost one hundred American cities were in flames as black communities throughout the country indicated an interest in the case. If ever there was a need for immediate and effective public action, the need was present and apparent on the days beginning with the evening of April 4. Yet on April 17 the FBI issued wanted posters charging Eric Galt with the crime. The fingerprints and the radio belonged to Ray not a man named Galt. One wonders if Huie ever contemplated the possibility that Ray had been given two weeks to leave the country by the FBI in the grand conspiracy which he had found to be directed against the United States of America.

If Ray had wanted the glory, even at the cost of spending the rest of his life in jail, he seems to have abandoned that aspiration. By insisting that he is innocent he lays no claim to the glory of having murdered Dr. King and suffers nevertheless the prospects of a lifetime spent in a rural Tennessee penitentiary.

As the reviewer assesses the two November 1968 articles, the April 1969 article, and *He Slew the Dreamer*, he is confronted by a great debate waged between Huie and Huie over the responsibility for the death of Dr. King. The earlier Huie offered facts, relevant interviews, and conclusions based upon the evidence he had presented. The subsequent Huie offered conclusions. In the first *Look* article, Ray was presented as a man who "was proud" that in all of his crimes he "had never hurt anybody." In *He Slew the Dreamer*, Ray was "an antisocial man capable of murder." The book was little more than an extension of Huie's April *Look* article, with a brief analysis of the sanitation workers' strike, and comment upon Huie's own commercial encounters with Ray and Percy Foreman.

Regarding the historic strike, Huie said that the city had been orderly: "Then agitators brought disorder." He added, "The mayor was winning this battle and the cheap laborers were losing when Dr. King came to help them."

Huie reported that on November 27, 1968, he had told Percy Foreman that he had made a mistake by getting involved in the Ray case. He said he told Foreman, "Now I wish that I had never gone into the case at all," and added:

> **And speaking of mistakes, I believe you've made one. This is not your sort of case. You let them get you to Memphis where the old fire horse couldn't resist another race to the fire. But a week after you begin trying to work with Ray you'll know that there is no defense, and you'll be as sick of the case as Hanes was. You did Art a favor by replacing him; you just haven't realized it yet.**

Yet Hanes was neither anxious to leave the case nor sick of it; he was, in fact, anxious and eager to try the case and confident that he would win it.

According to Huie:

> **Mr. Foreman liked my three-way contract with Ray. All he wanted was for Mr. Hanes to get out so he could have what Mr. Hanes had had. "I like the idea of owning 60 percent of one of your books," he said, "while you own only 40 percent. So you get Hanes out and let me in, then, goddamn it, get to work and write us a good book and make us a good movie and make us some money."**
>
> **"I don't mind you having the money," I said. "But your client hasn't met his obligations. I want to know how, why and when he decided to kill Dr. King."**
>
> **"He may be incapable of telling anybody that," Mr. Foreman said. "You know why he did it. I've seen him only briefly, and I already know why he did it."**

With Ray's biographer and lawyer convincing each other before trial that Ray was the assassin even in the absence of proof that he was, Ray's chances for a fair trial were severely diminished.

After Huie had seen the light he sought to convince both the defense lawyer and the trial judge of Ray's lone guilt. In his book Huie spoke of a conversation he had with Judge Battle which took place when it was presumed that the case was to be tried.

Huie said that he showed the judge the contract that he had entered into with Ray and then said:

I don't want any secrecy about this contract, Judge. I'm showing it to you, and I'll show it to any reporter who wants to see it. This contract is an effort to do what your court can't do: to find the truth about why Dr. King was murdered. When you try Ray your trial will be necessary but disappointing because you can establish only what is already known: that Ray came to Memphis and killed Dr. King. At great financial cost you will spend weeks hearing witnesses from five countries give testimonies which already has been published. And after your trial every thoughtful American, white and Negro, will feel cheated because you will not have answered the question that matters most: why?

Huie reported that "the judge broke in to agree with me," Judge Battle, according to Huie, said, "All we can get are a few facts and perhaps a conviction. But we can't get much truth."

According to Huie, Ray's biographer, defense lawyer, and trial judge had all reached a conclusion regarding the defendant's guilt before the trial began. And, according to Huie's account, he had played a part in the process which culminated in that result. Yet in three articles and in a book he was unable to offer any substantial basis for that conclusion.

Perhaps the most telling critique of Huie's work is to be found in his own book. There he stated that he decided that Ray had lied to him about an escape from prison. Huie said that he had deliberately published "false" material in the *Look* article to show Ray that he would publish "false" material in lesser crimes if "he would help me establish the truth about the murder." Huie never did explain why he thought Ray would be more inclined to tell the truth to a man who had not insisted upon it but who had, in fact, demonstrated his contempt for the truth by knowingly publishing a false statement. As we depart from Huie's odd work, are we not constrained in our analysis of his important role to ponder his peculiar approach to the truth and subject all of his writings on this matter to close scrutiny?

An examination of Huie's most recent statements, oral and written, reveals that he now supports the position that Ray acted alone. During February 1977, Huie also stated that he had heard from an informant that Ray's rifle had not been used to kill King and that a man, whom he

228

named, had purchased the real murder weapon. According to Huie, that man, the informant said, was connected with organized crime.

Huie followed his new revelation with the publication of an article in the March/April 1977 issue of *Skeptic*, appropriately subtitled "The Magazine of Opposing Views" in which he insisted that Ray alone had murdered King. Huie libeled those who wished that the matter be investigated, saying that those who called for such an inquiry were "publicity-seeking congressmen, bureaucrats and conspiracy racketeers." He attacked Dr. King as well stating that "his sexual track record" revealed that he had "exercised often with assorted maids, wives, and widows." He added that J. Edgar Hoover "may have been a homosexual." He concluded his article by asserting that those who doubted the FBI version of the murder were panderers and that "forced to choose between a murderer and a panderer, I'll support the murderer every time."

Huie's vacillation regarding the central question of conspiracy was perhaps never more apparent than in his attempt to inform the members of the grand jury in Memphis of his thoughts. Attorney General Phil Canale and his two assistants questioned Huie, who was then under oath. In that brief appearance on February 7, 1969, Huie swore that "I started with the assumption that a Negro might have been involved in it [the plot to kill Dr. King]." He also said that "I have never had the slightest doubt that Ray and Ray alone killed Dr. King." Then he insisted that "I still think Ray was assisted [in the murder of Dr. King]." After assuring the grand jury that Ray acted alone in the murder, Huie concluded by stating that "It is my belief that this [the conspiracy to kill Dr. King] is a simple story involving maybe no more than two men and no more than four."

Chapter Twenty-Seven

THE MAKING OF AN ASSASSIN

by Mark Lane

As the members of Congress contemplated the future and the proposed budget of the Select Committee on Assassinations, which promised to conduct the first thorough investigation into the murders of Dr. King and President Kennedy, they were able to read a review of *The Making of an Assassin* by George McMillan which was featured in the *Washington Star* on December 12, 1976. McMillan has been foremost among journalist-writers defending the official findings of the investigations of both the Kennedy and King assassinations; he gives evidence of having access to sensitive information sources far beyond the reach of most senior reporters, and has access to prestigious forums of American journalism, including the Op-Ed page of *The New York Times*. The task of reviewing McMillan's book was not assigned to an ordinary book reviewer but rather to Jeremiah O'Leary, an "investigative" and intelligence reporter for the *Washington Star,* who, as it turns out, is not an ordinary reporter either. He wrote:

> **Reflecting on the tidal wave of assassination books that erupted after the murders of President John F. Kennedy, Dr. Martin Luther King and Sen. Robert F. Kennedy, it is a professional pleasure to encounter a volume that reflects a solid six years of original research instead of ivory tower thumbsucking.**
>
> **It is especially timely that George McMillan is now in the book stores since a House Select Committee on Assassinations is about to embark on a full-scale investigation of the murders that shook the world in the 1960s. McMillan, unlike most of the assassination authors, did not rely almost wholly on the work of such entities as the Warren Commission, the FBI and various police departments.**

O'Leary added that McMillan did not bother to analyze "the official reports." O'Leary was quite correct there. There appears to be little indication in McMillan's work that he explored the documents, read witness' reports, examined the transcripts of the various hearings, listened to the illuminating Memphis police radio broadcasts, examined the crucial FBI ballistics reports, or glanced at the FBI and Memphis police fingerprint records. Why this approach should be considered a virtue becomes clear only when we learn more about O'Leary. But first to McMillan and his book. The review concludes.

The House Select Committee, among others, should take the reporting of George McMillan into account when it begins probing the murder of King. McMillan has done a good deal of the committee's work already when it comes to deciding whether the world knows all there is to know about Ray and why he set out to kill Dr. King and did so with nearly as much skill as the fictional "Jackal" of screen and novel. This is a most important book, and extremely timely, since the King assassination will soon be probed by a committee which does not have six years in which to reach a conclusion.

The reader who has come this far knows far more about the murder of Dr. King than does McMillan after his "solid six years of research," that is, if McMillan shared with his readers all he learned. A cursory examination of the index of *The Making of an Assassin* reveals that McMillan did not even mention Ed Redditt, the black detective who had been in charge of security for Dr. King in Memphis. The other police officer assigned to Dr. King, W. B. Richmond, is not mentioned either. The two black firemen so strangely detailed to another assignment on April 4, Floyd Newsum and N. E. Wallace, are not mentioned either. Lest the reader be given the impression that McMillan ignored the black witnesses only, we hasten to point out that he is indeed an equal opportunity omitter of relevant data. Neither Arthur Hanes, Sr., nor Arthur Hanes, Jr., the only two of Ray's lawyers who were familiar enough with the case and ready to try it, are mentioned in the book. Nor is Renfro Hays, who was the only responsible investigator for the defense. Nor is Percy Foreman, who entered Ray's pleas to the charge and who brought McMillan to Ray in an effort to make a deal for the remaining rights of his story. Ray refused to see him. Ray testified on November 22, 1969, in a civil action he had instituted against Huie and his former lawyers. At that time he explained why he would not see McMillan: "Well, the first time I saw Mr. Foreman in court after our court appearance dismissing Mr. Hanes, he brought in another writer. He wanted me to exchange information with George McMillan. I had heard his name and, of course, I had heard of this fellow's writing. I didn't want to get involved with any other writers and I thought we would just stick with Mr. Huie.''

McMillan did not mention Ralph Abernathy or Andrew Young or Jesse Jackson, or many of the other eyewitnesses. J. Edgar Hoover, who had wanted to destroy Dr. King, who had waged an unequal and secret war against him, was not mentioned. There is no reference to Frank Holloman, the director of the Memphis Police and Fire Departments, either.

If McMillan's book, published in 1976, was the result of six years of effort, then the work began in 1970, after he spoke with Martin Waldron, a *New York Times* reporter. *The New York Times* reported this illuminating remark by McMillan on March 13, 1969: ''I have always believed James Earl Ray did it alone,'' he said. ''This guy is a loner. And I have never investigated any aspect of a conspiracy, which has left me free to work on his biography.'' Fair enough. McMillan did not wish the facts of the crime to interfere with his work. In any event, he knew that Ray did it alone before his research began, so why should he have concerned himself with the evidence? His book reveals him to be a man of his word. Nowhere in the work is there any indication that he betrayed his original prejudice. Under the circumstances, I think we are entitled to know why O'Leary admired this book so much and why he recommended that a serious study of the crime by a Select Committee should begin with a frivolous bit of fluff.

Approximately one year after Dr. King was murdered, Hoover told a friendly news source that it was Robert Kennedy who had requested that Dr. King's telephone be covered by FBI electronic devices, but that Kennedy ''was persuaded by our people not to do it in view of the possible repercussions,'' and because Dr. King's constant traveling made a wiretap impractical. The friendly news source ran that false explanation of the episode, as Hoover requested. The Church committee examined the Hoover memorandum on the question and revealed the news source to be Jeremiah O'Leary.

On November 30, 1973, it was revealed that the CIA had forty full-time news reporters on the CIA payroll as undercover informants, some of them as full-time agents. Two months earlier William F. Colby, then the director of the CIA, ordered a review of the practice since legitimate reporters were concerned that agent-journalists seriously compromised the integrity of the American press in general and might cripple the ability of reporters to function overseas. It seems clear that an agent-journalist is really an agent, not a journalist. When a conflict arises between writing the truth or concealing it in what may be conceived of as the best interests of the intelligence agency, the latter concept must prevail if the reporter is to continue his relationship with the agency. Indeed his intelligence relationship is designed for the purpose of resolving such conflicts in that fashion. Another function of the agent-journalist is to publish false information which the agency writes to have released. The agent-journalist concept contravenes and endangers the fundamental principles of the First Amendment, for the right of the people to a free press includes not only the right to publish a newspaper but the right of the people to information that is not covertly manipulated by a secret police agency.

In 1973, the American press was able to secure just two of the forty names in the CIA file of journalists. The *Washington Star* and the *Washington Post* reported that one of the two was Jeremiah O'Leary.

The Making of an Assassin, to put it charitably, does not focus on the events of April 4th. Indeed, McMillan devotes just seven pages to those events. The allegations which comprise those pages are presented as if they were fact, but upon reflection it is clear that we are being treated instead to the imaginings of a biased mind. Let us, for example, examine McMillan's restatement of the final moments.

He [Ray] was going to make his shot from the bathroom. He raised the small window as far as he could, and knocked out the rusty screen. It fell two stories to the ground.

He rested the rifle on the windowsill and aimed it.

To do so meant that he had to stand in the bathtub, lean one arm against the wall. There was something inglorious in that, and something fatefully typical of Ray and his crimes. He was going to carry out the most important single act of his life and he had to do it with his feet in the old, stained, rooming house tub.

He watched through his binoculars until King came out on the balcony, until he was sure it was King. He aimed carefully and, at 6:01 P.M., he fired a single shot which hit Martin Luther King in his right jaw, shattering that side of his face, and which went on into his body to lodge in his vertebrae. King fell back on the balcony, mortally wounded.

Since McMillan claims that Ray was alone at that fateful moment and since Ray has consistently denied that he fired the shot, or was in the bathroom when it was fired, is it not fair to ask McMillan for his source? Quite obviously, there is no source—there can be no source.

Further in his recitation of events McMillan states, "Without telling King, Memphis police had put a security guard around the Lorraine." There are but two serious errors in that sentence. Dr. King's supporters had asked for police protection and knew that Redditt had been there. Redditt was then removed by the police officials and that removal was made without notification to Dr. King and his supporters.

As we turn from McMillan's brief but flawed recitation of the crucial events to his chosen thesis, the life and times of James Earl Ray, we are challenged again to decide whether his allegations in this area are real or imagined.

A major source of material for McMillan's book is Jerry Ray, James Earl Ray's brother. Indeed, Jerry Ray is quoted so often and in regard to such decisive matters that one wonders if the book could have been written without his remarks. Jerry has stated that he is convinced his brother is innocent and that he knows nothing that would indicate that his brother might be guilty. How then could McMillan make use of such a man in a book dedicated to the proposition of Ray's sole guilt? McMillan explains, "I would not place any value at all on any of the stories he told me about his brother's innocence." Yet, if McMillan was convinced that Jerry Ray lied regularly—"Of course he lied to me," he wrote—how could he rely upon him at all? Sociologists define as moral density the condition of those who can walk down a crowded street and, due to their rigid preconceptions, see only persons of their own class. Critics might observe that even authors may suffer from a strain of this tendency to select so capriciously.

According to McMillan's book, Jerry Ray had told him that he "agreed with Jimmy's ideas about King;" that "Jimmy was going to Birmingham to take out citizenship papers in Alabama;" that "he believed that if he killed King in Alabama, or killed him anywhere in the South, it would help if he showed he was a resident of Alabama;" that "Jimmy was getting caught up in the Wallace campaign;" that "he was talking as much that night in Chicago about getting Wallace in as he was about rubbing King out;" that "he had it in his head that it would help Wallace if King wasn't around." According to McMillan, Jerry and Jimmy spoke by telephone on the morning of April 4th. Without doubt, the most impressive words attributed to Jerry Ray by McMillan are those which reported Jimmy's last words to Jerry that morning. McMillan assures us that at that historic moment Jimmy had said, "Jerry, tomorrow it will be all over. I might not see you and Jack for a while. But don't worry about me. I'll be all right. Big Nigger has had it."

A serious evaluation of *The Making of an Assassin* requires, I believe, an interview with Jerry Ray. I spoke with him at some length. He denied making every serious quotation attributed to him by McMillan. His denials were not merely general but contained specific information to support his assertion that McMillan had invented the "quotations" which were attributed to him. He told me that it could not be said that he "agreed with Jimmy's ideas about King," since he had never discussed Dr. King with his brother. He said that not only did he say that "Jimmy was going to Birmingham to take out citizenship papers in Alabama," but that he did not even understand that sentence when he read McMillan's book since his brother was already a citizen: "How could he talk about citizenship papers? I don't understand that." He said that he never said that James was in the Wallace campaign; that he did not know if he ever worked for Wallace, and that the only indication that he had been in the campaign was that "I read that he was in one of those books but I never asked him about it." He also allowed that he was growing somewhat suspicious about books as reliable sources after his experiences with McMillan. He said that his brother had never mentioned Dr. King's name to him or in his presence and that he could not understand how Wallace's campaign for election might be improved by Dr. King's death.

Regarding the historic telephone call on the morning of April 4th, Jerry could also say that he was not the best source regarding James' calls that day since he did not speak with him by telephone or in person on April 4th and that he had not spoken with James for approximately three months before that day.

During several conversations with Jerry Ray I noticed that although his manner was informal in general, he referred to his brother almost invariably as James. Yet in McMillan's book, all of the reconstructed conversations attributed to Jerry find him referring to his brother as Jimmy.

If McMillan had merely exchanged Jimmy for James a few times in his text, no harm would have been done. I know that Jerry referred to his brother as James in talking to me because I tape recorded all of our conversations and subsequently listened to them and then reviewed the transcripts prepared from the tapes. I can not imagine any other responsible way to write a book based, at least in part, upon interviews. I wondered if McMillan had tape recorded his interviews with Jerry Ray as well. I began by asking Ray that question. He said that in his meetings with McMillan there never was a tape recorder visible. He said that McMillan may have had a hidden machine, but he doubted it. He said

McMillan might have tape recorded telephone calls. In fact, he said he suspected that McMillan did monitor telephone conversations. He added that he never discussed matters of substance with McMillan on the telephone.

Jerry Ray subsequently told me that he had just written to the House Select Committee on Assassinations and offered to testify before that body. He suggested that his sworn statement about what he contended were McMillan's fabrications be taken. He said that he agreed to take a lie detector test. He also told me that he had just been questioned by two men from the Department of Justice and asked about the statement attributed to him by McMillan. He said that he told them that McMillan had made up the quotations and that he was ready to accompany them to the FBI office and submit to a polygraph examination there.

It seemed inappropriate for me to publish Jerry Ray's allegations without securing and publishing in full the response of the author whose veracity and competence had been challenged. I called McMillan numerous times at the telephone listed for his address in Frogmore, South Carolina, which appeared on the last page of his book. No one answered. His publisher, Little, Brown, informed me that his "real address" could not be revealed. I then explained that a major source for the book Little, Brown had recently published had told me that McMillan had invented the statements attributed to him. I said that I was anxious to ask McMillan to comment upon Jerry Ray's charges and that I fully intended to publish his response. I was then given McMillan's telephone number in Cambridge, Massachusetts. On that day, December 20, 1976, I called him for the purpose of securing his denial that he had made up the Ray "quotations" and to discover whether he had any tape recordings or other proof to support his assertions. Our conversation was brief.

Lane: Hello. George McMillan?

McMillan: Yes.

Lane: This is Mark Lane. How are you today?

McMillan: Uh . . . (pause) . . . OK.

Lane: I'm doing a book about the murder of Dr. King. There will be a chapter in the book dealing with your book. I've talked with Jerry Ray who, obviously, is a very important source for you, and he denies telling you almost everything you quoted him as saying in the book. I wonder if you have any recordings of these interviews with him.

McMillan: Mr. Lane, I'd just rather not talk with you.

Lane: You'd rather not talk?

McMillan: Yep.

Lane: Well, will you tell me Mr. Ray is wrong when he denies that he made those statements to you?

McMillan: You must have not listened to me. I said I'd rather not talk.

Lane: You won't even deny that you made up what Mr. Ray says.

McMillan: You still must not have listened to me.

Lane: What did you say?

McMillan: I said, you must still have not listened to me.

Lane: Yes, I'm just asking if you will deny—

McMillan (interrupting): I said I'd rather not talk.

Lane: You'd rather not talk. And you won't even deny Ray's charge that you made up those quotations.

McMillan: Uh.

Lane: I mean, it couldn't take you very long to say you didn't make them up.

McMillan: You want me to hang up, or do you want to hang up?

Lane: Well, I don't want to hang up and I don't want you to hang up. I just want you to answer the question as to whether or not Mr. Ray's charge . . .

McMillan (interrupting): I've already told you I don't want to talk with you.

Lane: You won't even answer that question.

McMillan: I told you, I don't want to talk to you.

Lane: You have said that, yes.

McMillan: OK.

Lane: Very good. I'll send you a copy of the book.

McMillan: Thank you.

Lane: You're welcome.

McMillan did not deny Ray's charges. He did not claim to have any proof that his book was accurate. I was struck by the contrast between Jerry Ray's offer to make his statement under oath, before a possibly hostile body, while being monitored by a polygraph and to answer all questions put to him and McMillan's refusal to deny the Ray charges or to suggest that he had proof relating to the integrity of his book.

I spoke with Jerry Ray again and told him of my conversation with McMillan. I said that McMillan had seemed very tense. Ray was in an expansive mood and he said, "I wouldn't blame McMillan if he were mad at me." Ray then discussed his relationship with McMillan:

Ray: One time down in Atlanta, I was talking to him on the phone, and I had a couple people around me listening in. I told him that I really had something for him, that I had a couple of names that would make his book and would even help solve the case. I said that it was dangerous and I couldn't talk about it much around here. I'll give you a call. Later I called him, and he flew in from Cambridge and stayed at a hotel. I told him, "This is dangerous stuff I'm talking about. . . . I'm going to give you two names that will solve the case for you . . . One name is Rudolph Stroheim, you check him out. . . ."

Lane: Rudolph Stroheim? You made that up?

Ray: Yeh, I made that up. I said, check him up in Germany.

Lane: Did you tell him East or West?

Ray: I think I said Hamburg.

Lane: Oh.

Ray: So I said, "Check Emmett Daniels of Fort Leonard Wood, Missouri." But before I gave him the names, I made him give me a thousand dollars. I said that this was a dangerous business but that I would give him the names for a thousand dollars.

Lane: Is there an Emmett Daniels?

Ray: No such guy.

Lane: Well, then you made the whole thing up.

Ray: I made the whole damn thing up. So when he got back to Cambridge, he hired some guys, and he paid some guy over in Germany to check that out. So they checked all the old Nazi files, all the files they could check, and there wasn't any Rudolph Stroheim. So they checked with Fort Leonard Wood, and there was no Emmett Daniels. Then he called me up. "Jerry," he said, "I've spent so much money checking this stuff out—all these phone calls, and paying these guys—and there's no Stroheim over there that could be connected with him, and no Emmett Daniels within Fort Leonard Wood." I laughed, and said, "Well George, thanks for the thousand, and you come up again in another month, and I'll have another story for you."

Stroheim was a wrestler in Atlanta, that's how I thought of his name. And Emmett Daniels—I thought of Emmett Kelly, the clown, and I said to McMillan "you're a clown, and I just put Daniels on the back of it."

Then I laughed. Every time I took him for some money, he said, "Jerry, you shit on me. You shit on me again."

But he was so damn desperate with the book—I'd wait maybe eight or nine months and I'd give him a call again and say, "This time I'm on the level . . . no more bullshit." It'd take him awhile, and then he'd be on the plane back up. Last time—he thought I was bankrolling James when he got out. So he said to me, "If you show me some bankbooks or something. . ." Why, I've only had one bank account in my whole life, and that was in Missouri. So I said, "you come up here, and I'll show you the damn bankbook where it shows so many thousand dollars that I withdrew—I'll give you that bankbook." I said, "I'll go over and get it." So he's on the plane up—when he came up, I had asked him up on a Saturday afternoon, and the banks were closed—I told him that the president was out and I couldn't get my bankbook. But I got my money anyway. When he got back, he found out there was no such thing.

Lane: How much did he pay you for that?

Ray: I only got five hundred that time.

Lane: Five hundred? Not bad.

Ray: Then the last time I took him was in St. Louis a year ago this month. I went down to see James, and did a lot of traveling, and when I got back, I was a little short of money, so I called George up.

Lane: He's your banker?

Ray: Georgie-pie—I called him Georgie-pie. And he's always wanting some pictures of my family then. You know, mother, my dad, and James when he was a little kid. We got pictures like that, but we would never give them to him. I told him, "My sister left, and I'm holding all these damn pictures. If you want to buy some pictures, come on up." It took a while, but he finally flew up.

Lane: He flew from Cambridge again?

Ray: He flew up from Cambridge again . . .

Lane: To Chicago?

Ray: This was to St. Louis. I met him at the airport, and I had got these damn pictures from an antique shop. I didn't get them, my sister got them.

Lane: They weren't of your family?

Ray: Not one of them was.

Lane: —Old, yellow—

Ray: Yeh, these were old pictures, antique pictures. One was supposed to be my grandmother, and one was supposed to be Lucille when she was a baby—we had one picture that looked something like James. This was taken back in the Forties, and it was on a boat, but I had cut the picture half up where you couldn't see the boat. So I sold him all these pictures.

Lane: How much did you get for them?

Ray: I got two and a half for them. He keeps going down all the time, as he keeps getting taken for all that money.

He still thought they were genuine, and he went back, and I asked him if he was going to use them, and he said he didn't know. So I said, "Well, if you don't, send them back, because I paid a dollar for them at that damn antique shop." He was hotter than hell that time. He said, "No more money, because my book is finished anyway." I said, "Well, put in some good words about me in your book, because I'm your friend." Actually, what it was, he was so damn desperate.

Partial corroboration for Jerry Ray's assertions may be found in a letter sent to John Ray, another brother, by George McMillan on September 14, 1973. In that letter McMillan said that Jerry Ray had told him a lot of things. McMillan wrote that subsequently Jerry sent him a tape recording in which Jerry said he had conned McMillan. McMillan then, according to his signed letter, discarded the material from Jerry. However, as his deadline for the book approached, McMillan said that he reviewed and then changed his mind and finally decided to use it.

McMillan admitted that he was going to publish material that he had received from Jerry after his source, Jerry, told him the material was false.

McMillan pleaded with John to give him some information for his book as his deadline was fast approaching. He agreed to pay John for a statement adding the provision that he wouldn't pay in advance. McMillan closed by asking for photographs of the Rays. Evidently any picture of any one might do.

McMillan's letter raised a new question. Were the Department of Justice and the FBI assisting cooperative authors, who seemed certain to support the official version of the events, while denying access to relevant material to others? McMillan wrote that he was going to go to Memphis and see the FBI file on the case which was available to him.

When it became known in 1976 that the Department of Justice was conducting an inquiry into the murder of Dr. King, Donald Freed, a professor, researcher, author, screenwriter, and investigator in Los Angeles, wrote to the Department. Freed offered to share information with the investigation. The Justice office wrote back that it was Department policy not to share information with any private citizen.

After NBC announced that Abby Mann was writing an original screenplay on the life of Dr. King and it became clear that he was going to devote part of the drama to Dr. King's death, a woman lawyer in Los Angeles contacted Mann. She said that she wanted to arrange a meeting between Mann and Assistant Attorney General Stanley Pottinger. She told Mann that Pottinger could talk to him about the murder of Dr. King and another matter. Pottinger subsequently met with Mann in Los Angeles. Pottinger talked about the possibility of a conspiracy to kill Dr. King and about the investigation that the Justice Department had conducted. Pottinger has disclosed that the Department of Justice had asked for an advance copy of George McMillan's book which they thought might be helpful in the investigation.

Now one may ask, did the Justice Department decline to seek information from Freed, a private citizen, who together with his associates had conducted a serious and important investigation into the murder of Dr. King, while it sought out McMillan, a private citizen? According to McMillan, the FBI agreed to make its file available to him. Why? These questions focus on who George McMillan is.

McMillan led off the acknowledgments by thanking "my wife, Priscilla Johnson McMillan, without whom this book would not exist." There is no reason to doubt the accuracy of that statement. Priscilla Johnson McMillan and George McMillan have played a part, as a team and separately, in shaping events during the last decade in America. One researcher, Jerry Policoff of New York City, has closely followed, and on occasion commented upon, the assignments and undertakings of the McMillans. For his troubles the Boston law firm of Hausserman, Davidson and Shattuck, attorneys for George and Priscilla McMillan, have threatened to sue him.

In 1959, Priscilla McMillan, as Priscilla Johnson, first came to our attention after she had conducted an extensive interview in Moscow with

Lee Harvey Oswald, very soon after his arrival in the Soviet Union. This interview appears to be the longest ever given to any American journalist by Oswald. Soon after both the President and Oswald had been murdered, Johnson wrote about the origin of her interview for *Harper's Magazine.* "I had sought him out a few hours earlier on the advice of an American colleague in Moscow. A boy named Oswald was staying at my hotel, the Metropol, the friend casually remarked. He was angry at everything American and impatient to become a Russian citizen. 'He won't talk to anyone,' my colleague added, suggesting that, as a woman, I might have better luck."

Johnson's discretion in referring to the contact who led her to Oswald is apparent. He was in her story "an American colleague," "the friend," and finally "my colleague." The man who sent her to Oswald is John McVickar, who at that time was one of two officers in the consular section of the American embassy in Moscow. The "us" he referred to in his conversations with Johnson was the American Embassy in Moscow.

In June 1964, Richard Edward Snyder testified before the Warren Commission. He said that during 1959 he was employed at the American Embassy in Moscow as the consul and as the second secretary. He testified, "up until the time I left Moscow, Oswald was my baby." He also testified, "I know Priscilla Johnson talked to him." Snyder admitted under the questioning of Gerald R. Ford, then a member of the Congress and the Warren Commission, that he had sent out a dispatch to Washington in 1959 about Oswald's presence in Moscow and his desire to renounce his American citizenship which carried the notation "Press informed." He testified that "Priscilla Johnson, I think, was one of the first to be aware of Oswald." Although McVickar, the only other officer in the consul section of the Embassy in Moscow, had sent Johnson to Oswald, Snyder testified "just how she became aware of him, and just where I became aware of her knowledge of him, I don't know. But this, I think, was quite early in the game." Snyder indicated that on December 1, 1959, he sent an airgram to the State Department with intelligence about Oswald. Regarding that information he testified "this was the statement of the correspondent." When asked to identify "the correspondent" he replied, "This was Priscilla Johnson."

When McVickar testified, he referred to his debriefing of Johnson about the Oswald interview, an event which took place just after she had completed debriefing Oswald. McVickar asked how the American Embassy had learned when Oswald was going to leave his hotel and that he might be given training in electronics. In both instances McVickar said that Priscilla Johnson was the source. McVickar then produced a memorandum that he had prepared after debriefing Johnson. In it he said, "I pointed out to Miss Johnson that there was a thin line somewhere between her duty as a correspondent and as an American." He later wrote, "She seemed to understand this point."

When Johnson testified before the Warren Commission, she identified the man who suggested she interview Oswald as "Mr. McVickar, the consul." She testified that she believed McVickar told her about Oswald on November 16, 1959, "and that on coming home from the Embassy, coming to the Metropol, I went straight to Oswald's room, and therefore that would have placed my original conversation with Oswald probably on the 16th, my writing the story and my second conversation with McVickar on the 17th, and my filing of the story on the 18th."

Not long after the assassination, Priscilla Johnson entered into an agreement with Harper and Row to coauthor with Marina Oswald, the widow of Lee Harvey Oswald, a book about Marina. It was reported that the advance was $100,000. During that time Marina was being held in quasi-captivity and her contacts with the outside world were being monitored by the federal police authorities. I made several efforts to interview Marina Oswald but her agent and her lawyer, both provided by the United States Secret Service, said that I could not meet with her because the government wanted no one with her who could influence her testimony (other than the FBI agents who met with her regularly); they were concerned that some outsider might "plant" some documentary evidence for her to come upon; and above all, Marina should not talk to anyone about the facts until her book was published.

Priscilla Johnson did, however, meet with Marina Oswald before Marina had completed her testimony, and oddly enough Marina came upon an important document that she had evidently not seen before she was with Priscilla Johnson.

On September 6, 1964, Marina Oswald, still in what the government referred to as "protective custody," testified before the Warren Commission at the U.S. Naval Air Station in Dallas, Texas. Very much a matter of concern was the allegation that Oswald had gone to Mexico City and visited both the Soviet and Cuban Embassies while there. Years later it was revealed that the CIA had misled the Warren Commission about events surrounding those visits and had destroyed certain relevant evidence that might have demonstrated that Oswald had not been there. In 1964, however, the ill-informed Warren Commission was examining evidence about Oswald's Mexican trip.

Senator Richard Russell, then a member of the Commission, reminded Marina that she had previously testified that Lee had told her in

New Orleans that he said he was going to Mexico City. At that time Marina had no documentary evidence to support the allegation that Lee had actually gone to Mexico City. In September, however, Marina presented a ticket stub. She testified, "I found the stub of this ticket approximately two weeks ago when working with Priscilla Johnson on the book. Three weeks ago I found the stub among old magazines, Spanish magazines, and there was a television program also in Spanish and there was the stub of this ticket. But this was, you know, a piece of paper and I didn't know this was a ticket." She discovered that it was a ticket, she testified, when she showed it to Priscilla Johnson. Russell obviously did not believe the story. He asked why Lee would keep magazines in Spanish if, as Marina had previously testified, he could not read Spanish. Marina replied, "It was not a Spanish magazine." Russell asked how this document could possibly have escaped the extensive search of the FBI agents who were looking for such evidence and who had examined every scrap of paper. There was no responsive reply.

Priscilla Johnson's relationship with Marina Oswald for the purpose of writing a book which will tell Marina's story has been offered as the prime reason why Marina will not talk about the facts, many of which she alone knows. However, thirteen years after the contract was entered into, the book has not yet been published. A Warren Commission document (C.D. 49 page 24) which was supplied to the Commission by the FBI states, "On November 23, 1963, Mr. Jack Lynch, United States Department of Defense (USDS), Security office, telephonically advised Special Agent in Charge (SAC) Allen Gillies, Oswald had been contacted in Moscow by three employees of the State Department, whom he identified as John McVickar, Priscilla Johnson, and Mrs. Stanley G. Brown. Lynch indicated each of the above persons had interviewed Oswald in Moscow."

The law firm engaged by George and Priscilla in October 1975 for the purpose of threatening Jerry Policoff (the retraction demanded by the lawyers was not published and no legal action was taken) wrote to the editor of *New Times,* the magazine that published Policoff's article, stating, "As to the allegations of her being an undercover government employee throughout this period, there exists not even the slightest reasonable foundation for such an allegation. Mrs. McMillan has never seen the purported 'unpublished Warren Commission document listing her as a State Department employee.' "

The statement that Mrs. McMillan had not seen C.D. 49 is untrue. On May 11, 1975, I was a panelist, along with Priscilla J. McMillan and others, at the A. J. Liebling Counterconvention in New York City.

Anthony Lukas was the moderator. The proceedings were preserved by a tape recorder and a transcript from that record reveals:

> Lane: I wonder if I could just interject for a second, Tony. I think that Mrs. McMillan has played a really active part in this, being one of the few people to question Lee Harvey Oswald in Moscow, having access to Marina Oswald after some eleven years on a book which hasn't yet come out. And I know that you told me before I met you today for the first time that you were working for the North American Newspaper Alliance at the time you conducted that interview. I wonder if you've seen Commission Document 49, an FBI report which reads as follows: "on November 23rd, 1963, Mr. Jack Lynch, of the United States Department of State Security Office, telephonically advised Special Agent in Charge, Allen Gillies, Oswald had been contacted in Moscow by three employees of the State Department, whom he identified as John McVickar, Priscilla Johnson, and Mrs. Stanley G. Brown. Lynch indicated each of the above persons had interviewed Oswald in Moscow." I wonder if you were at any time, or at that time employed by the State Department, if you're familiar with this document, or if you've tried, if it's incorrect, if you've indicated to the Warren Commission that the United States Department of State's Security Officer had made a mistake when he gave that information to the FBI.

> McMillan: Well, no I'm not familiar with the uh doc . . . with the document. Uh, John McVickar was the vice-counsel who was present the first day Oswald went in to uh, put down his passport. And uh, he was, he did work for the State Department. Mrs. Brown was the wife of the Agricultural Attache, and she was sort of a receptionist in the consul's office, and I suppose she was authority in the State Department. But, uh, that was a mistake about me and I wouldn't bother to correct that mistake. I worked for the North American Newspaper Alliance and I didn't work for anyone else.

As soon as I read the document to Priscilla McMillan I passed it along to her so she could read it. Her lawyer's statement, made almost four months later, was based upon incorrect evidence given to him by his client or an error on his part.

When the Warren Report was issued during September 1964, two of its strongest supporters in the news media were Harrison Salisbury and Anthony Lewis, both of *The New York Times*. They wrote introductions to commercial publications of the report. Two months later, when the Commission published the twenty-six volumes of evidence, Lewis, who had had the volumes in his possession for just a few hours, wrote in a front page story for *The New York Times* saying all of the evidence they contained proved that Oswald was the lone assassin. Since it took me almost an entire year to read the volumes, I wondered how Lewis had been able to move through the material so quickly and then assure the readers of the *Times* that the evidence was consistent with the Commission's verdict, when it was not. Later Salisbury urged David Belin, the Warren Commission lawyer most committed to the preconception of Oswald's lone guilt, to write a book attacking the critics of the Warren Report and defending its essential findings. *The New York Times* published that book and Salisbury wrote the introduction. The book was then reviewed in *The New York Times Book Review* on November 10, 1973, by the team of Priscilla Johnson and George McMillan. Although Belin was the most vocal of the apologists for the Warren Report, the McMillans said of his book, "It is as if Lee Harvey Oswald had lived and there had been a trial." It would have perhaps been more accurate to suggest that it was as if Lee Harvey Oswald had died and there had been a lynching.

During April, 1967, the CIA staged one of the major coups in its history. It arranged for the defection from the Soviet Union of Svetlana Alliluyeva, the daughter of Joseph Stalin. When Alliluyeva arrived in the United States, the Voice of America, the broadcasting service of the United States Information Agency, sent news of her arrival all over the world, including the Soviet Union, where it was broadcast in Russian. Radio Free Europe, a "private broadcast operation" funded by the CIA, dispatched the word throughout Eastern Europe from its studios in Munich. During the great international brouhaha following her defection, Svetlana Alliluyeva spent her days in seclusion, at a site approved by American intelligence and the State Department, with George and Priscilla Johnson McMillan. The site was the home of Priscilla McMillan's parents. *The New York Times,* upon the arrival of Stalin's daughter, said that it would publish her forthcoming memoirs. Priscilla McMillan was assigned by Evan Thomas—who had edited William Manchester's defense of the Warren Report for Harper and Row and who would also supervise the editing of the Alliluyeva book—to translate Svetlana Alliluyeva's work for Harper and Row, the same publishers that had been waiting so patiently for Priscilla to finish the Marina Oswald biography. Alliluyeva and Lee Harvey Oswald had perhaps shared but one moment in common, both had been interviewed in Moscow by Priscilla Johnson McMillan before leaving for the United States.

When George McMillan's *The Making of an Assassin* was published, *The New York Times Book Review* assigned Anthony Lewis to review it. Before examining the Lewis review it is important to understand what the McMillan book claims to be. McMillan never even examined the voluminous files on the case maintained by Arthur Hanes, Sr., and Arthur Hanes, Jr.—the only lawyers who conducted an investigation and were prepared to try the case. There is, in my view, no way to review the case against James Earl Ray and his possible defense without making a thorough search through those files. Hanes Jr., told me, "I was astonished that McMillan did not come to our office as you did and spend days, as you did, going over the more relevant witnesses' statements, public reports, etc."

McMillan can, I suggest, be excused from failing to examine the evidence (although I would not elevate that failure to a virtue as did Jeremiah O'Leary) since he devoted almost none of his book to an assessment of the crime. He presented, instead, a biased biography of James Earl Ray and relied very substantially for that portrayal upon a man who now says that he falsified the record. Yet, even if McMillan were accurate where has he led us? He portrayed Ray as a racist, a man who had committed crimes, a man with a burning hatred of Dr. King and an obsession to do him harm. From this profile McMillan makes a quantum leap to the conclusion that Ray killed Dr. King and that he acted alone while doing so. McMillan's profile may describe Ray, although somewhat inexactly, but it would describe Hoover as if it were custom made for him. Ray may or may not have hated King, but unlike Hoover he never sent a letter to him encouraging him to kill himself.

Yet, if we were to presume that Ray wanted to kill King and that as McMillan states, his obsession to do so was rather widely known, have we established as fact that he did so and that he acted alone? Viable alternatives to McMillan's theory may rest upon McMillan's allegations as if they were fact. If Ray wanted to kill King, is it not possible that he organized a group to assist him? Is it not possible that a group planning to kill King picked up Ray because of his known propensities in that area and involved him, knowingly, in their effort? And is it not possible that a group planning to kill King picked up Ray and utilized him as the decoy and fall guy as he has insisted? To establish that Ray hated King and wished to kill him, which I suggest is contrary to the known evidence, is not to establish that he did so or that he acted alone and that there was no conspiracy.

Yet Lewis, in his major piece in *The New York Times Book Review*, concluded that McMillan's book "is a powerful, a devastating book" and then asks, "Will this brilliant piece of hard reportorial work end the attempt to find a conspiracy in the murder of Martin Luther King, Jr.?" He laments, "of course not," and explains, "as long as there are people unwilling to accept the pain of such deaths [President Kennedy, Robert Kennedy, and Dr. King] without some more satisfying reason—a political reason—the search will go on. And, I have to add, as long as there are self appointed 'investigators' who make an industry of finding conspiracies. The day I sat down to write this review, a newspaper carried a story about the latest theory of a man who got into the business in 1963. (I omit his name because publicity is gratification in this ghoulish business). The headline said: WAS DR. KING SET UP TO DIE?" Yet it is Lewis who attempted to buttress government dogma regarding the assassinations for thirteen years. His early and continuing advocacy of the conclusions of the Warren Report in stories in *The New York Times*, his book reviews and book prefaces, together with his panegyrical remarks in place of a critical analysis of the McMillan book established, I believe, an unblemished record of support for conventional and official doctrines regarding these assassinations that have been widely rejected.

The day I sat down to write this chapter the Gallup poll, published in the *Washington Post* on December 26, 1976, revealed that only 18 percent of the American people believed that James Earl Ray was the lone assassin of Dr. King and only 11 percent believed that Lee Harvey Oswald was the lone assassin of President Kennedy. Those statistics, in the face of the coordinated efforts of leaders of government, intelligence organizations, and their friendly media sources, stand as a monument to the good common sense of the people.

Unlike Anthony Lewis and George McMillan, James Earl Ray finds himself, on the issue of his lone guilt, among the majority of the American people.

Ray told me that "there are many statements in the McMillan book that are not true." Ray said,

McMillan makes me into a political activist for George Wallace. It's hard to discover the origin of a false statement here because Huie, McMillan, Foreman and the FBI all seem to feed from the

same trough. I was a fugitive, hiding out. I wasn't crazy enough to become active in a political campaign. I never even registered although once I considered registering under an assumed name to get a voter registration card because it is good identification. When you cross into Canada they always ask for a voter registration card. But I never did register or work in any political campaign under my right name or under an assumed name.

I asked Ray if he had any idea how McMillan or Huie had come upon the notion that he had been a political activist for Wallace. He said,

In December 1967, I took a woman to register to vote. She said she had a boy friend who was doing five years for marijuana. She registered and I think she did register for Wallace. That was the only time I was ever around any registration place. Later on she said to me that she wanted to get her boy friend out of jail, that she needed influential friends. I told her if she wanted help she should get into some organization that had influence. So she changed her registration to Republican. That was the extent of my political work. With a few more workers like me to depend on Wallace wouldn't even have gotten on the ballot.

Ray also spoke with me about McMillan's assertion that James and Jerry Ray had rendezvoused in a Chicago hotel the day after James had escaped from jail and talked there about killing Dr. King.

First of all when Jerry and I met in Chicago there were only the two of us there. We both know that we never talked about King. We talked about my getting out of the country. I was a fugitive trying to escape. Since there were just the two of us there and we both have always denied this charge about talking about King, what basis does McMillan have for his story? Ask him for some evidence for that charge—he won't have any, he can't; there isn't any.

I then asked Ray if his meeting took place in Chicago the day after he had escaped.

No, that's wrong too. It took me a week to get to Chicago after I escaped from Jeff City, Missouri. I walked. It takes a long time to walk on railroad ties. It takes a long time to cover fifty miles because you'd be surprised at how many houses are sitting right near railroad tracks. If there was a light in the house or if there were dogs there I'd circle around into the woods maybe for two or three miles. I slept during the day and walked at night. One time two railroad workmen came by on a handcar. I was under a trestle. It was April but it was cold so I had a little fire going. The fire attracted them, I imagine. They came over and talked to me. I imagine the FBI might have heard about that and checked it out and interviewed the men since I told Huie about it.

Ray expressed his dissent from *The New York Times* review in a letter he mailed to Anthony Lewis on December 29, 1976. There too Ray pointed to errors in the McMillan book.

Mr. Anthony Lewis; Co
Columnist
New York Times

re: Book review

Dear Goody Two-shoes:
Sometime ago I received a copy of the review you did on your New York Times fellow, George McMillian's, published novel titled "The making of an Assassin". And all of it's "brilliant revelations". It would appear that one of the most heretofore significant long suppressed (a Nixon conspiracy?) revelation's by McMillian was that yours truly, while in the Missouri big-house, used to rant and rave when Dr. King appeared on the tube shouting & sobbing, "somebody's gotta get him" "somebody's gotta get him". Now I didn't read ole Mac's novel (just the Time mag. article) but I guess he also has me devouring the proverbial carpet, ect. ect. Anthony, when Mac was spoon feeding you all these turkey droppings as revelations did he also tell you that TV'S were not permitted in the Missouri penitentiary during my entire sojourn therein?*

In *The Making of an Assassin,* McMillan had written:

In 1963 and 1964, Martin Luther King was on TV almost every day, talking defiantly about how black people were going to get their rights, insisting that they would accept with nonviolence all the terrible violence that white people were inflicting on them until the day of victory arrived, until they did overcome.

*Ray's letter to Lewis concluded:
"But having to assume legally that you do consider McMillan's novel the last word on the case I'll herein issue collectively to you and the above referred to literati an invitation to consider carrying your prissy asses before the select committee, and I shall do likewise with my midwest tobacco-road one, and we shall let under oath testimony determine the facts."

Ray watched it all avidly on the cellblock TV at Jeff City. He reacted as if King's remarks were directed at him personally. He boiled when King came on the tube. He began to call him Martin "Lucifer" King and Martin Luther "Coon." It got so that the very sight of King would *galvanize* Ray. "Somebody's gotta get him," Ray would say, his face drawn with tension, his fists clenched. "Somebody's gotta get him."
[Emphasis in original]

In this instance both McMillan's and Ray's allegations were susceptible to proof. In February 1977, I spoke with Bill Armontrout, the associate warden at the Missouri Penitentiary at Jefferson City. He told me that during 1963 and 1964 no television sets were available for any of the inmates. Television sets were placed in a TV room with limited access in 1966 and television sets were permitted in the cells and the cell-block for the first time in early 1970. Ray had escaped from that prison in 1967. Under those circumstances one wonders where McMillan, who had never spoken with James Earl Ray, but who did speak with Huie, who in turn had never spoken with Ray, secured his information. The allegation that Ray "boiled" when King was there on the tube in 1963 and 1964 was graphic enough, as was the charge that the sight of King would *"galvanize"* (emphasis present in the original) him but since these events never took place either McMillan or his informants must be credited with a lively imagination.

PART EIGHT

FOR A DAY IN COURT

Chapter Twenty-Eight

THE APPEAL
by Mark Lane

Although Ray was evidently threatened by the authorities and advised by his former lawyer not to proceed with an appeal, he did write to Judge Battle, as we have seen.

Battle neither responded to the letter nor treated it as an application to withdraw the plea previously entered, to set aside the conviction, to vacate the sentence or, in the alternative, to set a date for a hearing at which time such a formal application might be made. Ray was without counsel and his letter could have been considered by Battle as an attempt at a formal application. Instead Battle left for a vacation in Florida. When he returned on March 31, 1969, he found another letter from Ray waiting for him. In that letter dated March 26th, Ray asked Battle to consider it to be a formal application "for a reversal of the 99-year sentence." Ray also asked the judge to appoint "an attorney or the public defender to assist me in the proceeding." Ray wrote, "I understand on one avenue of appeal, I have only 30 days in which to file."

Battle showed the letter to James Beasley, the Assistant Attorney General who had presented the case against Ray. Three lawyers, J. B. Stoner, Richard J. Ryan, and Robert H. Hill, Jr., had all indicated that they were interested in representing Ray. Battle asked Beasley to find out who Ray wanted to represent him. It was improper, I believe, for Battle to involve the attorney who prosecuted Ray in an aspect of Ray's defense efforts. This act emphasized yet again the close working relationship between the court and the prosecuting authorities even as Ray's appeal was being initiated. The legal canons of ethics proscribe such conduct. Battle could not ethically call upon the prosecutor to play a role in the determination of counsel for Ray. Beasley should not have responded. Beasley said he determined that Ray wanted all three lawyers to represent him. He then called Battle to inform him of the fact. But Battle's telephone remained unanswered.

Just before Beasley called Battle, Richard J. Ryan had called upon the judge in his chambers. Ryan told me that he had asked the judge to set a hearing for Ray's application for a new trial. Battle responded, he said, by stating that he had the matter "under advisement."

At approximatley five o'clock Beasley visited Battle's chambers. He entered the room to find Judge Battle dead. He died, the medical examiner later reported, of a coronary insufficiency. He had fallen across his desk, his head on the last letter from James Earl Ray.

Ryan told me that with Battle's death he and the other lawyers for Ray were quite certain that their client was assured a new trial. Ryan said,

Ray's letter was an adequate application for a new trial. Just to be sure I perfected it by filing a formal application. We had thirty days to get it in and we filed it in a timely fashion. The law of Tennessee is really clear on this question. If a judge should die or go insane after an application for a new trial is filed and before he rules upon it the application is automatically granted. There has never been an exception in Tennessee since that statute was adopted by the legislature.

Judge Arthur J. Faquin emerged as Battles' successor. Ryan said,

He was working with Battle through the whole case. He just said at the hearing held at the end of May 1969 that Ray had pleaded guilty voluntarily and that was it. The laws of Tennessee just did not apply anymore. The reason is that there was a conspiracy to kill Dr. King, probably the FBI or CIA were in on it and they did not want this case being re-opened.

On January 9, 1970, Ray's application to the Supreme Court of Tennessee for a writ of *certiorari* was denied. The court, in a memorandum decision, denied the application with a vehemence rarely matched in appellate court opinions. The court pointed out that "the defendant was represented by privately retained able counsel." The court added that "The defendant upon the advice of his well-qualified and nationally known counsel pleaded guilty to murder in the first degree, the offense with which he was charged, a cold-blooded murder without an explained motive."

The court continued:

In Tennessee, as in all other liberty loving civilized countries, ambush killers are not looked upon with much favor, to say the least. In a country where you do not shoot a sitting duck or a fowl unless in flight; where a rabbit or other game of the field is allowed its chance to run; and where one does not shoot down his

fellowman unless that man has committed an overt act that would justify the defendant in so doing, jurors are inclined to deal harshly with such defendants.

And the court concluded that Ray

. . . willingly, knowingly and intelligently and with the advice of competent counsel entered a plea of guilty to murder in the first degree by lying in wait, and this Court cannot sit idly by while deepening disorder, disrespect for constituted authority, and mounting violence and murder stalk the land and let waiting justice sleep.

Judge Faquin had ruled against Ray in contravention, I believe, of Section 17-117 of the Tennessee Code Annotated, the relevant statute. The Court of Criminal Appeals of Tennessee refused to grant the petition and finally the Supreme Court of Tennessee refused to hear the arguments. Ray then chose to make an appeal to the federal court system. During April 1970, the lawyers who had been representing Ray withdrew from the case.

Bernard Fensterwald, Jr., a Washington, D.C., lawyer who was a native of Tennessee became counsel for Ray. He was associated in December 1972 as Ray's attorney with Robert Livingston, a Memphis lawyer, and James Lesar, then recently admitted to the bar in Washington, D.C.

There were at least two potential bases for Ray's application to the federal court system for a new trial: the allegation that Ray had been coerced into making his guilty plea and the allegation that important new evidence had subsequently been uncovered. In my opinion, the first was the weaker of the two, being inherently more difficult to establish and sustain. Much more compelling, and far easier to sustain, it seems to me, would have been an allegation that hitherto undeveloped evidence strongly suggested that there had been a conspiracy to murder Dr. King. The mysterious transfer of Detective Ed Redditt and the equally mysterious transfers of fireman Floyd Newsum and N. E. Wallace would, alone, have raised serious questions which the prosecution would have had difficulty answering.

Ray's attorneys brought their action for a writ of *habeas corpus* to the United States District Court for the middle district of Tennessee in the form of a petition and a supporting Memorandum of Facts. This Memorandum of Facts, hyperbolically headed "A Sham, A Farce, and a Mockery," was signed by Fensterwald, Lesar and Livingston. Where it adopted an aggressive and rhetorical tone (it concluded with the potentially offensive charge that Ray's treatment by the courts "was, in effect, a legal lynching"), it was doubtless designed to make the federal court sit up and take notice of the case. What other effects that may have had on the court's attitude can only be surmised.

At one point the memorandum referred to the narration of a lawyer as "perjury," although, since the lawyer had not made a statement under oath, the charge was incorrect. At another point, the memorandum charged that Judge Battle (then deceased) and others were "participants in these illicit meetings [which] have revealed, in part, this corruption of the judicial process."

But, as I have suggested, probably more important than what the memorandum did say was what it did not. By this time there existed a substantial number of leads that could, with further investigation, have developed new evidence that could have provided the basis for granting a new trial.

Harold Weisberg, the defense's investigator, had in 1971 written a book, *Frame-Up,* in which he referred only briefly to Detective Ed Redditt (whom Weisberg calls "Reddick"), dismissing him as a police spy and never inquiring into the matter of his removal from the scene shortly before Dr. King was shot. Similarly, he did not explore the importance of the observations of the other police officer on the scene, W. B. Richmond (whom Weisberg variously calls "Richardson" and "Richman"). He did not refer to either of the black firemen by name and summarized the twenty-five year high-level association of Memphis Fire and Police Departments Director, Frank Holloman, with the FBI merely by characterizing him as "a former FBI agent." At no point in *Frame Up* did Weisberg, who later claimed that he was the only one who had ever been Ray's investigator, claim to have interviewed any of these men.

On the strength of this, one may speculate that Ray's defense team was either unaware of the significance of these leads or simply did not choose to develop them. What is apparent is that they did not use them.

Ray's application to the District Court was denied. The matter was appealed to the United States Court of Appeals for the Sixth Circuit, which remanded the matter to the District Court for an evidentiary hearing. After the hearing it was again denied. On further appeal, the Court of Appeals affirmed the District Court's denial. It was finally submitted to the United States Supreme Court on a writ of *certiorari*. That application, too, was denied.

When I met with Ray, at his request, and interviewed him at the Brushy Mountain Penitentiary in Petros, Tennessee, Ray was receptive,

257

cordial, and outgoing. I told him that I was writing this book and he said that he hoped, unlike the others, that I wanted to be accurate. He wrote to me several times, and requested me to visit him again. I subsequently spent the major part of a weekend in February 1977 in Petros in extended conference with him.

This book is, of course, not intended to present the case for James Earl Ray. It focuses upon the events which transpired in Memphis on April 4, 1968, and the events which led up to the fateful moment that day as well as the incidents that followed. In the course of telling that story it becomes clear that James Earl Ray has been poorly treated, that his basic rights have been denied and that should he be granted a trial more of the facts about the murder of Dr. King might be known.

James Earl Ray was charged with a heinous crime. He and the American people have been denied the opportunity to witness an open inquiry into that murder, in which the evidence is offered under oath and subjected to the cross-examination required by our adversary system. Some may contend that Ray waived his right to a trial. Under the circumstances which prevailed I do not believe that such a waiver may be valid. In any event, the American people have entered into no such waiver and our right to know has been obliterated by actions seemingly beyond our power.

Chapter Twenty-Nine

THE BEGINNING
by Mark Lane

In February 1975, I founded the Citizens Commission of Inquiry (CCI). The CCI was mandated, through citizens' lobbies, to urge the Congress to reopen the investigation of the assassination of John F. Kennedy; further research revealed the need to pursue also the investigation of the death of Dr. Martin Luther King, Jr.

Many prominent citizens joined the CCI as advisers and active participants on our Executive Committee: among them John Adams, of the United Methodist Church and the Southern Christian Leadership Conference, a veteran of Kent State and Wounded Knee; Richard Barnet and Marcus Raskin, Directors of the Institute for Policy Studies; Robert Borosage, Director of the Center for National Security Studies; Morton Halperin, a former Assistant Secretary of Defense; researchers and writers Mary Ferrell, Donald Freed, L. Fletcher Prouty, and George O'Toole, a former computer specialist with the Central Intelligence Agency, and an author of several articles and books, including *The Assassination Tapes.* We were also joined by scientists and scholars interested in truth in government such as Nobel prize-winner Linus Pauling, astronomer Steven Soter, and philosopher Josiah Thompson.

As Director of the CCI—and while teaching at the Columbus School of Law, of the Catholic University of America—I was able to recruit a work force of student interns to conduct research and to assist in the formation of chapters of the CCI. The intern program was expanded to other colleges and universities, including the University of Massachusetts, Antioch College, Boston University, and the University of Pennsylvania.

The CCI was funded entirely by lecture fees I earned while speaking at colleges and universities throughout the United States; because the CCI lobbied as part of its program it was unable to achieve tax-exempt status and therefore could not attract foundation or other large gifts.

One advantage of my speaking at more than 180 institutions since 1975 was that at many of the schools a community-wide CCI chapter was formed. Each chapter, with guidance from the national CCI, operated autonomously, educating the community and motivating citizens to influence their Congressional representative to support a new investigation. We already knew that a majority of the American people did not believe the Warren Report and that the new information about Dr. King's death, and James Earl Ray's apparently induced guilty plea, had raised many additional questions. Now the old objections no longer had any meaning, and could not deter the determined citizenry—"What good would it do? It won't bring them back. Why stir it up? You can still have doubts about Lincoln's assassination, too." The people now insisted that their representatives, in whom the power had been vested, go to the enormous, complex, expensive, but worthwhile and necessary effort of determining the truth. The natural bent of most may be toward simplicity; but the Vietnam War and Watergate had shown that simplicity, while consonant with goodness and innocence, was not a match to the arabesque designs of the lie merchants. No sooner was one lie revealed than another took its place, and layer upon layer, like the integuments of an onion, needed to be removed before the truth could be approached.

CCI's first Congressional contact was Representative Henry B. Gonzalez of San Antonio, Texas, who had been in the Dallas motorcade on November 22, 1963, when President Kennedy was assassinated. Congressman Gonzalez had harbored doubts about the adequacy of the findings of the Warren Commission. Later he stated that he was also not satisfied with the official explanations of the deaths of Dr. King and Senator Robert F. Kennedy, and the attempted assassination of Governor George Wallace. Congressman Gonzalez believed that these assassinations were the responsibility of Congress to investigate, and ultimately to stop:

> **After all, these assassinations changed the course of history, thwarted democratic process, eliminated options, baited domestic unrest, and caused great harm to the collective national psyche—the extent of which I strongly feel it is the Congress' responsibility to assess.**

Gonzalez introduced House Resolution 204 in the United States House of Representatives on February 19, 1975, which called for a select committee of seven members of the House to study the assassinations of President Kennedy, Senator Robert Kennedy, Dr. King, and the attempted killing of Governor Wallace. The process of ultimately passing a resolution calls for the collection of sosponsors (other Congress persons who indicate their support of the bill). When a resolution goes through the Rules Committee, the greater the number of cosponsors, the greater may be the chance of the resolution being reported out of the Rules Committee to the floor of the House. The bill is then read, some debate may ensue, and a vote then takes place. Of course, before the vote, the work of vote gathering has already been done.

At first, Gonzalez's proposal was met with little enthusiasm. Representatives Stuart McKinney, Republican of Connecticut, and Henry Reuss, Democrat of Wisconsin, were among the 64 cosponsors who submitted letters to the Rules Committee in support of H.R. 204, but the majority of the Rules Committee was opposed to it.

Representative Thomas Downing, Democrat of Virginia, however, became interested enough to introduce H.R. 498 in May 1975 which proposed a select committee "That would study and investigate the circumstances surrounding the death of the President." In a "Dear Colleague" letter, a common form of correspondence between members of the House, Representative Downing asked that those "interested in knowing the truth" list themselves as cosponsors.

Downing also said, in the same letter, "It has surprised many of you, I know, that I have taken this interest. Let me assure you that this is not an emotional concern with me. I have seen sufficient evidence to indicate that the Warren Commission left unanswered a number of questions which I feel bear directly on the assassination."

Downing's interest was a surprise to many of his colleagues because, in his almost two decades on the Hill, he had generally expressed conservative viewpoints, and had stuck usually to the maintenance of his own Congressional First District in Virginia.

But this was to be Downing's last term on the Hill; he had announced his retirement and his desire to spend more time with his family. This foray into a subject of national interest was to be his swan song.

There were, then, two resolutions before Congress, and while some Congressmen supported both, there was a clear division between Gonzalez's and Downing's. Although Downing's resolution seemed to be gaining in the number of sponsors over Gonzalez, there were members of the House who felt that Downing's resolution would not pass without the support of the black members of the House, and the black members would also be in favor of investigating Dr. King's murder.

At the behest of Mr. Downing, I presented before members of the House and their aides many unanswered questions along with available evidence. The CCI conducted public seminars and conferences during the summers so that informed citizens could better persuade their Representatives on this subject.

Representative Bella Abzug, Democrat of New York, Chairperson of the Government Information and Individual Rights Subcommittee, in an Oversight Hearing of the National Archives and Records Service connected with Freedom of Information Requests and Declassification, contributed toward the hopes of passage of Resolutions 204 or 498. Her committee, in an open hearing on November 11, 1975, questioned Dr. James Rhoads, Archivist of the United States and Acting Chairman of the Interagency Classification Review Committee. The Committee was able to determine that the "Warren Commission was *never specifically given the power* by the President under the Executive Order to originally classify its transcripts and memos. In effect, then, hundreds of Warren Commission documents were withheld from the public for years when there was no sound, legal basis for it."

Representative Don Edwards, Democrat of California, Chairman of the Sub-Committee on the Civil and Constitutional Rights of the Judiciary, and a former FBI agent, conducted hearings on the FBI's involvement in the destruction of a note delivered by Lee Harvey Oswald to the Dallas FBI office shortly before the Kennedy assassination. The hearings established that an FBI official ordered Special Agent James Hosty, an FBI agent, to destroy the letter and that Hosty was then ordered by an assistant director of the FBI not to disclose that episode to the Warren Commission.

The CCI participated in the efforts of this committee, including the preparation of questions to witnesses. My association with Don Edwards dated back to the confirmation hearings, before the Senate and the House, for the designation of Gerald R. Ford to be Vice-President of the United States. During Ford's examination before the Senate Rules Committee he was asked whether he had used any classified material in the writing of his book, *Portrait of the Assassin.* Ford had responded, under oath, that all of his sources were those freely available to the public and unclassified. Before Ford went before the House Committee on the Judiciary for examination, Don Edwards called me in St. Paul, Minnesota, where I was trying the Wounded Knee case, and asked me if Ford's assertion was true. I replied that it was not, and at Edward's request flew to Washington, went to the National Archives and requested the material on which Ford had based his first chapter, "The Commission Gets Its First Shock." The Archivist, Marion Johnson, reported to me that the material, a transcript of a meeting of the Commission, was and always had been classified *Top Secret* and not available to the public. I gave this information to Don

Edwards, who then questioned Ford at the House confirmation hearing. Ford stated that he had made an "inadvertent error" in using the classified material for his book, for which he had received an advance of $10,000. Edwards then commented that Mr. Ford's unauthorized disclosure of the information was against the law and is covered by the "same statutes used to prosecute Dr. Ellsberg for allegedly releasing the Pentagon Papers." Edwards asked Ford to comment on his "apparent violation of the law or on the truthfulness of your testimony to the Senate?"

Senator Richard Schweiker, Republican of Pennsylvania, took a leading role in the discoveries of the Senate Committee on Intelligence Activities, chaired by Senator Frank Church, Democrat of Idaho, when it held hearings on illegal activities of the intelligence agencies in April 1976. The fifth and final report of the Select Committee particularly dealt with the performance of the intelligence agencies regarding the investigation of the assassination of President Kennedy.

Senator Schweiker became vitally interested in the subject and explored it fervently on his own; he gained access to the most restricted materials in the Archives, and became one of the most knowledgeable members of Congress on the assassination. CCI staff members conferred with the Senator while he gathered his information.

The Committee's final report stated that it had

developed evidence which impeaches the process by which the intelligence agencies arrived at their own conclusions about the assassination, and by which they provided information to the Warren Commission. This evidence indicates that the investigation of the assassination was deficient and that facts which might have substantially affected the course of the investigation were not provided the Warren Commission or those individuals within the FBI and the CIA, as well as other agencies of the Government, who were charged with investigating the assassination.

Once the Select Committee released its final report, however, its activities were concluded. Since that time the Senate has publicly indicated no desire to explore the matter any further.

In the months following the formation of the CCI, I briefed scores of members of Congress, hundreds of congressional aides, including legislative assistants and administrative assistants, and I lectured at almost 200 colleges, law schools, and universities. Almost 150 autonomous chapters of the CCI had helped to generate hundreds of thousands of letters, telegrams, and signatures on petitions to members of Congress. One hundred and thirty-seven members of Congress had sponsored either the Gonzalez resolution, the Downing resolution, or both. In March 1976, the resolutions were presented to the Rules Committee. The committee refused to refer the matter to the floor and the issue seemed inert for the 94th Congress.

We considered plans to begin again with the 95th Congress which would convene in January 1977.

Abby Mann had for sometime sought to write a screen play about the life of Dr. King. NBC television commissioned the work and Abby asked me to join him in Memphis to assist him in gathering some information about Dr. King's death.

Les Payne, a black newspaper reporter for *Newsday*, had written some unheralded stories about events in Memphis that had preceded the murder there. Donald Freed, the West Coast chairman of the CCI, had introduced me to Payne and I was impressed with his knowledge of the case and with his obviously determined and incisive reporting. Freed arranged for Payne and Mann to talk by telephone. Since Payne had written about Ed Redditt's removal from the scene his information was, I thought, of great importance. I agreed to meet Abby Mann in Memphis and to seek confirmation for Payne's observations.

I arrived at the Holiday Inn Rivermont two hours before Abby did. When he called my room from the lobby I told him to join us at once—for my long series of interviews with Ed Redditt had already begun. I introduced Abby to Ed Redditt and our investigation was underway. All that Payne had written was established again, confirmed in tape recorded interviews by the witnesses he had talked to, and corroborated by many additional witnesses he had not.

Together, in three days in Memphis, Abby and I interviewed Floyd Newsum and N. E. Wallace, the two firemen who had been so precipitously transferred from Fire Station Two; Frank Holloman, the former FBI official and former director of the Memphis Fire and Police Departments; Richard Ryan, a former lawyer for Ray; various officials of the fire and police departments; newspaper reporters; Reverend Samuel "Billy" Kyles, who was to have been Dr. King's host at a dinner at his home on April 4th; and others.

We left Memphis with a growing feeling that little of the truth about Dr. King's murder had ever been published. Together we called upon Coretta King following a Sunday service at the Ebenezer Baptist Church in Atlanta at which Daddy King, Martin's father and minister emeritus, delivered a moving sermon. In a small vestry room we shared the results of our incipient inquiry with Mrs. King. We talked about the need for an in-depth investigation by a Congressional committee armed with the power to subpoena witnesses and to examine all relevant documents and other physical evidence. Abby's commitment to a film about Dr. King's life and death took him to the cities and towns that Dr. King had visited and transformed—from Montgomery, Alabama, to Chicago, Illinois. My commitment to the facts about Dr. King's death took me within a few miles of the Canadian border to Constable, N.Y., where, with April Ferguson, the associate director of the CCI, we learned from Arthur Murtagh about the destroy-King squad maintained by the FBI in Atlanta.

In August 1976, I called upon three black members of Congress: Andrew Young of Georgia, now the United States Ambassador to the United Nations; Yvonne Burke of California, at that time the chairperson of the Black Congressional Caucus; and Walter Fauntroy, the delegate to Congress from Washington, D.C. I told them what we had learned in Memphis. I played a tape recording of the interview with Murtagh. I saw their growing anger transform itself into a desire for action. It was agreed that at the meeting of the Caucus that day a demand would be made for an investigation. The Caucus endorsed the demand unanimously and chose Fauntroy as its leader in the effort to create a Congressional inquiry.

As the presidential campaign was approaching its climax, a meeting was arranged with Coretta King, the leaders of the Caucus and the leaders of the Congress, Carl Albert, the Speaker, and Thomas P. (Tip) O'Neill, the heir apparent to that position in the 95th Congress. The leadership acceded to the requests, firmly put by the others present. At one point it had been suggested that "since we are in the closing days of the 94th Congress and there is so little time to act before the Congress expires why don't we wait for a few months until January?" Mrs. King, speaking, I am told, gently but without hesitation replied, "We have already waited more than eight years too long."

The leadership informed the Rules Committee that the resolution should be reported out. While CCI chapters helped to develop a mass campaign of support through meetings, radio and television programs, and a telephone network, Walter Fauntroy brilliantly maneuvered the newly-drafted resolution through the intricacies of the Congressional procedure. The new resolution, sponsored by Fauntroy, Gonzalez, and Downing, called for the establishment of a Select Committee on Assassinations to examine all of the facts surrounding the murders of President Kennedy and Dr. King.

The resolution cleared the Rules Committee on September 15, 1976, and reached the floor of Congress two days later. The people, some in the

Congress, others at colleges, union halls, churches, and in the streets had done their work well. The resolution passed by a vote of 280-65. A Select Committee had been formed, and within days, funded. Richard A. Sprague was chosen to be its general counsel and staff director. The investigation was underway.

Sprague brought with him the credentials of a long-time successful prosecutor, a real-life Philadelphia lawyer whose relentless investigative techniques and determination led to the classic investigation and presentation to a jury of a conspiracy to murder the Yablonski family in Pennsylvania. His work up to that time had won him the almost unanimous accolades of the news media. Sprague had served as an assistant to Arlen Specter, the Philadelphia District Attorney. Specter had played an important role as a Warren Commission lawyer; he had helped to design the implausible single bullet theory which provided the basis for the Commission's implausible conclusion.

Before the Committee's mandate had expired with the closing days of the 94th Congress the attacks upon the Committee and upon Sprague began.

Ben Franklin of the Washington bureau of *The New York Times*, who had written admiringly of Sprague, was taken off the assignment to cover the Committee. David Burnham, who had dealt with corruption or alleged corruption in Philadelphia politics, was given the assignment instead.

With Burnham leading the attack, and George Lardner, Jr., of the *Washington Post* and Jeremiah O'Leary of the *Washington Star* aiding and abetting his stories, what appeared to be a campaign against the Committee and its counsel was well underway. This trio ignored the work of the Committee to publish and then comment upon stories about Richard Sprague, some of them ten and fifteen years old, that Burnham had resurrected from the ancient clippings in the morgues of Philadelphia newspapers.

Among the stories that they did not cover as the events transpired was the action of the Memphis authorities after the announcement that a committee of Congress would investigate the assassination. The mayor ordered the police to burn all of the files—180 boxes of them—that comprised the entire history of the domestic intelligence division of the Memphis police. Why was Redditt pulled off his assignment? On September 10, 1976, the answer to that and a hundred other questions may have gone up in smoke. Why had the police protection been reduced? Were FBI agents surveilling Dr. King on the evening of April 4th? Why had the black firemen been transferred? Despite the best efforts of the

266

American Civil Liberties Union to prevent the official destruction of the files, the court order that they secured was served one hour too late; the records were gone. The facts could very likely be established only through a painful and careful reconstruction of the events.

Yet in January of 1977 the re-establishment of the Congressional committee with the authority to undertake such a project suddenly was in doubt with the new Congress. A *New York Times* editorial denouncing Sprague and questioning the wisdom of re-establishing the Committee was another blow to the hopes of the American people that at long last the facts might be uncovered and revealed. The stories of three newsmen had been effective. Why have *The New York Times*, the *Washington Post*, the *Washington Star*, and other major newspapers failed to meet and interview the relevant witnesses referred to earlier in these pages? Why have these publications instead focused upon the presumed errors of the Congressional investigators and published recurrent attacks, some of them containing dubious charges, against the committee's staff?

One of the black members of the Select Committee—Congressman Harold E. Ford of Memphis—charged that the FBI had hired former agents to lobby against the continuation of the investigation.

The stories, and the actions of the intelligence agencies, seriously eroded support for the investigation. In February 1977, the Rules Committee reported a compromise resolution to the floor. It placed the Select Committee on probation for two months; required that the committee adopt a modest budget; and stated that during the first week of April 1977, the Congress might decide to reestablish the Committee or perhaps forever end any hope of such an inquiry.

During the evening of February 1, 1977, on the eve of the vote, I spoke at Morse Auditorium at Boston University. Hours before I had telephoned Dick Gregory whom I had located in a dentist's chair in Boston where he was about to undergo dental surgery. I told him that I thought we should engage in an all night vigil in support of the resolution that night. He suggested the house in Brookline, Massachusetts, where John F. Kennedy was born. At the conclusion of my remarks at Boston University, I announced that Greg and I were going to walk to the house where John Kennedy was born and stand there in a silent vigil until the dawn brought in a new day with the hope that we might soon learn about his death. Two hundred people, students, professors, and others walked with us for the better part of an hour through that frigid winter night. When we arrived, it was nineteen degrees below freezing. Various reporters dropped in through the night. One person delivered a message that Steve Krause of the Boston office of the UPI wanted me to call him. I did so. I told him we were maintaining a silent prayerful vigil. He seemed receptive and almost supportive.

The next afternoon I arrived in Washington just in time to witness the debate on the resolution on the floor. The closing remarks were made by Representative Robert E. Bauman of Maryland.

He said that the *Washington Post* called the Select Committee "perhaps the worst example of Congressional unquiry run amok." Bauman then made a charge that caused considerable concern on the floor. He said:

> **I am well aware that this matter arouses certain passions. Last night the Speaker was subject to a public demonstration in Massachusetts warning that "They are watching Tip O'Neill, what you do in this matter," a statement from Mark Lane who has been a champion of such an investigation.**

When I inquired later that day, I discovered that Bauman based his allegation against me upon a UPI story. During the vigil I had not mentioned Tip O'Neill; I had not led a demonstration against him, or stated, or implied that we were watching him.

I secured a copy of the UPI story that had misled Bauman. It carried a Nicholas Daniloff by-line and read:

> **The night before the House debate, comedian and activist Dick Gregory and author Mark Lane led a group of about 200 people in an all-night vigil outside John F. Kennedy's birthplace in Brookline, Mass.**
>
> **"This vigil is to let Tip O'Neill know we're watching him," said Richard Feldman, a spokesman for the group.**

On February 4th, I wrote to Congressman Bauman and acquainted him with the facts. On February 7th he asked for and received unanimous consent from the House to correct the permanent record. On that occasion he admitted his error and apologized for any inconvenience to me that he may have caused. I wondered who Richard Feldman was. Clearly he was not a "spokesman" for the "group" since there was no formal group. I called Daniloff and asked him who Feldman was. He answered, "Feldman, you got me; who is he?" I referred him to the UPI story that carried his by-line. He read it and said, "I'll be damned. I did write the story but I never quoted Feldman, whoever he is, and I never put those words in there." I asked him who did quote Feldman and he said, "The only person who could have changed my story, and I can't imagine why she should, would be the overnight editor, Elizabeth Wharton." I called her and apprised her of the facts. She said, "That Feldman quote was not in there in Daniloff's story. He's right, he did not put it in there. And neither did I. This is the first I've heard of that quote and I saw the story when Daniloff wrote it. I did not change it and so far as I know it went out without any quote from Feldman. This is strange. This is very strange. All I can say, Mr. Lane, is that it could not have happened, but it did." It did. A phantom quote from a mystery person emerged in a UPI story from the Washington bureau in a fashion that remains an enigma to the Washington bureau of UPI and found its way onto the floor of Congress as a weapon against the investigation. The compromise resolution passed by the narrow margin of 237 to 165. The Committee was given a two month reprieve.

Nine years have passed since the death of Dr. King. The American people have not been given the details about the pathological hatred that Hoover's FBI betrayed toward Dr. King. Neither have we been told why the black witnesses were officially stripped from the scene the night before the murder nor why the police officer in charge was removed on an implausible pretext just before the fatal shot was fired. The witness and security stripping was directed by a former high-ranking FBI official. Mystery surrounds the failure of the FBI to seek James Earl Ray until April 19th, fifteen days after the murder in spite of the presence of the fingerprints on the presumed murder rifle.

The bullet taken from Dr. King's body was examined by an FBI agent whose conclusions raise more questions than they answer. The bullet has not yet been adequately tested. It may not have been fired from Ray's rifle.

Ray's claim that he was induced into entering a guilty plea is supported by much of the known evidence. His claim that a man named Raoul moved him about has never been tested by a comprehensive investigation and remains a viable theory.

The cover-up of facts surrounding the murder, including the publication of news stories, false information leads to authors of books and magazine articles, and direct lobbying against a Congressional investigation by intelligence and spy organizations requires that we ask what it is that is so feared by so few. And ask as well how powerful the few must be to influence and control so much.

The present available and known evidence leads inexorably to the conclusion, I believe, that persons employed by the Federal Bureau of Investigation in 1968 must be considered to be prime suspects in the murder of Dr. Martin Luther King, Jr. Even should the facts ultimately acquit those persons, to permit the FBI, under these circumstances, to conduct the only authorized investigation into the murder is, I believe, to profane our concept of justice and to betray our pretensions of decency. Indeed, an investigation conducted by the Department of Justice which relied upon the original FBI investigation would enjoy limited credibility.

Let the Congress act.

Let the truth be known.

POSTSCRIPT

POSTSCRIPT
by Mark Lane

"Just this morning, Mr. Speaker, one of the major wire services reported that the Justice Department after months of investigation had concluded that James Earl Ray acted alone in assassinating Martin Luther King, Jr." So spoke Representative James Quillen in leading off the debate in opposition to the resolution to establish a Select Committee to investigate the assassinations of President Kennedy and Dr. King.

Quillen was quickly challenged by Yvonne Burke, a member of Congress from California and formerly the Chairwoman of the Congressional Black Caucus.

> I have been trying to see that report. I have been advised that the material in that report is too sensitive. As a member of the Committee on Appropriations and a member of the Subcommittee on State, Justice, Commerce and the Judiciary, the committee that has jurisdiction over the Attorney General's office and the Justice Department, I find it very irregular that I have not been able to see that report.
>
> I also find it irregular that the Justice Department had 12 to 15 deputies originally assigned to this investigation, that those deputies came back with a report to Assistant Attorney General Pottinger concluding that there should be an independent investigation, but that as a result there was another person appointed, Michael Shaheen, and that person has now come up with a report that was on the former Attorney General's desk at least 2 weeks ago, although the Attorney General has been gone for some weeks. This morning, the report was leaked.
>
> The Justice Department told me this morning that they know nothing about the leak.

The alleged conclusion of the report prepared under the direction of a former Attorney General, Edward Levi, had been leaked to a news service, after a new Attorney General had taken office and on the very day that the Congress was to consider the matter. Members of Congress were unable to secure the report. The shadow of a previous administration had been conjured up to blur the distinctions between the present and past and between the executive and legislative branches of government.

The report, entitled *Report of the Department of Justice Task Force to Review the FBI Martin Luther King, Jr., Security and Assassination Investigation*, dated January 11, 1977, and leaked on February 2, 1977 (it was thereafter officially released on February 19, 1977, by the new Attorney General, Griffin Bell), was intended to be the final solution to the doubts that had been raised regarding the murder of Dr. King. Instead, it raised more questions than it could answer.

The mission of the task force, said the Department of Justice in its report, was to respond to the "widespread speculation on the possibility that the Bureau [FBI] may have had some responsibility in Dr. King's death and may not have done an impartial and thorough investigation of the assassination."

On November 24, 1975, Attorney General Levi directed Stanley Pottinger, the Assistant Attorney General in charge of the Civil Rights Division at Justice, to undertake a review of the files of the Department of Justice and the FBI to determine whether the investigation into the assassination of Dr. King should be reopened.

On April 9, 1976, Pottinger submitted a memorandum to Levi which embodied the results of his three-person study.

During May 1976, after Pottinger's work was completed, I became aware of the strange circumstances regarding the removal of Redditt two hours before Dr. King was killed and the transfer of Newsum and Wallace the night before. Don Freed, Les Payne, and I discussed the matter in New York City. Later Freed and I explored the matter with Abby Mann in Los Angeles. On June 13, 1976, Pottinger met with Mann in Los Angeles. The meeting had been arranged through a Los Angeles woman lawyer. At that meeting Mann expressed doubts about the official reconciliation of the facts by the FBI and the Department of Justice, citing as troubling examples of unexplained occurrences the transfer of the black firemen and the removal of the black police officer.

However, the report by the Department of Justice reveals that the question of Redditt's untimely removal and the Newsum and Wallace transfers was not even considered by the Department of Justice until July 1976, after Mann had raised the matters with Pottinger. More than eight years had passed since the assassination of Dr. King and the Department of Justice had not even contemplated the substantial questions raised by the witness and security stripping. Levi, then aware that the mysterious removal of the officer and firemen might be illuminated in Mann's NBC-TV screenplay and in this book, evidently began to prepare a defense against the facts.

The Department of Justice panel was established to continue the investigation, and Pottinger's assistant, Michael Shaheen, served as its investigator. Shaheen's work was incorporated into the final report issued by the Department of Justice.

The serious questions contemplated by the Justice Department inquiry were:

1. Why were only two police officers assigned to Dr. King on the evening of April 4, 1968?

2. Why was one of those officers, Redditt, removed so precipitously two hours before the murder?

3. Why were the only two black firemen removed from the scene of the murder the night before it occurred?

4. If Raoul did not provide Ray with funds as Ray claimed, where did Ray secure the many thousands of dollars that he expended from the time he escaped from the Missouri Penitentiary until his arrest in London?

Before the inquiry began it was necessary to determine who was to conduct it. A memorandum from Levi was published in the Justice Department's report on the King assassination. It referred to the earlier efforts made by Pottinger and reads, in part, as follows:

The review is not complete. Mr. Pottinger and all those who have commented upon his memorandum recommend that the review be completed. Mr. Pottinger also has made other recommendations upon which there is some difference of opinion. In my view, it is essential that the review be completed as soon as possible and in as thorough a manner as is required to answer the basic questions. In view of what has already been done, and the tentative conclusions reached, special emphasis should be given to the fourth question. In conducting this review you should call upon the Department to furnish to you the staff you need.

Levi had decided that the "thorough" investigation was to be conducted by his Department of Justice. Levi's delicate language regarding Pottinger's "recommendations" and the "difference of opinion" that existed tended to obfuscate the central question that Pottinger had raised.

On March 25, 1976, as Pottinger's survey of the records was nearing completion, he said that he would recommend that Levi appoint a committee made up of people outside the FBI, outside the Department of Justice, and *outside the government* to investigate the assassination of Dr. King. Pottinger said that new doubts and suspicions about possible FBI involvement in the murder required an independent inquiry. He said that for "reasons of credibility" the investigation should be conducted by persons independent of the Justice Department which has control over the FBI. Pottinger urged that the new committee look into such questions as whether there was any FBI complicity in the murder and whether the FBI violated any law in its harassment of Dr. King.

These were the "recommendations" that Pottinger had made. The "difference of opinion" that Levi referred to was his own categorical rejection of the Pottinger suggestion that anyone outside his department be entrusted to examine the evidence.

The Department of Justice embarked upon its secret investigation by establishing two categories of evidence for the Department of Justice report. Appendix A contained irrelevant or easily obtainable and previously published data for the most part, including the titles of several books about the assassination, maps of Memphis, a floor plan of the second floor of the rooming house, and various FBI memoranda. It purportedly consisted of eighteen exhibits. However exhibits 12, 17, and 18 were designated as "classified" and were not published.

The documents referred to in the Department of Justice report which seemed to bear some relationship to the case were all placed in Appendix B. All of the documents in Appendix B were classified and none can be examined by the public. Appendix B became a *Catch-22* kind of depository for all governmental doubtful propositions, for the evidentiary basis for all FBI speculations, and for all Justice Department theories.

Its *modus operandi* determined, the Levi task force began its work.

Why were only two police officers, Redditt and Richmond, assigned to Dr. King on the afternoon of April 4, 1968? In fact, did FBI agents witness the murder? The shameful record of FBI harassment of Dr. King established that he was subjected to electronic surveillance through telephone wiretaps and planted microphones in cities that he visited all over America, including Los Angeles, Washington D.C., and New York. He was followed and spied upon in cities throughout the country by an army of FBI agents. Does it seem likely that Dr. King was not subjected to any FBI surveillance at the time of his death and during the hours preceding his death? The report said only that the FBI "unequivocally assured the task force that there was no electronic surveillance of Dr. King in Memphis. It was explained [by the FBI] that Memphis was not in the mainstream of Dr. King's SCLC activities." The Justice Department task force relied entirely upon the suspect agency to resolve this important question. FBI records were apparently not examined. The FBI interview relied upon by the report was placed in Appendix B and is not available for examination. The explanation offered by the Bureau appears to be of little value since Dr. King's activities were subjected to continual electronic surveillance in many cities which were not in the mainstream of SCLC activities. In addition Dr. King's continuing commitment to the struggle of the sanitation workers, along with the efforts of his aides, Reverend Abernathy, Andy Young, Bernard Lee, and others, demonstrated yet again that Memphis was very much in the mainstream of SCLC activities. The report stated that "FBI agents did observe the sanitation workers' strike activities for intelligence purposes." Yet, nowhere in the report does the Department of Justice disclose if any of those agents observed Dr. King during the hours before his death or at the time of his death. The interviews relied upon by the report to establish the FBI position on this question were placed in Appendix B and cannot be seen.

Inspector G. P. Tines of the Memphis Police Department (MPD) told the task force that six or seven officers were assigned to place Dr. King under surveillance and to provide security for him on April 3rd. The report of Tines was made part of Appendix B and is unavailable. According to the report, the security detail of four or five men operated in the area of the Lorraine Motel "until they were ordered to headquarters by Chief J. C. Macdonald at approximately 5:05 P.M." on April 3, 1968. According to the report, Tine said "he was not conferred with and has no idea why the security detail was removed from Dr. King after 5:05 P.M." While the report asserted that Macdonald had ordered the security detail to leave the area of the Lorraine Motel, also according to the report, "Former Chief Macdonald has no present recollection of the security detail." The interview with Macdonald was made part of Appendix B and cannot be seen. The report stated that "the security detail was not resumed on April 4, 1968." It relied for that conclusion upon the secret reports of two MPD Inspectors which were incorporated in a document in appendix B.

On April 4, 1968, according to the report, Detective Ed Redditt and Patrolman W. B. Richmond were the only MPD officers in the vicinity of the Lorraine Motel. The Justice Department's investigation failed to determine if FBI agents were present at the time. It failed to investigate the possibility of FBI electronic surveillance at the time. The Justice Department was unable to discover why Redditt and Richmond were the only two police officers assigned to Dr. King on the evening of April 4, 1968. All of the evidence that the task force of the Justice Department examined regarding this aspect of the investigation was placed in Appendix B. None of it can be seen.

The second question considered by the Justice Department concerned the removal of Redditt from the scene two hours before the murder. The report stated:

> **At approximately 4:00 P.M., Redditt was ordered by telephone to leave the fire station and report to headquarters where he was advised that threats had been made on his life. He was, therefore, ordered to move his family into a motel under an assumed name by Frank Holloman, former Director of Police and Fire, Memphis, Tenn.**

Redditt stated that he was not called to headquarters as the result of a telephone call but that Lt. Arkin arrived on the scene and drove with him to headquarters. The source for the version published in the report is an interview with Frank Holloman. That interview remains secret and assigned to Appendix B. According to the report:

> **Redditt was taken home in a squad car, but refused to move his family because of a sick relative. At about the time the squad car arrived in front of Redditt's residence, it was announced on the radio that Dr. King had been shot. After a couple of days, Redditt did not hear any more about the threat on his life.**

An interview with Redditt was given as the source for that data. That interview also remains secret as part of Appendix B.

The matter was properly posed. The question before the task force was evident. Why was Redditt removed? The task force could not discover the answer. A secret report by Inspector Tines, filed in Appendix B, was given as the source for the story that a man named Philip R. Manuel, an investigator with Senator McClellan's investigating committee, had told the MPD that an informant in Mississippi said that the Mississippi Freedom Democratic Party (a liberal, nonviolent, interracial political movement within the Democratic Party) had made plans to kill a "Negro lieutenant" in Memphis and then later called to say that the "Negro lieutenant" was in Knoxville, not Memphis. This slender reed provided the only information the Justice Department could secure to form the basis for its conclusion regarding Redditt's removal. However, according to the report, "Philip R. Manuel neither has a present recollection of providing the information regarding the threat to the MPD, nor does he have a memorandum of the event."

The Manuel interview is, of course, secret and is, of course, in Appendix B. The reader may recall that Redditt told me, and very likely told the Justice Department as well, that he was introduced to the Secret Service agent by Holloman at MPD headquarters and that other law enforcement officials were present as well. Redditt's recollections appear to preclude the possibility that Manuel was the source of the information. Together with Manuel's own lack of independent support for the story, it appears to fall. The story attributed to Manuel regarding an unnamed "Negro lieutenant" in Memphis should not have led the Memphis police to Redditt in any event. Redditt was not a lieutenant. He was a detective with a rank of warrant officer. Following the publication of the Department of Justice's report I called Manuel and asked him if he had ever met Redditt. Manuel refused to discuss the matter with me, stating only, "I have made complete statements to the Department of Justice and the House Select Committee on Assassinations." Since the Department of Justice's statements are unavailable, stored in Appendix B, I visited Richard Sprague, the General Counsel and staff director to the House Select Committee on Assassinations. He said, "Manuel's statement was that he refused to talk to us unless we served him with a subpoena. We don't have that power now, so we have no statement from him." On March 1, 1977, I called Ed Redditt. He described for me the Secret Service agent he had seen on April 4, 1968, at Police Headquarters. Redditt said, "He was approximately 5 feet 11 inches tall; weighed about 200 pounds; light complexion; hair that was not dark, probably light brown." Later that evening I secured the description of Philip Manuel from an associate of his. He was described as being "approximately 5 feet 6 inches tall; 160 pounds in weight; an olive complexion and black hair." The Department of Justice's speculation that Manuel was the source for the story that led to Redditt's removal had apparently been refuted by the evidence. I wondered if the Department of Justice's investigators had confronted Redditt with Manuel or if they had even secured Redditt's description of the Secret Service agent from him. On March 3, 1977, I called Redditt and asked him about the Department of Justice's interview with him. He said, "They never asked me to describe the Secret Service agent who supposedly brought the death threat from Washington. They never showed me a picture of Manuel. They never told me that they had located a man who they thought had conveyed the threat." The Department of Justice had failed to conduct the most elementary investigation to determine if Manuel could have been the person who conveyed the threat to the Memphis authorities. The Department of Justice had failed to ask Redditt if he could identify Manuel. The Department of Justice had failed to send Redditt a copy of its report; I read relevant portions to him. When Redditt learned that Manuel had called the Memphis Police Department on April 5, 1958, "and advised them that a threat was on the life of a 'Negro lieutenant' in Knoxville, rather than Memphis" he was amused. He observed, "Yet headquarters did not release me from my 'house arrest' at that time—on April 5. They kept me there after that, still saying that I was the subject of a death threat. Manuel's story is a hoax, they evidently just won't tell the truth about why I was removed just before Dr. King was murdered." The report does not allege that Manuel called the Knoxville Police Department to inform them of the newly located threat or that the Memphis Police released Redditt from his protective custody status just after or as a result of the telephone call by Manuel to the Memphis Police Department in which he allegedly corrected his previous error.

Why were the only two black firemen assigned to Fire Station Two, which was located near the Lorraine Motel, removed from the scene of the murder the night before it occurred? Here again the investigation by the Department of Justice confirmed all of the findings of our investigation. The report reads:

As of April 3, 1968, Norvell E. Wallace and Floyd E. Newsum were the only black firemen assigned to Fire Station No. 2 of the Memphis Fire Department (MFD). Wallace was working the night shift on April 3rd and Newsum was scheduled to report for the day shift on April 4th. Both of these individuals actively supported the sanitation workers' strike, attending their rallies and making financial contributions.

In our interview of Wallace (Interview July 8, 1976, App. B.) he stated that at about 10:00 or 10:30 on the night of April 3rd his captain told him that a call had come in requesting that a man be detailed to Fire Station No. 33. He was immediately detailed to No. 33 although it was raining and he was preparing to go to bed. Wallace further stated that while Fire Station No. 33 was understaffed as a whole, there was no shortage of personnel for the pump truck on which he worked. Otherwise, he does not know why he was detailed.

Also, on the night of April 3rd Fireman Newsum, in a wholly personal capacity, attended a rally at the Mason Temple where

Dr. King made his last speech. When he returned home (about 10:30 P.M.) there was a message for him to call Lt. J. Smith at the fire department. When he called, Lt. J. Smith ordered him to report to Fire Station No. 31 on the morning of April 4th rather than Fire Station No. 2. Newsum claims that Fire Station No. 31 was overstrength at the time and his detail made his company short. Moreover, he says he never has received a satisfactory explanation why he was detailed. However, he did say that Lt. Barnett at one time told him he was detailed at the request of the police. (Interview of Floyd E. Newsum, July 8, 1976, App. B.)

Again the facts had posed the question. The Department of Justice could only report:

Interviews of past and present members of the MFD have failed to disclose the individual who initiated the order or the reason for detailing Wallace and Newsum.

The interviews of the past and present officers of the fire department are all secret. All have been made part of Appendix B. The investigation was able to establish that Wallace's Company at Fire Station Two "was operating at minimum strength after he was detailed; whereas Company No. 33 to which he was detailed operated at one over the minimum strength after the detail." Similarly, the records revealed that "Newsum's Company No. 55 at Fire Station 2 was operating at minimum strength after the detail but Company 31 to which he was detailed operated at one over minimum strength after the detail." The Department of Justice, failing to discover who initiated the order to remove Newsum and Wallace and failing to discover the reason for the order, was nevertheless willing to speculate:

Our investigation has not disclosed any evidence that the detail of Wallace and Newsum was in any way connected with the assassination of Dr. King.

The conclusion may be accurate since the investigation apparently uncovered no evidence regarding the cause for the transfer.

The report of the Department of Justice rejected out of hand Ray's claim that he had been financed by Raoul. The report concludeded;

Indeed, the overwhelming evidence indicates that Ray was almost totally alone during the year after his escape from the Missouri State Prison.

The evidence which impressed the Justice Department lawyers as being "overwhelming" was not shared with the readers of the Report. It too was placed in Appendix B.

If Raoul did not provide Ray with funds, who did?

The facts disclosed that Ray had traveled extensively after he escaped from the Missouri Penitentiary. The Department of Justice conceded that "in addition to normal living expenses, Ray made several substantial purchases, e.g., cars, photo equipment, dance lessons."

The report stated that:

These expenditures suggested that he had financial assistance and hence possible co-conspirators. Therefore, the Bureau was particularly interested in determining his sources of income.

Hoover went to extreme lengths in an effort to determine if Ray had been involved in any robberies or burglaries anywhere within the United States.

The report disclosed that,

On April 23, 1968, the Director advised all field divisions to consider Ray as a suspect in any unsolved bank robberies, burglaries or armed robberies occurring after April 23, 1967. The results were negative.

Six days later Hoover enlisted the entire law enforcement apparatus in the United States, federal, state and local, in another such effort.

On April 29, 1968, the Director in a teletype to all SAC's ordered that all law enforcement agencies which maintained unidentified latent fingerprints be contacted and requested that fingerprints of Ray be compared in order to determine his past whereabouts and possibly establish his source of funds. Again, negative results were obtained. The Director, on May 14, 1968, reminded all field divisions that Ray had spent a considerable amount of money from April 23, 1967, until April 4, 1968, and advised that a source for these monies had not been determined. The Director ordered that photographs of Ray be displayed to appropriate witnesses in unsolved bank robberies and bank burglaries. These efforts and all others to date, with one exception, have proved fruitless. The Bureau investigated the possibility that Ray participated in a bank robbery at Alton, Illinois, in 1967, but it was established that he was not a participant.

Hoover then involved the Canadian and Mexican police in an effort to explain Ray's income.

Reports from the Royal Canadian Mounted Police indicated no known robberies or burglaries which could be connected with Ray.

Unable to secure any evidence that Ray robbed or burglarized a single establishment in spite of its unprecedented efforts to do so the FBI fell back upon a guess:

It is the Bureau's opinion that Ray most likely committed on a periodic basis several robberies or burglaries during this period in order to support himself.

The Department of Justice concluded its report regarding Ray's "Sources of Funds" more enigmatically.

It held, "The sources for Ray's funds still remain a mystery today."

Indeed, to the Department of Justice every relevant area regarding the murder of Dr. King still remains a mystery today. The report confirmed the accuracy of our investigation. It posed to the American people the questions that our investigation had posed to the Department of Justice. Yet it provided not a single relevant answer.

A substantial portion of the report was devoted to a section designated IIC and titled "The Story of James Earl Ray." The Department of Justice relied upon Huie's book, *He Slew the Dreamer*, for many of his findings about Ray. In just the opening eight pages of Section IIC, it cited that book more than twenty times as the source of information about Ray. The report relied upon Huie's description of Ray's relationship with a Canadian woman who Ray considered asking for assistance in securing a passport. When Ray discovered that she was a government employee, he decided not to ask for her help. Huie had written in *He Slew the Dreamer* that when he interviewed the Canadian woman she told him that Ray was a racist. According to Huie, Ray had said to her that those people who "know niggers hate them." I asked Ray about that remark when I saw him in prison. He said that he had never made such a remark and that he doubted the Canadian woman told Huie that he had. The Canadian woman was reluctant to discuss this matter. I spoke with her attorney. He said, "We were going to sue Huie for attributing remarks to her that she did not make, but since Huie never mentioned her name in the book or articles I didn't think we had a legal case. If he had mentioned her name we would have sued because he made statements that were not true." The Department of Justice should have examined Huie's record in this matter thoroughly before relying upon him as the source. Huie's confusion of fact and fiction appears to have predated his work in the Ray case. In 1960, Huie brought an action in the United States District Court for a preliminary injunction against the National Broadcasting Company, Inc. (NBC), on his copyright on a story entitled "The Hero of Iwo-Jima." NBC had commissioned a television program entitled "The American" which Huie claimed was based upon his work. The court denied Huie's motion since in his book he claimed that the story was true, but before the court he demonstrated that episodes previously offered as fact were actually "the product of his imagination." Historical facts are not subject to copyright laws; works of fiction are. The court said that Huie was estopped to say that his book was fiction after having claimed in that book that it was true.

When the new Attorney General, Griffin Bell, released a report on February 18, 1977, he expressed reservations about its conclusions that Ray acted alone. His doubts encouraged members of the Congress to move on with their investigation into Dr. King's death. On Sunday, February 27, 1977, the *Washington Star* published a lengthy and strong defense of the report and in conclusion contained an attack upon the new Attorney General as well. The story that appeared on the front page of the editorial section of the newspaper was written by George McMillan. We had come full circle. The Department of Justice and Huie had provided information for McMillan's book. McMillan's book and Huie's book had been used by the Department of Justice's report. George McMillan then praised the report saying he liked it even better than the Warren Commission Report. On a personal note, McMillan added to his endorsement of the report that the critics of the official version had ignored him. He wrote, "The task force report takes on what has been a key point in the argument that the King assassination was a conspiracy: it is the myth that Ray was only a two-bit punk who had no motive and therefore must have been paid to kill King.

"I confess to having tried to lay this myth to rest myself. I spent six years on a biography of Ray—*The Making of an Assassin*—only to have my book treated among assassination buffs as if it did not exist." I trust that this book will help to remedy the situation of which McMillan complained. While McMillan was quite certain that the report concluded that Ray was not paid to kill Dr. King, the report itself was not so unequivocal on that point. In discussing motive, the report said, "Yet, Ray's apparent hatred for the civil rights movement, his possible yearning for recognition, 'and a desire for a potential quick profit' may have, as a whole, provided sufficient impetus for him to act, and to act alone."

On the afternoon of March 3, 1977, I met at the Department of Justice in Washington, D.C. with four of the five members of the Task Force and Michael Shaheen, who had directed their work. I informed them of Redditt's description of the Secret Service agent whom he had seen in

Memphis on April 4, 1968, and asked if that matched Manuel's description. The Task Force member who had interviewed Manuel said that he had never seen Manuel. He explained that, instead, he had talked briefly with Manuel by telephone. Manuel's physical attributes were relevant as was Redditt's description of the Secret Service agent, yet the Task Force members said that they had not inquired about the Secret Service agent when talking to Redditt and neither seen Manuel nor inquired about his physical description.

The report reveals that Redditt was interviewed on July 8, 1976; Tines, who related the Manuel story, was interviewed the following week. However, the telephone call to Manuel was not made until the end of September 1976. The Task Force member who had called Manuel asked me, "Why should I have conducted a long interview with Manuel? What could I have asked him after he said to me that he didn't remember the incident, had no memorandum about it, but was willing to accept the Memphis Police Department's account of it?" I said, "You might have asked him if he remembered calling the Knoxville Police Department to alert them to the threat. You might have asked him if he ever recalled telling any police department during his life that there was a contract out on one of its officers and if he thought it likely that he could forget such a dramatic moment. You might have asked him if he met Redditt on April 4th in the police station. You might have asked him for his height, weight, and hair color so that you could check that information out against Redditt's description of the Secret Service agent."

At that point, the Task Force member interrupted to say, "We do not interrogate witnesses." Another Task Force member said, "You don't have to tell us what questions to ask."

One of the younger Task Force members asked me what more could be done to investigate the Manuel story. I suggested that the Knoxville Police Department should be called to see if a threat had been relayed to that office on April 5, 1968; that a thorough investigation of the incredible story that the threat originated with the Mississippi Freedom Democratic Party should be made; that the Memphis police officials, including Holloman, should be asked why Redditt was confined to his house for days after the Memphis Police Department had been informed, on April 5, that he was not the presumed target and why Redditt had never been told, until I called him in March 1977, that he had in fact not been the target for the alleged contract killing. I noticed that no one associated with the Task Force made any notes.

I asked the government lawyers if they had determined in their search of the FBI's secret files whether Redditt, Newsum, Wallace, or Richmond had ever been questioned by the FBI in the investigation. Shaheen said that the FBI had not questioned any of the four men and that the first time any of the four had been questioned by federal employees was in July 1976.

Carl T. Rowan, perhaps America's most influential black journalist, wrote, in the *New York Post* on February 19, 1977, "Very clearly the FBI is suspect." He added, "We may never know the truth—but we must search for it." Rowan underscored the necessity for an investigation independent of the FBI and those associated with it in the Department of Justice by disclosing a startling fact. He wrote, "While James Earl Ray was fleeing some FBI operatives were trying to sell me the spurious line that Russians had killed King because of some hitch in his relations with 'Soviet spies.'" Within four hours after Dr. King was murdered the FBI had taken possession of Ray's rifle and binoculars which bore his fingerprints. Yet subsequently FBI personnel were alleging that Russians had killed King.

The Department of Justice did not examine, in its report, the failure of the FBI to seek Ray from the outset, in spite of the fingerprints which led inexorably to him. The report did not explore or disclose the fact that the original circulars advertising his escape from the Missouri Penitentiary inexplicably bore not Ray's, but another man's, fingerprints. The report did not disclose or explore the false stories circulated by the FBI regarding the suggested culprits, from Hoover's talk of "a jealous husband," to his employees' allegations about Russian spies.

Attorney General Bell reacted to the report, which was prepared during a previous Administration, by stating that it did not adequately answer the apparent questions. He felt, he said, that the question of a conspiracy to murder Dr. King survived the report and remained a viable one.

Indeed the report raised more questions than it answered. Only a serious, sober, and thorough investigation conducted by persons not afraid of what the evidence might reveal will suffice. And that investigation, to be effective, must not husband away its evidence beyond the perception of the people in a bin marked Appendix B.

APPENDIX

THE FUNERAL
by Dick Gregory

Martin Luther King had said time and time again that he would probably die fighting for civil rights. He felt that he was a likely target for the same type of violence that struck John F. Kennedy and others who tried to pave the way for freedom for all people. He had talked to his close friends about dying. He had mentioned to his wife, Coretta, that he, just like President Kennedy, was despised by many who were against integration, and that in a sick nation, violence was common. Martin Luther King died just the way he said he might; by an assassin's bullet; the way millions of Americans had hoped he wouldn't. He died in a town where he might not have been except for the garbage collectors' strike which was affecting blacks in Memphis in a way that was soon to be recognized as one of the single most important accomplishments of the civil rights movement. Martin Luther King died alone. He was not a victim of a bombing or a fire affecting a group of people, but rather he was the center of attraction. Reverend Andrew Young had always predicted that if violence ever struck the inner circle of civil rights leaders, it would probably hit them all at once. He felt that the entire movement and its leadership would be wiped out at the same time. It surprised him that Dr. King died alone with his close friends standing watch.

For more than ten years now, King had been under the constant pressure that had built up during his entire career in the civil rights movement. It had not been easy for this man who had lived with threats for such a long time. Many of the threats had become a regular part of his life along with the hatred and the lies that he and his family had to contend with.

King was labeled a national security threat and J. Edgar Hoover called him "The most notorious liar in the world." The FBI subjected King to massive and complete surveillance, smear campaigns, and blackmail. They tapped his phones. The way the FBI used to operate in the South was like a black guy would call them and tell them that the Ku Klux Klan was threatening his family. Two agents would come out to his house, warm their hands on the cross burning on the front lawn, take the black guy's fingerprints, and then leave. The FBI is hung up on fingerprints. If they can't get any fingerprints they can't solve anything. If a cat could figure out a way to rob banks just by using his feet, the FBI would never catch him! Black folks in America rate the FBI like they do the swine flu shots . . . "Use it at your own risk."

A secret FBI document dated March 4, 1968, issued this revealing directive:

Prevent the rise of a messiah who could unify, and electrify, the militant black nationalist movement. [Malcolm X] might have been such a messiah; he is a martyr of the movement today. [King could] be a real contender for this position should he abandon his supposed obedience to white liberal doctrines.

Maybe this accounts for what many have called his premonition of death. It was on the night of the Kennedy assassination that Mrs. Edith Scott Bagley in Atlanta recalls a statement made by King. She says he returned to his home all shook up, upset, and going to pieces. "This is the way I'm going," he said. He seemed to have even prepared his loved ones for the fate that would eventually come his way. They, too, lived in constant fear, and the pressure was building in all of them. Dr. King's younger brother, Reverend A. D. King, had taken the pulpit on the day of the funeral and cried out, "America, your day of death is coming."

It was hot and muggy the day of the funeral. Women were dressed in black with hats and gloves. Their bodies would soon feel the overwhelming heat and humidity of the warmer-than-usual spring day in Atlanta. Men, dressed in their best suits, knew that they would soon feel the urge to loosen their ties in order to find a bit of comfort fron the heat. But the atmosphere on this day soon made everyone unaware of the heat, and very much aware of the large crowd that poured into the church and onto the streets. Martin Luther King was dead, and for the first time since before the announcement of his death, the public was looking at him as his body lay at rest in the church where he had preached so many times.

More than a hundred thousand mourners crowded outside the Ebenezer Baptist Church and onto the streets. They also lined the sidewalks on the route leading to the campus of Morehouse State College where another memorial service would be held. There were hundreds of familiar faces. Celebrities were the first to begin pouring in. They hoped to get a good seat inside the church so they could see and hear the services. But there were just more people than the church could accommodate. There was seating space for 750 persons. Loud-speakers were set up so that those in the basement and those outside could hear. Among the celebrities I was able to see were Sammy Davis, Jr., Diana Ross, Eartha Kitt, James Brown, Lena Horne, Aretha Franklin, Nancy Wilson, Wilt Chamberlain, Mr. and Mrs. Harry Belafonte, Berry Gordy, Thurgood Marshall, Richard Nixon, Hubert Humphrey, Whitney Young, Roy Wilkins, Floyd Mc-Kissick, James Farmer, James Foreman, John Lewis, Julian Bond, Floyd Patterson, and Jackie Kennedy. Johnson Publishing Company President John H. Johnson and *Jet* Editor Bob Johnson were there. They had been a big force behind King's being built as a leader. For years *Jet* and *Ebony* had followed his cause, and now they would do tribute to the man who so often made their covers and filled their pages with news of the ongoing struggle for civil rights. As I watched the expressions of the SCLC members I knew that they were going through a special type of pain. They had walked with King, marched with him, and watched a whole movement turn a nation around; and now he was gone. I wondered how these ministers would be affected by it. Many of them I knew personally, people like Hosea Williams, James Bevel, Ralph Abernathy, Bernard Lee, C. T. Vivian, Fred Shuttlesworth, T. Y. Walker, Jesse Jackson, Walter Fauntroy, and Andrew Young.

During the first week of February Dr. King told his congregation at the Ebenezer Baptist Church what kind of eulogy he wanted at his funeral. One could say that King preached his own funeral before his death when he delivered the following sermon:

> **Every now and then I guess we all think realistically about that day when we will be victimized with what is life's final common denominator, that something we call death. We all think about it. And every now and then I think about my own death, and I think about my own funeral. And I don't think of it in a morbid sense. Every now and then I ask myself, "What is it that I would want said?" And I leave the word to you this morning.**
>
> **If any of you are around when I have to meet my day, I don't want a long funeral. And if you get somebody to deliver the eulogy, tell them not to talk too long. . . . Tell them not to mention that I have a Nobel Peace Prize, that isn't important. Tell them not to mention that I have three or four hundred other awards, that's not important. Tell him not to mention where I went to school.**
>
> **I'd like somebody to mention that day, that Martin Luther King, Jr., tried to . . . love somebody. I want you to say that day, that I tried to be right on the war question. I want you to be able to say that day that I did try to feed the hungry. I want you to be able to say that day that I did try in my life . . . to visit those who were in prison. I want you to say that I tried to love and serve humanity.**
>
> **Yes, if you want to say that I was a drum major, say that I was a drum major for . . . righteousness. And all of the other shallow things will not matter. I won't have . . . the fine and luxurious things of life to leave behind. But I just want to leave a committed life behind.**

AS HE DIED TO MAKE MEN HOLY, LET US DIE TO MAKE MEN FREE

A free man is a man with no fears. Martin Luther King, in life, was about setting men free. Martin Luther King was killed in the process of setting men free. President Emeritus of Morehouse College, Dr. Benjamin Mays gave the eulogy at Martin Luther King's funeral.

Eulogy of Dr. Martin Luther King, Jr.
Atlanta, Georgia — April 9, 1968
By Benjamin E. Mays

290

To be honored by being requested to give the Eulogy at the funeral of Doctor Martin Luther King, Jr., is like asking one to eulogize his deceased son—so close and so dear was he to me. Our friendship goes back to his student days at Morehouse College. It is not an easy task; nevertheless, I accept it, with a heavy heart and with full knowledge of my inadequacy to do justice to this man. It was my desire that if I pre-deceased Doctor King, he would pay tribute to me on my final day. It was his wish that if he pre-deceased me, I deliver the homily at his funeral. Fate has decreed that I eulogize him. I wish it might have been otherwise, for after all, I am three score and ten and Martin Luther is dead at thirty-nine.

Although there are some who rejoice in his death, there are millions across the length and breadth of this world who are smitten with grief that this friend of mankind—all mankind—has been cut down in the flower of his youth. So, multitudes here and in foreign lands, queens, kings, heads of governments, the clergy of the world, and the common man everywhere, are praying that God will be with the family, the American people, and the President of the United States in this tragic hour. We hope that this universal concern will bring comfort to the family—for grief is like a heavy load; when shared it is easier to bear. We come today to help you carry the load.

We have assembled here from every section of this great nation and from other parts of the world to give thanks to God that He gave to America, at this moment in history, Martin Luther King, Jr. Truly God is no respecter of persons. How strange! God called the grandson of a slave on his father's side, and said to him: Martin Luther, speak to America about war and peace; about social justice and racial discrimination; about its obligation to the poor; and about nonviolence as a way of perfecting social change in a world of brutality and war.

Here was a man who believed, with all of his might, that the pursuit of violence, at any time, is ethically and morally wrong; that God and the moral weight of the universe are against it; that violence is self-defeating; and that only love and forgiveness can break the vicious circle of revenge. He believed that nonviolence would prove effective in the abolition of injustice in politics, economics, in education, and in race relations. He was convinced, also, that people could not be moved to abolish voluntarily the inhumanity of man to man by mere persuasion and pleading, but that they could be moved to do so by dramatizing the evil through massive nonviolent resistance. He believed that nonviolent direct action was necessary to supplement the nonviolent victories won in the federal courts. He believed that the nonviolent approach to solving social problems would ultimately prove to be redemptive.

Out of this conviction, history records the marches in Montgomery, Birmingham, Selma, Chicago, and other cities. He gave people an ethical and moral way to engage in activities designed to perfect social change without bloodshed and violence; and when violence did erupt it was that which is potential in any protest which aims to uproot deeply entrenched wrongs. No reasonable person would deny that the activities and the personality of Martin Luther King, Jr., contributed largely to the success of the student sit-in movements; in abolishing segregation in downtown establishments; and that his activities contributed mightily to the passage of the civil-rights legislation of 1964 and 1965.

Martin Luther King, Jr., believed in a united America; that the walls of separation brought on by legal and de facto segregation, and discrimination based on race and color, could be eradicated. As he said in his Washington Monument address: "I have a dream!"

He had faith in his country. He died striving to desegregate and integrate America to the end that this great nation of ours, born in revolution and blood, conceived in liberty and dedicated to the proposition that all men are created free and equal, will truly become the lighthouse of freedom where none will be denied because his skin is black and none favored because his eyes are blue; where our nation will be militarily strong but perpetually at peace; economically secure but just; learned but wise; where the poorest—the garbage collectors—will have bread enough and to spare; where no one will be poorly housed, each educated up to his capacity; and where the richest will understand the meaning of empathy. This was his dream, and the end toward which he strove. As he and his followers so often sang: "We shall overcome someday; black and white together."

Let it be thoroughly understood that our deceased brother did not embrace nonviolence out of fear or cowardice. Moral courage was one of his noblest virtues. As Mahatma Gandhi challenged the British Empire without a sword and won, Martin Luther King, Jr., challenged the interracial wrongs of his country without a gun. And he had the faith to believe that he would win the battle for social justice. I make bold to assert that it took more courage for King to practice nonviolence than it took his assassin to fire that fatal shot. The assassin is a coward; he committed his foul act and fled. When Martin Luther disobeyed an unjust law, he accepted the consequences of his actions. He never ran away and he never begged for mercy. He returned to the Birmingham jail to serve his time.

Perhaps he was more courageous than soldiers who fight and die on the battlefield. There is an element of compulsion in their dying. But when Martin Luther faced death again and again, and finally embraced it, there was no external pressure. He was acting on an inner compulsion that drove him on. More courageous than those who advocate violence as a way out, for they carry weapons of destruction for defense. But Martin Luther faced the dogs, the police, jail, heavy criticism, and finally death; and he never carried a gun, not even a knife to defend himself. He had only his faith in a just God to rely on; and the belief that "thrice is he armed who has his quarrels just." The faith that Browning writes about when he says: "One who never turned his back, but marched breast forward: never doubted that clouds would break; never dreamed that right through worsted wrong would triumph; held we fall to rise, are baffled to fight better, sleep to wake."

Coupled with moral courage was Martin Luther King, Jr.'s capacity to love people. Though deeply committed to a program of freedom for Negroes, he had love and concern for all kinds of peoples. He drew no distinction between the high and the low; none between the rich and the poor. He believed especially that he was sent to champion the cause of the man farthest down. He would probably say that, if death had to come, I am sure there was no greater cause to die for than fighting to get a just wage for garbage collectors. He was supra race, supra nation, supra denomination, supra class, and supra culture. He belonged to the world and to mankind. Now he belongs to posterity!

But there is a dichotomy in all this. This man was loved by some and hated by others. If any man knew the meaning of suffering, King knew. House bombed; living day by day for thirteen years under constant threats of death; maliciously accused of being a Communist; falsely accused of being insincere and seeking the limelight for his own glory; stabbed by a member of his own race; slugged in a hotel lobby; jailed over twenty times; occasionally deeply hurt because friends betrayed him—and yet this man had no bitterness in his heart, no rancor in his soul, no revenge in his mind; and he went up and down the length and breadth of this world preaching nonviolence and the redemptive power of love. He believed with all his heart, mind, and soul that the way to peace and brotherhood is through nonviolence, love, and suffering. He was severely criticized for his opposition to the war in Vietnam. It must be said, however, that one could hardly expect a prophet of Doctor King's commitments to advocate nonviolence at home and violence in Vietnam. Nonviolence to King was total commitment not only in solving the problems of race in the United States, but in solving the problems of the world.

Surely this man was called of God to do this work. If Amos and Micah were prophets in the eighth century, B.C., Martin Luther King, Jr., was a prophet of the twentieth century. If Isaiah was called of God to prophesy in his day, Martin Luther was called of God to prophesy in his time. If Hosea was sent to preach love and forgiveness centuries ago, Martin Luther was sent to expound the doctrine of nonviolence and forgiveness in the third quarter of the twentieth century. If Jesus was called to preach the Gospel to the poor, Martin Luther was called to give dignity to the common man. If a prophet is one who interprets in clear and intelligible language the will of God, Martin Luther King, Jr., fits that designation. If a prophet is one who does not seek popular causes to espouse, but rather the causes which he thinks are right, Martin Luther qualified on that score.

No! he was not ahead of his time. No man is ahead of his time. Every man is within his star, each in his time. Each man must respond to the call of God in his lifetime and not in somebody else's time. Jesus had to respond to the call of God in the first century, A.D., and not in the twentieth century. He had but one life to live. He couldn't wait, even though he died young. How long do you think Jesus would have had to wait for the constituted authorities to accept him? Twenty-five years? A hundred years? A thousand? He died at thirty-three. He couldn't wait. Paul, Galileo, Copernicus, Martin Luther, the Protestant reformer, Gandhi and Nehru, couldn't wait for another time. They had to act in their lifetime. No man is ahead of his time. Abraham, leaving his country in obedience to God's call; Jesus dying on a cross; Galileo on his knees recanting; Lincoln dying of an assassin's bullet; Woodrow Wilson crusading for a League of Nations; Martin Luther King, Jr., dying fighting for justice for garbage collectors—none of these men were ahead of their time. With them the time was always ripe to do that which was right and that which needs to be done.

Too bad Martin Luther King, Jr., died so young. I feel that way, too. But, as I have said many times before, it isn't how long one lives, but how well. It's what one accomplishes for mankind that matters. Jesus died at thirty-three; Keats and Marlow at twenty-nine; Shelley at thirty; Dunbar before thirty-five; John Fitzgerald Kennedy at forty-six; William Rainey Harper at forty-nine; and Martin Luther King, Jr., at thirty-nine.

We all pray that the assassin will be apprehended and brought to justice. But, make no mistake, the American people are in part responsible for Martin Luther King, Jr.'s, death. The Memphis officials must bear some of the guilt for Martin Luther's assassination. The strike should have been settled several weeks ago. The lowest paid in our society should not have to strike for a more just wage. A century after Emancipation, and after the enactment of the 13th, 14th and 15th Amendments, it should not have been necessary for Martin Luther King, Jr., to stage marches in Montgomery, Birmingham and Selma, and go to jail over twenty times trying to achieve for his people those rights which people of lighter hue get by virtue of their being born white. We, too, are guilty of murder. It is time for the American people to repent and make democracy equally applicable to all Americans.

If we love Martin Luther King, Jr., and respect him, as this crowd testifies, let us see to it that he did not die in vain; let us see to it that we do not dishonor his name by trying to solve our problems through rioting in the streets. Violence was foreign to his nature. He warned that continued riots could produce a Fascist state. But let us see to it also that the conditions that cause riots are promptly removed, as the President of the United States is trying to get us to do. Let black and white alike search their hearts; and if there be any prejudice in our hearts against any racial or ethnic group, let us exterminate it and let us pray, as Martin Luther King, Jr. would pray if he could: "Father, forgive them for they know not what they do." If we do this, Martin Luther King, Jr., will have died a redemptive death from which all mankind will benefit. Morehouse College will never be the same because Martin Luther came by here, and the nation and the world will be indebted to him for centuries to come. It is natural that we here at Morehouse would want to memorialize him to serve as an inspiration to all students who study in this center.

I close by saying to you what Martin Luther King, Jr., believed, that if physical death was the price he had to pay to rid America of prejudice and injustice, nothing could be more redemptive. To paraphrase the words of the immortal John Fitzgerald Kennedy, permit me to say that Martin Luther King, Jr.'s, unfinished work on earth must truly be our own.

Appendix Two

SPEECH OF SENATOR ROBERT C. BYRD

SENATE—Friday, March 29, 1968

The Senate met at 9 o'clock a.m., on the expiration of the recess, and was called to order by the President pro tempore.

Rev. Edward B. Lewis, D.D., minister, Capitol Hill Methodist Church, Washington, D.C., offered the following prayer:

We come to Thee, Heavenly Father, with a very present need. We acknowledge that the bonds which hold the human family together have been broken. Our wisdom has been lacking, our hearts have become increasingly hard, our divisions between man and man, race and race, nation and nation are more apparent from day to day. None of us are free from fault. We have a deep hurt as we look at the world today.

Yet we must look up and see Thee longing to help us. This spring morning gives us new hope in Thy creation. From the dull earth of winter, we see nature reborn in splendor. We remember the words of Jesus, "Marvel not that I said unto you, 'You must be born again.' " Man's nature, O God, needs the touch of a new birth in Thee.

With a new birth in our hearts, our eyes are not dimmed by deep-seated prejudices that feed fear, our attitudes are not stirred by resentment. Our hope is in new opportunities of peace.

We pray for our worthy leaders. Give wisdom, patience, steadfastness, courage, and the gift of love. Here are our minds, our hearts, our lives. Make us anew. We pray in the name of our Lord and Master. Amen.

THE JOURNAL

Mr. LONG of Louisiana. Mr. President, I ask unanimous consent that the Journal of the proceedings of Thursday, March 28, 1968, be approved.

The PRESIDENT pro tempore. Without objection, it is so ordered.

MEMPHIS RIOTS AND THE COMING MARCH ON WASHINGTON

Mr. BYRD of West Virginia. Mr. President, we have been hearing for months now that Dr. Martin Luther King, Jr., has been planning a march on Washington and a "civil disobedience campaign" in the Nation's Capital in April.

Yesterday, Mr. President, the Nation was given a preview of what may be in store for this city by the outrageous and despicable riot that Martin Luther King helped to bring about in Memphis, Tenn.

If this self-seeking rabble-rouser is allowed to go through with his plans here, Washington may well be treated to the same kind of violence, destruction, looting, and bloodshed.

In Memphis, people were injured, stores were looted, property was destroyed, terror reigned in the streets, people were beaten by hoodlums, at least one Negro youth is known to have been killed, and massive rioting erupted during a march which was led by this man. It was a shameful and totally uncalled for outburst of lawlessness, undoubtedly encouraged to some considerable degree, at least, by his words and actions, and his presence. There is no reason for us to believe that the same destructive rioting and violence cannot, or that it will not, happen here if King attempts his so-called poor people's march, for what he plans in Washington appears to be something on a far greater scale than what he had indicated he planned to do in Memphis.

When the predictable rioting erupted in Tennessee, Martin Luther King fled the scene. He took to his heels and disappeared, leaving it to others to cope with the destructive forces he had helped to unleash.

He was due in Washington today, to conduct discussions in furtherance of the demonstration planned for this city. However, as a result of the tragic happening of yesterday, he canceled the conferences in Washington for today. Nonetheless, I do not believe that the implications of the ugly events of yesterday will be lost on local residents—despite the widespread sanction and support that has been offered to King by churches, the YMCA, and many other organizations in the Nation's Capital. I hope that well-meaning Negro leaders and individuals in the Negro community here will now take a new look at this man who gets other people into trouble and then takes off like a scared rabbit. If anybody is to be hurt or killed in the disorder which follows in the wake of his highly publicized marches and demonstrations, he apparently is going to be sure that it will be someone other than Martin Luther.

Mr. President, what occurred yesterday in Memphis was totally uncalled for—just as Martin Luther King's proposed march on Washington is totally uncalled for and totally unnecessary. He himself has been publicly quoted as saying that he thinks nothing constructive, so far as congressional action is concerned, can come out of his campaign here. Yet he says he is coming anyway. Why? To bring about another riot?

Mr. President, the main difference that I see now between what Martin Luther King plans here and what happened in Memphis yesterday is that the Memphis riot he precipitated might best be described as a hit-and-run riot, in view of his flight, while he was promised that his demonstration in the Federal City may last all summer.

Ostensibly, Martin Luther King went to Memphis to do the same sort of thing he has promised to do here—to "help poor people." He has billed his Washington march as a "poor people's crusade." In Memphis he went to lead striking garbage workers in a march to "help" them, but today, in the aftermath of Thursday's stupid and tragic occurrence, the Negroes he purportedly wanted to help are far worse off than they would have been if he had never gone there, for many are in jail and many are injured—and most certainly race relations have been dealt a severe setback across the Nation, as they have been in Memphis.

Is Washington now to be subjected to the same destruction and bloodshed?

Martin Luther King had no business in Memphis, he should never have gone there for the purpose of leading the protest march—just as he never should come here for the purpose of conducting a poor people's demonstration. There can be no doubt that he must be held directly responsible for much of what took place in Tennessee, and he will have to bear the onus for whatever takes place in Washington if he carries through on his threatened demonstration here.

King, himself, has talked of a crisis-packed situation in connection with his projected Washington demonstration and the erection of his proposed "shanty town," wherever it is to be located, whether among the Tidal Basin's cherry trees, on the Mall, in the District of Columbia Stadium, or elsewhere.

This man, who suffers from the delusion that only his eyes have the divine insight to detect what is wrong in our country, claims he wants to dramatize the plight of the poor. He has declared:

Bitter experience has shown that our Government does not act until it is confronted directly and militanty.

With this as his deceitful theme, King intends to demand greater and more unrealistic governmental subsidies in a year when the Federal Government is already spending over $25 billion annually to help the poor.

His plan for creating a crisis-packed situation, which he so often foments, is to bring 100 initial demonstrators to the Nation's Capital on April 22 to pressure Congress and Federal executives for more adequate health care and education, increases in jobs and incomes, and numerous other actions. Larger masses of people will begin moving in on April 26, according to a news story written by Willard Clopton, which was published in the *Washington Post,* of March 28, 1968.

Never before in history has an administration, a Congress, or a Nation's citizenry as a whole devoted as much effort and action toward alleviating the problems of poverty and discrimination. Yet, in the midst of this, the pious Dr. King ominously declares:

We have a national emergency. The prospects of cities aflame is very real indeed, but I would also remind America of the continuing violence perpetrated daily by racism in our society.

If King goes through with his plans now, he will indeed create a crisis-packed situation in Washington, just as his presence created an explosive situation in Memphis.

There are very real dangers, Mr. President—as yesterday's rioting clearly showed —in the sort of irresponsible actions King indulged in in Memphis, and in what he is planning here. The warning signals should be raised, if, indeed, they have not already been. There are dangers from the leader himself, as he so thoroughly demonstrated by not being able to keep down violence in Memphis despite his vaunted policy of nonviolence. And there is certainly danger in the type of gathering he envisions here.

Mr. President, I call attention to one paragraph in an article written again by Willard Clopton, entitled ''Riot Spurs Review of March Here,'' which was published in the *Washington Post* of this morning. The paragraph reads as follows:

One of the Campaign's organizers said of the Memphis eruption, "It looks like we were 'had' by the extremists . . . We weren't prepared."
He indicated that the SCLC's usual precautions against violence such as the posting of numerous marshals and monitors, were overlooked yesterday.

King intends to create a black hole of despair with people packed together with pigs and chickens in a ''shanty town'' lacking sanitation. Surely he must know that to change hearts it is not necessary to turn stomachs. It can be assumed that, however, if yesterday's flight by King from the disorder he had helped to generate was any indication of what he might do here, the ''Messiah'' himself will not share the squalor he plans and that instead he will be conducting a lay-in at a posh Washington hotel to dramatize some imaginary discrimination there.

In his typical fashion, King intends to build a powder keg village and then plead that no one play with matches nearby lest destruction occur. He lays down the fuses around such a situation, however, with his semantic storehouse of volatile phrases such as ''bloodless war,'' ''direct action program,'' ''crisis-packed situation,'' ''dramatic con-frontation,'' ''attention-getting activities,'' ''pressure,'' and ''civil disobedience.''

King's semantic gyrations have not fooled the American public, because violence has followed him like his shadow. Just as Shakespeare's Iago goaded Othello, the Moor, into committing outrage, King, the ever-correct phrasemaker, manages with saccharin words to produce sanguinary results.

He preaches nonviolence as a characteristic of disobedience. But the new civil disobedience is ''civil disturbance.'' Riots, bombing, and violent protest typify the civil disobedience of today.

The marches in Milwaukee and Chicago last year were chaotic, and the Memphis march Thursday was disastrous. King has called for nonviolence here, but there are people allied with the poor people's campaign who call for the overthrow of the American Government by violence. Martin Luther King may have been a powerful man in the civil rights movement up to now, but it seems almost impossible to expect that he can control such large groups of militant activists as those he expects to join him in the demonstration here. Or, Mr. President, does he really expect to control them?

Both Stokely Carmichael and H. Rap Brown, if he can get out of jail, have agreed to march with Dr. King on the latter's terms—nonviolence—but how can we, or King, be sure of this? How can we be sure that another Memphis will not erupt? How can we be sure that King's lieutenants will not again have to say, "It looks like we were 'had' by the extremists. We were not prepared."

It is a well-known fact that riots begin when there is some uniting spark to excite a mob. All it would take in a situation like a Washington camp-in would be for some incident to turn the modern Coxey's Army King is raising into an angry, and ugly mob.

If Dr. King's plans to obstruct passage into the departments of the Government and buildings on Capitol Hill are carried out, it is certain that these actions will be met with a counterforce. There would be violence, and there is a great possibility that someone could be injured or killed.

Washington citizens and businessmen are concerned about their city. They do not want Washington to be torn apart by riots or discord.

Washington businessmen have been meeting with District officials and among themselves to draw up plans for the possible coming of the campaign. Hotel Association President Hudson Moses was quoted in the Washington Post on March 1 on what the city might lose as a result of the demonstration. He said:

Several of our members told me they have had group cancellations specifically because of the march. . . . It will cost this city millions of dollars in indirect loss of business and taxes.

Martin Luther King's main target, in Washington, Mr. President, is the Congress, because it has not passed all of the broad legislation that he seeks.

From the beginning, this Washington march and demonstration—if it really seeks the goals that King claims for it—has been poorly conceived and poorly planned. It must be obvious to anyone that people who have to be recruited and trained will not be coming to Washington of their own volition. This will be no spontaneous demonstration, Mr. President, no grassroots movement. This task force he wants to bring here, by King's own admission, must be recruited and "trained."

Some of the recruits, it is said, will come from cities that went up in flames last summer. One can only assume that they will be riot-hardened veterans. One can properly ask, I think: What sort of "training" are they now being given?

Why, Mr. President, do citizens, if their cause and their grievances are just, have to be trained? It seems to me that there is something very sinister here. I am aware, as I have indicated before in these remarks, that Dr. King has said that his tactics will be nonviolent. But when he sets the stage for violence, how long can his "trained" army and the malcontents, disrupters, militants, and hoodlums already here be expected to remain nonviolent in Washington's long, hot summer?

Mr. President, they may have learned their lessons well from King, who once said:

I do feel that there are two types of laws. One is a just law and one is an unjust law. I think we all have moral obligations to disobey unjust laws. I think that the distinction here is that when one breaks a law that conscience tells him is unjust, he must do it openly, he must do it cheerfully, he must do it lovingly, he must do it civilly, not uncivilly, and he must do it with a willingness to accept the penalty.

King lovingly breaks the law like a boa constrictor. He crushes the very life from it. His willingness to accept the penalty, which is supposed to set him apart from the common lawbreaker, can be judged by his irritation at a court decision which upheld a 5-day jail sentence for King recently. Faced with the prospect of accepting the penalty, King intoned that the decision would "encourage riots and violence in the sense that it all but said that Negroes cannot redress their grievances through peaceful means without facing the kind of decision that we face." Analyze this comment, if you will. Although King states the court decision did not declare that Negroes could not redress their grievances, he seems to say just the opposite and warns that the dire consequences are riots and violence. The English language is like putty in King's hands, but his incantations are loaded with hidden land mines.

Apparently the hoodlums in Memphis yesterday followed King's advice to break laws with which they did not agree. This has been a cardinal principle of his philosophy—a philosophy that leads naturally to the escalation of nonviolence into civil disobedience—which is only a euphemism for lawbreaking and criminality and which escalates next into civil unrest, civil disorder, and insurrection.

Mr. President, I have previously urged, in discussing this matter with the Justice Department, that the Federal Government seek a court order to enjoin Martin Luther King and his pulpitless parsons from carrying out their planned poor people's campaign in the Nation's Capital. In the light of yesterday's bloody chapter of violence which erupted with the visit of Martin Luther King to Memphis, I again urge that the Federal Government take steps to prevent King from carrying out his planned harassment of Washington, D.C. An ounce of prevention is worth a pound of cure. It is time for our Federal Government —which in recent years has shown itself to be virtually spineless when it comes to standing up against the lawbreakers, the hoodlums, and the Marxist demonstrators—at least to let the Nation know, in no uncertain terms, that it will not allow this Nobel Peace Prize winner to create another Memphis in the city which serves as the seat of the Government of the United States.

Law-abiding citizens, both Negro and white, in Washington and elsewhere, deserve no less from a government, the first duty of which is to preserve law and order.

PERCY FOREMAN LETTER
to James Earl Ray

Dear James Earl:

You have heretofore assigned to me all of your royalties from magazine articles, book, motion picture or other revenue to be derived from the writings of Wm. Bradford Huie. These are my own property unconditionally.

However, you have heretofore authorized and requested me to negotiate a plea of guilty if the State of Tennessee through its District Attorney General and with the approval of the trial judge would waive the death penalty. You agreed to accept a sentence of 99 years.

It is contemplated that your case will be disposed of tomorrow, March 10, by the above plea and sentence. This will shorten the trial considerably. In consideration of the time it will save me, I am willing to make the following adjustment of my fee arrangement with you:

If the plea is entered and the sentence accepted and no embarrassing circumstances take place in the courtroom, I am willing to assign to any bank, trust company or individual selected by you all my receipts under the above assignment in excess of $165,000.00. These funds over and above the first $165,000.00 will be held by such bank, trust company or individual subject to your order.

I have either spent or obligated myself to spend in excess of $14,000.00, and I think these expenses should be paid in addition to a $150,000.00 fee. I am sure the expenses will exceed the $15,000.00, but I am willing to rest on that figure.

Yours truly,

/s/ Percy Foreman

Appendix Four

THE RIGHT TO KNOW
by Mark Lane

Early in the morning on Saturday, February 5, 1977, I began a drive from my home in Washington, D.C., to Brushy Mountain Penitentiary in Petros, Tennessee to visit with James Earl Ray. I picked up a copy of the *Washington Post* at a gasoline station and read a story published under the headline "Critics of Warren Report Objects of CIA Campaign." Sometime earlier I had brought an action against the CIA under the Freedom of Information Act for all of the documents about the Warren Report. On Friday, February 5th, a CIA officer informed me that some 900 pages of material was available. A student volunteer at the CCI drove to CIA headquarters at Langley, Virginia, and picked up the package Friday afternoon. I had planned to read the material upon my return from Petros. The CIA had evidently released the same material to the media and the *Washington Post* had published an Associated Press story. The Post version of the AP story said:

> **The documents show that the CIA examined copies of almost all books about the November, 1963, assassination, including one by then-Congressman Gerald R. Ford. A CIA officer called Ford's book "a re-hash of the Oswald case" and criticized its "loose" writing.**

On my next stop through Virginia I picked up a small local daily newspaper. There I read for the first time the complete version of the AP story, for the *Washington Post* story had excised all references to me (there were several in the AP Dispatch) and most of the most dramatic and startling admissions about illegal CIA conduct contained in the documents. The CIA was not concerned that Ford's book was a "re-hash of the Oswald case" but in the March 1, 1965, memorandum prepared for Richard Helms, then the Director of the CIA, the anonymous CIA source (his name was deleted before the documents were released) made that observation about the book and then expressed concern that Ford had disclosed material about Oswald's relationships to the FBI. He concluded, "I felt, therefore, that the chapter, as written, could be used by the Lefties, Mark Lane, *et al.*, to continue the campaign of which you are already aware." An examination of the newly-released CIA documents, the original AP story and the abbreviated and sanitized version of that story published by the

301

Washington Post, provided an indication that even as the CIA's illegal and improper conduct was at long last being bared, the *Washington Post* continued editing and deleting disclosures related to the assassinations.

CIA document number 1035-960 proposed a plan of action against the Warren Commission critics. It reads,

Action. We do *not* recommend that discussion of the assassination question be initiated where it is not already taking place. Where discussion is active however addressees are requested:

To discuss the publicity problem with liaison and friendly elite contacts (especially politicians and editors), pointing out that the Warren Commission made as thorough an investigation as humanly possible, that the charges of the critics are without serious foundation, and that further speculative discussion only plays into the hands of the opposition. Point out also that parts of the conspiracy talk appear to be deliberately generated by Communist propagandists. Urge them to use their influence to discourage unfounded and irresponsible speculation.

To employ propaganda assets to answer and refute the attacks of the critics. Book reviews and feature articles are particularly appropriate for this purpose. The unclassified attachments to this guidance should provide useful background material for passage to assets. Our play should point out, as applicable, that the critics are (i) wedded to theories adopted before the evidence was in, (ii) politically interested, (iii) financially interested.

The irrelevant and insulting questions that had followed me for a decade had been formulated and promulgated at CIA headquarters.

The document suggests that "a useful strategy may be to single out Epstein's theory for attack." Edward J. Epstein had written a book that tentatively raised some questions about the Warren Report. The CIA document explained that "Mark Lane's book" is "more difficult to answer as a whole." The three-page document urged that "reviewers" of books critical of the Warren Commission "might be encouraged to add to their account the idea that, checking back with the Report itself, they found it far superior to the work of its critics." Absurd arguments that have been put forth in the last decade in support of the Warren Report can be traced to the CIA document.

The CIA suggested that "in private or media discussion" various arguments "should be useful." Among those the CIA offered as most effective to destroy the impact of *Rush to Judgment* and other books critical of the Warren Report are these:

a. "No significant new evidence has emerged which the commission did not consider."

b. "Critics usually overvalue particular items and ignore others."

c. "Conspiracy on the large scale often suggested would be impossible to conceal in the United States."

d. "Oswald would not have been any sensible person's choice for a co-conspirator. He was a 'loner,' mixed-up, of questionable reliability and an unknown quantity to any professional intelligence service."

Reviewers and apologists for the Warren Commission offering themselves as freethinking iconoclasts have slavishly adopted the CIA's proposals and developed newspaper columns, major reviews and, on occasion, entire magazine articles around them. This has been so even though a wealth of newly-discovered significant evidence reveals that the Warren Commission did not secure the facts. The Select Committee on Intelligence of the United States Senate discovered that the CIA itself had withheld significant evidence from the Warren Commission. Conspiracies on a large scale, have of course, occured within the United States. The Watergate episode and its cover-up involved a President, an Attorney General and many others. The evidence now available discloses that Oswald worked for the FBI and with the CIA; perhaps that does call into question the professionalism of those services as the CIA document might suggest.

For those reviewers and publications not perceptive enough to understand the CIA line, the agency was kind enough to furnish more assistance. Regarding one long magazine article defending the Warren Commission and attacking the critics the CIA boasted: "This was pulled together by [name deleted] in close conjunction with [name deleted]. We furnished most of the source material, proposed many of the themes and provided general 'Expertise' on the case."

In addition the CIA prepared a book review of *Rush to Judgment* on August 2, 1966, *before* the book was published. It began, "I reviewed the attached proof copy of the above book per your request." The name of the CIA official who requested the review was deleted. Another memorandum dated August 25, 1966, addressed to the "Director of Central Intelligence" carried this heading, "Subject: New Book: *Rush to Judgment* by Mark Lane." That seven page review was dispatched by the CIA to eleven different CIA departments including its Plans Department, known as the "Department of Dirty Tricks" within the agency.

Another CIA report dated January 4, 1967, stressed the income that I had reportedly earned from the book. Although William Manchester had earned more than ten times the amount I did for his defense of the Warren Report, the CIA, taking note of his income, indicated that he should be exempt from criticism and said that he should not "be classed with critics of the Commission." A CIA letter dated October 1, 1964, was sent to J. Lee Rankin, then the General Counsel of the Warren Commission. It too dealt with a critic, Joachim Joesten. A copy of the letter was sent by the CIA to the FBI, Department of State, and the Immigration and Naturalization Service. Attached to the letter was a document dated, "Berlin, 8 November, 1937." The letterhead read "Secret State Police (Gestapo), Gestapo Headquarters." It was addressed to "The Chief of the SS and of the German Police in the Ministry of Interior." The document said that Joesten "has seriously transgressed against his duty to remain faithful to his [the German] people and State by his anti-German conduct in foreign countries." It seems that Joesten had fled from Hitler's Germany to warn the people of Denmark to arm against the Nazis. The Gestapo ordered that Joesten's "German citizenship be revoked and that his possessions be confiscated and declared as forfeited to the State."

The Gestapo also claimed that Joesten was a leftist, a charge not infrequently made by that police organization against democrats during that period. In its letter, the CIA parroted the Gestapo charge. Why the CIA felt compelled to share it and the Gestapo's joint conclusions about Joesten with the FBI, State Department, and Immigration and Naturalization Service is not clear. One can surmise, however, that it was not intended to substitute for a welcome wagon greeting. Why the CIA letter, signed by Richard Helms, then Deputy Director for Plans (Dirty Tricks Department) was sent to the Warren Commission remains a matter of conjecture. Joesten, no doubt, thought that he had left all of that behind when he fled from Nazi Germany. He never did envision that three decades later, three leading liberals, J. Lee Rankin, a pillar of the New York Bar, Norman Redlich, formerly general counsel for the Emergency Civil Liberties Committee and now dean of the School of Law at New York University, and Earl Warren, the Chief Justice of the United States, might one day pore over Gestapo documents to evaluate his political reliability. After all, Joesten did nothing more than question the conclusions of the Warren Commission Report.

I do not know how the CIA may react to this book or what demonic plans it may devise to interfere with the right of the American people to hear another view. I do not know who it may enlist knowingly or unwittingly in its crusade for darkness and its commitment to silence. It seems a pity that we may be required to wait yet another decade before that information becomes available to us. I think, in the circumstances, we are obligated to act against illegal and improper conduct rather than wait to read of it in anger and in sadness.

You have, I believe, the right to read this, and other serious and challenging books without the intervention of the CIA, the FBI, or other secretive government agencies. Perhaps we will soon view this time as a period from our troubled past. Perhaps the federal police will be forever restrained from poisoning the common well of knowledge that nourishes us only when our access to it is free.

304

Acknowledgments by Mark Lane

The deep concern for the truth of three members of the 94th Congress encouraged me to continue on with my work in investigating the death of Dr. King. I'm grateful to them—Yvonne Burke, Walter Fauntroy, and Andrew Young. Coretta King, Attorney General Griffin Bell, thousands of other Americans in cities and towns and at universities throughout the country, and scores of members of the 95th Congress have called for a thorough investigation of the circumstances of the murder. To all of them, my work is dedicated.

I am especially grateful to April Ferguson for her many suggestions and for her help in researching and editing.

Abby Mann and I were working in Memphis together when the pre-assassination scenario began to unfold. Abby's commitment to the truth and his love for Dr. King have influenced this work. Donald Freed has also helped to develop the facts of Memphis on April 4, 1968. His many helpful suggestions and leads are deeply appreciated. Les Payne's fine investigative reporting regarding those events and his published findings provided the basis for further inquiry. Jeff Cohen made useful discoveries in his trip to Memphis.

Jerry Policoff and George O'Toole provided ideas, information, and encouragement. Morton Halperin, John Shattuck, and the American Civil Liberties Union helped to establish the right of the people to know. Our access to the material referred to in the Appendix was essentially the result of their efforts.

James Earl Ray and Jerry Ray spoke with me on many occasions and answered the many questions that I asked without compensation.

Arthur Hanes, Sr., and Arthur Hanes, Jr., both opened their massive files to me and graciously answered all of the many questions I put to them. Orzell Billingsley spent many hours with Dick Gregory and me in an effort to re-create the hard days in Birmingham and the events surrounding the Tatum case.

I am particularly indebted to Arthur Murtagh whose painfully frank disclosures about life in the Federal Bureau of Investigation provided an invaluable insight into the operations of that organization.

Stonney Ray Lane, the warden at Brushy Mountain Penitentiary, made relaxed and informal interviews with James Earl Ray a reality as a result of his graciousness.

Students from Antioch College in Ohio, George Washington University and American University in Washington, D.C., and the University of Massachusetts served as interns with the Citizen's Committee of Inquiry and helped to research, type, and edit the manuscript. I am indebted to Lisa Freundlich, Helen Garrett, Jay Napolitan, O'Malley Pitcher, Adam Schneider, and Leona Zanetti.

Pamela Spack and Leona Zanetti journeyed to Memphis, remained there for four weeks, and uncovered evidence of value.

There could have been no comprehensive investigation without the witnesses who still vividly recall the days of April in Memphis. To all of them, especially Ed Redditt, Floyd Newsum, N. E. Wallace, Reverend Billy Kyles, Reverend Bernard Lee, and Reverend Ralph Abernathy we are, all of us, indebted.

And of course, I am grateful to my colleague and dear friend Dick Gregory.

Mark Lane
The Citizen's Commission
of Inquiry
105 Second Street, N.E.
Washington, D.C.

Acknowledgments by Dick Gregory

Whenever I begin research for a book, I inevitably reach back to previous experiences and people who have been helpful to me in the past. This book is no exception. It is, however, the first time I have coauthored a book. I am delighted that Mark Lane and I were able to merge our ideas with the facts to form what we feel will be the most accurate compilation of information surrounding the death of Martin Luther King, Jr.

Mark Lane's dedication to finding out the truth surrounding King's death makes it a pleasure to work with him. His years of extensive research have brought forth information which otherwise may have never been known. His diligence, his devotion, and his commitment to honest journalism made it possible for the two of us to put together this book.

In the beginning phases of my research, I depended on various people to assist me in sorting out the facts. I'd like to express special thanks to Charlene M. Mitchell, a television news reporter whose ability to gather information and patiently discern facts aided me greatly. I'd also like to thank my sister-in-law, Martha Smith, who sacrificed time away from her children, Elise, Suzanne, and John, to so generously give of her time and energy to help me complete the final portions of my research. The organizing skills of Charlene and Martha made it possible for me to comfortably trust their journalistic judgments.

My sincere appreciation goes to my wife, Lillian. She always makes herself available to help me when time is running out. Her willingness to lend a helping hand in organizing material speeded the completion of this book.

Each time I put together a new work of any sort, I look to Jim Sanders for another perspective. A brilliant comedy writer whose unique ability to uncover humor helps me to see the whimsical elements of situations that would otherwise not appear funny.

Special thanks go to Bob Lipsyte and Jim McGraw whose past writings and conversations helped me tremendously in recollecting the joys and triumphs of the civil rights movement and my visits with Martin Luther King.

Three people who were extremely influential in my initial interest in researching King's death were Robert Byron Watson, his mother, Mrs. Lillian Watson, and their attorney, Hudson John Myers. The Watsons took many risks which caused their family a lot of unnecessary suffering, but through their honest efforts I was able to obtain information which no one else could have provided.

Another person who played an important part in making public much of the information which I had collected was Reginald Eaves, Commissioner of Public Safety in Atlanta, Georgia. I feel that it was because of him that the first official investigation began outside of the federal government.

Several people in the field of communications were helpful to me during the course of my research. I'd like to thank John H. Johnson, Publisher of *Ebony*

307

and *Jet;* Bob Johnson, Editor of *Jet* magazine; Basil O. Phillipe, of the Johnson Publishing Company; Wesley South, of WVON-Radio in Chicago; Vernon Jarrett, of the *Chicago Tribune;* and Geraldo Rivera, of ABC-TV. These people helped to expose information which much of the news media tended to avoid. Through their reporting, millions of Americans became aware of the confusing and conflicting government reports surrounding King's death.

I'd also like to thank Al Duckett, Barbara Reynolds, George O'Hare, and George Curry for their willingness to help, and their constant availability throughout the course of my research.

I owe a special "thank you" to Reverend Ronald Carter, Director of the Martin Luther King Center at Boston University. He, along with his assistant, Verna Hart, supplied a wealth of information which was extremely helpful in the completion of my work. I'd also like to thank The Martin Luther King Center for Social Change in Atlanta, Georgia, for helping to make available to the public so much valuable information concerning the Martin Luther King era.

I also wish to thank E. Randall Osborn, Mercele E. Randolph, Earlene Carter, and Dyeatra Carter, whom I always felt free to call on whenever I needed extra help in finding information.

I owe special thanks to Reverend Ralph Abernathy and his wife, Juanita, C. T. Vivian, Hosea Williams, James Orange, Bernard Lee, James Bevel, and other members of the SCLC who provided insight into King's life, his career, and his death.

I'd also like to say thank you to Mike Watley, Alvin Banks, Richard Rodgers, and Dr. Alvenia Fulton. They provided patience and understanding during busy periods when I needed extra time to complete my work.

There are three very special people whose sincere interest and dedication made it possible for this work to be completed. I owe special thanks to Ralph Mann, Marge Weidenbacher, and Erica Spellman of International Creative Management in New York City.

Finally, I'd like to express my love and warm thanks to my wife, Lillian, and my children: Michelle, Lynne, Pamela, Paula, Stephanie, Gregory, Miss, Christian, Ayanna, and Yohance. Their understanding of my many days away from home, and their patience during times when I was preoccupied with work made it possible for me to work at a comfortable pace, and with ease.

Dick Gregory

INDEX

AD HOC WIRELESS NETWORKING

Network Theory and Applications

Volume 14

Managing Editors:

Ding-Zhu Du
University of Minnesota, U.S.A.

Cauligi Raghavendra
University of Southern Califorina, U.S.A.

WITHDRAWN
UTSA LIBRARIES

AD HOC WIRELESS NETWORKING

edited by

Xiuzhen Cheng
Department of Computer Science
The George Washington University
Washington, D.C. 20052
U.S.A.

Xiao Huang
Department of Computer Science
University of Minnesota
Minneapolis, MN 55455
U.S.A.

Ding-Zhu Du
Dept. of Computer Science
University of Minnesota
Minneapolis, MN 55455
U.S.A.

KLUWER ACADEMIC PUBLISHERS
Boston / Dordrecht / New York / London

Distributors for North, Central and South America:
Kluwer Academic Publishers
101 Philip Drive
Assinippi Park
Norwell, Massachusetts 02061 USA
Telephone (781) 871-6600
Fax (781) 871-6528
E-Mail <kluwer@wkap.com>

Distributors for all other countries:
Kluwer Academic Publishers Group
Post Office Box 322
3300 AH Dordrecht, THE NETHERLANDS
Telephone 31 78 6576 000
Fax 31 78 6576 474
E-Mail <orderdept@wkap.nl>

 Electronic Services <http://www.wkap.nl>

Library of Congress Cataloging-in-Publication

Cheng, Xiuzhen/ Huang, Xiao/ Du, Ding-Zhu
Ad Hoc Wireless Networking
ISBN 1-4020-7712-2

Copyright © 2004 by Kluwer Academic Publishers

All rights reserved. No part of this publication may be reproduced, stored in a retrieval system or transmitted in any form or by any means, electronic, mechanical, photo-copying, microfilming, recording, or otherwise, without the prior written permission of the publisher, with the exception of any material supplied specifically for the purpose of being entered and executed on a computer system, for exclusive use by the purchaser of the work.
Permissions for books published in the USA: permissions@wkap.com
Permissions for books published in Europe: permissions@wkap.nl
Printed on acid-free paper.

Printed in the United States of America

Library
University of Texas
at San Antonio

Contents

Foreword

Wireless networking enables two or more computers to communicate using standard network protocols without network cables. Since their emergence in the 1970s, *wireless networks* have become increasingly popular in the computing industry. In the past decade, wireless networks have enabled true mobility. There are currently two versions of mobile wireless networks. An *infrastructure network* contains a wired backbone with the last hop being wireless. The cellular phone system is an example of an infrastructure network. A *multihop ad hoc wireless network* has no infrastructure and is thus entirely wireless. A wireless sensor network is an example of a multihop ad hoc wireless network.

Ad hoc wireless networking is a technique to support robust and efficient operation in mobile wireless networks by incorporating routing functionality into mobile hosts. This technique will be used to realize the dream of "anywhere and anytime computing", which is termed *mobile computing*. Mobile computing is a new paradigm of computing in which users carrying portable devices have access to shared infrastructure in any location at any time. Mobile computing is a very challenging topic for scientists in computer science and electrical engineering. The representative system for ad hoc wireless networking is called MANET, an acronym for "Mobile Ad hoc NETworks". MANET is an autonomous system consisting of mobile hosts connected by wireless links which can be quickly deployed. For example, on the battlefield, the platoon of soldiers sent out on a mission can form a MANET if they are equipped with wireless communicators. Routing in MANET is a very critical problem. The IETF MANET working group is dedicated to the development of MANET routing specifications and introduction of routing protocols to the Internet Standards track.

Ad hoc wireless networks will revolutionize information gathering and processing in both urban environments and inhospitable terrain. MANETs are likely to be widely deployed in the future because they greatly extend our ability to monitor and control the physical environment from remote locations. Example applications of ad hoc wireless network include emergency search-and-rescue operations, decision making on the battlefield, data acquisition operations in inhospitable terrain, etc.

This book contains chapters dealing with various issues related to ad hoc wireless networking, including energy efficient ad hoc routing, location discovery in sensor networks, wireless security, routing challenges in large scale ad hoc networks, etc. Each chapter is self-contained, thus readers can pick any topic they are interested in with no need to start from the very beginning. Both experts and uninformed readers will find the book chapters stimulating and helpful.

We wish to thank all who made this book possible: the authors for their contributions, the referees for their reports, and the publishers for their support. In particular, we wish to thank Professors Yuguang "Michael" Fang, Srihari Nelakuditi, and Jie Wu for their constructive comments and suggestions.

Xiuzhen Cheng
in Washington, DC

Xiao Huang
in Minneapolis, MN

Ding-Zhu Du
in Minneapolis, MN

AD HOC WIRELESS NETWORKING
X. Cheng, X. Huang and D.-Z. Du (Eds.) pp. 1 - 44

A Lifetime-Optimizing Approach to Routing Messages in Ad-hoc Networks

Javed Aslam
Department of Computer Science
Dartmouth College, Hanover, NH 03755
E-mail: jaa@cs.dartmouth.edu

Qun Li
Department of Computer Science
Dartmouth College, Hanover, NH 03755
E-mail: liqun@cs.dartmouth.edu

Daniela Rus
Department of Computer Science
Dartmouth College, Hanover, NH 03755
E-mail: rus@cs.dartmouth.edu

Contents

1 Introduction

The proliferation of low-power analog and digital electronics has created huge opportunities for the field of wireless computing. It is now possible to deploy hundreds of devices of low computation, communication and battery power. They can create ad-hoc networks and be used as distributed sensors to monitor large geographical areas, as communication enablers for field operations, or as grids of computation. These applications require great care in the utilization of power. The power level is provided by batteries and thus it is finite. Every message sent and every computation performed drains the battery.

In this chapter we examine a class of algorithms for routing messages in wireless networks subject to power constraints and optimization. We envision a large ad-hoc network consisting of thousands of computers such as a sensor network distributed over a large geographical area. Clearly this type of network has a high degree of redundancy. We would like to develop a power-aware approach to routing messages in such a system that is fast, scalable, and is online in that it *does not know ahead of time the sequence of messages* that has to be routed over the network.

The power consumption of each node in an ad-hoc wireless system can be divided according to functionality into: (1) the power utilized for the transmission of a message; (2) the power utilized for the reception of a message; and (3) the power utilized while the system is idle. Table 1 lists power consumption numbers for several wireless cards. This suggests two complementary levels at which power consumption can be optimized: (1) minimizing power consumption during the idle time and (2) minimizing power consumption during communication. In this paper we focus only on issues related to minimizing power consumption during communication - that is, while the system is transmitting and receiving messages. We believe that efficient message routing algorithms, coupled with good solutions for optimizing power consumption during the idle time will lead to effective power management in wireless ad-hoc networks, especially for a sparsely deployed network.

Card	Tr	Rv	Idle	Slp	Power
	mA	mA	mA	mA	Sup. V
RangeLAN2-7410	265	130	n/a	2	5
WaveLAN(11Mbps)	284	190	156	10	4.74
Smart Spread	150	80	n/a	5	5

Table 1: Power Consumption Comparison among Different Wireless LAN Cards ([2, 15, 1]). For RangeLAN2, the power consumption for doze mode (which is claimed to be network aware) is 5mA. The last one is Smart Spread Spectrum of Adcon Telemetry.

Several metrics can be used to optimize power-routing for a sequence of messages. Minimizing the energy consumed for each message is an obvious solution that optimizes locally the power consumption. Other useful metrics include minimizing the variance in each computer power level, minimizing the ratio of cost/packet, and minimizing the maximum node cost. A drawback of these metrics is that they focus on individual nodes in the system instead of the system as a whole. Therefore, routing messages according to these metrics might quickly lead to a system in which nodes have high residual power but the system is not connected because some critical nodes have been depleted of power. We choose to focus on a global metric by maximizing the lifetime of the network. We model this as the time to the earliest time a message cannot be sent. This metric is very useful for ad-hoc networks where each message is important and the networks are sparsely deployed.

In this chapter we build on our previous work [26] and show that the online power-aware message routing problem is very hard (Section 3). This problem does not have a constant competitive ratio to the off-line optimal algorithm that knows the message sequence. Guided by this theoretical result, we propose an online approximation algorithm for power-aware message routing that optimizes the lifetime of the network and examine its bounds (Section 4). Our algorithm, called the *max-min* zP_{min} algorithm, combines the benefits of selecting the path with the minimum power consumption and the path that maximizes the minimal residual power in the nodes of the network. Despite the discouraging theoretical result concerning the competitive ratio for online routing, we show that the *max-min* zP_{min} algorithm has a good competitive ratio in practice, approaching the performance of the optimal off-line routing algorithm under realistic conditions.

Our proposed *max-min* zP_{min} algorithm requires information about the power level of each computer in the network. Having accurate knowledge of this information is not a problem in small networks. However, for large networks it is difficult to aggregate and maintain this information. This makes it hard to implement the *max-min* zP_{min} algorithm for large networks. Instead, we propose another online algorithm called *zone-based routing* that relies on *max-min* zP_{min} and is scalable (Section 5). Our experiments show that the performance of zone-base routing is very close to the performance of *max-min* zP_{min} with respect to optimizing the lifetime of the network.

Zone-base routing is a hierarchical approach where the area covered by the (sensor) network is divided into a small number of zones. Each zone has many nodes and thus a lot of redundancy in routing a message through it. To send a message across the entire area we find a "global" path from zone to zone and give each zone control over how to route the message within itself. Thus, zone-based power-aware routing consists of (1) an algorithm for estimating the power level of each zone; (2) an algorithm computing a path for each message across zones; and (3) an algorithm for computing the best path for the message within each zone (with respect to the power lifetime of the zone.)

The algorithm *max-min* zP_{min} has the great advantage of not relying on the message sequence but the disadvantage of being centralized and requiring knowledge of the power level of each node in the system. These are unrealistic assumptions for field applications, for example involving sensor networks, where the computation is distributed and information localized. The third type of routing we describe is a distributed version of our centralized algorithms, which require each node to use only local information, i.e., only the information about its neighbors. Distributed version of the *max-min* zP_{min} algorithm has the flavor of the distributed Bellman-Ford algorithm. This distributed algorithm requires n message broadcasts for each node if there is no clock synchronization, and only one message broadcast if the host clocks are synchronized.

We do not specifically address a mobile network although our algorithms can adapt to the mobile case if the required information in each protocol can be collected in a timely fashion. We also assume a link must be active when a packet is scheduled to be transmitted along that link. In case a node is in sleeping mode when a packet arrives, we require the underlying MAC protocol to guarantee the successful reception of the packet.

2   Related Work

We are inspired by exciting recent results in ad-hoc networks and in sensor networks. Most previous research on ad-hoc network routing [22, 18, 30, 31, 32, 37, 23, 28] focused on the protocol design and performance evaluation in terms of the message overhead and loss rate. To improve the scalability of routing algorithms for large networks, many hierarchical routing methods have been proposed in [24, 13, 29, 4, 16, 35]. In [21], zones, which are the route maintenance units, are used to find the routes. This previous work focused on how to find the correct route efficiently, but did not consider optimizing power while sending messages.

Singh et al. [38] proposed power-aware routing and discussed different metrics in power-aware routing. The metrics for power-aware routing include minimizing energy consumed per packet, maximizing time to network partition, minimizing variance in node power level, minimizing the ratio of cost and packet, and minimizing maximum node cost..

Minimal energy consumption was used in [36]. Their protocol reduces the searching complexity by removing all the edges that are not possibly on the minimum energy route. This can be achieved by using a localized algorithm for each node to eliminate the nodes in its relay regions from consideration and pick only those links in its immediate neighborhood to be the potential candidate. After the local searching, distributed Bellman-Ford algorithm can be applied on this pruned network graph.

Chang and Tassiulas [5] also proposed maximizing the lifetime of a network when the message rate is known. Their paper formalized the maximum lifetime problem and used the heuristic method to solve the problem by using flow augmenting algorithms and flow redirection algorithms. Stojmenovic and Lin proposed a localized power-aware algorithm in their paper series [39]. Their algorithm is novel in combining the power and cost into one metric and running only based on the local information.

Feeney [15] measured the energy consumption of a wireless network interface in an ad-hoc networking environment. The paper compared the power consumption of the Lucent IEEE 802.11 Wavelan PC card. The experiments showed that the power consumptions for idle mode and receive mode were considerably large compared to the transmit mode. For example, for 11Mbps card, the measured currents (which is proportional to the power consumption) for sleep mode, idle mode, receive mode, and transmit mode are 10mA, 156mA, 190mA, and 284mA respectively. It suggests it may attain a significant power saving by reducing the power consumption in idle mode. Jyn-Cheng Chen [7] did detailed analytical study to the energy efficiency of a number of MAC layer protocols. They used probabilistic analysis to examine the effectiveness of various media acquisition strategies in the presence of contention.

Ramanathan [34] proposed to adjust the transmit power to reduce spatial interference. They used heuristic distributed algorithms to maintain the network connectivity. This idea was further developed by Li Li [25] to use localized topology control. In their scheme, each node makes local decision about its transmission power and those local decisions collectively guarantee global connectivity. Each node increases its transmission power until it finds a neighbor node in every direction (they use cone with an angle) or it reaches its maximal transmission power. The resultant network topology maximizes the lifetime of the network and reduces the spatial interference because each node does not necessarily use its maximal power.

In [17], Gupta and Kumar discussed the critical power at which a node needs to transmit in order to ensure the network is connected. Energy efficient MAC layer protocols can be found in [12, 11].

Schemes optimizing power consumption during idle time rather than during the time of communicating messages were presented in [41, 6]. In Geographical Adaptive Fidelity (GAF), the network field is partitioned into virtual square grids such that the nodes in the adjacent grids are within their transmission ranges. GAF maintains the network connectivity by keeping at one node in each grid active. A node can be in sleeping, active, and discovery state. After sleeping for some time, the node wakes up and goes into the discovery state in which it decides whether it should go to active state to handle routing or it goes back to sleeping. An active node goes to discovery state after some time. The node in active or discovery state goes to sleeping again when it knows some other node in the grid handles the routing. Another protocol, SPAN [6] does not use geographical information of the nodes. It adaptively elects coordinators that stay awake continuously and perform routing. Other non-coordinator nodes remain in power-saving mode and periodically check if they should wakes up and becomes a coordinator. If a non-coordinator node finds its two neighbors cannot reach each other directly or via one or two coordinators, it should become the coordinator. In this way, the network is covered with sufficient coordinators. Multiple non-coordinator nodes may announce them to be the "coordinator node", which is called announcement congestion. Announcement congestion is resolved by using randomized back-off delay before becoming the coordinator. The back-off delay is related to the number of neighbors, the pairs of nodes that are connected after the node becomes the coordinator, and the remaining energy.

In a related work [40], Wu and Stojmenovic gave a solution by using connecting dominating sets, which generalize the idea of maintaining a connected network while keeping most of the nodes in sleeping mode. Other related work includes Virtual Backbone-Based Routing [10] and polynomial-time approximation scheme for minimum connected dominating set [9].

Related results in sensor networks include [33, 3, 20, 14, 27]. The high-level vision of wireless sensor networks was introduced in [33, 3]. Achieving energy-efficient communication is an important issue in sensor network design. Using directed diffusion for sensor coordination was described in [20, 14]. In [19] a low-energy adaptive protocol that uses data fusion was proposed for sensor networks. In [8], the problem on relay sensor placement in sensor networks was discussed aiming at maintaining network conectivity by using minimal number of sensors.

3   Formulation of Power-aware Routing

3.1   The Model

Power consumption in ad-hoc networks can be divided into two parts: (1) the idle mode and (2) the transmit/receive mode. The nodes in the network are either in idle mode or in transmit/receive mode at all time. The idle mode corresponds to a baseline power consumption. Optimizing this mode is the focus of [42, 6, 40]. We instead focus on studying and optimizing the transmit/receive mode. When a message is routed through the system, all the nodes with the exception of the source and destination receives a message and then immediately relay it. Because of this, we can view the power consumption at each node as an aggregate between transit and receive powers which we will model as one parameter. It may be possible that some neighboring nodes may overhear the packet for other nodes. We do not address this issue here; instead we assume that each node runs a sophisticated MAC protocol that can check the packet destination and goes to idle mode immediately after learning that the packet is for some other node.

More specifically, we assume an ad-hoc network that can be represented by a weighted graph $G(V, E)$. The vertices of the graph correspond to computers in the network. They have weights that correspond to the computer's power level. The edges in the graph correspond to pairs of computers that are in communication range. Each edge weight is the power cost of sending a unit message[1] between the two nodes. Our results are independent of the power consumption model as long as we assume the power consumption of sending a unit message between two nodes does not change during a run of the algorithm. That is, the weight of any edge in the network graph is fixed.

Although our algorithms are independent of the power consumption model, we fixed one model for our implementation and simulation experiments. Suppose a host needs power e to transmit a message to another host who is d distance away. We use the model of [15, 19, 36] to compute the power consumption for sending this message:

$$e = kd^c + a,$$

where k and c are constants for the specific wireless system (usually $2 \leq c \leq 4$), and a is the electronics energy that depends on factors such as digital coding, modulation, filtering, and spreading of the signal. Since our

---

[1]Without loss of generality, we assume that all the messages are unit messages. Longer messages can be expressed as sequences of unit messages.

algorithms can use any power consumption model, we use $a = 0$ to simplify the implementation. In a network with a fixed transmission range for all nodes, the power consumption e of a sender is simply the same for any message to any node within the sender's transmission range .

We focus on networks where power is a finite resource. Only a finite number of messages can be transmitted between any two hosts. We wish to solve the problem of routing messages so as to maximize the battery lives of the hosts in the system. The lifetime of a network with respect to a sequence of messages is the earliest time when a message cannot be sent due to saturated nodes. We selected this metric under the assumption that all messages are important. Our results, however, can be relaxed to accommodate up to m message delivery failures, with m a constant parameter.

3.2 Relationship to Classical Network Flow

Power-aware routing is different from the maximal network flow problem although there are similarities. The classical network flow problem constrains the capacity of the edges instead of limiting the capacity of the nodes. If the capacity of a node does not depend on the distances to neighboring nodes, our problem can also be reduced to maximal network flow.

We use the following special case of our problem in which there is only one source node and one sink node to show the problem is NP-hard. The maximal number of messages sustained by a network from the source nodes to the sink nodes can be formulated as linear programming. Let n_{ij} be the total number of messages from node v_i to node v_j, e_{ij} denote the power cost to send a message between node v_i to node v_j, and s and t denote the source and sink in the network. Let P_i denote the power of node i. We wish to maximize the number of messages in the system subject to the following constraints: (1) the total power used to send all messages from node v_i does not exceed P_i; and (2) the number of messages from v_i to all other nodes is the same as the number of messages from all other nodes to v_i, which are given below:

$$maximize \qquad \sum_j n_{sj} \ \ subject \ to$$

$$\sum_j n_{ij} \cdot e_{ij} \ \leq \ P_i \tag{1}$$

$$\sum_j n_{ij} \ = \ \sum_j n_{ji} \ \ (for \ i \neq s, \ t) \tag{2}$$

This linear programming formulation can be can be solved in polynomial time. However, we need the integer solution, but computing the integer solution is NP-hard. Figure 1 shows the reduction to set partition for proving the NP-hardness of the integer solution.

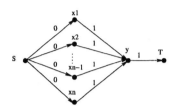

Figure 1: The integer solution problem can be reduced to set partition as follows. For any set of integers $S = a_1, a_2, \cdots, a_n$, we are asked to find A, a subset of S, such that $\sum_{a_i \in A} a_i = \sum_{a_i \in S-A} a_i$. Construct a network (as in the figure) based on the given set. The power of x_i is a_i for all $1 \leq i \leq n$, and the power of y is $\sum_{a_i \in A} a_i / 2$. The weight of each edge is marked on the network. The maximal flow of the network is $\sum_{a_i \in A} a_i / 2$, and it can only be obtained when the flow of $x_i y$ is a_i for all $a_i \in A$, and for all other $x_i y$, the flow is 0. That is, if we know the maximal flow of the network described, we can solve the set partition problem.

3.3 Competitive Ratio for Online Power-aware Routing

In a system where the message rates are unknown, we wish to compute the best path to route a message. Since the message sequence is unknown, there is no guarantee that we can find the optimal path. For example, the path with the least power consumption can quickly saturate some of the nodes. The difficulty of solving this problem without knowledge of the message sequence is summarized by the theoretical properties of its competitive ratio. The competitive ratio of an online algorithm is the ratio between the performance of that algorithm and the optimal off-line algorithm that has access to the entire execution sequence prior to making any decisions.

Theorem 3.1 *No online algorithm for message routing has a constant competitive ratio in terms of the lifetime of the network or the number of messages sent.*

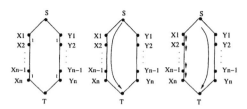

Figure 2: In this network, the power of each node is $1 + \epsilon$ and the weight on each edge is 1. The first figure gives the network; the center one is the route for the online algorithm; and the right one is the route for the optimal algorithm. Consider the message sequence that begins with a message from S to T, say, ST. Without loss of generality (since there are only two possible paths from S to T), the online algorithm routes the message via the route $SX_1X_2X_3\cdots X_{n-1}X_nT$. Then we further generate a message sequence of X_1X_2, X_2X_3, X_3X_4, $\cdots$, $X_{n-1}X_n$. It is easy to see that the optimal algorithm (see right figure) routes the first message through $SY_1Y_2Y_3\cdots Y_{n-1}Y_nT$, then routes the remaining messages through X_1X_2, X_2X_3, X_3X_4, $\cdots$, and $X_{n-1}X_n$. Thus the optimal algorithm can transmit n messages. The online algorithm (center) can transmit at most 1 message for this message sequence because the nodes $X_1, X_2, \cdots, X_n$ are all saturated after routing the first message. The competitive ratio is small when n is large.

Theorem 3.1, whose proof is shown in Figure 2, shows that it is not possible to compute online an optimal solution for power-aware routing.

4   Online Power-aware Routing with $max\text{-}min$ zP_{min}

4.1   The $max\text{-}min$ zP_{min} Algorithm

In this section we develop an approximation algorithm for online power-aware routing and show experimentally that our algorithm has a good empirical competitive ratio and comes close to the optimal.

We believe that it is important to develop algorithms for message routing that do not assume prior knowledge of the message sequence because for ad-hoc network applications this sequence is dynamic and depends on sensed values and goals communicated to the system as needed. Our goal is to increase the lifetime of the network when the message sequence is not known. We model lifetime as the earliest time that a message cannot be sent. Our assumption is that each message is important and thus the failure of delivering a message is a critical event. Our results can be extended to tolerate up to m message delivery failures, where m is a parameter. We focus the remaining of this discussion on the failure of the first message delivery.

Intuitively, message routes should avoid nodes whose power is low because overuse of those nodes will deplete their battery power. Thus, we would like to route messages along the path with the maximal minimal fraction of remaining power after the message is transmitted. We call this path the *max-min path*. The performance of max-min path can be very bad, as shown by the example in Figure 3. Another concern with the max-min path is that going through the nodes with high residual power may be expensive as compared to the path with the minimal power consumption. Too much power consumption decreases the overall power level of the system and thus decreases the life time of the network. There is a trade-off between minimizing the total power consumption and maximizing the minimal residual power of the network. We propose to enhance a max-min path by limiting its total power consumption.

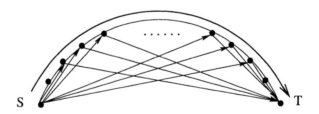

Figure 3: The performance of max-min path can be very bad. In this example, each node except for the source S has the power $20 + \epsilon$, and the weight of each edge on the arc is 1. The weight of each straight edge is 2. Let the power of the source be ∞. The network can send 20 messages from S to T according to max-min strategy by taking the edges on the arc (see the arc on the top). But the optimal number of messages follows the straight edges with black arrows is $10(n - 4)$ where n is the number of nodes.

The two extreme solutions to power-aware routing for one message are: (1) compute a path with minimal power consumption P_{min}; and (2) compute

0. Find the path with the least power consumption, P_{min}
    by using the Dijkstra algorithm.
1. Find the path with the least power consumption in the
    graph.
    If the power consumption $> z \cdot P_{min}$ or no path is found,
       then the previous shortest path is the solution, stop.
2. Find the minimal u_{tij} on that path, let it be u_{min}.
3. Find all the edges whose residual power fraction $u_{tij} \leq$
    u_{min}, remove them from the graph.
4. Goto 1.

Figure 4: *max-min* zP_{min}-path algorithm

a path that maximizes the minimal residual power in the network. We look
for an algorithm that optimizes *both* criteria. We relax the minimal power
consumption for the message to be zP_{min} with parameter $z \geq 1$ to restrict
the power consumption for sending one message to zP_{min}. We propose an
algorithm we call *max-min* zP_{min} that consumes at most zP_{min} while
maximizing the minimal residual power fraction. The rest of the section
describes the *max-min* zP_{min} algorithm, presents empirical justification
for it, a method for adaptively choosing the parameter z and describes some
of its theoretical properties.

The following notation is used in the description of the *max-min* zP_{min}
algorithm. Given a network graph (V, E), let $P(v_i)$ be the initial power level
of node v_i, e_{ij} the weight of the edge $v_i v_j$, and $P_t(v_i)$ is the power of the
node v_i at time t. Let $u_{tij} = \frac{P_t(v_i) - e_{ij}}{P(v_i)}$ be the residual power fraction after
sending a message from i to j.

Fig. 4 describes the algorithm. In each round we remove at least one
edge from the graph. The algorithm runs the Dijkstra algorithm to find
the shortest path for at most $|E|$ times where $|E|$ is the number of edges.
The running time of the Dijkstra algorithm is $O(|E| + |V| \log |V|)$ where
$|V|$ is the number of nodes. Then the running time of the algorithm is at
most $O(|E| \cdot (|E| + |V| \log |V|))$. By using binary search, the running time
can be reduced to $O(\log |E| \cdot (|E| + |V| \log |V|))$. To find the pure max-min
path, we can modify the Bellman-ford algorithm by changing the relaxation
procedure. The running time is $O(|V| \cdot |E|)$.

4.2 Adaptive Computation for z

An important factor in the $max\text{-}min$ zP_{min} algorithm is the parameter z which measures the trade-off between the max-min path and the minimal power path. When $z = 1$ the algorithm computes the minimal power consumption path. When $z = \infty$ it computes the max-min path. We would like to investigate an adaptive way of computing $z > 1$ such that $max\text{-}min$ zP_{min} that will lead to a longer lifetime for the network than each of the max-min and minimal power algorithms. Fig. 5 describes the algorithm for adaptively computing z. P is the initial power of a host. ΔP_t is the residual power decrease at time t compared to time $t - T$. Basically, $\frac{P}{\Delta P_t}$ gives an estimation for the lifetime of that node if the message sequence is regular with some cyclicity. The adaptive algorithm works well when the message distributions are similar as the time elapses.

4.3 Empirical Evaluation of $Max\text{-}min$ zP_{min} Algorithm

We conducted several experiments for evaluating the performance of the $max\text{-}min$ zP_{min} algorithm.

In the first set of experiments (Figure 6), we compare how z affects the performance of the lifetime of the network. In the experiments, a set of hosts are randomly generated on a square. For each pair of nodes, one message is sent in both directions for a unit of time. Thus there is a total of $n * (n - 1)$ messages sent in each unit time, where n is the number of the hosts in the network. Figure 6 (first) shows the number of messages transmitted until the first message delivery failure for different values of z. Using the adaptive method for selecting z with $z_{init} = 10$, the total number of messages sent increases to $12,207$, which is almost the best performance by $max\text{-}min$ zP_{min} algorithm. In the second experiment we generated the positions of hosts evenly distributed on the perimeter of a circle. The performance according to various z can be found in Figure 7 (first). By using the adaptive method, the total number of messages sent until reaching a network partition is $11,588$, which is much better than the most cases when we choose a fixed z. Figure 7 (second) shows the results obtained when the network consists of four columns where nodes are approximately aligned in each column. The same method used in experiment 1 varies the value of z.

These experiments show that adaptively selecting z leads to superior performance over the minimal power algorithm ($z = 1$) and the max-min algorithm ($z = \infty$). Furthermore, when compared to an optimal routing

0. Choose initial value z, the step δ.
1. Run the *max-min* zP_{min} algorithm for some interval T.
2. Compute $\frac{P}{\Delta P_t}$ for every host, let the minimal one be t_1.
3. Increase z by δ, and run the algorithm again for time T.
4. Compute the minimal $\frac{P}{\Delta P_t}$ among all hosts, let it be t_2.
5. **If** some host is saturated, exit.
6. **If** $t_1 < t_2$, **then** $t_1 = t_2$, goto 3.
7. **If** $t_1 > t_2$, **then** $\delta = -\delta/2$, $t_1 = t_2$, goto 3.

Figure 5: Adaptive *max-min* zP_{min} algorithm

algorithm, *max-min* zP_{min} has a constant empirical competitive ratio (see Figure 8 (first)). Figure 8 (second) shows more data that compares the *max-min* zP_{min} algorithm to the optimal routing strategy. We computed the optimal strategy by using a linear programming package[2]. We computed the ratio of the lifetime of the *max-min* zP_{min} algorithm to the optimal lifetime. Figure 8 shows that $max - min$ zP_{min} performs better than 80% of optimal for 92% of the experiments and performs within more than 90% of the optimal for 53% of the experiments. Since the optimal algorithm has the advantage of knowing the message sequence, we believe that *max-min* zP_{min} is practical for applications where there is no knowledge of the message sequence.

4.4 Analysis of the *Max-min* zP_{min} Algorithm

In this section we quantify the experimental results from the previous section in an attempt to formulate more precisely our original intuition about the trade-off between the minimal power routing and max-min power routing. We provide a lower bound for the lifetime of the *max-min* zP_{min} algorithm as compared to the optimal solution. We discuss this bound for a general case where there is some cyclicity to the messages that flow in the system and then show the specialization to the no cyclicity case.

Suppose the message distribution is regular, that is, in any period of time $[t_1, t_1 + \delta)$, the message distributions on the nodes in the network are the

---

[2]To compute the optimal lifetime, the message rates are known. The max-min algorithm does not have this information.

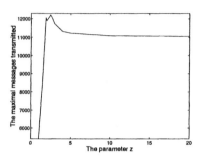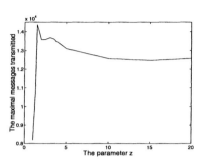

Figure 6: The effect of z on the maximal number of messages in a square network space. The positions of hosts are generated randomly. In the first graph the network scope is $10 * 10$, the number of hosts is 20, the weights are generated by $e_{ij} = 0.001 * d_{ij}^3$, the initial power of each host is 30, and messages are generated between all possible pairs of the hosts and are distributed evenly. In the second graph the number of hosts is 40, the initial power of each node is 10, and all other parameters are the same as the first graph.

same. Since in sensor networks we expect some sort of cyclicity for message transmission, we assume that we can schedule the message transmission with the same policy in each time slice we call δ. In other words, we partition the time line into many time slots $[0, \delta), [\delta, 2\delta), [2\delta, 3\delta), \cdots$. Note that δ is the lifetime of the network if there is no cyclical behavior in message transmission. We assume the same messages are generated in each δ slot but their sequence may be different.

Let the optimal algorithm be denoted by O, and the max-min zP_{min} algorithm be denoted by M. By optimal algorithm, we mean an algorithm that can give the maximal lifetime to the network among all the possible algorithms. In M, each message is transmitted along a path whose overall power consumption is less than z times the minimal power consumption for that message. The initial time is 0. The lifetime of the network by algorithm O is T_O, and the lifetime by algorithm M is T_M. The initial power of each node is: $P_{10}, P_{20}, P_{30}, \cdots, P_{(n-1)0}, P_{n0}$. The remaining power of each node at T_O by running algorithm O is: $P_{1O}, P_{2O}, P_{3O}, \cdots, P_{n-1O}, P_{nO}$. The remaining power of each node at T_M by running algorithm M is: $P_{1M}, P_{2M}, P_{3M}, \cdots, P_{n-1M}, P_{nM}$. Let the message sequence in any slot

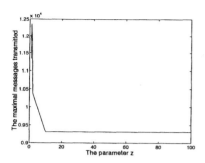 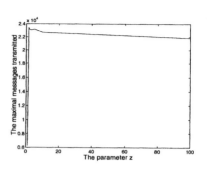

Figure 7: The first figure shows the effect of z on the maximal number of messages in a ring network. The radius of the circle is 20, the number of hosts is 20, the weights are generated by $e_{ij} = 0.0001 * d_{ij}^3$, the initial power of each host is 10 and messages are generated between all possible pairs of the hosts and are distributed evenly. The second figure shows a network with four columns of the size $1 * 0.1$. Each area has ten hosts which are randomly distributed. The distance between two adjacent columns is 1. The right figure gives the performance when z changes. The vertical axis is the maximal messages sent before the first host is saturated. The number of hosts is 40; the weight formula is $e_{ij} = 0.001 * d_{ij}^3$; the initial power of each host is 1; messages are generated between all possible pairs of the hosts and are distributed evenly.

be $m_1, m_2, \cdots, m_s$, and the minimal power consumption to transmit those messages be $P_{0m_1}, P_{0m_2}, P_{0m_3}, \cdots, P_{0m_s}$.

Theorem 4.1 *The lifetime of algorithm M satisfies*

$$T_M \geq \frac{T_O}{z} + \frac{\delta \cdot \left(\sum_{k=1}^n P_{kO} - \sum_{k=1}^n P_{kM} \right)}{z \cdot \sum_{k=1}^s P_{0m_k}} \tag{3}$$

Proof. We have

$$\sum_{k=1}^n P_{k0} = \sum_{k=1}^n P_{kM} + \sum_{k=1}^{M_{T_M}} P_{Mm_k} = P_M$$

where M_{T_M} is the number of messages transmitted from time point 0 to T_M. P_{Mm_k} is the power consumption of the k-th message by running algorithm

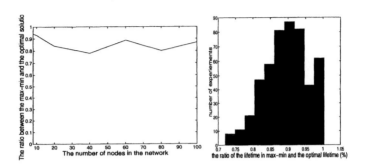

Figure 8: The first graph compares the performance of max-min zP_{min} to the optimal solution. The positions of hosts in the network are generated randomly. The network scope is $10 * 10$, the weight formula is $e_{ij} = 0.0001 * d_{ij}^3$, the initial power of each host is 10, messages are generated from each host to a specific gateway host, the ratio z is 100.0. The second figure shows the histogram that compares max-min zP_{min} to optimal for 500 experiments. In each experiment the network consists of 20 nodes randomly placed in a 10*10 network space. The cost of messages is given by $e_{ij} = 0.001 * d_{ij}^3$. The hosts have the same initial power and messages are generated for hosts to one gateway host. The horizontal axis is the ratio between the lifetime of the max-min zP_{min} max-min algorithm and the optimal lifetime, which is computed off-line.

M. We also have:

$$\sum_{k=1}^{n} P_{k0} = \sum_{k=1}^{n} P_{kO} + \sum_{k=1}^{M_{T_O}} P_{Om_k} = P_O$$

where M_{T_O} is the number of messages transmitted from time point 0 to T_O. P_{Om_k} is the power consumption of of the k-th message by running algorithm O.

Since the messages are the same for any two slots without considering their sequence, we can schedule the messages such that the message rates along the same route are the same in the two slots (think about divide every message into many tiny packets, and average the message rate along a route in algorithm O into the two consecutive slots evenly.). We have:

$$\sum_{k=1}^{M_{T_O}} P_{Om_k} = \frac{M_{T_O}}{s} \cdot \sum_{k=1}^{s} P_{Om_k} = \frac{T_O}{\delta} \cdot \sum_{k=1}^{s} P_{Om_k}$$

and

$$\sum_{k=1}^{M_{T_M}} P_{Mm_k} = \sum_{j=1}^{T_M/\delta} \sum_{k=1}^{s} P_{Mmkj}$$

So we have:

$$P_O = \sum_{k=1}^{n} P_{kO} + \frac{T_O}{\delta} \cdot \sum_{k=1}^{s} P_{Om_k}$$

$$P_M = \sum_{k=1}^{n} P_{kM} + \sum_{j=1}^{T_M/\delta} \sum_{k=1}^{s} P_{Mmkj}$$

and

$$P_O = P_M$$

P_{Mmkj} is the power consumption of the k-th message in slot j by running algorithm M. We also have the following assumption and the minimal power of P_{0mk}. For any $1 \leq j \leq \frac{T_M}{\delta}$ and k, we have only one corresponding l,

$$P_{Mmkj} \leq z \cdot P_{0m_l} \text{ and } P_{Om_k} \geq P_{0m_k}$$

Then,

$$P_O \geq \sum_{k=1}^{n} P_{kO} + \frac{T_O}{\delta} \cdot \sum_{k=1}^{s} P_{0m_k}$$

$$P_M \leq \sum_{k=1}^{n} P_{kM} + \frac{z \cdot T_M}{\delta} \cdot \sum_{k=1}^{s} P_{0m_k}$$

Thus,

$$\sum_{k=1}^{n} P_{kM} + \frac{z \cdot T_M}{\delta} \cdot \sum_{k=1}^{s} P_{0m_k} \geq \sum_{k=1}^{n} P_{kO} + \frac{T_O}{\delta} \cdot \sum_{k=1}^{s} P_{0m_k}$$

We have:

$$T_M \geq \frac{T_O}{z} + \frac{\delta \cdot (\sum_{k=1}^{n} P_{kO} - \sum_{k=1}^{n} P_{kM})}{z \cdot \sum_{k=1}^{s} P_{0m_k}}$$

$\square$

Theorem 4.1 gives us insight into how well the message routing algorithm does with respect to optimizing the lifetime of the network. Given a network topology and a message distribution, T_O, δ, $\sum_{k=1}^{n} P_{kO}$, $\sum_{k=1}^{s} P_{0m_k}$ are all fixed in Equation 3. The variables that determine the actual lifetime are $\sum_{k=1}^{n} P_{kM}$ and z. The smaller $\sum_{k=1}^{n} P_{kM}{}^3$ is, the better the performance lower bound is. And the smaller z is, the better the performance lower bound is. However, a small z will lead to a large $\sum_{k=1}^{n} P_{kM}$. This explains the trade-off between minimal power path and max-min path.

Theorem 4.1 can be used in applications that have a regular message distribution without the restriction that all the messages are the same in two different slots. For these applications, the ratio between δ and $\sum_{k=1}^{s} P_{0m_k}$ must be changed to $1/\sum_{k=1}^{r} P_{0m_k}$, where P_{0m_k} is the minimal power consumption for the message generated in a unit of time.

Theorem 4.2 *The optimal lifetime of the network is at most* $\dfrac{t_{SPT} \cdot \sum P_h}{\sum P_h - \sum P_h^{SPT}}$ *where t_{SPT} and P_h^{SPT} are the life time of the network and remaining power of host h by using the least power consumption routing strategy. P_h is the initial power of host h.*

Proof. $t_{OPT} \leq \dfrac{\sum P_h}{\sum P_m^{SPT}} = \sum P_h / \left(\dfrac{\sum P_h - \sum P_h^{SPT}}{t_{SPT}} \right) = \dfrac{t_{SPT} \cdot \sum P_h}{\sum P_h - \sum P_h^{SPT}}$ $\square$

5 Hierarchical Routing with $max\text{-}min\ zP_{min}$

Although it has nice theoretical and empirical properties, $max\text{-}min\ zP_{min}$ algorithm is hard to implement on large scale networks. The main obstacle is that $max\text{-}min\ zP_{min}$ requires accurate power level information for all the nodes in the network. It is difficult to collect this information from all the nodes in the network. One way to do it is by broadcast, but this would generate a huge power consumption which defeats our original goals. Furthermore, it is not clear how often such a broadcast would be necessary to keep the network data current. In this section we propose a hierarchical approach to power-aware routing that does not use as much information, does not know the message sequence, and relies in a feasible way on $max\text{-}min\ zP_{min}$.

We propose to organize the network structurally in geographical zones, and hierarchically to control routing across the zones. The idea is to group

---

[3]This is the remaining power of the network at the limit of the network.

together all the nodes that are in geographic proximity as a zone, treat the zone as an entity in the network, and allow each zone to decide how to route a message across[4]. The hosts in a zone autonomously direct local routing and participate in estimating the zone power level. Each message is routed across the zones using information about the zone power estimates. In our vision, a global controller for message routing manages the zones. This may be the node with the highest power, although other schemes such as round robin may also be employed.

If the network can be divided into a relatively small number of zones, the scale for the global routing algorithm is reduced. The global information required to send each message across is summarized by the power level estimate of each zone. We believe that in sensor networks this value will not need frequent updates because observable changes will occur only after long periods of time.

The rest of this section discusses (1) how the hosts in a zone collaborate to estimate the power of the zone; (2) how a message is routed within a zone; and (3) how a message is routed across zones. (1) and (2) will use our $max\text{-}min$ zP_{min} algorithm, which can be implemented in a distributed way by slightly modifying our definition of the $max\text{-}min$ zP_{min} path. The $max - min$ algorithm used in (3) is basically the Bellman-Ford algorithm, which can also be implemented as a distributed algorithm.

5.1 Zone Power Estimation

The power estimate for each zone is controlled by a node in the zone. This estimation measures the number of messages that can flow through the zone. Since the messages come from one neighboring zone and get directed to a different neighboring zone, we propose a method in which the power estimation is done *relative to the direction* of message transmission.

The protocol employed by the controller node consists of polling each node for its power level followed by running the $max\text{-}min$ zP_{min} algorithm. The returned value is then broadcast to all the zones in the system. The frequency of this procedure is inversely proportional to the estimated power level. When the power level is high, the power estimation update can be done infrequently because messages routed through the zone in this period will not change the overall power distribution in the entire network much.

---

[4]This geographical partitioning can be implemented easily using GPS information from each host.

When the power level is low, message transmission through the zone is likely to change the power distribution significantly.

Without loss of generality, we assume that zones are square so that they have four neighbors pointed to the North, South, East, and West[5]. We assume further that it is possible to communicate between the nodes that are close to the border between two zones, so that in effect the border nodes are part of both zones. In other words, neighboring zones that can communicate with each other have an area of overlap (see Figure 9 (first)).

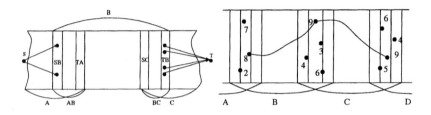

Figure 9: Three zones, A, B, and C. SB, SC are the source areas of B and C, and TA, TB are the sink areas of A and B. AB and BC are overlap border areas. The right figure shows how to connect the local path in zone B with the local path in zone C. The number next to each node is the number of paths passing through that node in the power evaluation procedure. The vertical stripes are the source and sink areas of the zones.

The power estimate of a zone can be approximated as follows. We can use the *max-min* zP_{min} algorithm to evaluate the power level, find the *max-min* zP_{min} path, simulate sending Δ messages through the path, and repeat until the network is saturated. Δ is chosen to be proportionate to the power level of the zone.

More precisely, consider Figure 9 (first). To estimate the power of zone B with respect to sending messages in the direction from A to C, let the left part of the overlap between A and B be the source area and the right part of the overlap between B and C the sink area. The power of zone B in the direction from A to C is the maximal number of messages that can flow from the source nodes to the sink nodes before a node in B gets saturated. This can be computed with the *max-min* zP_{min} algorithm (see Fig. 10). We start with the power graph of zone B and augment it. We create an

---

[5]this method can easily be generalized to zones with finite number of neighboring zones.

choose Δ for the message granularity. $P = 0$;
repeat{
        Find the *max-min* zP_{min} path for Δ messages
        send the Δ messages through the zone
        $P = P + \Delta$
} **until** (some nodes are saturated)
return P

Figure 10: An approximation algorithm for zone power evaluation.

imaginary source node S and connect it to all the source nodes. We create an imaginary sink node T and connect all the sink nodes to it. Let the weights of the newly added edges be 0. The *max-min* zP_{min} algorithm run on this graph determines the power estimate for zone B in the direction of A to C.

5.2 Global Path Selection

Given power-levels for each possible direction of message transmission, it is possible to construct a small zone-graph that models the global message routing problem. Figure 11 shows an example of a zone graph. A zone with k neighbors is represented by $k + 1$ vertices in this graph[6]. One vertex labels the zone; k vertices correspond to each message direction through the zone. The zone label vertex is connected to all the message direction vertices by edges in both direction. In addition, the message direction vertices are connected to the neighboring zone vertices if the current zone can go to the next neighboring zone in that direction. Each zone vertex has a power level of ∞. Each zone direction vertex is labeled by its estimated power level computed with the procedure in Section 5.1. Unlike in the model we proposed in Section 3.1, the edges in this zone graph do not have weights. Thus, the global route for sending a message can be found as the max-min path in the zone graph that starts in the originator's zone vertex and ends in the destination zone vertex for the message. We would like to bias towards path selection that uses the zones with higher power level. We can modify the Bellman-Ford algorithm (Fig. 12) to accomplish this.

---

[6]For square zones $k = 4 + 1$ as shown in Figure 11.

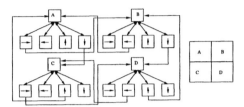

Figure 11: Four zones are in a square network field. The power of a zone is evaluated in four directions, left, right, up, and down. A zone is represented as a zone vertex with four direction vertices. The power labels are omitted from this figure.

5.3 Local Path Selection

Given a global route across zones, our goal is to find actual routes for messages within a zone. The *max-min zP_{min}* algorithm is used directly to route a message within a zone.

If there are multiple entry points into the zone, and multiple exit points to the next zone, it is possible that two paths through adjacent zones do not share any nodes. These paths have to be connected.

The following algorithm is used to ensure that the paths between adjacent zones are connected (see Figure 9 (right)). For each node in the overlap region, we compute how many paths can be routed locally through that node when zone power is evaluated. In order to optimize the message flow between zones, we find paths that go through the nodes that can sustain the maximal number of messages. Thus, to route a message through zone B in the direction from A to C we select the node with maximum message weight in the overlap between A and B, then we select the node with maximum message weight in the overlap between B and C, and compute the *max-min zP_{min}* paths between these two nodes.

5.4 Performance Evaluation for Zone-based Routing

The zone-based routing algorithm does not require as much information as would be required by *max-min zP_{min}* algorithm over the entire network. By giving up this information, we can expect the zone-based algorithm to perform worse than the *max-min zP_{min}* algorithm. We designed large experiments to measure how the zone-based algorithm does relative to the

Given graph $G(V, E)$, annotated with power level $p(v)$ for
each $v \in V$.
Find the path from s to t, $s = v_0, v_1, \cdots, v_{k-1}, v_k = t$ such
that $min_{i=1}^{k-1} p(v_i)$ is maximal.
for each vertex $v \in V[G]$ **do**
    If edge $(s, v) \in E[G]$ **then**
        $d[v] \leftarrow \infty$, $\pi[v] \leftarrow s$
      else $d[v] \leftarrow 0$, $\pi[v] \leftarrow NIL$
$d[s] \leftarrow \infty$

for $i \leftarrow 1$ **to** $|V[G]| - 1$ **do**
    for each edge $(u, v) \in E[G]$ and $u \neq s$ **do**
        if $d[v] < min(d[u], p[u])$ **then**
            $d[v] \leftarrow min(d[u], p[u])$
            $\pi[v] \leftarrow u$
return $\pi[t]$

Figure 12: Maximal minimum power level path

max-min zP_{min} algorithm. (In the following experiments, we only consider
the power consumption used for the application messages instead of the
control messages. Thus we can compare how much the performance of our
zone-based algorithm is close to that of the *max-min* zP_{min} algorithm
without the influence of the control messages.)

We disperse $1,000$ nodes randomly in a regular network space (see Figure 13). The zone partition is described in the figure. Each zone has av-
eragely 40 nodes. Each node sends one message to a gateway node in each
round (A round is the time for all the nodes to finish sending messages to
the gateway). The zone power evaluation protocol is executed after each
round. By running the *max-min* zP_{min} algorithm, we ran the algorithm
for about 41000 messages before one of the hosts got saturated. By running
the zone-based routing algorithm, we got about 39000 messages before the
first message could not be sent through. The performance ratio between the
two algorithms in terms of the lifetime of the network is 94.5%. Without the
zone structure, the number of control messages on the power of each node
in every information update is 1000, and they need to be broadcast to 1000

nodes. In zone-based algorithm, the number of control messages is just the number of the zones, 48 here, and they are broadcast to 24 zones after the zone power evaluation. And the zone-based routing dramatically reduces the running time to find a route in our simulation. In another experiment, we disperse 1240 sensors to a square field with size 6.2 ∗ 6.2. The sensors are distributed randomly in the field. Each sensor has an initial power of 400. The power consumption formula is $e_{ij} = 10 * d_{ij}^3$. The network field is divided by 5*5 squares each of which corresponds to four zones in four directions (left, right, up and down). The zone-based algorithm achieved 96% of the lifetime of the $max\text{-}min\ zP_{min}$ algorithm.

6   Distributed Routing with $max\text{-}min\ zP_{min}$

The algorithms discussed in the previous sections do not work for applications where it is impossible to control in a centralized way the message flow in the ad-hoc network. Applications in which nodes move frequently and unpredictably fall in this category. In this section we investigate a class of routing algorithms for which computation is distributed and information localized. We use the algorithms mainly for sensor networks in which all the messages are sent back to the base. The algorithms, however, can be adapted to ad-hoc networks in which messages can be sent between any two nodes by setting the destination node as base.

We introduce three new algorithms: a distributed minimal power algorithm, a distributed max-min power algorithm, and the distributed $max\text{-}min\ zP_{min}$ power-aware algorithm. The first two algorithms can be used to define the third, although they are very interesting and useful in their own right for applications in which the optimization criteria are the minimum power and the maximum residual power, respectively.

6.1   A Distributed Minimal Power Algorithm

We can develop a distributed version of Dijkstra's algorithm that is guaranteed to be a minimal-power path, by giving messages variable propagation delays. The idea is to have messages traveling along short paths move faster than messages traveling along long paths. Thus, messages traveling along shorter paths will arrive faster than messages traveling along longer paths— that is, the algorithm will select the shorter paths. In this case, the Dijkstra distance corresponds to power-consumption.

We can implement this idea by augmenting each message with a record of how far it traveled from the base to the current node. This information is represented by a variable attached to the message for the cost (distance representing power consumption). Fig. 14 is the resulting minimal power path algorithm.

We continue this section by arguing that Fig. 14 produces the minimal power-consumption path for each node. Furthermore, the running time of the algorithm is proportional to the longest shortest distance from the base node to any node.

We first examine a special case—when messages are time-sorted in the following sense. Suppose two messages carrying "distance" values v_1 and v_2 arrive at the same node at time t_1 and t_2. If for any two messages with $v_1 < v_2$, we have $t_1 < t_2$, the messages are *time-sorted*. Let n be the number of nodes in the network. In order to keep our proof simple, we assume that message transmission is instantaneous—this restriction can be relaxed.

Theorem 6.1 *If the messages are time-sorted, then Fig. 14 requires $O(n)$ broadcasting messages ($O(1)$ for each node).*

Proof. Let the message value of a message be the distance from the base station to the current node. Since the messages are time-sorted, the earliest message must carry the shortest distance from the base station to the current node. By line 9 of the algorithm, this message will be broadcast only once after the t_B waiting period has been completed. □

In Fig. 14 the messages are not time-sorted. However, the messages become time-sorted if we consider the broadcast time of a node as the message arrival time (because of the delays enforced by the algorithm) and by Theorem 6.1, Fig. 14 gives the shortest path within $O(n)$ broadcasts.

Note that the performance of our algorithm depends on the granularity at which we can measure power. Let the smallest measurement unit for power consumption be s. The parameter η, which can be chosen as the smallest time unit a node can distinguish, is the waiting time that corresponds to distance s. The running time of Fig. 14 is proportional to $1/s$ and to the size of the largest minimal power path. A large value for s results in a fast running time, but at the expense of precision. Say two messages that travel along paths with power consumption of P and $P + s_1$ (where $s_1 < s$) arrive at the same node in an interval less than η. The node may not distinguish them because the time difference is too small. Therefore, the running time is dependent on the precision of the required power consumption measurement. A better running time can be obtained by allowing a low measurement precision, that is, a large unit power consumption η. We can use these ideas to improve performance as described in Fig. 15.

Let P be the maximal minimal power consumption from the base station to any node. We divide $[0, P)$ into m slots, $[0, P/m), [P/m, 2P/m), \cdots,$ $[iP/m, (i+1)P/m), \cdots, [(m-1)P/m, P)$. When a node receives a message with value v, it first finds the ith slot such that $iP/m \leq v < (i+1)P/m$, waits till time $i\delta$, and then broadcasts the message to its neighbors. The running time of the algorithm $(m\delta)$ is proportional to m and the parameter δ, which is the time interval corresponding to P/m.

We can choose δ to be large enough so that any message traveling from the base station to any node in the network along a minimal power path with total message processing time $\epsilon < \delta$. (That is, the sum of the message processing time at each node on the minimal power path is less than δ).

Theorem 6.2 *For Fig. 15, the number of messages broadcast by each node is no greater than the maximal number of paths from the base to a node with the power consumption in the same slot as that of the minimal power path (that is, $[iP/m, (i+1)P/m)$ in which the minimal power consumption lies).*

Proof. Consider a message arriving at node A and scheduled to be broadcast in the slot $[i\delta, (i+1)\delta)$.

The message traveling along the minimal power path arrives at A at some time point before $i\delta + \epsilon$ since we assume the total message handling time (including message buffering, queuing, and propagation) is less than ϵ.

A message traveling along a path with power no less than $(i+1) \cdot \frac{P}{m}$ will not be scheduled to be broadcast because the node stops broadcasting at time $(i+1)\delta$.

There is no path with power consumption less than $i \cdot \frac{P}{m}$ to that node, so no message can be broadcast before $i\delta$ by that node.

Thus, only the messages traveling along the paths with power in the range of $[P_{min}, (i+1)\delta)$ can be scheduled to broadcast. $\square$

Theorem 6.3 *Fig. 15 gives the minimal power consumption route for each node.*

Proof. The message traveling along the minimal power path arrives at A at some time point before $i\delta + \epsilon < (i+1)\delta$ since we assume the total message handling time (including message buffering, queuing, and propagation) is less than ϵ. There is no path with power consumption less than $i \cdot \frac{P}{m}$ to that node, so no message can be broadcast before $i\delta$ by that node.

Thus, the message traveling along the minimal power path will be broadcast at each node. Then each node can look at the power consumption value carried by the message and set the node who broadcast the message as its route.   □

6.2 A Distributed Max-Min algorithm

The minimal power path algorithm does not consider the residual power of nodes when computing the route. Although a packet is routed along the minimal power path, some nodes on that path may be saturated very quickly. An alternative is to use the nodes with high power and avoid the nodes that are almost saturated, which leads to the max-min path for packet routing.

The max-min path is defined as the route from a node to the base on which the minimal residual power of the nodes is maximized among all the routes. The minimal residual power of a path $p(c,d)$ is $c = a_1, a_2, \cdots, a_k = d$, defined as $m_{p(c,d)} = min_{i=1}^{n-1} \frac{P(a_i) - e(a_i, a_{i+1})}{P(a_i)}$. The max-min value is $F_{(c,d)} = max_{all\ p(c,d)} m_{p(c,d)}$. For multiple routes with the same max-min residual power, we can resolve ties arbitrarily.

Max-min paths can be found by using a modified version of the distributed Bellman-Ford algorithm. Upon computing a new max-min value, each node broadcasts it. The neighbors compute their max-min value according to the new incoming value, and broadcast the result only if the value is changed. The number of message broadcasts may be $O(n^3)$ as in the case of the distributed Bellman-Ford algorithm.

To reduce the message broadcasts, we employ the same method as in Section 6.1 and add a variable waiting time on each node, which controls when the node broadcasts. Fig. 16 summarizes the resulting protocol. We assume all the nodes are synchronized well, so that they can decide locally the global time. Thus, a global clock is not needed to make this protocol work.

The max-min approximation, Fig. 16 considers the maximal residual power fraction of all nodes in the network F_{max} split into m slots $([0, F_{max}/m), [F_{max}/m, 2F_{max}/m), \cdots, [iF_{max}/m, (i+1)F_{max}/m), \cdots, [(m-1)F_{max}/m, F_{max}))$. The m slots are mapped to consecutive δ long time slots

$(s_1, s_2, \cdots, s_m.)$ In s_i the algorithm will find all the nodes whose max-min values are in slot $[(i-1)F_{max}/m, iF_{max}/m]$. The nodes found in the earlier slots have higher max-min values than those found in later slots.

We assume that the base has the maximal max-min value in the beginning of the algorithm. Thus, the base initiates the algorithm in the first slot s_1. Upon receiving the max-min values from the neighbors, nodes update their max-min value. Nodes wait until the time slot corresponding to the current max-min value, and then broadcast the value to their neighbors. If a node receives a new incoming value in some slot, say s_i, and finds that its max-min value should also be broadcast in this time slot, the broadcast is immediate. Thus, the nodes with max-min values in $[(i-1)F_{max}/m, iF_{max}/m)$ will be found as the messages go around the whole network.

If all the nodes have synchronized clocks, this algorithm performs $O(1)$ message broadcasts for each node. Otherwise, the base must initiate a synchronized broadcast to all the nodes to start a new slot and the number of broadcasts per node becomes $O(m)$.

Since each node broadcasts at most m messages, the running time of the algorithm is $m\delta$ where δ is the time for each round, which is at most n times the per message handling time. Furthermore, we can prove the following result using induction.

Theorem 6.4 *For each node, the algorithm gives a route with the minimal residual power fraction F, such that F and F^m are in the same slot where F^m is the max-min power fraction of the route from the base to that node. Then we have $|F - F^m| \le F_{max}/m$.*

Proof. We use induction. In the first round, the maximal max-min value is broadcast by the base node. Each node that has the max-min value in the slot will broadcast the message.

For any node B with max-min value F_B^m in slot i, it is impossible for B to broadcast its value in slots before i. That is, F_B must be no greater than F_B^m, the actual max-min value of node B. This can be derived by examining the computation of F_B.

Suppose each node who finishes broadcast has F and F^m in the same slot. For any node B whose max-min value is in slot i, let A be the upstream node on the max-min path from the base to B. If B broadcasts its max-min value before A, then B can determine A's slot. Otherwise, A must broadcast its max-min value before B and B will hear the max-min value of A. Thus, from the algorithm, we have (see Fig. 16)

$min(F_A^m, \frac{P(A)-e(A,B)}{P(A)}) = F_B^m \geq F_B \geq min(F_A, \frac{P(A)-e(A,B)}{P(A)})$. We know $min(F_A^m, \frac{P(A)-e(A,B)}{P(A)})$ and $min(F_A, \frac{P(A)-e(A,B)}{P(A)})$ are in the same slot, so F_B and F_B^m are in the same slot. $\qquad\square$

We can improve Fig. 16 using binary search. The running time can be reduced to $\delta \log m$, but the number of total messages sent is $n \log m$. The key idea is to split the range $[0, F_{max})$ in two, $[0, F_{max}/2)$ and $[F_{max}/2, F_{max})$. In the first epoch, the algorithm tries to find all the nodes within the highest half max-min values. In the second epoch, we split each range into two halves to get four ranges. The algorithm finds in parallel all the nodes with highest half max-min values for each range, etc.

6.3 Distributed *max-min* zP_{min}

We now derive the distributed version of the centralized online *max-min* zP_{min} algorithm. Like in the centralized case, our motivation is to define a routing algorithm that optimizes the overall lifetime of the network by avoiding nodes of low power, while not using too much total power. There is a trade-off between minimizing the total power consumption and maximizing the minimal residual power of the network. We propose to enhance a max-min path by limiting its total power consumption.

Recall that the network is described as a graph in which each vertex corresponds to a node in the network, and only two nodes within the transmission ranges of each other have an edge connecting them in the graph. The power level of a node a is denoted as $P(a)$, and the power consumption to send a message unit to one of its neighbors b is denoted as $e(a, b)$. Let $s(a)$ be the power consumption for sending a unit message from a to the base station along the least power consumption path. Let $r(a)$ be the minimum residual power fraction of the nodes on a's *mmz* path. Let P_a be the power consumption along the *mmz* path.

An *mmz* path has the following properties:

1. it consists of two parts: the edge connecting a to one of its neighbors and the *mmz* path of that neighbor;

2. its total power consumption is less then or equal to $z \cdot s(a)$; and

3. among all those paths defined by (1) and (2), the max-min value of the *mmz* path is maximized.

More precisely, $p(a)$ the mmz path of node a, is: (1) a simple path from a to the base station; (2) $P_a < z \cdot s(a)$; and (3) $p(a) = (a, b) \cup p(b)$, where b is a's neighbor such that for any other neighbor c $r(a) = min(r(b), \frac{P(a)-e(a,b)}{P(a)}) \geq min(r(c), \frac{P(a)-e(a,c)}{P(a)})$.

Theorem 6.5 *There is one node b_j such as $e(a, b_j) + f(b_j) \leq z \cdot s(a)$.*

Proof. Use induction. The case for base is obvious. Let b_j be the node on the shortest path from a to the base. $P_{b_j} \leq z \cdot s(b_j)$ and $e(a, b_j) + s(b_j) = s(a)$. So $e(a, b_j) + P_{b_j} \leq e(a, b_j) + z \cdot s(b_j) \leq z \cdot (e(a, b_j) + s(b_j)) = z \cdot s(a)$ $\qquad \square$

Note that $s(a)$ can be computed easily by using $s(a) = min \{s(b) + e(a, b)\}$ where b is a's neighbor.

The definition of the mmz path actually gives a constructive method for computing incrementally the mmz path by keeping track of $s(node), r(node), p(node)$ of each node because the computation only depends on these values at the node's neighbors. Let $n(node)$ be the next node on the path $p(node)$. The resulting algorithm is shown as Fig. 17. In the algorithm, the base station initiates the route exploration by broadcasting its route information ($s(base), r(base)$, and $n(base)$ to its neighbors). When a node's route information changes, it broadcasts its updated information. This broadcast triggers its neighbor nodes to check if their route information changes. Every time the route information of a node changes the information is broadcast until the system achieves equilibrium.

In our distributed version of the Max-min zP_{min} algorithm, we expect a total of $O(n^3)$ message broadcasts in the worst case.

It is possible to improve the number of message broadcasts by using timing variables to suppress some of the messages. We can also vary the timing granularity by dividing into slots. Two specific approaches are

- In the max-min part, let the message carry the total power consumption on the path, and use the power consumption to decide if the max-min value should be accepted.

- In the minimal power path part, incorporate the max-min value in the waiting time.

6.4   Experiments in simulation

We have implemented the distributed algorithms outlined in this section and studied the performance of the distributed $max\text{-}min\ zP_{min}$ algorithm. Furthermore, we compared this algorithm against a Greedy-style distributed algorithm.

Figure 18 shows the concept behind our greedy routing implementation. Periodically, nodes exchange power information with their neighbors. When there is a message at A for destination D, A finds the node B with the highest power level in the its transmission range centered at A with angle θ, which is bisected by line AD, and sends the message to B.

Figure 19 shows the performance comparison of the distributed $max\text{-}min\ zP_{min}$ algorithm and the distributed greedy algorithm. We conclude that $max\text{-}min\ zP_{min}$ outperforms a simple greedy algorithm for all values of z, and for some values of z the distributed $max\text{-}min\ zP_{min}$ doubles the performance. More specifically, peak of the $max\text{-}min\ zP_{min}$ algorithm is obtained when z=1.2, and the number of messages sent is 29078. When z=2, the number message sent is the lowest at 18935. The distributed greedy algorithm sent 14278 messages in total. The performance improvement is 103% in the best case when z=1.2 and 32.61% in the worst case.

We are currently collecting empirical data on the trade-offs between the various parameters we introduced to describe our algorithms.

7   Conclusion

We have described several online algorithms for power-aware routing of messages in large networks dispersed over large geographical areas. In most applications that involve ad-hoc networks made out of small hand-held computers, mobile computers, robots, or smart sensors, battery level is a real issue in the duration of the network. Power management can be done at two complementary levels (1) during communication and (2) during idle time. We believe that optimizing the performance of communication algorithms for power consumption and for the lifetime of the network is a very important problem.

It is hard to analyze the performance of online algorithms that do not rely on knowledge about the message arrival and distribution. This assumption is very important as in most real applications the message patterns are not known ahead of time. In this chapter we have shown that it is impossible to design an on-line algorithm that has a constant competitive ratio to the optimal off-line algorithm, and we computed a bound on the lifetime of a network whose messages are routed according to this algorithm. These results are very encouraging.

We developed an online algorithm called the $max\text{-}min$ zP_{min} algorithm and showed that it had a good empirical competitive ratio to the optimal off-line algorithm that knows the message sequence. We also showed empirically that $max\text{-}min$ zP_{min} achieves over 80% of the optimal (where the optimal router knows all the messages ahead of time) for most instances and over 90% of the optimal for many problem instances. Since this algorithm requires accurate power values for all the nodes in the system at all times, we proposed a second algorithm which is hierarchical. Zone-based power-aware routing partitions the ad-hoc network into a small number of zones. Each zone can evaluate its power level with a fast protocol. These power estimates are then used as weights on the zones. A global path for each message is determined across zones. Within each zone, a local path for the message is computed so as to not decrease the power level of the zone too much. Finally, we have developed a distributed version of the $max\text{-}min$ zP_{min}, in which all the decisions use local information only, and showed that this algorithm outperforms significantly a distributed greedy-style algorithm.

Acknowledgments. This work bas been supported in part by Department of Defense contract MURI F49620-97-1-0382 and DARPA contract F30602-98-2-0107, ONR grant N00014-01-1-0675, NSF CAREER award IRI-9624286, NSF award I1S-9912193, Honda corporation, and the Sloan foundation; we are grateful for this support. We thank the anonymous reviewers for their suggestions.

References

[1] Adcon Telemetetry, http://www.adcon.com.

[2] Range LAN, http://www.proxim.com/products/rl2/7410.shtml.

[3] Jon Agre and Loren Clare. An integrated architeture for cooperative sensing networks. *Computer*, pages 106 – 108, May 2000.

[4] A.D. Amis, R. Prakash, T.H.P. Vuong, and D.T. Huynh. Max-min d-cluster formation in wireless ad hoc networks. In *Proceedings IEEE INFOCOM 2000. Conference on Computer Communications*, March 2000.

[5] Jae-Hwan Chang and Leandros Tassiulas. Energy conserving routing in wireless ad-hoc networks. In *Proc. IEEE INFOCOM*, Tel Aviv, Israel, Mar. 2000.

[6] Benjie Chen, Kyle Jamieson, Hari Balakrishnan, and Robert Morris. Span: An energy-efficient coordination algorithm for topology maintenance in ad hoc wireless networks. In *7th Annual Int. Conf. Mobile Computing and Networking 2001*, Rome, Italy, July 2001.

[7] Jyh-Cheng Chen, Krishna M. Silvalingam, and Prathima Agrawal. Performance comparison of battery power consumption in wireless multiple access protocols. *Wireless Networks*, 5(6):445–460, 1999.

[8] X. Cheng, D.-Z. Du, L. Wang, and B. Xu. Relay sensor placement in wireless sensor networks. *submitted to IEEE Transactions on Computers.*

[9] X. Cheng, X. Huang, D. Li, and D.-Z. Du. Polynomial-time approximation scheme for minimum connected dominating set in ad hoc wireless networks. *submitted to Networks.*

[10] Xiuzhen Cheng and Ding-Zhu Du. Virtual backbone-based routing in ad hoc wireless networks. *submitted to IEEE Transactions on Parallel and Distributed Systems.*

[11] I. Chlamtac, C. Petrioli, and J. Redi. Energy-conserving access protocols for indetification networks. *IEEE/ACM Transactions on Networking*, 7(1):51–9, Feb. 1999.

[12] A. Chockalingam and M. Zorzi. Energy efficiency of media access protocols for mobile data networks. *IEEE Transactions on Communications*, 46(11):1418–21, Nov. 1998.

[13] B. Das, R. Sivakumar, and V. Bharghavan. Routing in ad hoc networks using a spine. In *Proceedings of Sixth International Conference on Computer Communications and Networks*, Sept. 1997.

[14] Deborah Estrin, Ramesh Govindan, John Heidemann, and Satish Kumar. Next century challenges: Scalable coordination in sensor networks. In *ACM MobiCom 99*, Seattle, USA, August 1999.

[15] Laura Maria Feeney and Martin Nilsson. Investigating the energy consumption of a wireless network interface in an ad hoc networking environment. In *INFOCOM 2001*, April 2001.

[16] M. Gerla, X. Hong, and G. Pei. Landmark routing for large ad hoc wireless networks. In *Proceedings of IEEE GLOBECOM 2000*, San Francisco, CA, Nov. 2000.

[17] Piyush Gupta and P. R. Kumar. Critical power for asymptotic connectivity in wireless networks. *Stochastic Analysis, Control, Optimization and Applications: A Volume in Honor of W.H. Fleming*, pages 547–566, 1998.

[18] Z. J. Haas. A new routing protocol for the reconfigurable wireless network. In *Proceedings of the 1997 IEEE 6th International Conference on Universal Personal Communications, ICUPC'97*, pages 562 –566, San Diego, CA, October 1997.

[19] W. Rabiner Heinzelman, A. Chandrakasan, and H. Balakrishnan. Energy-efficient routing protocols for wireless microsensor networks. In *Hawaii International Conference on System Sciences (HICSS '00)*, Jan. 2000.

[20] Chalermek Intanagonwiwat, Ramesh Govindan, and Deborah Estrin. Directed diffusion: A scalable and robust communication paradigm for sensor networks. In *Proc. of the Sixth Annual International Conference on Mobile Computing and Networks (MobiCOM 2000)*, Boston, Massachusetts, August 2000.

[21] Mario Joa-Ng and I-Tai Lu. A peer-to-peer zone-based two-level link state routing for mobile ad hoc networks. *IEEE Journal on Selected Areas in Communications*, 17, Aug. 1999.

[22] D. B. Johnson and D. A. Maltz. Dynamic source routing in ad-hoc wireless networks. In T. Imielinski and H. Korth, editors, *Mobile Computing*, pages 153 –181. Kluwer Academic Publishers, 1996.

[23] Y. B. Ko and N. H. Vaidya. Location-aided routing (LAR) in mobile ad hoc networks. In *Proceedings of ACM/IEEE MOBICOM'98*, pages 66 – 75, 1998.

[24] P. Krishna, N.H. Vaidya, M. Chatterjee, and D.K. Pradhan. A cluster-based approach for routing in dynamic networks. *Computer Communication Review*, 27, April 1997.

[25] L. Li, Y.M. Wang J. Halpern, V. Bahl, and R. Wattenhofer. Analysis of a cone-based distributed topology control algorithms for wireless multi-hop networks. In *ACM Symposium on Principle of Distributed Computing (PODC)*, August 2001.

[26] Qun Li, Javed Aslam, and Daniela Rus. Online power-aware routing in wireless ad-hoc networks. In *MOBICOM*, pages 97–107, Rome, July 2001.

[27] Qun Li, Ron Peterson, Michael DeRosa, and Daniela Ru. Reactive behavior in self-reconfiguring sensor network. *ACM Mobile Computing and Communications Review*, 2002.

[28] Qun Li and Daniela Rus. Sending messages to mobile users in disconnected ad-hoc wireless networks. In *MOBICOM*, pages 44–55, Boston, August 2000.

[29] A.B. McDonald and T.F. Znati. A mobility-based framework for adaptive clustering in wireless ad hoc networks. *IEEE Journal on Selected Areas in Communications*, 17, Aug. 1999.

[30] S. Murthy and J. J. Garcia-Luna-Aceves. An efficient routing protocol for wireless networks. *ACM/Baltzer Journal on Mobile Networks and Applications*, MANET(1,2):183 –197, October 1996.

[31] V. Park and M. S. Corson. A highly adaptive distributed algorithm for mobile wireless networks. In *Proceedings of INFOCOM'97*, Kobe, Japan, April 1997.

[32] C. E. Perkins and P. Bhagwat. Highly dynamic destination-sequenced distance-vector routing (DSDV) for mobile computers. *Computer Communication review*, 24(4):234 –244, October 1994.

[33] G. J. Pottie and W. J. Kaiser. Wireless integrated newtork sensors. *Communications of the ACM*, 43(5):51–58, May 2000.

[34] Ram Ramanathan and Regina Hain. Topology control of multihop wireless networks using transmit power adjustment. In *INFOCOM*, 2000.

[35] S. Ramanathan and M. Steenstrup. Hierarchically-organized, multihop mobile networks for multimedia support. *ACM/Baltzer Mobile Networks and Applications*, 3(1):101–119, June 1998.

[36] Volkan Rodoplu and Teresa H. Meng. Minimum energy mobile wireless networks. In *Proc. of the 1998 IEEE International Conference on Communications, ICC'98*, volume 3, pages 1633–1639, Atlanta, GA, June 1998.

[37] Elizabeth Royer and C-K. Toh. A review of current routing protocols for ad hoc mobile wireless networks. In *IEEE Personal Communication*, volume 6, pages 46 – 55, April 1999.

[38] S. Singh, M. Woo, and C. S. Raghavendra. Power-aware routing in mobile ad-hoc networks. In *Proc. of Fourth Annual ACM/IEEE International Conference on Mobile Computing and Networking*, pages 181–190, Dallas, TX, Oct. 1998.

[39] Ivan Stojmenovic and Xu Lin. Power aware localized routing in wireless networks. *IEEE Transactions on Parallel and Distributed Systems*, 12(11):1122–1133, November 2001.

[40] J. Wu, F. Dai, M. Gao, and I. Stojmenovic. On calculating power-aware connected dominating set for efficient routing in ad hoc wireless networks. *IEEE/KICS Journal of Communications and Networks*, 4(1):59–70, March 2002.

[41] Ya Xu, John Heidemann, and Deborah Estrin. Adaptive energy-conserving routing for multihop ad hoc networks. *Research Report 527 USC/Information Sciences Institute*, October 2000.

[42] Ya Xu, John Heidemann, and Deborah Estrin. Geography-informed energy conservation for ad hoc routing. In *7th Annual Int. Conf. Mobile Computing and Networking 2001*, Rome, Italy, July 2001.

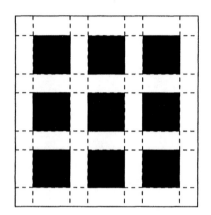   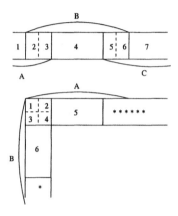

Figure 13: The scenario used for the zone-based experiment. The network space is a $10 * 10$ square with nine buildings blocking the network. Each building is of size $2 * 2$, and regularly placed at distance 1 from the others. The sensors are distributed randomly in the space nearby the buildings. Each sensor has an initial power of 4000. The power consumption formula is $e_{ij} = 10 * d_{ij}^3$. We partition the network space into 24 zones, each of which is of size $1*4$ or $4*1$, depending on its layout. For each zone, there is another corresponding zone with the same nodes but with opposite direction. For example, in the upper-right figure, areas $2, 3, 4, 5, 6$ constitute a zone, with 2 and 6 its source and sink areas; and $6, 5, 4, 3, 2$ constitute another zone with 6 and 2 its source and sink areas. We have a total of 48 zones. The right figures show the layout of the neighboring zones. In the upper figure, 3 is the sink area of the zone A, and 5 is the source area of zone C. The border area of A and B is $2, 3$; and the border area of B and C is $5, 6$. The lower figure shows two perpendicular zones. The source area of B is $1, 2$. The border area of A and B is $1, 2, 3, 4$.

1: **Initialization**;
2: Handshaking among neighbors; each node broadcasts its id, its position,
      and its current power level
3: $P_B = \infty$, $t_B = \infty$
4: **IF** I am base station
5:     initiate the message broadcasting
6: **ELSE IF** I am not base and my id is B
7:     Receive message (A, P_A); get the sender id A and P_A from the message
8:     Compute $P_B = min(P_A + e(A, B), P_B)$ and $t_B = min(t_B, \eta P_B)$
9:     Wait till t_B, broadcast the message (B, P_B) to its neighbors, and stop

---

Figure 14: *Minimal Power Path.* The input consists of a network system
in which each node can determine its location and its power level. The
output is the minimal-power routing table at each node (with respect to
communicating to the base.) The algorithm uses the following parameters:
η is the unit power for transforming the power level into waiting time; P_A is
the total power consumption of the optimal path found so far from A to the
base node; $e(A, B)$: the power consumption of sending one message from A
to B directly; t_B: the earliest time for B to broadcast the routing message;
N_B: the route of node B.

1: **Initialization**;
2: Handshaking among neighbors: each node broadcasts its id, its position,
      and its current power level
3: The base initiates the message broadcasting
4: **IF** I am not the base
5:      Let my id be B
6:      $P_B = \infty$. Initial time is 0
7:      Receive message (A, P_A); get the sender id A and the power P_A from
          the message
8:      Compute the new power $P_B = min(P_B, P_A + e(A, B))$, and find the
          proper slot $i = \lfloor m \cdot P_B/P \rfloor$
      IF $P_B == P_A + e(A, B)$
          $N_B = A$
9:      Set waiting timer to $i\delta$ (i.e. the time point when a broadcast happens)
10:     **IF** the current time is no less than the waiting time point
11:         broadcast the message (B, P_B) to its neighbors, and clear the
              timer. (We do that because there are may be several
              paths being broadcast to the node. But their time must
              be between $i\delta$ and $(i + 1)\delta$)
12:     **IF** the current time is $(i + 1)\delta$
13:         stop

Figure 15: The second minimal power path algorithm. The input is a network in which each node can determine its location and its power level. The
output is a routing table for each node. The parameters are P_A, the total
power consumption of the optimal path found so far from A to the base
node; $e(A, B)$, the power consumption of sending a message from A to B
directly; and δ, the unit time corresponding to each power slot (P/m), used
to transform the power level into waiting time; N_B: the route of node B.

1: **Initialization;**
2: Handshaking among neighbors: each node broadcasts its id, its position, and its current power level
3: For each node B, let $F_B = 0$, B does the following for $i = m - 1$, $m - 2, \cdots, 1, 0$.
4: The base node initiates the search and broadcasts the maximal max-min value
5: **IF** Node B receive a message $(A, P(A), F_A)$ from its neighbor A
6:     According to the power level of A and the distance between A and B, compute $F_B = max(F_B, min(F_A, \frac{P(A)-e(A,B)}{P(A)}))$
7:     **IF** $F_B == min(F_A, \frac{P(A)-e(A,B)}{P(A)})$
8:         $N_B = A$
9: **IF** $(i+1)F_{max}/m > F_B \geq iF_{max}/m$
10:     the max-min value of B is found
11:     B broadcasts the message $(B, P(B), F_B)$, the next node in the routing table is A, stop
12: After time δ, i=i-1; go to 5

Figure 16: Distributed Max-min Approximation. The input is a network in which each node can determine its location and its power level. The output is a routing table at each node. The parameters are: $P(A)$, the current power level of node A; $e(A, B)$, the power consumption of sending one message from A to B directly; and δ, the unit time corresponding to each power slot (P/m) used to transform the power level into waiting time.

1: Find the minimal power consumption path for each node
2: The base node 0 initiates the route discovery
3: $P_0 = 0; F_0 = \infty; N_0 = 0$
4: Node 0 sends route discovery request to its neighbors
5: Each node B receives message from its neighbors $A_1, A_2, \cdots, A_k$
6: It waits for time δ, then compute:

$$P_B = min(P_{A_1} + e(B, A_1), P_{A_2} + e(B, A_2), \cdots, P_{A_k} + e(B, A_k))$$

Find all the neighboring nodes such that $P_{A_i} + e(B, A_i) <= z P_{min}^{A_i}$
Among all those found neighbors, find the node with maximal
$min(F_{A_k}, (P_B - e(B, A_k))/P_B)$.
Let the node be N_B and the min value be F_B
7: Broadcast the P^B and F_B to its neighbors
8: Go to 5 until the routing table gets to equilibrium

Figure 17: Distributed *max-min* zP_{min}. The parameters are P_{min}^B, the minimal power consumption for node B to send a message to the base; P_B, the power consumption of the path discovered so far from the node to the base; $P(B)$, node B's current power level; F_B, the maximal min residual power level of the found route to base from node B; and N_B: the next node on B's found route; δ is an algorithm-dependent parameter; different implementations may have difference choices.

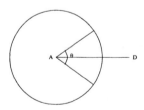

Figure 18: The greedy routing method sends messages the the nearest neighbor within transmission range, in a cone of directions captured by a parameter θ.

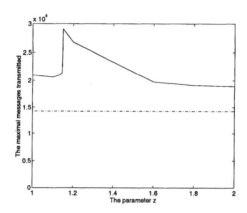

Figure 19: The performance comparison of distributed *max-min* zP_{min} algorithm and greedy algorithm. The dashed line shows the performance of the greedy algorithm and the solid line shows the performance of the *max-min* zP_{min} algorithm. The network includes 100 nodes. The network space is $100 * 100$, the transmission range is 20, the power consumption formula is $E = 2 * 10^{-6} * d^3$. The greedy algorithm uses a $\theta = \pi/3$. The routing protocol is run after every 100 messages. The neighbor information update in the greedy algorithm is updated every 100 messages.

AD HOC WIRELESS NETWORKING
X. Cheng, X. Huang and D.-Z. Du (Eds.) pp. 45 - 86

Improving TCP Performance in Mobile Ad hoc Networks

Rajendra V. Boppana
Department of Computer Science
University of Texas at San Antonio, San Antonio, TX 78249
E-mail: `boppana@cs.utsa.edu`

Thomas D. Dyer
Department of Computer Science
University of Texas at San Antonio, San Antonio, TX 78249
E-mail: `tdyer@cs.utsa.edu`

Contents

The performance of transport layer protocols will be a key factor in the successful extension of Internet applications and services to mobile ad hoc networks. The Transmission Control Protocol (TCP) is the most commonly used transport protocol for the Internet [33], so providing a high level of TCP performance in MANETs is of particular importance. While TCP has been extensively tuned for wireline networks, in its current form TCP does not perform well when used in MANETs. In this chapter, we investigate ways to improve TCP performance in MANETs.

The rest of the chapter is organized as follows. Section 1 describes the essential aspects of TCP and known techniques to improve TCP's performance in MANETs. Section 2 classifies techniques for TCP performance enhancement and describes two new techniques. Section 3 describes the simulation environment used for performance analyses. Section 4 presents results for 1 TCP connection. Section 5 analyzes the working of a proposed performance enhancement technique. Section 6 presents additional simulation results for varying number of TCP connections. Section 7 concludes the chapter.

1 Background

One of the services provided by transport layer protocols is to turn IP's best-effort level of service into a reliable packet delivery service. IP packets may be dropped, reordered, or duplicated on the way from sender to receiver. By contrast, the Transmission Control Protocol (TCP) [33] enables applications to establish reliable, full-duplex connections. TCP includes a flow control scheme by which the receiver can limit the rate at which the sender transmits data. TCP also implements a congestion control mechanism to keep TCP senders from overloading the network and possibly causing congestion collapse.

1.1   TCP fundamentals

In this section, we describe the key components of the TCP protocol that are germane to our work. This is not intended to be a comprehensive description of TCP, for which [35] is an excellent reference.

TCP utilizes a sliding window algorithm to guarantee reliable, in-order packet delivery and to enforce flow control. The sender can have at most a window's worth of outstanding packets, i.e. packets for which no acknowledgement (ACK) of their receipt has yet arrived from the TCP receiver. Since the transmission of new packets must await the acknowledgement of previously transmitted packets, TCP is said to be self-clocking. To implement flow control, the receiver includes an advertised window size in each ACK to inform the sender of the amount of free space left in its buffer. The size of the sender's window can never exceed the receiver's advertised window size. In addition, TCP keeps track of another parameter called congestion window size, which is increased or decreased based on the flow of ACKs. We should point out that TCP keeps track of bytes, not packets, so that window size is actually expressed as a number of bytes. For simplicity, however, we will talk about windows in terms of packets.

TCP's acknowledgements are cumulative meaning that the sender is guaranteed that all packets up to and including the packet being ACKed have been successfully delivered. If a packet is delivered out of order, the receiver resends the same ACK it sent previously. When the sender receives this duplicate ACK, it knows that a packet has left the network, but that the left-hand side of its window cannot yet be advanced.

Adjusting the size of the congestion window

If a TCP sender could determine how much network capacity was available for its use at any time, it would know how many packets it could safely have in flight and could set its window size accordingly. In the absence of such knowledge, TCP adopts the strategy of probing the network for additional bandwidth by steadily increasing its window size at the rate of roughly one packet for every window's worth of ACKs. This increase in the rate of transmission continues until a packet drop occurs. Because transmission losses are very infrequent in the wired Internet, a dropped packet is assumed to have occurred when some router's buffer filled up. Hence, packet losses are treated as signs of network congestion. In response to the perceived congestion, the sender immediately cuts its window size in half, and then begins again to steadily increase the size of its window. This process, called additive increase/multiplicative decrease (AI/MD), continually adjusts the size of the sender's window (called the congestion window) over the life of a connection.

When a TCP connection is first established, the sender has no idea what the network capacity might be. Increasing the window size linearly as in AI/MD is likely to take too long, so instead the sender increases the window size by one for every ACK it receives, effectively doubling the number of packets in transit every round trip time (RTT). (The RTT is the interval from packet transmission to receipt of the corresponding ACK.) This is the slow start phase, so named because the original practice was to transmit an entire advertised window's worth of packets all at once, which is likely to overwhelm the routers even if sufficient bandwidth is available. Slow start ends when a packet drop is observed. The congestion window is halved and the sender begins AI/MD.

Detecting and responding to packet loss

TCP has two mechanisms for detecting packet loss. Whenever an ACK arrives for a packet not previously acknowledged (a new ACK), a timer is set for a period of time called the retransmit timeout interval (RTO). If the retransmit timer expires before the next new ACK is received, TCP deduces that packet loss has occurred. The packet following the last consecutively ACKed packet is retransmitted, the retransmit timer is reset, the congestion window size is reduced to 1, and the sender enters slow start. Unlike at the beginning of a connection, the sender now has some idea of what network capacity is available based on the recent history of the congestion window. Before reducing the congestion window size to 1, TCP stores one-half the current window size in a variable called the slow start threshold. This time, TCP will leave the slow start phase and begin AI/MD as soon as the congestion window size reaches this threshold.

In prolonged periods of network congestion, it is possible that the re-transmitted packet will not be delivered either. The retransmit timer will expire again and the missing packet will be transmitted once more. To avoid adding to the network congestion, TCP doubles the RTO each time the timer expires. This exponential backoff of the RTO continues until the congestion is alleviated and packet flow is resumed. At that time, the RTO is reset to the current estimate of the RTT plus an additional amount to account for the sample variance of this estimate.

An additional method for detecting packet loss, called fast retransmit, is a heuristic intended to trigger a packet retransmission sooner than the regular retransmit timeout mechanism, which is often coarse-grained. When the sender receives a duplicate ACK, it knows that a packet has been delivered out of order. This suggests that an earlier packet may have been lost, in which case there is no need to wait for the retransmit timer to expire before retransmitting the dropped packet. However, the earlier packet may have only been delayed, so the sender waits until it sees some number of duplicate ACKs before retransmitting the missing packet. This number, let us call it the fast retransmit threshold, is normally set to three.

Collectively, these measures – AI/MD, slow start, and the retransmit timer – comprise TCP's congestion control mechanism. We consider the Reno version of TCP, which uses fast retransmit and fast recovery [35]. The TCP protocol has been tuned extensively from years of experience in the wired Internet. However, with the advent of wireless networking, it was soon evident that this mechanism does not work well in the wireless environment, and that TCP performance suffers as a consequence. The problem is that, in addition to congestion, packet losses in a wireless network can be caused by transmission errors and by node mobility [7]. Moreover, packet losses tend to be correlated; single, random packet losses are infrequent. A reduction in TCP's sending rate is not the appropriate response to these kinds of losses.

1.2 TCP performance in 1-hop wireless networks

A number of schemes were proposed to mitigate the ill effects caused by noncongestion-related losses on TCP performance in 1-hop wireless networks. These networks are often characterized by sporadic bursts of bit errors and temporary breaks in connectivity during handoffs. Balakrishnan et al. compared various mechanisms for improving TCP performance across wireless links [4]. These methods fell into one of three groups – split connections, link layer approaches, and end-to-end schemes. In their experiments, the TCP sender resides on the wired network and the receiver is a mobile host communicating with a base station over a wireless link.

Split connections

Split-connection protocols [2, 36] divide the TCP connection into two connections – a wired connection from the sender to the base station and a wireless connection from the base station to the receiver. Loss recovery over the wireless link is separated from that across the wired network, and so is hidden from the sender. Because ACKs can reach the source before the data packet arrives at the mobile host, split-connection protocols violate the end-to-end semantics of TCP acknowledgements. Another disadvantage of these schemes is the overhead of maintaining TCP state at the base station, which tends to make handoffs complicated and slow. While the split-connection approach does insulate the TCP sender from wireless losses, timeouts on the wireless link cause the sender to stall frequently, resulting in poor end-to-end throughput.

Link layer approaches

A link-layer approach evaluated in [4] was the snoop protocol [3]. In the snoop method, a TCP-aware agent at the base station caches the packets sent across the wireless link until they are ACKed so that local recovery is possible in the event of packet loss. By shielding the TCP sender from duplicate ACKs caused by wireless losses, the snoop protocol yielded increases of 10%-30% in throughput compared to a link-layer protocol with no knowledge of TCP. A disadvantage of this or any other technique that requires examination of TCP packet headers is that it will not work when encryption is used.

End-to-end schemes

The end-to-end schemes considered in [4] were selective acknowledgements and the addition of an explicit loss notification (ELN) option to TCP acknowledgements. Selective acknowledgements (SACK) allow the sender to handle multiple losses within a window more efficiently. ELN notifies the sender that a noncongestion-related loss has occurred so the sender can retransmit the lost packet without invoking congestion control. Two different SACK schemes were considered: a simple version of the SMART proposal [23], and an implementation based on RFC 2018 [27]. Compared to TCP Reno, the RFC 2018 SACK implementation yielded an increase in throughput of approximately 24%, while the fraction of packets successfully delivered (goodput) remained the same. The use of ELN increased throughput by about 25%, and again, goodput was unchanged. The combination of

SACK and ELN might be expected to increase throughput even more, but this was reserved for future work.

1.3 TCP performance in MANETs

An effective way to deal with wireless transmission losses is to use a reliable link-layer. In MANETs, the IEEE 802.11 MAC protocol provides reliable transmission of packets across wireless links. The MAC layer will retransmit a packet until either an ACK is received, indicating an error-free transmission, or the maximum number of retries is reached, in which case the link is declared to be broken. MANETs are still subject, however, to noncongestion-related losses induced by node mobility. Now, instead of delays during handoffs, we are faced with route failures and the loss of connectivity during route repair.

Since the root of the TCP performance problem in a MANET is its inability to distinguish between losses due to congestion and other types of packet losses, designing a mechanism by which TCP can determine that a loss was not caused by congestion, and thereby avoid congestion control, seems to be an obvious means of solving the problem. If the TCP sender is notified that a route failure has occurred, it can suspend its normal response to packet drops until the route has been reconstructed. Several researchers have taken exactly this approach.

TCP-F: Chandran et al. propose a feedback based scheme they call TCP-Feedback or TCP-F [8]. In this scheme, when an intermediate node detects the disruption of a route due to the mobility of the next host along that route, it explicitly sends a Route Failure Notification (RFN) to the TCP sender. Other nodes that receive the RFN invalidate that particular route and do not forward any packets intended for that destination. Upon receiving the RFN, the source suspends all packet transmissions and freezes its state, including the retransmission timeout interval and the congestion window. Eventually, an intermediate node that has previously forwarded the RFN learns of a new route to the destination. That node then sends a Route Re-establishment Notification (RRN) to the source. When the source receives the RRN, it restores its previous state and resumes transmission. The effect of this scheme was studied by simulating a single TCP connection over which 200-byte packets are transmitted at 12.8 Kbps. Periodic route failures were generated, followed by route re-establishment after some fixed period of time, the route re-establishment delay (RRD). For RRDs in excess of 2 seconds, an increase in throughput of roughly 45% to 75% was reported.

For a RRD of less than 1 second, however, essentially no benefit was derived from TCP-F. Three-fold increases in throughput were obtained when the transmission rate was increased to 128 Kbps.

ELFN: Holland et al. advocate the use of explicit link failure notification (ELFN) to significantly improve TCP performance in MANETs. In the ELFN scheme, when the TCP sender is informed of a link failure, it freezes its state (timers and window size) as in TCP-F. There is no route re-establishment notification, however. Instead, the source sends out packets (probes) at regular intervals to determine if a new route is available. Using the *ns-2* network simulator [12], they simulated a wireless network running TCP Reno and the DSR routing protocol. The TCP packet size was 1460 bytes, and the maximum window size was eight packets for both sender and receiver. They employed a random-waypoint network model, in which 30 nodes move toward randomly picked destinations in a 1500m x 300m flat, rectangular area. Upon reaching its destination, a node picks a new destination and continues onward without pausing. A total of 50 different mobility patterns were considered, and the mean speed at which the nodes travel was varied. For a mean node speed of 10 m/s, the throughput of a single TCP connection, averaged over the mobility patterns, was increased by 55% or more. Interestingly, an even greater increase in throughput (close to 100%) was obtained by simply turning off the DSR feature whereby intermediate nodes send out route updates based on the contents of their (often stale) route caches. In other words, avoiding DSR's stale route problem is of greater benefit than explicit notification of route failures.

TCP-BuS: In the TCP-BuS proposal [24], an explicit route disconnection message (ERDN) is generated at an intermediate node upon detection of a route failure. This message is propagated to the source which then stops transmission. Packet transmission is resumed after a partial path has been re-established from the node which detected the route failure to the destination and that information is relayed to the TCP sender in an explicit route successful notification (ERSN). During the course of a TCP connection, packets are buffered at the intermediate nodes along the path from sender to receiver. Nodes upstream from the failed link are able to forward these packets on to the destination once the route has been repaired, relieving the sender from having to retransmit these packets. This scheme is somewhat complex and would seem likely to have trouble with multiple route failures in quick succession, as in a high mobility network.

ATCP: In ATCP [26], a layer between TCP and the routing agent is proposed which, among other things, shields TCP from packet loss that is perceived to be non-congestion related. Upon learning of a route failure (by means of an ICMP *Destination Unreachable* message), ATCP places the TCP sender into *persist mode*, thus avoiding the invocation of congestion control measures. While in persist mode, TCP generates probe packets at exponentially increasing intervals up to a maximum of 60 seconds. Once the route is re-established and an ACK is received for one of the probe packets, TCP moves out of persist mode and resumes packet transmission.

To date, there has not been much reported in the way of evaluating TCP performance over different MANET routing protocols. Ahuja et al. [1] used *ns-2* to conduct a simulation-based comparison of TCP performance over several protocols, including AODV, DSR, and SSA. Only a single source of TCP traffic was simulated in their study. For low node mobility scenarios, the highest throughput was observed for DSR. As node mobility was increased, AODV performance became as good or better than that of DSR. Interestingly, for high node mobility scenarios, the SSA protocol achieved the highest TCP throughput. The authors attributed this to the fact that SSA selects routes on the basis of stability and stable routes experience fewer route failures. They concluded that the frequency of route failures, routing overhead, and delay in route establishment are the important determinants of TCP throughput in an ad hoc network. Like [18], they found that disabling route replies from cache actually improved TCP throughput for DSR by eliminating the effect of stale routes.

2 Techniques for improving TCP performance

We broadly group techniques for improving TCP performance in MANETs into three categories. This classification is based on which of the layers in the protocol stack are involved, and on what sources of feedback and other pertinent information are used.

- **Level 1: TCP layer.** These mechanisms are implemented in the TCP sender and/or the TCP receiver. No information is required from the routing layer or lower layers in the protocol stack. Existing TCP options, such as selective acknowledgements, are included in this level.

- **Level 2: Routing layer at TCP connection endpoints.** These mechanisms utilize feedback from the routing agents on the hosts where the TCP sender and receiver are running. Such methods may also use the MAC-layer information that is available to these routing agents.

- **Level 3: Routing agents on intermediate nodes.** Mechanisms at this level require feedback supplied by the routing agents running on one or more intermediate nodes along the route established by the TCP connection.

Level 1 solutions are considered to be end-to-end mechanisms since the modifications to protocols are confined to the transport layer level of the communicating nodes. The protocol stacks of intermediate nodes do not need to be modified. The other two types of solutions require protocols in the lower layers of the communicating nodes or intermediate nodes to be modified. So such solutions tend be more complex and may degrade the performance for other types of traffic. For these reasons, Level 1 solutions are preferred over Level 2 and 3 solutions when the performance benefits are about the same.

In the remainder of this section, we elaborate on the framework for TCP performance mechanisms outlined above and show where in this hierarchy existing methods and current research fit. We then describe two novel layer 1 techniques that we have designed and implemented.

2.1   TCP layer mechanisms

Even though MANET routing protocols are designed to repair broken routes quickly, route failure is often a source of packet delays and packet drops. Significant reordering of packets may occur as well. This suggests that mechanisms designed to avoid unnecessary retransmit timeouts, packet retransmissions, and reductions in the congestion window, may be promising means of improving TCP performance. TCP layer methods will generally require changes to the TCP sender, the TCP receiver, or both. We discuss below two existing TCP options that may be used to improve TCP performance in MANETs, selective acknowledgements and delayed acknowledgements.

Selective acknowledgments: In the Reno version of TCP, a duplicate ACK does not tell the sender which packet or packets are still outstanding, only that one or more packets have been dropped or delayed. The best the sender can do is retransmit at most one missing packet per round trip time (RTT) or risk retransmitting a packet that may already have been received. The selective acknowledgements (SACK) option allows the receiver to specify which non-consecutive packets have been received. Frequent route changes in a MANET can be expected to cause packet losses, and these losses may result in duplicate ACKs that trigger the TCP sender's fast retransmit mechanism. By enabling the sender to more accurately infer which packets are missing, SACK should reduce the number of unnecessary packet retransmissions.

Delayed acknowledgments: In networks where bandwidth is a scarce commodity, it makes sense to reduce traffic whenever possible. The use of delayed ACKs is expected to help by reducing the volume of ACK traffic in normal network conditions. In MANETS, delayed ACKs are also useful when routes break. During route reconstruction, data packets may be sitting in a queue at the source or at an intermediate node. If the route is repaired quickly enough that the data packets have not yet been flushed from the buffer, then all of these packets will arrive at the TCP receiver in quick succession. With delayed ACKs, the receiver is able to send fewer acknowledgements for these packets. This will, in turn, enable the TCP sender to increase its congestion window more quickly and retransmit fewer packets.

2.2 Routing layer mechanisms

These techniques require routing agents at TCP endpoints or in intermediate nodes to provide network information that is not directly available to TCP. If only the routing agents at the endpoints of a TCP connection provide additional feedback to TCP, then such mechanisms are classified as Level 2. If other routing agents are also involved, then such mechanisms are classified as Level 3.

2.2.1 Using feedback from routing agents at TCP connection end points

The routing agent running on the host where the TCP sender resides can be an immediate source of feedback to the sender. Likewise, the TCP receiver can get routing layer information directly from the agent running on its host. We give some examples of useful feedback that might be obtained from the routing layer.

Feedback to the TCP sender: When the sender's routing agent is unable to deliver a TCP data packet because the first link in the route to the destination is down, the agent can inform the sender of the route failure immediately. This is a "cheap" form of explicit link failure notification in that there are no route error packets involved. Similarly, when the routing agent learns through an update that the route has been re-established, this information can be passed directly to the sender.

Another useful item of information the routing agent has is the number of packets in the routing agent's send buffer waiting for routes. The number of packets in the MAC interface queue is also of interest. If the number of packets queued is high, the TCP sender may elect to reduce its sending rate until the level of buffering has dropped off.

Routing packets through a MANET is a store-and-forward process, so the number of packets that can profitably be in flight in a MANET is to some degree a function of the path length from sender to receiver. Therefore, the number of hops to the destination may be of interest to the TCP sender if that information can be used to set a reasonable size for the congestion window.

Feedback to the TCP receiver: If the TCP receiver can determine current conditions in the network from the "experience" of the data packets that have arrived recently, it can relay this information back to the TCP sender. Based on the earlier work on the DECbit scheme [34], the addition of Explicit Congestion Notification (ECN) to TCP was proposed for this purpose [15]. If a router along the path to the destination is congested or is close to congestion, it sets the ECN bit in the header of a data packet. The receiver echoes the notification to the sender in an ACK. This mechanism allows TCP to perform congestion control proactively.

2.2.2   Using feedback from routing agents at intermediate nodes

This is the level at which the solutions such as ELFN and TCP-F, proposed in the literature, see Section 1, fit in our hierarchy. These methods rely on route failure (and route re-establishment) notifications from intermediate nodes to reach the sender, which then modifies its behavior accordingly. Another possible level 3 approach to improving TCP performance might involve using knowledge of routing agent and/or MAC layer queue lengths at intermediate nodes, for example to adjust TCP's sending rate before congestion occurs.

2.3 Proposed TCP sender side options

The TCP sender is designed to adapt to network conditions by tracking the acknowledgements returned by the receiver. The timing of these ACKs and the order in which they are received are clues that the sender uses to infer what is occurring elsewhere in the network. How these clues are interpreted by the sender has a major impact on TCP performance. In MANETs, new heuristics can be used to elicit sender behavior that is conducive to good TCP performance. We have designed and implemented two mechanisms that use sender-based heuristics: the hold-down timer and the fixed RTO.

2.3.1 Hold-down timer

Sometimes the packet delay, as opposed to packet loss, due to a route failure can cause an ACK to arrive so late that the retransmit timer has already expired. In the description of the delayed acknowledgements option above, we noted that if route repair happens quickly, then any data packets that were buffered at the source or at an intermediate node will arrive at the receiver in rapid order. The same thing can happen for ACKs buffered during route repair. Once the route has been re-established, these ACKs will arrive at the TCP sender in quick succession. If the retransmit timer has expired, the packet corresponding to the first of the tardy ACKs will already have been retransmitted. If the ACKs arrive in order, the first one will trigger the retransmission of the packet corresponding to the second tardy ACK, the second one will trigger yet another retransmission, and so on.

In order to address this problem, we designed a method which utilizes a hold-down timer. Figure 1 illustrates the technique. When a timeout occurs, the length of this timer is set equal to the retransmit timeout interval (RTO) prior to the timeout. Since the RTO is doubled following a timeout, the hold-down period is one-half of the new timeout period. The first packet in the window is immediately retransmitted as usual. During the hold-down interval, any incoming ACKs are processed in the normal way except that they do not trigger further packet transmissions. If the hold-down timer expires before the first packet in the window has been acknowledged, then TCP reverts to its normal behavior during the second half of the retransmit timeout period, i.e. packets will be retransmitted when the outstanding ACK is received. Otherwise, any packets that are ACKed during the hold-down interval will not have to be retransmitted. If all the packets in the window are ACKed before the hold-down interval ends, the hold-down timer

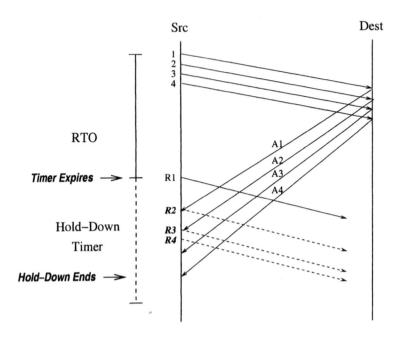

Figure 1: TCP data packet/ACK transmission diagram showing tardy ACKs arriving during the hold-down timer interval. The retransmit timer expires before the ACK for packet 1 arrives, so packet 1 is retransmitted (the event labeled **R1**). In normal TCP operation, the arrival of the ACK for packet 1 will trigger the retransmission of packet 2 (event **R2**), and the arrival of the ACK for packet 2 will trigger the retransmission of packets 3 and 4 (events **R3** and **R4**). With the hold-down timer, the tardy ACK for packet 1 does not cause packet 2 to be retransmitted. Similarly, the late-arriving ACK for packet 2 does not cause packets 3 and 4 to be retransmitted. Instead, since the ACKs for packets 2 - 4 are all received before the hold-down timer expires, no further packet retransmissions occur.

is cancelled and normal TCP operation is resumed.

2.3.2   Fixed retransmit timeout interval

In the event of a retransmit timeout, TCP retransmits the oldest unacknowledged packet and doubles the retransmit timeout interval (RTO). This process is repeated until an ACK for the retransmitted packet has been received. This exponential backoff of the RTO enables TCP to handle network congestion gracefully. However, in a MANET, the loss of packets (or ACKs) may be caused by temporary route loss as well as network congestion. Since routes are likely to be broken frequently in high node mobility environments, routing algorithms for MANETs are designed to repair broken routes quickly. To

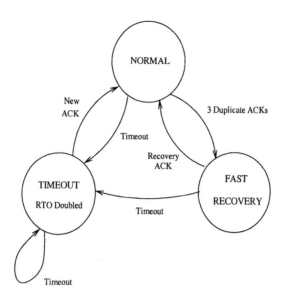

Figure 2: Simplified TCP state diagram illustrating normal operation of the TCP Reno protocol after the connection has been established. The RTO is doubled on the first timeout and every consecutive timeout thereafter.

take advantage of this capability, it is intuitive to let a TCP sender retransmit the unacknowledged packet at periodic intervals rather than having to wait increasingly long periods of time between retransmissions.

Therefore, we modified the TCP sender, employing a heuristic to distinguish between route failures and congestion, without relying on feedback from other network nodes. When timeouts occur consecutively, i.e. the missing ACK is not received before the second RTO expires, this is taken to be evidence of a route loss. The unacknowledged packet is retransmitted again but the RTO is not doubled a second time. The RTO remains fixed until the route is re-established and the retransmitted packet is acknowledged. The simplified state diagrams shown in Figures 2 and 3 highlight the change to the sender.

Under normal network conditions, there are no route breakages and the packet losses tend to be isolated and infrequent. So in such cases, the heuristic is seldom invoked and will not any impact on the performance.

3   Simulation Environment

For our simulations, we used the *ns-2* network simulator [12] with mobility extensions by Johnson et al. [28]. These extensions include the modeling of

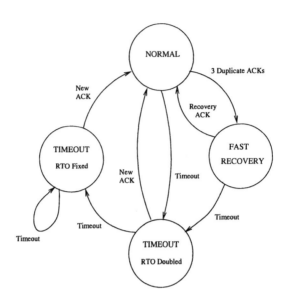

Figure 3: Simplified TCP state diagram illustrating the fixed-RTO protocol modification. The RTO is doubled on the first timeout, but remains fixed on succeeding consecutive timeouts.

an IEEE 802.11 wireless LAN [20]. To evaluate the effectiveness of various TCP heuristics, we used three routing protocols: two on-demand protocols, AODV and DSR, and one proactive protocol, ADV. We used the Monarch implementations of DSR, and all parameter values and optimizations used for DSR are as described by Broch et al. [6]. The AODV implementation is based on the version used by Das et al. [9] with the following parameter values: 50s active route timeouts; local route repair; 1, 2, and 7 for TTL_START, TTL_INCREMENT, and TTL_THRESHOLD, respectively. The ADV implementation was based on the version used by Boppana and Konduru [5] with all parameter values except the routing layer buffer timeout (which is set to 30s in this study) are set as in [5]. For all three routing protocols, link layer notification of broken links was used.

We simulated an ad hoc network comprised of 50 mobile nodes on a 1000m x 1000m field. The nodes move according to a mobility pattern based on the *random waypoint* model; to avoid clustering of nodes in the middle of the field, we let a node reaching an edge of the field to wraparound (instantaneously) and continue its movement in the same direction from the opposite edge of the field [19]. Since a MANET's performance is sensitive to movement patterns, 50 different mobility patterns (scenarios) were simulated and averaged for each data point presented in the plots. Node speeds were uniformly distributed between 0 m/s and 20/ms, yielding a mean node speed of 10 m/s, and only zero-length pause times were considered.

We simulated the *steady-state* conditions of a network with various background traffic loads generated by 10 and 40 constant bit rate (CBR) connections. The CBR packet sizes were fixed at 512 bytes. After a warm-up time of 100 seconds, one or more TCP connections were established over each of which an FTP file transfer with infinite backlog was conducted for 900 seconds. The TCP packet size was 1460 bytes, and the maximum size of both the send and receive windows was 8.

In each simulation run, we measured connect time, throughput, and goodput. Connect time is the time it takes to deliver the first TCP packet. Short connect times are important for some types of TCP traffic such as HTTP. Throughput is computed as the amount of data transferred by TCP divided by 900 seconds, the time interval from the end of the warm-up period to the end of the simulation. This does not include redundant packet receipts due to unnecessary packet retransmissions and packet replication in the network. Goodput is the ratio of TCP packets successfully delivered to the total number of TCP packets transmitted. In order to gauge the routing protocol overhead, we measured both the number of routing packets and the number of bytes of routing data transmitted per second at the IP layer. The overhead includes the routing of the background CBR traffic. For DSR, the number of bytes of routing data transmitted includes the routing information carried by data packets. We also measured the number of routing packets transmitted per second at the MAC layer, including all the IP layer routing packets and the RTS, CTS, and ACK control exchange packets used for transmitting unicast data *and* routing packets.

4   Analysis of TCP performance for 1 TCP connection

In this section we present simulation results for the case of 1 TCP connection with varying background UDP traffic. We analyze the results to see the impact of various TCP options and routing algorithms. In the next section, we present simulation results for multiple TCP connections.

We performed a series of five simulation runs. Each simulation run tested a different technique or combination of techniques: TCP Reno, Reno with SACK, Reno with SACK and delayed ACKs, fixed RTO on consecutive timeouts plus SACK and delayed ACKs, and a hold-down timer plus fixed RTO and SACK and delayed ACKs. In each run, a set of performance

Table 1: Percent increases in throughput of 1 TCP connection for various TCP options relative to TCP Reno. A 10-connection, 50 Kbps CBR background traffic is used.

Simulation Run	ADV	AODV	DSR
SACK	-1.3	0.7	-1.6
SACK + delayed ACKs	**3.7**	**5.1**	2.3
SACK + fixed RTO + delayed ACKs	**3.3**	**8.1**	**67.4**
SACK + fixed RTO + delayed ACKs + hold-down timer	2.2	**9.9**	**86.4**

Table 2: Percent increases in throughput of 1 TCP connection for various TCP options relative to TCP Reno. A 40-connection, 50 Kbps CBR background traffic is used.

Simulation Run	ADV	AODV	DSR
SACK	**-5.7**	0.6	**6.7**
SACK + delayed ACKs	1.6	4.1	**9.6**
SACK + fixed RTO + delayed ACKs	2.2	**15.6**	**47.8**
SACK + fixed RTO + delayed ACKs + hold-down timer	**3.7**	**20.4**	**59.9**

measurements were made for each of the three routing protocols at each of several background traffic loads from 10 CBR connections and from 40 CBR connections.

Tables 1 and 2 show the throughput of 1 TCP connection expressed as percent changes relative to the baseline TCP Reno results. The background traffic is 50 Kbps from 10 and 40 CBR connections. To compare the results from any two combinations of techniques, we paired the observed throughputs attained by these methods for each of the 50 scenarios and applied the paired t-test. Differences shown in bold print have 95% confidence intervals that do not include zero.

The data indicate that the selective acknowledgment (SACK) option did not provide significant benefit to any of the three routing algorithms. Selective acknowledgments will be useful in avoiding unnecessary timeouts if a packet is dropped occasionally by the network. Since multiple packets may be lost due to broken routes more frequently than a random drops by the network, SACK is not likely to be very useful in a MANET environment. The delayed acknowledgment (DACK) option provided modest performance gains to all three algorithms. With DACKs, the number of ACK packets are reduced, which in turn reduced the load on the path used by TCP sender and receiver.

The fixed-RTO option improved the throughputs of DSR significantly. Since each data packet must carry the path to destination in DSR routing, nodes snoop and learn routes. In a lightly loaded network such as the one used in these simulations, such routing information tends to be stale and incorrect. DSR does not use any aging mechanism to detect and remove such stale routes. So DSR suffers from the stale-route problem, especially for the TCP traffic [18]. With the fixed-RTO option, a TCP sender transmits TCP data packets more frequently in the event of a broken (or stale route at the routing layer level), which in turn forces the routing layer to learn fresh routes using route discovery. The stale route problem was not as severe for 40 connections as for 10 connections; so fixed-RTO has the most impact on DSR's performance for the 10 CBR connections case. AODV does not suffer from the stale route problem. However, fixed RTO improved AODV's performance. Since the overhead increases with the number of connections for AODV, its performance suffers with the increase in the number of connections. So fixed-RTO improved AODV's performance more for the 40-connections than the 10-connections case. ADV's performance was not impacted significantly by the fixed-RTO technique. We analyze this in depth in Section 5.

The hold-down timer option further improved the TCP throughputs for DSR, but not significantly for ADV or AODV. Additional simulations indicated that hold-down timer does not improve significantly the performance of the three routing algorithms with multiple TCP connections.

We now analyze the suitability of various TCP options and routing protocols using performance criteria such as TCP connect time, throughput, goodput ratio, and routing overhead. For this purpose, we use Figures 4 and 5, which show the connect times, throughputs, goodputs, and routing overheads observed for each of the protocols for a 100-Kbps background traffic load generated by 10 and 40 CBR connections.

4.1   Connect time

For all three algorithms, the base Reno version had the highest TCP connection times. Using the SACK option does not improve these times. For DSR, DACK, fixed-RTO and hold-down timer options provided consistent

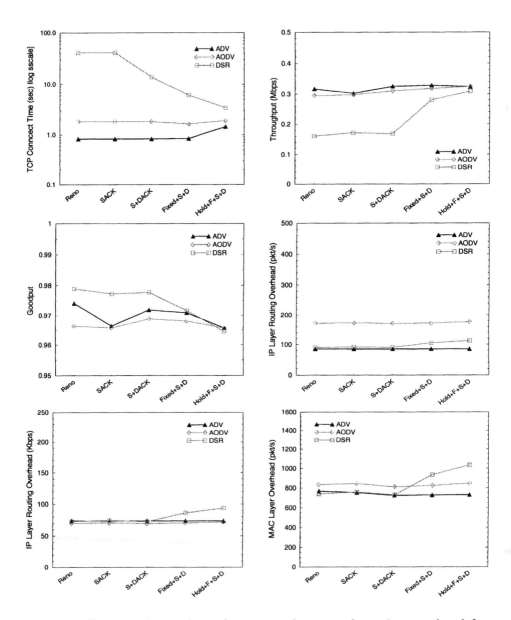

Figure 4: Connect times, throughputs, goodputs, and routing overhead for 1 TCP connection with a 100-Kbps background load from 10 CBR connections.

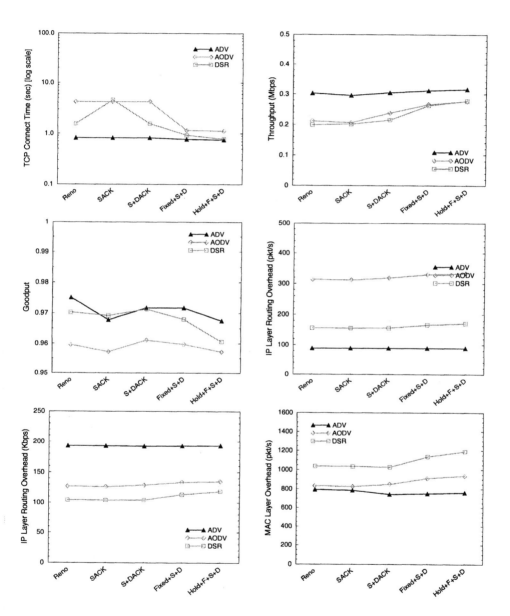

Figure 5: Connect times, throughputs, goodputs, and routing overhead for 1 TCP connection with a 100-Kbps background load from 40 CBR connections.

improvement in the connect times, nearly mitigating its stale-route problem, for both 10 and 40 CBR connections. For AODV and ADV the connect times were not improved by the various TCP options for the case of 10 CBR connections. In fact, the hold-down timer option increased the connect time by 10-20% for the case of 10 CBR connections. With 40 CBR connections, however, AODV benefited from the use of DACK, fixed-RTO and hold-down timer options. ADV's connect times were not improved by the various options for the case of 40 CBR connections. Looking at the absolute values of connect times, ADV provided under 1-second connect times, and AODV's connect times were about twice as large as ADV's. Owing to the stale route problem, however, DSR provided 40-second or 4-second connect times for the base Reno case with 10 or 40 CBRs, respectively. This clearly shows the detrimental effect of using regular TCP Reno tuned to treat any packet loss or delay as signs of congestion on top of a routing protocol with inherent weaknesses such as the stale-route problem.

4.2   Throughput

DSR's throughput improved dramatically with the use of fixed-RTO option, which is also seen for 50-Kbps background traffic in Tables 1 and 2. Hold-down timer provided additional, though less significant, improvements in throughput. The SACK option had no significant impact on the throughput, while the DACK option improved throughput marginally for 40 CBR connections. With 10 CBR connections and 100-Kbps background traffic, AODV's throughput was improved marginally by DACK, fixed-RTO and hold-down timer options. With 40 CBR connections, however, AODV benefited greatly with the use of DACK and fixed-RTO options. The reduction in number of TCP ACK packets by the DACK option seemed to be beneficial to AODV as the number of CBR connections was increased. ADV's throughput was not significantly impacted by any of the options we used.

The highest throughput achieved was 0.32 Mbps with 10 CBRs and 0.31 Mbps with 40 CBRs, when all four options were used. Looking at the results for the case of 40 CBR connections, both AODV and DSR's throughputs were improved by 30-40%.

4.3   Goodput and routing overhead

The goodput ratio indicates the efficiency of a given combination of transport and routing protocols in delivering data. All three protocols exhibited very high goodputs, ranging from 96% to 98%. It is noteworthy that

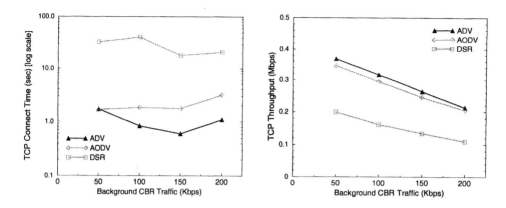

Figure 6: Connect times and throughputs for 1 TCP Reno connection with a 10-CBR background.

the proposed fixed-RTO technique did not significantly lessen the observed goodputs.

The routing overhead for DSR increased significantly in response to the fixed-RTO and hold-down timer techniques. A 20-33% increase in the MAC layer overhead was observed for DSR. The increased overhead is an expected result of the large gains in throughput seen for DSR. The routing overheads for ADV and AODV, on the other hand, were not affected by the different techniques.

Several simulations involving CBR traffic [6, 9, 5] seem to indicate that DSR and AODV have comparable MAC layer overheads. However, for the TCP traffic simulated in this work, AODV and ADV have lower overhead than DSR.

4.4 Comparison of routing algorithms

In order to compare the performances of the three routing algorithms, we conducted simulations of 1 TCP connection with various background traffics. At the transport layer, we used the base Reno and Reno with SACK, DACK, and fixed-RTO options. We denote combination of Reno with SACK, DACK and fixed-RTO as Reno-F. Figures 6 and 8 present the connect times and throughputs observed for each of the protocols for 1 TCP Reno connection with background traffic loads of 50, 100, 150, and 200 Kbps generated by 10 and 40 CBR connections. Figures 7 and 9 give the corresponding results for the Reno-F case. In addition, Figure 10 gives the routing overheads of the three routing algorithms with 40-CBR connections and Reno or Reno-F

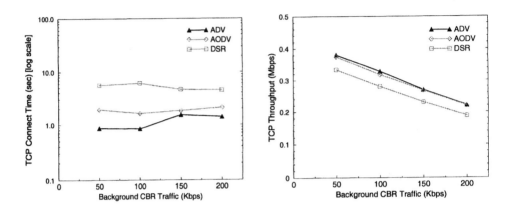

Figure 7: Connect times and throughputs for 1 TCP Reno-F connection with a 10-CBR background.

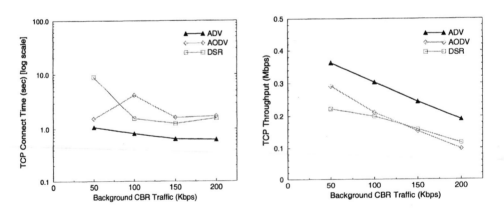

Figure 8: Connect times and throughputs for 1 TCP Reno connection with a 40-CBR background.

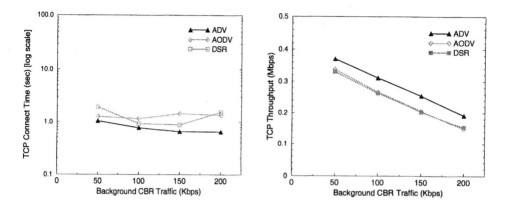

Figure 9: Connect times and throughputs for 1 TCP Reno-F connection with a 40-CBR background.

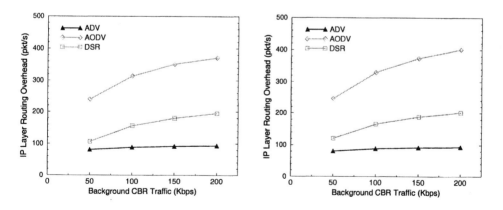

Figure 10: Routing overhead for the three routing algorithms with 1 TCP Reno (left) or Reno-F connection with a 40-CBR background.

used as the transport protocol.

Among the three routing algorithms, ADV provided consistently lower connect times, under 2 seconds with 10 CBRs and under 1 second with 40 CBRs, regardless of the traffic load. AODV also provided consistently low connect times, though always higher than those observed for ADV. For AODV and ADV, increasing the background traffic did not have a direct impact on the TCP connect time. For DSR, however, increasing the background traffic improved the connect times, especially with Reno as the transport protocol. Similarly, increasing the number of CBR connections for a given traffic load enabled DSR to provide significantly lower connect times since its stale route problem was alleviated somewhat by the need to store more active routes, which reduced the available route cache space for multiple, possibly stale, routes. The primary effect of Reno-F on connect times was to provide consistent connect times in the presence of increasing traffic load for given number of connections.

Keeping the number of CBR connections fixed at 10 or 40 and varying background traffic from 50 Kbps to 200 Kbps, reduced TCP throughputs for all three routing algorithms by 40-50%. In absolute terms, the loss in TCP throughput was about 150 Kbps, which is comparable to the increase in the background traffic load. Also, ADV provided the highest throughput among the three for all combinations of traffic loads, number of CBR connections and transport protocols. With 40 CBRs generating 200 Kbps traffic load and Reno as the transport protocol, ADV provided 80-100% higher throughput than AODV and DSR.

AODV suffered the most with increased number of CBR connections for a given traffic load. For example, increasing CBRs from 10 to 40 at 200 Kbps background traffic, with Reno as the transport protocol and AODV as the routing protocol, reduced TCP throughput by nearly 50%. In contrast, the reduction in throughput was about 9% with ADV as the transport protocol. As shown in Figure 10, AODV's routing overhead in terms of routing packets generated and processed by the routing protocol was high compared to the other two protocols. Furthermore, this routing overhead increases proportionately to the increase in the number of connections and traffic load. This seems to suggest that while AODV may perform well in light traffic loads with low number of connections, it needs to be evaluated carefully for other situations.

The impact of Reno-F is clear when throughputs in Figures 8 and 9 are compared. While ADV's throughput was nearly unchanged for all traffic loads, AODV and DSR's throughputs improved significantly for the case of 40 CBRs generating 200-Kbps traffic.

Finally, looking at the routing overheads generated by the three routing protocols, we note that ADV had the least routing overhead among the three, and its overhead is unchanged with increase in traffic load. On the other hand, both DSR and AODV tend to have higher overhead as the number of connections and background traffic is increased.

5   How fixed-RTO improves performance

The above analysis indicates that the combination of TCP's selective acknowledgements and delayed acknowledgements options with our proposed sender-side heuristic, fixed RTO, can yield substantial improvements in TCP performance. We call this combination of performance-enhancement techniques the TCP Reno-F protocol. While no TCP variant will succeed in utilizing all the available capacity of a MANET, the Reno-F protocol does a better job of adapting a TCP flow to the changes in a MANET's capacity than does TCP Reno.

To illustrate how Reno-F can impact the TCP performance of AODV while providing only a modest benefit to ADV, we analyze the TCP sender behavior for the worst-case mobility scenario among the 50 scenarios used in results given earlier. In this scenario, the length of the shortest possible path between the TCP sender and receiver nodes changed fairly frequently and tended to be a bit long, often 5 or 6 hops or more. There was a 50 Kbps background network load from 40 different CBR flows, and the single TCP connection was established after warming up the network for 100 seconds. To gain insight into the sender behavior, we examine the congestion window size, retransmissions, and repair times for broken routes at the sender. In Figures 11 and 12, the upper graph shows the congestion window size as a function of time along with two sets of hash marks; the upper (darker) hash marks denote retransmissions and the lower (lighter) hash marks denote transmission of a new packet by the sender. The size of the congestion window was limited to a maximum of eight. The lower graph shows the route repair times observed during the simulation; the horizontal dotted line indicates the average route repair time.

In Figure 11, at approximately time 375 a route failure occurs causing the congestion window size to drop to its minimum value of one. Retransmit timeouts follow at progressively longer intervals until the maximum of eight backoffs is reached. The upper hash marks indicate that the sender is probing the network at increasingly longer intervals; the lower hash marks indicate the lack of progress by the TCP sender. The route is not success-

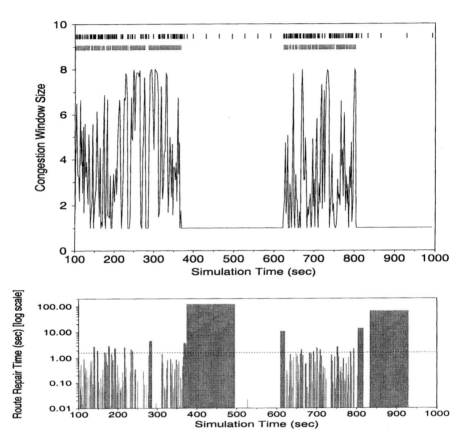

Figure 11: AODV congestion window sizes and route repair times for 1
TCP Reno connection with a 50 Kbps background load from 40 CBR
connections. The upper graph shows the congestion window size as a
function of time along with two sets of hash marks; the upper (darker)
hash marks denote retransmissions and the lower (lighter) hash marks
denote transmission of a new packet by the sender. Average route repair
time = 1.627 seconds. Throughput = 0.0914 Mbps.

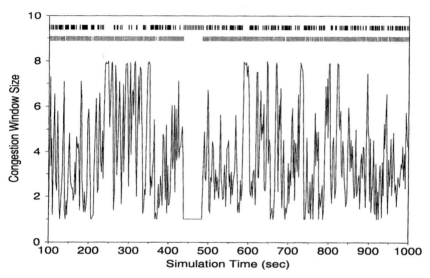

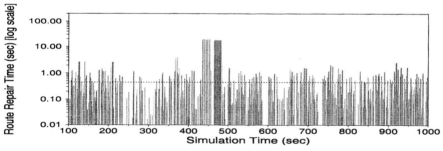

Figure 12: AODV congestion window sizes and route repair times for 1 TCP Reno-F connection with a 50 Kbps background load from 40 CBR connections. Average route repair time = 0.446 seconds. Throughput = 0.2023 Mbps.

fully re-established until about time 600, and during this period the observed route repair times shown in the lower graph are generally much longer than those before the route failure at time 375. Longer route repair times, along with fewer attempts to utilize a repaired route before node mobility breaks it again, cause the TCP sender to be stuck in retransmission mode as indicated by a congestion window of size 1 and the big gap in the lower hash marks. With the use of Reno-F in Figure 12, packet retransmissions due to timeouts are more frequent, which in turn stimulates AODV to discover new routes to the TCP receiver more frequently, thus reducing route repair time. Looking at the lower graphs, Reno-F reduces the average route repair delay (indicated by horizontal lines) by more than 70% and maximum route repair delay by 80%. So the TCP sender is able to utilize repaired routes quickly and keep the congestion window open. Additional analysis indicated that fixed-RTO improves DSR's performance also by improving its average and worst-case repair times.

In contrast, we see in Figure 13 that with TCP Reno, ADV is already doing a reasonable job of keeping the congestion window open and route repair times low. On average, ADV's proactive routing mechanism is able to repair routes in about half the time required by AODV. As a consequence, Reno-F produces almost no reduction in route repair time.

In summary, Reno-F, with its fixed-RTO heuristic, works well in situations where route failures are somewhat frequent and of long duration compared to the round-trip times for TCP packets. The performance benefits are greatest when an increased rate of packet retransmissions during route failure will stimulate the routing protocol's route repair mechanism to re-establish broken routes more quickly.

6   Analysis of TCP performance for multiple TCP connections

In the case of multiple TCP sources, we considered background traffic loads of 100 Kbps and 200 Kbps from 10 CBR and 40 CBR connections. The sender and receiver nodes were unique for each TCP connection, although in some cases a TCP endpoint was also the endpoint of one or more CBR flows. For the following discussion, we use results from simulations with 100-Kbps background traffic only, since the data from 200-Kbps simulations yield similar conclusions.

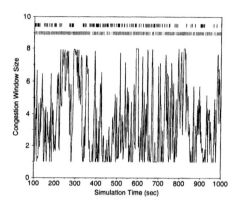

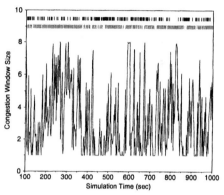

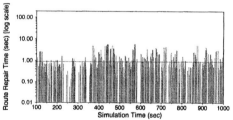

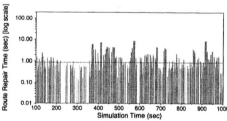

Figure 13: ADV congestion window sizes and route repair times for 1 TCP Reno connection with a 50 Kbps background load from 40 CBR connections. Average route repair time = 0.900 seconds. Throughput = 0.1702 Mbps.

Figure 14: ADV congestion window sizes and route repair times for 1 TCP Reno-F connection with a 50 Kbps background load from 40 CBR connections. Average route repair time = 0.879 seconds. Throughput = 0.1710 Mbps.

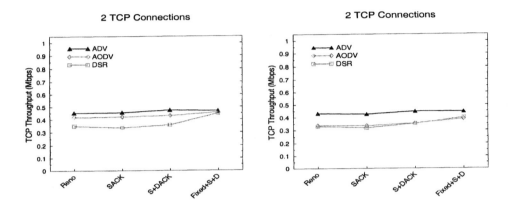

Figure 15: Throughputs for 2-TCP connections with 100-Kbps background
traffic generated by 10 (left) or 40 CBR connections.

6.1   Comparison of throughputs for different TCP options

The combined throughputs of 2, 5, and 10 TCP connections with a 100 Kbps
background traffic load are shown in Figures 15, 16 and 17.

As was observed previously for 1 TCP source, the addition of SACK and
delayed ACKs to TCP Reno resulted in modest gains (5-10%) in throughput. In most cases, ADV continued to provide the highest throughput. As
before, AODV showed decreased throughput relative to ADV and DSR as
the number of CBR connections increased from 10 to 40. Because AODV relies on its route discovery process to establish new routes and repair broken
routes, the larger number of connections results in considerably more work.
At the same time, a larger number of connections, as well as a higher volume
of traffic, enables DSR to use caching and snooping effectively to reduce this
route discovery overhead. For 5 and 10 TCP sources, DSR throughput was
observed to be nearly as high or even higher than that of AODV, particularly
for a larger number of CBR flows.

When the fixed-RTO technique (Reno-F) was employed, the performance
differences of the three protocols tended to be minimized. However, for more
than two TCP connections, the benefit of fixing the RTO in response to
consecutive timeouts became great enough that AODV and DSR provided
greater throughput than did ADV. For 10 TCPs with a 10-CBR background,
DSR throughput was 10% higher than ADV throughput. This effect became
even more pronounced when the background traffic load was increased to
200 Kbps.

As we show later, ADV provided significantly better CBR throughput

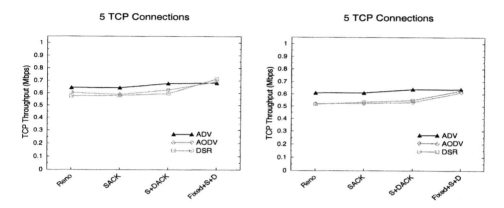

Figure 16: Throughputs for 5-TCP connections with 100-Kbps background traffic generated by 10 (left) or 40 CBR connections.

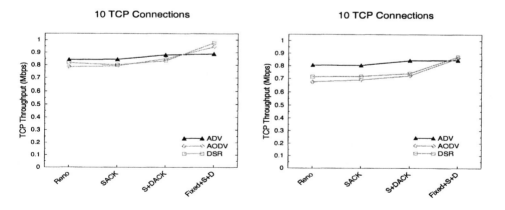

Figure 17: Throughputs for 10-TCP connections with 100-Kbps background traffic generated by 10 (left) or 40 CBR connections.

than the other protocols. Consequently, as the volume of CBR traffic increased, the impact of the background load on TCP throughput was largest for ADV. For the unmodified TCP sender (i.e., no fixed RTO), ADV and AODV throughputs were virtually the same and were higher than the DSR throughput, although this advantage decreased as the number of TCPs was increased. With 40 CBR connections, ADV continued to provide better throughput than AODV and DSR, which showed nearly identical performance.

6.2 TCP Reno vs. TCP Reno-F

The connect times, throughputs, goodputs, and routing overheads observed for the various number of TCP connections with a 100 Kbps background load from 10 CBR connections are shown in Figures 18 and 19. Given the relatively small throughput gains observed when using just the TCP options, we show only the results obtained using TCP Reno and TCP Reno-F (the combination of SACK, delayed ACKS, and fixed RTO).

For TCP Reno, the goodputs we observed for all three protocols were similar, ranging from about 96% to 98%. Reno-F decreased goodputs by about 2 percentage points.

AODV generated the highest number of routing packets, followed by DSR. Routing activity for AODV and DSR increased as more TCPs were added, but the rate of increase diminished as the number of connections grew. Due to its proactive nature, ADV generated the fewest routing packets, and ADV routing activity was constant with respect to both the number of TCP connections and the number of CBR connections.

Although the frequency of ADV routing updates remained constant, the amount of routing information contained in the updates did increase with the number of TCPs. When measured in Kbps, ADV routing overhead was quite a bit higher than that of the other protocols. For 1 TCP flow, ADV generated about twice as many routing bytes per second as AODV for 40 CBR connections, again a consequence of ADV's proactive routing. Several researchers have pointed out that the high cost of accessing the medium in a wireless network places a premium on a reduced number of routing packets. Hence, the larger number of ADV routing bytes may not be a concern.

6.3 UDP performance

The TCP performance afforded by a routing protocol should be weighed against how well the protocol is able to move non-TCP traffic at the same

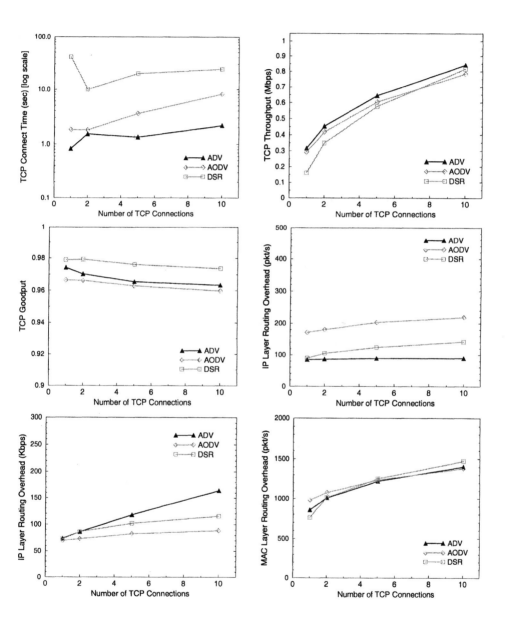

Figure 18: Connect times, throughputs, goodputs, and routing overhead for TCP Reno with a 100 Kbps 10-CBR background.

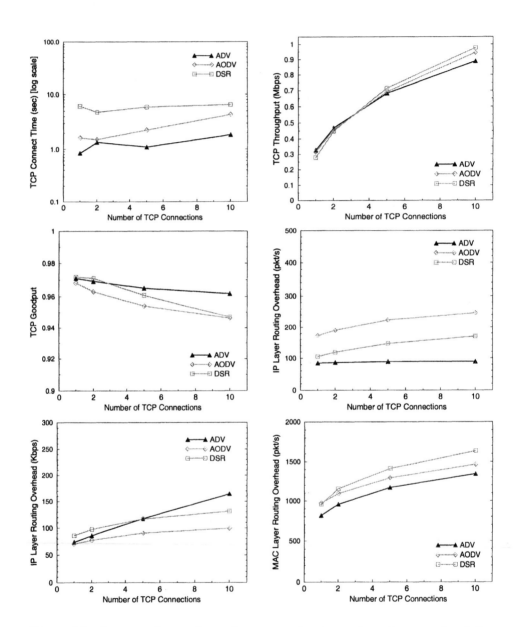

Figure 19: Connect times, throughputs, goodputs, and routing overhead for TCP Reno-F with a 100 Kbps 10-CBR background.

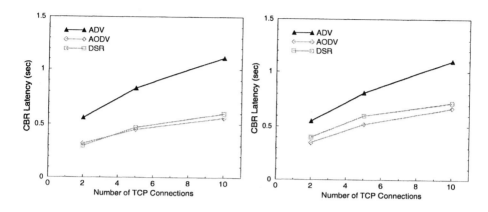

Figure 20: CBR packet latencies for TCP Reno and Reno-F with a 100 Kbps background load from 10 CBR connections

time. To assess the impact of TCP traffic on non-reactive CBR flows, we measured the average CBR packet latency and the fraction of CBR packets successfully delivered. The results observed for the various number of TCP connections with a 100 Kbps background load from 10 CBR connections are shown in Figures 20 and 21.

CBR packet latencies increased as more TCPs were added, but the increases were not enough to indicate saturation. For ADV, the use of a fixed RTO had essentially no effect on CBR latency compared to TCP Reno. For AODV and DSR, however, the increases in TCP throughput with a fixed RTO resulted in increased CBR packet latencies, which were 20% higher for 10 TCP connections. We found that ADV's buffer refresh time (buffer timeout) has a considerable impact on CBR latency. ADV latency was about twice that observed for the other protocols, which had nearly identical latencies, and for 10 TCP connections, ADV latency was slightly greater than 1 second compared to 0.5 second for DSR and AODV. This is in contrast to the results reported by [5], in which ADV latencies were lower than those of AODV and DSR. In that study, however, the CBR packet size was only 64 bytes, and a short buffer refresh time of 1 second was used for ADV.

Compared to the on-demand protocols, ADV did a much better job of handling the background CBR flows in terms of packet delivery fraction. With 10 TCP traffic sources, ADV delivered 70-75% of the CBR packets compared to about 60% for AODV and 50% for DSR. For only 2 TCPs, ADV achieved a delivery fraction above 90% for 10 CBR flows and in excess of 95% for 40 CBRs. AODV outperformed DSR in all cases, the observed

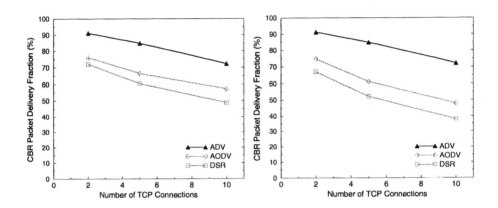

Figure 21: CBR packet delivery fractions for TCP Reno and Reno-F with a 100 Kbps background load from 10 CBR connections.

difference increasing with the number of TCP and CBR connections. As in the case of packet latency, the use of a fixed RTO had little or no effect on ADV's delivery fractions compared to TCP Reno. Packet delivery rates were 10-20% lower for AODV and DSR with a fixed RTO, again a result of the higher volume of TCP traffic.

7   Concluding remarks

We began this chapter by categorizing techniques for improving TCP performance in MANETs. We identified three levels at which one might attack the problem, and at each level we gave examples of potential methods for improving TCP performance. The highest level, level 1, is the class of techniques that are purely end-to-end at the transport layer. Such methods do not require information from or interaction with the routing layer or lower layers in the protocol stack, either at the connection endpoints or at intermediate nodes. Level 1 techniques have the advantage of being less complex and therefore easier to implement, requiring fewer modifications of existing network software. If adequate performance gains can be obtained with level 1 techniques, they are preferable.

We have considered several level 1 techniques for improving TCP performance in MANETs. Of these, our proposed TCP sender-side heuristic, the fixed-RTO technique, shows the most promise. We have combined fixed RTO with TCP's selective acknowledgements and delayed acknowledgements options to form the TCP Reno-F protocol. Reno-F works well in a variety of situations; for example, TCP performance benefits accrue with or without the presence of background network traffic. In the remainder of this section, we identify three main cases in which we have observed Reno-F to be helpful.

Reno-F works well with routing protocols having route discovery mechanisms that can be stimulated by an increased rate of packet transmissions, e.g. on-demand algorithms. Route stimulation can be useful in situations where route failures are frequent, or where route repairs are difficult, say due to a sudden, large increase in the number of hops between the TCP sender and receiver.

Reno-F tends to minimize the TCP performance differences among different MANET routing protocols, although it does not entirely eliminate these differences. In some cases, Reno-F can offset performance problems due to algorithmic shortcomings in a routing protocol. For example, an interesting effect of Reno-F is that it largely negates DSR's well-known problem with stale routes.

Among the three different routing algorithms we used in this study, the proactive ADV protocol outperforms both AODV and DSR in almost all cases except for the combination to Reno-F with a large number of TCP connections. The performance of ADV is particularly noteworthy when TCP Reno with no enhancement techniques is used. While AODV and DSR falter owing to high routing overhead or stale routes, ADV performs very well. This indicates that for consistently high performance, some form of proactive route maintenance should be considered to complement the route discovery used in on-demand routing protocols.

References

[1] A. Ahuja, S. Agarwal, J. P. Singh, and R. Shorey. Performance of TCP over different routing protocols in mobile ad-hoc networks. *Proc. IEEE Vehicular Technology Conference (VTC 2000)*, May 2000.

[2] A. Bakre and B. R. Badrinath. I-TCP: Indirect TCP for mobile hosts. In *Proc. 15th International Conf. on Distributed Computing Systems (ICDCS)*, pages 136–143, May 1995.

[3] H. Balakrishnan, S. Seshan, and R. H. Katz. Improving reliable transport and handoff performance in cellular wireless networks. *Wireless Networks* 1(4):469–481, Dec. 1995.

[4] H. Balakrishnan, V. N. Padmanabhan, S. Seshan, and R. H. Katz. A comparison of mechanisms for improving TCP performance over wireless links. *IEEE/ACM Trans. on Networking*, 5(6):756–769, Dec. 1997.

[5] R. V. Boppana and S. P. Konduru. An adaptive distance vector routing algorithm for mobile, ad hoc networks. In *Proc. 20th Annual Joint Conference of the IEEE Computer and Communications Societies (IEEE INFOCOM 2001)*, volume 3, pages 1753–1762, Mar. 2001.

[6] J. Broch, D. A. Maltz, D. B. Johnson, Y.-C. Hu, and J. Jetcheva. A performance comparison of multi-hop wireless ad hoc network routing protocols. In *Proc. 4th Annual ACM/IEEE International Conf. on Mobile Computing and Networking (ACM MobiCom '98)*, pages 85–97, Oct. 1998.

[7] R. Caceres and L. Iftode. Improving the performance of reliable transport protocols in mobile computing environments. *IEEE Journal on Selected Areas in Communications*, 13(5):850–857, June 1995.

[8] K. Chandran, S. Raghunathan, S. Venkatesan and R. Prakash. A feedback based scheme for improving TCP performance in ad-hoc wireless networks. In *Proc. 18th International Conf. on Distributed Computing Systems (ICDCS)*, pages 472–479, May 1998.

[9] S. R. Das, C. E. Perkins, and E. M. Royer. Performance comparison of two on-demand routing protocols for ad hoc networks. In *Proc. 19th Annual Joint Conference of the IEEE Computer and Communications Societies (IEEE INFOCOM 2000)*, volume 1, pages 3–12, Mar. 2000.

[10] T. D. Dyer and R.V. Boppana. A comparison of TCP performance over three routing protocols for mobile ad hoc networks. In *Proc. 2nd ACM International Symposium on Mobile Ad Hoc Networking and Computing (MobiHoc '01)*, pages 56–66, Oct. 2001.

[11] T. D. Dyer and R.V. Boppana. Routing HTTP traffic in a mobile ad hoc network. In *Proc. MILCOM 2002*, Oct. 2002.

[12] K. Fall and K. Varadhan. ns Manual. The VINT Project. UC Berkeley, LBL, USC/ISI, and Xerox PARC. Available from http://www.isi.edu/nsnam/ns/ns-documentation.html, Apr. 2002.

[13] S. Floyd, J. Mahdavi, M. Mathis, and M. Podolsky. An extension to the selective acknowledgement (SACK) option for TCP. RFC 2883, July 2000.

[14] S. Floyd. A report on recent developments in TCP congestion control. *IEEE Communications Magazine*, 39(4):84–90, Apr. 2001.

[15] S. Floyd. TCP and Explicit Congestion Notification. *ACM SIGCOMM Computer Communication Review*, 24(5):8–23, Oct. 1994.

[16] M. Gerla, K. Tang, and R. Bagrodia. TCP performance in wireless multi-hop networks. In *Proc. of 2nd IEEE Workshop on Mobile Computing Systems and Applications (WMCSA)*, pages 41–50, 1999.

[17] T. Goff, J. Moronski, D. S. Phatak, and V. Gupta. Freeze-TCP: A true end-to-end TCP enhancement mechanism for mobile environments. In *Proc. 19th Annual Joint Conference of the IEEE Computer and Communications Societies (IEEE INFOCOM 2000)*, volume 3, pages 1537–1545, Mar. 2000.

[18] G. Holland and N. Vaidya. Analysis of TCP performance over mobile ad hoc networks. In *Proc. 5th Annual ACM/IEEE International Conf. on Mobile Computing and Networking (ACM MobiCom '99)*, pages 219–230, Aug. 1999.

[19] Y.-C Hu and D. B. Johnson. Caching strategies in on-demand routing protocols for wireless ad hoc networks. In *Proc. 6th Annual ACM/IEEE International Conf. on Mobile Computing and Networking (ACM MobiCom '00)*, pages 231–242, Aug. 2000.

[20] IEEE Computer Society LAN/MAN Standards Committee. Wireless LAN medium access control (MAC) and physical layer (PHY) specifications. IEEE Standard 802.11-1999, 1999.

[21] IETF MANET Working Group Charter. http://www.ietf.org/html.charters/manet-charter.html.

[22] D. B. Johnson, D. A. Maltz, Y.-C. Hu, and J. Jetcheva. The dynamic source routing protocol for mobile ad hoc networks (DSR). IETF Internet Draft. http://www.ietf.org/internet-drafts/draft-ietf-manet-dsr-07.txt, Feb. 2002.

[23] S. Keshav and S. P. Morgan. SMART retransmission: performance with overload and random losses. In *Proc. 16th Annual Joint Conference of the IEEE Computer and Communications Societies (IEEE INFOCOM '97)*, volume 3, pages 1131–1138, 1997.

[24] D. Kim, C.-K. Toh, Y. Choi. TCP-BuS: Improving TCP performance in wireless ad hoc networks. *Journal of Communications and Networks*, 3(2):175–186, June 2001.

[25] S.-B. Lee, G.-S. Ahn, and A. Campbell. Improving UDP and TCP performance in mobile ad hoc networks with INSIGNIA. *IEEE Communications Magazine*, 39(6):156–165, June 2001.

[26] J. Liu and S. Singh. ATCP: TCP for mobile ad hoc networks. *IEEE Journal on Selected Areas in Communications*, 19(7):1300–1315, Jul. 2001.

[27] M. Mathis, J. Mahdavi, S. Floyd, and A. Romanow. TCP selective acknowledgment options. RFC 2018, Oct. 1996.

[28] Monarch Group. Wireless and mobility extensions to ns-2. Available from http://www.monarch.cs.rice.edu/cmu-ns.html, Oct. 1999.

[29] J. P. Monks, P. Sinha, and V. Bharghavan. Limitations of TCP-ELFN for ad hoc networks. In *Proc. 7th International Workshop on Mobile Multimedia Communications (MoMuC 2000)*, Oct. 2000.

[30] C. E. Perkins, E. M. Belding-Royer, and S. R. Das. Ad hoc on-demand distance vector (AODV) routing. IETF Internet Draft. http://www.ietf.org/internet-drafts/draft-ietf-manet-aodv-11.txt, Jun. 2002.

[31] C. E. Perkins and P. Bhagwat. Highly dynamic destination-sequenced distance vector (DSDV) for mobile computers. *ACM SIGCOMM Computer Communication Review*, 24(4):234–244, Oct. 1994.

[32] J. Postel. Internet Protocol. RFC 791, Sep. 1981.

[33] J. Postel. Transmission Control Protocol. RFC 793, Sep. 1981.

[34] K. K. Ramakrishnan and R. Jain. A binary feedback scheme for congestion avoidance in computer networks. *ACM Transactions on Computer Systems*, 8(2):158–181, May 1990.

[35] W. R. Stevens, *TCP/IP Illustrated, Volume 1: The Protocols*. Addison-Wesley, Reading, MA, 1994.

[36] R. Yavatkar and N. Bhagwat. Improving end-to-end performance of TCP over mobile internetworks. In *Proc. Workshop on Mobile Computing Systems and Applications*, pages 146–152, Dec. 1994.

AD HOC WIRELESS NETWORKING
X. Cheng, X. Huang and D.-Z. Du (Eds.) pp. 87 - 102

Energy Efficient Approaches in Wireless Networking

Mihaela Cardei [1] *Department of Computer Science and Engineering*
University of Minnesota, Minneapolis, MN 55455
E-mail: mihaela@cs.umn.edu

Ionut Cardei
Department of Computer Science and Engineering
University of Minnesota, Minneapolis, MN 55455
E-mail: ionut@cs.umn.edu

Ding-Zhu Du
Department of Computer Science and Engineering
University of Minnesota, Minneapolis, MN 55455
E-mail: dzd@cs.umn.edu

Contents

[1]Mihaela Cardei is supported by the University of Minnesota Graduate School Doctoral Dissertation Fellowship.

Abstract

Wireless networking is one of the fastest growing segments of the computer industry, being the platform of many critical applications in the military or in disaster recovery situations, where deployment of traditional wired networks is infeasible. Wireless devices are battery powered and therefore have a limited operational time. Recently, the optimization of energy utilization of wireless terminals has received significant attention. Different techniques for power management have been proposed at all layers of the network protocol stack. In this paper we survey recent advances in energy efficiency for Medium Access Control (MAC) protocols, ad-hoc routing and topology control mechanisms.

Key Words: wireless networks, energy efficiency, power aware protocols and algorithms.

1 Introduction

Wireless communications networks provide rapid access to information and computing, eliminating the barriers of distance, time and location for many applications in national security, civilian search and rescue operations, as well as in the area of personal communications.

Wireless networks are generally classified as (1) infrastructure based networks, where every host can directly communicate with a base station that coordinates communication and (2) ad hoc networks, where nodes are self configurable and able to forward packets so that end to end communication is achieved with multihop paths.

An important issue in mobile wireless networking recently receiving increased attention is power management. Wireless mobile stations are in general powered by electrochemical batteries, with a fairly reduced capacity, limited in part by constraints in size and weight. When replacing or recharging the battery is not feasible (for instance in military applications), the application success may depend on conserving energy resources. As research on battery technology did not produce significant advances in the last 30 year, the optimization of energy consumption in wireless terminal has received considerable attention. Energy efficiency has been addressed through low power design at the hardware level as well as through power-aware mechanisms at all layers of the network protocol stack. The paper [8] presents a survey of works that consider energy efficient techniques for each network layer.

For the purpose of network operation, energy is consumed for communication and computation. Computation energy is consumed by executing protocols and algorithms. Communication regards data transfer in the network. A mobile radio is equipped with a RF transceiver used for sending and receiving data. A mobile radio can be in one of the following states (modes): transmit, receive, idle and sleep. Generally, when a host is not sending or receiving packets, it is in the *idle* mode, with power consumption nearly as high as in receiving mode. Thus, in many papers the idle state is not differentiated from the receiving state. The highest power consumption is in transmit mode, and the lowest in the sleep mode, when a node turns off both its transmitter and receiver. For example, when the power supply is at 5V, the power consumption for transmit:receive:sleep modes for a 2 Mbps Digitan IEEE 802.11 Wireless LAN Module [9] is 1.9W:1.55W:0.75W, while for an 11 Mbps Lucent IEEE 802.11 WaveLAN PC [6] it is 1.4W:0.9W:0.05W. The work in [6] also describes a series of experiments on energy consumption with Lucent WaveLAN PC NICs in sending, receiving and discarding broadcast versus point-to-point data packets. Considering these characteristics, it is important to design protocols and algorithms that reduce transceiver energy consumption.

Mechanisms used to reduce energy consumption include: (1) having nodes enter sleep state as often and for as long as possible (2) choose routing paths that minimize energy consumption (3) selectively use nodes based on their energy status (4) construct communication and data delivery structures (e.g. broadcast/multicast tree, underlying topology) that minimize energy consumption (5) reduce networking overhead. Having nodes enter the sleep state is an important and efficient method to conserve energy resources. The idea is to enter a radio in the sleep state whenever it cannot send or receive data, to avoid overhearing transmissions not intended for itself. Routing protocols should use power-aware criteria in choosing the routing paths. If few nodes are overused, they can deplete their power earlier, triggering network partition. In order to prolong the network lifetime, it is important to select nodes based on their current power level. One method is to employ load-balanced routing. Underlying communication and data delivery structures are implicitly or explicitly used by the routing protocol and their maintenance should aim at minimizing the maximum energy consumption per node. Another important aspect of energy efficiency is reducing the networking overhead. For instance, contention at the MAC layer should be reduced, as it triggers retransmissions, thereby wasting energy. Also, the size and periodicity of background control packets need to be considered.

An emerging class of wireless networks is sensor networks, which promise to have a significant impact on a broad range of applications relating to surveillance, health care and environmental monitoring, etc. A sensor network usually consists of a large number of sensors collaborating to perform a common task. Since wireless sensors are battery powered, mechanisms for energy savings can effectively prolong their operational time.

In this paper we survey recent works that accomplish energy savings in medium access control (MAC) protocols, ad-hoc routing strategies and topology control mechanisms. The rest of the paper is structured as follows. Section 2 continues with methods at the MAC layer, section 3 presents routing related techniques, section 4 address topology control and section 5 concludes the paper.

2   Energy Efficient Scheduling of Node Activity

One efficient method for conserving energy is to schedule wireless node activity to alternate between *active* state (transmit or receive) and low-energy *sleep* state (also called *dozing* state). A node in the *sleep* mode is not aware of network activity and cannot participate in traffic exchange. The longer a node is in the sleep state, the longer it takes to consume its power reserves. As the transition time between the sleep mode and the active mode can be as high as $800\mu s$ [7], in order to reduce the number of transitions, it is recommended that the nodes schedule traffic into bursts in which a station can continuously transmit or receive data.

In this section we will present a few MAC layer protocols in wireless networks and wireless sensor networks which achieve energy savings by scheduling node activity to alternate between sleep and active modes.

2.1   Power Aware MAC Protocols in Wireless Networks

The IEEE 802.11 wireless standard [1] covers three functional areas of the MAC sublayer: reliable data delivery, medium access control and security. The data transfer mechanism is accomplished by a two frame exchange protocol: after every unicast data frame received successfully, the receiver sends an acknowledgment (ACK). To further enhance reliability, a four frame exchange protocol may be used for unicast frames as follows: the sender first sends a Request To Send (RTS) frame to the destination; the destination responds with a Clear To Send (CTS) frame; sender sends the data frame and the receiver replies with an ACK. The RTS/CTS scheme avoids the hidden terminal problem and is required by the 802.11 standard but may be disabled.

The basic medium access protocol is the Distributed Coordination Function (DCF) which implements medium sharing through the use of Carrier Sense Multiple Access with Collision Avoidance (CSMA/CA). Collision avoidance uses a binary exponential backoff procedure, which is invoked when a station that wants to transmit a frame detects a busy medium. Point Coordination Function (PCF) is an alternative access method build on top of DCF, with medium access controlled by a central point coordinator through polling.

The IEEE 802.11 standard [1] offers a power management technique. The basic concept is to have all stations that operate in power-save (PS) mode to synchronize and wake up at the same time. If a station receives an announcement about data to be delivered, it stays awake until receives the frame, otherwise may return to the dozing state. This mechanism is easily accomplished in infrastructure networks, where the point coordinator synchronizes all mobile stations and buffers the frames for stations in doze state. This is done by periodically sending a beacon, which contains both a time stamp as well as a Traffic Indication Map (TIM) which announces all u packets for stations in doze mode. The mobile stations that wake up to receive the beacon will determine if there is any pending traffic, in which case they will stay awake until the transmission is over. Power management for the DCF is accomplished in a distributed fashion. After the beacon interval, all mobile stations compete for sending the beacon, using the standard backoff algorithm. Packets for a station in doze state are buffered by the sender and announced using Ad-hoc TIMs (ATIMS) which are sent after the beacon during the ATIM window. All stations are awake during the ATIM window, therefore the announced receiver knows to stay awake until data transmission takes place. Both ATIMs and data packets are acknowledged and are sent using the standard backoff algorithm.

There are many publications in literature which further explore and look at different ways to improve the energy conservation mechanism proposed by IEEE 802.11. The Energy Conserving MAC (EC-MAC) protocol [12] was designed for a centrally controlled ATM network, having energy efficiency as the primary goal. After the schedule is transmitted by the base station (BS), the nodes in the network know when to be awake, only during the periods when they exchange traffic. This improve the energy consumption compared with 802.11, where the destination remains awake until the data transfer is completed. Also, by scheduling the exact order of data transfer, collisions are avoided and the number of retransmissions will be decreased. Further energy improvements are achieved when frames from or to the same station are allocated contiguous slots, by saving the transition energy between active-sleep states.

In [11], authors proposed PAMAS, a medium access control protocol for ad-hoc networks, based on the MACA protocol, with addition of a separate signaling channel. The signaling channel is used to send RTS/CTS control messages, and busy tones which are sent while a node receives a packet (at the beginning of message reception or when a receiving node gets a RTS from another station). The main way to save energy comes from nodes powering themself off when they overhear transmissions which were not directed to them. A node powers off when it cannot send or receive data: (1) has no data to transmit and one neighbor starts transmitting and (2) has data to transmit, but at least one neighbor is transmitting and another is receiving. In order for a station to determine the time to power off, the proposed probe protocol determines the longest transfer time for a sender or receiver neighbor. Experiments conducted on a random network topology, line topology and fully connected network topology, show power savings between $10-70\%$.

2.2 Energy Efficient MAC Techniques for Wireless Sensor Networks

Wireless sensors are devices equipped with sensing, processing and communication capabilities. The sensor nodes may communicate or forward data through multi-hop paths. This section presents approaches for power savings that apply to sensor networks.

In [17], authors proposed S-MAC, a MAC protocol for wireless sensor networks, having energy efficiency as the primary design objective. The modeled network has many sensor nodes capable of multi hop communication, deployed in an ad-hoc manner, which are inactive for long periods of time and become active when something is detected. This protocol assumes nodes collaborate for a common application, and adapts to changes to network size, density and topology.

The S-MAC protocol assumes the principal sources of energy waste are:

(1) collisions (2) message overhearing - receiving packets addressed to other nodes (3) control packet overhead and (4) idle listening. S-MAC uses the following mechanisms to reduce the energy waste from all the above sources. First, it lets nodes sleep periodically if they are in the idle listening mode. Neighboring nodes synchronize their sleep schedule, forming virtual clusters. In order to avoid the collisions, S-MAC follows a mechanism similar to 802.11, using RTS/CTS/DATA/ACK packet sequence. To avoid overhearing, S-MAC employs a mechanism similar with PAMAS, by putting the neighbors of both a sender and a receiver to sleep after they hear RTS or CTS packet, for the duration of the current transmission. Still S-MAC uses only one channel for data and signaling. The last mechanism used is message passing, where a long message is divided into many small packets, sent in a burst. Only one RTS/CTS packet sequence is used, but every data fragment is acknowledged to avoid the hidden terminal problem. These mechanisms may affect per-hop fairness and latency. The performance of this protocol is evaluated using Rene Motes, developed at University of California, Berkeley, and shows the energy savings of S-MAC compared with 802.11 DCF.

In [3], authors address the problem of energy efficiency in wireless sensor applications for surveillance of a set of targets with known locations. When ground access in that area is prohibited, one method is to deploy remotely (e.g. from an aircraft) a large sensor population, in targets' proximity. The sensors send the monitored information to a central processing node. Every target must be monitored at all times and every sensor is able to monitor all targets within its operational range. Energy savings are obtained by scheduling the sensor nodes transmission such that they are in the sleep mode as much as possible. The proposed method consists of dividing the set of sensors into disjoint sets, such that every set completely covers all targets. Then every set responsible for target monitoring is activated in a round-robin fashion. The nodes from the active set are in the active state, whereas all other nodes are in a low energy sleep state. This method also assures a balanced energy consumption among all sensor nodes. The lifetime of the network is extended proportional with the number of sets found. The paper presents an efficient heuristic for computing of a maximum number of disjoint sets. Once the sensors are deployed, they send their location information to the central node, which computes the disjoint sets and sends back the membership information. Knowing the set it belongs to and the total number of covers, every sensor is able to identify the time periods when will in active or sleep states. This mechanism can be implemented at MAC layer. In this case, the node synchronization is accomplished with periodic beacon messages transmitted by the central node. On the other hand, the medium access for the sensors within the same set can be implemented using any of the existing protocols, such as TDMA, FDMA or CDMA.

3 Energy Conservation in Ad-hoc Routing

Ah hoc wireless networks are infrastructure-less, with nodes establishing connections on-the-fly, without a centralized coordinator. All nodes have the ability to route packets, so that when the nodes are not within radio range of each other, they achieve end-to-end connectivity through multihop routes. This feature allows ad-hoc wireless networks to be very easy to deploy.

One difficulty is raised by the node mobility, which triggers frequent topology updates, therefore higher control message overhead. Methods to reduce the energy consumption include: consider battery resources when selecting the route, reduce overhead (e.g. frequency of control messages), efficient route reconfiguration mechanisms (as effect of topology change).

3.1 Power Aware Routing Protocols

Traditional routing metrics, such as minimum hop-count are not appropriate for ad-hoc wireless networking , as they may overuse the energy resources of a small set of nodes in favor of others. In order to increase node and network lifetime, the paper [16] introduces five new power-aware metrics for determining routes in ad-hoc wireless networks. Intuitively, it is desirable to route packets through lightly-loaded nodes, with sufficient power resources. The new metrics are:

1. Minimize energy consumed per packet: for any packet, the goal of this metric is to minimize the sum of energies consumed in every node involved in forwarding the packet from source to destination. One disadvantage is early energy consumption for some nodes, with impact on the network lifetime.

2. Maximize time to network partition. This can be accomplished by load balancing among the critical nodes. Optimizing this metric is difficult if application requires low delay and high throughput.

3. Minimize variance in node power levels. This is similar with load sharing, by keeping the amount of unfinished work in all nodes the same.

4. Minimize cost per packet. The cost of sending a packet along some path is defined as the sum of the costs of all nodes in path, where the cost of a node denotes the reluctance to forward packets. By incorporating the battery

characteristics in defining the node cost, different goal can be achieved such as avoiding nodes with depleted energy resources or increase the time to network partition.

5. Minimize maximum node cost, where the cost of a node is the cost of routing a packet. The goal is to increase the time until the first node fails.

The authors conducted simulations to validate the benefits of using these power-aware metrics. The authors compared the performance of shortest-hop routing versus shortest-cost routing as defined by the fourth metric, using three performance metrics: end-to-end packet delay, average cost/packet and average maximum node cost. The results indicated no difference in the end-to-end delay between the two routing methods. By using shortest-cost routing, some packets may have a longer delay when they avoid high cost nodes, but others have shorter delays by avoiding congested nodes. The experiments indicate higher cost savings for larger networks, for moderate network loads and in denser networks.

Performing routing such that the energy consumed along the selected path is minimized can result in overusing and power depletion of a small set of nodes. A better approach is to select a routing path with the objective of maximizing the network lifetime by balancing energy consumption among the nodes. This idea is explored in [5], where authors address the problem of routing in a static wireless network, having a set of source nodes generating packets that must reach a set of designated nodes. An instance of such a network is a sensor network, with sensors generating data that is sent to more powerful nodes for processing. Every node can participate in data forwarding, and can adjust its power within a range, resulting in a set of possible one-hop away neighbors. Considering the objective of maximizing the system lifetime, the authors proposed a class of flow augmentation algorithms and a flow redirection algorithm, that balance the energy consumption among network nodes, proportionally with their energy reserves. Performance evaluations with simulations show that the system lifetime is improved in average by 60% compared to minimum transmitted energy routing.

3.2 Power Aware Broadcast and Multicast Tree Construction

Broadcast and multicast are important functions for a routing protocol. An important issue in ad hoc wireless networks is the broadcast/multicast delivery structure. Traditional routing protocols for ad-hoc wireless networks used flooding for broadcast. In mobile ad-hoc wireless networks broadcast by flooding is usually very costly and results in serious redundancy, contention and collisions, referred to as the *broadcast storm problem* [13]. Alternative methods need to be designed for delivery of broadcast/multicast traffic considering the limitations in resource availability for a mobile node: energy, bandwidth, transceivers, etc.

Compared with wired networks where network links and their capacity are known apriori, in ad-hoc wireless networks links depend on factors such as the distance between nodes, transmission power and interferences. The wireless channel is characterized by the *broadcast* property and when omnidirectional antennas are used, all nodes within the sender's transmission range receive the message. The total power required to reach a set of nodes is the maximum power necessary to reach each individual node, whereas in wired networks, the cost for sending a message to a set of nodes is the sum of the costs of the individual transmissions. Therefore it is important to design algorithms and protocols which reflect the *node-based* model of wireless communications, compared with the *link-based* model of wired networks. These characteristics are pointed out in [15], where authors address the problem of constructing the minimum-energy source based broadcast and multicast trees, by determining which nodes belong to the tree and the power used by these nodes for transmission. The problem is addressed for a stationary network, when bandwidth and transceiver resources are considered unlimited. Every node, equipped with an omnidirectional antennae, can choose the transmission power from a range of values and has several transceivers, thus being able to support several multicast sessions simultaneously. There is a tradeoff in choosing the transmission power at a node. Higher transmission power results in a higher connectivity, with more nodes being reached in one hop at the cost of higher interference and higher energy usage. The authors design three algorithms for the broadcast tree construction: Broadcast Incremental Power (BIP) which uses a node-based cost, Broadcast Least-Unicast-cost(BLU) and Broadcast Link-based MST (BLiMST) that both use a link-based cost. BIP starts the broadcast tree construction from the source node and at every step adds a new node such that the additional power cost is minimum, in a manner similar to Prim's algorithm. BLU is constructed by superpositioning a minimum-cost path from the source node to every other node. BLiMST uses the standard Minimum Spanning Tree (MST) to build the tree, assuming a link cost between every two nodes. The transmission range of each node is then set to the distance to the farthest neighbor in the broadcast tree. A *sweep* operation can be applied to improve the broadcast trees performance by removing unnecessary transmissions. The solutions proposed for constructing the multicast tree use BIP or BLiMST by pruning transmissions not intended for multicast group members or use BLU by considering only the unicast paths to the desired destinations. Simulations show that BIP produces better results than the other two link-based algorithms.

Theoretical models and performance analysis of these protocols are further studied in [14]. By exploring geometric structures of Euclidean MSTs, authors showed that the approximation ratio of BIP is between 13/3 and 12 and the approximation ratio of MST is between 6 and 12. For the shortest path tree, the authors proved the approximation ratio to be at least $n/2$, where n is the number of nodes.

4 Energy Aware Connected Network Topology

The *topology* of a multihop wireless network is defined by the set of communication links between node pairs and is used mainly by the routing mechanism. Topology depends both on "uncontrollable" parameters such as node mobility, interference or weather, as well as on "controllable" parameters such as transmission power. Using a wrong topology may impact the network capacity, packet delay and may decrease robustness to node failure. A sparse topology may cause network partitioning and affects the end-to-end delay, whereas too dense a topology reduces bandwidth and spatial reuse with effect on aggregated network capacity. Because energy resources are limited, in order to extend the network lifetime, one important strategy is to control the node transmit power in order to achieve the desired topology qualities.

In the paper [10], the authors address the problem of controlling the network topology by adjusting the transmission power at each node in order to minimize the maximum node transmission power in the entire network, subject to the network being connected or biconnected. Biconnectivity provides two different paths between every pair of nodes, improving fault tolerance and load balancing. Two optimal centralized algorithms are proposed for static networks: CONNECT and BICONN-AUGMENT. CONNECT builds the topology first as a minimum spanning tree and then apply a post processing phase. In the second phase every node is considered and its power is decreased to the maximum possible extent which does not disconnect the induced graph. BICONN-AUGMENT algorithm employs a greedy technique, which starts from a connected network and adds links until the resulting topology is biconnected. A similar post processing phase is used to ensure per node minimality. For mobile networks, the authors propose two distributed heuristics which adaptively adjust the transmission power in order to maintain the desired topology considering the effect of mobility. Both heuristics do not require any special control messages. In the first heuristic, Local Information No Topology (LINT) every node gets the current neighbor information from the routing protocol and attempts to keep the number of neighbors bounded by increasing or decreasing its operational power. In the second heuristic, Local Information Link-State Topology (LILT) there are two mechanisms to control connectivity: the Neighbor Reduction Protocol (NRP) and the Neighbor Addition Protocol(NAP). When a node receives a routing update, it determines the status of the topology. If it is biconnected, no action is taken. If it is disconnected, the power is set to maximum. If it is connected, a timer is set proportional to the distance from the node to the first articulation point (a node whose removal partitions the network). After that time, if the network is not biconnected, the power is set to maximum. It is possible that the network overreacts, by having more nodes increasing their power, but this effect will be regulated by the NRP. Experiments are performed with a system that uses a flat link-state routing mechanism. The radio used is the Utilicom Longranger which has transmission power control and uses the CSMA channel access protocol. The performance metrics considered are throughput, end to end delay, maximum transmission power across all nodes (for static networks) and average transmission power (for static networks). The results show that for static networks, BICONN gives the best throughput and adapts very well to a changing node density. CONNECT suffers from congestion hotspots at low densities. BICONN uses significantly more power than CONNECT at lower densities, triggered by the isolated nodes. The conclusion is that at high densities it is better to use BICONN, whereas at lower densities the choice depends on which is more important: power or throughput. In mobile environments, LINT has a better throughput but a higher delay than LILT. This occurs mainly because the link-state database is often out of date, causing false alarms and power increases in LILT. Nevertheless, the experiments show that the performance of multihop wireless networks, in practice, can be substantially improved with topology control.

In [4] the authors address the problem of determining the transmission range for every node in a stationary ad-hoc wireless network such that the resulting network topology is strongly connected and the total transmission energy is minimized. Such a topology is used in all-to-all traffic such as background information exchange. The proposed optimization algorithm assumes that every node knows its location and broadcasts this information periodically. It can be applied to any spanning tree topology in order to improve the energy cost. This algorithm starts with a bidirectional graph, obtained from the spanning tree by replacing every undirected edge with two directed edges. Then, it identifies the critical paths with larger energy expenditure and replaces every such path with the corresponding closing edge, if the energy cost is improved. This centralized algorithm is executed by a leader node, designated apriori or determined by a leader-election protocol. The resulting topology is broadcasted by the leader periodically or only when updates occur. The authors applied this optimization algorithm to a MST topology and a Minimum Incremental Power (MIP) tree topology. MIP is similar with BIP, in that it starts from the root (leader node) and grows the tree such that every edge adds a minimum energy cost increase. It is known that MST produces a performance ratio-2 for the energy cost and minimizes the maximum transmission power, which has a positive effect on prolonging individual battery life. Performance evaluations for the optimization algorithm on MST and MIP structures show improvements of $10 - 25\%$ in energy cost.

Another strategy in prolonging the network lifetime, regarded as the time when the first node depletes its power resources, consists of strategic deployment of relay nodes in order to balance the energy consumption among wireless nodes. This technique is explored in [2]: having the location of n wireless nodes, the objective is to determine the deployment location of at most k relay nodes and the resulting interconnecting tree, such that the length of the longest edge is minimized. The proposed solution is a performance ratio $\sqrt{3} + \epsilon$ polynomial time approximation algorithm for this problem, known as the Bottleneck Steiner Tree problem. Having determined the interconnecting tree, the network topology is built by setting the transmission range at each node as the distance to its farthest neighbor.

5 Conclusion

In this paper we surveyed several recent mechanisms that address energy efficiency in wireless networking at the data link layer and above. Extending operation time of radio-equipped terminals is a particularly important issue in applications with size, weight and cost constraints, as well as when battery replacement of recharging is not feasible. The research results presented here can be broadly classified for using one of three main mechanisms for energy efficiency: (1) scheduling node activity, (2) power-aware routing and (3) topology control. These approaches provide benefits for particular environments and can be implemented at various layers in the protocol stack. They provide a solid basis for future developments but are not definitive answers to the problem of optimal energy usage in wireless networks.

References

[1] ANSI/IEEE, Standard 802.11, Wireless LAN Medium Access Control (MAC) and Physical Layer(PHY) specifications, 1999.

[2] I. Cardei, M. Cardei, L. Wang, B. Xu. D.-Z. Du, "Optimal Relay Location for Resource-Limited Energy-Efficient Wireless Communication", manuscript.

[3] M. Cardei, D.-Z. Du, "Improving Wireless Sensor Network Lifetime through Power Aware Organization", submitted to ACM Wireless Networks.

[4] M. Cardei, M. X. Cheng, J. Sun, L. Wang, Y. Xu, D.-Z. Du, "Minimum Energy Wireless Ad Hoc Networks", manuscript.

[5] J.-H. Chang, L. Tassiulas, "Energy Conserving Routing in Wireless Ad-hoc Networks", Proceedings IEEE INFOCOM, 2000.

[6] L. M. Feeney, M. Nilsson, "Investigating the Energy Consumption of a Wireless Network Interface in an Ad Hoc Networking Environment", IEEE INFOCOM 2001.

[7] P. J. M. Havinga, G. Smit, "Energy-efficient TDMA Medium Access Control Protocol Scheduling", Proceedings Asian International Mobile Computing Conference (AMOC 2000), November 2000.

[8] C. E. Jones, K. M. Sivalingam, "A survey of energy efficient network protocols for wireless networks", ACM/Baltzer Journal on Wireless Networks, vol. 7, No. 4, pp. 343 - 358, 2001.

[9] O. Kasten, Energy Consumption,
http://www.inf.ethz.ch/~kasten/research/bathtub/energy_consumption.htm

[10] R. Ramanathan, R. Rosales-Hain, "Topology Control of Multihop Wireless Networks using Transmit Power Adjustment", IEEE INFO-COM 2000.

[11] S. Singh, C.S. Raghavendra, "PAMAS-Power Aware Multi-Access protocol with Signaling for Ad Hoc Networks", Computer Communications Review Vol. 28, No. 3, July 1998.

[12] K. M. Sivalingam, J.-C. Chen, P. Agrawal, M. Srivastava, "Design and analysis of low-power access protocols for wireless and mobile ATM networks", ACM/Baltzer Wireless Networks, Vol. 6, No. 1, 2000.

[13] Y.-C. Tseng, S.-Y. Ni, Y.-S. Chen, J.-P. Sheu, "The Broadcast Storm Problem in a Mobile Ad Hoc Network", Wireless Networks, Vol. 8, pp 153-167, 2002.

[14] P.-J.Wan, G. Calinescu, X.-Y. Li, O. Frieder, "Minimum-Energy Broadcast Routing in Static Ad Hoc Wireless Networks", Proceedings IEEE INFOCOM, 2001.

[15] J. E. Wieselthier, G. D. Nguyen, A. Ephremides, "On the Construction of Energy-Efficient Broadcast and Multicast Trees in Wireless Networks", Proceedings IEEE INFOCOM, 2000.

[16] M. Woo, S. Singh, C.S. Raghavendra, "Power-Aware Routing in Mobile Ad Hoc Networks", Proceedings of ACM MobiCom 1998.

[17] W. Ye, J. Heidemann, D. Estrin, "An Energy-Efficient MAC Protocol for Wireless Sensor Networks", INFOCOM 2002, June 2002.

AD HOC WIRELESS NETWORKING
X. Cheng, X. Huang and D.-Z. Du (Eds.) pp. 103 - 136

Position Based Routing Algorithms For Ad Hoc Networks: A Taxonomy

Silvia Giordano
DIE-SUPSI CH-6928, Manno, Switzerland
E-mail: `Silvia.Giordano@die.supsi.ch`

Ivan Stojmenovic
SITE, University of Ottawa, Ottawa, Ontario K1N 6N5, Canada
E-mail: `ivan@site.uottawa.ca`

Contents

References

Recent availability of small inexpensive low power GPS receivers and techniques for finding relative coordinates based on signal strengths, and the need for the design of power efficient and scalable networks, provided justification for applying position based routing methods in ad hoc networks. A number of such algorithms were developed in last few years, in addition to few basic methods proposed about fifteen years ago. This article surveys known routing methods, and provides their taxonomy in terms of a number of characteristics: loop-free behavior, distributed operation (localized, global or zonal), path strategy (single path, multi-path or flooding based), metrics used (hop count, power or cost), memorization (memoryless or memorizing past traffic), guaranteed delivery, scalability, and robustness (strategies to handle the position deviation due to the dynamicity of the network). We also briefly discuss relevant issues such as physical requirements, experimental design, location updates, QoS, congestion, scheduling node activity, topology construction, broadcasting and network capacity.

1   Introduction

Mobile ad hoc networks (often referred to as MANETs) consist of wireless hosts that communicate with each other in the absence of a fixed infrastructure. They are used in disaster relief, conference and battlefield environments, and received significant attention in recent years [28, 49]. A class of wireless ad hoc networks that is currently subject of intensive research is sensor network. Wireless networks of sensors are likely to be widely deployed in the near future because they greatly extend our ability to monitor and control the physical environment from remote locations and improve our accuracy of information obtained via collaboration among sensor nodes and online information processing at those nodes. Networking these sensors (empowering them with the ability to coordinate amongst themselves on a larger sensing task) will revolutionize information gathering and processing in many situations. Sensor networks have been recently studied in [15, 24, 33]. Rooftop networks, proposed in [52], are not mobile, but are deployed very densely in metropolitan areas (the name refers to an antenna on each building's roof, for line-of-sight with neighbors) as an alternative to wired networking. Such a network also provides an alternative infrastructure in the event of failure of the conventional one, as after a disaster. A routing system that self-configures (without a trusted authority to configure a routing hierarchy) for hundreds of thousands of such nodes in a metropolitan area represents a significant scaling challenge. Commercial examples of static ad hoc networks include Metricom Ricochet [48] and Nokia Rooftop [51] systems. Other similar contexts where the material surveyed in this article is applicable are wireless local area networks, packet radio networks, home and office networks, spontaneous networks [17, 20] etc.

A widely accepted basic graph-theoretical model for all mentioned networks is the unit graph model, defined in the following way. Two nodes A and B in the network are neighbors (and thus joined by an edge) if the Euclidean distance between their coordinates in the network is at most R, where R is the transmission radius which is equal for all nodes in the network. Variation of this model include unit graphs with obstacles (or subgraph of unit graph), minpower graphs where each node has its own transmission radius and links are unidirectional or allowed only when bi-directional communication is possible. However, no credible research was done in literature on any model other than unit graph model (one important exception in [5]). Because of limited transmission radius, the routes are normally created through several hops in such multi-hop wireless network. For most algorithms reviewed here, the unit graph model is used in experiments, while the algorithm itself may be applied for arbitrary graph.

In this article we consider the routing task, in which a message is to be sent from a source node to a destination node in a given wireless network. The task of finding and maintaining routes in sensor and mobile networks is nontrivial since host mobility and changes in node activity status cause frequent unpredictable topological changes. The destination node is known and addressed by means of its location. Routing is performed by a scheme that is based on this information, that is generally classified as position-based scheme.

The distance between neighboring nodes can be estimated on the basis of incoming signal strengths. Relative coordinates of neighboring nodes can be obtained by exchanging such information between neighbors [9]. Alternatively, the location of nodes may be available directly by communicating with a satellite, using GPS (Global Positioning System), if nodes are equipped with a small low power GPS receiver. The surveys of protocols that do not use geographic location in the routing decisions are given in [7, 58, 59]. This survey will discuss only position-based approaches.

Qualitatively, the position-based schemes are more natural for ad hoc networks, as the address has some logic with the node. They are also more scalable, as do not request complex addressing schemes and more robust to the dynamic of the networks.

Qualitatively, there is not a simple way for a global comparison; neither between position-based schemes and traditional routing schemes, nor among position-based schemes themselves. In fact, (1) they have different conditions (e.g. addressing, address management), they starts from different assumptions, and are used for different purpose. Finally, on the practical side, for most of the position-based schemes, the code is not available, and this prevent from a complete simulation of them. However, as discussed in the next sections, some discussion is possible and this allows to deriving a taxonomy of position-based schemes.

2   Position-based Routing Protocols Taxonomy

Macker and Corson [49] listed qualitative and quantitative independent metrics for judging the performance of mobile ad hoc networks routing protocols. Desirable qualitative properties include: distributed operation, loop-freedom (to avoid a worst case scenario of a small fraction of packets spinning around in the network), demand-based operation, and 'sleep' period operation (when some nodes become temporarily inactive). We shall further elaborate on these properties and metrics. Our goal is to provide a taxonomy of existing position based routing algorithms in light of qualitative characteristics listed below.

a) *Loop-freedom*. The proposed routing protocols should be inherently loop-free, to avoid timeout or memorizing past traffic as cumbersome exit strategies. Proposed algorithms are therefore classified as having or not having loop free property.

b) *Distributed operation*. Localized algorithms [15] are distributed algorithms that resemble greedy algorithms, where simple local behavior achieves a desired global objective. In a localized routing algorithm, each node makes decision to which neighbor to forward the message based solely on the location of itself, its neighboring nodes, and destination. Non-localized algorithms can be classified as global or zonal ones. In a global routing algorithm, each node is assumed to know the position of every other node in the network. In addition, since nodes change between active and sleep periods, the activity status for each node is also required. When such global knowledge is available, the routing task becomes equivalent to the shortest path problem, if hop count is used as main performance metrics (such an algorithm is described in [4, 73]). If power or cost metrics are used instead, the shortest weighted path algorithm may be applied, as described in [57] for power and in [73] for cost metric. Between the two extremes is the zonal approach, where network is divided into zones, with localized algorithm applied within each zone, and shortest path or other scheme applied for routing between zones [29, 39]. Clearly, localized algorithms are preferred if they can nearly match the performance of non-localized ones. An expanded locality is sometimes considered. For example, if two hop neighbors are included, the algorithm is classified as 2-localized.

c) *Path strategy.* The shortest path route is an example of a single path strategy, where one copy of the message is in the network at any time. Arguably, the ideal localized algorithm should follow a single path. On the other extreme are flooding based approaches, where message is flooded through the whole network area (broadcasting solves routing, and in high mobility scenario this could be optimal solution [26], if optimized [55, 56, 70]), or portion of the area [3, 35]. The 'compromise' is multi-path strategy, that is route composed of few single recognizable paths. Some algorithms are combinations of two strategies, and are appropriately labeled (e.g. single-path/flooding, single-path/multi-path).

d) *Metrics.* The metrics that are used in simulations normally reflects the goal of designed algorithm, and is naturally decisive in the route selection. Most routing schemes use hop count as the metrics, where hop count is the number of transmissions on a route from a source to destination. This choice of metric agrees with the assumption that nodes cannot adjust (that is, reduce) their transmission radii in order to reach desired neighbor with minimal power. It also assumes that delay is proportional to hop count (when the impact of congestion is not significant), and that the (both energy and bandwidth) cost of starting communication with neighbor is considerable (this is supported by the analysis in [18, 19]). However, if nodes can adjust their transmission power (knowing the location of their neighbors) then the constant metric can be replaced by a power metric that depends on distance between nodes [14, 57, 24]. The goal is to minimize the energy required per each routing task. However, some nodes participate in routing packets for many source-destination pairs, and the increased energy consumption may result in their failure. Thus pure power consumption metric may be misguided in the long term, and longer path that passes through nodes that have plenty of energy may be a better solution. The cost metric (a rapidly increasing function of decreasing remaining energy at node) is used with the goal of maximizing the number of routing tasks that network can perform.

e) *Memorization.* Solutions that require nodes to memorize route or past traffic are sensitive to node queue size, changes in node activity and node mobility while routing is ongoing (e.g. monitoring environment). It is better to avoid memorizing past traffic at any node, if possible. However, the need to memorize past traffic is not necessarily a demand for significant new resources in the network for several reasons. First, a lot of memory space is available on tiny chips. Next, the memorization of past traffic is needed for short period of time, while ongoing routing task is in progress, and therefore after a timeout outdated traffic can be safely removed from memory. Finally, the creation of Quality-of-Service (QoS) path, that is, path with bandwidth, delay, and connection time [71] requirements, requires that the path is memorized in order to optimize the traffic flow and satisfy QoS criteria. This certainly includes the use of the best path found in the search process. Once destination is reached, the optimal path can be reported back to source.

f) *Guaranteed message delivery.* Delivery rate [7] is the ratio of numbers of messages received by destination and sent by senders. The primary goal of every routing scheme is to delivery the message, and the best assurance one can offer is to design routing scheme that will guarantee delivery. Wireless networks normally use single frequency communication model where a message intended for a neighbor is heard by all other neighbors within transmission radius of sender. Collisions are normally occurring in medium access schemes mostly used, such as IEEE 802.11. The guaranteed delivery property assumes the application of an ideal, collision free, medium access scheme, such as time division multiple access, or acknowledgement/retransmission scheme that is assumed to be always successful otherwise.

g) *Scalability.* The routing algorithms should perform well for wireless networks with arbitrary number of nodes. Sensor and rooftop networks, for instance, have hundreds or thousands of nodes. Scalable single-path strategies, such as shortest-path, have $O(\sqrt{n})$ overhead, where n is the number of nodes in the network. While other characteristics of each algorithms are easily detected, scalability is sometimes judgmental, and/or dependent on performance evaluation outcome. We shall apply a simplified (although arguable) criterion, that a routing scheme is scalable if it is loop-free, localized, and single-path. Note that, several schemes, are proved to guarantee the messages delivery (and to be loop free) in the static case. It is not clear how these schemes handle loops and perform delivery in the case of node mobility. We name these loops due to the position of some nodes as mobility-caused loops. These loops are in general temporary loops that appear because some nodes move in a position that causes the packet to loop.

This situation cannot be easily detected because it arises after the direction for packet has been chosen. In this work we classify as loop free and delivery guarantee, as traditionally done, all schemes that are proved to be loop free and which guarantee the message delivery, even if they are not proved for the mobility-caused loops.

h) *Robustness* The use of nodes' position for routing poses evident problems in terms of reliability. The accuracy of destination position is an important problem to consider. In some cases the destination is a fixed node (such as monitoring center known to all nodes, or the geographic area that is monitored), some networks are static which makes the problem straightforward, while the problem of designing location updates schemes to enable efficient routing in mobile ad hoc network appears to be more difficult than routing itself (see a recent survey [68]) and will not be discussed here unless it is integral part of presented method.

For small networks, in the absence of any useful information about destination location (that is, a clever location update scheme), the following simple strategy can be applied. If message is reasonably 'short', it can be broadcasted (that is, flooded), using an optimal broadcasting scheme [55, 56, 70]. If message is relatively 'long' then destination search (or route discovery [7]) can be initiated, which is a task of broadcasting short search message. Destination then reports back to source by routing a short message containing its position. The source then is able to route full message toward accurate position of destination.

However, in large networks, the algorithms that assume that the position of destination is 'reasonably' accurate are not able to deal with eventual position deviation, and impose high mobility tracking overhead. More robust and scalable routing algorithms must, by design, be able to cope with the network dynamicity or can have backup strategies that allow to reach a node even when the node deviated from the known position.

Another aspect of robust algorithms is their ability to deliver message when communication model deviates from unit graph, due to obstacles or noise. One such model is investigated in [5].

Performance of most algorithms surveyed in this paper will be discussed in terms of delivery rates and hop counts obtained in simulations, for graphs of various densities (measured by average degrees, that is, average number of neighbors of each node). This suffices for single-path strategies, but is misleading for flooding based or multi-path ones. Due to limited battery power, the communication overhead must be minimized if number of routing tasks is to be maximized. Purely proactive methods that maintain routing tables with up-to date routing information or global network information at each node are certainly unsatisfactory solution, especially when node mobility is high with respect to data traffic. For instance, shortest path based solutions are too sensitive to small changes in local topology and activity status (the later even does not involve node movement). Since localized algorithm should compete with the best (shortest path) algorithm (instead of competing with the worst, flooding, algorithm, as compared in [35]), the flooding rate was introduced in [64] as a measure of communication overhead. Flooding rate is the ratio of the number of message transmissions and the shortest possible hop count between two nodes. Each transmission in multiple routes is counted, and a message can be sent to all neighbors with one transmission. Note that the cost of location updates is not counted in the flooding rate, although it should be added to the total communication overhead.

We can distinguish seven main classes of existing position based routing schemes:

- Basic Distance, Progress, and Direction Based Methods

- Partial Flooding and Multi-Path Based Path Strategies

- Depth First Search Based Routing with Guaranteed Delivery

- Nearly Stateless Routing with Guaranteed Delivery

- Hierarchical Routing

- Assisted Routing

- Power and Cost Aware Routing

We will cover in this chapter the first six classes. For the large class of Power and Cost Aware Routing, we remand the reader to a recent survey [44]. The remaining of this paper is organized as follows: first we analyze the characteristic of each class and then describe and compare the schemes that present aspect of this class. Clearly, some schemes fall in more than one class and are, thus, discussed in more than one section. Finally, we summarize the described position based routing schemes behaviour with respect to the given taxonomy.

3 Basic Distance, Progress, and Direction Based Methods

The notion of progress is the key concept of several GPS based methods proposed in 1984-86. Given a transmitting node S, the progress of a node A is defined as the projection onto the line connecting S and the final destination of the distance between S and the receiving node A neighbor is in forward direction if the progress is positive (for example, for transmitting node S and receiving nodes A, C and F in Fig. 1); otherwise it is said to be in backward direction (e.g. nodes B and E in Fig. 1). Basic Distance, Progress, And Direction Based Methods use these concepts to select among neighbors the next routing step.

Schemes as the Random Progress Method [53], Most Forward within Radius [74], Nearest Forward Progress [25], the Greedy Scheme [16], the Nearest Closer [62] and all its variants (the 2-Hop Greedy Method [64] the Alternate Greedy method [45], the Disjoint Greedy method [45], and *GEDIR* [64]), and the Compass Routing method [34], fall in this class.

In the ***random progress method*** [53], packets destined toward D are routed with equal probability towards one intermediate neighboring node that has positive progress. The rationale for the method is that, if all nodes are sending packets frequently, probability of collision grows with the distance between nodes (assuming that the transmission power is adjusted to the minimal possible), and thus there is a trade-off between the progress and transmission success.

Takagi and Kleinrock [74] proposed MFR (most forward within radius) routing algorithm, in which packet is sent to the neighbor with the greatest progress (e.g. node A in Fig. 1). MFR is probed to be a loop-free algorithm [64]. MFR is the only progress-based algorithm competitive in terms of hop count.

In [25], the method is modified by proposing to adjust the transmission power to the distance between the two nodes. In this scheme, packet is sent to the nearest neighboring node with forward progress (for instance, to node C in Fig. 1).

In 1987, Finn [16] proposed, the greedy scheme as variant of random progress method, which 'allows choosing as successor node any node, which makes progress toward the packet's destination'. The optimal choice would be possible only with the complete topological knowledge of the network.. To bypass this problem, Finn adopted the greedy principle: select the node closest to the destination. In the example of Fig. 2, the sender S selects

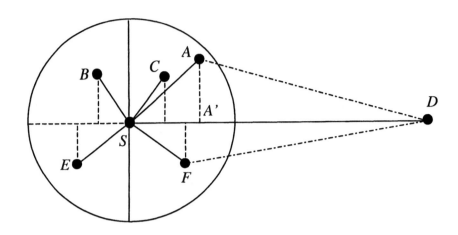

Figure 1: Positive and negative progress: C, A, F are in forward direction, with a positive progress (for example, A'D < SD); nodes B and E are in backward direction, with a negative progress.

node B which is closer to D than the other neighbor A. The path selected by the algorithm is SBEFGHID and consists of seven hops. When none of neighboring nodes is closer to the destination than current node C, Finn [16] proposes to search all n-hop neighbors (nodes at distance at most n hops from current node, where n is network dependent parameter) by flooding the nodes until a node closer to destination than C is found. The algorithm has non-trivial details and does not guaranty delivery, nor optimize flooding rate. The author argued that his algorithm has no loops, since it always forces message to make a step closer to the destination.

A variant of greedy algorithms, called **GEDIR**, is proposed in [64]. In this variant, the message is dropped if the best choice for a current node is to return the message to the node the message came from. It increases delivery rate by prolonging failure (that is, *GEDIR* does not always fail when *greedy* method fails). Message is dropped when a failure occurs. The same criterion can be applied to *MFR* method, and directional methods described below.

Greedy routing was applied as part of other routing schemes. For instance, in [1, 42], each node applies greedy routing scheme, but uses the last reported location of destination, which may be outdated, but, as the message progresses toward destination, closer nodes increase accuracy of destination information. Location updates schemes used in [1] is based on doubling size of circles of location updates. This idea has been rediscovered one year later in [42].

GEDIR is often used as basic ingredient in other routines. For instance, it is used in several location update schemes, such as quorum based [65] and home agent based schemes [2, 50, 54, 67, 80] (note that the later scheme was independently proposed in four papers).

In **2-hop greedy method** [64] node A selects the best candidate node C among its 1-hop and 2-hop neighbors according to the corresponding criterion. Then A forwards m to its best 1-hop neighbor in the set of neighbors of A and C. This basic idea is applicable also to most other methods listed in the sequel (the table presenting taxonomy includes only this one).

In the **alternate greedy** method [45], the i-th received copy of m is forwarded to i-th best neighbor, according to the selected criterion (it fails if number of copies exceeds number of neighbors). In the **disjoint greedy** method [45], each intermediate node, upon receiving m, will forward it to its best neighbor among those who never received the message (it fails if no such neighbor exists). These methods reduce failure rate compared to greedy method, by memorizing past traffic.

In the **compass routing** method (referred here to as the DIR method) proposed by Kranakis, Singh and Urrutia [34], the source or intermediate node A uses the location information of the destination D to calculate its direction. Then the message m is forwarded to the neighbor C, such that the direction AC closest to the direction AD. This process repeats until the destination is, eventually, reached. Consider the network on Fig. 2, where the radius is equal to edge EF. The direction SA is closer to direction SD than direction SB. The direction AC is closest to direction AD among candidate directions AS, AB, AC, and AP. The path selected by DIR method is SACJKLMND.

The MFR and greedy methods, in most cases, provide the same path to destination. Simulation in [64] revealed that nodes in greedy and MFR methods select the same forwarding neighbor in over 99cases, and, in the majority of the cases, the whole paths were identical (e.g. Fig. 2). The hop count for DIR method is somewhat higher than for *GEDIR*, while success rate is similar. All methods have high delivery rates for dense graphs, and low delivery rates for sparse graph (about half messages at average degrees below 4 are not delivered). When successful, hop counts of greedy and MFR methods nearly match the performance of the shortest path algorithm.

The DIR method, and any other method that includes forwarding message to neighbor with closest direction, such as DREAM [3], are not loop-

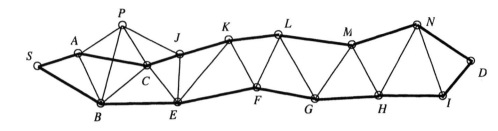

Figure 2: Paths selected by DIR (SACJKLMND) and GEDIR (SBEFGHID) algorithms

free, as shown in [64] using the counterexample shown in Figure 3. The loop consists of four nodes, denoted E, F, G and H. The graph is an unit graph and the radius is indicated in the figure. Let the source be any node in the loop, e.g. E. Node E selects node F to forward the message, because the direction of F is closer to destination D than the direction of its other neighbor H. Similarly node F selects G, node G selects H and node H selects E. Additional nodes can be taken outside the loop nodes, so that message can be delivered from E to D by alternate path.

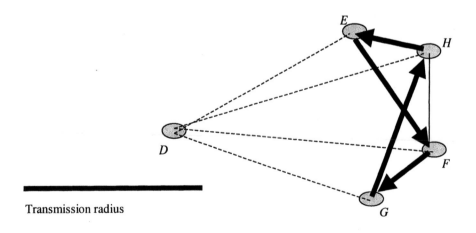

Transmission radius

Figure 3: A loop in the directional routing

Yeh [81] proposes several variable-radius routing protocols for achieving higher throughout, smaller latency at a given traffic load, and/or lower power consumption in ad hoc networks, by exploiting several unique characteristics of radio links.

Larsson [37] describes a forwarding method for routing in multi-hop networks which takes into account Raleigh fading and non-fading channels. The SDF (selection diversity forwarding) algorithm [37] makes forwarding decision based on multiple responses returned subsequent to that data being multicasted to a number of candidate relays. Subsequently, nodes addressed in the data packet header who successfully receive the data packet returns acknowledgements in consecutive order, e.g. as their addresses are listed in the packet header. In this manner, the problem of collisions between the acknowledgements is mitigated.

4 Partial Flooding and Multi-Path Based Path Strategies

In directional flooding-based routing methods, a node A transmits a message m to several neighbors whose direction (looking from A) is closest to the direction of destination D. In order to control flooding effect, flooding based method require nodes to memorize past traffic, to avoid forwarding the same message more than once.

DREAM [3], *LAR* KV, *V-GEDIR* [66], *CH-MFR* [66] belong to this class. Flooding can be partial because it is directed towards nodes in a limited sector of the network (e.g. in DREAM or in LAR) or because it is stopped after a certain number of hops (e.g. in flooding *GEDIR* family of schemes). Moreover, partial flooding can be used only for path discovery purpose (e.g. LAR) or for packet forwarding (e.g. DREAM).

In **DREAM** protocol [3], m is forwarded to all neighbors whose direction belongs to the selected range, determined by the tangents from A to the circle centered at D and with radius equal to a maximal possible movement of D since the last location update. *DREAM* algorithm [3] is a proactive protocol that uses a limited flooding of location update messages.

In the **location aided routing** (LAR) algorithm [35], the request zone (the area containing the circle and two tangents)is fixed from the source, and nodes, which are not in the request zone, do not forward a route request to their neighbors. In LAR scheme 2 [35], the source or an intermediate node A will forward the message to all nodes that are closer to the destination than A. The control part of LAR protocol is, essentially, equivalent to *DSR* flooding protocol [7], restricted to the request zone. Therefore all nodes inside an area receive the routing packet, and the algorithm is therefore of partial flooding nature, causing excessive flooding rates [11, 64].

[66] discusses **V-GEDIR** and **CH-MFR** methods in order to reduce flooding rate and provide loop-free behavior for a scheme that forwards m to several neighbors at each step. , The message m is forwarded to exactly those neighbors, which may be the best choices for the possible position of destination (using the distance or progress criterion, respectively). In V-GEDIR method, these neighbors are determined by intersecting the Voronoi diagram of neighbors with the circle (or rectangle) representing the possible positions of destination. The portion of the convex hull of neighboring nodes is analogously used in the *CH-MFR* method.

In order to avoid message dropping, [64] proposes a modification to greedy/GEDIR and *MFR* algorithms as follows: When the basic algorithm would drop the message at a 'concave' node A, in the modified version A floods it to all its neighbors. Then withdraws from the network for further copies of the same message m (that is, its neighbors do not forward m to A in future decisions). Since A is connected to D, at least one of its neighbors is also connected to D, therefore the algorithm guarantees the delivery of the message. The methods will be refereed to as *flooding greedy/GEDIR* (*GEDIR* variant in this case is better option, since flooding is postponed (that is: reduced) or avoided in some cases), and flooding MFR (abbreviated as *f-greedy, f-GEDIR, f-DIR* and *f-MFR*) [64]. In addition to guaranteed delivery and loop-free behavior, experiments in [64] report also reduced flooding rates compared to *LAR* [35] and *DREAM* [3] schemes. For dense graphs it approaches greedy method performance, providing delivery in rare failure events. For sparse graphs it does cause partial flooding. The method has been improved in [43]: In this solution, the message is forwarded to only one neighbor of each connected components of the sub-graph consisting of neighbors of concave node A. Since there are at most four connected components of neighbors of any concave node in unit graph model, the number of newly created components is at most three (note that one existing component terminates at concave node). However, while a new component is sometimes created, the creation of two or three components is a rare event in practice. The partial flooding impact of *f-GEDIR* is reduced to multi-path impact in this scheme, called the **component routing**. The creation of multiple 'parallel' paths is justified by the inability of a localized algorithm to decide which of global routes leads toward destination.

In the **multi-path** method [43], the source node S forwards m to c best neighbors according to distance from D. Each of c created copies afterwards follows the greedy, alternate, or disjoint method (these copies may interact since copy numbers are not communicated). Therefore one can consider *c-greedy*, *c-alternate* or *c-disjoint* methods [43]. The experiments indicate significant gain in delivery rate for $c=2$, some gain for $c=3$ and no significant gains for $c¿3$. The flooding rate increases with c, and it seems that only value $c=2$ justifies the use of additional resources.

5 Depth First Search Based Routing with Guaranteed Delivery

Single-path strategies that guarantee delivery of the message to the destination are very relevant for supporting loss sensitive traffic. *Geographic Routing Algorithm* [31] and the *Depth First Search Based Algorithm* proposed in [71] schemes are based on this concept.

Jain, Puri and Sengupta [31] proposed one such strategy called **geographic routing algorithm** (*GRA*), and it requires nodes to partially store routes toward certain destinations in routing tables. *GRA* applies greedy strategy in forwarding messages. However, sometimes node S may discover that it is closer to the destination D than any of its neighbors. That is, the packet may be 'stuck' at S. Under this condition, it starts the route discovery protocol. The route discovery finds a path from S to D and updates the routing tables toward D at any node on the path, with this information. After that the route discovery protocol is successfully completed, the stuck packet can be routed from S to D. The authors propose two route discovery strategies: breadth first search (which is equivalent to flooding) and depth first search (*DFS*). *DFS* yields a single acyclic path from S to D. Each node puts its name and address on the route discovery packet p. Then it forwards p to a neighbor who has not seen p before. This neighbor is one of all the neighbors which minimize $d(S,y)+d(y,D)$, where $d(x,y)$ is Euclidean distance between nodes x and y. If a node has no possibilities to forward the packet, it removes its name and address from the packet and returns the packet to the node from which it originally received it. Route discovery packets are kept for some time. Each node accepts given packet only once in forward mode, and later only accepts the same packet if returned to it. The authors investigate routing table sizes and present methods for taking into account positional errors, node failures and mobility.

Another *depth first search* based algorithm has been independently proposed in [71]. The algorithm does not use routing tables, and instead message follows the whole depth first search path from S to D. Next, each node

S minimizes $d(S,D)$, and therefore the algorithm is equivalent to greedy method whenever it exists a node closer to D than S. For dense graphs most of the paths generated by this method are the same as the paths obtained by the greedy method. The authors discuss also the application of this method for the creation of quality-of-service (QoS) paths, that is, paths that satisfy delay and bandwidth criteria. In particular, they propose to use, as criterion, the connection time, which is time node S predicts to have link with any of its neighbor based on speed and direction of movements of S and its neighbor. In a simplified model considered in [71], delay can be decomposed into propagation delay proportional to the hop count, and demand for additional bandwidth. In this model, edges with no sufficient bandwidth are simply ignored in the process. Additionally, the delay criterion reduces the search to finding a path with hop count no longer than a given maximum. When this maximum is reached, the greedy forwarding stops and the route discovery message is returned back in order to search another branch that might have shorter path. The nodes which remain on the created path memorize the forwarding and previous node on the path. When the so created path reaches the destination D, D can report it back to S along the path itself, and S can start sending to D. The algorithm can be evaluated in terms of length of route discovery path and length of created route.

6 Nearly Stateless Routing with Guaranteed Delivery

Nearly Stateless Routing with Guaranteed Delivery are schemes where nodes maintain only some local information to perform routing. The *Face Routing* and *GFG (Greedy-Face-Greedy)* schemes were described by Bose, Morin, Stojmenovic and Urrutia [8], subsequently improved in [13] by applying dominating set concept and adding a shortcut 2-hop procedure. Recently, Barriere, Fraigniaud, Narayanan and Opatrny [5] made them robust against intereferences. Karp and Kung [32] transformed GFG algorithm into *GPSR (Greedy Perimeter Stateless Routing)* protocol by including IEEE 802.11 medium access control scheme. They experimented with mobile nodes moving according to a random waypoint model, using ns-2 environment, and compared it with non-position based *DSR* protocol [7], assuming accurate destination information. *GPSR* protocol consistently delivered over 94disconnection) data packets successfully; it is competitive with *DSR* in this respect on 50 node networks, and increasingly more successful than *DSR* as the number of nodes increases. The routing protocol traffic generated by *GPSR* was constant as mobility increased, while *DSR* must query longer routes with longer diameter and do so more often as mobility increases (with less effective caching). Thus *DSR* generates drastically more routing protocol traffic in simulations with over 100 nodes [32]. Therefore the scalability seems to be the major advantage of this class of algorithms over source based protocols.

In order to ensure message delivery, the face algorithm [8] (called perimeter algorithm in [32]) constructs planar and connected so-called Gabriel subgraph of the unit graph, and then applies routing along the faces of the subgraph (e.g. by using the right hand rule) that intersect the line between the source and the destination.

If a face is traversed using the right hand rule then a loop will be created, since face will never be existed (see an illustration in Figure F). Forwarding in right hand rule is performed using directional approach. To improve the efficiency of the algorithm in terms of routing performance, face routing can be combined with greedy routing [16] to yield GFG algorithm. Routing is mainly greedy, but if a mobile host fails to find a neighbor closer than itself to the destination, it switches the message from 'greedy' state to 'face' state.

Nearly stateless schemes are likely to fail if there is some instability in the transmission ranges of the mobile host. Instability in the transmission range means that the area a mobile host can reach is not necessarily a disk and the range can vary between r=(1-e)R and R, e¿0. Barriere, Fraigniaud, Narayanan and Opatrny [5] considered such kind of instability, and proposed this model as a generalization of unit graph. With this model they are able to handle the unstable situations where nodes may or may not communicate directly. This situation occurs if there are obstacles (e.g. buildings, bad weather) that disrupt the radio transmission.

7 Assisted Routing

We classify in this category the schemes where some nodes help other nodes in performing their routing tasks. In these schemes, "supporter" nodes play a special role for the "supported" nodes, but are not special for the whole network, in line with the requirements of ad hoc networking.

A first example of assisted routing is the one taken in *Terminode routing* [6]. Terminode routing addresses by design the following objectives: scalability (both in terms of the number of nodes and geographical coverage); robustness; collaboration and simplicity of the nodes. In this scheme, a node can count on the assistance of some other nodes, called friends. The

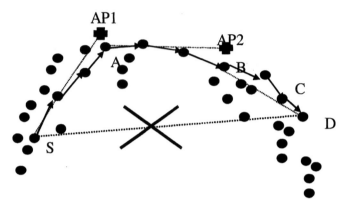

Figure 4: The Operation of AGPF

network is represented as a large graph, where the edges correspond to the "friend relationship". A node B is a friend of node A if (1) A thinks that it has a good path to B and (2) A decides to keep B in its list of friends. The resulting graph is highly clustered with a number of shortcut, with the characteristics of a small world graphs [36]. Small world graphs are very large graphs that tend to be sparse, clustered, and have a small diameter. As a friend is selected for being a collaborative node, the shortcuts are effective for the routing tasks, and in particular for selecting paths. When a source S wants to discover a path to destination D, it requests assistance from some friend. If this friend is in condition to collaborate, it tries to provide S with some path to D (it can have it already or try to find it, perhaps with the collaboration of its own friends).

The routing scheme is a combination of two protocols called Terminode Local Routing (TLR) and Terminode Remote Routing (TRR). TLR is a mechanism that allows to reaching destinations in the vicinity of a terminode and does not use location information for making packet forwarding decisions. TRR is used to send data to remote destinations and uses geographic information; it is the key element for achieving scalability and reduced dependence on intermediate systems. The major novelty is the Anchored Geodesic Packet Forwarding (*AGPF*) component of TRR. This is a source path based method designed to be robust for mobile networks: Instead of using traditional source paths, that is lists of nodes, it uses anchored paths. An anchored path is a list of fixed geographical points, called anchor. The packet loosely follows anchored path. At any point, the packet is sent in the direction of the next anchor in the anchored path by applying geodesic packet forwarding. When a terminode finds that the next anchor geographically falls within its transmission range, it deletes it from the anchored path and sends in the direction of the new next anchor. This is repeated until the packet is sent in direction of the final destination. Fig. 4 illustrates the operation of *AGPF*.

The figure presents how *AGPF* works when the source S has some data to send to a terminode D and there is no connectivity along the shortest line from S to D. S has an anchored path to D given by a list of geographical locations called anchored points: AP1, AP2. First, geodesic packet forwarding in the direction of AP1 is used. After some hops the packet arrives at a terminode A which finds that it is close to AP1. At A the packet is forwarded by using geodesic packet forwarding in the direction of AP2. Second, when the packet comes to B that is close to AP2, it starts sending the packet towards D. Last, when the packet comes to C it finds that D is TLR-reachable and forwards the packet to D by means of TLR.

GPF is both used between anchors in *AGPF* and as default method to send data to remote destinations when *AGPF* does not apply. Additionally, TRR has a component, Anchored Path Discovery (APD), which offers two methods to obtain anchored paths. In particular, Friend Assisted Path Discovery enables the source to learn the anchored path(s) to the destination using friends. The simulation results for mobile ad-hoc networks composed of several hundreds of terminode demonstrate benefits of the combination of TLR and TRR over an existing protocol that uses geographical information for packet forwarding [6].

Another example of assisted routing is presented in GRID [38]. Grid uses geographical forwarding to take advantage of the similarity between physical and network proximity. In order to support the geographical forwarding, the GRID scheme introduces an assisted location service: the Grid Location Server (GLS). GLS is based on the idea that a node maintains its current location in a number of location servers distributed throughout the network. These location servers are not specially designated; each node acts as a location server on behalf of some other nodes. The location servers for a node are relatively dense near the node but sparse farther from node; this ensures that anyone near a destination can use a nearby location server to find the destination, while also limiting the number of location servers for each node. On the other hand long distance queries are not too penalized: query path lengths are proportional to data path lengths.

8   Hierarchical Routing

The two main strategies used to combine nodes location and hierarchical network structures are the Zone Based Routing and the Dominating Set Routing.

The *Peer-To-Peer Zone-Based Two-Level Link State Routing* [29] and the *Online Power-Aware Routing* [39] schemes are example of the Zone Based Routing.

Joa-Ng and Lu [29] apply the shortest path algorithm on the hierarchical graph, where a network is divided into zones. Nodes within a zone update their location between themselves regularly and apply the shortest path routes between them. Each node also records the location of each zone (by treating it as a destination node positioned in the center of that zone). Routing begins by sending the message to destination if it is in the same zone as the sender. Otherwise, the sender initiates the search for the destination by sending route requests (that is, short messages, without the actual information), one to each other zone. The zone that contains the destination (more precisely, the first node from that zone reached on the way to the center of that zone) replies with the exact coordinates of the destination back to the sender node. The sender node then learns the path to the destination (i.e. the inter-zonal path) and sends the full message (containing all the information) toward the destination, using the inter-zonal path.

Li, Aslam and Rus [39] considered also zone-based routing alternative of their online power aware routing algorithm [39]. The hosts in a zone autonomously direct local routing and participate in estimating the zone power level. Each message is routed across the zones using information about the zone power estimates. In their vision, a global controller for message routing manages the zones. This may be the node with highest power, or round robin can be employed.

In [13] and [71], as well as in GRID algorithm [46] the Dominating Set concept is introduced in routing schemes. A *dominating set* is set of nodes so that each node is either in the set or a neighbor of node from the set. The nodes belonging to dominating sets are called internal nodes or gateway nodes. Several localized connected dominating set definitions are given in [79]. A node that does not have two unconnected neighbors is not in dominating set. Node A that has a neighbor B such that any path EAF can be replaced by the path EBF, and B has higher ID than A, can also be removed from dominating set. Finally, node A can be removed if it has two neighbors B and C such that any path EAF can be replaced by either path EBCF or ECBF, and B has lowest ID among the three, then B can be removed from the dominating set (but, in this case, the length of route may sometimes increase). Nodes in a dominating set are referred to as gateway nodes. The size of the dominating set is reduced in [70] by replacing the ID with the key (degree, ID). That way, the nodes with more neighbors have priority in entering dominating sets. Each node may decide whether or not it is in dominating set without any message exchanged with neighbors for that purpose. It suffices that each node knows its own location and location of all its neighbors (if location service is not available, then 2-hop neighboring information suffices). In order to decide which of neighbors are in dominating set, each node needs to know 2-hop information, or, alternatively, each node needs to add just one bit (referring to dominating status) in any message announcing its location to all its neighbors. In a dominating set based routing, if source is non-gateway node then it forwards message to the best gateway node neighbor, which routes the message toward D by considering only gateway nodes for forwarding. The message is delivered to if D when message reaches a gateway node neighbor of D for the first time. Such dominating set based routing was considered in [79] to reduce the size of routing tables in non-position based routing algorithms.

In order to reduce the length of route discovery path (which appears to be significant) in DFS and position based routing algorithm, [71] proposed to apply dominating set concept. The application of dominating set has considerably reduced the length of discovery route, as reported in [71]. The lengths of QoS paths constructed by DFS are close to the optimal length created by the shortest path algorithm.

GFG routing algorithm [8] has been improved in [13] by applying dominating nodes concept. While dominating sets did not improve the performance of greedy algorithm, they proved beneficial for the face mode of algorithm [8] by reducing the search space for face routing (thus shortening paths and providing energy savings). Another improvement made in [13] is the introduction of a shortcut procedure, which requires 2-hop neighborhood information. Instead of forwarding message directly to the next node B by current node A in face mode, A calculates few more hops in advance, if face mode is to be applied, until the next hop is to be made to a 2-hop neighbor C of A which is not any longer direct neighbor of A (thus further path calculation is no longer possible). The message then does not follow the calculated path, and can be forwarded directly from A to C, thus making a shortcut. Dominating set based routing was also applied in [61] to reduce power consumption and extend network life. These two improvements resulted in reducing the hop count, in excess of shortest path hop count, in about half for all densities.

Since network life is an important consideration, nodes in dominating sets perform more tasks and therefore reduce their remaining energy faster than other nodes. In order to address this issue, [78] suggested power aware dominating set definition. In this definition, each node has a key (power level, degree, id) for deciding dominating set status. Thus nodes use their power levels as the primary criterion, such that nodes with more power are preferred in the dominating set. If power levels are same, degrees are used as secondary key, and finally node ID to break ties. The further improvement is proposed in [72], where the primary key is a linear combination of power level and degree, that is $a * power_level + b * degree$, where a and b are parameters whose best values are to be experimentally determined and discussed in the ongoing work [72]. Dominating set concept was often used by authors without directly refereeing to it. For instance, the backbone consisting of clusterheads and border nodes (connecting two clusters) was applied in several non-position based routing algorithms (references are given in [79]). The maintenance of cluster structure, however, is nontrivial, since local moves may easily trigger global nontrivial updates (see [79, 70]).

Another example of applying dominating set concept is GRID routing algorithm proposed by Liao, Tseng and Sheu [46]. The geographic area is partitioned into a number of squares called grids. In each grid, one mobile host (if any) will be elected as the leader of the grid. Routing is then performed in a grid-by-grid manner through grid leaders, and non-leaders have no such responsibility. The size d of each grid depends on transmission radius R, and several options are proposed, with general idea of one leader being able to communicate directly with leaders in neighboring grids, and all nodes within each grid being connected to their leaders. Therefore, grid leaders form a dominating set. As discussed below, similar grid construction was rediscovered in [77] for scheduling node sleep periods. When a leader moves, another leader from the same grid replaces it by a handoff procedure. Routing tables contain grid IDs instead of host IDs. The authors use LAR [35] protocol for route discovery, although much better options are available, as already discussed in this survey. The use of LAR in GRID does not route discovery, has excessive flooding rate, and may create loops. The authors [46] do not elaborate on route maintenance required when a grid remains empty after its leader and only node leaves it.

9 Other Relevant Issues in Routing

A large class of routing algorithm was not included here. This is the class of cost and power aware algorithms. Hop count was traditionally used to measure energy requirement of a routing task, thus using constant metric per hop. However, if nodes can adjust their transmission power (knowing the location of their neighbors) then the constant metric can be replaced by a power metric that depends on distance between nodes [14, 57, 24]. While the computational power of the devices used in the network is rapidly increasing, the lifetime of batteries is not expected to improve much in the future. We see a clear need for improvement in power consumption in existing routing algorithms. Schemes that combine position based and power/cost aware routing are proposed in [57], [18], [19], [41], [40], [47], [14], [24], [73], [12], [21], [64], [62], [39], [61].

The experimental design to evaluate routing schemes has some issues that required clarification. There was a tendency in early papers on position based routing (following similar research on non-position based schemes) to compare hop count in proposed schemes against flooding instead of the shortest path [35], and to ignore flooding rate [3, 35]. Also, transmission radius was used as independent variable, hiding graph density. Good results in many experiments were obtained by varying transmission range so that obtained graphs were all sparse or all dense, whichever way better results emerged. The average degree was proposed in [49] as independent variable, and was first applied in [63] in experimenting with position based routing schemes. To generate random unit graphs, each of n nodes is initially chosen by selecting its x and y coordinates at random in an interval [0,m). In order to control the initial average node degree k (that is, the average number of neighbors), all n(n-1)/2 (potential) edges in the network are sorted by their length, in increasing order. The radius R that corresponds to chosen value of k is equal to the length of nk/2-th edge in the sorted order [63]. The parameter m is used in power aware routing, and can be fixed if hop count metric is used.

The network organization problem in wireless ad hoc and sensor networks received growing attention recently. Bluetooth is am emerging standard for short range wireless communication and networking. According to the standard, when two Bluetooth devices discover each other, one of them assumes the role of master and the other becomes slave. A master with up to seven slaves defines a piconet (each node is master for only one such piconet). Collection of piconets defines scatternet. The problem of scatternet formation to enable Bluetooth-based ad hoc networks was investigated recently [45].

Ad hoc routing requires that nodes cooperate to forward each others' packets through the network. This means that throughput available to each single node's applications is limited not only by the raw channel capacity, but also by the forwarding load imposed by distant nodes. This effect could seriously limit the usefulness of ad hoc routing. Gupta and Kumar [22] estimated per node capacity in ad hoc network. If node density is constant and route length grows as $O(\sqrt{n})$, where n is the number of nodes in the network, then end to end throughput available to each node is $O(1/\sqrt{n})$. Thus it approaches zero as the number of nodes increases. On the other hand, if average hop count does not increase with network size (that is, most communication remains local), per node throughput remains constant.

IEEE 802.11 defines two primary modes of operation for a wireless network interface: idle state and sleep state. A node in idle state is active, and can react to ongoing traffic by switching to receive or transmit mode. A node in sleep state, however, cannot be activated by neighbors, and can return to idle state only on its own, based on preset timer. Feeney and Nillson [19] and MIT researchers [60] concluded that the idle power consumption is nearly as large as that of receiving data. Nodes in ad hoc network spend about 20% more energy when receiving than when idle, and about 60% more energy in transmit than in idle mode. The error margin here is not small, as exact number depends on the equipment and defers in published articles, but rounded numbers given here are sufficient for problem description. A node in idle mode spends about 15-30 times more energy than if it is in sleep mode. Therefore it is most important to have as many as possible sleeping nodes in the network. The active nodes should be connected and should provide basic routing and broadcasting functionalities. The problem of designing sleep period schedules for each node in a localized manner was recently considered [10, 77]. [77] divides the sensor network area into small squares with side lengths $r = R/\sqrt{5}$, where R is the transmission radius, which ensures that two nodes which are in the same of two neighboring squares are connected. One node in each square is in idle mode, the others are in sleep mode. The idea is similar to one used in GRID routing algorithm [46]. If each node has lifetime of L time units, the algorithm is expected to extend network life to approximately Ln/M, where m is number of cells and n is number of nodes in the network (under uniform random node distribution). The SPAN algorithm [10] selects some nodes as coordinators. These nodes form dominating set. A node becomes coordinator if it discovers that two of its neighbors cannot communicate with each other directly or through one or two existing coordinators. This is essentially the definition of dominating sets proposed in [79]. The difference is that new and existing coordinators are not necessarily neighbors in [10], which, in effect, makes the design less energy efficient because of need to maintain the positions two or three hop neighbors in complicated *SPAN* algorithm. A simplified algorithm, which applies localized power aware dominating sets defined in [78], is proposed in [72].

10 Conclusion

Table 1 presents the summary and taxonomy of known position based routing algorithms. The last four columns in Table 1 summarize memory requirements, guaranteed delivery property, scalability, and robustness. The successful design of localized single-path loop-free algorithms with guaranteed delivery is encouraging start for future research. The search for localized routing methods that have excellent delivery rates, short hop counts, small flooding ratios and power efficiency is far from over. Since the battery power is not expected to increase significantly in the future and the ad hoc networks, on the other hand, are booming, power aware routing schemes need further investigation.

In QoS applications, memorization does not appear to require additional resources and is therefore acceptable. However, the research on QoS position based routing is scarce, in our knowledge, limited to [71], and will receive more attention in the future, since surveyed routing schemes which guarantee delivery are all very recent (except, of course, flooding).

Further research is needed to identify the best GPS based routing protocols for various network contexts. These contexts include nodes positioned in three-dimensional space and obstacles, nodes with unequal transmission powers, or networks with unidirectional links. One of the future goals in designing routing algorithms is adding congestion considerations, that is, replacing hop count performance measure by end-to-end delay. Algorithms need to take into account the congestion in neighboring nodes in routing decisions.

Finally, the mobility caused loop needs to be further investigated and solutions to be found and incorporated to position based routing schemes.

Acknowledgments

This research is partially supported by NSERC and CONACyT 37017-A grants, as well as by MobileMAN IST-2001-38113.

Table 1: A taxonomy of position based routing algorithms for wireless networks

Method	Loop-free	Distributed	Path Strategy	Metrics	Mem.	Guar.	Scal.	Rob.
shortest path [4, 73]	yes	global	single-path	hop count	no	yes	no	no
greedy [16], MFR [74]	yes[64]	localized	single-path	hop count	no	no	yes	no
compass [34]	no [64]	localized	single-path	hop count	no	no	yes	no
2-hop greedy [64]	yes	2-localized	single-path	hop count	no	no	yes	no
LAR [35], DREAM [3]	no [64]	localized	flooding	hop count	yes	no	no	no
V-GEDIR, CH-MFR [64]	yes	localized	flooding	hop count	yes	no	no	no
f-GEDIR, f-MFR [64]	yes	localized	single/flooding	hop count	yes	yes	Y/dense	no
component [45]	yes	localized	single/multi	hop count	yes	yes	Y/dense	no
alternate, disjoint greedy [45]	yes	localized	single-path	hop count	yes	no	yes	no
c-greedy, alternate, disjoint[45]	yes	localized	multi-path	hop count	yes	no	yes	no
GRA[31], gatewayDFS[71]	yes	localized	single-path	hop count	yes	yes	yes	no
zone based 2-level [29]	yes	zonal	single/flooding	hop count	no	yes	no	no
GRID [46]	yes	localized	single	hop count	yes	no	no	no
shortest power path [14, 57]	yes	global	single-path	power	no	yes	no	no
cluster power [24]	yes	global	single-path	power	no	no	no	no
shortest cost path [73]	yes	global	single-path	cost	no	yes	no	no
shortest power-cost path [12]	yes	global	single-path	power-cost	no	yes	no	no
route-redirect [21]	yes	global	multi-path	power-cost	no	no	no	no
max-min zP_min [39]	yes	global	single-path	power-cost	no	yes	no	no
zone based max-min [39]	yes	zonal	single-path	power-cost	no	yes	no	no
power aware [62]	yes	localized	single-path	power	no	no	yes	no
power-face-power [61]	yes	localized	single-path	power	no	yes	yes	no
cost aware [62]	yes	localized	single-path	cost	no	no	yes	no
cost-face-cost [61]	yes	localized	single-path	cost	no	yes	yes	no
power-cost aware [62]	yes	localized	single-path	power-cost	no	no	yes	no
Pc-F-Pc [61]	yes	localized	single-path	power-cost	no	yes	yes	no
face, GFG [8]	yes	localized	single-path	hop count	no	yes	yes	no
internal-shortcut-GFG [13]	yes	2-localized	single-path	hop count	no	yes	yes	no
robust GFG [5]	yes	localized	single-path	hop count	no	yes	yes	yes
Termonode Routing [6]	yes	localized	multi-path	hop count	no	yes	yes	yes

References

[1] K.N. Amouris, S. Papavassiliou, M. Li, A position based multi-zone routing protocol for wide area mobile ad-hoc networks, Proc. 49th IEEE Vehicular Technology Conference, 1999, 1365-1369.

[2] L. Blazevic, L. Buttyan, S. Capkun, S. Giordano, J.-P. Hubaux and J-Y. Le Boudec, Self-organization in mobile ad hoc networks: the approach of terminodes, IEEE Communication Magazine, June 2001, 166-175.

[3] S. Basagni, I. Chlamtac, V.R. Syrotiuk, B.A. Woodward, A distance routing effect algorithm for mobility (DREAM), Proc. MOBICOM, 1998, 76-84.

[4] S. Basagni, I. Chlamtac, V.R. Syrotiuk, Dynamic source routing for ad hoc networks using the global positioning system, Proc. IEEE Wireless Commun. and Networking Conf., New Orleans, September 1999.

[5] L. Barriere, P Fraigniaud, L. Narajanan, and J. Opatrny, Robust position based routing in wireless ad hoc networks with unstable transmission ranges, Proc. of 5th ACM Int. Workshop on Discrete Algorithms and Methods for Mobile Computing and Communications DIAL M01, 2001, 19-27.

[6] Lj. Blazevic, S. Giordano and J.Y. Le Boudec, Self organized terminode routing, TR DSC/2000/040, Swiss Federal Institute of Technology, Lausanne, December 2000.

[7] J. Broch, D.A. Maltz, D.B. Johnson, Y.C. Hu, J. Jetcheva, A performance comparison of multi-hop wireless ad hoc network routing protocols, Proc. MOBICOM, 1998, 85-97.

[8] P. Bose, P. Morin, I. Stojmenovic and J. Urrutia, Routing with guaranteed delivery in ad hoc wireless networks, 3rd int. Workshop on Discrete Algorithms and methods for mobile computing and communications, Seattle, August 20, 1999, 48-55; ACM/Kluwer Wireless Networks, 7, 6, November 2001, 609-616.

[9] S. Capkun, M. Hamdi, J.P. Hubaux, GPS-free positioning in mobile ad-hoc networks, Proc. Hawaii Int. Conf. on System Sciences, January 2001.

[10] B. Chen, K. Jamieson, H. Balakrishnan, R. Morris, Span: an energy-efficient coordination algorithm for topology maintenance in ad hoc wireless networks, Proc. MOBICOM, 2001, 85-96.

[11] D. Camara and A.F. Loureiro, A novel routing algorithm for ad hoc networks, Proc. HICSS, Hawaii, January 2000; Telecommunication Systems, 18, 1-3, September 2001.

[12] J.H. Chang and L. Tassiulas, Routing for maximum system lifetime in wireless ad-hoc networks, Proc. 37th Annual Allerton Conf. on Communication, Control, and Computing, Monticello, IL, Sept. 1999.

[13] S. Datta, I. Stojmenovic, J. Wu, Internal nodes and shortcut based routing with guaranteed delivery in wireless networks, Cluster Computing, 5, 2, 2002, 169-178.

[14] M. Ettus, System capacity, latency, and power consumption in multihop-routed SS-CDMA wireless networks, Proc. IEEE Radio and Wireless Conf., Colorado Springs, Aug. 1998.

[15] D. Estrin, R. Govindan, J. Heidemann, S. Kumar, Next century challenges: Scalable coordination in sensor networks, Proc. MOBICOM, 1999, Seattle, 263-270.

[16] G.G. Finn, Routing and addressing problems in large metropolitan-scale internetworks, ISI Research Report ISU/RR-87-180, March 1987.

[17] L.M. Feeney, B. Ahlgren and A. Westerlund, Spontaneous networking: An application oriented approach to ad hoc networking, IEEE Communications Magazine, June 2001, 176-181.

[18] L.M. Feeney, An energy-consumption model for performance analysis of routing protocols for mobile ad hoc networks, Mobile Networks and Applications, 6, 3, June 2001, 239-249.

[19] L.M. Feeney and M. Nilsson, Investigating the energy consumption of a wireless network interface in an ad hoc networking environment, Proc. IEEE INFOCOM, 2001.

[20] S. Giordano, Mobile ad hoc networks, in: Wireless Networks and Mobile Computing Handbook (I. Stojmenovic, ed.), John Wiley and Sons, 2002.

[21] J. Gomez, A.T. Campbell, M. Naghshineh, C. Bisdikian, Power-aware routing in wireless packet networks, proc. IEEE Int. Workshop on Mobile Multimedia Communication, San Diego, CA, Nov. 1999.

[22] P. Gupta and P.R. Kumar, The capacity of wireless networks, IEEE Trans. Information Theory, 46, 2, 388-404, March 2000.

[23] K. Gabriel and R. Sokal, A new statistical approach to geographic variation analysis, Systematic Zoology, 18, 1969, 259-278.

[24] W.R. Heinzelman, A. Chandrakasan and H. Balakrishnan, Energy-efficient routing protocols for wireless microsensor networks, Proc. HICSS, Hawaii, January 2000.

[25] T.C. Hou and V.O.K. Li, Transmission range control in multihop packet radio networks, IEEE Transactions on Communications, 34, 1, 1986, 38-44.

[26] C. Ho, K. Obraczka, G. Tsudik, and K. Viswanath, Flooding for reliable multicast in multihop ad hoc networks, 3rd Int. Workshop on Discrete Alg. and Methods for Mobile Comp. Comm. DIALM, August 1999.

[27] K. Obraczka, K. Viswanath, G. Tsudik, Flooding for reliable multicast in multihop ad hoc networks, Wireless Networks, 7, 6, Nov. 2001, 627-634.

[28] IETF Manet charter, http://www.ietf.org/html.charters/manet-charter.html .

[29] M. Joa-Ng and I. Lu, A peer-to-peer zone-based two-level link state routing for mobile ad hoc networks, IEEE J. Selected Areas in Communications, 17, 8, Aug. 1999, 1415-1425.

[30] D. Johnson, D. A. Maltz, Dynamic source routing in ad hoc wireless networks, in Mobile Computing (T. Imielinski and H. Korth, eds.), Kluwer Acad. Publ., 1996.

[31] R. Jain, A. Puri and R. Sengupta, Geographical routing using partial information for wireless ad hoc networks, IEEE Personal Communication, February 2001, 48-57.

[32] B. Karp and H.T. Kung, GPSR: Greedy perimeter stateless routing for wireless networks, Proc. MOBICOM, August 2000, 243-254.

[33] J.M. Kahn, R.H. Katz, K.S.J. Pister, Next century challenges: Mobile networking for 'smart dust', Proc. MOBICOM, 1999, Seattle, 271-278.

[34] E. Kranakis, H. Singh and J. Urrutia, Compass routing on geometric networks, Proc. 11th Canadian Conference on Computational Geometry, Vancouver, August, 1999.

[35] Y.B. Ko and N.H. Vaidya, Location-aided routing (LAR) in mobile ad hoc networks, MOBICOM, 1998, 66-75; Wireless Networks, 6, 4, July 2000, 307-321.

[36] Kleinberg, J., "The small-world phenomenon: an algorithmic perspective",Technical Report 99-1776, Cornell Computer Science,1999.

[37] P. Larsson, Selection diversity forwarding in a multihop packet radio network with fading channel and capture, Proc. ACM MobiHoc 2001, 279-282.

[38] Li. Li, J. Jannotti, D. S. J. De Couto, D. R. Karger, and R. Morris, A scalable location service for geographic ad hoc outing, ACM Mobicom 2000, Boston, MA.

[39] Q. Li, J. Aslam and D. Rus, Online power-aware routing in wireless ad-hoc networks, Proc. MOBICOM, 2001.

[40] Li Li, J.Y. Halpern, Minimum energy mobile wireless networks revisited, Proc. IEEE ICC, June 2001.

[41] Li Li, J.Y. Halpern, P. Bahl, Y.M. Wang, R. Wattenhoffer, Analysis of a cone-based distributed tolopogy control algorithm for wireless multi-hop networks, Proc. PODC, August 2001.

[42] J. Li, J. Jannotti, D.S.J. De Couto, D.R. Karger, R. Morris, A scalable location service for geographic ad hoc routing, Proc. MOBICOM 2000, 120-130.

[43] X. Lin, M. Lakshdisi and I. Stojmenovic, Location based localized alternate, disjoint, multi-path and component routing algorithms for wireless networks, Proc. ACM Symposium on Mobile Ad Hoc Networking and Computing MobiHoc, Long Beach, California, USA, October 4-5, 2001, 287-290.

[44] S. Lindsey, K. Sivalingam and C.S. Raghavendra, Power optimization in routing protocols for wireless and mobile networks, in: Wireless Networks and Mobile Computing Handbook (I. Stojmenovic, ed.), John Wiley and Sons, 2002, 407-424.

[45] X.-Y. Li, I. Stojmenovic, Partial Delaunay triangulation and degree limited localized Bluetooth scatternet formation, Proc. AD-HOC NetwOrks and Wireless (ADHOC-NOW), Fields Institute, Toronto, September 20-21, 2002, 17-32.

[46] W.H. Liao, Y.C. Tseng, J.P. Sheu, GRID: A fully location-aware routing protocols for mobile ad hoc networks, Proc. IEEE HICSS, January 2000; Telecommunication Systems, 18, 1-3, September 2001.

[47] Xiang-Yang Li, Peng-Jun Wan, Yu Wang and Ophir Fieder, Sparse power efficient topology for wireless networks, Proc. Hawaii Int. Conf. on System Sciences, 2002.

[48] Metricom Richonet wireless modem www.metricom.com

[49] J.P. Macker and M.S. Corson, Mobile ad hoc networking and the IETF, Mobile Computing and Communications Review, 2, 1, 1998, 9-14.

[50] R. Morris, J. Jannotti, F. Kaashoek, J. Li, D. Decouto, CarNet: A scalable ad hoc wireless network system, 9th ACM SIGOPS European Workshop, Kolding, Denmark, Sept. 2000.

[51] Nokia Rooftop wireless routing system. www.nwr.nokia.com

[52] T. Shepard, A channel access scheme for large dense packet radio networks, Proc. SIGCOMM Conf. on Communications Architectures, Aug. 1996.

[53] R. Nelson and L. Kleinrock, The spatial capacity of a slotted ALOHA multihop packet radio network with capture, IEEE Transactions on Communications, 32, 6, 1984, 684-694.

[54] G. Pei and M. Gerla, Mobility management for hierarchical wireless networks, Mobile Networks and Applications, 6, 4, August 2001, 331-337.

[55] Wei Peng, Xi-Cheng Lu, On the reduction of broadcast redundancy in mobile ad hoc networks, Proc. First Annual Workshop on Mobile and Ad Hoc Networking and Computing, Boston, USA, August 11, 2000, 129-130.

[56] A. Qayyum, L. Viennot, A. Laouiti, Multipoint relaying: An efficient technique for flooding in mobile wireless networks, RR-3898, IN-RIA, March 2000, www.inria.fr/RRRT/RR-3898.html , Proc. Hawaii Int. Conf. on System Sciences, 2002.

[57] V. Rodoplu and T.H. Meng, Minimum energy mobile wireless networks, IEEE Journal on Selected Areas in Communications, Vol. 17, No. 8, August 1999, 1333-1344.

[58] S. Ramanathan and M. Steenstrup, A survey of routing techniques for mobile communication networks, Mobile Networks and Applications, 1, 2, 1996, 89-104.

[59] E.M. Royer and C.K. Toh, A review of current routing protocols for ad hoc mobile wireless networks, IEEE Personal Communications, April 1999, 46-55.

[60] E. Shih, S.H. Cho, N. Ickes, R. Min, A. Sinha, A. Wang, A. Chandrakasan, Physical layer protocol and algorithm design for energy-efficient wireless sensor networks, Proc. MOBICOM 2001, 272-286.

[61] I. Stojmenovic, S. Datta, Power and cost aware routing with guaranteed delivery in ad hoc networks, Proc. Seventh IEEE Symposium on Computers and Communications ISCC, Taormina, Sicily, Italia, July 1-4, 2002, 31-36.

[62] I. Stojmenovic and Xu Lin, Power-aware localized routing in wireless networks, IEEE Transactions on Parallel and Distributed Systems, Vol. 12, No. 11, November 2001, 1122-1133.

[63] Ivan Stojmenovic and Xu Lin, Geographic distance routing in ad hoc wireless networks, Computer Science, SITE, University of Ottawa, TR-98-10, December 1998.

[64] Ivan Stojmenovic and Xu Lin, Loop-free hybrid single-path/flooding routing algorithms with guaranteed delivery for wireless networks, IEEE Transactions on Parallel and Distributed Systems, 12, 10, 2001, 1023-1032.

[65] I. Stojmenovic, A routing strategy and quorum based location update scheme for ad hoc wireless networks, Computer Science, SITE, University of Ottawa, TR-99-09, September 1999.

[66] I. Stojmenovic, Voronoi diagram and convex hull based geocasting and routing in wireless networks, SITE, University of Ottawa, TR-99-11, Dec. 1999. www.site.uottawa.ca/ ivan

[67] I. Stojmenovic, Home agent based location update and destination search schemes in ad hoc wireless networks, Computer science, SITE, University of Ottawa, TR-99-10, September 1999; in: Advances in Information Science and Soft Computing (A. Zemliak and N.E. Mastorakis, eds.), WSEAS Press, 2002, 6-11.

[68] I. Stojmenovic, Location updates for efficient routing in ad hoc networks, in: Handbook on Wireless Networks and Mobile Computing, Wiley, 2002, 451-472.

[69] M. Seddigh, J. Solano Gonzalez and I. Stojmenovic, RNG and internal node based broadcasting algorithms for wireless one-to-one networks, ACM Mobile Computing and Communications Review, 5, 2, 2001, 37-44.

[70] I. Stojmenovic, M. Seddigh, J. Zunic, Dominating sets and neighbor elimination based broadcasting algorithms in wireless networks, IEEE Transactions on Parallel and Distributed Systems, Vol 13, No. 1, January 2002, 14-25.

[71] I. Stojmenovic, M. Russell, and B. Vukojevic, Depth first search and location based localized routing and QoS routing in wireless networks, IEEE Int. Conf. on Parallel Processing, Aug. 21-24, Toronto, 173-180.

[72] J. Shaikh, I. Stojmenovic, and J. Wu, Sleep period sensor network schedules based on power aware dominating sets, in preparation.

[73] S. Singh, M. Woo, C.S. Raghavendra, Power-aware routing in mobile ad hoc networks, Proc. MOBICOM, 1998, 181-190.

[74] H. Takagi and L. Kleinrock, Optimal transmission ranges for randomly distributed packet radio terminals, IEEE Transactions on Communications, 32, 3, 1984, 246-257.

[75] Y.C. Tseng, S.L. Wu, W.H. Liao and C.M. Chao, Location awareness in wireless mobile ad hoc networks, IEEE Computer 34, 6, June 2001, 46-52.

[76] J. Urrutia, Routing with guaranteed delivery in geometric and wireless networks, in: Wireless Networks and Mobile Computing Handbook (I. Stojmenovic, ed.), John Wiley and Sons, 2002, 393-406.

[77] Ya Xu, John Heidemann and Deborah Estrin, Geography-informed energy conservation for ad hoc networks, Proc. MOBICOM 2001.

[78] J. Wu, F. Dai, M. Gao, and I. Stojmenovic, On calculating power-aware connected dominating sets for efficient routing in ad hoc wireless networks, IEEE/KICS Journal of Communication Networks, Vol. 4, No. 1, March 2002, 59-70.

[79] J. Wu and H. Li, On calculating connected dominating set for efficient routing in ad hoc wireless networks, Proc. DIAL M, Seattle, Aug. 1999, 7-14; Telecommunication Systems, 18, 1-3, Sept. 2001, 13-36.

[80] S.C.M. Woo and S. Singh, Scalable routing for ad hoc networks, TR 00.001, March 2000, Dept. of Elec. and Comp. Eng., Oregon State University, Corvallis, OR, USA; Wireless Networks, 7, 5, September 2001, 513-529.

[81] C. Yeh, Variable-radius routing protocols for high throughput, low power, and small latency in ad hoc wireless networks, IEEE Int. Conf. Wireless LANs and Home Networks, Dec. 2001.

AD HOC WIRELESS NETWORKING
X. Cheng, X. Huang and D.-Z. Du (Eds.) pp. 137 - 174

Location Discovery in Ad-hoc Wireless Sensor Networks

Farinaz Koushanfar
Department of Electrical Engineering and Computer Science
University of California at Berkeley, Berkeley, CA 94720
E-mail: `farinaz@eecs.berkeley.edu`

Sasa Slijepcevic
Department of Computer Science
University of California at Los Angeles, Los Angeles, CA 90095
E-mail: `sascha@cs.ucla.edu`

Miodrag Potkonjak
Department of Computer Science
University of California at Los Angeles, Los Angeles, CA 90095
E-mail: `miodrag@cs.ucla.edu`

Alberto Sangiovanni-Vincentelli
Department of Electrical Engineering and Computer Science
University of California at Berkeley, Berkeley, CA 94720
E-mail: `alberto@eecs.berkeley.edu`

Contents

Abstract

Location discovery is a fundamental task in wireless ad-hoc networks. Location discovery provides a basis for a variety of location-aware applications. The goal of location discovery is to establish the position of each node as accurately as possible, given partial information about location of a subset of nodes and measured distances between some pairs of nodes. Numerous approaches and systems for location discovery have been recently proposed. The goal of this Chapter is twofold. First is to summarize and systemize the already available location discovery approaches. Second is to present in great detail a new approach for location discovery in wireless ad-hoc sensor networks that resolve some of limitation of the current approaches and present a specific location discovery approach including all key technical details..

The new approach leverages on the insights and studies of the accuracy of atomic multilateration. We introduce a new and fast iterative improvement optimization mechanism that is amenable to a localized implementation. Furthermore, we illustrate how the approach and the algorithm are well-suited towards a number of other important tasks in wireless sensor and information networks such as calibration, skewing resilience and obstacle detection.

1 Introduction

Wireless ad-hoc sensor networks (WASNs) consist of a number of sensor nodes each equipped with a certain number of sensors and some amount of communication, storage and processing resources. The list of possible applications of WASNs includes many diverse problems, such as early fire detection in forests, indoor energy consumption monitoring [3], outdoor environmental monitoring [7], and target tracking on a battlefield. The applications, as well as a number of typical network management tasks, e.g. routing and coverage monitoring, require information about the locations of sensor nodes in the network. Nodes could acquire the estimates of their locations from outside sources. For example, GPS [15] is one of the primary candidates for location discovery is outdoor networks. However, due to the large number of nodes in a sensor network, it is not justifiable from an economic or energy preservation point of views to equip each node with a GPS receiver. Another scenario, in which the nodes are explicitly given their locations after deployment, is feasible only in WASNs consisting of a small number of nodes and deployed in easily accessible areas. Since most of the applications of WASNs assume a large number of nodes pseudorandomly deployed in remote areas, there is a need for a location discovery algorithm that can estimate the locations of all nodes from initial location estimates from a subset of nodes.

The location discovery problem can be stated at the informal and intuitive level in the following way. Given a WASN, some of the nodes have estimates of their locations. Neighboring nodes can exchange location estimates and they can measure (estimate) distances between themselves. The technical goal is to develop a procedure for locating each node such that the discrepancy between the distance measurements and the distances according to the computed locations is minimized. The main practical objective is to locate each node as accurately as possible with the given information with a certain amount of error about the distances between a subset of the nodes.

We start the Chapter by analyzing a number of proposed location discovery algorithms. We also discuss the advantages and limitations of each approach. Next, we justify the need for a new approach that addresses issues that are treated by the already existing approaches. Therefore, in the second part of the Chapter, we present a new location discovery algorithm that resolves a number of these issues. Another reason of presenting the new approach is provide insides in a number of technical problems associated with the location discovery process. The new location discovery method is distinguished from previous approaches in two ways. First, it is a location discovery procedure that not only runs on the wireless nodes in the network to estimate an erroneous location, but also a refinement and error correction strategy that guarantees a high quality location estimation in the presence of noisy data. Second, we introduce an efficient localized algorithm for the location discovery problem that employs local multilateration moves to locally compute the position of each node.

One new aspect of the localized approach is that it also contains an efficient way to locally accumulate the distance estimation between pairs of nodes in the network at the computing points of the network. The same efficient communication strategy can be used for information dissemination from the computation centers after the location discovery procedure returns its results.

The key highlights of the Chapter can be summarized in the following way.

- Summary of the history of location discovery technologies and methods. In particular, detailed description of the current state-of-the-art location discovery techniques and procedures in wireless ad-hoc sensor network.

- Introduction of the new algorithm that provides guaranteed tolerance against the errors, since the results are not just the location of the nodes, but also the level of confidence in the error values.

- Detailed insights from the atomic multilateration studies described in 2 and using the insights for developing more efficient localized algorithms. The insight can be used by many of popular location discovery algorithms to enhance their effectiveness.

- An intelligent initial localization solution to avoid extensive iterations through the network.

- A new comprehensive calibration scheme that uses the estimation of distances between all neighboring nodes in the network to properly scale the distances in such a way that the overall discrepancy is minimized. This task is accomplished in provably optimal way. The previously proposed calibration scheme was in the AHLoS system [24], where the calibration is done only using information between pairs of the anchor nodes and in [10] where calibration is performed only on a single pair of nodes at a time. The scheme can be used by many of popular location discovery algorithms to improve their effectiveness.

- Explicit treatment of error and flexibility of the proposed optimization algorithm that enables us to have obstacle detection and resiliency against malicious attacks.

The remainder of the Chapter is organized as followed. Section 2 presents basic information about the distance measurement techniques and atomic multilateration procedure and their place in the location discovery process. We also describe initial error modelling in our simulation environment used in the studies in Section 4. In Section 3, we give an overview of location discovery problems and solutions in wireless networks. We classify localization systems based on their required infrastructure and points of computation. Then we state the shortcoming of the current approaches and describe a new algorithmic method for location discovery that uses the multilateration studies and insights. Studies of the atomic multilateration procedure are described in Section 4. In Section 5 we give centralized and localized versions of the new location discovery algorithm. Next, we describe a number of important applications of the proposed location discovery algorithm in Section 6. Section 7 contains conclusions of the Chapter.

2   Background and overview of basic methods

Measuring distances or angles between the nodes is one of the most crucial components of any type of a location discovery system. In this Section, we first provide a brief summary of different distance and angle measurement and location estimation techniques. In addition, we present the error models commonly used in locations discovery simulations to capture the errors.

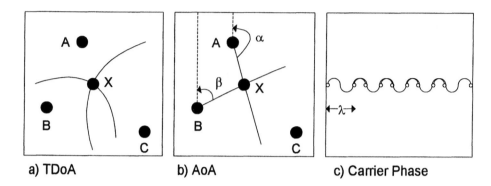

a) TDoA   b) AoA   c) Carrier Phase

Figure 1: Distance measurement methods, a) TDoA, b) AoA, and c) carrier phase method.

2.1 Distance and angle measurement techniques

Techniques proposed for distance measurement and, therefore, locating an object can be classified in terms of employed conceptual and physical mechanisms. Note that different technologies can be used to realize the same mechanism. There are several possible methods. Here, we list the most common approaches for distance and angle estimation, at both conceptual and technological levels. A more comprehensive survey is presented in [9].

- *Time of arrival (ToA)* methods measure the propagation time of a signal going from a transmitter to a receiver. Assuming that the speed of the signal in the medium is known, the distance could be estimated at the receiver to a certain accuracy. Since the system measures a time delay, it has to accurately synchronize the clocks on the sender and the receiver sides. Another way to conduct synchronization is to use two signals having different velocities. This method is often used in sensor networks location discovery systems. Another alternative way to cope with synchronization is to measure the round trip time of the signal, while it goes through a sender→receiver→sender path. This distance measurement method has been used in Radar sensory systems and the Global Positioning System (GPS).

- *Time difference of arrival (TDoA)* technique is similar to the ToA method. The only difference is in this approach the system assumes presence of simultaneously emitted signals from two beacons and finds the time difference between the two signals. An example is shown in Figure 1.a. The object X measures its distance to the Beacons A, B, and C. Note that synchronization between the beacon transmitters is required in order to ensure correct functionality.

- *Angle of arrival (AoA)* techniques measure the angle between a number of beacons (more than three) and an abject to determine the position of the object. An example is shown in Figure 1.b. The object X measures its angles to the Beacons A, B, and C. The precision of the AoA techniques diminishes with increasing the distances between the unknown object and the beacons, due to scattering effects of the environment. This technique is used in the Radar sensory system, in VHF omnidirectional range (VOR) used in aviation and, and in GSM sectors.

- *Received signal strength indicator (RSSI)* techniques works by observing the power of the received signal. Assuming that the original power of the received signal at a transmitter is known, the propagation loss can be used to estimate the distance between the transmitter and the receiver. The system should have a map between the loss and the distances, which is often either an empirical table or a equation-based model. The errors in this type of distance measurement can be quiet high, due to the obstacles and the multipath effects of the environment on the signal. This technique is mostly implemented with the radio frequency (RF) transmitter and receivers, and has been used with the GSM technology.

- *Carrier phase* technology has been used for accurate and longer range positioning in GPS. It has been long known that the rate of the amplitude distortion and decay is much higher than that of the frequency. For example, phase modulation communication techniques have much higher quality for longer ranges that amplitude modulation techniques. Since the technology is used for very long distances, it is difficult to measure the number of cycles of the carrier signal at the receiver. Thus, accurate devices are needed to maintain a continuous lock on the carrier signal. An example is shown in Figure 1.c.

The techniques mentioned so far are absolute distance estimation methods that find the distance of an object with respect to a number of beacons with known positions. It is also possible to estimate the relative distances.

For example, a set of wheelsensors, Velocity meter and accelerometer can be used to define the relative positions of moving objects, or a barometer can be used to find the relative height. These types of relative measurements have been used for aviation in Inertial Navigation System (INS).

Once we measure the distances between an object and a number of beacons, we also need a way to combine the measurements to find the actual position. The most common methods to combine the distance measurements from three or more beacons are triangulation, simple trilateration (multilateration), and atomic multilateration optimization:

- *Triangulation* is a method for finding the position of a node, when the angles are measured by AoA technique. An example of such a procedure is shown in Figure 2.a. The object X measures its angles with respect to the beacons A_1, A_2, and A_3. The measured angles form three straight lines along the directions XA_1, XA_2 and XA_3. The intersection between the three lines defines the location of the node X. The accuracy of this technique is heavily dependent upon the accuracy of the employed angle measurement technique.

- *Simple trilateration* is used when we have an accurate estimate of distances between a node and at least three beacon nodes. This simple method finds the intersection of three circles centered at beacons as the position of the node. The scenario is shown in Figure 2.b. Even though the conceptual simplicity makes this method very attractive, its accuracy requirements lead to its practical limited use. If the circles do not intersect at one point, the simple trilateration procedure is not be able to find the results. Therefore, more sophisticated atomic multilateration optimization procedure have been proposed to cope with the distance errors.

- *Atomic multilateration* is accepted as the most appropriate way to determine the location of a sensor node based on locations of beacons [23, 24, 4]. An example is shown in Figure 2.c, where the nodes A_1, A_2, A_3, and A_4 are beacons, with known estimates of their locations, while the node X estimates its location using a multilateration procedure. The procedure attempts to estimate the position of a node by minimizing the error and discrepancies between the measured values Therefore, to compute an estimate of the location of X, we define a multilateration objective function and select a local minimum of that

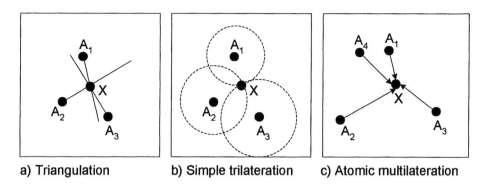

a) Triangulation   b) Simple trilateration   c) Atomic multilateration

Figure 2: The nodes A_1, A_2, A_3, and A_4 are beacons, while X is the node whose location is to be estimated. a) triangulation, b) simple trilateration, c) atomic multilateration.

function. In Section 4 we present three possible objective functions and compare their performances.

2.2   Error Modelling

We describe a practical approach for modelling of initial location and distance measurement in this subsection. We assume that simulations are performed in an X_{max} by Y_{max} rectangular area. The values of X_{max} and Y_{max} are function of the number of nodes in a simulation and the specified node density.

The real locations of sensor nodes A_i, i=0,..,n are represented as points $A_i(x_i, y_i)$. Coordinates x_i and y_i are generated from two uniform distributions, one on the interval $[0,X_{max}]$ and one on the interval $[0,Y_{max}]$. For each simulation, a subset of nodes that have initial estimates of their locations is randomly or according to user specified criteria selected. An initial location estimate is derived from a real location by superimposing an error to the real location. The error is represented as a pair $(\Delta x_i, \Delta y_i)$, where both Δx_i and Δy_i are generated from a zero mean Gaussian distribution $(0, \sigma_{loc}^2)$. Therefore, the location estimate for the node A_i is $\hat{A}_i(x_i + \Delta x_i, y_i + \Delta y_i)$.

The standard deviation σ_{loc} is a simulation parameter by that is adjusted to the value of the average initial location error, where the error is the distance between the real location and the initial location estimate for a node. The average initial location error is given as:

$$\mu_{error} = \int_{-\infty}^{\infty} \int_{-\infty}^{\infty} \sqrt{\Delta x^2 + \Delta y^2} P(\Delta x, \Delta y) dx dy \tag{1}$$

where $P(\Delta x, \Delta y)$ is the joint distribution of $(\Delta x, \Delta y)$. Since the distributions for Δx and Δy are independent with parameters $m = 0$ and σ_{loc}, we can state:

$$\mu_{error} = \int_{-\infty}^{\infty} \int_{-\infty}^{\infty} \sqrt{\Delta x^2 + \Delta y^2} P(\Delta x) P(\Delta y) dx dy \tag{2}$$

$$= \int_{-\infty}^{\infty} \int_{-\infty}^{\infty} \sqrt{\Delta x^2 + \Delta y^2} (\frac{1}{\sqrt{2\pi}\sigma})^2 e^{-\frac{\Delta x^2 + \Delta y^2}{2\sigma^2}} dx dy$$

After a transformation into polar coordinates and an application of the Gaussian integral $I_2(a)$ formula, we have

$$\mu_{error} = \frac{1}{2\pi\sigma^2} \int_0^{2\pi} \int_0^{\infty} \rho^2 e^{-\frac{\rho^2}{2\sigma^2}} d\rho d\theta = \frac{1}{\sigma^2} I_2(\frac{1}{2\sigma^2}) = \sqrt{\frac{\pi}{2}}\sigma_{loc} \tag{3}$$

Now, by selecting a corresponding σ_{loc}, we can generate a location error distribution with the desired mean value.

The distances measured in a WASN are susceptible to different sources of error, including obstacles, interference, and multipath effects. We model the distance measurement error as a function of the measured distance d. Since the errors from different sources exhibit different characteristics, we model the overall distance error as a sum of two components: a) $GAUSS\_ERROR(d_{ij})$ and b)$NLOS_{ij}(d_{ij})$.

a) $GAUSS\_ERROR(d_{ij}) = d_{ij} \times G(0, \sigma_{dist}^2)$

Since the signal goes through many different paths before arriving at the receiver, and the receiver adds on all of the small components to build the received signal, the model for this error is Gaussian Normal distribution according to the central limit theorem. Thus, the first component of the distance measurement error is a Gaussian white noise. It models the deviation of a particular measurement from the correct distance due to the propagation model imprecision, environmental changes in the area where the signal propagates, and noise. The order of magnitude of this component is controlled by σ_{dist}. The average absolute value of $G(0, \sigma_{dist})$ represents the average percentage for which the distances in the network are incorrectly measured due to the Gaussian white noise:

$$E(|x|) = \frac{2}{\sigma_{dist}\sqrt{2\pi}} \int_0^{\infty} x e^{-\frac{x^2}{2\sigma^2}} = \sqrt{\frac{2}{\pi}}\sigma_{dist} \tag{4}$$

b) $NLOS_{ij}(d_{ij}) = d_{ij} \times Un(0, NLOS_{max})$.

The second component of the error models non-line-of-sight error. The error is modelled as a percentage of the measured distance d_{ij}, same as for Gaussian noise. Since the line of sight is only along one dimension and it can be linearly estimated, we use a uniform distribution for this error term. The percentage of $NLOS$ error is drawn from a positive uniform distribution on the interval $(0, NLOS_{max})$. The average percentage for which the distance measurement error is increased due to $NLOS$ error is given as $NLOS_{max}/2$. The distance measurement $(\hat{d}_{ij})$ is therefore simulated as, $\hat{d}_{ij} = d_{ij} + G(d_{ij}) + NLOS(d_{ij})$.

3 History and State-of-the-Art Location Discovery Techniques

Location discovery has crucial practical importance and has long been a subject of active research. For example, Thales of Miletus, the first known scientist (6 century B.C.) had developed an ingenious scheme to locate a ship at sea by observing it and a corresponding set of points with known distances using a simple mechanical device. He had also developed a procedure to locate the top of pyramids. More recently, the first application of the least square error minimization is attributed to Gauss, who used the method for best-fitting the locations into a map [11]. In general, location discovery requires exceptional sophistication, not just in terms of practical engineering, but also in terms of the required theoretical foundations. For example, the GPS location system is one of very few devices that employs Einstein's theory of relativity [26].

A number of location discovery techniques had been developed for mobile wireless systems. The automatic vehicle location (AVL) systems [1] were the first class of proposed methods to determine the position of the moving vehicles using the wireless signal measurements in wireless distributed mobile systems. In this approach, several base stations derive their distance estimation from the moving vehicle by using the time-of-arrival (ToA) or time-difference-of-arrival (TDoA) of the signals. The most widely used and publicized location discovery system is GPS [15], which was implemented in 1993. The system consists of 24 satellites that emit radio frequency (RF) signals from space. The moving objects are equipped with special GPS receivers that receive the signal from at least four different satellites and estimate their location relative to the satellites using TOA. LORAN is a location discovery system very similar to GPS. However, the difference is that the LORAN base-stations are deployed on Earth [18]. The major limitations of GPS and LORAN are their inaccuracy in urban environments, cost of the receivers, and size and power consumption of the receivers that prevents their extensive use in small sensor nodes in WASN. Since 1996, the Federal Communication Commission (FCC) requires cellular service providers to provide a mechanism for determining subscriber location estimates for E-911 services. Following the initial order, several techniques were proposed for these services [6]. We do not go into the details of these services, since all of them function on the premise of a fixed base station.

In addition to the above proposed distance estimation approaches, a number of alternative distance measurement techniques exist. For example, electromagnetic sensing is a classical distance estimation method [22, 19]. These systems offer very accurate distance estimation. Their drawbacks include high implementation costs, sensitivity to metallic materials, short-distance ranging, and controllability. Hightower and Borriello [14] present a survey on different location systems for ubiquitous computing environments, including the wireless environments with fixed infrastructure.

In the remainder of this section, we present a brief summary of the current location discovery techniques and systems. We restrict our attention only to the techniques used in WASNs. In most of the location discovery systems, a few nodes usually called "beacons" are assumed to already have their location information. They serve as the reference point for the rest of the nodes within the network.

Active Badge and Active Bat systems. The first indoor badge sensing system was the Active Badge location system developed at Olivetti Research Laboratory, now AT&T Cambridge [27]. Active Badge tracks objects equipped with small infrared badge-like devices and stores them in a centralized location database. They also designed a comprehensive software architecture for handling the location data. A badge periodically transmits its ID to the fixed receivers. The location of the moving badges is then computed using a cellular proximity method. The disadvantages of active badge include the high cost and complexity of the infrastructure. The infrared diffusion systems additionally suffer from interferences from other light sources such as sunlight. Active Bat is a more recent location system developed at AT&T Cambridge [12]. Mobile objects are equipped with small wireless transmitters consisting of an RF transceiver, multiple ultrasonic transmitters, a microprocessor and an FPGA processor. Multiple fixed receivers are equipped with RF receivers and an interface to the serial data network and are deployed in a wired matrix and used for object detection. A central RF base-station synchronizes the transmitters and receivers by periodically sending RF messages to them. The approach uses the ultrasound time-of-flight multilateration technique to achieve greater accuracy than Active Badge. Each transmitter sends back an ultrasound pulse after receiving a message from the base-station. The receivers determine the TDoA of the RF signal from the base station and the ultrasound from each Bat to estimate the distances. The locations of the objects are then computed in a centralized database of distances. Centralized complex architecture and high cost are the drawbacks of this system.

RADAR. RADAR [2], is a radio frequency based system for location discovery from Microsoft. The emphasis of the RADAR project was placed on developing relatively large experimental testbed on one floor of a building. They placed two base station on one side of the floor, and one on the another. RADAR uses signal strength (RSSI) information from these three base stations to locate a mobile user's Pentium laptop. It combines empirical measurements with comprehensive signal propagation modelling of the environment to determine user location. The expensive infrastructure (fixed base-stations) and the inaccuracies due to using only three beacons are the main limitations of this system.

Cricket. Cricket [20] is an indoor location discovery system that uses information from a set of beacon nodes that are spread throughout the building and periodically broadcast messages out, to enable a set of listening nodes to deduce their locations. There is no explicit coordination between the beacons, but the location discovery procedure assumes that there are enough number of beacons at any point of time in the room. The beacons use a randomized algorithm to transmit the information to minimize collision and inferences among each other and use TDoA of the RF and ultrasonic signals to infer the distances to the nodes (similar to Bat [12]). Cricket achieves a granularity of 4 by 4 feet. Beacon placement plays an important role in enabling the listener nodes to correctly estimate their location. The cricket approach is mostly built following the principles of practical engineering and tuning the system parameters involved to have a functional solution with the current off-the-shelf technology. Some later approaches including the approach we discuss in Section 5, focus more on the optimization aspects of the location discovery task. More recently, the Cricket location discovery system has been used as a basis for building a software compass, a device that uses the location discovery process applied to several closely placed receivers on a single device to calculate its orientation [21].

SpotON. SpotON[13] is an approach for ad-hoc location sensing in ad-hoc wireless sensor networks. SpotON tags use radio signal strength information (RSSI) as a distance estimator to perform ad-hoc laterations. They first describe the details of building a hardware platform for location discovery and modelling the RSSI distance prediction model. The authors then present the details of calibrating the measured distances between the adjacent sensor nodes for adjusting their model to the environment. Again, the approach is a system engineering-based one, to minimize the local distance estimation error between the nodes using only the RSSI techniques, and not to minimize the location error of the network as a whole.

Bulusu et al. This approach [4] uses the connectivity information between the nodes that is more robust but less accurate than the measured distances. Each node receives RF signals from set of fixed beacons with known location, and estimates its location at the mean of the coordinates of the beacons it is hearing. The accuracy of the connectivity based approach is about 30% of the average distance between the beacon nodes.

Doherty et. al. The authors in [8] present a convex programming formulation of the location discovery problem in sensor networks and then tries to solve it using standard convex programming tools. The network edges are modelled as geometric constraints on the node's positions. The method is centralized and assumes that all of the nodes send their information to a central processing computer that does offline computations. Hence, the system is not very scalable. Also, the system is not robust to failures, when ambiguous measurements are involved.

AHLoS. AHLoS [24] is an iterative location discovery method proposed for WASN. It first compares different ranging methods to estimate the distance between the nodes in the network. In particular, AHLoS examines a signal strength (RSSI) and a Time difference of arrival (TDoA) for both RF and ultrasound signals. It finally adapts a range estimation method similar to the one described in BAT [12], that is measuring the TDoA between RF and ultrasound signals to measure the distances. The method uses a basic atomic multilateration procedure where a node without the location information estimates its distance to its neighbors using a standard linearized maximum likelihood (ML) method. Nodes that perform atomic multilaterations can estimate their location and become beacons, propagating their information to more nodes (collaborative multilaterations). The AHLoS algorithm iteratively uses the atomic multilaterations and collaborative multilaterations as its building blocks. The convergence of the iterative multilateration depends on the network connectivity and the availability of the beacon nodes. The authors evaluate their algorithm using methodology proposed in [16] to define the network connectivity, in terms of the number of beacons and the location discovery process.

The algorithm that we describe in Section 5 also uses the atomic multilaterations as the initial solution generator and iteratively improves its results in the improvement phase. However, there is a substantial difference between key optimization mechanism of the employed atomic multilaterations:

1. The method in Section 5 adopt several non-linear methods to optimize the multilateration results, whereas [24] just uses linear ML approximation.

2. AHLoS does not provide a stopping criteria or lower bound for the error in their iterative improvement algorithm whereas, Section 5 has a well-defined optimization goal.

3. AHLoS does not provide any order for the distributed algorithm that fixes the location of the nodes, as to which nodes should be fixed first: not only the method in Section 5 emphasis on the importance of the order of multilateration on error minimization, but also it integrate other results of the multilaterations studies into the iterative algorithm to make it more accurate.

Hop-TERRAIN The authors in [25] describe a positioning algorithm that is indifferent to which distance measurement method is used, although the distance measurement method has a profound impact on the cost, accuracy, and power consumption. Their algorithm is split into two phases: a start-up phase and a refinement phase. The start-up phase is called Hop-TERRAIN and is similar to the collaborative multilateration phase described in AHLoS in the sense that it propagates the anchor node's information throughout the network and each node finds an initial estimate of their location. Although Hop-TERRAIN has the advantage that it works with lower beacon densities. The refinement phase is also an iterative improvement algorithm. In order to mitigate error propagation they modified the refinement algorithm to include a confidence associated with the position of the nodes. This also results in the ability to identify loose connections in the network and avoid further inaccuracies caused by loose connections. The algorithm described in Section 5 is different from the algorithm described in [25] along several major dimensions, including:

1. Hop-TERRAIN considers only a single property atomic multilaterations (the number of neighbor nodes).

2. Section 5 uses calibration between the nodes to further enhance the accuracy of our measurements.

3. Section 5 uses optimization intensive procedure to conduct overall optimization.

HEAP and STROBE. THE USC/ISI researchers [5] identified density as an important parameter affecting the optimization quality of the location discovery systems. HEAP and STROBE are two algorithms to enable system self-configuration based on beacon density. The implementation of this method is on an RF proximity based localization system with constrained nodes. For sparse and medium density they propose HEAP, that identifies the regions with poor localization and selects candidate points to place new beacons. The drawback of HEAP is the beacon placer that requires external monitoring of the network. For dense beacon deployments, they propose STROBE that enables densely deployed beacons to coordinate without self-interferences and opportunistically conserving the energy. HEAP assumes an automatic placer that is central but the places for the beacons are defined locally. STROBE starts by assuming a very large density and then develops protocols of how to save energy to put the nodes in the large density network to the sleep. The objectives are, (1) to maintain a uniform localization granularity across the system and over time, (2) maximizing the lifetime of the system by minimizing the energy consumption of the system, and (3) to minimize the convergence time of the beacon infrastructure from an initial state where all the nodes are active to an energy efficient state. The drawback of this location discovery system is that it requires a dense network, otherwise it will encounter large errors.

The location discovery procedure that we describe in Section 5 is localized, error-tolerant, and automatically calibrated. It uses an iterative improvement phase that minimizes the overall error of the system and our algorithm works significantly better on sparse networks and has much more sophisticated error handling techniques. The approach further employs composite moves to avoid a greedy approach inside the new iterative multilateration procedure. The location discovery procedure in Section 5 differs from the previous discussions in several main aspects. It is the first procedure that targets error minimization as the goal for location discovery. Furthermore, it is also the first work that considers how atomic multilateration impacts the overall location discovery process.

Error handling enables a number of new applications of location discovery, including obstacle and skewing discovery and calibration. Note that although calibration was previously addressed [24], the calibration process presented in this chapter is significantly more powerful because it leverages on information from all measurements and is integrated within the location discovery algorithm.

4   Atomic Multilateration

In this section we describe the results of three studies of the atomic multilateration procedure. The goal of the studies is to give us an insight into the performance of the multilateration procedure under different conditions. We first analyze the impact of the multilateration objective function on the accuracy of the procedure. The goal of this study is to determine which objective function should be used in the multilateration procedure. In the next two studies, we examine how the number of available beacons and how the relative locations of the beacons and the node correspond to the accuracy of the procedure. Accuracy of the multilateration procedure directly impacts the effectiveness of a location discovery algorithm. We measure accuracy simply as the distance between the location estimates generated by multilaterations and the real locations of the nodes. From the results of the studies we infer how to estimate the accuracy of the results the procedure generates. With that knowledge, we build a location discovery algorithm that selectively uses the multilateration procedure results, relying more on results where the parameters of multilateration indicate higher accuracy.

4.1   Multilateration Objective Functions

The goal of a multilateration objective function is to calculate the location of a node based on the current measurements, such that the difference between the calculated location and the real location of a node is minimal. We compare three multilateration objective functions in terms of the accuracy they achieve: a) sum of residuals (L_1);
b) sum of squares of residuals (L_2);
c) min-max residual (L_∞).
As previously stated, the node whose location is determined is denoted as the node $A_0(X, Y)$, while the nodes $A_1(X_1, Y_1), .., A_N(X_N, Y_N)$ are beacons. The equations (1), (2), and (3) define the three candidate functions using the following notations for the measured distances between nodes:
$R_i(X, Y)$ - the estimated distance between the beacon $A_i(X_i, Y_i)$ and the node $A_0(X, Y)$;
$$D_i(X, Y) = \sqrt{(X_i - X)^2 + (Y_i - Y)^2}$$

$$L_1(X, Y) = \sum_{i=1}^{N} |D_i(X, Y) - R_i(X, Y)| \tag{5}$$

$$L_2(X, Y) = \sum_{i=1}^{N} (D_i(X, Y) - R_i(X, Y))^2 \tag{6}$$

$$L_\infty(X, Y) = \max_{(i=1,...,N)} (D_i(X, Y) - R_i(X, Y))/R_i(X, Y) \tag{7}$$

The location (X_0, Y_0) for which the value of the objective function is minimal is selected as the result of the multilateration procedure.

In this study, we randomly generate 2000 topologies with three beacons and the node A_0 whose location is to be estimated. The coordinates of the node A_0 are generated first, and then the coordinates of the three beacons are generated. If the distance from a beacon and the node A_0 is longer than the transmission range, that beacon is removed from the topology, and

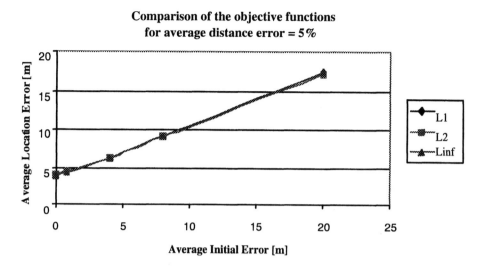

Figure 3: Average location error for the distance measurement error of 5% and the average initial location error from 0 m to 20 m.

a new one is generated. Those steps are repeated until all three beacons are within the transmission range of the node A_0. The coordinates of all nodes, distances, and errors are generated as described in Section 2. For each topology, we performed multilateration for each of the three objective functions. The average value of the utility function is calculated over 2000 topologies for each of the objective functions.

The whole experiment, with the same 2000 topologies, is repeated for a range of different average initial location errors and different average distance measurement errors. The results are given in Figure 3 and Figure 4. the X-axis in Figure 3, represents different values of the average initial location error for beacons. For each value on X-axis, the average utility function for 2000 topologies is calculated and represented as a value on Y-axis. For all the simulations given in Figure 3, the average distance measurement error is 5%, while the average initial location error for beacons ranges between 0 and 20 m, for a range of 100 m.

If we carefully examine the objective functions, we notice that L_∞ is tailored specifically for the model of the ranging error described in Section 2. The distance measurement error increases with the measured distance. At the same time, L_∞ estimates location of the node A_0 in such a way

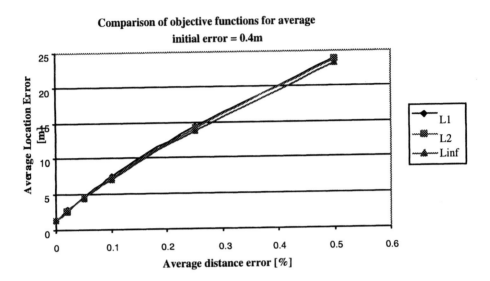

Figure 4: Average location error for the average initial error of 0.4 m and the distance measurement error from 0% to 50%

that it allows larger inconsistencies for longer distances than for shorter distances. For smaller values of initial location error, L_∞ achieves slightly better accuracy (up to 5%). However, as the initial location error increases, L_∞ loses its minimal advantage and L_2 achieves a better results.

We can see similar results in Figure 4. Here, the range is 100 m and the average initial location error is constant and relatively small, 0.4 m. Under these conditions, where the initial location error is small and the main source of error is the distance measurement error, L_∞ is consistently more accurate. Although, the average location error for the three objective functions is within 5%, L_∞ achieves the best results across the range of values of the initial location error and the distance measurement error. However, if the sources of error in a network are known in advance, and the initial location error dominates the distance measurement error, L_2 could be a better choice. The overall conclusion is that three error measures L_2, L_2, and L_∞ are essentially of the same quality. For other experiments in this paper, we use L_∞ as the multilateration objective function.

4.2 Number of Available Beacons

In the following study we examine how the accuracy of the multilateration depends on the number of available beacons. If there is a difference in accuracy when the number of beacons changes, then during the location discovery algorithm the result of a multilateration is trusted accordingly to the number of beacons involved in the multilateration. This is one of the mechanisms that the global location discovery algorithm uses to control the propagation of errors.

As in the previous study, the transmission range is 10 m. We generate 8000 different topologies. In each topology, 16 beacons are available. The average initial location error is 1m, while the average distance measurement error is 10%. We compare accuracy of the multilateration procedure with increasing number of beacons, starting from three. We use the following notation:

- A_0 - the node whose location is determined;

- (X_0^3, Y_0^3) an estimate of the location of the node A_0 when using three beacons;

- (X_0^n, Y_0^n) an estimate of the location of the node A_0 using n beacons;

- (X_0, Y_0) real location of the node A_0.

In each experiment we measure the relative average error (RAE) as the ratio of the location error with n beacons and the location error with three beacons.

$$RAE = \sqrt{(Y_0^n - Y_0)^2 + (X_0^n - X_0)^2} / \sqrt{(Y_0^3 - Y_0)^2 + (X_0^3 - X_0)^2} \quad (8)$$

Finally, the average value of RAE over 8000 topologies is the average improvement achieved, under the given values of the distance measurement error and beacons' location error, when n beacons are used compared to when only three beacons are used.

In Figure 5, we can see that the biggest improvement in accuracy is achieved when the number of beacons is increased from three to four; improvement is around 30%. For eight beacons, the location error reaches 40% of the error with three beacons, and then stays around 35% as the number of beacons increases. Depending on the density of the network, the number of available beacons has some limit, and since many beacons acquired their

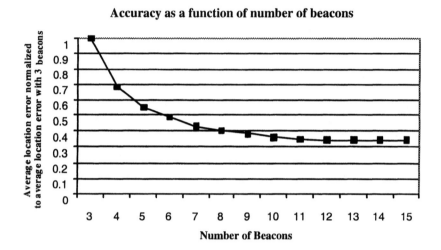

Figure 5: Average location error over all values of the distance measurement error and the initial location error for beacons.

locations through multilateration procedure, they have different estimates of location error. The results of this study allow a tradeoff between the expected improvement if more beacons are used and the possible decrease in accuracy if the additional beacons have larger location error than the rest of the beacons. To acquire a better understanding how the number of beacons impacts performance of multilateration on a case by case basis, in Figure 6, we show a distribution of absolute improvements in accuracy where the number of beacons used for a specific topology increases from three to six. In 1400 cases (17%), the error actually increases when six beacons are used instead of three. This scenario represents the cases where additional beacons have larger initial location error or distance measurement error. In another 1400 cases, accuracy does not change with additional beacons. On the other hand, 6% of the cases have an improvement larger than 5 m. This corresponds to the cases where three initial beacons had large errors. Therefore, to fully exploit improvement due to location error, it is necessary to estimate the error for used beacons, which is done in our global location discovery algorithm, where the beacons are mostly the nodes whose location estimates are calculated in previous multilaterations.

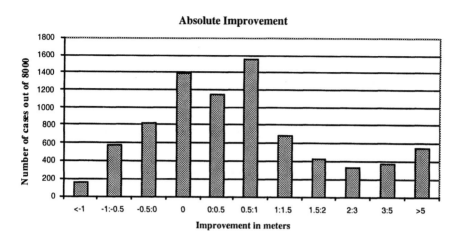

Figure 6: Absolute improvement measured in meters, when the number of beacons increases from three to six.

4.3 Relative Placement of Beacons

In this section, we examine how the accuracy of the triangulation procedure depends on the relative placement of the beacons and the node that estimates its location. The goal here is again to estimate the location error based on information available while the location discovery algorithm is executed. We compare two cases shown in Figure 7:

1. The location estimate is inside the triangle made by the beacons.

2. The location estimate is outside of the triangle made by the beacons.

For this study, we examined 2000 topologies with the node A_0 inside the triangle and 2000 topologies with the node A_0 outside of the triangle. The initial location error is set to 0, while the average distance measurement error ranges from 1% to 40%. Figure 8 displays the results of the simulation. A significant difference in accuracy when the two given cases are compared is noticeable only after the distance measurement error reaches 5%. For smaller distance measurement errors, two cases exhibit statistically same accuracy. It is important to notice that the placement of beacons is relative to estimate generated by multilateration. Therefore, if A_0 does not have any previous estimates of its location, it may try different combinations of available beacons until it acquires a location from beacons with acceptable

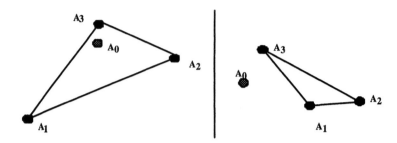

Figure 7: Examples of two different topologies: a) the node inside the triangle,b) the node outside the triangle

relative placement. However, if A_0 already has an estimate of its location, the estimate can be improved by choosing beacons with acceptable relative placement.

5   Fast Convergence Iterative Improvement Algorithm For Location Discovery

In this section, we present a new fast convergence iterative improvement algorithm (FCII) for the location discovery problem. From a conceptual point of view, the key novelty is that we rely on the conclusions from the studies of error induced by the atomic multilateration procedure to develop both suitable algorithmic objective functions and effective optimization mechanisms for the overall location discovery problem.

From the algorithmic point of view, the key new features of the FCII algorithm is that we use optimization intensive procedures for the creation of initial solution and explicit enabling moves to avoid local minima. The enabling moves both drastically reduce the required computation efforts and more importantly, the communication cost. We first introduce a centralized approach for solving the problem. After that, we explain how the centralized approach is used for developing a spectrum of localized version of the FCII algorithm.

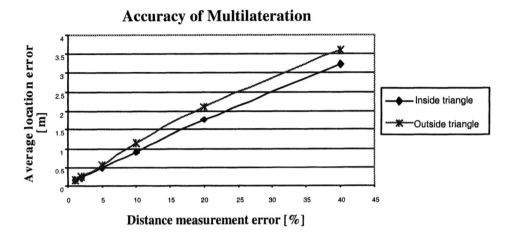

Figure 8: Accuracy of the multilateration procedure for two relative placements of the beacons and the location estimate.

5.1 Initial Solution Generation

Iterative improvement algorithms have been widely used for both continuous and combinatorial optimization due to their exceptional optimization effectiveness, simplicity of implementation, and intuitive appeal. The basic idea is simple: start with a randomly generated solution and keep altering small parts of the overall solution so that global objective function is improved. In traditional centralized iterative improvement algorithms, generating the initial solution is fully randomized. This is the proper decision since the number of improvement iterations is rarely a limiting factor. However, in localized algorithms, the number of hop communications defines the power consumption in the network. Since the power consumption is the most stringent limiting factor in WASN, it is crucial to avoid an excessively long iteration process. Therefore, we judiciously select an optimized initial solution that requires a significantly lower number of improvement step before achieving a high quality solution. The optimization intensive initial solution generator exploits the results of the atomic multilateration studies in order to generate a solution in the vicinity of the optimal solution. It functions in the following way: the solution generator assigns an initial objective function (IOF) to each node A_i in the network. The initial procedure then visits each vertex A_i in the network exactly once according to the priority defined by the IOF assigned to the nodes. The IOF itself is an additive composition of two factors:

$$IOF(A_i) = PTL(A_i) + ENB(A_i) \qquad (9)$$

Where the PTL is an indicator of the optimization potential of a node A_i, and ENB is an indicator of the enabling effect the node can have on the other nodes. In the following, we discuss each of these two components in more details.

5.1.1   Potential of a Node

As mentioned above, $PTL(A_i)$ is a quantitative measure of the optimization potential of the node A_i. In the case of location discovery, this component corresponds to the ability to conclude the accurate position of a node as a function of nodes that already determined their location, either because they have initial location estimates or estimates from the previous atomic multilateration steps of the algorithm.

Note that if we employ the potential of the node A_i as the only metric of consideration for the initial solution estimator, the initial step reduces to a greedy approach. Greedy algorithms are fast, but it is well known that they are inefficient for large scale optimization problems because of their tendency to get stuck at local minima. Therefore, to avoid a greedy optimization, we introduce a second term to the IOF that is a quantitative measure of the enabling potential of the node A_i to its neighboring nodes.

According to the presented atomic multilateration studies, a node A_i has potential to calculate its location with lower error than node A_j under the following conditions:

- A_i has shorter average measured distance to its neighbors than node A_j.

- A_i is inside the convex hull formed by its neighbors with known locations, while the node A_j is not,

- A_i has more neighbors with their location information than A_j.

Note that the last condition applies only if node A_j has less than nine neighbors due to the saturation point from the multilateration studies.

Specifically, the potential of the node A_i is defined as a function of closeness to the beacon neighbors $(CLS(A_i))$, being in the convex hull of the beacon neighbors $(CNX(A_i))$ and the degree of beacon neighbors $(DBN(A_i))$ for each vertex A_i in the network. More specifically, we write:

$$PTL(A_i) = \alpha \times CLS(A_i) + \beta \times CNX(A_i) + \gamma \times DBN(A_i). \qquad (10)$$

$CLS(A_i)$ is the ratio of the smallest possible distance between two nodes in the network divided by the average distance to the beacon neighbors to A_i. $CNX(A_i)$ is one, if the node A_i is inside the convex hull of its beacon neighbors and 0 otherwise. If A_i has b_i number of beacon neighbors, $DBN(A_i)$ is defined as:

if $b_i <= 7$ *then* $DBN(A_i) = b_i/7$; *else* $DBN(A_i) = 1$;

The weight factors: α, β and γ are set according to extensive experimentation to the following values: $\alpha=1$, $\beta=0.7$, and $\gamma=0.4$. The algorithm is very robust with respect to these values. Varying the weight factors over a wide range, we found less than 5% difference in the performances of both the initial step of the location discovery and in the overall effectiveness of the CFII location discovery algorithm.

5.1.2 Enabling Effect of a Node

The key idea of the enabling function is to try to assign a location to a node that will enable that as many neighbors as possible improve their PTL value. The enabling function also has three components:

$$ENB(A_i) = CLSN(A_i) + CNXN(A_i) + DBNN(A_i), \qquad (11)$$

where $CLSN(A_i)$ quantifies the closeness of A_i to its neighbors without location information. $CNX(A_i)$ is a measure of A_i forming convex hulls to the neighbors without their location information, and $DBNN(A_i)$ is a measure of how using the node A_i as a beacon could help the multilateration for its neighbors without location information. $CLSN(A_i)$ is the ratio of the smallest possible distance between two nodes in the network divided by the average distance to the non-beacon neighbors to A_i. $CNXN(A_i)$ is equal to the number of the non-beacon neighbors to A_i for which A_i forms a convex hull, divided by the total number of non-beacon neighbors of A_i. $DBNN(A_i)$ is the average of the $DBN(A_k)$, where the nodes A_k are the non-beacon neighbors to A_i. This function is weighted in the exactly the same way as the PTL objective function.

```
Procedure Iterative-localization-centralized
1. Generate the intelligent initial solution;
2. While (at least one improvement in the last k phases)
3. {   // (global objective function can be measured by L₁, L₂, or L∞)
4.    improvement = (GOF_now − GOF_old);
5.    if (improvement>0) then     //(iterative improvement round)
6.    {
7.       select the node v_i with the highest OOF and available   //(expired hold)
8.       atomic multilateration on A_i;
9.       start holding and aging A_i;
10.      update OOF's;
11.   }
12.   else   //(composite moves round)
13.   {
14.      select two available neighboring nodes with highest sum of OOF;
15.      do the composite improvement move on the two selected nodes;
16.      start holding and aging the composition of the visited couple;
17.      update OOF's;
18.   }
19.   Update GOF;
20. }
21. Last GASP;
```

Figure 9: Centralized iterative localization algorithm.

Finally, note that it is easy to randomize this procedure. For example, one way is to assign a new random component to both PTL and $CNLS$. If these values are relatively small, then we can get many high quality different initial solutions. We used this scheme to test the overall robustness of the CFII algorithm with respect to different initial solutions.

5.2   Global Flow of the Centralized Algorithm

Figure 9 presents the pseudocode of the new centralized iterative localization algorithm.

Line 1 is the generation of the intelligent initial solution presented in the previous subsection. The new iterative improvement algorithm starts at the line 2. The algorithm uses a global objective function (GOF) as the primary performance metric. The incremental change of the GOF is termed "improvement" and if positive, the new solution is better than the old one. If that is the case, the algorithm is in the "iterative" mode of operation. If "improvement" is negative, the algorithm is in the "composite move" mode of operation, where the goal is to escape a local minima. The main loop of the algorithm terminates when the algorithm stays in the "composite move" mode for k executions of the main loop as shown in line 2 of the algorithm.

In the beginning of each execution of the main loop (cycle) of the algorithm, the improvement is calculated as shown in line 4. The improvement is the difference between the values of GOF for the current solution and the value of GOF for the previous solution. There are a number of different choices for GOF. After extensive experimentation, we have decided to use the following three alternatives for measuring the GOF:

Global objective functions :
1. Sum of absolute residuals:

$$L_1(S) = \sum_{i=1}^{N} \sum_{j=1}^{i-1} \left| d(N_i, N_j) - \sqrt{(Y_j^S - Y_i^S)^2 + (X_j^S - X_i^S)^2} \right| \qquad (12)$$

2. Sum of squares of residuals:

$$L_2(S) = \sum_{i=1}^{N} \sum_{j=1}^{i-1} \left(d(N_i, N_j) - \sqrt{(Y_j^S - Y_i^S)^2 + (X_j^S - X_i^S)^2} \right)^2 \qquad (13)$$

3. Maximal residual:

$$L_\infty(S) = \max_{i=1...N; i \neq j} \left| d(N_i, N_j) - \sqrt{(Y_j^S - Y_i^S)^2 + (X_j^S - X_i^S)^2} \right| \qquad (14)$$

Where,

- (X_i^S, Y_i^S) is the estimated location of the sensor node i in the solution S;

- $d(N_i, N_j)$ is the measured distance between nodes i and j.

The "residual" is the difference, between the distances reported by the location discovery algorithm and the measured distances. Obviously, while the flow of the algorithm is the same for different choices of GOF, in general the final results depend on the overall objective to which GOF is tailored.

The iterative improvement round is shown in lines 5-11. As long as the value of the improvement is positive, the iterative improvement algorithm repeats the main optimization loop. However, if the improvement is negative, the algorithm goes through a round of composite moves shown in steps 13-18. After that, the algorithm updates GOF in the network in step 19.

When the main cycle terminates, the algorithm goes through a last round of optimization, called GASP, shown in line 21. During the GASP procedure, the algorithm visits each node once and examines each node for the possibility of one last improvement and then exits the program. The goal is to improve the solution to the extent that represents at least local minima.

Now we explain the details of the iterative improvement and the composite moves rounds. The iterative improvement round selects an available node that has the highest optimization objective function (OOF) and adjusts the location of that node using the atomic multilateration procedure. In order to avoid frequent repeat of steps of the iterative improvement procedure on the same node, the algorithm places a hold mark on the node that has just been adjusted. Every time we go through the main cycle, the hold function increases its age. A node becomes available for adjustment, once its age passes a certain threshold. In our implementation, the hold on one node expires after $N/3.5$ other nodes in the network are visited, where N is the total number of nodes in the network.

The OOF is based on the insights provided by the multilateration studies. For each node A_i, OOF is composed as the weighted sum of the following four components:

$$
\begin{aligned}
OOF(A_i) \;=\;& -w_1 \times CN(A_i) + w_2 \times CN(all A_k) \\
&+\; w_3 \times CNX(A_i) + w_4 \times CL(A_i).
\end{aligned}
\tag{15}
$$

where w_1, w_2, w_3 and w_4 are the weights for each component and are derived based on empirical multilateration studies. The function $CN(A_i)$ is a normalized measure of the consistency of A_i with respect to its neighbors and is the sum of differences between the estimated distance and the measured distance between the node and each of its neighbors. According to our studies, the percentage of improvement is higher for nodes with higher inconsistencies. The algorithm seeks to first improve the more inconsistent nodes, and hence, adds the consistency with a negative weight to the OOF. The notation all A_k in the second term denotes the average consistency function of the neighboring nodes of the node A_i. According to our studies, the more consistent the neighboring nodes are, the more improvement the results of the atomic multilateration would be. So $CN(all A_k)$ have a positive weight. The notion $CNX(A_i)$ determines the position of A_i with respect to the convex hull formed by its neighbors. $CNX(A_i)$ would be equal to one if A_i is inside the convex hull of its neighbors and zero otherwise. Since the nodes inside the convex hull are better optimization candidates, this term is added by a positive weight to OOF. The term $CL(A_i)$ is a measure of closeness of A_i to its neighbors. $CL(A_i)$ is the ratio of the smallest distance between two nodes in the network divided by the average distance to the neighboring nodes from A_i. The closer A_i is to its neighbors, the more accurately it can find its location. Thus, this term is also added by a positive weight.

If the improvement is negative, the algorithm enters the composite move round illustrated in lines 12-17. Since the location of a node affects the consistencies of its neighboring nodes, if no improvement occurs, the algorithm attempts to move two composite nodes together. The composite move runtime is the square of the runtime complexity of the multilateration procedure for a single node. The composite move has to search the space of two nodes at once. Therefore, the composite move would not be a wise move for a regular centralized algorithm.

However, our goal of developing centralized algorithm is to gain better insights for developing the localized location discovery algorithm. In localized algorithms, we assume that the communication costs put much more stringent constraints on the runtime and power consumption of the algorithm than the computation costs. Therefore, the attempt is not to optimize the computation parts of the algorithm, and thus composite moves are acceptable. The composite move is done on the two neighboring nodes that have the highest sum of OOF. The composite move also avoids adjusting the same pair of neighboring nodes. Hence, it also starts holding and aging the combination of two adjusted nodes using the same method as the iterative improvement phase.

The OOF's of the nodes are then updated and the algorithm exits the composite move round. After that, the GOF is reevaluated for defining the mode of the main loop at the next round. The algorithm continues within the two modes until the stopping condition of the main cycle is satisfied, i.e. until no negative improvement occurs for k consecutive cycles. When the main cycle terminates, the algorithm goes through the last GASP phase. During the last GASP phase, each node is adjusted for the last time, based on the priorities given by OOF, using the multilateration mechanism.

5.3 Localized FCII Location Discovery Algorithm

Two key constraints in wireless sensor network are communication bandwidth and energy consumption. In the current and pending technologies, energy consumption is dominated by needs for communication. Therefore, it is very important to develop algorithms that use as small level of communication as possible. Additionally, lower level of communication enhances both security and privacy. Therefore, there is a wide consensus that one of key research directions in wireless ad-hoc networks is development of localized algorithms - algorithms that require very low level of communication and that transmit information about themselves only to a small number of other nodes in the network. The natural way to measure to what extent some algorithm is localized is to analyze the required amount of single hop communication. Our goal in this section is to develop efficient localized algorithm for location discovery.

We make the following assumptions. The location discovery problem is not changed: we have n nodes and k of them (anchors) know their location. In addition, we know (with error) distances between nodes that can communicate. Furthermore, we assume that all nodes listen all the time and that any given point time exactly one node (with token) can talk. The token is initially assigned to a randomly selected node. The number of the nodes in the network is known in advance.

We directly use the CFII algorithm and atomic multilateration within it for location discovery calculation. Each Token node runs the CFII algorithm within its local realm. The key for low level of communication is to identify fast nodes that can accurately conclude their location and after that avoid assigning token to them again. Note that we assume that together with the token that the node transfers to one of its neighbors, each node transfers to all its neighbors information about all nodes in the network. This assumption can be changed, if dictated by security and privacy concerns. Once the node receives the token, it contacts all its neighbors using broadcast and they return to it their distances from the node. Therefore, the communication used for localized location discovery is simultaneously used for distance measurements.

In order to design efficient localized location discovery algorithm, one has to make two decisions: in which order to keep assigning the token, and when to estimate the location of a particular node. We make the first decision based on three criteria. The first is that we always prefer a node that has not been already visited or has been visited fewer times. The second criterion, in terms of its importance, is that we always prefer to visit an anchor node if it was not already visited. The final criterion is that at each step we try to learn as much as possible as soon as possible and therefore favor to assign the token to the neighbor that has the largest distance from the current node.

We determine the estimate of the location of the node when the following two conditions are satisfied: the node knows distances from at least four beacons (nodes that already have their locations estimated) and the node is inside of a convex hull formed by at least three of its neighbors. Important observation is that a node can estimate the location of other node when the conditions for other nodes are satisfied. In this case, the first node sends this information to that node at the end of the algorithm execution.

6 Applications

The global location discovery algorithm described in Section 5 is a general basis for location discovery. The algorithm does not assume any specific source of location error and the distance measurement error in the network. However, in certain scenarios, besides location discovery we may want to detect certain sources of distance inconsistencies in the network or we are aware in advance what are the sources of discrepancies, and we want to improve location discovery algorithm using that knowledge. For such cases we propose three extensions to a basic location discovery algorithm. Three applications that extend the location discovery algorithm are: calibration, skewing detection, and obstacles detection.

6.1 Calibration

Certain environmental conditions that prevail in the area where the network is deployed, can impact all or the majority of distance measurements in the network. For example, temperature variations in an area change the speed of sound, which is a parameter of some ranging techniques for sensor networks [10, 24]. To account for the impact of such conditions we scale all distance measurements in the network by a certain factor in order to adjust distance measurement consistencies so that their average value is 0.

If R_{ij} is the measured distance between the nodes A_i and A_j, and D_{ij} is the distance between location estimates for A_i and A_j in the current solution, then we determine the scaling coefficient K from:

$$\sum_{i=1}^{N}\sum_{j=1}^{N}(D_{ij} - KR_{ij}) = 0 \Rightarrow K = \sum_{i=1}^{N}\sum_{j=1}^{N}D_{ij}/\sum_{i=1}^{N}\sum_{j=1}^{N}R_{ij} \qquad (16)$$

Now, we multiply all distance measurements by K.

6.2   Skewing Detection

Skewing detection is designed for the cases where a small number of nodes report incorrect measurement. Incorrect measurements could be a result of the lack of calibration for a subset of nodes, or the result of several nodes intentionally sending incorrect measurements to all or to some of its neighbors. Our goal here is dual, as in the other two applications. We want to detect the nodes that interfere with the correct functioning of the network, while still aiming for an accurate estimate of the locations of nodes.

During an execution of the location discovery algorithm, we apply the objective function to a subset of distances and nodes. The eliminated distances and nodes outside the subset, are those highly inconsistent with the current solution. When a new solution is selected on the basis of the remaining distance measurements and nodes, the eliminated distances and nodes are considered again. For the next move, a new set of nodes and distances are eliminated from consideration.

6.3   Obstacles Detection

In many ways, obstacle detection is a special case of skewing detection. The most important difference is that instead of nodes sending incorrect information, there are obstacles in the area covered by the network. Obstacles impact distance measurements of the nodes in two distinctive ways. The distance measurement between two nodes can be incorrect, but those two nodes still communicate, or an obstacle can completely block the path between two nodes, so they do not have any distance measurements between themselves. The first case is detected when nodes whose distance between estimated locations is smaller than the transmission range, but they still cannot hear each other. The second case is detected when the distance measurements inconsistencies are located in the same area.

7   Conclusion

We have presented a survey of the key issues, trends and techniques for location discovery in wireless ad-hoc sensor networks. After describing the current state-of-the-art distance measurement methods and technologies, we discuss the main features of a number of the location discovery systems and algorithms proposed for an ad-hoc sensor networks. We elaborate on the relative advantages and limitations of each of the proposed solutions so far.

This analysis leads to the conclusion that there is a need for a location discovery method with a more sophisticated algorithmic structure. To address this needs, we propose a new location discovery algorithm that can bridge the gap between measurement inconsistencies and the overall performance of the location discovery. The approach is based on the insights about accuracy of atomic multilateration. It uses a new, non-greedy, iterative improvement algorithm that is well suited for localized implementation. Furthermore. The algorithm also can serve as a starting point and a building block for a number of important tasks in wireless sensor and information ad-hoc networks such as calibration, and skewing and obstacle detection.

References

[1] *AVL information Systems, Inc.*, (http://www.avlinfosys.com)

[2] P. Bahl and V. N. Padmanabhan, RADAR: an in-building RF-based user location and tracking system, *IEEE INFOCOM* Vol.2 (2000) pp.775-84.

[3] Smart sensors promise savings in electricity costs, *Berkeleyan, 6/7/2001.* (http://www.berkeley.edu/news/berkeleyan/2001/06/07_smart.html).

[4] N. Bulusu, J. Heidemann and D. Estrin, GPS-less Low Cost Outdoor Localization For Very Small Devices, *IEEE Personal Communications, Special Issue on "Smart Spaces and Environments"*, Vol.7 No.5 (2000) pp. 28-34.

[5] N. Bulusu, J. Heidemann, T. Tran, Self-configuring Localization Systems: Design and Experimental Evaluation. *Submitted for review to ACM Transactions on Embedded Computing Systems (ACM TECS)*, (August 2002).

[6] J. Caffery and G. Stuber, Overview of Radiolocation in CDMA Cellular Systems,*IEEE communication magazine*, (April 1999).

[7] A. Cerpa, J. Elson, D. Estrin, L. Girod, M. Hamilton and J. Zhao, Habitat monitoring: Application driver for wireless communications technology, *2001 ACM SIGCOMM Workshop on Data Communications in Latin America and the Caribbean*, (April 2001).

[8] L. Doherty, K. Pister and L. El Ghaoui. Convex Optimization Methods for Sensor Node Position Estimation *IEEE INFOCOM*, (2001) pp. 1655-1663.

[9] J. Gibson, *The mobile communications handbook*, IEEE Press (1999).

[10] L. Girod and D. Estrin, Robust range estimation using acoustic and multimodal sensing, *In Proceedings of the IEEE/RSJ International Conference on Intelligent Robots and Systems (IROS 2001)*, (October 2001).

[11] C. F. Gauss, *Theoria combinationis obsevationum erroribus minimis obnoxiae* Werke, Bd.4 (1810) p.1.

[12] A. Harter , A. Hopper, P. Steggles, A. Ward and P. Webster, The Anatomy of a Context-Aware Application, *ACM Sigmobile (Mobicom)*, (August 1999).

[13] J. Hightower, R. Want and G. Borriello, SpotON: An Indoor 3d Location Sensing Technology Based on RF Signal Strength, *UW CSE 2000-02-02, Univ. Washington, Seattle*, (Feb. 2000).

[14] J. Hightower and G. Borriello, Location Systems for Ubiquitous Computing, *IEEE Computer Magazine* Vol.34 No.8, (August 2001) pp. 57-66.

[15] B. Hofmann-Wellenhof, H. Lichtenegger, J. Collins, *Global Positioning System: Theory and Practice*, fourth edition, Springer Verlag (1997).

[16] F. Koushanfar. Iterative Fault-Tolerant Location Discovery in Ad-Hoc Wireless Sensor Networks, *MS thesis*, UCLA, (2001).

[17] S. Lin and B.W. Kernighan. An effective heuristic algorithm for the traveling-salesman problem. *Operations Research*, Vol.21 No.2 (1973) pp. 498-516.

[18] http://www.navcen.uscg.mil/loran/Default.htm#Link

[19] Technical Description of DC Magnetic Trackers, *Ascension Technology Corporation*, Burlington, Vt., (2001).

[20] N.B. Priyantha, A. Chakraborty and H. Balakrishnan, The Cricket Location-Support System, *ACM Sigmobile (Mobicom)*, (2000) pp. 32-43.

[21] N. Priyantha, A. Miu, H. Balakrishnan, and S. Teller. The Cricket Compass for Context-Aware Mobile Applications, *ACM Sigmobile (Mobicom)*, (2001) pp. 1-14.

[22] F. Raab et al., Magnetic Position and Orientation Tracking System, *IEEE Transactions on Aerospace and Electronic Systems*, (September 1979) pp. 709-717.

[23] C. Savarese , J. M. Rabaey and J. Beutel, Locationing In Distributed Ad-Hoc Wireless Sensor Networks. *ICASSP*, Vol.4 (2001) pp. 2037-2040.

[24] A. Savvides, C. Han and M. Srivastava, Dynamic Fine-Grained Localization in Ad-hoc Networks of Sensors, *ACM Sigmobile (Mobicom)*, (2001) pp. 166-179.

[25] C. Savarese , J. M. Rabaey, K. Langendoen, Robust Positioning Algorithms for Distributed Ad-Hoc Wireless Sensor Networks, *Usenix Annual Technical Conference*, (2001)

[26] G. Strang and K. Bore, *Linear Algebra, Geodesy, and GPS*, Wellesley-Cambridge, Wellesley, MA, (1997).

[27] R. Want, A. Hopper, V. Falcao and J. Gibbons, *The Active Badge Location System* ACM Transaction on Information Systems, (Jan. 1992), pp. 91-102.

Ad Hoc Wireless Networks: From Theory to Protocols[1]

P.R. Kumar
Department of Electrical and Computer Engineering, and
Coordinated Science Laboratory
University of Illinois, Urbana, IL 61801
E-mail: prkumar@uiuc.edu
and
Liang-Liang Xie
Institute of Systems Science
Chinese Academy of Sciences
Beijing 100080, China
E-mail: xie@mail.iss.ac.cn

Contents

[1]This material is based upon work partially supported by USARO under Contract Nos. DAAD19-00-1-0466 and DAAD19-01010-465, DARPA under Contract No. N00014-01-1-0576, AFOSR under Contract No. F49620-02-1-0217, DARPA/AFOSR unfer Contract No. F49620-02-1-0325, and NSF under Contract No. NSF ANI 02-21357. Any opinions, findings, and conclusions or recommendations expressed in this publication are those of the authors and do not necessarily reflect the views of the above agencies.

1   Introduction

Wireless networks simply consist of nodes radiating energy. Nodes can cooperate in complex manners to transport information. How then ought they to cooperate? Once this basic question is answered, one can determine what protocols are needed to execute the information transport strategy. Subsequently the task devolves to actually designing the particular protocols.

This chapter begins by addressing the fundamental strategic question of how wireless networks ought to be operated. By doing so, we address the longstanding gap, indeed chasm, between information theory and networks.

We provide a sound basis for current protocol development by showing that at least when the medium attenuates signals sufficiently, the current proposal of multi-hop transport with full decoding of packets at each hop, treating all interference as noise, is order optimal. This provides a bridge between the theory of what is ultimately achievable in wireless networks—network information theory, and the world of protocol development.

We then examine two protocols, for power control and media access control, which are necessitated by this strategy of simply treating interference as noise. We provide the reasoning behind and outline the details of the COMPOW protocol for power control, and the SEEDEX protocol for media access control.

In contrast, when the attenuation is sufficiently low, other strategies emerge as superior. One such is that of coherent multi-stage relaying with interference cancellation (CRIC). It is an intriguing question what situations allow such coherence to be realized. The emphasis in such scenarios is on the physical layer aspects of achieving coherence. Again this is an illustration of how information theory can point towards which protocols need to be designed.

Our work is applicable to all wireless networks where nodes can communicate by radios. This includes ad hoc networks as well as sensor networks. While the theoretical results in the first half of the chapter are applicable to both ad hoc networks as well as sensor networks, the emphasis of the protocol design in the latter half of the chapter is more geared towards ad hoc networks.

2 Two Fundamental Questions

Two questions one should ask about wireless networks are:

(i) How much traffic can they carry?

(ii) How should one operate them?

The first question is analogous to the question asked by Shannon [1] for a single link modeled as a discrete memoryless channel. Thus the answer to the question belongs to the realm of information theory for networks, which is also called multi-user information theory or network information theory. The reason for asking it is obvious. One should know what wireless networks can deliver, and also, importantly, what they cannot deliver. For example, if telephone modems are near the Shannon limit, then one can stop trying to build better telephone modems. So also for wireless networks.

The reason for asking the second question is also obvious, though the underlying reasons may be less so. Wireless networks, unlike wired networks, do not come with links. Rather, all that nodes do is simply radiate radio energy. Because of this, the ways in which nodes can possibly cooperate is huge. For example, a group of nodes could try to cancel the interference created by another group of nodes at a third group of nodes, rather than, more positively, relaying packets for each other. If our study of network information theory can point us to the right strategy for cooperation among the nodes, then we can determine what protocols are needed, and set about to design those protocols.

2.1   The Current Proposal for Ad Hoc Networks

The current proposal for operating ad hoc networks, around which a lot of activity is centered, is the following:

(i) Transport packets over multiple hops from their sources to their destinations.

(ii) Fully decode a packet at each hop, by treating all interference from other simultaneous transmissions as noise.

The first point gives us the abstraction of "wires in space," and makes wireless networks look like wired ones since each hop can be thought of as traversing a "link."

The second point has two aspects. To start with, it employs the notion of *digital regeneration*, which is at the heart of the whole digital revolution, since a packet is transmitted afresh at each hop. The other important feature is that when decoding the digital packet, all interfering transmissions are treated simply as noise, which leads to the classic problem of recovering a signal immersed in noise. The resulting receiver can therefore afford to be fairly simple, as opposed to, for example, other alternatives requiring interference cancellation, etc.

2.2   The Protocol Requirements that Emanate from the Current Proposal

The above proposal necessitates several protocols.

Since all interference is treated as noise, it gives rise to the need for *power control*. The reason is that one wants unwanted transmissions to not interfere too much, and so one wants the power of interfering transmissions to be properly regulated. (There are other reasons for power control too, such as the need to conserve battery energy).

Yet another protocol that is required is for *media access control*. The reason is that since all other transmissions are regarded as corrupting noise, one needs to regulate or avoid other simultaneous transmissions in the neighborhood of the receiver.

A third protocol that becomes necessary is for *routing*. Since one is using multiple hops to reach the desired destination, one needs to find a route to the destination.

2.3   The Need for a Theoretical Foundation of How to Operate Wireless Networks

It should be noted that the particular protocol suite that is required depends on how one chooses to operate wireless networks.

For example, if packets simply reached their destinations in one long hop by using a single high powered transmission, then there would be no need at all for any routing protocol.

Similarly, if nodes tried to cooperate by coherently transmitting to another node, then there would be a requirement for physical layer protocols for synchronizing the phase of signals.

The point is that the high level decision of how to operate wireless networks, (e.g., multi-hop transport with full decoding at each stage, treating all other interference as noise) determines what protocols need to be designed.

The fundamental issue that therefore arises *before* doing any protocol design is to determine, hopefully on a sound, theoretically well founded basis, what the mode of operation ought to be. This is the first goal of this chapter.

The difficulty, as we have already noted earlier, is that nodes in a wireless network simply radiate energy, and can therefore cooperate in rather complex ways. Technically, the design space for cooperation is infinite-dimensional. From this vast set of possibilities, one wants to find a particular best mode of operation. This is a notoriously difficult problem since it is an example of a problem in team theory, where different agents have different informations. In the specific communication context it belongs to the realm of network information theory.

Since the pioneering work of Shannon [1] on the rate at which information can be transferred over a single link, and how to do so, there has been much effort, for about the past five decades, to develop a similar theory for networks. Two situations that have been solved are: (i) the Gaussian broadcast channel where one node wants to simultaneously send different informations to several other nodes [2, 3, 4, 5], and (ii) the Gaussian multiple access channel where several nodes want to simultaneously send different informations to one node [6, 7]. However, in spite of much effort over the past thirty years, the capacity of even the three node network, where there is a single relay to help in information transfer, is unknown [8, 9]. So also is a system with two senders and two receivers; see [10, 11].

This void has led to a gap between the field of network information theory and the world of protocol development. In the next two sections we present recently obtained results [12] which help in bridging this gap, thus providing a sound basis for protocol development, at least under some attenuation scenarios.

3   A Theory of Information Transport in Wireless Networks

To make progress, we need to take more account of locations of nodes and distances between them than is usual, while still allowing for a general theory.

3.1   The Model of a Planar Network

Consider n nodes located on a plane. Let ρ_{ij} denote the distance between nodes i and j. We will suppose that nodes are separated by a distance of at least $\rho_{\min} > 0$. That is, $\rho_{ij} \geq \rho_{\min}$ for all i, j.

We also need to model how signals are attenuated as they traverse space. We will suppose that a signal's amplitude suffers an attenuation by a factor $ae^{-\gamma\rho}\rho^{-\delta}$ after it has traversed a distance ρ. The constant γ corresponds to *absorption*, and results in an attenuation of $(20\log_{10}e)\gamma$ db/meter. Generally, except in a vacuum [13], γ is positive, in which case we say that "there is absorption." However, we will also consider the case $\gamma = 0$ in our theory below. We will call the constant $\delta > 0$, the *path loss exponent*.

Let $x_i(t)$ be the signal transmitted by node i at discrete time instant t. Then the signal received by node j at time t, $y_j(t)$, is the superposition of attenuated transmissions by the other nodes, plus ambient white Gaussian noise of variance (i.e., power) σ^2. That is,

$$y_j(t) \;=\; \sum_{i \neq j} ae^{-\gamma\rho_{ij}}\rho_{ij}^{-\delta}x_i(t) + w_j(t),$$

where $w_j(t) \sim N(0, \sigma^2)$, and i.i.d.

We will consider one of two restrictions on the power available to nodes for their transmissions—either the total power available to all nodes for their transmissions is cumulatively bounded by P_{total}, or the individual powers available to nodes are each bounded by P_{ind}. That is, if P_i denotes the power used by node i, then either $\sum_{i=1}^{n} P_i \leq P_{total}$, or $P_i \leq P_{ind}$ for all i.

At time t, the signal transmitted by node i, $x_i(t)$, is allowed to depend on all its past observations $(y_i(0), y_i(1), \ldots, y_i(t-1))$ as well as any private information originating at node i destined for other destinations. This formulation is general in that it allows nodes to cooperate in any causal way. Similarly, a receiving node j can decode what was meant to be conveyed to it, based on all its past observations and any private information. Again, all manners of causal cooperation are allowed for in the formulation.

3.2 The Transport Capacity

Let (s, d) denote a source-destination pair, and suppose that $R = \{R_{sd} : 1 \leq s \leq n, 1 \leq d \leq n, s \neq d\}$ is a *feasible rate vector* that the wireless network can support for the $n(n-1)$ source-destination pairs. By this it is meant that given any tolerable probability of error $\epsilon > 0$, the network can send in a sufficiently long time interval $1 \leq t \leq T$, with probability of error not exceeding ϵ, TR_{sd} bits from source s to destination d, for each source-destination pair (s, d). This definition is standard in information theory; see [1]. The unit for measuring rate R_{sd} is bits/time unit, which we shall simply refer to as bits/sec, taking each time unit to be one second for simplicity.

Consider $\sum_{(s,d)} \rho_{sd} R_{sd}$, the distance weighted sum of rates over all the source-destination pairs. Its unit of measurement is bit-meters/second. We shall consider the maximum (or more precisely, supremum) value of this, over the set of all feasible rate vectors R,

$$C_T := \sup_{\text{Feasible rate vectors } R} \sum_{(s,d)} \rho_{sd} R_{sd}.$$

We call C_T the *transport capacity* of the network.

This transport capacity is analogous to the man-miles/year metric that airlines use. It is a natural metric giving credit for both bits hauled, as well as the distance over which they are hauled.

3.3 An Upper Bound on the Transport Capacity When $\gamma > 0$ or $\delta > 3$

The following theorem provides an information theoretic upper bound on what a planar network can deliver when either there is any absorption in the medium, i.e., $\gamma > 0$, or the path loss exponent $\delta > 3$.

Theorem 3.1 *If $\gamma > 0$ or $\delta > 3$, then*

$$C_T \leq \frac{c(a, \gamma, \delta, \rho_{\min})}{\sigma^2} P_{\text{total}}.$$

Or if each user is limited to P_{ind}, then

$$C_T \leq \frac{c(a, \gamma, \delta, \rho_{\min}) P_{\text{ind}}}{\sigma^2} \cdot n.$$

Here

$$
\begin{aligned}
c(a, \gamma, \delta, \rho_{min}) \quad &:= \quad \frac{a^2 2^{2\delta+7}}{\gamma^2 \rho_{min}^{2\delta+1}} \, e^{\frac{-\gamma\rho_{min}}{2}} \frac{\left(2 - e^{\frac{-\gamma\rho_{min}}{2}}\right)}{\left(1 - e^{\frac{-\gamma\rho_{min}}{2}}\right)} \quad \textit{if } \gamma > 0, \\[2mm]
&:= \quad \frac{a 2^{2\delta+5}(3\delta - 8)}{(\delta - 2)^2(\delta - 3)\rho_{min}^{2\delta-1}} \quad \textit{if } \gamma = 0 \textit{ and } \delta > 3.
\end{aligned}
$$

$$(1)$$

This shows that the transport capacity can, at best, scale linearly in the number of nodes. Note that the area A of the domain is $\Omega(n)$, since it grows at least linearly in the number of nodes when the distance between nodes is at least $\rho_{\min}$. Thus the scaling law is commensurate with the "square root scaling law" $0\left(\sqrt{An}\right)$ derived in [14], where the area of the domain was fixed as more nodes were added. Here we allow the area to grow with the number of nodes since attenuation does not simply scale with distance, and so, unlike in [14], the results cannot be scaled up or down by $\sqrt{A}$.

A few remarks on the square root scaling law derived in [14] are worth noting. The upper bound there was obtained under the assumption that interfering packets destructively collide with each other. However, that is not necessarily the case. To see this, consider two transmitters T_1 and T_2 simultaneously transmitting in the vicinity of a receiver R, as shown in Figure 1.

Suppose the receiver is really interested in the packet that T_1 is transmitting, which happens to be a low power transmission. Suppose, however, that T_2 is an interfering high power transmission. Then receiver R can first decode T_2's packet, since it is a high powered one. After that it can simply subtract T_2's signal, and recover T_1. Thus the receiver R has managed to successfully receive a low powered packet in the presence of high powered interference. The packets T_1 and T_2 certainly do not destructively collide.

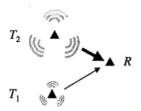

Figure 1: The low powered packet from T_1 and the high powered packet from T_2 do not collide at the receiver R.

The point that one should note is that interference is not interference—it is information.

Thus, the result obtained in the above Theorem, that the *same* order of the upper bound holds even when we do away with the assumption of destructive collisions, is striking. This, in fact, was the very reason we had to turn to information theory and establish that even when all modalities of cooperation are allowed, the "square root law" of [14] still holds.

3.4 The Optimality of Multi-Hop Transport When $\gamma > 0$ or $\delta > 3$

In many situations, as long as one can route traffic so that the load is evenly balanced with no bottlenecks, then one can indeed realize a linearly growing transport capacity $\Omega(n)$ by employing the multi-hop strategy outlined in Section 2.1. Since $O(n)$ is already known to be an upper bound for the case $\gamma > 0$ or $\delta > 3$, it therefore follows $\Theta(n)$ is indeed the optimal order for the transport capacity, and that the multi-hop strategy is order optimal. Thus, in such situations, we are able to identify the strategy around which further protocol work can be centered.

An example where such load balancing can be done is shown below.

Example

Consider n nodes located at the points with coordinates (i, j), $1 \leq i, j \leq \sqrt{n}$ in the plane, as shown in Figure 2.

Suppose every node on the left, i.e., nodes with coordinates $(1, j)$ for $1 \leq j \leq \sqrt{n}$, are $\sqrt{n}$ source nodes, and their corresponding destinations are the nodes on the right, located at $(\sqrt{n}, j)$, $1 \leq j \leq \sqrt{n}$, respectively. Then the straight line routing from left to right, shown in Figure 2, achieves load

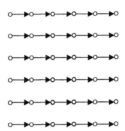

Figure 2: Multi-hop achieves a transport capacity of $\Omega(n)$ and is consequently order optimal.

balancing. Since there are $\sqrt{n}$ source-destination pairs, each sending $\Omega(1)$ bits/sec., over a distance $\sqrt{n}$, the transport capacity achieved is $\Omega(n)$. This is order optimal, since $O(n)$ is an upper bound as shown in Theorem 2.1, and it has been obtained by multi-hop transport with full decoding of each packet at each stage, assuming all interference is noise.

3.5 Near Optimal Multi-Hop Architecture for Randomly Located Nodes with Random Destinations

When $\gamma > 0$ or $\delta > 3$, it turns out due to the above results that we pretty much know how wireless networks should be operated.

Consider n nodes randomly (uniformly, i.i.d) located in a domain of area A square meters. Suppose that each node picks another randomly located point in the domain, and chooses the node nearest that point as its destination. Thus, we have the scenario of n randomly located nodes with a random choice of destination node for each of the n nodes.

This situation has been addressed in [14], under the collision model. Suppose we further restrict all nodes to have the same range r, and suppose a receiver successfully receives a packet from a transmitter when (i) the distance between the receiver and the transmitter is less than r, and (ii) there is no other simultaneous transmitter within a distance $(1 + \Delta)r$ of the receiver. Here $\Delta > 0$ models the requirement for a reception reasonably free of interference.

Then it has been shown in [14] that every node can be furnished a throughput of $\Theta\left(\frac{1}{\sqrt{n \log n}}\right)$ for its chosen destination, with probability approaching one as $n \to +\infty$. It is worth noting that this yields a transport capacity of $\Theta\left(\sqrt{\frac{n}{\log n}}\right)$ since the distances are about $\Theta\left(\sqrt{A}\right)$ on average, and there are a total of n source destination pairs.

This achieved transport capacity differs from the optimal achievable $O\left(\sqrt{n}\right)$ (in the case of a domain of fixed area) by at most a factor $\sqrt{\log n}$, which is relatively small in comparison to $\sqrt{n}$. Thus, it is nearly optimal. Moreover, it should be noted that this near optimality has been achieved by choosing a *common* range, or power, for all transmissions sent by all nodes in the network; there is no need for per-packet power control.

The next question is: What is the strategy which achieves this? This is also well understood [14]. Divide the domain into cells of roughly equal size, neither too thin nor too long, and such that each contains about $\Theta(\log n)$ nodes. Nodes can choose a range of about $\Theta\left(\sqrt{\frac{\log n}{n}}\right)$, which is chosen such that every node can communicate in one hop with all nodes in neighboring cells. Packets are relayed from cell to cell in a nearly straight line path, until they reach their destinations. Packet transmissions are scheduled to avoid collisions, which can also be done in a fair manner. This architecture is illustrated in Figure 3. It is nearly order optimal.

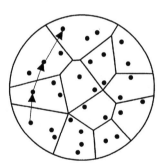

Figure 3: A nearly optimal architecture for wireless networks.

4   The Case of $\gamma = 0$ and Low δ

When there is absolutely no absorption, i.e., $\gamma = 0$, and δ is low, then another strategy, different from that in Section 2.1, emerges as optimal in some situations.

4.1   The CRIC Strategy

As earlier, the strategy we consider will have packets progressing from node to node. However, the scheme differs from that in Section 2.1 in two key ways. First, all upstream nodes *coherently* cooperate to send the packet to the next downstream node. Second, when a node is receiving packets, it *cancels the interference* from all packets being transmitted by other downstream nodes which it has already decoded. We call this strategy *coherent multi-stage relaying with interference cancellation* (CRIC).

At time k, node 1 sends a packet, say packet k, to node 2. Then nodes 1 and 2 coherently cooperate at time $k+1$ and send the packet k to node 3. Then nodes 1, 2, and 3, coherently cooperate at time $k+2$ and send the packet k to node 4, and so on.

To understand how decoding works, consider how node 3 decodes packet k. First, at time k, packet k is in transit from node 1 to node 2, packet $(k-1)$ is in transit to node 3, packet $(k-2)$ is in transit to node 4, and so on. Subsequently at time $(k+1)$ (see Figure 4), packet $(k+1)$ is in transit

Figure 4:   Coherent multi-stage relaying with interference cancellation (CRIC).

to node 2, packet k is in transit to node 3, packet $(k-1)$ is in transit to node 2, and so on. At time $(k+1)$, assume that node 3 has already successfully decoded packets $(k-1)$, $(k-2)$, $(k-3)$, ..., etc. Then it can decode packet k at time $(k+1)$ based on two receptions: receiving an attenuated version of packet k while it was being sent by node 1 to node 2 at time k, and subsequently at time $(k+1)$ receiving packet k from nodes 1 and 2 coherently cooperating with each other, in the presence of the interfering transmission of packet $(k+1)$ from node 1 to node 2. Both these receptions are additionally corrupted by the ambient noise.

4.2   Unbounded Transport Capacity for Finite Transmit Power

When $\gamma = 0$ and $\delta < \frac{3}{2}$, then it turns out that for any arbitrarly large value of c, there exists a network of nodes lying on a straight line, such that $C_T \geq c$ even when the total power used by all nodes for their transmission is restricted to being no more than P_{total}. Interestingly, the strategy which provides unbounded transport capacity is CRIC.

Thus we see that this different strategy emerges for our consideration under low attenuation scenarios. Essential to this strategy is (i) achieving coherence in transmissions, and (ii) cancelling interference. Both these require more physical layer attention than before. Thus, the burden on physical layer protocols is much higher than earlier.

Again, we see fundamental strategy providing the direction for protocol development and guiding it.

Whether such coherence can be achieved depends on node locations as well as channel conditions. Similarly, for performing interference cancellation, one needs good channel state information. Thus, it is intriguing whether and under what physical conditions this unbounded transport capacity can be approached.

4.3   Superlinear Scaling Under $\gamma = 0$ and $\frac{1}{2} < \delta < 1$ for Nodes Arranged on a Straight Line

In fact, when the nodes are on a straight line, and the path loss exponent is $\frac{1}{2} < \delta < 1$ with no absorption at all, then superlinear scaling of the transport capacity is feasible. Clearly with three-dimensional propagation, $\delta < 1$ is impossible to attain with $\gamma = 0$ since it corresponds to less than inverse square law attenuation. The challenge is thus to see if the examples shown in [12] can be generalized to planar or even three-dimensional layouts, but with $\delta > 1$.

The strategy for attaining such superlinear scaling in the case of networks with nodes lying on a straight line is once again CRIC.

5   Power Control: The COMPOW Protocol

We now turn to the design of a protocol for power control. The first problem that one faces is in deciding which layer to locate power control in. Should power control be regarded as a physical layer problem (as is done in cellular systems) because power influences signal quality? Or should power control be regarded as a network layer protocol because the choice of power levels determines which links will be available, and thus determines what routes can be used? Or should power control be regarded as a transport layer problem because power affects interference and thus congestion? Thus, the first issue that one faces is of conceptualization.

Our design begins by noting that bidirectional links are important for wireless networks. Assuming a relatively constant level of interference across the domain, such bidirectionality is attained when all nodes use the same power. This is so, even if the wireless footprint of transmissions is distorted by the presence of obstacles, etc., due to reciprocity in electromagnetic receptions.

Such bidirectional links are important since they allow link level ACKs, which we feel are important given the unreliability of the wireless medium, to reach the transmitter. Equal power level usage by all nodes also makes feasible the silencing feature of the IEEE 802.11 protocol, where a CTS packet is used to silence nodes near the receiver. The presumption is that only those nodes can interfere with the receivers as those that are reached by the CTS packet. This implicitly assumes equality of power levels. Similarly, bidirectional links are also important for the distributed Bellman-Ford algorithm to work properly with hop count as the metric.

Since a common power level adopted by all nodes makes bidirectionality feasible in the presence of roughly equal interference, let us adopt that strategy.

The next issue is the choice of the common power level. If it is too large then there is too much interference. If it is too small then it can lead to network disconnectivity. In fact, the theory of [14] shows that the smallest common power level at which the network is connected leads to the optimum transport capacity order.

It can additionally be shown that such a strategy also leads to energy efficient routes, see [15].

So let us strive to attain just such a power level—one at which the network is just connected. At this point, we immediately recognize that this is a *network layer problem*. The reason is that connectivity is a notion that arises only at the network layer—not below it. Also power control has to be solved at the network layer since routing depends on it. Thus, we need a joint solution for power control and routing situated at the network layer.

This can be done in a clean and modular way with any pro-active or table driven routing protocol, as follows. Consider a PCMCIA card, which has, say 6 power levels. (Such are available off the shelf currently). We will run several routing daemons in user space, one for each of the power levels. Such routing tables can be maintained by exchanging routing table updates with nearest neighbors, which is typically done by UDP. Thus, one simply gives each routing daemon a port number, and UDP port demultiplexing ensures that routing table updates at a certain power level reach the routing table being maintained for that power level.

Next, one simply scans the routing tables for each power level and compares the number of nodes for which connectivity is available with those that can be reached at the highest power level. Then one gives permission to the routing table of the lowest power level which has the same connectivity as that at the maximum power level to write itself into the kernel routing table.

This ensures that data packets are routed according to that routing table of lowest power level at which the node thinks it can get universal connectivity. This power level is informed to the driver as the default power level.

However routing table update packets carry special information which instructs the card to send them out at the power level corresponding to the routing table.

A scheduling algorithm is used to bunch packets of the same power level together to avoid frequent power changes.

This protocol, called COMPOW (for common power level), has been implemented on Linux laptops; see [15].

To summarize, COMPOW has the following properties:

(i) It exploits the theoretical result that a common power level which just provides connectivity is asymptotically optimal when nodes are uniformly distributed. Thus there is no need, asymptotically at least, for per-packet power control.

(ii) It is nearly optimal not only with respect to the transport capacity, but it also provides nearly optimal energy efficient routes.

(iii) It is a network layer protocol which can be employed in a plug and play fashion with any table driven, pro-active routing protocol.

(iv) The software architecture is modular (it uses parallel modality) and is easy to implement. It has, in fact, been implemented.

One could, however, envision scenarios where one faraway node drives all the other nodes to a higher common power level in COMPOW. Another protocol, called CLUSTERPOW, attempts to avoid this by clustering nodes; see [16]. Yet another protocol, MINPOW, simply finds routes of least-energy usage. It does so without any physical layer support or location information; see [16].

6   Media Access Control: The SEEDEX Protocol

We now turn to the design of a media access control protocol. The media access control problem is to restrict transmissions by other nodes in the vicinity of a receiver, in order to avoid destructive packet collisions.

The IEEE 802.11 protocol attempts to do so by a four phase RTS-CTS-DATA-ACK handshake. However, such a protocol is wasteful since it silences both the neighborhoods of the transmitter as well as the receiver, when only the neighborhood of the receiver needs to be silenced. In addition, to prevent ALOHA like instability (see [17]) caused by repeated retransmissions in congested situations, it employs exponential backoff counters, which have the potential to migrate to high values and thus provide low throughput.

Indeed, a scaling experiment reported in [18] showed that the per node throughput degraded according to a $\frac{c}{n^{1.68}}$ power law. In that experiment, there was no routing table overhead since routing tables were hardwired, and no TCP overhead since UDP was used. This points to a possible problem with the IEEE 802.11 protocol, which we suspect performs poorly due to the backoff counters and excessive silencing of nodes when faced with congestion. More recent efforts show that a model of the exponential backoff roughly explains a power law with exponent more than one, in the non-asymptotic regime.

We now describe the design of another MAC protocol, called SEEDEX, which attempts to avoid silencing two neighborhoods, as well as to make reservations without a handshake for each and every packet.

Let us suppose that nodes could publish their schedules to other nodes. By a "schedule," we mean a labeling of all future slots according to whether the node will be listening on that slot and refraining from transmission; or whether it may utilize that slot for transmission. One hopes that if all nodes know the schedules of all other nodes, then they can schedule their transmissions in such a way as to avoid or minimize collisions. Three questions arise: How should nodes choose their schedules? How can they efficiently publish them precisely to other interested parties? Last, how should nodes exploit knowledge of each other's schedules to determine when to transmit?

The question of how to choose a schedule has a simple answer. One can just choose a random schedule. That is, with probability p $(0 < p < 1)$ one can simply mark a slot as a "possibly transmit" slot, or with complementary probability $(1-p)$, mark it as a "definitely listen" slot. Calculations, see [19], show that a value of p around 0.2 is a good choice when nodes have about six neighbors each.

The next question of how to publish schedules also has a simple answer, given that schedules are chosen randomly. One only needs to publish the *seed* of one's own pseudo-random number generator to others. Other nodes can then reconstruct the schedule from the seed. (Actually, instead of publishing the seed, which is the initial state of the pseudo-random number generator, one can publish its current state. This avoids issues such as staleness, synchronization on what was the initial time, allowing entry of new nodes, etc). The remaining issue is whom to publish it to, and how.

Each node only needs to inform other nodes in its two-hop neighborhood of its schedule, since collisions only arise from neighbors of neighbors—the so called hidden terminal problem. Now, by doing a fan-in followed by a fan out of the seeds of one's one-hop neighbors, one determines all the seeds in one's two-hop neighborhood. Doing this periodically maintains the currency of the schedules.

Finally, how does one exploit knowledge of schedules? Suppose, in Figure 5, node T wishes to send a packet to node R in a slot. Suppose it knows

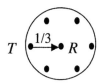

Figure 5: A node T with a packet to transmit in a "possibly transmit" state, transmits it with probability $\frac{1}{3}$, when there are 2 other neighbors of its receiver R also in a "possibly transmit" state (shown as darkened circles).

(through seed exchange) that there are m other neighbors of R also in a "possibly transmit" state. Then it could simply transmit the packet with probability $\frac{1}{m+1}$. The hope is that, if the other m neighbors of R also do the same, then there is a large chance that exactly one of the packets is transmitted in the slot. However, this is not completely accurate because another neighbor of R may be wanting to transmit its packet not to R, but to some other R', and the node R' may have a different number of its neighbors m' in a "possibly transmit" node. Such considerations do not, however, cause too much of a major difference, and so our reasoning is only approximate, but nevertheless sufficient for our purposes.

When the system is in light traffic, nodes may not have messages to transmit in a "possibly transmit" slot, and so a node with a message could be aggressive and choose to transmit with probability $\frac{\alpha}{m+1}$ where α is larger than 1.

This protocol, concerning which more details can be found in [19], is called the SEEDEX protocol. To summarize, it uses schedules, consisting of "possibly transmit" or "definitely listen" slots, which are randomly generated, and exchanged in a fan-in, fan-out procedure by exchanging periodically the states of pseudo-random number generators. A node then transmits its packet in a "possibly transmit" slot with a probability proportional to the reciprocal of the total number of neighbors of its intended receiver which are also in a "possibly transmit" slot.

This scheme can be further extended to employ an RTS-CTS-DATA-ACK four phase handshake, a la IEEE 802.11. This can be done by simply using SEEDEX for the RTS-CTS reservation part of the handshake. This protocol is referred to as SEEDEX-R.

This scheme has been implemented on our Linux laptops to show the proof of concept. Two difficulties were confronted in using existing off-the-shelf hardware. One was the inability to turn off the carrier sensing and subsequent retransmission efforts on the wireless PCMCIA cards used. This was circumvented by padding idle time before and after slots to ignore carrier sensing reverberations. A second difficulty was the need for clock synchronization to employ the slotted protocol. Since physical layer information is currently unavailable from the cards, it was necessary to do clock synchronization in software. Both these modifications are necessary with current hardware, but hopefully not with future hardware, and detract from throughput performance.

7 Concluding Remarks

The theme of this chapter is the connection between network information theory and protocol development.

When the propagation medium has any absorption ($\gamma > 0$) or has path loss exponent $\delta > 3$, then the transport capacity of wireless networks is bounded by the "square-root law". This square-root upper bound can, in fact, be attained in many situations by following multi-hop transport with full decoding of packets at each stage, treating all interference as noise. In all such cases, multi-hop transport attains the optimal order that the transport capacity can grow at. In fact, if nodes are randomly distributed, and the destinations are also randomly chosen, then such multi-hop transport is almost optimal. These results provide the critical connection between network information theory and protocol development.

These results are exploited in developing a power control protocol, COM-POW, and a media access control protocol, SEEDEX. Such protocols are necessitated by the strategy which treats interference as noise.

In contrast to the attenuation regime above, when there is no absorption at all ($\gamma = 0$), and the path loss exponent $\delta < \frac{3}{2}$, then other strategies emerge as superior. One such is the strategy of coherent multi-stage relaying with interference cancellation. Such a strategy requires more physical layer support, and points to the direction in which protocol efforts are to be directed in such attenuation regimes. It is an intriguing question what are the situations in which it can be utilized profitably.

References

[1] C. E. Shannon, "A mathematical theory of communication," *Bell Syst. Tech. J.*, vol. 27, pp. 379–423, 1948.

[2] T. Cover, "Broadcast channels," *IEEE Trans. Inform. Theory*, vol. 18, pp. 2–14, 1972.

[3] P. Bergmans, "Random coding theorem for broadcast channels with degraded components," *IEEE Trans. Inform. Theory*, vol. 19, pp. 197–207, 1973.

[4] P. Bergmans, "A simple converse for broadcast channels with additive white Gaussian noise," *IEEE Trans. Inform. Theory*, vol. 20, pp. 279–280, 1974.

[5] T. Cover, "Comments on broadcast channels," *IEEE Trans. Inform. Theory*, vol. 44, pp. 2524–2530, 1998.

[6] R. Ahlswede, "Multi-way communication channels," in *Proceedings of the 2nd Int. Symp. Inform. Theory (Tsahkadsor, Armenian S.S.R.),*

(Prague), pp. 23–52, Publishing House of the Hungarian Academy of Sciences, 1971.

[7] H. Liao, *Multiple access channels.* PhD thesis, University of Hawaii, Honolulu, HA, 1972. Department of Electrical Engineering.

[8] E. C. Van der Meulen, "Three-terminal communication channels," *Adv. Appl. Prob.*, vol. 3, pp. 120–154, 1971.

[9] T. Cover and A. E. Gamal, "Capacity theorems for the relay channel," *IEEE Trans. Inform. Theory*, vol. 25, pp. 572–584, 1979.

[10] C. E. Shannon, "Two-way communication channels," in *Proceedings of the 4th Berkeley Symp. Math. Stat. Prob.*, (Berkeley, CA), pp. 611–644, University of California Press, 1961.

[11] A. E. Gamal, "The capacity region of a class of deterministic interference channels," *IEEE Transactions on Information Theory*, vol. 28, pp. 343–346, 1982.

[12] L. Xie and P. R. Kumar, "A network information theory for wireless communication: Scaling laws and optimal operation." Submitted to *IEEE Transactions on Information Theory*, April 12 2002.

[13] M. Franceschetti, J. Bruck, and L. Schulman, "Microcellular systems, random walks and wave propagation." To appear in *Proceedings of the IEEE Symposium on Antennas and Propagation Society* (IEEE AP-S 2002, San Antonio, TX), June 2002.

[14] P. Gupta and P. R. Kumar, "The capacity of wireless networks," *IEEE Transactions on Information Theory*, vol. IT-46, pp. 388–404, March 2000.

[15] S. Narayanaswamy, V. Kawadia, R. S. Sreenivas, and P. R. Kumar, "Power control in ad-hoc networks: Theory, architecture, algorithm and implementation of the COMPOW protocol," in *European Wireless Conference – Next Generation Wireless Networks: Technologies, Protocols, Services and Applications*, (Florence, Italy), pp. 156–162, Feb 25–28 2002.

[16] V. Kawadia and P. R. Kumar, "Power Control and Clustering in Ad Hoc Networks." To appear in *Proceedings of INFOCOM2003*, San Francisco, March 30 - April 3, 2003.

[17] D. Bertsekas and R. Gallager, *Data Networks*. Englewood Cliffs, NJ: Prentice-Hall, 1987.

[18] P. Gupta, R. Gray, and P. R. Kumar, "An experimental scaling law for ad hoc networks." University of Illinois, May 16 2001.

[19] R. Rozovsky and P. R. Kumar, "SEEDEX: A MAC protocol for ad hoc networks," in *Proceedings of the 2001 ACM International Symposium on Mobile Ad Hoc Networking and Computing*, (Long Beach, CA), pp. 67–75, Oct 4-5 2001.

AD HOC WIRELESS NETWORKING
X. Cheng, X. Huang and D.-Z. Du (Eds.) pp. 197 - 264

Applications of Computational Geometry in Wireless Networks

Xiang-Yang Li
Department of Computer Science
Illinois Institute of Technology, Chicago, IL 60616
E-mail: `xli@cs.iit.edu`

Contents

1 Introduction

Ad Hoc Wireless Networks Due to its potential applications in various situations such as battlefield, emergency relief, and so on, wireless networking has received significant attention over the last few years. There are no wired infrastructures or cellular networks in *ad hoc* wireless network. Each mobile node has a transmission range. Node v can receive the signal from node u if node v is within the transmission range of the sender u. Otherwise, two nodes communicate through multi-hop wireless links by using intermediate nodes to relay the message. Consequently, each node in the wireless network also acts as a router, forwarding data packets for other nodes. In this survey, we consider that each wireless node has an omni-directional antenna. This is attractive because a single transmission of a node can be received by many nodes within its vicinity which, we assume, is a disk centered at the node. In addition, we assume that each node has a low-power Global Position System (GPS) receiver, which provides the position information of the node itself. If GPS is not available, the distance between neighboring nodes can be estimated on the basis of incoming signal strengths. Relative co-ordinates of neighboring nodes can be obtained by exchanging such information between neighbors [1].

Wireless ad hoc networks can be subdivided into two classes: *static* and *mobile*. In static networks, the position of a wireless node does not change or changes very slowly once the node was deployed. Typical example of such static networks includes sensor networks. In mobile networks, wireless nodes move arbitrarily. Since mobile wireless networks change their topology frequently and often without any regular pattern, topology maintenance and routing in such networks are challenging tasks. For the sake of the simplicity, we assume that the nodes are quasi-static during the short period of topology reconstruction or route finding.

We consider a wireless ad hoc network consisting of a set V of n wireless nodes distributed in a two-dimensional plane. By a proper scaling, we assume that all nodes have the maximum transmission range equal to one unit. These wireless nodes define a *unit disk graph* UDG(V) in which there is an edge between two nodes if and only if their Euclidean distance is at most one.

Computational Geometry Computational geometry emerged from the field of algorithms design and analysis in the late 70s. It studies various problems [2, 3, 4] from computer graphics, geographic information system, robotics, scientific computing, wireless networks recently, and others, in which geometric algorithms could play some fundamental roles. Most geometric algorithms are designed for studying the structural properties, searching, inclusion or exclusion relations, of a set of points, a set of hyperplanes, or both. For example, the structural properties include the convex hull, intersections, hyperplane arrangement, triangulation (Delaunay, regular, and so on), Voronoi diagram, and so on. The query operations often include point location, range searching (orthogonal, unbounded, or some variations) and so on.

In this survey, we concentrate on how to apply some structural properties of a point set for wireless networks as we treat wireless devices as two-dimensional points.

Networking and Routing It is common to separate the network design problem from the management and control of the network in the communication network literature. The separation is very convenient and helps to significantly simplify these two tasks, which are already very complex on its own. Nevertheless, there is a price to be paid for this modularity as the decisions made at the network design phase may strongly affect the network management and control phase. In particular, if the issue of designing efficient routing schemes is not taken into account by the network designers, then the constructed network might not be suited for supporting a good routing scheme. Wireless ad hoc network needs some special treatment as it intrinsically has its own special characteristics and some unavoidable limitations compared with traditional wired networks. Wireless nodes are often powered by batteries only and they often have limited memories. Therefore, it is more challenging to design a network topology for wireless ad hoc networks, which is suitable for designing an efficient routing scheme to save energy and storage memory consumption, than the traditional wired networks.

In technical terms, the question we deal with is therefore whether it is possible (if possible, then how) to design a network, which is a subgraph of the unit disk graph, such that it ensures both attractive network features such as bounded node degree, low-stretch factor, and linear number of links, and attractive routing schemes such as localized routing with guaranteed performances.

Network Structures in Wireless Networks The size of the unit disk graph could be as large as the square order of the number of network nodes. So we want to construct a subgraph of the unit disk graph $UDG(V)$, which is sparse, can be constructed locally in an efficient way, and is still relatively good compared with the original unit disk graph for routes' quality.

Unlike the wired networks that typically have fixed network topologies, each node in a wireless network can potentially change the network topology by adjusting its transmission range and/or selecting specific nodes to forward its messages, thus, controlling its set of neighbors. The primary goal of topology control in wireless networks is to maintain network connectivity, optimize network lifetime and throughput, and make it possible to design power-efficient routing. Not every connected subgraph of the unit disk graph plays the same important role in network designing. One of the perceptible requirements of topology control is to construct a subgraph such that the shortest path connecting any two nodes in the subgraph is not much longer than the shortest path connecting them in the original unit disk graph. This aspect of path quality is captured by the *stretch factor* of the subgraph. A subgraph with constant stretch factor is often called a *spanner* and a spanner is called a *sparse spanner* if it has only a linear number of links. In this survey, we review and study how to construct a spanner (a sparse network topology) efficiently for a set of static wireless nodes.

The other imperative requirement for network topology control in wireless ad hoc networks is the fault tolerance. To guarantee a good fault tolerance, the underlying network structure must be at least bi-connected, i.e., there are at least two disjoint paths for any pair of wireless nodes. Here, without doubt, we assume that the original unit disk graph is bi-connected.

Restricting the size of the network has been found to be extremely important in reducing the amount of routing information. The notion of establishing a subset of nodes which perform the routing has been proposed in many routing algorithms [5, 6, 7, 8]. These methods often construct a virtual backbone by using the connected dominating set [9, 10, 11], which is often constructed from dominating set or maximal independent set.

Routing Many routing algorithms were proposed recently for wireless ad hoc networks. The routing protocols proposed may be categorized as table-driven protocols or demand-driven protocols. A good survey may be found in [12].

Table-driven routing protocols maintain up-to-date routing information between every pair of nodes. The changes to the topology are maintained by propagating updates of the topology throughout the network. Destination-sequenced Distance-Vector Routing (DSDV) [13] and Zone-Routing Protocol (ZRP) [14, 15] are two of the table driven protocols proposed recently. The mobility nature of the wireless networks prevent these table-driven routing protocols from being widely used in large scale wireless ad hoc networks. Thus, on-demand routing protocols are preferred.

Source-initiated on-demand routing creates routes only when desired by the source node. The methodologies that have been proposed include the Ad-Hoc On-Demand Distance Vector Routing (AODV) [16], the Dynamic Source Routing (DSR) [17], and the Temporarily Ordered Routing Algorithm (TORA) [18]. In addition, the Associativity Based Routing (ABR) [19] and Signal Stability Routing (SSR) use various criteria for selecting routes.

Introducing a hierarchical structure into routing has also been used in many protocols such as the Clusterhead Gateway Switch Routing (CGSR)

[20], the Fisheye Routing [21, 22], and the Hierarchical State Routing [23]. Dominating set based methods were also adopted by several researchers [6, 7, 8]. To facilitate this, several methods [24, 9, 10, 25] were proposed to approximate the minimum dominating set or the minimum connected dominating set problems in centralized and/or distributed ways.

Route discovery can be very expensive in communication costs, thus reducing the response time of the network. On the other hand, explicit route maintenance can be even more costly in the explicit communication of substantial routing information and the usage of memory scarcity of wireless network nodes. The geometric nature of the multi-hop ad-hoc wireless networks allows a promising idea: localized routing protocols.

Localized routing does not require the nodes to maintain routing tables, a distinct advantage given the scarce storage resources and the relatively low computational power available to the wireless nodes. More importantly, given the numerous changes in topology expected in ad-hoc networks, no re-computation of the routing tables is needed and therefore we expect a significant reduction in the overhead. Thus localized routing is scalable. Localized routing is also uniform, in the sense that all the nodes execute the same protocol when deciding to which other node to forward a packet.

But localized routing is challenging to design, as even guaranteeing the successful arrival at the destination of the packet is a non-trivial task. This task was successfully solved by Bose et al. [26] (see also [27]) thus opening the way for a second stage of research, focusing on improving the *efficiency* of localized routings. Localized routing also has no built-in mechanism to avoid congestion by overloading nodes. Mauve *et al.* [28] conducted an excellent survey of position-based localized routing protocols.

Organization   The rest of the survey is organized as follows. In Section 2, we first review some definitions necessary for more detailed review of current progress of applying computational geometry techniques to wireless ad hoc networks. Specifically, we specify how the wireless network is modeled in this survey, review some geometry structures, define the graph spanners, and introduce the localized algorithm concept. In Section 3, we review in detail the geometry structures that are suitable for the topology control in wireless ad hoc networks, especially the structures with bounded stretch factor, or with bounded node degree, or planar structures. We also review the current status of controlling the transmission power so the total or the maximum transmission power is minimized without sacrificing the network connectivity. In Section 4, state of the art of constructing virtual backbone for wireless networks is reviewed. As there are many heuristics proposed in this area, we concentrate on the ones that have theoretic performance guarantees or are popular. After reviewing the geometric structures, we review the so called localized routing methods in Section 5. Many routing algorithms were proposed in the literature. We concentrate on the localized routing protocols as they utilize the geometry nature of the wireless ad hoc networks. Location service protocols are also discussed. Section 6 reviews the broadcasting protocols that apply the geometry nature to guarantee the performance. In Section 7, we review the current status of applying stochastic geometry to study the connectivity, capacity, etc, in wireless networks. We conclude the survey in Section 8 by pointing out some possible future research questions.

2   Preliminaries

2.1   Power-Attenuation Model

Energy conservation is a critical issue in *ad hoc* wireless network for the node and network life, as the nodes are powered by batteries only. Each mobile node typically has a portable set with transmission and reception processing capabilities. To transmit a signal from a node to the other node, the power consumed by these two nodes consists of the following three parts. First, the source node needs to consume some power to prepare the signal. Second, in the most common power-attenuation model, the power required to support the transmission between two nodes is dependent on their distance. Finally, when a node receives the signal, it needs consume some power to receive, store and then process that signal. The power cost $p(e)$ of a link $e = uv$ is then defined as the power consumed for transmitting signal from u to node v.

In the most common power-attenuation model, the power needed to support a link uv is $\|uv\|^\beta$, where $\|uv\|$ is the Euclidean distance between u and v, β is a real constant between 2 and 5 dependent on the wireless transmission environment. This power consumption is typically called *path loss*. In this survey, we assume that the path loss is the major part of power consumption to transmit signals.

Notice that, practically, there is some other overhead cost for each device to receive and then process the signal. For simplicity, this overhead cost can be integrated into one cost, which is almost the same for all nodes. Thus, we will use c to denote such constant overhead. In most results surveyed here, it is assumed that $c = 0$.

2.2   Geometry Structures

Several geometrical structures have been studied recently both by computational geometry scientists and network engineers. Here we review the definitions of some of them which could be used in the wireless networking applications. Let $G = (V, E)$ be a geometric graph defined on V.

The *minimum spanning tree* of G, denoted by MST(G), is the tree belong to E that connects all nodes and whose total edge length is minimized. MST(G) is obviously one of the sparsest possible connected subgraph, but its stretch factor can be as large as $n - 1$.

The *relative neighborhood graph*, denoted by RNG(G), is a geometric concept proposed by Toussaint [29]. It consists of all edges $uv \in E$ such that there is no point $w \in V$ with edges uw and wv in E satisfying $\|uw\| < \|uv\|$ and $\|wv\| < \|uv\|$. Thus, an edge uv is included if the intersection of two circles centered at u and v and with radius $\|uv\|$ do not contain any vertex w from the set V such that edges uw and wv are in E. Notice if G is a directed graph, then edges uw and wv also are directed in the above definition, i.e., we have $\overrightarrow{uw}$ and $\overrightarrow{wv}$ instead of uw and wv.

Let $disk(u,v)$ be the disk with diameter uv. Then, the *Gabriel graph* [30] GG(G) contains an edge uv from G if and only if $disk(u,v)$ contains no other vertex $w \in V$ such that there exist edges uw and wv from G satisfying $\|uw\| < \|uv\|$ and $\|wv\| < \|uv\|$. Same to the definition of RNG(G), if G is a directed graph, then edges uw and wv also are directed in the above definition of GG(G), i.e., we use $\overrightarrow{uw}$ and $\overrightarrow{wv}$ instead. GG(G) is a planar graph (that is, no two edges cross each other) if G is the complete graph. It is easy to show that RNG(G) is a subgraph of the Gabriel graph GG(G). For an undirected and connected graph G, both GG(G) and RNG(G) are connected and contain the minimum spanning tree of G.

The *Yao graph* with an integer parameter $k \geq 6$, denoted by $\overrightarrow{YG}_k(G)$, is defined as follows. At each node u, any k equally-separated rays originated at u define k cones. In each cone, choose the shortest edge uv among all edges from u, if there is any, and add a directed link $\overrightarrow{uv}$. Ties are broken arbitrarily. The resulting directed graph is called the Yao graph. See Figure 1 for an illustration. Let $YG_k(G)$ be the undirected graph by ignoring the direction of each link in $\overrightarrow{YG}_k(G)$. If we add the link $\overrightarrow{vu}$ instead of the link $\overrightarrow{uv}$, the graph is denoted by $\overleftarrow{YG}_k(G)$, which is called the *reverse* of the Yao graph. Some researchers used a similar construction named θ-graph [31], the difference is that, in each cone, it chooses the edge which has the shortest projection on the axis of the cone instead of the shortest edge. Here the axis of a cone is the angular bisector of the cone. For more detail, please refer to [31].

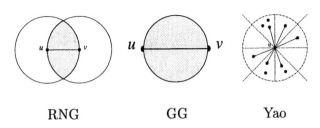

RNG   GG   Yao

Figure 1: The definitions of RNG, GG, and Yao on point set. Left: The lune using uv is empty for RNG. Middle: The diametric circle using uv is empty for GG. Right: The shortest edge in each cone is added as a neighbor of u for Yao.

Notice all these definitions are exactly the conventional definitions [32, 33, 34, 35] when graph G is the completed Euclidean graph $K(V)$. We will use RNG(V), GG(V), and Yao(V) to denote the corresponding resulting graph if G is the complete graph $K(V)$. Gabriel graph was used as a planar subgraph in the Face routing protocol [26, 36, 37] and the GPSR routing protocol [27] that guarantee the delivery of the packet. Relative neighborhood graph RNG was used for efficient broadcasting (minimizing the number of retransmissions) in one-to-one broadcasting model in [38].

We continue with the definition of Delaunay triangulation. Assume that there are no four vertices of V that are co-circular. A triangulation of V is a *Delaunay triangulation*, denoted by $Del(V)$, if the circumcircle of each of its triangles does not contain any other vertices of V in its interior. A triangle is called the *Delaunay triangle* if its circumcircle is empty of vertices of V. The *Voronoi region*, denoted by $Vor(p)$, of a vertex $p \in V$ is a collection of two dimensional points such that every point is closer to p than to any other vertex of V. The *Voronoi diagram* for V is the union of all Voronoi regions $Vor(p)$, where $p \in V$. The Delaunay triangulation $Del(V)$ is also the dual of the Voronoi diagram: two vertices p and q are connected in $Del(V)$ if and only if $Vor(p)$ and $Vor(q)$ share a common boundary. The shared boundary of two Voronoi regions $Vor(p)$ and $Vor(q)$ is on the perpendicular bisector line of segment pq. The boundary segment of a Voronoi region is called the *Voronoi edge*. The intersection point of two Voronoi edge is called the *Voronoi vertex*. The Voronoi vertex is the circumcenter of some Delaunay triangle.

Besides these geometric structures, some graph notations will also be used in this survey. A subset S of V is a *dominating set* if each node u in V is either in S or is adjacent to some node v in S. Nodes from S are called dominators, while nodes not is S are called dominatees. A subset C of V is a *connected dominating set* (CDS) if C is a dominating set and C induces a connected subgraph. Consequently, the nodes in C can communicate with each other without using nodes in $V - C$. A dominating set with minimum cardinality is called minimum dominating set, denoted by MDS. A connected dominating set with minimum cardinality is denoted by MCDS.

A subset of vertices in a graph G is an *independent set* if for any pair of vertices, there is no edge between them. It is a *maximal independent set* if no more vertices can be added to it to generate a larger independent set. It is a *maximum independent set* (MIS) if no other independent set has more vertices.

2.3 Spanners

Spanners have been studied intensively in recent years [39, 40, 41, 42, 43, 44, 45, 46, 34]. Let $G = (V, E)$ be a n-vertex connected weighted graph. The distance in G between two vertices $u, v \in V$ is the total weight (length) of the shortest path between u and v and is denoted by $d_G(u, v)$. A subgraph $H = (V, E')$, where $E' \subseteq E$, is a *t-spanner* of G if for every $u, v \in V$, $d_H(u, v) \leq t \cdot d_G(u, v)$. The value of t is called the *stretch factor*.

Spanners for Euclidean graphs is called *geometric spanners* or *Euclidean spanners*. It means the distance $d_G(u, v)$ in graph G between u and v is the Euclidean distance between vertices u and v. Geometric spanners were first introduced in computational geometry community by Chew [47]. Now they have numerous applications in computer science, such as VLSI, robotics motion planning, distributed systems, and communication networks. In this survey, we focus on their applications in wireless networks.

All previous algorithms that construct a t-spanner of the Euclidean complete graph $K(V)$ in computational geometry are centralized methods. The rapid development of the wireless communication presents a new challenge for algorithm designing and analysis. Distributed algorithms are favored than the more traditional centralized algorithms.

Consider any unicast $\Pi(u, v)$ in G (could be directed) from a node $u \in V$ to another node $v \in V$:

$$\Pi(u, v) = v_0 v_1 \cdots v_{h-1} v_h, \text{ where } u = v_0, \ v = v_h.$$

Here h is the number of hops of the path Π. The total *transmission power*

$p(\Pi)$ consumed by this path Π is defined as

$$p(\Pi) = \sum_{i=1}^{h} \|v_{i-1}v_i\|^{\beta}$$

Let $p_G(u, v)$ be the least energy consumed by all paths connecting nodes u and v in G. The path in G connecting u, v and consuming the least energy $p_G(u, v)$ is called the *least-energy path* in G for u and v. When G is the unit disk graph $UDG(V)$, we will omit the subscript G in $p_G(u, v)$.

Let H be a subgraph of G. The *power stretch factor* of the graph H with respect to G is then defined as

$$\rho_H(G) = \max_{u,v \in V} \frac{p_H(u, v)}{p_G(u, v)}$$

If G is a unit disk graph, we use $\rho_H(V)$ instead of $\rho_H(G)$. For any positive integer n, let

$$\rho_H(n) = \sup_{|V|=n} \rho_H(V).$$

Similarly, we define the length stretch factors $\ell_H(G)$ and $\ell_H(n)$. When the graph H is clear from the context, it is dropped from notations.

It was proved in [48] that, for a constant δ, $\rho_H(G) \leq \delta$ iff for any link v_iv_j in graph G but not in H, $p_H(v_i, v_j) \leq \delta\|v_iv_j\|^{\beta}$. It is then sufficient to analyze the power stretch factor of H for each link in G but not in H. It is not difficult to show that, for any $H \subseteq G$ with a length stretch factor δ, its power stretch factor is at most δ^{β} for any graph G. In particular, a graph with a constant bounded length stretch factor must also have a constant bounded power stretch factor, but the reverse is not true. Finally, the power stretch factor has the following monotonic property: If $H_1 \subset H_2 \subset G$ then the power stretch factors of H_1 and H_2 satisfy $\rho_{H_1}(G) \geq \rho_{H_2}(G)$.

2.4 Localized Algorithm

Due to the limited resources of the wireless nodes, it is preferred that the underlying network topology can be constructed in a localized manner. Here a distributed algorithm constructing a graph G is a *localized algorithm* if every node u can exactly decide all edges incident on u based only on the information of all nodes within a constant hops of u (plus a constant number of additional nodes' information if necessary). It is easy to see that the Yao graph $YG(V)$, the relative neighborhood graph $RNG(V)$ and the Gabriel graph $GG(V)$ can be constructed locally. However, the Euclidean minimum spanning tree EMST(V) and the Delaunay triangulation Del(V) can not be constructed by any localized algorithm. In this survey, we are interested in localized algorithms that construct sparse and power efficient network topologies.

3 Topology Control

In this section, we study the power stretch factor of several new sparse spanners for unit disk graph. A trade-off can be made between the sparseness of the topology and the power efficiency. The power efficiency of any spanner is measured by its power stretch factor, which is defined as the maximum ratio of the minimum power needed to support the connection of two nodes in this spanner to the least necessary in the unit disk graph.

3.1 RNG, GG, and Yao

Since the relative neighborhood graph has the length stretch factor as large as $n - 1$, then obviously its power stretch factor is at most $(n - 1)^2$. Li *et al.* [48] showed that it is actually $n - 1$.

Theorem 3.1 *[48]* $\rho_{RNG}(n) = n - 1$.

First $\rho_{RNG}(n)$ is at most $n - 1$. Consider the path between u and v in EMST(V). This path contains at most $n - 1$ edges and each edge has length at most $\|uv\|$. Thus, its total power consumption is at most $(n - 1)\|uv\|^\beta$. Notice $EMST(V) \subset RNG(V)$ if UDG(V) is connected. Thus,

$$\rho_{RNG}(n) \leq n - 1.$$

Then $\rho_{RNG}(n) \geq n - 1 - \varepsilon$ for any small positive ε by constructing an example illustrated in Figure 2.

They considered two cases. First consider even n, say $n = 2m$. The construction of the point set V is shown in Figure 2 (1), which was used in [42]. Let $\alpha = \frac{\pi}{3} + 2\delta, \theta = \frac{\pi}{3} - \delta$, where δ is a sufficiently small positive number which will be fixed later. The m points with odd subscripts $v_1, v_3,$ $v_5, \cdots, v_{2m-1}$ are collinear, so are the m points with even subscripts $v_2, v_4,$ $v_6, \cdots, v_{2m}$. As proved in [42], $RNG(V)$ is a path $v_1, v_3, v_5, \cdots, v_{2m-1},$ $v_{2m}, \cdots, v_6, v_4, v_2$. As $\delta \longrightarrow 0$, the length of each edge in $RNG(V)$ tends to $\|v_1 v_2\|$ from below, which implies $\frac{p_{RNG}(u,v)}{p(u,v)} \longrightarrow n - 1$. So we can find a sufficiently small $\delta > 0$ such that $\frac{p_{RNG}(u,v)}{p(u,v)} > n - 1 - \epsilon$, which implies $\rho_{RNG}(n) > n - 1 - \epsilon$.

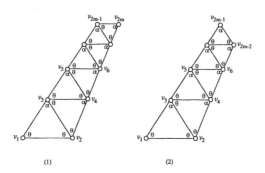

Figure 2: The Euclidean minimum spanning tree has large stretch factor.

When n is odd, the construction is shown in Figure 2 (2) and the existence can be proved by a similar argument.

The Gabriel graph has length stretch factor between $\frac{\sqrt{n}}{2}$ and $\frac{4\pi\sqrt{2n-4}}{3}$ [42]. Then its power stretch factor is at most $\left(\frac{4\pi\sqrt{2n-4}}{3}\right)^2$.

Theorem 3.2 *[48] The power stretch factor of any Gabriel graph is one.*

The Yao graph $YG_k(V)$ has length stretch factor $\frac{1}{1-2\sin\frac{\pi}{k}}$. Thus, its power stretch factor is no more than $(\frac{1}{1-2\sin\frac{\pi}{k}})^\beta$. Li *et al.* [48] proved a stronger result.

Theorem 3.3 *[48] The power stretch factor of the Yao graph $YG_k(V)$ is at most $\frac{1}{1-(2\sin\frac{\pi}{k})^\beta}$.*

See [48] for a detailed proof of this theorem. Li *et al.* [49] also proposed to apply the Yao structure on top of the Gabriel graph structure (the resulting graph is denoted by $\overrightarrow{YGG}_k(V)$), and apply the Gabriel graph structure on top of the Yao structure (the resulting graph is denoted by $\overrightarrow{GYG}_k(V)$). These structures are sparser than the Yao structure and the Gabriel graph structure and they still have a constant bounded power stretch factor. These two structures are connected graphs if the UDG is connected, which can be proved by showing that RNG is a subgraph of both structures.

We end this subsection by commenting a result by Wattenhofer *et al.* [50]. Their two-phased approach consists of a variation of the Yao graph followed by a variation of the Gabriel graph. They tried to prove that the constructed spanner has a constant power stretch factor and the node degree is bounded by a constant. Unfortunately, there are some bugs in their proof of the constant power stretch factor and their result is erroneous, which was discussed in detail in [48].

Li *et al.* [51] proposed a structure that is similar to the Yao structure for topology control. Each node u finds a power $p_{u,\alpha}$ such that in every cone of degree α surrounding u, there is some node that u can reach with power $p_{u,\alpha}$. Here, nevertheless, we assume that there is a node reachable from u by the maximum power in that cone. Then the graph G_α contains all edges uv such that u can communicate with v using power $p_{u,\alpha}$. It was proved in [51] that, if $\alpha \leq \frac{5\pi}{6}$ and the UDG is connected, then graph G_α is a connected graph. On the other hand, if $\alpha > \frac{5\pi}{6}$, they showed that the connectivity of G_α is not guaranteed by giving some counter-example [51].

3.2   Bounded Degree Spanners

Notice that although the directed graphs $\overrightarrow{YG_k}(V)$, $\overrightarrow{GYG_k}(V)$ and $\overrightarrow{YGG_k}(V)$ have a bounded power stretch factor and a bounded out-degree k for each node, some nodes may have a very large in-degree. The nodes configuration given in Figure 3 will result a very large in-degree for node u. Bounded out-degree gives us advantages when apply several routing algorithms. However, unbounded in-degree at node u will often cause large overhead at u. Therefore it is often imperative to construct a sparse network topology such that both the in-degree and the out-degree are bounded by a constant while it is still power-efficient.

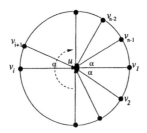

Figure 3: Node u has degree (or in-degree) $n - 1$.

3.2.1   Sink Structure

Arya *et al.* [40] gave an ingenious technique to generate a bounded degree graph with constant length stretch factor. In [48], Li *et al.* applied the same technique to construct a sparse network topology with a bounded degree and a bounded power stretch factor from $YG(V)$. The technique is to replace the directed star consisting of all links toward a node u by a directed tree $T(u)$ of a bounded degree with u as the sink. Tree $T(u)$ is constructed recursively. The algorithm is as follows.

Algorithm: Constructing-YG*

1. First, construct the graph $\overrightarrow{YG}_k(V)$. Each node u will have a set of in-coming nodes $I(u) = \{v \mid \overrightarrow{vu} \in \overrightarrow{YG}_k(V)\}$.

2. For each node u, use the following Tree$(u,I(u))$ to build tree $T(u)$.

Algorithm: Constructing-$T(u)$ Tree$(u,I(u))$

1. To partition the unit disk centered at u, choose k equal-sized cones centered at u: $C_1(u), C_2(u), \cdots, C_k(u)$.

2. Node u finds the nearest node $y_i \in I(u)$ in $C_i(u)$, for $1 \le i \le k$, if there is any. Link $\overrightarrow{y_i u}$ is added to $T(u)$ and y_i is removed from $I(u)$. For each cone $C_i(u)$, if $I(u) \cap C_i(u)$ is not empty, call Tree$(y_i, I(u) \cap C_i(u))$ and add the created edges to $T(u)$.

Figure 4 (a) illustrates a directed star centered at u and Figure 4 (b) shows the directed tree $T(u)$ constructed to replace the star with $k = 8$. The union of all trees $T(u)$ is called the *sink structure* $\overrightarrow{YG}_k^*(V)$.

Notice that, node u constructs the tree $T(u)$ and then broadcasts the structure of $T(u)$ to all nodes in $T(u)$. Since the total number of edges in the Yao structure is at most $k \cdot n$, where k is the number of cones divided, the total number of edges of $T(u)$ of all node u is also at most $k \cdot n$. Thus, the total communication cost of broadcasting the $T(u)$ to all its neighbors is still at most $k \cdot n$. Recall that k is a small constant.

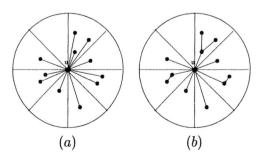

(a)   (b)

Figure 4: (a) Star formed by links toward to u. (b) Directed tree $T(u)$ sinked at u.

The algorithm uses a directed tree $T(u)$ to replace the directed star for each node u. Therefore, if nodes u and v are connected by a path in $\overrightarrow{YG}_k$, they are also connected by a path in $\overrightarrow{YG}_k^*$. It is already known that $\overrightarrow{YG}_k$ is strongly connected if UDG(V) is connected, so does $\overrightarrow{YG}_k^*$.

Theorem 3.4 *[48] The power stretch factor of the graph* $\overrightarrow{YG}_k^*(V)$ *is at most* $(\frac{1}{1-(2\sin\frac{\pi}{k})^\beta})^2$. *The maximum degree of the graph* $\overrightarrow{YG}_k^*(V)$ *is at most* $(k+1)^2 - 1$. *The maximum out-degree is* k.

Notice that the sink structure and the Yao graph structure do not have to have the same number of cones, and the cones do not need to be aligned. For setting up a power-efficient wireless networking, each node u finds all its neighbors in $YG_k(V)$, which can be done in linear time proportional to the number of nodes within its transmission range.

3.2.2 YaoYao Structure

In this section, we review another algorithm proposed by Li *et al.* [49] that constructs a sparse and power efficient topology. Assume that each node v_i of V has a unique identification number $ID(v_i) = i$. The identity of a directed link $\overrightarrow{uv}$ is defined as $ID(\overrightarrow{uv}) = (||uv||, ID(u), ID(v))$.

Node u chooses a node v from each cone, if there is any, so the directed link $\overrightarrow{vu}$ has the smallest $ID(\overrightarrow{vu})$ among all directed links $\overrightarrow{wu}$ in $YG(V)$ in that cone. The union of all chosen directed links is the final network topology, denoted by $\overrightarrow{YY}_k(V)$. If the directions of all links are ignored, the graph is denoted as $YY_k(V)$.

Theorem 3.5 *[49] Graph* $\overrightarrow{YY}_k(V)$ *is strongly connected if UDG(V) is connected and* $k > 6$.

It was proved in [52] that $\overrightarrow{YY}_k(V)$ is a spanner in civilized graph. Here a unit disk graph is civilized graph if the distance between any two nodes in this graph is larger than a positive constant λ. In [53], they called the civilized unit disk graph as the λ-precision unit disk graph. Notice the wireless devices in wireless networks can not be too close or overlapped. Thus, it is reasonable to model the wireless ad hoc networks as a civilized unit disk graph.

Theorem 3.6 *[49] The power stretch factor of the directed topology* $\overrightarrow{YY}_k(V)$ *is bounded by a constant* ρ *in civilized graph.*

The experimental results by Li *et al.* [49] showed that this sparse topology has a small power stretch factor in practice. They [49] conjectured that $\overrightarrow{YY}_k(V)$ also has a constant bounded power stretch factor theoretically in any unit disk graph. The proof of this conjecture or the construction of a counter-example remain a future work.

3.2.3 Symmetric Yao Graph

In [49], Li *et al.* also considered another undirected structure, called *symmetric Yao graph* $YS_k(V)$, which guarantees that the node degree is at most k. Each node u divides the region into k equal angular regions centered at the node, and chooses the closest node in each region, if any. An edge uv is selected to graph $YS_k(V)$ if and only if both directed edges $\overrightarrow{uv}$ and $\overrightarrow{vu}$ are in the *Yao graph* $\overrightarrow{YG}_k(V)$. Then it is obvious that the maximum node degree is k.

Theorem 3.7 *[48] The graph $YS_k(V)$ is strongly connected if UDG(V) is connected and $k \geq 6$.*

This was proved by showing that RNG is a subgraph of $YS_k(V)$ if $k \geq 6$. Notice that, Theorem 3.7 immediately implies the connectivity of the Yao graph, sink structure, and the YaoYao graph as RNG is also the subgraph of all these structures.

The experiment by Li *et al.* also showed that it has a small power stretch factor in practice. However, it was shown in [54] recently that $YS_k(V)$ is not a spanner theoretically. The basic idea of the counter example is similar to the counter example for RNG proposed by Bose *et al.* [42]. For the completeness of the presentation, we still review the counter example here.

Let nodes v_1 and v_0 have distance half unit from each other. Assume the ith cone of v_1 contains v_0, and the i'th cone of v_0 contains v_1. Then draw two lines $l_1 = v_1 v_3$ and $l_2 = v_0 v_2$ such that both the angles $\angle v_3 v_1 v_0$ and $\angle v_2 v_0 v_1$ are $\frac{\pi}{2} - \alpha$, where α is a very small positive number. Let's first consider even n, say $n = 2m$. Figure 5 illustrates the construction of the point set V. The node v_{2j} is placed on l_2 in the ith cone of v_{2j-1} and it is very close to the upper boundary of the ith cone of v_{2j-1}. The node v_{2j+1} is placed on l_1 in the i'th cone of v_{2j} close to the upper boundary of that cone. Using this method, place all nodes from v_2 to v_{2m} in order. Then it is easy to show that the $YS_k(V)$ does not contain any edge $v_{2j}v_{2j+1}$ and $v_{2j+1}v_{2j+2}$ for $0 \leq j \leq m - 1$. The nearest neighbor of v_{2j} is v_{2j+1}, but for v_{2j+1}, the nearest neighbor is v_{2j+2}. So although in $YS_k(V)$ there is a path from v_1 to v_2, its length is $\|v_1 v_{2m-1}\| + \|v_{2m-1} v_{2m}\| + \|v_{2m} v_2\|$. So when α is appropriately small, the length stretch factor of $Y S_k(V)$ cannot be bounded by a constant. Similarly, its power stretch factor cannot be bounded also. When n is odd, the construction is similar.

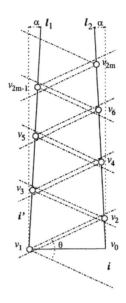

Figure 5: An example that $Y S_k(V)$ has a large stretch factor.

3.3 Planar Spanner

Given a set of nodes V, it is well-known that the Delaunay triangulation $Del(V)$ is a planar t-spanner of the completed graph $K(V)$. This was first proved by Dobkin, Friedman and Supowit with constant $t = \frac{1+\sqrt{5}}{2}\pi \approx 5.08$. Then Kevin and Gutwin improved the upper bound on t to be $\frac{2\pi}{3\cos\frac{\pi}{6}} = \frac{4\sqrt{3}}{9}\pi \approx 2.42$. However, it is not appropriate to require the construction of the Delaunay triangulation in the wireless communication environment because of the possible massive communications it requires. Given a set of points V, let UDel(V) be the graph of removing all edges of $Del(V)$ that are longer than one unit, i.e., $UDel(V) = Del(V) \cap UDG(V)$. Li et al. [35] considered the *unit Delaunay triangulation* UDel(V) for planar spanner of UDG, which is a subset of the Delaunay triangulation. It was proved in [35] that UDel(V) is a t-spanner of the unit disk graph UDG(V).

Theorem 3.8 *[35] For any two vertices u and v of V,*

$$||\Pi_{UDel(V)}(u,v)|| \le \frac{1+\sqrt{5}}{2}\pi \cdot ||\pi_{UDG(V)}(u,v)||$$

Notice that, Kevin and Gutwin [55] showed that the Delaunay triangulation is a *t*-spanner for a constant $t \approx 2.42$. This was proved by induction on the order of the lengths of all pair of nodes (from the shortest to the longest). It can be shown that the path connecting nodes *u* and *v* constructed by the method given in [55] also satisfies that all edges of that path is shorter than $||uv||$. Consequently, we know that the unit Delaunay triangulation $UDel(V)$ is a $\frac{4\sqrt{3}}{9}\pi$-spanner of the unit disk graph $UDG(V)$.

3.3.1 Localized Delaunay triangulation

Li *et al.* [35] gave a localized algorithm that constructs a sequence graphs, called *localized Delaunay* $LDel^{(k)}(V)$, which are supergraphs of UDel(V). We begin with some necessary definitions before presenting the algorithm.

Unit Gabriel graph It consists of all edges *uv* such that $||uv|| \le 1$ and the open disk using *uv* as diameter does not contain any vertex from *V*. Such edge *uv* is called the *Gabriel edge*. We denote the unit Gabriel graph by $GG(V)$ hereafter.

k-**localized Delaunay triangle** Triangle $\triangle uvw$ is called a *k-localized Delaunay triangle* if the interior of the circumcircle of $\triangle uvw$, denoted by $disk(u,v,w)$ hereafter, does not contain any vertex of *V* that is a *k*-neighbor of *u*, *v*, or *w*; and all edges of the triangle $\triangle uvw$ have length no more than one unit.

k-**localized Delaunay graph** The *k-localized Delaunay graph* over a vertex set *V*, denoted by $LDel^{(k)}(V)$, has exactly all unit Gabriel edges and edges of all *k*-localized Delaunay triangles.

When it is clear from the context, we will omit the integer *k* in our notation of $LDel^{(k)}(V)$. They originally conjectured that $LDel^{(1)}(V)$ is a planar graph and thus a planar *t*-spanner of $UDG(V)$ can be easily constructed by using localized approach. Unfortunately, as shown in [35], the graph $LDel^{(1)}(V)$ may contain some edges intersecting. On the other hand, $LDel^{(2)}(V)$ is a planar graph.

Theorem 3.9 *[35] $LDel^{(k)}(V)$ is a planar graph for any $k \ge 2$.*

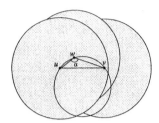

Figure 6: LDel: The circumcircle $disk(u, v, w)$ is not necessarily covered by unit disks centered at u and v. But it is empty of other vertices from $N_1(u) \cup N_1(v) \cup N_1(w)$.

Theorem 3.10 *Assume two triangles $\triangle uvw$ and $\triangle xyz$ of $LDel^{(k)}(V)$, $k \geq 1$, intersect, then either $disk(u, v, w)$ contains at least one of the nodes of $\{x, y, z\}$ or $disk(x, y, z)$ contains at least one of the nodes of $\{u, v, w\}$.*

Notice that, although $LDel^{(1)}(V)$ is not a planar graph, the following theorem proved in [35] guarantees that it is sparse.

Theorem 3.11 *Graph $LDel^{(1)}(V)$ has thickness 2.*

Although the graph $UDel(V)$ is a t-spanner for $UDG(V)$, it is unknown how to construct it locally. We can construct $LDel^{(2)}(V)$, which is guaranteed to be a planar spanner of $UDel(V)$, but a total communication cost of this approach is $O(m \log n)$ bits, where m is the number of edges in $UDG(V)$ and could be as large as $O(n^2)$. This is more complicated than some other non-planar t-spanners, such as the Yao structure [34] and the θ-graph [55] (although the lattes are not planar). In order to reduce the total communication cost to $O(n \log n)$ bits, they do not construct $LDel^{(2)}(V)$, and instead they extract a planar graph $PLDel(V)$ out of $LDel^{(1)}(V)$. They provided a novel algorithm to construct $LDel^{(1)}(V)$ using linear communications and then make it planar in linear communication cost. The final graph still contains $UDel(V)$ as a subgraph. Thus, it is a t-spanner of the unit-disk graph $UDG(V)$.

In the following, the order of three nodes in a triangle is immaterial.

Algorithm 1 *Localized Unit Delaunay Triangulation*

1. Each wireless node u broadcasts its identity and location and listens to the messages from other nodes.

2. Assume that node u gathered the location information of $N_1(u)$. It computes the Delaunay triangulation $Del(N_1(u))$ of its 1-neighbors $N_1(u)$, including u itself.

3. For each edge uv of $Del(N_1(u))$, let $\triangle uvw$ and $\triangle uvz$ be two triangles incident on uv. Edge uv is a Gabriel edge if both angles $\angle uwv$ and $\angle uzv$ are less than $\pi/2$. Node u marks all *Gabriel edges* uv, which will never be deleted.

4. Each node u finds all triangles $\triangle uvw$ from $Del(N_1(u))$ such that all three edges of $\triangle uvw$ have length at most one unit. If angle $\angle wuv \geq \frac{\pi}{3}$, node u broadcasts a message proposal(u, v, w) to form a 1-localized Delaunay triangle $\triangle uvw$ in $LDel^{(1)}(V)$, and listens to the messages from other nodes.

5. When a node u receives a message proposal(u, v, w), u accepts the proposal of constructing $\triangle uvw$ if $\triangle uvw$ belongs to the Delaunay triangulation $Del(N_1(u))$ by broadcasting message accept(u, v, w); otherwise, it rejects the proposal by broadcasting message reject(u, v, w).

6. A node u adds the edges uv and uw to its set of incident edges if the triangle $\triangle uvw$ is in the Delaunay triangulation $Del(N_1(u))$ and both v and w have sent either accept(u, v, w) or proposal(u, v, w).

It was proved that the graph constructed by the above algorithm is $LDel^{(1)}(V)$. Indeed, for each triangle $\triangle uvw$ of $LDel^{(1)}(V)$, one of its interior angle is at least $\pi/3$ and $\triangle uvw$ is in $Del(N_1(u))$, $Del(N_1(v))$ and $Del(N_1(w))$. So one of the nodes amongst $\{u, v, w\}$ will broadcast the message proposal(u, v, w) to form a 1-localized Delaunay triangle $\triangle uvw$.

As $Del(N_1(u))$ is a planar graph, and a proposal is made only if $\angle wuv \geq \frac{\pi}{3}$, node u broadcasts at most 6 proposals. And each proposal is replied by at most two nodes. Therefore, the total communication cost is $O(n \log n)$ bits. The above algorithm also shows that $LDel^{(1)}(V)$ has $O(n)$ edges, which we know from Theorem 3.11. Putting together the arguments above, we have:

Theorem 3.12 *[35] Algorithm 1 constructs $LDel^{(1)}(V)$ with total communication cost $O(n \log n)$ bits.*

We then review the algorithm to extract from $LDel^{(1)}(V)$ a planar subgraph.

Algorithm 2 *Planarize $LDel^{(1)}(V)$*

1. Each wireless node u broadcasts the Gabriel edges incident on u and the triangles $\triangle uvw$ of $LDel^{(1)}(V)$ and listens to the messages from other nodes.

2. Assume node u gathered the Gabriel edge and 1-local Delaunay triangles information of all nodes from $N_1(u)$. For two intersected triangles $\triangle uvw$ and $\triangle xyz$ known by u, node u removes the triangle $\triangle uvw$ if its circumcircle contains a node from $\{x, y, z\}$.

3. Each wireless node u broadcasts all the triangles incident on u which it has not removed in the previous step, and listens to the broadcasting by other nodes.

4. Node u keeps the edge uv in its set of incident edges if it is a Gabriel edge, or if there is a triangle $\triangle uvw$ such that u, v, and w have all announced they have not removed the triangle $\triangle uvw$ in Step 2.

They denoted the graph extracted by the algorithm above by $PLDel(V)$. Note that any triangle of $LDel^{(1)}(V)$ not kept in the last step of the Planarization Algorithm is not a triangle of $LDel^{(2)}(V)$, and therefore $PLDel(V)$ is a supergraph of $LDel^{(2)}(V)$. Thus,

$$UDel(V) \subseteq LDel^{(2)}(V) \subseteq PLDel(V) \subseteq LDel^{(1)}(V)$$

Similar to the proof that $LDel^{(2)}(V)$ is a planar graph, they showed that the algorithm does generate a planar graph. The total communication cost to construct the graph $PLDel(V)$ is a $O(\log n)$ times the number of edges of the graph $LDel^{(1)}(V)$, which by Theorem 3.11 is $O(n)$. Putting together all the arguments above and Theorem 3.8,

Theorem 3.13 *$PLDel(V)$ is planar $\frac{4\sqrt{3}}{9}\pi$-spanner of $UDG(V)$, and can be constructed with total communication cost $O(n \log n)$ bits.*

3.3.2   Partial Delaunay triangulation

Stojmenovic and Li [56] also proposed a geometry structure, namely the partial Delaunay triangulation (PDT), that can be constructed in a localized manner. Partial Delaunay triangulation contains Gabriel graph as its subgraph, and itself is a subgraph of the Delaunay triangulation, more precisely, the subgraph of the unit Delaunay triangulation UDel(V). The algorithm for the construction of PDT goes as follows.

Let u and v be two neighboring nodes in the network. Edge uv belongs to $Del(V)$ if and only if there exists a disk with u and v on its boundary, which does not contain any other point from the set V. First test whether $disk(u,v)$ contains any other node from the network. If it does not, the edge belongs to GG and therefore to PDT. If it does, check whether nodes exist on both sides of line uv or on only one side. If both sides of line uv contain nodes from the set inside $disk(u,v)$ then uv does not belong to $Del(V)$.

Suppose now that only one side of line uv contains nodes inside the circle $disk(u,v)$, and let w be one such point that maximizes the angle $\angle uwv$. Let $\alpha = \angle uwv$. Consider now the largest angle $\angle uxv$ on the other side of the mentioned circle $disk(u,v)$, where x is a node from the set S. If $\angle uwv + \angle uxv > \pi$, then edge uv is definitely not in the Delaunay triangulation $Del(V)$. The search can be restricted to common neighbors of u and v, if only one-hop neighbor information is available, or to neighbors of only one of the nodes if 2-hop information (or exchange of the information for the purpose of creating PDT is allowed) is available. Then whether edge uv is added to PDT is based on the following procedure.

Assume only $N_1(u)$ is known to u, and there is one node w from $N_1(u)$ that is inside $disk(u,v)$ with the largest angle $\angle uwv$. Edge uv is added to PDT if the following conditions hold: (1) there is no node from $N_1(u)$ that lies on the different side of uv with w and inside the circumcircle passing through u, v, and w, (2) $\sin \alpha > \frac{d}{R}$, where R is the transmission radius of each wireless node, d is the diameter of the circumcircle $disk(u,v,w)$, and $\alpha = \angle uwv$ (here $\alpha \geq \frac{\pi}{2}$).

Assume only 1-hop neighbors are known to u and v, and there is one node w from $N_1(u) \cup N_1(v)$ that is inside $disk(u,v)$ with the largest angle $\angle uwv$. Edge uv is added to PDT if the following conditions hold: (1) there is no node from $N_1(u) \cup N_1(v)$ that lies on the different side of uv with w and inside the circumcircle passing u, v, and w, (2) $\cos \frac{\alpha}{2} > \frac{d}{2R}$, where R is the transmission radius of each wireless node and $\alpha = \angle uwv$.

Obviously, PDT is a subgraph of $UDel(V)$. Thus, the spanning ratio of the partial Delaunay triangulation could be very large.

3.3.3   Restricted Delaunay Graph

Gao *et al.* [57] also proposed another structure, called *restricted Delaunay graph* RDG and showed that it has good spanning ratio properties and is easy to maintain locally. A restricted Delaunay graph of a set of points in the plane is a planar graph and contains all the Delaunay edges with length at most one. In other other words, they call any planar graph containing

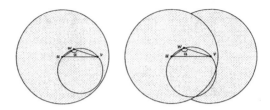

Figure 7: Left: Only one hop information is known to u. Then it requires $disk(u, v, w)$ to be covered by the transmission range of u (denoted by the shaded region) and is empty of neighbors of u. Right: Node u knows $N_1(u)$ and node v knows $N_1(v)$. The circumcircle $disk(u, v, w)$ is covered by the union of the transmission ranges of u and v and is empty of other vertices.

$UDel(V)$ as a restricted Delaunay graph. They described a distributed algorithm to maintain the RDG such that at the end of the algorithm, each node u maintains a set of edges $E(u)$ incident to u. Those edges $E(u)$ satisfy that (1) each edge in $E(u)$ has length at most one unit; (2) the edges are consistent, i.e., an edge $uv \in E(u)$ if and only if $uv \in E(v)$; (3) the graph obtained is planar; (4) The graph $UDel(V)$ is in the union of all edges $E(u)$.

The algorithm works as follows. First, each node u acquires the position of its 1-hop neighbors $N_1(u)$ and computes the Delaunay triangulation $Del(N_1(u))$ on $N_1(u)$, including u itself. In the second step, each node u sends $Del(N_1(u))$ to all of its neighbors. Let $E(u) = \{uv \mid uv \in Del(N_1(u))\}$. For each edge $uv \in E(u)$, and for each $w \in N_1(u)$, if u and v are in $N_1(w)$ and $uv \notin Del(N_1(u))$, then node u deletes edge uv from $E(u)$.

When the above steps are finished, the resulting edges $E(u)$ satisfy the four properties listed above. However, unlike the local Delaunay triangulation, the computation cost and communication cost of each node needed to obtain $E(u)$ is not optimal within a small constant factor.

3.4   Bounded Degree Planar Spanner

The structures discussed so far either have bounded degree, or is planar, or is spanner, but none of the structures has all these three properties together. We then review one recent result [60] that can construct a bounded degree planar spanner in a localized manner (total communication cost is $O(n)$ messages).

3.4.1   Centralized Construction for UDG

Our algorithms borrow some idea from the algorithm by Bose *et al.* [58] which constructs a bounded degree and planar spanner for a given points set V. For completeness of presentation, we review the basic steps of their algorithm.

First, it computes the Delaunay triangulation of V, $Del(V)$, and a degree-3 spanning subgraph $BDS(V)$ of $Del(V)$. Then, for each polygon P in $BDS(V)$, their algorithm first orders the nodes according to a geometry based breadth-first search, and processes the nodes of P in increasing order. It prunes this part of the Delaunay triangulation such that each node of P has low degree. The resulting graph is a planar spanner for the nodes of P. By combining all the spanners for each of the polygons, we get a planar spanner of bounded degree. Finally, they run a greedy algorithm in [59] on these structure to bound the total weight from a constant factor of the weight of the Euclidean minimum spanning tree.

They show that the length stretch factor of the final graph is $2\pi(\pi + 1)/((3\cos\pi/6)(1+\epsilon))$ and node degree is at most 27. The running time of their algorithm is $O(n\log n)$. However, their method is impossible to have a localized even distributed version, since they use BFS and many operations on polygons (such as degree-3 partitions). Notice that breadth-first-search may take $O(n^2)$ communications. In this section, we give a new method for constructing a planar spanner with bounded node degree for $UDG(V)$, and show that it can be converted to a localized method in Section 3.4.2. The basic idea of our method is to combine (localized) Delaunay triangulation and the ordered Yao structure [34].

Centralized Algorithm for UDG   We first study how to construct bounded degree planar spanner for UDG in a centralized approach.

Algorithm 3 *Centralized Construction of Planar Spanner with Bounded Degree for $UDG(V)$*

1. Compute the Delaunay triangulation $Del(V)$ of V.

2. Remove edges longer than 1 in $Del(V)$. Call the remaining graph unit Delaunay triangulation $UDel(V)$. For every node u, we know its unit Delaunay neighbors $N_{UDel}(u)$ and its node degree d_u in $UDel(V)$.

3. Then, find an order π of V as follows: Let $G_1 = UDel(V)$ and $d_{G,u}$ is the node degree of u in graph G. Remove the node u with the

smallest degree $d_{G_i,u}$ (smaller ID breaks tie) from graph G_i, and call the remaining graph G_{i+1}, for $1 \leq i \leq n$. Let $\pi_u = i$. Let P_v denote the predecessors of v in π, i.e., $P_v = \{u \in V : \pi_u < \pi_v\}$. Since G_i is always a planar graph, the smallest value of $d_{G_i,u}$ is at most 5. Then, in ordering π, node u has at most 5 edges to its predecessors P_u in $UDel(V)$.

4. Let E be the edge set of $UDel(V)$, E' be the edge set of the desired spanner. Initialize E' to be empty set and all nodes in V are unprocessed. Then, for each node u in V, following the increasing order π, run the following steps to add some edges from E to E' (only consider the unit Delaunay neighbors $N_{UDel}(u)$ of u):

   (a) For node u, let $v_1, v_2, \cdots, v_k$ be the unprocessed neighbors of u in $UDel(V)$ (see Figure 8). Here $k \leq 5$. Then k *open* sectors at node u are defined by rays emanated from u to the processed nodes v_i in $UDel(V)$. For each sector centered at u, we divide it into a minimum number of *open* cones of degree at most α, where $\alpha \leq \pi/3$ is a parameter.

   (b) For each cone, let $s_1, s_2, \cdots, s_m$ be the geometrically ordered neighbors of u in $N_{UDel}(u)$. Notice, $s_1, s_2, \cdots, s_m$ are *unprocessed* nodes. First add the shortest edge us_i in this cone to E', then add to E' all the edges $s_j s_{j+1}$, $1 \leq j < m$. Here edges $s_j s_{j+1}$ are not necessarily in $UDel(V)$.

   (c) Mark node u processed.

5. Repeat this procedure in the increasing order of π, until all nodes are processed. Let $BPS_1(UDG(V))$ denote the final graph formed by edge set E'.

Notice that in the algorithm we use *open* sectors, which means that we do not consider adding the edges on the boundaries. For example, in Figure 8, the cones do not include any edges uv_i. This guarantee the algorithm does not add any edges to node v_i after v_i has been processed. This approach, as we will show it later, bounds the node degree.

Analysis of Centralized Algorithm for UDG

Theorem 3.14 *The maximum node degree of the graph $BPS_1(UDG(V))$ is at most $19 + \lceil \frac{2\pi}{\alpha} \rceil$.*

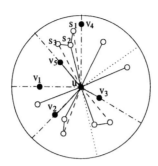

Figure 8: Constructing Planar Spanner with Bounded Degree for $UDG(V)$: Process node u.

For example, when $\alpha = \pi/3$, then the maximum node degree is at most 20. Method in [58] does not work for UDG.

Theorem 3.15 $BPS_1(UDG(V))$ *is a planar graph.*

Finally, we prove $BPS_1(UDG(V))$ is a spanner.

Theorem 3.16 *Graph* $BPS_1(UDG(V))$ *is a t-spanner, where*

$$t = \max\{\frac{\pi}{2}, \pi \sin \frac{\alpha}{2} + 1\} \cdot C_{del}.$$

For example, when $\alpha = \pi/3$, then the spanning ratio is at most $(\frac{\pi}{2} + 1) \cdot C_{del}$; when $\alpha = 2 \arcsin(\frac{1}{2} - \frac{1}{\pi}) \simeq 20.9^o$, then the spanning ratio is at most $(\frac{\pi}{2}) \cdot C_{del}$. We expect to further improve the bound on the spanning ratio by using the following property: all such Delaunay neighbors s_i is inside the circumcircle of the triangle uvv'. See [60] for the detail of the proof.

Notice that we can build Delaunay triangulation in $O(n \log n)$, and do ordering in time $O(n \log n)$ (using heap for the ordering based on degrees), and Yao structure in $O(n)$ (each edge is processed at most a constant times and there are $O(n)$ edges to be processed). Consequently, the time complexity of our centralized algorithm is $O(n \log n)$, same with the method by Bose *et al.* [58]. However, our algorithm has smaller bounded node degree, and (more importantly) our algorithm has potential to become a localized version for wireless networks application as we will describe next.

3.4.2 Localized Construction

In [63], Wang *et al.* showed that an algorithm presented in [40] does construct a bounded degree spanner for UDG with $O(n)$ messages (with unit

$\log n$ bits) under the broadcast communication model, Li *et al.* [35] presented the first algorithm that constructs a planar spanner using only $O(n)$ messages under the broadcast communication model. No localized method is known before for constructing a planar spanner with bounded node degree.

In this section, we reviewed the method in [60] that extended the algorithm presented in previous section to generate bounded degree planar spanner for UDG in a localized manner. The algorithm is based on a planar spanner $LDel^{(2)}(V)$ for UDG proposed by Li *et al.* [35]. They [35] cannot construct $LDel^{(2)}$ in $O(n)$ messages due to the difficulty of collecting the 2-hop neighbors for every node in $O(n)$ messages. Computing the 2-hop neighborhood is not trivial, as the UDG can be dense. The broadcast nature of the communication in ad hoc wireless networks is however very useful when computing local information. The approach (using $O(n)$ messages total) by Gruia [64] is based on the specific connected dominating set introduced by Alzoubi, Wan, and Frieder [65]. This connected dominating set is based on a maximal independent set (MIS). In the algorithm, each node uses its adjacent node(s) in the MIS to broadcast over a larger area relevant information. Listening to the information about other nodes broadcast by the MIS nodes enables a node to compute its 2-hop neighborhood.

Finally, the following lemma was proved in [60].

Lemma 3.1 *An edge uv is in $LDel^{(2)}(V)$ iff there is a disk passing through u, and v, which does not contain node from $N_2(u) \cup N_2(v)$ inside.*

Bound the Degree Locally   In the previous section, we described a localized algorithm to construct a planar spanner $LDel^{(2)}$ using $O(n)$ messages. However, some node in $LDel^{(2)}$ could have degree as large as $O(n)$. We [60] then gave an efficient method to bound the node degree.

Algorithm 4 *Localized Construction of Planar Spanner with Bounded Degree for $UDG(V)$*

1. First, compute the planar localized Delaunay triangulation $LDel^{(2)}(V)$, so that every node u knows its neighbors $N_{LDel^{(2)}}(u)$ and its node degree d_u in $LDel^{(2)}(V)$.

2. Build a local order π of V as follows: (Every node u initializes $\pi_u = 0$, i.e., unordered.)

(a) If node u has $\pi_u = 0$ and $d_u \leq 5$, then u queries [1] each node v, from its unordered neighbors, the current degree d_v. If node u has the smallest ID among all unordered neighbors v with $d_v \leq 5$, node u sets $\pi_u = \max\{\pi_v \mid v \in N_{LDel^{(2)}}(u)\} + 1$, and broadcasts π_u to its neighbors $N_{LDel^{(2)}}(u)$.

(b) If node u receives a message from its neighbor v saying that $\pi_v = k$, it updates its $d_u = d_u - 1$ and also updates the order π_v stored locally. So d_u represents how many neighbors are not ordered so far. If node u finds that $d_u \leq 5$ and $\pi_u = 0$, it goes to Step 2 (a). When node u finds that $d_u = 0$ and $\pi_u > 0$, it can go to step 3.

3. Build structures based on local order π as follows: (All nodes unprocessed initially.)

(a) If a unprocessed node u has the highest local order in its unprocessed neighbors in $LDel^{(2)}(V)$, let k be the number of processed neighbors [2] of u in $LDel^{(2)}(V)$. Node u divides its transmission range to k *open* sectors cut by the rays from u to these processed neighbors. Then divide each sector into a minimum number of *open* cones of degree at most α with $\alpha \leq \pi/3$. For each cone, let $s_1, s_2, \cdots, s_m$ be the ordered unprocessed neighbors of u in $N_{LDel^{(2)}}(u)$. For this cone, node u first adds an edge us_i, where s_i is the nearest neighbor of u in $s_1, s_2, \cdots, s_m$. Node u then tells s_j to add the edges $s_{j-1}s_j$, $s_j s_{j+1}$, $1 \leq j \leq m$. Node u marks itself processed, and tells all nodes in $N_{LDel^{(2)}}(u)$ that it is processed.

(b) If a unprocessed node v receives a message for adding edge vv' from its neighbor u, it adds vv'.

4. When all nodes are processed, the final network topology is denoted by $BPS_2(UDG(V))$.

Analysis of Localized Algorithm   We first show that the algorithm does process all nodes. First of all, the algorithm cannot stop at stage of ordering nodes locally. This can be shown by contradiction. Assume that there are some nodes are unordered. The graph formed by these unordered are

---

[1]If all unordered neighbors with $d_v \leq 5$ has larger ID, we call such query round a *failed round*. Node u performs a new round of queries only if it finds that the unordered neighbors have been reduced from previous failed round.

[2]There are at most 5 processed neighbors since $LDel^{(2)}(V)$ is planar.

planar, and thus it contains some nodes with at most 5 unordered neighbors. Among these nodes, the node with the smallest ID will perform step 2 (a), and reduces the number of unordered nodes consequently.

Notice that the ordering computed by our method is not a total ordering. Some nodes may have the same order. However, no two neighboring nodes in $LDel^{(2)}(V)$ receive the same order. Thus, after all nodes are ordered, the algorithm will process all nodes. Observe that the algorithm do not process two neighboring nodes at the same time. Assume that there are two nodes, say u and v are processed at the same time. Remember that we process a node only if it has the highest ordering among its unprocessed neighbors. Thus, nodes u and v must receive the same order, i.e., $\pi_u = \pi_v$, which is impossible in our ordering method.

Additionally, remember that our algorithm checks if $d_u \leq 5$ for computing an ordering locally. Here number 5 can be replaced by any integer larger than 5. Using larger integer may make the algorithm run faster, but on the other hand, it worsens the theoretical bound on the node degree. It is not difficult to show that the constructed final topology still has bounded node degree.

Theorem 3.17 *The maximum node degree of the graph $BPS_2(UDG(V))$ is at most $19 + \lceil \frac{2\pi}{\alpha} \rceil$.*

Notice that, the algorithms [58, 66] always add the edges in the Delaunay triangulation to construct a bounded degree planar spanner for a set of points. Thus, the planarity of the final structure is straightforward. The algorithm we proposed in Section 3.4.1 may add some edges (such as edges $s_i s_{i+1}$ added in step 4(b) of Algorithm 3) that do not belong to the $UDel(V)$. To prove the planarity of the structure $BPS_1(UDG(V))$, we show that no two added diagonal edges intersect. The property that edges, which possibly intersect $s_i s_{i+1}$ in the centralized algorithm, are all Delaunay edges is crucial in the proof of Theorem 3.15. This property does not hold anymore in the localized algorithm. We will show that $BPS_2(UDG(V))$ is a planar graph using a different approach.

Theorem 3.18 *$BPS_2(UDG(V))$ is a planar graph.*

Theorem 3.19 *Graph $BPS_2(UDG(V))$ is a t-spanner, where*

$$t = \max\{\frac{\pi}{2}, \pi \sin \frac{\alpha}{2} + 1\} \cdot C_{del}.$$

Theorem 3.20 *Algorithm 4 uses at most $O(n)$ messages, where each message has $O(\log n)$ bits.*

PROOF. Notice that it was shown in [64] that we can collect the 2-hop neighbor information for all nodes using total $O(n)$ messages. The communication cost of building $LDel^{(2)}$ is $O(n)$ since every node only has to propose at most 6 triangles and each propose is replied by two nodes.

The second step (local ordering) takes $O(n)$ messages, since every node only query at most 5 rounds, and at the ith round of query the node sends at most $6 - i$ query messages. For each query, only the queried node replies. After it was ordered, it broadcasts once to inform its neighbors.

The third step (bounded degree) also takes $O(n)$ messages, because every node only broadcasts twice: (1) tell its neighbors to add some edges, and (2) claims that it is processed. The total messages of telling neighbors to add some edges is $O(n)$ since the total added edges is $O(n)$ from the planar property of the final topology. So the total communication cost is bounded by $O(n)$. ◻

It is easy to show that the computation cost of each node is at most $O(d_2 \log d_2)$, where d_2 is the number of its 2-hop neighbors in UDG. This can be improved to $O(d_1 \log d_1 + d_2)$, where d_1 is the number of its 1-hop neighbors in UDG. The improvement is based on the fact that we only need the triangles $\triangle wuv$ in $LDel^{(2)}(V)$ that has angle $\angle wuv \geq \pi/3$. All such triangles are definitely in $LDel^{(1)}(V)$. Thus, we can construct the Delaunay triangulation $Del(N_1(u))$ instead. Then check each candidate triangle $\triangle wuv$ from $LDel^{(1)}(V)$ to see if they contain any node from $N_2(u)$ inside its circumcircle. If it does not, then it belongs to $Del(N_2(u))$.

Observe that, after each node u collects the 2-hop neighbors $N_2(u)$, our algorithms can be performed asynchronously. However, collecting $N_2(u)$ need synchronized communication since otherwise, a node cannot determine if it indeed already collected $N_2(u)$.

3.5 Examples of Geometry Structure

We then gave some concrete examples of the geometry structures introduced in the previous subsections.

3.6 Transmission Power Control

In the previous sections, we have assumed that the transmission power of every node is equal and is normalized to one unit. We relax this assumption

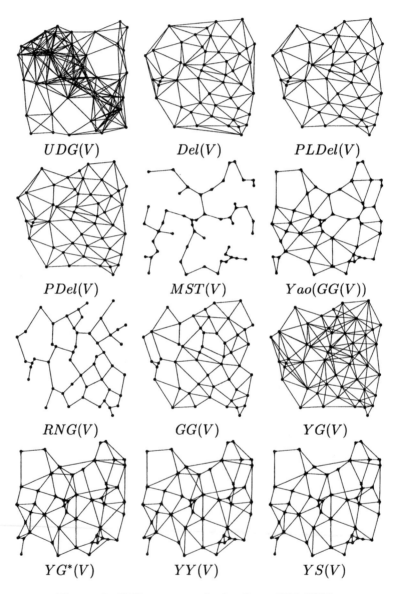

Figure 9: Different topologies from $UDG(V)$.

for a moment in this subsection. In other words, we assume that each node can adjust its transmission power according to its neighbors' positions. A natural question is then how to assign the transmission power for each node such that the wireless network is connected with optimization criteria being minimizing the maximum (or total) transmission power assigned.

A transmission power assignment on the vertices in V is a function f from V into real numbers. The *communication graph*, denoted by G_f, associated with a transmission power assignment f, is a directed graph with V as its vertices and has a directed edge $\overrightarrow{v_i v_j}$ if and only if $||v_i v_j||^\beta \leq f(v_i)$. We call a transmission power assignment f *complete* if the communication graph G_f is strongly connected. Recall that a directed graph is strongly connected if, for any given pair of ordered nodes s and t, there is a directed path from s to t.

The *maximum-cost* of a transmission power assignment f is defined as

$$mc(f) = \max_{v_i \in V} f(v_i).$$

And the *total-cost* of a transmission power assignment f is defined as

$$sc(f) = \sum_{v_i \in V} f(v_i).$$

The min-max assignment problem is then to find a complete transmission power assignment f whose cost $mc(f)$ is the least among all complete assignments. The min-total assignment problem is to find a complete transmission power assignment f whose cost $sc(f)$ is the least among all complete assignments.

Given a graph H, we say the power assignment f is induced by H if

$$f(v) = \max_{(v,u) \in E} ||vu||^\beta,$$

where E is the set of edges of H. In other words, the power assigned to a node v is the largest power needed to reach all neighbors of v in H.

Transmission power control has been well-studied by peer researchers in the recent years. Monks *et al.* [67] conducted simulations which show that implementing power control in a multiple access environment can improve the throughput performance of the non-power controlled IEEE 802.11 by a factor of 2. Therefore it provides a compelling reason for adopting the power controlled MAC protocol in wireless network.

The min-max assignment problem was studied by several researchers [68, 69]. Let EMST(V) be the Euclidean minimum spanning tree over a point set V. Both [68] and [69] use the power assignment induced by EMST(V). The correctness of using minimum spanning tree is proved in [68]. Both algorithms compute the minimum spanning tree from the fully connected graph. Notice that Kruskal's or Prim's minimum spanning tree algorithm has time complexity $O(m + n \log n)$, where m is the number of edges of the graph. Thus, the approach by [68] and [69] has time complexity $O(n^2)$ in the worst case. In addition, different distributed implementation of this algorithm is not feasible because of the information each node has to store and process. In contrast, we can give a simple $O(n \log n)$ time complexity centralized algorithm which can also be implemented efficiently for distributed computation.

For an optimum transmission power assignment f_{opt}, call a link uv the *critical link* if $\|uv\|^\beta = mc(f_{opt})$. It was proved in [68] that the longest edge of the Euclidean minimum spanning tree EMST(V) is always the critical link.

The best distributed algorithm [70, 71, 72] can compute the minimum spanning tree in $O(n)$ rounds using $O(m + n \log n)$ communications for a general graph with m edges and n nodes. The relative neighborhood graph, the Gabriel graph and the Yao graph all have $O(n)$ edges and contain the Euclidean minimum spanning tree. This implies the following theorem.

Theorem 3.21 *The distributed min-max assignment problem can be solved in $O(n)$ rounds using $O(n \log n)$ communications.*

The min-total assignment problem was studied by Kiroustis *et al.* [73] and by Clementi *et al.* [74, 75, 76]. Kiroustis *et al.* [73] first proved that the min-total assignment problem is *NP-hard* when the mobile nodes are deployed in a three-dimensional space. A simple 2-approximation algorithm based on the Euclidean minimum spanning tree was also given in [73]. The algorithm guarantees the same approximation ratio in any dimensions. Then Clementi *et al.* [74, 75, 76] proved that the min-total assignment problem is still NP-hard when the mobile nodes are deployed in a two dimensional space.

Recently, Călinescu *et al.* gave a method that achieves better approximation ratio than the approach by the minimum spanning tree by using idea from the minimum Steiner tree.

4 Clustering, Virtual Backbone

While all the structures discussed so far are flat structures, there are another set of structures, called hierarchical structures, are used in wireless networks. Instead of all nodes are involved in relaying packets for other nodes, the hierarchical routing protocols pick a subset of nodes that server as the routers, forwarding packets for other nodes. The structure used to build this virtual backbone is usually the connected dominating set.

4.1 Centralized Methods

Guha and Khuller [77] studied the approximation of the connected dominating set problem for general graphs. They gave two different approaches, both of them guarantee approximation ratio of $\Theta(H(\Delta))$. As their approaches are for general graphs and thus do not utilize the geometry structure if applied to the wireless ad hoc networks.

One approach is to grow a spanning tree that includes all nodes. The internal nodes of the spanning tree is selected as the final connected dominating set. They first pick the node (marked with *black*) with the maximum node degree and all of its neighbors as its children (marked with *gray*). They give two rules for selecting nodes (either gray node or a gray node and a white node adjacent to it) to grow the spanning tree: (1) the gray node with the maximum number of white neighbors; (2) two adjacent nodes, one is gray and one is white, with the maximum number of white neighbors. This approach has approximation ratio $2(H(\Delta) + 1)$, see [77].

The other approach is first approximating the dominating set and then connecting the dominating set to a connected dominating set. It runs in two phases. At the start of the first phase all nodes are colored white. Each time a vertex is included into the dominating set, we color it black. Dominators are colored gray. In this first phase, the algorithm picks a node at each step and colors it black and colors all its adjacent nodes gray (as dominators). A *piece* is defined as a white node, or a black connected component. At each step, pick a node to color black that gives the maximum non-zero reduction in the number of pieces. In the second phase, recursively connect pairs of black components by choosing a chain of vertices, until there is only one black connected component. The final connected dominating set is the set of black vertices. They [77] proved that this approach has approximation ratio $\ln \Delta + 3$.

One can also use the Steiner tree algorithm to connect the dominators. This straightforward method gives approximation ratio $c(H(\Delta) + 1)$, where c is the approximation ratio for the unweighted Steiner tree problem. Currently, the best ratio is $1 + \frac{\ln 3}{2} \simeq 1.55$, due to Robins and Zelikovsky [78].

By definition, any algorithm generating a maximal independent set is a clustering method. We first review the methods that approximates the maximum independent set, the minimum dominating set, and the minimum connected dominating set.

Hunt *et al.* [79] and Marathe *et al.* [80] also studied the approximation of the maximum independent set and the minimum dominating set for unit disk graphs. They gave the first PTASs for MDS in UDG. The method is based on the following observations: a maximal independent set is always a dominating set; given a square Ω with a fixed area, the size of any maximal dominating set is bounded by a constant C. Assume that there are n nodes in Ω. Then, we can enumerate all sets with size at most C in time $\Theta(n^C)$. Among these enumerated sets, the smallest dominating set is the minimum dominating set. Then, using the shifting strategy proposed by Hochbaum [81], they derived a PTAS for the minimum dominating set problem.

Since we have PTAS for minimum dominating set and the graph *VirtG* connecting every pair of dominators within at most 3 hops is connected [11], we have an approximation algorithm (constructing a minimum spanning tree *VirtG*) for MCDS with approximation ratio $3 + \epsilon$. Notice that, Berman *et al.* [82] gave an $\frac{4}{3}$ approximation method to connect a dominating set and Robins *et al.* [78] gave an $\frac{4}{3}$ approximation method to connect an independent set. Thus, we can easily have an $\frac{8}{3}$ approximation algorithm for MCDS, which was reported in [83]. Recently, Cheng *et al.* [84] designed a PTAS for MCDS in UDG. However, it is difficult to distributize their method efficiently.

4.2 Distributed Methods

Many distributed clustering (or dominating set) algorithms have been proposed in the literature [9, 85, 86, 87, 24, 88]. All algorithms assume that the nodes have distinctive identities (denoted by ID hereafter).

In the rest of section, we will interchange the terms cluster-head and dominator. The node that is not a cluster-head is also called *dominatee*. A node is called *white* node if its status is yet to be decided by the clustering algorithm. Initially, all nodes are white. The status of a node, after the clustering method finishes, could be *dominator* with color *black* or *dominatee* with color *gray*. The rest of this section is devoted for the distributed methods that approximates the minimum dominating set and the minimum connected dominating set for unit disk graph.

4.2.1 Clustering without Geometry Property

For general graphs, Jia *et al.* [89] described and analyzed some randomized distributed algorithms for the minimum dominating set problem that run in polylogarithmic time, independent of the diameter of the network, and that return a dominating set of size within a logarithmic factor from the optimum with high probability. Their best algorithm runs in $O(\log n \log \Delta)$ rounds with high probability, and every pair of neighbors exchange a constant number of messages in each round. The computed dominating set is within $O(\log \Delta)$ in expectation and within $O(\log n)$ with high probability. Their algorithm works for weighted dominating set also.

The method proposed by Das *et al.* [6, 90] contains three stages: approximating the minimum dominating set, constructing a spanning forest of stars, expanding the spanning forest to a spanning tree. Here the *stars* are formed by connecting each dominatee node to one of its dominators. The approximation method of MDS is essentially a distributed variation of the the centralized Chvatal's greedy algorithm [91] for set cover. Notice that the dominating set problem is essentially the set cover problem which is well-studied. It is then not surprise that the method by Das *et al.* [6, 90] guarantees a $H(\Delta)$ for the MDS problem, where H is the harmonic function and Δ is the maximum node degree.

While the algorithm proposed by Das *et al.* [6, 90] finds a dominating set and then grows it to a connecting dominating set, the algorithm proposed by Wu and Li [92, 7] takes an opposite approach. They first find a connecting dominating set and then prune out certain redundant nodes from the CDS. The initial CDS $\mathbb{C}$ contains all nodes that have at least two non-adjacent neighbors. A node u is said to be *locally redundant* if it has either a neighbor in $\mathbb{C}$ with larger ID which dominate all other neighbors of u, or two adjacent neighbors with larger ID which together dominates all other neighbors of u. Their algorithm then keeps removing all locally redundant nodes from $\mathbb{C}$. They showed that this algorithm works well in practice when the nodes are distributed uniformly and randomly, although no any theoretical analysis is given by them both for the worst case and for the average approximation ratio. However, it was shown by Alzoubi *et al.* [9] that the approximation ratio of this algorithm could be as large as $\frac{n}{2}$.

Stojmenovic *et al.* [8] proposed several synchronized distributed constructions of connecting dominating set. In their algorithms, the connecting dominating set consists of two types of nodes: clusterhead and border-nodes (also called gateway or connectors elsewhere). The clusterhead nodes are just a maximal independent set, which is constructed as follows. At each step, all white nodes which have the lowest *rank* among all white neighbors are colored black, and the white neighbors are colored gray. The ranks of the white nodes is updated if necessary. Here, the following rankings of a node are used in various methods: the ID only [86, 85], the ordered pair of degree and ID [93], and an ordered pair of degree and location [8]. After the clusterhead nodes are selected, border-nodes are selected to connect them. A node is a border-node if it is not a clusterhead and there are at least two clusterheads within its 2-hop neighborhood. It was shown by [9] that the worst case approximation ratio of this method is also $\frac{n}{2}$, although it works well in practice.

In [94, 95], Basagni *et al.* studied how to maintain the clustering in mobile wireless ad hoc networks. It uses a general *weight* as a criterion for selecting the node as the clusterhead, where the weight could be any criteria used before.

4.2.2 Clustering with Geometry Property

Notice that none of the above algorithm utilizes the geometry property of the underlying unit disk graph. Recently, several algorithms were proposed with a constant worst case approximation ratio by taking advantage of the geometry properties of the underlying graph. These methods typically use two messages similar to IamDominator and IamDominatee, and typically have the following procedures: a white node claims itself to be a dominator if it has the smallest ID among all of its white neighbors, if there is any, and broadcasts IamDominator to its 1-hop neighbors. A white node receiving IamDominator message marks itself as dominatee and broadcasts IamDomi-natee to its 1-hop neighbors. The set of dominators generated by the above method is actually a maximal independent set. Here, we assume that each node knows the IDs of all its 1-hop neighbors, which can be achieved by asking each node to broadcast its ID to its 1-hop neighbors initially. This approach of constructing MIS is well-known. For example, Stojmenovic *et al.* [8] also used this method to compute the MIS.

The second step of backbone formation is to find some *connectors* (also called *gateways*) among all the dominatees to connect the dominators. Then the connectors and the dominators form a *connected dominating set*. Recently, Wan, *et al.* [10] proposed a communication efficient algorithm to find connectors based on the fact that there are only a constant number of dominators within k-hops of any node. The following observation is a basis of several algorithms for CDS. After clustering, one dominator node can be connected to many dominatees. However, it is well-known that a dominatee node can only be connected to at most *five* dominators in the unit disk graph model.

Lemma 4.1 *In UDG, for every dominatee node v, it can be connected to at most 5 dominator nodes.*

Generally, it was shown in [10, 11] that for each node (dominator or dominatee), there are at most a constant number of dominators that are at most k units away.

Lemma 4.2 *For every node v, the number of dominators inside the disk centered at v with radius k-units is bounded by a constant* $\ell_k < (2k+1)^2$.

Lemma 4.3 *Given a dominating set S, let VirtG be the graph connecting all pairs of dominators u and v if there is a path in UDG connecting them with at most 3 hops. VirtG is connected.*

It is natural to form a connected dominating set by finding connectors to connect any pair of dominators u and v if they are connected in $VirtG$. This strategy is also adopted by Wan, *et al.* [10]. Notice that, in the approach by Stojmenovic *et al.* [8], they set any dominatee node as the connector if there are two dominators within its 2-hop neighborhood. This approach is very pessimistic and results in very large number of connectors in the worst case [9]. Instead, Wan *et al.* suggested to find only one unique shortest path to connect any two dominators that are at most three hops away.

We first briefly review their basic idea of forming a CDS in a distributed manner. Let $\Pi_{UDG}(u,v)$ be the path connecting two nodes u and v in UDG with the smallest number of hops. Let's first consider how to connect two dominators within 3 hops. If the path $\Pi_{UDG}(u,v)$ has two hops, then u finds the dominatee with the smallest ID to connect u and v. If the path $\Pi_{UDG}(u,v)$ has three hops, then u finds the node, say w, with the smallest ID such that w and v are two hops apart. Then node w selects the node with the smallest ID to connect w and v.

Wang and Li [11] and Alzoubi *et al.* [10] discussed in detail some approaches to optimize the communication cost and the memory cost. We briefly review the approaches proposed in [65, 11]. Notice that, for example, it is not obvious how node u can find such node w efficiently. In addition that, using the smallest ID is not efficient because we may have to postpone the selecting of connectors till the node collects the IDs of all its one-hop neighbors. Instead of using the intermediate node with the smallest ID, we pick any node that comes first to the notice of the node that makes the selection of connectors. Their method uses the following primitive messages (some messages are used in forming clusters):

- IamDominator(u): u tells its 1-hop neighbors that u is a dominator;

- IamDominatee(u, v): node u tells its 1-hop neighbors that u is a dominatee of node v;

- 2HopsPath(u, w, v): node u tells its 1-hop neighbors that u has a 2-hops path uwv and w is the unique node selected by u among all intermediate nodes that can connect u and v.

- 3HopsPath(x, u, w, v): node x tells its 1-hop neighbors that x has a 3-hops path $xuwv$ and u and w are the uniquely selected nodes among all intermediate nodes. Node u is selected by node x and node w is selected by node u.

The message IamDominator(u) is only broadcasted at most once by each node; IamDominatee(u, v) is only broadcasted at most five times by each node u for all possible dominators v from Lemma 4.1; from Lemma 4.2, we know that 2HopsPath(u, w, v) and 3HopsPath(x, u, w, v) are also broadcasted at most a constant times by each node for all possible dominator v.

To save the memory cost of each wireless node, they [11] also designed the following link lists for each node u:

- Dominators: it stores all dominators of u if there is any. Notice that if the node itself is a dominator, no value is assigned for Dominators.

- Connector2HopsPath: for each dominator v that are 2-hops apart from u, node u stores (w, v), where the intermediate node w is selected by u to connect u and v.

- Connector3HopsPath: for each dominator v that are 3-hops apart from u, node u stores (w, x, v) such that there is a path $uwxv$, and w is selected by u and x is the node selected by w to connect v.

Notice that for each node, there are at most five dominators. So the size of link list Dominators is at most five. Then from Lemma 4.2, for each node u, there are at most ℓ_k number of dominators v that are k-hops apart from u. Therefore, the sizes of link lists Connector2HopsPath, Connector3HopsPath are bounded by ℓ_2 and ℓ_3 respectively. Then we are in the position to review the distributed algorithm proposed in [65, 11] to find the connectors efficiently. Assume that a maximal independent set is already constructed by a cluster algorithm.

Algorithm 5 *Finding Connectors*

1. Every dominatee node w broadcasts to its 1-hop neighbors a message lamDominatee(w, v) for each dominator v stored at Dominators.

2. Assume node u receives a message lamDominatee(w, v) for the first time. If $u \neq v$, v is not in Dominators list of u, and there is no pair $(*, v)$ in Connector2HopsPath, then u adds (w, v) to Connector2HopsPath. Here $*$ denotes any node ID. If u is a dominatee, then it broadcasts message a 2HopsPath(u, w, v) to its 1-hop neighbors. If node u is a dominator, node u already knows a path uwv to connect a 2-hops apart dominator v.

   Node u will discard any message lamDominatee$(*, v)$ afterward.

3. When a node w (it must be a dominatee here) receives the message 2HopsPath(u, w, v), node w marks itself as a *connector*, if u is a dominator.

4. Assume a dominator x receives the message 2HopsPath(u, w, v), where $x \neq w$. If there is no triple $(*, *, v)$ in Connector3HopsPath, then x adds (u, w, v) to Connector3HopsPath and broadcasts the message 3HopsPath(x, u, w, v) to its 1-hop neighbors. Then node x already knows a path $xuwv$ to connect a 3-hops apart dominator v.

5. When a node u (it must be dominatee here) receives the message 3HopsPath(x, u, w, v), node u marks itself as a connector. Node u sends a message to node w asking w to be a connector.

Notice that it is possible that, given any two nodes u and v, the path found by node u to connect v is different from the path found by v to connect u. This increases the robustness of the backbone. When only one connecting path between any pair of dominators is needed, they suggested to add the following restrictions: a dominator node u stores a 2-hops or 3-hops path connecting it to another dominator node v if and only if node u has a smaller ID. In other words, the decision to select the connectors is always made by the node with smaller ID.

The graph constructed by the above algorithm **FindingConnectors** is called a CDS graph (or *backbone* of the network). If we also add all edges that connect all dominatees to their dominators, the graph is called extended CDS, denoted by CDS'.

Lemma 4.4 *The number of connectors found is at most ℓ_3 times of the minimum. The size of the connected dominating set found by the above algorithm is within a small constant factor of the minimum.*

Let *opt* be the size of the minimum connected dominating set. It was shown [80] that the size of the computed maximal independent set has size at most $4*opt+1$. We already showed that the size of the connected dominating set found by the above algorithm is at most $\ell_3 k + k$, where k is the size of the maximal independent set found by the clustering algorithm. It implies that the found connected dominating set has size at most $4(\ell_3 + 1) * opt + \ell_3 + 1$. Consequently, the computed connected dominating set is at most $4(\ell_3 + 1)$ factor of the optimum (with an additional constant $\ell_3 + 1$).

4.2.3 The Properties of Backbone

It was shown in [65, 11] that the CDS' graph is a sparse spanner in terms of both hops and length, meanwhile CDS has a bounded node degree.

Lemma 4.5 *The node degree of CDS is bounded by $\max(\ell_3, 5 + \ell_2)$.*

The above lemma immediately implies that CDS is a sparse graph, i.e., the total number of edges is $O(k)$, where k is the number of dominators. Moreover, the graph CDS' is also a sparse graph because the total number of the links from dominatees to dominators is at most $5(n - k)$. Notice that we have at most $n - k$ dominatees, each of which is connected to at most 5 dominators. The node degree in CDS is bounded, however, the degree of some dominator node in CDS' may be arbitrarily large.

After we construct the backbone CDS and the induced graph CDS', if a node u wants to send a message to another node v, it follows the following procedure. If v is within the transmission range of u, node u directly sends message to v. Otherwise, node u asks its dominator to send this message to v (or one of its dominators) through the backbone. They showed that CDS' (plus all implicit edges connecting dominatees that are no more than one unit apart) is a good spanner in terms of both hops and length.

Lemma 4.6 *The hops stretch factor of CDS' is bounded by a constant 3 and the length stretch factor of CDS' is bounded by a constant 6.*

Several routing algorithms require the underlying topology be planar. Notice in the formation algorithm of CDS, we do not use any geometry information. The resulting CDS maybe non-planar graph. Even using some geometry information, the CDS still is not guaranteed to be a planar graph. Then Li *et al.* [11] proposed a method to make the graph CDS planar without losing the spanner property of the backbone. Their method applies the localized Delaunay triangulation [35] on top of the induced graph from CDS, denoted by ICDS. It was proved in [35] that $LDel(G)$ is a spanner if G is a unit disk graph. Notice that ICDS is a unit disk graph defined over all dominators and connectors. Consequently, $LDel(ICDS)$ is a spanner in terms of length.

Lemma 4.7 *[11] The hops and length stretch factors of $LDel(ICDS)$ are bounded by some constants.*

5 Localized Routings

The geometric nature of the multi-hop ad-hoc wireless networks allows a promising idea: localized routing protocols. A routing protocol is *localized* if the decision to which node to forward a packet is based only on:

- The information in the header of the packet. This information includes the source and the destination of the packet, but more data could be included, provided that its total length is bounded.

- The local information gathered by the node from a small neighborhood. This information includes the set of 1-hop neighbors of the node, but a larger neighborhood set could be used provided it can be collected efficiently.

Randomization is also used in designing the protocols. A routing is said to be *memory-less* if the decision to which node to forward a packet is solely based on the destination, current node and its neighbors within some constant hops. Localized routing is sometimes called in the literature *stateless* [27], *online* [96, 61], or *distributed* [97].

5.1 Location Service

In order to make the localized routing work, the source node has to learn the current (or approximately current) location of the destination node. Notice that, for sensor networks collecting data, the destination node is often fixed, thus, location service is not needed in these applications. However, the help of a *location service* is needed in most application scenarios. Mobile nodes register their locations to the location service. When a source node does not know the position of the destination node, it queries the location service to get that information. In cellular networks, there are dedicated position severs. It will be difficult to implement the centralized approach of location services in wireless ad-hoc networks. First, for centralized approach, each node has to know the position of the node that provides the location services, which is a chicken-and-egg problem. Second, the dynamic nature of the wireless ad hoc networks makes it very unlikely that there is at least one location server available for each node. Thus, we will concentrate on distributed location services.

For the wireless ad hoc networks, the location service provided can be classified into four categorizes: *some-for-all*, *some-for-some*, *all-for-some*, *all-for-all*. Some-for-all service means that some wireless nodes provide location services for all wireless nodes. Other categorizations are defined similarly.

An example of all-for-all services is the location services provided in the Distance Routing Effect Algorithm for Mobility (DREAM) by Basagni *et al.* [98]. Each node stores a database of the position information for all other nodes in the wireless networks. Each node will regularly flood packets containing its position to all other nodes. A frequency of the flooding and the range of the flooding is used as a control of the cost of updating and the accuracy of the database.

Using the idea of *quorum* developed in the databases and distributed systems, Hass and Liang [99], Stojmenovic [100] developed quorum based location services for wireless ad-hoc networks. Given a set of wireless nodes V, a quorum system is a set of subset $(Q_1, Q_2, \cdots, Q_k)$ of nodes whose union is V. These subsets could be mutually disjoint or often have equal number of intersections. When one of the nodes requires the information of the other, it suffices to query one node (called the representative node of Q_i) from each quorum Q_i. A virtual backbone is often constructed between the representative nodes using a non-position-based methods such as [10, 9]. The updating information of a node v is sent to the representative node (or the nearest if there are many) of the quorum containing v. The difficulty of using quorum is that the mobility of the nodes requires the frequent updating of the quorums. The quorum based location service is often *some-for-some* type.

The other promising location service is based on the quadtree partition of the two-dimensional space [101]. It divides the region containing the wireless network into hierarchy of squares. The partition of the space in [101] is uniform. However, we notice that the partition could be non-uniform if the density of the wireless nodes is not uniform for some applications. Each node v will have the position information of all nodes within the same *smallest* square containing v. This position information of v is also propagated to up-layer squares by storing it in the node with the nearest identity to v in each up-layer square containing v. Using the nearest identity over the smallest identity can avoid the overload of some nodes. The query is conducted accordingly. It is easy to show that it takes about $O(\log n)$ time to update the location of v and to query another node's position information.

5.2   Localized Routing Protocols

We summarize some localized routing protocols proposed in the networking and computational geometry literature.

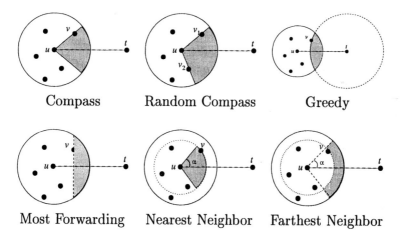

Figure 10: Various localized routing methods. Shaded area is empty and v is next node.

The following routing algorithms on the graphs were proposed recently.

Compass Routing Let t be the destination node. Current node u finds the next relay node v such that the angle $\angle vut$ is the smallest among all neighbors of u in a given topology. See[102].

Random Compass Routing Let u be the current node and t be the destination node. Let v_1 be the node on the above of line ut such that $\angle v_1 ut$ is the smallest among all such neighbors of u. Similarly, we define v_2 to be nodes below line ut that minimizes the angle $\angle v_2 ut$. Then node u randomly choose v_1 or v_2 to forward the packet. See[102].

Greedy Routing Let t be the destination node. Current node u finds the next relay node v such that the distance $\|vt\|$ is the smallest among all neighbors of u in a given topology. See [26].

Most Forwarding Routing (MFR) Current node u finds the next relay node v such that $\|v't\|$ is the smallest among all neighbors of u in a given topology, where v' is the projection of v on segment ut. See [97].

Nearest Neighbor Routing (NN) Given a parameter angle α, node u finds the nearest node v as forwarding node among all neighbors of u in a given topology such that $\angle vut \le \alpha$.

Farthest Neighbor Routing (FN) Given a parameter angle α, node u finds the farthest node v as forwarding node among all neighbors of u in a given topology such that $\angle vut \le \alpha$.

Greedy-Compass Current node u first finds the neighbors v_1 and v_2 such that v_1 forms the smallest counter-clockwise angle $\angle tuv_1$ and v_2 forms the smallest clockwise angle $\angle tuv_2$ among all neighbors of u with the segment ut. The packet is forwarded to the node of $\{v_1, v_2\}$ with minimum distance to t. See [61, 103]

Notice that it is shown in [26, 102] that the compass routing, random compass routing and the greedy routing guarantee to deliver the packets from the source to the destination if Delaunay triangulation is used as network topology. They proved this by showing that the distance from the selected forwarding node v to the destination node t is less than the distance from current node u to t. However, the same proof cannot be carried over when the network topology is Yao graph, Gabriel graph, relative neighborhood graph, and the localized Delaunay triangulation. When the underlying network topology is a planar graph, the right hand rule is often used to guarantee the packet delivery after simple localized routing heuristics fail [26, 97, 27].

Theorem 5.1 *[103] The greedy routing guarantees the delivery of the packets if the Delaunay triangulation is used as the underlying structure. The compass routing guarantees the delivery of the packets if the regular triangulation is used as the underlying structure. There are triangulations (not Delaunay) that defeat these two schemes. The greedy-compass routing works* *for all triangulations, i.e., it guarantees the delivery of the packets as long as there is a triangulation used as the underlying structure. Every oblivious routing method is defeated by some convex subdivisions.*

Here a triangulation is *regular triangulation* if it is the projection of the lower convex hull of some 3-dimensional polytopes P into the X-Y plane. Delaunay triangulation is a special regular triangulation in which all the vertices of P are on a paraboloid $z^2 = x^2 + y^2$. Another interesting triangulation is *greedy triangulation* which is constructed by adding edges in the increasing order of their lengths to avoid crossing edges. They [103] also study the localized routing for greedy triangulation. As the greedy triangulation can not be constructed locally or very efficiently in a distributed manner. We omit that part in this survey. It is easy to see that there is no memoryless routing method that works in the unit disk graph.

5.3 Quality Guaranteed Protocols

With respect to localized routing, there are several ways to measure the quality of the protocol. Given the scarcity of the power resources in wireless networks, minimizing the total power used is imperative. A stronger condition is to minimize the total Euclidean distance traversed by the packet. Morin *et al.* [61, 103] also studied the performance ratio of previously studied localized routing methods. They proved that none of the previous proposed heuristics guarantees a constant ratio of the traveled distance of a packet compared with the minimum. They gave the first localized routing algorithm such that the traveled distance of a packet from u to v is at most a constant factor of $\|uv\|$ when the Delaunay triangulation is used as the underlying structure.

Their algorithm is based on the proof of the spanner property of the Delaunay triangulation [62]. Without loss of generality, let $b_0 = u$, b_1, b_2, $\cdots$, b_{m-1}, $b_m = v$ be the vertices corresponding to the sequence of Voronoi regions traversed by walking from u to v along the segment uv. If a Voronoi edge or a Voronoi vertex happens to lie on the segment uv, then choose the Voronoi region lying above uv. See Figure 11. Given two nodes u and v, $tunnel(u,v)$ is defined as the collection of triangles that intersect the segment uv. The sequence of nodes b_i, $0 \le i \le m$, defines a path from u to v. In general, they [62] refer to the path constructed this way between some nodes u and v as the *direct DT path* from u to v.

Assume that line uv is the x-axis. The path constructed by Dobkin *et al.* uses the direct DT path as long as it is above the x-axis. Assume that

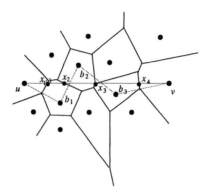

Figure 11: There is a good approximation path using the edges of $tunnel(u, v)$.

the path constructed so far has brought us to some node b_i such that b_i is above uv, and b_{i+1} is below uv. Let j be the least integer larger than i such that b_j is above uv. Notice that here j exists because $b_m = v$ is on uv. Then the path constructed by Dobkin et $al.$ uses either the direct DT path to b_j or takes a $shortcut$. See [62] for more detail about the condition when to choose the direct DT path from b_i to b_j, when to choose the shortcut path from b_i to b_j, and how the short-cut path is defined.

Bose and Morin basically use sort of binary search method to find which path is better. Refer [103] for more detail of finding the path. However, their algorithm needs the Delaunay triangulation as the underlying structure which is expensive to construct in wireless ad hoc networks. In [104], they further extent their method to any triangulations satisfying the diamond property. Here, a triangulation satisfying the diamond property if for every edge uv in the triangulation, either $\triangle uvw_1$ or $\triangle uvw_2$ is empty of other vertices, where w_i satisfying $\angle w_i uv = \angle w_i vu = \frac{\pi}{6}$, for $i = 1, 2$.

Localized routing protocols support mobility by eliminating the communication intensive task of updating the routing tables. But mobility can affect the localized routing protocols, in both the performance and the guarantee of delivery. There is no work so far to design protocols with guaranteed delivery when the network topology changes during the routing.

6 Broadcasting & Multicasting

Minimum-energy broadcast/multicast routing in a simple ad hoc networking environment has been addressed by the pioneering work in [105, 106, 107,

108]. To assess the complexities *one at a time*, the nodes in the network are assumed to be randomly distributed in a two-dimensional plane and there is no mobility. Nevertheless, as argued in [108], the impact of mobility can be incorporated into this static model because the transmitting power can be adjusted to accommodate the new locations of the nodes as necessary. In other words, the capability to adjust the transmission power provides considerable "elasticity" to the topological connectivity, and hence may reduce the need for hand-offs and tracking. In addition, as assumed in [108], there are sufficient bandwidth and transceiver resources. Under these assumptions, centralized (as opposed to distributed) algorithms were presented by [108] for minimum-energy broadcast/multicast routing. These centralized algorithms, in this simple networking environment, are expected to serve as the basis for further studies on distributed algorithms in a more practical network environment, with limited bandwidth and transceiver resources, as well as the node mobility.

6.1 Broadcasting

Three greedy heuristics were proposed in [108] for the minimum-energy broadcast routing problem: MST (minimum spanning tree), SPT (shortest-path tree), and BIP (broadcasting incremental power). The MST heuristic first applies the Prim's algorithm to obtain a MST, and then orient it as an arborescence rooted at the source node. The SPT heuristic applies the Dijkstra's algorithm to obtain a SPT rooted at the source node. The BIP heuristic is the node version of Dijkstra's algorithm for SPT. It maintains, throughout its execution, a single arborescence rooted at the source node. The arborescence starts from the source node, and new nodes are added to the arborescence one at a time on the minimum incremental cost basis until all nodes are included in the arborescence. The incremental cost of adding a new node to the arborescence is the minimum additional power increased by some node in the current arborescence to reach this new node. The implementation of BIP is based on the standard Dijkstra's algorithm, with one fundamental difference on the operation whenever a new node q is added. Whereas the Dijkstra's algorithm updates the node weights (representing the current knowing distances to the source node), BIP updates the cost of each link (representing the incremental power to reach the head node of the directed link). This update is performed by subtracting the cost of the added link pq from the cost of every link qr that starts from q to a node r not in the new arborescence.

They have been evaluated through simulations in [108], but little is known about their analytical performances in terms of the approximation ratio. Here, the approximation ratio of a heuristic is the maximum ratio of the energy needed to broadcast a message based on the arborescence generated by this heuristic to the least necessary energy by any arborescence for any set of points. The analytical performance is very essential and more convincing in evaluating these heuristics, because one may come up with several seemingly reasonable greedy heuristics. But it is hard to tell from simulation outputs which one is better or worse in the worst case scenario.

For a pure illustration purpose, another slight variation of BIP was discussed in detail in [109]. This greedy heuristic is similar to the Chvatal's algorithm [110] for the set cover problem and is a variation of BIP. Like BIP, an arborescence, which starts with the source node, is maintained throughout the execution of the algorithm. However, unlike BIP, many new nodes can be added one at a time. Similar to the Chvatal's algorithm [110], the new nodes added are chosen to have the minimal *average* incremental cost, which is defined as the ratio of the minimum additional power increased by some node in the current arborescence to reach these new nodes to the number of these new nodes. They called this heuristic as the Broadcast Average Incremental Power (BAIP). In contrast to the $1 + \log m$ approximation ratio of the Chvatal's algorithm [110], where m is the largest set size in the Set Cover Problem, they showed that the approximation ratio of BAIP is at least $\frac{4n}{\ln n} - o(1)$, where n is the number of receiving nodes.

Wan *et al.* [109, 111] showed that the approximation ratios of MST and BIP are between 6 and 12 and between $\frac{13}{3}$ and 12 respectively; on the other hand, the approximation ratios of SPT and BAIP are at least $\frac{n}{2}$ and $\frac{4n}{\ln n} - o(1)$ respectively, where n is the number of nodes. We then discuss in detail of their proof techniques.

Any broadcast routing is viewed as an arborescence (a directed tree) T, rooted at the source node of the broadcasting, that spans all nodes. Let $f_T(\mathbf{p})$ denote the transmission power of the node $\mathbf{p}$ required by T. For any leaf node $\mathbf{p}$ of T, $f_T(\mathbf{p}) = 0$. For any internal node $\mathbf{p}$ of T,

$$f_T(\mathbf{p}) = \max_{\mathbf{pq} \in T} \|\mathbf{pq}\|^\beta,$$

in other words, the β-th power of the longest distance between $\mathbf{p}$ and its children in T. The total energy required by T is $\sum_{\mathbf{p} \in P} f_T(\mathbf{p})$. Thus the minimum-energy broadcast routing problem is different from the conventional link-based minimum spanning tree (MST) problem. Indeed, while the MST can be solved in polynomial time by algorithms such as Prim's algorithm and Kruskal's algorithm [112], it is still unknown whether the minimum-energy broadcast routing problem can be solved in polynomial time. In its general graph version, the minimum-energy broadcast routing can be shown to be NP-hard [113], and even worse, it can not be approximated within a factor of $(1 - \epsilon) \log \Delta$, unless $NP \subseteq DTIME\left[n^{O(\log \log n)}\right]$, where Δ is the maximal degree and ϵ is any arbitrary small positive constant. However, this intractability of its general graph version does not necessarily imply the same hardness of its geometric version. In fact, as shown later in the survey, its geometric version can be approximated within a constant factor. Nevertheless, this suggests that the minimum-energy broadcast routing problem is considerably harder than the MST problem. Recently, Clementi *et al.* [105] proved that the minimum-energy broadcast routing problem is a NP-hard problem and obtained a parallel but weaker result to those of [109, 111].

Wan *et al.* [109, 111] gave some lower bounds on the approximation ratios of MST and BIP by studying some special instances in [109, 111]. Their deriving of the upper bounds relies extensively on the geometric structures of Euclidean MSTs. They first observed that as long as the cost of a link is an increasing function of the Euclidean length of the link, the set of MSTs of any point set *coincides* with the set of Euclidean MSTs of the same point set. In particular, for any spanning tree T of a finite point set P, parameter $\sum_{e \in T} \|e\|^2$ achieves its minimum if and only if T is an Euclidean MST of P. For any finite point set P, let $mst(P)$ denote an arbitrary Euclidean MST of P. The *radius* of a point set P is defined as

$$\inf_{\mathbf{p} \in P} \sup_{\mathbf{q} \in P} \|\mathbf{pq}\|.$$

Thus, a point set of radius one can be covered by a disk of radius one. A key result in [109, 111] is an upper bound on the parameter $\sum_{e \in mst(P)} \|e\|^2$ for any finite point set P of radius one. Note that the supreme of the total edge lengths of $mst(P)$, $\sum_{e \in mst(P)} \|e\|$, over all point sets P of radius one is infinity. However, the parameter $\sum_{e \in mst(P)} \|e\|^2$ is bounded from above by a constant for any point set P of radius one. They use c to denote the supreme of $\sum_{e \in mst(P)} \|e\|^2$ over all point sets P of radius one. The constant c is at most 12; see [109, 111].

Theorem 6.1 *[109, 111]* $6 \leq c \leq 12$.

The proof of this theorem involves complicated geometric arguments; see [109, 111] for more detail. Note that for any point set P of radius one, the length of each edge in $mst(P)$ is at most one. Therefore, Theorem 6.1 implies that for any point set P of radius one and any real number $\beta \geq 2$,

$$\sum_{e \in mst(P)} \|e\|^\beta \leq \sum_{e \in mst(P)} \|e\|^2 \leq c \leq 12.$$

The next theorem proved in [109, 111] explores a relation between the minimum energy required by a broadcasting and the energy required by the Euclidean MST of the corresponding point set.

Lemma 6.1 *[109, 111] For any point set P in the plane, the total energy required by any broadcasting among P is at least $\frac{1}{c} \sum_{e \in mst(P)} \|e\|^\beta$.*

PROOF. Let T be an arborescence for a broadcasting among P with the minimum energy consumption. For any none-leaf node $\mathbf{p}$ in T, let $T_\mathbf{p}$ be an Euclidean MST of the point set consisting $\mathbf{p}$ and all children of $\mathbf{p}$ in T. Suppose that the longest Euclidean distance between $\mathbf{p}$ and its children is r. Then the transmission power of node $\mathbf{p}$ is r^β, and all children of $\mathbf{p}$ lie in the disk centered at $\mathbf{p}$ with radius r. From the definition of c, we have

$$\sum_{e \in T_\mathbf{p}} \left(\frac{\|e\|}{r} \right)^\beta \leq c,$$

which implies that

$$r^\beta \geq \frac{1}{c} \sum_{e \in T_\mathbf{p}} \|e\|^\beta.$$

Let T^* denote the spanning tree obtained by superposing of all $T_\mathbf{p}$'s for non-leaf nodes of T. Then the total energy required by T is at least $\frac{1}{c} \sum_{e \in T^*} \|e\|^\beta$, which is further no less than $\frac{1}{c} \sum_{e \in mst(P)} \|e\|^\beta$. This completes the proof. ☐

Consider any point set P in a two-dimensional plane. Let T be an arborescence oriented from some $mst(P)$. Then the total energy required by T is at most $\sum_{e \in T_\mathbf{p}} \|e\|^\beta$. From Lemma 6.1, this total energy is at most c times the optimum cost. Thus the approximation ratio of the link-based MST heuristic is at most c. Together with Theorem 6.1, this observation leads to the following theorem.

Theorem 6.2 *[109, 111] The approximation ratio of the link-based MST heuristic is at most c, and therefore is at most 12.*

In addition, they derived an upper bound on the approximation ratio of the BIP heuristic. Once again, the Euclidean MST plays an important role.

Lemma 6.2 *[109, 111] For any broadcasting among a point set P in a two-dimensional plane, the total energy required by the arborescence generated by the BIP algorithm is at most $\sum_{e \in mst(P)} \|e\|^\beta$.*

6.2 Approximate MST of UDG Locally

The best distributed algorithm [70, 71, 72] can compute the minimum spanning tree in $O(n)$ rounds using $O(m + n \log n)$ communications for a general graph with m edges and n nodes. The relative neighborhood graph, the Gabriel graph and the Yao graph all have $O(n)$ edges and contain the Euclidean minimum spanning tree. This implies that we can construct the minimum spanning tree in a distributed manner using $O(n \log n)$ messages. Unfortunately, even for wireless network modeled by a ring, the $O(n \log n)$ number of messages is still necessary for constructing the minimum spanning tree.

Given a graph G, let $\omega_b(G) = \sum_{e \in G} \|e\|^b$. We [114] recently presented the first localized method to construct a bounded degree planar connected structure whose total edge length is within a constant factor of that of the minimum spanning tree. The total communication cost of our method is $O(n)$, and every node only uses its two-hop information to construct such structure. We showed that the energy consumption using this structure is within $O(n^{\beta-1})$ of the optimum, i.e., $\omega_\beta(H) = O(n^{\beta-1}) \cdot \omega_\beta(MST)$ for any $\beta \geq 1$. This improves the previously known "lightest" structure RNG by $O(n)$ factor since in the worst case $\omega(RNG) = \Theta(n) \cdot \omega(MST)$ and $\omega_\beta(RNG) = \Theta(n^\beta) \cdot \omega_\beta(MST)$.

Our low-weight structure is based on a modified relative neighborhood graph. Notice that, traditionally, the relative neighborhood graph will always select an edge uv even if there is some node on the boundary of $lune(u, v)$. Thus, RNG may have unbounded node degree, e.g., considering $n - 1$ points equally distributed on the circle centered at the nth point v, the degree of v is $n - 1$. Notice that for the sake of lowing the weight of a structure, the structure should contain as less edges as possible without breaking the connectivity. We then naturally extend the traditional definition of RNG as follows.

The modified *relative neighborhood graph* consists of all edges uv such that (1) the *interior* of $lune(u, v)$ contains no point $w \in V$ and, (2) there is no point $w \in V$ with $ID(w) < ID(v)$ on the boundary of $lune(u,v)$ and $\|wv\| < \|uv\|$, and (3) there is no point $w \in V$ with $ID(w) < ID(u)$ on the boundary of $lune(u,v)$ and $\|wu\| < \|uv\|$, and (4) there is no point $w \in V$ on the boundary of $lune(u,v)$ with $ID(w) < ID(u)$, $ID(w) < ID(v)$, and $\|wu\| = \|uv\|$. See Figure 12 for an illustration when an edge uv is not included in the modified relative neighborhood graph. We denote such structure by RNG' hereafter. Obviously, RNG' is a subgraph of traditional RNG. We [114] proved that RNG' has a maximum node degree 6 and still contains a minimum spanning tree as a subgraph.

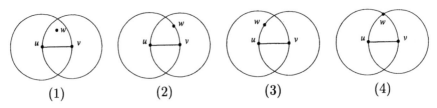

Figure 12: Which edges are not in the modified RNG.

So far RNG' is the previously best known connected structures that can be constructed locally and has a small total edge weight. As shown in [114], its total weight could still be as large as $O(n)$ times of $\omega(MST)$.

We then give the first localized algorithm that constructs a low-weighted structure using only some two hops information.

Algorithm 6 *Construct Low Weight Structure*

1. All nodes together construct the modified relative neighborhood graph RNG' in a localized manner.

2. Each node u locally broadcasts its incident edges in RNG' to its one-hop neighbors. Node u listens to the messages from its one-hop neighbors.

3. If node u received a message informing existence of edge xy from its neighbor x, for each edge uv in RNG', if uv is the longest among xy, ux, and vy, node u removes edge uv. Ties are broken by the label of the edges. Here assume that $uvyx$ is the convex hull of u, v, x, and y.

Let H be the final structure formed by all remaining edges in RNG', and we call it low weighted modified relative neighborhood graph. Obviously, if an edge uv is kept by node u, then it is also kept by node v.

Theorem 6.3 *[114] The total edge weight of H is within a constant factor of that of the minimum spanning tree.*

This was proved by showing that the edges in H satisfies the *isolation property* (defined in [115]). We [114] also showed that the final structure contains EMST of UDG as a subgraph. It was also shown in [114] that it is *impossible* to construct a low-weighted structure using only one hop neighbor information.

6.3 Forwarding Neighbors

The simplest broadcasting mechanism is to let every node retransmit the message to all its one-hop neighbors when receiving the first copy of the message, which is called *flooding* in the literature. Despite its simplicity, flooding is very inefficient and can result in high redundancy, contention, and collision. One approach to reducing the redundancy is to let a node only forward the message to a subset of one-hop neighbors who together can cover the two-hop neighbors. In other words, when a node retransmits a message to its neighbors, it explicitly ask a subset of its neighbors to relay the message.

Călinescu *et al.* [116] gave two practical heuristics for this problem (they called selecting forwarding neighbors). The first algorithm runs in time $O(n \log n)$ and returns a subset with size at most 6 times of the minimum. The second algorithm has an improved approximation ratio 3, but with running time $O(n^2)$. Here n is the number of total two-hop neighbors of a node. When all two-hop neighbors are in the same quadrant with respect to the source node, they gave an exact solution in time $O(n^2)$ and a solution with approximation factor 2 in time $O(n \log n)$. Their algorithms partition the region surrounding the source node into four quadrants, solve each quadrants using an algorithm with approximation factor α, and then combine these solutions. They proved that the combined solution is at most 3α times of the optimum solution.

Their approach assumes that every node u can collect its 2-hop neighbors $N_2(u)$ efficiently. Notice that, the 1-hop neighbors of every node u can be collected efficiently by asking each node to broadcast its information to its 1-hop neighbors. Thus all nodes get their 1-hop neighbors information by using total $O(n)$ messages. However, until recently, it is unknown how to collect the 2-hop neighbors information with $O(n)$ communications. The simplest broadcasting of 1-hop neighbors $N_1(u)$ to all neighbors u does let all nodes in $N_1(u)$ to collect their corresponding 2-hop neighbors. However, the total communication cost of this approach is $O(m)$, where m is the total number of links in UDG. Recently, Călinescu [64] proposed an efficient approach to collect $N_2(u)$ using the connected dominating set [10, 11] as forwarding nodes. Assume that the node position is known. He proved that the approach takes total communications $O(n)$, which is optimum within a constant factor.

7   Stochastic Geometry

In wireless ad hoc networks, one of the critical issues is that, for every pair of nodes, there is a path connecting them, i.e., the network is connected. With this in mind, Gupta and Kumar [117] studied what is the critical power at which each node has to transmit so as to guarantee the connectivity of the network asymptotically.

7.1   Background

Given an event Y, let $Pr\,(Y)$ be the probability of Y. Given a random variable X, we denote the expected value of X by $E[X]$, i.e., $E[X] = \sum_x x \cdot Pr\,(X = x)$ for discrete variables. As standard, we write log for base-2 logarithm and ln for natural logarithm. We say a function $f(n) \to a$ if $\lim_{n \to \infty} f(n) = a$.

A point set is said to a *random point process*, denoted by $\mathcal{X}_n$, if it consists of n independent points each of which is uniformly distributed over the region. The standard probabilistic model of *homogeneous Poisson process* is characterized by the property that the number of nodes in a region is a random variable depending only on the area (or volume in higher dimensions) of the region. In other words,

- The probability that there are exactly k nodes appearing in any region Ψ of area A is $\frac{(\lambda A)^k}{k!} \cdot e^{-\lambda A}$.

- For any region Ψ, the conditional distribution of nodes in Ψ given that exactly k nodes in the region is *joint uniform*.

Here after, we let $\mathcal{P}_n$ be a homogeneous Poisson process of intensity n on the unit cube $\mathcal{C} = [-0.5, 0.5] \times [-0.5, 0.5]$.

7.2   Connectivity

Given a finite set of n points V in a metric space and a positive real number r, let the r-graph, denoted by $G(V, r)$, be the graph with vertex set V

and with an edge connecting each pair of points separated by a distance of at most r. Two paths in a graph are said to be *vertex independent* if the only common vertices are the end-vertex of both paths. A graph is called k-vertex connected if, for each pair of vertices, there are k mutually vertex independent paths connecting them. Two paths are said to be *edge independent* if there is no common edge between them. Equivalently, a graph is called k-edge connected if, for each pair of vertices, there are k mutually edge independent paths connecting them. The *vertex connectivity*, denoted by $\kappa(G)$, of a graph G is the maximum k such that G is k vertex connected. The *edge connectivity*, denoted by $\xi(G)$, of a graph G is the maximum k such that G is k edge connected. The minimum degree of a graph G is denoted by $\delta(G)$ and the maximum degree of a graph G is denoted by $\Delta(G)$. Clearly, for any graph G,

$$\kappa(G) \le \xi(G) \le \delta(G) \le \Delta(G).$$

A graph property is called *monotone increasing* if G has such property then all graphs on the same vertex set containing G as a subgraph have this property. Let Q be any monotone increasing property of graphs, for example, the connectivity, the k-edge connectivity, the k-vertex connectivity, the minimum node degree at least k, and so on. The *hitting radius* $\varrho(V, Q)$ is the infimum of all r such that graph $G(V, r)$ has property Q. For example, $\varrho(V, \kappa \ge k)$ is the minimum radius r such that $G(V, r)$ is at least k vertex connected; $\varrho(V, \delta \ge k)$ is the minimum radius r at which the graph $G(V, r)$ has the minimum degree at least k. It is obvious that, for any V,

$$\varrho(V, \kappa \ge k) \ge \varrho(V, \delta \ge k).$$

Let $P_k(\mathcal{X}_n, r(n))$ be the probability that a graph in $\mathcal{G}(\mathcal{X}_n, r(n))$ is k-connected.

It was proved by Penrose [118] that, given any metric l_p with $2 \le p \le \infty$ and any positive integer k,

$$\lim_{n \to \infty} Pr\left(\varrho(\mathcal{X}_n, \kappa \ge k) = \varrho(\mathcal{X}_n, \delta \ge k)\right) = 1.$$

This result says that, if n is large enough, then with high probability, if we start with isolated n random points $\mathcal{X}_n$ in C, and add the edges in order of the increasing length to connect the points of $\mathcal{X}_n$, the resulting graph becomes k vertex connected at the moment when the minimum degree of the graph becomes k. This result is analogous to the well-known results in the graph theory [119] that graph becomes k vertex connected when it achieves the minimum degree k if we add the edges randomly and uniformly from $\binom{n}{2}!$ possibilities. Similarly, instead of considering $\mathcal{X}_n$, Penrose also considered a homogeneous Poisson point process with intensity n on the unit-cube $\mathcal{C}$. Penrose gave loose upper and lower bound on the hitting radius $r_n = \varrho(\mathcal{X}_n, \delta \geq k)$ as

$$\frac{\ln n}{2d+1} \leq n \cdot r_n^d \leq d! \cdot 2 \cdot \ln n$$

for homogeneous Poisson point process on a d-dimensional unit cube.

The connectivity of random graphs, especially the geometric graphs and its variations, have been considered in the random graph theory literature [119] in the stochastic geometry literature [120, 121, 118, 122], and the wireless ad hoc network literature [123, 117, 124, 125].

Let $\mathcal{B}(n, p(n))$ be the set of graphs on n nodes in which each edge of the completed graphs K_n is chosen independently with probability $p(n)$. Then it has been shown that the probability that a graph in $\mathcal{B}(n, p(n))$ is connected goes to one if $p(n) = \frac{\ln n + c(n)}{n}$ for any $c(n) \to \infty$. Notice that, although their asymptotic expressions are the same with that by Gupta and Kumar [117], but we can not apply this to the wireless model as, in wireless network, the existences of two edges are not independent, and we do not choose edges from the completed graph using Bernoulli model.

Bollobás and Thomason proved that, if $c(n) \to \infty$, $c(n) \leq \ln \ln \ln n$ and $p(n) = \frac{\ln n + (k-1) \ln \ln n - c(n)}{n}$, then almost no graph from $\mathcal{B}(n, p(n))$ contains a non-trivial $(k-1)$-separator. Notice that a graph with minimum degree k is k-connected unless it contains a non-trivial $(k-1)$-separator. Thus, this result by Bollobás and Thomason implies that if $p(n) = \frac{\ln n + (k-1) \ln \ln n - c(n)}{n}$ then graphs from $\mathcal{B}(n, p(n))$ almost surely have minimum degree $k-1$ and thus almost surely are k-connected.

Another closely related question is the *coverage* problem: disks of radius r are placed in a two-dimensional unit-area disk $\mathcal{D}$ with centers from a Poisson point process with intensity n. A result shown by Hall [126] implies that, if $\pi \cdot r^2 = \frac{\ln n + \ln \ln n + c(n)}{n}$ and $c(n) \to \infty$, then the probability that there is a vacancy area in $\mathcal{D}$ is 0 as n goes infinity; if $c(n) \to -\infty$, then the probability that there is a vacancy in $\mathcal{D}$ is at least $\frac{1}{20}$. Thus, for $c(n) \to +\infty$,

$$\pi \cdot \varrho(P, \kappa)^2 \leq 4 \frac{\ln n + \ln \ln n + c(n)}{n}.$$

Given n nodes V *randomly and independently* distributed in a unit-area disk $\mathcal{D}$, Gupta and Kumar [117] showed that the graph $G(V, r(n))$ is connected almost surely if $\pi \cdot r_n^2 \geq \frac{\ln n + c(n)}{n}$ for any $c(n)$ with $c(n) \to \infty$

as n goes infinity. This bound is tight as they also proved that the graph $\mathcal{G}(\mathcal{X}_n, r(n))$ is asymptotically disconnected with positive probability if

$$\pi \cdot r(n)^2 = \frac{\ln n + c(n)}{n}$$

and $\limsup_n c(n) < +\infty$. Notice, they actually derived their results for a homogeneous Poisson process of points instead of the independent and uniform point process. They showed that the difference between them is negligible. This result is essentially the same as [120], which was developed earlier by mathematicians, but not introduced to the computer science community.

8 Conclusion

Wireless ad hoc networks has attracted considerable attentions recently due to its potential wide applications in various areas and the moreover, the ubiquitous computing. Many excellent researches have been conducted to study the electronic part of the wireless ad hoc networks, the networking part of the wireless ad hoc networks. For networking, there are also many interesting topics such as topology control, routing, energy conservation, QoS, mobility management, and so on. In this survey, we present an overview of the recent progress of applying computational geometry techniques to solve some questions, such as topology construction and localized routing, in wireless ad hoc networks. Nevertheless, there are still many excellent results are not covered in this survey due to space limit.

9 Acknowledgment

The author would like to thank the anonymous reviewers for the helpful suggestions to improve this survey.

References

[1] S. Capkun, M. Hamdi, and J.P. Hubaux, "Gps-free positioning in mobile ad-hoc networks," in *Proc. Hawaii Int. Conf. on System Sciences*, 2001.

[2] Franco P. Preparata and Michael Ian Shamos, *Computational Geometry: an Introduction*, Springer-Verlag, 1985.

[3] H. Edelsbrunner, *Algorithms in Combinatorial Geometry*, Springer-Verlag, 1987.

[4] Paul-Louis George and Houman Borouchaki, *Delaunay Triangulations and Meshing*, HERMES, 1998.

[5] P. Sinha, R. Sivakumar, and V. Bharghavan, "Cedar: Core extraction distributed ad hoc routing," in *Proc. of IEEE INFOCOMM '99*, 1999.

[6] B. Das and V. Bharghavan, "Routing in ad-hoc networks using minimum connected dominating sets," in *1997 IEEE International Conference on on Communications (ICC'97)*, 1997, vol. 1, pp. 376–380.

[7] Jie Wu and Hailan Li, "A dominating-set-based routing scheme in ad hoc wireless networks," *the special issue on Wireless Networks in the Telecommunication Systems Journal*, vol. 3, pp. 63–84, 2001.

[8] Ivan Stojmenovic, Mahtab Seddigh, and Jovisa Zunic, "Dominating sets and neighbor elimination based broadcasting algorithms in wireless networks," *IEEE Transactions on Parallel and Distributed Systems*, vol. 13, no. 1, pp. 14–25, 2002.

[9] Khaled M. Alzoubi, Peng-Jun Wan, and Ophir Frieder, "New distributed algorithm for connected dominating set in wireless ad hoc networks," in *HICSS, Hawaii*, 2002.

[10] Peng-Jun Wan, Khaled M. Alzoubi, and Ophir Frieder, "Distributed construction of connected dominating set in wireless ad hoc networks," in *INFOCOM*, 2002.

[11] Yu Wang and Xiang-Yang Li, "Geometric spanners for wireless ad hoc networks," in *Proc. of 22nd IEEE International Conference on Distributed Computing Systems (ICDCS)*, 2002.

[12] E. Royer and C. Toh, "A review of current routing protocols for ad-hoc mobile wireless networks," *IEEE Personal Communications*, Apr. 1999.

[13] C.E. Perkins and P. Bhagwat, "Highly dynamic destination-sequenced distance-vector routing (dsdv) for mobile computers," *Computer Communications Review*, pp. 234–244, October 1994.

[14] Mario Joa-Ng and I-Tai Lu, "A peer-to-peer zone-based two-level link state routing for mobile ad hoc networks," *IEEE Journal on Selected Areas in Communication*, vol. 17, no. 8, pp. 1415–1425, August 1999.

[15] Haas Z.J. and Pearlman M.R., "The zone routing protocol(zrp) for ad hoc networks," in *Internet draft - Mobile Ad hoc NETworking (MANET), Working Group of the Internet Engineering Task Force (IETF)*, Novermber 1997.

[16] C.E. Perkins and E.M.Royer, "Ad-hoc on demand distance vector routing," in *Proceedings of the 2nd IEEE Workshop on Mobile Computing Systems and Applications, New Orleans, LA*, February 1999, pp. 90–100.

[17] J. Broch, D. Johnson, and D. Maltz, "The dynamic source routing protocol for mobile ad hoc networks," 1998.

[18] Vincent D. Park and M. Scott Corson, "A highly adaptive distributed routing algorithm for mobile wireless networks," in *IEEE INFOCOM*, 1997.

[19] C-K. Toh, "A novel distributed routing protocol to support ad-hoc mobile networks," in *Proc 1996 IEEE 15th Annual Int'l. Phoenix Conf. Comp. and Commun.*, Mar 1996, pp. 480–86.

[20] C.C. Chiang, "Routing in clustered multihop, mobile wireless networks with fading channel," in *Proceedings of IEEE SICON'97*, Apr. 1997, pp. 197–211.

[21] G. Pei, M. Gerla, and T.-W. Chen, "Fisheye state routing: A routing scheme for ad hoc wireless networks," in *Proceedings of ICC 2000*, 2000.

[22] G. Pei, M. Gerla, and T.-W. Chen, "Fisheye state routing in mobile ad hoc networks," in *Proceedings of Workshop on Wireless Networks and Mobile Computing, Taipei, Taiwan, Apr*, 2000.

[23] A. Iwata, C.-C. Chiang, G. Pei, M. Gerla, and T.-W. Chen, "Scalable routing strategies for ad hoc wireless networks," *JSAC99, IEEE Journal on Selected Areas in Communications*, vol. 17, no. 8, pp. 1369–1379, August 1999.

[24] Ji-Cherng Lin, Shi-Nine Yang, and Maw-Sheng Chern, "An efficient distributed algorithm for minimal connected dominating set problem," in *Proc. of the Tenth Annual International Phoenix Conference on Computers and Communications 1991*, 1991, pp. 204–210.

[25] Jie Wu, F. Dai, M. Gao, and I. Stojmenovic, "On calculating power-aware connected dominating sets for efficient routing in ad hoc wireless networks," *IEEE/KICS Journal of Communication and Networks*, vol. 4, no. 1, pp. 59–70, 2002.

[26] P. Bose, P. Morin, I. Stojmenovic, and J. Urrutia, "Routing with guaranteed delivery in ad hoc wireless networks," *ACM/Kluwer Wireless Networks*, vol. 7, no. 6, pp. 609–616, 2001, 3rd int. Workshop on Discrete Algorithms and methods for mobile computing and communications, 1999, 48-55.

[27] B. Karp and H. T. Kung, "Gpsr: Greedy perimeter stateless routing for wireless networks," in *ACM/IEEE International Conference on Mobile Computing and Networking*, 2000.

[28] Martin Mauve, Jorg Widmer, and Hannes Harenstein, "A survey on position-based routing in mobile ad hoc networks," *IEEE Network Magazine*, vol. 15, no. 6, pp. 30–39, 2001.

[29] Godfried T. Toussaint, "The relative neighborhood graph of a finite planar set," *Pattern Recognition*, vol. 12, no. 4, pp. 261–268, 1980.

[30] K.R. Gabriel and R.R. Sokal, "A new statistical approach to geographic variation analysis," *Systematic Zoology*, vol. 18, pp. 259–278, 1969.

[31] Tamas Lukovszki, *New Results on Geometric Spanners and Their Applications*, Ph.D. thesis, University of Paderborn, 1999.

[32] H. N. Gabow, J. L. Bently, and R. E. Tarjan, "Scaling and related techniques for geometry problems," in *ACM Symposium on Theory of Computing*, 1984, pp. 135–143.

[33] J. Katajainen, "The region approach for computing relative neighborhood graphs in the lp metric," *Computing*, vol. 40, pp. 147–161, 1988.

[34] A. C.-C. Yao, "On constructing minimum spanning trees in k-dimensional spaces and related problems," *SIAM J. Computing*, vol. 11, pp. 721–736, 1982.

[35] Xiang-Yang Li, G. Calinescu, and Peng-Jun Wan, "Distributed construction of planar spanner and routing for ad hoc wireless networks," in *21st Annual Joint Conference of the IEEE Computer and Communications Societies (INFOCOM)*, 2002, vol. 3.

[36] S. Datta, I. Stojmenovic, and J. Wu, "Internal node and shortcut based routing with guaranteed delivery in wireless networks," *Cluster Computing*, vol. 5, no. 2, pp. 169–178, 2002.

[37] I. Stojmenovic and S. Datta, "Power and cost aware localized routing with guaranteed delivery in wireless networks," in *Proc. Seventh IEEE Symposium on Computers and Communications ISCC*, 2002.

[38] Mahtab Seddigh, J. Solano Gonzalez, and I. Stojmenovic, "Rng and internal node based broadcasting algorithms for wireless one-to-one networks," *ACM Mobile Computing and Communications Review*, vol. 5, no. 2, pp. 37–44, 2002.

[39] Sunil Arya, Gautam Das, David M. Mount, Jeffrey S. Salowe, and Michiel Smid, "Euclidean spanners," in *Proceedings of the twenty-seventh annual ACM symposium on Theory of computing*, 1995.

[40] S. Arya, G. Das, D. Mount, J. Salowe, and M. Smid, "Euclidean spanners: short, thin, and lanky," in *Proc. 27th ACM STOC*, 1995, pp. 489–498.

[41] S. Arya and M. Smid, "Efficient construction of a bounded degree spanner with low weight," in *Proc. 2nd Annu. European Sympos. Algorithms (ESA), volume 855 of Lecture Notes in Computer Science*, 1994, pp. 48–59.

[42] P. Bose, L. Devroye, W. Evans, and D. Kirkpatrick, "On the spanning ratio of gabriel graphs and beta-skeletons," in *Proceedings of the Latin American Theoretical Infocomatics (LATIN)*, 2002.

[43] Barun Chandra, Gautam Das, Giri Narasimhan, and Jos Soares, "New sparseness results on graph spanners," in *Proceedings of the eighth annual symposium on Computational geometry*, 1992.

[44] Gautam Das and Giri Narasimhan, "A fast algorithm for constructing sparse euclidean spanners," in *Proceedings of the tenth annual symposium on Computational geometry*, 1994.

[45] Menelaos I. Karavelas and Leonidas J. Guibas, "Static and kinetic geometric spanners with applications," in *Proceeding of the Twelfth Annual Symposium on Discrete algorithms*, 2001, pp. 168–176.

[46] Christos Levcopoulos, Giri Narasimhan, and Michiel Smid, "Efficient algorithms for constructing fault-tolerant geometric spanners," in *Proceedings of the thirtieth annual ACM symposium on Theory of computing*, 1998.

[47] P.L. Chew, "There is a planar graph as good as the complete graph," in *Proceedings of the 2nd Symposium on Computational Geometry*, 1986, pp. 169–177.

[48] Xiang-Yang Li, Peng-Jun Wan, and Yu Wang, "Power efficient and sparse spanner for wireless ad hoc networks," in *IEEE Int. Conf. on Computer Communications and Networks (ICCCN01)*, 2001, pp. 564–567.

[49] Xiang-Yang Li, Peng-Jun Wan, Yu Wang, and Ophir Frieder, "Sparse power efficient topology for wireless networks," in *IEEE Hawaii Int. Conf. on System Sciences (HICSS)*, 2002.

[50] Roger Wattenhofer, Li Li, Paramvir Bahl, and Yi-Min Wang, "Distributed topology control for wireless multihop ad-hoc networks," in *IEEE INFOCOM'01*, 2001.

[51] Li Li, Joseph Y. Halpern, Paramvir Bahl, Yi-Min Wang, and Roger Wattenhofer, "Analysis of a cone-based distributed topology control algorithms for wireless multi-hop networks," in *ACM Symposium on Principle of Distributed Computing (PODC)*, 2001.

[52] Yu Wang and Xiang-Yang Li, "Distributed spanner with bounded degree for wireless ad hoc networks," in *International Parallel and Distributed Processing Symposium: Parallel and Distributed Computing Issues in Wireless networks and Mobile Computing*, April 2002.

[53] Harry B. Hunt III, Madhav V. Marathe, Venkatesh Radhakrishnan, S. S. Ravi, Daniel J. Rosenkrantz, and RichardE. Stearns, "NC-approximation schemes for NP- and PSPACE -hard problems for geometric graphs," *J. Algorithms*, vol. 26, no. 2, pp. 238–274, 1999.

[54] M. Grünewald, T. Lukovszki, C. Schindelhauer, and K. Volbert, "Distributed maintenance of resource efficient wireless network topologies," 2002, Submitted for publication.

[55] J. M. Keil and C. A. Gutwin, "Classes of graphs which approximate the complete euclidean graph," *Discr. Comp. Geom.*, vol. 7, pp. 13–28, 1992.

[56] Xiang-Yang Li, Ivan Stojmenovic, and Yu Wang, "Partial delaunay triangulation and degree limited localized bluetooth scatternet formation," in *AdHocNow*, 2002.

[57] J. Gao, L. J. Guibas, J. Hershburger, L. Zhang, and A. Zhu, "Geometric spanner for routing in mobile networks," in *Proceedings of the 2nd ACM Symposium on Mobile Ad Hoc Networking and Computing (MobiHoc 01)*, 2001.

[58] Prosenjit Bose, Joachim Gudmundsson, and Michiel Smid, "Constructing plane spanners of bounded degree and low weight," in *Proceedings of European Symposium of Algorithms*, 2002.

[59] Joachim Gudmundsson, Christos Levcopoulos, and Giri Narasimhan, "Improved greedy algorithms for constructing sparse geometric spanners," in *Scandinavian Workshop on Algorithm Theory*, 2000, pp. 314–327.

[60] Xiang-Yang Li and Yu Wang, "Localized construction of bounded degree planar spanner for wireless networks," 2003, Submitted for publication.

[61] P. Bose and P. Morin, "Online routing in triangulations," in *Proc. of the 10 th Annual Int. Symp. on Algorithms and Computation ISAAC*, 1999.

[62] D.P. Dobkin, S.J. Friedman, and K.J. Supowit, "Delaunay graphs are almost as good as complete graphs," *Discr. Comp. Geom.*, pp. 399–407, 1990.

[63] Yu Wang, Xiang-Yang Li, and Ophir Frieder, "Distributed spanner with bounded degree for wireless networks," *International Journal of Foundations of Computer Science*, 2002, Accepted for publication.

[64] Gruia Călinescu, "Computing 2-hop neighborhoods in ad hoc wireless networks," 2002, Submitted for publication.

[65] Khaled Alzoubi, Peng-Jun Wan, and Ophir Frieder, "Message-optimal connected-dominating-set construction for routing in mobile ad hoc networks," in *3rd ACM International Symposium on Mobile Ad Hoc Networking and Computing (MobiHoc'02)*, 2002.

[66] Xiang-Yang Li and Yu Wang, "Efficient construction of low weight bounded degree planar spanner," 2002, Submitted for publication.

[67] J. Monks, V. Bharghavan, and W.-M Hwu, "Transmission power control for multiple access wireless packet networks," in *IEEE Conference on Local Computer Networks (LCN)*, 2000.

[68] R. Ramanathan and R. Rosales-Hain, "Topology control of multihop wireless networks using transmit power adjustment," in *IEEE INFOCOM*, 2000.

[69] M. Sanchez, P. Manzoni, and Z. Haas, "Determination of critical transmission range in ad-hoc networks," in *Multiaccess, Mobility and Teletraffic for Wireless Communications (MMT'99)*, 1999.

[70] M. Faloutsos and M. Molle, "Creating optimal distributed algorithms for minimum spanning trees," Tech. Rep. Technical Report CSRI-327 (also submitted in WDAG '95), 1995.

[71] R. Gallager, P. Humblet, and P. Spira, "A distributed algorithm for minimumweight spanning trees," *ACM Transactions on Programming Languages and Systems*, vol. 5, no. 1, pp. 66–77, 1983.

[72] J. A. Garay, S. Kutten, and D. Peleg, "A sub-linear time distributed algorithms for minimum-weight spanning trees," in *Symp. on Theory of Computing*, 1993, pp. 659–668.

[73] L. Kirousis, E. Kranakis, D. Krizanc, and A. Pelc, "Power consumption in packet radio networks," in *Symposium on Theoretical Aspects of Computer Science (STACS) '97.*, 1997.

[74] Andrea E.F. Clementi, Paolo Penna, and Riccardo Silvestri, "On the power assignment problem in radio networks," 2000.

[75] A. Clementi, P. Penna, and R. Silvestri, "The power range assignment problem in radio networks on the plane," in *XVII Symposium on Theoretical Aspects of Computer Science (STACS'00), LNCS(1770):651–660,*, 2000.

[76] A. Clementi, P. Penna, and R. Silvestri, "Hardness results for the power range assignment problem in packet radio networks," in *II International Workshop on Approximation Algorithms for Combinatorial Optimization Problems (RANDOM/APPROX'99), LNCS(1671):197–208,*, 1999.

[77] Sudipto Guha and Samir Khuller, "Approximation algorithms for connected dominating sets," in *European Symposium on Algorithms*, 1996, pp. 179–193.

[78] G. Robins and A. Zelikovsky, "Improved steiner tree approximation in graphs," in *Proceedings of ACM/SIAM Symposium on Discrete Algorithms*, 2000, pp. 770–779.

[79] H.B. Hunt, M. V. Marathe, V. Radhakrishnan, S. Ravi, D. J. Rosenkrantz, and R. E. Stearns, "Nc-approximation schemes for np and pspace hard problems for geometric graphs," *Journal of Algorithms*, vol. 26, pp. 238–274, 1998.

[80] Madhav V. Marathe, Heinz Breu, Harry B. Hunt III, S. S. Ravi, and Daniel J. Rosenkrantz, "Simple heuristics for unit disk graphs," *Networks*, vol. 25, pp. 59–68, 1995.

[81] Dorit S. Hochbaum and Wolfgang Maass, "Approximation schemes for covering and packing problems in image processing and vlsi," *Journal of ACM*, vol. 32, pp. 130–136, 1985.

[82] P. Berman, M. Furer, and A. Zelikovsky, "Applications of matroid parity problem to approximating steiner trees," Tech. Rep. 980021, Computer Science, UCLA, 1998.

[83] Khaled M. Alzoubi, *Virtual Backbone in Wireless Ad Hoc Networks*, Ph.D. thesis, Illinois Institute of Technology, 2002.

[84] Xiuzhen Cheng, "A polynomial time approximation algorithm for connected dominating set problem in wireless ad hoc networks," 2002.

[85] Chunhung Richard Lin and Mario Gerla, "Adaptive clustering for mobile wireless networks," *IEEE Journal of Selected Areas in Communications*, vol. 15, no. 7, pp. 1265–1275, 1997.

[86] I. Chlamtac and A. Farago, "A new approach to design and analysis of peer to peer mobile networks," *Wireless Networks*, vol. 5, pp. 149–156, 1999.

[87] Alan D. Amis, Ravi Prakash, Dung Huynh, and Thai Vuong, "Max-min d-cluster formation in wireless ad hoc networks," in *Proc. of the Nineteenth Annual Joint Conference of the IEEE Computer and Communications Societies INFOCOM*, 2000, vol. 1, pp. 32–41.

[88] Alan D. Amis and Ravi Prakash, "Load-balancing clusters in wireless ad hoc networks," in *Proc. of the 3rd IEEE Symposium on Application-Specific Systems and Software Engineering Technology*, 2000.

[89] Lujun Jia, Rajmohan Rajaraman, and Torsten Suel, "An efficient distributed algorithm for constructing small dominating sets," in *ACM PODC*, 2000.

[90] R. Sivakumar, B. Das, and V. Bharghavan, "An improved spine-based infrastructure for routing in ad hoc networks," in *IEEE Symposium on Computers and Communications*, Athens, Greece, June 1998.

[91] V. Chvatal, "A greedy heuristic for the set-covering problem," *Mathematics of Operation Research*, vol. 4, no. 3, pp. 233–235, 1979.

[92] Jie Wu and Hailan Li, "Domination and its applications in ad hoc wireless networks with unidirectional links," in *Proc. of the International Conference on Parallel Processing 2000*, 2000, pp. 189–197.

[93] G. Chen, F. Garcia, J. Solano, and I. Stojmenovic, "Connectivity based k-hop clustering in wireless networks," in *CD Proc. IEEE Hawaii Int. Conf. System Science*, 2002.

[94] S. Basagni, "Distributed clustering for ad hoc networks," in *Proceedings of the IEEE International Symposium on Parallel Architectures, Algorithms, and Networks (I-SPAN)*, 1999, pp. 310–315.

[95] S. Basagni, I. Chlamtac, and A. Farago, "A generalized clustering algorithm for peer-to-peer networks," in *Workshop on Algorithmic Aspects of Communication*, 1997.

[96] P. Bose, A. Brodnik, S Carlsson, E. D. Demaine, R. Fleischer, A. Lopez-Ortiz, P. Morin, and J. I. Munro, "Online routing in convex subdivisions," in *International Symposium on Algorithms and Computation*, 2000, pp. 47–59.

[97] Ivan Stojmenovic and Xu Lin, "Loop-free hybrid single-path/flooding routing algorithms with guaranteed delivery for wireless networks," *IEEE Transactions on Parallel and Distributed Systems*, vol. 12, no. 10, 2001.

[98] S. Basagni, I. Chlamtac, V.R. Syrotiuk, and B.A. Woodward, "A distance routing effect algorithm for mobility (dream)," in *Proceedings of ACM/IEEE MobiCom'98*, 1998.

[99] Z. Haas and B. Liang, "Ad-hoc mobility management with uniform quorum systems," *IEEE/ACM Transactions on Networking*, vol. 7, no. 2, pp. 228–240, 1999.

[100] I. Stojmenovic, "A routing strategy and quorum based location update scheme for ad hoc wireless networks," Tech. Rep. TR-99-09, Computer Science, SITE, University of Ottawa, 1999.

[101] J. Li, J. Jannotti, D. De Couto, D. Karger, and R. Morris, "A scalable location service for geographic ad-hoc routing," in *Proceedings of the 6th ACM International Conference on Mobile Computing and Networking (MobiCom '00)*, 2000, pp. 120–130.

[102] E. Kranakis, H. Singh, and J. Urrutia, "Compass routing on geometric networks," in *Proc. 11 th Canadian Conference on Computational Geometry*, 1999, pp. 51–54.

[103] P. Morin, *Online routing in Geometric Graphs*, Ph.D. thesis, Carleton University School of Computer Science, 2001.

[104] P. Bose and P. Morin, "Competitive online routing in geometric graphs," in *Proceedings of the VIII International Colloquium on Structural Information and Communication Complexity (SIROCCO 2001)*, 2001, pp. 35–44.

[105] A. Clementi, P. Crescenzi, P. Penna, G. Rossi, and P. Vocca, "On the complexity of computing minimum energy consumption broadcast subgraphs," in *18th Annual Symposium on Theoretical Aspects of Computer Science, LNCS 2010*, 2001, pp. 121–131.

[106] A. Clementi, P. Penna, and R. Silvestri, "On the power assignment problem in radio networks," *Electronic Colloquium on Computational Complexity*, 2001, To approach. Preliminary results in APPROX'99 and STACS'2000.

[107] L. M. Kirousis, E. Kranakis, D. Krizanc, and A. Pelc, "Power consumption in packet radio networks," *Theoretical Computer Science*, vol. 243, pp. 289–305, 2000.

[108] J. Wieselthier, G. Nguyen, and A. Ephremides, "On the construction of energy-efficient broadcast and multicast trees in wireless networks," in *Proc. IEEE INFOCOM 2000*, 2000, pp. 586–594.

[109] Peng-Jun Wan, G. Calinescu, Xiang-Yang Li, and Ophir Frieder, "Minimum-energy broadcast routing in static ad hoc wireless networks," in *IEEE Infocom*, 2001.

[110] V. Chvátal, "A greedy heuristic for the set-covering problem," *Mathematics of Operations Research*, vol. 4, no. 3, pp. 233–235, 1979.

[111] Peng-Jun Wan, G. Calinescu, Xiang-Yang Li, and Ophir Frieder, "Minimum-energy broadcast routing in static ad hoc wireless networks," *ACM Wireless Networks*, 2002, Preliminary version appeared in IEEE INFOCOM 2000.

[112] T. J. Cormen, C. E. Leiserson, and R. L. Rivest, *Introduction to Algorithms*, MIT Press and McGraw-Hill, 1990.

[113] M. R. Garey and D. S. Johnson, *Computers and Intractability*, W.H. Freeman and Co., NY, 1979.

[114] Xiang-Yang Li, "Efficient local construction of low weight topology and its applications in broadcast for wireless networks," 2002, Submitted for publication.

[115] Gautam Das, Giri Narasimhan, and Jeffrey Salowe, "A new way to weigh malnourished euclidean graphs," in *ACM Symposium of Discrete Algorithms*, 1995, pp. 215–222.

[116] Gruia Călinescu, Ion Măndoiu, Peng-Jun Wan, and Alexander Zelikovsky, "Selecting forwarding neighbors in wireless ad hoc networks," in *ACM DialM*, 2001.

[117] P. Gupta and P. R. Kumar, "Critical power for asymptotic connectivity in wireless networks," *Stochastic Analysis, Control, Optimization and Applications: A Volume in Honor of W.H. Fleming, W. M. McEneaney, G. Yin, and Q. Zhang (Eds.)*, 1998.

[118] Mathew Penrose, "On k-connectivity for a geometric random graph," *Random Structures and Algorithms*, vol. 15, pp. 145–164, 1999.

[119] B. Bollobás, *Random Graphs*, Cambridge University Press, 2001.

[120] Mathew Penrose, "The longest edge of the random minimal spanning tree," *Annals of Applied Probability*, vol. 7, pp. 340–361, 1997.

[121] Mathew Penrose, "Extremes for the minimal spanning tree on normally distributed points," *Advances in Applied Probability*, vol. 30, pp. 628–639, 1998.

[122] Mathew Penrose, "A strong law for the longest edge of the minimal spanning tree," *Annals of Probability*, vol. 27, pp. 246–260, 1999.

[123] Matthias Grossglauser and David Tse, "Mobility increases the capacity of ad-hoc wireless networks," in *INFOCOMM*, 2001, vol. 3, pp. 1360 –1369.

[124] P. Gupta and P. Kumar, "Capacity of wireless networks," Tech. Rep., University of Illinois, Urbana-Champaign, 1999.

[125] Olivier Dousse Patrick, "Connectivity in ad-hoc and hybrid networks," in *IEEE INFOCOM*, 2002.

[126] P. Hall, *Introduction to the Theory of Coverage Processes*, J. Wiley and Sons, New York, 1988.

AD HOC WIRELESS NETWORKING
X. Cheng, X. Huang and D.-Z. Du (Eds.) pp. 265 - 318

Channel-Adaptive Ad Hoc Routing

Xiao-Hui Lin
Department of Electrical and Electronic Engineering
The University of Hong Kong, Pokfulam, Hong Kong
E-mail: `xhlin@eee.hku.hk`

Yu-Kwong Kwok
Department of Electrical and Electronic Engineering
The University of Hong Kong, Pokfulam, Hong Kong
E-mail: `ykwok@eee.hku.hk`

Vincent K. N. Lau
Department of Electrical and Electronic Engineering
The University of Hong Kong, Pokfulam, Hong Kong
E-mail: `knlau@eee.hku.hk`

Contents

1 Introduction

On-demand routing is important for mobile devices, when they are out of each other's transmission range, to communicate in a wireless network. As a prominent example, wireless LANs, based on the IEEE 802.11b standard, are becoming ubiquitous because of the almost seamless integration with wireline Ethernet LANs. Nevertheless, it is widely envisioned that a huge potential of wireless networking is yet to be realized until we can deploy a robust and large scale *ad hoc* mobile computing network. Specifically, in an ad hoc network, devices join and leave the network at will and in a totally asynchronous manner. Thus, such a wireless network can provide truly "any-time any-where" computation due to its robustness and inherent fault-tolerance. Furthermore, many peer-to-peer applications (e.g., location based services) can be supported in such a network [16, 24]. However, to make such an ad hoc mobile computing network feasible, we have to meet a number of challenges related to wireless infrastructure problems. Most notably, for example, when the devices in an IEEE 802.11b wireless LAN are operating in a peer-to-peer manner (i.e., invoking the distributed coordination function) to form an ad hoc mobile computing system [2, 22, 25], we need to tackle the problem of finding optimized ad hoc routes to enable point-to-point communications between two devices that are possibly out of each other's range.

There are two major classes of ad hoc routing protocols: reactive on-demand and proactive table-based [16, 12]. As many researchers have pointed out [1, 11, 16] table-based algorithms are notoriously inefficient in that they require periodic update of the routing information stored in the routing tables, even when there is no data traffic. The major merit of table-based algorithms, as compared with on-demand algorithms, is that the set up delay for a data transfer is expected to be shorter because a route is presumably stored in the table for use. However, such routes may no longer exist or have become unusable when the actual data transfer is to be taken place for at least two reasons. First, due to the mobility of the mobile devices in the network, their geographical locations may have changed when a data transfer is required, rendering a previously set up route useless. The second reason, which, we believe, is a more important one, is that the quality of the channels among the mobile devices is inevitably time-varying (due to shadowing and fast fading [15]), and thus, the links in a route may no longer be usable (i.e., the error rate on the link is too high) even if the geographical locations do not change much.

Much research has been done on designing ad hoc routing protocols and some well known protocols are also being implemented in practical situations. However, one major drawback in existing state-of-the-art protocols, such as the AODV (ad hoc on demand distance vector) routing protocol, is that the time-varying nature of the wireless channels among the mobile terminals is completely ignored, let alone exploited. This is a rather serious design drawback because the varying channel quality can lead to very poor overall route quality, in turn result in low data throughput. In our study, we consider on-demand routing algorithms for ad hoc networks. In particular, we are interested in studying the behavior and performance of routing protocols when the time-varying nature of wireless channels is taken into account. Indeed, because modern wireless communication environments, such as the IEEE 802.11b standard [6], typically provides multi-rate services with different rates supported by different modulation schemes, it is useful to dynamically change routes by selecting links that can use higher bandwidth modulation schemes.

In this chapter, we propose a new ad hoc routing algorithm that can be applied in an IEEE 802.11b based wireless LAN as well as in general peer-to-peer wireless network (as will be elaborated later, we use a CDMA based system as an example also). Our algorithm, called RICA (receiver-initiated channel-adaptive) routing, works by proactively changing routes through judicious selection of links that can support higher data rates. After introducing some state-of-the-art ad hoc routing techniques in Section 2, the features and design considerations of the RICA protocol are detailed in Section 3. To illustrate the effectiveness of the RICA protocol, we extensively tested it in a simulated IEEE 802.11b wireless LAN environment and compared it with two well-known protocols—ABR (associativity based routing) [21, 23] and AODV (ad hoc on-demand distance vector routing) [20] protocols—that are not channel-adaptive. The results are included in Section 4. To investigate the performance of the RICA protocol in a more general wireless environment, we have also performed a detailed simulation study for a CDMA based ad hoc wireless network. These results are presented in Section 5. The last section concludes this chapter.

2   State-of-the-Art Protocols

2.1   The ABR Protocol

ABR (Associativity Based Routing) [21, 23] is a source-initiated on-demand routing protocol—a mobile device in the network does not need to keep a route to every other device. The major distinctive characteristic of ABR is that the route is not chosen on a shortest-path basis as in other protocols, but on a long-lived basis. Selecting a long-lived route has much merits, such as the chosen route is more robust (not easy to break due to mobility), the maintenance of route is easier, and the number of route reconstruct (RRC) messages is reduced (thus, the routing overhead is reduced and more bandwidth is saved). In ABR, longevity of a route is put at the first place, whereas in other protocols, such as Link State and AODV (described below), the primary goal is to find the shortest path. However, in the latter protocols, data flow transmission interruptions occur more often and more route reconstructions are needed. The essence of ABR is that as a mobile device moves, its associativity with the neighbor devices also changes, and this associativity can be quantified by using associativity ticks. In ABR, each mobile device periodically transmits beacons (such as hello messages) to signify its existence. When these beacons are received by its neighbor devices, these beacons cause the associativity of this device with its neighbor devices increase. The greater the associativity is, the more stable of this device will be. A high associativity of the device means a low mobility of a device. If a device moves out of the transmission range of another device, the associativity record of the former in the latter device is reset. It should be noted that the most fundamental objective of ABR is to derive a long-lived route between the source and destination devices.

2.2 The AODV Protocol

AODV (Ad-hoc On-Demand Distance Vector) [20] is a purely reactive routing protocol. In this protocol, each device does not need to keep a view of the whole network nor a route to every other device. Nor does it need to periodically exchange route information with the neighbor devices. Furthermore, only when a mobile device has packets to send to a destination does it need to discover and maintain a route to that destination device. Being considered by the IETF as a standard ad hoc routing protocol [18], AODV's major distinctive characteristics are:

- routes are discovered or maintained only when necessary (or on an as-needed basis);

- AODV is loop-free [20] at all time, this is accomplished through the use of device sequence number which is increased monotonically (this technique also ensures that the most current route is always used when discovering a route);

- AODV is a bandwidth efficient routing algorithm, which greatly reduces the use of limited bandwidth (the number of route broadcasts are minimized on as-needed basis);

- AODV responds very quickly to the topology changes of the network and can recover a broken route in a timely manner; and

- AODV has a low storage requirement on the device because it only need to maintain the active neighbors information instead of a full route to the destination.

In AODV, each device contains a route table for a destination. Route table stores the following information: destination address and its sequence number, active neighbors for the route, hop count to the destination, and expiration time for the table. The expiration time is updated each time as this route is used. If this route has not been used for a specified period of time, it is discarded.

2.3 Link State Routing Protocol

Link state routing protocol was originally designed for wireline networks [16]. In this protocol, each mobile device keeps its own view of the whole network. When a mobile device has a packet to forward, it uses a shortest path algorithm to determine the next hop to forward that packet to its destination. Every mobile device must keep an up-to-date view of the network. When a mobile device finds a link cost change (due to the change in channel quality) with one of its neighbors, it floods this change throughout the network. Once this flooding packet is received by a mobile device, this mobile device updates its view of the network accordingly. Here, it can be seen that asynchronous updates cause transient routing loop, but this loop is eliminated eventually as the flooding packet is propagated throughout the network.

2.4 DSDV Routing Protocol

The DSDV (Destination Sequenced Distance Vector) routing protocol [17] is an improvement of the original distributed Bellman-Ford routing protocol by using a destination sequence number for each node [16]. Each terminal maintains a routing table containing entries for all the terminals in the network. Each entry contains the following information: the destinations address, the distance, and the next terminal to the destination, and the sequence number as time stamped by the destination. In DSDV, in order to keep the routing table completely updated at all time, each terminal periodically broadcasts routing message to its neighbor terminals. In this routing message, a monotonically increasing even sequence number for the node is included. Thus the sequence number is disseminated in the network via update messages. This sequence number is used to address the freshness of a route. The largest sequence number is always adopted to update routing entry. If the sequence number is the same, the one with smaller distance metric is used.

By using the concept of sequence number, DSDV avoids the long-lives routing loop and counting-to infinity problems. For the proof of this and detailed description of DSDV, the interested readers can refer to [17]. When a terminal B finds that its route to a destination D has broken, it advertises the route to D with an infinite distance metric and a sequence number (odd) one greater than its original sequence number for the route that that has broken. This causes any terminal A routing packets through B to the corresponding destination update its routing entry by making the distance metric as infinite until node A gets a new route to D with a higher sequence number [1]. To take the channel quality fluctuating influence on routing into consideration, we make some revisions to DSDV. In our simulation of DSDV, each node keeps a record table of channel quality based link cost with its neighbors. Periodically (every one second in our simulation), each node broadcasts a channel quality checking packets to its neighbors. When a neighbor receives this checking packet and knows the current link cost to the node, it compares this value with the corresponding value stored in its record table. If the neighbor node finds a change in the value, it updates this value and recompute the distance metric of the route which includes this link in the routing table.

3 Receiver Initiated Channel-Adaptive (RICA) Routing

The major feature of the proposed RICA is to make use of the time-varying property of the wireless channel in that the routing between the source and destination devices is adaptive to the change in *channel state information* (CSI). Specifically, in the RICA algorithm, it is possible that the entire route is changed in response to a change in CSI. Before describing the proposed protocol in detail, we introduce the channel model below.

3.1 Channel Model

The wireless link between two mobile devices is characterized by two components, namely the *fast fading* component and the *long-term shadowing* component [15]. Fast fading is caused by the superposition of multipath components and is therefore fluctuating in a very fast manner (on the order of a few msec). Long-term shadowing is caused by terrain configuration or obstacles and is fluctuating only in a relatively much slower manner (on the order of one to two seconds). To illustrate, a sample of measured fading signal is shown in Figure 1.

Let $c(t)$ be the combined channel fading which is given by:

$$c(t) = c_l(t)c_s(t)$$

where $c_l(t)$ and $c_s(t)$ are the long-term and short-term fading components, respectively. Both $c_s(t)$ and $c_l(t)$ are random processes with a *coherence time* (time separation between two uncorrelated fading samples) on the order of a few milli-seconds and seconds, respectively.

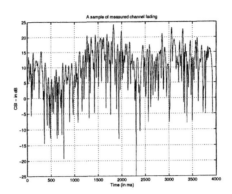

Figure 1: A sample of channel fading with fast fading superimposed on long-term shadowing.

Short-Term Fading. Without loss of generality, we assume $\mathcal{E}[c_s^2(t)] = 1$ where $\mathcal{E}[]$ denotes the expected value of a random variable. The probability distribution of $c_s(t)$ follows the Rayleigh distribution which is given by:

$$f_{c_s}(c_s) = c_s \exp\left(-\frac{c_s^2}{2}\right)$$

In this chapter, we assume the mean and maximum speeds of the mobile device are around 20 km/hr and 40 km/hr, respectively. Thus, the Doppler spread [15], $f_d \approx 100$ Hz. It follows that the coherence time, denoted by T_c, is approximately given by:

$$T_c \approx \frac{1}{f_d} \tag{1}$$

which is about ten msec.

Long-Term Fading. The long-term fading component, $c_l(t)$, is also referred to as the *local mean* [15], which, as shown by field test measurement, obeys the *log-normal* distribution, $f_{c_l}(c_l)$. That is,

$$f_{c_l}(c_l) = \frac{4.34}{\sqrt{2\pi}\sigma_l c_l} \exp\left(-\frac{(c_l(dB) - m_l)^2}{2\sigma_l^2}\right)$$

where m_l, σ_l are the mean (in dB) and the variance of the log-normal distribution, i.e., $c_l(dB) = 20\log(c_l)$. Since $c_l(t)$ is caused by terrain configuration and obstacles, the fluctuation is over a much longer time scale. Again, from field test results, the order of time span for $c_l(t)$ is about one second. Since mobile devices are scattered geographically across the whole wireless network and are moving independently of each other, we assume the channel fading experienced by each mobile device is independent of each other.

To exploit the time-varying nature of the wireless channel, typically a variable-throughput channel-adaptive physical layer is incorporated in the transceiver of a mobile device such that variable amount of data redundancy is incorporated in the information packet for error protection, according to different channel conditions. In our study, we consider several channel-adaptive physical layer designs [4, 10, 6, 13]. The one we employ is a 6-mode ABICM (Adaptive Bit-by-Bit Interleaved Channel Modulation) scheme[1], which is illustrated in Figure 2(a). Channel state information (CSI), $c(t)$, which is estimated at the receiver, is fed back to the transmitter via a low-capacity *feedback channel*. Based on the CSI, the level of redundancy and the modulation constellation applied to the information packets are adjusted accordingly by choosing a suitable transmission mode. Thus, the instantaneous throughput is varied according to the instantaneous channel state. Using a channel adaptive physical layer is one of major distinctive features of our approach in contrast to existing work in ad hoc routing that uses simple channel model. Transmission modes with *normalized throughput*[2] varying from 1/2 to 5 are available depending on the channel condition.

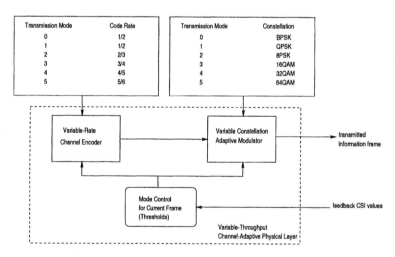

Transmission Mode	Code Rate
0	1/2
1	1/2
2	2/3
3	3/4
4	4/5
5	5/6

Transmission Mode	Constellation
0	BPSK
1	QPSK
2	8PSK
3	16QAM
4	32QAM
5	64QAM

Figure 2: A conceptual block diagram of the variable-throughput channel adaptive physical layer.

We assume the coherence time of the short-term fading is around ten

---

[1]Note that the usage of the ABICM scheme [10] is just for illustration purposes only; other adaptive physical layer schemes, such as MQAM [4] can also be used with our ad hoc routing protocol.

[2]Normalized throughput refers to the number of information bits carried per modulation symbol.

msec which is much longer than an information slot duration. Thus, the
CSI remains approximately constant within a frame and it follows that the
transmission mode for the whole frame is determined only by the current
CSI level. Specifically, transmission mode q is chosen if the feedback CSI, $\hat{c}$,
falls within the *adaptation thresholds*, (ζ_{q-1}, ζ_q). Here, the operation and the
performance of the ABICM scheme is determined by the set of adaptation
thresholds $\{\zeta_0, \zeta_1, \ldots\}$. In this chapter, we assume that the ABICM scheme
is operated in the *constant BER* mode [10]. That is, the adaptation thresholds are set optimally to maintain a target transmission error level over a
range of CSI values. When the channel condition is good, a higher mode
could be used and the system enjoys a higher throughput. On the other
hand, when the channel condition is bad, a lower mode is used to maintain
the target error level at the expense of a lower transmission throughput.
Note that when the channel state is very bad, the adaptation range of the
ABICM scheme can be exceeded such that the throughput (mode-0) becomes so low, making it impossible to maintain the targeted BER level.
This adverse situation is illustrated in Figure 3(a).

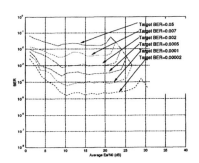

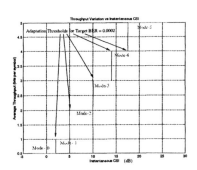

(a) instantaneous BER and the adap-   (b) instantaneous throughput vs.
tation range   CSI

Figure 3: BER and throughput of ABICM scheme.

Given the above considerations about the channel state, the instantaneous throughput offered to the access control layer, denoted by ρ, is also
variable and is therefore a function of the CSI, $c(t)$, and the target BER, P_b,
denoted by $\rho = f_\rho(c(t), P_b)$. Figure 3(b) illustrates the variation of ρ with
respect to the CSI.

In practical wireless communication standards, variants of variable throughput physical layer are also implemented. Indeed, in view of the need to support higher data rate wireless transmission, in 1998 the IEEE 802.11b working group adopted complementary code keying (CCK) [5] as the basis for the high rate physical layer extension to transmit data rates up to 11 Mbps [6]. Specifically, through the adoption of the concept of adaptive modulation [10], an IEEE 802.11b wireless channel can provide multi-rate direct sequence spread spectrum (DSSS) [8] transmission at 1, 2, 5.5, and 11 Mbps, corresponding to differential binary phase shift keying (DBPSK), differential quaternary phase shift keying (DQPSK) (for both 2 and 5.5 Mbps), and CCK, respectively. Thus, each mobile device transmits data at an appropriate data rate using a particular modulation mode based on the perceived signal-to-noise ratio (SNR) of the immediately previous frame in the frame exchange process. For details about the IEEE 802.11b standard, the reader is referred to [6, 13]

We define a CSI based "hop" in the following manner. For example, based on the CSI (can be detected from the SNR of the received signal), we can classify the channel quality into four classes: A, B, C, and D, corresponding to data rates of 11 Mbps, 5.5 Mbps, 2 Mbps, and 1 Mbps, respectively, as specified in the IEEE 802.11b standard. Thus, if a link between two mobile devices with channel quality of class A (i.e., able to support the data rate of 11 Mbps), then the distance between these two devices is defined as ONE hop. We then use this "distance" as a baseline as follows. If a link between two mobile devices has a channel quality of class B (with a data rate of 5.5 Mbps), the distance between two devices is two hops because now the transmission delay is two times that of a class A link. In summary, the distance between two devices, with a link having class A (11 Mbps), class B (5.5 Mbps), class C (2 Mbps), or class D (1 Mbps), is 1, 2, 5.5, and 11 hops, respectively.

3.2 Route Discovery

The RICA protocol is a reactive and on-demand algorithm in that a source mobile device does not permanently keep a route to any destination. The source device will try to determine a route only when it has packets to send to a particular destination. When the source device has packets to transmit, it generates a *route request* (RREQ) packet which includes the following information: type of the packet, source sequence number and address, destination sequence number and address, hop count from the source (initialized to zero), hop distance based on CSI (initialized to zero), broadcast identifier (ID) of the RREQ, and a list of intermediate nodes (initialized to an empty list). Whenever the source generates a RREQ, the broadcast ID is increased by one. Thus, the source and destination addresses together with the broadcast ID uniquely identify a RREQ. The source broadcasts the RREQ to all devices within the transmission range. These neighboring devices will relay the RREQ to other farther devices in the following fashion. An intermediate device upon receiving the RREQ first checks whether it has seen this packet before by looking up its RREQ cache. If the RREQ is in the cache (indexed by the source and destination addresses, as well as the broadcast ID), the newly received copy is discarded; otherwise, the RREQ is stored in the cache and is forwarded to the neighbors after the following modifications are done:

- The intermediate device inserts its sequence number in the list of intermediate devices in the RREQ packet.

- The intermediate device increments the hop count field in the RREQ packet.

- The CSI based hop distance is also updated as follows: the intermediate device measures the CSI of the link through which the RREQ is transmitted and computes the CSI-based hop distance from the upstream device. The intermediate device then resets the hop distance to the original hop distance plus this CSI-based hop distance to the upstream device.

This RREQ relaying process continues until the RREQ reaches the destination. In order not to let a device be unfairly burdened, the RICA protocol also requires that a device under a heavy traffic load (e.g., being the hot-spot pivot devices for two distinct connections) just discards the newly received RREQ. Thus, within a short time frame in the future all new route will not include such a heavily burdened device.

Figure 4(a) illustrates the broadcast of the RREQ in an ad hoc mobile computing network. As can be seen, eventually the destination device receives several copies of the RREQ from the same source via all possible routes. The destination can determine its CSI-based hop distance (as defined earlier) from the source on all the routes and thus, it can choose a route with the minimum distance. As shown in Figure 4(a), the RREQ reaches the destination device through four distinct routes (note that the links are labeled with the channel classes) with the hop count distance 8.5, 13, 5, and 15, respectively (with respect to the IEEE 802.11b standard). The destination device then generates a *route reply* (RREP) which includes the following information: type of the packet, source sequence number and

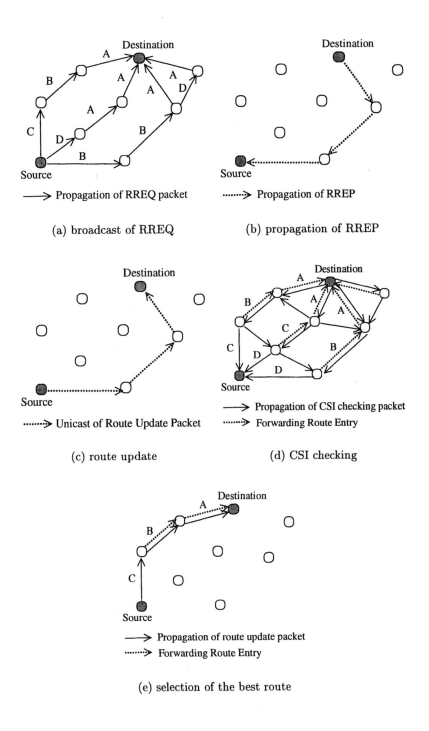

Figure 4: Illustration of the routing mechanisms in the RICA protocol.

address, destination sequence number and address, route reply ID (corresponding to the broadcast ID of the RREQ), hop distance (CSI-based) and hop count of the route, and the list of intermediate devices. The destination device unicasts the RREP along the selected route to the source device (note that each device can identify its upstream neighbor to which the RREP is forwarded) as shown in Figure 4(b). Please note that during the transmission of RREP from the destination to the source, the CSI-based hop distance field in RREP has to be recomputed as before. After receiving the RREP, the source device can decide whether to update the route based on the RREP or not. If the source decides to update the route, it has to construct a route update packet and send it along the selected route to the destination (as depicted in Figure 4(c)). This process is elaborated in the following section.

3.3   Broadcast of CSI-Checking Packets

Because the channel quality between two devices is a time-varying function, the throughput of the route to the destination is also changing all the time. Thus, the prime goal of the RICA algorithm is to maintain a route between a communicating source-destination pair such that the highest throughput is achieved. Essentially, to attain this goal, a route will have to be updated, possibly frequently, according to the changing channel conditions. Our idea is to let the destination device broadcast a CSI-checking packet periodically (the period depends on the coherence time of the fading/shadowing conditions; typically one to two seconds is acceptable). The CSI-checking packet, acting as a probe, is used for measuring the CSI of every link it is transmitted through. Thus, an updated CSI-based hop distance can be obtained. During the life time of a communication session, the source could receive several CSI-checking packets periodically from the destination and thus, it can update the route accordingly. We explain this process in more detail with the help of Figures 4(d) and 4(e).

First, the destination device generates a CSI-checking packet which includes the following information: type of the packet, source sequence number and address, destination sequence number and address, hop count and hop distance field (the latter is CSI-based and both are initialized to zero), time-to-live (TTL) field, checking packet ID. Whenever the destination broadcasts a new CSI-checking packet within the same communication session, the checking packet ID is increased by one. The TTL field is used for limiting the broadcast scope of the packet because exhaustive flooding should be avoided to save bandwidth. Specifically, the TTL field is set to the originally known hop count (not based on CSI) of the path plus one. Every time the packet is rebroadcast, the TTL field is decremented and when TTL becomes zero, the checking packet is discarded. The destination first broadcasts the CSI-checking packet to its neighboring devices. When a neighbor device receives the checking packet, it updates several fields of the packet as follows: measures the CSI of the link from which the checking packet is transmitted and computes the hop distance based on the measured CSI; resets hop count to the original value plus one and decrements the TTL, and then relays the checking packet to its neighbors. Based on the received checking packet, an intermediate device also sets up a forwarding route entry including these fields: source and destination sequence numbers, route entry ID and downstream device, which is the device from which the intermediate device receives the checking packet. This implies that the forwarding route entry points to the device from which the checking packet is transmitted. The route entry ID is equal to the value of CSI checking packet ID. The forwarding route entry also has a life-time. The life-time of the route entry is set to the broadcast period of the CSI checking packet. After the life-time has elapsed, the forwarding route entry is deleted.

Note that within the same CSI-checking process, an intermediate device only relays a CSI-checking packet once in that further received copies are simply discarded. Moreover, as in the route discovery process, a device under a heavy traffic load also does not forward the CSI-checking packet and simply discard it. Eventually, the source device receives several checking packets from all possible routes as shown in Figure 4(d), then the source device selects the shortest path and uses it to replace the original route. For example, in Figure 4(d), there are three candidate routes with hop distance 8.5, 17.5, and 14, respectively. The source device can then choose the shortest one (the top one), which has a hop distance of 8.5, by using a route update packet. The route update packet includes the following fields: type of the packet, source sequence number and address, destination sequence number and address, hop count, update sequence number, and route entry ID. The route entry ID is equal to the CSI-checking packet ID. The updated sequence number is used for identifying a new route update from the source to destination. The sequence number is increased monotonically in the course of successive updating. On receiving the route update entry, the downstream device updates its routing table by setting the next device to the destination as the one in its forwarding route entry (i.e., the downstream device in the entry), then passes the route update packet to its downstream device. We will further explain the route updating process in the subsequent sections. It should be noted that:

- the original route eventually might automatically expire, probably because of no traffic for a specified time-out period, and be deleted; and

- the breaking of the link in original route has no impact to the data transmission in the current route if the link is not in the current route (this is illustrated below).

3.4   Route Maintenance

In the RICA protocol, the updating of the routing table can be quite frequent and thus, an upstream device has to be sensitive to the status of the connection with its downstream device. The feedback information from the physical layer [9, 10] can be used to detect the connectivity of the link. When a device notifies that its downstream device has moved out of its transmission range, the device generates a *route error* (REER) packet, which includes the following information: type of the packet, source sequence number and address, destination sequence number and address, last route update sequence number. The device then unicasts the REER to the upstream device. The upstream device first checks whether the device unicasting the REER is its downstream device or not, by looking up its routing table route entry and the related route update sequence number. If either one of these two fields does not match, the device ignores this REER because such an REER comes from a broken route which is out of date and is useless on the data transmission that is going on in the current route. On the other hand, if both fields match, the upstream device also unicasts the RRER to its upstream device. This process continues until the REER reaches the source.

For example, as shown in Figure 5, mobile device C finds that the link to the destination is broken and thus, it sends a REER to A. However, mobile device A ignores this REER because it knows that device C is not its downstream device and the REER comes from an old link that is not used by the current route. If the device unicasting the REER is its current downstream device, it also unicasts this REER to its upstream device. The process continues, and if the REER reaches the source, then the source can decide whether it should initiate another route discovery process based on two considerations:

1. The source device is now receiving CSI-checking packets and thus, the source device ignores the REER and chooses the shortest route based on CSI checking packet; and

2. If the source device is not receiving CSI-checking packets, it then

broadcasts a RREQ in search of the destination and waits for a RREP, there are three possible scenarios:

- if the RREP reaches the source together with the CSI checking packets (the source device waits for a certain time period so that it may receive all the CSI checking packets, during this period, RREP also reaches the source), the source selects the shortest route based on both the CSI checking packets and RREP packet; or

- if the CSI checking packets arrive before the RREP, the source decides the route based on these CSI checking packets, and afterwards, if RREP also arrives and is with a shorter hop distance, the source chooses the route based on RREP (some communications may have already been taken place); or

- if the RREP arrives before CSI checking packet, the source chooses route based on RREP, and afterwards, when the CSI checking packets arrive, and the route is decided based on CSI checking packets (again some communications may have already been taken place).

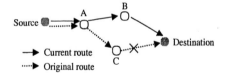

Node	Upstream node	Downstream node	Last route update sequence number
A	S	B	96
B	A	D	96
C	A	D	94

D-Destination

Figure 5: Route updating induced by the breaking of a link.

3.5 Route Updating

As described above, the updating of a route might be based on the CSI checking packets or RREP packets. However, these two updating mechanisms can lead to different results. If the route updating is based on RREP packet, the route update packet has the format of: type of the packet, source sequence number and address, destination sequence number and address, hop count, update sequence number, and list of intermediate devices. Because the route update could be based on CSI checking packet or RREP, routing loops [3] might be formed. To avoid the formation of loops and to differentiate the two cases of route updating based on RREP and on CSI checking packet, an update sequence number is also used. Each source and destination connection pair is related to an update sequence number. Each time the source device decides to have a route update, the route update sequence number is incremented. When the intermediate device receives such a route update packet, it first compares the update sequence number in the packet with the last related route update sequence number it has seen before. If the update sequence number in the packet is greater, it unicasts the route update packet to the next downstream device (note that there is a list intermediate devices in the route update packet) and updates its routing table entry (recording its next upstream and downstream device). If the update sequence number is smaller, the device can just ignore the route update packet. If the route update is based on CSI checking packet, the related route update packet has the format: type of the packet, source sequence number and address, destination sequence number and address, hop count, update sequence number, the intermediate device's (the device sending this packet) address, and route entry ID. If an intermediate device receives such a route update packet, it also compares the update sequence number as mentioned above. If the sequence number in the packet is greater, it further checks the route entry ID in the packet to see whether it matches the one kept in its forwarding route entry (to assure the freshness of the route). If the checking is positive, the device unicasts the packet to the downstream device as indicated in its forwarding route entry, and updates its routing table so as to record the next upstream and downstream devices of the route.

The route updating process is illustrated in Figures 6 and 7. The solid arrows depict the propagation of CSI checking packets, while the dotted arrows represent the setup of forwarding route entries. As can be seen from Figure 6, when the route update packet reaches the destination, a new route from the source to destination is set up. The route entry corresponding to a source-destination pair in each device is shown in Figure 6(c). We can see that the current full route is S-2-5-D and each device in the route is with the greatest last route update sequence number (i.e., 93) in its route entry. Note that the greater this number is, the fresher the route would be. As time goes by, the link quality may change and the destination device initiates another round of broadcast of CSI checking packet and a new route is set up as illustrated in Figure 7. The updating process is the same as that described above. Now the full route is S-1-6-D and each device in the route has a greater last route update sequence number (i.e., 94) in its new route entry. Note that some old route entries may automatically expire and be deleted because they are obsolete after a specified period of time has elapsed.

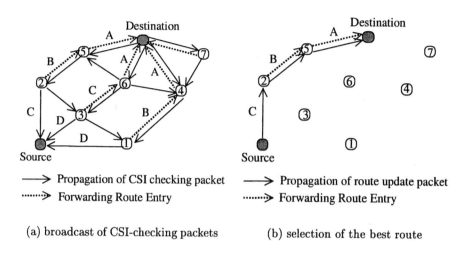

(a) broadcast of CSI-checking packets   (b) selection of the best route

Node	Upstream node	Downstream node	Last route update sequence number
S	---	2	93
1	S	4	91
2	S	5	93
3	S	6	92
4	1	D	91
5	2	D	93
6	3	D	92
7*	---	---	---
D	5	---	93

* The routing table entry has expired.

(c) routing table

Figure 6: Illustration of the route updating mechanism based on the CSI-checking packets.

3.6 Comparison with Other Protocols

It is useful to compare the key characteristics of the RICA protocol with other contemporary protocols. Table 1 below summarizes the comparison.

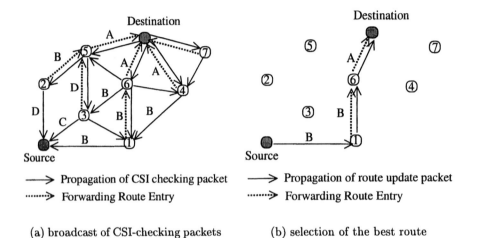

(a) broadcast of CSI-checking packets   (b) selection of the best route

Node	Upstream node	Downstream node	Last route update sequence number
S	---	1	94
1	S	6	94
2	S	5	93
3	S	6	92
4	---	---	---
5	2	D	93
6	1	D	94
7*	---	---	---
D	6	---	94

* The routing table entry has expired.

(c) routing table

Figure 7: Illustration of the route updating mechanism based on the CSI-checking packets with a slightly different broadcasting sequence.

Table 1: Summary of protocol characteristics.

Feature	ABR [21]	AODV [20]	Link State [16]	BGCA [12]	RICA
Power Consumption	Low	Low	High	Low	Medium-High
Loop Free?	Yes	Yes	No	Yes	Yes
Routing Metric	Associativity of device and link load	Shortest path	Shortest path	Shortest path (CSI-based)	Shortest path (CSI-based)
Alternative Route Available?	No	No	Yes	No	No
Adaptive to CSI?	No	No	Yes	Yes	Yes
Protocol Type	Demand-Driven	Demand-Driven	Table-Driven	Demand-Driven	Demand-Driven

4 Performance Results in an IEEE 802.11b Ad Hoc Network

In this section, we present the results obtained in our extensive simulations using the IEEE 802.11b environment implemented in NS-2 [14] for comparing the three protocols (RICA, ABR, and AODV) considered in this chapter. We first introduce the simulation environment.

4.1 Simulation Environment

In our simulation environment, we use an indoor wireless channel model, which captures the fast fading and long-term shadowing factors. The maximal transmission ranges for 4 modulation schemes are specified as: 70 meters for 1 Mbps, 60 meters for 2 Mbps, 45 meters for 5.5 Mbps, and 35 meters for 11 Mbps. To model an ad hoc network, we also use the distributed coordination function (DCF) in the simulated IEEE 802.11b wireless LAN. Using a collision avoidance scheme and handshaking with request-to-send/clear-to-send (RTS/CTS) exchanges between the sender and receiver, and acknowledgment (ACK) from the receiver, packets can be reliably unicast between any two neighbors within an appropriate range. Through the exchange of RTS/CTS/DATA/ACK, the MAC protocol can detect any data link disconnection with its neighbor and report this to the network layer. In all the simulations, the broadcast packets (e.g., RREQ) and control packets such as RTS/CTS and ACK are transmitted at the basic data rate set, (i.e., 1 Mbps). Other simulation parameters we used are as follows:

- testing field: 200m × 200m (such large fields can model the environment in a shopping mall or an exhibition center);

- mobile speed: uniformly distributed between 0 and MAXSPEED (will be elaborated later);

- mobility model: when the device reaches its destination, it pauses for 3 seconds, then randomly chooses another destination point within the field (this is the random ray point model defined in the movement file in NS-2);

- traffic load: 10 source-destination pairs for the 50-device scenarios and 20 pairs for the 100-device scenarios; in the former test cases, the traffic load is varied as 10, 20, 30, and 50 packets/sec; in the latter test cases, the traffic loads are 10 and 15 packets/sec;

- simulation time: 600 seconds.

Furthermore, the data packet size is 512 bytes and the capacity of data buffer size is set to 50 packets. The transmission of packets is a store-and-forward process. When a packet reaches an intermediate device, it waits in the queue for service in a first-come-first-served (FCFS) manner. Each packet is allowed to be kept in the buffer for no more than 3 seconds such that if it has not been transmitted during this period, it will be discarded. Such a relatively short time-out period is chosen because we would like to exert a high pressure on the routing protocols to test their responsiveness in dealing with congested routes (possibly due to poor channel qualities in some links). Finally, the generation of data packets in each source device is a Poisson arrival, i.e., the inter-arrival of two packets is exponential distribution. Each simulation scenario is repeated 50 times with a different random seed and each data point is the average of these 50 trials.

To evaluate the routing algorithms, we compare them using three major metrics:

- Average End-to-End Delay: Measured in msec, the end-to-end delay includes the processing time and queuing time of packet in each device in the route.

- Successful Percentage of Packet Delivery: This is the ratio of packets reaching the destination to total packets generated in the sources. A packet may be dropped if there is not enough data buffer due to the congestion, or has stayed in the buffer for more than 30 seconds.

- Routing Control Overheads: This parameter reflects the efficiency of the routing protocol and is measured in bps (bit per second). We count the total number of routing control packets in each round of simulation. These control overheads include routing packets, ARP packets, and RTS/CTS/ACK packets. We then average the amount of routing control overheads (in bits) to the whole simulation time.

4.2 Average End-to-End Delay

The first set of results is the average packet end-to-end delay against mobile speed with the traffic load increased from 10 packets/sec to 50 packets/sec for 50 deviecs with 10 source-destination pairs. The mean mobile speed is varied from 0 to 14.4 km/hr and thus, the MAXSPEED is varied between 0 and 28.8 km/hr. This speed range can reasonably model a stationary user, a user moving with pedestrain speed, as well as a running user. As can be seen in Figure 8, taking the CSI into consideration can greatly shorten the end-to-end delay from the source to the destination in the RICA protocol, which outperforms the other two on-demand protocols for the following reasons.

1. The source can update the route to the destination timely and adaptively according to the change of the CSI of the links in a route. Indeed, a chosen route is temporally the shortest one with a much better channel quality than those found by the ABR and AODV protocols. Thus, the transmission of the packet is greatly speeded up.

2. The periodic update of the route is adaptive to the geographically sensitive changes of the CSI, which occurs frequently in an indoor environment. Thus, packets for the same source-destination pair (i.e., in the same session) can travel through different routes. Load balancing is therefore automatically achieved. Indeed, in the RICA protocol, a busy device will refrain from forwarding RREQ and CSI checking packets, thereby shifting the load to other devices with less burdens. Such a load balancing effect can help keeping the packet queue short and hence, reduce the overall queueing delay.

3. Using CSI checking mechanism, a full broadcast in search of a route can sometimes be avoided. Thus, the data queuing delay at the source will be reduced because the source device can swiftly choose a route to destination based on the CSI-checking packets. Furthermore, the CSI checking mechanism can also result in shorter routes (with a smaller hop count) and thus, the propagation delay of the packets will also be reduced.

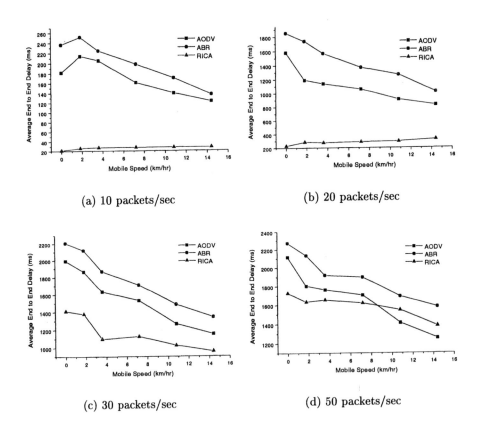

(a) 10 packets/sec

(b) 20 packets/sec

(c) 30 packets/sec

(d) 50 packets/sec

Figure 8: End-to-end delay of all protocols (50 devices with 10 source-destination pairs).

In all three routing algorithms, the end-to-end delay decreases with the increase of the speed of mobile devices. The reason is that all these three protocol are tested under a rather heavy traffic load (at least 10 packets/sec) and thus, a long queue in each device is very easy to form because a route is long-lived when the mobility is low. Each device must compete for the channel to transmit the packets in its long queue. On the other hand, when the mobile speed increases, a long queue is not easy to form because link break happens more often and most packets in a broken route are dropped (recall that a packet is allowed to stay in the buffer for no more than 3 seconds), thus decreasing the queuing delay, at the expense of a much higher packet loss rate. The same phenomenon was also observed in simulations reported by Per Johansson et al. [7] and Perkins et al. [19].

Another observation is that in general, ABR has the longest end-to-end delay. This can be explicated as follows:

- The ABR protocol emphasizes the longevity of routes. The route in ABR is not necessarily the shortest in number of hops as in AODV and thus, packet may need to pass through more devices before reaching its destination (see also Section 4.8). This can add further traffic loads in the network as a whole and the average end-to-end delay will increase.

- Because routes chosen by ABR are usually long-lived. Packet queues can be long in the devices. A higher delay will also result.

- In ABR, local search is employed to find a partial route when a link breaks. During the searching process, packets must wait in the device performing the local search and thus, a long queue is formed. This can also increase the end-to-end delay.

4.3 Successful Percentage of Packet Delivery

From Figure 9, we can see that taking CSI into consideration contributes to the reliability of packet delivery in that the RICA protocol outperforms the ABR and AODV protocols. Based on a scrutiny of the behaviors of the RICA protocol, we find that:

1. Usually, links chosen by RICA are with a higher throughput (see also Section 4.7) and this can help avoiding the discarding of packets due to buffer full.

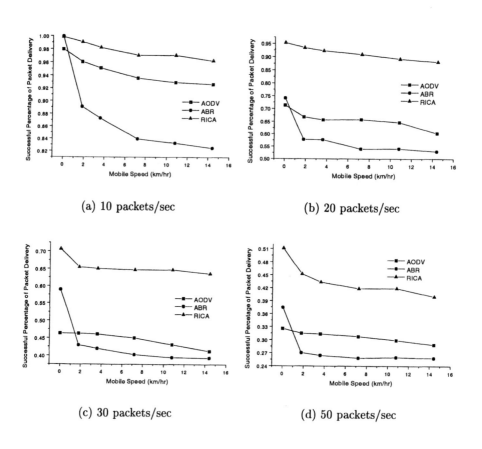

(a) 10 packets/sec

(b) 20 packets/sec

(c) 30 packets/sec

(d) 50 packets/sec

Figure 9: Packet delivery success rates of all protocols (50 devices with 10 source-destination pairs).

2. Frequent and adaptive updates of the route and load balancing can make the traffic evenly distributed in the network and thus, no link is particularly overloaded.

The performance improvement is more obvious as we increase the traffic loads. The ABR and AODV protocols do not take the CSI into consideration and, therefore, they cannot respond timely enough to the change of link throughput which fluctuates with time. Long queue is thus easier to form when the channel quality of some links is not good. Congestion and data loss will result.

4.4 Control Overhead

To study the efficiency of the routing protocols, we also measure the control overhead incurred at the MAC and network layer. Specifically, the control overhead includes all the routing overhead at the IP layer, and the ACK, RTS, and CTS control messages, which are used to exchange information to unicast data and perform routing. The results are shown in Figure 10. We can see that the overhead incurred by the RICA protocol is higher while the ABR protocol's control overhead is the smallest. The reason is that ABR is much less proactive in improving routes, while in RICA the destination broadcasts CSI-checking packets periodically and with much more data packets delivered, and thus RICA incurs a higher control overhead.

4.5 Scalability

To demonstrate the scalability of the protocols, a larger population of devices (i.e., 100 devices in a field) is used. The number of source-destination pairs is increased to 20. The traffic loads used are 10 and 15 packets/sec. The average end-to-end delay, packet delivery success rate, and control overhead, respectively, are depicted in Figures 11 and 12. As can be seen, RICA still outperforms AODV and ABR in that higher data throughput and shorter end-to-end delay are achieved.

4.6 Varying Offered Traffic Load

To test the network performance under different offered loads, we increase the load until the network gets saturated. All the three protocols are tested in two rectangular fields of different populations with number of source-destination pairs of 10 and 20. The mobile speed is fixed at 7.2 km/hr, which is a reasonable pedestrian speed. The average end-to-end delay, aggregate

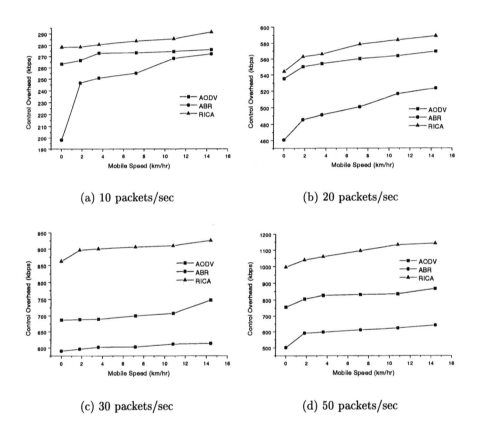

(a) 10 packets/sec

(b) 20 packets/sec

(c) 30 packets/sec

(d) 50 packets/sec

Figure 10: Control overheads of all protocols (50 devices with 10 source-destination pairs).

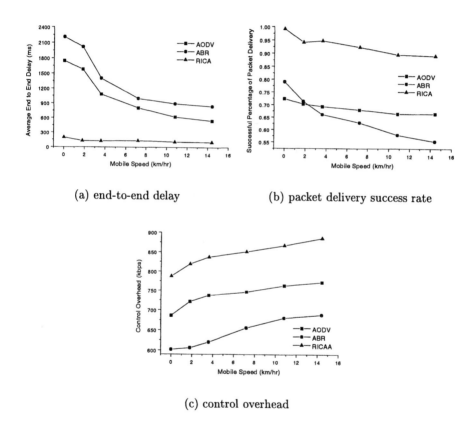

(a) end-to-end delay (b) packet delivery success rate

(c) control overhead

Figure 11: Performance of all protocols under a high traffic load (100 devices with 20 source-destination pairs; 10 packets/sec).

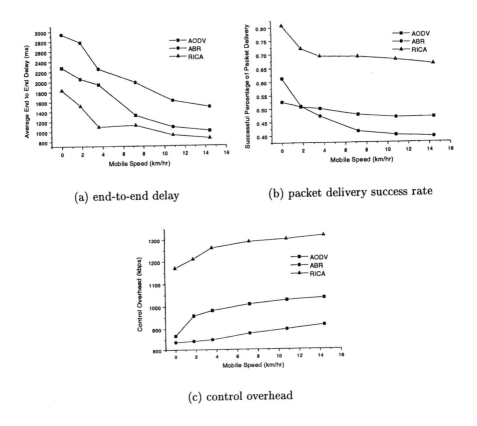

(a) end-to-end delay

(b) packet delivery success rate

(c) control overhead

Figure 12: Performance of all protocols under a high traffic load (100 devices with 20 source-destination pairs; 15 packets/sec).

network throughput, and control overhead, against offered load are shown in Figures 13 and 14. Aggregated network throughput here refers to total amount of data (in bits) reaching the destination devices per second.

Figure 13 depicts the performance of protocols with different offered loads for 50 devices with 10 source-destination pairs. As can be seen, RICA has much greater aggregate network throughput than AODV and ABR. At the offered load of 1500 kbps, AODV and ABR begin to saturate, while RICA saturates at offered load of about 2200 kbps. The network capacity of RICA is about 1.4 and 1.7 times of that of AODV and ABR, respectively. ABR has the lowest aggregate throughput because of the longer route length. Thus, under the same offered load, the network has to consume more limited bandwidth to transmit the data packets and the network is easier to be saturated. For the end-to-end delay, RICA again outperforms the other two due to the higher channel quality (see Section 4.7). Again, the price to pay is that the control overhead in RICA is higher than AODV and ABR. At the extreme offered load, the amount of overhead in RICA is about 1.2 times and 1.4 times of that incurred by AODV and ABR, respectively. The results of 100 devices with 20 source-destination pairs show similar trends and are not shown here due to space limitations. Similar trends can be observed in Figure 14 which shows the results of 100 devices with 20 source-destination pairs.

4.7 Quality of Routes

It is also interesting to compare the quality of the routes selected by different protocols. Figure 15(a) shows the average link throughput, which are defined as the total bandwidth of the links that all packets reaching destinations have traversed, divided by the total number of hops. This parameter reflects the quality of the selected links in each routing algorithm. As can be seen, the average link throughputs in ABR and AODV are very close to each other and are the lowest among all protocols because these two algorithms have not taken the channel quality into consideration when choosing a route.

4.8 Average Number of Hops

Figure 15(b) shows the average number of hops of the route in each algorithm. It is defined as the average number of hops all the data packets traverse to reach their destinations. As can be seen, the routes in RICA have on average the lowest number of hops because this algorithm can continuously find the shortest route when the network is in mobility. The length

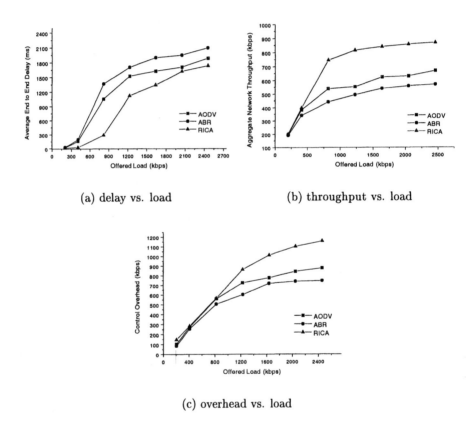

(a) delay vs. load   (b) throughput vs. load

(c) overhead vs. load

Figure 13: Performance of all protocols under various different traffic loads (50 devices with 10 source-destination pairs).

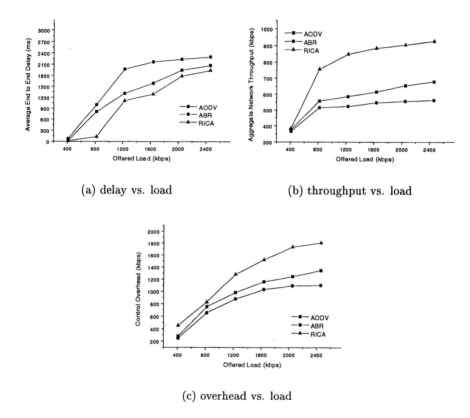

(a) delay vs. load   (b) throughput vs. load

(c) overhead vs. load

Figure 14: Performance of all protocols under various different traffic loads (100 devices with 20 source-destination pairs).

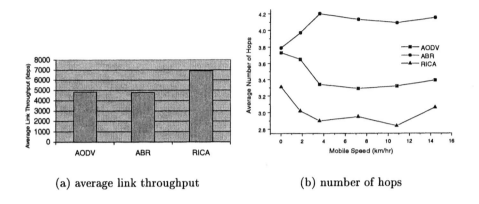

| (a) average link throughput | (b) number of hops |

Figure 15: Quality of routes of all protocols (50 devices with 10 source-destination pairs).

of the route in ABR is the longest than the other two because ABR inclines to select routes with higher stability.

4.9   Throughput Variations

Finally, we also record the throughput variations of the protocols during the whole simulation time periods. These results can indicate the stability of the protocols. As can be seen from Figure 16, the RICA protocol exhibits a rather stable behavior.

5   Performance Results in a CDMA Based Ad Hoc Network

In this section, we present the results obtained in our extensive simulations using a more general CDMA based ad hoc wireless network for comparing the five algorithms considered in this chapter. We first introduce the simulation environment.

5.1   Simulation Environment

In the simulated CDMA based ad hoc network, each terminal pair is assigned a unique pair of PN codes for transmission data in two directions between them. For example, PN code PN(A, B) is assigned to terminal A to transmit

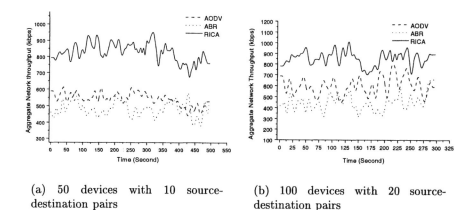

(a) 50 devices with 10 source-destination pairs

(b) 100 devices with 20 source-destination pairs

Figure 16: Throughput variations.

data to terminal B, and PN(B, A) is assigned to terminal B to transmit data to terminal A. Each terminal keeps a database which includes a set of terminal sequences and PN codes. So when a terminal needs to transmit data to another terminal, it only needs to know that terminals sequence and maps this information to its database, then it knows the corresponding PN code to use to transmit data. This also means that each PN code has been pre-assigned to some terminal to transmit data to some another terminal, or PN code can be a function of two terminals sequences. All this information (terminal sequence and function) is stored in the database of each terminal. So each data transmission is independent of another without collision even if one receiver can hear another transmission which is going on because different PN codes are involved. This is quite different from that in IEEE 802.11b (Wi-Fi) in which only one PN code is used and at any time only one transmission is allowed and other is prohibited to avoid collision.

The simulation parameters we used are as follows:

- number of terminals: 50;

- testing field: 1000 m × 1000 m;

- mobile speed: uniformly distributed between 0 and MAXSPEED (will be elaborated later);

- mobility model: when the terminal reaches its destination, it pauses for 3 seconds, then randomly chooses another destination point;

- radio transmission range: 250 m;

- channel model: characterized by fast fading and long-term shadowing components, with throughput 250 kbps, 150 kbps, 75 kbps, 50 kbps, as provided by the adaptive channel coding and modulator ABICM;

- bandwidth of the common channel: 250 kbps, we suppose this channel is robust that can withstand deep fading and interference;

- MAC of common channel: unslotted CSMA/CA based on CDMA [8];

- traffic load: 10 terminal pairs, in each pair, we change the traffic load for 10, 15, 20, 60 packets/sec respectively.

Furthermore, the size of the data packet is 512 bytes and the capacity of data buffer size is set to be 10 packets for one connection of two adjacent mobile terminals when traffic load is low (i.e., at 10, 15, 20 packets/sec) and 50 packets when the load is high (i.e., at 60 packets/sec), respectively. This is because we would like to have a fair comparison of the protocols under different load and we do not want the buffer size to become the bottleneck of the protocol performance when the load is extremely high. Furthermore, we do not set the buffer size to a great value, and this means that when the link is in deep fading, the packets cannot be sent out timely, congestion results and lead to the drop of the packets. The aim of such experiment is to test all the algorithms under the same channel fading wireless environment.

The transmission of packet is described as a store-and-forward process. When packet reaches an intermediate terminal, it waits in the queue for service (FCFS). Each packet is allowed to be kept in the buffer for no more than three seconds, and if it has not been transmitted in this period, it is discarded. The generation of data packets in each source terminal follows a Poisson arrival process, i.e., the inter-arrival of two packets is exponential distribution. Each simulation is run for 500 seconds (simulation time) and repeated for 25 trials. We compute the average of the results of these 25 sets of data.

For the link state protocol, at the beginning of each simulation run, an accurate view of the network topology is installed in each mobile terminal. When the mobile terminal finds the bandwidth with its neighbor change (due to CSI change or link break), it floods this change throughout the network. The aim is to test the performance of the protocol and see whether it can converge or adapt to this time-varying wireless environment. Figure 17 shows the parameters we used for each protocol in our simulations.

Parameter values in ABR

Hello interval	1 s
Hello message missed before link declared broken	2
Association stability threshold	500/(Average mobile speed)
Maximum relaying load on a link	2 connections
Local search timeout	0.5 s
Maximum time a data packet buffered before sent	3 s

(a) parameter values of ABR

Parameter values in AODV

Route discovery timeout	2 s
Route expiration timeout	2 s
Reverse route timeout	2 s
Maximum times a unicast retries	3
Broadcast Hello message	No
Mac layer link breakage detection	Yes
Maximum time a data buffer before sent	3 s

(b) parameter values of AODV

Parameter values in DSDV

Periodical route update interval	6 s
Periodical update missed before link declared broken	2
Mac layer link breakage detection	Yes
Maximum time a unicast retries	3
Route advertisement aggregation time	0.5 s

(c) parameter values of DSDV

Parameter values in Link State

Hello interval	1 s
Hello message missed before link declared broken	2
Routing metric	Hop count (CSI based)
Shortest routing algorithm	Dijkstra algorithm
Maximum time a data packet buffered before sent	3 s

(d) parameter values of Link State

Parameter values in RICA

CSI interval	1 s
Route expiration timeout	1 s
PN code detection time for possible upstream terminal	100 ms
MAC layer link breakage detection	Yes
Maximum time a unicast reties	3

(e) parameter values of RICA

Figure 17: Parameter values of the five protocols in the CDMA environment.

5.2   Average End-to-End Delay

The first set of results is the average end-to-end delay against the mobile speed for the traffic load from 10 packets/sec to 20 packets/sec (in increments of 5), then to 60 packets/sec which is used for testing the performance of the protocols under an extremely heavy load. We varied the mean mobile speeds from 0 to 72 km/hr, and thus, the value of MAXSPEED was varied from 0 to 144 km/hr. As can be seen in Figure 18, taking the CSI into consideration can greatly shorten the transmission delay from the source to destination as in RICA, which outperforms the other four algorithms for the following reasons.

1. The source can update the route to the destination very frequently and usually this route is temporally the shortest one, and this greatly speeds up the transmission of the data packets.

2. The periodical update of the route is adaptive to the regional changes of the CSI, and this happens very frequently, so in this sense, the packets may reach the destination through different routes. This means that load balancing can be achieved in RICA and each link is not overloaded for a long time, thus the queue length is decreased and transmission delay is also shortened.

3. CSI checking packets sometimes make the full broadcast in search of a route unnecessary, this reduces the data queuing delay at the source because source terminal can choose a route to destination based on CSI checking packets.

In RICA, the delay decreases with the increase of the mobile terminal. This is because when the mobile speed increases, the long queue is not easy to form (because link break happens more often), thus decreasing the queueing delay, but at the same time the number of dropped packets also increases, as detailed below. In ABR, however, delay increases with the mobile speed because of the local search. When the link breaks, the packets accumulate in the upstream terminal performing the local search until a partial route is found, thus the long queue forms and queuing time increases.

We also observe one interesting phenomenon that when in low mobility ABR outperforms AODV, but in high mobility AODV outperforms ABR in end-to-end delay. This is because ABR takes the load and propagation delay of the link into consideration when selecting the route (by not choosing links with heavy load), thus balancing the link load and decreasing the delay.

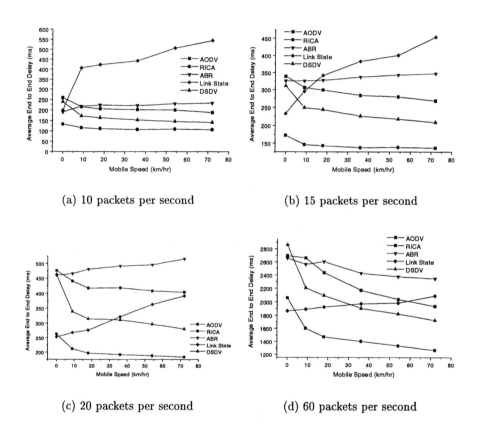

(a) 10 packets per second

(b) 15 packets per second

(c) 20 packets per second

(d) 60 packets per second

Figure 18: Average end-to-end delays of all protocols.

While in AODV, the destination responds only the first RREQ and chooses the path this RREQ has gone through although this route is usually not the shortest one or the some links in the route may be congested. But as the mobility increases and the link is easier to break due to the mobility, in AODV, the source terminal performs a full broadcast in search of a new route, and packets in the original broken route usually is discarded, so the long queue wont be easy to form.

However, in ABR, a LQ (local query) is implemented to find a partial route and data packets have to wait in the terminal performing LQ, so the long queue is formed, and this increases the end- to-end delay, but on another side, the packet delivery rate of ABR is also greater than that in AODV as shown later (usually in AODV a great portion of data packets is dropped due to link break as observed in our experiments). Another reason is that usually, the link in ABR is robust than that in AODV, so the long queue is easier to form in the link with low throughput (50 kbps or 75 kbps). Long queue is also formed in link with low throughput in AODV, but frequent link break often eliminates these long queues. Normally, route in ABR is longer than that in AODV (as will be seen in Section 5.5 due to different route selection criteria, making the delay in ABR longer.

From Figure 18, it can be seen that, the end-to-end delay in link state protocol increases more sharply with the mobility due to the formation of routing loop. In the link state protocol, the change of the link is broadcast throughout the network. This idea is very effective in the wire-line network where the link cost is relatively stable and the algorithm can quickly converge. However, in an ad hoc wireless network, this is not the case because the CSI or network topology changes too frequently, and each change has to be flooded as routing packet throughout the network through the common channel. This flooding leads to an inefficient use of the common channel and the frequent collisions of the packets. The consequence is that at last the status of the network in each mobile terminal can be very inconsistent and thus, the algorithm takes a long time to converge.

Furthermore, as the mobile terminal's mobility increases, the link break event happens more frequently but this information cannot be propagated timely throughout the network due to collisions (we observe in the simulations that the common channel is very congested for the link state protocol), and thus, a routing loop is formed. The routing loop, in turn, causes:

- the increase of the packet delay; and

- the severe contention of the data buffer and eventually the drop of packets.

We observe that when the network is static or in low mobility, the delay of the packet is very low (even the lowest in some scenarios). This is due to two reasons:

1. At the beginning of each simulation, a correct view of the network has been installed in each mobile terminal and the network topology is relatively stable during the simulation time due to the low mobility. This may be "unfair" to other protocols.

2. Usually the bandwidth of the links that the packet has gone through are very high due to the property of Dijkstra algorithm's route selection criteria (as further elaborated in Section 5.5).

We also observe an interesting phenomenon that as the traffic load increased (from 10 packets/sec to 20 packets/sec), average end-to-end delay of the packets decrease (when the mobile terminals are in motion). This is utterly different from other routing protocols. The reason is simple: as the mobile terminal is in motion, the routing loops are formed in the network. Usually a loop lasts for several seconds from our observations, and thus, when we increase the traffic load, congestion is much more easier to form in the loop because of the limited data buffer size (10 for these three scenarios). Consequently, the packets in the loop are dropped with a much higher probability and the average time a packet staying in the loop decreases. Eventually, those packets reaching the destination are from a loop-free route or a route with loop with a short life-time. This interesting phenomenon also reinforces our conclusion that the mobility of mobile terminals is the main cause of the formation of the loop (note that as the network is static, the delay in link state protocol increases with the increase of the traffic load as in other protocols). Furthermore, as we have expected, in all other 4 algorithms, the end-to-end delay increased as we add the traffic load from 10 packets/sec to 60 packets/sec.

Finally, it can be seen that the end to end delay in DSDV also decreases with the increase of mobility as in other protocols. This is because as the mobility increases, the long queue is not easy to form and the waiting time in the queue is shortened. Unlike another table-driven link state routing protocol, DSDV is loop-free and end to end delay is shorter than link state. The end to end delay is even shorter than AODV and ABR because in DSDV, each terminal can exchange routing information with its neighboring terminals and change the next hop to the destination dynamically. This means that the traffic is shifted to different links and the link in DSDV is not as burdened as in AODV and ABR. Another reason is that when a terminal finds that its distance metric to destination is infinite due to the link break, it usually has to drop the packets destined to that destination until it gets a new route with a greater sequence number originated from that destination. During this waiting period, the terminal can not send any packets to that destination. Due to this, the whole network is so burdened as in AODV and ABR. Compared with RICA, the end to end delay in DSDV is greater than RICA due to the quality of the route. This is discussed in the subsequent section.

5.3   Successful Percentage of Packet Delivery

From the simulation results shown in Figure 19, we can see that taking CSI into consideration also contributes to the reliability of packet delivery. Again in terms of successful delivery percentages, RICA outperforms the other four algorithms for the following reasons.

1. Usually links in RICA are with high throughput (see Section 5.5) and this ensure that data packets will not be discarded due to the long queue (not enough buffer).

2. Frequent and adaptive update of the route can make the traffic evenly distributed in the network, thus no link is unfairly overburdened and link congestion does not happen.

3. Packets do not accumulate in a particular terminal because of load balancing, thus long queue seldom forms in a link and the drop of large amount of queuing packets because link break seldom happens.

The gain is more obvious as we increase the traffic loads. ABR and AODV do not take the CSI into consideration, so their routing can not adapt to the change of link throughput which fluctuates with time and long queue is easier to form.

Normally the main causes of data loss are: link congestion and not enough data buffer; and link break. In these two algorithms, long queue is very easy to form in the link with low throughput especially when the traffic load is high (for example 20 packets/sec or 60 packets/sec). We have observed the saturation of the data buffers in this circumstance for many times in our experiments. To ensure the reliability of packet delivery, long queue should be avoided. As seen from the results of delivery rate, ABR performs better than AODV because:

- the routes in ABR are more robust than those in AODV;

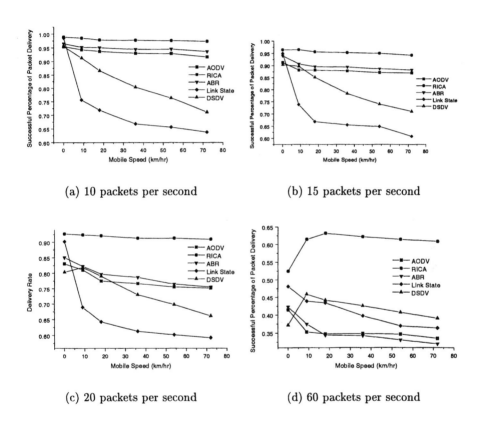

(a) 10 packets per second

(b) 15 packets per second

(c) 20 packets per second

(d) 60 packets per second

Figure 19: Percentages of successful packet delivery.

- ABR takes the link load into consideration when choosing the route; and

- ABR performs LQ to find a partial route at the broken point, so the probability of packets being dropped in the upstream route is reduced.

As what we have expected, packet delivery rate decreases with increase of the mobility (only with one exception as described below) and traffic loads in three on-demand routing protocols because the link break happens more often and congestion and long queue are easier to form.

In the link state routing protocol, the packet delivery rate drops more sharply with the increase of the mobile speed due to the formation of the routing loop. The higher the mobile speed, the easier for a routing loop to form (see Section 5.5). This illustrates that link state protocol is not suitable for a mobile wireless ad hoc network. The common channel is overused and the routing packets cannot be propagated efficiently throughout the network.

We further increase the traffic load to 60 packets/sec to test the performance of all five algorithms under this extreme condition (now the traffic load is 245.76 kbps for a mobile terminal pair). We observe an interesting phenomenon: when the network is static, the packet delivery rate in RICA is the lowest. The optimal value is about 20 km/hr. A plausible explanation: now the network is rather congested and many links are saturated (note that the maximal throughput of the link is 250 kbps) and thus, a great portion of packets are dropped. As we further increase the mobile speed, the topology of the network changes much faster and the RICA algorithm finds more new routes. More traffic load is then shifted to these new routes. Consequently, the traffic distribution is more uniform and some links are not so much overloaded (does not increase the packet delivery rate).

In this extreme condition, link state protocol outperforms ABR and AODV protocols in packet delivery rate. This is due to the fact that the average link throughput is normally rather high in link state protocol compared with that of ABR and AODV (as illustrated below), and the links in link state routing protocol are not so congested as in ABR and AODV although loops still exist in link state protocol.

We observe that when mobility is increased, AODV begins to outperform ABR in packet delivery rate. This is because now the traffic load of the link is extremely high and most links in AODV and ABR are saturated (note that they cannot adapt to the CSI change of the link), and the average length of the route in ABR is longer than that in AODV (as shown in Section 5.5). In this extreme condition, the longer the route, the higher the packet being dropped.

Finally, it can be seen that the packet delivery rate in DSDV is not satisfactory due to the inherent property of DSDV. When a link breaks, this causes the routes including this link breaks temporarily until the corresponding destination issues a new sequence number. This also means that DSDV lacks an initiative mechanism to recover the broken route. This is even worse when the traffic is time-sensitive such as video or audio. When the network load is not heavy (10, 15, 20 packets/sec), the successful packet delivery rate decreases with the increase of mobility because route break happens more often and more packets are dropped. But in extremely heavy load (60 packets/second), the delivery rate is the lowest when all the terminals are stationary and the optimal value for delivery rate is about 10 km/hr. This is because now most links are saturated. A stationary network means the routes are relatively fixed and links are extremely burdened. In this situation, most packets are dropped due to the congestion. As the mobility is increased, the topology changes faster and the terminals can find more new links to destination. Then the traffics are shifted to these new links. This is also a kind of load balancing and decreases the extent of congestion in the network.

5.4 Routing Overhead

Routing overhead is defined as the average bit rate required for sending/receiving the routing messages. The results on routing overhead are shown in Figure 20. In RICA, taking CSI into consideration when choosing a route can improve the network performance in the sense of delay and packet delivery rate, but the cost is that it also adds more routing overhead. If we use the amount of routing overhead in AODV as baseline, RICA generates about 4 times of overhead. The reason is obvious: in RICA, the destinations broadcast CSI checking packets periodically to the source so that the sources can master the CSI changes timely and change the routes adaptively. As seen from the plots, ABR generates the least amount of routing overhead because:

- the route in ABR is long-lived so the break of link happens not so frequent as in other routing algorithm; and

- even when the link breaks, the intermediate terminal perform local search instead of a full broadcast.

Thus, ABR is a bandwidth efficient algorithm. On the contrary, the amount of routing overhead in link state protocol is much higher than in

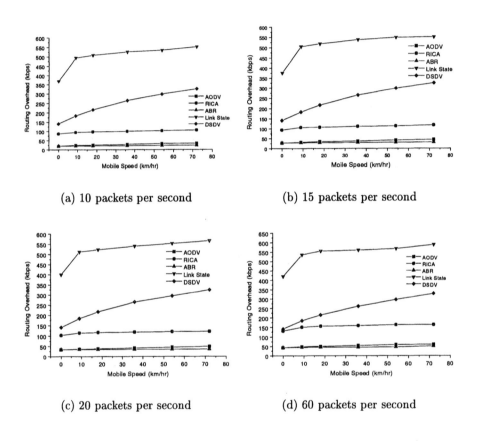

Figure 20: Routing control overhead (average bit rate of routing control packets) of all protocols.

other protocols. In link state protocol, each change of the link cost is broadcast throughout the network even though much routing information is useless. This causes a tremendous amount of routing overhead. This inefficient use of channel causes congestion and can increase the consumption of the limited battery power in each mobile terminal [22].

Just as expected, in all algorithms, routing overhead increases with the mobility because link break is more frequent and this increases the load of route maintenance. It is also observed that increasing the load of data traffic has a little influence on the routing overhead because more data acknowledgments are generated.

It can be seen that the amount of routing overhead in DSDV is very huge just like that of link state protocol. This is a typical drawback of table-driven kind routing protocols. In order to maintain a consistent routing table, each terminal has to periodically broadcast all its routing information to it neighbors. Usually, the whole routing table is huge and much information in the routing table has never been used. Doing so is a waste of limited bandwidth of common channel. And it is even worse when the number of terminals is further increased. For these reasons, DSDV is not suitable for an ad hoc wireless environment.

Although in DSDV, CSI fluctuating property is taken into consideration when routing packets, the performance of DSDV is still unsatisfactory: low packet delivery rate and tremendous amount of routing overhead. CSI of the link is transient with the lasting time in the order of several seconds. This puts a great challenge in designing an efficient routing protocol adaptive to this environment. In this sense, DSDV is not good and can not converge. Although the CSI is taken into consideration, usually by the time the update message is received by other terminals, CSI of the link now again changes! This means that it is hard or impossible for DSDV to be convergent especially when the number of terminals is large because it takes more time for routing message to reach very remote terminals and the routing message is easier to be out of date.

Through comparing on-demand and table driven protocols, we find that on-demand routing protocols are more superior to table-driven kinds even CSI fluctuating property is taken into consideration. In order to make the routing table be up-to-date all the time, table-driven protocols generate more routing overhead. This is an inefficient use of limited wireless bandwidth and battery power. Although such great amount of routing overhead is generated, the performance of table-driven protocols is not satisfactory. In link state protocol, routing loop is very easy to form especially when the mobility is high. This causes a long end to end delay of the packet and high packet drop rate. While in DSDV, there lacks a route-reconstruction mechanism when a link breaks. This causes the destinations through this link temporarily unreachable, thus the successful packet delivery rate is low compared to those of on-demand kinds. Another drawback of DSDV is that convergence is hard to get due to the inefficiency of routing updates.

5.5 Quality of Routes

It is also interesting to compare the quality of the routes selected by different algorithms. Figure 21(a) shows the average link throughput, which is defined as the total bandwidth of the links that all packets reaching destinations have passed through, divided by the total number of hops that these packets have passed through. This parameter reflects the quality of the selected link in each routing algorithm. As can be seen, the link throughputs in ABR and AODV are very close to each other and are the lowest among all protocols because these two algorithms have not taken the CSI of the link into consideration when choosing a route. In RICA, the average link throughputs are much higher than those in ABR and AODV because the former two are adaptive to the CSI change of the link when routing packets. This is the major reason of the algorithms' ability in reducing the packet delay. Link state routing protocol has the highest average link throughput due to the route selection criteria of the Dijkstra algorithm (when a mobile terminal need to forward packets, it uses this algorithm to compute the next hop, normally the link throughput between the mobile terminal and next hop is very high, for example 250 or 150 kbps). This observation may seem to be contradictory to the results of link state protocol but in fact, there is another counter-acting factor, as detailed below.

Figure 21(b) shows the average number of hops of the route in each algorithm. The testing mobile speed is 72 km/hr for each algorithm. As can be seen, the route in link state protocol has the highest number of hops due to the formation of the routing loop. This leads to a bad deterioration of the performance even though it has the highest average link throughput. That is, even the throughput is high, the propagation delay is so high that it offsets the gain from a higher throughput. The route in RICA has the lowest number of hops because this algorithm can continuously find the shortest route. The length of the routes in ABR are longer than the other three on-demand routing protocols and DSDV because ABR inclines to select the route with the highest stability and normally such a route has a greater number of hops.

In order to test the influence of mobile speed of mobile terminals on the

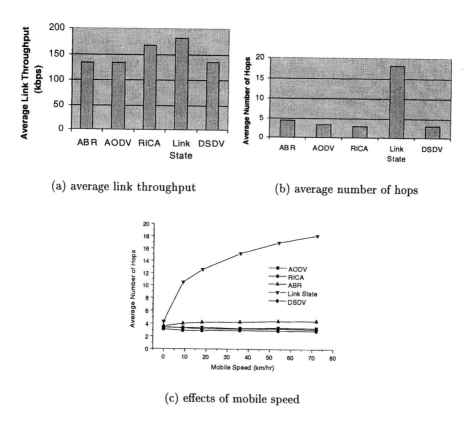

(a) average link throughput

(b) average number of hops

(c) effects of mobile speed

Figure 21: Comparison of route quality of all protocols.

route length in all protocols (in particular, the link state protocol), we also performed more experiments with various mobile speeds, and the results are shown as in Figure 21(c). We can see that for the Link State protocol, the number of hops in each route in general increases with the mobile speed. This is because when mobile speed increases, the faster the topology changes, and the harder the algorithm converges (it may take longer time for a loop being eliminated). Thus, the longer the loops persist. The consequence is that the end-to-end delay and number of packets being dropped due to congestion increase. We have also tested this on the other algorithms and found that the average number of hops in the route in these algorithms doesn't fluctuate greatly with the mobile speed and remains relatively stable.

Finally, as shown in Figure 22, we also measured overall throughput, which is defined as the amount of data reaching destination terminals in every 4 seconds (simulation time). As can be seen, RICA consistently outperforms the other protocols in this aspect.

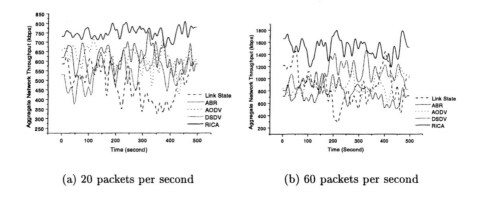

(a) 20 packets per second   (b) 60 packets per second

Figure 22: Throughput variations of all protocols over the entire simulation time period.

6 Concluding Remarks

We have presented a channel-adaptive ad hoc routing protocol that works by dynamically updating routes through judiciously selecting links with higher bandwidths. Under a wide range of performance metrics, including delays, packet delivery rates, overheads, scalability, offered load, and route quality, the proposed protocol, called RICA (receiver-initiated channel-adaptive) protocol, is found to outperform several contemporary well-known protocols. We are currently investigating the effectiveness of using the proposed RICA protocol to perform multipath load balancing in carrying high data rate traffic in an ad hoc network.

Acknowledgments

The authors would like to thank Professors Xiuzhen Cheng, Xiao Huang, and Ding-Zhu Du for their encouragements in writing this chapter. This research was supported by the Hong Kong Research Grants Council under project number HKU 7024/00E. A preliminary version of portions of this chapter appears in the Proceedings of the 3rd IEEE Wireless Communications and Networking Conference (WCNC'2002), vol. 1, pp. 433–439, Orlando, Florida, USA, March 2002, and the Proceedings of the IEEE 22nd International Conference on Distributed Computing Systems (ICDCS'2002), pp. 84-91, Vienna, Austria, July 2002.

References

[1] J. Broch, D. A. Maltz, D. B. Johnson, Y.-C. Hu, and J. Jetcheva, "A Performance Comparison of Multi-Hop Wireless Ad Hoc Network Routing Protocols," *Proc. MOBICOM'98*, pp. 85–97, July 1998.

[2] M. S. Corson, J. P. Macker, and G. H. Cirincione, "Internet-Based Mobile Ad Hoc Networking," *IEEE Internet Computing*, July/Aug. 1999, pp. 63–70.

[3] J. J. Garcia-Luna-Aceves and S. Murthy, "A Path-Finding Algorithm for Loop-Free Routing," *IEEE/ACM Trans. Networking*, vol. 5, no. 1, pp. 148–160, Feb. 1997.

[4] A. J. Goldsmith and S.-G. Chua, "Variable-Rate Variable-Power MQAM for Fading Channels," *IEEE Trans. Communications*, vol. 45, no. 10, pp. 1218–1230, Oct. 1997.

[5] K. Halford, S. Halford, M. Webster, and C. Andren, "Complementary Code Keying for RAKE-Based Indoor Wireless Communication," *Proceedings of the 1999 IEEE International Symposium on Circuits and Systems*, vol. 4, pp. 427–430, 1999.

[6] IEEE Standard 802.11b/D5.0, *Wireless LAN Medium Access Control (MAC) and Physical Layer (PHY) Specifications: Higher Speed Physical Layer (PHY) Extension in the 2.4G Hz Band*, Apr. 1999.

[7] P. Johansson and T. L. Larsson, "Scenario-Based Performance Analysis of Routing Protocols for Mobile Ad-hoc Networks," *Proceedings of MOBICOM'1999*, pp.195–206, July 1999.

[8] K. I. Kim, *Handbook of CDMA System Design, Engineering, and Optimization*, Prentice-Hall, 2000.

[9] Y.-K. Kwok and V. K. N. Lau, "A Quantitative Comparison of Multiple Access Control Protocols for Wireless ATM," *IEEE Transactions on Vehicular Technology*, vol. 50, no. 3, pp. 796–815, May 2001.

[10] V. K. N. Lau, "Performance Analysis of Variable Rate: Symbol-By-Symbol Adaptive Bit Interleaved Coded Modulation for Rayleigh Fading Channels," *IEEE Transactions on Vehicular Technology*, vol. 51, no. 3, pp. 537–550, May 2002.

[11] S.-J. Lee, M. Gerla, and C.-K. Toh, "A Simulation Study of Table-driven and On-demand Routing Protocols for Mobile Ad Hoc Networks," *IEEE Network*, vol.13, no.4, pp. 48–54, July-Aug. 1999.

[12] X.-H. Lin, Y.-K. Kwok, and V. K. N. Lau, "BGCA: Bandwidth Guarded Channel Adaptive Routing for Ad Hoc Networks," *Proceedings of the 3rd IEEE Wireless Communications and Networking Conference (WCNC'2002)*, vol. 1, pp. 433–439, Mar. 2002.

[13] R. van Nee, G. Awater, M. Morikura, H. Takanashi, M. Webster, and K. W. Halford, "New High-Rate Wireless LAN Standards," *IEEE Communications Magazine*, vol. 37, no. 12, pp. 82–88, Dec. 1999.

[14] The Network Simulator—NS-2, http://www.isi.edu/nsnam/ns/, 2002.

[15] J. D. Parsons, *The Mobile Radio Propagation Channel*, Second Edition, Wiley, 2000.

[16] C. E. Perkins (Ed.), *Ad Hoc Networking*, Addison-Wesley, 2000.

[17] C. E. Perkins and P. Bhagwat, "Highly Dynamic Destination Sequenced Distance Vector Routing (DSDV) for Mobile Computers," *Proceedings of SIGCOMM'94*, pp. 234-244.

[18] C. E. Perkins, E. M. Royer and S. R. Das, "Ad Hoc On-Demand Distance Vector (AODV) Routing," *IETF Internet Draft*, `draft-ietf-manet-aodv-10.txt`, Feb. 2002 (work in progress).

[19] C. E. Perkins, S. R. Das, E. M. Royer, and M. K. Marina, "Performance Comparison of Two On-demand Routing Protocols for Ad Hoc Networks," *IEEE Personal Communications*, vol. 8, no. 1, pp. 16–28, Feb. 2001.

[20] C. E. Perkins and E. M. Royer, "Ad-hoc On-Demand Distance Vector Routing, Mobile Computing Systems and Applications," *Proceedings of WMCSA'99*, pp. 90–100, 1999.

[21] E. M. Royer and C.-K. Toh, "A Review of Current Routing Protocols for Ad Hoc Mobile Wireless Networks," *IEEE Personal Communications*, vol. 6, no. 2, pp. 46–55, April 1999.

[22] A. P. Sista, O. Wolfson, and Y. Huang, "Minimization of Communication Cost Through Caching in Mobile Environments," *IEEE Transactions on Parallel and Distributed Systems*, vol. 9, no. 4, pp. 378–390, Apr. 1998.

[23] C.-K. Toh, "A Novel Distributed Routing Protocol to Support Ad-Hoc Mobile Computing," *Proceedings of the 1996 IEEE Fifteenth Annual International Phoenix Conference on Computers and Communications*, pp. 480–486, 1996.

[24] C.-K. Toh, *Ad Hoc Mobile Wireless Networks: Protocols and Systems*, Prentice-Hall, 2002.

[25] M. Zorzi and R. R. Rao, "Error Control and Energy Consumption in Communications for Nomadic Computing," *IEEE Transactions on Computers*, vol. 46, no. 3, pp. 279–289, Mar. 1997.

AD HOC WIRELESS NETWORKING
X. Cheng, X. Huang and D.-Z. Du (Eds.) pp. 319 - 364

A Survey of Wireless Security in Mobile Ad Hoc Networks: Challenges and Available Solutions [1]

Wenjing Lou and Yuguang Fang
Department of Electrical and Computer Engineering
University of Florida, Gainesville, FL 32611
E-mail: {wjlou@,fang@ece.}ufl.edu

Contents

[1]This work was supported in part by the Office of Naval Research under Young Investigator Award N000140210464 and under grant N000140210554, and the NSF under Faculty Early Career Development Award ANI-0093241 and under grant ANI-0220287.

1   Introduction

A mobile ad hoc network (MANET) is a self-configurable, self-organizing, infrastructureless multi-hop wireless network. By self-configurable and self-organizing, we mean that an ad hoc network can be formed, merged together or partitioned into separated networks on the fly depending on the networking needs, and few administrative actions need to be performed for network setup and maintenance. By infrastructureless, we mean that an ad hoc network can be promptly deployed without relying on any existing infrastructure such as base stations for wireless cellular networks. By multi-hop wireless, we mean that in an ad hoc network the routes between end users may consist of multi-hop wireless links, as compared to the single wireless hop in a wireless LAN or a cellular network, where only the last hop, e.g. from the end user to the access point or the base station, is wireless, all the links beyond that point remain wired. In addition, each node in a mobile ad hoc network is capable of moving independently and forwarding packets to other nodes. The rapidly deployable and self-organizing features make mobile ad hoc networking very attractive in military applications, where fixed infrastructures are not available or reliable, and fast network establishment and self-reconfiguration are necessary. Primary applications of mobile ad hoc networks include the tactical communications in battlefields and disaster rescue after an earthquake, for example, where the environments are hostile and the operations are security-sensitive, yet fast and reliable deployments are a must. Recently, due to the availability of wireless communication devices that operate in the ISM (Industrial, Scientific and Medical) bands and other unlicensed band, the interest in mobile ad hoc networks has been extended to civilian life such as on-the-fly setup for conferencing and home-area wireless networking.

Although mobile ad hoc networks have attracted tremendous attention in the last few years, most research efforts have been focused on the development of the network architecture itself, particularly in the network routing protocol and medium access control (MAC) protocol design. We observe that relatively little works have been carried with the security consideration. Lessons we learned from the recent history of the Internet and cellular networks tell us that if a given network architecture is not designed with security from the very start, the security vulnerabilities will be exploited by malicious users, and the network might be paralyzed by various types of attacks. Moreover, addressing security issues as an after thought can be very painful, expensive, and also inefficient ([24]). Thus, incorporation of security aspects into the currently formalized ad hoc networking architecture is of paramount importance.

Computer network and information security has been extensively studied in the wired Internet context in the past. A number of effective security mechanisms are already in place. However, due to the salient (e.g. infrastructureless, wireless, mobile, self-organizing) features of mobile ad hoc networks, the security approaches that are valid in the Internet may not be fully applicable in mobile ad hoc networks. Many new challenges that restrict the applicability of security mechanisms for this new environment arise. First of all, the wireless channels suffer from poor protection and are more susceptible to various forms of attacks such as passive eavesdropping, active signal interference, and jamming. Secondly, most ad hoc network routing protocols are co-operative in nature and rely on an implicit trust relationship among participating nodes to route packets. The co-operative nature makes it much easier for data tampering, impersonation, and denial of service (DoS) attacks. Thirdly, the lack of a fixed infrastructure and a central concentration point makes some conventional security mechanisms difficult to apply. For example, it makes it difficult for an intrusion detection system to collect audit data, and also impedes the deployment of wide spread asymmetric cryptography due to the lack of a PKI (Public Key Infrastructure), where a centralized certificate authority is needed. Fourthly, mobile devices tend to have limited memory, slow processing, low battery power, as well as finite radio transmission bandwidth, which limit the practical deployment of computationally intensive or more comprehensive security schemes in MANET environments. Finally, continuous and unpredictable ad hoc network mobility clouds the distinction between normalcy and anomaly, thus makes the detection of malicious behaviors difficult.

In this chapter, we focus on various security issues in mobile ad hoc networks. We start with an overview of some new challenges: how the security aspects (i.e. attacks, mechanisms, and services) differ in an ad hoc network from those in a wired network. Then, we present a comprehensive survey of currently available solutions for mobile ad hoc networks, which answers the question: how are these new challenges tackled? Some recent proposals on key management and secure routing protocols are presented in more details because of their importance and tremendous interest. We hope this chapter could serve as a key to open the door for readers who are interested in grasping and understanding the security related issues in mobile ad hoc networks.

2 Security Challenges

In the computer network and information security context, when there are needs to assess security, to evaluate various network mechanisms, and to choose security products or policies, the following three aspects are usually considered: *security attacks*, *security mechanisms*, and *security services* ([63]). The salient features of mobile ad hoc networks pose new challenges in each of these aspects of security when compared to their wired network counterparts. In this section, we discuss the possible impacts of those ad hoc networking features (e.g. the lack of infrastructure, the node mobility, etc.) on these three aspects of security.

2.1 Security Attacks

A security attack is any action that compromises the security of information illegally or in an unauthorized way. The attacks can be classified into two categories: *passive attacks* and *active attacks*. A passive attack obtains information without proper authorization, while an active attack involves some type of information interruption, modification, or fabrication. Examples of passive attacks are information leakage (via eavesdropping) and traffic analysis (traffic monitoring). Some types of active attacks include masquerade (impersonating), replay, modification of messages, and denial of service (DoS).

Virtually all kinds of attacks possible in wired networks are possible in a MANET. However, an ad hoc network is generally deployed within a specific area. It is an isolated intranet unless it is connected to the Internet. Such confined communication system actually isolates attackers who are not local to the area. Attackers may exploit the weaknesses of such unique system architecture. It turns out that the mobile ad hoc networking approach does provide some unique vulnerability that an attacker can exploit.

The first vulnerability comes from the wireless channel. The wireless channel is broadcast in nature so it is more susceptible to various forms of attacks such as passive eavesdropping, active signal interference, jamming, and so on. Messages transmitted over the air can be eavesdropped or faked messages can be injected into the network from anywhere without having the physical access to the network components. In addition, the nodes in ad hoc networks are also vulnerable to physical attacks since the nodes usually reside in an open and hostile environment rather than a physically protected place. In a battlefield scenario, the node itself may be captured or compromised.

Traffic monitoring and analysis can be deployed by adversaries to identify the communicating parties and maybe their functionalities. For example, in a tactical MANET without precaution against traffic analysis, an adversary node or nodes may monitor the traffic activities, the nodes with heavy traffic might be the commanding nodes or critical nodes for network connectivity. With this knowledge, the adversaries may be able to take out the important nodes to disable the network. Although many MANET designs have taken the LPI/LPD (low probability of intercept and low probability of detection) into consideration, the LPI/LPD may not be enough against the network penetration, and a passive internal attack is still a possibility.

Another vulnerability made worse by the ad hoc networking approach is attacks on network protocols, both routing protocols and media access control protocols. Restricted by the limited bandwidth, many ad hoc routing protocols are on-demand, which makes them different from the routing protocols used in Internet. All the nodes in an ad hoc network are responsible for routing and forwarding packets. Many ad hoc routing protocols are co-operative in nature and rely on an implicit trust relationship among participating nodes to relay packets. Their co-operative nature makes them more vulnerable to data tampering, impersonation, and denial of service (DoS) attacks ([21, 22, 57]). Moreover, the wireless medium makes it easier for an attacker to inject false information into the network, while the unpredictable and frequent topological changes make it difficult to distinguish between faked routing information generated by malicious nodes and out-of-date routing information caused by topological changes. Finally, the MAC protocols used in MANET are also co-operative in nature. In either contention-based or reservation-based MAC protocols, all the nodes are supposed to follow the predefined rule to gain the channel access. However, in reality, it is easy for a selfish node to take advantage of this weak point by not following the rules ([36]). For example, it is hard to detect a malicious node who always uses the minimum backoff window size in an MANET using IEEE 802.11 MAC protocol.

2.2   Security Mechanisms

A security mechanism is a mechanism that is designed to provide one or more security services by detecting, preventing, or recovering from one or more security attacks. There is no single mechanism that can provide all the services required in a network and information system. A variety of security mechanisms have been proposed, widely used, and proved effective in the wired Internet. However, certain characteristics of mobile ad hoc networks impede the practical deployment of some security mechanisms that are valid in the wired Internet.

First of all, the lack of a fixed infrastructure or a central concentration point in a mobile ad hoc network makes some conventional security mechanisms based on centralized online servers inapplicable in mobile ad hoc networks. For example, the conventional authentication and encryption schemes using public-key cryptography are based on a centralized trusted certificate authority and intrusion detection systems need a central concentration point to collect audit data. These requirements contradict the infrastructureless and the self-organizing nature of ad hoc networks.

Secondly, nodes in a MANET can move continuously in an unpredictable way. This type of MANET mobility precludes any security solution with a static configuration. In addition, it clouds the distinction between normalcy and anomaly, which makes the detection of the malicious behaviors difficult. For example, as we mentioned before, the mobility causes frequent topological changes, it is very difficult to distinguish between faked routing information and stale routing information. Moreover, as the fundamental security mechanism in virtually all networks, a good cryptographic scheme requires proper management and safe keeping of a small number of cryptographic keys. This design objective is very hard to accomplish in a MANET where nodes can move independently and connectivity is not guaranteed

([24]).

Finally, in MANETs, mobile devices tend to have limited processing power (CPU cycles), limited memory (buffer space), limited transmitting power, limited network bandwidth, and limited battery energy. This severely restricts the practical deployment of more comprehensive or computational intensive, yet more effective, security schemes in MANET environments.

2.3   Security Services

A security service is a service that enhances the security of the network and the information transferred over the network. A number of various security functions have been desirable in a network information system. Based on their objectives, the security services can be categorized into: *Confidentiality, Authentication, Integrity, Non-repudiation, Access Control, and Availability* ([63]). These services are intended to counter one or more attacks, and make use of one or more security mechanisms to achieve their goals. We examine their security properties in a MANET environment next. We present them in a different order, as this often reflects their actual importance in MANETs ([62]).

Availability

Availability requires the network services to be available to authorized parties whenever needed. A variety of denial of service (DoS) attacks can result in the loss of or reduction in availability. Particularly, in a MANET, an adversary could jam the radio frequencies to interfere with signals on physical channels; it could interact with a node in an otherwise legitimate way, but for no other purpose than to deplete others' battery power (it is a more powerful threat than CPU exhaustion for a mobile node ([62]); it could disrupt routing to cripple the network; or it could bring down higher layer services, such as the key management service, a fundamental service for any cryptographic scheme.

Authentication

Authentication ensures that the origin and the destination of a message is correctly identified, with an assurance that the identities between two communicating parties are not falsified. Without authentication, an adversary could masquerade a node, interfere with other nodes' communication, or gain unauthorized transmission and reception. Mobile devices are susceptible to loss, theft, and capture (in a battle field), thus frequent re-authentication becomes necessary. Again, the absence of an online server poses a fundamental problem in MANETs because the usual authentication mechanisms involve a centralized system entity.

Confidentiality

Confidentiality is the protection of transmitted data from passive attacks, such as eavesdropping. Sensitive information, such as tactical military information or strategic information, requires confidentiality. Leakage of such information to enemies could cause devastating consequences. The other aspect of confidentiality is the protection of traffic flow from analysis. Routing information needs to remain confidential in certain cases, because the source and destination, frequency, length, or other characteristics of the traffic might be helpful for enemies to identify and to locate their targets in a battlefield, or to infer certain tactical information.

Integrity

Integrity ensures that the transmitted information is not illegally modified. Modification includes changing, deleting, creating, delaying or replaying of the transmitted messages. Certain modification could be caused by benign failures, such as the radio propagation impairments. Others are caused by malicious attacks. The integrity of the routing information, particularly the cost metrics, is of great importance in maintaining the proper functioning of the network.

Non-repudiation

A non-repudiation service guarantees that neither the sender nor the receiver of a message is able to deny the transmission. Non-repudiation helps to detect and punish compromised or misbehaving nodes.

Access Control

Access control is the ability to limit and control access to devices and applications via communication links. Each entity attempting to gain access must first be authenticated.

3 Available Security Solutions

In this section, we present proposed security solutions for tackling each of the challenges described in the previous section. In the first five subsections we focus on the security mechanisms and schemes that are proactive and preventive in nature to protect the security of a MANET. In the last two subsections, we summarize the detective and reactive approaches.

3.1 Defending Against Physical Attacks

Mobile devices are susceptible to loss and theft because they are small, light, and easy to carry. In a battle field scenario, they are at risk of being hijacked or captured. It is necessary to protect the physical safety of the mobile devices. The conventional solution to the physical attacks is to implement a security module that is tamper-resistant, i.e. that contains measures to keep data secret and uncorrupted even under physical attacks ([53]). An example is the use of the smart card, which is basically a safe containing a microprocessor and necessary cryptographic information ([1]). The smart card performs all the relevant cryptographic operations and could be inserted into or removed from the device easily. The safe has lid switches and circuitry, which interrupts power to memory, thus key material will be erased when the lid is opened. The advantage of using a removable card is that it allows a user to change devices while keeping his/her own private data. In addition, the sensitive information is protected by the smart card and it can be removed at will. However, when all the information is stored in the smart card, there is still a problem, for example, the device may be stolen with the smart card in it.

An additional protection scheme can be designed to detect whether a device has fallen into the wrong hands. This could be done through user identification and authentication. Some well known techniques include PINs (personal identification numbers), passphrases, and biometics. By requiring user identification periodically and/or for each security-critical transaction, an adversary can be prevented from making a stolen device operational. However, frequent re-authentication is somewhat troublesome and discourages users from activating the security mechanism. Recently a zero-interaction authentication was proposed ([14]), in which a user wears a small authentication token that communicates with the mobile device (such as a laptop) over a short-range wireless link. Whenever the mobile device needs decryption authority (DA), it acquires the DA from the token. The system is automatically protected (re-encrypted) when the user is not around and the decryption authority cannot be acquired. The system can be restored in seconds once it detects the user's return. The DA is only retained while it is needed. This scheme secures the mobile device from a physical attack while recovering full performance before a returning user resumes to work.

3.2   Enforcing Confidentiality

The wireless channel in MANETs is broadcast in nature. It suffers from poor protection and is particularly vulnerable to passive eavesdropping attacks. This vulnerability is not specific to mobile ad hoc network, but common to all wireless communication networks. In these environments, confidentiality may consists of two aspects: one is to protect the the identity of nodes (either users' identity or the communications entities' functionalities), the other is to protect the transmitted messages from disclosure. The former is particularly important in military applications, in which a node's functionality (e.g. a command node) should be hidden away from non-participating nodes. In what follows in this subsection, we will address both aspects.

3.2.1   Hiding the Nodes' Transmissions

One of the most effective ways to protect the identities of communications entities is to conceal their communications effectively. This can be achieved in the physical layer, where many solutions have been proposed to protect the wireless channel. For example, spread spectrum technologies (e.g. frequency hopping or direct sequence), which either spread the energy in time and/or frequency in a random fashion to make signal capture difficult or spread the energy to a wider spectrum so that transmission power is hidden behind the noise level, can make it difficult to detect or jam signals. The characteristics of LPI/LPD (low probability of intercept/low probability of detection) are highly desirable in military applications. Directional antennas can also be deployed due to the fact that the communication techniques can be designed to spread the signal energy in space. We will not discuss these solutions further as we mainly focus on solutions in high layers.

3.2.2   Securing the Communications Path

One common approach, not unique for MANETs but effective, is to secure the communication path. The basic idea is to encrypt all messages exchanged between communication entities (either point-to-point or end-to-end). However, due to resource (time, frequency and space) constraints, the full version of security schemes used in wired networks may not be effective in MANETs, instead, light weight versions may have to be developed to fulfill the needs ([17, 52, 67]).

3.2.3 Enhancing Confidentiality via Multipath Routing

As we mentioned earlier, the traditional way of providing a confidentiality service is to apply data encryption/decryption to the information transmitted over the networks. However, the computational burden may pose a serious problem in resource limited environments. Moreover, as we will discuss later in this chapter, key management in MANETs is also problematic due to the infrastructureless architecture.

Another approach enhancing a confidentiality service is to utilize the salient features of MANETs such as the mobility of the network architecture. The fundamental idea comes from the following observation: a messenger who carries the full message from one place to another across hostile ground may reveal the message easier if he/she is captured, while the message will not be fully recovered if multiple messengers are deployed to carry only partial information and go through different routes across the hostile ground. We ([40, 39]) recently developed such a scheme to enhance the confidentiality service on top of any security scheme suitable for the deployed MANET. The proposed scheme, namely, *SPREAD: Secure enhancement Protocol for REliable dAta Delivery*, is based on secret sharing and multipath routing. The basic idea is described as follows. Using a (T, N) secret sharing algorithm, we generate multiple (N) shares of a message (or messages) to be protected, such that from any T or more shares, we can easily recover the message (or messages), while from any $T - 1$ or fewer shares, it is computationally impossible to recover the message (messages). Then, using a multipath routing algorithm, we find multiple paths with minimal overlaps (e.g., independent node-disjoint paths) and then we send the N shares over such multiple paths towards the destination. From a network point of view, if a whole message follows a single path to its destination, a hacker can intercept all the necessary information to recover that message at any intermediate node. However, with the SPREAD scheme, the hacker has to compromise a number of nodes on a number of independent paths to obtain at least T different shares. Reduced information interception ratio can be expected from SPREAD.

To better understand the scheme, we give a brief introduction to the threshold secret sharing system, which is also used later for the key management, details can be found in [59]. Suppose that we have a system secret K to be protected, we use it to generate N pieces, S_1, S_2, ..., S_N, called *shares* or *shadows*. Each of N participants of the system, P_1, P_2, ..., P_N, hold one share of the secret, respectively. The generation of the secret shares guarantees that any less than T participants cannot learn anything about the system secret K, while with an effective algorithm, any T out of N participants can reconstruct the system secret K. This is called a (T, N) *threshold secret sharing scheme* ([60, 4, 61]). A secret sharing scheme consists of two algorithms. The first is called the *dealer*, which generates and distributes the shares among the participants. The second is called the *combiner*, which collects shares from the participants and recomputes the secret, i.e., it produces the secret K from any T correct shares. A combiner fails to recompute the secret if the number of the correct shares is less than T. For illustration purposes, we take Shamir's Lagrange interpolating polynomial scheme as an example. The dealer obtains the ith participant's share by evaluating a polynomial of degree $(T - 1)$:

$$f(x) = (a_0 + a_1 x + a_2 x^2 + \cdots + a_{T-1} x^{T-1}) \bmod p$$

at $x = i$:

$$S_i = f(i)$$

which is given to the participant P_i, where p is a large prime number greater than any of the coefficients and is made available to both the dealer and the combiner, and the coefficient $a_0 = K$ is the secret while other coefficients a_1, a_2, ..., a_{T-1} are all randomly chosen. Then, at a combiner, once T shares have been obtained, the combiner can reconstruct the original blocks by solving a set of linear equations over a finite field. For example, assume that the received T shares are $f(i_1)$, $f(i_2)$, ..., and $f(i_T)$, let

$$A = \begin{pmatrix} a_0 \\ a_1 \\ a_2 \\ \vdots \\ a_{T-1} \end{pmatrix}, B = \begin{pmatrix} 1 & 1 & 1 & \cdots & 1 \\ i_1 & i_2 & i_3 & \cdots & i_T \\ i_1^2 & i_2^2 & i_3^2 & \cdots & i_T^2 \\ \vdots & \vdots & \vdots & \ddots & \vdots \\ i_1^{T-1} & i_2^{T-1} & i_3^{T-1} & \cdots & i_T^{T-1} \end{pmatrix}, F = \begin{pmatrix} f(i_1) \\ f(i_2) \\ f(i_3) \\ \vdots \\ f(i_T) \end{pmatrix}$$

then, the original secret $a_0 = K$ can be recovered by solving the following linear equations in matrix form

$$B'A = F$$

where B' denotes the matrix transpose of the matrix B. It is known that this equation has a unique solution over the finite field $GF(p)$.

The SPREAD scheme works as follows: if a source node wants to send a message to a destination node securely in a MANET, depending on the security level, the source can use a multipath routing algorithm to find multiple paths from the source to destination with certain properties (for example, disjoint paths in a certain sense), then the source determines a secret sharing scheme, say, a (T, N) threshold scheme, according to the message security level and the availability of the paths with the desirable non-overlapping property. The source will be the dealer in this case, and will choose the a_0 as the message and choose other coefficients randomly on the finite field $GP(p)$, where p is appropriately chosen. Finally, the source node will generate the message shares as discussed earlier and send them over the multiple paths found from the source to the destination. The destination will be a combiner, upon receiving T shares, it is able to recover the original secure message. We observe that SPREAD is built on top of any security scheme, hence it only enhances the confidentiality. Since the multiple paths are chosen in a way that any eavesdropper cannot physically be at two paths, hence he/she will find it hard to collect enough shares for that particular message. Due to the mobility of nodes, even the multiple paths from one node to another will constantly change, which makes possible collusion difficult. Thus, unless a malicious node knows all mobility patterns of the secure communication parties (source and destination), it will be difficult to capture the message flow from the source to the destination when both ends are highly mobile.

A few remarks are in order. First, the SPREAD scheme cannot address confidentiality alone in MANETs, it only statistically enhances this service. For example, a node which can hear all path transmissions can recover the secure message, this is the case if a node near either the source or the destination knows also the spreading codes or hopping pattern used by either the source or destination. The multiple paths in this scenario can be achieved by combining it with either encryption algorithm or directional antenna. Second, if a message is too large compared to the chosen prime number p, the message can be chopped up as we normally do in the transport layer. During this process, some scrambling may be helpful. Third, depending on the number of paths used, SPREAD seems to waste a lot of bandwidth. To save the network bandwidth, in SPREAD all the coefficients a_0, a_1, a_2, ..., a_{T-1} can be assigned messages, so that multiple messages can be delivered simultaneously. Finally, SPREAD can be made adaptive in the sense that the source node could make final decisions whether a message is delivered at a certain time instant according to the security level and the availability of multiple paths. Moreover, the chosen set of multiple paths may be changed from time to time to avoid any potential capture of those multiple paths by adversaries.

Many variations of SPREAD can be designed according to the above few remarks. Due to the inherited redundancy in SPREAD scheme, we also develop a redundant SPREAD scheme (where $T < N$), which can improve data reliability as the multipath routing has been shown coping with frequent topological changes well, and improving overall throughput ([64, 68]), although it consumes more network bandwidth. In addition, by embedding the cheater detection and identification mechanisms in a secret sharing scheme, the SPREAD scheme is also helpful in identifying malicious or compromised nodes. When combined with the conventional cryptographic schemes, it can reduce computation by using partial share encryption. The major drawback of the SPREAD scheme is that it is limited by the available multiple paths in the MANETs.

3.2.4 Preventing Traffic Analysis

Another threat related to confidentiality is traffic analysis. Traffic analysis is basically the attempt to discover the pattern of traffic between parties. Conventionally, traffic analysis is prevented by link encryption and hiding the real traffic pattern using dummy traffic to form a uniform traffic cloud ([47]). Typically, there are two types of encryption used in a packet-switching network: end-to-end encryption and link encryption. End-to-end encryption is performed at or above the transport layer in the two end systems. When the packets are transmitted over the network, the payload of each transport layer segment, i.e. message content, is encrypted except the header. So the eavesdropper is able to acquire end-to-end flow traffic pattern information such as the source and destination, frequency, duration, and so on. This information can help the adversary to locate the target or to infer the activity or intention of the communication parties. For example, in a military network, a significant change of traffic pattern may imply the deployment of troops, chains of command, level of readiness, etc. In contrast, link encryption is performed at the data link layer by encrypting the payload of each frame. Since multiple end-to-end flows may be multiplexed on each link, an eavesdropper would not be able to distinguish the traffic pattern of end-to-end flows, although the link flow traffic is still observable. Due to the broadcast nature of the wireless channel, the eavesdropper could easily intercept data in an mobile ad hoc network. Thus, link encryption is a more suitable security mechanism for hiding the end-to-end traffic flow information. The wired equivalent privacy (WEP) encryption scheme defined in IEEE 802.11 wireless LAN standard uses link encryption. Moreover, some high level security schemes, which combine multi-path routing, traffic rerouting, and traffic padding techniques, have been proposed to protect end-to-end traffic patterns in a conventional network ([47, 66, 19]).

Recently, a few attempts have been made to prevent traffic analysis specifically for mobile ad hoc networks. The basic strategy to prevent traffic analysis is to create security clouds in a way that each node under a security cloud is identical in terms of traffic generation. In [26] and [27], Jiang, Vaidya and Zhao discussed different methods of constructing a traffic cover mode, e.g., the end-to-end cover mode and the link cover mode. The purpose of the cover mode is to hide the changes of an end-to-end flow traffic pattern as certain tactical information might be inferred from the unusual changes in the traffic pattern. They formulate the construction of the optimal cover mode into an optimization problem and present a solution based on flow rerouting. Their solution is able to find an optimal cover mode for a number of predefined operation modes. However, node mobility and its impact on the calculation of the cover mode are not considered in their solutions. In [28], the authors proposed another approach to hide the source and destination information using the dynamic mix method (DMM). The mix method was originally proposed in [13], which achieves the anonymity of the message delivery via a cryptographic method and "mix" nodes in the network. Due to the dynamic topology changes, when applying the mix method in a MANET, the network performance degrades. The proposed DMM improves the network performance by allowing the communicating nodes to choose mix node dynamically at run time.

3.3 Key Management

Key management is possibly the most critical and complex issue when talking about security in a mobile ad hoc network. The applicability of many other security services, such as confidentiality and authentication, relies on effective and efficient key management. For efficiency reasons, the parties involved in a secure communication usually need to share a common secret key. Public key cryptography has made key distribution easier among those parties in the wired Internet. For example, some public key cryptography based key exchange algorithms, such as the Diffie-Hellman key exchange algorithm ([16]), have been widely adopted to establish the session keys between parties without transmitting the keys themselves in the network. However, the management of the public keys usually involves a centralized trusted control point, called a *certificate authority (CA)*. Such centralized trust control contradicts the design goal of MANETs, where there is no infrastructure. Some research have been carried out to address the public key management issue in MANETs. Basically, there are two major research directions along this line. One is to retain the certificate authority concept, but distribute its functionality into multiple servers (or trusted nodes) ([42, 30, 75]). In this way, both the availability and the security of the CA can be improved. Another approach is to discard the centralized CA, and instead, create a totally distributed and self-organized key management system ([24]). We will discuss the key management issue in more detail in section 4.

3.4 Authentication

To guarantee secure communication, a node in a MANET has to make sure the party it communicates with is what it claims to be. The process of this verification is authentication, which is done via a challenge process: if the node shares a secret with the other party, the node can issue a challenge message to request the correct answer; or if both parties do not share a secret, a trusted third party (certificate authority) can be used for the verification with the understanding that both parties share secrets with the CA, then the challenge process will be carried out between both parties with the CA. In the traditional Internet, centralized CAs in the fixed infrastructure exist, hence more comprehensive authentication processes can be launched without too many concerns. However, in a MANET, the trust model in the Internet is no longer valid. Mobile devices are powered on and off, move in and out a certain networking domain often, and there is no fixed infrastructure to be trusted, therefore a new trust model has to be developed ([67]). Due to the resource limitations, signaling traffic due to authentication has to be minimized ([37, 38]). The latter issue has been ignored for MANETs in the current literature, while the former issue attracts some attention in conjunction with key management for MANETs ([24, 42, 30, 62, 75]), various distributed trust models have been proposed. Some distributed trust models are developed based on the salient features of MANETs. In [62], the trust model is based on *imprinting*: a duckling recognizes whomever it sees at first sight as its mother and will always obey its mother. Thus, a node will always trust whichever gives its secret and becomes a slave of a mother node, hence authentication can be verified by the mother node. In a distributed public-key trust model ([75]), a selected set of nodes is used as servers (CAs) and collaboratively manages the public keys. Whenever a node needs to have its public key signed, the node has to contact a subset of servers to gain the certificate of its public key, which could be used in the authentication process when communicating with other nodes. Instead of pre-selecting a set of nodes as the CAs, the authors of [24] suggested a self-organized public-key infrastructure based on a chain of trust. Whenever a node wants to communicate to another party, the trust repositories of both parties will be merged and a search for a trust chain is initiated. Depending on the web of the trust in a MANET, authentication signaling traffic may be huge for both trust models. In [42, 30], Lu and his colleagues proposed a localized distributed trust model: at the very beginning, a system secret key is shared by all nodes in a MANET, each node obtains a share via a threshold sharing scheme with threshold, say, k, i.e., any k shares can recover the original secret. A node can obtain the security services by contacting at least k nearest nodes. In this way, all authentication processes can be localized.

Recently, Weimerskirch and Thonet ([67]) proposed a light-weight authentication model based on the observation that "no model ensures authentication for an ad-hoc network in every environment" and that "depending on the situation users can select the appropriate system". Their proposed trust model targets low-value transactions: it does not make a transaction perfectly secure, but rather makes the attacker's cost to get falsely authenticated higher than the value of the transaction! The trust model is based on human behavior. Assume that a node, say, A wants to authenticate another node, say, B. A can ask some questions (such as a secret or a recent transactions), if the answer is yes, A can trust B. Otherwise, A starts to solicit A's trusted friendly nodes for recommendation, or asks B to provide a list of references for verification. If A's trusted friend node says yes or a reference from B can be authenticated by A and tells A that B is trusted, then A can trust B. This authentication model is useful for MANETs consisting of less powerful processors. More details can be found in [67].

3.5 Protecting Routing Protocols

Protecting routing protocols is another important issue in a mobile ad hoc network. As discussed in Section 2.1, routing in ad hoc networks is more vulnerable than its counterpart in wired networks. Correct routing can be disrupted in many ways or be disabled by denial of service attacks (see section 5.1). Great efforts have been made to protect routing protocols. Several secure routing protocols that aim to protect the correctness of routing protocols have been proposed. Traditional source authentication and message integrity measures have been adopted ([57]). In response to the key management difficulty and the limited resource restrictions, authentication mechanisms without using public key cryptography are also proposed

([21, 22]). Different mechanisms have been proposed for different types of ad hoc routing protocols (table-driven and on-demand, distance vector and source routing). Both preventive schemes and reactive schemes are developed. Due to their importance, section 5 of this chapter will be dedicated to securing routing protocols in more details.

3.6 Handling Node Misbehavior

A less severe attack in MANETs is the node misbehavior caused by selfishness. In an ad hoc network, all basic functions, such as routing and packet forwarding, are collaboratively carried out by all participating nodes. The effectiveness of the MANET design relies heavily on mutual trust and mutual collaboration in sharing the network resources (such as time, frequency, space, code and battery power). It is expected that all participants follow the rules according to the MANET design objective. However, there might exist selfish nodes that do not want to provide services to other nodes for some reasons, e.g. to save their own battery energy ([45]). Or some nodes may want to grasp more bandwidth or demand less delay for their own packets ([36]). Although the selfish node does not perform active attacks, the misbehaviors can cause significant network performance degradation because the MANET depends on the co-operation of all participants to provide services to each other. For example, if $10\% - 40\%$ of the nodes in the network agree to forward packets but fail to do so, the average throughput may degrade by $16\% - 32\%$ ([45]). In this section, we discuss some solutions proposed in the current literature to handle such misbehaviors due to selfishness.

3.6.1 Network Layer Misbehavior

The selfishness in the network layer appears as not forwarding packets for others. Although routing and packet forwarding are two closely related functions in the network layer, the correctness of the routing information does not guarantee the correct forwarding of a packet. Two types of solutions have been proposed to deal with reluctant or even erroneous packet forwarding problems. The first type is reactive in nature. The misbehaving nodes are detected and corresponding reactions are carried out. The other type is to create a incentive mechanism to encourage the cooperation of the nodes.

In [45], Marti et al proposed two techniques that improve throughput in the presence of nodes that agree to forward traffic but fail to do so. A *watchdog* is used to identify misbehaving nodes and a *pathrater* is then designed to help routing protocols avoid these nodes. The watchdog's mechanism is based on the promiscuous mode of radio interface: the receiver of one node could listen to the transmission of any of its neighbors, regardless of the intended destination of that transmission. Thus, when a node forwards a packet, the node's watchdog verifies that the next node in the path also forwards the packet by overhearing the next node's transmission. If the next node does not forward the packet(s), then it is misbehaving. The pathrater then uses this knowledge to rate the nodes and chooses network paths to avoid the use of misbehaving nodes, thus the packets are most likely to be delivered. This scheme is more for avoiding the problem than facing the problem. If there are too many such misbehaving nodes, the pathrater may not be able to find a feasible path, which will degrade the network performance severely. Some award and punishment strategy may have to be developed and incorporated into this scheme to make it more effective.

Another protocol, using the same type of approach, is the *CONFIDANT (Cooperation Of Nodes: Fairness In Dynamic Ad-hoc NeTworks) protocol* ([7, 8]). The CONFIDANT protocol consists of four major components: the *Monitor*, the *Reputation system*, the *Path manager*, and the *Trust manager*. The monitor performs a similar function as a watchdog, observing the transmission of the next node on the path or observing the routing protocol behaviors. By keeping a copy of a packet while listening to the transmission of the next node, it could also detect any content changes in the frame. If the function that is being monitored provides an acknowledgment message (e.g. the Route Reply message of the DSR protocol), reputation information can be gathered about the nodes that are not within the radio range of the monitoring node. The reputation system rates each node in the network according to the observations about its routing and forwarding behavior, including the first hand observation of neighboring nodes and the trusted second hand observations reported from other nodes. The path manager then performs functions such as path re-ranking according to the reputation of the nodes in the path, deletion of paths containing malicious nodes, action upon receiving a request for a route from a malicious node (e.g. ignore, do not send any reply), and action upon receiving a request for a route containing a malicious node in the source route (e.g. ignore, alert the source). Finally, the trust manager deals with the ALARM messages: it sends out an ALARM message to friends (friendly nodes) when it experiences, observes, or receives a report of malicious behaviors, it also makes a decision on the trustworthiness of an incoming ALARM message.

The CONFIDANT protocol is similar to [45] in the sense that each is a reactive protocol dealing with node selfishness. It improves the detection mechanism by letting nodes learn not only from their own experience, by observing their neighbors, but also by exchanging experience with their neighbors. However, as we mentioned earlier, the reactive scheme proposed in [45] does not punish malicious nodes that do not cooperate, but rather relieves them of the burden of forwarding for others. The CONFIDANT protocol in contrast isolates the detected selfish nodes so that misbehavior is punished and co-operation is rewarded.

In [9], a different approach was proposed to handle node selfishness. Relying on the observation that sophisticated transactions are usually based on some form of currency, Buttyan and Hubaux proposed a mechanism based on a virtual currency called *"nuglet"*. Nodes pay for the service they receive from a MANET and are paid for service they provide to the other nodes. Two payment models are proposed: *Packet Purse model* and *Packet Trade model*. In the packet purse model, when a node originates a packet, it puts an estimated amount of nuglets in the packet purse attached to that packet. Each node forwarding the packet would then take a certain number of nuglets from that packet purse. If the packet runs out of nuglets in its packet purse, it is dropped. In this way, nodes are given incentive to cooperate by collecting more nuglets for future uses and are discouraged from overloading the network. In a later version of this scheme ([12]), the packet purse is removed from the packet, instead, a *nuglet counter* is implemented in each node. Whenever a packet is originated, the number of nuglets is reduced from the nuglet counter in the source. When a node forwards a packet for others, its nuglet counter is increased. This approach requires a tamper-resistant security module (hardware) in each node to handle the nuglets so that the nuglet counter cannot be changed in an illegal way. It also requires the estimation of the cost from source to destination.

In the packet trade model, the packet does not carry nuglets. Instead, it trades for nuglets with intermediate nodes (neighbors). Each intermediate node buys the packet from the upstream node for nuglets and sells it to the downstream node for more nuglets. The destination actually pays off all the cost. A drawback of this model is that it actually encourages nodes to overload the network since the source does not have to pay.

3.6.2   MAC Layer Misbehavior

Node misbehavior could also happen at the MAC layer. The current wireless LAN MAC protocol IEEE 802.11 (DCF mode) is a contention based protocol. Nodes share the same channel and follow the same exponential backoff procedure when contending for the channel access. The priority that a node wins the contention depends on its backoff value which further heavily depends on the contention window size selected by that node. If a small contention window size is selected, the average deferring time for that node would be short while if a large contention window size is selected, the node might have to back off for a long time period. Therefore, the node misbehavior at the MAC layer typically appears as unfairly obtaining a higher share of the channel or experiencing shorter delay by selecting small backoff value or small contention window size. In [36], Kyasanur and Vaidya proposed a MAC layer node misbehavior detection and correction scheme. The backoff mechanism used in the current 802.11 standard is modified to simplify the misbehavior detection. In the current IEEE 802.11 standard, the backoff value of each station is selected by the station itself, thus other nodes have difficulty in judging if the node follows the backoff procedure or not. In the modified version, the backoff value to be used by a sender for the next transmission to a receiver is selected by that receiver during the current transmission between the sender and receiver. This change allows the receiver to detect the deviation of the actual waiting slots of the sender from the expected waiting slots accurately and promptly. Once a certain number of deviations are detected within a window of certain packets from a node, the node is designated to be misbehaving. Then, a certain amount of backoff time is calculated and added as the penalty to the next backoff time assigned to that node. This correction scheme is actually very weak as it again requires the co-operation of the misbehavior node.

Another approach handling the MAC layer node misbehavior is to develop MAC protocols that are resilient to misbehavior. Game theory seems to be a viable design technique along this direction. According to game theory, the protocol could be designed to reach an optimal operating mode called the *"Nash equilibrium"*. Thus, no node can improve its own interest (such as bandwidth or delay) by changing its own strategy while other nodes' strategies remain fixed. However, the use of game theory in designing self-configuring protocols for wireless mobile ad hoc network has not been well understood. In addition, working at the Nash equilibrium might be far from optimal from the network performance point of view. More work needs to be done along this direction although a few works have demonstrated the applicability of such an approach ([43, 31, 32, 10]).

3.7 Intrusion Detection

In the previous sections, we have focused mainly on the preventive mechanisms to protect network security. As we know, a prevention-only strategy only works if the prevention mechanisms are perfect. Otherwise, someone may be able to find a way to get around them ([58]). Most of the threats have been the results of bypassing prevention mechanisms. Intrusion detection and response mechanisms in this case provide a second line of defense.

Intrusion detection is based on the assumption that the behavior of the intruder differs from that of a legitimate user in ways that can be quantified ([56]). Generally speaking, there are two approaches detecting an intrusion: misuse (or rule-based) detection and (statistical) anomaly detection. The misuse detection attempts to define improper behavior based on the patterns of well-known attacks. Examples of misuse detection systems include IDIOT ([33]) and STAT ([25]). The misuse detection system can accurately and efficiently detect the known attacks, but it lacks the ability to detect unknown attacks. Statistical anomaly detection attempts to define normal, or expected, behavior. It involves the collection of data relating to the behavior of legitimate users over a period of time. Then, statistical tests are applied to determine with a high level of confidence whether an observed behavior deviates from a legitimate user behavior. An example of anomaly detection system is IDES ([41]). The anomaly detection can be used for a more general purposed protection, including unknown new attacks. However, such systems might cause more false alarms. In practice, both approaches may be combined to be effective against a broader range of attacks.

The intrusion detection systems (IDSs) designed for wired networks do not function well in MANETs. The most important reason is that the intrusion detection systems rely on real time traffic analysis of traces collected at switches, routers, or gateways, while in a MANET environment, there is no such traffic concentration points from which one can collect audit data for the entire network. In addition, MANET mobility, which allows nodes to move freely and independently, complicates the detection because it is harder to distinguish anomaly and normalcy. Other constraints include the availability of only local and partial audit traces, fully distributed requirement, and resource (such as power) limitations ([73]).

In [73, 74], Zhang, Lee and Huang proposed a new "Distributed and Cooperative Intrusion Detection" architecture suitable for mobile ad hoc networks. In this model, an IDS agent runs independently on each node. The IDS agent conceptually consists of six modules: local data collection, local detection engine, local response, global response, cooperative detection engine, and secure communication. The local data collection monitors local activities and collects useful audit data, such as system and user activities within the mobile node, communication activities by this node, and communication activities within the radio range and observed by this node. The local detection engine detects intrusion from these local traces. It includes both misuse detection and anomaly detection. If a known attack or anomaly with strong evidence is detected, the node can determine independently that the network is under attack. If an anomaly with weak evidence is detected and a broader investigation is required, the node will use the cooperative detection engine to initiate a cooperative global intrusion detection procedure. This procedure includes propagating the intrusion detection state information among nodes and a distributed consensus algorithm to make a decision based on the information received from other nodes. Once an intrusion is determined, the response modules, both the local one and the global one, are responsible for taking actions. The local response module triggers action local to this node while the global one coordinates actions among neighboring nodes. The exact actions taken depend on the type of intrusion, type of network protocols and applications, and the confidence in the evidence. For example, re-authentication between certain nodes or the re-organization of the whole network might be required. Finally, the secure communication module provides a highly secure communication channel among IDS agents.

The proposed intrusion detection architecture is fully distributed and collaborative, and well suitable for MANET environments. In general, it is applicable to all network layers, or in an integrated cross-layer manner. However, intrusion detection heavily depends on the definition of proper behavior or improper behavior that further relies on different applications, protocols, and attacks. As MANET networking is still under active development, we do not yet know what is a "typical" application or scenario. The authors proposed an anomaly detection model for detecting attacks on MANET routing protocols, because routing protocols in MANET are fundamental and well studied. As pointed out by the authors themselves, the more pressing tasks now are to better understand the potential applications for MANETs, and to define realistic benchmarks. Otherwise, it will be very difficult to use intrusion detection in MANETs.

4 Key Management

As we mentioned earlier, key management plays very critical role in addressing any effective security issue. Intensive research has been carried out for MANETs in the last few years. In this section, we present more comprehensive discussions of key management.

4.1   Fundamentals and Overview

Cryptography is the fundamental security technique used in addressing almost all aspects of security. It provides the basis for many security services such as the confidentiality and integrity of messages whenever they are exposed to potential attacks, for example, during the transmission across the networks that are vulnerable to eavesdropping and message tampering. There are two main classes of cryptographic algorithms in general use. The first class is symmetric (or secret-key) cryptography, where the sender and the receiver use the same secret key to encrypt and decrypt the information transmitted between them. The secret key used in this class of algorithms should only be known to the sender and receiver, but not be revealed to anyone else. The second class is asymmetric (or public-key) cryptography, where each participant has a public/private key pair. The public keys are made public to everyone while each participant keeps his/her private key secret. When sending a message, the sender uses the receiver's public key to encrypt the message. The public-key algorithm ensures that only the intended receiver can decrypt the message with his/her private key. The public key algorithm is also used to sign the digital signature for authentication and non-repudiation purpose. When sending a message, the sender signs the message with his/her own private key. The receiver can verify the sender's digital signature with the sender's public key.

Cryptography is widely used in the construction of secure distribution systems. The strength of any cryptographic system depends on proper key management. In symmetric cryptography, if an attacker compromises the keys used in encryption/decryption, then all encrypted messages will be compromised. In asymmetric cryptography, although private keys are not transmitted in the open, the distribution of public keys also causes problem. For example, malicious Tracy could use her public key to replace Alice's public key in a certain key directory to trick Bob to send messages to her. Without proper protection of secret keys in symmetric cryptography or the public keys in asymmetric cryptography, the whole cryptographic system can be easily defeated. Due to the computational complexity of the security schemes, in practice, symmetric cryptography is widely used for bulk data encryption while asymmetric cryptography is used to distribute cryptographic keys as its performance is inadequate for the encryption of bulk data (typically requires 100 to 1000 times as much processing power as symmetric cryptographic algorithms). Moreover, key management for an asymmetric cryptography is also problematic. The management problem here is basically the distribution of public keys. After the public keys have been distributed or become accessible, well-defined algorithms based on public key cryptography could be applied to sign the digital signature or to distribute session keys for symmetric data encryption, e.g. using key exchange algorithms such as the Diffie-Hellman technique ([16]) or simply encrypting the secret key generated by one party with the public key of the other party. Thus, the problem, key management here, is how to make the public key accessible to all concerned parties without potential abuse of the public key distribution system.

One approach providing public key management service in wired networks or wireless cellular networks is the deployment of a Public Key Infrastructure (PKI). The most important component in a PKI is the *certificate authority* (CA), a trusted entity with its public key known to everyone in the system. The CA is then responsible for issuing, validating and distributing the public keys (in the form of digital certificates) for others. The success of a PKI depends on the availability and security of the CA. However, a PKI does need a central control point, which everybody trusts, this is possible only when certain fixed infrastructure exists. Thus, the difficulty in applying a PKI in a MANET is that such a central control point is not available. Even when available, it cannot be well protected in MANETs and would become the most vulnerable point in the system. To deal with this problem, a distributed and cooperative CA was proposed ([75]). The basic idea is that, by secret sharing, the service and the trust of a CA is distributed into a set of nodes (also called servers), which can be trusted to a certain extent, a certain number of nodes cooperatively perform the functions of a CA, so that the service remains available and correct even if a small number of such nodes or servers become unavailable or compromised. Substantial work has been carried out in this direction recently ([75, 76, 30, 70]). We will elaborate this approach in Section 4.2.

Another approach is to deploy distributed key management without a CA. Distributed key management, as used in PGP (Pretty Good Privacy) ([63, 59]), solves the "no CA" problem with introducers. The introducers are other users of the system who sign their friends' public keys. The basic idea is as follows. If A knows B, then A signs B's key and gives B a copy of the signature. When B meets a stranger C, B presents his key with the signature of A. If C also knows and trusts A, C has reason to trust B. By this means, the users sign each other's key and over time, each one will collect many introducers. Then, they have high probability of verifying each other's key by one of their introducers. A similar approach as in PGP was adopted in [24], where the authors proposed a self-organized public key management system for fully self-organized mobile ad hoc networks. We will discuss this approach in Section 4.3.

It is worth noting that providing a security service always starts from a certain *prior context*, consisting of the well defined name space, each node's security requirement, and some prior trust relationship ([2]). For example, the centralized PKI system with CA is based on the prior trust between each node and CA while the distributed key management, as used in PEP, is based on the prior trust between friends (e.g. authentic nodes in MANETs). These prior trusts must be done out-of-band, through possibly non-cryptographic ways, such as physical contact or other secure channel. Security techniques can help only in transforming and transferring the trust assumptions in the prior context. They cannot create trust.

More key management mechanisms based on different types of prior context have been proposed. In [2], Asokan and Ginzboorg proposed a solution for key agreement for a MANET conferencing scenario. It is assumed that there is no public key infrastructure or physically secure communication channels. However, all the participants are able to choose and share a fresh password (e.g. by writing it on a blackboard). Starting from this weak shared password, the authors proposed a password-based authenticated key exchange to establish a stronger shared key among participants. However, this proposal assumes that the participants in the conference do not change during the session. If the members are dynamic, the session keys needs to be updated when the composition of the group changes. In another paper [46], Montenegro and Castelluccia proposed using a crypto-based identifier (CBID) to simplify the key management and provide an auto-configurable foundation for nodes to engage in verifiable information exchanges with each other. The idea is to have an implicit cryptographic binding between a node's identifier and its public key (or certificate). Ideally, in identity-based public key cryptography ([59]), the binding should be done by generating public/private key pair based on the node's ID. However, the mathematics of these sorts of schemes turns out to be infuriatingly complicated to make secure ([59]). Otherwise, a trusted authority is required to establish the private keys among the users. In [46], the authors proposed the binding by generating the node's ID from self-generated public key. However, this actually poses another challenge, that of managing the name (ID) space of the MANET, which is not desirable.

For a critical survey on key establishment protocols in a mobile communications network with infrastructure, readers are referred to [6].

4.2 Distributed and Cooperative Certificate Authority

PKI is the most popular public key management system. In the PKI system, the public keys are distributed in the form of public-key certificates. A public-key certificate is a node's public key signed by a trusted entity, which also contains information about that node. The trusted entity is a certificate authority (CA). Prior trust between the CA and each node is assumed (the initial authentication can be done by non-cryptographic means such as physical contact). Then, it is up to the CA to manage the public-key certificate of each node with proper authentication. The major certification services provided by a CA include certificate issue, renewal, revocation, and certificate directory service ([70]).

CA is a centralized control mechanism. Its success depends on the availability and the security of the CA. In a MANET, due to the frequent change of topology , it is not easy to guarantee that a single node is always accessible. Moreover, setting up a single node as a CA would provide the adversaries a single most vulnerable point. Once the CA is compromised, the whole system will be subverted. Based on these considerations, a distributed and cooperative CA model was proposed recently by Zhou and Haas ([75]).

In this proposed model, the distribution of trust is achieved by using threshold cryptography. As we introduced in section 3.2.3, an $(n, t + 1)$ (denoted as (T, N) in Section 3.2.3) threshold cryptography scheme allows n parties to share the ability to perform a cryptographic operation, so that any $t + 1$ or more parties can perform this operation jointly, though it is infeasible for t or fewer parties to do so, even by a possible collusion. With an $(n, t + 1)$ configuration ($n \geq 3t + 1$), there are n special nodes, called *servers*, collectively perform the functions of a CA. The system private key K is divided into n shares $(s_1, s_2, \ldots, s_n)$, each share is given to each server. Each server has its corresponding private/public key pair and stores the public keys of all the nodes in the network. In particular, each server knows the public keys of all other servers.

For the service to sign a certificate, each server generates a partial signature for the certificate using its private key share and submits the partial signatures to a combiner. With $t + 1$ correct partial signature, the combiner is able to compute the signature for the certificate. However, with t or fewer partial signatures, it is computationally impossible to compute the signature of the certificate. Thus, to subvert the CA, the enemy has to compromise at least $t + 1$ servers. It is worth noting that the signing process here is not the generation of an commom digital signature. In order to maintain the property of the secret sharing, when a secret share is used in signing partial certificate, it is treated as an exponent in RSA algorithm. More details about the signing process was described in [30].

To tackle the mobile adversaries attack, in which an adversary compromises one server and then moves to the next victim, the authors proposed to use *share refreshing*. Share refreshing allows the servers to compute new shares from the old shares in collaboration without disclosing the system private key to any server. Share refreshing is based on the following homomorphic property. If $(s_{11}, s_{21}, \ldots, s_{n1})$ are the $(n, t + 1)$ secret shares of K_1 and $(s_{12}, s_{22}, \ldots, s_{n2})$ are the $(n, t + 1)$ secret shares of K_2, then $(s_{11} + s_{12}, s_{21} + s_{22}, \ldots, s_{n1} + s_{n2})$, where " $+$ " is the addition operation on a finite field, are the $(n, t + 1)$ secret shares of key $K_1 + K_2$. If K_2 is 0, then a new $(n, t + 1)$ secret shares of K_1 are obtained. The new shares are independent of the old ones, so the mobile adversary has to compromise at least $t + 1$ servers during one refreshing period. A share refreshing process is also proposed, and it requires only $t + 1$ subshares to generate the new shares. In addition, the configuration of the system could be changed from $(n, t + 1)$ to $(n', t' + 1)$ adaptively, if necessary.

The proposed distributed CA model has been implemented in COCA (Cornell Online CA) ([76]), although it is not dedicated to MANET. A similar approach has been adopted in [30] and [70]. In [30], a self-initialization protocol is proposed to handle dynamic node membership (i.e. joins and leaves) and secret share updates. The nice feature of this approach is that providing the security services can be localized and the trust can be made more robust (see also [42]).

4.3 Self-organized Public Key Management

As we mentioned before, PGP, a widely used Email security system, uses a distributed approach for key management. There is no centralized key certification authority. Instead, PGP supports a "web of trust". Every user generates and distributes his/her own public key. Users sign each other's public keys, creating an interconnected community of PGP users. Similar to that used in PGP, an alternative key management system, *the self-organizing public key management system*, was proposed by Hubaux and his colleagues in their TERMINODES project for fully self-organized mobile ad hoc networks ([5, 18, 24]).

In this proposed system, each user maintains a local certificate repository that contains a limited number of certificates selected by the user according to some algorithm. When user u wants to obtain or verify the public key of user v, the user u will merge the local certificate repositories of both user u

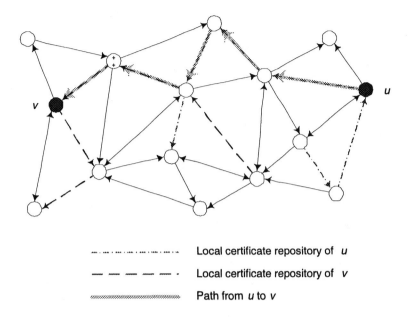

--- .. .. -   Local certificate repository of *u*

— — — — — ·   Local certificate repository of *v*

▨▨▨▨▨▨▨▨▨▨▨▨▨▨▨   Path from *u* to *v*

Figure 1: Merging subgraphes of node *u* and *v* for chain of trust between them ([24])

and user v, and tries to find an appropriate certificate chain from u to v in the merged repository. The authors use a directed graph $G(V, E)$, called a *trust graph*, to represent the trust relationship between users. As shown in Figure 1, if user u issues a public-key certificate to user v, there would be a directed edge from vertex u to vertex v in the graph. Then, a directed path from vertex u to vertex v indicates a certificate chain from user u to user v.

The local certificate repository maintained at each node is represented as a subgraph of that node. The success of this approach depends on the construction of the local certificate repositories and the characteristics of the trust graph. The size of each local repository should be kept small compared with the total number of users in the system for scalability. On the other hand, when combining their repositories, any pair of legal users should be able to find a certificate chain between them with high probability. Two algorithms are proposed for users to build their local certificate repositories: *shortcut hunter algorithm* and *star shortcut hunter algorithm*. Here, a *shortcut* is defined as an edge, such that once it is removed, the shortest undirected path between the nodes previously connected by that edge becomes strictly larger than two. The basic idea of the shortcut hunter al-

gorithm is to build a subgraph that consists of a single out-bound path and
a single in-bound path. Path selection is similar for both paths. It starts
from the node itself. In each round, it selects a node among neighbors of the
last selected vertex. The selection criterion is to choose the one that has the
highest number of shortcuts. The star shortcut hunter algorithm modified
the pure shortcut hunter algorithm a little bit. Instead of finding a single
out-bound and a single in-bound path, it builds a subgraph that consists of
several vertex disjoint out-bound paths and several vertex disjoint in-bound
paths.

This is a fully distributed and also scalable approach to the key management system. However, it only provides probabilistic guarantees. In
addition, this approach assumes that trust is transitive, which is often not
the case in practice. In order to alleviate this problem, the authors proposed
using multiple certificate paths and using authentication. Similar to PGP,
the weakest link of this whole system is key revocation, which was briefly
addressed in their work.

5   Secure Routing Protocols

Routing is of paramount importance in a mobile ad hoc network because
traditional Internet routing protocols are no longer effective due to the frequent topological changes. A great effort has been made within the Internet Engineering Task Force (IETF) mobile ad hoc networking (MANET)
working group in order to develop a routing framework for IP-based protocols in MANETs. A number of routing protocols have been proposed and
widely evaluated. The proposed routing protocols can be generally divided
into two main categories: *table-driven (proactive)* and *on-demand (reactive)*
([55]). Similar to the routing protocols used in wired networks, table-driven
routing protocols [50] attempt to maintain consistent, up-to-date route information from each node to every other node, regardless of the need for
such routes. They respond to changes in topology by propagating updates
throughout the network. An on-demand routing protocol ([29, 49]) differs
from this in that it attempts to discover a route to a destination only when it
has a packet to forward to the destination. Discovered routes are maintained
by a route maintenance procedure until either the destination becomes in-
accessible along every path from the source or until the route is no longer
desired. In addition, some ad hoc routing protocols are hybrid with a combination of the table-driven and on-demand mechanisms ([20]). These routing
protocols are generally designed with the objective of keeping up with the

frequent and unpredictable changes in topology. More sophisticated protocols consider routing scalability, route stability, energy efficiency, and so on. Most of the designs assume a trusted environment and the co-operation of each participating node. Relatively little research has been done in a more realistic setting where an adversary may attempt to disrupt operation.

5.1 Vulnerabilities Analysis of Mobile Ad Hoc Routing Protocols

As mentioned in Section 2.1, without incorporating protection mechanisms, ad hoc network routing protocols are more vulnerable to many types of attacks. Generally speaking, the attacks to a routing protocol can be first divided into two classes: *passive attacks* and *active attacks*. The passive attacks on routing protocols are eavesdropping only, but not endangering message transmissions. It is mainly a threat to the message confidentiality, and does not affect the proper functioning of the routing protocols. The passive attacks on routing protocols can be readily protected in the same way as for data traffic. So we do not discuss it further here. The active attacks, however, can be further classified into two classes: *external attacks* and *internal attacks*. External attacks are from outsiders, such attacks are limited when encryption and source authentication are in place. A special case of external attacks is the wormwhole attack, which will be discussed shortly. Internal attacks, coming from internal nodes (e.g. compromised nodes), are more severe attacks because an internal node has all the necessary credentials for authentication and so on. A single node or multiple nodes could launch an attack individually without collusion, or multiple nodes could also launch attacks as a team with shared information and coordinated collaboration. Most of the secure routing protocols proposed in the current literature can only prevent individual attacks, either from internal or from external sources, but have limited capability to handle collusion attacks.

With this classification, we are now ready to identify and classify the possible attacks to routing protocols ([57, 22]). We discuss the protection against the attacks briefly.

5.1.1 Modification of Routing Information

A general attack to disrupt routing function is to modify the routing information. Here, by modification, we assume that the source and destination nodes are trusted while the attack is performed by any intermediate node while processing the transit routing information. For example, for a table-driven protocol, a malicious node could send out false routing updates, or for an on-demand protocol, a malicious node could alter the information contained in the route request or route reply in a route discovery process. The altered routing information could cause legitimate traffic to be redirected to a black hole or an inefficient detour (a black hole is where all the packets are dropped except routing packets), or a routing loop is formed, or even a network partition may be caused ([22]). Any information field in a routing message could be exploited by an attacker. For example, the *destination_sequence_number* is widely used in a mobile ad hoc network routing protocol to indicate the freshness of the routes. A malicious node could simply modify the *destination_sequence_number* to make other routing information invalid while making itself the freshest route, or it could modify the hop counts to claim the shortest path to any destination, or in protocols such as DSR, any intermediate node could simply modify the replied routes, or a malicious node could also illegally modify its IP and/or MAC address to impersonate another node (spoofing).

This type of modification attack is basically an attack by illegally modifying the content in the routing messages, carried out by either an external attacker or an internal attacker. This type of attack can be prevented by source authentication and message integrity services. The illegal modification of the stationary fields such as the node address or *destination_sequence_number* can be protected by message integrity measures such as a message authentication code (MAC). While protection of the integrity of the routing metric (e.g. hop count) for a hop-by-hop routing protocol and the complete route (node lists) information contained in some on-demand routing protocols is a little different, as such information is allowed to change at each hop. Much effort has been made along this line to guarantee the correctness of the routing operation and routing information. Several secure routing protocols have been proposed that are robust to these attacks when performed by individual attackers. We will discuss the proposed secure routing protocols in Section 5.2.

5.1.2 Fabrication of Routing Information

Another form of attack is to fabricate false topology information. By fabrication, we mean that the false routing information is initiated by a malicious node. This happens particularly for route maintenance processes. For example, in any routing protocols such as DSDV ([50]), AODV ([49]) or DSR ([29]), a malicious node can fabricate routing updates or route error messages to claim the inaccessibility of another node. Source authentication can limit this type of attacks to the extent that the malicious node could only claim the inaccessibility to its own neighbors. Thus, this attack actually causes less significant damage to the network, as the effect of this attack is the isolation of the malicious node itself. This type of attack cannot be prevented for an internal attacker. However, non-repudiation protection can be applied to facilitate the detection of such attackers ([57]).

5.1.3 Replay

A replay attack captures a data unit passively and then retransmits it to produce an unauthorized effect. One of the replay attacks in MANETs is to create a *wormhole* ([23]). In a wormhole attack, the attacker records packets, particularly routing control packets, at one location in the network, tunnels them to another location, and then retransmits them into the network there. It could be either an external attack or an internal attack. This attack is dangerous because the source may fail to find routes or find routes that actually do not exist. An individual wormhole attack is shown in Figure 2(a) where a malicious node M simply replay the routing request and reply message between node S and T without showing itself. Thus, an actually non-exist path S-T would be replied to S. Figure 2(b) shows a collusive wormhole attack, where two malicious nodes M_1 and M_2 collaborate to make the tunneled packets arrive sooner than other packets traveling over a normal multihop route. In order to minimize the delay introduced by the wormhole, the attack(s) can replay the packet bit by bit without storing the whole packet, or can use some long-distance wireless link or even wired link to tunnel the packet ([23]).

A subtler replay type of attacks is *tunneling* ([57]). A tunneling attack is where two or more nodes may collaborate to encapsulate and exchange messages between them along existing data routes. This attack requires the collusion of internal attackers. An example of the tunneling attack is shown in Figure 3, where malicious node M_1 and M_2 tunnels RREQ and RREP messages using the data path M_1-B-C-M_2. However, the source would wrongly consider route S-M_1-M_2-D to be a shorter path.

The external wormhole attack can be partially prevented at the physical layer, e.g, by using a secret modulation method, RF watermarking, or tamper-resistant hardware ([23]). However, if the attackers manage to capture and replicate the waveform, this approach is likely to fail. Prevention of such an attack by a software-only approach is difficult, if not impossible, as the attack takes advantage of the operation of the routing protocols. How-

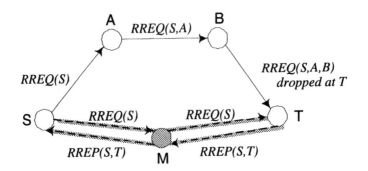

(a). Individual attack

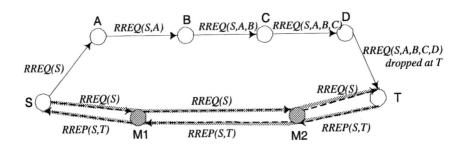

(b). Collaborative attack (collusion)

Figure 2: Wormhole attack

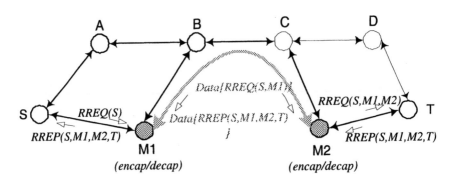

Figure 3: Tunneling attack

ever, detection of such an attack is possible by using some unalterable and independent physical metric such as time delay or geographical location. We will discuss a mechanism dealing with this problem in the next section.

5.1.4 Denial of Service (DOS)

The DoS attack on a routing protocol could take many forms, but all result in the unavailability of the routing service. The consequences of many of the above attacks are denial of service. Besides disrupting routing, an attacker could also launch a DoS attack by excessively consuming network resources. For example, a malicious node could initiate excessively unnecessary route discovery processes or it could inject extra packets into network with the sole purpose of wasting other nodes' energy when processing and forwarding the packets. This type of attacks, if performed by an internal node, is difficult to prevent. However, as pointed out in [22], an attack is considered a DoS attack only if the ratio between the total work performed by nodes in the network and the work performed by the attacker is on the order of the number of nodes in the network. e.g., a single packet sent by the attacker results in a packet flood throughout the network. Thus the DoS attack can be efficiently limited by preventing an attacker from inserting routing loops, or enforcing a maximum route length a packet can traverse. Moreover, an active detection scheme could also be applied to identify such attacks ([65]), as we will discuss in the next subsection.

5.2 Protection of Routing Protocols

Much of the effort in providing security in mobile ad hoc networks has been spent on protecting routing protocols. In general, a secure routing protocol should implement some kind of authentication and integrity schemes so that the correctness of the routing information, particularly, the node identity, the *destination_sequence_number*, and the cost metric, can be protected. Several secure routing protocols have been proposed along this line, each with different authentication schemes and for different types of routing protocols.

5.2.1 Hop-by-hop Authentication

For distance vector routing protocols such as DSDV and AODV, due to their operational features, the correctness of the routing information has to be provided on a hop-by-hop basis. Moreover, the correct accumulation of the routing metric has to be guaranteed, i.e. an internal malicious node should not be able to reduce the routing metric from itself to any other destination. In [21], Hu, Johnson and Perrig proposed a *Secure Efficient Distance Vector (SEAD)* routing protocol to provide authentic routing information for the proactive DSDV protocols. The authors suggested several options for neighbor authentication, such as computing an Message Authentication Code (MAC) for each neighbor with each routing update, to protect fields such as source identity and destination sequence number. Particularly, they proposed using a one-way hash chain to protect the metric field. The one-way hash chain is a series of data generated from a one-way hash function, which is easy to compute in one way while infeasible to do in the reverse. Thus, in a one-way hash chain, any following datum can be calculated from a previous datum, however, a previous datum cannot be derived from a following datum. In the proposed scheme, the one-way hash chain is generated from one direction, but used in the reverse direction. A hash value corresponding to both the sequence number and the metric is used to authenticate each entry in the routing update. Due to the one-way nature of the hash chain, any intermediate node is not able to modify a route to some destination with a lower metric. This scheme does not use the computationally intensive asymmetric cryptographic operations. However, it does require some mechanism for a node to distribute an authentic element from its generated hash chain initially and periodically when necessary, as the authentication of a value in the hash chain is based on an earlier authentic value. A similar approach has been used in S-AODV ([72]) as an extension of the AODV routing protocol. A one-way hash chain is used for each route discovery to secure the hop count information while public key cryptography (digital signature) is used to authenticate the sources as well as other non-mutable fields of the messages. In [57], Sanzgiri et al implemented the hop-by-hop authentication for the route control messages of AODV and DSR. The protocol uses public key cryptography (digital signature) to guarantee message authentication, integrity and non-repudiation. It provides end-to-end authentication by disabling the option in a route discovery process to reply from intermediate node. The assumption of the existence of a centralized CA in the proposed protocol limits the applicable scenarios to classroom or conference type of managed-open environments.

5.2.2   End-to-end Authentication

For source routing based protocols such as DSR, authentication can be done on an end-to-end basis because the end nodes have knowledge of the complete route. However, the integrity of the routes (e.g., the complete and correct node list in the route) needs to be carefully protected in this case. In [48], Papadimitratos and Haas proposed a secure routing protocol (SRP) to provide end-to-end authentication for source routing based protocols. The correctness of the replied routes is protected by adding message authentication codes (MACs) at the source to the route requests, and at the destination to the route reply messages. The scheme assumes a prior security association (SA) between source and destination while the existence of SAs with any of the intermediate nodes is not necessary. In [22], Hu, Perrig and Johnson proposed another secure routing protocol (Ariadne) based on DSR. The authentication also relies on the message authentication code and is end-to-end in nature. The destination node authenticates the route request messages. In addition, a per-hop hashing technique is presented to verify that no node is missing from the node list in the Route Request message and that all the nodes listed in the Route Request are legitimate nodes. They introduced the use of a broadcast authentication scheme, called *TESLA* ([51]), which requires loose time synchronization, to provide the authenticity of the routing information for the DSR protocol. Because the authentication is end-to-end in nature, both schemes require the route replies from the destination while disabling the route replies from intermediate nodes. This might cause performance degradation of routing protocols ([44]).

5.2.3 Reactive Approach

The afore-mentioned basic mechanisms are generally proactive and preventive methods to secure routing protocols. The objective is to secure the correctness of the exchanged routing information as well as the routing operation. More mechanisms are proposed to enhance routing security using reactive approaches. One motivation of using reactive mechanism is to protect the attacks that are difficult to prevent. In [23], Hu, Perrig and Johnson proposed a mechanism, namely *packet leashes*, to defend against the wormhole attacks (it also applies to tunneling attacks). The basic idea is to use additional timing and/or location information so that a receiver can determine if the packet has traveled a route that is not realistic for the specific network technology used. Two types of packet leashes are considered: geographical leashes and temporal leashes. The temporal leashes rely on extremely precise time synchronization and extremely precise timestamps in each packet, while the geographical leashes use location information and loose time synchronization.

The network layer plays two major functions: routing and packet forwarding. They are closely related: the packet forwarding is based on the routing decision. A reactive approach can monitor the behaviors of both the routing function and the forwarding function. So another motivation for a reactive approach is to provide unified network layer protection. In [69], Yang, Meng and Lu proposed such a unified network-layer security protocol that protects both routing and forwarding functions in the context of AODV. In their design, each authentic node is assigned a temporary token to participate in the network. The routing and packet forwarding behavior of each node is constantly monitored by his/her neighbors. Once the token is expired, the neighbors collaboratively renew the node's token based on a threshold secret sharing scheme ([42]). Only when the node's behavior is approved by a certain number (threshold) of neighbors, is the node able to renew its token. Otherwise, it will be isolated from the network. This scheme takes a fully localized design without completely trusting any individual node. In [65], Venkatraman and Agrawal proposed a model that combines both external attack prevention and internal attack detection for AODV. The message authentication code is used to prevent external attacks, while an internal detection and response module is designed to identify the misbehaving nodes, and then isolate them. Their detection mechanism is similar to a rule-based intrusion detection system and both the routing and packet forwarding behaviors are monitored. The AODV protocol is modified so that two-hop routing information is maintained at each node for each route. Each node constantly monitors and analyzes the behavior of its neighbors based on certain predefined attack patterns. The fabrication attacks are monitored in their scheme. Work adopting a similar approach can also be found in [3], where a protocol consisting of both the preventive mechanism and the fault detection mechanism was proposed. However, the objective of the detection is to detect Byzantine behavior, which is defined as any action by an authenticated node that results in disruption or degradation of the routing service. The detection is result based, without considering the reason that causes the fault. An adaptive probing technique was proposed, which is based on acknowledgments of the data packets.

In [71], Yi, Naldurg and Kravets presented a *security-aware routing (SAR)* protocol. Nodes are assumed to have different trust levels and the SAR is designed to find the path consisting of only nodes with a required trust level. Nodes with the same level of trust share the same secret keys. Nodes with different trust levels are not able to process the routing control messages. SAR is actually not a secure routing protocol in the strict sense, but an approach more to quality of service (QoS) routing in which the security is treated as a QoS parameter.

6　Conclusions

Security is an important issue in mobile ad hoc networks. The current research and development in this area is still in its infancy. In this chapter, we examine the security aspects and present a comprehensive survey on the state-of-the-art development in the security related issues in mobile ad hoc networks. We discuss many security issues, mainly from a network perspective, and present the recently proposed solutions. Two major research focuses, key management and secure routing protocols, are presented in more details. Due to the space limitations, only the novel and fundamental idea of each approach is presented here. The readers are referred to each individual paper for the mechanism or protocol details as well as the performance evaluations.

References

[1] R. Anderson, M. Kuhn, "Tamper resistance - a cautionary note," *Proceedings of the Second USENIX Workshop on Electric Commence*, pp. 1-11, Oakland, CA, November 1996.

[2] N. Asokan and P. Ginzboorg, "Key agreement in ad-hoc networks," *Computer Communications*, **23**:1627-1637, 2000.

[3] B. Awerhuch, D. Holmer, C. Nita-Totaru and H. Rubens, "An on-demand secure routing protocol resilient to Byzantine failure," *ACM WiSe'02*, September 2002.

[4] G.R. Blakley, "Safeguarding Cryptographic Keys," *Proc. AFIPS 1979 National Computer Conference*, vol.48, pp.313-317, New York, June 1979.

[5] L. Blazevic, L. Buttyan, S. Capkun, S. Giordano, J.-P. Hubaux and J.-Y. Le Boudec, "Self-organization in mobile ad hoc networks: the approach of terminodes," *IEEE Communication Magazine*, vol. 39, issue 6, pp. 166-174, June 2001.

[6] C. Boyd and A. Mathuria, "Key establishment protocols for secure mobile communications: a critical survey," *Computer Communications*, 23:575-587, 2000.

[7] S. Buchegger and J.-Y. Le Boudec, "Performance analysis of the CONFIDENT protocol," *Proceedings of the 3rd ACM International Sym-*

posium on Mobile Ad Hoc Networking and Computing (MobiHOC'02), June 2002.

[8] S. Buchegger and J.-Y. Le Boudec, "Nodes bearing grudges: towards routing security, fairness, and robustness in mobile ad hoc networks," *Proceedings of 10th Euromicro Workshop on Parallel, Distributed and Network-based Processing (EUROMICRO-PDP)*, pp. 403-410, 2002.

[9] L. Buttyan and J.-P. Hubaux, "Enforcing service availability in mobile ad hoc networks," *Proceedings of the 1st ACM International Symposium on Mobile Ad Hoc Networking and Computing (MobiHOC'00)*, pp. 87-96, 2000.

[10] L. Buttyan and J.-P. Hubaux, "Rational exchange - a formal model based on game theory," *Proceedings of the 2nd International Workshop on Electrical Commerce (WELCOM)*, November 2001

[11] L. Buttyan and J-P. Hubaux, "Report on a working session on security in wireless ad hoc networks," *ACM Mobile and Computing and Communication Review*, vol.6, no.4, 2002.

[12] L. Buttyan and J.-P. Hubaux, "Stimulating co-operation in self-organizing mobile ad hoc networks," *ACM/Kluwer Mobile Networks and Applications (MONET)*, to appear 2002.

[13] D. Chaum, "Untraceable electronic mail, return addresses, and digital pseudonyms," *Communications of the ACM*, vol. 24, no. 2, pp. 84-88, February 1981

[14] M. D. Corner and B. D. Noble, "Zero-interaction authentication," *the 8th ACM International Conference on Mobile Computing and Networking (MobiCom'02)*, pp. 1-11, Atlanta, GA, September 2002.

[15] H. Deng, W. Li and D. P. Agrawal, "Routing security in wireless ad hoc networks," *IEEE Communications Magazine*, pp. 70-75, October 2002.

[16] W. Diffie and M. Hellman, "New direction in cryptography," *IEEE Transaction on Information Theory*, pp.644-654, 1976.

[17] A. Fox and S. Gribble, "Security on the move: indirect authentication using Kerberos," *IEEE/ACM MobiCom'96*, New York, 1996.

[18] T. Gross, J.-P. Hubaux, J.-Y. Le Boudec and M. Vetterli, "Toward self-organized mobile ad hoc networks: the terminodes project," *IEEE Communication Magazine*, vol. 39, issue 1, pp. 118-124, January 2001.

[19] Y. Guan, X. Fu, D. Xuan, P. U. Shenoy, R. Bettati and W. Zhao, "NetCamo: Camouflaging network traffic for QoS-guaranteed mission critical applications," *IEEE Transactions on Systems, MAN, and Cybernetics - Part A: Systems and Humans*, pp. 253-265, vol.31, no.4, July 2001.

[20] Z. J. Haas, M. R. Pearlman and P. Samar, "The zone routing protocol (ZRP) for ad hoc networks," IETF Internet draft, draft-ietf-manet-zone-zrp-04.txt, July 2002

[21] Y.-C. Hu, D. B. Johnson and A. Perrig, "SEAD: secure efficient distance vector routing for mobile wireless ad hoc networks," *The 4th IEEE Workshop on Mobile Computing Systems and Applications (WMCSA'02)*, pp. 3-13, June 2002.

[22] Y.-C. Hu, A. Perrig and D. B. Johnson, "Ariadne : a secure on-demand routing protocol for ad hoc networks," *the 8th ACM International Conference on Mobile Computing and Networking (MobiCom 2002)*, pp. 12-23, September 2002.

[23] Y.-C. Hu, A. Perrig and D. B. Johnson, "Packet leashes: A defense against wormhole attacks in wireless ad hoc networks," Technical Report TR01-384, Department of Computer Science, Rice University, Dec 2001.

[24] J-P. Hubaux, L. Buttyan and S. Capkun, "The quest for security in mobile ad hoc networks," *Proceedings of the 2nd ACM International Symposium on Mobile Ad Hoc Networking and Computing (MobiHOC'01)*, 2001.

[25] K. Ilgun, R. A. Kemmerer and P. A. Porras, "State transition analysis: a rule-based intrusion detection approach," *IEEE Transaction on Software Engineering*, 21(3):181-199, March 1995.

[26] S. Jiang, N. Vaidya and W. Zhao, "Routing in packet radio networks to prevent traffic analysis," *Proceedings of the IEEE Information Assurance and Security Workshop*, pp. 96-102, West Point, NY, July 2000.

[27] S. Jiang, N. H. Vaidya and W. Zhao, "A dynamic mix method for wireless ad hoc networks," *IEEE Military Communications Conference (Milcom'01)*, pp. 873-877, McLean, VA, October 2001.

[28] S. Jiang, N. Vaidya and W. Zhao, "Preventing traffic analysis in packet radio networks," *DARPA Information Survivability Conference & Exposition II (DISCEX'01)*, vol.2, pp. 163-158, 2001

[29] D. B. Johnson, D. A. Maltz, Y-C. Hu and J. G. Jetcheva, "The dynamic source routing protocol for mobile ad hoc networks," IETF Internet Draft, draft-ietf-manet-dsr-07.txt, February 2002.

[30] J. Kong, P. Zerfos, H. Luo, S. Lu and L. Zhang, "Providing robust and ubiquitous security support for manet," *Proceedings of the 9th IEEE International Conference on Network Protocols(ICNP)*, pp. 251 -260, 2001.

[31] J. Konorski, "Protection of fairness for multimedia traffic streams in a non-cooperative wireless LAN setting," PROMS 2001, vol. 2213 of LNCS, Springer

[32] J. Konorski, "Multiple access in ad-hoc wireless LANs with non-cooperative stations," NETWORKING 2002, vol. 2345 of LNCS, Springer

[33] S. Kumar and E. H. Spafford, "A software architecture to support misuse intrusion detection," *Proceedings of the 18th National Information Security Conference*, 1995.

[34] Y. Kwon, Y. Fang, and H. Latchman, "A novel medium access control protocol for wireless local area networks," *IEEE INFOCOM'2003*, San Francisco, California, March/April 2003.

[35] Y. Kwon, Y. Fang, and H. Latchman, "Fast collision resolution (FCR) MAC algorithm for wireless local area networks," *IEEE Globecom'2002*, Taipei, Taiwan, November 2002.

[36] P. Kyasanur and N. H. Vaidya, "Detection and handling of MAC layer misbehavior in wireless networks," Technical Report, CSL, UIUC, Aug 2002

[37] Y.-B. Lin and Y.K. Chen, "Reducing authentication signaling traffic in third generation mobile network," To appear in *IEEE Transactions on Wireless Communications*.

[38] Y.-B. Lin, S. Mohan, N. Sollenberger and H. Sherry, "Adaptive algorithms for reducing PCS network authentication traffic," *IEEE Transactions on Vehicular Technology*, 46(3):588-596, 1997.

[39] W. Lou and Y. Fang, "SPREAD: Improving network security by multipath routing in ad hoc networks," Technical Report, Dept. of Electrical and Computer Engineering, University of Florida, 2002.

[40] W. Lou and Y. Fang, "A multipath routing approach for secure data delivery," *IEEE Military Communications Conference (Milcom'01)*, vol. 2, pp. 1467 -1473, McLean, VA, October 2001.

[41] T. Lunt, A. Tamaru, F. Gilham, R. Jagannathan, P. Neumann, H. Javitz, A. Valdes and T. Garvey, "A real-time intrusion detection expert system (IDES) - final technical report", Technical Report, Computer Science Laboratory, SRI International, Menlo Park, CA, February 1992.

[42] H. Luo and S. Lu, "Ubiquitous and robust authentication services for ad hoc wireless networks," Technical Report UCLA-CSD-TR-200030, Department of Computer Science, UCLA, 2000.

[43] A. B. MacKenzie and S. B. Wicker, "Game theory and the design of self-configuring, adaptive wireless networks," *IEEE Communication Magazine*, pp. 126-131, November 2001.

[44] D. A. Maltz, J. Broch, J. Jetcheva and D. B. Johnson, "The effects of on-demand behavior in routing protocols for multihop wireless ad hoc networks," *IEEE Journal on Selected Areas in Communications*, vol.17, no.8, pp.1439-1453, August 1999.

[45] S. Marti, T. Giuli, K. Lai and M. Baker, "Mitigating routing misbehavior in mobile ad hoc networks," *the 6th annual ACM/IEEE International Conference on Mobile Computing and Networking (MobiCom'00)*, pp.255-265, Boston, MA, USA, August 2000.

[46] G. Montenegro and C. Castelluccia, "Statistically unique and cryptographically verifiable (SUCV) identifiers and addresses," *Proceedings of the 9th annual network and distributed system security symposium (NDSS)*, February 2002.

[47] R. E. Newman-Wolfe and B. R. Venkatraman, "High level prevention of traffic analysis," *Proceedings of the 7th Annual Computer Security and Applications Conference*, pp. 102-109, December 1991.

[48] P. Papadimitratos and Z. J. Haas, "Secure routing for mobile ad hoc networks," *Proceedings of the SCS communication networks and distributed systems modeling and simulation conference (CNDS 2002)*, San Antonio, TX, January 2002.

[49] C. E. Perkins, E. M. Belding-Royer and S. R. Das, "Ad hoc on-demand distance vector (AODV) routing," IETF Internet draft, draft-ietf-manet-aodv-12.txt, November 2002.

[50] C. E. Perkins and P. Bhagwat, "Highly dynamic destination-sequenced distance-vector routing (DSDV) for mobile computers," *Computer Communication Review*, October 1994, pp. 234-244.

[51] A. Perrig, R. Canetti, D. Tygar and D. Song, "Efficient authentication and signature of multicast streams over lossy channels," *Proceedings of the IEEE Symposium on Security and Privacy*, May 2000.

[52] A. Perrig, R. Szewczyk, J.D. Tygar, V. Wen, and D.E. Culler, "SPINS: security protocols for sensor networks," *ACM Wireless Networks*, 8(5), 521-534, September 2002.

[53] A. Pfitzmann, B. Pfitzmann and M. Waidner, "Trusting mobile user devices and security modules," *IEEE Computer*, February 1997.

[54] B. Radosavljevic and B. Jajek, "Hiding traffic flow in communication networks," *IEEE Military Communications Conference (Milcom'92)*, October 1992.

[55] E. M. Royer and C-K Toh, "A review of current routing protocols for ad hoc mobile wireless networks," *IEEE Personal Communications*, pp.46-55, April 1999.

[56] D. Samfat and R. Molva, "IDAMN: an intrusion detection architecture for mobile networks," *IEEE JSAC*, vol.15, no.7, pp.1373-1380, 1997.

[57] K. Sanzgiri, B. Dahill, B. N. Levine, C. Shields and E. M. Belding-Royer, "A secure routing protocol for ad hoc networks," *the 10th IEEE International conference on network protocols (ICNP)*, November 2002.

[58] B. Schneier, *Secrets and Lies: Digital Security in a Network World*, John Wiley & Sons, 1st edition, 2000.

[59] B. Schneier, *Applied Cryptography: Protocols, Algorithms, and Source Code in C*, John Wiley & Sons, 2nd edition, 1996.

[60] A. Shamir, "How to Share a Secret," *Communications of the ACM*, 22(11):612-613, November 1979.

[61] G. J. Simmons, "An Introduction to Shared Secret and/or Shared Control Schemes and The Application," *Contemporary Cryptology: The Science of Information Integrity*, IEEE Press, pp.441-497, 1992.

[62] F. Stajano and R. Anderson, "The resurrencting duckling: security issues for ad-hoc wireless networks," *Proceedings of the 7th International Workshop on Security Protocols, Lecture Notes in Computer Science 1796*, pp. 172-182, Springer-Verlag, Berlin, 1999.

[63] W. Stallings, *Cryptography and Network Security: Principles and Practice*, 2nd edition, Prentice Hall, 1999.

[64] A. Tsirigos and Z.J. Haas, "Multipath routing in the presence of frequent topological changes," *IEEE Communication Magazine*, pp. 132-138, November 2001.

[65] L. Venkatraman and D.P. Agrawal, "Strategies for enhancing routing security in protocols for mobile ad hoc networks," *Journal of Parallel and Distributed Computing*, to appear.

[66] B. R. Venkatraman and R. E. Newman-Wolfe, "Transmission schedules to prevent traffic analysis," *Proceedings of the 9th Annual Computer Security and Applications Conference*, pp. 108-115, December 1993.

[67] A. Weimerskirch and G. Thonet, "A distributed light-weight authentication model for ad-hoc networks," *Lecture Notes in Computer Science*, No. 2288, pp.341-354, 2002.

[68] K. Wu and J. Harms, "Performance study of a multipath routing method for wireless mobile ad hoc networks," *the 9th International Symposium on Modeling, Analysis and Simulation of Computer and Telecommunication Systems*, pp. 99-107, 2001.

[69] H. Yang, X. Meng and S. Lu, "Self-organized network-layer security in mobile ad hoc networks," *ACM WiSe'02*, September 2002.

[70] S. Yi and R. Kravets, "Key management for heterogeneous ad hoc wireless networks," Technical Report No. UIUCDCS-R-2002-2290, UIUC, July 2002.

[71] S. Yi, P. Naldurg and R. Kravets, "Security-aware ad-hoc routing for wireless networks," Report No. UIUCDCS-R-2001-2241, Department of Computer Science, UIUC, Aug 2001.

[72] M. G. Zapata, "Secure ad hoc on-demand distance vector (SAODV) routing," Internet draft, draft-guarrero-manet-saodv-00.txt, Aug 2002

[73] Y. Zhang and W. Lee, "Intrusion detection in wireless ad hoc networks," *Proceedings of the 6th ACM International Conference on Mobile Computing and Networking (MobiCom'00)*, August 2000.

[74] Y. Zhang, W. Lee and Y. Huang, "Intrusion detection techniques for mobile wireless networks," *ACM/Kluwer Mobile Networks and Applications (MONET)*, to appear.

[75] L. Zhou and Z. J. Haas, "Securing ad hoc networks," *IEEE Network Magazine*, vol. 13, no. 6, pp. 24-30, November/December 1999.

[76] L. Zhou, F. B. Schneider and R. V. Renesse, "COCA: a secure distributed on-line certification authority," *ACM Transactions on Computer Systems*, to appear.

AD HOC WIRELESS NETWORKING
X. Cheng, X. Huang and D.-Z. Du (Eds.) pp. 365 - 382

Location Related Issues in Mobile Network Systems

Xiaobin Ma
Department of Computer Science and Engineering
University of Minnesota, Minneapolis, MN 55455
E-mail: `xiaobin@cs.umn.edu`

Contents

1   Introduction

The fact that large fixed network infrastructures exist seems to limit the usefulness of other forms of communication systems such as ad hoc networks. In many situations, however, ad hoc networks are preferred. Currently mobile network system has attracted more and more attention because of great benefit from the mobile network such as the mobility and flexibility. Mobile network users can move anywhere with almost no restriction to communicate with other people or access the network. Also, if they like, they can construct their own ad hoc network to share their information among them with their small computers and/or even their PDAs.

Mobile network system is tightly related to location information because of its inherent mobile characteristics. The location related issues such as acquisition of location information of mobile host, the routing techniques based on location information and the location management and query techniques that can or will be used in mobile network or provided by mobile network are of more and more importance.

This paper is organized as following. First, we discuss how we can get the location information through various devices and architectures. In location related service, this is the first and basic step. Second, we introduce the location based, especially GPS based, routing protocols. Routing is one of most important issues in network system. Because of the mobile characteristics in mobile network system, it introduces more difficulty. Third, mobile user's location information management is discussed. Because location user has inherent mobile quality, his information is related to his location. For more efficient access of mobile user's information, location data management approaches must be taken effectively. We will also address the query of location related information in mobile network in order to better serve the mobile user.

2   Navigation/Position Identification

In location related system, the acquisition of objects' locations is the critical step for the effective and smooth working procedures. This task has two aspects. First our concern is the location acquisition devices that help mobile users to get absolute or relative physical distance or angular information in reference to some known objects. The second step is to develop a mathematical model to calculate the specific location for an indicated object.

2.1 Location Acquisition System

There are many kinds of location acquisition systems developed to get the object's location. They can be grouped into two categories that are outdoor positioning system and indoor positioning system. Global Positioning System (GPS) is a representative of outdoor positioning system. When GPS signal is not available to object inside building, indoor positioning system is needed to detect the object's location.

Outdoor Positioning System

The Global Positioning System (GPS) is a satellite-based navigation system consisting of a network of 24 orbiting satellites that are orbiting in space eleven miles from Earth. Each satellite sends a signal that containing three parts that are the satellite number, the space position and the satellite local time that the signal was sent. The receiver accepts this signal and decodes it, then the decoded time is compared to receiver's local time to compute the distance information. Finally after some mathematic computations, object's location information is formed. In the next section, some location sensing techniques will be introduced. It is worth noting that GPS system can provide not only instantaneous position that can include latitude, longitude and altitude but also object's velocity. GPS system can provide positioning accuracy ranging from 100 meters to 5 or 10 meters, depending on specific GPS receivers. The more GPS signals the receiver gets from different satellites, the better the accuracy will be.

There is a kind of more accurate GPS that can provide more accurate signals and be named as differential GPS. Differential GPS resorts to ground base reference station and spatial coherent property that states that the error in one location is similar to the errors within nearby locations, which is called autocorrelation in spatial statistics. Its accuracy can even get to 2cm.

Indoor Positioning System

Inside a building where the GPS signal is unavailable, some other positioning techniques need be developed. Some widely used systems are infrared sensor system and short-range radio system that both can be used for short range positioning system.

Infrared radiation is the region of the electromagnetic spectrum between microwaves and visible light. In infrared communication system, many LED transmitters are set up in various places inside a building and these transmitters automatically transmit the infrared signal as bursts of non-visible light in which the transmitters' IDs have been packed. In the receiver end, a photoreceptor detects and captures these light pulse. This way the computing device can determine its position. Infrared sensors are low cost and low power consuming device. However, it is easy to be blocked like visible light.

Short-range radio sensors can be transmitted omni-directionally. As a positioning device, it is very suitable. But if it is used as data transmission device, the information is easy to be eavesdropped. Bluetooth, however, is a kind of newly developed short-range wireless communication system. Since its each communication link has been coded and protected against both eavesdropping and interference, bluetooth can be considered as a secure short-range wireless network.

2.2   Location Sensing Techniques   [2]

Location system such as mobile networking system need know some location information about the mobile users. There are three principal location sensing techniques that are triangulation, scene analysis and proximity. They are widely used to detect the user's location individually or combinatorially.

Triangulation

Triangulation consists of two kinds of approaches that use the geometric properties of triangles to compute the location of objects. The lateration uses only the distance information, however the angulation uses angle and distance information that are collected from some devices.

Lateration In mathematic theory, distance information from 3 non-collinear positions are required to compute two dimensional objects' locations and distance information from 4 non-coplanar points are required to compute a three dimensional objects' locations. Three appraaches can be used to get the distance information. Direct distance measurement uses physical movement to detect the distance. Time-of-Flight calculates the travel time between the object and point. For example, in GPS system, first the receiver locks on a satellite and then shifts its internal clock to the locked satellite. This way, the two clocks in satellite and receiver respectively are synchronized. After lock-on to the satellite, the receiver can determine the travel time of the received signal by its own internal clock. Then the distance can be estimated. There are three difficulties in this approach. The timer resolution, reflective and subtractive signals, and synchronization between different timers will affect the measuring precision. The most famous time-of-flight location sensing system is the well-known GPS system. The third approach used to calculate distance is to use the signal attenuation properties. That will ask for a better mathematic model. Other factors such as environment around objects will also affect the calculation precision.

Angulation It also uses triangle's mathematic properties to compute object's location. Unlike lateration, it uses the angular information in addition. Sometimes the angular information is easier to get than the distance information.

Scene Analysis

The bigger problem with triangular technique is that the object's information is known to others to some extend in order to get distance or angle information. This means the user's privacy might not be guaranteed. In scene analysis, the system is self-contained, which means it does not need to interact with other parties. In static scene analysis, system stores a well computed dictionary about the environment. As the observed environment changes, the system just looks up the dictionary to get the pre-computed location information. The differential scene analysis computes the difference between different scene and then induces the location according to a known location and observer's movement properties. This technique is in fact implementing a signature system to the travel areas and is a kind of pattern matching technology. The obvious drawback is that the changed environment will affect the computed result dramatically.

Proximation

Referring to some known object's location, the location of unknown objects that communicates with the known object can be estimated using some sensing techniques such as pressure sensing and wireless communication sensing. Sometimes this system need incorporate an identification system.

3   Location Aware Routing Protocols

In mobile network literatures about routing protocols, traditionally routing protocols are classified into two groups that are table-driven or proactive protocols and on-demand or reactive protocols. This classification comes from criteria such as route discovery and route maintenance because they are key issues in ad hoc network. In location aware routing protocols, however, location information is incorporated into the routing protocols so most of these location aware routing protocols are on-demand or reactive protocols that need less space for previously established routing tables and more suitable for dynamic ad hoc networks because the mobile nodes frequently change their locations such that the network topology is also changed. In this scenario, especially in the environment with even more frequently moving mobile users, the route maintenance will take on most network bandwidth. Most exchanged packages are served for discovering new routes or maintaining existing routes. In location aware routing protocols, most attentions are paid to how to use the location information efficiently, which will be conceived in routing protocols' message forwarding strategies. In this section, different location aware routing protocols are introduced according to their package forwarding techniques that mostly depends on how the routing protocols utilize the mobile node's location information. Commonly, location service used by one end of the communication to determine the other end has been divided into two groups, the GPS-based service and the GPS-free service [6] [7].

3.1   Selective Directional Flooding

Generally, in mobile ad hoc network route discovery procedure is implemented by message flooding though part or the entire network. Dynamic source routing (DSR) [9] and ad hoc on-demand distance vector routing (AODV) [10] both are based on message flooding routing discovery. Although they both propose some optimization in order to decrease routing discovery overhead, they still suffer from taking much time on it. In worst case, they are reduced to simple flooding.

LAR [1] and DREAM [8] are two similar message forwarding technique that uses GPS-based location service to restrict the message flooding range from message sender towards the message destination. LAR suggests an approach to utilize location information to decrease overhead of routing discovery and improve the performance of routing protocols for mobile ad hoc networks. LAR limits the routing discovery to a request zone according to some expected zone based on location of destination. This protocol assumes that the message sender S knows about the location of the destination D. Based on the knowledge of location of destination D at time t0, the sender S, at time t1 thought that the expected zone of message destination would be around D the circle area which area is v(t1-t0) and v is maximum velocity of receiver node D. After determining the expected zone, sender should determine what region the route request message should go. This region is the request zone. The request zone should include the expected zone. For the case where the expected zone is the potential entire communication space, the request zone is also the potential entire communication space. In [1], several schemes are proposed to determine the requested zone. In figure 1(a), r is the maximum distance that node D can move within time t1-t0. X is the distance from sender S to destination node D at time t0.

In DREAM [8], apart from the similar approach using the location information to find the message route, it introduces two important properties that can be used to further decrease the routing discovery overhead.

distance effect: The greater the distance separating two nodes, the slower they appear to be moving with respect to each other [8]. So far away nodes need send less new location information to each others.

mobility rate: The faster a node moves, the more often it must communicate its location [8]. This property makes the more frequent moving mobile users to report their locations more frequently than the slower mobile users.

Figure 1(b) shows the expected zone in DREAM.

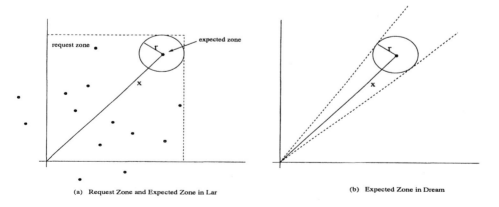

(a) Request Zone and Expected Zone in Lar   (b) Expected Zone in Dream

Figure 1: LAR and DREAM Communication Zone

3.2   Greedy (Directional) Routing Algorithm

Selective directional routing selection algorithm is a kind of on-demand algorithm in that the protocol does not require to pre-establish a route from source to destination. Some greedy routing algorithms are also on-demand algorithm. It selects next transmitting host by some metrics such as Euclidean distance. Like selective directional routing protocols, this algorithm also assumes that every node knows the physical positions of other nodes in the ad hoc network. Generally, this position information is latitude, longitude and possibly altitude. Also like selective directional flooding protocols, the selection of the next transmitting host is partly dependent on the direction of the destination although some do not consider direction of destination intentionally in order to avoid collision. The difference between these two is that greedy algorithm generally select one next host as intermediate node but directional flooding selects all nodes within some range of transmitting direction.

MRF [16] and Geographic Distance Routing(GEDIR) [15] are two similar proposed greedy routing algorithms that use position information. Their purpose is to minimize the transmitting host along the transmitted route. They both use a concept *progress* to select the next transmitting hop. *Progress* is defined as the distance between the transmitting node and receiving node projected onto a line drawn from transmitter toward the final destination [15]. The *progress* is positive if the neighbor is in the forward direction.; otherwise, the *progress* is negative if it is in the backward direction. In MRF, a circle around node that likes to transmit package is drawn. The node with maximum forward *progress* within the circle is selected to be next transmitting hop. However, in GEDIR all neighbors are candidate next transmitting hops in 1-hop strategy. The node with maximum forward *progress* within all neighbors is selected. It is proved that these two routing algorithms are loop-free if comparing the distances among all candidate nodes, including current node. Even if the current node is not considered, in this case the local loop might be created, it is easy to detect the loop.

Another algorithm is Compass [17] routing algorithm that tries to minimize the transmitted distance by selecting the host that is closest to the straight line connected source and destination. The original version is not a loop-free algorithm, however the modified version is loop-free.

3.3 Hierarchical Routing

As more and more mobile nodes join the ad hoc networks, how to manage the whole ad hoc network becomes a serious challenging problem. Like traditional internet, some form of hierarchy can allow the ad hoc networks to scale to a very large network system consisting a large number of nodes. Some position-based hierarchical routing protocols appear to be promising approaches for a very large ad hoc network.

Grid [11] [12] and zone-based [13] [14] ad hoc routing protocols provide an opportunity to establish a very large mobile ad hoc networks.

Analogically, the Grid routing protocol developed in MIT is kind of like currently used mobile cell phone system in that all mobile devices communicate to each other via a known location proxy/server. Any mobile device knowing his own location would be potential location proxy. A location ignorant node selects a nearby location aware node as its location proxy. When sending message, it reports the location proxy's address as its own address to destination. When receiving message, it gets message sent to it via the location proxy. Thus, a location ignorant node has to know some route to the location proxy and the location proxy has to know the route to the location ignorant node. Moreover, among the location proxies, some routes have to exist for them to communicate either via other location proxies or via some location ignorant nodes. The consequences are that not only the scalability of the ad hoc network has been guaranteed but also location ignorant nodes in the ad hoc network can communicate to other nodes in the same ad hoc network.

Zone-based [13] position routing protocol is derived from zone based routing protocol and incorporates the location information into the protocol. In [13], each node is aware of its geographic position and geographic zone is formed with geographic circle with radius R(i). It uses proactive routing strategy. Thus if the destination node is within the geographic zone, the route exists. If the destination node is out of geographic zone, the message is sent to core-zone border router with minimum angular distance from straight line connecting current node and destination node. This selected border router continues this procedure until message reaches the destination or timeout.

4   Location Related Data Management and Query

In mobile ad hoc network system, when the location dependent routing protocols are used to forward the information packets, the location of mobile objects becomes a critical information for the feasibility and effectiveness of these protocols. Thus, some information management system is needed for storing and querying the mobile objects' location information. How to organize these mobile database is a very important task. For this reason, it is not like in the traditional computing environment in which the database management systems are located in a static location and connected to other components with static topology. In mobile computing environment, database systems are connected or disconnected to whole system from time to time. So the new architecture of the database system organization need be proposed. Further more, traditionally database system is used to store and retrieve large amount of information efficiently and is just proposed and developed to deal with constant and stable data that are assumed to be unchanged for a period of time. However, the location of mobile objects is changed frequently, which imposes even more research challenges on the underlying database system. Another important aspect worth noting is that the database query of the location information and location related information such as "where is the nearest gas station from me?". This is also strictly coupled with the location information of the mobile objects. In traditional approaches of managing data, the relationship between the data and the geographical location of the organization it represents is usually ignored. This is a kind of "location transparency" implementation. After mobility property has been introduced to data management system, it is replaced by "location dependency". The correct answer to a query in this kind of system need consider the mode of issuing query data. In other words, the role of geographical location related to the query is very important for this kind of queries.

4.1   Mobility Management System Architecture

Home Location Registers (HLR) and Visitor Location Registers (VLR) [20] [21] are two conventional schemes that allow limited mobile communications to some extend. Mobile host's location information is registered in the HLR/VLR databases that reside in the fixed infrastructure networks through location update procedure. When a mobile host needs to communicate to other parties, its location information can be retrieved by other parties through location query procedure. Then information packets are sent via optimal routes, and possibly parts of them are through wired network to or from mobile hosts.

Conventional schemes just provide some limited wireless communication ability. For pure ad hoc mobile networks it is not useful because there is no fixed network infrastructure that can be used as bridge for communication parties. In centralized ad hoc mobility management schemes [22] [23] [24], some pre-defined nodes comprise backbone of the ad hoc network. All packets among communication parties are sent through these backbone nodes which then transmitted the packets to destination. Here the apparent drawbacks are that the large communication burdens are imposed on these backbone nodes, the failure, for example, that they are disconnected to the network, which happens frequently in ad hoc network, of these nodes will cause huge problems to the whole network and their ability will dramatically affect the performance of the whole network.

In [18] [19], some new ad hoc mobility management systems of distributed scheme are proposed to deal with the new challenges in ad hoc mobile network. Both of them use some dynamically allocated ad hoc nodes as virtual bone that plays similar role as backbone in centralized scheme. These virtual bone nodes are dynamically distributed among the flat ad hoc network instead of hierarchical network as in centralized scheme. Location database resides in these virtual bone nodes. However the information packets are not necessarily transmitted through these nodes. Instead, their function is just provide the location of the mobile hosts within some range. In [18], a quorum system is proposed such that the nodes are dynamically allocated to play the role of location database and a mobile node can use any location database randomly among the virtual bone nodes. A quorum consists a set of mobile nodes and every two quorums are intersected. No one quorum is completely contained in another quorum. Mobile nodes location information are contained within all databases of the quorum. Any mobile node is dynamically assigned to any quorum according to the topology changes or other factors. A information packet is routed with the location information from any randomly chosen quorum of databases. This way, the operation and responsibility are distributed among the whole quorums. In [19], unlike in [18] where any two quorums are intersected at a constant databases, given virtual backbone with n location databases and a group size k, a Randomized Database Group (RDG) is formed by choosing any k location databases randomly. When the average duration of database disconnection is expected to last for a long time, the requirement for constructing location database groups in Uniform Quorum System are possibly not satisfied. In this situation, the RDG distributed scheme is a very good candidate to provide better performance against such instability.

4.2   Location Dependent Data Modeling and Query

Location Dependent Data (LDD) refers to data whose values depend on locations where the data reside. In traditional centralized database, only one copy of the data object exists. In the distributed database, different copies might be located in the different parts of the whole database system. According to different semantics, the different copy values might be allowed. But for the most strictly semantics, only one copy has the correct value of the object. With location dependent data, the values of one object might vary, depending on different locations. For example, same TV program such as CNN might have be broadcast on different local cable TV channels. So multiple copies of a data object might have different correct values and these values are not forced to be same within the whole mobile database. These statements explain that the spatial components introduced into the DBMS complicate the data management. New data model and data management approaches need to be proposed to handle these new conditions.

There are two different approaches that incorporate spatial and temporal information into the database management system. First is the Moving Objects Spatial-Temporal (MOST) model [25] [26] that models the moving objects and proposes some corresponding query processing approaches for the new moving objects. The other model [28] [29] [30] does not put specific location information in the database. Instead, this model partitions the whole database into regions [30]. Each region includes correct value of a data object for this region. Several corresponding issues related to this partition method have been addressed.

4.2.1   Managing Moving Objects

In ad hoc environment, some new characteristics of data management are presented such as frequently disconnected location databases, frequently changed locations of the moving mobile nodes. Nowadays, existing database management systems are supposed to support constant data very well. However, they are not well equipped to store and retrieve the frequently changing data. Some new challenges are in front of the database researches.

In [25] [26], some issues related to moving object database are analyzed and some solutions are proposed as the parts of DOMINO project. First issue is the location modeling issue. In existing DBMS's that assume that the data in database are constant and will be updated explicitly, frequently changing data are hard to represent. In DOMINO, a dynamic attributes approach is proposed to model moving object and enable the DBMS to predict the future location of the moving object to some extend. This way, the location data need not be updated too often because the update information can be calculated from information stored in the dynamic attributes whose value changes continuously as time goes by, which is reasonable assumption for a moving object location. Second, the moving mobile objects have both spatial and temporal attributes. So a spatial temporal language is required to query these objects related information in the moving objects location database. In [26], a temporal query language called Future Temporal Logic (FTL) is introduced for this purpose. Third, traditional spatial index is not enough for the spatial temporal objects. In DOMINO, this problem is decomposed into two sub-problem. First is geometric representation of a dynamic attribute value. In this sub-problem, multidimensional space is constructed to accommodate moving objects, all moving objects in that space are mapped into a region and all queries are also mapped into some region in that space. The query result is expressed as an intersected region. Second sub-problem is handle efficient search for the intersected region. Fourth, considering the uncertainty of the moving objects location, heuristics are used to deal with the moving objects and its related queries. For example, different kinds of semantics of query language are developed for "may" and "must" query set. Thus the uncertainty problems are solved to some extend.

In [27], a detailed description of the spatial temporal DBMS data model and query language are proposed. This framework mainly focuses on the data type model for moving objects. These abstract data types include base types, spatial types, time types and their temporal and spatial temporal versions. The detailed embedding query language is also described formally.

4.2.2 Location Dependent Data Management By Partitioning Region Method

In MOST [25] model, explicit location information are coded in dynamic attribute and then brought into the DBMS. In the partitioning method [30], database is referred to as partitioned into locations and each partition contains the correct value for that location. Data in the whole database are viewed as location dependent data whose values strongly dependent on location. For a specific data object, its correct values are possibly different, depending on the location from which the mobile users intend to get data.

Data region is defined as logic area within geographic domain, within which one correct value exists for a data object [30]. The whole geographic domain on which the database is defined is partitioned into different data regions. Within one data region, there is only one correct value for a data object. All data values for one data object are called spatial replica of that data object. No only one correct value constraint is imposed on these values. Instead, spatial consistency indicating that all data values of a spatial replication are associated with one and only data region introduces another constraint. Thus there is one to one mapping between data value set and the region it services.

In LDD model, each service provider maintains its own local database for one data region. When a query is issued by mobile user, it is bound with location information. This query with location information is then forwarded to corresponding service provider to get the correct query result.

Location dependent data leaves the local database schema to local service provider, which will reduce the table size that need to be searched by a query and thus improve efficiency. This kind of autonomy gives the whole system better scalability and maintainability by distributing the responsibility to many local service provider. Still, a global service provider is needed to provide mobile users a global view of the whole system.

In [30], some other issues such as data caching and transaction management are also briefly discussed. But the further research is worth to be continued for the completeness of whole framework because the mobile data management introduces more complexity into DBMS.

5   Conclusions

Mobility of information system brings much more convenience to people. It also offers more new research challenges to different fields in computer science. IEEE 802.11 protocol gives a framework for ad hoc mobile networks. But more research is still needed to develop more efficient, scalable and robust routing protocols to deal with increasing complexity of mobile computing environment. Next, the information retrieval and exchange in this mobile network are also needed. The extension to current database system is a critical issue because the traditional database including distributed database system is not directly usable in the mobile network system.

We introduce some key issues related to mobile network system and some current research achievements on these issues. We believe that these issues are and will be hot topics in the related research domains in the near future.

References

[1] Y.-B. Ko and N.H. Kung, Location-Aided Routing (LAR) in Mobile Ad Hoc Networks, *ACM/Baltzer WINET J.* (2000), pp. 307-321.

[2] Jeffrey Hightower and Gaetano Borriello, Location Sensing Techniques, *University of Washington UW-CSE-01-07-01*, August (2001).

[3] James J. Caffery and Gordon L. Stuber, Overview of Radiolocation in CDMA Cellular Systems, *IEEE Communication Magazine*, April (1998).

[4] Nirupama Bulusu, John Heidemann and Deborah Estrin, GPS-less Low Cost Outdoor Localization For Very Small Devices, *IEEE Personal Computers*, Vol.7 No.5 (2000) pp. 28-34.

[5] S. Ramanathan and Martha Steenstrup, A Survey of Routing Techniques for Mobile Communications Networks, *ACM/Baltzer Mobile Networks and Applications*, Vol.1 No.2 (1996) pp. 89-104.

[6] S. Capkun, M. Hamdi and J. Hubaux, GPS-free Positioning in Mobile Ad Hoc Networks, *Proc. Hawaii Int'l Conf. System Sciences*, Jan (2001).

[7] Quality Engineering and Service Technology Ltd, *GPS Tutor*, http://www.mercat.com/QUEST/Intro.htm/ (1998).

[8] Stefano Basagni, Imrich Chlamtac, Violet R. Syrotiuk and Barry A. Woodward, A Distance Routing Effect Algorithm for Mobility (DREAM), *ACM MOBICOM 98* (1998).

[9] D. Johnson and D.A. Maltz, Dynamic source routing in ad hoc wireless networks, *Mobile Computing*, Kluwere Academic Publishers (1996).

[10] C.E. Perkins and E.M. Royer, Ad hoc on demand distance vector(AODV) routing, *Proc. 2nd IEEE Workshop Mobile Comp. Sys. App*, Feb (1999) pp. 90-100.

[11] Jinyang Li, John Jannotti and Douglas S. J. De Couto et al., A Scalable Location Service for Geographic Ad Hoc Routing, *MOBICOM*, August (2000).

[12] Douglas S. J., De Couto and Robert Morris, Location proxies intermediate node forwarding for practical geographics forwarding, *Tech. rep.MIT-LCS-TR824, MIT Lab. Comp Sci* June (2001).

[13] Konstantinos N. Amouris, Symeon Papavassiliou and Miao Li, A Position-based Multi-zone Routing Protocol for Wide Area Mobile Ad-Hoc Networks, *Proc. 49th IEEE Vehicular Technology Conference* (1999) pp.1365-1369.

[14] Z. J. Haas and M. R. Perlman, The zone routing protocol: A hybrid framework for routing in ad hoc networks, *Ad Hoc Networks* (Addison-Wesley, 2000).

[15] Xu Lin and Ivan Stojmenovic, *GPS based distributed routing algorithms for wireless networks*, (University of Ottawa), August (2001).

[16] H. Takagi and L. Kleinrock, Optimal transmission ranges for randomly distributed packet radio terminals, *IEEE Transactions on Communications*, (1984) pp. 246-257.

[17] E. Kranankis, H. Singh and J. Urrutia, Compass routing on geometric networks, *Proc. 11th Canadian Conference on Computational Geometry*, August (1999).

[18] Zygmunt J. Haas and Ben Liang, Ad hoc mobility management with uniform quorum systems, *IEEE/ACM Transactions on Networking*, Vol.7 No.2 (1999).

[19] Zygmunt J. Haas and Ben Liang, Ad hoc mobility management with randomized database groups, *IEEE ICC*, June (1999).

[20] S. Mohan and R. Jain, Two users location strategies for personal communications services, *IEEE Personal Communications*, First Quarter (1994).

[21] Zygmunt J. Haas and Y-B Ling, On optimizing the location update costs in the presence of database failures, *ACM/Baltzer Wireless Networks Journal*, Vol.4 No.5 (1998).

[22] A. Ephremides, J.E. Wieselthier and D. J. Baker, A design concept for reliable mobile radio networks with frequency hopping signaling, *Proceedings of IEEE*, Vol.75 No.1 (1987).

[23] B. Das and V. Bharghavan, Routing in ad-hoc networks using minimum connected dominating sets, *IEEE Intl. Conf. on Communications*, June (1997).

[24] J. Sharony, A mobile radio network architecture with dynamically changing topology using virtual subnets, *MONET*, Vol.1 No.1 (1996).

[25] A. Prasad Sistla, Ouri Wolfson, Sam Chambelain and Son Dao, Modeling and querying moving objects, *Proc. of ICDE*, June (1997).

[26] Ouri Wolfson, Bo Xu, Sam Chamberlain and Liqin Jiang, Moving objects databases: issues and solutions, *In International Conference on Scientific and Statistical Database Management, (SSDBM'98)*, July (1998).

[27] Ralf Hartmut Guting, Michael H Bohlen, Martin Erwig and Christian S Jensen et al, A foundation for representing and querying moving objects, *ACM Transactions on Database Systems*, March (2000).

[28] V. Kumar and M.H. Dunham, Defining location data dependency, transaction mobility and commitment, *Sothern Methodist University* (1998).

[29] A.Y. Seydim, M.H. Dunham and V. Kumar, Location dependent query processing, *Second ACM International Workshop on Data Engineering for Mobile and Wireless Access, MobiDE'01*, May (2001).

[30] M.H. Dunham and V. Kumar, Location dependent data and its management in mobile databases", *Ninth International Workshop on Database and Expert System Applications*, August (1998).

[31] M.H. Dunham and V. Kumar, An architecture for location dependent query processing, *Proc. of 4th International Workshop on Mobility in Databases and Distributed Systems (MDDS 01) in 12th International Conference on Database and Expert System Applications (DEXA 2001)*, September (2001).

[32] A.Y. Seydim and M.H. Dunham, A location dependent benchmark with mobility behavior, *International Database Engineering and Applications Symposium* (2002).

AD HOC WIRELESS NETWORKING
X. Cheng, X. Huang and D.-Z. Du (Eds.) pp. 383 - 446

Power-Conserving Algorithms and Protocols in Ad Hoc Networks

Hung Q. Ngo
Computer Science and Engineering Department,
State University of New York at Buffalo, Amherst, NY 14260, USA.
E-mail: hungngo@cse.buffalo.edu

Dazhen Pan
Computer Science and Engineering Department,
State University of New York at Buffalo, Amherst, NY 14260, USA.
E-mail: dpan@cse.buffalo.edu

Vikas P. Verma
Computer Science and Engineering Department,
State University of New York at Buffalo, Amherst, NY 14260, USA.
E-mail: vpverma@cse.buffalo.edu

Contents

1 Introduction

Wireless networking in recent years has become more and more popular. It has rapidly emerged into a major component of the networking infrastructure. The global market for mobile wireless devices and services has met great demand. In the year of 2002, there are about a billion wireless communication devices in use, and more than 200 million wireless telephone handsets are purchased annually.

As we become more and more accustomed to the "anytime, anywhere" type of computing, mobile devices and applications will be indispensable even at times and places where the usual networking infrastructure is not available. The term *ad hoc network* refers precisely to this type of network: a wireless network of (mostly mobile) devices that can be set up dynamically on the fly without resorting to the existing Internet or any other network infrastructure.

Ad hoc networking has enormous commercial and military potential, supporting applications such as mobile conferencing, battle field communications, sensor dust, home networking, emergency services, personal area networks and Bluetooth, embedded computing, to name a few.

Obviously the infrastructureless environment poses a lot of challenging issues never encountered in the normal networking case. The reader is referred to [5, 20, 49, 74] for more discussions on many of these issues.

In this chapter, we shall be focusing only on energy consumption issues in ad hoc networking. This issue is unique to ad hoc networking. In the infrastructured case we often assume limitless power at each node, while in an ad hoc environment the mobile nodes operate on battery power. The state-of-the-art technologies on battery power are still fairly limited in terms of durability. While the power spent on transmitting and receiving normal data can be argued not to be part of being "ad hoc," the power consumed on *relaying* or *forwarding* data is clearly a main discriminator of ad hoc (multi-hop) networks. It makes more sense and even more economical to allow nodes to forward data, i.e. serves as routers as in wired networks. For one thing, without forwarding nodes the network may be disconnected due to limited transmission range. Secondly, even when nodes can transmit over long range to reach any other node, we desire simultaneous transmissions at the same channel and thus we would like to limit transmission range. Reducing transmission range saves power consumption, and sometimes also reduces potential interference at receiving nodes, which further reduces collisions and retransmissions, leading to further saving in power usage. Last but not least, allowing nodes to forward data may also saves total energy consumed overall.

In a laptop, for example, beside typical energy consumers like the LCD, CPU, hard drives, ... it has been determined that the wireless network interface card also plays an important role. Researches on power saving from the perspective of the physical, transport and application layers can be found in various recent surveys, books, papers, and technical specifications

[20, 32, 33, 35, 49]. In this chapter, we only focus on power-aware protocols at the MAC and network layers.

With recent intense attention of researchers on power-aware protocols, there is a huge literature on the topics at hand. We cannot expect a single chapter to cover the topics from all possible angles. We have chosen to cover problems, approaches, results, and open research directions, which we feel most representative of the recent wave of research on power-aware protocols. It should also be noted that the terms *power-aware*, *power-efficient*, *power-sensitive*, and *power-conserving* have been used more or less interchangeably in the literature. We make no attempt to fix a particular terminology here.

The rest of this chapter is organized as follows. Section 2 discusses power-conserving protocols and algorithms at the MAC layer. Section 3 presents power-conserving unicast protocols and algorithms. Section 4 is on multicasting and broadcasting. Lastly, section 5 provides a few concluding remarks on the chapter. We assume that the reader is familiar with basic concepts on wireless networking, such as those found in a typical textbook on wireless networking [49, 51].

2   MAC layer protocols

2.1   Overview

Medium access control (MAC) layer protocols can broadly be classified into single channel and multiple channel protocols.

In *single channel* algorithms, all nodes transmit on the same channel, and conflicts are resolved by either a random access, a coordinated access or a scheduling scheme. As far as power-awareness is concerned, *random access* (aloha-type protocols) and scheduling protocols have not been pursued much. *Coordinated access* is currently the major scheme for conflict resolution in wireless networks, as evident in IEEE 802.11 specification. However, improvements to IEEE 802.11 is still an active research direction. Several power conserving modifications have been proposed. In addition, other coordination based protocols have been proposed in recent years, such as power aware multiple access scheme (PAMAS) [56] and power control multiple access (PCMA) [45], as shall be discussed in more details later.

In *multiple channel* algorithms, the nodes transmit on separate channels. A single channel is subdivided into multiple channels with a variety of multiple access division technologies, such as code devision multiple access (CDMA), time division multiple access (TDMA), frequency division multiple access (FDMA), orthogonal frequency division multiple access (OFDM), etc. The MAC layer algorithm in this case is responsible for assigning the available channels to different nodes in such a way that no two nodes whose transmissions could result in a collision would be allowed to transmit on the same channel. Also, the channel assignment algorithm should aim to maximize the number of simultaneous transmissions. This can be achieved in a distributed as well as centralized fashion. Transmitting on separate channels avoids collisions and retransmission, which implies power-conservation.

The rest of this section is organized as follows. Sub-section 2.2 first elaborates on the criteria which a power-aware MAC layer protocols is expected to fulfill. Often these objectives are conflicting with each other, and conflicting with the overall goal of saving power. Hence, balancing all the trade-offs is one of the most challenging and important aspect of protocol designing. Next, sub-section 2.3 outlines several common approaches on designing our kind of protocols. The rest of the sub-sections go slightly further into the details of several proposed protocols, classified based on the approaches listed earlier. It is impossible to go over all available protocols, as the literature is quite large for the limitation of this chapter. We have attempted to pick the protocols which we feel more representative of the topic under consideration.

2.2 Common objectives of a power conserving MAC layer protocol

Many of the following desired objectives of MAC layer protocols form trade-offs that protocol designers have to take into account when designing new MAC layer power-aware protocols. For each criterion listed below, we hence briefly analyze the involved trade-offs with the overall objective of power-conserving.

- **Distributivity**. This is an important criterion for virtually every networking protocol. The reasons for desiring distributivity are standard: avoiding bottlenecks, single points of failure, more robust, and more realistic. We shall not attempt to analyze this point further as they are pretty much well known. Obviously centralized protocols are easier to design and often lead to more optimal solutions, however they come at great costs.

- **Avoiding global synchronization**. This is somewhat overlapping with the previous criterion, but it is worth mentioning. Global synchronization usually happens when we have reservation and scheduling types of algorithms. Doing so imposes a great deal of delay and dependency on certain services or technologies, such as the global positioning system (GPS). Since ad hoc networking is essentially infrastructure-less, one should not make use too much of this kind of assumption. Even when synchronization could be done distributively, the overhead is often too high, not only with respect to power consumption.

- **Avoiding control packet overhead.** Packet overhead in transmission, like request-to-send (RTS) or clear-to-send (CTS) type of packets, (e.g. RTS, CTS) should not be over-used even though they could be of great utility for a number of purposes. The point is that the control packets reduce the energy per useful bit transmitted, an important optimizing parameter for power-aware protocols.

- **Minimizing collisions/retransmissions.** Again, retransmissions contribute to lower energy per useful bit transmitted.

- **Quality of Service (QoS) support.** Reliability, efficiency, low delay and high throughput are the first things that come to mind. Channel utilization should be optimized by allowing as many simultaneous transmissions as possible. Care should be taken that the transmission on one link should not disrupt the transmission on another nearby link by decreasing its SINR (Signal to Interference plus Noise Ratio) below the threshold value. Bandwidth utilization is another key QoS factor which should be taken into consideration.

- **Adaptation to mobility.** It could be argued that this is THE most difficult criterion to be satisfied by any ad hoc wireless network protocol. Mobility imposes great pressures on protocols to re-synchronize information, re-establishment of routes, neighbor lists, and other related data. This leads to more overhead and thus increases greatly the total power usage.

2.3   Approaches for designing power-aware MAC protocols

In this section, we outline various approaches of MAC protocol designs. The approaches, although listed individually, are not necessarily exclusive from each other. We expect future good protocols to employ a balanced, and improved combination of the common-sense strategies listed here.

The first approach is to **vary transmission power** for both data and control packets. Energy consumed while transmission is proportional to the transmission power. Hence, reducing transmission power is the first obvious way to reduce energy usage. Transmission at low power also reduces interference at other neighboring receivers. The draw back include increase in error rate (lower the transmission power higher the error rate) and increase in control packet overhead, which comes from the exchange of signaling packets to determine the minimum transmission power level, and possibly more control packets to facilitate multi-hop transmissions due to smaller transmission range.

In this approach, some protocols propose to find optimal transmission powers so as to maintain a threshold level of SINR at all the receiving nodes [19]. Maintaining optimal transmission power levels sometime require power level information exchange [45]. between the sender and the receiver. Another approach on a similar line of attack involves the piggybacking of the ratio of the received signal strength, of the signaling/data packets, to the minimum signal strength that is acceptable by this receiver, in the header of the signalling/data packet to be sent. A node receiving this ratio stores this information for some number of past transmissions and applies the typical exponential averaging to predict future power-levels [1].

The second approach is to try **lessen potential collisions** at the receivers due to heterogenous transmission powers. This approach often results in minimizing retransmissions and thus saving the additional energy overhead induced by retransmissions.

To implement this idea, one could allocate transmissions on multiple channels. Every node transmits on its uniquely assigned channel. This reduces the work of a MAC layer protocol to the task of a channel assignment scheduler. After running the scheduling algorithm, the protocol simply notifies the nodes of their channel of transmission [27]. Another less extreme scheme is to separate signaling and data channels to eliminate collisions between control packets and data packets. The obvious problem with the two schemes just listed is that it could result in inefficient bandwidth utilization [56]. It is also apparent that bit error rates (BER) and packet lengths (which also effect BER) are major factors contributing to retransmissions. One could also try to balance transmission power and these parameters to reduce collisions [18].

In order to improve the overall durability of the network, especially in collaborative-types of networks, nodes with less power left should be allowed to do less work to lengthen their lives. A scheme along this line of thought makes use of the propagation of CTS from the low power nodes to high power nodes at a distance for them to forbear any transmission at maximum power. When a network comprises of nodes with varying degrees of powers, nodes with low power are not able to reach those with high power but the reverse is true. Hence, a high power node may not need to receive RTS-

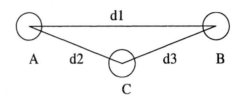

Figure 1: As power-consumption is proportional to d^α and $d_1^\alpha > d_2^\alpha + d_3^\alpha$, route AC-CB is more efficient then single hop AB

CTS messages from its low power peer and might initiate a transmission disrupting communication at the low power node. For this purpose, one could try to propagate the CTS messages by the low power nodes up to a certain distance to make sure that every possible interfering node learns about the transmission [50]. The disadvantage of this scheme lies in the overhead incurred for the propagation, which possibly outweighs the benefit of reaching distant nodes and power-conserving.

The third approach involves **powering off nodes** at appropriate times. In this type of scheme, a node which is neither transmitting nor receiving sleeps for a certain period of time which obviously conserves power. PAMAS [56] is built on this principle. The node either sleeps for a predefined time period or it has a separate wake up radio, which senses packet arrival and wakes up the main radio. The drawbacks of this scheme is that it is hard to predetermine or predict the right amount of sleeping time. Sleeping for too long could result in unnecessary transmissions by other nodes, or even network disconnectivity. Sleeping for too short is not worth the trouble of maintaining the scheduling. The overhead involved in the sleep-scheduling algorithm and/or hardwares is another factor to be reckoned with.

There have also been various proposals on mechanisms to include **power control in IEEE 802.11** The proposals were built upon the framework of IEEE 802.11, and they mainly attempted to modify or slightly improve the specification with respect to power-awareness. We shall review some of these proposals in a later section.

A few other works can be classified under the **miscellaneous** category. We briefly overview some of them as follows. One idea is to cross the network/MAC layer barrier, allowing the network layer module to *overhear* ongoing transmission [17]. The node then estimates if it could possibly improve the route with respect to (locally) total power usage of the nodes involved. A scenario of route improvement is shown in Figure 2.3. If improvement is possible, the node informs participating nodes for a possible change in routes. Another work examined the possibility of transmission at a minimum common power level for all the nodes [46]. With the right power level, it might be possible to improve throughput, battery life and reduce collision at the MAC layer all at the same time.

2.4 Collision and error rate dependent protocols

In this section, we briefly describe a few representative protocols which aim to reduce collisions and also control power based on error rates and packet sizes. For each paper under review, we discuss the problem, idea for solution, and its pros and cons.

2.4.1 A low power distributed MAC for ad hoc sensor radio network

This is an overview of the work in [27].

Problem

The paper addressed the problem of devising power-conversing MAC protocols on sensor networks. Sensor networks are limited mobility, high density, large-scale systems of sensors, which are also very limited in power supply. MAC protocols for sensor networks should be scalable, distributive, and robust, in the sense that a few link failures should not affect overall functionality of the network. Most importantly, MAC protocols on sensor networks must be low power consuming, because many sensor networks are made such that they exist only until they run out of battery power. For example, in some applications the nodes are buried inside the walls, which makes them useless once the batteries get depleted. Consequently, power conservation in such networks is a major issue.

Idea

A single channel can be divided into multiple channels using standard channel division schemes such as CDMA, TDMA, FDMA, etc. The channels can be distributed among the various transmitting nodes. Communications on multiple channels reduce collisions and retransmissions. The control packet overhead is limited to the channel distribution phase, not with individual packet transmission. In addition, a wakeup radio scheme is presented in which nodes use two separate radios: one of which is a low-quality, low-power consuming radio which always stays on; the other is a normal transmitting/receiving radio. The nodes are powered off during idle (monitoring) times and are powered on with the help of the wakeup radio.

Description

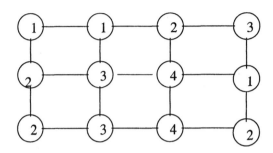

Figure 2: A possible channel assignment where no two-hop neighbors are assigned with the same channel.

Channel Assignment: this is the problem of distributing channels among communicating nodes in such a way that any two-hop neighbors do not transmit on the same channel. The assignment is to be done "locally," in a distributive manner. Also, it is done on a separate control channel, simplifying the scheduling algorithm. Each node has information about the available set of free channels. A node picks one channel arbitrarily from the pool and sends out this information in a signaling packet. The single hop neighbors receive this packet and re-broadcast it so that the two-hop neighbors of the original node also get the information. Every node maintains a table containing the two-hop neighbor channel information. Once a node receives the re-broadcasted packet of a two-hop neighbor, it updates this information on the table. As the algorithm converges every node has a complete picture of channels picked by its two-hop neighbors. Figure 2.4.1 shows a possible channel assignment. While transmitting a node sends out the data packets, without any signaling packet for coordination on the channel that has been assigned to it. This way, collision free communications are guaranteed.

Wake up radio: in a typical scenario, more than 90% of the energy is spent on channel monitoring, when nothing is being transmitted or received. A two-radio model is considered with the front-end radio capable of transmitting and receiving packets, while the back-end radio is responsible for channel monitoring. As the back-end radio only does carrier sensing, it is not required to have high quality, power consuming hardwares. Typically, a wake-up receiver radio operation only take around 1uW, compared to 10uW for a CDMA radio in monitoring mode. If any node wants to communicate with the sleeping node it sends out a wakeup beacon which is sensed by the wake up radio, which in turn awakens the node.

Disadvantages

The obvious disadvantage of any type of fixed-bandwidth channel division multiple access scheme is the potential inefficiency in bandwidth utilization. This is especially true under low load and/or bursty traffics. When mobility is taken into account, the scheme also incur high cost on control overhead, as channel assignments have to be refreshed and updated when network topology changes.

Results and Conclusions

Simulation results show the protocol to reduce power consumption by 10-100 times the existing MAC with traditional radios. Moreover, the proposed scheme is distributive, scalable and robust under high load and low mobility.

2.4.2   Power controlled MAC (PCM)

This is an overview of the work in [36].

Problem

Typically, the nodes within the transmitting range of a sender and receiver pair sense and decode the RTS-CTS packets. These nodes refrain from receiving and transmitting respectively, for the duration of the ongoing transmission. Certain nodes which are not within the transmission range of the sender and receiver can just sense a possible RTS-CTS handshake but cannot decode it. Hence they refrain for only a fixed brief period of time. Once this period gets over and the data transmission starts at the minimum transmission power level, these nodes can no longer sense the channel and are free to initiate a transmission. This might cause collision at the sender and receiver of the original RTS-CTS. This scenario is often referred to as the hidden terminal problem.

Idea

The idea is for communicating nodes to transmit data intermitantly at maximum power to inform far away nodes of an ongoing transaction. This prevents them from starting any new communication and thus avoids collision.

Description

Before describing the proposed solution, we need a few definitions. The *transmission range* (TR) is the range within which any node can listen and decode every packet sent by the sender. The *carrier sensing range* (CSR) is the range within which any node can sense a signal. (It should be noted that TR is a sub-area of CSR.) The *carrier sensing zone* (CSZ) is the space between the transmission range circle and the carrier sensing range circle. Within a CSZ, any node can sense a signal but cannot decode it.

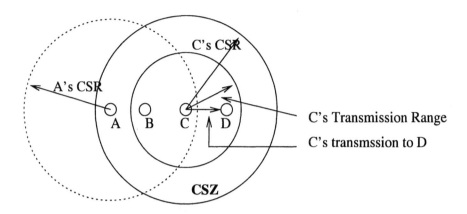

Figure 3: C transmits data to D. B overhears and decodes the RTS and refrains from transmitting RTS from C. On the other hand, A is in the CSZ of C and can sense the RTS but cannot decode it. As it cannot determine the duration of transmission between C and D, it refrains the transmission for EIFS period and then transmits the RTS which collides with the ACK at C.

Upon hearing an RTS-CTS, nodes within the TR determine the time interval for data transmission and refrain from transmission for that period. On the other hand, nodes in the CSZ, upon hearing a RTS-CTS which they cannot decode, refrain from sending any data for a fixed interval of time called the *extended inter frame space* (EIFS). Now, if the data-acknowledgement transmission continues at the maximum power level, then the node will further refrain from sending any packets even after the EIFS period ends. However, in order to save power nodes should reduce their transmission range once a data-acknowledgement transmission begins. If the power level for data-acknowledgement decreases the nodes in the CSZ cannot determine this ongoing transmission and begin a fresh transmission with the maximum power level. This could cause collision of the data packets at the receiver and acknowledgement at the source. As a simple solution to the above problem, data is transmitted intermitantly at maximum power so as to inform the nodes in the CSZ to refrain from sending RTS-CTS. The interval of transmission with maximum power is equal to EIFS, which is the time period for which the nodes in CSZ refrain from sending. Figure 2.4.2 illustrates the positioning of the nodes in different ranges and zones in our problem.

Disadvantages

Obviously, periodic maximum power transmissions require more power than needed to transmit data. If the nodes around are idle, this power is lost. Moreover, the energy required in transition from lower power level to higher power level and back may outwit the benefit of having this scheme.

Results and Conclusions

The proposed scheme does partially solve the original problem. It is also quite simple to implement. The trade-off to be made is between power wasted on maximum power transmissions and the prevention of collision due to the hidden terminal problem. There is also a balance between a typical data duration and EIFS size, which should be carefully analyzed and experimented.

2.4.3 Power control based on packet length and error rate

This is an overview of the work in [18].

Problem

Minimizing the output power does not necessarily minimize the energy consumed in transmitting a packet. Transmitting with low power increases the chances of packet error depending on the channel conditions. This then requires retransmission which incurs additional energy. Hence, the over all energy spend in transmitting a packet increases. Also, large packets are more prone to error then small packets. Thus, greater transmission power is required to transmit bigger packets than smaller packets. It is desirable to find optimal transmission powers under such network scenarios considering the error rates and packet lengths.

Idea

The output transmission power is adjusted to maximize energy savings. The total energy saving is calculated taking into consideration the energy spent in high power transmission as well as energy spent in re-transmissions (which are inversely proportional to the transmission power). Also, the transmission power is adjusted taking into consideration the size of the MAC layer packet. The approach is designed to work for wireless LAN, but the concept could be well adapted to ad hoc networks.

Description

The BER (bit error rate) for a given transmission power level, based on *link budget analysis* [58], is given by the following formula:

$$\text{BER} = \frac{1}{2}\exp\left(-10^{\frac{P_{tx}+G_{tx}+G_{rx}-L-L_{fade}-N-N_{rx}}{10}}\frac{B_T}{R}\right),$$

where P_{tx} (in dBm) is the transmission power; G_{tx} and G_{rx} are transmitter's and receiver's antenna gain, respectively; L (in dB) denotes the path loss for line of sight wave propagation; L_{fade} (in dB) is the fade margin, an amount of power added to the transmission power in advance to signify the fact that signal cancellation because fading is not complete; N (in Watt) is the thermal noise; and lastly N_{rx} (in dB) is the circuit noise at the receiver The essence of the formula is that BER is inversely and exponentially proportional to the transmission power, assuming all else are equal.

On the other hand, the total energy spent in transmitting one bit is given as

$$E_{bit\_res} = \frac{P_{tx} \cdot T_{bit}}{\eta_{pr}}.$$

Here, η_{pr} is the number of successful bits transmitted per number of transmitted bits, and T_{bit} is the amount of time it takes to transmit one data bit.

The optimum transmission power for different packet size is then calculated for which E_{bit_res} is minimum. The calculation is simulation based, in which the number of successful bits and the total number of bits are measured for different power levels. From this the optimal power level is calculated for the packet of that size. Simulation study for varying packet sizes with the optimal power show greater energy saving when the packet is transmitted at optimal transmission power than the case of one fixed power level.

Results and Conclusions

Having fixed transmission power level for every packet size increases energy consumption. If the power level used for the transmission is less than the optimal then the energy usage increases due to retransmission. If the power level exceeds the minimum required then again the energy saving decrease. Hence, an optimum power level pertaining to different packets is required for transmission. The results only hold for a particular channel model. More work need to be done, in the same direction or not, to cope with other common channel models.

2.5 Protocols based on varying transmission powers

2.5.1 Joint scheduling and power control

This is an overview of the work in [19].

Problem

Every node in a wireless network is required to transmit with a minimum power level to reach the receiver. If the power of transmission exceeds this minimum level then the signal to interference ratio (SIR) at all the neighbouring links decreases. This leads to increased error and collision rate at the near by receivers.

Idea

The idea is to seek an optimal transmission power level such that if nodes adjust their transmitter power level to that level then the SIR at all the neighbouring links remains above a threshold value. The optimal power vector for transmission in case of infrastructured cellular networks can be applied to MANET given the same scenario of operation. The paper also investigates the difference and similarity between cellular and ad-hoc networks to incorporate the optimal transmission power vector for nodes in ad-hoc networks.

Protocol Description

The basic approach is to first centrally schedule the transmissions of all nodes. This is done via the scheduling phase. This phase is responsible for coordinating transmissions among users to eliminate strong levels of interference. The power control phase finds the optimum power vector of transmission for every node, such that the SINR at every receiver is above a threshold value. If such a power vector exists then nodes transmit with that optimal power, otherwise the scheduling phase starts all over again with some of the nodes forced to defer transmission. The two phases are described below in more detail:

Scheduling : This phase determines the nodes that are allowed to transmit in a given time slot. The scheduling algorithm is run at the start of every slot and is responsible for finding the valid transmission scenario for the nodes . A transmission scenario is valid if it satisfies the following 3 conditions

1. A node is not allowed to transmit and receive simultaneously.

2. A node cannot receive from more than one neighbour at a time.

3. A node receiving from a neighbor should be spatially seperated from any other transmitter by at least a certain distance D, which depends on the SINR threshold value at the receiver.

Also, having this phase makes the problem structure similar to cellular networks, which follows the similar 2 phase pattern.

Power Control : This phase is responsible for finding the optimal power vector for the nodes scheduled to transmit obtained from the first phase.

Finding the optimal power vector is a step by step process. Every node increases its power in steps following the following power incremental equation

$$P_i(N+1) = \min\left(P_{max}, \frac{\beta}{\text{SINR}_i(N)} P_i(N)\right),$$

where P_i is the transmission power for node i; N is step number; $SINR$ is the signal to interference plus noise ratio measured at the receiver; β is the threshold value of SINR which every receiver is supposed to maintain so as to receive packets without error. It can be seen from the power equation that the next step power increases if the β value is greater than the SINR at the receiver and decreases otherwise.

Disadvantages

Making the phases distributive will require too much control packet overhead. The complexity of both the scheduling and power control problems is exponential with the number of users and is impractical to implement.

Results and Conclusions

The multiple access problem in wireless ad-hoc networks is solved using scheduling and power control, increasing the average slot throughput and minimizing energy consumption by transmitting at optimal power.

2.5.2 Power controlled multiple access (PCMA) protocol

This is an overview of the work in [45].

Problem

The RTS-CTS exchange in current IEEE 802.11 acquires the channel over the maximum range over which any hidden terminal can cause collision. The data and acknowledgement transmission take place at minimumum power level. Due to the maximum range channel acquiring by the RTS-CTS packet the possibility of another possible simultaneous transmission is eliminated. Every node that hears this RTS-CTS transmission fails to intiate another transmission, i.e. suffers the exposed terminal problem. This effects the throughput of the system. The problem is well explained in figure 2.5.2.

Idea

Instead of nodes refraining transmission after hearing an RTS/CTS (as with typical coordination based protocol), they reduce their transmission power level, with the help of power information sent through the RTS/CTS, so as to increase simultaneous transmissions (channel re-use).

Description

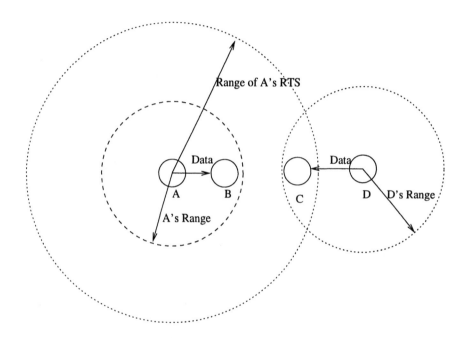

Figure 4: A transmission scenerio in which D is unable to communicate with node C even when it is possible to have simultaneous transmission between A-B and D-C. This is because the transmission range of A's RTS covers C and hence it will refrain from receiving anything from D.

The source sends an RPTS packet to intiate a transmission. The RPTS packet contains information about the transmitted power P_t and noise level P_{ns} measured at its interface. With the help of these parameters and the received power level of the RPTS packet P_r the receiver calculates the optimum power P_{t_o} that the source node should use for data transmission. It includes P_{t_o} in an APTS packet (CTS as in MACA). The APTS packet is transmitted using the minimum transmission power, calculated with the help of P_r and P_{ns} contained in the RPTS packet. The source node then transmits the packet with this value of P_{t_o}.

Also, every receiver is supposed to maintain its SINR above a thresold value for error free reception of packets. The noise tolerance level E_j at the receiver is defined to be the noise and interference required to drop the SINR at the receiver below the threshold value. To refrain other transmitting nodes from achieving this, the receiver transmits a busy tone on a separate channel with a power level inversely proportional to its noise tolerance. Any nearby node initiating a transmission who receives this busy tone decreases its transmission power level in proportion to the received power level of the busy tone.

Results and Conclusions

It is shown via simulations that PCMA protocol allows more simultaneous transmissions and increases aggregate bandwidth by a factor of 2 against IEEE 802.11 for high-density networks.

2.6 Power control using sleep mode

2.6.1 Power aware multiple access scheme (PAMAS)

This is an overview of the work in [56].

Problem

Multiple access with collision avoidance (MACA), the protocol for medium access solves the (in)famous hidden terminal problem but it creates some others. One of them is the collision of the control packets with the data packets. This reduces overall throughput and energy savings. Secondly, nodes that are neither receiving nor transmitting stay in their idle mode. Even in the idle mode the power consumption of the nodes are considerable. What we would like to power off such nodes at appropriate times.

Idea

The first problem of collision of data packets with control packets is solved using a separate signaling channel for data and control packets. The

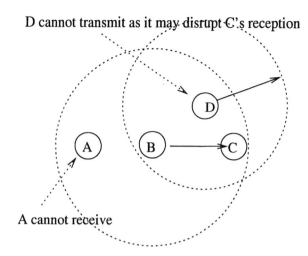

Figure 5: Various tranmission scenarios. Node D can sleep as it can neither transmit nor receive. Similarly, A cannot receive and if it does not have any data packets to transmit, it can sleep too.

second problem is addressed by powering off nodes not actively transmitting or receiving packets. The length of a sleeping period is determined appropriately before a node goes to sleep.

Description

Nodes spend a considerable amount of power receiving packets not destined to them. This happens when there is an ongoing transmission in the neighborhood and the nodes are within the transmission range of the sender. At this moment it cannot receive data from any other node. Similarly, if there is an ongoing transmission and the receiver is within the transmission range of a node then the node is not allowed to transmit even though it may have packets to transmit. Both these problems are illustrated in figure 2.6.1. The aim is to power off these nodes, which are unable to transmit and receive.

The first question is "when to power off?" A node powers off when

- it does not have packets to transmit and is unable to receive because a neighbourhood node has begun transmission.

- there is an ongoing transmission and both the transmitter and receiver are within the transmission range of the node, in which case the node cannot transmit or receive.

Its easy to determine if a node is unable to receive by sensing the data channel. For a node to determine if any reciever is receiving in the neighbourhood, the following approach is followed. A receiver sends out a busy tone as soon as it over hears an RTS-CTS handshake. After receiving this busy tone the node who wishes to transmit learns that there is an ongoing transmission in the neighborhood.

The second question is "How long should the sleeping period be?" If a node decides to sleep when a packet transmission just began in the neighborhood then in knows the length of the transmission. If it decides to sleep in the middle of some on going transmission it sends a t_probe(l) signaling packet where l is the maximum packet length. Every node who finishes its transmission within $[l/2, l]$ replies to the signal packet. If the response collides then the node assumes that there are more than one node finishing in that interval and hence tries a sub interval of the interval previously sent. For example if the probe packet $[l/2, l]$ collides then it probes with time period $[3l/4, l]$. If there is no response then it tries altogether different interval. So the interval $[l/2, 3l/4]$ will be probed if the $[3l/4, l]$ generates no response. In this way a node determines when the ongoing transmissions end and can wakeup after that.

Disadvantages

Using seperate signaling and data channels decreases effective bandwidth utilization. If a node sleeps and wakes up for one packet duration then the energy consumed in transition may reduce the over all power savings.

Results and Conclusions

The protocol shows power savings ranging from 10%, in sparsely connected networks to 50%, in fully connected networks. The difference comes from the fact that more number of nodes can sleep in case there is a transmission in the neighborhood, which is more frequent when the network is dense.

2.7 Energy efficient IEEE 802.11

IEEE 802.11 is the current standard MAC layer protocol specification for wireless LANs and ad hoc wireless networks. Various solutions have been proposed to improve power conserving behaviour of 802.11. This section gives a short description of the protocol operation related to power saving, followed by a few representative proposals to improve 802.11's power efficiency.

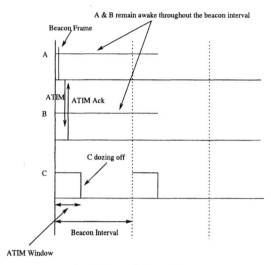

Figure 1. DCF operation in IEEE 802.11.

Figure 6: DCF operation in IEEE 802.11

2.7.1 Introduction

IEEE 802.11 works in two modes viz *point coordination function* (PCF) and *distributed coordination function* (DCF). PCF requires a central *access point* for coordination, whereas DCF is a fully distributed protocol. IEEE 802.11 specifies power saving mechanisms for both PCF and DCF. As DCF is a single hop ad-hoc operation mode, we will discuss DCF operation only. In DCF, time is divided into *beacon intervals* (BI). The nodes are synchronized in a distributed fashion through the transmission of beacon frames at the begining of each BIs. Any node hearing a beacon must set its clock to the time stamp included in the beacon frame plus the additional propagation delay. The power saving mechanism specified for DCF requires each node to stay awake at the start of each BI for a length of ATIM (ad hoc traffic indication map) interval. The purpose of the ATIM window is to let nodes announce that they have buffered packets to transmit. The transmitter and the receiver of the ATIM frame both stay awake for the entire BI. All other nodes go back to the power saving (PS) mode, i.e. the sleep mode. The BI structure and the operation of IEEE 802.11 in power saving mode is illustrated in Figure2.7.1.

Presented below are several approaches to make IEEE 802.11 power efficient.

2.7.2 Adapting IEEE 802.11 for power saving

This is an overview of the work in [63].

Problem

The existing standard of IEEE 802.11 assumes that there is a clock synchronization mechanism and the network is fully connected. This may not be true in case of multi hop ad hoc networks with unpredictable mobility. Hence, it is difficult to predict when another host will wake up to receive packets. If the nodes are not synchronized, then the BIs of different nodes will not overlap perfectly. This in turn may result in some node being unaware of its neighbours because it missed some neighbours' beacon. Most current routing protocols rely on accurate neighbour information and hence will be effected.

Idea

More beacons: in order to make other nodes aware of its presence, a node should transmit some beacons even after it hears a beacon frame. Note that with the existing standards a node should inhibit from transmitting a beacon frame if it has heard a beacon from some other node.

Overlapping BIs: a mechanism is provided to make sure that the BIs of any two nodes overlap each other. Hence, eliminating the need of a global clock synchronization.

Wake-up prediction: A node is required to predict the wake up pattern of another node by hearing its beacon. This informaton is needed if the node wants to transmit to another node in its PS mode.

Description

Every BI begins with an active window. The active window consists of a beacon window followed by an MTIM window. (Similar to ATIM in the existing IEEE 802.11. Here, the initial 'M' stands for "multihop".). A node transmits its beacon in the beacon window and any MTIM frame if it has, in the MTIM window. After the active window if a node does not have any packet to transmit or receive it goes back to the PS mode. The entire BI structure is represented in Figure 2.7.2.

The following three protocols are designed to implement the given solution.

Dominating awake interval (DAI)

This protocol requires a node to remain awake for at least half of the BI, i.e the active window spans at least half the BI. This property allows the beacon window of one node to be completely overlapped with any neighbouring nodes active window in at least every other BI, no matter how much

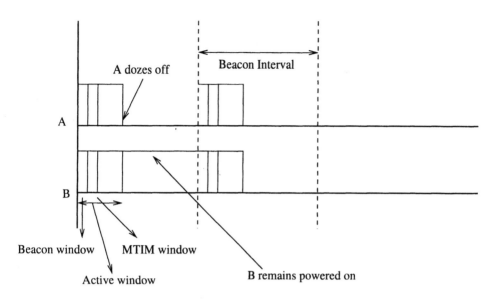

Figure 7: Beacon Interval layout

their clocks drift away. A proof of this fact could be found in [63]. With this property every node will receive its neighbours' beacon frames within two BIs, resulting in faster neighbour discovery. The disadvantage is that the node has to stay awake for more than half of the BIs thus resulting in poor power conserving behaviour.

Periodically fully awake interval (PFAI)

As the name suggests, this protocol requires a node to have several consequtive low-power intervals in which a node sleeps as soon as the MTIM window closes. Thus AW = BW + MTIM. After every T intervals, a low-pwer interval is followed by a fully awake interval in which the node continues to stay awake during the entire BI. Lower power interval is meant for the node to send out beacon frames to let other nodes learn of its existance and the fully awake interval is for the node to learn about its neighbours. The advantage of this approach lies in the greater power saving but the drawback is that the neighbour discovery process is delayed by T intervals.

Quorum based (QB)

In a QB protocol, the BIs for each node are organized in a mesh like structure. The node selects an arbitary pair of a row and a column as its awake BI. This guarantees that given perfect synchronization between nodes, any node's BI will overlap with any other node's BI at least twice

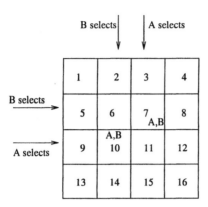

Figure : Quorum structure. Each cell represents a BI.
A and B has BIs overlap at cell 7 and 10.

Figure 8: Quorum structure. Each cell represents a BI. A and B overlap at cell 7 and 10

every n^2 times where n is the length of the BI mesh. Figure 2.7.2 explains the process. This approach is the best in terms of power saving as the nodes are awake only in $2n$ intervals out of every n^2 intervals. However, the neighbour discovery is slow as compared to the previous protocols.

Results and Conslusions

The QB protocol spends the least amount of power in transmitting beacons. The PFAI and the QB protocols' active (awake) ratios are quite small. The PFAI protocol requires nodes to remain awake every T BIs, while the QB protocol requires the nodes to remain awake for $2n$ out of n^2 intervals. The DAI protocol is most sensitive to neighbor changes where as QB protocol is least sensitive. The decision of selecting the appropriate protocol is made considering the network characterstics. For highly mobile nodes where neighbour discovery should happen quick enough the DAI protocol should be used. On the contrary, if the network is considerably static and power consumption is required, then QB or PFAI protocol should be used.

2.7.3 Dynamic power saving mechanism (DPSM)

This is an overview of the work in [36].

Problem

Current implementations of IEEE 802.11 have fixed ATIM window size, resulting in poor performance in several situations with respect to throughput and energy saving. When the ATIM window size is too small then it may not be sufficient to announce all the buffered packets. On the other hand, if it is too large, then there may be less time remaining for actual data transmission which takes place once the ATIM window gets over. Also, idle ATIM windows result in higher energy consumption.

In addition, both the transmitter and the receiver remain awake for the entire BI even after the transmission ends. This is unnecessary as it consumes additional power.

Idea

We dynamically adjust the size of ATIM window according to the network traffic. A higher network load needs many ATIM frames exchanges hence requires the size of the ATIM window to be proportional.

As a solution to the second problem a node returns to the PS mode once it completes its packet transfer. This is done when the energy saving in returning to the PS mode is greater than the energy spent in transition from the awake to the sleep mode. The approach has been followed for wireless LANs. With some modifications this could be used for mobile ad hoc networks.

Description

The protocol defines certain rules to decrease and increase the size of the ATIM window dynamically:

(i) If there are pending packets that could not be announced in the current ATIM window, it was suggestted that the ATIM window is small and the node increases its ATIM window in the next BI.

(ii) Each node is supposed to piggyback their ATIM window size on the transmitted packets. Upon hearing a larger window size a node increases its own window size so as to synchronize the ATIM windows.

(iii) If a node receives an ATIM frame after the end of its ATIM window it increases the size of its ATIM window. The following situation could happen when any node is having an ongoing transmission after its ATIM window closes and it receives an ATIM frame from some other node. It indicates that its ATIM window is too small to receive all the ATIM frames and hence needs an increase.

(iv) If a node is unable to successfully transmit an ATIM frame within one ATIM window, then it marks the ATIM frame and transmits it in the next BI. The receiver upon receiving this marked packet learns that its ATIM window is too small to receive an ATIM frame in the first attempt and thus increases its window size. Similarly, a node decreases its ATIM window sizes when it transmits all its ATIM frames well within the ATIM window and none of the above rules are satisfied.

Results and Conclusions

The simulation results showed that the above rules of increasing and decreasing the ATIM window size to improve energy savings and increase the throughput.

3   Unicast routing protocols

3.1   Introduction

Ad hoc networks are dynamically formed by moving nodes without any existing infrastructure. This nature of ad hoc networks makes it difficult to design a good routing protocol which takes every possible trade-off parameter into consideration. There have been a multitude of unicast routing protocols proposed in the literature. However, most of the proposed protocols have focused on minimizing delay and increasing network throughput, just as in the case of traditional routing protocols. The dominant routing metric has been the hop count.

When power-consumption is taken into account, hop count may not be the best routing metric. For instance, a few nodes in the "middle" of a topology may serve heavy traffics for many connections, draining quickly their own power, resulting in network disconnectivity. In many applications, network life-time is much more important than throughput or delay. In addition, given the normally limited power resources for ad hoc networks, power-conserving routing is a critical issue in ad hoc networking.

Incorporating power consumption into protocol design brings about many new unique problems as compared to the already quite complex routing problem in ad hoc networks. This problem is especially challenging when mobility is taken into consideration.

The rest of this section is organized as follows. Section 3.2 addresses the problems which arise when we take power consumption in consideration when designing routing protocols. Section 3.3 presents a few representative routing metrics with respect to power conserving. Section 3.4 describes various approaches which have been proposed in the literature, and a few other related issues. Sections 3.5, 3.6, 3.7, 3.8, and 3.9 discuss in more details a few protocols,

3.2 Issues for power-conserving routing protocols

- *New routing metrics.* What metrics should we use to select route? It should be intuitively obvious that conventional metrics such as the hop count or end-to-end delay are not satisfactory, as we have briefly analyzed earlier.

- *Mobility.* Coping with mobility is almost always the most challenging problem to be dealt with, whatever our concern is. Currently, most power saving protocols assume static topologies, which works fine for wireless LANs or other static ad hoc networks such as networks of sensors. In fact, as far as we understand, there is no protocol which deals with mobility in a satisfactory manner.

- *Resource sharing.* Because power is a valuable resource, nodes may not be willing to expend their power to forward network traffic. Co-operation and resource sharing is an important issue in power saving ad hoc networks. This is similar to a typical game theoretic problem.

- *Interaction with other layers.* The functionality of network layer and the MAC layer is fairly well separated in a wired environment. In ad hoc networks, especially with power conservation in mind, there need be much more interaction between the two layers, and even the physical layer. The traditional OSI or TCP/IP layering scheme is far from sufficient to deal with this problem. A new protocol stack structure is needed in this case.

- *Modeling of the physical layer.* Yet another problem is on wireless network physical layer modeling. Currently, different protocols make different assumptions about the underlying nature of the physical layers. Even in simulated environments, popular simulation packages like ns2 [47] and GloMoSim [25] have different modeling factors for the physical layer. For instance, these two packages were compared [60] and it was shown that they yield quite different results when configured with the same set of protocols. The discrepancies come from different assumptions made at the physical layer. In fact, the results coming out of the two simulation packages can even change the relative ranking of routing protocols for specific scenarios.

3.3 Power conserving routing metrics

One important problem in network layer is how to decide if one route is "better" than another. In our case, "better" means less power consumption. In traditional ad hoc network routing protocols, commonly used metrics have been the number of hops or end-to-end delay. However, solely using these metrics may have a negative affect on the network. In [57], five metrics with respect to battery power consumption have been discussed:

1. *Minimize energy consumed per packet.* The first metric which comes to mind is to attempt to save as much power as possible. A route consuming the least power seems to be a good choice. Suppose a packet j is transmitted through a route consisted of nodes $n_1, \ldots, n_k$. Let $T(a, b)$ be the energy consumed in transmitting (and receiving) one packet over one hop from a to b. Then, the total energy consumed for packet j on this route will be:

$$e_j = \sum_{i=1}^{k-1} T(n_i, n_{i_1})$$

   This simple metric suffers from the drawback that other factors effecting power consumption have not been taken into account. For example, if a route goes through a congested area of the network, there might be a lot of retransmissions needed. Retransmission might also be caused by environmental factors which affect bit error rate, which is significant in ad hoc networks. The power consumed by retransmissions is not at all negligible. Also, power aware routing algorithms tend to select route with more hops which further accumulates the error if we don't have link error control. In [6], a more accurate link energy consumption function $T(a, b)$ was proposed based on link error probability and the power consumption. The new cost function gives us a better estimation of how much energy will be consumed on a single link.

   Another problem is that this new metric, or any other metric for that matter, may force the overuse of some nodes in the network, draining their power quickly, leading to network disconnection and unfair division of labor.

   Two attempts to fix the problems are discussed next.

2. *Maximize time to network partition.* Normally, we define the life time of a network as the expected time until the network is partitioned, or

disconnected. This metric deals with the network life time. For a given network topology and a pair of nodes (u, v), we can use the max-flow min-cut Theorem [16] to find the minimal set of nodes (the cut set) the removal of which will disconnect the network. A route between u and v must go through one node in this set. To achieve maximum network life time, we need to alternate routes between these nodes. By doing so, we alleviate the load on the critical nodes, thus extend the network life time .

3. *Minimize the variance in node power levels.* This is actually dealing with the node life time or the fairness of power consumption. This metric treats all the nodes in the network equally and every node should keep the same level of power. Unlike in the previous metric, this metric is not so much concerned with the nodes in the cut set. We can reduce the variance in node power level by balancing the work load. In [57], it was suggested to use a routing procedure where each node sends packets through a neighbor with the least amount of data waiting to be transmitted.

4. *Minimize cost per packet.* Besides the energy consumed per packet (link cost function), we also need some other metric to measure the node cost per packet. Let f_i be a function that denotes the node cost of node n_i. Then, the cost of sending a packet j along a route of $n_1, \ldots, n_k$ is

$$C_j = \Sigma_{i=1}^{k-1} f_i.$$

The goal of this metric is to minimize C_j. Intuitively, f_i could be a node's reluctance to forward packets. The function f_i can also be tailored to represent a battery's remaining life time [57].

5. *Minimize maximum node cost Min-max battery cost routing* was proposed in [57]. Let $c_i(t)$ be the battery capacity of host n_i at time t. We define the node cost function $f_i(t) = 1/c_i(t)$. So, the less capacity it has, the more reluctant it is to forward traffic. The route r_j cost function is defined to be

$$R(r_j) = \max_{n_i \in r_j} f_i(t)$$

We select a route that minimizes the route cost. This approach will choose route whose weakest node has the highest residual power among all routes. A side effect is that the variance in node power level is also reduced. The protocol does not consider the total power in this route, hence may choose a route which consumes a lot of power.

Another work [62] gives a hybrid approach which first selects all the routes whose nodes are above some threshold, then choose the route which consumes the least power. If all the routes have nodes whose power is below threshold, then we apply the *min-max battery cost routing*. The approach is sound, but it is not easy to decide the threshold, which is important as the protocol's performance totally depends on it.

There is still yet another problem. If a node is willing to accept all route requests only because it currently has enough residual battery capacity, much traffic load will be injected through that node. In this sense, the actual drain rates of power consumption of the node will tend to be high, resulting in a sharp reduction of battery power. Another metric name *drain rate* [61] was proposed to address this problem. Each node monitors its energy consumption and maintains its battery power drain rate value DR_i by averaging the amount of energy consumption and estimating the energy dissipation per second during the given past interval. Let

$$DR_i = \alpha \cdot DR_{old} + (1 - \alpha) \cdot DR_{sample},$$

then the ratio $C_i = \frac{RBP_i}{DR_i}$ tells us when the remaining battery of node n_i is exhausted. Here, RBP_i denotes the *residual battery power* at node n_i, We can then maximize the minimum C_i to select a route. Using DR_i can avoid situations in which a few nodes allow too much traffic to pass through themselves, simply because their remaining battery capacity is temporarily high. However, it still cannot guarantee the minimum power consumption.

3.4   Other approaches for designing routing protocols

There are mainly two kinds of routing protocols in ad hoc networks: *on demand* and *table driven*. On demand routing protocols discover routes whenever needed, and are source initiated. Table driven protocols rely on periodic broadcasting or limited broadcasting to update routing tables at all nodes to keep up with the changes in network topology. The periodic maintenance of routing tables may waste a lot of energy, hence not suitable for power conservation, especially when network mobility is high. On demand protocols are more practical under high mobility. On the other hand,

Card	Transmit (mA)	Receive (mA)	Idle (mA)	Sleep (mA)	Voltage (V)
RangeLAN2-7410	265	130	n/a	2	5
WaveLAN(11Mbps)	284	190	156	10	4.74
Smart Spread	150	80	n/a	5	5

Table 1: Power consumption comparison between several typical wireless devices in different modes.

when mobility is low, we do not have to update routing tables too frequently. Hence, a table driven protocol is a better choice in this case.

In the previous section, we have discussed several metrics for route selection. In what follows, we shall discuss several other more special approaches for unicast routing protocols with power saving.

1. **Sleep and wake up.** Even when the node is in the idle mode, the power consumption is still comparable to that of the transmitting or receiving mode. Table 1 gives us some idea about the power consumption of some typical wireless devices in different modes. From the table we can see that even when the devices are idle, they still consume significant energy.

   One approach is to put the device into sleeping mode whenever possible, and wake it up when needed. PAMAS [56] uses this idea at the MAC layer. (See Section 2 for more details.) The protocols proposed in [12, 59, 73] are routing protocols which have taken this idea. They utilize information at the application layer to decide when to turn off the radio interface module. The difficulty of this approach is to decide when to wake up. Nodes can sleep for a fixed period or adaptively update the sleeping period according to the activity history. Waking up too early wastes power. Waking up late makes the node unable to receive a coming packet, causing unnecessary retransmission, leading to power waste and higher delay. It should also be emphasize that the trade-off between power conservation and network delay is another central problem in designing power sensitive protocols.

2. **Topology control.** The topology in an ad hoc network is often dynamic. When viewed as a directed graph, there is an edge from node i to node j if j is in the transmission range of i. Changing power levels thus leads to a topological change, which induces changes in network

connectivity, diameter, node degrees and other important network parameters. Connectivity is an important parameter, if not the most. The larger the power assigned to each node, the more connected the network is, and the smaller the network diameter is. In some sense, network diameter is a direct indication of average network delay. This trade-off between power consumption and connectivity/delay is a central problem in designing power saving protocols. Higher power also increases the interference and decreases the life time of the nodes. It is thus important to balance topology control and power consumption.

The purpose of topology control is just to reduce the power consumption and, at the same time, to get a good topology (higher connectivity, lower end-to-end delay, etc.). Intuitively, this approach does not work well under high mobility, in which case the network would spend most of its time computing the topology and adjust the power level. In [7], an investigation of the connectivity of a wireless multi-hop network with homogeneous random node distribution was conducted. An analytical expression was derived to the determine the transmission range r_0 that creates, for a given node density ρ, an almost surely k-connected network. (For graph theoretic terminologies, the reader is referred to [67].) If the maximum value of r_0 is given, then we can decide how many nodes are needed to cover a certain area with a k-connected network. The papers [41, 54] introduce the concept of *minimum power topology* which is the smallest subgraph of the given graph that contains the shortest path between all pairs of nodes. The work described in [42] presents a nice formulation of topology control problem. In general, a topology control problem can be specified by a triple of the form (M,P,O), where M∈{DIR, UNDIR} represents the graph model (directed or undirected), P is the desired graph property and O is the minimization objective. Typically, we can take O∈{MAXP, TOTALP} (max power and total power). For instance, in the (DIR, STRONGLY CONNECTED, MAXP) problem powers must be assigned to nodes so that the resulting directed graph is strongly connected and the maximum power assigned to a node is minimized.

3. **Clustering.** Since nodes in ad hoc networks tend to move in groups, where the relative location of the members in a particular group does not change much during movement, it makes sense select a coordinator from each group to form a backbone network. Non-coordinator members shall send all traffic to their corresponding coordinator. The

backbone could be considered to be a typical mobile ad hoc network, where any routing protocol could be employed. The drawback of this approach is that the coordinator's powers shall be drained out very quickly. Consequently, we need to select coordinators with higher power and alternate the role assignment inside the group.

Besides routing packets, coordinator can also schedule the sleep/wakeup of group members and buffer the packets when the destination node is sleeping. An algorithm for the *connected dominating set* problem [59, 72] can be used to select the coordinator. (A dominating set S of a graph G is a set of vertices for which each vertex of G is either in S or is incident to a vertex in S. A connected dominating set is a dominating set which forms an induced connected subgraph of G. It should be clear that a connected dominating set of small size is a good candidate for the set of coordinators.) Moreover, since the price of changing states from transmitting to receiving is high. We want the transmission to be as long as possible before a state change. A scheduling scheme can be used to schedule the nodes who want to transmit. One such scheme is given in [23], which addresses the problem in wireless LANs. In clustered ad hoc networks, we can use the cluster center to do such scheduling. The paper [30] further studies the topology control mechanisms for ad hoc networks with directional antennas.

4. **Cooperation in ad hoc networks.** Cooperation is very important in ad hoc networks, because we do not have any dedicated routers as in wired network. All the routing need the "sacrifice" of intermediate nodes to relay packets. As power is a very valuable resource, the intermediate nodes may not wish to forward the to much traffic. Such a node may report a false low remaining battery power or a much higher power consumption of forwarding to escape the duty of forwarding, or simply refuse to forward. If a lot of the nodes in the network behave like that, the delay will increase and the throughput will deduce drastically. In [43], methods to identify misbehaving users and to avoid routing through these nodes were studied. There is also a way to "force" the intermediate nodes to cooperate [8, 9]. This method is based on the introduction of a virtual currency called *nuggets*. Each node needs to pay *nuggets* to send out messages and middle nodes can earn *nuggets* when they are relaying messages. Clearly the price to implement such a scheme is the additional communication overhead induced. Moreover, a node may not be able to get enough reward

to transmit if few routes go through it because of its position in the network.

5. **Making use of the global positioning system (GPS).** Recent technological development has made GPS devices available at affordable prices. They are also small and power efficient enough to be used in ad hoc networks. Through broadcasting, nodes can send their locations to their neighbors, or even to the entire network. GPS is not the only approach here. Many algorithms, protocols mentioned above rely on GPS or can use GPS technique to enhance their performance. From the power saving point of view, GPS devices can be used as long as the power consumed by GPS devices is less than the power we can save with their help. This technique may not be applicable to sensor networks, where the cost of adding GPS devices will far exceed the cost of the network itself.

So far, we have discussed several power saving issues and approaches in ad hoc networks. It can be seen that there are numerous angles from where one can attack the power consumption problem. It is easy to make twists and turns here and there to come up with a new protocol. However, such protocols are very difficult to evaluate analytically, or even experimentally if the experiments are to be done in a comprehensive manner. There are simply too many factors involved, which are application dependent. To illustrate this point, a few protocols are presented in more details in the next few sections.

3.5   Maximizing network life time

We will first introduce a protocol proposed in [44] which combines several routing metrics mentioned above. Denote B_i as the residual battery power at node i, and E_{ij} as the transmission energy required by node i to transmit a packet over link (i, j). For reliable transmission, a transmission energy metric of the following form [6] was suggested:

$$E_{ij} = \frac{T_{ij}}{(1 - p_{ij})^L},$$

where p_{ij} is the link's packet error probability, T_{ij} is the energy involved in a single packet transmission attempt from node i to node j, and L is a parameter which determines how much weight we put on the error probability component. Then, we can define a *node-link metric* C_{ij} for the link (i, j) as follows.

$$C_{ij} = \frac{B_i}{E_{ij}}.$$

Note that this metric combines both the properties of node i and link (i, j). Using the max-min approach, we can define the life time of a route p to be the weakest link in this route:

$$\text{Life}_p = \min_{(i,j) \in p} \{C_{ij}\}$$

and select the route which has the maximum life time.

In [39], another max-min algorithm was proposed, which works as follows.

1. Find a path with the least power consumption P_{min} by using the Dijkstra algorithm [16].

2. Find a path with the least power consumption P_0 in the whole network.

3. If $P_0 > z \cdot P_{min}$, then the previous shortest path is the solution, in which case we stop. The role of the parameter z is explained later.

4. Find the minimal residual power fraction on the path which gives P_0. Let it be u_{min}.

5. Find all the edges whose residual power fraction u_{ij} is at most u_{min}, remove them from the graph.

6. Back to step 1.

The parameter z in this algorithm serves the role of deciding the maximal power we can use on the route we are looking for. We do not want to sacrifice a lot of power just to save one single node. Hence, the algorithm tries to balance the minimal residual power and the total power consumption on the path.

In fact, all current power aware routing algorithms use one or a combination of several of the five metrics we introduced earlier. It should be apparent that a common analytical model is missing to which new routing algorithms should be compared to. As we have emphasized earlier, it is easy to come up with a new metric or a combination of known metrics. It is very difficult, on the other hand, to make a point that a new metric is superior to the old ones in a convincing manner.

3.6   Coordinated power conservation

Coordinated Power Conservation (CPC) [59] is a clustered-based approach
which saves energy by turning off some nodes.

Construction of the backbone: CPC uses the *virtual dynamic backbone
protocol* (VDBP) [37] for backbone construction to achieve lower number
of nodes comprising the backbone. The VDBP protocol consists of the
following three phases:

- *Backbone Selection Process (BSP).* We select a dominating set of nodes
  using local one-hop away information. (See section 3.4 for a brief
  discussion on dominating sets.) We normally want a dominating set
  of size as small as possible. Unfortunately, the minimum connected
  dominating set problem has been shown to be NP-hard. Nodes decide
  on their own, based on the neighbor information, to participate in a
  dominating set or not.

- *Backbone connecting process (BCP).* A backbone is constructed by
  connecting the dominating set nodes we got from the first phase.

- *Backbone maintenance process (BMP).* BMP collaboratively works
  with the BCP to maintain the connectivity of the backbone in case
  of nodes' movements or changes in nodes' status.

The role of backbone nodes: after the backbone is known, there are two
schemes we could use to decide the role of the nodes on the backbone.

- *Backbone forwarded.* In this approach, the backbone is used for both
  power coordination and packet forwarding. Power coordination is just
  to schedule the sleeping and wakeup of non-backbone nodes. This
  approach would save more power for non-backbone nodes, but it will
  also increase coordinators' number of activities and thus increase the
  variance of power level in the network and the bandwidth is limited
  too.

- *Backbone coordinated.* The backbone is only used for power coordination. CPC uses this approach.

For power coordination, a backbone node will periodically check whether
there are suspending requests from client nodes within it coverage area and
then decide which nodes should be put into sleep mode, along with a suitable sleeping interval. This is done based on the dynamics of the network,

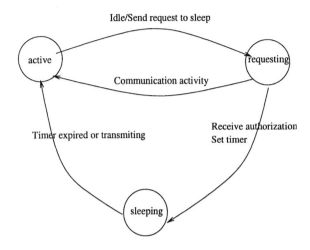

Figure 9: Operational cycle of a CPC non-backbone node

the ratio of number of active nodes per sleeping node, and the remaining energy level of client nodes. The backbone node selects more stable nodes as candidate sleeping nodes.

The role of non-backbone nodes: the operational cycle of such nodes is depicted in Figure 3.6. Being a non-backbone node, it starts up in the active state. If it has any ongoing communication activity, it will stay in this state. Otherwise, it will send a request for sleeping to its dominating node which decides if it should authorize this request. If the request is authorized, then the client node will set up a wake up timer, turn off its radio interface, and go to the sleeping mode. Sleeping nodes wake up when the timer expires or when a higher layer wants to access the channel.

Comment and Related works: clustering approach tends to quickly use up backbone nodes' power. Because of the selection of backbone nodes, they are normally nodes at critical positions, whose death will dramatically reduce the network life time. An improvement can be done by rerunning the backbone selection algorithm periodically and forcing the previous backbone nodes to be non-backbone nodes. Clearly this "quick fix" imposes more overhead. There should also be some bound to the size of the backbone. Small sized backbones are hard to construct, and suffer from the above problem. Large size backbones negate the clustering advantage. There are several recent works which addressed connected nominating set problem, such as those of [3, 4, 71].

Similar solutions include SPAN [12] and GAF [73]. GAF (geographical

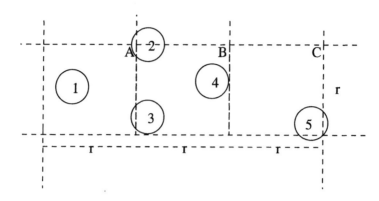

Figure 10: An example of virtual grid in GAF. Note that if the nominal radio range is R, then, to satisfy the condition that any node in adjacent grid can communicate with each other, we must have $r^2 + (2r)^2 \leq R^2$. (For node 2 and 5 to communicate.)

adaptive fidelity) uses geographic location information to divide the world into fixed square grids. The size of each grid stays constant, regardless of node density. In the definition of the grid, it is required that any node in an adjacent grid can communicate with each other. Figure 3.6 illustrates an idea of such virtual grid. All nodes in each grid are equivalent for routing. Nodes within a grid can switch between sleeping and listening, as long as we guarantee that there is at least one node in each grid stays awake to route packets. To avoid the abuse of coordinators' power, SPAN rotates the coordinators. It also attempts to minimize the number of nodes elected as coordinators, so that the network shall not suffer a significant loss of capacity or an increase in latency.

3.7   Minimum power topology

The concept of *minimum power topology*, introduced in [38, 40, 54], is very important in topology control for wireless ad hoc networks. The works in [38, 40] were based on the formulation and idea of [54]. In this section, we will first review the some of the main ideas in [54] and its extensions in [38, 40] later.

The minimum power topology G_m is the smallest subgraph of of a graph G that contains the shortest paths between all pairs of nodes. [54] gives a localized protocol to calculate G_m. To simplify the problem, a node was taken to be the information sink (*master site*) for all nodes in the network.

Hence, in effect their algorithm gives a minimum power topology between one node and all the other nodes. Though we can calculate such topology for each node from their approach, it was not discussed on how to calculate the global optimal topology from these individual topologies. To introduce their algorithm, we will first give some definitions:

Relay Region. The relay region of a transmit-relay node pair (i, r) is define to be

$$R(i, r) = \{(x, y) \mid P_{i \to r \to (x,y)} < P_{i \to (x,y)}\},$$

where $P_{i \to r \to (x,y)}$ denotes the power required to transmit information from node i to (x, y) through the relay node r, and $P_{i \to (x,y)}$ is the power required to transmit information from i to (x, y) directly. Hence, i should use r to relay its messages if the destination is in the relay area.

Enclosure region and neighbor. The enclosure region of a node i is defined as:

$$\varepsilon_i = \bigcap_{k \in N(i)} R^c(i, k),$$

and

$$N(i) = \{n \in \mathcal{N} \mid (x_n, y_n) \in \varepsilon_i, n \neq i\},$$

where $R^c(i, k)$ is the complement area for relay region $R(i, k)$, and $\mathcal{N}$ is the node set. Each element in $N(i)$ will be the neighbor of i. Figure 3.7 illustrates the notions of relay regions, enclosures and neighbors.

Enclosure Graph. The enclosure graph of a set of nodes $\mathcal{N}$ is the graph whose vertex set is $\mathcal{N}$ and whose edge set is

$$\bigcap_{i \in \mathcal{N}} \bigcap_{k \in N(i)} l_{i \to k},$$

where $l_{i \to k}$ is the direct communications link from i to k. It can be shown that that the enclosure graph of $\mathcal{N}$ is strongly connected [54].

From the above definitions we can see that, in order to get the minimum power topology we could first find the enclosure graph of the node set; then, for each node we eliminate all nodes in its relay region, and choose a few links in its immediate neighborhood to be the potential candidates.

The protocol can be divided into two phases: *search for enclosure* and *cost distribution*. In the first phase, each node starts the search by sending out a beacon search signal which includes the position information for this node (GPS or some similar device is a requirement). When a node i receives such searching signals, it will use the location information of the neighbors to calculate the relay region for them. If a node is found to be in the relay

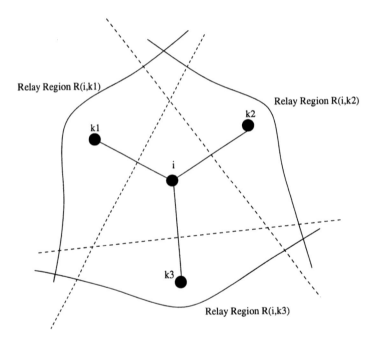

Figure 11: Enclosure and neighbors of node i

regions of previously found node, we will mark it as "dead". If a node is not in other's relay regions, we mark it as "alive". So when the searching algorithm terminates, the set of alive nodes will be the set of neighbors for node i. It can be shown that the resulting $(\varepsilon_i, N(i)))$ is correct and also unique. In the second phase, each node will broadcast its power consumption cost to its neighbors and then we use the distributed Bellman-Ford shortest path algorithm on the enclosure graph using this cost metric. The power consumption cost is defined to be the minimum power necessary for node i to establish a path to the master-site. Of course, at the very beginning of the algorithm, we can assign any cost value to i (of course, the cost of the master site will always be zero), and it will converge eventually. Let $n \in N(i))$, then when i receives the broadcasted cost of n, it computes

$$C_{i,n} = cost(n) + P_{transmit}(i, n) + P_{receiver}(n),$$

where $P_{transmit}(i, n)$ is the power required to transmit from i to n, and $P_{receiver}(n)$ is the additional receiver power that i's connection to n would induce at n. Then, i computes

$$cost(i) = min_{n \in N(i))}C_{i,n}$$

and picks the link corresponding to the minimum cost neighbor. The algorithm repeats until it converges.

Paper [40] gave a slightly modified version of this algorithm. In the first phase of this modified version, when a node is marked "alive", it won't be mark "dead" anymore. This is unlike that in the original algorithm, where it could happen that a node is marked dead after being marked alive. It was claimed that this modification can significantly improve the performance, and make the computation simpler.

In [38], instead of finding nodes that can not be served as relay nodes, it was suggested to try to find the nodes that are guaranteed to be the neighbors of i which greatly reduces the time and space complexity. A similar algorithm was proposed in [66]. In the neighbors search phase, nodes keep increasing transmission power until there is at least one neighbor in every cone of α degrees or the maximum transmission power is reached. The second phase remains the same.

3.8 Clustering schemes

A cluster is a set of nodes with a distinguished *master* node and the rest are *slave* nodes. The clustering approach involves the partitioning of the entire network into clusters. Each individual cluster has one master node and several slave nodes. Node communication is between master and slave only. Slaves do not communicate with each other. The master within a cluster is responsible for routing packets to other clusters.

Problem. The task here is to form efficient clusters such that no call gets dropped. A call gets dropped when for some node there is no master. Also, the cluster area should be as small as possible such that the energy consumption of the network is minimized.

Description. Two clustering mechanisms were introduced in [28]:

Single clustering : To form a cluster master node pages at its maximum power level on a common control channel. Slaves receiving this page acknowledge back to the master, piggybacking the received power level of the page. The master allocates the channel that it has to the slaves on the basis of the received power level (and hence the distance of the slave node from the master). This keeps the cluster size as small as possible. The slaves that do not get any connections result in a dropped call and are not a part of the network.

Double clustering : The first phase of this protocol is similar to the single clustering scheme. Once the master assigns channels to slave nodes if it has any channels left, then they are re-paged onto the common control channel. The slaves whose call gets dropped during the first call can re-acknowledge them in the second phase thus further reducing the call drop rate.

Disadvantage The clustering algorithms were proposed with the static network assumption. Hence, they do not deal well with mobility. The channel division is not bandwidth efficient.

3.9   Energy aware routing for sensor networks

Problem. If a source-destination pair always uses the lowest energy path for data transmission, then it might result in the depletion of energy reserve for nodes within that path. This creates an imbalance of energy resources in the network.

Idea. Instead of transmitting on a single path, multiple paths should be chosen for data delivery, which has the effect of balancing out energy reserves among network nodes and thus increases time to network partition [55].

Description. Apart from the optimal route, every node maintains a set of k optimal paths and chooses one of them while transmitting. The protocol is designed to run for ad hoc sensor networks. The data exchange usually involves queries like "Send the temperature for room 5". So the

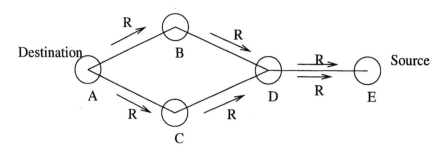

Figure 12: Route discovery process. The destination A floods the request packet R in the direction of E (the source). Intermediate node B stores E_{AB}, the energy required for link AB, as the cost for that path. Node D stores $E_{AB} + E_{BD}$, $E_{AC} + E_{CD}$, the cost of two different paths for reaching the destination.

sensor nodes located in room 5 start the transfer. Here the sensor nodes are the transmitters. It can be seen that the route formation is done from destination to source. While the routes are determined, every intermediate node stores the energy of the sub-path from that node to the destination. It includes this value to the request and forwards it further. The procedure is represented in figure 3.9. While transmitting data, every node has several options for selecting the onward path to send the data. A node can select the route based on a probability function which is inversely proportional to the energy requirement of the path. Hence the most optimal route has the highest probability of getting selected. The probability of route selection is determined as follows.

$$P_{N_j, N_i} = \frac{1/C_{N_j, N_i}}{\sum_{k \in FT_j} 1/C_{N_j, N_k}} \tag{1}$$

Here, P_{N_j, N_i} is the probability of node j picking neighbor i to forward packets, C_{N_j, N_i} is the cost for choosing that path, FT_j represents the forwarding table of node j. The cost function is proportional to the energy requirement for that path.

Results and Conclusions. Simulation results showed that the protocol was able to reduce the average energy consumed per node by around 21% and increase the average lifetime by 40%.

4   Multicast and broadcast routing protocols

In many typical ad hoc network applications such as mobile conferencing, emergency services, and battle field communications, multicasting and/or broadcasting are the most natural communication primitives. Multicasting is a fundamental generalization of both unicasting and broadcasting. On the other hand, many unicasting protocols, whether or not they are power-aware, rely on broadcasting to communicate routing data, to discover routes, etc. Consequently, the problems of devising efficient multicast, broadcast protocols are of tremendous importance in ad hoc wireless networking.

In this section, we shall discuss problems, results, approaches, and open questions relating to power-aware multicast and broadcast protocols and algorithms on wireless ad hoc networks. The precise descriptions of the problems shall be presented later. Let us first briefly discuss the types of problems and solutions relating to energy-aware multicast and broadcast algorithms.

The power-aware broadcasting and multicasting problem we are facing is assumed to be source initiated, namely some distinguished node among a set of given nodes initiates the process of finding a power assignment vector which indicates the transmission power level at each node in the network. Here we assume omnidirectional antennas are used so that given a power assignment at a node, say u, all nodes within a certain radius of u are reachable from u in a single hop. The assignment is such that all nodes in the network are reachable, possibly in several hops, from the source in the broadcasting case, or the nodes in a multicast group are reachable from the source in the multicasting case.

We would like to reduce the total power in the power assignment vector. Initially, several authors have casted this problem in terms of building a multicast/broadcast tree rooted at the source [65, 68, 69]. In fact, the trees are *directed rooted trees*, also called *arborescences*, where there is a directed edge from u to v if and only if the power assigned at node u is large enough to reach v in one transmission hop. In reality, given a power assignment vector we could form a *reachability graph* which is a directed graph with an edge from u to v if and only if the power assigned at u is large enough to reach v in one hop. The reachability graph is not an arborescence in general. What we would like is to have a directed path from the root to every node in a specified set of nodes, while keeping the total assigned power as small as possible.

One fundamental feature which distinguishes this problem in ad hoc wireless network to the same problem in the wired case is that transmission power cost is node-based. In the wired environment, transmission costs are on a link by link basis. On the contrary, when some power level is assigned to a node in an ad hoc network, that cost is fixed no matter how many potential links are created by that power assignment. This is due to the omnidirectional antenna assumption we have made.

In wired networks, it is often advantageous to build multicast/broadcast trees which use multiple short hops to reach the group members. This may not be the case is ad hoc networks. A large power assignment to a node could save more power than small power assignments to many nodes to reach the same set of group members.

Although the literature on this problem is quite large, as shall be subsequently reviewed , there is still little progress toward a reasonably practical solution. The problem of finding an energy-optimal reachability graph is NP-Hard [10, 11, 41]. The first step has been to find some analytically and/or experimentally good heuristic and approximation algorithm for the centralized version of the problem. In sections 4.2.1 and 4.3.1 we shall discuss known algorithms on the centralized version of the problem. The second natural step is to extend the ideas and algorithms obtained from studying the centralized version to devise distributed algorithms for the same problem. Results obtained thus far are very limited and impractical. We review some of them in sections 4.2.2 and 4.3.2. Before all of that, we mathematically formulate the problem, review related results and show that it is NP-Complete in section 4.1. It should be noted that the issue of mobility has not been properly addressed at all. All related works thus far have focused on static ad hoc networks, which is already quite challenging.

4.1 Problem formulation and NP-Completeness results

As mentioned earlier, we assume that all nodes are equipped with omnidirectional antennas. The antennas' power levels are adjustable. There are two different basic assumptions: (1) the power levels can continuously be adjusted from 0 to some level p_{max}; (2) the power levels can only be chosen from a given discrete set $\{0, p_1, \ldots, p_m\}$ of power levels. In fact, when the nodes are heterogeneous it is possible that each node has its own power level set in case (2). To simplify our discussion, we shall mostly restrict ourselves to case (1). Many algorithms and protocols with assumption (1) can easily be extended to handle case (2). A simple strategy is to assume (1) and then "round" an assigned power level up to the next available level from the given set. In particular, algorithms' performances are not changed by much if the granularity of the power level set is fine enough. The readers are referred to [70] for a discussion on the effect of different granularities of power level sets on energy-efficient broadcast protocols.

The most common, admittedly simplistic, attenuation model assumes that signal power falls proportional to d^α, where d is the signal traveling distance, and α is an environmentally dependent real constant between 2 and 6. Suppose a node u is transmitting with power p_u. A node v of distance d_{uv} from u can properly receive the signal from u if $p_u \geq \gamma d_{uv}^\alpha$. Here, γ represents the receiver's power threshold for signal detection, often normalized to be unity. Thus, from here on we assume that v can properly receive u's signal if and only if $p_u \geq d_{uv}^\alpha$.

Let us continue with the u, v example above. If $p_{max} < d_{uv}^\alpha$, then it is impossible to get from u to v via a single hop. In this case, multi-hop transmission is necessary. In many cases, multi-hop transmission also saves the total power usage of the nodes involved.

Given the basic communication model described above, we are now ready to define our broadcast and multicast problems. We first describe the problem in a highly general setting, then discuss their specializations leading back to our original problems. Graph theoretic terminologies we use here are fairly standard. The reader is referred to [67] for more details. Terminologies and concepts for NP-Complete theory and approximation algorithms can be found in [24, 29].

4.1.1   The minimum energy consumption broadcast subgraph (MECB problem

In this problem, we are given a directed graph $G = (V, E)$ with a symmetric cost function $c : E \to \mathbb{R}^+$ on its edges, namely $c(u, v) = c(v, u), \forall (u, v) \in E$. A distinguished vertex $r \in V$, called the source node, is also given. A power assignment vector is a function $p : V \to \mathbb{R}^+$, which assigns to each node of G some "power level". The reachability graph $G_p = (V, E_p)$ given a power assignment vector p is defined as follows. The directed graph G_p has the same set of vertices as G. There is an edge from u to v in G_p if and only if $p_u \geq c(u, v)$, that is, the power assigned to u is at least the cost to reach v.

Our problem is to find a power assignment vector p such that there is a directed path from r to every node in G_p, so as to minimize the sum $\sum_{v \in V} p_v$. A more realistic variation of the problem also has a given $p_{max} > 0$ and requires that $p_v \leq p_{max}, \forall v \in V$.

When the nodes of the graph G are points on a d-dimensional Euclidean space, $d \geq 1$, and $c(u, v) = d_{uv}^\alpha$, $\alpha \in [2, 6]$, we denote the problem as MECBS[N_d^α]. The case when $d = 2$ is of most interest, and is where most known results come from.

There are overwhelmingly more results on the broadcast version than the multicast version. Particularly due to the fact that the broadcast version is already difficult enough. Secondly, one can always build the broadcast graph and then prune it to a multicast graph. However, it has been shown that the pruning may not give good approximation ratios [64].

Wieselthier et al. [68] studied several simple heuristics and experimentally studied their performances for the MECBS$[N_2^2]$ problem. The algorithms under their study include: MST (minimum spanning tree), BIP (Broadcast Incremental Power), and SPT (Shortest Path Tree). Wan et al. [65] and Clementi et al. [14] gave upper and lower bounds on the performance ratios of several of these heuristics. In particular, the MST heuristic for MECBS$[N_2^2]$ was shown to have approximation ratio between 6 and 12; the BIP heuristic for the same problem has approximation ratio between $\frac{13}{3}$ and 12; the SPT approximation ratio is at least $\frac{n}{2}$. One can envision applying the same heuristic as Chvatal's approximation algorithm for the weighted SET-COVER problem [13] to solve MECBS$[N_2^2]$ or MECBS$[N_d^\alpha]$ in general. Let us refer to this heuristic as the ABIP (Average Broadcast Incremental Power) algorithm. Unfortunately, ABIP has performance ratio at least $\frac{4n}{\ln n} - o(1)$ in the worst case [65] for the MECBS$[N_2^2]$ problem. On the positive side, Ngo et al. [48] has devised a modified version of ABIP called MABIP (modified ABIP) which works very well on average, beating both MST and BIP. Cagalj et al. [10] came up with an algorithm called EWMA (Embedded Wireless Multicast Advantage) which tries to modify an MST to form a better reachability graph. One biggest advantage of EWMA is that it is a better modification of MST, hence its performance ratio is at least as good as MST, which is upper bounded by 12 for the MECBS$[N_2^2]$ problem. The authors also showed experimentally that it works better than BIP on average.

For the general version of MECBS, Caragiannis et al. [11] found a approximation algorithm with performance ratio of $10.8 \ln n$, by a reduction of MECBS to the *node-weighted connected dominating set* problem, which has a $1.35 \ln n$-approximation [26]. In the same paper, the author also devised a polynomial time solution to the MECBS$[N_1^\alpha]$ problem. Liang [41] also addressed the same problem by a reduction to the Steiner Tree problem [31], however the approximation ratio is about $O(\log^3 n)$, which is not as good.

As far as negative results are concerned, unless NP $\subseteq$ DTIME$(n^{O(\log \log n)})$, MECBS can be shown to be inapproximatable within a ratio of $(1 - \epsilon) \ln n$ by a reduction to MINIMUM SET COVER [14] or to CONNECTED DOMINATING SET [65].

4.1.2   The minimum energy consumption multicast subgraph (MECMS) problem

In the MECMS problem, in addition to r, we are also given a non-empty subset $M \subseteq V - \{r\}$ of nodes which form a multicast group. Instead of requiring every node in V to be reachable from r in G_p, we are only required that there is a directed path from r to each member of M. The rest of the problem is the same. We also have the important special cases MECMS[N_d^α].

In terms of the general problem, Liang [41] showed that his reduction to Steiner tree has performance ratio of about $O(|M|^\epsilon)$. Given the nature of this problem as seen thus far, an approximation of logarithmic ratio is expected.

Since MECBS is a special case of MECMS, all complexity results of MECBS can be applied to MECMS, including the fact that it is NP-hard and likely inapproximatable within $(1 - \epsilon) \ln n$, for any $\epsilon > 0$.

As far as our original problem MECMS[N_2^2] is concerned, all broadcast algorithms discussed in the previous section can be modified to get multicast algorithms by "pruning" the broadcast graph back to a multicast graph. We shall be more precise in later sections. For now, the reader could think of this pruning as the normal multicast tree pruning. Naming-wise, we shall add a P, for pruned, in front of the broadcast algorithms' names, such as P-MST, P-BIP, P-SPT, ... Wan and Calinescu [64] gave some negative results to the pruned versions. In particular, P-MST, P-SPT, and P-BIP were shown to have worst cast approximation ratios at least $(n - 1)/2$, $(n - 1)$, and $(n - 2) - o(1)$ respectively. They also proposed two new algorithms: SPF (shortest path first) and MIPF (minimum incremental path first), which were shown to have constant approximation ratios between 6 and 24, and $\frac{13}{3}$ and 24, respectively.

4.1.3   Hardness results

Let us first consider the general MECBS problem. This problem is not only NP-Complete, it is not approximatable within a ratio of $(1 - \epsilon) \ln n$, for any $\epsilon > 0$, unless NP $\not\subseteq$ DTIME($n^{O(\log \log n)}$). To show this fact, we reduce to MECBS the MINIMUM SET COVER optimization problem [34], which is not approximatable within a factor of $(1 - \epsilon) \ln n$ unless P=NP [21]. Note that since MECBS is a special case of MECMS, the MECMS problem is also not approximatable within a factor of $(1 - \epsilon) \ln n$. Let us formally put this as a theorem:

Theorem 4.1. *The MECBS problem is not approximatable within a factor* *of* $(1 - \epsilon) \ln n$, *for any* $\epsilon > 0$, *unless* $NP \not\subseteq DTIME(n^{O(\log \log n)})$.

Proof. The MINIMUM SET COVER (MSC) problem is defined as follows. Given a universe set $\mathcal{U}$, and a collection $\mathcal{S} = \{S_1, S_2, \ldots, S_n\}$ of subsets of $\mathcal{U}$. The problem is to find a smallest sized sub-collection $\{S_i \mid i \in I\}$ of $\mathcal{S}$, such that

$$\bigcup_{i \in I} S_i = \mathcal{U}.$$

The reduction from MSC to MECBS goes as follows. Given an instance $(\mathcal{U}, \mathcal{S})$ of MSC, we construct a directed graph $G = (V, E)$, where

$$V = \{r\} \cup \mathcal{S} \cup \mathcal{U},$$

and

$$E = \{(r, u) \mid u \in \mathcal{U}\} \cup \{(S, u) \mid S \in \mathcal{S}, u \in S\}.$$

The vertex r is the broadcast source. The cost function c assigns 1 to every edge of G.

We claim that the MSC instance has a set cover of size at most k, i.e. $|I| \leq k$, if and only if there is a power assignment vector p for G with total power at most $k + 1$.

Firstly, consider a set cover $\{S_i \mid i \in I\}$ of $\mathcal{U}$, where $|I| \leq k$. We assign a power of 1 to r, and a power of 1 to each vertex S_i, with $i \in I$. It is clear that all vertices in $\mathcal{S}$ are covered by r, and all vertices in $\mathcal{U}$ are covered by the S_i, $i \in I$. The total power we used is at most $k + 1$.

Conversely, suppose there is a power assignment of total power at most $k + 1$ to G, then the collection of subsets of $\mathcal{S}$ with assigned power at least 1 have to cover all vertices in $\mathcal{U}$. In other words, this collection is also a set cover in the MSC problem. As the total power is at most $k + 1$, and r has to be assigned with power at least 1 to cover all the vertices in $\mathcal{S}$, the sub-collection of $\mathcal{S}$ we picked is of size at most k as desired. $\square$

Corollary 4.2. *The MECMS problem is not approximatable within a factor of* $(1 - \epsilon) \ln n$, *for any* $\epsilon > 0$, *unless* $NP \not\subseteq DTIME(n^{O(\log \log n)})$.

The conclusion of MSC not approximatable within a factor of $(1 - \epsilon) \ln n$ was based on the assumption that NP $\not\subseteq$ DTIME($n^{O(\log \log n)}$). If we only take the common "conjecture" that P $\neq$ NP, then we know that MSC is not approximatable within a factor of $c \log n$ for any constant $c > 0$ [52], so is MECSB. We have the following corollary:

Corollary 4.3. *The MECBS and the MECMS problem are not approximatable within a factor of* $c \log n$, *for any* $c > 0$, *unless* $P = NP$.

One can also show that MECBS[N_d^α] is NP-Hard for $d \geq 2$, and $\alpha >$ 1. For a complete proof, see [14] which uses a reduction from MINIMUM VERTEX COVER on planar cubic graphs, which is known to be APX-complete [2], i.e. there is no polynomial time approximation scheme for this problem, unless P = NP. The reduction is almost the same as the argument used in [15] for the power assignment problem in radio networks.

4.2 Power-aware broadcast routing

Now that we know that the problem MECBS[N_2^α], our main broadcasting problem, is NP-hard. The next step would be to find good approximation algorithms for this problem, and then try to distributize them. The distributed version is difficult and there have not been many promising results on it. For the centralized versions, there are a number of algorithms known, as introduced in Section 4.1.1. We shall review some of them here, and discuss the distributed version in the next section.

4.2.1 The centralized version

Given a set S of nodes on the plane, define a complete graph G_S with the same set of nodes, and each edge (u, v) is weighted with the minimum power to for v to be in the transmission range of u (and vice versa).

The first heuristic is to compute a minimum spanning tree (MST) $T = \mathrm{mst}(S)$ of G_S, then direct edges out from the broadcast source r so that T becomes an arborescence. Then, assign to each internal node v of T to be the weight of the heaviest directed edge coming out of v. All leaf nodes are assigned with power 0. Obviously, this MST algorithm yields a valid solution to our broadcasting problem. The hard part is to compute its approximation ratio. A simple example could be used to show that the approximation ratio of MST is at least 6 [65]. As for the upper bound, we need a few technical lemmas. The *radius* of a set S of points on the plane is defined to be

$$\inf_{s \in S} \sup_{t \in S} |st|.$$

Lemma 4.4. *Let P be a set of points of radius 1, then we have*

$$\sum_{e \in mst(S)} |e|^\alpha \leq 12,$$

for $\alpha \geq 2$.

The proof of this lemma is quite technical, and the reader is referred to [65] for details. We now can use this lemma to estimate the approximation ratio of MST.

Theorem 4.5. *For the MECBS[N_2^α] problem, the MST heuristic has approximation ratio at most 12.*

Proof. Consider an instance of the problem with point set S, and the broadcast source s. Let p be an optimal power assignment vector for nodes in S, with node $u \in S$ assigned with power p_u. For a node u with $p_u \neq 0$, let S_u be the set of nodes within the transmission range p_u of u, and let $T_u = \text{mst}(S_u)$. Let r_u be the distance from u to the farthest node in s_u. Then, it is easy to see that

$$\sum_{e \in T_u} \left(\frac{|e|}{r_u} \right)^\alpha \leq 12.$$

In other words,

$$\sum_{e \in T_u} |e|^\alpha \leq 12|r_u|^\alpha = 12p_u.$$

Again, we turn all the T_u into arborescences by directing the edges from u toward the leaves, and then superpose all T_u together to form an arborescence of T, with total power cost at least the MST solution. The superposition cost is at most 12 times the sum of all p_u, which completes the proof. $\square$

One advantage of MST is that it does have a guaranteed approximation ratio, as shown above. Another one is that minimum spanning trees are such fundamental combinatorial objects on point sets that the analyses of other algorithms could use its approximation ratio as a basis to compare to. We shall see an example of this fact below.

The second heuristic is the BIP algorithm, which works as follows. Recall Prim's algorithm for computing minimum spanning trees, which starts from a node in a graph G, and each step adds a new node with least distance to the existing covered set of nodes. The MST heuristic above could be programmed with Prim's algorithm. The problem with this approach is that it is link-based, which does not take into account the wireless multicast advantage (WMA), namely once a certain power is assigned to a node u, all nodes within that radius is covered by u, not only the node of the specific distance constituting that power.

The BIP algorithm attempts to take advantage of WMA by simulating Prim's algorithm. The only difference is that a new node with imposes the least "incremental" power to the existing set of nodes is added to the set.

The incremental distance is the difference between the new power assigned to a node and the old one, in order to cover the new node.

The BIP algorithm's approximation ratio could also be upper bounded by 12, as the following theorem shows.

Theorem 4.6. *For the MECBS[N_2^α] problem, the BIP heuristic has approximation ratio at most 12.*

Proof. Consider the graph G_S, with source s, as defined earlier. Grow a spanning tree, using Prim's algorithm, starting from s. Let $s = s_1, \ldots, s_n$ be the sequence of nodes added to the MST during the execution.

Define a new complete graph H_S on S with the weight between s_i and s_{i+1} being the incremental weight when adding s_{i+1} to the set of covered nodes $\{s_1, \ldots, s_i\}$ during the execution of Prim's algorithm above. The rest of the weights are the same as those in G_S.

Clearly, the weight of each edge in H_S is at most that in G_S. Execute Prim's algorithm on H_S starting from $s = s_1$, we get the path $s_1, \ldots, s_n$, with weight exactly the weight of the MST we got earlier, which is also the total weight of edges in the tree returned by BIP.

The total power of the tree returned by BIP is at most its tree's weight, which is in turn at most the MST's weight, which we know is at most 12 times the optimal solution.   □

The last algorithm we shall review is the EWMA algorithm. This algorithm takes advantage, again, of the fact that MST returns a approximation ration bounded solution. EWMA starts by building an MST. Then, starting from the root s of the arborescence, we can look at all children of a particular neighbor u of s. Increasing s's power to cover all these children might actually save some power, since u does not have to cover any of them anymore, and this new power assignment to s might additionally cover some more children of s's children other than u. For every child u of s, we calculate the potential saving in power by forcing s to cover all of u's children. The child u inducing the best power saving is chosen to extend s's power. This process could be repeated for each of the non-zero assigned power (new) children of s, until we reach all the leaves. Simulations show that EWMA is superior to both BIP and MST. More over, EWMA has approximation ratio at most 12 as well, because it is just as good as MST.

4.2.2   The distributed version

One advantage of MST is that it could be distributized by a standard algorithm, such as that in [22]. The disadvantages include the fact that the distributed version for MST is quite complicated, require lots of overhead. The version given in [22] is not even source initiated. A source-initiated version requires many more message passing rounds, and thus converges much slower than the corresponding parallel version.

The BIP algorithm could be distributized in much the same way as the MST algorithm. It suffers from the same kind of problem, namely slow to converge and too much overhead. No one to date has done some proper evaluation of distributed implementations of these algorithms, which would be of tremendous interest. They many not give good results, but they shall serve as benchmarks to compare future algorithms to.

A distributed version of the EWMA algorithm could also be implemented, by first building the MST distributively, and perform each of EWMA's step locally among two-hop neighbors. Obviously, all the disadvantages mentioned above still hold, as the MST step is still there. Moreover, the second distributed step involving two-hop neighbors are even more complex than the MST step.

It is sensible that any distributed version for our problem involves a step where we would like to add a new node u with minimum "distance" to an existing set of U nodes. This could be considered a communication primitive. Implementing this step in an entirely distributive manner could yield very high cost.

One solution, with high cost, is for each node in U to calculate the "distance", whatever that might be, to each of its neighbors. Then, some sort of controlled broadcasting is done amongst U to decide who has the best neighbor to expand U from. The controlled broadcasting step could be done along some spanning subgraph of U, which we have built during the process of constructing U. That is the reason why it was called "controlled" in the first place. Some experimental and analytical study on the cost of this basic communication primitive should be studied in more details. This will benefit all later solutions to our problem.

Another solution, with possible lower cost but pays the price of possible non-optimal outcomes, is for each node in U to independently attempts to expand U from itself. Each node in U could try to delay the expansion proportional to the cost of expansion. Thus, the node with lowest expansion cost has the best chance to go first. The problem with this approach is that during the delay time, each node has to monitor its neighbors to see if any of them has been included in the possible expansion from some other node in U. The monitoring has to be synchronized, in some manner, in order for nodes in U to update its cost function, and then delay for the new appropriate amount of time. We do not know if doing so is more beneficial than the first controlled broadcasting solution amongst U.

4.3   Power-aware multicast routing

Unlike the broadcasting case, the multicasting case has very few proposals for solutions so far, even partial and centralized ones. We briefly review some solutions proposed thus far.

In the ad hoc networking environment, it has often been assumed that multicasting (and broadcasting) are source initiated, in contrast to the normal Internet case, where nodes are allowed to join and leave multicast groups dynamically with the Internet group management protocol (IGMP). This assumption comes from the fact that many ad hoc network protocol designers have applications such as battle field communications, sensor network communications in mind, while the Internet multicast applications are more entertainment, service-oriented.

There is also an important distinction between bursty traffic and real-time traffic, which has a huge effect on the kind of protocols we choose. While real-time traffic requires QoS support such as bandwidth reservation, data rate insurance, etc., bursty traffic could be connection-less, allowing greater flexibility in reserving network resources. Most current works focus on connection-oriented traffic, and so do we in this section.

Before designing a protocol, we have to determine all factors affecting our objective function. The one we have mentioned involves the total energy consumed by all nodes in a multicast sub-graph. However, other factors such as network life time, mobility, etc. are also important and should be taken into consideration eventually. In this section though, we shall only focus on the simplest measure of total energy consumed by a fixed-source multicast subgraph. This problem is already difficult enough, and also it is parallel to the broadcast counterpart we discussed earlier. More information on other factors could be found in [20].

4.3.1   The centralized version

The easiest approach to build a multicast sub-graph is to first build a broadcast sub-graph and *prune* it back, in much the same way as the Internet-like multicast protocol such as distance vector multicast routing protocol (DVMRP), protocol independent multicast (PIM), or multicast open shortest path first (MOSPF).

It should be noted that many authors used the term multicast tree instead of multicast sub-graph. We use "sub-graph" here to emphasize the fact that due to the wireless multicast advantage (WMA) feature induced by the omnidirectional antenna assumption, the "trees" are not necessarily trees. They become trees when forwarding paths are fixed after a particular power assignment vector has been decided up on.

Wieselthier et al. [68] have experimented the P-BIP, P-SPT, P-MST heuristics, and found out that for very small group sizes, P-SPT outperforms the other two algorithms, while for moderate to large group sizes, P-BIP performs the best. This result is quite reasonable, since SPT finds shortest paths from the source to the destination without resorting much to the WMA feature, while BIP does take into account the feature but it grows the graph "globally" without taking the group memberships into account.

Wan and Calinescu [64] have done a theoretical evaluation of these algorithms, and found out that in the worst case P-MST, P-SPT, and P-BIP have linear performance ratios in terms of the number of nodes in the network. Hence, they do not perform well theoretically. In the same paper, the authors also proposed an analog of MST for the multicast case, called the shortest path first (SPF) algorithm. The algorithm starts from the source s, grows out a set of covered nodes S with $S = \{s\}$ initially, and each time it finds a shortest path in G_S from any node in S to any uncovered node in M - the multicast members. This way, after each iteration at least a new node in M is covered. This algorithm can be done quite effectively by first running an all-pairs shortest path algorithm, such as the Floyd-Warshall algorithm [16].

Another algorithm based on Steiner minimum trees (SMT) [31] was also given in the same paper. The analog for BIP was called minimum incremental path first (MIPF), which works in much the same way as SPF, but we pick a new path which yields the least incremental power. It could be shown that both SPF and MIPF have approximation ratios at most 24, in the same spirit that MST and BIP have approximation ratios at most 12. The SMT-based algorithm, on the other hand, was shown to have approximation ratio at most $12 \left(1 + \frac{\ln 3}{2}\right)$, based on a relatively new result on SMT by Robins and Zelikovsky [53]. One drawback of the SMT algorithm is that it is quite complicated and somewhat impractical for our purpose.

Lastly, the generalized problem of MECMS$[N_d^\alpha]$ for general values of α and d have not been addressed properly at all. We know that for $d = 2$, there are constant approximation-ratio algorithms, as discussed earlier. Other than that, there is not much known at present. The only result is that of Liang [41], who showed, by a reduction to the Steiner tree problem, that it is approximatable within a factor of $O(|M|^\epsilon)$. We suspect that, like the broadcasting case, some $\ln |M|$ approximation algorithm exsits.

4.3.2   The distributed version

As we have mentioned a few times earlier, the distributed version for the multicasting problem lies in pretty much un-charted territory. One can always try to devise a distributed broadcasting protocol first and prune the graph or tree back. However, as discussed in the previous section, pruning, albeit being simple and fairly well-known, does not necessarily yield decent solution in the worst case.

On the other hand, distributizing theoretically better algorithms such as SMT, MIPF, and SPF faces a major problem of being overly complicated, or requires a lot of rounds to converge. A complicated algorithm, even when it has good performance guarantee, might negates all the positives it brings in terms of power-saving.

Given the fact that multicasting is of tremendous importance in ad hoc networks, this problem needs more attention from researchers in the near future. We have not even discussed the mobility issue, which shall make our problem ever more challenging and interesting.

5   Conclusions

Ad hoc networks are wireless networks of devices that can be set up dynamically on the fly without resorting to the existing Internet or any other network infrastructure. Ad hoc networking has enormous commercial and military potential, supporting applications such as mobile conferencing, battle field communications, sensor dust, home networking, emergency services, personal area networks and Bluetooth, embedded computing, to name a few.

In this chapter, we have introduces problems, algorithms, protocols, open problems relating to energy consumption issues in ad hoc networking. We focused on the MAC and the network layers' protocols. It can be seen that there are a lot of open problems and questions, contributing to the fact that ad hoc networking is somewhat slacking behind the fast pacing emergence of wireless networking as a whole into the communications and networking infrastructure.

The problems we have discussed are very interesting and challenging however. We expect more and more works from researchers on various fields on these problems in the near future, opening up the enormous commercial and military potential of ad hoc networks.

References

[1] S. AGARWAL, S. V. KRISHNAMURTHY, R. H. KATZ, AND S. K. DAO, *Distributed power control in ad-hoc wireless networks*, in Proceedings of the 2001 IEEE International Symposium on Personal, Indoor and Mobile Radio Communications (PIMRC), IEEE, 2001.

[2] P. ALIMONTI AND V. KANN, *Hardness of approximating problems on cubic graphs*, in Algorithms and complexity (Rome, 1997), vol. 1203 of Lecture Notes in Comput. Sci., Springer, Berlin, 1997, pp. 288–298.

[3] K. ALZOUBI, O. FRIEDER, AND P.-J. WAN, *Distributed construction of connected dominating set in wireless ad hoc networks*, in Proceedings of the Twenty-First Annual Joint Conference of the IEEE Computer and Communications Societies (INFOCOM), vol. 3, IEEE, 2002, pp. 1597–1604.

[4] K. M. ALZOUBI, P.-J. WAN, AND O. FRIEDER, *Message-optimal connected dominating sets in mobile ad hoc networks*, in Proceedings of the third ACM international symposium on Mobile ad hoc networking and computing (MOBICOM), Lausanne, Switzerland, 2002, ACM Press, pp. 157–164.

[5] N. BAMBOS, *Toward Power-Sensitive Network Architectures in Wireless Communications: Concepts, Issues, and*, IEEE Personal Communications, 5 (1998), pp. 50–59.

[6] S. BANERJEE AND A. MISRA, *Minimum energy paths for reliable communication in multi-hop wireless networks*, in Proceedings of the third ACM International Symposium on Mobile Ad Hoc Networking & Computing (MOBIHOC), Lausanne, Switzerland, 2002, ACM Press, pp. 146–156.

[7] C. BETTSTETTER, *On the minimum node degree and connectivity of a wireless multihop network*, in Proceedings of the third ACM Symposium on Mobile Adhoc Networking and Computing (MOBIHOC), Lausanne, Switzerland, June 9–11 2002, pp. 80–91.

[8] L. BUTTYAN AND J. P. HUBAUX, *Stimulating cooperation in self-organizing mobile ad hoc networks*, Tech. Rep. DSC/2001/046, EPFL-DI-ICA, August 2001.

[9] L. BUTTYN AND J.-P. HUBAUX, *Enforcing service availability in mobile ad-hoc wans*, in Proceedings of the first ACM international symposium on Mobile and ad hoc networking & computing (MOBIHOC), Boston, Massachusetts, 2000, IEEE Press, pp. 87–96.

[10] M. CAGALJ, J.-P. HUBAUX, AND C. ENZ, *Minimum-energy broadcast in all-wireless networks: NP-completeness and distribution issues*, in Proceedings of the 8th annual international conference on Mobile computing and networking (MOBICOM), Atlanta, Georgia, USA, 2002, ACM Press, pp. 172–182.

[11] I. CARAGIANNIS, C. KAKLAMANIS, AND P. KANELLOPOULOS, *New results for energy-efficient broadcasting in wireless networks*, in Proceedings of the 13th International Symposium 2002 on Algorithms and Computation (ISAAC '02), Springer Verlag, Lecture Notes in Computer Science, Nov 2002, pp. 332–343.

[12] B. CHEN, K. JAMIESON, H. BALAKRISHNAN, AND R. MORRIS, *Span: An energy-efficient coordination algorithm for topology maintenance in ad hoc wireless networks*, in Proceedings of the seventh annual international conference on Mobile computing and networking, Rome, Italy, 2001, ACM Press, pp. 85–96.

[13] V. CHVÁTAL, *A greedy heuristic for the set-covering problem*, Math. Oper. Res., 4 (1979), pp. 233–235.

[14] A. E. F. CLEMENTI, P. CRESCENZI, P. PENNA, G. ROSSI, AND P. VOCCA, *On the complexity of computing minimum energy consumption broadcast subgraphs*, in STACS 2001 (Dresden), vol. 2010 of Lecture Notes in Comput. Sci., Springer, Berlin, 2001, pp. 121–131.

[15] A. E. F. CLEMENTI, P. PENNA, AND R. SILVESTRI, *On the power assignment problem in radio networks*, Electronic Colloquium on Computational Complexity (ECCC), (2000).

[16] T. H. CORMEN, C. E. LEISERSON, R. L. RIVEST, AND C. STEIN, *Introduction to algorithms*, MIT Press, Cambridge, MA, second ed., 2001.

[17] S. DOSHI AND T. X. BROWN, *Minimum energy routing schemes for a wireless ad hoc network*, in Proceedings of the Twenty-First Annual Joint Conference of the IEEE Computer and Communications Societies (INFOCOM), vol. 2, New York, NY, June 23–27 2002, pp. 1162–1171.

[18] J. EBERT, B. STREMMEL, S. ECKHARDT, AND W. ADAM, *An energy-efficient power control approach for WLANs*, Journal of Communications and Networks (JCN), 2 (2000), pp. 197–206.

[19] T. ELBATT AND A. EPHREMIDES, *Joint scheduling and power control for wireless ad-hoc networks*, in Proceedings of the Twenty-First Annual Joint Conference of the IEEE Computer and Communications Societies (INFOCOM), vol. 2, 2002, pp. 976–984.

[20] A. EPHREMIDES, *Energy concerns in wireless networks*, IEEE Wireless Communications, 9 (2002), pp. 48–59.

[21] U. FEIGE, *A threshold of* ln n *for approximating set cover*, J. ACM, 45 (1998), pp. 634–652.

[22] R. GALLAGER, P. HUMBLET, AND P. SPIRA, *A distributed algorithm for minimum-weight snapping trees*, ACM Trans. on Prog. Lang. and Systems, 5 (1983), pp. 66–77.

[23] A. E. GAMAL, C. NAIR, B. PRABHAKAR, E. UYSAL-BIYIKOGLU, AND S. ZAHEDI, *Energy-efficient scheduling of packet transmissions over wireless networks*, in Proceedings of the Twenty-First Annual Joint Conference of the IEEE Computer and Communications Societies (INFOCOM), vol. 3, New York, NY, June 23–27 2002, pp. 1773–1782.

[24] M. R. GAREY AND D. S. JOHNSON, *Computers and intractability*, W. H. Freeman and Co., San Francisco, Calif., 1979. A guide to the theory of NP-completeness, A Series of Books in the Mathematical Sciences.

[25] GLOMOSIM. http://pcl.cs.ucla.edu/projects/glomosim/.

[26] S. GUHA AND S. KHULLER, *Improved methods for approximating node weighted Steiner trees and connected dominating sets*, Inform. and Comput., 150 (1999), pp. 57–74.

[27] C. GUO, L. C. ZHONG, AND J. M. RABAEY, *Low power distributed mac for ad hoc sensor radio networks*, in Proceedings of the 2001 Global Telecommunications Conference (GLOBECOM '01), vol. 5, IEEE, 2001, pp. 2944 –2948.

[28] J. HEE RYU, S. SONG, AND D.-H. CHO, *New clustering schemes for energy conservation in two-tiered mobile ad-hoc networks*, in Proceedings of the IEEE International Conference on Communications (ICC), vol. 3, Helsinki, Finland, Jun 2001, pp. 862–866.

[29] D. S. HOCHBAUM, ed., _Approximation Algorithms for NP Hard Problems_, PWS Publishing Company, Boston, MA, 1997.

[30] Z. HUANG, C.-C. SHEN, C. SRISATHAPORNPHAT, AND C. JAIKAEO, _Topology control mechanisms for ad hoc networks with directional antennas_, in Proceedings of the 11th International Conference on computer Communications and Networks (ICCCN), Miami, Florida, October 14-16 2002.

[31] F. K. HWANG, D. S. RICHARDS, AND P. WINTER, _The Steiner tree problem_, vol. 53 of Annals of Discrete Mathematics, North-Holland Publishing Co., Amsterdam, 1992.

[32] INTEL AND M. CORPORATIONS, _Advanced power management (APM), BIOS interface specifications rev. 1.2_, Feb 1996.

[33] M. INTEL AND T. CORPORATIONS, _Advanced configuration and power interface (ACPI) specification_, Feb 1999.

[34] D. S. JOHNSON, _Approximation algorithms for combinatorial problems_, J. Comput. System Sci., 9 (1974), pp. 256–278. Fifth Annual ACM Symposium on the Theory of Computing (Austin, Tex., 1973).

[35] C. E. JONES, K. M. SIVALINGAM, P. AGRAWAL, AND J.-C. CHEN, _A survey of energy efficient networkprotocols for wireless and mobile networks_, ACM/Baltzer Journal on Wireless Networks, 7 (2001), pp. 343–358.

[36] E.-S. JUNG AND N. H. VAIDYA, _An energy efficient mac protocol for wireless lans_, in Proceedings of the Twenty-First Annual Joint Conference of the IEEE Computer and Communications Societies (INFO-COM), vol. 3, New York, NY, June 23–27 2002, pp. 1756–1764.

[37] U. C. KOZAT, G. KONDYLIS, B. RYU, AND M. K. MARINA, _Virtual dynamic backbone for mobile ad hoc networks_, in Proceedings of the IEEE International Conference on Communications (ICC), vol. 1, Helsinki, Finland, Jun 2001, pp. 250–255.

[38] L. LI AND J. Y. HALPERN, _Minimum-energy mobile wireless networks revisited_, in Proceedings of the IEEE International Conference on Communications (ICC), vol. 1, Helsinki, Finland, Jun 2001, pp. 278–283.

[39] Q. Li, J. Aslam, and D. Rus, *Online power-aware routing in wireless ad-hoc networks*, in Proceedings of the seventh annual international conference on Mobile computing and networking (MOBICOM), Rome, Italy, 2001, ACM Press, pp. 97–107.

[40] X.-Y. Li and P.-J. Wan, *Constructing minimum energy mobile wireless networks*, ACM SIGMOBILE Mobile Computing and Communications Review, 5 (2001), pp. 55–67.

[41] W. Liang, *Constructing minimum-energy broadcast trees in wireless ad hoc networks*, in Proceedings of the third ACM international symposium on Mobile ad hoc networking & computing (MOBIHOC), Lausanne, Switzerland, 2002, ACM Press, pp. 112–122.

[42] E. L. Lloyd, R. Liu, M. V. Marathe, R. Ramanathan, and S. S. Ravi, *Algorithmic aspects of topology control problems for ad hoc networks*, in Proceedings of the third ACM international symposium on Mobile ad hoc networking & computing (MOBIHOC), Lausanne, Switzerland, 2002, ACM Press, pp. 123–134.

[43] S. Marti, T. Giuli, K. Lai, and M. Baker, *Mitigating routing misbehavior in mobile ad hoc networks*, in Proceedings of the 6th annual international conference on Mobile computing and networking (MOBICOM), EPFL Lausanne, Swizerland, August 2000, pp. 255–265.

[44] A. Misra and S. Banerjee, *MRPC: Maximizing network lifetime for reliable routing in wireless environments*, in Proceedings of IEEE Wireless Communications and Networking Conference (WCNC), vol. 1, Mar 2002, pp. 129–134.

[45] J. Monks, V. Bharghavan, and W. Hwu, *A power controlled multiple access protocol for wireless packet networks*, in Proceedings of the Twentieth Annual Joint Conference of the IEEE Computer and Communications Societies (INFOCOM), Los Alamitos, CA, Apr 22–26 2001, IEEE Computer Society, pp. 219–228.

[46] S. Narayanaswamy, V. Kawadia, R.S.Sreenivas, and P. Kumar, *Power control in ad-hoc networks: Theory, architecture, algorithm and implementation of the COMPOW protocol*, in Proceedings of European Wireless, Florence, Italy, Feb 2002, pp. 156–62.

[47] Network Simulator NS2. http://www.isi.edu/nsnam/ns/.

[48] H. Q. NGO, D. PAN, AND V. VERMA, *A class of algorithms and protocols on power-aware broadcasting in ad hoc wireless neteworks*, (2002). Preprint.

[49] C. E. PERKINS, *Ad Hoc Networking*, Pearson Education, New Jersey, USA, Dec 2000.

[50] N. POOJARY, S. V. KRISHNAMURTHY, AND S. DAO, *Medium access control in a network of ad hoc mobile nodes with heterogeneous power capabilities*, in Proceedings of the IEEE International Conference on Communications (ICC), vol. 3, Jun 2001, pp. 872–877.

[51] T. RAPPAPORT, *Wireles Communications: Principles and Practices*, Prentice Hall PTR, New Jersey, USA, second ed., Dec 2001.

[52] R. RAZ AND S. SAFRA, *A sub-constant error-probability low-degree test, and a sub-constant error-probability PCP characterization of NP*, in STOC '97 (El Paso, TX), ACM, New York, 1999, pp. 475–484 (electronic).

[53] G. ROBINS AND A. ZELIKOVSKY, *Improved Steiner tree approximation in graphs*, in Proceedings of the Eleventh Annual ACM-SIAM Symposium on Discrete Algorithms (San Francisco, CA, 2000), New York, 2000, ACM, pp. 770–779.

[54] V. RODOPLU AND T. H. MENG, *Minimum energy mobile wireless networks*, IEEE Journal on Selected Areas in Communications, 17 (1999), pp. 1333–1344.

[55] R. C. SHAH AND J. RABAEY, *Energy aware routing for low energy ad hoc sensor networks*, in Proceedings of IEEE Wireless Communications and Networking Conference (WCNC), vol. 1, Mar 2002, pp. 350–355.

[56] S. SINGH AND C. S. RAGHAVENDRA, *Pamas – power aware multi-access protocol with signalling for ad hoc networks*, ACM SIGCOMM Computer Communication Review, 28 (1998), pp. 5–26.

[57] S. SINGH, M. WOO, AND C. S. RAGHAVENDRA, *Power-Aware Routing in Mobile Ad Hoc Networks*, in the Fourth Annual ACM/IEEE International Conference on Mobile Computing and Networking, Dallas, TX, October 1998, pp. 181–190.

[58] B. SKLAR, *Digital Communications: Principles and Applications*, Prentice Hall PTR, New Jersey, USA, international ed., 1988.

[59] C. SRISATHAPORNPHAT AND C.-C. SHEN, *Coordinated power conservation for ad hoc networks*, in Proceedings of the IEEE International Conference on Communications (ICC), vol. 5, New York, NY, Apr 2002, pp. 3330–3335.

[60] M. TAKAI, J. MARTIN, AND R. BAGRODIA, *Effects of wireless physical layer modeling in mobile ad hoc networks*, in Proceedings of the second ACM International Symposium on Mobile ad hoc networking and computing (MOBIHOC), Long Beach, CA, USA, 2001, ACM Press, pp. 87–94.

[61] ——, *Effects of wireless physical layer modeling in mobile ad hoc networks*, in Proceedings of the 2001 ACM International Symposium on Mobile ad hoc networking & computing (MOBIHOC), Long Beach, CA, USA, 2001, ACM Press, pp. 87–94.

[62] C.-K. TOH, *Maximum battery life routing to support ubiquitous mobile computing in wireless ad hoc networks*, IEEE Communications Magazine, 39 (2001), pp. 138–147.

[63] Y.-C. TSENG, C.-S. HSU, AND T.-Y. HSIEH, *Power-saving protocols for ieee 802.11-based multi-hop ad hoc networks*, in Proceedings of the Twenty-First Annual Joint Conference of the IEEE Computer and Communications Societies (INFOCOM), vol. 1, New York, NY, June 23–27 2002, pp. 200–209.

[64] P.-J. WAN AND G. CALINESCU, *Minimum-energy multicast in routing in static ad hoc wireless networks*, 2001. manuscript.

[65] P.-J. WAN, G. CALINESCU, X.-Y. LI, AND O. FRIEDER, *Minimum-energy broadcast routing in static ad hoc wireless networks*, in Proceedings of the Twentieth Annual Joint Conference of the IEEE Computer and Communications Societies (INFOCOM), vol. 2, IEEE, 2001, pp. 1162–1171.

[66] R. WATTENHOFER, L. LI, P. BAHL, AND Y.-M. WANG, *Distributed topology control for power efficient operation in multihop wireless ad hoc networks*, in Proceedings of the Twentieth Annual Joint Conference of the IEEE Computer and Communications Societies (INFOCOM), vol. 3, Anchorage, Alaska, April 2001, pp. 1388–1397.

[67] D. B. WEST, *Introduction to graph theory*, Prentice Hall Inc., Upper Saddle River, NJ, 1996.

[68] J. E. WIESELTHIER, G. D. NGUYEN, AND A. EPHREMIDES, *On the construction of energy-efficient broadcast and multicast trees in wireless networks*, in Proceedings of the Nineteenth Annual Joint Conference of the IEEE Computer and Communications Societies (INFOCOM), vol. 2, IEEE, 2000, pp. 585–594.

[69] ——, *Algorithms for energy-efficient multicasting in static ad hoc wireless networks*, Mobile Networks and Applications, 6 (2001), pp. 251–263.

[70] ——, *The effect of discrete power levels on energy-efficient wireless broadcast in ad hoc networks*, in Proceedings of the 13th IEEE International Symposium on Personal, Indoor and Mobile Radio Communications, vol. 4, IEEE, 2002, pp. 1655–1659.

[71] J. WU, F. DAI, M. GAO, AND I. STOJMENOVIC, *On Calculating Power-Aware Connected Dominating Set for Efficient Routing in Ad Hoc Wireless Networks*, vol. 5, 2002, pp. 169–178.

[72] J. WU AND H. LI, *A Dominating-Set-Based Routing Scheme in Ad Hoc Wireless Networks*, Wireless Networks in the Telecommunication Systems, 3 (2001), pp. 63–84.

[73] Y. XU, J. HEIDEMANN, AND D. ESTRIN, *Geography-informed energy conservation for ad hoc routing*, in Proceedings of the 7th annual international conference on Mobile computing and networking (MOBICOM), Rome, Italy, July 2001, pp. 70–84.

[74] M. ZORZI, ed., *Energy Management in Personal Communications and Mobile Computing*, vol. 5 of IEEE Personal Communications Special Issue, IEEE, Jun 1998.

Secure Communication in Adverse Mobile Ad Hoc Networks[1]

Panagiotis Papadimitratos
School of Electrical and Computer Engineering
Cornell University, Ithaca, NY 14853
E-mail: `papadp@ece.cornell.edu`

Zygmunt J. Haas
School of Electrical and Computer Engineering
Cornell University, Ithaca, NY 14853
E-mail: `haas@ece.cornell.edu`

Contents

[1]Reprinted with permission from "Handbook of Ad Hoc Wireless Networks," chapter 31, CRC Press 2003. Copyright Zygmunt J. Haas.

1 Abstract

The vision of nomadic computing with its ubiquitous access has stimulated much interest in the Mobile Ad Hoc Networking (MANET) technology. Those infrastructure-less, self-organized networks that either operate autonomously or as an extension to the wired networking infrastructure, are expected to support new MANET-based applications. However, the proliferation of this networking paradigm strongly depends on the availability of security provisions, among other factors. The absence of infrastructure, the nature of the envisioned applications, and the resource-constrained environment pose some new challenges in securing the protocols in the ad hoc networking environments. Moreover, the security requirements can differ significantly from those for infrastructure-based networks, while the provision of security enhancements may take completely different directions as well. In particular, practically any node in the open, collaborative MANET environment can abuse the network operation and disrupt or deny communication. In this paper we introduce our approach to this multifaceted and intriguing problem: a set of protocols that secure the fundamental networking operations of routing and data transmission. Moreover, we survey solutions that address the management of trust in ad hoc networks.

2 Introduction

Mobile ad hoc networks comprise freely roaming wireless nodes that cooperatively make up for the absence of fixed infrastructure, with the nodes themselves supporting the network functionality. Nodes form transient associations with their peers that are within the radio connectivity range of their transceiver, and implicitly agree to assist in provision of the basic network services. These associations are dynamically created and torn down, often without prior notice or the consent of the communicating parties. The MANET technology targets networks that can be rapidly deployed or formed in an arbitrary environment to enable communications or to serve, in some cases, a common objective dictated by the supported application. Such networks can be highly heterogeneous, with various types of equipment, usage, transmission, and mobility patterns.

Secure communication, being an important aspect of any networking environment, becomes an especially significant challenge in ad hoc networks. This is due to the particular characteristics of this new networking paradigm and due to the fact that traditional security mechanisms may be inapplicable.

The peer-to-peer node interaction opens MANET protocols to abuse. The MANET paradigm seeks to enable communication across networks whose topology and membership may change very frequently, based on the cooperative support of the network functionality. Malicious nodes can disrupt or even deny the communications of potentially any node within their ad hoc networking domain. This is so, exactly because each and every node is not only entitled, but is, in fact, required to assist the network operation.

With migrating nodes joining and leaving MANET domains and transient associations between nodes constantly established and torn down, it is particularly difficult to distinguish which nodes are trustworthy and supportive. First, the practically invisible or non-existent administrative boundaries encumber the a priori classification of a subset of nodes as trusted. Second, it is impractical, in such a volatile communication environment, to determine which nodes can be trusted based on the network interaction - the overhead and especially the delay to make such an inference would be prohibitive, with additional overhead and complexity imposed if such inferences were to propagate in the form of recommendations or accusations. In most cases, transiently associated nodes will assist each other with the provision of basic networking services, such as route discovery and data forwarding. As a result, the nodes, or, practically the users of the devices, may have no means to establish a trust relationship, since not all mobile nodes would necessarily pursue collectively a common mission.

In other words, in mobile ad hoc networks, the particular challenge is to safeguard the correct operation of the network layer protocols. Nodes may be designated as trusted or non-trusted at the application layer - for example, access to a service or participation to its collaborative support would be allowed only to nodes that present the necessary credentials. However, only closed, mission-oriented networks could satisfy such an assumption of full trust. Thus, the reliance on trusted nodes solely would drastically narrow the scope and limit the potential of ad hoc networking.

We first outline the primary goals of security enhancements for MANET and shed light on the commensurate challenges. In Section 5 we present the Secure Routing Protocol (SRP) and the Secure Link State Protocol (SLSP), which safeguard the discovery of routing information assisted by the Neighbor Lookup Protocol (NLP). The Secure Message Transmission (SMT) protocol, which enhances the security and robustness of the data transmission, follows in Section 6. Next, we discuss approaches for managing trust in the MANET environment in Section 7, briefly survey related work in Section 8 and conclude with a discussion.

3 Security Goals

The overall problem of securing a distributed system comprises the security of the networked environment, and the security of each individual network node. The latter issue is important due to the pervasive nature of MANET, which does not allow us to assume that networked devices will always be under the continuous control of their owner. As a result, the physical security of the node becomes an important issue, leading to the requirement of tamper-resistant nodes [43], if comprehensive security is to be provided. However, security problems manifest themselves in a more emphatic manner in a networked environment, and especially in mobile ad hoc networks. This is why in this work we focus on the network-related security issues.

Security encompasses a number of attributes that have to be addressed: availability, integrity, authentication, confidentiality, non-repudiation and authorization. These goals, which are not MANET-specific only, call for approaches that have to be adapted to the particular features of MANET.

Availability ensures the survivability of network services despite misbehavior of network nodes; for instance, when nodes exhibit selfish behavior or when denial-of-service (DoS) attacks are mounted. DoS attacks can be launched at any layer of an ad hoc network. For example, an adversary could use jamming to interfere with communication at the physical layer, or, at the network layer, it could disable the routing protocol operation, by disrupting the operation of the route discovery procedure. Moreover, an adversary could bring down high-level services. One such target is the key management service, an essential service for an implementation of any security framework.

Integrity guarantees that an in-transit message is not altered. A message could be altered because of benign failures, such as radio propagation impairments, or because of malicious attacks on the network. Integrity viewed in the context of a specific connection, that is, the communication of two or more nodes, can provide the assurance that no messages are removed, replayed, re-ordered (if re-ordering would cause loss of information), or unlawfully inserted.

Authentication enables a node to ensure the identity of the peer node that it is communicating with. Without authentication, an adversary could masquerade a node, possibly gain unauthorized access to resources and sensitive information, and interfere with the operation of other nodes.

Confidentiality ensures that certain information is never disclosed to unauthorized entities. Confidentiality is required for the protection of sensitive information, such as strategic or tactical military information. However, confidentially is not restricted to user information only; routing information may also need to remain confidential in certain cases. For example, routing information might be valuable for an enemy to identify and to locate targets in a battlefield.

Non-repudiation ensures that the origin of a message cannot deny having sent the message. Non-repudiation is useful for detection and isolation of compromised nodes. When a node A receives an erroneous message from a node B, A can use this message to accuse B and to convince other nodes that B is compromised.

Finally, authorization establishes rules that define what each network node is or is not allowed to do. In many cases, it is required to determine which resources or information across the network a node can access. This requirement can be the result of the network organization, or the supported application, when, for instance, a group of nodes or a service provider wishes to regulate the interaction with the rest of the network. Another example could be when specific roles are attributed to nodes in order to facilitate the network operation.

The security of mobile ad hoc networks has additional dimensions, such as privacy, correctness, reliability, and fault-tolerance. In particular, the resilience to failures, which in our context can be the result of malicious acts, and the protection of the correct operation of the employed protocols are of critical importance and should be considered in conjunction with the security of the mobile ad hoc network.

4   Threats and Challenges

Mobile ad hoc networks are vulnerable to a wide range of active and passive attacks that can be launched relatively easily, since all communications take place over the wireless medium. In particular, wireless communication facilitates eavesdropping, especially because continuous monitoring of the shared medium, referred to as promiscuous mode, is required by many MANET protocols. Impersonation is another attack that becomes more feasible in the wireless environment. Physical access to the network is gained simply by transmitting with adequate power to reach one or more nodes in proximity, which may have no means to distinguish the transmission of an adversary from that of a legitimate source. Finally, wireless transmissions can be intercepted, and an adversary with sufficient transmission power and knowledge of the physical and medium access control layer mechanisms can obstruct its neighbors from gaining access to the wireless medium.

Assisted by these "opportunities" the wireless communication offers, malicious nodes can meaningfully alter, discard, forge, inject and replay control and data traffic, generate floods of spurious messages, and, in general, avoid complying with the employed protocols. The impact of such malicious behavior can be severe, especially because the cooperation of all network nodes provides for the functionality of the absent fixed infrastructure. In particular, as part of the normal operation of the network, nodes are transiently associated with a dynamically changing, over time, subset of their peers; that is, the nodes within the range of their transceiver, or the ones that provide routing information and implicitly agree to relay their data packets. As a result, a malicious node can obstruct the communications of potentially any node in the network, exactly because it is entitled, or, even, expected to assist in the network operation.

In addition, freely roaming nodes join and leave MANET sub-domains independently, possibly frequently, and without notice, making it difficult in most cases to have a clear picture of the ad hoc network membership. In other words, there may be no ground for an a priori classification of a subset of nodes as trusted to support the network functionality. Trust may only be developed over time, while trust relationships among nodes may also change, when, for example, nodes in an ad hoc network dynamically become affiliated with administrative domains. This is in contrast to other mobile networking paradigms, such as Mobile IP or cellular telephony, where nodes continue to belong to their administrative domain, in spite of mobility. Consequently, security solutions with static configuration would not suffice, and the assumption that all nodes can be bootstrapped with the credentials of all other nodes would be unrealistic for a wide range of MANET instances.

From a slightly different point of view, it becomes apparent that nodes cannot be easily classified as 'internal' or 'external,' that is, nodes that belong to the network or not; i.e., nodes that are expected to participate and be dedicated to supporting a certain network operation and those that are not. In other words, the absence of an infrastructure impedes the usual practice of establishing a line of defense, separating nodes into trusted and non-trusted. As a result, attacks cannot be classified as internal or external either, especially at the network layer. Of course, such a distinction could be made at the application layer, where access to a service, or participation to its collaborative support, may be allowed only to authorized nodes. In the latter example, an attack from a compromised node within the group, that is, a group node under the control of an adversary would be considered as an internal one.

The absence of a central entity makes the detection of attackers a very difficult problem, since highly dynamic large networks cannot be easily monitored. Benign failures, such as transmission impairments, path breakages, and dropped packets, are naturally a fairly common occurrence in mobile ad hoc networks, and, consequently, malicious failures will be more difficult to distinguish. This will be especially true for adversaries that vary their attack pattern and misbehave intermittently against a set of their peers that also changes over time. As a result, short-lived observations will not allow detection of the adversaries. Moreover, abnormal situations may occur frequently, because nodes behave in a selfish manner and do not always assist the network functionality. It is noteworthy that such behavior may not be malicious, but only necessary when, for example, the node shuts its transceiver down in order to preserve its battery.

Most of the currently considered MANET protocols were not originally designed to deal with malicious behavior or other security threats. Thus they are easy to abuse. Incorrect routing information can be injected by malicious nodes that respond with or advertise inexistent or stale routes and links. In addition, compromised routes, i.e., routes that are not free of malicious nodes, may be repeatedly chosen with the "encouragement" provided by the malicious nodes themselves.[2] The result being that the pair of the communicating end-nodes will experience DoS, and they may have to rely on cycles of time-out and new route discovery to find operational routes, with successive query broadcasts imposing additional overhead. Or, even

---

[2]For instance, by the malicious nodes claiming that they possess an inexpensive (short) route to the destination.

worse, the end nodes may be easily deceived for some period of time that the data flow is undisrupted, while no actual communication takes place. For example, the adversary may drop a route error message, "hiding" a route breakage, or it can corrupt both the data and their checksum, or forge network and transport layer acknowledgments.

Finally, mobile or nomadic hosts have limited computational capabilities, due to constraints stemming from the nature of the envisioned MANET applications. Expensive cryptographic operations, especially if they have to be performed for each packet and over each link of the traversed path, make such schemes implausible for the vast majority of mobile devices. Cryptographic algorithms may require computation delays ranging from one to several seconds [7, 14]. Such delays, imposed, for example, by the generation or verification of a single digital signature, affect the data rate of secure communication. But, more importantly, mobile devices become ideal targets of DoS attacks due to their limited computational resources. An adversary would generate bogus packets, forcing the device to consume substantial portion of its resources. Worse even, a malicious node with valid credentials would generate control traffic, such as route queries, at a high rate not only to consume bandwidth, but also to impose cumbersome cryptographic operations on sizable portion of the network nodes.

5 Secure Routing

The secure operation of the MANET routing protocol is of central importance, primarily because of the absence of a fixed infrastructure. Attackers can "effectively" obstruct the flow of data by systematically disrupting the discovery of routing information and thus distorting or even dictating the topology knowledge of benign nodes.

Protocols proposed to secure Internet routing share goals with MANET secure routing protocols, seeking to safeguard the correct operation of the topology discovery. However, they cannot be readily transplanted into the MANET context, since they are designed to operate in a fundamentally different networking environment. They establish a line of defense, separating the fixed routing infrastructure from all other network entities. Routers are equipped with credentials (public keys, certificates) that signify the router's authority to act within the limits of the employed protocol (e.g., advertise certain routes), and allow all routing traffic to be authenticated, not repudiated and protected from tampering [33]. Clearly, the volatility and the salient features of the MANET environment, as discussed in Section 4, impede such an approach.

Our design seeks to overcome such limitations and furthermore provide protocols applicable to a wide range of MANET instances. More specifically, we do not require that each node be able to present and validate credentials, such as public keys, for all other network nodes. In addition, the operation of our protocols does not rely on any assumption on the network membership, which may change frequently. At the same time, we do not make any assumption on the node mobility, node equipment (such as Global Positioning System (GPS)), and network size. Finally, our protocols do not rely on intrusion detection or monitoring techniques and do not assume any regularity or patterns of malicious behavior in order to identify and isolate adversarial nodes. Instead, they are capable of operating in the presence of adversaries that actively disrupt the discovery and distribution of routing information.

The scope of the proposed protocols is broadened by their ability to operate under the least restrictive assumptions. Nevertheless, differing operational conditions may call for different topology discovery approaches. First, we propose a reactive routing protocol, the Secure Routing Protocol (SRP). Additionally, a proactive protocol, the Secure Link State Protocol (SLSP), is presented. Finally, we introduce the Neighbor Lookup Protocol (NLP), which can complement and strengthen both SRP and SLSP.

NLP addresses the correctness of communication with the node's immediate neighbors, that is nodes within its transceiver range. In essence, NLP is responsible for countering attackers that exploit the wireless communication over the shared medium. Its purpose is to identify traffic that violates specific criteria, and notify the conceptually overlying routing protocol. As a result, the routing protocol discards such traffic.

The goal of both SRP and SLSP is to safeguard the acquisition of topological information by countering attacks that disrupt or exploit the route discovery operation to deny communication. In particular, they provide correct, i.e., factual, up-to-date and authentic topology information, and they robust against individual Byzantine adversaries.

5.1   The Neighbor Lookup Protocol

The Neighbor Lookup Protocol (NLP), which can be an integral part of the routing protocol, is responsible for the following tasks: (*i*) it maintains a mapping of MAC and IP layer addresses of the node's neighbors, (*ii*) it identifies potential discrepancies, such as the use of multiple IP addresses by a single data-link interface, and (*iii*) it measuring the rates at which control packets are received from each neighbor, by differentiating the traffic primarily based on MAC addresses. The measured rates of incoming control packets are provided to the routing protocol. This way, control traffic originating from nodes that selfishly or maliciously attempt to overload the network can be discarded.

Basically, NLP extracts and retains the 48-bit hardware source address for each received (overheard) frame, along with the encapsulated IP address. This requires a simple modification of the device driver [50], so that the data link address is "passed up" to the routing protocol along with each packet. With nodes operating in promiscuous mode, the extraction of such pairs of addresses from all overheard packets leads to a significant reduction in the use of the neighbor discovery and query/reply mechanisms for medium access control address resolution.

Each node updates its neighbor table by retaining both, the data-link and the network interface addresses. The mappings between the two addresses are retained in the table as long as transmissions from the corresponding neighboring nodes are overheard; a lost neighbor timeout period [3] is associated with each table entry.

NLP issues a notification to the routing protocol, according to the content of a received packet, in the event that: (i) a neighbor used an IP address different from the address currently recorded in the neighbor table, (ii) two neighbors used the same IP address (that is, a packet appears to originate from a node that may have "spoofed" an IP address), (iii) a node uses the same medium access control address as the detecting node (in that case, the data link address may be "spoofed"). Upon reception of the notification, the routing protocol discards the packet bearing the address that violated the aforementioned policies.

Each notification is used by the routing protocol to discard the corresponding transmission originating from the node suspected to be misbehaving. This is the primary goal of NLP, which can be secondarily used to identify the attacker itself. The unambiguous identification of the attacker and the later use of such information to protect the network is a particularly difficult task for MANET. Its feasibility depends on the underlying trust between nodes, among other factors. On the other hand, the prompt detection of traffic that can harm the network operation individually at each node avoids such limitations and can be readily beneficial.

---

[3]The lost neighbor timeout should be longer than the timeout periods associated with the flushing of routing information (link state, routing table entries), related to the particular neighbor.

The operation of NLP can be adjusted to the requirements of the routing protocol, by employing cryptography or not. This depends on the requirements and operation of the routing protocol. For example, in the context of SRP that assumes solely an end-to-end security association, NLP would not be expected to utilize cryptography. Nevertheless, the cryptographic operation of NLP can be orthogonal to end-to-end security associations. Such an example is SLSP, which requires a portion of its traffic to be cryptographically validated by immediate neighbors and thus strengthen NLP.

5.2 The Secure Routing Protocol

The Secure Routing Protocol (SRP) [31] for mobile ad hoc networks provides correct end-to-end routing information over an unknown, frequently changing network, in the presence of malicious nodes. We require that any two nodes that wish to employ SRP have a Security Association (SA) instantiated by a symmetric shared secret key. Communication takes place over a broadcast medium, with no need for cryptographic operations on control traffic at intermediate nodes, two factors that render the scheme efficient and scalable. SRP places the overhead on the end nodes, an appropriate choice for a highly decentralized environment, and contributes to the robustness and flexibility of the scheme.

The novelty of SRP lies in the verification of the correctness of the discovered route(s) from the route "geometry" itself. False or corrupted control traffic is discarded in parts by the end nodes, thanks to the end-to-end security association, and in parts by the intermediate benign nodes, without cryptographic processing in the latter case. Basically, route requests propagate verifiably to the sought trusted destination and route replies are returned strictly over the reversed route, as accumulated in the route request packet. Moreover, intermediate nodes do not relay route replies unless their downstream node had previously relayed the corresponding query. In order to guarantee this crucially important functionality, the interaction of the protocol with the IP-related functionality is explicitly defined. An intact reply implies that (*i*) the reported path is the one placed in the reply packet by the destination, and (*ii*) the corresponding connectivity information is correct, since the reply was relayed along the reverse of the discovered route and consists of all nodes that participated in both phases of the route discovery.

The securing of the route discovery deprives the adversarial nodes of an "effective" means to systematically disrupt the communications of their peers. Despite our minimal trust assumptions, attackers cannot impersonate the destination and redirect data traffic, cannot respond with stale or corrupted routing information, are prevented from broadcasting forged control packets to obstruct the later propagation of legitimate queries, and are unable to influence the topological knowledge of benign nodes. To that extent, SRP provides very strong assurances on the correctness of the link-level connectivity information as well. It precludes adversarial nodes from controlling multiple potential routes per source-destination pair, and from forming "dumb" relays, that is, from not placing themselves in a route whose discovery they assisted.

The security features of SRP do not undermine its efficiency, that is, the ability of nodes to quickly respond to topological changes and discover correct routes. In addition, the protocol retains its ability to operate when under attack, with adversaries actively disrupting the route discovery. Furthermore, its low cryptographic processing overhead renders SRP applicable for nodes with very limited computational resources. Finally, the reliance on the basic and widely accepted reactive route discovery mechanism (broadcasted route query packets traverse the network as the relaying intermediate nodes append their identifier (IP address)) allows SRP to naturally extend a number of existing protocols. In particular, the IERP [16] of the Zone Routing Protocol (ZRP) [17] framework, the Dynamic Source Routing (DSR) [20], and ABR [48] are protocols that can incorporate the features of SRP with minimal or limited modifications.

5.2.1   The Generation of Route Requests

A source node S maintains a query sequence number Q_{SEQ} for each destination it securely communicates with. The 32-bit Q_{SEQ} increases monotonically, for each request generated by S, and allows T to detect outdated route requests. The sequence number is initialized at the establishment of the SA and although it is not allowed to wrap around, it provides approximately a space of four billion query requests per destination. If the entire space is used, a new security association has to be established.

For each outgoing *ROUTE REQUEST*, S generates a 32-bit random Query Identifier Q_{ID}, which is used by intermediate nodes as a means to identify the request. Q_{ID} is the output of a secure pseudo-random number generator [28]; its output is statistically indistinguishable from a truly random one and is unpredictable by an adversary with limited computational power. Since intermediate nodes have limited memory of past queries, uniqueness and randomness can be efficiently achieved, by using a one-way function (e.g., SHA-1 [42] or MD5 [41]) and a small random seed as input.

This renders the prediction of the query identifiers practically impossible, and combats the following attack: malicious nodes simply broadcast fabricated requests only to cause subsequent legitimate queries to be dropped.

Along with Q_{ID} and Q_{SEQ}, the *ROUTE REQUEST* header includes a Message Authentication Code (MAC). The MAC is a 96-bit long field, generated by a keyed hash algorithm [9], which calculates the truncated output of a one-way or hash function. The one-way function input is the entire IP header, the route request packet and most importantly, $K_{S,T}$ the key shared by the two communicating nodes. However, the packet fields where the addresses of the intermediate nodes are accumulated as the packet propagates towards the destination are excluded.

The querying node regulates the rate of queries it generates in order to avoid overloading the network. It can also indicate the number of route replies per query the destination should return by including a field protected the request MAC. This value may be increased in case of a failed route discovery or when the node needs to enrich its view of the network topology.

5.2.2 The Processing of Route Requests

Nodes parse received *ROUTE REQUEST* packets to determine whether an SRP header is present. If the SRP header is not present the packet is dropped. Intermediate nodes extract the Q_{ID} value to determine if they have already relayed a packet corresponding to the same request. If not, they compare the last entry in the accumulated route to the IP datagram source address, which belongs to the neighboring node that relayed the request. Request packets are dropped in the case of a mismatch or if an NLP provides a notification that the relaying neighbor violated one of the enforced policies. Otherwise, the packet is relayed (re-broadcasted), with the intermediate node inserting its IP address.

The Q_{ID}, the source and the destination address field values are placed in the query table. In addition, intermediate nodes retain the IP addresses of their neighbors overheard forwarding (re-broadcasting) the query, in a *FORWARD LIST* associated with the query table entry. As it will be explained below, this information ensures that intermediate nodes cannot hide themselves from a discovered route.

In order to guarantee the responsiveness of the routing protocol, nodes maintain a priority ranking of their neighbors according to the rate of queries observed by NLP. The highest priority is assigned to the nodes generating (or relaying) requests with the lowest rate and vice versa. Quanta are allocated proportionally to the priorities and not serviced low-priority queries are eventually discarded. Within each class, queries are serviced in a round-robin manner.

Selfish or malicious nodes that broadcast requests at a very high rate are throttled back, first by their immediate neighbors and then by nodes farther from the source of potential misbehavior. On the other hand, non-malicious queries, that is, queries originating from benign nodes that regulate in a non-selfish manner the rate of their query generation, will be affected only for a period equal to the time it takes to update the priority (weight) assigned to a misbehaving neighbor. In the mean time, the round robin servicing of requests provides the assurance that benign requests will be relayed even amidst a "storm" of malicious or extraneous requests.

When requests arrive at the sought destination, they are validated thanks to the security binding with the querying node. First, Q_{SEQ} is compared to $S_{MAX}(S)$, the latest (highest) query sequence number received from S, within the lifetime of the S-T SA. If $Q_{SEQ} < S_{MAX}(S)$, the request is discarded as outdated or replayed. If $Q_{SEQ} \geq S_{MAX}(S)$, T verifies the integrity and authenticity of the origin of the request packet. It generates a route reply, up to the point it has responded to the number of valid requests indicated by the query packets.

5.2.3   The Generation and Processing of Route Replies

The $ROUTE$ $REPLY$ is identified by the Q_{SEQ} and Q_{ID} of the corresponding $ROUTE$ $REQUEST$. The reverse of the route accumulated in the request packet is used as the source route of the reply packet. The destination calculates, using KS,T, and appends a MAC covering the entire SRP header, and the source route of the reply packet. The reply is routed strictly along the reverse of the discovered route. This way, the source is provided with evidence that the request had reached the destination and that the reply was indeed returned along the reverse of the discovered route.

As the reply propagates along the reverse route, each intermediate relaying node check whether the source address of the $ROUTE$ $REPLY$ datagram is the same as the address of its downstream node, as reported in the reply. If not, or if and NLP notification has been received, the reply packet is discarded. Clearly, replies are discarded if the corresponding request is not previously received and relayed, that is, there is no entry in the node's query table.

Additionally, the reply packet is discarded if it originates from a node that is not listed in $FORWARD$ $LIST$. This last control practically eliminates the possibility of a "dumb" or "Byzantine" relay, if a malicious node relayed both the route request and route reply while 'hiding' itself from the discovered route. This further strengthens the defense provided by NLP, which would issue a notification upon receiving the packet that the malicious node would relay attempting to mount the attack. If NLP is employed alone, a collision at the receiver (benign node) could prevent the detection of the first stage of the attack. On the other hand, such a collision could lead to discarding a benign reply, but it ensures that the Byzantine link attack cannot be mounted. The choice of either or both countermeasures is clearly a design decision, dependent on the envisioned networking environment.

Ultimately, the source validates the reply: it first checks whether it corresponds to a pending query. Then, it suffices to validate the MAC, and extract the route from the IP source route of the *ROUTE REPLY*, which already provides the (reversed) discovered route.

5.2.4 The SRP Extension

The basic operation of SRP can be extended in order to allow for nodes, other than the destination, to provide route replies or feedback on the status of utilized routes. This may be possible if a subset of nodes share a common objective, belong to the same group G and mutually trust all the group members.

In that case, the mutual trust could be instantiated by all group members sharing a secret key K_G. In that case, a querying node can append to each query an additional MAC calculated with the group key K_G, which we call Intermediate Node Reply Token (INRT). The functionality of SRP remains as described above, with the following addition: each group member maintains the latest query identifier seen from each of its peers, and can thus validate both the freshness and origin authenticity of queries generated from other group nodes.

Nodes other than the sought destination respond to a validated request, if they have knowledge of a route to the destination in question. The replies are generated as above, except for the MAC calculation that uses KG. The correctness of such a route is conditional upon the correctness of the information provided by the intermediate node, regarding the second portion of the route. When the reply is generated by the destination, an additional $MAC(K_G, ROUTE\ REPLY)$ is appended, apart from the end-to-end $MAC(K_{S,T}, ROUTE\ REPLY)$. This would allow an intermediate node V that is part of the route and a member of the group G to utilize the discovered route suffix (i.e., the V to T part).

The INRT functionality can be provided independently from and in parallel with the one relying solely on the end-to-end security associations. For example, it could be useful for frequent intra-group communication; any two members can benefit from the assistance of their trusted peers, which may already have useful routes. Finally, the shared KG can be utilized for purposes that are beyond the discovery of routes. One example is the authentication of *ROUTE ERROR* messages, as explained below.

5.2.5   The Route Maintenance Procedure

Intermediate node that fails to deliver a data packet to the next hop generate a *ROUTE ERROR* packet which is strictly source-routed back to the source node S along the prefix of the route being reported as broken. The upstream nodes, with respect to the point of breakage, check if the source address of the *ROUTE ERROR* datagram is the same as the one of their downstream node, as reported in the broken route. If there is no NLP notification that the relaying neighbor violated one of the enforced policies, the packet is relayed towards the source.

The source node compares the source-route of the error message to the prefix of the corresponding active route. This way, it verifies that the provided route error message refers to the actual route, and that it is not generated by a node that is not part of the route. The correctness of the feedback (i.e., whether it reports an actual failure to forward a packet) cannot be verified though. As a result, a malicious node lying on a route can mislead the source by corrupting error messages generated by another node, or by masking a dropped packet as a link failure. However, this allows it to harm only the route it belongs to, something that was possible in the first place, if it simply dropped or corrupted in-transit data packets.

If the reporting intermediate node does not have a security association with the source node, *ROUTE ERROR* messages do not include a MAC. This allows an adversary that can spoof a data link address and lies within one hop of an end-to-end data flow (route) to inject a *ROUTE ERROR*. This would be possible if it impersonated a node that is part of the route. Although the NLP of the victim would issue a notification, the forged error packet would be in-transit towards the source.

Consequently, *ROUTE ERROR* messages can be used in the following cases: (*i*) an end-to-end secure mechanism is present and thus the source node can infer the status of the utilized route(s), and (*ii*) the intermediate issuing node has a security association with the source node. In case (*i*) holds but (*ii*) does not, route errors can be used in a complementary manner. For example, the Secure Message Transmission (SMT) protocol which we describe Section 6, can utilize unauthenticated *ROUTE ERROR* messages to update the 'rating' of the utilized route(s) only when the end-to-end secure feedback reports a failed transmission. In case (*ii*), an intermediate node, which is for example member of the same group as the source of the broken route, can use the group key to generate a MAC that covers the entire route error packet and its IP source route.

5.3   The Secure Link State Protocol

The Secure Link State Protocol (SLSP) for mobile ad hoc networks [34] is responsible for securing the discovery and distribution of link state information. The scope of SLSP may range from a secure neighborhood discovery to a network-wide secure link state protocol. SLSP nodes disseminate their link state updates and maintain topological information for the subset of network nodes within R hops, which is termed as their zone [38]. Nevertheless, SLSP is a self-contained link state discovery protocol, even though it draws from, and naturally fits within, the concept of hybrid routing.

Each node is equipped with a public/private key pair, namely E_V and D_V, and with a single network interface per node within a MANET domain.[4] Key certification can be provided in a number of ways, as we explain in detail in Section 7.

Nodes are identified by their IP addresses, which may be assigned by a variety of schemes, e.g., dynamically or even randomly [12, 15]. Although E_V does not need to be tied to the node's IP address, it could be beneficial to use IP addresses derived from the nodes' public keys [29]. Nodes are equipped with a one-way or hash function H and a public key cryptosystem (e.g., [40]).

To counter adversaries, SLSP protects link state update (*LSU*) packets from malicious alteration, as they propagate across the network. It disallows advertisements of non-existent, fabricated links, stops nodes from masquerading their peers, strengthens the robustness of neighbor discovery, and thwarts deliberate floods of control traffic that exhausts network and node resources.

To operate efficiently in the absence of a central key management, SLSP provides for each node to distribute its public key to nodes within its zone. Nodes periodically broadcast their certified key, so that the receiving nodes validate their subsequent link state updates. As the network topology

---

[4]To support operation with multiple interfaces, one key pair should be assigned to each interface.

changes, nodes learn the keys of nodes that move into their zone, thus keeping track of a relatively limited number of keys at every instance.

SLSP defines a secure neighbor discovery that binds each node V to its Medium Access Control (MAC) address and its IP address, and allows all other nodes within transmission range to identify V unambiguously, given that they already have E_V. Each node commits its Medium Access Control (MAC) address and its IP address, the (MAC_V, IP_V) pair, to its neighbors by broadcasting signed hello messages. Receiving nodes validate the signature and retain the information; in the case of SUCV addresses [29] the confirmation for the IP address can be done in a memory-less manner.

5.3.1   The Link State Updates

Nodes advertise the state of their incident links by broadcasting periodically signed link state updates. SLSP restricts the propagation of the LSU packets to within the zone of their origin node. Receiving nodes validate the updates, suppress duplicates, and relay previously unseen updates that have not already propagated R hops. Link state information acquired from validated LSU packets is accepted only if both nodes incident on each link advertise the same state of the link.

Link state updates are identified by the IP address of their originator and a 32-bit sequence number, which provides an ample space of approximately four billion updates. To ensure that the LSU's propagate only within the zone of its origin, i.e., R hops away, the node selects a random number X and calculates a hash chain: $X_i = H^i(X)$, $i = 1, ..., R$, $H^0(X) = X$. It places X_R and X_1 in the *zone radius* and the *hops traversed* fields of the LSU header,[5] respectively, and sets TTL equal to $R - 1$, with R placed in the R_{LSU} field. Finally, a signature is appended.

Receiving nodes check if they have the public key of the originating node, unless the key is attached to the LSU (see Section 5.3.2 below). For an LSU that has already travelled over i hops ($i = R - TTL$), if i is less than the radius of the originating node, the packet is not relayed unless $H^{R-i}(hops\ traversed)$ equals *zone radius*. Each relaying node sets *hops traversed* equal to $H(hops\ traversed)$, decrements TTL, and rebroadcasts the LSU.

The provided information is discarded after a $confirm_{LS}$ timeout, unless both nodes incident on a link report the same state. Finally, NLP notifications result in discarding an update relayed by a misbehaved node. The

---

[5]Hash chains have a wide range of applications; in the MANET context, they have been used to assist in hop count authentication [52].

flooding of the LSU packets renders the protocol resilient against malicious failures (e.g., packet dropping, alteration, or modification of the packet's *hops traversed* field). Meanwhile, the localized flooding keeps the transmission and processing overhead low.

5.3.2 The Public Key Distribution

Nodes use Public Key Distribution (PKD) packets, or attach their certified keys to LSU packets. PKD packets are flooded throughout the zone, or they may be distributed less frequently throughout an extended zone.

Alternatively, the keys can be distributed attached to LSU packets. This approach can provide for timely acquisition of the key and thus validation of routing information to nodes that move into a new zone. It can also reduce to a great extent the transmission of PKD packets, thus reducing the message complexity. On the other hand, the distribution within an extended zone can reduce the delay of validating new keys when nodes outside a zone eventually enter the zone.

Key broadcasts are timed according to the network conditions and the device characteristics. For example, a node can rebroadcast its key when it detects a substantial change of the topology of its zone; that is, if at least some percentage of nodes has departed from the node's neighborhood since the last key broadcast.

The node's certificate "vouches" for the public key. Additionally, the authenticity and freshness of the PKD packet are verified by a signature from the node that possesses and distributes the key. The PKD sequence number is set to the next available value, following the increasing values used for LSU packets. When the LSU-based key broadcast is used, no additional PKD signature is required.

Nodes validate PKD packets only if they are not already aware of the originator's public key. Upon validation, E_V and the corresponding source IP address are stored locally, along with the corresponding sequence number.[6] Each node can autonomously decide whether to validate a key broadcast or not. For example, if it communicates with a nearby destination, it might have no incentive to validate a PKD that originates from a node a large distance away. Similarly, a validation could be avoided if the node

---

[6]This information is maintained in a FIFO manner. If the entire sequence is covered, a new key is generated and distributed, after the node voluntarily remains "disconnected" for a period equal to NLP's *neighbor lost*. This temporary disconnection ensures that the possible change of the node's IP address does not cause neighbors to perceive this as a possible attack (i.e., spoofing of an IP address).

considers its topology view broad enough, or sufficient to support its communication. This could happen for a dense network or zone, when not all physically present links are necessary.

Malicious floods of spurious PKD packets are countered by several mechanisms: (*i*) NLP imposes a bottleneck thanks to the lost neighbor timeout, (*ii*) PKD packets will not propagate more than R hops, unless they are "carried" farther by adversaries (e.g., when they don't update the *hops traversed* field), (*iii*) nodes can autonomously decide whether to validate a public key or not (e.g., for an very high R), and (*iv*) PKD packets are also subject to restrictions imposed by the above-mentioned penalizing priority mechanism.

6 Secure Data Forwarding

No secure routing protocol, including SRP and SLSP, can guarantee that the nodes along a correctly discovered route will indeed relay the data as expected. An adversary may misbehave in an intermittent manner, that is, initially provide correct routing information during the route discovery stage, and later forge or corrupt data packets during the data forwarding stage.

Clearly, upper layer mechanisms, such as reliable transport protocols, or mechanisms currently assumed by MANET routing protocols, such as reliable data link or acknowledged routing, cannot cope with malicious disruptions. In fact, the communicating nodes may be easily deceived for long periods of time that the data flow is undisrupted, with no actual communication taking place.[7]

To cope with such attacks, the integrity of the exchanged traffic can be cryptographically protected. However, cryptographic protection of the data cannot shield the communication against denial of service (DoS). Compromised routes, i.e., routes that are not free of malicious nodes, may be repeatedly chosen, and to communicate nodes may have to rely on long cycles of disconnection detection and new route discovery, with the successive query broadcasts imposing additional overhead.

Below, we present a simple, efficient and effective protocol, the Secure Message Transmission (SMT) protocol, to secure the flow of data traffic in the presence of malicious nodes, after the routes between the source and the destination have been discovered. We emphasize that the goal of SMT is

---

[7]For example, the adversary can corrupt the data and their checksum, forge network or transport layer acknowledgments, or, it may drop a route error message and "hide" a route breakage.

not to securely discover routes in the network - this is achieved by protocols such as the SRP and SLSP.

6.1 The Secure Message Transmission Protocol

SMT is a secure end-to-end data forwarding protocol that safeguards the communication across an unknown frequently changing network, in the presence of adversaries [32]. SMT can counter attacks against the data transmission without network monitoring and misbehavior detection, which would impose complexity and excessive overhead to the network operation. At the same time, such an improvement is achieved without restrictive assumptions on the trust, membership and size of the network, or the types of misbehavior. As a result, SMT is a practical, broadly applicable protocol.

Furthermore, SMT is capable of supporting real-time traffic, while adapting to the frequently changing network conditions. SMT can be continuously reconfigured to provide either enhanced security and resilience, or highly efficient operation in a relatively safer environment. Finally, the proposed SMT, a network layer protocol, does not rely on restrictive assumptions on cross-layer interactions, providing a self-contained solution tailored to the MANET characteristics.

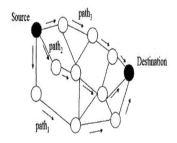

Figure 1: The Secure Message Transmission Protocol makes use of multiple diverse paths connecting the source and the destination. In particular, the Active Path Set (APS) contains paths that have not been detected as failed, either due to path breakage or because of the presence of an adversary on the path.

The basic idea behind the SMT protocol is to combine efficient end-to-end security services and a robust feedback mechanism, with dispersion of transmitted data and simultaneous usage of multiple paths. At the same time, continuous reconfiguration driven by an easy-to-implement method allows the adaptation of SMT to the requirements of the networking environment.

6.2 The SMT Operation

Our protocol determines a set of diverse routes, as shown in Figure 1. It disperses each outgoing message by introducing limited redundancy and dividing the data with the redundant information into a number of pieces. The information dispersal is based on the algorithm proposed in [39], which is in essence an error correction code.

Due to the message dispersion, the reception of a sufficient number of pieces allows successful reconstruction at the receiver's side. A low-cost cryptographic header is appended to each piece and the dispersed message is transmitted across a set of diverse, preferably node-disjoint paths. Diversity is welcome, so that a malicious node cannot harm more than one piece.

The receiver validates the incoming packets and acknowledges the successfully received packets, with the feedback cryptographically protected as well. If a sufficient number of pieces were received, the receiver reconstructs the message. Otherwise, it awaits the additional needed packets to be retransmitted by the sender. Once the message is successfully reconstructed, it is passed to the upper protocol layers.

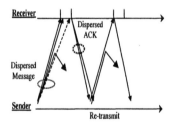

Figure 2: Simple example of the SMT protocol operation.

An illustrative example of a single message transmission is shown in Figure 2. The sender disperses the message, so that any three out of four packets are sufficient for successful reconstruction. The four packets are routed over four disjoint paths and two of them arrive intact at the receiver. The remaining two packets are compromised by malicious nodes lying on the corresponding paths; for example, one packet is dropped, and one (dashed arrow) is modified.

The receiver extracts the information from the first incoming validated packet and waits for subsequent packets, while setting a reception timer. When the fourth packet arrives, the cryptographic integrity check reveals the data tampering and the packet is rejected. At the expiration of the timer, the receiver generates an acknowledgement reporting the two successfully received packets and transmits it across the two operational paths.

It is sufficient for the sender to receive and cryptographically validate only one acknowledgement, ignoring duplicates. The two missing pieces are then retransmitted; however, one of the two packets is lost, for example, because of intermittent malicious behavior, or a benign path breakage. The receiver acknowledges the successful reception immediately, before the timer expiration, since an adequate number of packets have been received. In all cases, the sender sets a retransmission timer, so that total loss of all the message pieces or of all the acknowledgments is detected.

The two communicating end nodes make use of the Active Path Set (APS), comprising diverse paths that are not deemed failed. The sender invokes the underlying route discovery protocol, updates its network topology view, and then determines the APS for a specific destination. This model can be extended to multiple destinations, with one APS per destination. At the receiver's side, the APS is used for the feedback transmission, but if links are not bi-directional, the destination will have to determine its own "reverse" APS.

The routing decisions are made by the querying node, based on the feedback that the destination and the underlying secure routing protocol provide. At the same time, no additional processing overhead is imposed on intermediate nodes, which do not perform any cryptographic operation but simply relay the message pieces.

The dispersion of messages is coupled to the APS characteristics, and with the appropriate selection of the dispersion algorithm parameters discussed below. Once dispersed, the message pieces are transmitted across APS in cryptographically protected packets. If the message cannot be reconstructed at the destination, the source re-transmits the pieces that were not received, according to the feedback that is verifiably provided by the destination.

Message pieces are re-transmitted by SMT a maximum number of times, $Retry_{MAX}$, which is a protocol-selectable parameter. If all re-transmissions fail, the message is discarded. This way, a number of re-transmissions by SMT enhance its efficiency, by alleviating the overhead from re-transmitting the entire amount of data. On the other hand, SMT does not assume the role of a transport or application layer protocol; its goal is to promptly detect and tolerate compromised transmissions, while adapting its operation to provide secure data forwarding with low delays.

The transmission of data is continuous over the APS, with re-transmissions placed at the head of the queue upon reception of the feedback. The continuous usage of the APS allows SMT to update fast its assessment on the quality of the paths. Moreover, the simultaneous routing over a number of paths, if not the entire APS, provides the opportunity for low-cost probing of the paths. The source can easily tolerate the loss of a piece that was transmitted over a low-rated path, and the benefit from doing so can be two-fold: either the piece will be lost but the rating of a failing path will be further decreased and removed from the APS, or, the piece will be successfully received and contribute to the re-construction of the message, if an adversary lying on the path misbehaves intermittently.

6.3   The SMT Adapation

The protocol can continuously adapt its configuration in order to achieve both enhanced robustness in a highly adverse environment and efficiency in low-risk conditions. The adaptation of SMT takes into consideration the network state and the requirements of the supported application.

Intuitively, path diversity is the primary goal to meet in order to provide increased protection by disallowing any single malicious node to compromise more than one data flow. In general, the sender needs to determine a sufficiently high number of paths in order for the dispersed message to be successfully received. Although this is the most obvious solution, one cannot expect that in every occasion a high number of paths will be found. In low connectivity conditions (small number of disjoint paths), the sender could increase the transmission redundancy in order to provide increased assurance.

More specifically, the protocol adaptation is the result of the interplay among the following parameters: (i) K, the (sought) cardinality of the APS, (ii) k, the (S,T)-connectivity, i.e., the maximum number of $S \rightarrow T$ node-disjoint paths from the source (S) to the destination (T), (iii) r, the redundancy factor of the information dispersal, and (iv) x, the maximum number of malicious nodes.

If we assume that no more than $X\%$ of the nodes may act maliciously at any time instance, then $x = X \times a$, with the number of network nodes denoted by a. In particular, nodes may either estimate or be given an estimate or prediction of the percentage of malicious nodes, which can be viewed as the probability that any single node is malicious. Instead of a, a node can use the number of nodes in its topology view.

If M out of N transmitted packets are required for successful transmission, $r = N/M$, and, for an allocation of one piece per path, K should be at least N. The larger K is, the higher the number of faults that can be tolerated. Equivalently, the higher x is, the larger K should be for a fixed r. For an APS of K paths, the required number of packets is K/r. The relationship among the interacting parameter values is shown by the condition for successful reception, which is $x \leq \lceil K \times (1 - r^{-1}) \rceil$.

Our protocol adapts its operation as follows: K, the required number of paths, is determined as a function of r, so that the probability of successful transmission is maximized. In order to do so, the source starts by constructing an APS of k node-disjoint paths, depending on the actual node connectivity of its topology view. This can be done by constructing k node-disjoint paths connecting the two end nodes, using an algorithm such as [46] with the number of hops as cost, so that the shortest k-path set has the minimum sum of the path lengths. Alternatively, a minimum-cost maximum-flow algorithm [1] with unit node capacities and a fixed goal of k paths can yield the same result. We should note that other cost measures could be used as well.

Then, let P_{GOAL} be the target probability of successful reconstruction of a dispersed message. P_{GOAL} can be provided from the application layer and correspond to the features of the supported application for example. The source determines the sought number of paths and redundancy factor to achieve a secure transmission. The calculation of the probability of success as a function of r and K can use the approximation provided in [43]. Given P_{GOAL} and k, the node calculates the corresponding redundancy factor, r_{GOAL}. Then, outgoing messages are dispersed with the redundancy value closest or equal to r_{GOAL}. Note that the source may achieve similar results with different values of M and N, a flexibility that is proven valuable.

If $N < k$, the node selects the N paths of the APS with the highest rating. Similarly, the few first most highly rated paths are selected for retransmissions, that is, transmission of fewer than M pieces. As this process continues, paths will be deemed failed, thus reducing k. Then, the node repeats the above-mentioned algorithm.

On the other hand, if $k \ll K$, then the sender can enhance the resilience of the communication by determining additional, partially disjoint paths.

Given a set of k node-disjoint paths, additional $K - k$ paths can be calculated, partially overlapping with the node-disjoint ones. If less than k malicious nodes lie on the selected paths, at least one or more packets will reach the destination. For any additional non-disjoint path, the number of faulty paths that can be tolerated increases in practice, but no guarantee can be provided for the worst case, without knowing the actual overlapping information. If the adversarial nodes constitute a cut of cardinality C_X, the result would be either a partitioned network ($C_X \geq k$) as seen by S and T, or a mere failure to reconstruct the message at the receiver ($C_X \geq k - M$).

While transmitting across the APS, the source updates the rating of the paths. For each successful or failed piece, the rating of the corresponding path is increased or decreased, respectively. When the rating drops below a threshold, the path is discarded, which implies that its constituent links are discarded as well. This last procedure implies that the determination of the APS by SMT is performed in parallel and it can contribute to the update of the topology view of the node. The reverse interaction is also possible, if for example route error messages are taken into consideration, in a complementary manner, to update the path rating. Furthermore, an alternative implementation could reduce a metric for each of the path's constituent links, when it is removed from APS, and discard links only when their metric drops below a threshold. We should note that in all cases it is desirable to promptly discard connectivity that corresponds to non-operational paths.

7 Trust Management

The use of cryptographic techniques is necessary for the provision of any type of security services, and mobile ad hoc networks are not an exception to this rule. The definition and the mechanisms for security policies, credentials, and trust relationships, i.e., the components of what is collectively identified as trust management, are a prerequisite for any security scheme. A large number of solutions have been presented in the literature for distributed systems, but they cannot be readily transplanted into the MANET context, since they rely on the existence of network hierarchy and on the existence of a central entity. Envisioned applications for the ad hoc networking environment may require a completely different notion of establishing a trust relationship, while the network operation may impose additional obstacles to the effective implementation of such solutions.

For small-scale networks, of the size of a personal or home network, trust can be established in a truly ad hoc manner, with relationships being static and sporadically reconfigured manually. In such an environment, the owner of a number of devices or appliances can imprint them, that is, distribute their credentials along with a set of rules that determine the allowed interaction with and between devices [43]. The proposed security policy follows a master-slave model, with the master device being responsible for reconfiguring slave devices, issuing commands or retrieving data. The return to the initial state can be done only by the master device, or by some trusted key escrow service.

This model naturally lends itself to represent personal area networking, in particular network instances such as Bluetooth [6], in the sense that within a Piconet the interactions between nodes can be determined by the security policy. The model can be extended by allowing partial control or access rights to be delegated, so that the secure interaction of devices becomes more flexible [44]. However, if the control over a node can be delegated, the new master should be prevented from eradicating prior associations and assuming full control of the node.

A more flexible configuration, independent of initial bindings, can be useful when a group of people wish to form a collaborative computing environment [13]. In such a scenario, the problem of establishing a trust relationship can be solved by a secure key agreement, so that any two or more devices are able to communicate securely. The mutual trust among users allows them to share or establish a password using an off-line secure channel or perform a "pre-authentication" step through a localized channel [3]. Then, they can execute a password-based authenticated key exchange over the insecure wireless medium. Schemes that derive a shared symmetric key could use a two- or a multi-party version of the password authenticated Diffie-Hellman key-exchange algorithm [4, 11].

The human judgment and intervention can greatly facilitate the establishment of spontaneous connectivity among devices. Users can select a shared password or manually configure the security bindings between devices, as seen above. Furthermore, they could assess subjectively the 'security' of their physical and networking environment and then proceed accordingly. However, human assistance may be impossible for the envisioned MANET environment with nodes acting as mobile routers, even though the distinction between an end device and a router may be only logical, with nodes assuming both roles. Frequently, the sole requirement for two transiently associated devices will be to mutually assist each other in the provision of basic networking services, such as route discovery and data forwarding. This could be so since mobile nodes do not necessarily pursue collectively a common goal. As a result, the users of the devices may have no means to establish a trust relationship in the absence of a prior context.

There is no reason to believe that a more general trust model would not be required in the MANET context. For instance, a node joining a domain may have to present its credentials in order to access an available service, and, at the same time, authenticate the service itself. Similarly, two network nodes may wish to employ a secure mode of, possibly multi-hop, communication and verify each other's identity. Clearly, support for such types of secure interaction, either at the network or at the application layer, will be needed.

A public key cryptosystem can be a solution, with each node bound to a pair of keys, one publicly known and one private. However, the deployment of a public key infrastructure (PKI) requires the existence of a certification authority (CA), a trusted third party responsible for certifying the binding between nodes and public keys. The use of a single point of service for key management can be a problem in the MANET context, especially because such a service should always remain available. It is possible that network partitions or congested links close to the CA server, although they may be transient, cause significant delays in getting a response. Moreover, in the presence of adversaries, access to the CA may be obstructed, or the resources of the CA node may be exhausted by a DoS attack. One approach is not to rely on a CA and thus abolish all the advantages of such a facility. Another approach is to instantiate the CA in a way that answers the particular challenges of the MANET environment.

The former approach can be based on the bootstrapping of all network nodes with the credentials of every other node. However, such an assumption would dramatically narrow the scope of ad hoc networking, since it can be applied only to short-lived mission-oriented and thus closed networks. An additional limitation may stem from the need to ensure a sufficient level of security, which implies that certificates should be refreshed from time to time, requiring, again, the presence of a CA.

Alternatively, it has been suggested that users certify the public keys of other users. One such scheme proposes that any group of K nodes may provide a certificate to a requesting node. Such a node broadcasts the request to its one-hop neighborhood, each neighbor provides a partial certificate, and if sufficient K such certificates are collected, the node acquires the complete certificate [53, 24]. Another scheme proposes that each node selects a number of certificates to store, so that, when a node wants the public key of one of its peers, the two certificate repositories are merged, and if a chain of certificates is discovered, the public key is obtained [19].

The solution of a key management facility that meets the requirements of the MANET environment has been proposed in [53]. To do so, the proposed instantiation of the public key infrastructure provides increased availability and fault-tolerance. The distributed certification authority (CA) is equipped with a private/public key pair. All network nodes know the public key of the CA, and trust all certificates signed by the CA's private key. Nodes that wish to establish secure communication with a destination, query the CA and retrieve the required certificate, thus being able to authenticate the other end, and establish a secret shared key for improved efficiency. Similarly, nodes can request an update from the CA, that is, change their own public key and acquire a certificate for the new key.

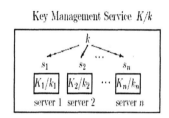

Figure 3: The configuration of a key management service comprising n servers. The service, as a whole, has a public/private key pair K/k. The public key is known to all nodes in the network, whereas the private key k is divided into n shares $s_1, s_2, \ldots s_n$, with one share for each server. Moreover, each server has a public/private key pair K_i/k_i and knows the public keys of all nodes. Reprinted with permission from [L. Zhou and Z.J. Haas. "Securing Ad Hoc Networks," *IEEE Network Magazine,* vol. 13, no. 6, November/ December 1999] ©1999 IEEE.

The CA is instantiated by a set of nodes (servers), as shown in Figure 3, for enhanced availability. However, this is not done through nave replication, which would increase the vulnerability of the system, since the compromise of a single replica would be sufficient for the adversary to control the CA. Instead, the trust is distributed among a set of nodes, which share the key management responsibility. In particular, each of the n servers has its own pair of public/private key and they collectively share the ability to sign certificates. This is achieved with the use of threshold cryptography, which allows any $t+1$ out of n parties to perform a cryptographic operation, while t parties cannot do so. To accomplish this, the private key of the service, as a whole, is divided into n shares, with each of the servers holding one share. When a signature has to be computed, each server uses its share and generates a partial signature. All partial signatures are submitted to a combiner, a server with the special role to generate the certificate signature out of the collected partial signatures, as shown in the example of Figure 3. This is possible only with at least $t+1$ valid partial signatures.

The application of threshold cryptography provides protection from compromised servers, since more than t servers have to be compromised before it assumes control of the service. If less than $t+1$ servers are under the control of an adversary, the operation of the CA can continue, since purposefully invalid partial signatures, 'contributed' by rogue servers, will be detected. Moreover, the service provides the assurance that the adversary will not be able to compromise enough servers over a long period of time. This is done with the help of share refreshing, a technique that allows the servers to calculate new shares from the old ones without disclosing the private key of the service. The new shares are independent from the older ones and cannot be combined with the old shares in an attempt to recover the private key of the CA. As a result, to compromise the system, all t+1 shares have to be compromised within one refresh period, which can be chosen appropriately short in order to decrease vulnerability. The vulnerability can be decreased even further, when a quorum of correct servers detects compromised or unavailable servers and re-configures the service, that is, generates and distributes a new set of n' shares, $t'+1$ of which need be combined now to calculate a valid signature. It is noteworthy that the public/private key pair of the service is not affected by share refreshing and re-configuration operations, which are transparent to all clients.

The threshold cryptography key management scheme can be adapted further by selecting different configurations of the key management service for different network instances. For example, the numbers of servers can be selected according to the size or the rate of membership changes of the network; for a large number of nodes within a large coverage area, the number of servers should also be large, so that the responsiveness of the service can be high. Nodes will tend to interact with the closest server, which can be only a few hops away, or with the server that responds with the least delay. Another possibility is to alternate among the servers within easy reach of the client, something that can happen naturally in a dynamically changing topology. This way, the load from queries and updates will be balanced among different servers, and the chances of congestion near one

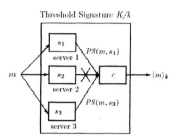

Figure 4: The calculation of a threshold signature. As an example, the service consists of three servers a $(3, 2)$ threshold cryptography scheme. K/k is the public/private key pair of the service and each server has a share s_i of the service private key. To calculate the threshold signature on a message m, each server generates a partial signature $PS(m, s_i)$ and correct servers 1 and 3 forward their signatures to a combiner c. Even though server 2 fails to submit a partial signature, c is able to generate the signature $< m >_k$ of m signed by service private key k. Reprinted with permission from [L. Zhou and Z.J. Haas. "Securing Ad Hoc Networks," *IEEE Network Magazine,* vol. 13, no. 6, November/ December 1999] ©1999 IEEE.

of the servers will be reduced. At the same time, the storage requirements can be traded off for inter-server communication, by storing at each server a fraction of the entire database.

Additionally, the efficient operation of the CA can be enhanced, when it is combined with secure route discovery and data forwarding protocols. Such protocols could, in fact, approximate the assumption of reliable links between servers in [47] even in the presence of adversaries. In particular, the above-discussed protocols SRP, SLSP and SMT, lend themselves naturally to this model. Any two servers [8] can discover and maintain routes to each other, and forward service-related traffic, regardless of whether intermediate nodes are trusted or not.

---

[8] Any two servers of the key management service have a mutual security binding.

8 Related Work

A number of secure routing protocols for MANET have appeared in the literature and are related to our protocols. They fall mainly into two categories: solutions that target to secure the route discovery, or solutions to mitigate malicious or selfish behavior regarding the forwarding of data.

In the former category, it has been proposed to tackle the protection of the route discovery by classifying nodes into different trust and privilege levels [51]. At each trust level, nodes share symmetric encryption and decryption keys to provide protection (e.g., integrity) of the routing protocol traffic against adversaries outside a specific trust level.

A number of works proposed the enhancement of existing MANET routing protocols with cryptographic primitives. Such schemes require that each node has obtained and trusts the credentials of all other nodes in the network.

It has been proposed to extend the Ad Hoc On-demand Distance Vector (AODV) routing protocol [36] with public key signatures. [52] authenticates control traffic at each relaying and utilizes a hash chain mechanism to protect the path length (hop count). [10] proposes an onion-like digital signature scheme to protect control traffic and a two-phase discovery of possibly the shortest path to the destination.

The authentication of all nodes that relay control traffic has also been proposed to secure the route discovery of the DSR protocol [18]. The scheme utilizes a broadcast authentication technique, which was initially introduced for the protection of multicast traffic flows, and requires that all nodes are equipped with synchronized clocks.

Secure link state routing protocols proposed for the "wired" Internet bear resemblance to SLSP but have additional requirements or features pertinent to the fixed-infrastructure routing. For example, [36] utilizes a robust flooding protocol and a central entity to distribute all keys throughout the network, along with the reliable flooding of link state updates throughout the entire network. [30] enhances the security of OSPF and seeks to synchronize the topology maps across all nodes or to support the full exchange of link state databases. [35] provides nodes with credentials to prove their authorization to advertise specific routing information due to the continuously changing network connectivity and membership. Finally, a number of non-link state protocols, which we review in [33], authorize the participation of nodes in routing based on their possession of credentials.

The Internet security architecture (IPsec) [21] provides authentication and integrity [22], confidentiality [23], or their combination, in addition to a framework [27] for the establishment of keys for the participating entities. The IPsec protocols that assume the existence of a fixed routing infrastructure may not be applicable to MANET. [9] Nevertheless, the goals such as the end-to-end protection of packets, and in particular, authentication, integrity and replay protection apply equally to the MANET context as well.

Transport layer protocols such as [45] relies on the services of IPsec and bear some remote resemblance to SMT. Another transport protocol [5], which utilizes the Information Dispersal Algorithm (IDA) [39] to introduce redundancy, protects against dropped ATM (Asynchronous Transfer Mode) cells to avoid TCP segments to be dropped.

As for security solutions targeting MANET, it has been proposed to detect misbehaving nodes and report such events to the rest of the network [26]. [8] takes the same direction, but, additionally, all nodes are assumed capable to authenticate traffic from all other network nodes. Both of the two previously mentioned schemes seek to detect the misbehaving nodes, i.e., nodes that do not forward packets. Similarly, [2] proposes to test each utilized path, after a threshold rate of failures has been observed, to determine where the failure occurred, without exchanging alerts. A different approach [9] provides incentive to nodes, so that they comply with protocol rules and properly relay user data.

9 Discussion

The fast development of the mobile ad hoc networking technology over the last few years, with satisfactory solutions to a number of technical problems, supports the vision of widely deployed mobile ad hoc networks with self-organizing features and without the necessity of a pre-existing infrastructure. In this context, the secure operation of such infrastructure-less networks becomes a primary concern. Nevertheless, the provision of security services is dependent on the characteristics of the supported application and the networked environment, which may vary significantly. At one extreme, we can think of a library or an Internet caf, which provide short-range wireless connectivity to patrons, without any access constraint other than the location of the mobile device. At the other extreme, a military or law enforcement unit can make use of powerful mobile devices, capable to per-

---

[9]The "Router Implementation" of IPsec does not make sense within a MANET domain. Similarly, the "Tunnel Mode" will not be applicable, unless a master/slave association exists (e.g., Bluetooth [6]), even though the dependent devices would be practically invisible at the routing layer.

form expensive cryptographic operations. Such devices would communicate only with the rest of the other trusted devices.

Between these two ends of the spectrum, a multitude of MANET instances will provide different services, assume different modes of interaction and trust models, and admit solutions such as the ones surveyed above. However, it is probable that instead of a clear-cut distinction among network instances, devices and users with various security requirements will coexist in a large, open, frequently changing ubiquitous network.

The circumstantial co-existence of disparate nodes, or the requirement of fine-grained trust relationships call for solutions that can adapt to specific context and support the corresponding application. However, although the requirements of the application are expected to dictate the characteristics of the required security mechanisms, some aspects of security, such as confidentiality, may not be different at all in the MANET context. Instead, the greatest challenge is to safeguard the basic network operation.

In particular, the securing of the network topology discovery and data forwarding is a prerequisite for the secure operation of mobile ad hoc networks in any adverse environment. Additionally, the protection of the functionality of the networking protocols will be in many cases orthogonal to the security requirements and the security services provided at the application layer. For example, a transaction can be secured when the two communicating end nodes execute a cryptographic protocol based on established mutual trust, with the adversary being practically unable to attack the protocol. But this does not imply that the nodes are secure against denial of service attacks; the adversary can still abuse the network protocols, and in fact, do it with little effort compared to the effort needed to compromise the cryptographic protocol.

The self-organizing networking infrastructure has to be protected against misbehaving nodes, with the use of low-cost cryptographic tools, under the least restrictive trust assumptions. Moreover, the overhead stemming from such security measures should be imposed mostly, if not entirely, on nodes that communicate in a secure manner and that directly benefit from these security measures. Furthermore, we believe that the salient MANET features and the unique operational requirements of these networks call for security mechanisms that are primarily present at, and closely interwoven with, the network-layer operation, in order to realize the full potential of this promising new technology.

10 Acknowledgements

This work has been supported in part by the DoD Multidisciplinary University Research Initiative (MURI) program administered by the Office of Naval Research under the grant number N00014-00-1-0564, the DoD Multidisciplinary University Research Initiative (MURI) program administered by the Air Force Office of Scientific Research under the grant number F49620-02-1-0233, and by the National Science Foundation grant number ANI-9980521.

References

[1] R.K. Ahuja, T.L. Magnati, and J.B. Olin, "Network Flows," *Prentice Hall,* Upper Saddle River, NJ, 1993

[2] B. Awerbuch, D. Holmer, C. Nita-Rotaru and H. Rubens, "An On-Demand Secure Routing Protocol Resilent to Byzantine Failures," in Proceedings of the *ACM Workshop on Wireless Security,* Atlanta, GA, Sept. 2002

[3] D. Balfanz, D.K. Smetters, P. Stuart, and H.C. Wang, "Talking to Strangers: Authentication in Ad Hoc Networks," in Proceedings of the *Network and Distributed System Security Symposium (NDSS),* San Diego, CA, Feb. 2002

[4] S.M. Bellovin and M. Merritt, "Encrypted Key Exchange: Password-based protocols secure against dictionary attacks," in Proceedings of the *IEEE Symposium on Security and Privacy,* Oakland, CA, May 1992

[5] A. Bestavros and G. Kim, "TCP-Boston: A Fragmentation-Tolerant TCP Protocol for ATM networks," in Proceedings of the *IEEE Infocom 1997,* Kobe, Japan, Apr. 1997

[6] Bluetooth Special Interest Group, "Specifications of the Bluetooth System," *http://www.bluetooth.com*

[7] M. Brown, D. Cheung, D. Hankerson, J.L. Hernadez, M. Kirkup and A. Menezes, "PGP in Constrained Wireless Devices," in Proceedings of the *9th USENIX Symposium,* Denver, CO, Aug. 2000

[8] S. Buchegger and J.Y. LeBoudec, "Performance Evaluation of the CONFIDANT protocol," in Proceedings of the *Third ACM International Symposium on Mobile Ad Hoc Networking and Computing (Mobihoc),* Lausanne, Switzerland, Jun. 2002

[9] L. Buttyan and J.P. Hubaux, "Enforcing Service Availability in Mobile Ad Hoc WANs," in Proceedings of the *First ACM International Symposium on Mobile Ad Hoc Networking and Computing (Mobihoc)*, Boston, MA, Aug. 2000

[10] B. Dahill, B.N. Levine, E. Royer and C. Shields, "A Secure Routing Protocol for Ad Hoc Networks," *Technical Report UM-CS-2001-037*, Dept. of EE and CS, Univ. of Michigan, August 2001

[11] W. Diffie and M.E. Hellman, "New directions in cryptography," *IEEE Transactions in Information Theory*, Vol IT-22, No 6, p. 644-654, 1976

[12] R. Droms, "Dynamic Host Configuration Protocol," *IETF RFC 2131*, Mar. 1997

[13] L.M. Feeney, B. Ahlgren and A. Westerlund, "Spontaneous Networking: An Application-Oriented Approach to Ad Hoc Networking," *IEEE Communications Magazine*, vol. 39, No. 6, p. 176-181, Jun. 2001

[14] V. Gupta and S. Gupta, "Securing the Wireless Internet," *IEEE Communications Magazine*, p. 68-74, December 2001

[15] M. Hattig, Editor, "Zero-conf IP Host Requirements," *draft-ietf-zeroconf-reqts-09.txt*, IETF MANET Working Group, Aug. 31st, 2001

[16] Z.J. Haas, M.R. Pearlman, P. Samar, "The Interzone Routing Protocol (IERP) for Ad Hoc Networks," *draft-ietf-manet-zone-ierp-02.txt*, IETF MANET Working Group, Jul. 2002

[17] Z.J. Haas, M.R. Pearlman, P. Samar, "The Zone Routing Protocol (ZRP) for Ad Hoc Networks," *draft-ietf-manet-zrp-02.txt*, IETF MANET Working Group, Jul. 2002

[18] Y.C. Hu, A. Perrig and D. Johnson, "Ariadne: A Secure on demand routing protocol," in Proceedings of the *The Eighth Annual International Conference on Mobile Computing and Networking (Mobicom)*, Atlanta, GA, Sept. 2002

[19] J.P. Hubaux, L. Buttyan and S. Capkun, "The quest for security in mobile ad hoc networks," in Proceeding of the *Second ACM International Symposium on Mobile Ad Hoc Networking and Computing (Mobihoc)*, San Diego, CA, Oct. 2001

[20] D. Johnson et al, "The Dynamic Source Routing Protocol," *draft-ietf-manet-dsr-07.txt*, IETF MANET Working Group, Jul. 2002

[21] S. Kent and R. Atkinson, "Security Architecture for the Internet Protocol," *IETF RFC 2401*, Nov. 1998

[22] S. Kent and R. Atkinson, "IP Authentication Header," *IETF RFC 2402*, Nov. 1998

[23] S. Kent and R. Atkinson, "IP Encapsulating Security Payload," *IETF RFC 2406*, Nov. 1998

[24] J. Kong, P. Zerfos, H. Luo, S. Lu and L. Zhang, "Providing Robust and Ubiquitous Security Support for Mobile Ad-Hoc Networks," in Proceedings of the *IEEE International Conference on Network Protocols (ICNP)2001*, Riverside, CA, Nov. 2001

[25] L. Lamport, "Password Authentication with Insecure Communication," *Communications of the ACM*, 24 (11), pp. 770-772, Nov. 1981

[26] S. Marti, T.J. Giuli, K. Lai and M. Baker, "Mitigating Routing Misbehavior in Mobile Ad Hoc Networks," in Procedings of the *The Sixth Annual International Conference on Mobile Computing and Networking (Mobicom)* Boston, MA, Aug. 2000

[27] D. Maughan, M. Schertler, M. Schneider and J. Turner, "Internet Security Association and Key Management Protocol," *IETF RFC 2408*, Nov. 1998

[28] A. Menezes, P.V. Oorschot and S. Vanstone, "Handbook of Applied Cryptography," *CRC Press*, Oct. 1996 (5th reprinting Aug. 2001)

[29] G. Montenegro and C. Canstellucia, "SUCV Identifiers and Addresses," *draft-montenegro-sucv-02.txt*, Internet Engineering Task Force (IETF), Jul. 2002

[30] S. Murphy et al, "Retrofitting Security into Internet Infrastructure Protocols," in Proceedings of the *DARPA Information Survivability Conference and Exposition (DISCEX'00)*, 2000

[31] P. Papadimitratos and Z.J. Haas, "Secure Routing for Mobile Ad Hoc Networks," in Proceedings of the *SCS Communication Networks and Distributed Systems Modeling and Simulation Conference (CNDS 2002)*, San Antonio, TX, Jan. 2002

[32] P. Papadimitratos and Z.J. Haas, "Secure Message Transmission in Mobile Ad Hoc Networks," *Submitted for publication*

[33] P. Papadimitratos and Z.J. Haas, "Securing the Internet Routing Infrastructure" *IEEE Communications Magazine,* Vol. 40, No. 10, Oct. 2002

[34] P. Papadimitratos and Z.J. Haas, "Secure Link State Routing for Mobile Ad Hoc Networks" in Proceedings of the *IEEE CS Workshop on Security and Assurance in Ad hoc Networks, (in conjunction with the 2003 International Symposium on Applications and the Internet),* Orlando, FL, Jan. 2003

[35] C. Partridge et al, "FIRE: flexible Intra-AS routing environment," *ACM SIGCOMM Computer Comm. Review,* Vol. 30, Issue 4, Aug. 2000

[36] C.E. Perkins, E.M. Royer and S.R. Das, "Ad hoc On-Demand Distance Vector Routing," *draft-ietf-manet-aodv-08.txt,* IETF MANET Working Group, Jun. 2001

[37] R. Perlman, "Interconnections: Bridges, Router, Switches and Internetworking Protocols," *Addisson-Wesley,* 2000

[38] M.R. Pearlman and Z.J. Haas, "Determining the Optimal Configuration of for the Zone Routing Protocol," *IEEE JSAC, special issue on Ad-Hoc Networks,* vol. 17, no.8, Aug. 1999

[39] M.O. Rabin, "Efficient Dispersal of Information for Security, Load Balancing, and Fault Tolerance." *Journal of ACM,* Vol. 36, No. 2, pp. 335-348, Apr. 1989

[40] R. Rivest, A. Shamir and L. Adleman, "A method for obtaining Digital Signatures and Public Key Cryptosystems," *Communications of the ACM,* Vol. 21, No 2, pp. 120-126, Feb. 1978

[41] R. Rivest, "The MD5 Message-Digest Algorithm," *IETF RFC 1321,* Apr. 1992

[42] "Secure Hash Standard," *Federal Information Processing Standard,* FIPS 180-2, Aug. 2002

[43] F. Stajano and R. Anderson, "The Resurrecting Duckling: Security Issues for Ad Hoc Wireless Networks," in Proceedings of the *7th International Workshop on Security Protocols,* LNCS, Springer-Verlag, 1999

[44] F. Stajano, "The Resurrecting Duckling - What next?" in Proceedings of the *8th International Workshop on Security Protocols*, LNCS, Springer-Verlag, 2000

[45] R. Stewart et al, "Stream Control Transmission Protocol," *IETF RFC 2960*, Oct. 2000

[46] J.W. Suurballe, "Disjoint Paths in a Network," *Networks*, vol. 4, p. 125-145, 1974

[47] S. Thomson and T. Narten, "IPv6 Stateless Address Autoconfiguration," *IETF RFC 2462*, Dec. 1998

[48] C.K. Toh, "Associativity-Based Routing for Ad-Hoc Mobile Networks," *Wireless Personal Communications*, Vol. 4, No. 2, pp. 1-36, Mar. 1997

[49] A. Tsirigos and Z.J. Haas, "Multipath Routing in the Presence of Frequent Topological Changes," *IEEE Communications Magazine*, p. 132-138, Nov. 2001

[50] G.R. Wright and W. Stevens, "TCP/IP Illustrated, vol.2, the implementation." *Addison-Wesley*, Feb. 1997

[51] S. Yi, P. Naldurg and R. Kravets, "Security-Aware Ad-Hoc Routing for Wireless Networks," *Technical Report UIUCDCS-R-2001-2241*, Aug. 2001

[52] M.G. Zapata and N. Asokan, "Securing Ad hoc Routing Protocols," in Proceedings of the *ACM Workshop on Wireless Security*, Atlanta, GA, Sept. 2002

[53] L. Zhou and Z.J. Haas, "Securing Ad Hoc Networks," *IEEE Network Magazine*, vol. 13, no.6, Nov./Dec. 1999

AD HOC WIRELESS NETWORKING
X. Cheng, X. Huang and D.-Z. Du (Eds.) pp. 487 - 528

The Role of Proactivity in Wireless and Ad Hoc Networks

Dhananjay S. Phatak
Department of Computer Science and Electrical Engineering
University of Maryland Baltimore County, Baltimore, MD 21250
E-mail: phatak@umbc.edu

Tom Goff
Department of Computer Science and Electrical Engineering
University of Maryland Baltimore County, Baltimore, MD 21250
E-mail: tgoff1@umbc.edu

Contents

This work was supported in part by NSF grants ECS-9875705 and CDA 800828.
Portions of this work have appeared in [1], [2], and [3].

1   Introduction

The vast strides made in VLSI technology and the emergence of the Internet
as a global communication infrastructure undoubtedly rank amongst the
most profound developments of recent times. Advances in VLSI have made
computer hardware faster, cheaper, smaller, and lighter with each passing
year. Not only has this made computers more useful and affordable, it has
also made them easily portable so that more and more people are beginning
to carry them (in the form of PDAs, electronic organizers or notebooks,
web-enabled cell-phones, etc.) on an almost permanent basis.

  We have already witnessed a shift in computing paradigm from institu-
tional, where only institutions could afford computers and they were shared
among many users, to personal, where individuals can afford and do have
their own computers. A continuation of that trend can now be seen in the
shift towards ubiquitous computing where computers are getting so cheap
and portable that people have continuous access to them (almost) anytime,
anywhere. As the shift towards ubiquitous computing continues and the
use of richer media content (audio, images, and video besides text) spreads,
there is an ever increasing need for networks that support user mobility and
high performance, not just raw bandwidth but low latency and predictable
quality of service.

Given the overall information explosion and the dramatic increase in wireless services subscribers, it is natural that supporting user mobility in the Internet is a hot and exciting issue. User mobility also raises interesting networking issues. So far the trend has been for technologies to appear, experience explosive growth and mature faster and faster. If the silicon revolution is still evolving 50 years after the invention of the transistor, the information revolution will probably unfold even faster. In keeping with this trend, since it's beginnings in the early 1990s, within a short span of about a decade, Mobile IP has already matured to a stage where it is being proposed as a standard by the IETF as evidenced by [4, 5, 6, 7] and other RFCs (Requests for Comments). Now that the basic mobile IP protocol is more or less standardized, researchers are beginning to focus on performance enhancing mechanisms at all layers of the networking stack in order to deliver high performance at the end-user level.

Unfortunately, however, the Internet was not conceived with mobility, security, or QoS issues in mind. Hence adding these services and features is in some sense a continual *"retrofitting"* job. As a result, simply adopting TCP and/or IP (the main protocols at the heart of the Internet Suite) and other Internet protocols in mobile environments can lead to bad performance or even complete failures. For example running TCP on a CDPD connection often leads to so many disconnections that for all practical purposes it could be considered a complete failure [8].

One of the fundamental reasons for this poor performance in mobile environments is the fact that wireless environments are almost the exact antithesis of wired scenarios: they are characterized by frequent disconnections, low bandwidth, periodic losses and random error bursts as opposed to almost no disconnections, reliable high bandwidth links with low bit error rates typical of wired networks. Perhaps the most damaging phenomenon is short, frequent disconnections. Instead of *reacting* to a disconnection after the fact why not *anticipate* a disconnection and take proactive actions to compensate for it or at least mitigate its effect? We discuss such proactive strategies at the network (IP) and transport (TCP) layers and present our analysis and experimental evaluation of a couple of such techniques. The reason we concentrate on network and transport layers is straightforward: above the transport layer is the application layer and given the wide spectrum of applications, it is beyond the scope of a "networks perspective" to investigate the role of proactivity in the wide variety of applications. Furthermore many applications may not need to be aware of the underlying communication links. A solution transparent to the applications has several

advantages, the biggest one being interoperability with the existing infrastructure.

Likewise, the MAC layer starts getting medium and hardware specific.
Moreover, most MAC level protocols for wireless environments already incorporate retransmissions and some proactive mechanisms. For instance,
implementing the CSMA-CA mechanism and continually sensing the channel to monitor RTS-CTS exchanges in order to mitigate the effects of hidden
and exposed terminals can be thought as being tantamount to proactive actions that avoid potential medium access conflicts.

From a networks perspective, it is therefore more interesting to look at
how proactivity would benefit the network and transport layers. It should
be noted that in the context of routing (network layer), the term "proactive"
is typically used to refer to table-driven routing protocols that attempt to
keep track of the topology of a network on a continual basis independent of
whether or not there are active connections (e.g., [9, 10, 11, 12, 13]). This is
in contrast with the "on-demand" or reactive routing protocols (for instance
[14, 15, 16]) that search for a route from source to destination only when
the source initiates the establishment of a connection.

We use the term "proactivity" at the network layer in a different sense.
We do not mean continual topology updates, rather proactivity refers to
compensatory or remedial actions taken in anticipation of a disconnection,
in a proactive manner, rather than reacting to a disconnection after the fact.
We use the term "proactive" in the context of the transport layer in the exact
same sense. In the following we illustrate two proactive mechanisms: one at
the transport layer, and one for the network layer in ad hoc networks. We
then discuss the overall effectiveness of proactivity and outline directions for
future work.

2   Proactivity at the Transport Layer: Freeze-TCP [1]

TCP is a vital component at the transport layer of the Internet protocol
suite. It is intended to provide reliable connection oriented service over
an underlying unreliable network. It is therefore not surprising that TCP
has received a lot of attention and many researchers have tried to optimize
and improve TCP for different environments characterized by heterogeneous
subnetworks with widely different bandwidths and latencies (for instance
TCP over wireless links, satellite links, slow serial links, etc.).

In the following, we first outline the problems with TCP in mobile environments. Next, we summarize the proposed solutions, indicating their strengths and weaknesses. We then explore the "Freeze-TCP" mechanism to enhance TCP for mobile environments and identify its advantages and drawbacks.

2.1 TCP's Window Management and Problems in Mobile Environments

TCP uses a sliding window mechanism to accomplish reliable, in-order delivery and flow/congestion control. Figure 1 shows this graphically, with the window sliding towards the right. The window size (W) is determined as the minimum of receiver's advertised buffer space, and the perceived network bandwidth delay product, taking into account congestion. The sender allows up to W outstanding or unacknowledged packets at a time. This results in a "usable window" size equal to W minus the number of outstanding packets.

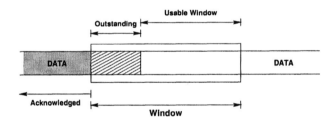

Figure 1: TCP Window Management

Under normal conditions, the right edge of the window stays fixed (when packets from the current window remain unacknowledged), or advances to the right followed by the left edge of the window, as outstanding packets are acknowledged. If the consuming process at the receiver end is slower than the sender, the receiver's buffers will begin to fill causing it to advertises progressively smaller window sizes. Eventually the receiver may run out of buffer space, in which case it advertises a window size of zero.

Upon seeing an advertised window size of zero, the sender should freeze all retransmit timers and enter a persist mode. This involves sending probes (called the Zero Window Probes or ZWPs) until the receiver's window opens up. In a strict sense, each ZWP should contain exactly one byte of data [17] but many TCP implementations do not include any data in their ZWPs. The interval between successive probes grows exponentially (exponential back-off) until it reaches 1 minute, where it remains constant. Because these probes are not delivered reliably, the sender *does not* drop its congestion window if a Zero Window Probe itself gets lost. Eventually the receiver responds to a ZWP with a non-zero window size, and the sender will continue transmission using a window size consistent with the advertised value.

An exception to this normal window management operation can occur if the receiver "shrinks" its advertised window, that is moves the right edge towards the left. This can suddenly create a negative usable window size which might confuse the sender. While this behavior is discouraged, the sender must be able to recover it occurs. As stated in [18] and [19], the sender is allowed to retransmit any outstanding packets (up to W) when an advertised window shrinks, but should not send new data. Also, any lost packets from the old window (and now to the right of the new window because the right edge moved leftward) should not cause the congestion window to drop. This means that if the receiver shrinks its window to zero, all outstanding packets can be lost without affecting the sender's congestion window and the sender should enter the persist mode described above.

2.2   Problems with TCP in Mobile Environments

TCP was conceived for wired, fixed topologies which are fairly reliable. Hence it operates on the assumption that any losses are due to congestion, which is reasonable for a reliable infrastructure. In mobile environments, however, losses are more often caused by: (i) the inherently higher bit error rate (BER) of the wireless links, and (ii) temporary disconnections (due to signal fading or other link errors; or because a mobile node moves, etc.).

To better illustrate the second item above, it should be noted that mobility is distinct from wireless connectivity. For instance, a user working in the office on a notebook wants to move (with the notebook) to a laboratory or a meeting room at the other end of a building or in the next building, where the IP addresses can be on different subnets; possibly across one or more firewalls. FTP, Telnet sessions and other connections can certainly remain alive for a few minutes it might take to go from one end of a building to another. The idea behind mobility is that such open connections should be retrieved seamlessly despite the move and a change of the underlying IP address.

Even if a single packet is dropped for any reason, current standard implementations of TCP assume that the loss was due to congestion and transmission is throttled by reducing the size of the congestion window. This, possibly coupled with TCP's slow-start mechanism, means that the sender unnecessarily holds back, slowly growing the transmission rate, even though the receiver often recovers quickly form the temporary, short disconnection. Network capacity can therefore remain underutilized for some time after a successful reconnection.

2.3 Existing Solutions

Several approaches have been proposed to overcome these shortcomings of standard TCP. The Berkeley Snoop module [20, 21] resides on an intermediate host, preferably the base station, near the mobile user. It caches packets from the sender and inspects their TCP headers. If the module, using the snooped information, determines that a packet has been lost, it retransmits a buffered copy to the mobile node (which is intended to be a local retransmission over one or a few links). The Snoop module maintains it's own timers for retransmission of buffered packets, implements selective retransmissions, etc.

Indirect TCP (I-TCP) [22] proposes to split the connection between a fixed sender host (FS) and mobile host (MH) at a mobility support station (which should ideally be the base station, BS). The data sent to MH is received, buffered and ACKed by BS. It is then the responsibility of BS to deliver the data to MH. On the link between BS and MH, it is not necessary to use TCP. One can use any other protocol optimized for wireless links. MTCP proposed in [23] is similar to I-TCP and also splits a TCP connection into two: one from MH to BS and the other from BS to FH. The MH to BS connection passes through a session layer protocol which can employ a selective repeat protocol (SRP) over the wireless link.

In [24], a method is proposed to alleviate the performance degradation as a result of disconnections due to handoffs. If packets are lost during handoff, the standard TCP at the sender end drops its congestion window and starts a timeout. If this timeout period is longer than the handoff disconnection, the mobile client does not receive any data until the timeout period is over. To reduce this waiting period, [24] makes the mobile host retransmit 3 copies of the ACK for the last data segment it received prior to the disconnection, immediately after completing the handoff. This causes the sender to immediately retransmit one segment, which eliminates the waiting period.

In [25] it is proposed to delay the duplicate ACKs for a missing packet (which could trigger a fast retransmission from the sender) in order to allow any special local retransmissions on the wireless links to work, before forcing the sender to fast-retransmit the missing packet(s). In [26] an explicit bad-state notification (EBSN) scheme is presented, wherein, for each failed attempt to send a packet to a MH, the base station (BS) sends an explicit bad-state notification to the sender. Upon the receipt of each EBSN, the sender resets its retransmit timers to their original values. The idea is that these explicit notifications prevent the sender from dropping its congestion window, when the TCP code on the sender side is modified accordingly.

It is possible to exploit TCP's response to a receiver shrinking its window to zero in order to enhance performance in presence of frequent disconnections. The main advantage is that when the sender enters persist mode, it freezes all packet retransmit timers and does not drop the congestion window so that the idle time during the slow-start phase can be avoided. M-TCP proposed in [27] uses this idea. It also splits up the connection between a sender (FH) and mobile receiver (MH) in two parts: one between FH and BS (base station/mobility support station) and one between BS and MH, which uses a customized wireless protocol.

Whenever the base station (BS) detects a disconnection or packet loss, it sends back an ACK to the sender (FH) with a zero window size to force the sender into persist mode, and not drop it's congestion window. To maintain end-to-end semantics, the BS relays ACKs back to the sender only when the receiver (MH) has ACKed data. This can lead to problems: for instance, assume that the sender has transmitted one widow full of packets and is waiting for ACKs. Suppose the receiver receives them all and ACKs the last transmission (TCP ACKs are cumulative) and then immediately gets disconnected. If the BS relays back the ACK to sender, it will keep transmitting eventually leading to packet loss and congestion window throttling. One could send a duplicate ACK for the last segment, advertising a window size of zero, but such duplicate ACKs may be ignored by the sender. Hence, the M-TCP scheme proposes that the base station hold back the ACK to the last byte so that if a disconnection is detected, that ACK can be relayed back to the sender with a zero window size.

2.4   Strengths and Drawbacks of Existing Solutions

Next we consider major factors, not necessarily in the order of importance, that should be considered in assessing any TCP enhancement scheme.

(1) One of the main considerations is inter-operation with the existing infrastructure. To realize this goal, ideally, no changes should be required at intermediate routers or the sender because these are likely to belong to other organizations, making them unavailable for modifications. All approaches that split the connection into two parts (this includes all the schemes mentioned in the previous subsection, with the exception of [25] and [26]) require substantial modification and processing at an intermediate node (BS). Some schemes, such as EBSN [25], also require modifications at the sender side.

(2) The second important issue is encrypted traffic. As more attention is being paid to network security, encryption is likely to be widely adopted. For instance, IPSEC is an integral part of IPv6, the next generation IP protocol. In such cases the whole IP payload is encrypted, so that the intermediate nodes may not even know that the traffic being carried in the payload is TCP. Any approach (such as SNOOP, I-TCP, MTCP, M-TCP, etc.) which depends on the base station doing a lot of mediation will fail when the traffic is encrypted.

(3) Even more serious, sometimes data and ACKs can take different paths, for instance in satellite networks. Schemes based on intermediary involvement will have serious problems in such a case.

(4) Yet another consideration is maintaining true end-to-end semantics. I-TCP and MTCP do not maintain true end-to-end semantics. M-TCP in [27] does maintain end-to-end semantics, but requires a substantial base-station involvement nonetheless. Thus there is a need for true end-to-end signaling without involving any intermediary.

(5) Even if one assumes that issues (1)–(4) above are not relevant, and that an intermediary (such as a base station) can be brought in for performance enhancements; there is still a need to consider whether the intermediary will become the bottleneck. It is clear that the base stations (BS) in SNOOP, I-TCP, MTCP, M-TCP will all have to buffer at least some amount of data (to perform local retransmission, etc.) and do some extra processing for each connection going through them. If hundreds or thousands of nodes are mobile in the domain of a base station, it could get overwhelmed from processing traffic associated with each connection. This might cause some packets to be lost, resulting in the sender dropping its congestion window which would

defeat the original purpose of the whole endeavor.

	SNOOP [20, 21]	ITCP [22] and MTCP [23]	M-TCP [27]	Delayed Duplicate ACKs [25]	EBSN [26]	Freeze-TCP
Modifications Required at Intermediaries	Yes	Yes	Yes	No	Yes	No
Encrypted Traffic Handled	No	No	No	Yes	No	Yes
End-to-end TCP Semantics Maintained	Yes	No	No	Yes	No	Yes
Long Disconnections Handled	No	May Run Out of Buffers	Yes	No	Yes	Yes
Frequent Disconnections Handled	No	Handoff Costly	Handoff May be Costly	No	Yes	Yes
High BER Handled	Yes	Yes	Yes	No	No	No

Table 1: Characteristics of Various Mobile TCP Solutions

On the positive side, if the above issues can be ignored, then most of the proposed solutions (especially M-TCP) do yield performance improvements (although holding back a byte in the M-TCP scheme might force repacketization at the sender end, thereby degrading the performance). In [27] it was observed that SNOOP, I-TCP, MTCP handle bit-errors well but do not effectively deal with frequent disconnections of sizable duration or frequent handoffs. The delayed duplicate ACKs scheme [25] was found to improve performance in presence of occasional transmission losses, but it can degrade performance in case of actual congestion losses [26]. Likewise, the explicit bad-state notification (EBSN) scheme works well if the "bad state" lasts for significant duration or when large error bursts occur. However, it may not be as effective as the SNOOP method for random occasional errors [26]. We have summarized the characteristics of some of the proposed solutions in Table 1.

A very good summary of current state-of-the-art approaches to optimizing the transport layer for mobile environments can be found in the Internet Draft [28]. In that draft only SNOOP plus SACK is being recommended for adoption, after issues related to IP encrypted payloads (such as those in IPSEC) have been resolved. Some recommendations from the draft to resolve these issues are: (i) make the SNOOPing base station a party to the security association between the client and the server, or (ii) terminate the IPSEC tunneling mode at the SNOOPing base station. The draft also recommends adopting delayed duplicate acknowledgments when that technique eventually stabilizes through further research and experimentation. Likewise, the draft recommends only those schemes that require changes at base stations and mobile ends be further researched.

2.5 The Freeze-TCP Approach

The main idea behind Freeze-TCP is to move the onus of signaling an impending disconnection to the client. A mobile node can certainly monitor signal strengths in the wireless antennas and detect an impending handoff; and in certain cases, might even be able to predict a temporary disconnection (if the signal strength is fading, for instance). In such a case, it can advertise a zero window size, to force the sender into the ZWP mode and prevent it from dropping its congestion window. As mentioned earlier, even if one of the zero window probes is lost, the sender does not drop the congestion window [17]. To implement this scheme, only the client's TCP code needs to change and there is no need for an intermediary (no code changes are required at the base station or the sender).

If the receiver can sense an impending disconnection, it should try to send a few (at least one) acknowledgments, wherein it's window size is advertised as zero (let an ACK with a zero receiver window size be abbreviated "ZWA", i.e., Zero Window Advertisement). The question is: how much in advance of the disconnection should the receiver start advertising a window size of zero? This period is in a sense the "warning period" prior to disconnection. Ideally, the warning period should be long enough to ensure that exactly one ZWA gets across to the sender. If the warning period is any longer, the sender will be forced into Zero Window Probe mode prematurely, thereby leading to idle time prior to the disconnection. If the warning period is too small, there might not be enough time for the receiver to send out a ZWA which will cause the sender's congestion window to drop due to packets lost during the disconnection which will in turn lead to network underutilization.

Given this, a reasonable warning period is the round-trip-time (RTT). During periods of continuous data transfer, this allows the sender to transmit a packet and then receive its acknowledgment. Experimental data corroborates this: warning periods longer or shorter than RTT led to worse average performance in most cases we tested. Note that Freeze-TCP is only useful if a disconnection occurs while data is being transfered (as opposed to when the receiver is idle for some time and then gets disconnected), which is the most interesting scenario in any case.

Since the ZWPs are exponentially backed off, there is the possibility of substantial idle time after a reconnection. This could happen, for instance, if the disconnection period was long and the reconnection happened immediately after losing a ZWP from the sender. In that case, the sender will go into a long back-off before sending the next probe. In the meantime the receiver has already reconnected, but the connection remains idle until the sender transmits its next probe. To avoid this idle period, we also implement the scheme suggested in [24]. As soon as a connection is reestablished, the receiver sends 3 copies of the ACK for the last data segment it received prior to the disconnection. This scheme is henceforth abbreviated as "TR-ACKs" (Triplicate Reconnection ACKs). Note that even in standard TCP, packet retransmissions are exponentially backed off. Therefore the post reconnection idle time can occur there as well. For a fair comparison, the standard TCP on the receiver side was also modified to optionally send TR-ACKs. This way, the effect of the Freeze-TCP mechanism (i.e., forcing the sender into ZWP mode *prior* to a disconnection) can be isolated.

Unlike M-TCP, there is no advantage to holding back the ACK to the last byte. For M-TCP it was useful because even when the mobile client was disconnected, the base station could still signal the sender on behalf of the client. In the case of Freeze-TCP, since changes are restricted to the client end, holding back the ACK for the last byte does not help. Note that Freeze-TCP will avoid any repacketization penalty at the sender end (which M-TCP might incur because it holds back the ACK to the last byte).

Figures 2 and 3 help estimate the performance gain possible due to the Freeze-TCP technique. In Figure 2, t_s is the time required to "write the packet on the wire", RTT is the total round trip delay including the t_s delays at sending, receiving as well as any intermediate nodes; and W is the sender's window. From the figure, it is seen that if any idle periods are to be avoided:

$$W \cdot t_s \geq \text{RTT} \quad \text{or} \quad W \geq \frac{\text{RTT}}{t_s}. \tag{1}$$

Since $t_s \approx \frac{\text{packet size}}{\text{bandwidth}}$ (ignoring processing/queuing delays internal to the host, collisions in case of shared medium, etc.) it is seen that the [delay ×

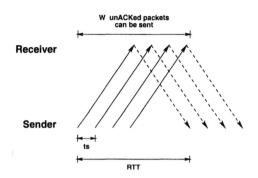

Figure 2: Relationship Between t_s, RTT, and W

bandwidth] product is important in determining how big the congestion window W needs to be if underutilization of network capacity is to be avoided. Assuming $RTT/t_s \gg 1$, then

$$W \gg 1 \qquad (2)$$

is required for full network capacity utilization. Figure 3 pictorially illustrates the increased throughput under this condition, when Freeze-TCP prevents sender side window, W, from dropping and regrowing (due to packet losses).

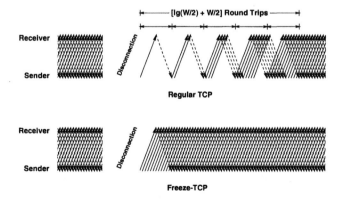

Figure 3: Illustration of Increased Throughput Due to Freeze-TCP

From the figure it can be seen that the (approximate) number of *extra* packets transferred by the Freeze-TCP scheme is given by

$$\text{Extra Segments} = \frac{W^2}{8} + W \lg W - \frac{5W}{4} + 1 \qquad (3)$$

In addition to (2), the above expression (3) also assumes that upon a disconnection (and the loss of packets), regular TCP drops the congestion window down to 1 segment, and first grows it by a factor of 2 each time an ACK is received, until it reaches $W/2$. From there on, it is incremented by 1 each time an ACK is received until it reaches the same size W prior to disconnection. These congestion window growth mechanisms are dubbed slow-start and congestion avoidance respectively, and were adopted in 4.3 BSD Reno release and onwards [17]. It should be noted that (3) is an approximate expression, ignoring collisions, and other factors that might affect the traffic.

2.6   Experimental Setup

We carried out experiments by modifying the Linux 2.1.101 TCP source code. The receiver side Freeze-TCP mechanism was implemented on a PC designated to emulate the mobile host. All performance measurements used client-server programs specifically written to emulate frequent disconnections during data transfer and measure the resulting data transfer rates and delays.

The server is on the "sender side" without any changes to its underlying TCP code. It runs as a normal user process without any special privileges. The server could be operated in two modes: (i) continually send data until the client disconnects, or (ii) only send a stream of specified length to the client. In either mode the segment size can be specified by the client. In addition, Each segment has its own serial number included as data, along with a check-sum. This way, the client can easily monitor corrupt or missing packets.

The client runs on the "receiver side" which emulates a mobile node implementing the Freeze-TCP scheme. The client maintains a time ordered list of events to be executed in course of the experiment; such as FreezeOn (start advertising a zero window size), InterfaceOff (simulate a disconnection), FreezeOff, InterfaceOn, Count (which prints the amount of data received since last Count event as well as cumulative time and data bytes since the start of the experiment); etc. In addition, the client can be operated in two modes: (i) send a triplicate ACK (TR-ACK) after a reconnection, i.e., immediately after every InterfaceOn event, and (ii) non-TR-ACK or standard mode, where the receiver does *not* send extra ACKs after a re-connection, it just waits for the next segment from the sender. Between FreezeOn and InterfaceOff events (i.e., in the warning interval prior to disconnection) data segments from the sender are accepted as usual, but the receiver window size is advertised as zero in all acknowledgments sent out during this period.

2.7 Experimental Data

As mentioned above, the performance of the Freeze-TCP scheme depends on the RTT/t_s ratio which is proportional to [delay × bandwidth]. The higher this ratio, the more effective this mechanism can be. To illustrate these trends we consider the following environments which span a large range and variety of bandwidths: 10 Mbps Ethernet, 100 Mbps Ethernet, and 38.4 Kbps PPP. Local (in the same room) as well as distant (across the county) servers were used to vary the round-trip delay of the 1000 byte packets used.

The 10 Mbps Ethernet experiments were performed to emulate a mobile host in a wireless Ethernet cell, where, under light load conditions, the bandwidth available can be comparable to wired Ethernet. In this scenario a local server running Solaris 2.6 and a distant server running AIX 4.2 were used. Each experiment was repeated 10 times with the base and Freeze-TCP cases running alternately to ensure that similar network conditions were experienced by corresponding scenarios. The results are shown in Tables 2 and 3.

Table 2 shows that the Freeze-TCP scheme enhances performance substantially. The results presented are the average of ten experimental runs, each run experiencing 10 disconnections with a one second period between disconnection events. In all cases 10 MB of data was transfered and the effective throughput of the client's 10 Mbps Ethernet connection was around 1 MB/sec. Therefore, the warning period was 2.6 msec corresponding to the approximate RTT. Besides the overall gain, i.e. the performance of Freeze-TCP with TR-ACKs compared to standard TCP, we have also evaluated the performance enhancement for the TR-ACK and non-TR-ACK cases separately. This helps isolate the performance enhancement due to the Freeze-TCP mechanism from that due to TR-ACKs. The data demonstrates that the Freeze-TCP mechanism by itself can yield a sizable increase in performance. In addition, Freeze-TCP can be used in conjunction with other beneficial techniques, such as TR-ACKs, to further enhance the overall

| Disconnect | Transfer Time (sec) | | | | Overall Gain |
| Time | With TR-ACKs | | Without TR-ACKs | | of |
(sec)	TCP	Freeze-TCP	TCP	Freeze-TCP	Freeze-TCP
0.0026	18.7	13.0 (+30.4%)	18.6	17.1 (+8.1%)	+30.1%
0.03	17.9	13.2 (+26.2%)	17.8	16.9 (+5.4%)	+25.8%
0.1	18.4	13.8 (+25.2%)	18.7	17.5 (+6.3%)	+26.2%
0.5	19.4	17.3 (+10.9%)	21.2	21.8 (−3.2%)	+18.4%
1.0	25.7	22.4 (+12.7%)	28.2	28.6 (−1.5%)	+20.6%
2.0	40.0	32.5 (+16.6%)	66.1	66.6 (−0.8%)	+50.8%
5.0	71.0	63.6 (+10.4%)	116.3	95.0 (+18.4%)	+45.3%
10.0	143.8	116.6 (+18.9%)	190.6	184.3 (+3.3%)	+38.8%

Table 2: Freeze-TCP Performance: Local Server (3 Hops Away), 10 Mbps
Client Connection

gain.

Table 3 shows the results obtained in experiments with a quite remote
host: 17 hops, and geographically across the country. In this case there were
8 disconnections per run, the effective throughput of the client's 10 Mbps
Ethernet connection was around 10 KB/sec, and a warning period of 85 msec
was used. Once again, it is seen that Freeze-TCP leads to better performance
in almost all cases. Here, there is more variability in the data which is
attributable to the unpredictable traffic conditions in the Internet at large.
However, the main trends are same as those seen in Table 2. Notice that in
most cases using Freeze-TCP leads to substantially higher performance.

The experiments with remote hosts clearly demonstrate the interoperability of Freeze-TCP with the existing infrastructure: the server can be
anywhere and all the changes to TCP code are confined to the client which
was under our control. As both tables show, in the cases where Freeze-TCP
does not give better results, the loss is very small (no more than 3.2%).
This is the main advantage of Freeze-TCP; most of the time it leads to better performance and the enhancement can be substantial, while for the few
times when it leads to worse results, the loss is marginal.

To illustrate how the results vary with bandwidth, the next set of experiments were done on a local 100 Mbps Ethernet segment. The number
of disconnections per run varied between 8 and 11, with an interval of 50–
160 msec between disconnections resulting in 10–20 MB of data being transfered. The effective throughput of the client's 100 Mbps Ethernet connection

Disconnect Time (sec)	Transfer Time (sec) With TR-ACKs		Freeze-TCP Gain
	TCP	Freeze-TCP	
0.0026	103.4	88.9	+14.1%
0.03	114.2	90.8	+20.6%
0.1	109.3	90.1	+17.6%
0.5	109.9	92.2	+16.1%
1.0	113.0	96.6	+14.5%
2.0	116.1	106.8	+8.10%
5.0	140.4	134.8	+3.99%

Table 3: Freeze-TCP Performance: Remote Server (17 Hops Away), 10 Mbps Client Connection

was about 10 MB/sec and a warning period of 0.3 msec was used. As expected, Table 4 shows that the benefits of using Freeze-TCP are significant in high bandwidth environments. Also, the 100 Mbps TR-ACKs results illustrate better improvements on average than the 10 Mbps TR-ACKs data. The substantial performance gains are facilitated by the high bandwidth, which leads to a higher [delay × bandwidth] product (and higher RTT/t_s ratio). Since the [delay × bandwidth] product required to "fill the pipe" is greater than that of 10 Mbps Ethernet, higher window sizes are required to saturate the network. Consequently, the gain that can be realized when such a large congestion window is prevented from dropping is also higher. This is consistent with equation (3) which shows that the gain grows (essentially) quadratically with the window size W.

The final set of experiments emulate a mobile client connecting via a wireless modem; resulting in data rates that are much lower than wireless Ethernet LANs. To simulate such low link speeds we connected the receiver, emulating the mobile client, to a router with a serial link using the PPP protocol. The results are shown in Table 5, where there were 100 disconnections with 5 sec between disconnection events and 200 KB transfered per run. The effective throughput of the client's 38.4 Kbps PPP connection was around 3.2 KB/sec, and the warning period was 780 msec. As the experimental data shows, the current implementation of Freeze-TCP can enhance performance in several cases. It rarely performs significantly worse than normal TCP, although it does appear to yield almost similar performance in many cases. This is mainly due to the lower RTT/t_s ratio of this PPP scenario. The

Disconnect Time (msec)	Transfer Time (sec) With TR-ACKs		Freeze-TCP Gain
	TCP	Freeze-TCP	
0.4	2.35	1.45	+38.4%
1.0	23.5	14.5	+38.1%
10.0	1.98	1.13	+43.3%
100.0	3.40	2.30	+32.4%
400.0	8.81	6.12	+30.6%
1000.0	13.1	9.96	+23.9%
2000.0	26.3	17.9	+31.8%

Table 4: Freeze-TCP Performance: Local Server (2 Hops Away), 100 Mbps Client Connection

network can be saturated fairly quickly, with small sized windows. Consequently, the gain that can accrue from preventing the congestion window from falling is not as high as Ethernet environments where the ratio is much higher.

Disconnect Time (sec)	Transfer Time (sec)				Overall Gain of Freeze-TCP
	With TR-ACKs		Without TR-ACKs		
	TCP	Freeze-TCP	TCP	Freeze-TCP	
0.0026	76.9	75.0 (+2.5%)	73.4	78.7 (−7.3%)	−2.18%
0.03	81.1	76.8 (+5.2%)	74.7	75.6 (−1.2%)	−2.81%
0.1	78.6	76.1 (+3.1%)	77.2	80.2 (−3.8%)	+1.42%
0.5	87.3	86.2 (+1.2%)	92.8	93.5 (−0.7%)	+7.11%
1.0	95.5	97.9 (−2.5%)	106.6	103.7 (+2.7%)	+8.16%
2.0	111.4	110.5 (+0.8%)	124.0	114.1 (+8.0%)	+10.9%
5.0	153.9	135.8 (+11.7%)	182.9	178.3 (+2.5%)	+25.8%

Table 5: Freeze-TCP Performance: Remote Server (24 Hops Away), 38.4 Kbps Client Connection

We would like to point out that for all the data presented, the number of disconnections was kept equal in both base and Freeze-TCP cases, even though the base case typically takes a longer time to execute than the corresponding Freeze-TCP case. In reality, connections with longer transfer times are likely to suffer more disconnections. This means the data is highly pessimistic and illustrates a worst-case scenario. The main point is that even when Freeze-TCP is not effective, it does not worsen performance by a noticeable amount. The few cases in which it loses, the losses are marginal. This indicates that the overhead due to the Freeze-TCP mechanism is very small: even if it fails to enhance performance, it will at least render baseline (standard TCP like) performance. *This is a win, no-loss situation!*

3 Network Layer Proactivity: Preemptive Routing in Ad Hoc Networks [3, 2]

3.1 Preemptive Route Maintenance

In traditional mobile and wired-network routing algorithms, a change of path occurs when a link along the path fails or a shorter path is found. A link failure is costly because multiple retransmissions or timeouts are required to detect the failure and a new path has to be found. Since paths fail so infrequently in wired networks, this is not an important cost. However, routing protocols in mobile networks follow this model despite the significantly higher frequency of path disconnections that occur in this environment.

Preemptive route maintenance is therefore an extension to on-demand routing protocols in ad hoc networks. With preemptive maintenance, recovery is initiated early by detecting that a link is likely to break and finding and using an alternative path before the cost of a link failure is incurred. This technique is similar to soft-handoff techniques used in cellular phone networks as mobiles move across cells [29]. When extended with preemptive maintenance, an on-demand routing algorithm consists of two components: (i) detecting that a path is likely to be disconnected soon; and (ii) finding a better path and switching to it. Note the similarity to pure on-demand protocols: path failure is replaced, with the likelihood of failure as the trigger mechanism for route discovery. Note that it is possible to add preemptive maintenance to table-driven protocols as well to avoid the cost of detecting a path failure.

By using preemptive route maintenance the cost of detecting a broken path (the retransmit/timeout time) is eliminated if another path is found successfully before the path breaks. In addition, the cost for discovering an alternate path is reduced (or eliminated) since the path discovery is initiated before the current path was actually broken. This can be expected to reduce the latency and jitter. Among the disadvantages, a higher number of path discoveries may be initiated since a path may become suspect but never actually break. However, if only high quality paths are accepted; they are likely to last longer, reducing the number of rediscoveries needed.

A critical component of the proposed scheme is determining when path quality is no longer acceptable, which in turn generates a preemptive warning. The path quality can incorporate several criteria such as signal strength, the age of a path, the number of hops, and rate of collisions. Currently we restrict the path quality (and hence the preemptive warnings) to be a function of the signal strength of received packets with the number of hops being used as secondary measure. Since most breaks can be attributed to link failures due to *node motion* in a typical network with mobility, the signal strength offers the most direct estimate of the ability of the nodes to reach each other. It is important that signal power fluctuations due to fading and other transient disturbances do not generate erroneous preemptive warnings. The next section examines these issues in more detail describing our approach to mitigating the effects of transient signal fades.

3.2   Generating the Preemptive Warning

A preemptive warning is generated when the signal power of a received packet drops below some *preemptive threshold*. The value of this threshold is critical to the efficiency of the algorithm – if the value is too low, there will not be sufficient time to discover an alternative path before the path breaks. Conversely, if the value is too high, the warning is generated early with the following negative side-effects: (i) unnecessary route discoveries are generated increasing overhead; (ii) early switches to what is actually a lower quality path are possible; and (iii) increasing the preemptive threshold effectively limits the range of the mobile nodes and false network partitioning can occur. Generating the preemptive warning is complicated due to transient fading that can cause sudden variations in the received signal power. The remainder of this section derives the criteria for selecting good threshold values under ideal conditions, then addresses link state estimation in the presence of channel fading and other random interference.

Figure 4 demonstrates the preemptive region around a source. For example, as node C in the figure enters this region, the signal power of received packets from the source A falls below the preemptive threshold, generating a warning packet to A. A initiates route discovery action, and discovers a route through D; A switches to this route avoiding the failure of the path as C moves out of direct range of A. We now develop an estimate for the optimal size of the preemptive region and, relate it to the signal power threshold under ideal conditions.

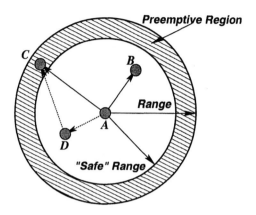

Figure 4: Preemptive Region

The recovery time from a broken path, $T_{recover}$, depends on the size and topology of the network, the load on the network as well as the path being recovered. In a realistic implementation, we assume that each node keeps a running estimate of the (possibly path specific) recovery time, and uses that as its preemptive threshold. The optimal value for the signal threshold will warn the source $T_{recover}$ seconds before the path breaks; this allows just enough time to discover a new path. Hence the warning interval T_w, that is the time between a route warning and path break, should be set to $T_{recover}$.

Given two mobile nodes with a vector distance X between them, moving with vector speeds, V_1 and V_2, the distance between the two nodes is $X + t(V_2 - V_1)$. The time until the absolute distance between them becomes greater than the range of the source is a function of their relative location and velocity. In the worst case the sources are moving at their maximum speeds away from each other. This case can be used to derive a conservative estimate on the preemptive region.

Consider a typical land-based network where the maximum speed of a node is 20 m/s, and a recovery time estimate of 0.1 sec (this value is used for illustration; it is in the typical range observed empirically). The preemptive region would start 4 meters from the maximum range; even if the two nodes are moving away from each other at maximum speeds (a relative velocity of 40 m/s), a distance of 4 meters will give the source the 0.1 second necessary to find a new path. If the nodes were actually drifting apart at a relative speed of 20 m/s, then 0.2 seconds would be available for the route discovery.

3.2.1   Relating the Preemptive Region to Signal Power

Because an explicit estimate of the preemptive region requires the nodes to exchange location and velocity information, we use the signal power of received packets to estimate the distance between them. Moreover, in a real environment, the distance between nodes does not correlate well with the received power due to obstacles, fading, and other interference. The recovery time can be related to the power threshold as follows. We consider devices operating in the ISM bands, such as Lucent WaveLANs. In this case, the transmission power is restricted by the FCC to less than 250 milliwatts at a distance of 3 meters from the transmitter (e.g., a 280 milliwatt transmit power using the omni-directional antennas of the WaveLAN cards [30]). The signal power drops such that

$$P_r = \frac{P_0}{r^n} \tag{4}$$

at a distance r from the transmitter, where P_0 is the transmitted power and n is typically between 2 and 4.

The signal power at any point is the sum of the main signal transmitted by the antenna and other components of the signal that reflect off surrounding features (the multipath effect) [29]. In an open environment, the main secondary component is the strong reflection of the transmitted signal from the ground, known as the two-ray propagation model. Equation 4 represents an idealized model for the channel. Usually, $n = 2$ near the source until a certain distance where n transitions to 4. Such an equation cannot account for general channel fading, which can cause sudden sharp fluctuations in signal power, since fading is highly dependent on the specific surrounding terrain. Stable power estimates in the presence of fading is considered in the following subsection.

We assume the $1/r^4$ drop in signal power with distance model [31] throughout the preemptive region (since the preemptive region is near the maximum range of the devices). More specifically,

$$P_{received} = \frac{P_0}{r^4} \tag{5}$$

where P_0 is a constant for each transmitter/receiver pair, based on antenna gain and height. The minimum power receivable by the device is the resulting power at the maximum transmission range, P_{range}, and is $\frac{P_0}{range^4}$. This value is characteristic of the specific device being used (e.g., $3.65 \cdot 10^{-10}$ Watts for WaveLANs [30]). Similarly, the preemptive signal power threshold is the signal power at the edge of the preemptive region. In addition, for a preemptive region of width of w, the signal power threshold is

$$P_{threshold} = \frac{P_0}{r_{preemptive}^4}. \tag{6}$$

Note that $r_{preemptive}$ is equal to $(range - w)$ where $w = (relative\ speed) \cdot T_w$. The preemptive ratio, δ is then defined as

$$\delta = \frac{P_{threshold}}{P_{range}} = \frac{\frac{P_0}{(range-w)^4}}{\frac{P_0}{range^4}} = \left(\frac{range}{range - w}\right)^4. \tag{7}$$

For example, WaveLAN cards have a range of 250 meters in open environments in the 900MHz band [30]. The preemptive ratio for a preemptive region of width 4 meters is $\left(\frac{250}{250-4}\right)^4 = 1.07$. This value corresponds to a signal threshold of $1.07 \cdot P_{range} = 3.9 \cdot 10^{-10}$ Watts.

3.2.2 Mitigation of Channel Fading and Other Transient Interferences

In practice, the received signal power may experience sudden and substantial fluctuations due to channel fading, multipath effects and Doppler shifts [29]. These fluctuations might then trigger false preemptive route warnings, causing unnecessary route request floods. The overhead of unnecessary route request floods can adversely affect performance as the network becomes saturated. Furthermore, route switches to lower quality routes may be initiated.

The problem is not as significant as may appear at first. For most networks, the preemptive region is sufficiently narrow making the probability of a transient fade changing the received power within the preemptive range small. Moreover, there are established mechanisms to produce stable power estimates developed for power control in cellular networks. For example, maintaining an exponential average of the signal power to trigger the warning mechanism. Alternatively, quicker power estimates can be achieved by sending a warning whenever the instantaneous power drops below the preemptive threshold, and checking the received power of the warning packet. In general, a more stable average can be generated by having any number of ping pong rounds using query packets of minimal size to sample the signal strength. The number and duration of these pings should be related to the expected duration of possible fading phenomena, which depends on the channel and the surrounding environment.

The two mechanisms can be mixed by using the exponential average if the packet reception rate is high, and resorting to ping pong rounds if it is not. Finally, for mobile nodes equipped with GPS systems, a warning packet can include the location/velocity of its sender so that a recipient can compute whether the sender is actually moving out of range. This approach is interesting since cellular phones will soon be required to provide location information due to the FCC's "911" mandate [32]. The source can also apply a dead reckoning calculation using its own location and velocity information to estimate when the path will be broken and when the optimal time to start corrective action is. However, we believe the use of geographical information will be complicated by environmental factors, such as non-uniform topology and obstacles.

Another potential problem occurs when the transmission rate along a path is low or bursty. A node may move into the preemptive region during a quiet interval. No warning will be generated until the next packet is sent, because route warnings are triggered only when the signal strength of a received packet falls below the threshold. By that time the path may have already broke, or there might not be enough time remaining to complete a route discovery. To avoid this situation a null (empty) packet can be sent along idle but active paths. The period of this heart-beat probe can be related to the width of the preemptive region to balance overhead against recovery time. The preemptive region could also be extended to account for this sampling period.

For example, consider the case when sources generate traffic at a fixed rate, the constant bit-rate (CBR) model. The inter-packet interval T_{pkt} is therefore

$$T_{\text{pkt}} \approx \frac{1}{\text{CBR}}. \tag{8}$$

No preemptive warning will be generated unless a packet happens to be received when a node is in the preemptive region (see Figure 4). This indicates that to be able to "sample" the preemptive region, the CBR should satisfy the constraint:

$$T_{\text{pkt}} = \frac{1}{\text{CBR}} < \text{Time to traverse the preemptive region}$$

$$= \frac{w}{\text{average relative speed}} = T_{recover} \qquad (9)$$

$$\text{or} \quad \text{CBR} > \frac{1}{T_{recover}}.$$

3.3 TCP in Ad Hoc Networks

Packets in flight along a path that breaks are often dropped, unless some form of intermediate salvaging is applied. In addition, a period of disconnection is suffered while an alternative path is found. These two factors can cause significant degradation of TCP performance especially when mobility is high [33]. Since TCP was designed for wired networks, it assumes that packet losses are due to congestion. Therefore, when a packet is lost TCP applies "congestion avoidance" mechanisms and slows its transmission rate by reducing the congestion window and exponentially backing off its retransmit timers [34]. The disconnection time may result in multiple failed retransmits, and a large exponential backoff on the timer. Thus, when the path is eventually reestablished, a long timeout value may be suffered before packet transmission resumes.

Consequently, packet losses due to mobility and transmission errors cause TCP to perform poorly in wireless environments [21, 35]. When packets are lost due to either of these reasons, there is no need to initiate congestion avoidance/control procedures, since congestion is not what caused the loss. This is, unfortunately, how TCP reacts in such as case. Thus, a path break leads to underutilization of bandwidth for the following reasons:

(1) When packets are lost, the retransmission timers are exponentially backed off as part of the standard congestion avoidance procedures in TCP. Upon a path break the source initiates a route discovery, and if a route is found just when TCP has entered a long retransmit back-off period packets will be unnecessarily delayed.

(2) In response to packet losses due to retransmission timeouts TCP drops its congestion window. In most TCP implementations, the window size will be dropped to one segment and the slow start mechanism invoked, as seen in Figure 3.

In last-hop wireless environments, mobility causes packets to be lost due to hand-offs as a mobile node moves out of range from one base station and into the range of another [27, 1]. Packets lost during such transitions also initiate TCP's congestion avoidance. Several researchers have addressed optimizing TCP in wireless last-hop environments [21, 27, 1, 36]. Similarly, in ad hoc networks if any of the hops constituting a path fail due to intermediate node mobility, TCP packets will be dropped and congestion avoidance initiated. Since the routing algorithm is responsible for finding paths between communicating nodes, its performance has a direct influence on the frequency of packet losses due to mobility. Other work has focused on reducing the false congestion avoidance effect in ad hoc networks by using techniques such as explicit loss notification and randomized congestion avoidance [37, 38, 33]. Since preemptive maintenance eliminates most disconnections, there is reason to believe that it will achieve a similar improvement in TCP performance which is beyond any benefit obtained from better routing, and does not require changes to TCP.

3.4   Preemptive Route Maintenance Case Studies

As was noted previously, preemptive maintenance can be added to any ad hoc routing protocol, although we have only investigated on-demand ones. In order to evaluate preemptive route maintenance, the Dynamic Source Routing (DSR) protocol and Ad Hoc On Demand Distance Vector (AODV) protocols were modified to incorporate preemptive path maintenance. We call the modified versions Preemptive DSR (PDSR) and Preemptive AODV (PAODV), respectively. We focus on DSR for the sake of brevity and to allow a more detailed analysis. AODV is used to illustrate that the results are not specific to DSR.

3.4.1   Preemptive Route Warning Generation

As outlined above, if a received packet's signal strength is below $\delta \cdot P_{range}$ (where δ is the preemptive ratio from (7)) the receiving node starts pinging the node which sent the packet. A reply is then sent immediately in response to such a signal strength ping, and the process may repeat so that a total of n ping-pong pairs are used to monitor the signal strength. During this monitoring period, if the total number of low signal strength packets is above a certain threshold value, k, then a route warning is sent back to the source. A route warning is also generated when there is no response to a ping within a timeout period $T_{\text{ping-timeout}}$. Thus the total length of time for which the state of a link is monitored may be as large as $n \cdot T_{\text{ping-timeout}}$.

Upon receiving a route warning, the source initiates a route discovery to find a higher quality path. From experiments, it was observed that multiple packets will cause repeated route warning messages for the same failing link. To prevent this behavior, a "signal-strength-threshold" field was added to the DSR header. If a node receives a packet with a signal strength below this value, it initiates link monitoring, and if necessary sends a route warning back to the source. Initially the source sets the signal-strength-threshold for a path to $\delta \cdot P_{range}$. After receiving a route warning the signal-strength-threshold is reduced to zero for outgoing packets which use the afflicted path. Note that this mechanism reduces the number of redundant route warnings generated, and does not require intermediate nodes to store any additional path information.

When a route discovery query flood is generated in response to a warning from a given path, the first new path found is immediately used. Any paths subsequently discovered are compared against the path in use, and the shorter path is chosen. Many alternatives to this selection algorithm are possible that discriminate between paths based on other factors, for example using the less congested path.

Since the route discovery flood is generated while the original bad path is still active, it is possible to (re)discover a path that might soon be broken. To avoid this situation and find only high quality paths, route queries are tagged with a minimum signal strength threshold for each link of a path. This threshold is currently set to the preemptive threshold, although it could assume any higher value. Intermediate nodes that receive a path request packet with a signal strength below this threshold do not respond, equivalent to if they did not receive the path query. This effectively limits the range of the nodes, so that if all available paths are below the desired threshold no alternative paths will be discovered. A more general implementation might have the route reply phase of the query maintain the minimum power of discovered routes. The source could then select the best path available even when the desired threshold is not satisfied.

An additional DSR modification was made to change how cached routes were managed. Nodes would not respond to route requests with cached routes, in other words only paths discovered first-hand were allowed. In addition, a source would kept only one path for each active destination. This aspect of the implementation could be significantly optimized to reduce both the number of route discoveries and the cost per discovery by using an effective caching strategy with a higher success rate. For example Hu and Johnson analyzed how several parameters affected cache performance [39]. Other work explored localized query floods based on previous path [40] or location information [41] to reduce query costs. To demonstrate that the results are not due to the modified cache behavior alone, AODV [16] cache management was not changed since it generally performed well.

3.5 Experimental Study

An extended version of UCB/LBNL network simulator NS-2 [42] was used for the experimental study. NS-2 is a discrete event simulator that was developed as part of the VINT project at the Lawrence Berkeley National Laboratory. The extensions implemented by the CMU Monarch project [43] enable it to simulate mobile nodes connected by wireless network interfaces. The NS-2 DSR protocol implementation was extended with preemptive maintenance as per the previous description.

To simulate the effects of Rayleigh fading and other transients, we modified the two-state error model provided by NS-2 to reflect a channel experiencing fading, or not. Packets received while a channel was in the fading state had their signal strength reduced by a multiplicative factor chosen randomly between 2 and 100. The received power was not modified for packets received when the channel was not in the fading state. This model approximates a typical fading scenario such as the one illustrated in [29, page 71] and accounts for deep fades up to 20dB, i.e., a signal strength reduction by a factor of 100. The period of time a channel remained in each state was determined by an exponentially distributed random variable, with the mean duration for remaining in the non-fading state set to 20,000 packets. Likewise the mean stay in the fading state was set at 2 packets. This corresponds to a mean packet error rate of 10^{-4}. This approximates a moderate quality wireless channel, i.e. a BER of around 10^{-6} and bursty errors. Note that not every fade results in an actual error (dropped packet) since when the initial received strength is high a reduction by a factor of up to 100 can still leave the packet above the detection threshold.

For an unbiased comparison, scenarios similar to those previously studied [44, 45] were selected and simulated with and without proactivity. More specifically, we considered scenarios with a set of 35 nodes in an area of 700 meters by 700 meters. Nodes randomly pick a location within the simulated area and start moving towards it. There were 10 source nodes transmitting to 10 destination nodes at a Constant Bit Rate (CBR) with 5 packets/sec.

In addition, two mobility scenarios were considered: (i) low mobility (max. node speed 10 m/s); and (ii) high mobility (max. node speed 20 m/s). Note that both the selected CBR values represent significant load on the network given the large number of nodes sharing a relatively small area – the immediate range of a node ($\pi \cdot range^2$) represents nearly 40% of the whole area.

The experimental signal strength probing parameters used were as follows. The timeout period associated with each ping was $T_{\text{ping-timeout}} = 0.04$ seconds. A maximum of 3 pings were sent (i.e., $n = 3$) and $k = 3$, meaning that if 3 packets with a strength below the preemptive threshold were received within this window a route warning was generated. Note that since the average duration of the bad state due to temporary fadings is 2 packets, we require 3 low-strength packets to indicate that a link is bad with sufficient consistency to warrant a route warning. However, all of these values were chosen somewhat arbitrarily and could benefit from empirical tuning. In general, depending upon the congestion, traffic rate, observed link state, and other variables it is possible to dynamically adjust any of these parameters. Such online adaptation is a topic for future work.

3.5.1   Preemptive Routing Analysis

The direct effect of preemptive routing can be seen by examining the number of broken paths in Figure 5(a). The horizontal lines on each figure correspond to baseline DSR (with no modifications whatsoever) under high mobility and low mobility. The number of broken paths is shown as the preemptive ratio (δ) is increased. Note that he case with $\delta = 1$ corresponds to *non-preemptive PDSR* which is equivalent to DSR with the modified cache behavior previously described. Thus, the non-preemptive PDSR results isolate the effects of the cache modifications from those due to proactivity. At the knee of the curve, the proactivity threshold provides sufficient time to initiate rediscovery; lower values cannot avoid all path breaks while higher values restrict the effective range and increase the overhead unnecessarily. We note that the optimal preemptive threshold increases with mobility and CBR rate, to allow more time to recover from a path break given the higher speed of nodes and longer latency respectively.

It is evident that preemptive routing drastically reduces the number of broken paths, eliminating most of them for the low CBR case. With a high CBR, collisions are more frequent and large variability in latencies can be experienced due to the exponential back-off initiated when a collision oc-

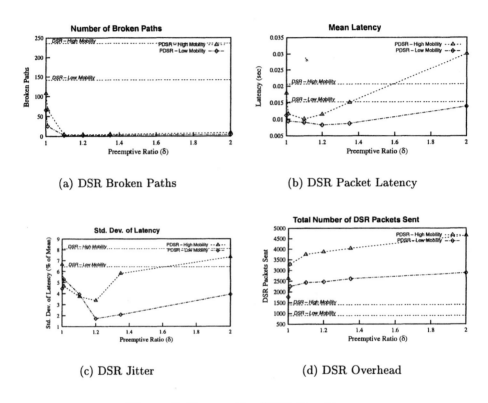

(a) DSR Broken Paths   (b) DSR Packet Latency

(c) DSR Jitter   (d) DSR Overhead

Figure 5: Preemptive DSR Results

curs [46]. Under these conditions, the preemptive warning may not provide sufficient time for path discovery. Accordingly, while proactivity significantly reduces the number of broken paths, the number remains higher than the low CBR case. Proactivity is even more successful for the high mobility scenarios where paths break more frequently. Very high proactivity thresholds are inefficient, for example a proactivity threshold of 4 corresponds to limiting the effective range by 28% and coverage area by 48%. In practice, the useful range of proactivity should be restricted to below $\delta = 2$. An alternative measure of the effectiveness of proactivity is the total recovery time experienced by broken paths; we observed this value going down drastically as well under preemptive routing implementations.

Figure 5(b) shows the mean overall packet latency. Significant reductions in latency can be observed in the best case, e.g. at $\delta \approx 1.2$ which is close to the optimal preemptive threshold. The reduction in latency is largely due to avoiding the delays associated with path breaks. In fact, latencies on established paths can be expected to increase slightly because proactivity limits the effective range slightly since a shorter path with a link below the proactivity threshold is rejected in favor of a longer path with higher quality links. Figure 5(c) plots the standard deviation in latency (jitter) as a percentage of the mean latency. Please note that these jitter values must be taken with a grain of salt since variance in the delays is expected due to variations in path length and due to congestion. Ideally, the jitter would be measured on a per-connection basis. However, by eliminating the very high delays for disconnected paths, the overall jitter values are improved.

Figure 5(d) shows the overhead of PDSR compared to DSR. While the overhead of PDSR is higher, we note that most of the overhead was also experienced by the non-preemptive version of PDSR ($\delta = 1$, corresponding to DSR with caching disabled) and increased only slightly for preemptive ratios in the practical range. This indicates that most of the overhead is due to the modified cache behavior (no path replies from cache) and not due to the addition of proactivity. There is reason to believe that the overhead will drop with an effective caching strategy.

To illustrate that the results are not specific to DSR, we incorporated preemptive path maintenance into AODV, a distance vector based routing algorithm for ad hoc networks. Figure 6(a) and Figure 6(b) show the number of broken paths and the packet latency for the same CBR traffic scenarios. Again, the number of broken paths is drastically reduced, and the latency is improved by up to 30% in the best case. We note that the number of broken paths for baseline AODV is less than that for baseline DSR (potentially due to the better caching scheme). Figure 6(c) shows number of AODV packets introduced. As can be expected, the overhead increases with preemptive routing due provocative searches that are proved unnecessary. However, we note that the increase is significantly lower than the increase in the DSR case. This strengthens the claim that the increased DSR overhead was mainly due to the modified cache behavior.

3.5.2 TCP Analysis

We consider two TCP traffic scenarios to assess how preemptive route maintenance might affect applications: (i) telnet, where pairs of nodes simulate telnet sessions and small messages are exchanged with "human delays" between them; and (ii) ftp, where a sender transmits a continuous data stream

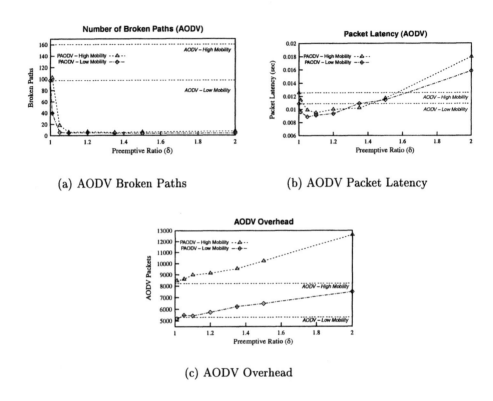

(a) AODV Broken Paths   (b) AODV Packet Latency

(c) AODV Overhead

Figure 6: Preemptive AODV Results

to a receiver at the maximum rate possible for the duration of the experiment. Latency is the main performance metric for telnet scenarios, while for ftp throughput is the appropriate measure of performance.

Figures 7(a) and 7(b) show the average packet latency in the telnet scenarios. Baseline DSR is the left most point on each plot. Again, the performance of baseline DSR is significantly lower than PDSR with no preemptive maintenance due to the bad caching behavior exhibited by DSR. Adding preemptive maintenance further improved the latency by up to 40%. An interesting observation about the behavior of baseline DSR is that the latency improved as the number of senders increased. A possible explanation is that the cache behavior is improved as nodes listen to traffic and route requests from other paths which makes their caches fresher. Thus, the caches benefit from a better sampling of the network state. The throughput

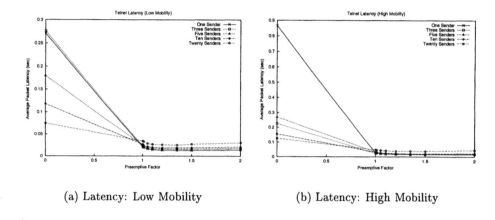

(a) Latency: Low Mobility   (b) Latency: High Mobility

Figure 7: Telnet Performance

was almost identical in all cases since the offered load is relatively light.

The packet latency for the FTP scenarios are shown in Figure 8(a). The latency is marginally improved in the one sender case when preemptive path maintenance is used. The small improvement relative to the telnet case can be explained by the low number of packets affected by path disconnects, relative to the high volume of ftp data traffic. Since ftp represents a high network load (a single ftp connection has been observed to saturate a wireless LAN in experimental settings [47]), the more frequent path discoveries in PDSR can escalate congestion in this already high load scenario. This is especially true when multiple active ftp connections are considered. Moreover, we observed a fairness problem in multiple-sender ftp case which skews these results. This can occur, for example, when ftp data traffic from one flow effectively monopolizes the available bandwidth blocking route request packets from other flows which can in turn cause TCP to timeout and exponentially backoff. If this happens for successive route requests, a significant bandwidth disparity will develop between the active flows. Figure 8(b) shows the throughput for the FTP scenario. The multiple-sender fairness problem again distorts the 3-sender case, while a small improvement (around 10%) in throughput is achieved due to preemptive maintenance in the single sender case.

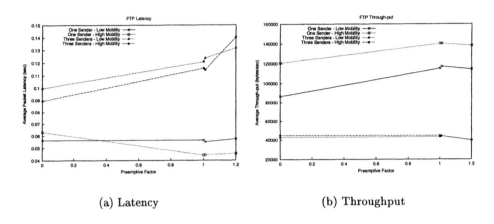

(a) Latency   (b) Throughput

Figure 8: FTP Performance

4   Discussion and Conclusions

We illustrated the use of proactive mechanisms at network and transport
layers to mitigate the effects of disconnections. At the transport level the
Freeze-TCP mechanism is designed to prevent the congestion window from
falling so that the sender can resume transmission at the same rate it had
adopted just prior to the disconnection. At a more fundamental level, the
question is whether it is appropriate to restart transmission at this full rate
from the old window size upon entering a new, unknown network environment? TCP itself implements slow-start at the beginning of a connection
precisely because it wants to sample the congestion state before it decides
to increase the transmission rate. While this is true in general, there are
many situations in mobile environments where the disconnections are not
caused by any fundamental or substantial changes in the traffic or congestion state of the network. This can happen for instance, due to temporary
obstructions or fades that the mobile client may experience. In such cases,
it should be safe to resume transmission with the same window size as prior
to a disconnection.

   This issue is resolved when Freeze-TCP is used against a peer whose
TCP implementation complies with the recommendations of RFC 2581 [48].
In such scenarios, Freeze-TCP should be effective when brief periods of
interruption are encountered, while initiating slow-start when recovering

from a longer interval of disruption. Specifically, RFC 2581 [48] states that TCP connections which have not sent data within the last retransmission timeout (RTO) period should perform slow-start. This limits the influence of Freeze-TCP to periods of interruption which last for less time than RTO, where RTO typically equals $RTT + 4 \cdot V$ for a smoothed round-trip time RTT and smoothed variation in round-trip time V.

Another possible drawback of Freeze-TCP is that it needs the receiver to predict impending disconnections. However, if a disconnection cannot be predicted the behavior and performance will be exactly that of standard TCP. Simulation results highlight the importance of *proactive* action and signaling by the mobile-host. The data indicates that in many cases, a *proactive* mechanisms such as Freeze-TCP can yield better performance than those that simply *react after* a disconnection occurs.

An alternate approach can be used when Explicit Congestion Notification (ECN) [49, 50] is supported by both communicating TCP peers, as well as by intermediate wireless routers. In general, the use of ECN should reduce the number of packets lost due to congestion, since TCP can invoke congestion avoidance procedures before any loss actually occurs. This allows TCP implementations operating in wireless environments to assume that losses occurring without prior ECN warnings (or perhaps all losses) are due to random wireless effects such as temporary signal fades [51, 52, 53]. This provides a simple mechanism for TCP to infer the cause of packet loss, and consequently only invoke congestion avoidance when there is explicit knowledge that the network is currently congested.

At the network layer we proposed proactively searching for alternate paths if the path in use becomes suspect but before it actually breaks. Our initial implementation of this preemptive routing strategy relied on signal strength as the only metric of path quality. Note that the path-quality metric can be easily extended to include other attributes such as latency, jitter, etc., which naturally leads to QoS issues. Another interesting future study would be to deploy the proactive Transport and Network level mechanisms simultaneously, i.e., to employ a proactive TCP (such as Freeze-TCP) on top of preemptive routing which has the potential of further improving performance.

Fundamentally we believe that the strict layering implicit in the network stack design must in some ways be relaxed to facilitate the flow of information between layers in order to allow protocols to work more efficiently in mobile environments. For example, Transport layer entities such as TCP cannot be completely oblivious to the characteristics of the links underneath, otherwise poor performance results. Likewise, applications should also adapt to the environment they find themselves in, for example a browser could disable the automatic downloading of graphics-rich content if the only network connection available is a low bandwidth wireless link. In other words a tighter vertical integration across the layers of the networking stack is necessary to cope with mobile and ad hoc environments.

Such a need for vertical integration manifests itself in many other cases where performance is critical. Consider systems incorporated into NASA spacecraft sent on long voyages. In such a case performance and reliability are critical and warrant sacrificing the convenience afforded by the strict partitioning of network layers. A similar analogy can be drawn from computers in their early days: in the 1960s and early 70s, computer technology was just taking off. Hence it was necessary for one entity (IBM, CDC, etc.) to build the hardware, write the operating systems to manage the hardware, and also provide application software. There was tight vertical integration in order to extract maximum performance out of the available technology. As the technology matured, separate vendors began to supply independent hardware, systems software, and application software. This kind of "layering" is natural as any technology develops and the performance of each individual component of a system reaches a level where the overhead of abstraction is negligible and necessary to better manage overall complexity.

When disruptive events occur, such as the emergence of mobile computing, a reexamination of the strict layering vs. vertical integration issue is necessary. We believe that attempting to integrate mobility, security, and QoS attributes into the Internet is a continual retrofit job which is bound by the backward compatibility chains imposed by such an enormous existing infrastructure. Any such patchwork will probably provided only a temporary fix, while what is really needed is radical redesign rather than a series of increasingly diminishing incremental enhancements to TCP and IP.

References

[1] T. Goff, J. Moronski, D. S. Phatak, and V. Gupta, " Freeze-TCP: a true end-to-end TCP enhancement mechanism for mobile environments," in *Proceedings of the IEEE INFOCOM'2000, Tel-Aviv, Israel*, vol. 3, pp. 1537–1545, Mar. 2000.

[2] T. Goff, N. Abu-Ghazaleh, D. S. Phatak, and R. Kahvecioglu, "Preemptive Routing in Ad Hoc Networks," in *Proceedings of the ACM*

MOBICOM'2001, Rome, , pp. 43–52, July. 2001.

[3] T. Goff, N. Abu-Ghazaleh, D. S. Phatak, and R. Kahvecioglu, "Preemptive Routing in Ad Hoc Networks," *Journal of Parallel and Distributed Computing (JPDC), Special issue on mobile and Wireless Networks.* To Appear.

[4] C. Perkins, Editor, *IP Mobility Support,* October 1996. RFC 2002.

[5] C. Perkins, *IP Encapsulation within IP,* October 1996. RFC 2003.

[6] C. Perkins, *Minimal Encapsulation within IP,* October 1996. RFC 2004.

[7] J. Solomon, *Applicability Statement for IP Mobility Support,* October 1996. RFC 2005.

[8] S. Avancha, V. Korolev, A. Joshi, T. Finin, and Y. Yesha, "On experiments with a transport protocol for pervasive computing environments," *Computer Networks,* vol. 40, pp. 515–535, June 2002.

[9] C. Chiang, M. Gerla, and L. Zhang, "Routing in clustered multihop, mobile wireless networks with fading channel," in *Proceedings of IEEE SICON 97,* pp. 197–211, April 1997.

[10] P. Jacquet, P. Muhlethaler, T. Clausen, A. Laoulti, A. Qayyum, and L. Viennot, "Optimized link state routing protocol for ad hoc networks," in *IEEE INMIC 2001,* pp. 62–68, December 2001.

[11] S. Murthy and J. J. Garcia-Luna-Aceves, "An Efficient Routing Protocol for Wireless Networks," *ACM Mobile Networks and Applications Journal,* pp. 183–197, Oct. 1996.

[12] G. Pei and M. Gerla, "Fisheye state routing in mobile ad hoc networks," in *Proceedings of ICC 2000,* pp. D71–D78, 2000. Internet Draft available at: `http://www.ietf.org/internet-drafts/draft-ietf-manet-fsr-00.txt`.

[13] C. Perkins and P. Bhagwat, "Highly dynamic destination-sequenced distance-vector routing (dsdv) for mobile computers," in *ACM SIG-COMM'94 Conference on Communications Architectures, Protocols and Applications,* pp. 234–244, Aug. 1994.

[14] D. Johnson, D. Maltz, Y. Hu, and J. Jetcheva, "The dynamic source routing protocol for mobile ad hoc networks." Internet Draft, Internet Engineering Task Force, March 2001. `http://www.ietf.org/internet-drafts/draft-ietf-manet-dsr-05.txt`.

[15] V. Park and S. Corson, "Temporally-ordered routing algorithm (TORA) version 1 functional specification." Internet Draft, Internet Engineering Task Force, November 2000. `http://www.ietf.org/internet-drafts/draft-ietf-manet-tora-spec-03.txt`.

[16] C. Perkins, E. Royer, and S. Das, "Ad hoc on-demand distance vector (AODV) routing." Internet Draft, Internet Engineering Task Force, March 2001. `http://www.ietf.org/internet-drafts/draft-ietf-manet-aodv-08.txt`.

[17] W. R. Stevens, *TCP/IP Illustrated, Volume 1*. Addison Wesley, 1994.

[18] J. Postel, *Transmission Control Protocol*, Sep 1981. RFC 0793.

[19] E. R. Braden, *Requirements for Internet Hosts - Communication Layers*, October 1989. RFC 1122.

[20] H. Balakrishnan, V. N. Padmanabhan, and R. Katz, "Improving Reliable Transport and Handoff Performance in Cellular Wireless Networks," *Wireless Networks*, vol. 1, Dec. 1995.

[21] H. Balakrishnan, V. N. Padmanabhan, S. Seshan, and R. Katz, "A Comparison of Mechanisms for Improving TCP performance over wireless links," in *Proceedings of ACM SIGCOMM'96, Palo Alto, CA*, pp. 256–269, Aug 1996.

[22] A. Bakre and B. Badrinath, "I-TCP: Indirect TCP for mobile hosts," tech. rep., Rutgers University, May 1995. `http://www.cs.rutgers.edu/~badri/journal/contents11.html`.

[23] R. Yavatkar and N. Bhagawat, "Improving end-to-end performance of tcp over mobile internetworks," in *IEEE Workshop on Mobile Computing Systems and Applications*, (Santa Cruz, CA, US), Dec. 1994. `http://snapple.cs.washington.edu/mobile/mcsa94.html`.

[24] R. Cceres and L. Iftode, "Improving the performance of reliable transport protocols in mobile computing environments," *IEEE JSAC Special*

Issue on Mobile Computing Network, 1994. http://www.cs.rutgers.edu/~badri/journal/contents11.html.

[25] M. Mehta and N. H. Vaidya, "Delayed duplicate acknowledgments: A proposal to improve performance of tcp on wireless links," tech. rep., Texas A&M University, Dec. 1997. http://www.cs.tamu.edu/faculty/vaidya/Vaidya-mobile.html.

[26] N. Vaidya. Overview of work in mobile-computing (transparencies) available at http://http://www.cs.tamu.edu/faculty/vaidya/slides.ps.

[27] K. Brown and S. Singh, "M-TCP: TCP for Mobile Cellular Networks," *ACM Computer Communications Review (CCR)*, vol. 27, no. 5, 1997.

[28] G. Montenegro and S. Dawkins, "Wireless Networking for the MNCRS, Internet Draft, work in progress," Aug. 1998. http://www.ietf.org/internet-drafts/draft-montenegro-mncrs-00.txt.

[29] S. S. Rappaport, *Wireless Communication Systems*. Prentice Hall, 1996.

[30] Lucent Technologies, *WaveLAN/PCMCIA Card User's Guide*.

[31] J. B. Andersen, T. S. Rappaport, and S. Yoshida, "Propagation measurements and models for wireless communications channels," *IEEE Communication Magazine*, vol. 33, pp. 42–49, Jan. 1995.

[32] Federal Communications Commission (FCC), Enhanced 911 (e911) mandate, 2001 http://www.fcc.gov/911/enhanced.

[33] G. Holland and N. H. Vaidya, "Analysis of TCP Performance over Mobile Ad Hoc Networks," in *Proceedings of MOBICOM, Seattle*, Aug. 1999.

[34] V. Jacobson, "Congestion avoidance and control," in *Symposium proceedings on Communications architectures and protocols*, pp. 314–329, ACM Press, 1988.

[35] S. Biaz and N. H. Vaidya, "Distinguishing Congestion Losses from Wireless Transmission Losses," in *7th International Conference on Computer Communications and Networks (IC3N), New Orleans*, Oct 1998.

[36] N. Vaidya, "Tutorial on TCP for Wireless and Mobile Hosts." Presented at MobiCom '99, 1999. `http://www.crhc.uiuc.edu/~nhv/seminars/tcp-wireless-tutorial.ppt`.

[37] A. Boukerche, S. K. Das, and A. Fabbri, "Analysis of Randomized Congestion Control with DSDV Routing in Ad Hoc Wireless Networks," *Journal of Parallel and Distributed Computing (JPDC)*, vol. 61, pp. 967–995, July 2001.

[38] M. Gerla, K. Tang, and R. Bagrodia, "TCP performance in wireless multi-hop networks," in *Proceedings of IEEE WMCSA 99, New Orleans, LA*, February 1999.

[39] Y.-C. Hu and D. Johnson, "Caching strategies in on-demand routing protocols for wireless ad hoc networks," in *Proceedings of the International Conference on Mobile Computing and Networks (MobiCom 00)*, pp. 231–242, August 2000.

[40] R. Castaneda and S. Das, "Query localization techniques for on-demand routing protocols in Ad Hoc networks," in *Proceedings of the International Conference on Mobile Computing and Networking (MobiCom 99)*, August 1999.

[41] Y. Ko and N. H. Vaidya, "Location-Aided Routing (LAR) Mobile Ad Hoc Networks," in *Proceedings of MOBICOM'98, Dallas*, Oct. 1998.

[42] UCB/LBNL/VINT Network Simulator, web-site `http://www-mash.CS.Berkeley.EDU/ns`.

[43] NS-2 with Wireless and Mobility Extensions, available via web-site `http://www.monarch.cs.cmu.edu`.

[44] J. Broch, D. A. Maltz, D. B. Johnson, Y.-C. Hu, and J. Jetcheva, "A Performance Comparison of Multi-Hop Wireless Ad Hoc Network Routing Protocols," in *Proceedings of ACM/IEEE MOBICOM'98 Dallas*, Oct. 1998.

[45] D. A. Maltz, J. Broch, J. Jetcheva, and D. B. Johnson, " The Effects of On-Demand Behavior in Routing Protocols for Multi-Hop Wireless Ad Hoc Networks," *IEEE Journal on Selected Areas in Communications, pecial issue on mobile and wireless networks*, Aug. 1999.

[46] J. Geier, *Wireless LANs: Implementing Interoperable Networks*. McMillan Technical Publishing, 1999.

[47] D. Tang and M. Baker, "Analysis of a Local-Area Wireless Network," in *Proceedings of the International Confernece on Mobile Computing and Networks (MobiComm 00)*, pp. 1–10, 2000.

[48] M. Allman, V. Paxson, and W. Stevens, *TCP Congestion Control*, April 1999. RFC 2581.

[49] S. Floyd, "TCP and Explicit Congestion Notification," *ACM Computer Communication Review*, vol. 24, pp. 10–23, October 1994.

[50] K. Ramakrishnan, S. Floyd, and D. Black, *The Addition of Explicit Congestion Notification (ECN) to IP*, September 2001. RFC 3168.

[51] R. Ramani and A. Karandikar, "Explicit Congestion Notification (ECN) in TCP Over Wireless Network," in *IEEE International Conference on Personal Wireless Communications*, pp. 495–499, December 2000.

[52] F. Peng, S. Cheng, and J. Ma, "An Effective Way to Improve TCP Performance in Wireless/Mobile Networks," in *IEEE/AFCEA EUROCOMM 2000. Information Systems for Enhanced Public Safety and Security.*, pp. 250–255, May 2000.

[53] J. Liu and S. Singh, "ATCP: TCP for Mobile Ad Hoc Networks," *IEEE Journal on Selected Areas in Communications*, vol. 19, pp. 1300–1315, July 2001.

AD HOC WIRELESS NETWORKING
X. Cheng, X. Huang and D.-Z. Du (Eds.) pp. 529 - 560

Hybrid Routing: The Pursuit of an Adaptable and Scalable Routing Framework for Ad Hoc Networks[1]

Prince Samar
School of Electrical and Computer Engineering
Cornell University, Ithaca, NY 14850
E-mail: samar@ece.cornell.edu

Marc R. Pearlman
School of Electrical and Computer Engineering
Cornell University, Ithaca, NY 14850
E-mail: pearlman@ece.cornell.edu

Zygmunt J. Haas
School of Electrical and Computer Engineering
Cornell University, Ithaca, NY 14850
E-mail: haas@ece.cornell.edu

Contents

---

[1]Reprinted with permission from "Handbook of Ad Hoc Wireless Networks," chapter 14, CRC Press 2003. Copyright Zygmunt J. Haas.

Abstract

Advances in ad hoc network research have opened the door to an assortment of promising military and commercial applications for ad hoc networks. However, because each application has unique characteristics (such as traffic behavior, device capabilities, mobility patterns, operating environments, etc.), routing in such a versatile environment is a challenging task and numerous protocols have been developed to address it. While many protocols excel for certain types of ad hoc networks, it is clear that a single basic protocol cannot perform well over the entire space of ad hoc networks. To conform to any arbitrary ad hoc network, the basic protocols designed for various extremes of the ad hoc network design space need to be integrated into a tunable framework.

The Zone Routing framework demonstrates how multi-scoping can provide the basis for a hybrid routing protocol framework. Zone Routing proactively maintains routing information for a local neighborhood called the routing zone, while reactively acquiring routes to destinations beyond the routing zone. In this paper, we review the Zone Routing concept and propose Zone Routing with independently sized routing zones capability. With this capability, each of the nodes in the network can adaptively configure its own optimal zone radius in a distributed fashion. We show that the performance of Zone Routing is significantly improved by the ability to provide fine-tuned adaptation to spatial and temporal variations in network characteristics.

1 Ad Hoc Networks Overview

An ad hoc network is a self-organizing wireless network made up of mobile nodes and requiring no fixed infrastructure. The limitations on power consumption imposed by portable wireless radios result in a node transmission range that is typically small relative to the span of the network. To provide communication throughout the entire network, nodes are designed to serve as routers. The result is a distributed multi-hop network with a time-varying topology.

Because ad hoc networks do not rely on existing infrastructure and are self-organizing, they can be rapidly deployed to provide robust communication in a variety of hostile environments. This makes ad hoc networks very appropriate for providing tactical communication for the military, law enforcement and emergency response efforts. Ad hoc networks can also play a role in civilian forums, such as the electronic classroom, convention centers, and construction sites. With such a broad scope of applications, it is not difficult to envision ad hoc networks operating over a wide range of coverage areas, node densities, mobility patterns and communication behaviors.

This potentially wide range of ad hoc network operating configurations poses a challenge for developing efficient routing protocols. On one hand, the effectiveness of a routing protocol increases as network topology information becomes more detailed and up-to-date. On the other hand, in an ad hoc network, the topology may change quite often, requiring large and frequent exchanges of control information among the network nodes. This is in contradiction with the fact that all updates in the wireless communication environment travel over the air and are, thus, costly in resources.

2 Brief Survey of Basic Ad Hoc Routing Protocols

Existing routing protocols can be classified either as *proactive* or as *reactive*. Proactive protocols continuously evaluate the routes within the network, so that when a packet needs to be forwarded, the route is already known and can be immediately used. Early applications of proactive routing schemes for ad hoc networks were Distance Vector protocols based on the Distributed Bellman-Ford (DBF) algorithm [2]. Modifications to the basic DBF algorithm (i.e., [4], [7], and [29]) were proposed to address inherent problems of convergence and excessive traffic (both of which can be quite severe problems in ad hoc networks, where bandwidth is scarce and topologies are often very dynamic). The convergence problem has also been addressed by the application of Link State protocols such as TBRPF [1], STAR [8], ALP [9], and GSR [3] to the ad hoc environment. In general, Link State protocols converge faster than Distance Vector protocols, but may lead to a lot of control traffic. Motivation to both improve protocol convergence and to reduce control traffic has led to the development of proactive path finding algorithms, which combine the features of the Distance Vector and Link State approaches. Realizations of the path finding algorithms, like the Wireless Routing Protocol (WRP) ([21] and [22]), are able to eliminate the "counting-to-infinity" problem and to reduce the occurrence of temporary loops, often with less control traffic than traditional Distance Vector schemes.

In contrast, reactive protocols[2] invoke a route determination procedure on an on-demand basis. The reactive route discovery is usually based on a query-reply exchange, where the route query uses some flooding-based process to reach the desired destination. In the case of the Temporally Ordered Routing Algorithm (TORA) [23], the route replies are also flooded, in a controlled manner, distributing routing information in the form of directed acyclic graphs (DAGs) rooted at the destination. In contrast, the Dynamic Source Routing (DSR) [17] and Ad hoc On Demand Distance Vector (AODV) [30] protocols unicast the route reply back to the querying source, along a path constructed during the route query phase. In the case of DSR, the routing information is accumulated in the query packet and the complete sequence of nodes is returned to the source (to be used for source routing of the actual user data). AODV, on the other hand, distributes the discovered route in the form of next-hop information stored at each node in the route. The on-demand discovery of routes can result in much less traffic than the standard proactive Distance Vector or Link State schemes, especially when innovative route maintenance schemes are employed. However, the reliance on flooding of the reactive schemes may still lead to considerable control traffic in the highly versatile ad hoc networking environment. Moreover, due to the large increase in control traffic at the times of route discovery, the delay of the route-discovery process in reactive protocols can be significant.

---

[2]*Reactive protocols* are also referred to as *on-demand protocols*.

3   Multi-scope Routing

All else being equal, the value of information decreases with respect to the distance from the information source. For example, a node cannot compute routes without knowing any of its neighbors. On the other hand, a node may make near-optimal forwarding decisions, even in spite of outdated or missing *distant* state information.

This relationship between information value and distance is extremely valuable for routing protocol design. Simply distributing the same information, at the same rate to all nodes in the network does not provide the most "bang for the buck." There is more value in providing nearby nodes with more frequent update and/or detailed information, at the expense of keeping more distant nodes less informed.

To some extent, most basic protocols exhibit some degree of multi-scope behavior. Many proactive routing protocols monitor the status of neighbor connectivity through neighbor broadcast HELLO beacons, which occur at a faster rate than the global link state (or distance vector) advertisements. In many reactive routing protocols, route discovery is based on querying on a global scale, whereas subsequent route repair utilizes local querying, constrained by a time-to-live (TTL) packet hop counter

The high quality local route information provided by multi-scope routing can be used to provide an assortment of new and enhanced services. By identifying overlaps in local connectivity, broadcast messages can be distributed to all nodes more efficiently (e.g., OLSR's multipoint relay [6]). Moreover, local exchange of route information can be further exploited to provide a *bordercast* query distribution service, in which only a subset of the network's nodes needs to be queried. Such a service can be applied to global route discovery, name-address translation, and general database lookups. In the case of global reactive protocols, once a route has been discovered, changes in local connectivity can be quickly identified, allowing for either proactive route repair or proactive route shortening [25]. Local multi-hop feedback of link layer acknowledgments can be used to discover and reliably use unidirectional links [26]. Intelligent node participation/sleep-mode algorithms can use local route information to determine if a node's absence would compromise the network connectivity.

Perhaps the most familiar examples of multi-scope routing are the various flavors of hierarchical routing [16] [5] [28]. In basic clustered routing, nodes are aggregated into subnets. Each node knows the topology of its subnet through a local proactive protocol. On a global scale, each subnet is represented by a clusterhead, which knows the connectivity to other subnets' clusterheads, but not the details of the other subnets' topologies. Nodes are located in the hierarchy through relative addressing that associates nodes with clusterheads. This two level example can be easily extended by grouping clusterheads into intermediate level subnets, thus creating a deeper hierarchy.

A variation on clustered routing is landmark routing (e.g. LANMAR [10]). As in the previous example, nodes are organized into local subnets and assume hierarchical addresses. However, the clusterheads are replaced with globally visible landmarks. A global distance vector routing protocol is used to provide all nodes with routes to the landmarks. The role of the landmark is to identify the general location of the associated subnet. Data packets are forwarded toward the landmark, until they reach the subnet, at which point the subnet nodes can forward the packet directly to the destination.

Another hierarchical routing approach is based on the concept of a *core*. In these schemes, local topology is proactively monitored for the purpose of selecting a set of core nodes, such that every node has at least one core node neighbor. The purpose of the core nodes is to determine routes on behalf of the nodes that they cover. This is generally accomplished through global route discovery that is carried through the core. Although the route discovery occurs in the core, the core nodes apply knowledge of their local topology to construct routes that do not necessarily pass through the core. In addition to this basic operation, the CEDAR protocol [33] introduces an interesting local scoping behavior by advertising higher quality links (e.g. high capacity links) over greater distances. The Dynamic Virtual Backbone scheme [18] also employs a similar concept by restricting the route queries within the virtual backbone, thus reducing the control traffic overhead.

Specialized node roles and regional node addressing help hierarchical routing protocols to scale with network size, especially when there is structure in the underlying network connectivity (for example, group mobility) that can be exploited [19]. However, as network behavior becomes less coordinated, the overhead of the hierarchy maintenance (e.g. clusterhead election, node re-addressing) becomes a limiting factor for scaling. In addition, hierarchical routing may introduce uneven resource utilization, traffic hotspots, and in some cases, sub-optimal routing.

It is also possible to provide multi-scope routing without the limitations and overhead of hierarchy management. For example, in FSR [27] a node's link state is distributed over various distances (scopes), with longer distance updates occurring at lower frequencies. This provides each node with a fresh view of the surrounding topology, but a more dated view of farther network regions. The less accurate distant views effectively serve as land-marks, getting data packets forwarded in the right general direction. As the data packets approach the destination, the path to the destination becomes more accurate and the forwarding more refined.

Additional benefits of multi-scope routing can be realized when larger scope protocols are able to exploit the information provided by a smaller scope. Two protocols that exhibit this kind of scope integration are OLSR and Zone Routing. In OLSR [6], an extended neighbor discovery provides each node with the topology of its surrounding two hops. This local infor-mation is used to provide an efficient global link state broadcast, based on *multipoint relay*. Multipoint relay identifies a "minimal" subset of neighbors needed to relay a message, such that all nodes two hops away will receive the message. In the case of Zone Routing, a proactive routing protocol is used to provide each node with a view of its surrounding "routing zone" topol-ogy. This local information enables an efficient query distribution service (bordercasting), which is used by a global reactive route discovery protocol.[3] For Zone Routing, the global protocol efficiency increases with the size of the local "zone." The cost of local vs global scope can be traded-off, and ultimately optimized, through the adjustment of a single parameter – the zone radius.

4 Protocol Hybridization

The diverse applications of ad hoc networks pose a challenge for a single protocol that operates efficiently across a wide range of operational condi-tions and network configurations. Each of the purely proactive or purely reactive protocols described above performs well in a limited region of this range. For example, reactive routing protocols are well suited for networks where the "call to mobility" ratio is relatively low. Proactive routing pro-tocols, on the other hand, are well suited for networks where this ratio is relatively high. Figure 1 shows the ad hoc network design space with node mobility and call rate as the two dimensions and the approximate regions where each of these two kinds of protocols performs well. The performance of either class of protocols degrades when they are applied to regions of ad hoc network space between the two extremes.

Given multiple protocols, each suited for a different region of the ad hoc network design space, it makes sense to capitalize on each protocol's strengths by combining them into a single framework (i.e., hybridization).

---

[3]The Zone Routing framework is described in more detail later in this paper.

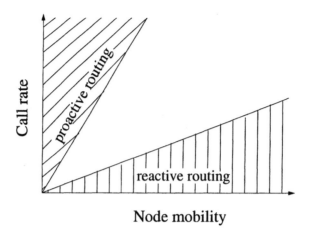

Figure 1: The ad hoc network design space and the applicability of proactive vs. reactive routing.

In the most basic hybrid framework, one of the protocols would be selected based on its suitability for the specific network's characteristics. Although not an elegant solution, such a framework would perform as well as the best suited protocol for any scenario, and outperform either protocol over the entire ad hoc network design space. However, by not using both protocols together, this approach fails to capitalize on the potential synergy that would make the framework perform as well *or better* than either protocol *for any given scenario.*

A more promising approach for protocol hybridization is to have the base protocols operate simultaneously, but with different "scopes." For the case of a two-protocol framework, protocol A would operate locally, while the operation of protocol B would be global. The key to this framework is that the local information acquired by protocol A is used by protocol B to operate in a more efficient manner. This framework can be tuned to network behavior simply by adjusting the size of protocol A's scope. In one extreme configuration, the scope of protocol A is reduced to nothing, leaving protocol B to run by itself. As the scope of protocol A is increased, more information becomes available to protocol B, thereby reducing the overhead produced by protocol B. At the other extreme, protocol A is made global, eliminating the load of protocol B altogether. So, at either extreme, the framework defaults to the operation of an individual protocol. In the wide range of intermediate configurations, the framework performs better than either protocol on its own.

5 Framework Tuning

The motivation behind hybrid routing and multi-scope routing is to provide a framework that can be configured to match the network's operational condition and configuration. Therefore, an integral component of the framework is a tuning mechanism. In particular, the three basic ingredients for tuning are a means for measuring relevant network characteristics, a mapping of these measurements to a framework configuration, and a scheme to update the configurations of affected nodes.

The most basic approach to tuning is to determine the network characteristics and proper configuration offline, prior to the network deployment. Typically, the configurations are determined through network simulation and subsequent parameter optimizations. The nodes are loaded with the proper configuration and then activated. When it is not possible to pre-configure all nodes individually, a small number of nodes may be configured and this configuration can be shared with other nodes as part of an automatic configuration procedure.

The main advantages of pre-configuration are that it requires limited network intelligence and low real-time processing overhead and it ensures stable and consistent configuration. However, for many applications, pre-configuration is not an option. Pre-configuration requires a central configuration authority, which may not exist for distributed applications. In addition, the network characteristics may not be known a priori, or may vary over time, preventing the offline analysis and reducing the effectiveness of the static configuration.

Ad hoc networks naturally lend themselves to dynamic reconfiguration. Through the course of normal operation, nodes directly measure (or infer) local network characteristics. Each node may use its own local measurements for independent self-configuration. Alternatively, the measurements could be relayed to a central configuration node or shared with surrounding nodes for a distributed configuration approach.

At first glance, centralized dynamic reconfiguration may appear to prevent inconsistent configuration, as is the case for centralized static configuration. However, the multi-hop nature of ad hoc networks makes it impossible to reliably perform tightly synchronized configuration updates for all nodes. This means that, for some period of time, the network could be in an inconsistent state. As this also affects distributed and independent reconfiguration, it is necessary that a dynamically tunable routing framework be able to deal with, and potentially exploit, non-uniform node configurations. The way in which a routing framework supports non-uniform configuration

depends on its particular design. We will later see how non-uniform configuration is supported in the Zone Routing framework.

With support for non-uniform configuration, reconfiguration decisions
and associated measurement/control traffic can be localized, thereby providing for scalable framework tuning. Furthermore, the framework can be
fine-tuned to adapt to changes in regional, and even nodal, behavior rather
than broadly tracking average network behavior. This can lead to significant
performance improvements, especially in the case of networks where node
behavior has regional dependencies.

6 The Zone Routing Framework

Protocol hybridization, multi-scope operation, and dynamic reconfiguration,
the key features of adaptable and scalable routing, form the basis of the Zone
Routing framework [15]. At a local level, a proactive routing protocol provides a detailed and fresh view of each node's surrounding local topology
(the *routing zone*). The knowledge of local topology is used to support services such as proactive route maintenance, unidirectional link discovery, and
guided message distribution. One particular message distribution service,
called *bordercasting*, directs queries throughout the network across overlapping routing zones. Bordercasting is used in place of traditional broadcasting
to improve the efficiency of a global reactive routing protocol.

The benefits provided by routing zones, compared with the overhead of
proactively tracking routing zone topology, determine the optimal framework configuration. As network conditions change, the framework can be
dynamically reconfigured through adjustment of each node's routing zone.

In the following sections, we describe the routing and dynamic configuration components of the Zone Routing framework in more detail.

6.1 Local Proactive (Intrazone) Routing

In Zone Routing, the Intrazone Routing Protocol (IARP) proactively maintains routes to destinations within a local neighborhood, which we refer to
as a routing zone. More precisely, a node's routing zone is defined as a collection of nodes whose minimum distance in hops from the node in question
is no greater than a parameter referred to as the *zone radius*. Note that each
node maintains its own routing zone. An important consequence is that the
routing zones of neighboring nodes overlap.

Figure 3 illustrates the routing zone concept with a routing zone of radius
2 hops. This particular routing zone belongs to node S, which we refer to as

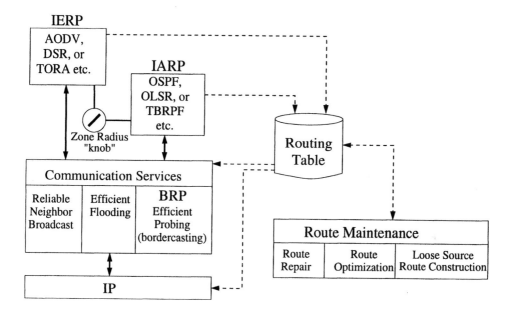

Figure 2: Architecture of the Zone Routing Framework.

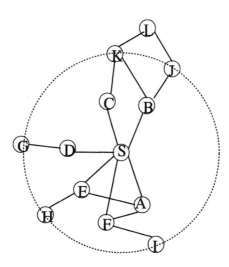

Figure 3: A Routing Zone of radius 2 hops. Reprinted with permission from [M. Pearlman and Z.J. Haas, "Determining the Optimal Configuration for the Zone Routing Protocol," *IEEE JSAC*, vol. 17, no. 8, August 1999] ©1999 IEEE.

the central node of the routing zone. Nodes A through K are members of S's routing zone. Node L, however, is three hops away from S, and is therefore outside of S's routing zone. An important subset of the routing zone nodes is the collection of nodes whose minimum distance to the central node is exactly equal to the zone radius. These nodes are aptly named *peripheral nodes*. In our example, nodes G-K are peripheral nodes of node S. We typically illustrate a routing zone as a circle centered around the central node. However, one should keep in mind that the zone is not a description of physical distance, but rather nodal connectivity (hops).

The construction of a routing zone requires a node to first know who its neighbors are. A neighbor is defined as a node with whom direct (point-to-point) communication can be established and is, thus, one hop away. Identification of a node's neighbors may be provided directly by the media access control (MAC) protocols, as in the case of polling-based protocols. In other cases, neighbor discovery may be implemented through a separate Neighbor Discovery Protocol (NDP). Such a protocol typically operates through the periodic broadcasting of "hello" beacons. The reception (or quality of reception) of a "hello" beacon can be used to indicate the status of a connection to the beaconing neighbor.

Neighbor discovery information is used as a basis for IARP. IARP can be derived from globally proactive link state routing protocols that provide a complete view of network connectivity (for example, OSPF [20], OLSR [6], or TBRPF [1] as shown in Figure 2). The base protocol needs to be modified to ensure that the scope of the routing updates is restricted to the radius of the node's routing zone [13]. In this paper, IARP is based on a simple, timer-based, link state protocol. To track the topology of R-hop routing zones, each node periodically broadcasts its link state for a depth of R hops (controlled by a time-to-live (TTL) field in the update message).

6.2   Bordercast-Based Global Reactive (Interzone) Routing

Route discovery in the Zone Routing framework is distinguished from standard broadcast based route discovery through a message distribution service known as *bordercasting* [14]. Rather than blindly broadcasting a route query from a neighbor to a neighbor, bordercasting allows the query to be directed outward, toward regions of the network (specifically, toward peripheral nodes) that have not yet been "covered" by the query. (A covered node is one that belongs to the routing zone of a node that has received a route query). The query control mechanisms reduce route query traffic by directing query messages outward from the query source and away from covered routing zones, as illustrated in Figure 4.

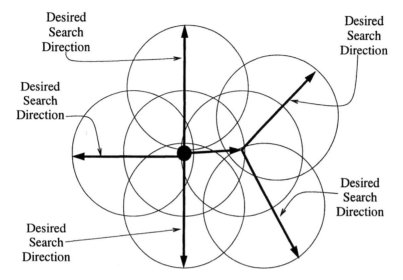

Figure 4: Guiding the search in desirable directions. Reprinted with permission from [M. Pearlman and Z.J. Haas, "Determining the Optimal Configuration for the Zone Routing Protocol," *IEEE JSAC*, vol. 17, no. 8, August 1999] ©1999 IEEE.

A node can determine local query coverage by noting the addresses of neighboring nodes that have forwarded the query. In the case of multiple channel networks, a node can only detect query packets that have been directly forwarded to it. For single channel networks, a node may be able to detect any query packet forwarded within the node's radio range (i.e., through eavesdropping in promiscuous reception mode). When a node identifies a query forwarding neighbor, all known members of that neighbor's routing zone (i.e., those members which belong to both the node's and neighbor's routing zones) are marked as covered.

When a node is called upon to relay a bordercast message, it again uses its routing zone topology to construct a bordercast tree, that is rooted at itself and spans its uncovered peripheral nodes. The message is then forwarded to those neighbors in the bordercast tree. By virtue of the fact that this node has forwarded the query, all of its routing zone members are marked as covered. Therefore, a bordercasting node will not forward a query more than once.

Query detection can be enhanced by introducing a random delay prior to construction of the bordercast tree. During this time, the waiting node benefits from the opportunity to detect the added query coverage from other bordercasting neighbors. This, in turn, promotes a more thorough pruning of the bordercast tree. Increasing the average delay can significantly improve performance, up to a point. Once the bordercast delays are sufficiently spread out, further increases in delay have only a negligible impact on query efficiency.

The use of *short* random delays does not necessarily result in extra route discovery delay. Many route discovery protocols use random pre-transmission jitter to dilute the "instantaneous" channel load of neighboring query retransmissions. This forwarding jitter may be scheduled any time between query packet reception and query packet retransmission, including just prior to bordercast tree construction.

Given the implementation of an underlying bordercast service, the operation of Zone Routing's global reactive Interzone Routing Protocol (IERP) is quite similar to standard route discovery protocols. An IERP route discovery is initiated when no route is locally available to the destination of an outgoing data packet. The source generates a route query packet, which is uniquely identified by a combination of the source node's address and request number. The query is then relayed to a subset of neighbors as determined by the bordercast algorithm. Upon receipt of a route query packet, a node records its ID in the route query packet. The sequence of recorded node IDs specifies an accumulated route from the source to the current node. If a valid route for the destination is not known (i.e., the destination is not in the node's routing zone and an active route does not appear in the node's route cache), then the node bordercasts the query. This process continues until the query reaches a node that has a valid route to the destination or until the query reaches the destination itself. In that case, a route reply is sent back to the source, along the path specified by reversing the accumulated route. The operation of IERP is sufficiently general, so that many existing reactive protocols can be used as an IERP with minimal modification [12]. In particular, the DSR [17] or the AODV [30] can be incorporated into the Zone Routing framework as its reactive component (IERP), as shown in Figure 2.

7 Motivation for Independent Zones

According to the description of Zone Routing in the previous section, every node participating in network routing should have the same value of the zone-radius. This means that before the network becomes operational, all the nodes in the network should come to a consensus on the optimal value of the zone-radius by some extraneous means. Also, any node joining the network later or undergoing rebooting should be able to infer the correct value of the zone-radius at which the rest of the network is operating.

Most applications of ad hoc networks require that the network be formed and be operational quickly and nodes be free to join and leave the system at their own will, without the need for any external configuration. In such networks, the constraint of having uniform zone radius for all the nodes may not be desirable. Having independent zones capability within the Zone Routing framework would allow nodes to dynamically, distributedly, and automatically configure their optimal zone-radii making the framework truly flexible.[4]

Intuition, confirmed by simulation results of Zone Routing, suggests that high mobility and/or low call rates favor smaller zone radius. And vice versa, low mobility and/or high call rates favor larger zone radius. Now consider a network where different parts of the network have different mobility and call rate patterns. Due to these differences, it may turn out that the different sections may have different *optimal* zone-radii. This motivates the development of the Zone Routing framework with independent zones capability, such that different nodes are possibly assigned different zone radii. It is quite likely that such a framework would perform better than the single zone size case, as it can be fine-tuned to the local conditions of the network. Furthermore, if the network characteristics change over time, such a framework can easily and quickly adapt to the changing conditions of the network.

All these points motivate the development of Zone Routing with the capability to have independently sized routing zones. Such a framework would help determine the appropriate balance of contributions from the proactive and reactive components, which is just right for the specific characteristics and operational conditions of the network. The balance of proactive and reactive contributions can easily be changed over time and location by changing a single parameter – the zone radius of each node. Such a framework would not only reduce the routing overhead, but would be responsive to the needs of the network traffic as well.

---

[4]We will later see how a node determines the optimal value of its zone-radius in a distributed fashion.

8 IZR Introduction

In the Independent Zone Routing (IZR) framework, different nodes may
have differently sized "routing zones." What does it mean for the nodes
to have independent routing zones and how does such a routing protocol
operate? Before exploring these issues, we begin by re-defining some terms
in the IZR context.

- *Routing Zone or Receive Zone:* The *neighborhood* around each node
  about which a node proactively maintains routing information is called
  its routing zone. A node maintains this information by receiving proactive updates from these nodes in the neighborhood, hence this zone
  is also called its receive zone. This neighborhood consists of the set
  of all nodes, whose minimum distance, in hops, from the node is not
  more than the *zone radius, R*.

- *Send Zone:* All the nodes which require proactive updates from the
  node in question, in order to maintain their intra-zone routing information, belong to the node's send zone. A node is expected to broadcast
  proactive updates to the members of its send zone.

- *Peripheral Nodes:* The farthest members of a node's routing zone,
  whose minimum distance from the node is R hops, are called its peripheral nodes.

We have seen that in the case of equally sized routing zones, a node
broadcasts proactive routing information to all the members of its zone and
also receives the same from each one of them. Thus, the send zone of a
node is the same as its receive zone, when all nodes have equal zone-radius.
However, when the nodes in the network are allowed to have independently
sized routing zones, this may not be the case.

In IZR, the routing zone or the receive zone is also *regular* in shape – that
is, it can be represented by a circle of radius proportional to the zone-radius
of the node. All nodes with lesser number of hops from the node lie inside
this circle and the peripheral nodes lie on the circle. In contrast, in IZR, the
send zones may not have such a regular shape. The members of the send
zone of a particular node S consist of all nodes of which S is a routing zone
member (so that they expect to receive a routing update from S). Because
nodes in S's send zone may have different receive zone radii, S's resulting
send zone may be irregularly-shaped. It is to be noted that the send zone
may not even be a connected (contiguous) area.

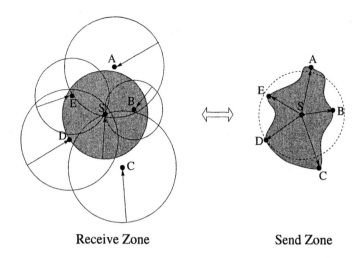

Receive Zone   Send Zone

Figure 5: The receive zone is regular in shape but the send zone may not be.

Figure 5 shows the routing or receive zones of nodes S, A, B, C, D, and E, which are regular in shape. As S is a routing zone member of A, B, C, D, and E, they belong to its send zone, which turns out to be irregular in shape.

9 IZR Details

The basic operation of IZR is similar to Zone Routing as discussed above. If a source node has a packet to send to a destination node which is not a member of its routing zone, it bordercasts a route query packet. However, due to the presence of unequal routing zones in the network, a somewhat different bordercasting scheme is used. As unequal routing zones imply that the send zone of a node may be irregular in shape, the Intrazone Routing Protocol (IARP) has to be modified in order to distribute the proactive updates in such a send zone. Below, we discuss the IARP and the Bordercast Resolution Protocol (BRP) for the Independent Zone Routing framework. Note that as the receive zones are still of regular shape, there is no need for any changes in the operation of IERP.

9.1 Intrazone Routing Protocol (IARP)

Each node maintains proactive routing information about the members of its routing or receive zone. For this to happen, each node needs to broadcast its proactive updates to the members of its send zone. As the send zone may be irregular in terms of the distance in hops to the "boundary" nodes, a node first needs to infer the size and shape of its send zone.

Consider a scenario where each node floods "zone building packets" in its routing zone. As the routing zones are regular in shape, this can easily be done by setting the time-to-live (TTL) field of the update packet equal to the node's zone-radius, R. The value in the TTL field is decremented by one, each time the packet travels one hop. If the TTL value reaches zero, the packet is dropped, else it is rebroadcasted. In Figure 5, nodes A, B, C, D, E, and S broadcast their zone building packets to the members of their routing zones (marked by a circle around each of them). Thus, each node will receive a zone building packet from all those nodes to whose routing zone it belongs. In particular, S would receive A, B, C, D, and E's zone building packets as it is a member of each of their routing zones. Note that all these nodes whose zone building packets are received by a node will belong to that node's send zone – A, B, C, D, and E belong to S's send zone, as in Figure 5.

Based on the above discussion, in the general case of independent routing zones, a node can find out the size and extent of its send zone. The following scheme is used by the nodes to distribute the proactive updates in their send zones. Along with the zone-radius field and the dynamic time-to-live TTL field, an update packet also has a field which contains the initial value of TTL at the source, the TTL_0 field. The source node sets the value of the TTL and TTL_0 fields equal to the distance in hops to the farthest member of its send zone.

Initializing the TTL field to the above value makes the updates reachable to all the members of a node's send zone. For example, in Figure 6, B sets the TTL (and TTL_0) field equal to the distance in hops to one of the farthest members of its send zone (node C, E or G). However, this may lead to some extra overhead, due to the updates being broadcasted in the area marked by the horizontal lines in the figure (which lies outside B's send zone). In order to reduce this overhead, each of the peripheral nodes of B maintains information about members of B's send zone which lie further away from B than itself. That is, A maintains information about C, D about E, and F about G. B's other peripheral nodes, H, J, and K do not have any such nodes. Hence, when A, D, and F receive B's proactive updates, they send it towards C, E, and G respectively. When H, J, and K receive B's updates, they do not forward the update packets, thus reducing the extra overhead.

This information to reduce the overhead is maintained as follows. A node A maintains a list of all nodes for whom it serves as a peripheral node. For each node B in this list, A maintains another list called the *expecting_nodes_list*, which consists of all nodes C, whose "zone building packets" are received by A such that the value of TTL in the packet is not less than the zone radius of B. (This implies that B lies in C's routing zone, or equivalently, C lies in B's send zone.)

Now a peripheral node A of a node B does not forward a proactive update packet originated at B, if A has no nodes in the *expecting_nodes_list* for node B. This reduces unnecessary traffic going beyond the peripheral nodes, if there are no nodes in that region which have B in its routing zone. Note that all these conditions can be checked by using the TTL, TTL_0, and the zone radius values available in the update packets or the zone building packets.

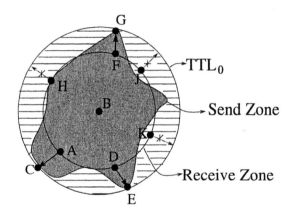

Figure 6: The irregular send zone of node B, which is marked by the grayed area.

Using the above scheme, each node in the network broadcasts proactive update packets by initializing the values of TTL and TTL_0 as above. Propagation of unnecessary update packets may be terminated by the peripheral nodes, if no nodes beyond them are *expecting* these packets, as found by examining the maintained lists.

It is to be noted that there is no need to broadcast separate "zone building packets" by the nodes – these packets can be combined with the proactive update packets to reduce the overhead. Also, the broadcasting of the proactive updates by IARP can be based on one of the strategies proposed in [31] for more efficient performance.

9.2   Bordercast Resolution Protocol (BRP)

With independently sized routing zones in the network, it is possible that
some of the nodes in the bordercast tree of the source node have a routing
zone which is small, so that it lies completely within the source node's
routing zone. Such nodes may not be able to reconstruct the source node's
bordercast tree and may not be able to correctly judge who to forward the
query packets to. In order to deal with situations like these, a different
bordercasting mechanism is used.

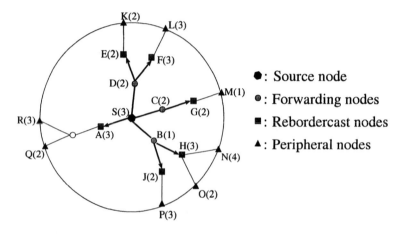

Figure 7: The bordercast tree of the source node S. Numbers in parentheses
next to the node labels indicate the zone radii of the nodes.

Figure 7 shows the bordercast tree of the source node S, which has a
zone radius of 3. Nodes $A, B, C,$ and D are the bordercast tree neighbors
of S. The zone radius of A is 3 and its zone extends beyond S's routing
zone. However, as the zone radii of $B, C,$ and D are small (1, 2, and 2,
respectively), their routing zones lie completely inside S's routing zone. So,
S examines the nodes which are two hops from it in the bordercast tree
downstream from $B, C,$ and D. It finds that the routing zones of $E, F, G, H,$
and J include newer regions outside its own routing zone, and so they get
selected. S then sends the route query packet to $A, E, F, G, H,$ and J (via
forwarding through one-hop neighbors, if needed). These nodes bordercast
the query again, covering unexplored regions of the network.

Formally, we define the following two kinds of nodes, which a bordercasting node identifies after constructing the bordercast tree to its *uncovered*
peripheral nodes.

- *Rebordercast Node:* The node closest to the source node on the bordercast path[5] from the source node to a peripheral node, such that its routing zone extends beyond the source node's routing zone, is called a rebordercast node of the source node corresponding to that peripheral node. For example, in Figure 7, H is a rebordercast node corresponding to O and N, J is a rebordercast node corresponding to P, etc. Mathematically, the following condition holds true for a source node s and its rebordercast node b:

$$\mathcal{H}(s,b) + \mathcal{R}(b) > \mathcal{R}(s), \tag{1}$$

where $\mathcal{H}(s,b)$ is the minimum distance in hops between the source node s and the rebordercast node b, and $\mathcal{R}(b)$ is the routing zone radius of b.

- *Forwarding Node:* Nodes lying on the bordercast-path between the source node and a rebordercast node belong to the set of forwarding nodes corresponding to that rebordercast node. For example, B is a forwarding node corresponding to J and H, while A does not have any forwarding node. Note that if a node's routing zone is no larger than the routing zones of all its bordercast tree neighbors, the set of forwarding nodes is empty.

The following bordercasting mechanism is used by the nodes in order to guide a route query "outwards", toward unexplored regions of the network.

1. Source node S constructs the bordercast tree to *uncovered* peripheral nodes.

2. S chooses rebordercast nodes corresponding to each of its *uncovered* peripheral nodes.

3. S then sends the query packet to each of these rebordercast nodes via the forwarding nodes, if any.

4. When the rebordercast nodes receive the query packet, they become the bordercast nodes and go back to step 1.

For query control, when a node receives a query packet, it marks certain members of its zone as *covered* and tries to steer the query away from such nodes. The following rules are used by a node for identifying such covered regions of its routing zone:

---

[5]Bordercast path is a path on the bordercast tree.

- A forwarding node marks all the members of its zone as covered.

- A rebordercast node marks

  - the nodes lying in the intersection of its zone with the zone of the bordercasting node as covered, if the bordercasting node is a member of its zone.[6]

  - the nodes lying in the intersection of its zone with the zone of the last forwarding node as covered, if the bordercasting node does not lie in its zone.[7]

The above mechanism ensures that the query always gets bordercasted by nodes whose routing zones covers newer, unexplored regions. A correctness proof of the Independent Zone Routing framework in included in [32].

9.3   Zone Radius Determination Algorithm

In order to determine the optimal zone radius of each node in the network independently, the algorithm for zone radius determination should depend only on the local measurements made at the node. A hybrid of *Min Searching* and *Adaptive Traffic Estimation* schemes described in [24] is used to determine the optimal zone radius of each node dynamically and independently.

The Min Searching scheme involves iteratively searching for the minima of the routing control traffic curve by incrementally increasing or decreasing the routing zone radius of a node by one hop. During each estimation interval, the amount of routing traffic is measured. If the amount of routing traffic in the current estimation interval is less than that in the previous interval, the zone radius is further incremented/decremented in the same direction. Otherwise, the direction of zone radius change is reversed. The process continues until a minimum is detected, as shown in Figure 8. The Min Searching scheme converges to the local minima, provided that the network characteristics do not change substantially during the search and that the estimation interval is long enough to provide a good measurement of the routing control traffic.

---

[6]As the bordercasting node is a member of the rebordercasting node's routing zone, the rebordercasting node knows the bordercasting node's position relative to the other members of its routing zone and thus can infer the intersection of their routing zones.

[7]The last forwarding node will be a member of the rebordercasting node's routing zone and, thus, it has the required information to mark the intersection of their routing zones as covered.

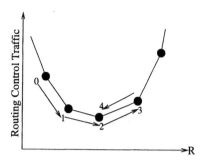

Figure 8: Min Searching to determine the minima of the routing control traffic curve. The algorithm starts at t=0 and converges to the optimal value at t=4. Reprinted with permission from [M. Pearlman and Z.J. Haas, "Determining the Optimal Configuration for the Zone Routing Protocol," *IEEE JSAC*, vol. 17, no. 8, August 1999] ©1999 IEEE.

The optimal zone radius of a node lies in a region where the total routing control traffic is neither predominantly reactive nor predominantly proactive. The Adaptive Traffic Estimation scheme exploits the fact that close to the minimum the amount of these two traffic types is relatively equal. The scheme involves iteratively changing the routing zone radius based on the relative proportions of reactive and proactive components in the total routing overhead generated in each estimation interval. Let $\Gamma(R)$ be the ratio of reactive (IERP) traffic to proactive (IARP) traffic at zone radius R during a certain estimation interval. Adjustments to the zone radius are made by comparing this ratio with a predetermined threshold, Γ_{thres}. If $\Gamma(R) > \Gamma_{thres}$, increase the zone radius; if $\Gamma(R) < \Gamma_{thres}$, decrease the zone radius. However, possibly changing the zone radius after each estimation interval could lead to too frequent adaptation of the zone radius and to possible network instability. Hence, a triggering mechanism is introduced by a hysteresis term, so that if $\Gamma(R) > \Gamma_{thres} \cdot H$, increase the zone radius; if $\Gamma(R) < \Gamma_{thres}/H$, decrease the zone radius. In this scheme, the decision to change the zone radius is based on the measurements made in the current estimation interval only. This is desirable as the scheme can better track the changes in the network and the dependence on the need for correlation between successive intervals is reduced.

A combination of Min Searching and Adaptive Traffic Estimation schemes is used for IZR zone radius determination. Initially, the Min Searching algorithm is applied, which starts from a zone radius of one and searches for the zone radius which would cause the least overhead. Once the minimum

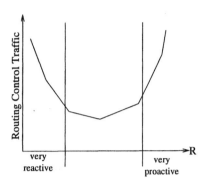

Figure 9: Location of optimal zone radius is the region where the routing control traffic is neither very reactive or very proactive. Reprinted with permission from [M. Pearlman and Z.J. Haas, "Determining the Optimal Configuration for the Zone Routing Protocol," *IEEE JSAC*, vol. 17, no. 8, August 1999] ©1999 IEEE.

of the control traffic curve is reached, Min Searching is replaced with Adaptive Traffic Estimation which adaptively tracks the changing characteristics of the network. Also, whenever the zone radius R reaches one, zone radius determination reverts back to Min Searching. This is done because at a zone radius of one, the proactive component of the routing control traffic is, by definition, zero (implying $\Gamma(1) = \infty$). Thus, without any additional control, the Adaptive Traffic Estimation scheme would be misled by the highly reactive traffic at zone radius of one, possibly resulting in an oscillation between $R = 1$ and $R = 2$. When the Min Searching scheme increments R beyond two hops, control can be switched back to the Adaptive Traffic Estimation scheme.

The stability of the zone radius determination process has been shown in [32].

10   Performance Evaluation

The $OPNET^{TM}$ simulation environment was used to simulate the Independent Zone Routing framework. Link-state based IARP, described in [13] was used as the proactive component and a source-route based IERP described in [12] was used as the reactive component. Neighbor discovery is based on the reception of $HELLO$ beacons transmitted at random intervals of mean T_{beacon}. If a new beacon fails to arrive within $2 \cdot T_{beacon}$ of the most recent beacon, a link failure is reported. We assume that neighbor discovery beacons are given highest transmission priority and are not destroyed by collisions. This prevents the inaccurate reporting of link failures for the allowed $2 \cdot T_{beacon}$ window.

The network consists of 50 nodes, spread randomly in an area of 1000 × 1000 $meter^2$. A node moves at a constant speed v and is assigned an initial direction θ, which is uniformly distributed between 0 and 2π. When a node reaches an edge of the square simulation region, it is reflected back into the coverage area by setting its direction to $-\theta$ (horizontal edges) or $\pi - \theta$ (vertical edges). The magnitude of its velocity is not altered. In the absence of packet collision, we assume that background channel interference and receiver noise limit the transmission range of packets to a physical radius of 225 $meters$.

Measurements of routing control traffic are reported in terms of control traffic packets. The total routing overhead is viewed as the sum of the IARP route update packets and IERP request/reply packets. A node's session with a randomly chosen destination consists of sending a certain number of packets; the number of packets per session is exponentially distributed with an average of 25 packets. The interarrival time between sessions are exponentially distributed. As different simulation runs were performed for different zone radius settings, the network behavior was made to remain exactly the same; i.e., the nodes move in exactly the same path and start sessions with exactly the same nodes at the very same instants. No data was collected for the first 5 sec of the simulations, while the initial intrazone route discovery process stabilized.

Figure 10 (a) shows the amount of routing control traffic generated during a simulation duration of 180 seconds. The scenario consists of 50 nodes, half of which (Set I) move at a constant speed (v) of 14 m/sec and have a mean session interarrival delay (MSID) of 1 sec. The other half (Set II) move at a speed of 1 m/sec and have a mean session interarrival delay of 0.1 sec. From the plot, it can be seen that Independent Zone Routing with dynamic radius configuration leads to about 50% reduction in routing control traffic as compared to regular Zone Routing (with uniform zone sizes for all nodes). The plot also shows the amount of routing control traffic for IZR with fixed but different zone radius (R) assignments for the two sets of nodes. The reduction in control traffic for this case reinforces our belief that different zone radii may be preferable for nodes with different characteristics.

For the scenario reflected in Figure 10 (b), the speed of Set I nodes is slowed to 7 m/sec, while the other parameters remain the same. This reduction in Set I nodes' velocity translates to a decrease in the overall control traffic for regular ZRP as well as IZR, though their relative performance

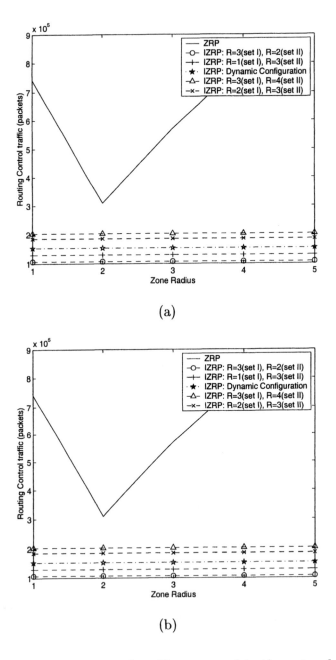

Figure 10: Total routing control traffic generated in the network consisting of 50 nodes divided into two sets (a)Set I: $v = 14\ m/sec$, MSID $= 1\ sec$ and Set II: $v = 1\ m/sec$, MSID $= 0.1\ sec$; (b)Set I: $v = 7\ m/sec$, MSID $= 1\ sec$ and Set II: $v = 1\ m/sec$, MSID $= 0.1\ sec$

remains the same.

Both Figures 10 (a) and (b) show the reduction in routing control traffic as compared to Zone Routing, when IZR with dynamic zone radius configuration or IZR with fixed but different zone radii for the two sets of nodes are used. Also, the total amount of routing overhead generated for IZR with dynamic zone radius configuration is between the different values for IZR with fixed but different zone radii combinations. The reason why IZR with dynamic zone radius configuration does not produce the best results is that the zone radius configuration scheme only assures performance *close* to the optimal (but not necessarily the best possible), in a region where the reactive and proactive components of routing overhead are relatively equal. Further, some noise introduced due to imperfect estimates of the control traffic during an estimation interval may introduce some extra overhead.

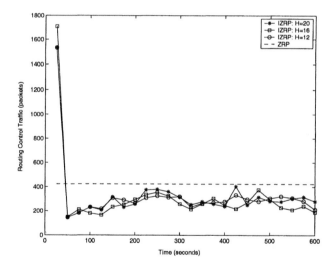

Figure 11: The variation in routing control traffic for IZR with dynamic zone radius configuration. The points correspond to routing overhead generated over a window of last 25 seconds.

Figure 11 shows how the routing control traffic generated in the network varies as time progresses. The points on the curves represent the amount of control traffic generated over a window of 25 seconds. Initially, the amount of traffic generated is high, as the network is operating at sub-optimal routing zone radii values. Soon, the zone radius determination algorithm is able to find optimal values of the zone radii for the nodes and the routing overhead decreases to below the level of regular Zone Routing. The routing control traffic values for the case of IZR with dynamic zone radius configuration in

Figures 10 (a) and (b) do not include this initial overhead of the scheme during its stabilization . Γ_{thres} has been set equal to 1 (corresponding to equal proactive and reactive components) for these curves. The curves for different hysteresis (H) values are pretty close, indicating that the dependence on H is not strong in the indicated range. Further simulation studies for a variety of scenarios have confirmed this result [32].

These results have demonstrated that IZR enhances the Zone Routing framework by enabling each node in the network to independently and adaptively configure its optimal zone radius. Furthermore, it can lead to a reduction in routing control traffic as well, as observed from the simulation results. IZR enables setting the zone radius of each of the nodes to its optimal value over time and space. This can improve the efficiency and increase the scalability of the routing protocol.

11   Conclusions

Hybridization, multi-scope operation, and local tuning form the basis for scalable, adaptable routing, as demonstrated by the Zone Routing framework. Zone Routing provides a flexible solution to the challenge of discovering and maintaining routes in a wide variety of ad hoc networking environments, by adapting the balance of proactive and reactive routing based on network conditions. With independent zone sizing capability, Zone Routing can be fine tuned to the local conditions of the network. Each of the nodes in the network can dynamically, distributedly, and automatically configure its zone radius to the temporally and spatially optimal value. This configuration is done at each node by analyzing just the local route control traffic, making the tuning mechanism itself scalable. All these factors lead to significant performance improvements and increase the scalability and robustness of the routing protocol.

Possible future directions consist of extending the hybrid routing framework into additional dimensions, for example balancing the trade-offs between bandwidth efficiency and local processing/storage requirements. The impact of multi-scope routing on providing Quality of Service (QoS) in the network may also be investigated. The performance of the Zone Routing framework may further be enhanced by incorporating multi-scoped proactive (IARP) and reactive (IERP) components. Another potential area that needs to be explored further is the application of hybridization to hierarchical routing. Integration of security into the Zone Routing framework is another area on which work is in progress.

12 Acknowledgements

This work has been supported in part by the DoD Multidisciplinary University Research Initiative (MURI) program administered by the Office of Naval Research under the grant number N00014-00-1-0564, the DoD Multidisciplinary University Research Initiative (MURI) program administered by the Air Force Office of Scientific Research under the grant number F49620-02-1-0233, and by the National Science Foundation grant number ANI-0081357.

References

[1] Bellur, B., and Ogier, R.G., "A Reliable, Efficient Topology Broadcast Protocol for Dynamic Networks," *IEEE INFOCOM,* March 1999.

[2] Bertsekas, D., and Gallager, R., *Data Networks*, Second Edition, Prentice Hall, Inc., 1992.

[3] Chen, T.-W., and Gerla, M., "Global State Routing: A New Routing Scheme for Ad-hoc Wireless Networks," *IEEE ICC'98*, Atlanta, GA, Jun. 1998.

[4] Cheng, C., Reley, R., Kumar, S.P.R., and Garcia-Luna-Aceves, J.J., "A Loop-Free Extended Bellman-Ford Routing Protocol without Bouncing Effect," *ACM Computer Communications Review*, vol. 19, no. 4, 1989, pp. 224-236.

[5] Chiang, C.-C., "Routing in Clustered Multihop, Mobile Wireless Networks with Fading Channel," *IEEE SICON'97*, Apr.1997.

[6] Clausen, T., Jacquet, P., Laouiti, A., Minet, P., Muhlethaler, P., Qayyum, A., Viennot, L., "Optimized Link State Routing Protocol (OLSR)," *IETF MANET,* Internet Draft, October 2001.

[7] Garcia-Luna-Aceves, J.J., "Loop-Free Routing Using Diffusing Computations," *IEEE/ACM Transactions on Networking*, vol. 1, no. 1, February 1993, pp. 130-141.

[8] Garcia-Luna-Aceves, J.J., and Spohn, M., "Efficient Routing in Packet-Radio Networks Using Link-State Information," *IEEE WCNC 99*, August 1999.

[9] Garcia-Luna-Aceves, J.J., and Spohn, M., "Scalable Link-State Internet Routing," *IEEE International Conference on Network Protocols (ICNP 98)*, Austin, Texas, October 14-16, 1998.

[10] Gerla, M., Hong,X., Pei, G., "Landmark Routing for Large Ad Hoc Wireless Networks," *IEEE GLOBECOM 2000*, San Francisco, CA, Nov. 2000.

[11] Haas, Z.J., and Pearlman, M.R., "The Performance of Query Control Schemes for the Zone Routing Protocol," *ACM/IEEE Transactions on Networking*, vol. 9, no. 4, pp. 427-438, August 2001.

[12] Haas, Z.J., Pearlman, M.R., and Samar, P., "The Zone Routing Protocol (ZRP) for Ad Hoc Networks," *IETF MANET* Internet Draft, July 2002.

[13] Haas, Z.J., Pearlman, M.R., and Samar, P., "The Interzone Routing Protocol (IERP) for Ad Hoc Networks," *IETF MANET,* Internet Draft, July 2002.

[14] Haas, Z.J., Pearlman, M.R., and Samar, P., "The Intrazone Routing Protocol (IARP) for Ad Hoc Networks," *IETF MANET,* Internet Draft, July 2002.

[15] Haas, Z.J., Pearlman, M.R., and Samar, P., "The Bordercast Resolution Protocol (BRP) for Ad Hoc Networks," *IETF MANET,* Internet Draft, June 2001.

[16] Iwata, A., Chiang, C.-C., Pei, G., Gerla, M., and Chen, T.-W., "Scalable Routing Strategies for Ad Hoc Wireless Networks," *IEEE JSAC, special issue on Ad-Hoc Networks*, vol. 17, no.8, August 1999.

[17] Johnson, D.B., and Maltz, D.A., "Dynamic Source Routing in Ad hoc Wireless Networking," in *Mobile Computing*, T. Imielinski and H. Korth, editors, Kluwer Academic Publishing, 1996.

[18] Liang, B., and Haas, Z.J., "Hybrid Routing in Ad Hoc Networks with a Dynamic Virtual Backbone", to appear in *Transactions on Wireless Communications*.

[19] McDonald, A.B., and Znati, T., "Predicting Node Proximity in Ad-Hoc Networks: A Least Overhead Adaptive Model for electing Stable Routes," *MobiHoc 2000*, August 4th, Boston.

[20] Moy, J., "OSPF version 2," RFC 2178, March 1997.

[21] Murthy, S. , and Garcia-Luna-Aceves, J.J., "A Routing Protocol for Packet Radio Networks," Proc. of ACM Mobile Computing and Networking Conference, *MOBICOM'95*, Nov. 14-15, 1995.

[22] Murthy, S., and Garcia-Luna-Aceves, J.J., "An Efficient Routing Protocol for Wireless Networks," *MONET*, vol.1, no.2, pp.183-197, October 1996.

[23] Park, V.D., and Corson, M.S., "A Highly Adaptive Distributed Routing Algorithm for Mobile Wireless Networks," *IEEE INFOCOM '97*, Kobe, Japan, 1997.

[24] Pearlman, M.R., and Haas, Z.J., "Determining the Optimal Configuration for the Zone Routing Protocol," *IEEE JSAC, special issue on Ad-Hoc Networks*, vol. 17, no.8, August 1999.

[25] Pearlman, M.R., Haas, Z.J. and S.I. Mir, "Using Routing Zones to Support Route Maintenance in Ad Hoc Networks," *IEEE WCNC 2000*, Chicago, IL, Sept. 2000.

[26] Pearlman, M.R., Haas, Z.J. and B.P. Manvell, "Discovering and Reliably Communicating over Unidirectional Links in Ad Hoc Networks," *IEEE WCNC 2000*, Chicago, IL, Sept. 2000.

[27] Pei, G., Gerla, M., and Chen, T.-W., "Fisheye State Routing: A Routing Scheme for Ad Hoc Wireless Networks," *ICC 2000*, New Orleans, LA, Jun. 2000.

[28] Pei, G., Gerla, M., Hong, X., and Chiang, C.-C., "A Wireless Hierarchical Routing Protocol with Group Mobility," *IEEE WCNC'99*, New Orleans, LA, Sep. 1999.

[29] Perkins, C.E., and Bhagwat, P., "Highly Dynamic Destination Sequenced Distance-Vector Routing (DSDV) for Mobile Computers," *ACM SIGCOMM*, vol.24, no.4, Oct. 1994, pp.234-244.

[30] Perkins, C.E. and Royer, E.M., "Ad Hoc On-Demand Distance Vector Routing," *IEEE WMCSA '99*, New Orleans, LA, Feb. 1999.

[31] Samar, P., and Haas, Z.J., "Strategies for Broadcasting Updates by Proactive Routing Protocols in Mobile Ad hoc Networks," in Proceedings of IEEE MILCOM 2002, Anaheim, CA, Oct. 2002.

[32] Samar, P., Pearlman, M.R., and Haas, Z.J., "Independent Zone Routing: An Adaptive Hybrid Routing Framework for Ad Hoc Wireless Networks," under review.

[33] Sivakumar, P., Sinha, R., Bharghavan, V., "CEDAR: A Core Extraction Distributed Routing Algorithm," *IEEE JSAC, special issue on Ad-Hoc Networks*, vol. 17, no.8, August 1999.

AD HOC WIRELESS NETWORKING
X. Cheng, X. Huang and D.-Z. Du (Eds.) pp. 561 - 622

Scalability of Routing in Ad Hoc Networks: Principles and Practice

César A. Santiváñez
Internetwork Research Department
BBN Technologies (A Verizon Company), Cambridge, MA 02138
E-mail: `csantiva@bbn.com`

Ram Ramanathan
Internetwork Research Department
BBN Technologies (A Verizon Company), Cambridge, MA 02138
E-mail: `ramanath@bbn.com`

Contents

1   Introduction

Recent years have witnessed a surge in the interest in ad hoc networks. Spurred by ever-decreasing form-factors and cost of wireless transceivers and processors, a multitude of new applications are emerging. These include short-range ad hoc wireless networks for ubiquitous computing, larger range indoor wireless LANs that operate in ad hoc mode, metropolitan area networks and sensor networks. Standards such as Bluetooth, HomeRF, and IEEE 802.11 are giving impetus to the growth in the number of ad hoc communication enabled devices. Propelled by these trends, ad hoc networks with a large number (e.g. 1000s) of nodes are moving rapidly from the realm of imagination to that of reality.

Deploying such large-scale networks requires *scalable* ad hoc routing protocols. There are a number of questions that arise when considering routing scalability, including: *what does scalability really mean, what factors does scalability depend on, how scalable are current-day ad hoc networks routing protocols*, etc. Answering these questions is of paramount importance in understanding and evaluating the set of mechanisms available for improving ad hoc routing scalability, including, for example: hierarchical routing, efficient flooding, limited search/local repair (for reactive protocols), limited dissemination, etc.

This chapter addresses the scalability of routing in ad hoc networks from a fundamental viewpoint, and covers the state of the art in the metrics, methodology, and techniques for designing highly scalable protocols. Both the *principles* underlying routing scalability, and the protocols that put them into *practice* are presented in a balanced manner. The intention is to provide the reader with an insight into the scalability of and tradeoffs inherent in a particular protocol, and introduce him or her to the design of highly scalable protocols.

Ad hoc routing protocols can be broadly classified into proactive (or table-driven) and reactive (or on-demand). While our treatment is mostly in terms of proactive protocols, we emphasize that the basic principles are quite generic and may well be applied to reactive protocols. In other words, we present scalability principles in a given context but the principles in general are not tied to that context.

This chapter is organized as follows. Section 2 presents a brief overview of current ad hoc routing protocols and provides a more detailed description of a selected set of representative protocols that will be used for comparison purposes. Section 3 presents a theoretical foundation for the study of scalability, defining a routing scalability metric and a framework that has proven to be useful in developing tractable models and obtaining closed form expressions for ad hoc routing protocols. Section 4 presents the results obtained when applying the methodologies described in Section 3 to the set of representative protocols described in Section 2.

These results shed a new light into our understanding of scalability. They provide the reader with a better understanding of the interactions and combined effect of increasing the network size, mobility, and/or traffic load. An important result is that limited-dissemination flat routing techniques, as well as hierarchical routing techniques, present the best scalability properties regarding network size. Thus, an important question arises: *Which approach is preferable : hierarchical or flat routing?* And, *Under what circumstances is each of these approaches better?* Section 5 answers these questions. Section 5 starts by discussing the design approaches for making ad hoc routing protocols highly scalable. These approaches can be broadly classified into "flat" and "hierarchical". Using an exemplary protocol in each class, we discuss the merits/demerits of each approach and then compare their theoretical and experimental performance. Finally, Section 6 presents some conclusions and future research directions.

2   Overview of Ad Hoc Routing Protocols

The surge of interest in ad hoc networks has given rise to a plethora of ad hoc routing protocols. To individually study each of them would constitute a gigantic task. Fortunately, from a scalability point of view, we can group protocols together into classes, and therefore focus on representative protocols in each class.

Routing protocols can typically be classified as *proactive* and *reactive*. Proactive protocols attempt to constantly build routes to destinations, so that they are readily available when needed. Standard Link State (SLS) [1], Distance Vector (DV) algorithms based on the Distributed Bellman-Ford (DBF) algorithm[2], Optimized Link State Routing Protocol (OLSR)[3], and Topology Broadcast Based on Reverse Path Forwarding (TBRPF)[4] are examples of proactive routing protocols. Reactive protocol build routes upon request (from the upper layers) so they do not waste bandwidth transmitting routing information when this information is not needed. Ad Hoc On-Demand Distance Vector (AODV)[5, 6], Dynamic Source Routing (DSR)[7], Associativity-Based Routing (ABR)[8], Temporally Ordered Routing Algorithms (TORA)[9], and Distance Routing Effect Algorithm for Mobility (DREAM)[10] are examples of reactive protocols.

Due to its simplicity, quick convergence, well understood dynamics, and good performance, SLS is a good representative of the class of *pure flat* proactive protocols. SLS will be used in the remainder of this chapter as a representative of the class of pure proactive protocols. However, it should be kept in mind that most of the conclusions hold for all the protocols in the same class. Similarly, DSR is chosen as the representative of pure reactive protocols, mainly due to its simplicity and the fact that this is the reactive protocol that has received most attention in the literature. Indeed, DSR is typically the benchmark most reactive routing protocol designers use to compare its designs against.

As size increases, flat routing techniques such as SLS and DSR are no longer efficient. A typical solution (for both proactive and reactive) protocols has been to build a hierarchical structure to limit the control overhead at the expense of route degradation. Hierarchical Link State (HierLS)[11], Hierarchical State Routing (HSR)[12], Link Cluster Architecture (LCA)[13],

Clusterhead-Gateway Switch Routing (CGSR)[14], Multimedia support for Mobile Wireless Networks (MMWN)[15], and Adaptive Routing using Clusters (ARC)[16] are examples of hierarchical routing protocols.

The Hierarchical Link State algorithm presented in [11] is a good representative of hierarchical routing techniques. It captures the essence of the hierarchical approaches followed in [15, 12], still it is broad enough to allow analyzing a wide range of design choices for hierarchical routing, mainly regarding location management.

Besides the traditional definition of proactive versus reactive or flat versus hierarchical, there are hybrid protocols. Zone Routing Protocol (ZRP)[17, 18] is an example of such an hybrid approach. ZRP presents a proactive and a reactive component. It successfully adapts its components to different values of mobility over traffic activity radius[19], thus exhibiting a behavior that ranges from pure proactive to pure reactive. Furthermore, even though no hierarchy is being built or maintained, no node aggregation takes place and therefore all the nodes belong to the same level, ZRP behaves as a 2-level reactive hierarchical scheme. ZRP will be used as a representative of the class of hybrid approaches.

More recently, a new class of "limited information" protocols has been proposed. These protocols are flat in the sense that they do not aggregate routing information, and therefore they have the same memory requirements as SLS. But in the other hand, they limit the rate and scope of information dissemination so that the bandwidth consumed by routing updates propagation is reduced. Global State Routing (GSR)[20], and Source-Tree Adaptive Routing (STAR)[21] are examples of protocols in this class that limit the rate of information generation. Fisheye State Routing (FSR[12], and Hazy Sighted Link State (HSLS)[22] are examples of routing protocols that limit not only the generation rate but also the propagation scope of the routing information dissemination. HSLS presents the best performance among protocols in this class and therefore will be use as its representative.

Finally, from a conceptual point of view it is interesting to consider a mechanism that does not use a structured routing algorithm: Plain Flooding (PF). The consideration and comparison of plain flooding will help illustrate the point (network scenario) at which routing protocols break and, it becomes more efficient to just flood each data packet without attempting to locate/keep track of the destination (mobility).

In the remainder of this section a brief description of each of the routing protocols representative of its class is presented. The reader familiar with these protocols (PF, SLS, DSR, HierLS, ZRP, and HSLS) may skip this reading and proceed directly to Section 3.

2.1 Plain Flooding (PF)

In Plain Flooding, a source node S willing to send a packet to a destination D broadcasts this packet to all its neighbors, regardless of the destination identity. Node S's neighbors, in turn rebroadcast the packet once (and just once) to their neighbors, and so on. Every node in the network (unless the network is partitioned) will receive at least one copy of the packet (typically more) and will re-broadcast the packet only once. In particular, the destination node D will receive the packet and deliver it to it upper layers.

In PF, nodes then must keep track of the packets previously sent to avoid sending a packet more than once.

The flooding mechanism described above is typically used to propagate routing control messages inside a network. Flooding is not typically used for normal data packet delivery. However, if the network size is small, the traffic load is small and the mobility rate is very high, PF may be the best routing alternative. Thus, PF can be used as a benchmark against other routing protocols under extremely high mobility.

2.2 Standard Link State (SLS)

SLS and its variants are good representatives of proactive protocols. SLS was initially used in the ARPANET[1] as the replacement of the original Distance-Vector based routing protocol. Since then, several link state protocols have been developed and are being used over different networks, including OSPF, IS-IS, and NLSP, among others. SLS's success was a consequence of its being simple yet robust, and having predictable dynamics and quick convergence in the presence of topology changes.

In SLS, a node sends (floods) a Link State Update (LSU) containing a list of its current neighbors (and their associated link costs) to the entire network each time it detects a link status change. A node also sends periodic, soft-state LSUs every T_p seconds. Each node stores a copy of the latest LSU received from each node in the network in a local database referred to as *topology table*. The *topology table* provides each node with information about the entire network connectivity.

To find a route to a destination node D, the source node (as well as each intermediate node along the route) may apply Dijkstra's Shortest Path First (SPF) algorithm[23] over its local copy of the *topology table*.

2.3 Dynamic Source Routing without Route Cache (DSR-noRC)

DSR[7] is a good representative of reactive protocols. DSR has received considerable attention in the literature, especially due to the easy availability of source code for different platforms. Today, DSR is the typical benchmark used to compare against other ad hoc on-demand routing protocols.

In DSR, no proactive information is exchanged. A source node S builds a route to a destination node D by flooding the network with a route request (RREQ) message. When a RREQ message reaches node D (or a node with a cached route towards the destination, if the route-cache option is enabled) a route reply message is sent back to the source node S, including the newly found route. Node S attaches the new route to the header of all subsequent packets destined to node D, and any intermediate node along the route uses this attached information to determine the next hop in the route.

2.4 Hierarchical Link State (HierLS)

As the size of a network increases, maintaining full topology information may become prohibitively expensive. The bandwidth consumed in propagating up-to-date topology information to each node in the network may grow too large. Also, the memory required to store all this information may exceed the node capabilities. Finally, the processing power required to compute routes (for example executing the Dijkstra's algorithm in a link state protocol) in a timely fashion may also exceed the node's processing capabilities.

A hierarchical approach is a technique for aggregating information. Nodes are grouped in sets, several sets are grouped in supersets, and so on, forming a hierarchy. This reduces the size and frequency of information dissemination, and reduces table sizes and processing requirements. All of this is at the cost of reducing the quality (optimality) of the routes.

In this subsection we will discuss the implementation of this aggregation paradigm in a link state context. We will focus on a generic class of hierarchical algorithms named Hierarchical Link State (HierLS) routing[11]. However, the reader should keep in mind that the hierarchical paradigm may be applied to other routing techniques, not only proactive (e.g. Distance Vector-based) but also reactive. Also, different HierLS algorithms may represent (abstract) higher level elements in the virtual topology differently. This discussion focuses on the *virtual node* abstraction.

In the *m-level* HierLS routing[11, 15], network nodes are regarded as level

1 nodes, and level 0 clusters. Level i nodes are grouped into level i clusters, which become level $i + 1$ nodes, until the number of highest level nodes is below a threshold and therefore they can be grouped (conceptually) into a single level m. Thus, the value of m is determined dynamically based on the network size, topology, and threshold values.

Link state information inside a level i cluster is aggregated (limiting the rate of LSU generation) and transmitted only to other level i nodes belonging in the same level i cluster (limiting the scope of the LSU). Thus, a node link change may not be sent outside the level 1 cluster (if they do not cause a significant change to higher levels aggregated information), thus reducing the proactive overhead.

HierLS for mobile networks relies on the Location Management service to inform a source node S of the address of the highest level cluster that contains the desired destination D and does not contain the source node S.[1] For example, consider a 4-level network as shown in Figure 1. S and D are level 1 nodes; $X.1.1$, $X.1.2$, etc. are level 2 nodes (level 1 clusters); $X.1$, $X.2$, etc. are level 3 nodes (level 2 clusters); X, Y, V, and Z are level 4 nodes (level 3 clusters); the entire network forms the level 4 cluster. The Location Management (LM) service provides S with the address of the highest level cluster that contains D and does not contain S (e.g. the level 3 cluster Z in Figure 1). Node S can then construct a route toward the destination. This route will be formed by a set of links in node S level 1 cluster ($X.1.1$), a set of level 2 links in node S level 2 clusters ($X.1$), and so on. In Figure 1 the route found by node S is : $S - n_1 - n_2 - X.1.5 - X.1.3 - X.2 - X.3 - Y - Z - D$. When a node outside node S level 1 cluster receives the packet, the node will likely produce the same high-level route towards D, and will 'expand' the high-level links that traverse its cluster using lower level (more detailed) information. In Figure 1 this expansion is shown for the segment $Z - D$. The Location Management (LM) service can be implemented in different ways, whether proactive (location update messages), reactive (paging), or a combination of both.

---

[1]Traditional, wireline-based hierarchical routing protocols do not need a location management service, since the address of the node is associated with its location. For example, in the IP protocol the first part of a node address contains the identity of the subnet the node belongs to.

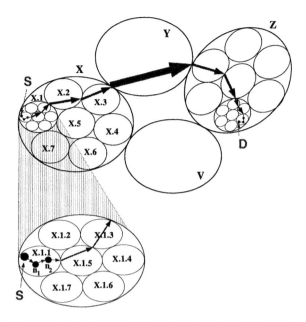

Figure 1: A Source (S) - Destination (D) path in HierLS.

2.5   Zone Routing Protocol (ZRP)

ZRP is a hybrid approach, combining a proactive and a reactive part, trying to minimize the sum of their respective overheads. In ZRP, a node disseminates event-driven LSUs to its k-hop neighbors (nodes at a distance, in hops, of k or less). The set of k-hop neighbors constitute the node's *zone*. Each node has full topology information of nodes inside its *zone* and may forward packets to any node within it. When a node needs to forward a packet outside its *zone*, it sends a route request to a subset of the nodes in the network, namely the 'border nodes'. The 'border nodes' will have enough information about their own *zones* (i.e. k-hop neighborhoods) to decide whether to reply to the route request or to forward it to its own set of 'border' nodes. The route formed will be described in terms of the 'border' nodes only.

The maintenance of the zone structure allows for a reduction in the cost of the route discovery procedure, since instead of flooding the entire network with route request (as done in DSR) ZRP pokes a selected subset of ('border') nodes only. Also, the fact that routes are specified in terms of border nodes only allows 'border' nodes in a path to locally recover from individual link failures, reducing the overhead induced by the route maintenance procedure.

ZRP may dynamically adjust its zone size by increasing or decreasing the value of k to balance the proactive (i.e. propagation information inside the zone) and reactive (i.e. route discovery and maintenance) overheads. ZRP may morph from a fully proactive (k tends to infinity) protocol when a high traffic load is the main challenge to network survivability, all the way to fully reactive (k equal to 1) protocol if the network scenario changes to having node mobility as the main factor limiting network performance. For typical, non-degenerated values of k (i.e. $k > 1$, but smaller than the network diameter) ZRP will resemble a two-level hierarchical network.

2.6 Hazy Sighted Link State (HSLS)

HSLS is based on the observation that nodes that are far away do not need to have complete topological information in order to make a good next hop decision. Thus, propagating every link status change over the entire network may not be necessary. In a highly mobile environment, a node running HSLS will transmit - provided that there is a need to - a LSU only at particular time instants that are multiples of t_e seconds. Thus, potentially several link changes are 'collected' and transmitted every t_e seconds. The *Time To Live* (TTL) field of the LSU packet is set to a value (which specifies how far the LSU will be propagated) that is a function of the current time index as explained below. After one global LSU transmission – LSU that travels over the entire network, i.e. TTL field set to infinity, as for example during initialization – a node 'wakes up' every t_e seconds and sends a LSU with TTL set to 2 if there has been a link status change in the last t_e seconds. Also, the node wakes up every $2t_e$ seconds and transmits a LSU with TTL set to 4 if there has been a link status change in the last $2t_e$ seconds. In general, a node wakes up every $2^{i-1}t_e$ ($i = 1, 2, 3, ...$) seconds and transmits a LSU with TTL set to 2^i if there has been a link status change in the last $2^{i-1}t_e$ seconds. If a packet TTL field value (2^i) is greater than the distance from this node to any other node in the network (which will cause the LSU to reach the entire network), the TTL field of the LSU is reset to infinity (global LSU), and the algorithm is re-initiated.

Nodes that are at most two hops away from a node, say X, will receive information about node X's link status change at most after t_e seconds. Nodes that are more than 2 but at most 4 hops away from X will receive information about any of X links change at most after $2t_e$ seconds. In general, nodes that are more than 2^{i-1} but at most 2^i hops away from X will receive information about any of X links change at most after $2^{i-1}t_e$

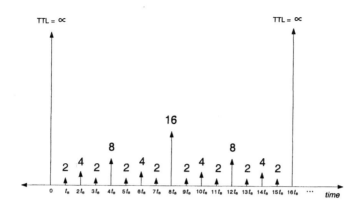

Figure 2: HSLS's LSU generation process (when mobility is high).

seconds. Figure 2 shows an example of HSLS's LSU generation process when mobility is high and in consequence LSUs are always generated. An arrow with a number over it indicates that at that time instant a LSU (with TTL field set to the indicated value) was generated and transmitted. Figure 2 assumes that the node executing HSLS computes its distance to the node farthest away to be between 17 and 32 hops, and therefore it replaces the TTL value of 32 with the value infinity, resetting the algorithm at time $16t_e$. The reader is referred to [22] and [24] for more details about HSLS.

HSLS is a flat routing protocol since each node is represented by an entry in the (distributed) topology table at each node and routes are built by applying Dijkstra's algorithm over the entire set of nodes in the network (high processing and memory requirements). However, HSLS differs from traditional flat protocols in that each node's vision of the topology table is different. Besides, the propagation of the topology information is not done by flooding the entire network each time but by sending information to smaller areas of the network more frequently and gradually increasing the areas' size while decreasing the frequency of propagation, resembling the information dissemination method employed in a multilevel hierarchical approach.

3 Routing Scalability : Theoretical Background

There is a wide consensus on the importance of understanding the scalability limits of both ad hoc networks and their related routing protocols. Surprisingly, however, there is not a consensus of a well defined routing scalability

metric. Adding to the chaos, there is sometimes a confusion between the
routing protocol scalability and the *network scalability* of the network the
protocol is run over.

In this section, we review a promising metric, the *total overhead*, that
captures the main impact of increasing network limiting parameters on performance of routing protocol running on bandwidth-limited networks. The
limiting parameters of a network are those parameters – as for example mobility rate, traffic rate, and network size, etc. – whose increase causes the
network (and oftentimes the routing protocol) performance to degrade. On
the remainder of this chapter only limiting parameters will be considered,
and therefore the terms 'parameter' and 'limiting parameter' will be used
indistinctly.

The *Total Overhead* metric enables the derivation of tractable models
and closed form expressions, providing us with the understanding of the
scalability properties of different ad hoc routing protocols.

3.1   Scalability Aspects of Ad Hoc Routing Protocols

When a network limiting parameter such as the network size increases, it
impacts the network at several, concurrent levels. For example, if the network is running the Standard Link State (SLS) protocol, where each node
advertises its set of neighbors to all other nodes in the network, the increase
in the network size will cause:

- An increase in the rate of the Link State Updates (LSU) sent through
  the network, and therefore an increase in the bandwidth consumed by
  the control messages of the routing protocol.

- An increase in the memory requirements of each node, since each node
  must store a local copy of the *Topology Table*, which contains an entry
  per node in the network.

- An increase in the processing requirements of each node, since the time
  complexity of the route computation algorithm (e.g. Dijkstra's) used
  for finding the best route to a given destination increases monotonically with the number of entries in its *topology table* (i.e. the number
  of nodes in the network). Thus, more operations will need to be done
  per unit of time, which may require the use of faster processors.

- Since more processing is being done, and more packets are being transmitted, the power consumption also increases. Thus, the battery re-

quirements of a mobile node also increases.

- Since the network diameter (i.e. maximum distance - in hops - between two nodes in the network) also increases, the average delay for delivering a packet to its destination – assuming uniform traffic distribution, i.e. non-local traffic profile – also increases. [2] Also, since the control packets (LSUs) and the data packets share the same transmission medium, the aforementioned increase on the number of LSUs will cause the data packets contending for access to the same channel experiencing a longer delay before succeeding. As size increases the delay may grow so large that real time applications like voice and video can no longer be supported on the network.

Thus, an increase in network size has an impact on several aspects of scalability. Which one of these aspects (bandwidth, memory, processing power, energy consumption, delay, etc.) is the most important depends on the characteristics of the network under study. In particular it depends on which resource is the most scarce, or depleted first. Ad hoc networks tend to be bandwidth-limited, i.e. bandwidth is the most scarce resource, but emerging applications such as sensor networks may well shift the relative importance of the scalability aspects to the point that processing power or battery life become the more important ones.

It is extremely hard to define a metric that simultaneously encompasses the effect of an increase in network parameters on all of the aforementioned scalability aspects. Therefore, in order to build tractable models we must be content with metrics that address each of these scalability aspects independently. Thus, when referring to the bandwidth aspect we can talk about the communication overhead or communication complexity of a protocol. Similarly, when referring to the processing or memory requirements aspect we can talk about the time or memory complexity of the protocol, respectively, and so forth.

As mentioned before, a large class of ad hoc networks are bandwidth-limited, that is, bandwidth is the most scarce resource. In other words, as network parameters increase, it is the lack of additional bandwidth which causes the network to collapse. While a bandwidth-related metric may not fully characterize all the performance aspects relevant to specific scenario

---

[2]Although in this case (using SLS) the increase in the delay is independent of the routing protocol being used, it is not rare to observe routing protocols (e.g. on-demand ones) where the packet delay increase is caused by latency in the route discovery procedure. This latency is dependent on the network size.

(for example it may fail to capture variation on packet delays) it does capture the main performance degradation due to a network parameter increase. Moreover, a bandwidth related metric is proportional to energy and processing requirements and it has been shown that even delay constraints can be expressed in terms of equivalent bandwidth[25]. In the remainder of this chapter we will present the state-of-the-art in the study of the bandwidth aspect of scalability. Theoretical results and insight into the scalability limits of ad hoc routing were enabled by the introduction of the *Total Overhead* metric in [22, 11].

The reader interested in other aspects of scalability, as for example memory requirements may want to take a look at [26].

3.2   Communication Overhead: Conventional Notions

Traditionally, the term *(communication) overhead* has been used in relation to the *control overhead*, that is, the amount of bandwidth required to construct and maintain a route. Thus, in proactive approaches such as Standard Link State (SLS) and Distance Vector (DV) the communication overhead has been expressed in terms of the number of packets exchanged between nodes in order to maintain the node's forwarding tables up-to-date. In reactive approaches such as Dynamic Source Routing (DSR) and Ad hoc On Demand distance Vector (AODV), the communication overhead has been described in terms of the bandwidth consumed by the route request/reply messages (global or local). A primary goal of ad hoc routing protocol research has been to design protocols that keep this control overhead low.

While it is true that the control overhead significantly affects the protocol behavior, it does not provide enough information to facilitate a proper performance assessment of a given protocol since it fails to include the impact of suboptimal routes on the protocol's performance. As the network size increases above, say, 100 nodes, keeping route optimality imposes an unacceptable cost under both the proactive and reactive approaches, and suboptimal routes become a fact of life in any scalable routing protocol.

Suboptimal routes are introduced in reactive protocols because they try to maintain the current source-destination path for as long as it is valid, although it may no longer be optimal. Also, local repair techniques try to reduce the overhead induced by the protocol at the expense of longer, non optimal paths. Proactive approaches introduce suboptimal routes by limiting the scope of topology information dissemination (e.g. hierarchical routing [15, 12]) and/or limiting the time between successive topology information updates dissemination so that topology updates are no longer instantaneously event-driven (e.g GSR [20]).

This leads to the question : how can we define *overhead* so that it includes the effect of suboptimal routes in capacity limited systems? We need to do this since *suboptimal routes not only increase the end-to-end delay but also result in a greater bandwidth usage than required*. This extra bandwidth is an overhead that may be comparable to the other types of overhead. Approaches that attempt to minimize only the control overhead may lead to the (potentially erroneous) conclusion that they are "scalable" by inducing a fixed amount of control overhead, while in practice the resulting performance is seriously degraded as the extra bandwidth overhead induced by suboptimal routes increases with the network size. In the next subsections we discuss a more comprehensive definition of overhead that is more useful in the comparative analysis of protocols.

3.3 Emerging concept: Total (Communication) Overhead

In order to quantify the effect of a routing protocol on the network performance, the *minimum traffic load* of the network as a routing protocol-independent metric is defined as follows:

Definition 3.1 *The* **minimum traffic load** *of a network, is the minimum amount of bandwidth required to forward packets over the shortest distance (in number of hops) paths available, assuming all the nodes have instantaneous* **a priori** *full topology information.*

The above definition is independent of the routing protocol being employed, since it does not include the control overhead but assumes that all the nodes are provided *a priori* global information. This might be possible in fixed networks when a node is provided with static optimal routes, and therefore there is no bandwidth consumption above the *minimum traffic load*. On the other hand, in mobile scenarios this is not possible. Due to the unpredictability of the movement patterns and the topology they induce, even if static routes are provided so that no control packets are needed, it is extremely unlikely that these static routes remain optimal during the entire network lifetime. In an actual mobile ad hoc network, the bandwidth usage would be greater than the *minimum traffic load* value. This motivated the following definition of the *total overhead* of a routing protocol.

Definition 3.2 *The* **total overhead** *induced by a routing protocol X is the difference between the total amount of bandwidth actually consumed by the network running X minus the* **minimum traffic load.**

Thus, the actual bandwidth consumption in a network will be the sum of a protocol independent term, the *minimum traffic load*, and a protocol dependent one, the *total overhead*. Obviously, effective routing protocols should try to reduce the second term (*total overhead*) as much as possible. The different sources of overhead that contribute to the *total overhead* may be classified into *reactive, proactive,* and *suboptimal routing overhead.*

The *reactive overhead* of a protocol is the amount of bandwidth consumed by the specific protocol to build paths from a source to a destination, *after* a traffic flow to that destination has been generated at the source. In static networks, the reactive overhead is a function of the rate of generation of new flows. In dynamic (mobile) networks, however, paths are (re)built not only due to new flows but also due to link failures in an already active path. Thus, in general, the reactive overhead is a function of both the traffic *and* the rate topology change.

The *proactive overhead* of a protocol is the amount of bandwidth consumed by the protocol in order to propagate route information *before* it is needed. This may take place periodically and/or in response to topological changes.

The *suboptimal routing overhead* of a protocol is the difference between the bandwidth consumed when transmitting data from all the sources to their destinations using the routes determined by the specific protocol, and the bandwidth that would have been consumed should the data have followed the shortest available path(s). For example, consider a source that is 3 hops away from its destination. If a protocol chooses to deliver one packet following a k ($k > 3$) hop path (maybe because of out-of-date information, or because the source has not yet been informed about the availability of a 3 hop path), then $(k - 3) * packet\_length$ bits will need to be added to the suboptimal routing overhead computation.

The *total overhead* provides an unbiased metric for performance comparison that reflects bandwidth consumption. Despite increasing efficiency at the physical and MAC-layers, bandwidth is likely to remain the limiting factor in terms of scalability.

3.4 Overhead: Achievable Regions and Operating Points

Having defined a fair metric for overhead, we now ask : is a pure proactive or a pure reactive protocol the best approach for routing scalability? What is the desirable relation/balance between the different classes of overhead in a scalable routing protocol?

We begin by noting that the three different overhead sources mentioned above are locked in a 3-way trade-off since, in an already efficient algorithm, the reduction of one of them will most likely cause the increase of one of the others. For example, reducing the 'zone' size in the Zone Routing Protocol (ZRP) [17, 18] will reduce ZRP's proactive overhead, but will increase the overhead induced when 'bordercasting' new route request, thus increasing ZRP's reactive overhead. The above observation leads to the definition of the *achievable region* of overhead as the three dimensional region formed by all the values of proactive, reactive, and suboptimal routing overheads that can be achieved (induced) by any protocol under a given scenario (traffic, mobility, etc.). Figure 3 shows a typical 2-dimensional transformation of this 'achievable region' where two sources of overhead (reactive and suboptimal routing) have been added together for the sake of clarity. The horizontal axis represents the proactive overhead induced by a protocol, while the vertical axis represents the sum of the reactive and suboptimal routing overheads.

It can be seen that the achievable region is convex [3], lower-bounded by the curve of overhead points achieved by the 'efficient' (i.e. minimizing some source of overhead given a constraint being imposed on the others) protocols. For example, point P is obtained by the best pure proactive approach given that optimal routes are required – that is, given the constraints that the suboptimal and reactive overheads must be equal to zero. Similarly, point R is achieved for the best protocol that does not use any proactive information. Obviously, the best protocol (in terms of overhead) is the one that minimizes the *total overhead* achieving the point *Opt* (point tangent to the line $x + y = K$, where K is a numerical constant).

Different scenarios result in different slopes of the boundary of the achievable region and consequently different positions for *Opt*. For example, if the traffic increases (more sessions) or diversifies, R moves upward (pure reactive protocol induces more overhead) and, if mobility is low P moves to the

---

[3]To see that the achievable region is convex, just consider the points P_1 and P_2 achieved by protocols $\mathcal{P}_1$ and $\mathcal{P}_2$. Then, any point $\lambda P_1 + (1 - \lambda)P_2$ can be achieved by engaging protocol $\mathcal{P}_3$ that behaves as protocol P_1 a fraction λ of a (long) period of time and as protocol P_2 the remainder of the time.

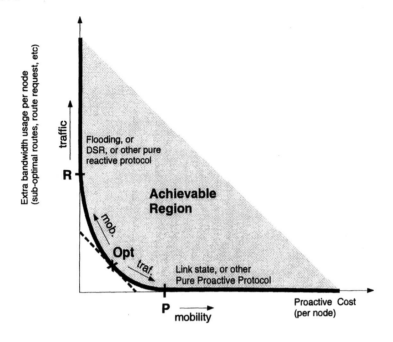

Figure 3: Overhead's achievable region.

left (pure proactive protocol induces less overhead) and may cause *Opt* to coincide with the point *P* (pure proactive protocol with optimal routes). The reverse is also true as the mobility rate increases and the traffic diversity/intensity decreases. Figure 4 shows how the boundary of the achievable region is (re)shaped as the network size increases. The lower curve corresponds to the boundary region when the network size is small. The effect of increasing the network size is to 'pull' the boundary region up. However, the region displacement is not uniform along the X and Y axes as will be discussed next.

Pure proactive protocols, such as SLS, may generate a control message (in the worse case) each time a link change is detected. Each control message will be retransmitted by each node in the network. Since both the generation rate of control messages and the number of message retransmissions increases linearly with network size (N), the total overhead induced by pure proactive algorithms (that determine the point P) increases as rapidly as N^2. Pure reactive algorithms, such as DSR without the route cache option, will transmit route request (RREQ) control messages each time a new session is initiated. The RREQ message will be retransmitted by each node in

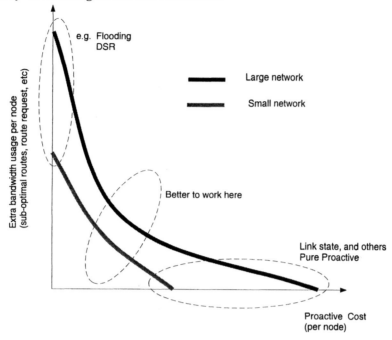

Figure 4: Change in achievable region due to size.

the network. Since both the rate of generation of RREQ and the number of retransmissions required by each RREQ message increases linearly with N, the total overhead of a purely reactive protocol (the point R) increases as rapidly as N^2.

On the other hand, the overhead of protocols at 'intermediate points', such as HierLS and ZRP, may increase more slowly with respect to N. In [11] it is shown that under a reasonable set of assumptions HierLS's and ZRP's overhead grows with respect to N is roughly $N^{1.5}$ and $N^{1.66}$, respectively.

Summarizing, it can be seen that points P and R increase proportionally to $\Theta(N^2)$ whereas an 'intermediate' point as HierLS increases almost as $\Theta(N^{1.5})$. [4] Referring again to Figure 4, it is easy to see that the extreme points are stretched "faster" than the intermediate points. Thus, *as size increases, the best operating point is in the "middle" region where the proactive, reactive, and suboptimal routing overheads are balanced.* One might

---

[4]Standard asymptotic notation is employed. A function $f(n) = \Omega(g(n))$ [similarly, $f(n) = O(g(n))$] if there exists constants c_1 and n_1 [similarly, c_2 and n_2] such that $c_1 g(n) \leq f(n)$ [similarly $f(n) \leq c_2 g(n)$] for all $n \geq n_1$ [similarly, $n \geq n_2$]. Also, $f(n) = \Theta(g(n))$ if and only if $f(n) = \Omega(g(n))$, and $f(n) = O(g(n))$.

reasonable argue that in order to achieve high scalability, one should operate in the intermediate region where suboptimal routes are present. In other
words, suboptimal routes are a fact of life for ultimate scalability.

3.5   A Formal Definition of Scalability

As mentioned before, there is no established scalability metric for ad hoc
networks. In this chapter we will follow the definitions and framework presented in [11] since they provide us with tractable models that capture the
bandwidth aspects of routing protocol's scalability and properly distinguish
a routing protocol scalability properties and limits from the scalability properties and limits inherent to the network (independent of the routing algorithm – if any[5] – run over it).

The key idea here is to separate out the concepts of *network* scalability
and *protocol* scalability. Some networks are inherently unscalable and some
are inherently scalable. It is only for the latter class that demanding protocol scalability – as traditionally understood the term – makes sense. We
elaborate on this below.

Let's start by the intuitive definition of scalability:

Definition 3.3 Scalability *is the ability of a network to support the increase of its limiting parameters.*

Thus, scalability is a property. In order to quantify this property, the
concept of *minimum traffic load* presented in Subsection 3.3, definition 3.1,
is used to define the *network scalability factor*:

Definition 3.4 *Let* $Tr(\lambda_1, \lambda_2, \ldots)$ *be the* **minimum traffic load** *experienced by a network under parameters* $\lambda_1, \lambda_2, \ldots$ *(e.g. network size, mobility
rate, data generation rate, etc.). Then, the* **network scalability factor** *of
such a network, with respect to a parameter* λ_i *(* Ψ_{λ_i} *) is defined to be :*

$$\Psi_{\lambda_i} \stackrel{\text{def}}{=} \lim_{\lambda_i \to \infty} \frac{\log Tr(\lambda_1, \lambda_2, \ldots)}{\log \lambda_i}$$

The *network scalability factor* is a number that asymptotically relates the
increase in network load to the different network parameters. For example,

---

[5]Since the concepts are generic, they cover even the case of static networks which may
use static, pre-defined routes.

let's consider the most efficient wireless ad hoc networks : the class of topology controlled ad hoc networks. For this class of networks the *minimum traffic load* $Tr(\lambda_{lc}, \lambda_t, N)$ as a function of the per node rate of link change λ_{lc}, per node traffic λ_t, and network size N is $\Theta(\lambda_t N^{1.5})$, [6] and therefore $\Psi_{\lambda_{lc}} = 0$, $\Psi_{\lambda_t} = 1$, and $\Psi_N = 1.5$.

The *network scalability factor* may be used to compare the scalability properties of different networks (wireline, mobile ad hoc, etc.), and as a result of such comparisons we can say that one class of networks scales better than the other. However, if our desire is to assess whether a network is *scalable* (an adjective) with respect to a parameter λ_i, then the *network rate* dependency on such a parameter must be considered.

Definition 3.5 *The* **network rate** R^{net} *of a network is the maximum number of bits that can be simultaneously transmitted in a unit of time. For the* **network rate** *(*R^{net}*) computation, all successful link layer transmissions must be counted, regardless of whether the link layer recipient is the final network-layer destination or not.*

Definition 3.6 *A network is said to be* **scalable** *with respect to the parameter* λ_i *if and only if, as the parameter* λ_i *increases, the network's* **minimum traffic load** *does not increase faster than the* **network rate** *(*R^{net}*) can support. That is, if and only if:*

$$\Psi_{\lambda_i} \leq \lim_{\lambda_i \to \infty} \frac{\log R^{net}(\lambda_1, \lambda_2, \ldots)}{\log \lambda_i}$$

For example, it has been proved that in mobile ad hoc networks at most $\Theta(N)$ successful transmissions can be scheduled simultaneously (see for example [27, 28]). The class of ad hoc networks considered before (i.e. resulting from applying power control techniques) are precisely the class of networks that achieves that maximum *network rate*. Thus, in order for this class of ad hoc network to be regarded as scalable with respect to network size, we would need that $\Psi_N \leq 1$. Unfortunately, this is not the case (recalling that for these networks $\Psi_N = 1.5$) and as a consequence this (wide) class of ad hoc networks are not *scalable* with respect to network

---

[6]Each node generate λ_t bits per seconds, that must be retransmitted (in average) L times (hops). Thus, each node induce a load of $\lambda_t L$, which after adding all the nodes results in a $Tr(\lambda_{lc}, \lambda_t, N) = \lambda_t N L$. Since, L, the average path length, is $\Theta(\sqrt{N})$, the above expression was obtained in [11].

size. [7] Fully connected wireline networks, on the other hand, exhibit a *network scalability factor* $\Psi_N = 1$ while its network rate R^{net} increases as fast as $\Theta(N^2)$, and therefore they are scalable with respect to network size (in the bandwidth sense). Note, however, that this scalability requires the nodes' degree to grow with the network size which may become prohibitely expensive.

Similarly, since the *network rate* does not increase with mobility or traffic load, then a network will be scalable w.r.t. mobility and traffic if and only if $\Psi_{\lambda_{lc}} = 0$ and $\Psi_{\lambda_t} = 0$, respectively. Again, considering topology-controlled ad hoc networks we notice that they are *scalable* w.r.t. mobility ($\Psi_{\lambda_{lc}} = 0$), but are not *scalable* w.r.t. traffic ($\Psi_{\lambda_t} = 1$).

Note that similar conclusions may be drawn for scalability w.r.t. additional parameters as for example network density, transmission range ℓ, etc. that are not being further considered in this chapter. For example, as transmission range increases (and assuming an infinite size network with regular density) the spatial reuse decreases and as a consequence *network rate* decreases as rapidly as ℓ^2. Thus, Ψ_ℓ should be lower than -2 for the network to be deemed *scalable*. Since the *minimum traffic load* will only decrease linearly w.r.t. ℓ (paths are shortening), $\Psi_\ell = -1$, and therefore ad hoc networks are not scalable w.r.t. transmission range. This observation is the main reason behind our focusing on networks with power control, where the transmission range is kept in line so that the network degree is kept bounded.

Now, after noticing that mobile ad hoc networks are not *scalable* with respect to size and traffic, one may ask : what does it mean for a routing protocol to be *scalable*?. The remaining of this subsection will clarify this meaning.

Definition 3.7 Routing protocol's scalability *is the ability of a routing protocol to support the continuous increase of the network parameters without degrading network performance.*

In other words, the scalability of a routing protocol is dependent on the scalability properties of the *network* the protocol is running over. That is,

---

[7]It has been shown in [28] that if the network applications can support infinitely long delays and the mobility pattern is completely random, then the average path length may be reduced to 2 ($\Theta(1)$) regardless of network size and, as a consequence, that network *scalability factor* with respect to network size Ψ_N is equal to 1. Thus, those ad hoc networks (random mobility and capable of accepting infinitely long delays) are the only class of ad hoc networks that are scalable with respect to network size.

the network's scalability properties provide the reference level as to what to expect of a routing protocol. If the overhead induced by a routing protocol grows faster than the *network rate* (eventually depleting the available bandwidth) but slower than the *minimum traffic load*, the routing protocol is not degrading network performance, which is being determined by the *minimum traffic load*. Roughly speaking, if a type of network can handle thousands of nodes, then an *scalable* routing protocol for this type of networks should be able to run over the thousand-node network without collapsing. But, if the network can only handle hundreds of nodes, the fact that a routing protocol collapses when run over thousand of nodes does not mean that the routing protocol is not scalable for this type of network. The routing protocol is not degrading network performance at the 100-node level. Performance is being dominated by the network limitations (*minimum traffic load* versus *network rate*). There is no point in requiring the routing protocol to operate at a point where the network collapses on its own!.

From the above discussion it is clear that a routing protocol may be deem to be scalable or not only in the context of the underlying network the protocol is running over. This chapter covers the scalability of routing protocol running over wireless ad hoc networks; specifically the (wide) class of networks defined by assumptions a.1-a.8.

To quantify a *routing protocol scalability*, the respective scalability factor is defined, based on the *total overhead* concept presented in Subsection 3.3, definition 3.2, as follows:

Definition 3.8 *Let* $X_{ov}(\lambda_1, \lambda_2, \ldots)$ *be the* **total overhead** *induced by routing protocol X, dependent on parameters* $\lambda_1, \lambda_2, \ldots$ *(e.g. network size, mobility rate, data generation rate, etc.). Then, the Protocol X's* **routing protocol scalability** **factor** *with respect to a parameter* λ_i *(* $\rho_{\lambda_i}^X$ *) is defined to be :*

$$\rho_{\lambda_i}^X \overset{\text{def}}{=} \lim_{\lambda_i \to \infty} \frac{\log X_{ov}(\lambda_1, \lambda_2, \ldots)}{\log \lambda_i}$$

The *routing protocol scalability factor* provides a basis for comparison among different routing protocols. Finally, to assess whether a routing protocol is *scalable* the following definition is used:

Definition 3.9 *A routing protocol X is said to be* **scalable** *with respect to the parameter* λ_i *if and only if, as parameter* λ_i *increases, the* **total**

overhead *induced by such protocol (X_{ov}) does not increase faster than the* network's **minimum traffic load.** *That is, if and only if:*

$$\rho_{\lambda_i}^X \leq \Psi_{\lambda_i}$$

Thus, for the class of topology-controlled ad hoc networks, a routing protocol X is *scalable* with respect to network size if and only if $\rho_N^X \leq 1.5$; it is *scalable* w.r.t. mobility rate if and only if $\rho_{\lambda_{lc}}^X \leq 0$; and it is *scalable* w.r.t. traffic if and only if $\rho_{\lambda_t}^X \leq 1$.

Using the above definitions, we are now ready to assess the scalability of protocols described in Section 2.

4   Results on Scalability of Ad Hoc Routing Protocols

In this section, we present an overview of the main results for bandwidth-related scalability for the representative set of routing protocols described in Section 2. The interested reader is referred to [22, 11] for more information about the derivations.

4.1   Scalability Dimensions

Scalability is often interpreted as the ability to handle increasing *size*. While the size of an ad hoc network is a key parameter affecting the scalability, it is by no means the only one. Other scalability dimensions include mobility (for *mobile* ad hoc networks), network density, network diameter, traffic diversity, energy etc. These parameters may influence the design of the network control mechanisms at various layers. For instance, an increase in the diameter of a network implies a higher latency for control information propagation, leading to a greater risk of inconsistent routes and instability. Similarly, an increase in density results in decreased spatial reuse of the spectrum and consequent reduction in capacity.

Figure 5 shows some key scalability dimensions and their effect on the lower four layers of the ad hoc network stack. Different protocols may exhibit different levels of scalability with respect to each of these dimensions, and an understanding of this is essential to an informed choice of a protocol for a given application.

Out of the different parameters shown, we observe that size, density, diameter, and transmission range (not shown) are related. For a given net-

dimension layer	Size	Mobility	Density	Diameter
Transport		**X**		**X**
Network	**(X)**	**(X)**	**X**	**X**
Link/MAC		**X**	**X**	
Physical		**X**		

Figure 5: Scalability dimensions and the layers. An 'X' indicates that the scalability problem involving the dimension representing the column manifests itself at the layer representing the row. A circle around an 'X' indicates combinations that we address in this chapter.

work size and density, different transmission power levels will result in different combinations of node degree and network diameter (longer transmission range will result in higher node degree and smaller network diameters). The state of the art in the area of topology control for ad hoc networks provides effective algorithms which adjust the transmission power in order to obtain more advantageous topologies. It is well understood that in order to increase the overall network performance, the average node degree must remain bounded except when required to improve connectivity (a reasonable goal is to have a biconnected network). Thus, the density dimension can be addressed by means of effective topology control algorithms (see for example [29]). For this reason, in the remainder of this chapter we will consider topology-controlled networks where the density is not a limiting factor and where the network diameter and size are mutually dependent. Thus, we will only consider the network size and mobility dimensions in our discussion of scalability. Of course no treatment of scalability would be complete without addressing the third scalability dimension (not shown in the figure for being self-evident at every layer) : traffic load.

4.2 Network Model

In order to obtain concrete, closed-form expressions for total overhead induced by the representative set of protocols described in Section 2 it is necessary to refine the class of network under study. This refinement was done favoring the most common, but challenging types of networks. Alternatively expressions can be derived for other classes of network if they are of interest.

However, in order to maintain focus and obtain the desired insight, in the remainder of this chapter we will follow the work in [11] and will restrict our attention to the (broad) class of networks defined by the assumptions presented below.

Let N be the number of nodes in the network, d be the average in-degree, L be the average path length over all source destination pairs, λ_{lc} be the expected number of link status changes that a node detects per second, λ_t be the average traffic rate that a node generates in a second (in bps), and λ_s be the average number of new sessions generated by a node in a second. The following assumptions, motivated by geographical reasoning and the availability of desirable topology control techniques, define the kind of scenarios under consideration:

a.1 As the network size increases, the average in-degree d remains constant.

a.2 Let A be the area covered by the N nodes of the network, and $\sigma = N/A$ be the network average density. Then, the expected (average) number of nodes inside an area A_1 is approximately $\sigma * A_1$.

a.3 The number of nodes that are at distance of k or less hops away from a source node increases (on average) as $\Theta(d * k^2)$. The number of nodes exactly at k hops away increases as $\Theta(d * k)$.

a.4 The maximum and average path length (in hops) among nodes in a connected subset of n nodes both increase as $\Theta(\sqrt{n})$. In particular, the maximum path length across the whole network and the average path length across the network (L) increases as $\Theta(\sqrt{N})$.

a.5 The traffic that a node generates in a second (λ_t), is independent of the network size N (number of possible destinations). As the network size increases, the total amount of data transmitted/received by a single node will remain constant but the number of destinations will increase (the destinations diversity will increase).

a.6 For a given source node, all possible destinations ($N - 1$ nodes) are equiprobable and – as a consequence of a.5 – the traffic from one node to every destination decreases as $\Theta(1/N)$.

a.7 Link status changes are due to mobility. λ_{lc} is directly proportional to the relative node speed.

a.8 Mobility models : time scaling.

Let $f_{1/0}(x, y)$ be the probability distribution function of a node position at time 1 second, given that the node was at the origin $(0, 0)$ at time 0. Then, the probability distribution function of a node position at time t given that the node was at the position (x_{t_0}, y_{t_0}) at time t_0 is given by $f_{t/t_0}(x, y, x_{t_0}, y_{t_0}) = \frac{1}{(t-t_0)^2} f_{1/0}\left(\frac{x-x_{t_0}}{t-t_0}, \frac{y-y_{t_0}}{t-t_0}\right)$.

Similarly, let $g_{0/1}(x, y)$ be the probability distribution function of a node position at time 0, given that it is known that the node position at time 1 will be $(0, 0)$. Then, the probability distribution function of a node position at time $t < t_1$ given that the node will be at the position (x_{t_1}, y_{t_1}) at time t_1 is given by $g_{t/t_1}(x, y, x_{t_1}, y_{t_1}) = \frac{1}{(t_1-t)^2} g_{0/1}\left(\frac{x-x_{t_1}}{t_1-t}, \frac{y-y_{t_1}}{t_1-t}\right)$.

For a discussion on the rationale behind these assumptions (besides the existence of an underlying topology control mechanism) the reader is referred to [22, 11].

4.3 Asymptotic Behavior of Ad Hoc Routing Protocols

Table 1 shows asymptotic expressions for the proactive, reactive and sub-optimal routing overhead (in bps) for the protocols described in Subsection 2 when run over the (wide) class of networks determined by assumptions a.1 through a.8.

PF induces no proactive or reactive overhead. But each packet generated (there are $\lambda_t N$ such packets per second) is flooded to the entire network (retransmitted N times), and therefore its sub-optimal routing overhead is linearly dependent on the traffic rate and on the square of the network size.

SLS builds optimal routes proactively, so there is no reactive or suboptimal routing overhead associated with it. Each time there is a link change ($\lambda_{lc} N$ times per second) an LSU is flooded throughout the entire network (N retransmissions) resulting in a proactive overhead that increases linearly with the rate of per node link changes and the square of the network size.

DSR-noRC has no proactive component. Its reactive overhead is lower bounded by the overhead induced by the route discovery procedures in response to new sessions ($\lambda_s N$ new sessions per unit of time). DSR-noRC

Protocol	Proactive Overhead	Reactive Overhead	Suboptimal Routing Overhead
PF	–	–	$\Theta(\lambda_t N^2)$
SLS	$\Theta(\lambda_{lc} N^2)$	–	–
DSR-noRC	–	$\Omega(\lambda_s N^2)$ $O((\lambda_s + \lambda_{lc})N^2)$	$\Omega(\lambda_t N^2 \log_2 N)$
HierLS	$\Omega(s N^{1.5} + \lambda_{lc} N)$	–	$\Theta(\lambda_t N^{1.5+\delta})$
ZRP	$\Theta(n_k \lambda_{lc} N)$	$\Omega(\lambda_s N^2/\sqrt{n_k})$	$O(\lambda_t N^2/\sqrt{n_k})$
HSLS	$\Theta(N^{1.5}/t_e)$	–	$\Theta((e^{\lambda_{lc} t_e K_4} - 1)\lambda_t N^{1.5})$

Table 1: Asymptotic results for several routing protocol for mobile ad hoc networks.

reactive overhead is upper bounded by assuming that each link change will trigger a new route maintenance procedure and that each route maintenance procedure will cause a global flooding (i.e. local repair did not succeed). The combined effect of these assumptions is that each link change event has the same effect as a new session event and therefore the combined rate of events – $(\lambda_s + \lambda_{lc})N$ new sessions plus link changes per second – results in the upper bound shown in table 1. Finally, DSR-noRC sub-optimal routing overhead's lower bound shown in Table 1 was derived by considering the extra bits $\Theta(\sqrt{N}log_2 N)$ required to add the source route to each packet. Recall that $log_2 N$ bits are required to specify a node address, and that the average route length is $L = \Theta(\sqrt{N})$.

Regarding HierLS, depending on the location management approach being used, HierLS may or may not induce reactive overhead. For example, if the location management approach requires that a node pages one or more location servers in order to find the current location of a destination and be able to build routes towards him, then the paging packet(s) will contribute to the reactive overhead. Table 1 shows HierLS's overhead results when a pure proactive location management is employed and therefore there is no reactive overhead associated with HierLS. In a pure proactive location management scheme (referred to as LM1 elsewhere in this chapter) each node S has a local copy of a location table where there is a map between every node in the network and the highest level cluster that contains the node but does not contain node S. The advantage of such a scheme is that there is no location server that may constitute single-point-of-failure for the entire network.

For HierLS-LM1, table 1 shows that there is no reactive overhead and that the proactive overhead is dominated by the location update cost $\Theta(sN^{1.5})$ – where s is the average node speed – which is far greater than the LSU propagation cost $\Theta(\lambda_{lc}N)$. This shows that in HierLS, for higher levels in the hierarchy, it is more likely to have cluster membership changes (due to node movements being unrelated to the cluster selection) than it is to have virtual link changes (since individual link changes get buffered out by the large number of links forming a virtual link). The sub-optimal routing overhead is determined by observing that for a fixed number of hierarchical levels, the average path length is a percentage above the optimal path length, and therefore the sub-optimal routing overhead was proportional to the actual rate of traffic transmission (hop-by-hop, not source-destination)i of $\Theta(\lambda_t N^{1.5})$. Further observing that the percentage of sub-optimality of the routes increased with the number of hierarchical levels, which in turn increased with the network size, determined the inclusion of the value δ (a small constant value dependent on the number of nodes in a cluster) in the sub-optimal routing expression.

For ZRP, the proactive overhead is dependent of the size of a node's *zone* (n_k). The bigger the zone the larger number of proactive control message that will need to be retransmitted. The reactive overhead, on the contrary, will decrease with the zone size. However, the reactive overhead does not vary inversely proportional to the *zone* size n_k but it depends on the square root of it. To understand this, consider that increasing the zone size will increase the area that each border node 'covers'. The larger the zone size the smaller the number of border nodes required to cover the entire network will be. Even though the border node zones are overlapping, still it is true that the number of border nodes required will be $\Theta(N/\sqrt{n_k})$. Thus, as the zone size increases a source node S in ZRP will need to poke a smaller number of 'border' nodes. However, the distance between border nodes also increases (in average $\Theta(\sqrt{n_k})$) resulting in the expression shown in Table 1. For ZRP's sub-optimal routing overhead an upper bound is provided that shows that ZRP's sub-optimal overhead does not affect ZRP's total overhead expression since it (sub-optimal routing) is (asymptotically) dominated by the reactive overhead. The sub-optimal routing upper bound is derived by considering the maximum route length after subsequent local repair procedures for long lived sessions. Since two border nodes, non-adjacents, in a ZRP's source route may not belong to each other zone (otherwise the route may be shortcutted) then the number of border nodes in a path is at most

N/n_k. Since border nodes are $\Theta(\sqrt{n_k})$ hops away from each other, then the maximum length of a packet roue to its destination is $\Theta(N/\sqrt{n_k})$, resulting in the expression shown in Table 1.

For HSLS, it is obvious that the proactive overhead will be inversively proportional to the LSU generation period $1/t_e$. However, the dependency on network size is not so obvious. t can be understood if we consider that in HSLS, the proactive overhead is dominated by the global LSUs, that is, LSUs that traverse the entire network. The next type of LSU in order of importance for the proactive overhead computation is the LSUs with the next higher time-to-live field. This is due to the fact that decreasing the time-to-live field by a factor of 2 reduces the number of LSU retransmissions by a factor of 4 while only increasing the frequency of transmissions by a factor of 2, providing a combined effect of reducing the proactive overhead induced by these LSUs by a factor of 2. When considering the global LSUs, we may notice that their generation rate according to HSLS rules is inversely proportional to the network diameter, which is $\Theta(\sqrt{N})$, resulting in the expression on Table 1

HSLS has no reactive overhead. Determination of HSLS sub-optimal routing overhead is not trivial, but the result can be understood by considering that for a given mobility rate and generation period, the probability of making an erroneous next-hop decision is bounded independently of the distance to the destination. This independence of the distance to the destination is a consequence of the LSU generation/propagation mechanism used in HSLS, which imposes a quasi-linear relationship between distance and routing information latency. Thus, the ratio of information latency (related to position uncertainty) over distance is bounded and so is the uncertainty about the destination angular position, which is the only critical information required to make a best next hop decision. Finally, having a bounded probability of a bad next hop decision, regardless of distance, ensures that the paths built by HSLS are just a fraction from optimal. This fraction depends on λ_{lc} and t_e as shown in Table 1.

As we may see from Table 1 and the above discussion, ZRP and HSLS behavior depends on configurable parameters. Table 2 shows the *total overhead* obtained when the routing protocol parameters are chosen to optimize performance. Values on Table 2 represents the best each protocol can do.

These asymptotic expressions provide valuable insight about the behavior of several representative routing protocols. They help network designers to better identify the class of protocols to engage depending on their operating scenario. For example, if the designer's main concern is network

Protocol	Total overhead (best)	Cases
PF	$\Theta(\lambda_t N^2)$	Always
SLS	$\Theta(\lambda_{lc} N^2)$	Always
DSR-noRC	$\Omega(\lambda_s N^2 + \lambda_t N^2 \log_2 N)$	Always
HierLS	$\Omega(sN^{1.5} + \lambda_{lc}N + \lambda_t N^{1.5+\delta})$	LM1
ZRP	$\Omega(\lambda_{lc} N^2)$	if $\lambda_{lc} = O(\lambda_s/\sqrt{N})$
	$\Omega(\lambda_{lc}^{\frac{1}{3}}\lambda_s^{\frac{2}{3}} N^{\frac{5}{3}})$	if $\lambda_{lc} = \Omega(\lambda_s/\sqrt{N})$ and $\lambda_{lc} = O(\lambda_s N)$
	$\Omega(\lambda_s N^2)$	if $\lambda_{lc} = \Omega(\lambda_s N)$
HSLS	$\Theta(\sqrt{\lambda_{lc}\lambda_t} N^{1.5})$	if $\lambda_{lc} = O(\lambda_t)$
	$\Theta(\lambda_{lc} N^{1.5})$	if $\lambda_{lc} = \Omega(\lambda_t)$

Table 2: Best possible total overhead bounds for mobile ad hoc networks protocols.

size, it can be noted that HierLS and HSLS scale better than the others. Moreover, by observing the asymptotic expressions we may notice that when information dissemination (either link state, route request, or data itself) is flood to the entire network, the routing protocol scalability factor with respect to network size is equal to 2. Splitting the information dissemination at two different levels, like in 2-level hierarchical routing, NSLS, ZRP, and DREAM, can achieve a reduction in the routing protocol scalability factor down to 1.66. Allowing the number of levels of information dissemination grow as required when the network size increases, as done explicitly by m-level HierLS and implicitly by HSLS, can further achieve a reduction of the scalability factor down to 1.5, which seems to be the limit on performance for routing protocols for ad hoc networks defined by a.1 through a.8.

If traffic intensity is the most demanding requirement, then SLS, and ZRP are to be preferred since they scale better with respect to traffic (*total overhead* is independent of λ_t); HSLS follows as it scales as $\Theta(\sqrt{\lambda_t})$, and PF, DSR, and HierLS are the last since their *total overhead* increases linearly with traffic. ZRP scales well with respect to traffic load since it can adapt its zone size, increasing it to the point that ZRP's behaves a a pure proactive algorithm (e.g. as SLS). HSLS scales better than PF, DSR, and HierLS since as traffic load increases, HSLS increases the value of its LSU generation rate $(1/t_e)$, which causes more LSUs to be injected into the network, reducing routing information latency and improving the quality of the routes. This points out two observations: (1) as traffic load increases, the quality of the routes becomes more and more important; (2) as traffic increases, more bandwidth should be allocated for dissemination of routing information, so that the quality of the routes are improved. **The second observation contradicts the widely held belief that as traffic load is increased, less bandwidth should be allocated to control traffic and let more bandwidth available for user data.**

With respect to the rate of topological change, we observe that PF may be preferred (if size and traffic are small and the rate of topological change increases too rapidly), since its *total overhead* is independent of the rate of topological change. Provably next will be ZRP and DSR since their lower bounds are independent of the rate of topological changes. The bounds are not necessarily tight, and ZRP's and DSR's behavior should depend somewhat of the rate of topological change. Finally, for SLS, HierLS, and HSLS we know (as opposed to DSR and ZRP where we suppose) that their *total overheads* increase linearly with the rate of topological change.

It is interesting to note that when only the traffic or the mobility is increased (but not both), ZRP can achieve almost the best performance in each case. However, if mobility and traffic increase at the same rate; that is, $\lambda_{lc} = \Theta(\lambda)$ and $\lambda_t = \Theta(\lambda)$ (for some parameter λ), then ZRP's *total overhead* ($\Omega(\lambda N^{1.66})$)) will present the same scalability properties as HSLS's ($\Theta(\lambda N^{1.5})$)) and HierLS's ($\Theta(\lambda N^{1.5+\delta})$)) with respect to λ, with the difference that ZRP does not scale as well as the other two with respect to size.

These and more complex analyses can be derived from the expression presented, when different parameters are modified simultaneously according to the scenario the designer is interested in.

Comparing HSLS and HierLS results, it is counter-intuitive to observe that HSLS –a flat, relatively easy to implement protocol – has better asymptotic properties than HierLS with respect to network size. This means that as size increases HSLS eventually outperforms HierLS. **This contradicts the widely held belief that as size increases the only routing solution is to shift from a flat to a hierarchical paradigm.** However, this section discussion suggests that building/maintaining/managing a complex routing hierarchy (a potential implementation nightmare) may not be necessary. The next section goes deeper into this issue, comparing flat and hierarchical routing techniques for ad hoc networks, trying to answer the question *which is better: flat or hierarchical?*.

5 Flat vs. Hierarchical Routing

Perhaps the most significant result from previous sections is this: a protocol that restricts the scope of control messages and takes the penalty of sub-optimal routes is more scalable than one that insists on "full information". For instance, as the network size grows while the available bandwidth remains fixed, traditional routing protocols such as SLS and DV quickly collapse, since they waste all the available bandwidth in disseminating routing protocol control messages. On the other hand, all of the protocols with sub-exponent-2 asymptotic scalability (ZRP, HierLS, FSLS) are "limited information" protocols.

Within this class of limited information protocols however, it appears that one can achieve the scalability goal using either a "flat" routing approach or a hierarchical approach. The question then is: *Is the hierarchical approach better or flat?* Or, more specifically: *Under which circumstances does a flat approach outperform a hierarchical one?*

In this section, we compare and contrast the two approaches, bringing out the advantages and disadvantages of each. We take a representative protocol from each class – namely HSLS for flat, and HierLS for hierarchical – for a direct comparison using simulation. In a sense then, this section is the "finals" of a tournament, where all but the best have been eliminated and the interest zooms in on the two best.

This section is organized as follows. In the first subsection we present a taxonomy of the hierarchical approaches, and comment on the different sub-classes from a bandwidth-scalability and implementation-complexity perspective. In the second subsection, we describe the main techniques for scaling flat routing protocols. Emphasis is on the most promising class of techniques, the FSLS family of algorithms, particularly the optimal algorithm in this class, namely the HSLS algorithm.

We then proceed, in the third subsection, to compare hierarchical and flat routing. In order to obtain concrete results, a representative protocol for each routing approach is chosen. HSLS, the best algorithm in the FSLS family, is picked as the representative of flat routing techniques. A highly efficient m-level hierarchical routing protocol based on MMWN is chosen as the representative of hierarchical routing. This protocol, while using the *virtual gateway* abstraction, sets the cost of each virtual link at a given hierarchical level to the same value, behaving as if the *virtual node* abstraction was used. Thus, this protocol behaves as belonging to the class of HierLS routing algorithm. This protocol was chosen since it presents good scalability properties without demanding an unreasonably high implementation cost.

We present a simulation study under moderate stress conditions in order to capture behavior that could be overlooked by the theoretical analysis. By virtue of the simulations, practical issues affecting hierarchical and flat routing protocol performance differently are identified. The level of incidence of these issues in a given network may shift the relative performance of the hierarchical and flat routing techniques. Finally, the last subsection discusses our conclusions from the comparison.

5.1   Hierarchical Routing Techniques

The core of a hierarchical algorithm consists in aggregating nodes into (level-1) clusters, clusters into superclusters (level-2 clusters) and so on. This grouping of nodes allows for an abstraction of the routing information. For example consider the HierLS algorithm presented in subsection 2.4. In HierLS a node may consider all clusters (level-1 and up) as virtual nodes in a virtual topology. In such a topology the set of links between two such clusters conform a virtual link. In such case, individual link variations will have a small impact in the virtual (aggregated) link state. If the routing algorithm restricts the generation of updates such that only changes above a predetermined threshold trigger updates, then the rate of updates sent as a response to virtual links' changes is significantly reduced.

It should be noted that the virtual topology may be built in a different manner. For example, MMWN [15] chooses the set of links between two clusters (namely virtual gateways) to become the virtual nodes. MMWN then chooses the set of nodes inside a cluster, needed to traverse from a virtual gateway to another in the same cluster, as the virtual link.

Whatever the definition of the virtual topology is, the main characteristics of a hierarchical approach is:

- Nodes are grouped in clusters. Clusters in Superclusters, and so on. Each cluster defines a cluster leader for coordinating functions.

- Information about nodes far away is aggregated, resulting in smaller memory requirements for storing topology information, lower processing requirements to build routes, and lower bandwidth requirements for propagating traditional (i.e. excluding location management) routing information updates.

- Due to mobility, a location management scheme is required. Note that this is a main difference between hierarchical schemes for fixed (e.g. IP networks) and mobile (e.g. ad hoc) networks.

Hierarchical approaches may then be classified by its cluster and cluster leader selection algorithm; by the abstraction used to map virtual nodes and virtual links to the actual elements of the physical world; and by the location management technique being used. In the next subsections, we present a quick overview of the current techniques used for hierarchical routing. Readers interested in a more extensive treatment of the subject will find reference [30] to be an excellent starting point.

5.1.1 Cluster and Cluster Leader Selection Methods

Clustering techniques may be classified by the radius of the cluster formed; by the affiliation method used; by the objective (gain) function used in the affiliation method; and by the cluster leader selection method used.

Cluster Radius
There is a class of clustering techniques that impose the restriction that the cluster radius (distance, in hops, from the cluster leader or center to any other node in the cluster) be at most 1 (e.g. LCA[13], CGSR[14], and ARC[16]). Thus, two cluster leaders belonging to neighboring clusters will be at most 2 hops away. The intermediate node in the 2-hop path is called a gateway node. The advantage of this kind of clustering techniques, especially if only two levels are being formed, is its simplicity. There are efficient algorithms that only require local (i.e. one-hop) information in order to make clustering decisions. These kind of techniques, however, will result in a large number of level-1 clusters. And, if higher level clusters are to be constructed by the same procedure, one finds that most of the simplicity advantage is lost. Thus this method is not particularly scalable. This technique is also used to build clusters for purposes other than routing: control of access to the shared medium (i.e. scheduling transmissions), efficient flooding of information (including routing related information as for example LSUs), etc.

The other class of clustering techniques does not require the cluster leader to be in direct communication (e.g. one hop away) from the cluster leader (e.g. HierLS[11], HSR[12], and MMWN[15]). Still, usually they impose a maximum limit on the distance between a cluster leader and nodes in the cluster boundaries, mainly for performance reasons. The HierLS algorithm presented in Subsection 2.4 belongs to this class. An advantage of this class of clustering techniques is that the clustering size (as well as other parameters) can be adjusted to optimize performance. For example, if a 2-level network must be formed out of 10000 nodes, a good clustering technique will result in roughly 100 clusters of 100 nodes each. Of course, for this cluster size, it will be even better to increase the number of levels in the network (although it should be kept in mind that building and maintaining a 3-level hierarchy is as complex as a m-level hierarchy, which is much more complex than a 2-level one).

Cluster Affiliation Method

Cluster affiliation refers to the way nodes are assigned to clusters. In some techniques, this decision is left to the node itself. In others, it is the cluster leader which assigns the nodes to its cluster.

The main advantage of leaving the 'joining' decision to the nodes, is that it allows for distributed algorithm implementation. On the other hand, the lack of a centralized control, and the latency in propagating control information may result in unpredictable dynamics causing, for example, cluster size to increase to unacceptable levels. This in turn may induce the splitting of a cluster, which may result (again due to information propagation latency) in a cluster that is too small and nodes rejoining the cluster, etc. In general, clustering affiliations where each node makes its own decisions are more susceptible to instabilities.

The other approach is to let the cluster leader to make the clustering assignments (it may 'grab' a set of nodes or may assign nodes previously in its cluster to another clusters). This approach may require the cluster leader to collect information about nodes more than one hop away, in order to decide which nodes to 'grab'. Also, the leader may decide to sequentially 'grab' nodes in the boundary of the cluster (resembling the dynamics of the previous technique when nodes 'join' the cluster) or it may grab a large set of nodes at once. The latter will speed up convergence time but require the leader to have up-to-date information about nodes outside of its cluster.

Performance objective

Clustering techniques may also be classified by the performance objective they target. Although one may expect that throughput or a routing performance metric be the goal of every clustering techniques, in reality the difficulty of mapping clustering parameters into actual routing performance metrics results in different hierarchical schemes targeting intermediate goals that are *suspected* to have a positive impact on performance.

Some protocols target clusters with balanced size. For example, MMWN defines a minimum and a maximum size for a cluster, and engages 'join' or 'split' procedures if these boundaries are crossed.

Other protocols target a desired level of connectivity inside the cluster (i.e. that the nodes inside the cluster form a k-connected) set. Similarly, the objective may be maximize connectivity of the nodes forming a virtual gateway (see MMWN [15]). The idea in targeting k-connectivity is to avoid the cluster to become partitioned in the near future. K-connectivity provide alternative paths in case of link failures. The idea of maximizing path availability inside a cluster is further explored in [31], where the authors propose a cluster formation technique (the (α, t) clustering) that targets the formation of clusters such that the probability that there will always be a path between two nodes inside the cluster for the next t seconds is at least α. The (α, t) clustering technique is mobility adaptive. Since a path availability is the product of the availabilities of the links forming the path; then the longer the path the lower the availability. Thus, higher speeds (and consequently smaller link availability) will result in smaller cluster diameter (and size). Lower speeds (and therefore lower link volatility) will allow the cluster diameter (and size) to grow.

Other performance objectives include a minimum level of 'affiliation' between a candidate node and the cluster. The 'affiliation' may be defined as the composite bandwidth between the node and all other nodes in the cluster; the distance to the cluster leader; a measure of similarity between the candidate node and the node inside the cluster (based on pre-assigned, task dependent role); or a linear combination of all the above.

Cluster leader selection

Clustering techniques for homogeneous networks usually do not distinguish between individual nodes, and therefore the identity of the cluster leader is not relevant. These techniques, however, require the leader selection to be unique, and therefore they need a common criteria for determining the cluster leader or a mechanism to solve conflicts if they occur.

A usual common criteria for cluster leader selection consists of picking the node with the lowest id among its unclustered neighbors. Since the id of the nodes do not follow any rational order, this amounts to having a random leader selection technique. Actually, there are clustering techniques where the selection of the leader is explicitly made at random (e.g. NTDR [32]).

At the other hand there are clustering techniques where the leader selection is preassigned, based on additional knowledge about the scenario. For example, LANMAR [33] preassigns the cluster leaders based on knowledge of the mobility patterns of the nodes. In LANMAR the nodes are assumed to exhibit group mobility, and the group leaders are selected as cluster leaders. Similarly, extra knowledge about a node capabilities: battery power, extra bandwidth, low mobility/high stability, extra processing power, susceptibility to destruction, mission role, etc. may be used in pre-determining the identity of the cluster leader.

Another cluster leader selection technique is based on picking as leader the node that maximizes a gain function among all the other nodes in its cluster (which initially may just be its 1-hop neighbors). A good gain function to maximize is the node degree, since a cluster leader with a higher degree assures that the cluster leader will likely remain connected to the cluster nodes over time. Besides, high degrees are usually associated with advantaged nodes (e.g. higher power, higher elevation, etc.). Even if there are no advantaged nodes, picking nodes with higher degree will result is cluster with smaller diameter, which improves performance. An obvious extension of this criteria is to define the gain function to be equal to the number of k-neighbors of a node, where k is the expected radius of the cluster. These gain functions, however, consider the network topology as something static, and therefore may choose the cluster leader (and the cluster around him) that is appropriate for a short period of time. Thus, a better gain function should take into account (as much as possible) node mobility patterns, and based on this knowledge pick up as cluster leaders those nodes that will maximize the expected number of k-neighbors over time. SOAP [34, 24] is an example of an algorithm implementing such a gain function. It should be noted that cluster (leader) selection techniques that take into account the mobility patterns as in LANMAR and SOAP has the potential to reduce or even eliminate the location management cost associated with hierarchical routing if the nodes mobility presents strong patterns, such as group mobility. As we saw in the previous section the location management cost dominates the link state information dissemination cost for HierLS approaches, so reducing this former cost will greatly improve performance and may even enable us to improve HierLS asymptotic performance, by trading off an increase in the (now small) proactive overhead for a reduction in sub-optimal routing overhead, resulting in a smaller combined total overhead.

Finally, the gain function may also be a weighted combination of the aforementioned quantities, plus additional quantities such as available power, processing speed, memory available, role, vulnerability, etc. that need to be pre-configured in each node.

Thus, there is a plethora of criteria for cluster formation. This diversity is symptomatic of our lack of understanding of the dynamics involved in clustering formation and maintenance and its impact in the generation of link state and location management information, the generation of clustering management messages, and the transient latencies incurred due to the handling of exception situations (e.g. a cluster leader is destroyed or is temporary partitioned from the cluster). The obscure nature of the impact of clustering in network performance has been the main obstacle to the design of highly efficient hierarchical algorithms.

5.1.2 Topology Abstraction Methods

Once the network nodes are organized in the clustering hierarchy, this structure is used to reduce the topology information that needs to be propagated inside the network. However, different techniques may be employed.

The HierLS algorithm presented in Subsection 2.4 is an example of a hierarchical system using the *virtual node* abstraction. In the virtual node abstraction, level-m clusters are considered level-m nodes. Real nodes are considered level-0 nodes. The set of links connecting real nodes in neighboring level-m cluster forms a level-m virtual link. A node keeps track of all the level-m virtual node and virtual links inside its level-$m + 1$ cluster. Thus, routing information is reduced since a node does not need information about level-m virtual nodes outside its level-$(m + 1)$ cluster. Subsection 2.4 presents a more detailed explanation of routing using the virtual node abstraction.

MMWN[15] is a protocol that uses the *virtual gateway* abstraction instead of the virtual node abstraction. To illustrate the way the virtual gateway abstraction works, consider a network formed by four clusters A, B, C, and D aligned horizontally as follows: $A - B - C - D$. A $-$ between B and C, for example, represents that there are some (physical) links connecting (physical) nodes in cluster B with nodes in cluster C. In the virtual gateway abstraction, each set of links connecting different clusters is called a virtual gateway and constitute level-1 nodes. Thus, at the level-1 the aforementioned network has three nodes: $A.B$, $B.C$, and $C.D$. Now, the level-1 link joining, for example, nodes $A.B$ and $B.C$ is formed by an aggregation of all the paths from nodes in $A.B$ to nodes in $B.C$. For example, if the link metric of interest is available bandwidth (for QoS-based routing), then this level-1 link metric is not associated with the number of nodes and links inside node B, but with the maximum flow from $A.B$ to $B.C$. Similar aggregation may be achieved if the link metric of interest is delay, etc.. Similarly, virtual gateways among level-2 cluster constitute level-2 nodes and aggregation of paths between these virtual gateways constitute level-2 links, and so for. Route computation is performed almost as in HierLS, with the difference being that the objective is to find a virtual gateway neighboring the destination cluster, as opposed to looking for the destination cluster itself. For example, if a node inside cluster A in the above example is looking for a node inside cluster D, its Dijkstra's computation will stop when the virtual gateway $C.D$ is found. The route obtained will be $source-$level-0 nodes$-A.B-B.C-C.D$, instead of $source-$ level-0 nodes $-B-C-D$ which would be the case if the virtual node abstraction were used. Intermediate nodes in the path will expand the route as necessary, similar to the virtual node abstraction case (e.g. HierLS).

The virtual node abstraction is more intuitive and therefore easier to analyze, implement, and debug. However, if QoS constraints are to be satisfied (as for example a minimum required bandwidth) the virtual gateway abstraction provides better link information aggregation. In the virtual node abstraction, clusters won't be able to properly estimate the virtual link cost because: (1) virtual links include links in two different clusters, and a cluster only has information about link inside itself, thus it only has information about half the link. And (2) the cost of traversing a cluster is dependent on the entry and exit points. For example, in the case of the $A-B-C-D$ network discussed before, the cost of going from A to C depends on the cost of traversing cluster B having $A.B$ as an entry point and $B.C$ as an exit point. The virtual node abstraction will estimate this cost as the sum of $A-B$ and $B-C$, where the cost of $A-B$ is computed without knowledge of the next link in the path (i.e. $B-C$) resulting in a lower quality estimate. Roughly speaking, the virtual node abstraction's link cost estimates will – at best – be equivalent to assuming that all paths go through the cluster leaders, which is a bad estimate. Thus, in general, the virtual gateway abstraction will produce routes of better quality than the virtual node abstraction. Of course, the price we pay is the extra complexity in maintaining the virtual gateway structure in addition to the clusters: some node inside the virtual gateway must to be chosen as leader and should propagate link state updates with the latest (virtual) link cost.

Besides the virtual node and virtual gateway abstractions, other techniques to exploit the hierarchical structure formed include the *quasi-hierarchic algorithm*[35, 39] and *Landmark routing*[36]. Both techniques try to maintain optimal (or good) paths toward higher level clusters. Therefore, some link changes may result in network wide propagation of updates. Thus, if propagation is event driven, these updates result in higher control overhead consumption. On the other hand, if information propagation is done periodically, the effect of these long-impact changes is long latency in routing information propagation which results in poor response to network dynamics.

5.1.3 Location Management Methods

The core of hierarchical routing consists on aggregating information by efficiently using the clusters built. Therefore, a node no longer has complete information about how to reach a node outside its level-1 cluster. To determine how to route packets to nodes outside its (level-1) cluster, a node needs to know the identity of a cluster associated with the destination. The service that provides the nodes with this information is referred to as *Location Management (LM)*. The need of a *LM* service is a main difference between hierarchical approaches for static (wireline) and mobile networks. In static networks, a LM service was not needed since the address of a node was tied to its location in the hierarchy. Due to mobility, this is no longer the case.

The LM service can be implemented in different ways, whether proactive (location update messages), reactive (paging), or a combination of both. Typical choices are:

LM1 Pure reactive. Whenever a node changes its level-i clustering membership but remains in the same level-$(i+1)$ cluster, this node sends an update to all the nodes inside its level-$(i + 1)$ cluster. As an example let's consider Figure 1, if node n_2 moves inside cluster $X.1.5$, i.e. it changes its level-1 cluster membership but does not change its level-2 cluster membership (cluster $X.1$), then node n_2 will send a location update to all the nodes inside cluster $X.1$. The remaining nodes will not be informed.

LM2 Local paging. In this LM technique, one node in each level-1 cluster assumes the role of a LM server. Also, one node among the level-1 LM servers inside the same level-2 cluster assumes the role of a level-2 LM server, and so on up to level-m. The LM servers form a hierarchical tree. Location updates are only generated and transmitted between nodes in this tree (LM servers). When a node D changes its level-i clustering membership, the LM server of its new level-i cluster will send a location update message to the level-$(i + 1)$ LM server, which in turn will forward the update to all the level-i LM servers inside this level-$(i + 1)$ cluster. Additionally, the level-$(i + 1)$ LM server checks if the node D is new in the level-$(i + 1)$ cluster, and if this is the case it will send a location update to its level-$(i + 2)$ LM server, and so on.

When a level-i LM server receives a location update message regarding node D from its level-$(i + 1)$ LM server, it updates its local database with node D's new location information and forwards this information to all the level-$(i-1)$ LM servers inside its level-i cluster. Each of these level-$(i - 1)$ LM servers forwards the location update message to the level-$(i - 2)$ servers in its level-$(i - 1)$ cluster, and so on until all the level-1 LM servers (inside node D's level-$(i + 1)$ cluster) are informed of the new level-i location information of node D. When a node needs location information about any node in the network, the node pages its level-1 LM server for this information.

For example, if node n_2 in Figure 1 moves inside cluster $X.1.5$, then the level-2 location server of cluster $X.1$ will be notified, who in turn will notify the location servers of clusters $X.1.1$ through $X.1.7$. Alternatively, if node n_2 had moved inside cluster $X.4$ instead, then the location server of cluster X would have been notified, and he in turn would have trigger notifications to all level-2 and level-1 location servers inside cluster X. And so on.

LM3 Global paging. LM3 is similar to LM2. In LM3, however, when a level-i LM server receives a location update from a higher level-$(i + 1)$ LM server, it does not forward this information to the lower level (i.e. level-$(i - 1)$) LM servers. Thus, a lower level (say level $j < i$) LM server does not have location information for nodes outside its level-j cluster. A mechanism for removing outdated location information about nodes that left a level-i cluster need to be added to the level-i clusters LM servers. Basically, a level-1 LM server that detects that a node left its level-1 cluster will remove the entry corresponding to this node from its own database, and will inform its level-2 LM server. The level-2 LM server will wait for a while for a location update from the new level-1 cluster (if inside the same level-2 cluster) and if no such an update is received it will remove the node entry and will inform its level-3 LM server, and so on until arriving to a LM server that already has information about the new location of the node. For example, if node n_2 in Figure 1 moves inside cluster $X.1.5$, then the location server of that cluster will notify the level-2 location server of cluster $X.1$. Additionally, the location server of cluster $X.1.1$ will also notify the level-2 location server that node n_2 does not belong to that cluster anymore. No other location server will be notified. Alternatively, if node n_2 had moved inside cluster $X.4$ instead, then the location servers of clusters $X.1.1$, $X.1$, and X would had been updated. Location servers on clusters $X.1.1$ and $X.1$ would learn that node n_2 does not belong to their clusters anymore, and the location server of cluster X would know that node n_2 belonged to cluster $X.4$.

When a node needs location information about any node in the network, the node pages its level-1 LM server for the information. If the level-1 LM does not have the required information, it (the level-1 LM server) pages its level-2 LM server, who in turn pages its level-3 LM server, and so on, until a LM server with location information about the desired destination is found.

The LM1 technique is the simplest of the three, but it may consume significant bandwidth for propagating location update messages. Technique LM2 reduces the bandwidth consumption for reasonable rates of new session (requiring a local page to the local location server) arrivals but at the expense of complexity (selection and maintenance of LM servers) and an increase in the latency for route establishment. However, the asymptotic characteristics of the hierarchical protocol do not change whether we use approach LM1 or approach LM2[11, 24].

Approach LM3 is the more complex to implement and analyze. It will induce a fair amount of reactive overhead (susceptible to traffic), but will significantly reduce the amount of overhead induced by mobility. However, it is expected that the bandwidth consumption of approach LM3 is the smallest of the three for typical operating conditions. The price we pay is increased latency when building new routes, a high paging cost under high traffic load and diversity, much higher implementation complexity, and network susceptibility to single points of failure.

To summarize, we observe that there are a large number of variants of hierarchical routing. Each variant represents a different trade off between complexity and performance. We will expect the more complex approaches to present better performance. However, due to the unpredictable nature of the hierarchical routing dynamics, we can not be sure of this until after analyzing the protocol through extensive simulations. Thus, it is not clear until after a protocol has been designed, debugged, and tested whether or not the extra complexity has a payoff. This points out the need of theoretical models of performance. For example, from the results shown in Table 2, we get the insight that jumping from a 2-level hierarchy to a m-level hierarchy (not a small jump in implementation complexity) will allow us to reduce the protocol scalability factor with respect to network size from 1.66 to 1.5. Whether this reduction justifies the extra complexity will be a decision that the designer will make based on his perception of how large a network the protocol is intended to support.

Finally, the experience of working with hierarchical routing approaches, especially its high degree of complexity, has motivated a renovated interest for alternative approaches. Thus, there has been a surge of research for efficient flat routing algorithms whose performance (with respect to increase to network size) may be competitive (under a cost-benefit analysis) with hierarchical approaches. The next subsection presents a survey of these techniques. Some of them, specifically HSLS, has been shown to have better asymptotic scalability properties than some hierarchical algorithms (see Table 2).

5.2   Flat Routing Techniques

The term "flat routing" is used to contrast basic routing techniques from hierarchical routing applying a topology abstraction. Unlike hierarchical routing, there are no "boundaries" imposed between groups of nodes, nor is there an addressing scheme based on hierarchy.

In flat routing, then, there are no abstractions and no virtual nodes or links. Each node and link in the topology table of a flat algorithm represents an actual (physical) node or link. Thus, the topology table may grow large as the network size increases. However, in a flat routing scheme we do not need *all* the nodes and links be present in the topology table. Specifically, some links may be hidden if they are not expected to affect a node's route computation. Similarly, nodes may not be included in the topology table if they have no consequence for reaching destinations. Notwithstanding all of the above, as the network size increases, flat routing usually requires much more memory and processing power than its hierarchical counterparts. More importantly, if not carefully designed, flat routing techniques may result in much more bandwidth consumption than hierarchical approaches.

As previously discussed, except for very specific applications, the state of the art on microelectronics allows inexpensive memory chips inside the network nodes. These chips provide sufficient memory space to handle even tens of thousands of nodes. Processing power is not so inexpensive, but efficient (incremental) algorithms still allow network with reasonable priced processors to handle the route computation algorithms when run over a large topology. Thus, the main challenge to network survivability as size increases is the excessive bandwidth consumption. So, it is not surprising that significant effort has been directed in reducing this bandwidth consumption.

The techniques for bandwidth consumption reduction for flat routing can be classified into: efficient flooding, limited generation, limited dissemination. These techniques can be used in isolation or in combination.

5.2.1 Efficient Flooding

Most proactive and reactive algorithms rely on flooding of control packets to a subset of nodes in the network. However, classical flooding is a very inefficient technique, resulting in each node receiving the same packet several times.

Efficient flooding techniques reduce the number of times a flooded message is retransmitted, and at a minimum, each intended recipient receives each flooded packet at least once. For example, a technique may consist of finding a tree in the topology such that the set of nodes in the tree covers (i.e. is neighbor of) all the nodes in the network. An effective flooding technique may then consist of propagating the message across all the nodes in the tree. Every node in the tree will have to transmit the message once.

Optimized Link State Routing (OLSR) [3], Topology Broadcast based on Reverse Path Flooding (TBRPF)[4], and Core Extraction Distributed Ad Hoc Routing (CEDAR)[37] are examples of protocols implementing efficient flooding algorithms.

Typically, the performance improvements obtained by using efficient flooding techniques increases with the average node degree of the network. Thus, these techniques are especially useful for networks with high density. However, as pointed out earlier in this chapter, high density scenarios are better handled by means of a topology (power) control algorithm which reduces the average node degree to an acceptable level. If topology control mechanisms are in place and the network is of the kind defined by assumptions a.1 through a.8, then the performance improvement obtained by efficient flooding will be a constant factor independent of the network

size, and therefore this technique will not affect the asymptotic behavior of
the protocol being run. Thus, for bounded node degree, effective flooding
techniques – while helpful – do not solve the routing protocol scalability
problem and can not be used in lieu of hierarchical routing.

5.2.2   Limited Generation

Limited generation techniques limit the amount of control information being
generated.

For example, Global State Routing (GSR)[20], and Discretized Link
State (DLS)[22] routing limit routing update generation to times which are
multiples of a base period t_e. At such times, all the changes since the last update are collected and sent to all other nodes in the network. This technique
is effective for high mobility.

Source-Tree Adaptive Routing (STAR)[21] limits the update generation
by only triggering updates for link state changes that affect another node's
best route selection. Most other limited generation techniques (e.g. the one
used in OLSR[3]) reduce the amount of control information by operating on
a network subgraph formed by all the nodes and a subset of the links in such
a way that the resulting subgraph is connected. The level of performance
improvement that can be obtained with these *partial-topology* techniques is
not easy to analyze. However, it is expected to be above the one achieved
by efficient flooding, but below the one obtained by limited dissemination
techniques.

5.2.3   Limited Dissemination

In limited dissemination techniques, most routing information updates are
not sent to the entire network but to a smaller subset. The subset may
change over time.

For example, ZRP[17] and NSLS[22] protocols limit the event-driven link
state update propagation to their k-neighbors only.

In Fisheye State Routing[12], a node divides the set of nodes into the
in-scope and the out-of-scope subsets. A node then propagates information
about nodes in its in-scope subset with a pre-configured frequency. Information about out-of-scope nodes is propagated with a smaller frequency.
In other words, most of the messages propagating routing information have
been stripped of information related to the out-of-scope nodes.

The family of Fuzzy Sighted Link State (FSLS) algorithms[22] limits the LSU generation to multiples of a base time t_e. When a LSU is sent it does not (in general) travel to the entire network. Instead, it traverses the number of hops specified in the LSU's packet Time To Live (TTL) field. The value of the TTL field will depend on the current time index. Given its potential for scalability, the family of FSLS algorithm will be described in detail in the next subsection.

Limited dissemination techniques, by reducing the depth of propagation of routing updates to a small fraction of the network, hold better promise for scalability improvement for networks with a large diameter, as is the case when the network size increases and the average node degree is kept bounded. The challenge here is to do so in a way that does not overly compromise route optimally.

One technique, namely HSLS[22], – a member of the FSLS family – produces a significant change in link state asymptotic properties, reducing its scalability factor w.r.t. network size from 2 to 1.5, rendering the algorithm indeed scalable w.r.t. network size. Thus, remarkably, HSLS presents *even better* scalability properties than hierarchical routing approaches.

5.2.4   The family of Fuzzy Sighted Link State (FSLS) algorithms

In the FSLS family of algorithms[22], the frequency of Link State Updates (LSUs) propagated to distant nodes is reduced based on the observation that in hop-by-hop routing, changes experienced by nodes far away tend to have little impact in a node's 'local' next hop decision.

In a highly mobile environment, under a Fuzzy Sighted Link State (FSLS) protocol a node will transmit - provided that there is a need to - a Link State Update (LSU) only at particular time instants that are multiples of t_e seconds. Thus, potentially several link changes are 'collected' and transmitted every t_e seconds. The *Time To Live* (TTL) field of the LSU packet is set to a value (which specifies how far the LSU will be propagated) that is a function of the current time index as explained below. After one global LSU transmission – LSU that travels over the entire network, i.e. TTL field set to infinity, as for example during initialization – a node 'wakes up' every t_e seconds and sends a LSU with TTL set to s_1 if there has been a link status change in the last t_e seconds. Also, the node wakes up every $2 * t_e$ seconds and transmits a LSU with TTL set to s_2 if there has been a link status change in the last $2 * t_e$ seconds. In general, a node wakes up every $2^{i-1} * t_e$ ($i = 1, 2, 3, ...$) seconds and transmits a LSU with TTL set to s_i if there has been a link status change in the last $2^{i-1} * t_e$ seconds.

If the value of s_i is greater than the distance from this node to any other node in the network (which will cause the LSU to reach the entire network), the TTL field of the LSU is set to infinity (global LSU), and all the counters and timers are reset. In addition, as a soft state protection on low mobility environments, a periodic timer may be set to ensure that a global LSU is transmitted at least each t_b seconds. The latter timer has effect in low mobility scenarios only, since in high mobility ones, global LSUs are going to be transmitted with high probability.

Figure 6 shows an example of FSLS's LSU generation process when mobility is high and consequently LSUs are always generated every t_e seconds. Note that the sequence $s_1, s_2, \ldots$ is non-decreasing. For example consider what happens at time $4t_e$ (see figure 6). This time is a multiple of t_e (associated with s_1), also a multiple of $2t_e$ (associated with s_2) and $4t_e$ (associated with s_3). Note that if there has been a link status change in the past t_e or $2t_e$ seconds, then this implies that there has been a link change in the past $4t_e$ seconds. Thus, if we have to set the TTL field to at least s_1 (or s_2) we also have to increase it to s_3. Similarly, if there has not been a link status change in the past $4t_e$ seconds, then there has not been a link change in the past t_e or $2t_e$ seconds. Thus, if we do not send a LSU with TTL set to s_3, we do not send a LSU at all. Thus, at time $4t_e$ (as well at times $12t_e$, $20t_e$ any other time $4 * k * t_e$ where k is an odd number) the link state change activity during the past $4t_e$ seconds needs to be checked and, if there is any, then an LSU with TTL set to s_3 will be sent. Thus, in the highly mobile scenario assumed on figure 6, a LSU with TTL equal to s_3 is sent at times $4t_e$ and $12t_e$.

The above approach guarantees that nodes that are s_i hops away from a tagged node will learn about a link status change at most after $2^{i-1}t_e$ seconds. Thus, the maximum 'refresh' time ($T(r)$) as a function of distance (r) is as shown in Figure 7. The function $T(r)$ will determine the latency in the link state information, and therefore will determine the performance of the network under a FSLS algorithm.

Different approaches may be implemented by considering different $\{s_i\}$ sequences. Of particular interest are Discretized Link State (DLS), Near Sighted Link State (NSLS), and Hazy Sighted Link State, discussed next.

DLS is obtained by setting $s_i = \infty$ for all i (see Figure 8 left). DLS is similar to the Standard Link State (SLS) algorithm and differs only in that under DLS a LSU is not sent immediately after a link status change is detected but only when the current t_e interval is completed. Thus, several link status changes may be collected in one LSU. DLS is a modification of

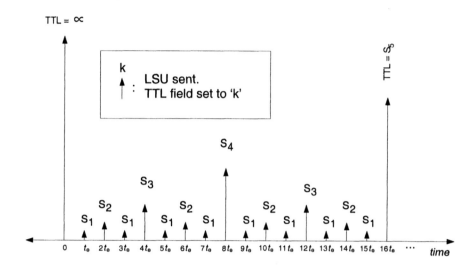

Figure 6: Example of FSLS's LSU generation process

SLS that attempts to scale better with respect to mobility.

NSLS is obtained by setting $s_i = k$ for $i < p$ and $s_p = \infty$ (for some p integer), as shown in Figure 8 (right). In NSLS, a node receives information about changes in link status from nodes that are less than 'k' hops away (i.e. inside its sight area), but it is not refreshed with new link state updates from nodes out-of-sight. NSLS has similarities with ZRP, DREAM, and FSR.

Suppose that initially, a node has knowledge of routes to every destination. In NSLS, as time evolves and nodes move, the referred node will learn that the previously computed routes will fail due to links going down. However, the node will not learn of new routes becoming available because the out-of-sight information is not being updated. This problem is not unique to NSLS but it is common to every algorithm in the FSLS family. NSLS, however, represents its worst case scenario. To solve this problem, NSLS (and any algorithm in the FSLS family) uses the 'memory' of past links to forward packets in the direction it 'saw' the destination for the last time. As the packet gets to a node that is on the 'sight' of the destination, this node will know how to forward the packet to the destination. The above is achieved by building routes beginning from the destination and going backwards until getting to the source; without removing old entries that although inaccurate, allows tracing the destination. NSLS has similarities with ZRP, DREAM, and FSR.

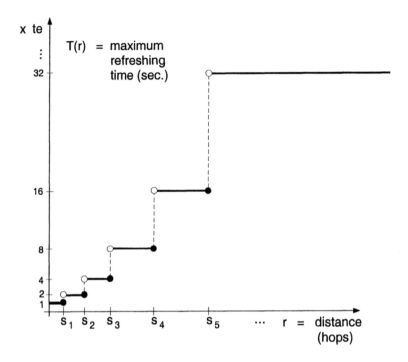

Figure 7: Maximum refresh time $T(r)$ as a function of distance from link event.

Finally, the family of Fuzzy Sighted Link State algorithms is based on the observation that nodes that are far away do not need to have complete topological information in order to make a good next hop decision, thus propagating every link status change over the network may not be necessary. The sequence $\{s_i\}$ must be chosen as to minimize the total overhead (as defined in the previous section). The total overhead is greatly influenced by the traffic pattern and intensity. However, the choice of $\{s_i\}$ is solely determined by the traffic locality conditions. Based on the uniform traffic distribution (assumptions a.1 - a.8) among all the nodes in the network, the best values of $\{s_i\}$ were found (see [22]) to be equal to $\{s_i\} = \{2^i\}$. FSLS with $\{s_i = 2^i\}$ is called the Hazy Sighted Link State (HSLS) algorithm[22]. Figure 2 shows an example of HSLS's LSU generation process. HSLS induces an almost linear relationship between route information latency and the distance in hops. This in turn causes the uncertainty in the relative angular position of the distant node to be roughly constant independent of the distance. Since in hop-by-hop routing a node is only concerned with the

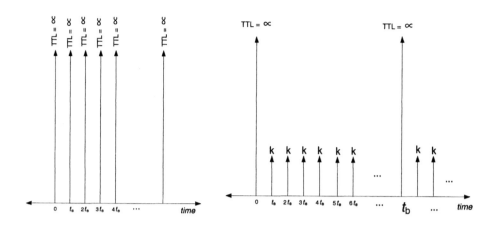

Figure 8: DLS's (left) and NSLS's (right) LSU generation process.

next hop decision, and the probability of making a wrong decision depends mainly in the angular uncertainty, which was roughly constant independent of the distance, we end up with a probability of making a bad next hop decision to be also roughly constant independent of the distance. Out of all possible assignments of probability of error versus distance, it turns out that the best performance is obtained when all the values are balanced. That is, the probability of error is roughly constant independent of the distance. Thus, HSLS's dissemination results in a linear relationship between latency and distance represent the optimal balance between proactive and sub-optimal routing overhead. If the latency versus distance curve grows faster than linear, too many mistakes are made when forwarding packets to nodes far away. If the curve grows slower than linear, we make fewer mistakes when finding routes for nodes far away than when finding routes to nodes close by, but the proactive overhead increases a fair amount since global LSUs would be sent more frequently (to reduce the latency in routing information for nodes far away).

5.3   Comparing HierLS and HSLS

The theoretical results in Table 2 shows that both HierLS and HSLS present good scalability with respect to network size. This result may be explained by the fact that both protocols induce a multi-level information dissemination technique. HSLS outperforms HierLS since HSLS's routes' quality does not degrade with network size. HSLS's angular displacement uncertainty is mainly dependent on the nodes speed and the timer period t_e, which is optimally set based on the mobility and traffic rates (regardless of network size). HierLS's routes's quality suffer small degradation each time the number of hierarchical levels is increased. Moreover, HSLS is able to improve the quality of its routes as a response to an increase in traffic load. HierLS's route quality, on the other hand, is dependent on the number of hierarchical levels, which depend on the cluster size, a parameter that is independent of the traffic load, leaving HierLS powerless to react to an increase in traffic load. Thus, HSLS present better scalability properties than HierLS.

However, the constants involved in the asymptotic expression may be too large, preventing HSLS from outperforming HierLS under real life scenarios. Therefore, HierLS and HSLS were compared through simulation.

Table 3 shows the simulation results obtained by OPNET for a 400-node network where nodes are randomly located on a square of area equal to 320 square miles (i.e. density is 1.25 nodes per square mile). Each node chooses a random direction among 4 possible values, and moves in that direction at 28.8 mph. Upon reaching the area boundaries, a node bounces back. The radio link capacity was 1.676 Mbps. Simulations were run for 350 seconds, leaving the first 50 seconds for protocol initialization, and transmitting packets (60 8kbps streams) for the remaining 300 seconds. The HierLS approach simulated was the DAWN project [38] modification of the MMWN clustering protocol [15]. Following the taxonomy presented in this paper, this protocol can be classified as a m-level hierarchy[8] with a cluster radius greater than one. The node affiliation decisions were performed by the cluster leaders with the goal of balancing cluster sizes with a lower and upper bound on the cluster sizes of 9 and 35. The cluster leader selection criteria was to choose the node in the cluster with the largest number of (unassigned) k-hop neighbors. The virtual gateway method of topology abstraction was used.

The metric of interest is the throughput (i.e. fraction of packets successfully delivered). Table 3 shows the throughput obtained under two different MAC protocols: unreliable and reliable CSMA. For reliable CSMA, packets were retransmitted up to 10 times if a MAC-level ACK was not received in a reasonable time. We can see that in both cases HSLS outperforms HierLS, although the relative difference is reduced under the reliable MAC case. This can be explained considering that the high rate of collisions expe-

---

[8]Although m-level can be formed, since the network size was relatively small, only 2 levels were formed during the simulations.

Protocol	UNRELIABLE	RELIABLE
HSLS	0.2454	0.7991
HierLS-LM1	0.0668	0.3445

Table 3: Throughput of a 400-node network.

rienced under unreliable CSMA favored shorter paths. For nodes close by, HSLS may provide almost optimal routes while HierLS routes may be far from optimal if the destination belongs to a neighboring cluster. Thus, we can see that an unreliable MAC biases performance towards HSLS. Another factor to take into account is the latency to detect link up/downs. Under HierLS this information is synchronized among all the nodes in the cluster and therefore some latency is enforced to avoid link flapping. In HSLS, on the other hand, each node may have its own view of the network, and as a consequence a node may be more aggressive in temporarily taking links down without informing other nodes. As a consequence, HSLS is more aggressive and reacts much faster to link degradation, using alternate paths if available.

The simulation results presented do not represent a comprehensive study of the relative performance of HierLS versus HSLS under all possible scenarios. They just present an example of a real-life situation to complement the theoretical analysis. The theoretical analysis focuses on asymptotically large networks, heavy traffic load, and saturation conditions where the remaining capacity determines the protocol performance. The simulation results, on the other hand, refer to medium size networks with moderate loads, where depending on the MAC employed, other factors such as the quality of the links that neighbor discovery declares up, the latency on detecting link failures, etc., may have more weight over the protocols' performance.

Thus, whether HSLS or HierLS should be preferred for a particular scenario, depends on the particular constraints. For example, if memory or processing time is an issue, HierLS may be preferred since it requires a smaller topology table to be stored/processed. On the other hand, if implementation complexity is an issue, then HSLS should be preferred.

5.4 Discussion

Traditionally, as network size increases it was believed that the best alternative for routing scalability was the inclusion of hierarchical routing techniques. Several such techniques were designed, as for example the work done under DARPA's SURAN project (see [39, 40] for a survey).

Hierarchical routing solutions, however, quickly showed their drawbacks. For one, their implementations proved too complex, having to handle too many exception situations, especially in scenarios –as in the military – where nodes chosen for special functions (e.g. cluster leaders, location management servers, etc.) are susceptible to attack/destruction. In these scenarios, the routing protocol has to specify mechanisms for backup selection and activation. Another drawback is that the overhead induced for maintaining the hierarchy and for keeping up-to-date location management information reduces the bandwidth savings achieved due to reduction of link state information dissemination. These drawbacks have played a large part in the fact that in practice no multilevel hierarchical protocols has been implemented in real life networks. All current hierarchical routing implementations limit its number of hierarchical levels to 2, which in turn puts a limit to its scalability.

The difficulty in the implementation of hierarchical routing motivated the search of alternative, simpler techniques to improve routing protocol scalability with respect to network size, including but not limited to efficient flooding, limited generation, limited dissemination, and a combination thereof. This section presented a comparison of these new techniques against the classical hierarchical routing approach.

The theoretical analysis showed that there is no fundamental advantage provided by hierarchical routing over an efficient combination of these techniques, as for example, the HSLS algorithm. Indeed, HSLS scalability properties with respect to network size are not worse than that achieved by hierarchical routing. Furthermore, HSLS presented better scalability properties with respect to traffic rate.

The experimental study also pointed out that hierarchical routing implementations, while extremely more complex than HSLS's implementation, are not guaranteed to achieve better performance than HSLS. The relative performance of the protocols depends on other factors, such as the link layer latency on detecting link failures, or the MAC layer susceptibility to collisions between control and data packets.

Thus, we conclude that limited dissemination techniques are good candidates for achieving scalable routing protocols. Regarding which protocol should be preferred in a practical situation, we realize that this determination depends on several factors. We may say that when network size, mobility, and traffic increases; an efficient MAC is used; or implementation complexity is one of the main concerns; limited dissemination techniques as HSLS should tend to be preferred over hierarchical approaches.

But, in scenarios unfavorable to limited dissemination techniques such as HSLS, hierarchical approaches should tend to be preferred. Scenarios unfavorable to HSLS include scenarios where storage capacity at each node is limited, the topology is sparse, or there is a large amount of hostile misbehaving nodes. It was already noted that HSLS requires more storage space than hierarchical approaches. Sparse, tree-like topologies present a challenge to HSLS, since link status changes of links on shortest paths will have an effect on routing decisions taken by nodes several hopes away from the node experiencing the link status change. Roughly speaking, instead of 'locally repairing' the broken route, the network will have to back the old route up until reaching a node (maybe even the source) from where a new route segment to the destination node may be built. Since HSLS link state dissemination to nodes more than 2 hops away is not immediate but a latency is induced, this may result in temporary routing loops. The impact of these routing loops (other than rendering the destination unreachable) on the network performance depends on the loop detection/removal capabilities available on the network. Additionally, since in SLS a node receives 2 LSUs each time there is a link status change (one from each node at each extreme of the link) a node can validate routing information sent by misbehaving nodes. In HSLS – depending on the distance to the node experiencing a link status change – only one LSU may be received, making the problem of detecting misbehaving nodes more difficult.

Finally, the reader should keep in mind that hierarchical routing's relative performance (against limited dissemination techniques) may increase in scenarios different to the homogeneous network considered in this chapter (defined by assumptions a.1-a.8). For example if the network is formed by some low power terrestrial nodes and some high power/aerial nodes with much better coverage. Or if the network is formed by nodes whose movements are not uncorrelated but follow well defined group patterns. In these cases, a desirable property of the hierarchical routing technique would be to be able to extract the underlying network structure and mimic it in its cluster formation process. If successful, the clustering mechanism will significantly reduce the bandwidth consumed by the location management procedure, resulting in improved scalability with respect to the results shown in Table 2, where assumptions a.1 through a.8 were valid. These scenarios may provide hierarchical routing approaches an edge above limited dissemination flat techniques that do not try to exploit the underlying network structure.

6   Conclusions and Future Research Directions

This chapter addressed the issue of the scalability of routing protocol for bandwidth-constrained ad hoc networks from a fundamental viewpoint. It presented concepts, metrics, and methodologies for the study of routing protocols. Analytical results for the scalability of a representative set of routing protocols were discussed, providing a deeper understanding of the characteristics and tradeoffs associated with various classes of routing protocols for mobile networks. This treatment of the subject is not all-inclusive. Several (valid) assumptions about the networking scenario were adopted in order to achieve closed form expressions. We hope, however, to have succeeded in providing the reader with the necessary tools for performing his/her own analysis and performance assessment under the particular networking scenario he/she is interested in.

In particular, as a consequence of the fundamental analysis two common misconceptions were exposed:

- **Misconception 1:** As traffic load increases, the bandwidth allocated to routing information dissemination should decrease.

- **Misconception 2:** As network size increases the best option is to engage a hierarchical routing algorithm.

The analysis also pointed out the best performing approaches in the context of scalability with respect to network size: limited dissemination flat routing, and m-level hierarchical routing. Thus, a more in depth analysis of these 'winner' approaches were presented.

The treatment of hierarchical routing approaches showed that they are not only extremely complex to implement but they are also hard to analyze, to the point of not being clear if the performance improvement to be achieved with a particular hierarchical routing approach would justify the implementation headache. This disappointment with hierarchical routing complexity has motivated a surge of interest in the study of scalable non-hierarchical protocols.

We presented the main techniques to improve scalability for flat routing. We compare the (probably) best of this techniques against an average hierarchical routing technique and the result was that the flat routing scheme, while much easier to implement, outperforms the hierarchical approach under the high stress (asymptotic) regime and also under the moderate stress scenario.

In conclusion, it seems that imposing an arbitrary hierarchy in homogeneous ad hoc networks provides no scalability advantage (over flat-routing scalability-improving techniques). It seems that hierarchical routing would justify its high implementation complexity only if the hierarchy built was a response/reflection of an underlying hierarchy/structure in the network.

Future research should extend the results shown in Section 4 for scenarios different to the ones defined by assumptions a.1-a.8. Of particular interest are the group mobility scenarios, since it appears that they are likely to be present due to patterns on human motion following streets, highways, etc., and the task requirements of automated systems (robots, etc.). For these scenarios the theory can be easily extended, and should be used to help in the design of structure-learning gain functions for cluster formation, like the one developed in SOAP[24].

This chapter has addressed the scalability challenge from a bandwidth point of view. As ad hoc networks used become widespread, different applications will need to be supported. A particular challenge is posed by QoS demanding applications, where the question is not to get the best route to a destination but whether a particular QoS constraint can be satisfied (Call Admission Control) by the network and how. Call Admission Control (CAC) usually requires more information than say, minimum hop routing. Moreover, the impact of routing information latency or imprecision into system performance is not easy to evaluate. Defining a metric that captures the effect of routing protocols (control overhead, route information latency, etc.) in QoS related performance (as *Total Overhead* does for bandwidth related performance) is not an easy task. However, this task is paramount for the proper design of routing protocols enabling large ad hoc network running application with demanding QoS constraints such as voice and videoconferencing. Support of such applications may well be the rite of passage required for ad hoc networking technology in order to reach the mass market, and as such it may define the future of this technology.

References

[1] J. McQuillan, I. Richer, and E. Rosen, " The new routing algorithm for the ARPANET," *IEEE Transactions on Communications*, 28(5):711-719, May 1980.

[2] R. Gallager, D. Bertsekas, *Data Networks*. Prentice Hall, New Jersey, 1992.

[3] P. Jacquet, P. Muhlethaler, and A. Quayyum, "Optimized Link State Routing Protocol", draft-ietf-manet-olsr-05.txt, Internet Draft, IETF MANET Working Group, Nov. 2000. Work in Progress.

[4] B. Bellur, R. Ogier, "A Reliable, Efficient Topology Broadcast Algorithm for Dynamic Networks," *Proc. IEEE INFOCOM*, 1999.

[5] C. Perkins. "Ad-Hoc On-Demand Distance Vector Routing". MILCOM'97 panel on Ad-Hoc Networks, Monterey, CA, November 3, 1997.

[6] C. Perkins and E. M. Roger, "Ad-Hoc On-Demand Distance Vector Routing ," *Proceedings of IEEE WMCSA'99*, New Orleans, LA, Feb. 1999, pp. 90-100.

[7] D. B. Johnson and D. Maltz,*"Dynamic Source Routing in Ad Hoc Wireless Networks."*, In Mobile Computing, edited by Tomasz Imielinski and Hank Korth. Kluwer Academic Publishers, 1995.

[8] C-K Toh, " Associativity Based Routing For Ad Hoc Mobile Networks," *Wireless Personal Communications Journal*, Special Issue on Mobile Networking & Computing Systems, Vol. 4, No. 2, March 1997.

[9] V.D. Park and M.S. Corson, "A highly adaptive distributed routing algorithm for mobile wireless networks," in *IEEE INFOCOM '97*, pp. 1405-1413, 1997.

[10] S. Basagni, I. Chlamtac, V.R. Syrotiuk, and B.A. Woodward, "A Distance Routing Effect Algorithm for Mobility (DREAM)," in *Proceedings of ACM/IEEE MobiCom'98*, Dallas, Tx, 1998.

[11] C. Santivanez, A. B. McDonald, I. Stavrakakis, S. Ramanathan. "On the Scalability of Ad Hoc Routing Protocols," in *Proceedings of IEEE Infocom'2002*, New York, USA, June 2002.

[12] B. A. Iwata, C.-C. Chiang, G. Pei, M. Gerla, and T.-W. Chen, "Scalable Routing Strategies for Ad Hoc Wireless Networks". *IEEE Journal of Selected Areas on Communications*, vol. 17, no. 8, pp. 1369-1379, Aug. 1999.

[13] D. J. Baker and A. Ephremides, "The Architectural Organization of a Mobile Radio Network via a Distributed ALgorithm," *IEEE Transactions on Communications*, 1981, 29(11): 1694-1701.

[14] C. -C. Chiang and M. Gerla, " Routing and Multicast in Multihop, Mobile Wireless Networks," *Proceeding of the IEEE UCUPC'97*, San Diego, CA, Oct. 1997.

[15] S. Ramanathan, M. Steenstrup, "Hierarchically-organized, Multihop Mobile Networks for Multimedia Support", *ACM/Baltzer Mobile Networks and Applications*, Vol. 3, No. 1, pp 101-119.

[16] E. M. Belding-Royer, "Hierarchical Routing in Ad Hoc Mobile Networks," *Wireless Communications & Mobile Computing*, No. 5, Vol. 2, August 2002.

[17] Z. Haas, " A New Routing Protocol for the Reconfigurable Wireless Networks," *Proceedings of ICUPC'97*, San Diego, CA, Oct. 12, 1997.

[18] Z. Haas and M. Pearlman, "The performance of query control schemes for the zone routing protocol," in *ACM SIGCOMM*, 1998.

[19] M. R. Pearlman and Z. J. Haas, "Determining the Optimal Configuration for the Zone Routing Protocol," *IEEE Journal of Selected Areas on Communications*, vol. 17, no. 8, pp. 1395-1414, Aug. 1999.

[20] T. Chen and M. Gerla, " Global State Routing: A New Routing Scheme for Ad-hoc Wireless Networks ," *Proceedings of IEEE ICC '98*, 1998.

[21] J.J. Garcia-Luna-Aceves and M. Spohn, "Source-Tree Routing in Wireless Networks,", *Proc. IEEE ICNP 99: 7th International Conference on Network Protocols*, Toronto, Canada, October 31–November 3, 1999.

[22] C. Santivanez, S. Ramanathan, and I. Stavrakakis,"Making Link State Routing Scale for Ad Hoc Networks", In *Proceedings of MobiHOC'2001*, Long Beach, CA, Oct. 2001.

[23] E. W. Dijkstra, "A Note on Two Problems in Connection with Graphs," *Numerische Math.*, 1:269-271, 1959.

[24] C. Santiváñez, "A framework for multi-mode routing in wireless ad hoc networks: theoretical and practical aspects of scalability and dynamic adaptation to varying network size, traffic and mobility patterns," *Doctoral thesis*, Electrical and Computing Engineering Department, Northeastern University, Boston, MA, November 2001.

[25] R. Guerin, et. al., "Equivalent Capacity and Its Applications to Bandwidth Allocation in High Speed Networks," *IEEE Journal of Selected Areas on Communications*, vol. 9, no. 7, pp. 968-981, Sept. 1991.

[26] X. Hong, K. Xu, and M. Gerla, "Scalable Routing Protocols for Mobile Ad Hoc Networks," *IEEE Network Magazine*, Special Issue on Scalabili in Communication Networks, No. 4, Vol. 16, July/August 2002, pp. 11-21.

[27] P. Gupta and P.R. Kumar. "The Capacity of Wireless Networks", *IEEE Transaction on Information Theory*, 46 (2):388-404, March 2000.

[28] M. Grossglauser and D. Tse. "Mobility Increases the Capacity of Ad-hoc Wireless Networks", in *Proceedings of IEEE Infocom'2001*, Anchorage, Alaska, April 2001.

[29] S. Ramanathan and R. Hain, "Topology Control of Multihop Radio Networks using Transmit Power Adjustment," in *Proceedings of IEEE Infocom'2000*, Tel Aviv, Israel, 2000

[30] M. Steenstrup, "Cluster-Based Networks," In *Ad Hoc Networking*, C. E. Perkins, Ed., Chapter 4, Addison-Wesley, 2001, pp. 75-138.

[31] A. B. McDonald and T.F. Znati. "A Mobility Based Framework for Adaptive Clustering in Wireless Ad Hoc Networks". *IEEE Journal of Selected Areas on Communications*, col. 17, no. 8, pp. 1466-1487, Aug. 1999.

[32] J. Zavgren, "NTDR Mobility Management Protocols and Procedures," In *Proceedings of IEEE MILCOM'97*, Nov. 1997.

[33] G. Pei, M. Gerla and X. Hong, "LANMAR: Landmark Routing for Large Scale Wireless Ad Hoc Networks with Group Mobility", in *Proceedings of ACM Workshop on Mobile and Ad Hoc Networking and Computing MobiHOC'00*, Boston, MA, August 2000.

[34] C. Santiváñez and I. Stavrakakis, " SOAP : a Self-Organizing, Adaptive Protocol for routing in large, highly mobile ad-hoc networks", *Technical Report TR-CDSP-99-50, CDSP center*, Ece Dept., Northeastern University, Boston, MA, 1999.

[35] L. Kleinrock and F. Kamoun, "Hierarchical Routing for Large Networks," *Computer Networks*, No. 1, January 1977, pp. 155-174.

[36] P. F. Tsuchiya, " Landmark Routing : Architecture, Algorithms, and Issues," *Technical Report MTR-87W00174*, Cambridge, MA: MITRE Corporation, September 1987.

[37] R. Sivakumar, P. Sinha, and V. Bharghavan, " CEDAR: a Core-Extraction Distributed Ad hoc Routing algorithm," *Proceedings of INFOCOM'99*, New York, 1999.

[38] http://www.ir.bbn.com/projects/dawn/dawn-index.html

[39] G. Lauer, " Packet Radio Routing," In *Routing in Communications networks*, edited by Martha E. Steenstrup, Chapter 11, pages 351-396. Prentice Hall, Englewood Cliffs, New Jersey, 1995.

[40] G. Lauer, " Hierarchical Routing Design for SURAN," *Proceedings of ICC'86*, 1986, pages 93-101.